Addison-Wesley

Algebra and Trigonometry

Solutions Manual

Stanley A. Smith
Randall I. Charles
John A. Dossey
Mervin L. Keedy
Marvin L. Bittinger

Addison-Wesley Publishing Company

Menlo Park, California • Reading, Massachusetts • New York
Don Mills, Ontario • Wokingham, England
Amsterdam • Bonn • Sydney • Singapore • Tokyo
Madrid • San Juan

ISBN   0-201-25362-3

3 4 5 6 7 8 9 10 · ML-95 94 93

To the Teacher

This Solutions Manual provides answers for all the exercises in the student textbook *Algebra and Trigonometry* by Smith, Charles, Keedy, Dossey, and Bittinger (code number 25383). The answers are also given in the Teacher's Edition (code number 25384), either in blue print on the pages where the exercises occur, in the margins, or in the Teacher's Answer Section in the front of the Teacher's Edition.

This Solutions Manual contains more complete answers than the Teacher's Edition. In the Teacher's Edition, there is rarely enough space to show graphs, proofs, or step-by-step solutions on the pages where these exercises occur. The blue pages in the front of the Teacher's Edition provide graphs and some of the more space-consuming answers, but the Solutions Manual is more detailed in its presentation.

In every chapter of the student textbook there are Try This exercises that exactly match and immediately follow the Examples. Complete step-by-step solutions for the Try This exercises are given in the Solutions Manual for each lesson.

Answers are given for the A-level exercises; complete solutions are provided for all Critical Thinking, Challenge, and Mixed Review Exercises as well as for all Chapter Summary and Review and Test Sections.

Contents

CHAPTER 1

READY FOR REAL NUMBERS, ALGEBRA, AND PROBLEM SOLVING?

1. $\frac{16}{5}$ **2.** $\frac{103}{20}$ **3.** $\frac{1}{25}$ **4.** $\frac{1001}{1000}$ **5.** 0.55 **6.** 0.72

7. 3.6 **8.** $4.\overline{142857}$ **9.** 37.37 **10.** 10.19 **11.** 1.47

12. 0.166 **13.** 12.8 **14.** 3.978 **15.** 2.5 **16.** 0.375

17. $\frac{14}{15}$ **18.** $4\frac{11}{12}$ **19.** $\frac{1}{14}$ **20.** $\frac{11}{12}$ **21.** $\frac{5}{48}$ **22.** $2\frac{1}{4}$

23. $\frac{16}{15}$ **24.** $2\frac{1}{2}$ **25.** 33.12 **26.** 6.25 **27.** 83.2

28. 2 **29.** > **30.** < **31.** > **32.** = **33.** 7:1

34. 13:3 **35.** 23:2 **36.** 4:11

pp. 5–8   1-1 TRY THIS

a. Rational; the numeral ends **b.** Rational; $\sqrt{49} = 7$
c. Rational; the numeral repeats
d. Irrational; $-\sqrt{32}$ is not a perfect square

e. Rational; ratio of integers, $\frac{a}{b}$, $b \neq 0$

f. Irrational; the numeral does not repeat
g. $-8 + (-9) = -17$ **h.** $-8.9 + (-9.7) = -18.6$

i. $-\frac{6}{5} + \left(\frac{-23}{10}\right) = \frac{-12}{10} + \left(\frac{-23}{10}\right) = -\frac{35}{10} = -\frac{7}{2}$

j. $14 + (-28) = -14$ **k.** $-4.5 + (7.8) = 3.3$

l. $\frac{3}{8} + \left(\frac{-5}{6}\right) = \frac{9}{24} + \left(\frac{-20}{24}\right) = -\frac{11}{24}$

m. $8 - (-9) = 8 + 9 = 17$ **n.** $23.7 - 5.9 = 17.8$

o. $-\frac{11}{16} - \left(-\frac{23}{12}\right) = -\frac{33}{48} + \frac{92}{48} = \frac{59}{48}$

pp. 7–8   1-1 EXERCISES

1. Rational **2.** Rational **3.** Rational **4.** Rational

5. Rational **6.** Irrational **7.** Rational **8.** Irrational

9. Rational **10.** Irrational **11.** Rational **12.** Irrational

13. -28 **14.** -29 **15.** -16 **16.** 5 **17.** 5

18. -7 **19.** -15 **20.** -24 **21.** -34 **22.** 1.2

23. -13.26 **24.** $\frac{1}{7}$ **25.** $-\frac{2}{3}$ **26.** $-\frac{4}{3}$ **27.** $\frac{1}{10}$

28. -2 **29.** -3 **30.** -12 **31.** -21 **32.** 5 **33.** 5

34. 15 **35.** 44 **36.** -11.6 **37.** -7.7 **38.** -29.25

39. -34.8 **40.** $-\frac{7}{2}$ **41.** $-\frac{13}{5}$ **42.** $-\frac{5}{12}$

43. $2:\text{II}$, $\sqrt{4}$, $(\sqrt{2})^2$, $\sqrt[3]{8}$, $\frac{8}{4}$; Answers may vary.

44. $10:\text{X}$, $\sqrt{100}$, $(\sqrt{10})^2$, $\sqrt[3]{1000}$, $\frac{20}{2}$; Answers may vary.

45. $0.5:\frac{1}{2}$, $\sqrt{\frac{1}{4}}$, $\frac{8}{16}$, $\sqrt[3]{\frac{1}{8}}$, $\frac{2}{4}$; Answers may vary.

46. $-3:-\sqrt{9}$, $-(\sqrt{3})^2$, $-(\sqrt[3]{27})$, $-\frac{18}{6}$, $\left(-\frac{1}{3}\right)^{-1}$;

Answers may vary.

47. Two unrelated sets of digits appear, each 6 times, with a different starting digit for each ratio.
Set 1:

$\frac{1}{13} = 0.076923076923\ldots = 0.\overline{076923}$

$\frac{10}{13} = 0.76923076923\ldots = 0.\overline{769230}$

$\frac{9}{13} = 0.6923076923\ldots = 0.\overline{692307}$

$\frac{12}{13} = 0.923076923\ldots = 0.\overline{923076}$

$\frac{3}{13} = 0.23076923\ldots = 0.\overline{230769}$

$\frac{4}{13} = 0.3076923\ldots = 0.\overline{307692}$

Set 2:

$\frac{2}{13} = 0.153846153846\ldots = 0.\overline{153846}$

$\frac{7}{13} = 0.53846153846\ldots = 0.\overline{538461}$

$\frac{11}{13} = 0.3846153846\ldots = 0.\overline{384615}$

$\frac{5}{13} = 0.846153846\ldots = 0.\overline{846153}$

$\frac{6}{13} = 0.46153846\ldots = 0.\overline{461538}$

$\frac{8}{13} = 0.6153846\ldots = 0.\overline{615384}$

Other patterns are possible.

48. a. $\begin{aligned} 10n &= 6.\overline{6} \\ n &= 0.\overline{6} \\ \hline 9n &= 6 \\ n &= \frac{6}{9} = \frac{2}{3} \end{aligned}$

b. $\begin{aligned} 10n &= 7.\overline{7} \\ n &= 0.\overline{7} \\ \hline 9n &= 7 \\ n &= \frac{7}{9} \end{aligned}$

c. $\begin{aligned} 100n &= 82.\overline{2} \\ 10n &= 8.\overline{2} \\ \hline 90n &= 74 \\ n &= \frac{74}{90} = \frac{37}{45} \end{aligned}$

49. $0.909009000900009\ldots$, for example.

50. a. No
b. No
c. No
d. No
e. Densely ordered
f. Densely ordered

51. $\frac{5}{12} - \frac{1}{8} = \frac{10}{24} - \frac{3}{24} = \frac{7}{24}$ **52.** $1.103 + 2.908 = 4.011$

53. $\frac{7}{10} + \frac{3}{8} = \frac{28}{40} + \frac{15}{40} = \frac{43}{40}$ **54.** $38.9 + 17.6 = 56.5$

55. $(12.7)(20.4) = 259.08$ **56.** $\frac{2}{7} \cdot \frac{7}{11} = \frac{14}{77} = \frac{2}{11}$

57. $\frac{1}{2} \cdot \frac{2}{3} \cdot \frac{3}{4} = \frac{6}{24} = \frac{1}{4}$ **58.** $\frac{1}{2} + \frac{2}{3} + \frac{3}{4} = \frac{6}{12} + \frac{8}{12} + \frac{9}{12} = \frac{23}{12}$

59. $\frac{2}{3} \div \frac{1}{3} = \frac{2}{3} \times \frac{3}{1} = \frac{6}{3} = 2$

60. $\begin{aligned} 8 &= 2^3 \\ 20 &= 2^2 \cdot 5 \\ \text{GCF} &= 2^2 = 4 \end{aligned}$ **61.** $\begin{aligned} 27 &= 3^3 \\ 64 &= 4^3 \\ \end{aligned}$ No common factors so the GCF $= 1$

62. $\begin{aligned} 256 &= 2^8 \\ 512 &= 2^9 \\ \text{GCF} &= 2^8 = 256 \end{aligned}$ **63.** $\begin{aligned} 6 &= 2 \cdot 3 \\ 20 &= 2^2 \cdot 5 \\ \text{LCM} &= 2^2 \cdot 3 \cdot 5 = 60 \end{aligned}$

64. $15 = 3 \cdot 5$
$35 = 5 \cdot 7$
LCM $= 3 \cdot 5 \cdot 7 = 105$

65. $11 = 11$
$36 = 2^2 \cdot 3^2$
LCM $= 2^2 \cdot 3^2 \cdot 11 = 396$

pp. 9–11   **1-2 TRY THIS**

a. $-4 \cdot 6 = -24$ **b.** $-8.1 \times -3.5 = 28.35$

c. $9.1(-4.7) = -42.77$ **d.** $\left(\dfrac{-3}{4}\right)\left(\dfrac{-5}{6}\right) = \dfrac{15}{24} = \dfrac{5}{8}$

e. $\dfrac{24}{-8} = -3$ **f.** $-\dfrac{10}{5} = -2$ **g.** $\dfrac{-10}{-40} = \dfrac{1}{4} = 0.25$

h. $-\dfrac{3}{4} \div \dfrac{7}{8} = -\dfrac{3}{4} \cdot \dfrac{8}{7} = -\dfrac{24}{28} = -\dfrac{6}{7}$

i. $-\dfrac{12}{5} \div \left(-\dfrac{7}{15}\right) = \left(-\dfrac{12}{5}\right)\left(-\dfrac{15}{7}\right) = \dfrac{180}{35} = \dfrac{36}{7}$

j. $\dfrac{0}{8}$; Possible   **k.** $\dfrac{0}{0}$; Not possible, cannot divide by 0.

l. $\dfrac{8}{0}$; Not possible, cannot divide by 0.

m. $\dfrac{17}{2x - 2x} = \dfrac{17}{0}$; Not possible, cannot divide by 0.

pp. 12–13   **1-2 EXERCISES**

1. -21 **2.** -40 **3.** -8 **4.** -45 **5.** 16 **6.** 21

7. 126 **8.** 136 **9.** -34.2 **10.** 42.7 **11.** 26.46

12. -71.04 **13.** 2 **14.** 3 **15.** 60 **16.** 432 **17.** 24

18. 0 **19.** $-\dfrac{12}{35}$ **20.** $-\dfrac{55}{12}$ **21.** 1 **22.** $\dfrac{65}{14}$ **23.** $-\dfrac{8}{27}$

24. $-\dfrac{64}{125}$ **25.** $\dfrac{1}{5}$ **26.** -2 **27.** -8 **28.** -7

29. -4 **30.** -9 **31.** 7 **32.** 8 **33.** -7 **34.** 0.3

35. 0.7 **36.** -6 **37.** -3 **38.** 5 **39.** 110

40. $-\dfrac{3}{14}$ **41.** $-\dfrac{1}{10}$ **42.** 8 **43.** $\dfrac{5}{4}$ **44.** $-\dfrac{14}{3}$

45. $-\dfrac{4}{3}$ **46.** Not possible   **47.** Possible   **48.** Possible

49. Not possible   **50.** $\dfrac{1}{8}$ **51.** $-\dfrac{1}{2}$ **52.** $-\dfrac{9}{25}$ **53.** -2

54. No   **55.** Yes

56. Answers may vary. For example, multiply all numbers whose absolute values are reciprocals.

$\left(-\dfrac{1}{6}\right)(-6) \cdot \left(\dfrac{1}{5}\right)(5) \cdot \left(\dfrac{1}{4}\right)(-4) \cdot \left(-\dfrac{1}{3}\right)(-3) \cdot \left(-\dfrac{1}{2}\right)(2) \cdot$
$(-1) = 1 \cdot 1 \cdot (-1) \cdot 1 \cdot (-1)(-1)$

There are an odd number of negative signs, so the result is -1.

57. $2\left(-\dfrac{1}{2}\right) = -1$

58. Rational: the reciprocal of a rational number $\dfrac{p}{q}$, where p and q are integers, and $p \neq 0$ and $q \neq 0$ is $\dfrac{q}{p}$.

59. a. The reciprocal of a percent is the percent we multiply it by to get 1.

b. $40\% = 0.4$, $\dfrac{1}{0.4} = 2.5 = 250\%$

c. $125\% = 1.25$, $\dfrac{1}{1.25} = 0.8 = 80\%$

60. $x \cdot (-8) = |-2|$
$-8x = 2$

$x = -\dfrac{2}{8}$

$x = -\dfrac{1}{4}$

61. 7.875 **62.** 5.0625 **63.** $-4.\overline{66}$ **64.** Irrational

65. Rational   **66.** Rational   **67.** $3 + (-6) = -3$

68. $-5.1 + (-4.3) = -9.4$ **69.** $8 - 11 = -3$

70. $3 - (-4) = 3 + 4 = 7$ **71.** $\dfrac{2}{9} + \left(-\dfrac{7}{9}\right) = -\dfrac{5}{9}$

72. $-\dfrac{2}{3} - \left(-\dfrac{2}{3}\right) = -\dfrac{2}{3} + \dfrac{2}{3} = 0$

73. $\dfrac{3}{5} - \dfrac{1}{10} = \dfrac{6}{10} - \dfrac{1}{10} = \dfrac{5}{10} = \dfrac{1}{2}$

74. $\dfrac{2}{3} + \left(-\dfrac{1}{6}\right) = \dfrac{4}{6} + \left(-\dfrac{1}{6}\right) = \dfrac{3}{6} = \dfrac{1}{2}$

75. $|-37| + |12| = 37 + 12 = 49$

76. $-\dfrac{5}{6} + \dfrac{2}{3} = -\dfrac{5}{6} + \dfrac{4}{6} = -\dfrac{1}{6}$

77. $|0| - |1| - |2| = 0 - 1 - 2 = -3$

78. $-\dfrac{1}{2} + \dfrac{1}{3} - \dfrac{1}{4} + \dfrac{1}{5} = -\dfrac{30}{60} + \dfrac{20}{60} - \dfrac{15}{60} + \dfrac{12}{60}$

$= -\dfrac{45}{60} + \dfrac{32}{60} = -\dfrac{13}{60}$

79. 81 **80.** 81 **81.** $2(5.75) + 2(3.50) = \$18.50$

pp. 15–17   **1-3 TRY THIS**

a. $5x - y$; $x = 10$, $y = 5$
$5(10) - 5 = 50 - 5 = 45$
b. $-(-y)$; $y = -8 - (-(-8)) = -8$
c. $|x| - 2|y|$; $x = -16$, $y = -4$
$|-16| - 2|-4| = 16 - 2(4) = 16 - 8 = 8$
d. $-5x - 3y = -5x + (-3y)$ **e.** $17m - 45 = 17m + (-45)$
f. $-6p + 5t = -6p - (-5t)$
g. $(8m + 5n) + 6p = 8m + (5n + 6p)$
h. $(17x)(-9t) = (-9t)(17x)$ **i.** $9p(4q \cdot 16r) = 16r(4q \cdot 9p)$

j. $\dfrac{19t}{3x} \cdot \dfrac{9}{9} = \dfrac{171t}{27x}$ **k.** $\dfrac{10yz}{5z} = \dfrac{5 \cdot 2 \cdot yz}{5z} = \left(\dfrac{5z}{5z}\right) \cdot \dfrac{2y}{1} = 2y$

l. $8a - b$; $x - x = 0$
$8a - b + 0 = 8a - b + (x - x) = 8a + x - b - x$

pp. 18–19   **1-3 EXERCISES**

1. 54 **2.** -63 **3.** 11 **4.** -109 **5.** 103 **6.** 124

7. -4 **8.** 8 **9.** -17 **10.** 12 **11.** $-2 - 4a$

12. -14 **13.** -15 **14.** -3 **15.** 6 **16.** 43

17. 115 **18.** 12 **19.** 30 **20.** 37 **21.** $8y + (-9x)$

22. $16m + (-56)$ **23.** $t + (-34s)$ **24.** $-18x + (-5y)$

25. $9x - (-7)$ **26.** $23x - (-12y)$ **27.** $-18m - (-n)$

28. $-65k - (-15h)$ **29.** $73x + 9y$ **30.** $(9a \cdot 6b) \cdot 12c$

31. $(12x + 9y) + 89z$ **32.** $(-12b)(32a)$

33. $(6x + 90) + \dfrac{y}{8}$, etc.   **34.** $9x \cdot (8z \cdot 12y)$, etc.

35. $\dfrac{96x}{184y}$ **36.** $\dfrac{171a}{9b}$ **37.** $\dfrac{714}{35xy}$ **38.** $\dfrac{90xz}{16xy}$ **39.** $\dfrac{y}{x}$

40. $\dfrac{x}{2}$ **41.** $\dfrac{5}{-2x}$ **42.** $\dfrac{1}{7}$ **43.** $5 + |x|$ **44.** $-x + |x|$

45. $-|2a|$ **46.** $|a + b|$ **47.** $|p| + |q|$ **48.** $|x - y| > 5$

49. $3|p| = 8$ **50.** $|x + y| < (x + y)^2$

51. Examples are $x - 3y$, $4x - 2y$, $7x - y$.

52. No, $9 @ 2 = 3(9) - 2 = 27 - 2 = 25$,
$2 @ 9 = 3(2) - 9 = 6 - 9 = -3$; $-3 \neq 25$

53. Yes, $a \oplus b = a^2 + b^2$, $4 \oplus 2 = 4^2 + 2^2 = 16 + 4 = 20$,
$2 \oplus 4 = 2^2 + 4^2 = 4 + 16 = 20$; $20 = 20$, commutative

54. $4.2 + (-6.8) = -2.6$ **55.** $6(-9) = -54$

56. $-3.2(-4.1) = 13.12$ **57.** $-8 \div 2 = -4$

58. $-4 - 9 = -13$ **59.** $-9(-3) = 27$

60. $40 \div (-5) = -8$ **61.** $-8 + 27 = 19$

62. $7 - 11 = -4$ **63.** $-\frac{3}{16} + \frac{8}{16} = \frac{5}{16}$

64. $\frac{3}{5} - \frac{3}{10} = \frac{6}{10} - \frac{3}{10} = \frac{3}{10}$ **65.** $-\frac{4}{5} \cdot \frac{1}{2} = -\frac{4}{10} = -\frac{2}{5}$

66. $-5 = \frac{-5}{1}$ **67.** $9.1 = 9\frac{1}{10} = \frac{91}{10}$ **68.** $\frac{2.8}{4.5} = \frac{28}{45}$

69. $\frac{-0.2}{0.05} = -4 = \frac{-4}{1}$ **70.** Rational   **71.** Irrational

72. Rational   **73.** Rational   **74.** Irrational

p. 19   CALCULATOR INVESTIGATION

a. As x gets smaller, the value of the expression gets larger.
b. As n gets smaller, the expression gets larger.

pp. 20–23   1-4 TRY THIS

a. $5(x + 9) = 5x + 45$ **b.** $8(y - 10) = 8y - 80$
c. $a(x + y - z) = ax + ay - az$ **d.** $2l + 2w = 2(l + w)$
e. $ac - ay = a(c - y)$ **f.** $6x - 12 = 6(x - 2)$
g. $-25y + 15w + 5 = 5(-5y + 3w + 1)$
h. $9x + 11x = (9 + 11)x = 20x$
i. $5x - 12x = (5 - 12)x = -7x$
j. $22x - 2.5 + 1.4x + 6.4 = 22x + (-2.5) + 1.4x + 6.4$
= $22x + 1.4x + (-2.5) + 6.4$
= $(22 + 1.4)x + (-2.5) + 6.4 = 23.4x + 3.9$
k. $-(7x) = -1(7x) = (-1 \cdot 7)x = -7x$
l. $-(y + 10) = -1(y + 10) = -1(y) + (-1)(10)$
= $y + (-10) = -y - 10$
m. $-(-3x - 2y + 1) = -1(-3x - 2y + 1)$
= $-1(-3)x + (-1)(-2)y + (-1)(1) = 3x + 2y - 1$
n. $-(-2x - 5z + 24) = 2x + 5z - 24$
o. $-\left(\frac{1}{4}t + 41w - rd + 23\right) = -\frac{1}{4}t - 41w + rd - 23$
p. $6x - (3x - 8) = 6x + [-(3x - 8)] = 6x + [(-3x) + 8]$
= $6x - 3x + 8 = 3x + 8$
q. $x - 2(y + x) = x + [-2(y + x)] = x + [-2(x + y)]$
= $x + [-2x - 2y] = x - 2x - 2y = -x - 2y$
r. $3x - 5(2y - 4x) = 3x - [5(2y - 4x)] = 3x - (10y - 20x)$
= $3x + [-1(10y - 20x)] = 3x + [-10y + 20x]$
= $3x + [20x - 10y] = 23x - 10y$
s. $15x - \{2[2(x - 5) - 6(x + 3)] + 4\}$
= $15x - \{2[2x - 10 - 6x - 18] + 4\}$
= $15x - \{4x - 20 - 12x - 36 + 4\}$
= $15x - \{4x - 12x - 20 - 36 + 4\}$
= $15x - \{-8x - 52\} = 23x + 52$
t. $9a + \{3a - 2[(a - 4) - (a + 2)]\}$
= $9a + \{3a - 2[a - 4 - a - 2]\}$
= $9a + \{3a - 2[-6]\} = 9a + \{3a + 12\}$
= $9a + 3a + 12 = 12a + 12$

pp. 24–25   1-4 EXERCISES

1. $3a + 3$ **2.** $8x + 8$ **3.** $4x - 4y$ **4.** $9a - 9b$

5. $-10a - 15b$ **6.** $-6c - 10d$ **7.** $2ab - 2ac + 2ad$

8. $5xy - 5xz + 5xw$ **9.** $2\pi rh + 2\pi r$ **10.** $P + Prt$

11. $\frac{1}{2}ha + \frac{1}{2}hb$ **12.** $\pi r + \pi rs$ **13.** $8(x + y)$

14. $7(a + b)$ **15.** $9(p - 1)$ **16.** $12(x - 1)$ **17.** $7(x - 3)$

18. $6(y - 6)$ **19.** $x(y + 1)$ **20.** $a(b + 1)$

21. $2(x - y + z)$ **22.** $3(x + y - z)$ **23.** $3(x + 2y - 1)$

24. $4(a + 2b - 1)$ **25.** $a(b + c - d)$ **26.** $x(y - z - w)$

27. $\pi r(r + s)$ **28.** $\frac{1}{2}h(a + b)$ **29.** $9a$ **30.** $12x$

31. $-3b$ **32.** $-3c$ **33.** $15y$ **34.** $14x$ **35.** $11a$

36. $14x$ **37.** $-8t$ **38.** $-5x$ **39.** $10x$ **40.** $-6x$

41. $13a - 10b$ **42.** $2c + 10d$ **43.** $7a + 9b$

44. $22x + 18$ **45.** $9p + 12$ **46.** $5a - 21b$ **47.** $4b$

48. $5x$ **49.** $-a - 2$ **50.** $-b - 9$ **51.** $-b + 3$

52. $-x + 8$ **53.** $-t + y$ **54.** $-r + s$ **55.** $-a - b - c$

56. $-x - y - z$ **57.** $-8x + 6y - 13$ **58.** $-9a + 7b - 24$

59. $2c - 5d + 3e - 4f$ **60.** $4x - 8y + 5w - 9z$

61. $-a - 5$ **62.** $-4x - 9$ **63.** $m + 1$ **64.** $a + 3$

65. $5d - 12$ **66.** $13x - 16$ **67.** $-7x + 14$

68. $-15y - 45$ **69.** $-9x + 21$ **70.** $-12y + 24$

71. $44a - 22$ **72.** $47b - 51$ **73.** -190 **74.** -1449

75. $-12y - 145$ **76.** $-11b + 217$ **77.** $17x + 14y + 129$

78. $23a - 18b + 184$ **79.** $-42x - 360y - 276$

80. $-102y - 980z - 301$ **81.** $-[-(-(-9))] = -[-(9)] = 9$

82. $-\{-[-(-(-10))]\} = -\{-[-(10)]\} = -\{10\} = -10$

83. $-\{-[-(-(-(-8)))]\} = -\{-[-(-8)]\} = -\{-[8]\} = \{8\} = 8$

84. $\frac{2}{3}[2(x + y) + 4(x + 4y)] = \frac{2}{3}[2x + 2y + 4x + 16y]$

$= \frac{2}{3}[6x + 18y] = 4x + 12y$

85. $-4[3(x - y - z) - 3(2x + y - 5z)]$
= $-4[3x - 3y - 3z - 6x - 3y + 15z]$
= $-4[-3x - 6y + 12z] = 12x + 24y - 48z$

86. $P = \$120$, $r = 12\%$, $t = 1$ yr;
$P + Prt = 120 + (120)(0.12)(1) = 120 + 14.40$
= $\$134.40$

87. $P = \$500$, $r = 14\%$, $t = \frac{1}{2}$ yr;

$P + Prt = 500 + (500)(0.14)\left(\frac{1}{2}\right) = 500 + (250)(0.14)$

= $500 + 35.00 = \$535.00$

88. No, not distributive.
$|-3 + 5| \neq |-3| + |5|$

89. $[-7a - b) - (a + 5b)] - \left[2\left(a + \frac{1}{2}b\right) + 3\left(7a - \frac{5}{3}b\right)\right]$

= $[-7a + b - a - 5b] - [2a + b + 21a - 5b]$
= $-8a - 4b - 23a + 4b = -31a$

90. $0.01\{0.1(x - 2y) - [0.001(3x + y) - (0.2x - 0.1y)]\}$
$- (x - y) = 0.01\{0.1x - 0.2y - [0.003x + 0.001y - 0.2x$
$+ 0.1y]\} - x + y$
= $0.01\{0.1x - 0.2y - [-0.197x + 0.101y]\} - x + y$
= $0.01\{0.1x - 0.2y + 0.197x - 0.101y\} - x + y$
= $0.01\{0.297x - 0.301y\} - x + y$
= $0.00297x - 0.00301y - x + y$
= $-0.99703x + 0.99699y$

91. The answer is positive for an even number of minus signs, negative for an odd number of minus signs.

92. $(x - y)(y - x) = (x - y)(-1)(-y + x)$
= $(x - y)(-1)(x - y) = -1(x - y)(x - y) = -(x - y)^2$

93. $-(s - 4t)$, $s = -4$, $t = 15$; $-(-4 - 60) = -(-64) = 64$

94. $-3x + 6y = 6y - 3x$ **95.** $8x(9x \cdot 17z) = (9y \cdot 8x)17z$

96. $12\% = 0.12$ **97.** $50\% = 0.5$ **98.** $\frac{2}{5} = \frac{4}{10} = 0.4$

99. $\frac{1}{0.7} = 0.7\overline{)1.000000} = 1.\overline{428571}$ (quotient 1.42857)

100. $10\% = \frac{1}{10}$ **101.** $0.45 = \frac{45}{100} = \frac{9}{20}$

102. $10.5 = \frac{105}{10} = 10\frac{1}{2}$ or $\frac{21}{2}$ **103.** $125\% = \frac{125}{100} = \frac{5}{4}$

pp. 27–28   1-5 TRY THIS

a.
$$13 = -25 + y$$
$$13 + (25) = -25 + 25 + y$$
$$13 + 25 = 0 + y$$
$$38 = y$$

b.
$$-4x = 64$$
$$-\frac{1}{4} \cdot -4x = -\frac{1}{4} \cdot 64$$
$$1 \cdot x = -\frac{64}{4}$$
$$x = -16$$

c.
$$9x - 4 = 8$$
$$9x - 4 + 4 = 8 + 4$$
$$9x = 12$$
$$\frac{1}{9} \cdot 9x = 12 \cdot \frac{1}{9}$$
$$1 \cdot x = \frac{12}{9}$$
$$x = \frac{4}{3}$$

d.
$$-\frac{1}{4}y + \frac{3}{2} = \frac{1}{2}$$
$$-\frac{1}{4}y + \frac{3}{2} + \left(-\frac{3}{2}\right) = \frac{1}{2} + \left(-\frac{3}{2}\right)$$
$$-\frac{1}{4}y = -1$$
$$-\frac{1}{4}y \cdot -4 = -1 \cdot -4$$
$$1 \cdot y = 4$$
$$y = 4$$

e.
$$5y - 8 = -8 - 4y - 4$$
$$5y + 4y = -8 + 8 - 4$$
$$9y = -4$$
$$y = -\frac{4}{9}$$

f.
$$5x - 12 - 3x = 7x - 2 - x$$
$$2x - 6x = 12 - 2$$
$$-4x = 10$$
$$x = -\frac{10}{4} = -\frac{5}{2}$$

pp. 28–29   1-5 EXERCISES

1. -3 **2.** -9 **3.** 40 **4.** 26 **5.** -15 **6.** -56

7. -14 **8.** 4 **9.** 39 **10.** 4 **11.** 7 **12.** -9

13. -9 **14.** 8 **15.** -9 **16.** 40 **17.** 36 **18.** $\frac{81}{2}$

19. 18 **20.** 19 **21.** 5 **22.** 9 **23.** 24 **24.** 14

25. 7 **26.** 11 **27.** 8 **28.** 12 **29.** 21 **30.** 13

31. 2 **32.** -2 **33.** 2 **34.** -6 **35.** $\frac{18}{5}$ **36.** 4

37. 0 **38.** 0 **39.** $\frac{4}{5}$ **40.** -8

41. All real numbers.   **42.** $x = 0$ **43.** No solution

44. All real numbers.   **45.** $w = 0$

46.
$$4x - 2x - 2 = 2x$$
$$0x = 2$$
$$x = \frac{2}{0}; \text{ No solution}$$

47.
$$2x + 4 + x = 4 + 3x$$
$$3x + 4 = 4 + 3x; \text{ All real numbers}$$

48.
$$-\frac{3}{4}x + \frac{1}{8} = -2$$
$$-\frac{3}{4}x + \frac{1}{8} - \frac{1}{8} = -2 - \frac{1}{8}$$
$$-\frac{3}{4}x = -2\frac{1}{8}$$
$$-\frac{4}{3} \cdot -\frac{3}{4}x = -\frac{17}{8} \cdot -\frac{4}{3}$$
$$1 \cdot x = \frac{68}{24}$$
$$x = \frac{17}{6}$$

49.
$$y - \frac{1}{3}y - 15 = 0$$
$$\frac{2}{3}y - 15 + 15 = 15$$
$$\frac{2}{3}y = 15$$
$$\frac{3}{2} \cdot \frac{2}{3}y = 15 \cdot \frac{3}{2}$$
$$1 \cdot y = \frac{45}{2}$$
$$y = \frac{45}{2}$$

50.
$$\frac{3x}{2} + \frac{5x}{3} - \frac{13x}{6} - \frac{2}{3} = \frac{5}{6}$$
$$\frac{9x + 10x - 13x}{6} = \frac{5}{6} + \frac{2}{3}$$
$$\frac{6x}{6} = \frac{5 + 4}{6}$$
$$x = \frac{9}{6} = \frac{3}{2}$$

51.
$$3x + 2^2 = x + 3^2$$
$$3x + 4 = x + 9$$
$$2x = 5$$
$$x = \frac{5}{2}$$

52.
$$2^3 \cdot x + 9 = 2^2 \cdot x - 23$$
$$8x + 9 = 4x - 23$$
$$4x = -32$$
$$x = -\frac{32}{4} = -8$$

53. True, if $a + c = b + c$, then $a + c + (-c) = b + c + (-c)$. It is given $a \ne b$, hence $a + c \ne b + c$.

54.
$$2(x - 3) + 5 = 3(x - 2) + 5$$
$$2x - 6 + 5 = 3x - 6 + 5$$
$$2x - 1 \ne 3x - 1; \text{ No}$$

55.
$$3(x - 4) = 3x - 4$$
$$3x - 12 \ne 3x - 4; \text{ No}$$

56.
$$\frac{3y - 1}{y^2 - y} - \frac{2}{y - 1} = \frac{1}{y}$$
$$\frac{3y - 1}{y(y - 1)} - \frac{2}{y - 1} = \frac{1}{y}$$
$$\frac{3y - 1 - 2y}{y(y - 1)} = \frac{1}{y}$$
$$\frac{y - 1}{y(y - 1)} = \frac{1}{y}$$
$$\frac{1}{y} = \frac{1}{y}; \text{ Yes}$$

57.
$$7(x - 3) \cdot \frac{1}{7} = x - 3$$
$$7 \cdot \frac{1}{7} = 1$$
therefore, $x - 3 = x - 3$; Yes

58. $4a - 7(3a - 9) = 4a - 21a + 63 = -17a + 63$

59.
$$[5(a + 2) + 6a] - \{8[2(5a - 4)] + 17a\}$$
$$= 5a + 10 + 6a - \{8(10a - 8) + 17a\}$$
$$= 5a + 10 + 6a - \{80a - 64 + 17a\}$$
$$= 5a + 10 + 6a - 80a + 64 - 17a$$
$$= -86a + 74$$

60. $9c + 12b - 3a = 3(3c + 4b - a)$

61. $8n - 8m = 8(n - m)$ **62.** $14t - 7 = 7(2t - 1)$

63. $6n + 12 = 6(n + 2)$ **64.** $2m + 4n; m = -6, n = 2$
$$2(-6) + 4(2) = -12 + 8 = -4$$

65. $4(m + 3) - 15; m = 2$
$$4(2 + 3) - 15 = 4(5) - 15 = 20 - 15 = 5$$

66. Answers may vary.   **67.** Answers may vary.

Ex: $2x \cdot \frac{1}{2}x \cdot 5y \cdot \frac{1}{5}y$ Ex: $2x + \frac{1}{2}x + 5y + \frac{1}{5}y$

p. 29   PROBLEM FOR PROGRAMMERS

```
1    REM      Chapter 1 Problem
10   INPUT "For ax + b = c,
enter a, b, c "; A, B, C
20   PRINT "x = "; (C - B) / A
30   END
```

a. $x = 0.70 + (14)(4)(0.12)$
$x = 0.70 + 6.72$
$x = 7.42$
The total cost of a 14-km ride is $7.42.

b. $x = 1.82 - [(1995 - 1930)0.0035]$
$x = 1.82 - [(65)0.0035]$
$x = 1.82 - 0.2275$
$x = 1.5925$
The record will be about 1.593 min, or 1 min, 35.5 s.

c. $y \cdot \dfrac{1}{100} \cdot 350{,}000 = 525{,}000$

$y \cdot \dfrac{350{,}000}{100} = 525{,}000$

$3500y = 525{,}000$

$y = \dfrac{525{,}000}{3500}$

$y = 150$; 150% of the station's goal was reached.

d. $y \cdot \dfrac{1}{100} \cdot \dfrac{3}{4} = \dfrac{1}{12}$

$\dfrac{3y}{400} = \dfrac{1}{12}$

$36y = 400$

$y = 11.1$; 11.1% of your original amount of rye flour will remain.

1. $14.75   **2.** $18.13   **3.** $169.60   **4.** $4.00

5. 48,000,000 mi   **6.** $11.00   **7.** 341 m

8. $2{,}516{,}667$ km^2 **9.** $622.45°F$ **10.** $520{,}000{,}000$ km^2

11. 37.2 seconds   **12.** 39.6 seconds   **13.** 43.92 seconds

14. 964,000   **15.** $\approx 85.3\%$ **16.** $\approx 5.3\%$

17. $\approx 288.2\%$ **18.** $744

19.
x = original price
$x - 50$ = sale price
$10(x - 50) = 5x + 900$
$10x - 500 = 5x + 900$
$5x = 1400$ cents
$x = 2.80
The original price of a disk was $2.80.

20.
x = Delia's age
$6x$ = Reggie's age
$6x + 2$ = Kirra's age

$\dfrac{x + 6x + 6x + 2}{3} = 9\dfrac{1}{3}$

$x + 6x + 6x + 2 = 28$
$13x + 2 = 28$
$13x = 26$
$x = 2$
Delia is 2; Reggie is 6(2) or 12; Kirra is 6(2) + 2 or 14.

21. $\dfrac{3}{5}$ of the wall area remains after the 1st gallon.

The second gallon covers $\dfrac{1}{3}$ of the wall area.

$\dfrac{1}{3}$ is what percent of $\dfrac{3}{5}$?

$\dfrac{1}{3} \div \dfrac{3}{5} = \dfrac{1}{3} \times \dfrac{5}{3} = \dfrac{5}{9} \approx 0.556$

The second gallon will cover $\approx 55.6\%$ of the remaining wall area.

22. Answers will vary. For example, the price of a VCR was cut to $10 more than half of its original price. Its original price was $570. What is the new price?

23.
$55t = 40(t + 2)$
$55t = 40t + 80$
$15t = 80$

$t = 5\dfrac{1}{3}$ hours

8:00 + 5:20 = 1:20 p.m.
The Heisers expect to overtake the Wongs at 1:20 p.m.

24. Let x = ones digit,
$x + 3$ = tens digit.

$2[10(x + 3) + x] - \dfrac{1}{2}(10x + x + 3) = 108$

$2[10x + 30 + x] - \dfrac{1}{2}(11x + 3) = 108$

$2[11x + 30] - \dfrac{1}{2}(11x + 3) = 108$

$22x + 60 - 5.5x - 1.5 = 108$
$16.5x + 58.5 = 108$
$16.5x = 49.5$
$x = 3$
$x + 3 = 6$

The original number is 63.

25. $11t + 4t = 15t$ **26.** $3c + 4c - 9c = -2c$

27. $x - 9x = -8x$

28. $y + 6 = 14$
$y = 8$

29. $2m + 5 = 4$
$2m = -1$

$m = -\dfrac{1}{2}$

30. $34t - 7 = 10$
$34t = 17$

$t = \dfrac{17}{34} = \dfrac{1}{2}$

31. $\dfrac{1}{2}r + 13 = 20$

$\dfrac{1}{2}r = 7$

$r = 14$

32. $6a + 18 = 54$
$6a = 36$
$a = 6$

33. $-9w = 27$

$w = -\dfrac{1}{9}(27)$

$w = -3$

34. $5(n - 2) = -65$
$5n - 10 = -65$
$5n = -55$
$n = -11$

35. $9c + 4 = 31 + 18c$
$-9c = 27$
$c = -3$

36. $4w + 5 = 6w + 1$
$-2w = -4$
$w = 2$

37. $8 - 5y = 11y - 8$
$16 = 16y$

$y = \dfrac{16}{16} = 1$

38. $7c + 15 = 16c - 3$
$18 = 9c$
$c = 2$

a. $(8x)^3 = 8x \cdot 8x \cdot 8x = 512x^3$
b. $(-3m)^4 = -3m \cdot -3m \cdot -3m \cdot -3m = 81m^4$
c. $9^2 = (9 \cdot 9) = 81$

d. $9(3y)^3 = 9 \cdot 3y \cdot 3y \cdot 3y = 243y^3$ **e.** $10^{-4} = \dfrac{1}{10^4} = \dfrac{1}{10{,}000}$

f. $(-4)^{-3} = \dfrac{1}{(-4)^3} = -\dfrac{1}{64}$ **g.** $(5y)^{-3} = \dfrac{1}{(5y)^3} = \dfrac{1}{125y^3}$

h. $(-5)^{-4} = \dfrac{1}{(-5)^4} = \dfrac{1}{625}$ **i.** $\dfrac{1}{4^3} = 4^{-3}$ **j.** $\dfrac{1}{-5^4} = (-5)^{-4}$

k. $\dfrac{1}{(2x)^6} = (2x)^{-6}$ **l.** $\dfrac{1}{(-8x)^{-5}} = (-8x)^5$

1. $27y^3$ **2.** $16x^4$ **3.** 1   **4.** -81 **5.** $6m$ **6.** $180x^2$

7. -125 **8.** -64 **9.** $\dfrac{1}{9^5}$ **10.** $\dfrac{1}{16^2}$ **11.** $\dfrac{1}{11^1}$

12. $\frac{1}{(-4)^3}$ **13.** $\frac{1}{(6x)^3}$ **14.** $\frac{1}{(-5y)^2}$ **15.** $\frac{1}{(3m)^4}$ **16.** $\frac{x^2}{y^3}$

17. $\frac{2a^2}{b^5}$ **18.** $\frac{a^2c^4}{b^3d^5}$ **19.** x^2y^2 **20.** $\frac{a^2y^2}{x^3b^3}$ **21.** 3^{-4}

22. 9^{-2} **23.** $(-16)^{-2}$ **24.** $(-8)^{-6}$ **25.** $(5y)^{-3}$

26. $(5x)^{-5}$ **27.** $\frac{y^{-4}}{3}$ **28.** $\frac{b^{-3}}{4}$ **29.** $\frac{x^2y}{z^7} = x^2yz^{-7}$

30. $\frac{20}{4xy} = 5x^{-1}y^{-1}$ **31.** $\frac{b^{-10}}{x^{10}y^{10}} = b^{-10}x^{-10}y^{-10}$

32. $\frac{a^2b^{-3}}{x^3y^{-2}} = a^2b^{-3}x^{-3}y^2$

33. $x^{-4}; x = 2$

$$2^{-4} = \frac{1}{2^4} = \frac{1}{16}$$

34. $m^{-3} + 7; m = -0.25 = -\frac{1}{4}$

$$\frac{1}{\left(-\frac{1}{4}\right)^3} + 7 = \frac{1}{\left(-\frac{1}{64}\right)} + 7 = -64 + 7 = -57$$

35. $x^3 + y^{-2}; x = -3, y = 4$

$$(-3) \cdot (-3) \cdot (-3) + \left(\frac{1}{4} \cdot \frac{1}{4}\right) = -27 + \frac{1}{16} = -26\frac{15}{16}$$

36. Answers may vary. Examples are 1, 1; 4, 2; 9, 30

37. $(-2)^0 - (-2)^3 - (-2)^{-1} + (-2)^4 - (-2)^{-2}$

$$= 1 - (-2)(-2)(-2) - \left(-\frac{1}{2}\right)$$

$$+ (-2)(-2)(-2)(-2) - \left(-\frac{1}{2}\right)\left(-\frac{1}{2}\right)$$

$$= 1 - (-8) + \frac{1}{2} + 16 - \frac{1}{4}$$

$$= 1 + 8 + 16 + \frac{1}{2} - \frac{1}{4} = 25\frac{1}{4}$$

38. $2(6^1 \cdot 6^{-1} - 6^{-1} \cdot 6^0) = 2\left(6 \cdot \frac{1}{6} - \frac{1}{6} \cdot 1\right)$

$$= 2\left(1 - \frac{1}{6}\right) = 2\left(\frac{5}{6}\right) = \frac{10}{6} = \frac{5}{3}$$

39. $\frac{(-8)^{-2} \cdot (8 - 8^0)}{2^{-6}} = \frac{\left(-\frac{1}{8}\right)\left(-\frac{1}{8}\right) \cdot (8-1)}{\frac{1}{64}} = \frac{\frac{1}{64} \cdot 7}{\frac{1}{64}} = 7$

40. $(x - y)(x^{y-x} - y^{x-y}); \quad x = 1, y = -2$
$(1 - (-2))(1^{-2-1} - (-2)^{1-(-2)}) = (1 + 2)(1^{-3} + 2^3)$
$$= (3)(1 + 8) = 3(9) = 27$$

41. $7^5 = 16,807$ **42.** $ab + mb - xb = b(a + m - x)$

43. $17 - 51y^2 = 17(1 - 3y^2)$

44. $20k^3a^2 - 16k^2a^3 = 4k^2a^2(5k - 4a)$

45. $9 - 3y = 5y - 23$ **46.** $5c + 3c = 16$
     $32 = 8y$ $8c = 16$

     $y = \frac{1}{8} \cdot 32$ $c = \frac{1}{8} \cdot 16$

     $y = 4$ $c = 2$

47. $-21t = 21$

     $t = -\frac{1}{21} \cdot 21$

     $t = -1$

pp. 38–42   **1-8 TRY THIS**

a. $8^{-3}8^7 = 8^{-3+7} = 8^4 = 4096$
b. $(-3x^{-4})(25x^{-10}) = (-3)(25)x^{-4-10} = -75x^{-14}$

c. $(5x^{-3}y^4)(-2x^{-9}y^{-2})(5)(-2)x^{-3-9}y^{4-2} = -10x^{-12}y^2$
d. $(5x^my^n)(6x^7y^4) = (5)(6)x^{m+7}y^{n+4} = 30x^{m+7}y^{n+4}$
e. $\frac{5^4}{5^{-2}} = 5^{4-(-2)} = 5^6$ **f.** $\frac{10^{-2}}{10^{-8}} = 10^{-2+8} = 10^6$
g. $\frac{42y^7x^6}{-21y^{-3}x^{10}} = -2y^{7+3}x^{6-10} = -2y^{10}x^{-4}$, or $\frac{-2y^{10}}{x^4}$
h. $\frac{33a^5b^{-2}}{22a^7b^{-4}} = \frac{3a^{5-7}b^{-2+4}}{2} = \frac{3b^2}{2a^2}$, or $\frac{3}{2}a^{-2}b^2$
i. $\frac{56y^{ab}}{-7y^{ab}} = -8y^{ab-ab} = -8y^0 = -8$ **j.** $(3^7)^6 = 3^{42}$

k. $(x^2)^{-7} = x^{-14}$ or $\frac{1}{x^{14}}$ **l.** $(t^{-3})^{-2} = t^6$

m. $(2xy)^3 = 8x^3y^3$ **n.** $(-2x^4y^2)^5 = -32x^{20}y^{10}$

o. $(10x^{-4}y^7z^{-2})^3 = 1000x^{-12}y^{21}z^{-6}$, or $\frac{1000y^{21}}{x^{12}z^6}$

p. $\left(\frac{x^{-3}}{y^4}\right)^{-3} = \frac{x^9}{y^{-12}} = x^9y^{12}$ **q.** $\left(\frac{3x^2y^{-3}}{2y^{-1}}\right)^2\frac{9x^4y^{-6}}{4y^{-2}} = \frac{9x^4}{4y^4}$, or $\frac{9x^4y^{-4}}{4}$

r. $3 \cdot 2^2 + 4 = (3 \cdot 4) + 4 = 12 + 4 = 16$
s. $3 \cdot (2^2 + 4) = 3 \cdot (4 + 4) = 3(8) = 24$
t. $\{[(3 + 2)^2 - 3 + 2^2 + 1] \div 9\}^3$
$$= \{[(5)^2 - 3 + 4 + 1] \div 9\}^3$$
$$= \{[25 - 3 + 4 + 1] \div 9\}^3$$
$$= (27 \div 9)^3 = 3^3 = 27$$

pp. 42–43   **1-8 EXERCISES**

1. 5^9 **2.** 6^8 **3.** $8^{-4} = \frac{1}{8^4}$ **4.** $9^{-2} = \frac{1}{9^2}$ **5.** $8^{-6} = \frac{1}{8^6}$

6. $9^{-7} = \frac{1}{9^7}$ **7.** $b^{-3} = \frac{1}{b^3}$ **8.** a **9.** a^3 **10.** 1

11. $6x^5$ **12.** $18y^5$ **13.** $-28m^5n^5$ **14.** $-18x^7y$

15. $-14x^{-11} = \frac{-14}{x^{11}}$ **16.** $-24v^{-12}v = -\frac{24y}{x^{12}}$

17. $-30(x^{a+5})(y^{b+9})$ **18.** $72(x^{m+n})(y^{p+6})$ **19.** 6^5 **20.** 7^5

21. 4^5 **22.** 5^{11} **23.** $\frac{1}{10^9}$ **24.** $\frac{1}{12^{12}}$ **25.** 9^2 **26.** $\frac{1}{2^2} = \frac{1}{4}$

27. a^5 **28.** y^9 **29.** 1   **30.** $-3ab^2$ **31.** $-\frac{4x^9}{3y^2}$

32. $-\frac{7b^2}{4a^4}$ **33.** $\frac{3x^3}{2y^2}$ **34.** $\frac{7a^{16}b^5}{9}$ **35.** $-10x^{5a}$ **36.** $6x^{11y}$

37. $-3x^{a-2}y^{b-5}$ **38.** $4x^{4a}y^{-11}$ **39.** 4^6 **40.** 5^{20} **41.** 8^{-12}

42. 9^{-12} **43.** 6^{12} **44.** 7^{40} **45.** $27x^6y^6$ **46.** $32a^{15}b^{20}$

47. $\frac{1}{4}x^{-6}y^8$ **48.** $-\frac{1}{27}a^{-6}b^{15}$ **49.** $\frac{1}{36}a^4b^{-6}c^{-2}$

50. $\frac{1}{4096}x^{16}y^{-20}z^{-8}$ **51.** $\frac{1}{4^9 \cdot 3^{12}}$ **52.** $\frac{1}{5^6 \cdot 4^9}$ **53.** $\frac{8x^9y^3}{27}$

54. $\frac{5^4y^{24}}{(-4)^4x^{20}}$ **55.** 10   **56.** 18   **57.** 24   **58.** -65

59. $\frac{(2^{-2})^{-4}(2^3)^{-2}}{(2^{-2})^2(2^5)^{-3}} = \frac{(2^8)(2^{-6})}{(2^{-4})(2^{-15})} = \frac{2^2}{2^{-19}} = 2^{2+19} = 2^{21}$

60. $\left[\frac{(-3x^2y^5)^{-3}}{(2x^4y^{-8})^2}\right]^2 = \left[\frac{2^2x^{-6}y^{-15}}{3^3x^{-8}y^{16}}\right]^2 = \frac{2^4x^{-12}y^{-30}}{3^6x^{-16}y^{32}} = \frac{2^4x^4}{3^6y^{62}}$

61. $\left[\left(\frac{a^{-2}}{b^7}\right)^{-3} \cdot \left(\frac{a^4}{b^{-3}}\right)^2\right]^{-1} = \left[\left(\frac{a^b}{b^{-21}} \cdot \frac{a^8}{b^{-6}}\right)\right]^{-1}\left(\frac{a^{14}}{b^{-27}}\right)^{-1}$

$$= \frac{a^{-14}}{b^{27}} = \frac{1}{a^{14}b^{27}}$$

62. $\left[\frac{(-4x^2y^3)(-2xy)^{-2}}{(4x^4y^2)(-2x^5y)}\right]^{-2} = \left[\frac{-4x^2y^3}{(4x^4y^2)(-2xy)^2(-2x^5y)}\right]^{-2}$

$$= \left[\frac{-4x^2y^3}{(4x^4y^2)(-2x^5y)(4x^2y^2)}\right]^{-2}$$

$$= \left[\frac{-4x^2y^3}{-32x^{11}y^5}\right]^{-2} = \left[\frac{1}{8x^9y^2}\right]^{-2}$$
$$= 64x^{18}y^4$$

63. $\dfrac{(3xy)^2(6x^2y^2) \times 4x^4y^4}{(4xy)^2 \times 13x^2y^2} = \dfrac{9x^2y^2(6x^2y^2) \cdot 4x^4y^4}{(16x^2y^2)(13x^2y^2)} = \dfrac{216x^8y^8}{208x^4y^4}$
$$= \dfrac{27x^4y^4}{26}$$

64. Suppose we substitute $-n$ for n in Theorem 1-11, which states

$(a^m b^n)^p = a^{mp}b^{mp}$. Then $(a^m b^{-n})^p = a^{mp}b^{-np}$. Since $b^{-n} = \dfrac{1}{b^n}$ and

$b^{-np} = \dfrac{1}{b^{np}}$, we have $\left(a^m \cdot \dfrac{1}{b^n}\right)^p = a^{mp} \cdot \dfrac{1}{b^{np}}$, or $\left(\dfrac{a^m}{b^n}\right)^p = \dfrac{a^{mp}}{b^{np}}$.

65. $(x^y \cdot x^{2y})^3 = (x^{3y})^3 = x^{9y}$ **66.** $(y^x \cdot y^{-x})^4 = (y^0)^4 = (1)^4 = 1$

67. $(a^{b+x} \cdot a^{b-x})^3 = (a^{2b})^3 = a^{6b}$

68. $(m^{a-b} \cdot m^{2b-a})^p = (m^b)^p = m^{bp}$

69. $(x^b y^a \cdot x^a y^b)^c = (x^{a+b} \cdot y^{a+b})^c = x^{ca+cb}y^{ca+cb}$

70. $(m^{x-b}n^{x+b})^x(m^b n^{-b})^x = (m^{x^2-bx}n^{x^2+bx})(m^{bx}n^{-bx}) = m^{x^2}n^{x^2}$

71. $\left[\dfrac{(2x^a y^b)^3}{(-2x^a y^b)^2}\right]^2 = \dfrac{(2x^a y^b)^6}{(-2x^a y^b)^4} = \dfrac{(2x^a y^b)^6}{(2x^a y^b)^4} = (2x^a y^b)^2$
$$= 4x^{2a}y^{2b}$$

72. $\left[\left(\dfrac{x^r}{y^s}\right)^2\left(\dfrac{x^{2r}}{x^{3s}}\right)^{-2}\right]^{-2} = \left[\left(\dfrac{x^{2r}}{y^{2s}}\right)\left(\dfrac{x^{-4r}}{y^{-6s}}\right)\right]^{-2} = \left(\dfrac{x^{-2r}}{y^{-4s}}\right)^{-2} = \dfrac{x^{4r}}{y^{8s}}$

73. $t(3t + 5); \; t = 4$
$4[3(4) + 5] = 4(12 + 5) = 4(17) = 68$

74. $-3x + 7 + 2x; \; x = 5$
$-3(5) + 7 + 2(5) = -15 + 7 + 10 = 2$

75. $\left(-\dfrac{1}{2}\right)\left(-\dfrac{2}{3}\right)\left(-\dfrac{3}{4}\right)\left(-\dfrac{4}{5}\right) = \dfrac{24}{120} = \dfrac{1}{5}$

76. $(200)(-4)\left(-\dfrac{3}{2}\right)(0)(0.974) = 0$

77. $3(x + 17) - 3(17 + x) = 3x + 51 - 51 - 3x = 0$

78. $7(14x - 15x) + 4(x + x) = 7(-x) + 4(2x) = -7x + 8x = x$

pp. 45–46   1-9 TRY THIS

a. $460,000,000,000 = 4.6 \times 10^{11}$
b. $0.000000001235 = 1.235 + 10^{-9}$
c. $0.0000000000000000000000017 = 1.7 \times 10^{-24}$ g
d. $150,000,000 = 1.5 \times 10^8$ km
e. $7.893 \times 10^{11} = 789,300,000,000$
f. $5.67 \times 10^{-5} = 0.0000567$
g. $(9.1 \times 10^{-17})(8.2 \times 10^3) = 74.62 \times 10^{-14} = 7.462 \times 10^{-13}$
h. $\dfrac{4.2 \times 10^5}{2.1 \times 10^2} = 2.0 \times 10^3$
i. $\dfrac{1.1 \times 10^{-4}}{2.0 \times 10^{-7}} = 0.55 \times 10^3 = 5.5 \times 10^2$
j. $830,000,000 \times \dfrac{0.0000012}{3,100,000} = \dfrac{(8.3 \times 10^8)(1.2 \times 10^{-6})}{3.1 \times 10^6}$
$$\approx \dfrac{(8)(1)}{3} \times 10^{8+(-6)-6} \approx 3 \times 10^{-4}$$

pp. 47–48   1-9 EXERCISES

1. 4.7×10^{10} **2.** 2.6×10^{12} **3.** 8.63×10^{17}
4. 9.57×10^{17} **5.** 1.6×10^{-8} **6.** 2.63×10^{-7}
7. 7×10^{-11} **8.** 9×10^{-11} **9.** 9.11×10^{-28} gram
10. 2.4×10^8 **11.** 4.8×10^{-10} eu   **12.** 1.3×10^{-9} ft^3
13. 1×10^{-9} **14.** 3.664×10^9 mi   **15.** 3.0699×10^5 lbs
16. $\$3.6628 \times 10^{12}$ **17.** 0.0004 **18.** 0.00005

19. $673,000,000$ **20.** $92,400,000$ **21.** 0.0000000008923
22. 0.07034 **23.** 9.66×10^{-5} **24.** 3.38×10^{-4}
25. 1.3338×10^{-11} **26.** 2.6732×10^{-11} **27.** 8.32×10^{10}
28. 3.1411×10^{16} **29.** 2.5×10^3 **30.** 1.5×10^3
31. 5×10^{-4} **32.** 3×10^{-5} **33.** 3×10^{11} **34.** 4×10^{-16}
35. 4.5×10^2 **36.** 1.6×10^{-17} **37.** 1.1×10^{11}
38. 3×10^1 **39.** 6.5×10^1 **40.** 1×10^3
41. $3,871.5403 = 3.8715403 \times 10^3$
42. $510.0036 = 5.100036 \times 10^2$
43. $20,000,000.029 = 2.0000000029 \times 10^7$
44. $71.428571 = 7.1428571 \times 10^1$
45. $0.0025 \times 5.8 \times 10^{14}$
$= 2.5 \times 10^{-3} \times 5.8 \times 10^{14} \approx 1.4 \times 10^{12}$ mi
46. $C = 2\pi r$
$C = 2(3.14)(9.3 \times 10^7) = 58.404 \times 10^7 \approx 5.8 \times 10^8$ mi
47. $500,000,000$
48. $8 \times 10^{-90}, \; 0.9 \times 10^{-90}$; 8×10^{-90} is larger by 7.1×10^{-90}.

49. $\dfrac{1 \text{ ft}}{\text{sec}} = \dfrac{\frac{1}{5280} \text{ mi}}{\frac{1}{3600} \text{ hr}} = \dfrac{1}{5280} \div \dfrac{1}{3600} = \dfrac{1}{5280} \times \dfrac{3600}{1}$
$$= 0.681818 \approx 6.82 \times 10^{-1} \text{ mi/h}$$

50. $\dfrac{25 \text{ ft}}{\text{sec}} = \dfrac{\frac{25}{2580} \text{ mi}}{\frac{1}{3600} \text{ hr}} = \dfrac{5}{1056} \div \dfrac{1}{3600} = \dfrac{5}{1056} \times 3600$
$$\approx 17.04 \approx 1.7 \times 10 \text{ mi/hr}$$

51. $\dfrac{5280 \text{ ft}}{226.32 \text{ sec}} = 23.329798 \approx 2.33 \times 10^1$ ft/sec
52. $\dfrac{300 \text{ ft}}{9.0 \text{ sec}} = 33.3 = 3.33 \times 10^1$ ft/sec
53. $\begin{array}{r} 3.33 \times 10^1 \\ -2.33 \times 10^1 \\ \hline 1 \times 10^1 \end{array} \quad \dfrac{1 \times 10^1}{2.33 \times 10^1} = 0.42918 \approx 42.9\%$
54. 1.86×10^5 mi/sec $\cdot 5.28 \times 10^3$ ft/mi $\approx 9.82 \times 10^8$ ft/sec
9.82×10^8 ft/sec $\cdot 60$ sec/min $\cdot 60$ min/hr $\cdot 24$ hr/day
$= 8.485 \times 10^{13}$ ft/day $\approx 8.5 \times 10^{13}$ ft/day
55. 1.86×10^5 mi/sec $\cdot 1.76 \times 10^3$ yd/mi $= 3.27 \times 10^8$ yd/sec
$\dfrac{100}{3.27 \times 108} = 3.05 \times 10^{-7}$ sec
56. $6y - [8 - 11(9y + 4)] = 6y - [8 - 99y - 44]$
$\qquad\qquad\qquad\qquad\qquad = 6y + 36 + 99y = 105y + 36$
57. $[9(y + 2) + 8y] - \{6[(3y - 5) - (6y + 11)] + 16\}$
$[9y + 18 + 8y] - \{6[3y - 5 - 6y - 11] + 16\}$
$= 9y + 18 + 8y - 18y + 30 + 36y + 66 - 16$
$= 35y + 98$
58. $\left(\dfrac{5^{-6}}{3^2}\right)^4 = \dfrac{5^{-24}}{3^8} = 5^{-24}3^{-8}$, or $\dfrac{1}{5^{24}3^8}$
59. $[6(9 - 4) + 3] \cdot (4 - 3 \cdot 8) \div 5$
$= [6(5) + 3] \cdot (-20) \div 5$
$= [30 + 3] \cdot -4$
$= 33 \cdot -4 = -132$
60. $(4t)^3 = 64t^3$ **61.** $(-t)^2 = t^2$
62. $5(-3m)^2 = 5(9m^2) = 45m^2$
63. $4a - 5b - 6a + 3b = -2a - 2b = -2(a + b)$
64. $9m - 5n + 3n - 12m = -3m - 2n = -(3m + 2n)$
65. $\dfrac{wx}{2} - \dfrac{yx}{2} = \dfrac{x}{2}(w - y)$

66. $\frac{1}{3a} + \frac{1}{6b} - \frac{1}{12c} = \frac{1}{12}\left(\frac{4}{a} + \frac{2}{b} - \frac{1}{c}\right)$

67. $\frac{3y}{5} + 6 = 3\left(\frac{y}{5} + 2\right)$

pp. 50–51   1-10 TRY THIS

a. Associative property of addition
b. Distributive property
c. Identity property of addition
d. Identity property of multiplication and property of multiplicative inverses
e. No, the set has no multiplicative inverse.
f. Yes   **g.** Distributive property

pp. 52–53   1-10 EXERCISES

1. Distributive property

2. Associative property of addition

3. Property of additive inverses

4. Distributive property

5. None; subtraction theorem

6. Associative property of multiplication

7. Associative property of addition

8. None; division theorem

9. Symmetric property of equality

10. Reflexive property of equality

11. Commutative property of addition

12. Associative property of addition

13. None; subtraction theorem

14. Distributive property

15. Commutative property of addition

16. Transitive property of equality

17. No, there is no additive or multiplicative inverse.

18. No, there is no multiplicative inverse.

19. Yes   **20.** No, there is no additive inverse.

21. Associative property of addition.
    Identity property of addition.

22. 1. Commutative, associative properties of addition
    2. Property of additive inverses
    3. Identity property of addition
    4. Property of additive inverses

23. 1. $-(a - b) = -(a + (-b))$ Theorem 1-1
    2. $= -1(a + (-b))$ Identity property of multiplication
    3. $= (-1)(a) + (-1)(-b)$ Distributive property
    4. $= -a + b$ Multiplicative property of -1
    5. $= b + (-a)$ Commutative property of addition
    6. $= b - a$ Theorem 1-1
    7. $-(a - b) = b - a$ Statements 1–6

24. 1. $a - a = a + (-a)$ Theorem 1-1
    2. $a - a = 0$ Additive inverse property
    3. $a + (-a) = 0$ Theorem 1-1
    4. $a = -(-a)$ Reflexive property of equality, Statements 1–3

25. 1. $\frac{a}{b} = \frac{a \cdot 1}{1 \cdot b}$ Identity property of multiplication

    2. $= \frac{a}{1} \cdot \frac{1}{b}$ Associative property of multiplication

    3. $= a \cdot \frac{1}{b}$ Identity property of multiplication

    4. $\frac{a}{b} = a \cdot \frac{1}{b}$ Statements 1–3

26. 1. $\frac{a}{a} = a \cdot \frac{1}{a}$ Division theorem

    2. $a \cdot \frac{1}{a} = 1$ Property of multiplicative inverses

    3. $\frac{a}{a} = 1$ Statements 1–2

27. Yes, No, No, Yes, Yes   **28.** Yes

29. $5x(y + 3z) = 5xy + 15xz$ **30.** $3a(2b + 3c) = 6ab - 9ac$

31. $2w(1 - 3x) = 2w - 6xw$ **32.** $6^2 \cdot 6^4 = 6^6$

33. $m^{-8} \cdot m^5 = m^{-3}$ **34.** $y^3 \cdot y^{-7} \cdot y^2 = y^{-2} = \frac{1}{y^2}$

35. $x^{13} \cdot x^{-9} = x^4$

36. $m - 31 = 19$ **37.** $z - 64 = 241$ **38.** $23x = 368$
    $m = 50$ $z = 305$ $x = \frac{368}{23}$

                                           $x = 16$

39. $-\frac{7}{16}y = \frac{7}{4}$

    $y = \frac{7}{4}\left(-\frac{16}{7}\right) = -\frac{112}{28} = -4$

40. $0.85 \times x = 238$ **41.** $44 - 25 = 19$
     $x = \frac{238}{0.85}$ $19 \cdot 2 = 38$
                         $38 + 10 = \$48$
     $x = 280$ $\$280$

42. $\frac{1.28 \times 10^{-3}}{6.4 \times 10^{-1}} = \frac{1.28}{6.4} \times \frac{10^{-3}}{10^{-1}} = .2 \times 10^{-2} = 2 \times 10^{-3}$

43. $\frac{7.29 \times 10^2}{8.1 \times 10^4} = \frac{7.29}{8.1} \times \frac{10^2}{10^4} = .9 \times 10^{-2} = 9 \times 10^{-3}$

44. $\frac{10^4}{8 \times 10^4} = \frac{1}{8} \times \frac{104}{104} = 0.125 \times 10^0 = 1.25 \times 10^{-1}$

p. 55   1-11 PROBLEM SOLVING: STRATEGIES

1. Strategy: Draw a diagram

   A wheel has 16 spokes if there are 16 spaces between spokes.

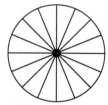

2. Strategy: Write an equation
   125 is what percent of 280?
   $125 = x \cdot 280$

   $\frac{125}{280} = x$

   280
   $0.446 \approx x$
   The child's dosage is about 45% of the adult dosage.

3. Strategy: Draw a diagram

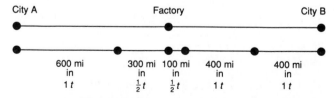

   Let $t =$ the time it takes Train A to go 600 miles. Train B goes 400 miles in t. Train A goes the 900 miles to the factory in $\frac{3}{2}t$.

   Train B goes $\frac{3}{2} \cdot 400$ miles, or 600 miles in this time, so Train B needs a 300-mile head start.

4. Strategy: Write an equation
p = population 10 years ago
$1.35p$ = population today
$1.35p = 105,030$
$p \approx 77,800$
The population 10 years ago was 77,800.

5. Strategy: Draw a diagram

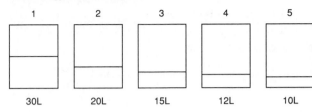

There will be 10 liters at 5 hours, so there would be less than 10 liters after 5 hours.

pp. 56–58   CHAPTER 1 SUMMARY AND REVIEW

1. No, no, yes, yes   **2.** Rational   **3.** Rational   **4.** Rational

5. $-\dfrac{7}{5} + \left(-\dfrac{13}{10}\right) = -\dfrac{14}{10} + \left(-\dfrac{13}{10}\right) = -\dfrac{27}{10}$

6. $8.7 + (-7.9) = 0.8$ **7.** $-\dfrac{7}{8} + \dfrac{5}{6} = -\dfrac{21}{24} + \dfrac{20}{24} = -\dfrac{1}{24}$

8. $-\dfrac{6}{7} - \left(-\dfrac{2}{5}\right) = -\dfrac{6}{7} + \dfrac{2}{5} = -\dfrac{30}{35} + \dfrac{14}{35} = -\dfrac{16}{35}$

9. $-13.8 - 5.9 = -13.8 + (-5.9) = -19.7$

10. $16.56 - (-15.72) = 16.56 + 15.72 = 32.28$

11. $-4(2.1) = -8.4$ **12.** $-\dfrac{5}{6}\left(-\dfrac{18}{7}\right) = \dfrac{15}{7} = 2\dfrac{1}{7}$

13. $(-6.01)(-1000) = 6010$ **14.** $-\dfrac{18.72}{3.6} = -5.2$

15. $-\dfrac{7}{8} \div \left(-\dfrac{3}{4}\right) = -\dfrac{7}{8}\left(-\dfrac{4}{3}\right) = \dfrac{7}{6}$

16. $\dfrac{2}{3} \div \left(-\dfrac{8}{5}\right) = \dfrac{2}{3}\left(-\dfrac{5}{8}\right) = -\dfrac{5}{12}$

17. $4x \cdot 7y = 7y \cdot 4x$ **18.** $\left(\dfrac{x}{3} + 5\right) + 2y = \dfrac{x}{3} + (5 + 2y)$

19. $\dfrac{10(x-2)}{24(x-2)} = \dfrac{5}{12}$

20. $2x + 1 - 3y$ for $x = 3$ and $y = -2$
$= 2(3) + 1 - 3(-2)$
$= 6 + 1 - (-6)$
$= 7 + 6$
$= 13$

21. $-(x - 1 - y)$
$= -(3 - 1 - (-2))$
$= -(2 + 2)$
$= -4$

22. $2|x - 4| - |y| = 2|3 - 4| - |-2|$
$= 2|-1| - 2$
$= 2(1) - 2$
$= 0$

23. $6(x - y - z) = 6x - 6y - 6z$

24. $-3(k - 2t + w) = -3k + 6t - 3w$

25. $12\left(\dfrac{a}{2} - \dfrac{b}{3} + \dfrac{c}{4}\right) = \dfrac{12a}{2} - \dfrac{12b}{3} + \dfrac{12c}{4} = 6a - 4b + 3c$

26. $ax - ay = a(x - y)$

27. $-20x + 5y - 10z = -5(4x - y + 2z)$

28. $2ab - 6ac - 8ad = 2a(b - 3c - 4d)$

29. $-6y - 8z - 4y + 3z = -10y - 5z$

30. $2.3y - 8 - 4y + 7.6x - 5.8x = 1.8x - 1.7y - 8$

31. $-(r - t) = -r + t$ **32.** $-(-4x + 3y) = 4x - 3y$

33. $2a - (3a - 4) = 2a - 3a + 4 = -a + 4$

34. $y - 3(2y - 4x) = y - 6y + 12x = -5y + 12x$

35. $5x - [2x - (3x + 2)] = 5x - [2x - 3x - 2]$
$= 5x - [-1x - 2]$
$= 5x + 1x + 2 = 6x + 2$

36. $8x - \{2x - 3[(x - 4) - (x + 2)]\}$
$= 8x - \{2x - 3[x - 4 - x - 2]\}$
$= 8x - \{2x - 3(-6)\} = 8x - 2x - 18 = 6x - 18$

37. $5x - 3 = 27$
$5x - 3 + 3 = 27 + 3$
$5x = 30$
$5x \cdot \dfrac{1}{5} = 30 \cdot \dfrac{1}{5}$
$x = 6$

38. $6y + 3 = y - 12$
$6y + 3y = y - 12 - y$
$5y + 3 = -12$
$5y + 3 - 3 = -12 - 3$
$5y = -15$
$\dfrac{1}{5} \cdot 5y = \dfrac{1}{5} \cdot -15$
$y = -3$

39. $3t - 8 - t = 7t - 8 + 2t$
$2t - 8 = 9t - 8$
$2t - 8 - 2t = 9t - 8 - 2t$
$-8 = 7t - 8$
$-8 + 8 = 7t - 8 + 8$
$0 = 7t$
$0 \cdot \dfrac{1}{7} = 7t \cdot \dfrac{1}{4}$
$0 = t$

40. $7(27) + (840 \times .35)$
$= 189 + 294 = \$483$

41. $\dfrac{1}{8^3} = 8^{-3}$ **42.** $\dfrac{1}{(-3)^2} = (-3)^{-2}$ **43.** $\dfrac{1}{3y^5} = (3y^5)^{-1}$, or $\dfrac{y^{-5}}{3}$

44. $\dfrac{1}{(3y)^5} = (3y)^{-5}$ **45.** $(-4)^{-3} = \dfrac{1}{(-4)^3} = -\dfrac{1}{64}$

46. $\dfrac{x^3}{y^{-4}} = x^3y^4$ **47.** $3a^3c^{-5} = \dfrac{3a^3}{c^5}$ **48.** $w^3x^{-2}y^5z^{-6} = \dfrac{w^3y^5}{x^2z^6}$

49. $(7x^3y^{-1})(-2x^{-4}y) = \dfrac{7x^3}{y} \cdot -\dfrac{2y}{x^4} = -\dfrac{14}{x}$

50. $\dfrac{a^{-2}}{a^{-4}} = \dfrac{a^4}{a^2} = a^2$ **51.** $-\dfrac{54x^{-5}y^4}{18x^3y^{-1}} = -\dfrac{3y^5}{x^8}$

52. $(-3x^2y^3)^4 = 81x^8y^{12}$ **53.** $(-2x^3)^{-3} = \dfrac{1}{(-2x^3)^3} = -\dfrac{1}{8x^9}$

54. $\left(-\dfrac{2x^3y^{-6}}{3y^4}\right)^2 = \left(\dfrac{4x^6y^{-12}}{9y^8}\right) = \dfrac{4x^6}{9y^{20}}$

55. $80,000,000 = 8 \times 10^7$ **56.** $0.00000074 = 7.4 \times 10^{-7}$

57. $(1.8 \times 10^{12})(2.1 \times 10^{-3}) = 3.78 \times 10^9$

58. $\dfrac{6.25 \times 10^{-6}}{2.5 \times 10^3} = 2.5 \times 10^{-9}$

pp. 58–59   CHAPTER 1 TEST

1. Irrational   **2.** Rational   **3.** Irrational   **4.** Rational
5. Irrational   **6.** Rational   **7.** Irrational   **8.** Rational

9. $-4.9 + (-3.08) = -7.98$

10. $\dfrac{9}{16} + \left(-\dfrac{7}{10}\right) = \dfrac{45}{80} + \left(-\dfrac{56}{80}\right) = -\dfrac{11}{80}$

11. $-\dfrac{4}{9} + \dfrac{7}{12} = -\dfrac{16}{36} + \dfrac{21}{36} = \dfrac{5}{36}$

12. $-0.74 - (-11.8) = -0.74 + 11.8 = 11.06$

13. $\frac{8}{9} - \left(-\frac{5}{6}\right) = \frac{16}{18} + \frac{15}{18} = \frac{31}{18}$

14. $-30.7 - 6.1 = -30.7 + (-6.1) = -36.8$

15. $-0.9(3.1) = -2.79$ **16.** $-\frac{2}{7}\left(-\frac{10}{3}\right) = \frac{20}{21}$

17. $0.43(-100) = -43$ **18.** $\frac{4}{3} \div \left(-\frac{8}{15}\right) = \frac{4}{3}\left(-\frac{15}{8}\right) = -\frac{5}{2}$

19. $-\frac{6.09}{0.29} = -21$ **20.** $\frac{-7.2}{-0.4} = 18$

21. $(x \cdot 2y) \cdot 8z = x \cdot (2y \cdot 8z)$ **22.** $5y + 3x = 3x + 5y$

23. $\frac{12xyz}{8y} = \frac{3xz}{2}$

24. $3x - y + 7$ **25.** $-(y - x + 1)$
  $= 3(-1) - (5) + 7$ $= -(5 - (-1) + 1)$
  $= -3 + (-5) + 7$ $= -(5 + 1 + 1)$
  $= -8 + 7$ $= -7$
  $= -1$

26. $3|x + 1| - |y|$ **27.** $-4(x - y + 8)$
  $= 3|-1 + 1| - |5|$ $= -4x + 4y - 32$
  $= 3 \cdot 0 - 5$
  $= 0 - 5$
  $= -5$

28. $a(3b - c - d) = 3ab - ac - ad$

29. $6\left(3x - \frac{y}{2} - \frac{z}{4}\right) = 18x - 3y - \frac{3}{2}z$

30. $2xy - xz = x(2y - z)$

31. $6ab - 8bc - 4bd = 2b(3a - 4c - 2d)$

32. $3xy - 6xyz = 3xy(1 - 2z)$ **33.** $9x - 5x - 6x + 7x = 5x$

34. $3.2y - 9 - 5y + 4.8x - 5.7x = -1.8y - 0.9x - 9$

35. $-(-2t) = 2t$ **36.** $-(-5 - 3x) = 5 + 3x$

37. $-(6 - 5y) = -6 + 5y$

38. $3t - (5t - 6) = 3t - 5t + 6 = -2t + 6$

39. $9y - [4y - (2y - 5)] = 9y - [4y - 2y + 5]$
  $= 9y - [2y + 5] = 7y - 5$

40. $2x - 5(3 - 2x) - 5 = 2x - 15 + 10x - 5 = 12x - 20$

41. $3 - 2x = 7$
  $(-3) + 3 - 2x = 7 + (-3)$
  $-2x = 4$

  $-\frac{1}{2} \cdot (-2x) = 4 \cdot \left(-\frac{1}{2}\right)$

  $x = -2$

42. $5y - 2 = y - 10$
  $5y - 2 + 2 - y = y - 10 + y + 2$
  $4y = -8$

  $\frac{1}{4} \cdot 4y = \frac{1}{4} \cdot (-8)$

  $y = -2$

43. $5x - 2 + 3x = 9 - 2x - 11$
  $8x - 2 = -2x - 2$
  $8x - 2 + 2 + 2x = -2x - 2 + 2 + 2x$
  $6x = 0$

  $\frac{1}{6} \cdot 6x = \frac{1}{6} \cdot 0$

  $x = 0$

44. $\$10 + \$7.50(3.5) = \$10 + \$26.25 = \$36.25$ **45.** $\frac{1}{a^3} = a^{-3}$

46. $3^2 = \frac{1}{3^{-2}}$ **47.** $x^n = \frac{1}{x^{-n}}$ **48.** $\frac{1}{3x^2} = (3x^2)^{-1} = \frac{x^{-2}}{3}$

49. $(-2)^{-2} = \frac{1}{(-2)^2} = \frac{1}{4}$ **50.** $x^{-2}y^3 = \frac{y^3}{x^2}$ **51.** $2a^{-2}c^4 = \frac{2c^4}{a^2}$

52. $\frac{1}{-x^{-5}} = -x^5$ **53.** $(-5x^3)(-6x^5) = 30x^8$

54. $\frac{63y^4z^9}{9y^2z^3} = 7y^2z^{12}$ **55.** $\frac{2x^{-4}}{8x^{-2}} = \frac{1}{4x^2}$

56. $(-4x^2y^4)^3 = -64x^6y^{12}$ **57.** $(-3x^4y)^{-3} = \frac{1}{-27x^{12}y^3} = -\frac{1}{27x^{12}y^3}$

58. $\left(\frac{3x^2y^3}{12x^{-1}y^{-6}}\right)^2 = \left(\frac{x^3y^9}{4}\right)^2 = \frac{x^6y^{18}}{16}$ **59.** $90,400,000 = 9.04 \times 10^7$

60. $0.00000752 = 7.52 \times 10^{-6}$

61. $\frac{2 \times 10^{-4}}{5 \times 10^3} = \frac{2}{5} \times \frac{10^{-4}}{10^3} = .4 \times 10^{-7} = 4 \times 10^{-8}$

CHAPTER 2

p. 60   READY FOR EQUATIONS AND INEQUALITIES?

1. $>$ **2.** $=$ **3.** $<$ **4.** 0 **5.** -3.6 **6.** $-\frac{13}{24}$

7. 13 **8.** -22.9 **9.** $-\frac{2}{21}$ **10.** -24 **11.** -47

12. 6 **13.** $3(x - 6)$ **14.** $5(x - 2y + 3)$

15. $2(2x - 4 + 3y)$ **16.** $4a(3b + c - 4d)$ **17.** $5y - 20$

18. $2a - ab$ **19.** $cx + cy - cz$ **20.** $-3x + 3y - 3$

21. $-x$ **22.** $7y + 2$

pp. 62–64   2-1 TRY THIS

a. $\frac{2}{3} - \frac{5}{6}y = \frac{1}{3}$

  $6\left(\frac{2}{3} - \frac{5}{6}y\right) = 6\left(\frac{1}{3}\right)$ Multiplying by 6

  $6 \cdot \frac{2}{3} - 6 \cdot \frac{5}{6}y = 6 \cdot \frac{1}{3}$

  $4 - 5y = 2$
  $-5y = -2$

  $y = \frac{2}{5}$

b. $6.3x - 9.6 = 3$
  $10(6.3x - 9.6) = 10(3)$ Multiplying by 10
  $63x - 96 = 30$
  $63x = 126$
  $x = 2$

c. $3(y - 1) - 1 = 2 - 5(y + 5)$
  $3y - 3 - 1 = 2 - 5y - 25$
  $3y - 4 = -5y - 23$
  $8y = -19$

  $y = -\frac{19}{8}$

d. $(x - 19)(x + 5) = 0$
  $x - 19 = 0$ or $x + 5 = 0$
    $x = 19$ or $x = -5$
  Solution set is $\{19, -5\}$.

e. $x(3x - 17) = 0$
  $x = 0$ or $3x - 17 = 0$
        $3x = 17$

        $x = \frac{17}{3}$

  Solution set is $\left\{0, \frac{17}{3}\right\}$.

f. $(9x + 2)(-6x + 3) = 0$
  $9x + 2 = 0$ or $-6x + 3 = 0$
    $9x = -2$ or $-6x = -3$

$$x = -\frac{2}{9} \quad \text{or} \quad x = \frac{-3}{-6}$$

$$x = \frac{1}{2}$$

Solution set is $\left\{ -\frac{2}{9}, \frac{1}{2} \right\}$.

pp. 64–65   **2-1 EXERCISES**

1. $\frac{4}{3}$ **2.** 2   **3.** $\frac{37}{5}$ **4.** $\frac{49}{9}$ **5.** 13   **6.** $-\frac{502}{100}$

7. 2   **8.** 3   **9.** 2   **10.** 1   **11.** 7   **12.** 7   **13.** 5

14. 7   **15.** $-\frac{51}{31}$ **16.** $\frac{39}{14}$ **17.** 5   **18.** 6   **19.** 2

20. $-\frac{37}{5}$ **21.** $\{-2, 5\}$ **22.** $\{-4, 8\}$ **23.** $\{8, 9\}$ **24.** $\{3, 7\}$

25. $\left\{ \frac{3}{2}, \frac{2}{3} \right\}$ **26.** $\left\{ \frac{4}{3}, \frac{1}{4} \right\}$ **27.** $\{0, 8\}$ **28.** $\{0, 5\}$

29. $x(x - 1)(x + 2) = 0$
$x = 0 \quad \text{or} \quad x - 1 = 0 \quad \text{or} \quad x + 2 = 0$
$\qquad\qquad\qquad x = 1 \quad \text{or} \qquad x = -2$
Solution set is $\{0, 1, -2\}$.

30. $y(y - 4)(y + 2) = 0$
$y = 0 \quad \text{or} \quad y - 4 = 0 \quad \text{or} \quad y + 2 = 0$
$\qquad\qquad\qquad y = 4 \quad \text{or} \qquad y = -2$
Solution set is $\{0, 4, -2\}$.

31. $\frac{1}{7}(a - 3)(7a + 4) = 0$

$(a - 3) = 0 \quad \text{or} \quad (7a + 4) = 0$
$\quad a = 3 \quad \text{or} \qquad 7a = -4$

$$a = -\frac{4}{7}$$

Solution set is $\left\{ 3, -\frac{4}{7} \right\}$.

32. $24\left(\frac{x}{6} - \frac{1}{3} \right) = x - 24$

$4x - 8 = x - 24$
$3x = -16$

$$x = -\frac{16}{3}$$

33. $0.5(x - 2) - 2(x - 5) = 0.4(x - 5) - 5(x - 2)$
$10[0.5(x - 2) - 2(x - 5)] = 10[0.4(x - 5) - 5(x - 2)]$
$\qquad\qquad\qquad\qquad\qquad\qquad\qquad$ (Multiplying by 10)
$5(x - 2) - 20(x - 5) = 4(x - 5) - 50(x - 2)$
$5x - 10 - 20x + 100 = 4x - 20 - 50x + 100$
$-15x + 90 = -46x + 80$
$31x = -10$

$$x = -\frac{10}{31}$$

34. $8x + 3 = c$
$\quad 8x = c - 3$

$$x = \frac{c - 3}{8}$$

35. $16x - 4 = f$
$\quad 16x = f + 4$

$$x = \frac{f + 4}{16}$$

36. $cx + 3h = 5a$
$\quad cx = 5a - 3h$

$$x = \frac{5a - 3h}{c}$$

37. $7x - 3 = ax + 5b$
$7x - ax = 5b + 3$
$x(7 - a) = 5b + 3$

$$x = \frac{5b + 3}{7 - a}$$

38. $ax - bx = 12$
$\quad x(a - b) = 12$

$$x = \frac{12}{a - b}$$

39. $5x + ax = 19$
$\quad x(5 + a) = 19$

$$x = \frac{19}{5 + a}$$

40. By first clearing decimals, the equation is easily solvable. Without first clearing the decimals, long division of decimals has to be done. With a calculator, there is no need to clear decimals.

41. Answers may vary. Ex: $x^2 + x - 56 = 0$

42.
$x \cdot x = 1$
$x^2 - 1 = 0$
$(x + 1)(x - 1) = 0$
$x + 1 = 0$
or $x - 1 = 0$
$x = -1$ or $x = 1$
Solution set is $\{-1, 1\}$.

43.
$x \cdot x = x$
$x^2 - x = 0$
$x(x - 1) = 0$
$x = 0 \quad \text{or} \quad x - 1 = 0$
$x = 1$
Solution set is $\{0, 1\}$.

44. $x(x - 1) = x$
$x^2 - x - x = 0$
$x^2 - 2x = 0$
$x(x - 2) = 0$
$x = 0 \quad \text{or} \quad x - 2 = 0$
$\qquad\qquad\qquad x = 2$
Solution set is $\{0, 2\}$.

45. $x(x - 1) = x(x + 1)$
$x^2 - x = x^2 + x$
$-2x = 0$
$x = 0$
Solution set is $\{0\}$.

46.   a. {the integers greater than or equal to zero}.
b. {the positive integers}
c. {the negative integers}
d. {the even integers and zero}
e. {the integers that are multiples of 10 and zero}
f. {the integers}

47. $4^2 \cdot 4^3 \cdot x^0 =$
$4^{2+3} \cdot 1 =$
4^5

48. $(-y)^3(-y)^2 =$
$(-y)^{3+2} =$
$(-y)^5$

49. $x^3 \cdot x^{-5} =$
$x^{3-5} =$
x^{-2}

50. $(3c^2)^3 =$
$27c^6$

51. $390,000 = 3.9004 \times 10^5$

52. $0.000421 = 4.21 \times 10^{-4}$

53. $24.072 = 2.4072 \times 10^1$

54. $4.03 \times 10^{-6} = 0.00000403$

55. $-8.22 \times 10^6 = -8,220,000$

pp. 66–68   **2-2 TRY THIS**

a. $x + 3x = 23$
$\quad 4x = 23$

$x = 5\frac{3}{4}; 3x = 17\frac{1}{4}$

$5\frac{3}{4}$ ft; $17\frac{1}{4}$ ft

b. $6 - 7x = 5x$
$\quad 6 = 12x$

$\frac{1}{2} = x$

The number is $\frac{1}{2}$.

c. $3x + 30 = 5x$
$\quad 30 = 2x$
$\quad 15 = x$; \$15

d. $x - 0.25x = 93$
$0.75x = 93$
$x = 124$; \$124

e. $x + 0.12x = 812$
$1.12x = 812$
$x = 725$; \$725

f. $x + (x + 2) = 36$
$2x + 2 = 36$
$2x = 34$
$x = 17$; 17 and 19

g. (1) $2x + 2(x + 1) = 46$
$2x + 2x + 2 = 46$
$4x = 44$
$x = 11$
Harold 22; Gunther 24

(2) Harold 11; Gunther 12

pp. 69–70   **2-2 EXERCISES**

1. 8 cm; 4 cm   **2.** 6 m; 4 m;   **3.** $1\frac{3}{5}$ m; $2\frac{2}{5}$ m

4. $1\frac{7}{8}$ m; $3\frac{1}{8}$ m   **5.** 5   **6.** 8   **7.** \$45   **8.** \$500

9. \$650   **10.** \$800   **11.** $32°, 96°, 52°$ **12.** $25°, 100°, 55°$

13. Length is 31 m; width is 17m

14. Length is 110 m; width is 45 m

15. 11, 13, and 15   **16.** 14 and 16   **17.** \$15,000

18. \$43,000   **19.** \$3644

20. Ground school portion costs \$375; flight portion costs \$1875

21. $(93 + 89 + 72 + 80 + 96 + x) \div 6 = 88$
$(430 + x) \div 6 = 88$
$6(430 + x) \div 6 = 6(88)$
$430 + x = 528$
$x = 98; 98\%$

22. Let x be the initial population. Then in three consecutive years the population changes by a factor of 1.2, 1.3, and 0.8, respectively:
$\{([(x)1.2]1.3)0.8\} = [(x)1.2](1.04) = 1.248x \approx 1.25x$, a 25% increase over x.

23. $x, 3x - 6, \dfrac{2}{3}(3x - 6) + 2$ are the three numbers.

$x + (3x - 6) + \left[\dfrac{2}{3}(3x - 6) + 2\right] = 172$

$6x - 6 - 2 = 172$
$6x - 8 = 172$
$6x = 180$
$x = 30$
$(3x - 6)$ is the largest number: $3(30) - 6 = 90 - 6 = 84$

24. The price of each TV set can be represented as $x + 60(n - 1)$, where x is the price of the least expensive set and n is the set's ranking in order from least to most expensive set. Solve for x.
$x + 60(2 - 1) + x + 60(6 - 1) = x + 60(13 - 1)$
$x + 60 + x + 60(5) = x + 60(12)$
$2x + 60 + 300 = x + 720$
$2x - x = 720 - 60 - 300$
$x = 360; \$360$

25. 7.5% of 2000 gallons: $0.075(2000) = 150$ "gallons" salt. 150 gallons is 7% of what amount? $150 \text{ g} = 0.07x$

$$\frac{150 \text{ g}}{0.07} = x$$

$2143 \text{ g} = x$
Add 143 gallons of fresh water to the tank.

26. $x + (x + 2) = 137$
$2x + 2 = 137$
$2x = 135$

$x = \dfrac{135}{2}$; not an integer. No solution.

27. Since the perimeter of one square is 12 cm longer than that of another square, we know that each side of the larger square is $\dfrac{12}{4} = 3$ cm longer than the sides of the smaller square.
$(x + 3)^2 = x^2 + 39$
$x^2 + 6x + 9 = x^2 + 39$; $6x + 9 = 39$; $6x = 30$; $x = 5$
The smaller square is of side 5, the larger of side $5 + 3 = 8$.
The perimeters of the squares are $4(5) = 20$ cm, $4(8) = 32$ cm.

28. Answers may vary. Ex: A 36-ft rope is cut into two pieces. One piece is 3 ft longer than the other. How long are the pieces?

29. Let l represent the number of years in Diophantos' life. Then he is $\left[\left(\dfrac{1}{6} + \dfrac{1}{12} + \dfrac{1}{7}\right)l + 5\right]$ years older than his son. Since his son died at half his father's final age, 4 years before Diophantos did, he is also $\left(\dfrac{l}{2} - 4\right)$ years older than his son.

$\left[\left(\dfrac{1}{6} + \dfrac{1}{12} + \dfrac{1}{7}\right)l + 5 = \dfrac{l}{2} - 4\right]; \left(\dfrac{14 + 7 + 12}{84}\right)l + 9 = \dfrac{42l}{84};$

$\dfrac{9(84)}{84} = \left(\dfrac{42 - 14 - 7 - 12}{84}\right)l; 9(84) = (42 - 33)l;$

$9(84) = 9l; 84 = l.$

30. $x^2 + 3 + (-2x^2) + 4 = -x^2 + 7$

31. $x^4 + x^2y + 2x^4 + 2yx^2 - xy^2 = 3x^4 + 3x^2y - xy^2$

32. $a^3b + 2a^2b - 6ab^2 - 3a^3b + 2ab^2 - a^2b$
$= -2a^3b + a^2b - 4ab^2$

33. $a^2 + b^2 + c^2 - (-a^2 - b^2 - c^2) = 2a^2 + 2b^2 + 2c^2$

34. $2x^2 + 2x$
$= 2x(x + 1)$

35. $3a^2b^2 - 9ab^2$
$= 3ab^2(a - 3)$

36. $12a^2 - 4a^3$
$= 4a^2(3 - a)$

37. $30x^2y + 6xy^2 - 12x^3y$
$= 6xy(5x + y - 2x^2)$

38. $3x - [2x - 3 - (-x - 4)]$
$= 3x - 2x + 3 - x - 4$
$= -1$

39. $(8.2 \times 10^{-3})(2 \times 10^5) = 16.4 \times 10^2$
$= 1.64 \times 10^3$

p. 71   2-3 TRY THIS

a. $A = \dfrac{1}{2}bh$ **b.** $P = \dfrac{3}{5}(c + 10)$

$2A = bh$ $\dfrac{5}{3}P = \dfrac{5}{3} \cdot \dfrac{3}{5}(c + 10)$

$\dfrac{2A}{h} = b$ $\dfrac{5}{3}P = c + 10$

$\dfrac{5}{3}P - 10 = c$

c. $H = 2r + 3m$ **d.** $Q = 3r + 5p$
$H - 2r = 3m$ $-p = 3r - Q$

$\dfrac{H - 2r}{3} = m$ $p = -\dfrac{(3r - Q)}{5}$

$p = \dfrac{Q - 3r}{5}$

e. $T = Q + Qiy$ **f.** $x = G - Gr^2p$
$T = Q(i + iy)$ $x = G(1 - r^2p)$

$Q = \dfrac{T}{1 + iy}$ $G = \dfrac{x}{1 - r^2p}$

p. 72   2-3 EXERCISES

1. $l = \dfrac{A}{W}$ **2.** $w = \dfrac{A}{l}$ **3.** $I = \dfrac{W}{E}$ **4.** $E = \dfrac{W}{I}$

5. $m = \dfrac{F}{a}$ **6.** $a = \dfrac{F}{m}$ **7.** $t = \dfrac{I}{Pr}$ **8.** $P = \dfrac{I}{rt}$

9. $m = \dfrac{E}{c^2}$ **10.** $c^2 = \dfrac{E}{m}$ **11.** $l = \dfrac{P - 2w}{2}$

12. $w = \dfrac{P - 2l}{2}$ **13.** $a^2 = c^2 - b^2$ **14.** $b^2 = c^2 - a^2$

15. $r^2 = \dfrac{A}{\pi}$ **16.** $\pi = \dfrac{A}{r^2}$ **17.** $F = \dfrac{9}{5}C + 32$

18. $h = \dfrac{2}{11}W + 40$ **19.** $r^3 = \dfrac{3V}{4\pi}$ **20.** $\pi = \dfrac{3V}{4r^3}$

21. $h = \dfrac{2A}{(a + b)}$ **22.** $b = \dfrac{2A}{h} - a$ or $\dfrac{2A - ha}{h}$

23. $m = \dfrac{rF}{v^2}$ **24.** $v^2 = \dfrac{rF}{m}$

25. $s = v_1t + \dfrac{1}{2}at^2$

$s - v_1t = \dfrac{1}{2}at^2$

$2(s - v_1t) = at^2$

$\dfrac{2(s - v_1t)}{t^2} = a$

$a = \dfrac{2(s - v_1t)}{t^2}$ or $\dfrac{2s - 2v_1t}{t^2}$

26. $A = \pi rs + r^2$
$A + r^2 = \pi rs$

$\dfrac{A - r^2}{\pi r} = s$

$s = \dfrac{A - r^2}{\pi r}$

27. $t = \dfrac{1}{Pr}$ 　　**28.** $P = \dfrac{1}{rt}$

$t = \dfrac{3}{75(0.10)}$ 　　$P = \dfrac{6}{(0.12)\left(\dfrac{2}{3}\right)}$

$t = 0.4$ of a year 　　$P = 75;\ \$75$

29. Answers may vary. Enter the numerical value of a^2, then press the square root function key. The value of r^3 can be found in a similar way.

30. $\left(\dfrac{P_1 V_1}{T_1}\right)T_1 = \left(\dfrac{P_2 V_2}{T_2}\right)T_1$ 　　**31.** $\dfrac{P_1 V_1}{T_1} = \dfrac{P_2 V_2}{T_2}$

$P_1 V_1 = \dfrac{T_1 P_2 V_2}{T_2}$ 　　$\dfrac{T_2 P_1 V_1}{T_1} = P_2 V_2$

$V_1 = \dfrac{T_1 P_2 V_2}{P_1 T_2}$ 　　$T_2 = \dfrac{T_1 P_2 V_2}{P_1 V_1}$

32. $(x^2)^2 = x^4$ 　　**33.** $(6^3)^{-2} = 6^{-6}$ 　　**34.** $(2m^2 n)^2 = 4m^4 n^2$

35. $(8^{-2})^{-3} = 8^6$

36. $\dfrac{3}{5} + \dfrac{t}{2} = \dfrac{5}{4}$ 　　**37.** $\left(\dfrac{11}{2}\right)m - 3 = \dfrac{13}{2}$

$\dfrac{12}{20} + \dfrac{10t}{20} = \dfrac{25}{20}$ 　　$\dfrac{11}{2}m - \dfrac{6}{2} = \dfrac{13}{2}$

$\dfrac{10t}{20} = \dfrac{13}{20}$ 　　$\dfrac{11}{2}m = \dfrac{19}{2}$

$10t = 13$ 　　$11m = 19$

$t = \dfrac{13}{10}$ 　　$m = \dfrac{19}{11}$

38. $\left(-\dfrac{1}{8}\right)t + \dfrac{1}{6} = -\dfrac{1}{12}$ 　　**39.** $4n - (3n + 6) = -1$

$\left(-\dfrac{3}{24}\right)t + \dfrac{4}{24} = -\dfrac{2}{24}$ 　　$n - 6 = -1$

$\left(-\dfrac{3}{24}\right)t = -\dfrac{6}{24}$ 　　$n = 5$

$-3t = -6$

$t = 2$

40. $0.4n + 2.7 = 5.1$

$0.4n = 2.4$

$n = 6$

41. $(x - 4)(x + 5) = 0$

$x - 4 = 0$ 　or 　$x + 5 = 0$

$x = 4$ 　or 　$x = -5$

pp. 73–76 　　**2-4 TRY THIS**

a. $3 - x < 2;\ 4$

$3 - 4 < 2$

$-1 < 2$ 　　4 is a solution

b. $3y + 2 > -1;\ -2$

$3(-2) + 2 > -1$

$-6 + 2 > -1$

$-4 > -1$ 　　-2 is not a solution

c. $3x + 2 \le 4x - 3;\ 5$

$3(5) + 2 \le 4(5) - 3$

$15 + 2 \le 20 - 3$

$17 \le 17$ 　　5 is a solution

d.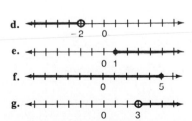

e.

f.

g.

h.

i.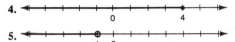

j. $5y \le \dfrac{3}{2}$ 　　**k.** $-2y > \dfrac{5}{6}$ 　　**l.** $-\dfrac{1}{3}x \le -4$

$10y \le 3$ 　　$-12y > 5$ 　　$-x \le -12$

　　　　　　　　　　　　　　　　$x \ge 12$

$y \le \dfrac{3}{10}$ 　　$y < -\dfrac{5}{12}$

m. $6 - 5y \ge 7$ 　　**n.** $3x + 5x < 4$ 　　**o.** $17 - 5y \le 8y - 5$

$-5y \ge 1$ 　　$8x < 4$ 　　$17 - 13y \le -5$

　　　　　　　　　　　　　　　　$-13y \le -22$

$y \le -\dfrac{1}{5}$ 　　$x < \dfrac{1}{2}$ 　　$y \ge \dfrac{22}{13}$

p. 77 　　**EXERCISES 2-4**

1. Solution 　　**2.** Solution 　　**3.** Not a solution

4.

5.

6.

7.

8. $x > -5$ 　　**9.** $x > -3$ 　　**10.** $y < 6$ 　　**11.** $y < 6$

12. $a \le -21$ 　　**13.** $a \le -20$ 　　**14.** $t \ge -5$

15. $x \le 19$ 　　**16.** $y > -6$ 　　**17.** $y > -9$ 　　**18.** $x \le 9$

19. $y \le 14$ 　　**20.** $x \ge 3$ 　　**21.** $t < -9$ 　　**22.** $x < -60$

23. $x < 50$ 　　**24.** $x \le 0.9$ 　　**25.** $y \ge -0.4$ 　　**26.** $x \le \dfrac{5}{6}$

27. $y \ge \dfrac{9}{10}$ 　　**28.** $x < 6$ 　　**29.** $y > 3$ 　　**30.** $y \le -3$

31. $x \le 4$ 　　**32.** $y > \dfrac{2}{3}$ 　　**33.** $x < -\dfrac{2}{5}$ 　　**34.** $x \ge 11.25$

35. $y < 5$

36. $3x - \dfrac{1}{8} \le -\dfrac{3}{8} + 3x$

$-\dfrac{1}{8} \le -\dfrac{3}{8}$

$\dfrac{1}{8} \ge \dfrac{3}{8};$ No solution

37. $2x - 3 < \dfrac{13}{4}x + 10 - 1.25x$

$\dfrac{8}{4}x - \dfrac{13}{4}x + 1.25x < 10 + 3$

$-\dfrac{5}{4}x + \dfrac{5}{4}x < 13$

$0 < 13$ 　　Real number line

38. $4(3y - 2) \ge 9(2y + 5)$

$12y - 8 \ge 18y + 45$

$-6y \ge 53$

$y \le -\dfrac{53}{6};$ or $y \le -8\dfrac{5}{8}$

39. $4m + 5 \ge 14(m - 2)$

$4m + 5 \ge 14m - 28$

$-10m \ge -33$

$m \le \dfrac{33}{10}$ or $3\dfrac{3}{10}$

40. Answers may vary. Example: $x < -5,\ 3x + 2 < -13$

41. For $(y + 3)(y - 3) < 0$ either $y + 3 < 0$ and $y - 3 > 0$ or $y + 3 > 0$ and $y - 3 < 0$. If $y + 3 < 0$ and $y - 3 > 0$, then $y < -3$ and $y > 3$. If $y + 3 > 0$ and $y - 3 < 0$, then $y > -3$ and $y < 3$.

42. If $y(y + 5) > 0$, then either $y > 0$ and $y + 5 > 0$ or $y < 0$ and $y + 5 < 0$. If $y > 0$ and $y + 5 > 0$, then $y > 0$ and $y > -5$. If $y < 0$ and $y + 5 < 0$, then $y < 0$ and $y < -5$. Thus, $y > 0$ or $y < -5$.

43. If $\dfrac{x + 3}{x - 3} > 0$, then $x + 3 > 0$ and $x - 3 > 0$ or $x + 3 < 0$ and $x - 3 < 0$. If both are larger than zero, then both equations are satisfied by $x > 3$. If both are smaller than zero, then both equations are satisfied by $x < -3$. Hence, $\{x \mid x < -3 \text{ or } x > 3\}$.

44. $\{x \mid -1 < x < 2\}$

45. a. False; for $a = 4$, $b = 5$, $c = 1$, $d = 4$, $4 - 5 \not< 1 - 4$
b. False; $-3 < -2$ but $9 > 4$.

46. $a^5 \cdot a^{-3} \cdot a^2 = a^{5-3+2} = a^4$ **47.** $(6x^3y^5)^2 = 36x^6y^{10}$

48. $(2m^5)^2 = 4m^{10}$ **49.** $\dfrac{20n^{3t}}{5n^t} = 4n^{3t-1} = 4n^{2t}$

50. $\left(\dfrac{x^2}{y^2}\right)^3 = \dfrac{x^6}{y^6}$ **51.** $n + (n + 1) + (n + 2) = 2n + 65$
$$3n + 3 = 2n + 65$$
$$n = 62$$
62, 63, and 64

pp. 79–80   2-5 TRY THIS

a. $91 + 86 + 73 + 79 + x \geq 400$
$x \geq 71$; a source of 71 or higher

b. $500 + 15n > 20n$
$-5n > -500$
$n < 100$; less than 100 hours

pp. 80–81   2-5 EXERCISES

1. Less than 620.5 miles   **2.** 84 or more   **3.** $20,000

4. $5000   **5.** Less than $2.00 ($1.99)

6. More than $15,000   **7.** Less than 10 hours

8. More than 40 hours

9. $12000 \leq 10000 + 10000(2)\,(r)$
$12000 \leq 10000 + 20000r$
$2000 \leq 20000r$
$r \geq 0.10$; 10% interest

10. $(75 + 95 + 91 + x) \div 4 \geq 89$
$(261 + x) \div 4 \geq 89$
$261 + x \geq 356$
$x \geq 95$
You need a score of 95 or more.

11. $\dfrac{(75 + 95 + 91 + 2x)}{5} = 89$
$75 + 95 + 91 + 2x = 445$
$261 + 2x = 184$
$2x = 184$
$x = 92$
You need to average 92 or more.

12. $\dfrac{75 + 90 + 91 + 90x}{3 + x} = 89$
$75 + 90 + 91 + 90x = 89x + 267$
$261 + 90x = 89x + 267$
$x = 6$; 6 tests remain.

13. $w \leq 4.5$ cm and cannot be negative.

14. $S = -16t^2 + v_0t + S_0$
$3072 < -16t^2 + 448t$
$-192 > t^2 - 28t$
$0 > t^2 - 28t + 192$
$0 > (t - 12)(t - 16)$
$12 < t < 16$; between 12 and 16 seconds

15. Never. From the answer to Exercise 14, you know that the projectile will reach its maximum height between 12 and 16 seconds. At 14 seconds:
$S = -16(14)^2 + 448(14) + 0$

$= -3136 + 6272$
$= 3136$
The projectile will never exceed an altitude of 3136 feet.

16. $rx - f < (r - 5)x$ **17.** $rx - 2f > (r - 7.50)x$
$rx - f < rx - 5x$ $\quad\quad rx - 2f > rx - 7.50x$
$-f < -5x$ $\quad\quad\quad -2f > -7.50x$

$\dfrac{f}{5} > x$ $\quad\quad\quad\quad \dfrac{f}{3.75} < x$

less than $\dfrac{f}{5}$ hr   greater than $\dfrac{f}{3.75}$ hr

18. $2a + b = c$ **19.** $x = \dfrac{1}{yz}$
$2a = c - b$
$\quad\quad xyz = 1$
$a = \dfrac{c - b}{2}$
$\quad\quad z = \dfrac{1}{xy}$

20. $ab + cd = ef = g$ **21.** $r = \dfrac{A}{2\pi(1 + h)}$
$cd = g - ab - ef$
$c = \dfrac{g - ab - ef}{d}$

pp. 83–85   2-6 TRY THIS

a.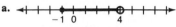

b.

c. $-2 \leq 3x + 4 \leq 7$
$-2 - 4 \leq 3x + 4 - 4 \leq 7 - 4$
$-6 \leq 3x \leq 3$
$-2 \leq x \leq 1$
$\{x \mid -2 \leq x \leq 1\}$

d. $4 \geq -x + 3 > -6$
$1 \geq -x > -9$
$-1 \leq x < 9$
$\{x \mid -1 \leq x < 9\}$

e.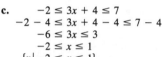

f.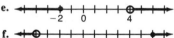

g. $x - 4 < -3$ or $x - 4 \geq 3$
$x < 1$ or $x \geq 7$
$\{x \mid x < 1$ or $x \geq 7\}$

h. $-2x + 4 \leq -3$ or $x + 5 < 3$
$-2x \leq -7$ or $x < -2$
$x \geq \dfrac{7}{2}$ or $x < -2$
$\left\{x \mid x < -2 \text{ or } x \geq \dfrac{7}{2}\right\}$

pp. 85–86   2-6 EXERCISES

1.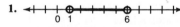

2.

3.

4.

5. $-4 < x < 6$ **6.** $-2 < x \leq 5$ **7.** $-2 < y \leq 2$

8. $0 \leq x \leq 1$ **9.** $-\dfrac{5}{3} \leq x \leq \dfrac{4}{3}$ **10.** $\dfrac{11}{2} \geq x > -\dfrac{7}{2}$

11. $0 < x < 14$ **12.** $-5 \leq x < 5$

13.

14.
       −2 0

15.
    −3   0 1

16.
    −1 0   3

17.
  −8   −2 0

18.
  −10   −5   0

19. $x < -9$ or $x > -5$ **20.** $x < -13$ or $x > -5$

21. $x \le \dfrac{5}{2}$ or $x \ge 11$

22. $x \le 5$ or $x \ge 3$ (any real number)

23. $x < \dfrac{4}{3}$ or $x > 15$ **24.** $x < -1$ or $x > 16$

25. $x \ge 2$ and $x > 5$
$\{x \mid x > 5\}$ satisfies both inequalities.

26. No solution   **27.** $x > 1$ **28.** All real numbers

29. $x < 0$

30. $4a - 2 \le a + 1 \le 3a + 4$
    $4a - 2 \le a + 1$ and $a + 1 \le 3a + 4$
       $-3 \le -3a$ and $-2a \le 3$

         $1 \ge a$ and $a \ge -\dfrac{3}{2}$

       $-\dfrac{3}{2} \le a \le 1$

31. $4m - 8 > 6m + 5$ or $5m - 8 < -2$
     $-2m > 13$ or $5m < 6$

     $m < -\dfrac{13}{2}$ $m < \dfrac{6}{5}$

        $m < \dfrac{6}{5}$

32. $-\dfrac{2}{15} \le \dfrac{2}{3}x - \dfrac{2}{5} < \dfrac{2}{15}$

  $-\dfrac{2}{15} \le \dfrac{2}{3}x - \dfrac{2}{5}$ and $\dfrac{2}{3}x - \dfrac{2}{5} < \dfrac{2}{15}$

  $-\dfrac{2}{15} \le \dfrac{10}{15}x - \dfrac{6}{15}$ and $\dfrac{10}{15}x - \dfrac{6}{15} < \dfrac{2}{15}$

     $\dfrac{4}{15} \le \dfrac{10}{15}x$ and $\dfrac{10}{15}x < \dfrac{8}{15}$

      $\dfrac{4}{10} \le x$ and $x < \dfrac{8}{10}$

      $\dfrac{2}{5} \le x$ and $x < \dfrac{4}{5}$

      $\dfrac{2}{5} \le x < \dfrac{4}{5}$

33. $2x - \dfrac{3}{4} < -\dfrac{1}{10}$ or $2x - \dfrac{3}{4} > \dfrac{1}{10}$

  $2x - \dfrac{30}{40} < -\dfrac{4}{40}$ or $2x - \dfrac{30}{40} > \dfrac{4}{40}$

    $2x < \dfrac{26}{40}$ or $2x > \dfrac{34}{40}$

    $x < \dfrac{26}{80}$ or $x > \dfrac{34}{80}$

    $x < \dfrac{13}{40}$ or $x > \dfrac{17}{40}$

34. $3x < 4 - 5x < 5 + 3x$
   $3x < 4 - 5x$ and $4 - 5x < 5 + 3x$
    $8x < 4$ and $-8x < 1$

      $x < \dfrac{1}{2}$ and $x > -\dfrac{1}{8}$

    $-\dfrac{1}{8} < x < \dfrac{1}{2}$

35. $(x + 6)(x - 4) > (x + 1)(x - 3)$
   $x^2 + 2x - 24 > x^2 - 2x - 3$
        $4x > 21$

        $x > \dfrac{21}{4}$

36. True   **37.** True   **38.** False   **39.** False   **40.** False

41. False

42. Answers may vary.
   Ex: $(x < 0$ or $x > 2)$ and $(x > 1$ or $x < -1)$.

43. $[4x - 2 < 8$ or $3(x - 1) < -2]$ and $-2 \le 5x \le 10$

   $[4x < 10$ or $3x - 3 < -2]$ and $-\dfrac{2}{5} \le x \le 2$

    $\left[x < \dfrac{10}{4}\right.$ or $\left. 3x < 1\right]$ and $-\dfrac{2}{5} \le x \le 2$

    $\left[x < \dfrac{5}{2}\right.$ or $\left. x < \dfrac{1}{3}\right]$ and $-\dfrac{2}{5} \le x \le 2$

    $-\dfrac{2}{5} \le x \le 2$

44. $-2 \le 4m + 3 < 7$ and $[m - 5 \le 4$ or $3 - m > 12]$
   $-2 \le 4m + 3$ and $4m + 3 < 7$ and $[m \le 9$ or $-m > 9]$
   $-5 \le 4m$ and $4m < 4$ and $[m \le 9$ or $m < -9]$

   $-\dfrac{5}{4} \le m$ and $m < 1$

   $-\dfrac{5}{4} \le m < 1$ and $[m \le 9$ or $m < -9]$

   $-\dfrac{5}{4} \le m < 1$

45. $x + 4 < 2x - 6 \le x + 12$
   $x + 4 < 2x - 6$ and $2x - 6 \le x + 12$
     $10 < x$ and $x \le 18$
     $10 < x \le 18$

46. $x \le -\dfrac{1}{5}$ or $x \ge 0$

47. a. 1   **48.** a. q (all of the statements)
    b. p (all of the statements)   b. 1

49. $-3t - 21$ for $t = -8$ **50.** $4|x + y|$ for $x = 3, y = -9$
   $24 - 21 = 3$ $4|3 - 9| = 4|-6| = 24$

51. $3(m - 5) + 2$ for $m = -1$
   $3(-1 - 5) + 2 = 3(-6) + 2$
              $= -18 + 2 = -16$

52. $3a(2b - 3c)$ for $a = 2, b = 3, c = -1$
   $3(2)(2(3) - 3(-1)) = 6(6 + 3) = 54$

53. $(-3w)^2 = 9w^2$ **54.** $-6(-4c)^2 = -6(16c^2) = -96c^2$

55. $(-4a^2b)^3 = -64a^6b^3$ **56.** $|-2048| = 2048$

57. $4(3)(8) + 25 = 96 + 25 = \$121$

p. 86   PROBLEM FOR PROGRAMMERS

```
10   REM        Chapter 2 Problem
20   DR = - 1
30   INEQ$ = "<"
40   PRINT "For AX + B > or < C"
50   INPUT "Input A  ";A
60   INPUT "Input B  ";B
70   INPUT "Input < OR >  ";LTGT$
80   INPUT "Input C  ";C
90   IF LTGT$ = "<"  THEN DR = 1
100    IF SGN  (A)*  DR = -1  THEN INEQ$ = ">"
110    PRINT "X";INEQ$;"";(C - B) / A
120  END
```

```
10  REM       Chapter 2 Challenge Problem
20  DR = - 1
30  INEQ$ = "<"
40  EQ$ = " "
50    PRINT "For AX + B <, >, <=, or >= C"
60    INPUT "Input A    ";A
70    INPUT "Input B    ";B
80    INPUT "Input <,   >,   <=,   >= ";LTGT$
90    INPUT "Input C    ";C
100 IF LEFT$  (LTGT$,1) = "<" THEN DR = 1
110 IF   SGN (A)   * DR = -1  THEN INEQ$ = ">"
120 IF  RIGHT$ (LTGT$,1) = "=" THEN EQ$ = "="
130 PRINT "X  ";INEQ$;EQ$; (C - B) / A
140 END
```

pp. 88–90   2-7 TRY THIS

a. $|7x| = 7|x|$ **b.** $|x^8| = x^8$ **c.** $|5a^2b| = 5a^2|b|$

d. $\left|\dfrac{7a}{b^2}\right| = \dfrac{7}{b^2}|a|$ **e.** $|-9x| = 9|x|$ **f.** $|-6 - (-35)| = 29$

g. $|19 - 14| = 5$ **h.** $|-3 - 17| = 20$

i. $\{6, -6\}$

j. $\left\{\dfrac{1}{2}, -\dfrac{1}{2}\right\}$

k. $\{x \mid -5 < x < 5\}$

l. $\{x \mid -6.5 \le x \le 6.5\}$

m. $\{y \mid y \le -8 \text{ or } y \ge 8\}$

n. $\left\{x \mid x < -\dfrac{1}{2} \text{ or } x > \dfrac{1}{2}\right\}$

o. $\left\{x \mid x = -\dfrac{13}{3} \text{ or } x = \dfrac{5}{3}\right\}$

p. $\{x \mid -2 \le x \le 5\}$

q. $\left\{x \mid x < -\dfrac{3}{2} \text{ or } x > \dfrac{11}{2}\right\}$

p. 91   2-7 EXERCISES

1. $3|x|$ **2.** $4|x|$ **3.** y^8 **4.** x^6 **5.** $9x^2y^2|y|$

6. $10a^4b^6|b|$ **7.** $\dfrac{a^2}{|b|}$ **8.** $\dfrac{y^4}{|m|}$ **9.** $16|m|$ **10.** $9|t|$

11. $t^2|t|$ **12.** $p^4|p|$ **13.** 34   **14.** 27   **15.** 11   **16.** 36

17. 33   **18.** 19   **19.** 5   **20.** 23

You may wish to have students write answers in set notation. For example, the answer to Exercise 21 would be $\{-3, 3\}$ and the answer to Exercise 23 would be $\{x \mid -3 < x < 3\}$.

21. $-3, 3$

22. $-5, 5$

23. $-3 < x < 3$

24. $-5 \le x \le 5$

25. $x \le -2 \text{ or } x \ge 2$

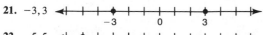

26. $y < -8 \text{ or } y > 8$

27. $t \le -5.5 \text{ or } t \ge 5.5$

28. $m \ne 0$

29. $-9, 15$

30. $-\dfrac{4}{3}, \dfrac{8}{3}$

31. $-\dfrac{1}{2} \le x \le \dfrac{7}{2}$

32. $-1 \le x \le \dfrac{1}{5}$

33. $y < -\dfrac{3}{2} \text{ or } y > \dfrac{17}{2}$

34. $y < -\dfrac{4}{3} \text{ or } y > 4$

35. $x \le -\dfrac{5}{4} \text{ or } x \ge \dfrac{23}{4}$

36. $y < -\dfrac{15}{9} \text{ or } y > \dfrac{19}{9}$

37. $x > -\dfrac{3}{5} \text{ or } x < -1$

38. $|m + 5| + 9 \le 16$
$\quad |m + 5| \le 7$
$\quad\quad m + 5 \le 7 \text{ and } m + 5 \ge -7$
$\quad\quad\quad m \le 2 \text{ and } \quad\quad m \ge -12$
$\quad\quad -12 \le m \le 2$

39. $|t - 7| + 3 \ge 4$
$\quad |t - 7| \ge 1$
$\quad t - 7 \le -1 \text{ or } t - 7 \ge 1$
$\quad t \le 6 \text{ or } \quad\quad t \ge 8$

40. $|g + 7| + 13 = 4$
$\quad |g + 7| = -9$
$\quad$ No solution

41. $2|2x - 7| + 11 = 25$
$\quad 2|2x - 7| = 14$
$\quad |2x - 7| = 7$
$\quad\quad 2x - 7 = 7 \text{ or } 2x - 7 = -7$
$\quad\quad\quad 2x = 14 \text{ or } \quad\quad 2x = 0$
$\quad\quad\quad\quad x = 7 \text{ or } \quad\quad\quad x = 0$

42. No. Ex: $|3 - 5| \ne |3| - |5|$

43. $|3x - 4| > -2$
$\quad 3x - 4 < 2 \text{ or } 3x - 4 > -2$
$\quad\quad 3x < 6 \text{ or } \quad\quad 3x > 2$

44. $|x - 6| \le -8$
$\quad$ No solution

16 *Algebra and Trigonometry*

$$x < 2 \quad \text{or} \quad x > \frac{2}{3}$$

All real numbers

45. $\left|\frac{5}{9} + 3x\right| < \frac{1}{6}$

$\frac{5}{9} + 3x < \frac{1}{6}$ and $\frac{5}{9} + 3x > \frac{-1}{6}$

$\frac{10}{18} + 3x < \frac{3}{18}$ and $\frac{10}{18} + 3x > \frac{-3}{18}$

$3x < \frac{-7}{18}$ and $3x > \frac{-13}{18}$

$x < \frac{-7}{54}$ and $x > \frac{-13}{54}$

46. $1 - \left|\frac{1}{4}x + 8\right| > \frac{3}{4}$

$-\left|\frac{1}{4}x + 8\right| > -\frac{1}{4}$

$-\frac{1}{4}x - 8 > -\frac{1}{4}$ and $-\frac{1}{4}x - 8 < \frac{1}{4}$

$-\frac{1}{4}x > \frac{31}{4}$ and $-\frac{1}{4}x < \frac{33}{4}$

$x < -31$ and $x > -33$

47. $|x + 5| > x$

$x + 5 > x$ or $x + 5 < -x$

$5 > 0$ or $2x < -5$

$5 > 0$ or $x < -\frac{5}{2}$ All real numbers

48. $2 \le |x - 1| \le 5$

$|x - 1| \ge 2$

$x - 1 \ge 2$ or $x - 1 \le -2$

$x \ge 3$ or $x \le -1$ and

$|x - 1| \le 5$

$x - 1 \le 5$ and $x - 1 \ge -5$

$x \le 6$ and $x \ge -4$

so $-4 \le x \le -1$ or $3 \le x \le 6$

49. $|7x - 2| = x + 4$

$7x - 2 = -x - 4$ or $7x - 2 = x + 4$

$8x = -2$ or $6x = 6$

$x = -\frac{1}{4}$ or $x = 1$

50. $|x - 1| - 2 = |2x - 5|$

If $2x - 5 \ge 0$ then $x - 1 \ge 0$.

Then $x - 1 - 2 = 2x - 5$

$x - 3 = 2x - 5$

$x = 2$

But $2(2) - 5 < 0$, so 2 is not a solution.

If $2x - 5 \le 0$, then

$x - 1 - 2 = -2x + 5$ or $-x + 1 - 2 = -2x + 5$

$x - 3 = -2x + 5$ or $-x - 1 = -2x + 5$

$3x = 8$ or $x = 6$

$x = \frac{8}{3}$ or $x = 6$

But $2\left(\frac{8}{3}\right) - 5 > 0$, so $\frac{8}{3}$ is not a solution, and $2(6) - 5 > 0$ so

5 is not a solution.

No solution

51. $|x + 1| \le |x - 3|$

If $x - 3 \ge 0$, then $x + 1 \ge 0$.

Then $x + 1 \le x - 3$

$1 \le -3$, so $x - 3 \le 0$

$x + 1 \le -x + 3$ or $-x - 1 \le -x + 3$

$2x \le 2$ or $-1 \le 2$

$x \le 1$ is the only solution.

52. $n^{-8} \cdot n^{12} = n^{-8+12} = n^4$ **53.** $\frac{m^3}{m^5} = m^{3-5} = m^{-2}$

54. $\frac{y^5}{y^{-3}} = y^{5+3} = y^8$ **55.** $\frac{-56w^8}{7n^6} = -8w^8n^{-6}$

56. $1.8t = -3.6$ **57.** $12c + 6 = 9c$

$t = -2$ $3x = -6$

$c = -2$

58. $5a - (3a - 10) = 4a$

$2a + 10 = 4a$

$-2a = -10$

$a = 5$

59. Answers may vary;
$ab + (d + c)$,
$(c + d) + ab$,
$ba + (c + d)$.

60. Answers may vary;
$(yz \times xy)x^2$,
$x^2(zy \times yx)$,
$x^2(xy \times yz)$.

pp. 92–96   **2-8 TRY THIS**

a. If $3x + 5 = 20$, then $x = 5$.
1. $3x + 5 = 20$ — 1. Assume hypothesis
2. $3x = 15$ — 2. Addition property
3. $x = 5$ — 3. Multiplication property
4. If $3x + 5 = 20$, then $x = 5$ — 4. Statements 1–3

b. If $-3x + 8 > 23$, then $x < -5$.
1. $-3x + 8 > 23$ — 1. Assume hypothesis
2. $-3x > 15$ — 2. Addition property
3. $x < -5$ — 3. Multiplication property
4. If $-3x + 8 > 23$, then $x < -5$ — 4. Statements 1–3

c. If $x = 10$, then $3x + 7 = 37$.

d. If $x > 12$, then $x > 15$.

e. If $x = 5$, then $3x + 5 = 20$.
1. $x = 5$ — 1. Assume hypothesis
2. $3x = 15$ — 2. Multiplication property
3. $3x + 5 = 20$ — 3. Addition property
4. If $x = 5$, then $3x + 5 = 20$ — 4. Statements 1–3

f. (1) If $x < -5$, then $-3x + 8 > 23$.
1. $x < -5$ — 1. Assume hypothesis
2. $-3x < 15$ — 2. Multiplication property
3. $-3x + 8 = 23$ — 3. Addition property
4. If $x < -5$, then $-3x + 8 > 23$ — 4. Statements 1–3

(2) Solution sets of antecedent and consequent are the same: $\{x | x < -5\}$

g. 1. $7x - 1 > 34$ — 1. Hypothesis
2. $7x > 35$ — 2. Addition property
3. $x > 5$ — 3. Multiplication property

Converse:
1. $x > 5$ — 1. Hypothesis
2. $7x > 35$ — 2. Multiplication property
3. $7x - 1 > 34$ — 3. Addition property

h. (1) Statement
1. $9x - 5 = 103$ — 1. Hypothesis
2. $9x = 108$ — 2. Addition property
3. $x = 12$ — 3. Multiplication property

Converse
1. $x = 12$ — 1. Hypothesis
2. $9x = 108$ — 2. Multiplication property
3. $9x - 5 = 103$ — 3. Addition property

(2) $9x - 5 = 103$
$9x = 108$
$x = 12$
$9(12) - 5 = 103$ Substituting
$108 - 5 = 103$
$103 = 103$

i. Yes   **j.** No   **k.** Yes   **l.** Yes   **m.** No   **n.** No

1. $7x - 12 = 37$

1. $7x = 49$	1. Addition principle
2. $x = 7$	2. Multiplication principle

2. $5y + 16 = 88 - 3y$

1. $8y + 16 = 88$	1. Addition principle
2. $8y = 72$	2. Addition principle
3. $y = 9$	3. Multiplication principle

3. $15x - 5 \geq 11 - 2x$

1. $17x \geq 16$	1. Addition principle
2. $x \geq \frac{16}{17}$	2. Multiplication principle

4. $13x + 12 < 15x - 7$

1. $-2x < -19$	1. Addition principle
2. $x > \frac{19}{2}$	2. Multiplication principle

5. If $6y = 10$, then $3y = 5$.

6. If $2x + 5 = 14$, then $5x + 3 = 17$.

7. If $x < 20$, then $x < 12$.

8. If $4y + 2 < 8y + 1$, then $3y + 5 > 17 - y$.

9. If $x = 7$, then $7x - 12 = 37$.

10. If $y = 9$, then $5y + 16 = 88 - 3y$.

11. If $x \geq \frac{16}{17}$, then $15x - 5 \geq 11 - 2x$.

12. If $x \geq \frac{19}{2}$, then $13x + 12 < 15x - 7$.

13. $\left\{ x \mid -\frac{9}{2} < x \right\}$ **14.** $\left\{ y \mid \frac{7}{3} \geq y \right\}$ **15.** $-\frac{4}{7}$

16. -7 **17.** $-\frac{17}{2}$ **18.** 1 **19.** $-\frac{5}{3}$ **20.** $\frac{7}{5}$

21. Yes   **22.** No   **23.** Yes   **24.** Yes   **25.** No

26. Yes   **27.** Yes   **28.** Yes

29.

1. $a = b$	Hypothesis
2. $a - a = 0$	Prop. of additive inverses
3. $a - b = 0$	Statements 1 and 2 (substitution)
4. $a - b + 0 = 0$	Additive identity property
5. $a - b + c - c = 0$	Prop. of additive inverses
6. $a + c - b - c = 0$	Commutative property
7. $a + c - (b + c) = 0$	Inverse of a sum property
8. $a + c = b + c$	Prop. of additive inverses

30.

1. $a = b$	Hypothesis
2. $a(1) = b(1)$	Mult. identity property
3. $a\left(\frac{c}{c}\right) = b\left(\frac{c}{c}\right)$	Property of 1
4. $\frac{ac}{c} = \frac{bc}{c}$	Multiplication
5. $\frac{ac}{c} - \frac{bc}{c} = 0$	Addition principle
6. $\frac{1}{c}(ac - bc) = 0$	Distributive property
7. $c\left[\frac{1}{c}(ac - bc)\right] = 0$	Prin. of zero products
8. $\frac{c}{c}[(ac - bc)] = 0$	Associative property
9. $1(ac - bc) = 0$	Property of 1
10. $ac - bc = 0$	Mult. identity property
11. $ac = bc$	Addition principle

31. Part 1. If $a = 0$ or $b = 0$ then $ab = 0$

1. $a = 0$	Hypothesis
2. $ab = 0(b)$	Mult. principle
3. $ab = 0$	Mult. prop. of zero
4. If $a = 0$ then $ab = 0$	Statements 1–3
5. $b = 0$	Hypothesis
6. $ab = a(0)$	Mult. principle
7. $ab = 0$	Mult. prop. of zero
8. If $b = 0$ then $ab = 0$	Statements 5–7
9. If $a = 0$ or $b = 0$ then $ab = 0$	Statements 4 and 8

Part 2. If $ab = 0$ then $a = 0$ or $b = 0$

1. $ab = 0(a \neq 0)$	Hypothesis
2. $\frac{1}{a} \cdot ab = \frac{1}{a} \cdot 0$	Mult. principle
3. $1(b) = 0$	Prop. of reciprocals
4. $b = 0$	Mult. identity prop.
5. If $ab = 0$ and $a \neq 0$ then $b = 0$	Statements 1–4
6. $ab = 0(b \neq 0)$	Hypothesis
7. $ab \cdot \frac{1}{b} = 0 \cdot \frac{1}{b}$	Mult. principle
8. $a(1) = 0$	Prop. of reciprocals
9. $a = 0$	Mult. identity prop.
10. If $ab = 0$ and $b \neq 0$ then $a = 0$	Statements 6–9
11. If $ab = 0$ then $a = 0$ or $b = 0$	Statements 5 and 10

32. Answers may vary. If $x < 3$ then $x + 5 < 8$.
If $x = 0$ then x is an integer.

33.

1. $a < b$	Hypothesis
2. $a - a < b - a$	Addn. prin. for ineq.
3. $0 < b - a$	Additive inv. prop.
4. $b < c$	Hypothesis
5. $b - b < c - b$	Addn. prin. for ineq.
6. $0 < c - b$	Additive inv. prop.
7. $0 < (b - a) + (c - b)$	Addn. of pos. #'s is pos.
8. $0 < c - a + b - b$	Comm. prop.
9. $0 < c - a$	Additive inverse prop.
10. $0 + a < c - a + a$	Addn. prin. for ineq.
11. $a < c$	Add. ident. add. inv. prop.
12. If $a < b$ and $b < c$ then $a < c$	Statements 1, 4, 11

34.

1. $a < b$	Hypothesis
2. $0 < b - a$	Defn. of $<$
3. $0 < b - a + 0$	Add. identity
4. $0 < b - a + c - c$	Add. inverse prop.
5. $0 < (b + c) - (a + c)$	Comm. and dist. props.
6. $a + c < b + c$	Defn. of $<$
7. If $a < b$ then $a + c < b + c$	Statements 1–6

35. Part 1. $(c > 0)$

1. $a < b$	Hypothesis
2. $0 < b - a$	Defn. of $<$
3. $0 < c(b - a)$	Prod. of pos. #'s is pos.
4. $0 < cb - ca$	Dist. prop.
5. $ca < cb$	Defn. of $<$
6. If $a < b$ and $c > 0$ then $ac < bc$	Statements 1–5

Part 2. $(c < 0)$

1. $a < b$	Hypothesis
2. $0 < b - a$	Defn. of $<$
3. $0 > c(b - a)$	Prod. of neg. and pos. #'s is neg.
4. $0 > cb - ca$	Dist. prop.
5. $ca > cb$	Defn. of $>$
6. If $a < b$ and $c < 0$ then $ac > bc$	Statements 1–5

36. If x is an integer, then x is a rational number. If x is a rational number, then x is an integer.

37. If x is a quitter, then x never wins. If x never wins, then x is a quitter.

38. Part 1.

1. $a > b$	Hypothesis
2. $0 > b - a$	Add. princ.
3. $-b > -a$	Add. princ.
4. $-a < -b$	Commut. prop.
5. If $a > b$, then $-a < -b$.	Statements 1–4

Part 2.

1. $-a < -b$	Hypthesis
2. $0 < -b + a$	Add. princ.
3. $b < a$	Add. princ.
4. $a > b$	Commut. prop
5. If $-a < -b$, then $a > b$.	Statements 1–4

Combining the two parts of the proof, $a > b$ if and only if $-a < -b$. Thus the two statements are equivalent.

39. $\dfrac{1}{m^3} = \dfrac{1}{2^3} = \dfrac{1}{8}$ **40.** $m - \dfrac{4}{5} = \dfrac{1}{2} - \dfrac{4}{5} = \dfrac{5}{10} - \dfrac{8}{10} = -\dfrac{3}{10}$

41. $\dfrac{m}{3} = \dfrac{\frac{1}{2}}{3} = \dfrac{1}{2} \cdot \dfrac{1}{3} = \dfrac{1}{6}$

42. $\dfrac{1}{3} + 3m = \dfrac{1}{3} + 3\left(\dfrac{1}{2}\right) = \dfrac{1}{3} + \dfrac{3}{2} = \dfrac{2}{6} + \dfrac{9}{6} = \dfrac{11}{6}$

43. $16n + 8n = 312$
$24n = 312$
$n = 13$

44. $-16 = 4c + 6$
$-22 = 4c$
$c = -\dfrac{22}{4} = -\dfrac{11}{2}$

45. $r - 16r = 645$
$-15r = 645$
$r = -43$

p. 99   2-9 PROBLEM SOLVING: STRATEGIES

1. Strategy: Write an equation
$54.50 \geq 600(0.04) + x(0.1\ 0)$
$54.50 \geq 24 + 0.10x$
$30.50 \geq 0.10x$
$305 \geq x$ They would use 905 kwh.

2. Strategy: Write an equation

$1800 = x + \dfrac{1}{3}x + \dfrac{1}{2}\left(\dfrac{1}{3}x\right)$

$1800 = \dfrac{3}{5}x + \dfrac{1}{3}x + \dfrac{1}{6}x$

$1800 = \dfrac{6}{6}x + \dfrac{2}{6}x + \dfrac{1}{6}x$

$1800 = \dfrac{9}{6}x$

$10{,}800 = 9x$
$1200 = x$
Model C = \$1200; Model E = \$400; Model P = \$200

3. Strategy: Write an equation
1st 2 years
$x = 275(0.15) + 275$
$= 316.25$

2nd 2 years
$x = 316.25(0.15) + 316.25$
$= 363.68$

There will be about 364 customers after 4 years.

4. Strategy: Draw a diagram

11 pieces

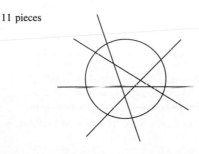

5. Strategy: Draw a diagram
Answers may vary.

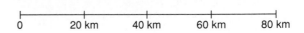

They need to divide the 80 kilometers into four sections so that the combined length of the first and third is the same as the combined length of the second and fourth. One possible solution is 20 km, 40 km, and 60 km.

p. 101   PROBLEM SOLVING: APPLICATION

1. $\dfrac{1}{4} + \dfrac{140}{140} + \dfrac{1}{4} = 1.5$ hr   Internal

$\dfrac{1}{12} + \dfrac{140}{100} + \dfrac{1}{12} = 1.56$ hr   External

Internal loading is preferable.

2. $\dfrac{1}{4} + \dfrac{110}{140} + \dfrac{1}{4} = 1.28$ hr   Internal

$\dfrac{1}{12} + \dfrac{110}{100} + \dfrac{1}{12} = 1.26$ hr   External

External loading is preferable.

3. $\dfrac{1}{4} + \dfrac{118}{140} + \dfrac{1}{4} = 1.342$ hr   Internal

$\dfrac{1}{12} + \dfrac{118}{100} + \dfrac{1}{12} = 1.346$ hr   External

Internal loading is preferable.

4. $\dfrac{1}{4} + \dfrac{100}{200} + \dfrac{1}{4} = 1.00$ hr   Internal

$\dfrac{1}{8} + \dfrac{100}{150} + \dfrac{1}{8} = 0.92$ hr   External

External loading is preferable.

5. $\dfrac{1}{4} + \dfrac{250}{200} + \dfrac{1}{4} = 1.75$ hr   Internal

$\dfrac{1}{8} + \dfrac{250}{150} + \dfrac{1}{8} = 1.92$ hr   External

Internal loading is preferable.

6. Internal $\dfrac{1}{4} + \dfrac{D}{200} + \dfrac{1}{4} = \dfrac{D}{200} + \dfrac{1}{2}$

External $\dfrac{1}{8} + \dfrac{D}{150} + \dfrac{1}{8} = \dfrac{D}{150} + \dfrac{1}{4}$

$\dfrac{D}{200} + \dfrac{1}{2} = \dfrac{D}{150} + \dfrac{1}{4}$

$\dfrac{D}{200} - \dfrac{D}{150} = -\dfrac{1}{4}$

$\dfrac{3D}{600} - \dfrac{4D}{600} = -\dfrac{1}{4}$

$\dfrac{-D}{600} = -\dfrac{1}{4}$

$D = 150$ Same
$D > 150$ Internal loading preferable
$D < 150$ External loading preferable

pp. 102–103   CHAPTER 2 SUMMARY AND REVIEW

1. $\dfrac{1}{4} + \dfrac{1}{2}x = \dfrac{5}{4}$

$4\left(\dfrac{1}{4} + \dfrac{1}{2}x\right) = 4\left(\dfrac{5}{4}\right)$

$1 + 2x = 5$
$1 + (-1) + 2x = 5 + (-1)$
$2x = 4$

$$\frac{1}{2} \cdot 2x = \frac{1}{2} \cdot 4$$
$$x = 2$$

2.
$$\frac{2}{3}x + \frac{1}{6} = 9$$
$$6\left(\frac{2}{3}x + \frac{1}{6}\right) = 6 \cdot 9$$
$$4x + 1 = 54$$
$$4x + 1 + (-1) = 54 + (-1)$$
$$4x = 53$$
$$x = \frac{53}{4} = 13\frac{1}{4}$$

3.
$$0.6x + 1.5 = 2.1$$
$$10(0.6x + 1.5) = 10 \cdot 2.1$$
$$6x + 15 = 21$$
$$6x + 15 + (-15) = 21 + (-1)$$
$$6x = 6$$
$$\frac{1}{6} \cdot 6x = \frac{1}{6} \cdot 6$$
$$x = 1$$

4.
$$2.9y - 4.6 = 0.6y$$
$$10(2.9y - 4.6) = 10 \cdot 0.6y$$
$$29y - 46 = 6y$$
$$29y - 46 + (-29y) = 6y + (-29y)$$
$$-46 = -23y$$
$$-\frac{1}{23} \cdot -46 = -\frac{1}{23}(-23y)$$
$$2 = y$$

5.
$$300(x + 7) = 350$$
$$300x + 2100 = 350$$
$$300x + 2100 + (-2100) = 350 + (-2100)$$
$$300x = -1750$$
$$\frac{1}{300} \cdot 300x = \frac{1}{300}(-1750)$$
$$x = -\frac{1750}{300} = -\frac{175}{30} = -\frac{35}{6} = -5\frac{5}{6}$$

6.
$$\frac{1}{4}(3x - 5) = 10 - \frac{3}{4}(x - 1)$$
$$4 \cdot \frac{1}{4}(3x - 5) = 4\left(10 - \frac{3}{4}(x - 1)\right)$$
$$3x - 5 = 40 - 3(x - 1)$$
$$3x - 5 = 40 - 3x + 3$$
$$3x - 5 + 3x = 43 - 3x + 3x$$
$$6x - 5 = 43$$
$$6x - 5 + 5 = 43 + 5$$
$$6x = 48$$
$$\frac{1}{6} \cdot 6x = \frac{1}{6} \cdot 48$$
$$x = 8$$

7. $(x + 4)(x - 3) = 0$
$x + 4 = 0$ or $x - 3 = 0$
$x = -4$ $x = 3$

8. $(2x - 5)(3x + 4) = 0$
$2x - 5 = 0$ or $3x + 4 = 0$
$2x = 5$ $3x = -4$
$x = \frac{5}{2}$ $x = -\frac{4}{3}$

9. $x + 5x + (x - 2) = 180$
$7x - 2 = 180$
$7x = 182$
$x = 26°$
$5x = 130°$
$x - 2 = 24°$

10. $y - .2y = 120$
$10y - 2y = 1200$
$8y = 1200$
$y = \$150$

11. $A = \frac{1}{2}bh$
$$2A = 2 \cdot \frac{1}{2}bh$$
$$2A = bh$$
$$\frac{2A}{h} = b$$

12. $v = ab + at$
$v = a(b + t)$
$$\frac{v}{b + t} = a$$

13.
$$y + 3 \geq 4$$
$$y + 3(-3) \geq 4 + (-3)$$
$$y \geq 1$$

14.
$$2x + 7 > x - 9$$
$$2x + 7 - x - 7 > x - 9 - x - 7$$
$$x > -16$$

15. $\frac{1}{3}x \geq -9$
$$x \geq -27$$

16. $-9y \geq -45$
$$y \leq 5$$

17. $-\frac{2}{3}x \geq -20$
$$x \leq 30$$

18.
$$3x - 8 \leq 7x + 5$$
$$3x - 8 + (-3x) - 5 \leq 7x + 5 + (-3x) - 5$$
$$-13 \leq 4x$$
$$-\frac{13}{4} \leq x$$

19. $x + (x + 2) + (x + 4) < 20$
$$10 < 3x + 6 < 20$$
$$4 < 3x < 14$$
$$\frac{4}{3} < x < \frac{14}{3}$$
$$x = 3$$
$$x + 2 = 5$$
$$x + 4 = 7$$

20. $-3 < x < 5$

21. $x < -5$ or $x > 3$

22. $-7 < 2x - 1 < 3$
$-6 < 2x < 4$
$-3 < x < 2$

23. $x + 1 < -1$ or $x + 1 > 2$
$x < -2$ or $x > 1$

24. $y^2|y|$ **25.** $x^2|xy|$ **26.** $3x^2y^2$

27. $|-9 - 17|$
$= |-26|$
$= 26$

28. $|-40 - (-23)|$
$= |-40 + 23|$
$= |-17|$
$= 17$

29. $|-18 - 3|$
$= |-21|$
$= 21$

30. $x = 6$ or $x = -6$

31. $-4 < y < 4$

32. $x \geq 2$ or $x \leq -2$

33. $|x - 3| \geq 5$
$x - 3 \geq 5$ or $3 - x \geq 5$
$\quad x \geq 8 \qquad\qquad -x \geq 2$
$\qquad\qquad\qquad\qquad\quad x \leq -2$

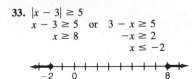

34. $|3x + 5| < 7$
$3x + 5 < 7$ or $-3x - 5 < 7$
$\quad 3x < 2 \qquad\qquad -3x < 12$
$\quad x < \dfrac{2}{3} \qquad\qquad x > -4$

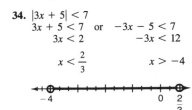

p. 103   CHAPTER 2 TEST

1. $r - 17 = 20$ **2.** $-9n = 450$ **3.** $3y + 10 = 16$
$\quad r = 37 \qquad\qquad\quad n = -50 \qquad\qquad\quad 3y = 6$
$\qquad\qquad\qquad\qquad\qquad\qquad\qquad\qquad\qquad\quad y = 2$

4. $-2z + 5 = 7$ **5.** $0.8x - 3.7 = 0.3$
$\quad -2z = 2 \qquad\qquad\qquad 8x - 37 = 3$
$\qquad z = -1 \qquad\qquad\qquad\quad 8x = 40$
$\qquad\qquad\qquad\qquad\qquad\qquad\quad x = 5$

6. $\dfrac{1}{5}y - \dfrac{2}{3} = 6$ **7.** $8(x + 9) = 112$
$\qquad\qquad\qquad\qquad\quad 8x + 72 = 112$
$3y - 10 = 90 \qquad\qquad 8x = 40$
$\quad 3y = 100 \qquad\qquad\quad x = 5$
$\quad\, y = \dfrac{100}{3}$

8. $8y - (5y - 9) = -160$ **9.** $(3x + 5)(2x - 6) = 0$
$\quad 3y + 9 = -160 \qquad\qquad\quad 3x + 5 = 0$ or $2x - 6 = 0$
$\quad 3y = -169 \qquad\qquad\qquad\quad 3x = -5 \qquad\qquad 2x = 6$
$\quad y = -\dfrac{169}{3} \qquad\qquad\qquad\quad x = -\dfrac{5}{3} \qquad\qquad x = 3$

10. $y + 5 \geq 8$ **11.** $4x \geq 28$ **12.** $-8y \leq -40$
$\quad\, y \geq 3 \qquad\qquad\quad x \geq 7 \qquad\qquad\quad y \geq 5$

13. $4 + 7y \leq 39$ **14.** $2x - 9 \leq 9x + 4$
$\quad 7y \leq 35 \qquad\qquad\qquad -9 \leq 7x + 4$
$\quad\, y \leq 5 \qquad\qquad\qquad\, -13 \leq 7x$
$\qquad\qquad\qquad\qquad\qquad\, -\dfrac{13}{7} \leq x$

15. $-4x - 6 > 7x - 14$ **16.** $x + (x + 4) = 14$
$\quad -6 > 11x - 14 \qquad\qquad\quad 2x + 4 = 14$
$\quad 8 > 11x \qquad\qquad\qquad\qquad\quad 2x = 10$
$\quad \dfrac{8}{11} > x \qquad\qquad\qquad\qquad\qquad x = 5m$
$\qquad\qquad\qquad\qquad\qquad\qquad x + 4 = 9m$

17. $Q = P - Prt$
$\quad Q = P(1 - rt)$
$\quad \dfrac{Q}{1 - rt} = P$

18. $x^4 y^4 |x|$

19. $\dfrac{81 + 76 + 82 + x}{4} \geq 80$
$\quad 239 + x \geq 320$
$\qquad\quad x \geq 81$
81

20. $|33 - (-12)|$
$= |33 + 12|$
$= 45$

21. $-3 < x + 1 < 8$
$\quad -4 < x < 7$

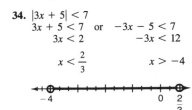

22. $y \leq -8$ or $y \geq 8$

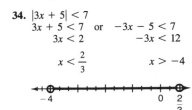

---

23. $|x - 2| \leq 6$
$x - 2 \leq 6$ or $2 - x \leq 6$
$\quad x \leq 8 \qquad\qquad -x \leq 4$
$\qquad\qquad\qquad\qquad\quad x \geq -4$

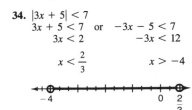

24. $|2x + 7| < 9$
$2x + 7 < 9$ or $-2x - 7 < 9$
$\quad 2x < 2 \qquad\qquad -2x < 16$
$\quad x < 1 \qquad\qquad\quad x > -8$

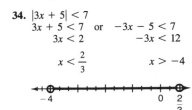

CHAPTER 3

pp. 104   READY FOR RELATIONS, FUNCTIONS, AND GRAPHS?

1. -4 **2.** -9 **3.** -6.2 **4.** 7 **5.** -5.7 **6.** $\dfrac{1}{15}$

7. -5 **8.** 4 **9.** -20 **10.** 7 **11.** 4 **12.** 3

13. $\dfrac{1}{6}$ **14.** $-\dfrac{13}{12}$ **15.** $-\dfrac{12}{5}$ **16.** 24 **17.** -4 **18.** $\dfrac{11}{3}$

19. 3 **20.** $x < 4$ **21.** $y \geq 8$ **22.** $y \leq -2$ **23.** $x < -2$

24. $x > 3$ **25.** $y \leq \dfrac{1}{7}$ **26.** $y < 1$ **27.** $x \leq 2$

pp. 106–108   3-1 TRY THIS

a. $A \times B = \{(d, 1), (d, 2), (e, 1), (e, 2)\}$
b. $C \times C = \{(x, x), (x, y), (x, z), (y, x), (y, y), (y, z), (z, x), (z, y), (z, z)\}$
c. $\{(1, 1), (2, 2)\}$
d. Domain: $\{a, b, c, e\}$,   **e.** Domain: $\{1, 2\}$ **f.** $\{6\}$
    Range: $\{1, 2, 3\}$ Range: $\{1, 2, 3\}$
g. $\{(3, 4), (3, 5), (4, 4), (4, 5), (5, 4), (5, 5)\}$

pp. 108–109   3-1 EXERCISES

1. {(chili, cheese), (chili, onions), (chili, peppers), (pizza, cheese), (pizza, onions), (pizza, peppers), (salad, cheese), (salad, onions), (salad, peppers)}

2. {(omelette, bacon), (omelette, sausage), (scrambled, bacon), (scrambled, sausage)}

3. $\{(x, 1), (x, 2), (y, 1), (y, 2), (z, 1), (z, 2)\}$

4. $\{(5, a), (5, z), (7, a), (7, z), (10, a), (10, z)\}$

5. $\{(5, 5), (5, 6), (5, 7), (5, 8), (6, 5), (6, 6), (6, 7), (6, 8), (7, 5), (7, 6), (7, 7), (7, 8), (8, 5), (8, 6), (8, 7), (8, 8)\}$

6. $\{(-2, -2), (-2, 0), (-2, 2), (-2, 4), (0, -2), (0, 0), (0, 2), (0, 4), (2, -2), (2, 0), (2, 2), (2, 4), (4, -2), (4, 0), (4, 2), (4, 4)\}$

7. $\{(-7, -3), (-7, 1), (-7, 2), (-7, 5), (-3, 1), (-3, 2), (-3, 5), (1, 2), (1, 5), (2, 5)\}$

8. $\{(5, -7), (5, -3), (5, 1), (5, 2), (2, 1), (2, -3), (2, -7), (1, -3), (1, -7), (-3, -7)\}$

9. $\{(-7, -7), (-7, -3), (-7, 1), (-7, 2), (-7, 5), (-3, -3), (-3, 1), (-3, 2), (-3, 5), (1, 1), (1, 2), (1, 5), (2, 2), (2, 5), (5, 5)\}$

10. $\{(5, 5), (5, 2), (5, 1), (5, -3), (5, -7), (2, 2), (2, 1), (2, -3), (2, -7), (1, 1), (1, -3), (1, -7), (-3, -3), (-3, -7), (-7, -7)\}$

11. $\{(-7, -7), (-3, -3), (1, 1), (2, 2), (5, 5)\}$

12. $\{(-7, -3), (-7, 1), (-7, 2), (-7, 5), (-3, -7), (-3, 1), (3, 2), (-3, 5), (1, 1), (1, -3), (1, 2), (1, 5), (2, -7), (2, -3), (2, 1), (2, 5), (5, -7), (5, -3), (5, 1), (5, 2)\}$

13. Domain: $\{5, 6, 8\}$;   **14.** Domain: $\{7, 8, 9\}$,
    Range: $\{2, 4, 6\}$ Range: $\{1, 2, 5\}$

15. Domain: $\{6, 7, 8\}$;
Range: $\{0, 5\}$

16. Domain: $\{8, 10, 6\}$;
Range: $\{2, 1, 3\}$

17. Domain: $\{8, 5\}$;
Range: $\{1\}$

18. Domain: $\{6, 2, -3\}$;
Range: $\{2, 0\}$

19. Domain: $\{5\}$;
Range: $\{6\}$

20. Domain: $\{7\}$;
Range: $\{-4\}$

21. $\{8, 10, 12\}$ **22.** $\{4, 6, 8\}$ **23.** $\{2, 8, 10, 12\}$

24. $\{(2, 2), (2, 3)\}$ **25.** $\{(5, 2), (5, 3)\}$ **26.** $\{(2, 3), (3, 3)\}$

27. $\{(2, 4), (2, 5), (3, 4), (3, 5)\}$ **28.** $\{(3, 2)\}$ **29.** $\{(3, 3), (3, 4)\}$

30. **a.** $D \times D = \{(-1, -1), (-1, 0), (-1, 1), (-1, 2), (0, -1),$
$(0, 0), (0, 1), (0, 2), (1, -1), (1, 0), (1, 1), (1, 2),$
$(2, -1), (2, 0), (2, 1), (2, 2)\}$
b. $\{(x, y) \mid x \neq y\} = \{(-1, 0), (-1, 1), (-1, 2), (0, -1), (0, 1),$
$(0, 2), (1, -1), (1, 0), (1, 2), (2, -1),$
$(2, 0), (2, 1)\}$
c. Since we are taking a Cartesian product of a set D with itself,
the domain and range will contain all of the elements of D.
Domain: $\{-1, 0, 1, 2\}$;
Range: $\{-1, 0, 1, 2\}$
This is also true for the relation $\neq$.
d. $\{(-1, -1), (0, 0), (1, 1), (2, 2), (-1, 1), (1, -1)\}$

31. **a.** $E \times E = \{(-1, -1), (-1, 1), (-1, 3), (-1, 5), (1, -1), (1, 1),$
$(1, 3), (1, 5), (3, -1), (3, 1), (3, 3), (3, 5), (5, -1),$
$(5, 1), (5, 3), (5, 5)\}$
b. $\{(x, y)/x \leq y\} = \{(-1, -1), (-1, 1), (-1, 3), (-1, 5), (1, 1),$
$(1, 3), (1, 5), (3, 3), (3, 5), (5, 5)\}$
c. Domain: $\{-1, 1, 3, 5\}$;
Range: $\{-1, 1, 3, 5\}$
d. $\{(x, y)/|x| < |y|\} = \{(-1, 3), (-1, 5), (1, 3), (1, 5), (3, 5)\}$

32. Answers may vary. Examples are
$A \times B$ where $A = \{\text{chili}\}$ and $B = \{\text{chili}\}$.

33. Possible answers:
$(3, 1, 1),$
$(3, 2, 4),$
$(3, 3, 9),$
$(3, 4, 16),$
$(3, 5, 25)$
The general form of these ordered triples is $(3, a, a^2)$ where a
is any positive real number.

34. Possible answers:
To construct any member of this set, simply pick a negative real
number and substitute it for a in this ordered triple: $(2a, a, a^3)$.
$(-2, -1, -1),$
$(-4, -2, -8),$
$(-6, -3, -27),$
$(-8, -4, -64),$
$(-10, -5, -125)$

35. $(a + b)^2 = (3 + (-5))^2 = (3 - 5)^2 = (-2)^2 = 4$

36. $4a - 3b = 4(3) - 5(-5) = 12 - (-15) = 27$

37. $b^4 = (-1)^4 = 1$

38. $-a|2b| = -4(|2(-1)|) = -4(|-2|) = -4(2) = -8$

39. $c^{-4} \cdot c^3 \cdot c^7 = c^{-4+3+7} = c^6$

40. $(-4x^2 y^{-3})(2x^3 y^2) = -4(2)x^{(2+3)} y^{(-3+2)}$
$= -8x^5 y^{-1}$

41. $\left(\dfrac{1}{3}\right)y + 5 > \left(\dfrac{3}{4}\right)y$
$\left(\dfrac{1}{3} - \dfrac{3}{4}\right)y > -5$
$-\dfrac{5}{12}y > -5$
$y < 12$

42. $-4 < x - 3 < 5$
$-4 + 3 < x < 5 + 3$
$-1 < x < 8$

43. $-5t - \dfrac{1}{8} < \dfrac{1}{2} - 3t$
$-5t + 3t < \dfrac{1}{2} + \dfrac{1}{8}$
$-2t < \dfrac{4}{8} + \dfrac{1}{8}$
$-2t < \dfrac{5}{8}$
$t > -\dfrac{5}{16}$

pp. 111–114   3-2 TRY THIS

a.

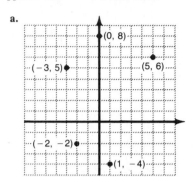

b.

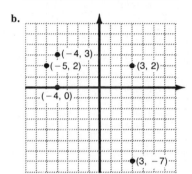

c. $(1, 7)$

$y = 2x + 5$	
7	$2 \cdot 1 + 5$
7	$2 + 5$
7	7

The equation becomes true, so $(1, 7)$ is a solution.

$(2, 9)$

$y = 2x + 5$	
9	$2 \cdot 2 + 5$
	$4 + 5$
	9

The equation becomes true, so $(2, 9)$ is a solution.

d. $(-1, 4)$

$y = -2x + 5$	
4	$-2 \cdot -1 + 5$
4	$2 + 5$
4	7

The equation becomes false, so $(-1, 4)$ is not a solution.

$(0, 6)$

$y = -2x + 5$	
6	$-2(0) + 5$
6	5

The equation becomes false, so $(0, 6)$ is not a solution.

e. $(-2, 5)$

$y = x^2$	
5	$(-2)^2$
5	4

22   *Algebra and Trigonometry*   Lessons 3-1–3-2

The equation becomes false, so $(-2, 5)$ is not a solution.

$(3, 9)$

$y = x^2$

$\dfrac{9}{9} \quad \dfrac{(3)^2}{9}$

The equation becomes true, so $(3, 9)$ is a solution.

f. 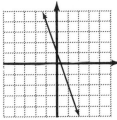 **g.**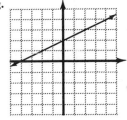

h. 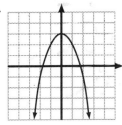 **i.**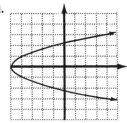

7. 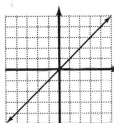 **8.**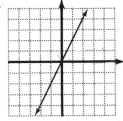

9. Yes; no   **10.** Yes; yes   **11.** No; no   **12.** No; yes

13. Yes; yes   **14.** Yes; no   **15.** Yes; no   **16.** Yes; yes

17. Yes; no   **18.** Yes; yes   **19.** No; yes   **20.** No; no

21. 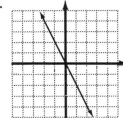 **22.**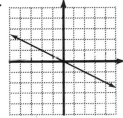

23. 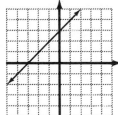 **24.**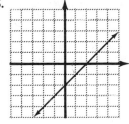

pp. 114–115   3-2 EXERCISES

1. 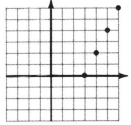 **2.**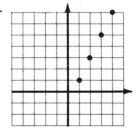

25. 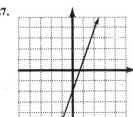 **26.**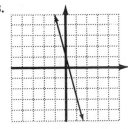

3. 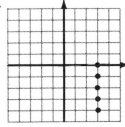 **4.**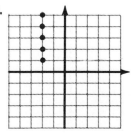

27. 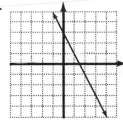 **28.**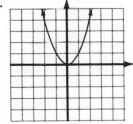

5. 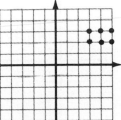 **6.**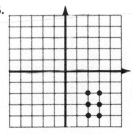

29. 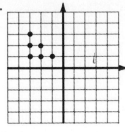 **30.**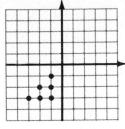

31.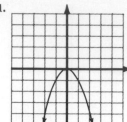

32.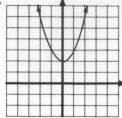

33.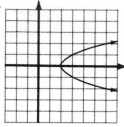

34.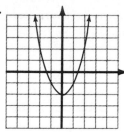

35.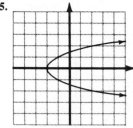

36. $y = x^2$

There is no restriction on x, so the domain consists of all real numbers.

Domain is $\{x \mid x$ is a real number$\}$.

Since $y = x^2$ it cannot be negative; therefore the range consists of all positive real numbers and zero.

Range is $\{y \mid y \geq 0\}$.

37. $y = -x^2$

Domain is $\{x \mid x$ is a real number$\}$.

Since y is equal to the negative of a square, it can attain only negative values or zero.

Range is $\{y \mid y \leq 0\}$.

38. $y = x^2 + 2$

Domain is $\{x \mid x$ is a real number$\}$.

Since x^2 is always positive, y is equal to a positive number plus 2; therefore, y cannot be less than 2.

Range is $\{y \mid y \geq 2\}$.

39. $y = x^2 - 2$

There is no restriction on x.

Domain is $\{x \mid x$ is a real number$\}$.

Since x^2 is always a positive number, the minimum value it can attain is zero; therefore, the minimum value that y can attain is zero minus 2.

Range is $\{y \mid y \geq -2\}$.

40. $x = y^2 + 2$

Since y^2 is always positive, x is equal to a positive number plus 2; therefore x cannot be less than 2.

Domain is $\{x \mid x \geq 2\}$.

There is no restriction on y.

Range is $\{y \mid y$ is a real number$\}$.

41. $x = y^2 - 2$

Since y^2 is always a positive number, the minimum value it can attain is zero; therefore, the minimum value that x can attain is zero minus 2.

Domain is $\{x \mid x \geq -2\}$.

There is no restriction on y.

Range is $\{y \mid y$ is a real number$\}$.

42.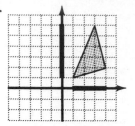

a. From the shaded area on the x-axis we see that $x \geq 1$ and $x \leq 4$; therefore, the domain $= \{x \mid 1 \leq x \leq 4\}$.

b. From the shaded area on the y-axis we see that $y \geq 1$ and $y \leq 6$; therefore, the range $= \{y \mid 1 \leq y \leq 6\}$.

43.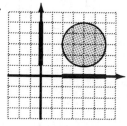

Some reference points to draw the circle are $(4, 1)$, $(4, 5)$, $(2, 3)$, and $(6, 3)$.

a. From the shaded area on the x-axis we see that $x \geq 2$ and $x \leq 6$; therefore, the domain $= \{x \mid 2 \leq x \leq 6\}$.

b. From the shaded area on the y-axis, we see that $y \geq 1$ and $y \leq 5$; therefore the range $= \{y \mid 1 \leq y \leq 6\}$.

44.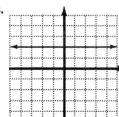

45.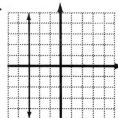

46.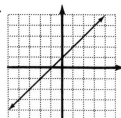

47.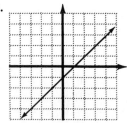

48.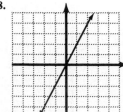

49.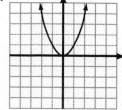

50.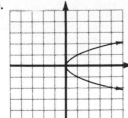

51.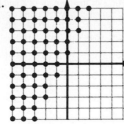

52.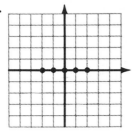

53.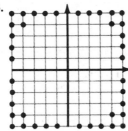

54.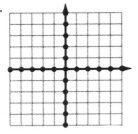

55. Answers may vary.
Ex: $x + y = -1$; $x + 2y = 0$; $-x + y = 3$

56.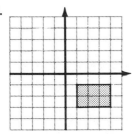

57.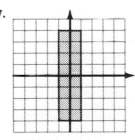

58.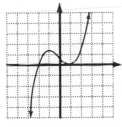

59.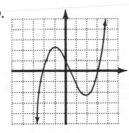

60. $|a - 11| - 7 = -2$
$|a - 11| = 5$
$a - 11 = -5$ or $a - 11 = 5$
$a = 6$ $a = 16$

61. $2(y^2 - y) = \frac{1}{2}(4y^2 + 10)$

$2y^2 - 2y = 2y^2 + 5$
$-2y = 5$

$y = -\frac{5}{2}$

62. $x = $ 1st odd integer, $\quad x + (x + 2) + (x + 4) = 41 + 2$
$x + 2 = $ 2nd odd integer, $\quad\quad 3x + 6 = 41 + 2$
$x + 4 = $ 3rd odd integer, $\quad\quad\quad\quad x = 35$
$35, 37, 39$

63. $x = $ length of longer piece,

$\frac{1}{4}x = $ length of shorter piece.

$x + \frac{1}{4}x = 30$

$\frac{5}{4}x = 30$

$x = 24$
24 in., 6 in.

64. $A = $ amount invested at 6%,
$B = $ amount invested at 8%.
$A + B = 500 - B$
$A = 500 - B$
$A(0.06) + B(0.08) + 500 = 535$

Substituting for A
$(500 - B)(0.06) + B(0.08) = 535 - 500$
$30 - 0.06B + B(0.08) = 35$
$B(0.02) = 5$
$B = 250$
Amount in account $B = \$250$
Amount in account $A = 500 - 250 = \$250$

WRITING TO LEARN p. 115

Answers may vary.
The axes are formed from the real number system. Since the real numbers are infinite, so is the cartesian coordinate system.

pp. 116–119   3-3 TRY THIS

a. A is not a function; $(9, 0)$ and $(9, 1)$ have the same first coordinate. B, C, D, and E are functions.
b. (1) Yes, (2) Yes, (3) Yes, (4) No
c. Since we have the ordered pairs $(9, 1)$, $(6, 6)$, and $(0, -2)$ in the set h, we have $h(9) = 1$; $h(6) = 6$; and $h(0) = -2$.
d. $f(0) = 3 \cdot 0^2 + 1 = 0 + 1 = 1$
e. $f(1) = 3 \cdot 1^2 + 1 = 3 + 1 = 4$
f. $f(-1) = 3 \cdot (-1)^2 + 1 = 3 + 1 = 4$
g. $f(2a) = 3 \cdot (2a)^2 + 1 = 3 \cdot 4a^2 + 1 = 12a^2 + 1$
h. $g(x)$ is undefined when $(x - 1)(x + 3) = 0$.
$x - 1 = 0$ or $x + 3 = 0$
$x = 1$ $x = -3$
Domain is $\{x \mid x \neq 1 \text{ and } x \neq -3\}$.
i. $h(x)$ is defined for any x.
Domain is $\{x \mid x \text{ is a real number}\}$.
j. $p(x)$ is undefined when $3x = 0$.
$3x = 0$
$x = 0$
Domain is $\{x \mid x \neq 0\}$.

pp. 119–121   3-3 EXERCISES

1. Yes   **2.** Yes   **3.** No   **4.** No   **5.** Yes
6. No, unless $a = -1$ **7.** Yes   **8.** Yes   **9.** No
10. No   **11.** Yes   **12.** Yes

13. a. 1
b. -3
c. -6
d. 9

14. a. 0
b. 4
c. -7
d. -8

15. a. 0
b. 1
c. 57
d. $5t^2 + 4t$

16. a. 0
b. 5
c. 21
d. $3t^2 - 2t$

17. a. 15
b. 32
c. 20
d. 4

18. a. 35
b. 2
c. 7
d. 20

19. a. $\dfrac{2}{3}$
b. $\dfrac{10}{9}$
c. 0
d. Not possible

20. a. $\dfrac{26}{25}$
b. $\dfrac{2}{9}$
c. Not possible
d. $-\dfrac{7}{3}$

21. The set of real numbers   **22.** The set of real numbers

23. $\{x \mid x \neq 0\}$ **24.** $\{x \mid x \neq 3\}$ **25.** $\left\{x \mid x \neq -\dfrac{8}{5}\right\}$

26. $\{x \mid x \neq 3 \text{ and } x \neq 0\}$ **27.** $\{x \mid x \neq 0, x \neq -2, \text{ and } x \neq 1\}$

28. R

29. a. $f(2) = \dfrac{1}{2}$ b. $f(3) = \dfrac{1}{3}$ c. $f(-2) = -\dfrac{1}{2}$

   d. $f(0)$; Not possible because division by zero is undefined.

30. This function is undefined when $x - 4 = 0$; 4.

31. This function is undefined when $x^2 - x = 0$; 0 and 1.

32. This function is undefined when $-x = 0$; 0.

33. No. For example, $A = \{$the rational numbers$\}$ and $B = \{$the rational numbers$\}$, the function $y = \dfrac{1}{x - 3}$ is a function from A to B. The function is undefined when $x = 3$.

34. a. $(f \oplus g)(5) = f(5) + g(5)$
$= 2 \cdot 5 + 3 + 5 - 5$
$= 13$
   b. $(f \oplus g)(-6) = f(-6) + g(-6)$
$= 2(-6) + 3 + (-6) - 5$
$= -12 + 3 - 6 - 5$
$= -20$
   c. $(f \oplus g)(0) = f(0) + g(0)$
$= 2 \cdot 0 + 3 + 0 - 5$
$= -2$
   d. The set of all real numbers
   e. $(f \oplus g)(x) = f(x) + g(x)$
$= 2x + 3 + x - 5$
$= x - 5 + 2x + 3$
$= g(x) + f(x)$
$= (g \oplus f)(x);$ Yes

35. a. $(f \oplus g)(1) = f(1) + g(1)$
$= \dfrac{1}{1} + \dfrac{1}{1 - 2}$
$= 0$
   b. $(f \oplus g)(2) = f(2) + g(2)$
$= \dfrac{1}{2} + \dfrac{1}{2 - 2}$
$= \dfrac{1}{2} + \dfrac{1}{0}$
Not possible
   c. $(f \oplus g)(0) = f(0) + g(0)$
$= \dfrac{1}{0} + \dfrac{1}{0 - 2}$
Not possible
   d. The domain of $(f \oplus g)(x)$ is the intersection of the domains of $f(x)$ and $g(x)$.
Domain of $f(x)$: $\{x \mid x \neq 0\}$
Domain of $g(x)$: $\{x \mid x \neq 2\}$
Domain of $(f \oplus g)(x)$: $\{x \mid x \neq 0 \text{ and } x \neq 2\}$

36. For x in the domain of f and g, $(f \oplus g)(x) = [f(x)][g(x)]$.

37. $|-14 - (-22)| = |22 - 14| = 8$

38. $|-2 - 8| = |-10| = 10$ **39.** $|0 - 47.5| = 47.5$

40. $|-24 - (-2)| = |-24 + 2| = 22$

41. $-x + 2 < -1$ or $0.3x < 0.6$

$-x < -3$ or $x < \dfrac{0.6}{0.3}$

$x > 3$ or $x < 2$

42. $2x + 4 < 3x + 2$ and $3x + 2 < 29$
$4 - 2 < 3x - 2x$ and $3x < 27$
$2 < x$ and $x < 9$
$2 < x < 9$

43. $-\dfrac{9}{2} < -\dfrac{1}{2}x + 1 < -2$

$-\dfrac{9}{2} - 1 < -\dfrac{1}{2}x < -2 - 1$

$-\dfrac{11}{2} < -\dfrac{1}{2}x < -3$

$-2\left(-\dfrac{11}{2}\right) > -2\left(-\dfrac{1}{2}\right)x > -3(-2)$

$11 > x > 6$

44. $x \div \dfrac{0}{x} = x \div 0$, not possible; none

45. $\dfrac{2(3x - 6)}{2(3x - 6) - 3(2x - 4)} = \dfrac{2(3)(x - 2)}{2(3)(x - 2) - 3(2)(x - 2)}$

$= \dfrac{6(x - 2)}{6(x - 2)[1 - 1]}$

$= \dfrac{1}{0}$, not possible; none

46. The expression is undefined when
$x - 2 = 0$ or $2 - x = 0$
$x = 2$ $2 = x$
All real numbers except $x = 2$.

p. 121   PROBLEM FOR PROGRAMMERS

```
10   REM Chapter 3 Problem
20   FLAG$ = "is"
30   FOR X = 1 TO 10
40   PRINT "Input ordered pair x";X;", y";X
50   INPUT A(X),B(X)
60   FOR TST = 1 TO X
70   IF TST = X THEN 120
80   IF A(X) = A(TST) THEN 100
90   GOTO 120
100  IF B(X) = B(TST) THEN 120
110  FLAG$ = "is not"
120  NEXT TST
130  NEXT X
140  PRINT "The relation ";FLAG$;" a function."
150  END
```

pp. 122–125   3-4 TRY THIS

a. Linear—all variables are first degree with no products of variables or variables in denominators.
b. Linear
c. Not linear—y is raised to the second power and there is a product of two variables.

d. Not linear—y is in the denominator.
e. Not linear—there is a product of two variables.
f. Linear
g. $2x - 6y = -2$

y-intercept: $\quad 2 \cdot 0 - 6y = -2$
$$-6y = -2$$
$$y = \frac{-2}{-6}$$
$$y = \frac{1}{3}$$

x-intercept: $\quad 2x - (6 \cdot 0) = -2$
$$2x = -2$$
$$x = -\frac{2}{2}$$
$$x = -1$$

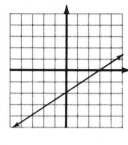

h. $3y = 2x - 6$

y-intercept: $\quad 3y = 2 \cdot 0 - 6$
$$3y = -6$$
$$y = -\frac{6}{3}$$
$$y = -2$$

x-intercept: $\quad 3 \cdot 0 = 2x = 6$
$$2x = 6$$
$$x = \frac{6}{2}$$
$$x = 3$$

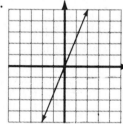

i.

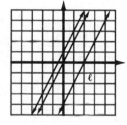

j.

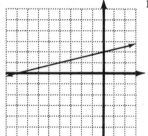

k. $y = 2x \qquad y = 2x + 1$

x	y
1	2
-1	-2
0	0

x	y
0	1
-1	-1
1	3

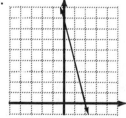

The graph of $y = 2x + 1$ is a line moved up 1 unit from $y = 2x$.

l. $y = 2x - 4$

x	y
0	-4
1	-2
2	0

The graph of $y = 2x - 4$ is a line moved down 4 units from the graph of $y = 2x$.

m–o.

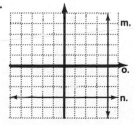

---

1. Yes   **2.** Yes   **3.** No; 2nd degree

4. No; product of variables   **5.** Yes   **6.** No; 2nd degree

7. Yes   **8.** No; variable in denominator   **9.** Yes   **10.** Yes

11.

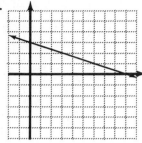

12.

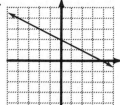

13.

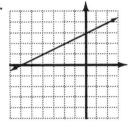

14.

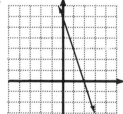

15.

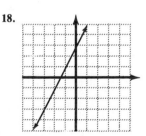

16.

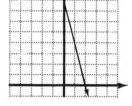

17.

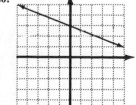

18.

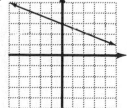

19.

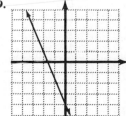

20.

21.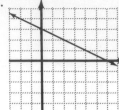

22.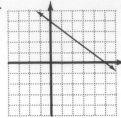

33.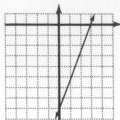

34.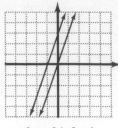

$y = 3x + 3$ is 3 units above $y = 3x$.

23.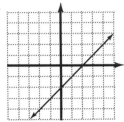

24.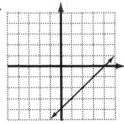

35.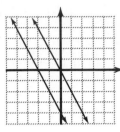

36.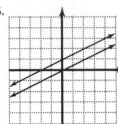

$y = -2x - 4$ is 4 units below $y = -2x$.

$y = y = \frac{1}{2}x + 1$ is 1 unit above $y = \frac{1}{2}x$.

25.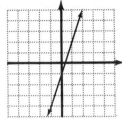

26.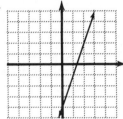

27.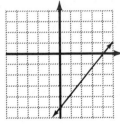

28.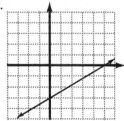

37.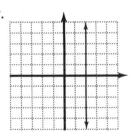

38.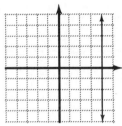

39.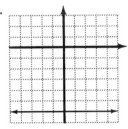

40.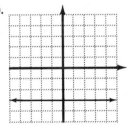

29.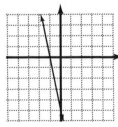

30.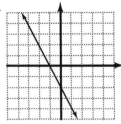

41.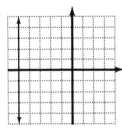

42.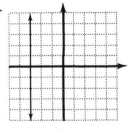

31.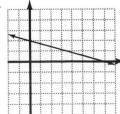

32.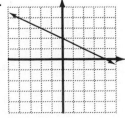

43.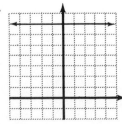

44.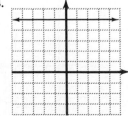

45. 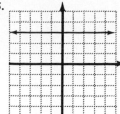 **46.**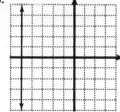

x-intercept: $x = -\dfrac{7}{3}(0) - \dfrac{2}{11}$

$$x = -\dfrac{2}{11}; \left(-\dfrac{2}{11}, 0\right)$$

53. The graphs of exercises 39, 40, 43, 44, 45, and 48 are horizontal lines and are therefore functions.

54. Answers may vary.
When $x = 3$, $y = 0$ and when $x = -3$, $y = 0$. Connecting the points $(3, 0)$ and $(-3, 0)$ will give the x-axis as the graph.

55. a. Answers may vary.
b. All of these lines contain the point $(3, 2)$.
c. $y - 3 = k(x + 5)$

56. $(-2x^3y^2)^2(-xy)^4(x^{-2}y^{-1})^{-2}$
$= (-2)^2x^{3+2}y^{2+2}(-1)^4x^4y^4(x^{-2\cdot-2}y^{-1\cdot-2})$
$= 4x^6y^4(x^4y^4)(x^4y^2)$
$= 4x^{14}y^{10}$

57. $\left(\dfrac{1}{a^{-2}}\right)^3 = \dfrac{1}{a^{-2\cdot3}} = \dfrac{1}{a^{-6}} = a^6$

58. $b^3\left(\dfrac{b}{b^{-2}}\right) = b^{-3}\left(\dfrac{b^{-1}}{b^{-2\cdot-1}}\right)$

$= b^3\left(\dfrac{b^{-1}}{b^2}\right)$

$= \dfrac{b^3}{b^3} = 1$

59. $A \times B = \{(a, 0), (a, 1), (b, 0), (b, 1), (c, 0), (c, 1)\}$

60. $B \times A = \{(0, a), (0, b), (0, c), (1, a), (1, b), (1, c)\}$
$C \times C = \{(-1, -1), (-1, 0), (-1, 1), (0, -1), (0, 0), (0, 1),$
$(1, -1), (1, 0), (1, 1)\}$

61. $<$ for $C \times C = \{(-1, 0), (-1, 1), (0, 1)\}$

49. $2x + 5y + 2 = 5x - 10y - 8$
$10y + 5y = 5x - 2x - 8 - 2$
$15y = 3x - 10$
y-intercept: $15y = 3 \cdot 0 - 10$
$15y = -10$
$$y = -\dfrac{10}{15} = -\dfrac{2}{3}; \left(0, -\dfrac{2}{3}\right)$$
x-intercept: $15 \cdot 0 = 3 \cdot x - 10$
$3x = 10$
$$x = \dfrac{10}{3}; \left(\dfrac{10}{3}, 0\right)$$

50. $\dfrac{1}{8}y = -x - \dfrac{7}{16}$

y-intercept: $\dfrac{1}{8}y = -0 \cdot \dfrac{7}{16}$

$y = -\dfrac{8 \cdot 7}{16}$

$$y = -\dfrac{7}{2}; \left(0, -\dfrac{7}{2}\right)$$

x-intercept: $\dfrac{1}{8} \cdot 0 = -x - \dfrac{7}{16}$

$$x = -\dfrac{7}{16}; \left(-\dfrac{7}{16}, 0\right)$$

51. $0.4y - 0.004x = -0.04$
y-intercept: $0.4y - 0.004(0) = -0.04$
$0.4y = -0.04$
$$y = -\dfrac{0.04}{0.4} = -0.1; (0, -0.1)$$
x-intercept: $0.4(0) - 0.004x = -0.04$
$$x = \dfrac{0.04}{0.004} = 10; (10, 0)$$

52. $x = -\dfrac{7}{3}y - \dfrac{2}{11}$

y-intercept: $0 = -\dfrac{7}{3}y - \dfrac{2}{11}$

$\dfrac{7}{3}y = -\dfrac{2}{11}$

$y = \dfrac{3}{7} \cdot \left(-\dfrac{2}{11}\right)$

$$y = -\dfrac{6}{77}; \left(0, -\dfrac{6}{77}\right)$$

pp. 128–130   **3-5 TRY THIS**

a. $m = \dfrac{14 - 1}{12 - 1} = \dfrac{13}{11}$ **b.** $m = \dfrac{10 - 9}{4 - 3} = \dfrac{1}{1} = 1$

c. $m = \dfrac{7 - (-4)}{5 - 0} = \dfrac{11}{5}$ **d.** $m = \dfrac{3 - 2}{6 - 7} = \dfrac{1}{-1} = -1$

e. $m = \dfrac{y_2 - y_1}{x_2 - x_1} = \dfrac{-5 - (-5)}{1 - 0} = \dfrac{0}{1} = 0$

f. $m = \dfrac{y_2 - y_1}{x_2 - x_1} = \dfrac{-2 - 3}{17 - 17} = \dfrac{-1}{0}$; No slope

g. $(y - y_1) = m(x - x_1)$
$y - 4 = -3(x - (-2))$
$y - 4 = -3(x + 2)$
$y - 4 = -3x - 6$
$y = -3x - 2$

h. $(y - y_1) = m(x - x_1)$
$y - (-10) = \dfrac{1}{4}(x - (-4))$

$y + 10 = \dfrac{1}{4}(x + 4)$

$y + 10 = \dfrac{1}{4}x + 1$

$y = \dfrac{1}{4}x - 9$

i. $(y - 0) = -\dfrac{1}{2}(x - 5)$

$y = -\dfrac{1}{2}x + \dfrac{5}{2}$

pp. 131–132   **3-5 EXERCISES**

1. 8 **2.** 1 **3.** -1 **4.** 0 **5.** $-\dfrac{1}{2}$ **6.** $\dfrac{4}{3}$

7. 2 **8.** $\dfrac{6}{5}$ **9.** $\dfrac{3}{7}$ **10.** $-\dfrac{2}{5}$ **11.** $\dfrac{1}{2}$ **12.** $\dfrac{5}{2}$

13. $\dfrac{2}{5}$ **14.** $-\dfrac{1}{4}$ **15.** No slope **16.** 0 **17.** No slope

47. 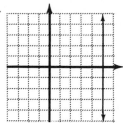 **48.**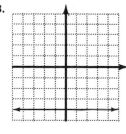

Algebra and Trigonometry 29

18. No slope   **19.** 0   **20.** 0   **21.** No slope   **22.** No slope

23. 0   **24.** 0   **25.** No slope   **26.** No slope   **27.** 0

28. 0   **29.** 0   **30.** No slope   **31.** No slope   **32.** 0

33. $y = 4x - 10$ **34.** $y = -2x + 15$ **35.** $y = -x - 7$

36. $y = 3x + 2$ **37.** $y = \frac{1}{2}x + 7$ **38.** $y = -\frac{4}{3}x + 3$

39. $y = -7$ **40.** $y = 0$

41. $m = \dfrac{0.83 - 0.08}{0.47 - 0.04} = \dfrac{0.75}{0.43} \approx 1.7441860$

42. $m = \dfrac{0.8 - (-0.04)}{0.02 - (-0.2)} = \dfrac{0.84}{0.22} = 3.\overline{81}$

43. $y - (-2.563) = 3.516(x - 3.014)$
$y + 2.563 = 3.516x - 10.597224$
$y = 3.516x - 13.1602$

44. $m = \dfrac{11.012 - 2.443}{8.114 - 1.103}$

$= \dfrac{8.569}{7.011} = 1.\overline{22}$, or ≈ 1.22

$y - 2.443 = 1.2222(x - 1.103)$
$y = 1.2222x - 1.34808 + 2.443$
$y = 1.22x + 1.0949$

45. $m_{\overline{AB}} = \dfrac{4 - 2}{9 + 1} = \dfrac{2}{10} = \dfrac{1}{5}$

$m_{\overline{BC}} = \dfrac{3 - 2}{4 + 1} = \dfrac{1}{5}$

Since the slopes are equal, the points lie on a line.

46. $m_{\overline{AB}} = \dfrac{2 + 1}{2 + 1} = 1$

$m_{\overline{BC}} = \dfrac{2 + 4}{2 + 3} = \dfrac{6}{5}$

The slopes are not equal. These points are not on the same line.

47. $\dfrac{3a + a}{-2 - 4} = \dfrac{4a}{-6} = -\dfrac{2a}{3}$

$-\dfrac{2a}{3} = -\dfrac{5}{12}$

$-2a = 3\left(-\dfrac{5}{12}\right)$

$-2a = -\dfrac{5}{4}$

$a = -\dfrac{5}{4}\left(-\dfrac{1}{2}\right)$

$a = \dfrac{5}{8}$

48. a. $m = \dfrac{-c - (-6c)}{b - 5b} = \dfrac{-c + 6c}{-4b} = -\dfrac{5c}{4b}$

b. $m = \dfrac{(d + e) - d}{b - b} = \dfrac{e}{0}$; No slope

c. $m = \dfrac{a + d - (-a - d)}{c + f - (c - f)} = \dfrac{a + d + a + d}{c + f - c + f}$

$= \dfrac{2a + 2d}{2f} = \dfrac{a + d}{f}$

49. Answers may vary

$m = \dfrac{4 - 0}{-100 - 0} = -\dfrac{4}{100} = -\dfrac{1}{25}$

$y = \dfrac{1}{25}x$ since the x- and y-intercepts are at $(0, 0)$.

Possible points are $(-25, 1), (-50, 2), (-75, 3), (25, -1)$.

50. $2x + 3y = 6$
$3y = 6 - 2x$

$y = \dfrac{6}{3} - \dfrac{2}{3}x$

$y = 2 - \dfrac{2}{3}x$

$m = \dfrac{0 - 2}{3 - 0} = -\dfrac{2}{3}$

x	y
0	2
3	0

51. $2x + 5y + 2 = 5x + 10y - 8$
$5y - 10y = 5x - 2x - 8 - 2$
$-5y = 3x - 10$

$y = -\dfrac{3}{5}x + 2$

$m = \dfrac{2 - (-1)}{0 - 5} = -\dfrac{3}{5}$

x	y
0	2
5	-1

52. Their graphs are either entirely in the 1st and 3rd quadrants or entirely in the 2nd and 4th quadrants.

53. $m_{\overline{AB}} = \dfrac{2 - 0}{8 - 0} = \dfrac{2}{8} = \dfrac{1}{4}$

$m_{\overline{CD}} = \dfrac{6 - 4}{11 - 6} = \dfrac{2}{8} = \dfrac{1}{4}$ $m_{\overline{AB}} = m_{\overline{CD}}$

$m_{\overline{BC}} = \dfrac{6 - 2}{11 - 8} = \dfrac{4}{3}$

$m_{\overline{DA}} = \dfrac{4 - 0}{3 - 0} = \dfrac{4}{3}$ $m_{\overline{BC}} = m_{\overline{DA}}$

Figure $ABCD$ is a parallelogram and its opposite sides are parallel.

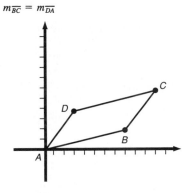

54. $m_{\overline{EG}} = \dfrac{-2 - (-5)}{7 - (-2)} = \dfrac{3}{9} = \dfrac{1}{3}$

$m_{\overline{FH}} = \dfrac{-2 - (-5)}{2 - 3} = \dfrac{3}{-1} = -3$

Figure $EFGH$ is a rhombus and its diagonals are perpendicular. The slopes of $\overline{EG}$ and $\overline{FH}$ are negative reciprocals.

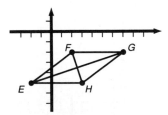

55. a. grade $= \dfrac{50}{1250} = 0.04$ or   4%

$y = $ grade (x)
$y = 0.04x$

b. grade $= \dfrac{920.58}{13,740} = 0.067$ or   6.7%

$y = $ grade (x)
$y = 0.067x$

56. $f(x)$ is undefined when $\dfrac{3}{x}$ is undefined.

Domain: $\{x \mid x \neq 0\}$

57. $f(x)$ is defined for all values of x.
Domain is $\{x \mid x$ is a real number$\}$.

58. $5(n + 2) + 12 = 5(4 + 2) + 12$
$= 5(6) + 12$
$= 30 + 12$
$= 42$

59. $n(6 - n) + 7 = 4(6 - 4) + 7$
$= 4(2) + 7$
$= 8 + 7$
$= 15$

60. $(3n)^2 = 3^2(4)^2 = 9(16) = 144$

61. $c + \dfrac{2}{3} = \dfrac{1}{2}$

$c = \dfrac{1}{2} - \dfrac{2}{3}$

$c = \dfrac{3 - 4}{6}$

$c = -\dfrac{1}{6}$

62. $v - \dfrac{1}{2} = \dfrac{2}{5}$

$v = \dfrac{1}{2} + \dfrac{2}{5}$

$v = \dfrac{5 + 4}{10}$

$v = \dfrac{9}{10}$

63. $-\dfrac{k}{9} = \dfrac{4}{5}$

$k = \dfrac{4}{5}(-9)$

$k = -\dfrac{36}{5}$

64. $9c = \dfrac{2}{5}$

$c = \dfrac{2}{5}\left(\dfrac{1}{9}\right)$

$c = \dfrac{2}{45}$

pp. 133–136   **3-6 TRY THIS**

a. $y - 4 = \dfrac{-2 - 4}{3 - 1}(x - 1)$

$y - 4 = \dfrac{-6}{2}(x - 1)$

$y - 4 = -3(x - 1)$
$y = -3x + 3 + 4$
$y = -3x + 7$

b. $y - 4 = \dfrac{-6 - 4}{3 - 0}(x - 0)$

$y - 4 = \dfrac{-10}{3}x$

$y = -\dfrac{10}{3}x + 4$

c. $y = -5x + \dfrac{1}{3}$

$m = -5$

$y\text{-intercept} = \dfrac{1}{3}$

d. $-2x + 3y - 6 = 0$
$3y = 2x + 6$

$y = \dfrac{2}{3}x + 2$

$m = \dfrac{2}{3}$

$y\text{-intercept} = 2$

e. $2y - 6 = 0$
$2y = 6$

$y = \dfrac{6}{2}$

$y = 3 = 0 \cdot x + 3$
$m = 0$
$y\text{-intercept} = 3$

f. $y\text{-intercept} = -1$
$m = 3$

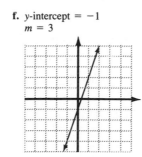

g. $7y = -4x - 21$

$y = -\dfrac{4}{7}x - \dfrac{21}{7}$

$y = -\dfrac{4}{7}x - 3$

$y\text{-intercept} = -3$

$m = -\dfrac{4}{7}$

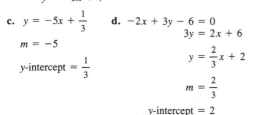

h. $6x = -5y - \dfrac{5}{2}$

$5y = -6x - \dfrac{5}{2}$

$y = -\dfrac{6}{5}x - \dfrac{1}{2}$

$y\text{-intercept} = -\dfrac{1}{2}$

$m = -\dfrac{6}{5}$

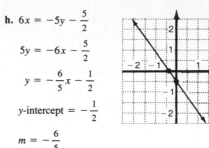

i. $5y = \dfrac{1}{2} + 5x$

$5x - 5y + \dfrac{1}{2} = 0$

$m = -\dfrac{-5}{5} = 1$

j. $8x = 10 + 5y$
$8x - 5y - 10 = 0$

$m = -\dfrac{8}{-5} = \dfrac{8}{5}$

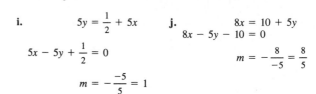

pp. 136–137   **3-6 EXERCISES**

1. $y = \dfrac{1}{2}x + \dfrac{7}{2}$ **2.** $y = -\dfrac{5}{2}x + 11$ **3.** $y = x$

4. $y = x$ **5.** $y = \dfrac{5}{2}x + 5$ **6.** $y = \dfrac{1}{2}x - 3$

7. $y = \dfrac{1}{4}x + \dfrac{17}{4}$ **8.** $y = \dfrac{1}{5}x + \dfrac{26}{5}$ **9.** $y = \dfrac{2}{5}x$

10. $y = \dfrac{3}{7}x$ **11.** $y = 3x + 5$ **12.** $y = \dfrac{3}{2}x$

13. $m = 2; b = 3$ **14.** $m = 3; b = 4$

15. $m = -4; b = 9$ **16.** $m = -5; b = -7$

17. $m = -1; b = 6$ **18.** $m = -1; b = 7$

19. $m = -3; b = 5$ **20.** $m = 4; b = -2$

21. $m = \dfrac{3}{4}; b = -3$ **22.** $m = -\dfrac{5}{2}; b = -\dfrac{7}{2}$

23. $m = -3; b = 4$ **24.** $m = \dfrac{2}{3}; b = -\dfrac{5}{3}$

25. $m = -\dfrac{7}{3}; b = -3$ **26.** $m = -\dfrac{8}{5}; b = -\dfrac{7}{5}$

27. $m = 0; b = 7$ **28.** $m = 0; b = 9$

29. $m = 0; b = -\dfrac{10}{3}$ **30.** $m = 0; b = -\dfrac{11}{4}$

31.

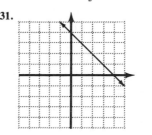

32.

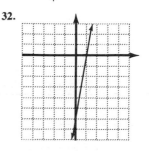

33.

34.

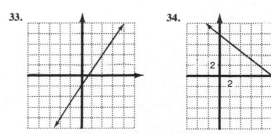

35.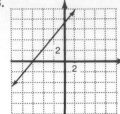

36.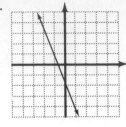

37. $4x - y - 8 = 0; m = 4$ 　　**38.** $6x - y - 2 = 0$　$m = 6$

39. $2x - y + 3 = 0$　$m = 2$ 　　**40.** $x - 2y + 1 = 0$　$m = \dfrac{1}{2}$

41. $x - 6 = 0$　no slope 　　**42.** $y - 9 = 0$　$m = 0$

43. $x + y - 2 = 0$　$m = -1$ 　　**44.** $4x - y + 4 = 0$　$m = 4$

45. $2x - 6 = 0$　no slope 　　**46.** $y = 0$　$m = 0$

47. Not a linear equation

48. $y = -4x + 3$ 　　**49.** $y = \dfrac{2}{5}x - 4$ 　　**50.** $y = 75x - 18$

51. $y = -0.36x + 10$

52.
$$m = \frac{0.7 - (-0.3)}{-0.2 - (-0.7)} = \frac{1}{0.5} = 2$$
$$y - 0.7 = 2(x - (-0.2))$$
$$y - 0.7 = 2(x + 0.2)$$
$$y - 0.7 = 2x + 0.4$$
$$y = 2x + 1.1$$

53.
$$m = \frac{\dfrac{1}{2} - (-2)}{\dfrac{1}{11} - \left(-\dfrac{10}{11}\right)} = \frac{\dfrac{5}{2}}{1} = \frac{5}{2}$$
$$y - \frac{1}{2} = \frac{5}{2}\left(x - \frac{1}{11}\right)$$
$$y - \frac{1}{2} = \frac{5}{2}x - \frac{5}{22}$$
$$y = \frac{5}{2}x - \frac{5}{22} + \frac{1}{2}$$
$$y = \frac{5}{2}x + \frac{3}{11}$$

54. $3x + 4y - 10 = 0$
$$y = \frac{-3}{4}x + \frac{5}{2}$$
$$m = -\frac{3}{4}$$
$$y - (-3) = -\frac{3}{4}(x - 2)$$
$$y + 3 = -\frac{3}{4}x + \frac{3}{2}$$
$$y = -\frac{3}{4}x - \frac{3}{2}$$

55. $y - (-4) = -2(x - 3)$,　$y = -2x + 2$
$$y + 4 = -2x + 6$$
$$y = -2x + 2$$
$$8 = -2x + 2 \qquad b = -2(5) + 2$$
$$-2a = 6 \qquad\quad b = -10 + 2$$
$$a = -3 \qquad\quad b = -8$$

56.
$$m = \frac{\dfrac{2}{5} - 0}{0 - (-3)} = \frac{\dfrac{2}{5}}{3} = \frac{2}{15}$$
$$y - 0 = \frac{2}{15}(x - (-3))$$
$$y = \frac{2}{15}x + \frac{2}{5}$$

57. Equation (*b*) does not belong. It has a negative slope.

58. Let $y = 0$:　$\dfrac{x}{a} + \dfrac{0}{b} = 1$
$$\frac{x}{a} = 1$$
$$x = a, \text{ the } x\text{-intercept}$$
　　Let $x = 0$:　$\dfrac{0}{a} + \dfrac{y}{b} = 1$
$$\frac{y}{b} = 1$$
$$y = b, \text{ the } y\text{-intercept}$$

59.　$5x - 4y - 7 = 0$　$m = \dfrac{5}{4}$
$$x - \frac{4}{5}y = \frac{7}{5}$$
$$\frac{x}{4} + \frac{y}{-5} = \frac{7}{20}$$
$$\frac{x}{\dfrac{7}{20}(4)} + \frac{y}{\dfrac{7}{20}(-5)} = \frac{\dfrac{7}{20}}{\dfrac{7}{20}}$$
$$\frac{x}{\dfrac{7}{5}} + \frac{y}{-\dfrac{7}{4}} = 1$$
$$a = \frac{7}{5}; b = -\frac{7}{4}; m = \frac{5}{4}$$

60.　$2y - 3x = 4$　$m = -\left(-\dfrac{3}{2}\right) = \dfrac{3}{2}$
$$y - \frac{3}{2}x = 2$$
$$\frac{y}{3} - \frac{1}{2}x = \frac{2}{3}$$
$$\frac{y}{\dfrac{2}{3}(3)} - \frac{x}{\dfrac{2}{3}(2)} = \frac{\dfrac{2}{3}}{\dfrac{2}{3}}$$
$$\frac{x}{-\dfrac{4}{3}} + \frac{y}{2} = 1; a = -\frac{4}{3}; b = 2; m = \frac{3}{2}$$

61.　$1.25y + 7.8x = 4.2x - 18$
$$1.25y + 3.6x = -18 \qquad m = -\frac{3.6}{1.25} = -2.88$$
$$y + \frac{3.6x}{1.25} = \frac{-18}{1.25}$$
$$\frac{y}{3.6} + \frac{x}{1.25} = \frac{-18}{1.25(3.6)} = -4$$
$$\frac{y}{-4(3.6)} + \frac{x}{-4(1.25)} = 1$$
$$\frac{y}{-14.4} + \frac{x}{-5} = 1; a = -5; b = -14.4; m = -2.88$$

62. $Ax + By + C = 0$
$$By = -Ax - C$$
$$y = -\frac{A}{B}x - \frac{C}{B}$$

This is the slope-intercept equation of the line, so $m = -\dfrac{A}{B}$, where $B \neq 0$.

63. Function 　　**64.** Not a function 　　**65.** Function

66. Function 　　**67.** Not a function 　　**68.** Domain: $\{-1, 0, 1, 2\}$; Range: $\{0, 7\}$

69. Domain: {1}
Range: {2, 6}

70. Domain is $\{x \mid x$ is a real number$\}$.
Range is $\{y \mid y$ is a real number$\}$.

71. Domain is $\{x \mid x$ is a real number$\}$
Range is {3}

72. Domain is {2};
Range is $\{y \mid y$ is a real number$\}$.

73. $\dfrac{9.34 + 9.40 + 9.25 + a}{4} \geq 9.45$

$$\dfrac{28 + a}{4} \geq 9.45$$

$$28 + a \geq 4(9.45)$$
$$a \geq 37.8 - 28$$
$$a \geq 9.8; \; 9.80 \text{ or more}$$

pp. 139–141 **3-7 TRY THIS**

a. $y = x + 4; \; y - x = -3$
$\qquad\qquad\quad y = x - 3$
The slopes are the same; the y-intercepts are different; the lines are parallel.

b. $y + 4 = 3x; \qquad 4x - y = -7$
$\quad y = 3x - 4 \qquad\quad y = -4x + 7$
The slopes are different; the lines are not parallel.

c. $y = 4x + 5; \qquad 2y = 8x + 10$
$\qquad\qquad\qquad\quad y = 4x + 5$
No, the equations have the same graph.

d. $2y + 8x = 6$
$\quad 2y = -8x + 6$
$\quad\;\; y = -4x + 3; \; m = -4$
$y - (-4) = -4(x - (-2))$
$\quad y + 2 = -4x - 8$
$\qquad\; y = -4x - 12$

e. $2y - x = 2 \qquad\qquad y + 2 = 4$
$\quad 2y = x + 2 \qquad\qquad y = -2x + 4; \; m = -2$
$\quad\; y = \dfrac{1}{2}x + 2; \; m = \dfrac{1}{2}$

$\left(\dfrac{1}{2}\right) \cdot (-2) = -1$; the lines are perpendicular.

f. $3y = 2x + 15 \qquad\qquad 2y = 3x + 10$
$\quad y = \dfrac{2x}{3} + \dfrac{15}{3} \qquad\qquad y = \dfrac{3x}{2} + \dfrac{10}{2}$
$\quad y = \dfrac{2}{3}x + 5; \; m = \dfrac{2}{3} \qquad y = \dfrac{3}{2}x + 5; \; m = \dfrac{3}{2}$

$\left(\dfrac{2}{3}\right) \cdot \left(\dfrac{3}{2}\right) - 1$; the lines are not perpendicular.

g. $\qquad y = \dfrac{7}{8}x - 2$

The slope of the perpendicular line is $-\dfrac{8}{7}$.

$$y - 2 = -\dfrac{8}{7}(x - (-1))$$

$$y - 2 = -\dfrac{8}{7}x - \dfrac{8}{7}$$

$$y = -\dfrac{8}{7}x + \dfrac{6}{7}$$

h. $4 - y = 2x$
$\quad -y = 2x + 4$
$\quad\;\; y = -2x - 4$

The slopes the perpendicular line is $\dfrac{1}{2}$.

$$y - 4 = \dfrac{1}{2}(x - 3)$$

$$y - 4 = \dfrac{1}{2}x - \dfrac{3}{2}$$

$$y = \dfrac{1}{2}x + \dfrac{5}{2}$$

pp. 141–142 **3-7 EXERCISES**

1. Yes **2.** Yes **3.** No **4.** No **5.** Yes

6. Yes **7.** $y = -\dfrac{1}{2}x + \dfrac{17}{2}$ **8.** $y = 3x + 3$

9. $y = \dfrac{5}{7}x - \dfrac{17}{7}$ **10.** $y = -2x - 13$

11. $y = \dfrac{1}{3}x + 4$ **12.** $y = -\dfrac{5}{2}x - \dfrac{35}{2}$

13. Yes **14.** No **15.** No **16.** Yes

17. $y = \dfrac{1}{2}x + 4$ **18.** $y = -3x + 12$ **19.** $y = \dfrac{4}{3}x - 6$

20. $y = -\dfrac{2}{5}x - \dfrac{31}{5}$ **21.** $y = \dfrac{5}{2}x + 9$ **22.** $y = -2x - 10$

23. $\qquad m = \dfrac{4 - (-3)}{-1 - 2} = -\dfrac{7}{3}$

$$y - (-2) = -\dfrac{7}{3}(x - 4)$$

$$y + 2 = -\dfrac{7}{3}x + \dfrac{28}{3}$$

$$y = -\dfrac{7}{3}x + \dfrac{22}{3}$$

24. $\qquad m = -\dfrac{1}{\dfrac{7 - (-5)}{-2 - 3}} = -\dfrac{1}{-\dfrac{12}{5}} = \dfrac{5}{12}$

$$y - 3 = \dfrac{5}{12}(x + 1)$$

$$y = \dfrac{5}{12}x + \dfrac{41}{12}$$

25. $m_1 = \dfrac{9 - 7}{6 + 2} = \dfrac{2}{8} = \dfrac{1}{4}$

$m_2 = \dfrac{9 - 4}{6 - 3} = \dfrac{5}{3}$

$m_3 = \dfrac{7 - 4}{-2 - 3} = -\dfrac{3}{5}$

The side that contains $(3, 4)$ and $(6, 9)$ has slope $\dfrac{5}{3}$. The side that contains $(-2, 7)$ and $(3, 4)$ has slope $-\dfrac{3}{5}$. Since $\dfrac{5}{3}\left(-\dfrac{3}{5}\right) - -1$, these two sides are perpendicular.

26. $6x - 3y = 1$
$\quad -3y = -6x + 1$
$\qquad\;\; y = 2x - \dfrac{1}{3}; \; m = 2$

$$y - \dfrac{5}{7} = 2(x - 0)$$

$$y = 2x + \dfrac{5}{7}$$

27. $6x - 3y = 1$
$\quad\; 3y = 6x - 1$
$\qquad y = 2x - \dfrac{1}{3}; \; m = 2$

The slope of the perpendicular line is $-\dfrac{1}{2}$.

$$y - 0 = -\dfrac{1}{2}(x - (-1.2))$$

$$y = -\dfrac{1}{2}(x + 1.2)$$

$$y = -\dfrac{1}{2}x - 0.6$$

$$y = -0.5x - 0.6$$

28. Since the lines are not vertical, they cannot be parallel to the
x- or y-axis, nor do they coincide with these axes. Therefore,
each line must cross the x- and y-axis once. Since the lines
have opposite slopes, they pass through all 4 quadrants.

29. **a.** The lines are parallel; the slopes are the same.
   b. None; the lines are parallel.
   c. Since the lines are parallel, the slopes are the same and the
   y-intercept are different. $y = mx + c; c \neq b$

30. $5y = ax + 5$ $\frac{1}{4}y = \frac{1}{10}x - 1$

$y = \frac{a}{5}x + 1$ $y = \frac{4}{10}x - 4$

$\frac{a}{5} = \frac{2}{5}$ $y = \frac{2}{5}x - 4$

$a = 2$

31. $x + 7y = 70$ $y + 3 = kx$
    $7y = -x + 70$ $y = kx - 3$

$y = -\frac{1}{7}x + 10$

$k = -\dfrac{1}{-\dfrac{1}{7}}$

$k = -(-7)$
$k = 7$

32. No   **33.** Yes   **34.** No   **35.** Yes

36. No

x	y = 3x + 5	
−1	2	Yes
0	5	No
−50	−145	Yes
50	155	No

37. $f(0) = 3(0)^3 - 2 \cdot 0 + 6 = 6$

38. $f(-2) = 3(-2)^2 - 2 \cdot (-2) + 6 = 22$

39. $f(3) = 3(3)^2 - 2 \cdot 3 + 6 = 27$

40. $f(1) = 3(1)^2 - 2 \cdot 1 + 6 = 7$

41. $f(-6) = 3(-6)^2 - 2 \cdot (-6) + 6 = 126$

42. $f(6) = 3(6)^2 - 2 \cdot 6 + 6 = 102$

p. 145   **3-8 TRY THIS**

a. 1. Given: $(0, 10.43), (63, 9.93)$

$m = \dfrac{9.93 - 10.43}{63 - 0} = \dfrac{-0.5}{63} = -0.0079t$

$R - 10.43 = -0.0079(t - 0)$
$R = -0.0079t + 10.43$

2. In 2000, $t = 80$
    $R = -0.0079(80) + 10.43$
      $= -0.63 + 10.43$
      $= 9.80$ seconds
  In 2050, $t = 130$.
    $R = -0.0079(130) + 10.43$
      $= -1.03 + 10.43$
      $= 9.40$ seconds

3. $9.0 = -0.008(x) + 10.43$
    $0.008x = 10.43 - 9.0$
    $0.008x = 1.43$
        $x = 178.75$
  $1920 + x = 1920 + 178.75 = 2098.75$
         ≈ 2099

b. Given: $(5, 75)$ and $(30, 200)$

$m = \dfrac{200 - 75}{30 - 5} = \dfrac{125}{25} = 5$

$T - 75 = 5(t - 5)$
   $T = 5t + 50$
   $T = 5(8) + 50$
   $T = 90°$
  $60 = 5t + 50$
  $5t = 10$
   $t = 2$ min

1. **a.** $E = \dfrac{3}{20}t + 72$ **2. a.** $E = \dfrac{3}{20}t + 65$
   b. 78.45 years in 1993   **b.** 71.9 years in 1996
      80.7 years in 2008   73.55 years in 2007

3. **a.** $D = \dfrac{1}{5}t + 20$
   b. 28.2 quadrillion joules in 1991
      31 quadrillion joules in 2005

4. **a.** $R = -0.0075t + 3.85$ **5. a.** $R = -0.075t + 46.8$
   b. 3.37 minutes in 1994   **b.** 41.85 seconds in 1996
      3.3175 minutes in 2001   41.325 seconds in 2003
   c. ≈ 2003 **c.** 2021

6. **a.** $C = m + 1.3$ **7. a.** $C = 0.15m + 15$
   b. $8.30   **b.** $45.00
   c. 18.7 miles

8. Given: $(8, 24)$ and $(75, 560)$.

$m = \dfrac{560 - 24}{75 - 8} = \dfrac{536}{67} = 8$

$T - 24 = 8(I - 8)$
    $T = 8I - 40$
    $T = 8(55) - 40$
    $T = 400$
  $240 = 8I - 40$
    $8I = 280$
     $I = 35$ (in thousands)

9. Given: $(2, 0.95)$ and $(32, 8.99)$

$m = \dfrac{8.99 - 0.95}{32 - 2} = \dfrac{8.04}{30} = 0.268$

$P - 0.95 = 0.268(O - 2)$
     $P = 0.268O + 0.414$
     $P = 0.268(24) + 0.414$
     $P = \$6.85$
  $13.99 = 0.268O + 0.414$
 $0.268O = 13.58$
     $O = 50.7$ oz.

10. time $= t$, value $= V$.
  Data points: $(0, 5200), (2, 4225)$

$$V - V_1 = \frac{V_2 - V_1}{t_2 - t_1}(t - t_1)$$

$$V - 5200 = \frac{4225 - 5200}{2 - 0}(t - 0)$$

$V = -487.5t + 5200;$
After 8 years $V = -487.5(8) + 5200 = \$1300$.

11. Data points: $(32°, 0°), (212°, 100°)$

$$C - 0 = \frac{100 - 0}{212 - 32}(F - 32)$$

$$C = \frac{5}{9}(F - 32)$$

At $F = 70°, C = \dfrac{5}{9}(70° - 32°) = 21.1°$

12. Number of units sold $= s$, income $= I$.
  Data points: $(7,000, 22,000), (8,000, 25,000)$

$$I - 22,000 = \frac{25,000 - 22,000}{8,000 - 7,000}(s - 7,000)$$

    $I = 3(s - 7,000) + 22,000$
    $I = 3s + 1000;$
  At $s = 10,000, I = 3(10,000) + 1,000 = \$31,000.$

13. Temperature $= t$, length of pipe $= \ell$.
  Date points: $(18, 100), (20, 100.00356)$

$$\ell - 100 = \frac{0.00356}{2}(t - 18)$$

    $\ell = 0.00178t + 99.96796$
At $t = 40°, \ell = 0.00178(40) + 99.96796$
         $= 100.03916$ cm
At $t = 0°, \ell = 0 + 99.96796 = 99.96796$ cm

14. a. Data points: $(-1, 3), (2, 4)$

$$y - 3 = \frac{1}{3}(x + 1)$$

$$y = \frac{1}{3}x + 3 + \frac{1}{3}$$

$$f(x) = \frac{1}{3}x + 3\frac{1}{3}$$

b. $f(3) = \frac{1}{3}(3) + 3\frac{1}{3} = 4\frac{1}{3}$

c. $f(a) = \frac{1}{3}a + 3\frac{1}{3} = 100$

$$\frac{1}{3}a = 96\frac{2}{3}$$

$$a = 290$$

15. Answers may vary. By solving the equation for t. The equation would become

$$t + \frac{1}{7}c + \frac{32}{7}.$$

16. Income is a function of gross sales plus base salary:
  a. Plan A: $E_a = 0.04x + 600$
     Plan B: $E_b = 0.06(x - 10,000) + 700$, where $x \geq 10,000$.
       $= 0.06x + 100$
  b. $E_b = 0.06x + 100 \geq 0.04x + 600 = E_a$
     $0.06x - 0.04x \geq 600 - 100$
       $0.02x \geq 500$
         $x \geq 25,000$

17. a. $M(45) = 2.89(45) + 70.64$
       $= 130.05 + 70.64$
       $= 200.69$ cm
  b. $F(45) = 2.75(45) + 71.48$
       $= 123.75 + 71.48$
       $= 195.23$ cm
  c. $2.89x + 70.64 = 2.75x + 71.48$
     $(2.89 - 2.75)x = 71.48 - 70.64$
       $0.14x = 0.84$
         $x = 6$
    $M(6) = 2.89(6) + 70.64 = 87.98$ cm
    $F(6) = 2.75(6) + 71.98 = 87.98$ cm

18. $3y = -12$ **19.** No slope
    $y = 0 \cdot x - 4$
    Slope = 0

20. $y - (-4) = 1(x - (-1))$ **21.** $y - 3 = -1(x - 2)$
     $y + 4 = x + 1$ $y - 3 = -x + 2$
        $y = x - 3$ $y = -x + 5$

22. $y - 2 = 0(x - 4)$ **23.** $9c - 16c = -7c$
     $y = 2$

24. $4m + 2m - m = m(4 + 2 - 1) = 5m$

25. $7x + 5 + (4 - 2x) = 5x + 9$ **26.** $t + t + t = 3t$

27. $4(3r) - 12s + 2r = 12r + 2r - 12s = 14r - 12s$

28. $6(y + 4y) + 3y = 6y + 24y + 3y = 33y$

29. $(p^2 \cdot p^2)^2 \cdot p^{-4} = (p^4)^2 \cdot p^{-4} = p^8 \cdot p^{-4} = p^4$

pp. 149–150   3-9 TRY THIS

a.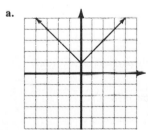

b.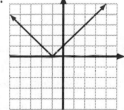

c-d.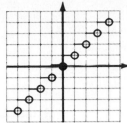

e. $f(g(2)) = f(2 - 7) = 2(-5) = -10$
f. $g(f(2)) = g(2 \cdot 2) = 4 - 7 = -3$
g. $g(f(0)) = g(2 \cdot 0) = 0 - 7 = -7$
h. $f(g(-5)) = f(-5 - 7) = 2 \cdot (-12) = -24$
i. $f(g(x)) = f(x - 4) = -3(x - 4) = -3x + 12$
j. $g(f(x)) = g(-3x) = -3x - 4$
k. $f(f(x)) = f(-3x) = -3(-3x) = 9x$
l. $g(g(x)) = g(x - 4) = (x - 4) - 4 = x - 8$

pp. 150–151   3-9 EXERCISES

1.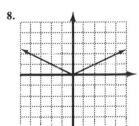

2–3.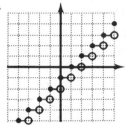

4.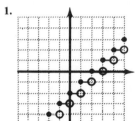

5.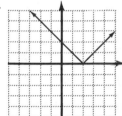

6.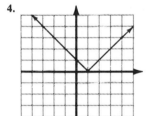

7.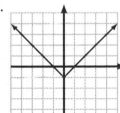

8.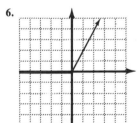

9.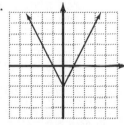

10. 1   **11.** 0   **12.** 8   **13.** 64   **14.** -4 **15.** 35

16. 36   **17.** -52 **18.** $(x - 1)^2$ **19.** $4x - 1$ **20.** $16x^2$

21. $x^2 - 1$ **22.** $x - 2$ **23.** x^4 **24.** $4x^2$ **25.** $16x$

26. a. $A = \left[\dfrac{547}{3}\right] = [182.3] = 182$

b. $A = \left[\dfrac{4621}{27}\right] = [171.15] = 171$

27. Domain: $\{x: x > 0\}$
Range: $\{y: y = 25 + 20n,$
n a whole number$\}$

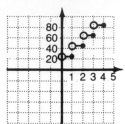

28.

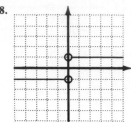

29. $f(g(-5)) = f(2 \cdot (-5)) = |-10| = 10$

30. $g(f(-6)) = g(|-6|) = 2 \cdot 6 = 12$

31. $f(g(-18)) = f(2 \cdot (-18)) = |-36| = 36$

32. $(f \circ g)(-3) = f(7 \cdot (-3)) = -(-21) = 21$

33. $(f \circ g)(7) = f(7 \cdot 7) = -(49) = -49$

34. $(g \circ f)(0) = g(-0) = 7 \cdot 0 = 0$

35. $f(g(h(1))) = f(g(-2 \cdot 1)) = f(-2 - 3) = -(5)^2 = -25$

36. $g(h(f(0))) = g(h(-(0)^2)) = g(-2 \cdot 0) = 0 - 3 = -3$

37. $h(g(f(4))) = h(g(-(4)^2)) = h(-16 - 3) = -2 \cdot (-19) = 38$

38. $h(h(h(2))) = h(h(-2 \cdot 2)) = h(-2 \cdot (-4)) = -2 \cdot 8 = -16$

39. $f(g(h(x))) = f(g(x + 5)) = f(2(x + 5) - 1)$
$= f(2x + 9)$
$= 5(2x + 9)$
$= 10x + 45$

40. $g(g(h(x))) = g(g(x + 5)) = g(2(x + 5) - 1)$
$= g(2x + 9)$
$= 2(2x + 9) - 1$
$= 4x + 17$

41. $h(g(f(x))) = h(g(5x)) = h(2(5x) - 1)$
$= h(10x - 1)$
$= (10x - 1) + 5$
$= 10x + 4$

42. $f(g(f(x))) = f(g(5x)) = f(2(5x)) - 1$
$= f(10x - 1)$
$= 5(10x - 1)$
$= 50x - 5$

43. a. $K = 273 + C$

$F = \dfrac{9}{5}(C) + 32$

$\dfrac{9}{5}C = F - 32$

$C = \dfrac{5}{9}F - \dfrac{160}{9}$

$K(F) = K\left(\dfrac{5}{9}F - \dfrac{160}{9}\right)$

$= \dfrac{5}{9}F - \dfrac{160}{9} + 273$

$= \dfrac{5}{9}F + 255\dfrac{2}{9}$

b. $K(F) = \dfrac{5}{9}(-13) + 255\dfrac{2}{9}$

$= 248K$

44. $f(x) = -|x|$

45.

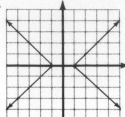

46.

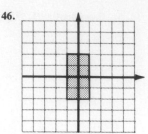

47. No. If $x = 0$, then there are an infinite number of values of y that satisfy the relation.

48. No

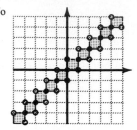

49. $f(g(x)) = f(3x + b) = 2(3x + b) + 7$
$= 6x + 2b + 7$
$g(f(x)) = g(2x + 7) = 3(2x + 7) + b$
$= 6x + 21 + b$
$f(g(x)) = g(f(x))$
$6x + 2b + 7 = 6x + 21 + b$
$b = 14$

50. $f(f(x)) = f(ax + b) = a(ax + b) + b$
$= a^2x + ab + b$

51. $m = \dfrac{13 - 3}{6 - 1} = \dfrac{10}{5} = 2$

$y - 3 = 2(x - 1)$
$y = 2x - 2 + 3$
$y = 2x + 1$

52. $m = \dfrac{3 - (-1)}{3 - (-1)} = 1$

$y - 3 = x - 3$
$y = x$

53. $m = \dfrac{-3 - 0}{2 - 0} = -\dfrac{3}{2}$ **54.** $\dfrac{1}{5^4}$

$y - 0 = -\dfrac{3}{2}(x - 0)$

$y = -\dfrac{3}{2}x$

55. $\dfrac{1}{(2w)^3}$ **56.** $\dfrac{m^2}{n^9}$

57. $0.8a = -2.4$

$a = \dfrac{-2.4}{0.8} = -3$

58. $1.02 + c = -0.85$
$c = -0.85 - 1.02$
$c = -1.87$

59. $|3x - 5| = 19$
$3x - 5 = -19$ or $3x - 5 = 19$
$3x = -14$ or $3x = 24$
$x = -\dfrac{14}{3}$ or $x = 8$

60. $8700(0.25) = 2175$
$8700 - 2175 = 6525$
Valerie must pay $6525 in monthly payments over 3 years.
$3 \cdot 12 = 36$ months
$\dfrac{6525}{36} = \$181.25$ per month

1. Strategy: Make an organized list

Number of $9.50 tapes ($6)	1	2	3	4	5	6	7	8
Cost	6	12	18	24	30	36	42	48

Number of $8.25 tapes ($4)	1	2	3	4	5	6	7	8	9	10	11	12
Cost	4	8	12	16	20	24	28	32	36	40	44	48

$6 tapes	$4 tapes
8	0
6	3
4	6
2	9
0	12

The announcer could spend all of the money in 5 ways.

2. Strategy: Write an equation
   Guess, check, revise
   Let A = area of the floor
   $2A = 442$
   $A = 221$
   The area is 221 sq. ft.
   $13 \times 17 = 221$
   The dimensions of the floor are 13 ft by 17 ft.

3. Strategy: Draw a diagram

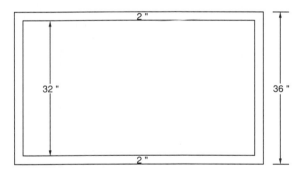

   2″ letters plus 1″ of space = 3″
   $32 \div 3 = 10$ R 2 (1″ of space if not needed under the last line.)
   There can be 11 rows of letters on the poster.

4. Strategy: Make an organized list
   WWW   WWLLW
   WWLW   WLLWW
   WLWW   LLWWW
   LWWW   WLWLW
            LWLWW
            LWWLW
   There are 10 ways to win 3 out of 5 games.

5. Strategy: Guess, check, revise
   Try 72 people. $72 \div 2 = 36$ dishes of rice
                    $72 \div 3 = 24$ dishes of noodles
                    $72 \div 4 = \underline{18}$ dishes of meat
                                 78 dishes — too high
   Revise guess. $60 \div 2 = 30$ dishes of rice
   Try 60 people. $60 \div 3 = 20$ dishes of noodles
                    $60 \div 4 = \underline{15}$ dishes of meat
                                 65 dishes — correct
   There could be 60 people at the party. (Note: You can show that there could also be 59 people at the party. Since 2, 3, and 4 divide evenly into 60, each bowl of each type would be used with no extra dishes. For 59 people, 65 dishes would still be needed, but there would be extra dishes.)

6. Strategy: Draw a diagram

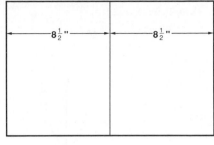

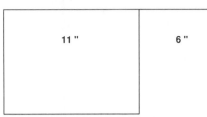

   First, draw a segment 17″ long by using the $8\frac{1}{2}$″ side of the paper twice.
   Then lay the 11″ side on the 17″ segment. The difference is 6″.

7. Strategy: Guess, check, revise
   Guess 3 quarters. This is the most he can have without having change for a dollar. Then he can have up to 4 dimes. If he has 4 dimes he cannot have any nickels. He can have 4 pennies. You can also start by guessing 9 dimes. Grant had $1.19 (3 quarters, 4 dimes, and 4 pennies or 1 quarter, 9 dimes, and 4 pennies).

8. Strategy: Make an organized list
   2358   3258   5238   8235
   2385   3285   5283   8253
   2538   3528   5328   8325
   2583   3582   5382   8352
   2835   3825   5823   8523
   2853   3852   5832   8532
   There are 24 possible codes.

9. Strategy: Use logical reasoning
   If 3 machines produce 3 pairs in 3 hours, then in 9 hours they would produce 3 times that, or 9 headphones. Since there are 3 times as many machines, there will be three times as many headphones, 3×9, or 27 headphones.

1. Buckle-Up $90 + 37.50 = \$127.50$
   Rent-A-Roadster $42 + 56.25 = \$98.25$
   Choose Rent-A-Roadster.

2. Buckle-Up $90 + 120 = \$210$
   Rent-A-Roadster $42 + 180 = \$222$
   Choose Buckle-Up.

3. Buckle-Up $360 + 300 = \$660$
   Rent-A-Roadster $168 + 450 = \$618$
   Choose Rent-A-Roadster.

4. $30 + .1x = 14 + 0.15x$
   $16 = 0.05x$
   $320 = x$

5. $x > 100$ and $x < 100$
   $25 + 0.2(x - 100) < 30 + 0.1x$ $25 < 30 + 0.1x$
   $250 > x$ $-5 < 0.1x$
                                         $-50 < x$
   Swift is cheaper than Buckle-Up for all mileage under 250.
   for $x > 100$ and   for $x < 100$
   $25 + 0.2(x - 100) < 14 + 0.15x$ $25 < 14 + 0.15x$
   $180 > x > 100$ $11 < 0.15x$
                                            $73 < x$
   Swift is cheaper than Rent-A-Roadster for mileage under 180 and greater than 73. For Problems 1–3, Swift is more expensive in each situation.

1. $\{(a,1),(a,2),(b,1),(b,2),(c,1),(c,2)\}$

2. $\{(1,0),(1,-1),(1,-2),(0,-1),(0,-2),(-1,-2)\}$

3. Domain: $\{-6,-1,0,1,2\}$ **4.** $\{0,3\}$
Range: $\{-4,1,2,4,5\}$

5. 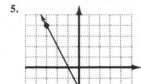   **6.**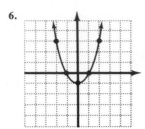

7. No   **8.** Yes   **9.** Yes   **10.** No   **11.** Yes   **12.** No

13. 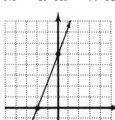   **14.**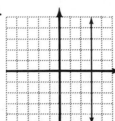

15.   **16.** $m = \dfrac{2-(-3)}{8-(-4)} = \dfrac{5}{12}$

17. $y - 2 = \dfrac{1}{2}(x-(-4))$

$y - 2 = \dfrac{1}{2}x + 2$

$y = \dfrac{1}{2}x + 4$

18. $m = \dfrac{-3-2}{-4-8} = \dfrac{5}{12}$ **19.** $-5x + 2y = -4$
                                                    $2y = -4 + 5x$

$y - 2 = \dfrac{5}{12}(x-8)$ $y = -2 + \dfrac{5}{2}x$

$y - 2 = \dfrac{5}{12}x - \dfrac{10}{3}$

$y = \dfrac{5}{12}x - \dfrac{4}{3}$ $m = \dfrac{5}{2}$ $y\text{-intercept} = -2$

20. $5x + 2y - 7 = 5y - 11$
$5x - 3y - 7 = -11$

$5x - 3y + 4 = 0$ $m = \dfrac{5}{3}$

21. a. $m = -\dfrac{5}{3}$

$y - 7 = -\dfrac{5}{3}(x-(-3))$

$y - 7 = -\dfrac{5}{3}x - 5$

$y = -\dfrac{5}{3}x + 2$

b. $m = \dfrac{3}{5}$

$y - 7 = \dfrac{3}{5}(x-(-3))$

$y - 7 = \dfrac{3}{5}x + \dfrac{9}{5}$

$y = \dfrac{3}{5}x + \dfrac{44}{5}$

22. Given: $(0, 20.8)$ and $(25, 20.1)$

$m = \dfrac{20.1 - 20.8}{25} = -\dfrac{.7}{25} = -.028$

$R - 20.8 = -.028(t-0)$
$R = -.028 + 20.8$

23. $R = -.028(74) + 20.8$ **24.** $18.5 = -.028t + 20.8$
$R = 18.728$ sec $-.028t = -2.3$
                                                 $t = 82$
                                           $1920 + 82 = 2002$

25. 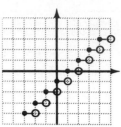   **26.**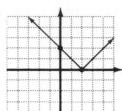

27. $g(3) = 3^2 - 1 = 8$ **28.** $f(2) = 2(2) = 4$
$f(8) = 2(8) = 16$ $g(4) = 4^2 - 1 = 15$
                                           $h(15) = 15 + 1 = 16$

29. $h(x) = x + 1$
$g(h(x)) = (x+1)^2 - 1 = x^2 + 2x$
$f(g(h(x))) = 2(x^2 + 2x) = 2x^2 + 4x$

p. 157   CHAPTER 3 TEST

1. $\{(-1,p),(-1,q),(1,p),(1,q),(3,p),(3,q),(7,p),(7,q)\}$

2. $\{(-4,-4),(-4,-2),(-4,0),(-4,2),(-2,-2),(-2,0),$
$(-2,2),(0,0),(0,2),(2,2)\}$

3. Domain: $\{-2,-1,1,2\}$ **4.** $\{-5,0\}$ **5.** $(3,-1)$
Range: $\{-3,-2,3,4\}$

6. 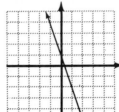   **7.**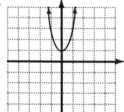

8. No   **9.** Yes   **10.** No   **11.** No   **12.** Yes   **13.** Yes

14. 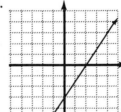   **15.**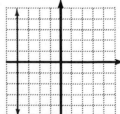

16.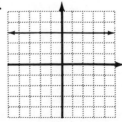

17. $m = -\dfrac{2-4}{5-(-3)} = -\dfrac{6}{8} = -\dfrac{3}{4}$

18. $y + 3 = -\dfrac{3}{4}(x + 2)$

$y + 3 = -\dfrac{3}{4}x - \dfrac{3}{2}$

$y = -\dfrac{3}{4}x - \dfrac{9}{2}$

19. $m = -\dfrac{5 - (-6)}{2 - (-3)} = \dfrac{1}{5}$

$y + 5 = \dfrac{1}{5}(x - 2)$

$y + 5 = \dfrac{1}{5}x - \dfrac{2}{5}$

$y = \dfrac{1}{5}x - \dfrac{27}{5}$

20. $-3x + 5y - 6 = 0$

$5y = 6 + 3x$

$y = \dfrac{6}{5} + \dfrac{3}{5}x \qquad m = \dfrac{3}{5}$

$y\text{-intercept} = \dfrac{6}{5}$

21. $y = -\dfrac{3}{5}x - \dfrac{8}{5}$

$5y = -3x - 8$

$3x + 5y + 8 = 0$

$m = -\dfrac{3}{5}$

22. $m = \dfrac{3}{2}$

$y + 3 = \dfrac{3}{2}(x - 4)$

$y + 3 = \dfrac{3}{2}x - 6$

$y = \dfrac{3}{2}x - 9$

23. $m = -\dfrac{2}{3}$

$y + 3 = -\dfrac{2}{3}(x - 4)$

$y + 3 = -\dfrac{2}{3}x + \dfrac{8}{3}$

$y = -\dfrac{2}{3}x - \dfrac{1}{3}$

24. Given: $(100, 40)$ and $(150, 48.50)$

$m = \dfrac{48.50 - 40}{150 - 100} = \dfrac{8.50}{50} = 0.17$

  a. $C - 40 = 0.17(m - 100)$

      $C = 0.17M + 23$

  b. $C = 0.17(200) + 23$

      $C = 57$

  c. $\quad 91 = 0.17m + 23$

      $0.17m = 68$

      $m = 400$

25.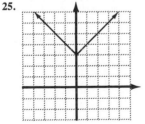

26.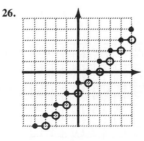

27. $h(-2) = 2 - (-2) = 2 + 2 = 4$

28. $f(2) = -2(2) + 1 = -3$
$g(f(2)) = (-3)^2 = 9$

29. $g(-1) = (-1)^2 = 1$
$h(g(-1)) = 2 - 1 = 1$
$f(h(g(-1))) = -2(1) + 1 = -1$

30. $f(x) = -2x + 1$
$h(fx) = 2 - (-2x + 1) = 2 + 2x - 1 = 1 + 2x$
$g(h(f(x))) = (1 + 2x)^2 = 1 + 4x + 4x^2$

CHAPTER 4

p. 158   READY FOR SYSTEMS OF EQUATIONS AND PROBLEM SOLVING?

1. 8   **2.** -7 **3.** $-\dfrac{3}{4}$ **4.** 0   **5.** $-\dfrac{7}{12}$ **6.** 0

7. -12 **8.** 10   **9.** $-\dfrac{22}{15}$ **10.** 4.9

11.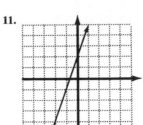

12.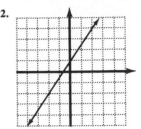

13.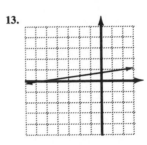

14.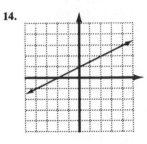

15.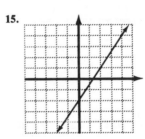

16.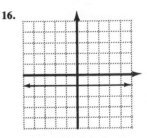

17. $\quad 3y - 1 > y - 3$

$3y - 1 - y > y - 3 - y$

$\quad 2y - 1 > -3$

$2y - 1 + 1 > -3 + 1$

$\quad\quad 2y > -2$

$\quad\quad \dfrac{2y}{2} > -\dfrac{2}{2}$

$\quad\quad\quad y > -1$

18. $\quad 2x - 3 > 5$

$2x - 3 + 3 > 5 + 3$

$\quad\quad 2x > 8$

$\quad\quad \dfrac{2x}{2} > \dfrac{8}{2}$

$\quad\quad\quad x > 4$

19. $\quad |x + 2| \le 6$

$x + 2 \le 6 \quad\text{and}\quad x + 2 \ge -6$

$x + 2 - 2 \le 6 - 2 \qquad x + 2 - 2 \ge -6 - 2$

$\quad x \le 4 \quad\text{and}\quad\quad x \ge -8$

20. $\quad -7 \le 2x - 7 < 7$

$-7 + 7 \le 2x - 7 + 7 < 7 + 7$

$\quad\quad 0 \le 2x < 14$

$\quad\quad \dfrac{0}{2} \le \dfrac{2x}{2} < \dfrac{14}{2}$

$\quad\quad 0 \le x < 7$

$\quad\quad 0 \le x \quad\text{and}\quad x < 7$

21. $\frac{1}{2}x - 5y = 3$

$$\frac{\frac{1}{2}x}{5} - \frac{5y}{5} = \frac{3}{5}$$

$$\frac{x}{10} - y = \frac{3}{5}$$

$$\frac{x}{10} - \frac{x}{10} - y = \frac{3}{5} - \frac{x}{10}$$

$$-y = \frac{3}{5} - \frac{x}{10}$$

$$y = -\frac{3}{5} + \frac{x}{10}$$

$$y = \frac{x}{10} - \frac{3}{5}$$

Slope is $\frac{1}{10}$.

$$-2x + 10y = 1$$
$$-2x + 2x + 10y = 1 + 2x$$
$$10y = 1 + 2x$$

$$\frac{10y}{10} = \frac{1}{10} + \frac{2x}{10}$$

$$y = \frac{1}{10} + \frac{x}{5}$$

$$y = \frac{x}{5} + \frac{1}{10}$$

Slope is $\frac{1}{5}$.

Lines are not parallel because the slopes are not the same.

p. 160   4-1 TRY THIS

a. $x + y = 11$
$3x - y = 5$

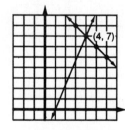

Check

$x + y = 11$	$3x - y = 5$
$4 + 7$ | 11	$12 - 7$ | 5
11 | 11	5 | 5

b. $2x - y = 7$
$-x + 2y = -5$

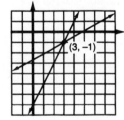

Check

$2x - y = 7$
$2(3) - (-1)$ | 7
$6 + 1$ | 7
7 | 7

$-x + 2y = -5$
$-(3) + 2(-1)$ | -5
$-3 - 2$ | -5
-5 | -5

p. 161   4-1 EXERCISES

1. $(3, 1)$ **2.** $(4, 1)$ **3.** $(3, 2)$ **4.** $(2, -1)$ **5.** $(1, -5)$

6. $\left(3, \frac{3}{2}\right)$ **7.** $(2, 1)$ **8.** $(-3, -2)$ **9.** $\left(\frac{5}{2}, -2\right)$

10. $(7, 2)$ **11.** $(3, -2)$ **12.** $(4, 0)$

13.
$$3x - y = -5$$
$$3x - 3x - y = -5 - 3x$$
$$-y = -5 - 3x$$
$$y = 5 + 3x$$
$$y - 3x = -2$$
$$y - 3x + 3x = -2 + 3x$$
$$y = 3x + 2$$

No solution

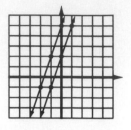

14.
$$y = -3x + 5$$
$$4y + 12x = 20$$
$$4y + 12x - 12x = -12x + 20$$
$$4y = -12x + 20$$
$$y = -3x + 5$$
Infinitely many solutions;
any point on line $y = -3x + 5$.

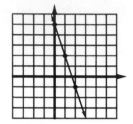

15. Answers may vary.
   a. $x + y = 6$ **b.** $x + 2y = -1$
      $x - y = 4$ $x + 3y = 2$
   c. $x + y = 3$ **d.** $x + y = 3$
      $x + y = 1$ $2x + 2y = 6$

16.
$$x - y = 0$$
$$x - x - y = 0 - x$$
$$-y = -x \qquad y = x^2$$
$$y = x$$

x	y		x	y
1	1		0	0
0	0		-1	1
-3	-3		1	1
			-2	4
			2	4

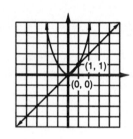

Solutions: $(1, 1)$ or $(0, 0)$.

17.
$$x - y = 0 \qquad y = |x|$$
$$x - x - y = 0 - x \qquad y = x \text{ and } y = -x$$
$$-y = -x$$
$$y = x$$

x	y		x	y
0	0		-1	1
1	1		1	1
-2	-2		-2	2
2	2		2	2
			0	0

$\{(x, y) \mid x = y \text{ and } x \geq 0\}$

18.

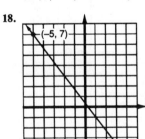

   a. $(4, -5)$ is another solution.
   b. Infinitely many solutions
      must exist.

19. $f(3) = 2(3^2) - 3$ **20.** $f(0) = 2(0^2) - 0$
     $= 2(9) - 3$ $= 0$
     $= 18 - 3$
     $= 15$

21. $f(-1) = 2(-1^2) - (-1)$ **22.** $f(1) = 2(1^2) - 1$
      $= 2 + 1$ $= 2 - 1$
      $= 3$ $= 1$

23. $f(-3) = 2(-3^2) - (-3)$
$= 2(9) - (-3)$
$= 21$

24. $f(2) = 2(2^2) - 2$
$= 8 - 2$
$= 6$

25. $6x + 3y - 12 = 0$
$3y = -6x + 12$
$$\frac{3y}{3} = \frac{-6x + 12}{3}$$
$y = -2x + 4$
Slope $= -2$;
y-intercept is 4.

26. $-9 < 3t < 6$
$-3 < t < 2$

27. $|5a - 1| > 9$
$5a - 1 > 9$ or $5a - 1 < -9$
$5a > 9 + 1$ $\quad 5a < -8$
$5a > 10$
$a > 2 \quad a < -\dfrac{8}{5}$
$\left\{ a \mid a > 2 \text{ or } a < -\dfrac{8}{5} \right\}$

28. $3.2(1.5 + m) = 19.2$
$3.2 \cdot 1.5 + 3.2m = 19.2$
$4.8 + 3.2m = 19.2$
$3.2m = 14.4$
$m = 4.5$

pp. 162–165 4-2 TRY THIS

a. $2y + x = 1$
$x = 1 - 2y$
$3y - 2x = 12$
$3y - 2(1 - 2y) = 12$ $\quad$ Substituting $1 - 2y$ for x
$3y - 2 + 4y = 12$
$7y = 14$
$y = 2$
$x = 1 - 2(2)$ $\quad$ Substituting 2 for y
$x = 1 - 4$
$x = -3$
$(-3, 2)$

b. $5x + 3y = 6$
$x - y = -1$
$x = -1 + y$
$5(-1 + y) + 3y = 6$ $\quad$ Substituting -1 for x
$-5 + 5y + 3y = 6$
$-5 + 8y = 6$
$8y = 11$
$y = \dfrac{11}{8}$
$x = -1 + \dfrac{11}{8}$ $\quad$ Substituting $\dfrac{11}{8}$ for y
$x = \dfrac{3}{8}$
$\left(\dfrac{3}{8}, \dfrac{11}{8} \right)$

c. $5x + 3y = 17$
$-5x + 2y = 3$
$5y = 20$ $\quad$ Adding
$\dfrac{5y}{5} = \dfrac{20}{5}$
$y = 4$
$5x + 3(4) = 17$ $\quad$ Substituting 4 for y
$5x + 12 = 17$
$5x + 12 - 12 = 17 - 12$
$5x = 5$
$\dfrac{5x}{5} = \dfrac{5}{5}$
$x = 1 \quad (1, 4)$

d. $6x + 2y = -16$
$-12x - 5y = 31$
$12x + 4y = -32$ $\quad$ Multiply equation ① by 2.
$-12x - 5y = 31$
$-y = -1$
$y = 1$
$6x + 2(1) = -16$ $\quad$ Substituting 1 for y
$6x = -18$
$x = -3$
$(-3, 1)$

e. $3x + 5y = 30$
$5x + 3y = 34$
Multiply equation ① by -5 and equation ② by 3.
$-5(3x + 5y) = -5(30) \rightarrow -15x - 25y = -150$
$3(5x + 3y) = 3(34) \rightarrow 15x + 9y = 102$
$-16y = -48$
$y = 3$
$3x + 5(3) = 30$ $\quad$ Substituting 3 for y
$3x + 15 = 30$
$3x + 15 - 15 = 30 - 15$
$3x = 15$
$x = 5$
$(5, 3)$

f. $0.2x + 0.3y = 0.1$
$0.03x - 0.01y = 0.07$
$100(0.03x) - 100(0.01y) = 100(0.07)$ $\quad$ Multiply equation ① by 10.
$10(0.02x) + 10(0.3y) = 10(0.1)$ $\quad$ Multiply equation ② by 100.
$2x + 3y = 1$
$3x - y = 7$
Multiply equation ② by 3.
$2x + 3y = 1$
$9x - 3y = 21$
$11x = 22$
$x = 2$
$2(2) + 3y = 1$ $\quad$ Substituting 2 for x
$4 + 3y = 1$
$3y = -3$
$y = -11$
$(2, -1)$

g. $\dfrac{3}{5}x + \dfrac{2}{3}y = 14$
$\dfrac{3}{4}x - \dfrac{1}{3}y = 14$
Multiply equation ① by 15 and equation ② by -12.
$9x + 10x = 210$
$-9x + 4y = -168$
$14y = 42$
$y = 3$
$9x + 10(3) = 210$ $\quad$ Substituting 3 for y
$9x + 30 = 210$
$9x = 180$
$x = 20$
$(20, 3)$

pp. 166–167 4-2 EXERCISES

1. $(2, -2)$ $\quad$ **2.** $(2, -7)$ $\quad$ **3.** $(-2, 1)$ $\quad$ **4.** $(4, -1)$

5. $(1, 2)$ $\quad$ **6.** $(2, 7)$ $\quad$ **7.** $(3, 0)$ $\quad$ **8.** $(10, 2)$ $\quad$ **9.** $(-1, 2)$

10. $\left(\dfrac{1}{2}, -5 \right)$ $\quad$ **11.** $(-3, 2)$ $\quad$ **12.** $(4, 5)$ $\quad$ **13.** $(6, 2)$

14. $(1, 3)$ $\quad$ **15.** $(3, -3)$ $\quad$ **16.** $(2, 3)$ $\quad$ **17.** $\left(\dfrac{1}{2}, -\dfrac{1}{2} \right)$

18. $(-2, -9)$ $\quad$ **19.** $\left(-\dfrac{4}{3}, -\dfrac{19}{3} \right)$ $\quad$ **20.** $(10, 5)$

21. $(90.91, -90.91)$ $\quad$ **22.** $(-20, 20)$

23. Let $u = \dfrac{1}{x}$, $v = \dfrac{1}{y}$

Then
$$u - 3v = 2$$
$$6u + 5v = -34$$
$$-6u + 18v = -12$$
$$6u + 5v = -34$$

Add:
$$0 + 23v = -46$$
$$v = -2$$

Substitute: $u - 3(-2) = 2$
$$u + 6 = 2$$
$$u = -4$$

Substitute for u and v: $u = -4 = \dfrac{1}{x}$
$$v = -2 = \dfrac{1}{y}$$

Therefore, $x = -\dfrac{1}{4}$, $y = -\dfrac{1}{2}$.

24. $u = \dfrac{1}{x}$, $v = \dfrac{1}{y}$

$$2u + v = 0$$
$$5u + 2v = -5$$
$$-4u - 2v = 0$$
$$5u + 2v = -5$$

Add:
$$u + 0 = -5$$
$$u = -5$$

Substitute: $2(-5) + v = 0$
$$-10 + v = 0$$
$$v = 10$$

Substitute for u and v: $u = -5 = \dfrac{1}{x}$; $v = 10 = \dfrac{1}{y}$.

$$x = -\dfrac{1}{5}, \quad y = \dfrac{1}{10}$$

25. Let $u = |x| = \sqrt{x^2}$; $v = |y| = \sqrt{y^2}$.

Then ① $3u + 5y = 30$
② $5u + 3y = 34$
$$15u + 25v = 150 \qquad \text{Multiply ① by 5}$$
$$-15u - 9v = -102 \qquad \text{Multiply ② by } -3$$
$$0 + 16v = 48$$
$$v = 3$$

Substituting: $\sqrt{y^2} = 3$
$$y^2 = 9$$
$$y = \pm 3$$

Substituting in ①: $3u + 15 = 30$
$$3u = 15$$
$$u = 5$$

Substituting: $\sqrt{x^2} = 5$
$$x^2 = 25$$
$$x = \pm 5$$

Solutions: $\{(5, 3) (-5, 3) (5, -3) (-5, -3)\}$

26. Both lines in each set are perpendicular. System B cannot be solved by linear combinations.

27. $y = mx + b$

Substituting:
$$2 = m + b$$
$$4 = -3m + b$$

Subtracting: $-2 = 4m + 0$
$$-\dfrac{1}{2} = m$$

Substituting: $2 = -\dfrac{1}{2}(1) + b$
$$\dfrac{5}{2} = b$$

Substituting: $y = -\dfrac{1}{2}x + \dfrac{5}{2}$

28. Substituting: $3 = a(0) + c \rightarrow 3 = 0 + c$
$$3 = a(-2^2) + c \rightarrow 3 = 4z + c$$

Subtracting $\quad 0 = -4a + 0$
$$0 = a$$

Substituting: $\quad 3 = 0 + c$
$$3 = c$$

29. $\quad 2x + 6 = y$ **30.** $\quad\quad y = -7$
$\quad 2x - y + 6 = 0$ $\quad\quad 0x + y + 7 = 0$

31. Not linear because cannot be written in form $y = mx + b$.

32. Not linear **33.** Not linear

34. $y + x = 2x + 1$
$$y = x + 1 \quad \text{Linear}$$

35. $A + B = 5000$ ①
$0.10A + 0.08B = 435$ ②
Multiply ① by 0.10.
$$0.10A + 0.10B = 500$$
$$0.10A + 0.08B = 435$$
$$0.02B = 65$$
$$B = 3250$$
She invested \$3250 in fund B.

p. 167 PROBLEM FOR PROGRAMMERS

```
10  REM Chapter 4 Problem
20  INPUT "For ax + by = c; enter a,b,c ";A,B,C
30  INPUT "For dx + ey = f; enter d,e,f ";D,E,F
40  Y = (F * A - C * D) / (E * A - B * D)
50  X = (C - B * Y) / A
60  PRINT "x = ";X;",y = ";Y
70  END
```

```
10  REM Chapter 4 Challenge Problem
20  INPUT "For ax + by = c; enter a,b,c ";A,B,C
30  INPUT "For dx + ey = f; enter d,e,f ";D,E,F
40  DY = F * A - C * D
50  D = E * A - B * D
60  IF D = 0 THEN 110
70  Y = DY / D
80  X = (C - B * Y) / A
90  PRINT "x = ";X;",y = ";Y
100  GOTO 150
110  IF DY = 0 THEN 140
120  PRINT "No solutions"
130  GOTO 150
140  PRINT "Unlimited solutions"
150  END
```

pp. 169–171 4-3 TRY THIS

a. $x = $ 1st number
$y = $ 2nd number
$$x = 4y$$
$$x + y = 175$$
$$x - 4y = 0$$
$$x + y = 175$$
$$-5y = -175$$
$$y = 35$$
$$x = 4(35)$$
$$x = 140$$
The numbers are 35 and 140.

b. $x + y = 100 \rightarrow y = 100 - x$
$0.05x + 0.15y = 0.12(100)$
Substituting: $0.05x + 0.15(100 - x) = 0.12(100)$
$$0.05x + 15 - 0.15x = 12$$
$$15 - 0.10x = 12$$
$$-0.10x = -3$$
$$x = 30$$
Substituting: $\quad\quad 30 + y = 100$
$$y = 70$$

30 liters of 5%, 70 liters of 15%

c.

	D	R	T
Slow train	d	35	$x + 1$
Fast train	d	40	x

$$d = 35(x + 1)$$
$$d = 40x$$
$$40x = 35x + 35$$
$$5x = 35$$
$$x = 7$$
$$d = 40(7) = 280 \text{ km}$$

pp. 171–173   4-3 EXERCISES

1. $5, -47$ 2. $-52, -11$ 3. $24, 8$ 4. $29, 18$

5. 150 lb soybean meal, 200 lb cornmeal

6. 4 L of 25% solution, 6 L of 50% solution   7. 5 L of each

8. $12\frac{1}{2}$ L of A, $7\frac{1}{2}$ L of B 9. \$4100 at 14%, \$4700 at 16%

10. \$6800 at 9%, \$8200 at 10%

11. \$725 at 12%, \$425 at 11%

12. \$12,500 at 10%, \$14,500 at 12%   13. 375 km   14. 3

15. $1\frac{3}{4}$ 16. 2   17. 8 white, 22 yellow

18. 12 white, 28 printed   19. 13 at \$9.75, 32 at \$8.50

20. 84 adult, 33 children   21. Maria 20, Carlos 28

22. Paula 32, Bob 20   23. $l = 160$ m, $w = 154$ m

24. $l = 76$ m, $w = 19$ m   25. $l = 31$ cm, $w = 12$ cm

26. $l = 137$ m, $w = 55$ m

27. Let $x =$ Mr. Irwin, $y =$ Mr. Lippi.
$$x + y = 46$$
$$x - 2 = 2.5(y - 2)$$
Solve for x in second equation: $x = 2.5y - 3$
Substitute: $2.5y - 3 + y = 46$
$$3.5y = 49$$
$$y = 14$$
Substitute: $x + 14 = 46$
$$x = 32$$
Mr. Irwin = 32 yr, Mr. Lippi = 14 yr.

28. Let $x =$ walking distance, $y =$ jogging distance.
$$x + y = 6$$
By the formula $d = rt, \dfrac{d}{r} = t.$
$$\frac{x}{4} + \frac{y}{8} = 1$$
Clearing of fractions: $2x + y = 8$
Subtracting: $\underline{x + y = 6}$
$$x = 2$$
Substituting: $2 + y = 6$
$$y = 4 \text{ km}$$

29. Let $x =$ tens digit, $y =$ ones digit.
$$x = 2 + 3y$$
$$10y + x = \frac{1}{2}(10x + y) - 13$$
Substitute: $10y + (2 + 3y) = \frac{1}{2}[10(2 + 3y) + y] - 13$
$$13y + 2 = \frac{31}{2}y - 3$$
$$5 = \frac{5}{2}y$$
$$y = 2, x = 3(2) + 2 = 8$$
The number is $10(8) + y = 82$.

30. Let $x =$ number of books sold for \$12,
$y =$ number sold for \$8.
$$x + y = 880$$
$$12x + 8y = 9840$$
$$\underline{\begin{array}{l} -8x - 8y = -7040 \\ 12x + 8y = 9840 \end{array}}$$
$$4x = 2800$$
$$x = 700; \quad y = 880 - 700 = 180 \text{ members}$$

31. x and y are supplementary angles.
$$x + y = 180$$
$$x = 8 + 3y$$
Substitute: $8 + 3y + y = 180$ $x = 180 - 43$
$$4y + 8 = 180 \qquad x = 137°$$
$$4y = 172$$
$$y = 43$$

32. Answers may vary.

33. Radiator contains 30% of 16 L, or 4.8 L, of antifreeze. We want 50% of 16, or 8 L of antifreeze. We need $3\frac{1}{5}$ additional liters of antifreeze.
Let $x =$ amount drained and replaced.
The amount lost in draining is $(0.3)x$.
The net gain refilling is $x - 0.3x = 0.7x$.
$$0.7x = 3\frac{1}{5}$$
$$\frac{7}{10}x = 3\frac{1}{5}$$
$$\frac{7}{10}x = \frac{16}{5}$$
$$x = 4\frac{4}{7} \text{ liters drained}$$

34. Let $x =$ speed of first train,
$y =$ speed of second train
It takes x 3 h and y 2 h to meet.
$$3x + 2y = 216$$
Also, it would take x $1\frac{1}{2}$ h and y 3 h to meet.
$$1\frac{1}{2}x + 3y = 216$$
Solving: $3x + 2y = 216$
$$\underline{1\frac{1}{2}x + 3y = 216} \to \text{Multiply this by } -2$$
$$-3x - 6y = -432$$
Add: $\underline{3x + 2y = 216}$
$$-4y = -216$$
$$y = 54$$
$$\overline{3x + 2(54) = 216}$$
$$x = 36$$
First train: 36 km/h; Second train: 54 km/h

35. m^4 36. $|-3| \cdot |t| = 3|t|$ 37. $w^6|w|$

38. $|m^4| \cdot |m| \cdot |n^4| = m^4 n^4 |m|$ 39. $|75a^2| \cdot |a| = 75a^2|a|$

40. $m = \dfrac{y_2 - y_1}{x_2 - x_1}$ 41. $m = \dfrac{3.2 - 2.4}{1.1 - 1.9}$ 42. $m = \dfrac{5 - (-3)}{-2 - 2}$

$m = \dfrac{2 - 2}{3 - (-5)}$ $m = -1$ $m = -2$

$m = 0$

43. $y = -x + 1$
Since parallel lines have the same slope, $m = -1$.
Then $y - 1 = -(x - 2)$;
$$y = -x + 3.$$

44. $g(1) = \dfrac{1}{2}(1) + 1$
$$= \frac{3}{2}$$
$$f\left(\frac{3}{2}\right) = 2\left(\frac{3}{2}\right) - 1$$
$$= 2$$
$$\therefore f(g(1)) = 2$$

45. $f(g(x)) = 2\left(\dfrac{1}{2}x + 1\right) - 1$
$$= x + 1$$

46.
$$f(1) = 2(1) - 1$$
$$f(1) = 1$$

$$g(1) = \frac{1}{2}(1) + 1$$

$$g(1) = \frac{3}{2}$$

$$\therefore g(f(1)) = \frac{3}{2}$$

47. $g(f(x)) = \frac{1}{2}(2x - 1) + 1$

$$g(f(x)) = x - \frac{1}{2} + 1$$

$$g(f(x)) = x + \frac{1}{2}$$

p. 177   **4-4 TRY THIS**

a. $x + 2y - z = 5$ ①
$2x - 4y + z = 0$ ②
$3x + 2y + 2z = 3$ ③
−1② + 2①:
$x + 2y - z = 5$ ①
$8y - 3z = 10$ ②
$3x + 2y + 2z = 3$ ③
−1③ + 3①:
$x + 2y - z = 5$ ①
$8y - 3z = 10$ ②
$4y - 5z = 12$ ③
−2③ + ②:
$x + 2y - z = 5$
$8y - 3z = 10$
$7z = -14$
$z = -2$
Substitute $z = -2$ in ②.
$8y - 3(-2) = 10$

$$y = \frac{1}{2}$$

Substitute $z = -2$ and $y = \frac{1}{2}$ in ①.

$$x + 2\left(\frac{1}{2}\right) - (-2) = 5$$

$$x = 2$$

$\left(2, \frac{1}{2}, -2\right)$ is the solution.

b. $x + y + z = 2$ ①
$x - 2y - z = 2$ ②
$3x + 2y + z = 2$ ③
−1② + ①:
$x + y + z = 2$ ①
$3y + 2z = 0$ ②
$3x + 2y + z = 2$ ③
−1③ + 3①:
$x + y + z = 2$ ①
$3y + 2z = 0$ ②
$y + 2z = 4$ ③
−3③ + ②:
$-4z = -12$
$z = 3$
Substitute $z = 3$ in ②.
$3y + 2(3) = 0$
$y = -2$
Substitute $y = -2$ in ①.
$x + (-2) + 3 = 2$
$x = 1$
$(1, -2, 3)$ is the solution.

c. $x + y - z = 2$ ①
$x - y - 2z = 2$ ②
$2x + 3y + z = 9$ ③
−1① + ②:

$x + y - z = 2$ ①
$-2y - z = 0$ ②
$2x + 3y + z = 9$ ③
−2① + 3:
$x + y - z = 2$ ①
$-2y - z = 0$ ②
$y + 3z = 5$ ③
3② + ③:
$x + y - z = 2$ ①
$-6y - 3z = 0$ ②
$y + 3z = 5$ ③
$-5y = 5$
$y = -1$
Substitute $y = -1$ in ③.
$-1 + 3z = 5$
$3z = 6$
$z = 2$
Substitute $y = -1$, $z = 2$ in ①.
$x + (-1) - 2 = 2$
$x = 5$
$(5, -1, 2)$ is the solution.

pp. 178–179   **4-4 EXERCISES**

1. $(1, 2, 3)$ **2.** $(4, 0, 2)$ **3.** $(-1, 5, -2)$

4. $(2, -2, 2)$ **5.** $(3, 1, 2)$ **6.** $(3, -2, 1)$

7. $(-3, -4, 2)$ **8.** $(7, -3, -4)$ **9.** $(2, 4, 1)$

10. $(2, 1, 3)$ **11.** $(-3, 0, 4)$ **12.** $(2, -5, 6)$

13. $(2, 2, 4)$ **14.** $(-2, -1, 4)$ **15.** $\left(\frac{1}{2}, 4, -6\right)$

16. $(3, -5, 8)$ **17.** $\left(\frac{1}{2}, \frac{1}{3}, \frac{1}{6}\right)$ **18.** $\left(\frac{3}{5}, \frac{2}{3}, -3\right)$

19. $4a + 9b = 8$ ①
$8a + 6c = -1$ ②
$6b + 6c = -1$ ③
−2① + ②:
$4a + 9b = 8$ ①
$-18b + 6c = -17$ ②
$6b + 6c = -1$ ③
−1③ + ②:
$4a + 9b = 8$ ①
$-6b - 6c = 1$ ②
$-18b + 6c = -17$ ③
$-24b = -16$

$$b = \frac{2}{3}$$

Substitute $b = \frac{2}{3}$ in ②.

$$-6\left(\frac{2}{3}\right) - 6c = 1$$

$$-6c = 5$$

$$c = -\frac{5}{6}$$

Substitute $b = \frac{2}{3}$.

$$4a + 9b = 8$$

$$4a + 9\left(\frac{2}{3}\right) = 8$$

$$4a = 2$$

$$a = \frac{1}{2}$$ $\left(\frac{1}{2}, \frac{2}{3}, -\frac{5}{6}\right)$ is the solution.

20. $3p + 2r = 11$ ①
  $q - 7r = 4$ ②
  $p - 6q = 1$ ③
  $-3③ + ①$:
  $3p + 2r = 11$ ①
  $q - 7r = 4$ ②
  $18q - 2r = 8$ ③
  $-18② + ③$:
  $3p + 2r = 11$ ①
  $-18q + 126r = -72$ ②
  $18q + 2r = 8$ ③
  $128r = -64$
  $r = -\dfrac{1}{2}$

Substitute $r = -\dfrac{1}{2}$ in ③.

$18q + 2\left(-\dfrac{1}{2}\right) = 8$

$18q = 9$

$q = \dfrac{1}{2}$

Substitute $r = -\dfrac{1}{2}$ in ①.

$3p + 2\left(-\dfrac{1}{2}\right) = 11$

$3p = 12$
$p = 4$

$\left(4, \dfrac{1}{2}, -\dfrac{1}{2}\right)$ is the solution.

21. $6\left(\dfrac{x+2}{3} - \dfrac{y+4}{2} + \dfrac{z+1}{6}\right) = 0 \cdot 6$ ①

$12\left(\dfrac{x-4}{3} + \dfrac{y+1}{4} - \dfrac{z-2}{2}\right) = -1 \cdot 12$ ②

$4\left(\dfrac{x+1}{2} + \dfrac{y}{2} + \dfrac{z-1}{4}\right) = \dfrac{3}{4} \cdot 4$ ③

$2x + 4 - 3y - 12 + z + 1 = 0$ ①
$4x - 16 + 3y + 3 - 6z + 12 = -12$ ②
$2x + 2 + 2y + z - 1 = 3$ ③

Combine like terms:
$2x - 3y + z = 7$ ①
$4x + 3y - 6z = -11$ ②
$2x + 2y + z = 2$ ③
$-2① + ②$:
$-4x + 6y - 2z = -14$
$4x + 3y - 6z = -11$
$9y - 8z = -25$
$2x - 3y + z = 7$ ①
$9y - 8z = -25$ ②
$2x + 2y + z = 2$ ③
$③ - ①$:
$2x + 2y + z = 2$
$2x - 3y + z = 7$
$5y = -5$
$y = -1$
Substitute $y = -1$ in ②.
$9(-1) - 8z = -25$
$z = 2$
Substitute $y = -1$, $z = 2$ in ①.
$2x - 3(-1) + 2 = 7$
$x = 1$
$(1, -1, 2)$ is the solution.

22. $10(0.2x + 0.3y + 1.1z) = 10(1.6)$ ①
  $10(0.5x - 0.2y + 0.4z) = 10(0.7)$ ②
  $10(-1.2x + y - 0.7z) = 10(-0.9)$ ③
  $2x + 3y + 11z = 16$ ①
  $5x - 2y + 4z = 7$ ②
  $-12x + 10y - 7z = -9$ ③
  $5① - 2②$:
  $10x + 15y + 55z = 80$
  $10x - 4y + 8z = 14$
  $19y + 47z = 66$
  $2x + 3y + 11z = 16$ ①
  $19y + 47z = 66$ ②
  $-12x + 10y - 7z = -9$ ③
  $6① + ③$:
  $12x + 18y + 66z = 96$
  $-12x + 10y - 7z = -9$
  $28y + 59z = 87$

$2x + 3y + 11z = 16$ ①
$19y + 47z = 66$ ②
$28y + 59z = 87$ ③
$19③ - 28②$:
$2x + 3y + 11z = 16$ ①
$532y + 1121z = 1653$ ②
$532y + 1316z = 1848$ ③
$-195z = -195$
$z = 1$
Substitute $z = 1$ in ②.
$532y + 1121 = 1653$
$532y = 532$
$y = 1$
Substitute $z = 1$, $y = 1$ in ①.
$2x + 3 + 11 = 16$
$2x = 2$
$x = 1$
$(1, 1, 1)$ is the solution.

23. $w + x + y + z = 2$ ①
  $w + 2x + 2y + 4z = 1$ ②
  $w - x + y + z = 6$ ③
  $w - 3x - y + z = 2$ ④
  $-1③ + ④$:
  $-w + x + y - z = -6$
  $w - 3x - y + z = 2$
  $-2x - 2y = -4$
  $w + x + y + z = 2$ ①
  $w + 2x + 2y + 4z = 1$ ②
  $-2x - 2y = -4$ ③
  $w - 3x - y + z = 2$ ④
  $-1① + 4$:
  $-w - x - y - z = -2$
  $w - 3x - y + z = 2$
  $-4x - 2y = 0$
  $w + x + y + z = 2$ ①
  $w + 2x + 2y + 4z = 1$ ②
  $-2x - 2y = -4$ ③
  $-4x - 2y = 0$ ④
  $-1④ + 3$:
  $-2x - 2y = -4$
  $4x + 2y = 0$
  $2x = -4$
  $x = -2$
Substitute $x = -2$ in ③. $-2(-2) - 2y = -4$
  $4 - 2y = -4$
  $y = 4$
Substitute $x = 2$ and $y = 4$ in ① and ②.
  $w + (-2) + 4 + z = 2$
  $w + 2(-2) + 8 + 4z = 1$
  $w + z = 0$
  $w + 4z = -3$
Subtract: $-3z = 3$
  $z = -1$
Substitute in ①.
  $w + x + y + z = 2$
  $w + (-2) + 4 - 1 = 2$
  $w = 1$
$(1, -2, 4, -1)$ is the solution.

24. Subtract 3rd equation from 2nd equation.
  $w + x - y + z = 0$
  $w - 3x - y + z = 4$
  $4x = -4$
  $x = -1$
Substitute $x = -1$. $w - 1 - y + z = 0$ ①
  $w + 2 - 2y - z = -5$ ②
  $w + 3 - y + z = 4$ ③
  $2w + 1 - y + 3z = 7$ ④

Regroup: $w - y + z = 1$ ①
$w - 2y - z = -7$ ②
$w - y + z = 1$ ③
$2w - y + 3z = 6$ ④
Equations ① and ③ are the same.
$w - y + z = 1$ ①
$w - 2y - z = -7$ ②
$2w - y + 3z = 6$ ③
① − ②: $y + 2z = 8$
$w - y + z = 1$ ①
$y + 2z = 8$ ②
$2w - y + 3z = 6$ ③
2① − ③: $-y - z = -4$
$w - y + z = 1$ ①
$y + 2z = 8$ ②
$-y - z = -4$ ③
② + ③: $z = 4$
Substituting in ②: $y + 2(4) = 8$
$y = 0$
Substituting in ①: $w - 0 + 4 = 1$
$w = -3$
$(-3, -1, 0, 4)$ is the solution.

25. Let $u = \dfrac{1}{x}$, $v = \dfrac{1}{y}$, $w = \dfrac{1}{z}$.
$2u - v - 3w = -1$ ①
$2u - v + w = -9$ ②
$u + 2v - 4w = 17$ ③
① − ②: $-4w = 8$
$w = -2$
Substituting in ② and ③:
$2u - v - 2 = -9$
$u + 2v + 8 = 17$
Regroup: $2u - v = -7$ ①
$u + 2v = 9$ ②
① − 2②: $2u - v = -7$
$\underline{2u + 4v = 18}$
$-5v = -25$
$v = 5$
Substituting in ①: $2u - 5 + 6 = -1$
$2u = -2$
$u = -1$
$\left(-1, \dfrac{1}{5}, -\dfrac{1}{2}\right)$ is the solution.

26. Let $u = \dfrac{1}{x}$, $v = \dfrac{1}{y}$, $w = \dfrac{1}{z}$.
$2u + 2v - 3w = 3$ ①
$u - 2v - 3w = 9$ ②
$7u - 2v + 9w = -39$ ③
① − 2②: $6v + 3w = -15$
$2u + 2v - 3w = 3$ ①
$6v + 3w = -15$ ②
$7u - 2v + 9w = -39$ ③
7① − 2③: $18v - 39w = 99$
$2u + 2v - 3w = 3$ ①
$6v + 3w = -15$ ②
$18v - 39w = 99$ ③
3② − ③: $48w = -144$
$w = -3$
Substitute in ②: $6v + 3(-3) = -15$
$6v = -6$
$v = -1$
Substitute in ①: $2u + 2(-1) - 3(-3) = 3$
$2u = -4$
$u = -2$
$\left(-\dfrac{1}{2}, -1, -\dfrac{1}{3}\right)$ is the solution.

27. False. Answers may vary.
Example: If $(x, y, z) = (1, 2, 3)$,
$x + y + z = 6 \qquad 2x + 2y + z = 0$
$2x + y + z = 7 \qquad 3x + 2y + z = 10$
$3x + y + z = 8 \qquad 3x + y + 2z = 11$

28. Substitute $(2, 3, -4)$ in equations.
$2a + 3b - 4c = -11$ ①
$-4a + 2b - 3c = -19$ ②
$2a + 4b + 3c = 9$ ③
① − ③: $-b - 7c = -20$
$2a + 3b - 4c = -11$ ①
$-4 + 2b - 3c = -19$ ②
$-b - 7c = -20$
2① + ②: $8b - 11c = -41$
$2a + 3b - 4c = -11$ ①
$8b - 11c = -41$ ②
$-b - 7c = -20$ ③
2① + ②: $8b - 11c = -41$
$2a + 3b - 4c = -11$ ①
$8b - 11c = 41$ ②
$-b - 7c = -20$ ③
8③ + ②: $-67c = -201$
$c = 3$
Substituting in ③: $-b - 21 = -20$
$-b = 1$
$b = -1$
Substituting in ①: $2a - 3 - 12 = -11$
$2a - 15 = -11$
$2a = 4$
$a = 2$
$a = 2$, $b = -1$, $c = 3$

29. $A + \dfrac{3}{4}B + 3C = 12$ ①
$\dfrac{4}{3}A + B + 2C = 12$ ②
$2A + B + C = 12$ ③
$4A + 3B + 12C = 48$ ①
$4A + 3B + 6C = 36$ ②
$2A + B + C = 12$ ③
① − ②: $6c = 12$
$c = 2$
Substituting in ① and ③:
$4A + 3B + 12 = 36$
$2A + B + 2 = 12$
$4A + 3B = 24$
$2A + B = 10$
① − 2②: $B = 4$
Substituting in ①: $4A + 12 + 24 = 48$
$4A = 12$
$A = 3$
Substituting in $Ax + By + Cz = 12$:
The equation is $3x + 4y + 2z = 12$.

30. Substituting values in $z = b - mx - ny$, we have:
$2 = b - m - n$ ①
$6 = b - 3m + n$ ②
$1 = b - \dfrac{3}{2}m - n$ ③
Multiplying ③ by 2:
$2 = b - m - n$ ①
$6 = b - 3m + n$ ②
$2 = 2b - 3m - 2n$ ③
① − ②: $-4 = 2m - 2n$
$2 = b - m - n$ ①
$-4 = 2m - 2n$ ②
$2 = 2b - 3m - 2n$ ③
2① − ③: $m = 2$

Substituting in ②: $-4 = 2(z) - 2n$
$$-8 = -2n$$
$$4 = n$$
Substituting in ①: $2 = b - 2 - 4$
$$8 = b$$
The equation is $z = 8 - 2x - 4y$.

31. $y - 3x = 2$
$$y = 3x + 2$$

Line 1 would have slope $-\dfrac{1}{3}$.

$$y - 1 = -\dfrac{1}{3}(x - 5)$$

$$y = -\dfrac{1}{3}x + \dfrac{8}{3}$$

32. All real numbers   **33.** $\{x \mid x \neq 0\}$ **34.** $\{x \mid x \neq 5\}$

35. $-2x + 4y + 8 = 0$; $y = \dfrac{1}{2}x - 2$

36. $x - 3y - 5 = 0$; $y = \dfrac{1}{3}x - \dfrac{5}{3}$

37. a. $c - 42 = \left(\dfrac{73.5 - 42}{13 - 6}\right)(d - 6)$

$$c - 42 = \left(\dfrac{31.50}{7}\right)(d - 6)$$

$$7c - 294 = 31.5d - 189 + 294$$
$$7c = 31.5d + 105$$
$$c = 4.5d + 15$$

b. $c = 4.5(26) + 15$
$$c = \$132$$

p. 180   **4-5 TRY THIS**

a. $A + B + C = 287$ ①
  $A \qquad + C = 197$ ②
  $A + B \qquad = 202$ ③
  ① − ③: $C = 85$
  Substitute $C = 85$ in ②.
  $$A = 112$$
  Substitute $C = 85$, $A = 112$ in ①.
  $$B + 197 = 287$$
  $$B = 90$$

pp. 181–182   **4-5 EXERCISES**

1. $17, 9, 79$ **2.** $16, 19, 22$ **3.** $4, 2, -1$ **4.** $8, 21, -3$

5. $A = 34°, B = 104°, C = 42°$ **6.** $P = 30°, Q = 90°, R = 60°$

7. $T = 25°, U = 50°, V = 105°$ **8.** $F = 32°, G = 96°, H = 52°$

9. \$21 on Thur., \$18 on Fri., \$27 on Sat.

10. 20 on Mon., 35 on Tues., 32 on Wed.

11. First score: 74.5, second score: 68.5, third score: 82

12. A: 1500, B: 1900, C: 2300   **13.** A: 2200, B: 2500, C: 2700

14. A: 900 gal/hr; B: 1300 gal/hr; C: 1500 gal/hr

15. Todd 10, Don 12, Carla 15

16. Let T = Tammy's age, D = Dennis's age,
  C = Carmen's age, M = Mark's age.
  $$T = C + D$$
  $C = 2 + D + M$ and $T + C + D + M = 42$
  $$D = 4M$$
  Tammy is 20 yr old.

17. Let x = 1st digit, y = 2nd digit, and z = 3rd digit.
  $x + y + z = 14$ ①
  $y = 2 + x$ ②
  $x = z$ ③

Substituting y and z in ①: $x + 2 + x + x = 14$
$$3x = 12$$
$$x = 4$$
$$x + 2 = 6$$
The number is 464.

18. Let H = Hal's tickets, T = Tom's tickets, J = Jorge's tickets.
  Hal: $2[2(H - T - J)]$
  Tom: $2[(T + T) - (H - T - J + 2J)]$
  Jorge: $2(2J) - 2(H - T - J) - [(T + T) - (H - T - J - 2J)]$
  Combining terms:
  $$-4H - 4T - 4J = 40$$
  $$-2H + 6T - 2J = 40$$
  $$-H - T + 7J = 40$$
  Tom had 35 tickets.

19. Let C = Children's tickets, A = Adults' tickets,
  S = Senior citizens' tickets

$$C + S = 30 + \dfrac{1}{2}A$$

$$S = 5 + 4C$$
$$5.5A + 4S + 1.5C = 14{,}970$$

Regrouping: $-\dfrac{1}{2}A + C + S = 30$

$$-4C + S = 5$$
$$5.5A + 1.5C + 4S = 14{,}970$$
Clearing of fractions and decimals:
$$-A + 2C + 2S = 60$$
$$-4C + S = 5$$
$$55A + 15C + 40S = 149{,}700$$
Adults': 2050; senior citizens': 845; children's: 210

20. $t = \dfrac{d}{r}$

$$\dfrac{2}{U} + \dfrac{15}{L} + \dfrac{5}{D} = 1.5$$

$$\dfrac{6}{U} + \dfrac{9}{L} + \dfrac{1}{D} = 1.4$$

$$\dfrac{8}{U} + \dfrac{3}{L} + \dfrac{8}{D} = 1.6$$

Substitute $x = \dfrac{1}{U}$, $y = \dfrac{1}{L}$, $z = \dfrac{1}{D}$

$$2x + 15y + 5z = 1.5$$
$$6x + 9y + z = 1.4$$
$$8x + 3y + 8z = 1.6$$
$$2x + 15y + 5z = 1.5$$

$3① − ②$ $36y + 14z = 3.1$
$4① − ③$ $57y + 12y = 4.4$
           $2x + 15y + 5z = 1.5$
           $36y + 14z = 3.1$

$19② − 12③$ $122z = 6.1$

So $z = \dfrac{6.1}{122} = \dfrac{1}{20}$, $36y + 14\left(\dfrac{1}{20}\right) = 3.1$

$$36y + 0.7 = 3.1$$

$$36y = 2.4, y = \dfrac{2.4}{36} = \dfrac{1}{15}$$

$$2x + 15\left(\dfrac{1}{15}\right) + 5\left(\dfrac{1}{20}\right) = 1.5$$

$$2x + 1.25 = 1.5, 2x = 0.25, x = \dfrac{0.25}{2} = \dfrac{1}{8}$$

$(x, y, z) = \left(\dfrac{1}{8}, \dfrac{1}{15}, \dfrac{1}{20}\right)$, so $(U, L, D) = (8, 15, 20)$

Uphill: 8 mi/h; Level: 15 mi/h; Downhill: 20 mi/h

21. $g(3) = 3 + 2 = 5$ **22.** $f(3) = 9$
  $f(g(3)) = 5^2 = 25$ $g(f(3)) = 9 + 2 = 11$

23. $g(2) = 4$ **24.** $h(-1) = -2$ **25.** $h(2) = 4$
  $h(g(2)) = 8$ $f(h(-1)) = 4$ $g(h(2)) = 6$

26. Rewriting equations in form $y = mx + b$:

$$y = -4x + 9 \text{ and } y = -4x + \frac{9}{2}$$

Slope of each is -4, $\therefore$ lines are parallel.

27. Rewriting equations in form $y = mx + b$:

$$y = \frac{2}{3}x - \frac{4}{3} \qquad y = \frac{3}{2}x - 2$$

Slopes $\neq$, $\therefore$ lines are not parallel.

28. A linear function does not fit the data.

pp. 184–186 **4-6 TRY THIS**

a.
$$3x - y = 2 \;\text{①}$$
$$6x - 2y = 3 \;\text{②}$$
$$-2\text{①} + 2\text{:}$$
$$-6x + 2y = -4$$
$$\underline{6x - 2y = 3}$$
$$0 = -1$$

This is a false statement. Inconsistent

b.
$$x + 4y = 2 \;\text{①}$$
$$2x - y = 1 \;\text{②}$$
$$\text{①} + 4\text{②:}$$
$$x + 4y = 2$$
$$\underline{8x - 4y = 4}$$
$$9x = 6$$
$$x = \frac{2}{3}$$

Substituting: $\frac{2}{3} + 4y = 2$

$$4y = \frac{4}{3}$$
$$y = \frac{1}{3}$$

Solution is $\left(\frac{2}{3}, \frac{1}{3}\right)$. Consistent

c.
$$x + 2y + z = 1 \;\text{①}$$
$$3x + 3y + z = 2 \;\text{②}$$
$$2x + y = 2 \;\text{③}$$
$$-3\text{①} + 2\text{②:}$$
$$-3x - 6y - 3z = -3$$
$$\underline{3x + 3y + z = 2}$$
$$-3y - 2z = -1$$
$$x + 2y + z = 1 \;\text{①}$$
$$-3y - 2z = -1 \;\text{②}$$
$$2x + y = 2 \;\text{③}$$
$$-2\text{①} + 3\text{:}$$
$$-2x - 4y - 2z = -2$$
$$\underline{2x + y = 2}$$
$$-3y - 2z = 0$$
$$\begin{array}{ll} x + 2y + z = 1 \;\text{①} & \text{②} + \text{③:} \\ -3y - 2z = -1 \;\text{②} & 0 \neq -1 \\ -3y - 2z = 0 \;\text{③} & \text{Inconsistent} \end{array}$$

d.
$$x + z = 1 \;\text{①}$$
$$y + z = 1 \;\text{②}$$
$$x + y = 1 \;\text{③}$$
$$\text{①} - \text{③:}$$
$$x + z = 1$$
$$\underline{x + y = 1}$$
$$z - y = 0$$
$$x + z = 1 \;\text{①}$$
$$y + z = 1 \;\text{②}$$
$$-y + z = 0 \;\text{③}$$

② + **③:**
$$2z = 1$$
$$z = \frac{1}{2}$$

Substituting: $x + \frac{1}{2} = 1$

$$x = \frac{1}{2}$$
$$y + \frac{1}{2} = 1$$
$$y = \frac{1}{2}$$
$$\left(\frac{1}{2}, \frac{1}{2}, \frac{1}{2}\right)$$

Consistent

e.
$$3x - 2y = 1 \;\text{①} \quad \text{Slope-intercept forms of}$$
$$-6x + 4y = -2 \;\text{②} \quad \text{the equations are}$$
$$\text{①} \; y = \frac{3}{2}x - \frac{1}{2}$$
$$\text{②} \; y = \frac{3}{2}x - \frac{1}{2}$$
Dependent

f.
$$x - y = 2 \;\text{①}$$
$$x + y = 4 \;\text{②}$$
$$\text{①} + \text{②:}$$
$$2x = 6$$
$$x = 3$$
Substituting: $3 - y = 2$
$$y = 1$$
$(1, 3)$ Not dependent

g.
$$x + y + 2z = 1 \;\text{①}$$
$$x - y + z = 1 \;\text{②}$$
$$2x + 3z = 2 \;\text{③}$$
$$\text{①} + \text{②:}$$
$$x + y + 2z = 1$$
$$2x + 3z = 2$$
$$2x + 3z = 2$$
Dependent

h.
$$x + y + 2z = 1 \;\text{①}$$
$$x - y + z = 1 \;\text{②}$$
$$x + 2y + z = 2 \;\text{③}$$
$$\text{①} - \text{③:}$$
$$x + y + 2z = 1 \;\text{①}$$
$$x - y + z = 1 \;\text{②}$$
$$-y + z = -1 \;\text{③}$$
$$\begin{array}{ll} \text{①} - \text{②:} & x + y + 2z = 1 \;\text{①} \\ & 2y + z = 0 \;\text{②} \\ & -y + z = -1 \;\text{③} \end{array}$$
② − **③:** $3y = 1$
$$y = \frac{1}{3}$$

Substituting: $-\frac{1}{3} + z = -1$

$$z = -\frac{2}{3}$$
$$x + \frac{1}{3} - \frac{4}{3} = 1$$
$$x = 2$$
$\left(2, \frac{1}{3}, -\frac{2}{3}\right)$ Not dependent

pp. 186–187 **4-6 EXERCISES**

1. Inconsistent   **2.** Inconsistent   **3.** Consistent

4. Consistent   **5.** Consistent   **6.** Consistent

7. Inconsistent **8.** Inconsistent **9.** Consistent

10. Consistent **11.** Dependent **12.** Dependent

13. Not dependent **14.** Not dependent **15.** Dependent

16. Dependent **17.** Not dependent **18.** Not dependent

19. Dependent **20.** Dependent

21.
$$\frac{9x - 3y}{3} = \frac{15}{3} \ \textcircled{1}$$

$$\frac{6x - 2y}{2} = \frac{10}{2} \ \textcircled{2}$$

$$3\left(\frac{9x - 3y}{3}\right) = \left(\frac{15}{3}\right) \cdot 3$$

$$2\left(\frac{6x - 2y}{2}\right) = \left(\frac{10}{2}\right) \cdot 2$$

$3x - y = 5$
$3x - y = 5$
Same line with infinite solutions on the line
$(0, -5)\,(1, -2),\,(-1, -8)$

22. $2s - 3t = -9 \ \textcircled{1}$
$4s - 6t = 9 \ \textcircled{2}$
$2\textcircled{1} - \textcircled{2}:$
$4s - 6t = 18$
$\underline{4s - 6t = 9}$
$\quad\quad 0 \neq 9 \quad$ Subtracting
No solution

23. $x + 2y - z = -8 \ \textcircled{1}$
$2x - y + z = 4 \ \ \ \textcircled{2}$
$8x + y + z = 2 \ \ \ \textcircled{3}$
$2\textcircled{1} - \textcircled{2}: 2x + 4y - 2z = -16$
$\quad\quad\quad\quad \underline{2x - y + z = 4}$
$\quad\quad\quad\quad\quad 5y - 3z = -20$
$x + 2y - z = -8 \ \textcircled{1}$
$\quad 5y - 3z = -20 \ \textcircled{2}$
$8x + y + z = 2 \ \ \ \textcircled{3}$
$8\textcircled{1} - \textcircled{3}: 8x + 16y - 8z = -64$
$\quad\quad\quad\quad\ \underline{8x + y + z = 2}$
$\quad\quad\quad\quad\ 15y - 9z = -66$
$2x + 4y - 2z = -16 \ \textcircled{1}$
$\quad\quad 5y - 3z = -20 \ \textcircled{2}$
$\quad\ 15y - 9z = -66 \ \textcircled{3}$
$3\textcircled{1} - \textcircled{3}: 15y - 9z = -60$
$\quad\quad\quad\quad \underline{15y - 9z = -66}$
$\quad\quad\quad\quad\quad 0 = 6 \quad$ No solution

24. $2x + y + z = 0 \ \textcircled{1}$
$\ x + y - z = 0 \ \textcircled{2}$
$x + 2y + 2z = 0 \ \textcircled{3}$
$\textcircled{2} - \textcircled{3}: -y - 3z = 0$
$2x + y - z = 0 \ \textcircled{1}$
$\ x + y - z = 0 \ \textcircled{2}$
$\quad -y - 3z = 0 \ \textcircled{3}$
$\textcircled{1} - 2\textcircled{2}: \quad 2x + y + z = 0$
$\quad\quad\quad\ \underline{-2x + 2y + 2z = 0}$
$\quad\quad\quad\quad\quad -y - z = 0$
$2x + y + z = 0 \ \textcircled{1}$
$\quad -y - 3z = 0 \ \textcircled{2}$
$\quad -y - z = 0 \ \textcircled{3}$
$\textcircled{2} - \textcircled{3}: -y - 3z = 0$
$\quad\quad\quad \underline{-y - z = 0}$
$\quad\quad\quad\quad -2z = 0$
$\quad\quad\quad\quad\quad z = 0$
Substitute $z = 0$ in $\textcircled{2}$. $\quad -y = 0$
$\quad\quad\quad\quad\quad\quad\quad\quad\quad\quad y = 0$
Substitute $z = 0$, $y = 0$ in $\textcircled{1}$.
$x = 0 \ (0, 0, 0)$ is the solution.

25. $2x + 4y + 8z = 5 \ \textcircled{1}$
$\ x + 2y + 4z = 13 \ \textcircled{2}$
$4x + 8y - 16z = 10 \ \textcircled{3}$
$\textcircled{1} - 2\textcircled{2}: 2x + 4y + 8z = 5$
$\quad\quad\quad\quad \underline{2x + 4y + 8z = 26}$
$\quad\quad\quad\quad\quad 0 = -21 \quad$ No solution

26. $\quad x + y + z = 4 \ \textcircled{1}$
$5x + 5y + 5z = 15 \ \textcircled{2}$
$2x + 2y + 2z = 6 \ \ \textcircled{3}$
$2\textcircled{1} - \textcircled{3}: 2x + 2y + 2z = 8$
$\quad\quad\quad\quad \underline{2x + 2y + 2z = 6}$
$\quad\quad\quad\quad\quad 0 = 2 \quad$ No solution

27. 21: Consistent and dependent
23: Inconsistent
25: Inconsistent

28. 22: Inconsistent
24: Consistent, not dependent
26: Inconsistent

29. There is no solution. Each vertex satisfies 2 equations, but not the third. The system is inconsistent. It is not dependent.

30. Write in slope-intercept form.
$\quad 6x - 9y = -3 \quad\quad\quad -4x + 6y = k$
$\quad\quad -9y = -6x - 3 \quad\quad\quad 6y = 4x + k$

$$y = \frac{2}{3}x + \frac{1}{3} \quad\quad \frac{6y}{6} = \frac{4x}{6} + \frac{k}{6}$$

$$y = \frac{2}{3}x + \frac{k}{6}$$

Intercepts must be equal, so $\frac{1}{3} = \frac{k}{6}$; $k = 2$.

31. Write in slope-intercept form.
$\quad 8x - 16y = 20 \quad\quad 10x - 20y = k$
$\quad\quad -16y = -8x + 20 \quad -20y = -10x + k$

$$y = \frac{1}{2}x - \frac{5}{4} \quad\quad \frac{-20y}{-20} = \frac{-10x}{-20} + \frac{k}{-20}$$

$$y = \frac{1}{2}x + \frac{k}{-20}$$

Intercepts must be equal, so $-\frac{5}{4} = \frac{k}{-20}$; $k = 25$.

32. $2x = 1 - 3y \quad\quad 4x = 2 - 6y$
$$x = \frac{1 - 3y}{2} \quad\quad x = \frac{1 - 3y}{2}$$
$$\left(\frac{1 - 3y}{2}, y\right)$$

33. $-6x = -4y + 10 \quad\quad 3x = 2y - 5$
$$x = \frac{2y - 5}{3} \quad\quad x = \frac{2y - 5}{3}$$
$$\left(\frac{2y - 5}{3}, y\right)$$

34. When $x = 2$, denominator is 0. $\{x \,|\, x \neq 2\}$

35. When $x = 1$ or $x = 0$, denominator is 0.
$\{x \,|\, x \neq 1 \text{ and } x \neq 0\}$

36. $-4y = -3x - 11$
$$y = \frac{3}{4}x + \frac{11}{4} \quad \text{Slope} = \frac{3}{4},$$
$$y\text{-intercept} = \frac{11}{4}$$

37. $9y = 6x + 15$
$$y = -\frac{2}{3}x + \frac{5}{3} \quad \text{Slope} = -\frac{2}{3}, \ y\text{-intercept} = \frac{5}{3}$$

38. $y = 0x + 4 \quad$ Slope $= 0$, y-intercept $= 4$

39. $y = \frac{5}{2}x + \frac{11}{2}$ Slope $= \frac{5}{2}$, y-intercept $= \frac{11}{2}$

40. $y = -2x + 3$ Slope $= -2$, y-intercept $= 3$

41. $11 - 35m = -59$ **42.** $t + 4.2t = 156$
$-35m = -70$ $5.2t = 156$
$m = 2$ $t = 30$

43. $-3c = 18$
$c = -6$

p. 187   CONNECTIONS: GEOMETRY

1. All intersect at 1 point.   **2.** All intersect in 1 line.

3. The three planes are parallel.

4. Two planes are parallel, the third intersects each of the others in a line.

5. The three planes coincide.

6. Two planes coincide; the third intersects them in a line.

7. Two planes coincide; the third is parallel to them.

8. Each plane intersects with each one of the others, forming a 3-d triangle.

pp. 187–191   4-7 TRY THIS

a.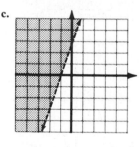

b.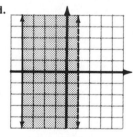

c.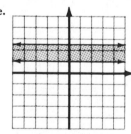

d.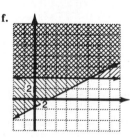

e.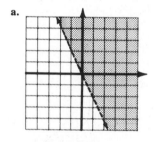

f.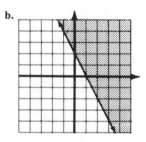

g.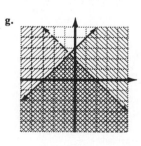

h.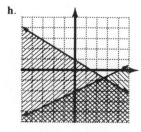

i.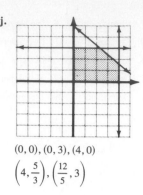

$\left(-\frac{1}{2}, \frac{3}{2}\right)$

j.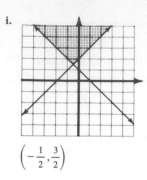

$(0, 0), (0, 3), (4, 0)$
$\left(4, \frac{5}{3}\right), \left(\frac{12}{5}, 3\right)$

p. 192   4-7 EXERCISES

1.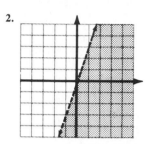

2.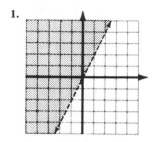

3.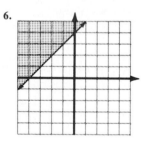

4.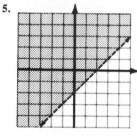

5.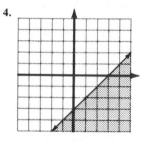

6.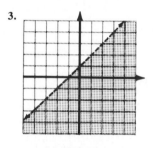

7.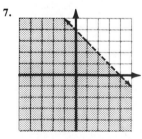

8.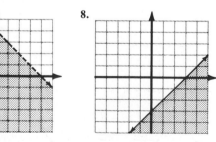

9.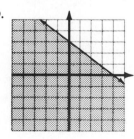

10.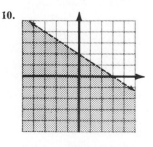

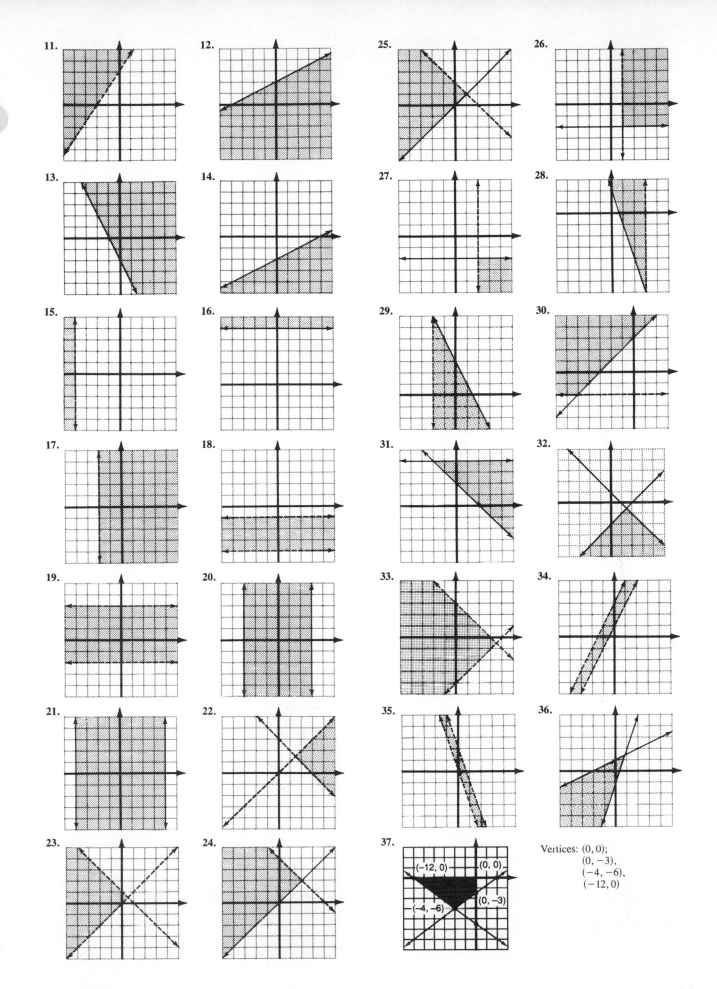

11.

12.

13.

14.

15.

16.

17.

18.

19.

20.

21.

22.

23.

24.

25.

26.

27.

28.

29.

30.

31.

32.

33.

34.

35.

36.

37. (−12, 0) (0, 0) (−4, −6) (0, −3)

Vertices: (0, 0);
(0, −3),
(−4, −6),
(−12, 0)

38.

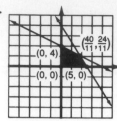

Vertices: $(0, 0)$,
$(0, 4)$,
$\left(\frac{40}{11}, \frac{24}{11}\right)$,
$(5, 0)$

39.

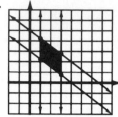

Vertices: $\left(1, \frac{9}{4}\right), \left(1, \frac{25}{6}\right),$
$\left(3, \frac{3}{4}\right), \left(3, \frac{5}{2}\right)$

40.

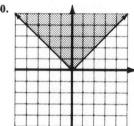

41.

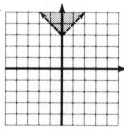

42.

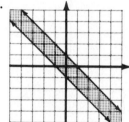

43.

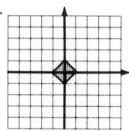

44.

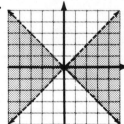

45.

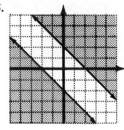

46. Answers may vary.
  a. $0 \le x \le 3$ **b.** $y \le -x + 4$
  $0 \le y \le 3$ $x \ge 0$
                 $y \ge 0$
  c. $y \le x$ **d.** $0 \le y \le 2$
  $y \ge x - 5$ $y \le x$
  $0 \le y \le 5$ $y \ge -x + 10$

47. Yes, for example, $y > 2x + 1$
       $y < 2x + 1$

48. $y + 2 = 3(x - 3)$ **49.** $y + 2 = -2(x - 3)$
  $y + 2 = 3x - 9$ $y + 2 = -2x + 6$
  $y = 3x - 11$ $y = -2x + 4$

50. $y + 2 = \frac{1}{2}(x - 3)$ **51.** $y + 2 = \frac{4}{5}(x - 3)$

  $y + 2 = \frac{1}{2}x - \frac{3}{2}$ $y + 2 = \frac{4}{5}x - \frac{12}{5}$

  $y = \frac{1}{2}x - \frac{7}{2}$ $y = \frac{4}{5}x - \frac{22}{5}$

52. $y + 2 = -\frac{2}{3}(x - 3)$ **53.** $3m + 13 = 1 + m$
                    $2m = -12$
  $y + 2 = -\frac{2}{3}x + 2$ $m = -6$

  $y = -\frac{2}{3}x$

54. $16 - 4t = 3 - 3t$ **55.** $-3.6 = 16a$
    $-t = -13$ $-0.225 = a$
     $t = 13$

p. 194   **4-8 TRY THIS**

a. Let $x =$ number of hamburgers,
  $y =$ number of hot dogs.
  The profit is $P = 0.33x + 0.21y$, subject to these constraints:
  $10 \le x \le 40$
  $30 \le y \le 70$
  $x + y \le 90$

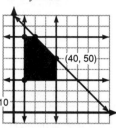

(40, 50)

Vertices: (x, y) Profit: $P = 0.33x + 0.21y$
     $(10, 30)$ $P = 9.6$
     $(10, 70)$ $P = 18$
     $(20, 70)$ $P = 21.30$
     $(40, 30)$ $P = 19.51$
     $(40, 50)$ $P = 23.70$
The snack bar will make a profit of $23.70 by selling
40 hamburgers and 50 hot dogs.

p. 195   **4-8 EXERCISES**

1. $5 \le A \le 10$ Vertices: $M = 4A + 7B$
  $3 \le B \le 10$ $(5, 3)$ $= 41$
  $A + B \le 18$ $(5, 10)$ $= 90$
    $A > 0$ $(10, 3)$ $= 61$
    $B > 0$ $(10, 8)$ $= 96$
       $(8, 10)$ $= 102$

(8, 10)

You must correctly answer 8 Type A
and 10 Type B questions for
a maximum score of 102.

2. $3 \le A \le 12$ Vertices: $M = 10A + 25B$
  $4 \le B \le 15$ $A > 0$ $(3, 15)$ $= 405$
  $A + B \le 20$ $B > 0$ $(5, 15)$ $= 425$
         $(12, 8)$ $= 320$
         $(12, 0)$ $= 120$
         $(3, 0)$ $= 55$

(5, 15)

You must correctly answer 5 Type A
and 15 Type B questions for a
maximum score of 425.

3. $2000 \leq X \leq 14{,}000$

$0 \leq Y \leq 15{,}000$

$X + Y \leq 22{,}000$

Vertices:	$M = 0.06X + 0.065Y$
$(2000, 0)$	$= 12{,}000$
$(14{,}000, 0)$	$= 840$
$(14{,}000, 8000)$	$= 1360$
$(7000, 15{,}000)$	$= 1395$
$(2000, 15{,}000)$	$= 1095$

$7000 must be invested at Bank X and $15,000 at Bank Y for a maximum income of $1395.

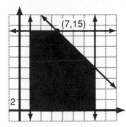

4. Let X = Corporate bonds, Y = Municipal bonds

$6000 \leq X \leq 22{,}000$

$0 \leq Y \leq 30{,}000$

$X + Y \leq 40{,}000$

Vertices:	$M = 0.08X + 0.075Y$
$(6, 0)$	$= 480$
$(22, 0)$	$= 1760$
$(22, 18)$	$= 3110$
$(10, 30)$	$= 2250$
$(6, 30)$	$= 2730$

$22,000 should be invested in corporate bonds and $18,000 in municipal bonds to make a maximum income of $3110.

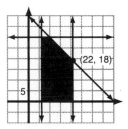

5. Let k = number of knit suits made; w = number of worsted suits made. 20 hr per day are available for cutting, 16 hr per day for sewing.

$$2k + 4w \leq 20$$
$$4k + 2w \leq 16$$

Since it is impossible to manufacture a negative number of suits, $k \geq 0$ and $w \geq 0$. Upon graphing the two inequalities, we find:
Vertices: Set up a system of equations: $2(2k + 4w) = (20)\,(2)$

$$\underline{\quad 4k + 2w = 16 \quad}$$
$$6w = 24$$
$$w = 4$$

There is a vertex at $(2, 4)$. (and $\therefore k = 2$)

Other vertices are the w- and k-intercepts of the two inequalities.

Vertices: (k, w)	Profit: $P = 34k + 31w$
$(0, 0)$	0
$(4, 0)$	136
$(2, 4)$	192 maximum
$(0, 5)$	155

2 knit suits and 4 worsted suits maximized profit at $192.

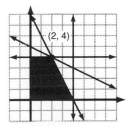

6. The profit for $(40, 120)$ or $(60, 100)$ is $16,000, since the number produced must be an integer. The number of mopeds can be any integer from 40 to 60; the number of bicycles is 160 minus the number of mopeds.

7. Let x = number of P-1 planes
n = number of P-2 planes
f = first class
t = tourist class
e = cconomy class
$f \geq 2000$, $t \geq 1500$, $e \geq 2400$ and the capacities of x and y are:
x: $40f$, $40t$, $120e$
y: $80f$, $30t$, $40e$

Since $f \geq 2000$, we have $40x + 80 \geq 2000$
Similarly for t and 3, $\quad 40x + 30y \geq 1500$
$$120x + 40y \geq 2400$$
Vertices: $\quad 40x + 80y = 2000$
$$\underline{\quad 40x + 30y = 1500 \quad}$$
$$50y = 500;\ y = 10 \text{ and } x = 30$$
$$120x + 40y = 2400$$
$$\underline{3(40x + 30y) = 3(1500)}$$
$$-50y = -2100;\ y = 42 \text{ and } x = 6$$
The other vertices are the x-and y-intercepts that are farthest from $(0, 0)$.

Vertices: (x, y)	Cost: $12,000x + $10,000y
$(0, 60)$	$600,000
$(6, 42)$	$492,000
$(30, 10)$	$460,000 minimum
$(50, 0)$	$600,000

30 P-1 airplanes and 10 P-2 airplanes should be used to minimize the cost at $460,000.

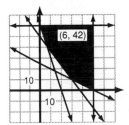

8. $19c + 57 = 76$
$19c = 19$
$c = 1$

9. $14 < 3r + 2$
$12 < 3r$
$4 < r$
$r > 4$

10. $-2c > -18$
$c < 9$

p. 197 COLLEGE ENTRANCE EXAMS

1. $x + 2y = 6$ ①
$3x + y = 3$ ②
① + ②: $4x + 3y = 9$
$2(4x + 3y) = 2(9)$
$8x + 6y = 18$
(A)

2. $5x - 3y = 6$ ①
$x = \dfrac{4y}{5}$ ②
$5 \cdot$ ②: $5x = 4y$
$5x - 3y = 6$ ①
$\underline{5x - 4y = 0}$ ②
① − ②: $y = 6$
(C)

3. $3x + 3y = 7$ ①
$x + 4y = 3$ ②
① − 3②: $\quad 3x + 3y = 7$
$$\underline{-3x - 12y = -9}$$
$$-9y = -2$$
$$y = \frac{2}{9}$$

$$3x + 3\left(\frac{2}{9}\right) = 7$$
$$3x = \frac{19}{3}$$
$$x = \frac{19}{9}$$

$$\frac{4\left(\frac{19}{9}\right) + 7\left(\frac{2}{9}\right)}{5} = \frac{\frac{76}{9} + \frac{14}{9}}{5} = \frac{10}{5} = 2$$
(B)

4. $x + 4y = 5$ ①
$4x + 3y = 4$ ②
$-4$①$+$②$: -4x - 16y = -20$

$$\underline{ 4x + 3y = 4}$$
$$-13y = -16$$
$$y = \frac{16}{3}$$

Substituting: $x + 4\left(\frac{16}{13}\right) = 5$

$$x = \frac{1}{13}$$

$$10\left(\frac{1}{13}\right) + 14\left(\frac{16}{13}\right) = 18$$

(D)

5. $\quad x + y = 3$ ① $\qquad$ **6.** $\quad 4x - 3y = 10$
$\quad\ x - y = 3$ ②
①$+$②$: 2x = 5$ $\qquad\qquad\qquad x = \frac{74}{4}$

$$x = \frac{5}{2}$$

$$6x = 15 \qquad\qquad 4\left(\frac{7y}{4}\right) - 3y = 10$$
(A)
$$4y = 10$$
$$y = \frac{5}{2}$$
$$2y = 5$$
(D)

7. $x + 2y = 3$ ①
$2x + y = 1$ ②
$-2$①$+ 2: -2x - 4y = -6$

$$\underline{ 2x + y = 1}$$
$$-3y = -5$$
$$y = \frac{5}{3}$$

Substituting: $x + 2\left(\frac{5}{3}\right) = 3$

$$x = -\frac{1}{3}$$

$$9\left(-\frac{1}{3}\right) + 9\left(\frac{5}{3}\right) = 12$$

(E)

8. $5x + 3y = 8$ ①
$3x + y = 4$ ②
①$- 3$②$: \ 5x + 3y = 8$

$$\underline{-9x - 3y = -12}$$
$$-4x = -4$$
$$x = 1$$

Substituting: $5 + 3y = 8$
$$y = 1$$
$$4(1) + 2(1) = 6$$
(D)

9. $\qquad\qquad 3x + 5y = 44$ ①
$$\underline{\qquad\qquad 2x - 5y = -29 \ ②}$$
①$+$②$: \qquad\quad 5x = 15$
$$x = 3$$
Substituting: $9 + 5y = 44$
$$5y = 35$$
$$y = 7$$
$$5(3) + 5(7) = 50$$
(E)

10. $ax + by = c$
$$\underline{ax - by = d}$$
$$2ax = c + d$$
$$2x = \frac{c + d}{a}$$
(C)

---

1. $(0, 1)$ $\qquad$ **2.** $(3, 3)$

3. $-y = -9 - 2x \qquad 3x - 8(9 + 2x) = -7 \qquad y = 9 + 2(-5)$
$\quad\ y = 9 + 2x \qquad\ 3x - 72 - 16x = -7 \qquad y = 9 - 10$
$\qquad\qquad\qquad\qquad -72 - 13x = -7 \qquad y = -1$
$\qquad\qquad\qquad\qquad\qquad\ -13x = 65$
$\qquad\qquad\qquad\qquad\qquad\qquad\ x = -5$

Solution is $(-5, -1)$.

4. $\qquad\qquad y = x + 2$
$\qquad\qquad x + y = 6$
$\qquad\ x + (x + 2) = 6$
$\qquad\qquad\ 2x + 2 = 6$
$\qquad\qquad\quad\ 2x = 4$
$\qquad\qquad\qquad x = 2$
$\qquad\qquad\qquad y = 4 \qquad$ Solution is $(2, 4)$.

5. $\qquad\qquad\ y = 7 - x$
$\qquad\qquad 2x - y = 8$
$\qquad 2x - (7 - x) = 8$
$\qquad\ 2x - 7 + x = 8$
$\qquad\qquad 3x - 7 = 8$
$\qquad\qquad\qquad 3x = 15$
$\qquad\qquad\qquad\ x = 5$
$\qquad\qquad y = 7 - 5 = 2 \qquad$ Solution is $(5, 2)$.

6. $2x + 7y = 2 \qquad 3(2x + 7y) = 3(2) \qquad 6x + 21y = 6$
$3x + 5y = -8 \qquad -2(3x + 5y) = -2(-8) \qquad \underline{-6x - 10y = 16}$
$\qquad\qquad\qquad\qquad\qquad\qquad\qquad\qquad\qquad 11y = 22$
$\qquad\qquad\qquad\qquad\qquad\qquad\qquad\qquad\qquad\ y = 2$

$2x + 7(12) = 2$
$2x + 14 = 2$
$\quad\ 2x = -12$
$\qquad x = -6 \qquad$ Solution is $(-6, 2)$.

7. $\quad 5x + 3y = 17$
$$\underline{-5x + 3y = 3}$$
$$\qquad\quad 6y = 20$$
$$y = \frac{20}{6} = \frac{10}{3}$$

$5x + 3\left(\frac{10}{3}\right) = 17$
$\quad 5x + 10 = 17$
$\qquad\quad\ 5x = 7$
$$x = \frac{7}{5} \qquad \text{Solution is } \left(\frac{7}{5}, \frac{10}{3}\right).$$

8. $-3a + 2b = 0$
$$\underline{\ 3a - 4b = -1}$$
$$-2b = -1$$
$$b = \frac{1}{2}$$

$-3a + 2\left(\frac{1}{2}\right) = 0$
$\quad -3a + 1 = 0$
$\qquad\quad -3a = -1$
$$a = \frac{1}{3} \qquad \text{Solution is } \left(\frac{1}{3}, \frac{1}{2}\right).$$

9. Let C be Carol's speed. Then $C + 17$ is Ellie's speed. Using distance = rate · time, then $264 = (C + 17)t$ and $198 = Ct$. Solving for t in both cases,

$$\frac{264}{C + 17} = \frac{198}{C}$$

$264C = 198(C + 17)$
$264C = 198C + (198)(17)$
$\ 66C = 3366$
$\quad\ C = 51$

Carol's speed is 51 km/h and Ellie's speed is 68 km/h.

10. $\quad 2x - y + z = 7$
$\quad\ x + 2y + 2z = 3 \qquad -2$②$+$①
$\quad 7x - 3y - 3z = 4 \qquad -2$③$+ 7$①

$$\begin{aligned}2x - y + z &= 7\\-5y - 3z &= 1\\-y + 13z &= 41\end{aligned} \qquad -5\circled{3} + \circled{2}$$

$$\begin{aligned}2x - y + z &= 7\\-5y - 3z &= 1\\-68z &= -204\\z &= 3\end{aligned}$$

$$\begin{aligned}z &= 3\\-5y - 3(3) &= 1\\-5y - 9 &= 1\\-5y &= 10\\y &= -2\end{aligned}$$

$$\begin{aligned}2x - y + z &= 7\\2x - (-2) + 3 &= 7\\2x + 5 &= 7 \qquad \text{Solution is } (1, -2, 3).\\2x &= 2\\x &= 1\end{aligned}$$

11.
$$\begin{aligned}2a + b - 4c &= 0\\a - b + 2c &= 5 \qquad -2\circled{2} + \circled{1}\\3a + 2b + 2c &= 3 \qquad -2\circled{3} + 3\circled{1}\end{aligned}$$

$$\begin{aligned}2a + b - 4c &= 0\\3b - 8c &= -10\\-b - 16c &= -6 \qquad 3\circled{3} + \circled{2}\end{aligned}$$

$$\begin{aligned}2a + b - 4c &= 0\\3b - 8c &= -10\\-56c &= -28\end{aligned}$$

$$c = \frac{1}{2}$$

$$3b - 8\left(\frac{1}{2}\right) = -10$$

$$\begin{aligned}3b - 4 &= -10\\3b &= -6\\b &= -2\end{aligned}$$

$$2a + (-2) - 4\left(\frac{1}{2}\right) = 0 \qquad \text{Solution is } \left(2, -2, \frac{1}{2}\right).$$

$$\begin{aligned}2a - 4 &= 0\\2a &= 4\\a &= 2\end{aligned}$$

12.
$$\begin{aligned}A + B + C &= 86\\A + B &= 59 \qquad -1\circled{2} + \circled{1}\\A + C &= 58 \qquad -1\circled{3} + \circled{1}\end{aligned}$$
$$\begin{aligned}A + B + C &= 86\\C &= 27\\B &= 28\end{aligned}$$

$$\begin{aligned}A + 28 + 27 &= 86\\A &= 31\end{aligned}$$

13.
$$\begin{aligned}2x - y &= 4\\2x - y &= 6 \qquad \text{The system is inconsistent.}\end{aligned}$$

14.
$$\begin{aligned}x - 2y &= 3 \qquad -4\circled{1} + 2 \qquad\qquad 0 = 0\\4x - 8y &= 12 \qquad\qquad\qquad\quad 4x - 8y = 12\end{aligned}$$
The system is dependent.

15.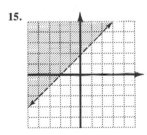

16.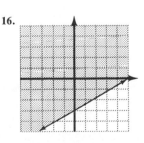

17.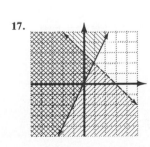

18.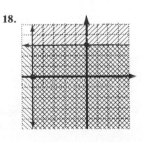

19.
$$\begin{aligned}F + B &= 60,000\\12,000 &< F < 30,000\\10,000 &< B \le 40,000\\T &= 0.10F + 0.12B\end{aligned}$$

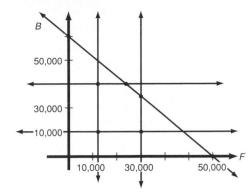

Vertices are $(12,000, 10,000), (12,000, 40,000), (30,000, 10,000)$, $(30,000, 30,000), (20,000, 40,000)$.
The maximum is $(20,000, 40,000)$ or \$20,000 in mutual funds and \$40,000 in municipal bonds. The maximum income is \$6800.

p. 200 **CHAPTER 4 TEST**

1.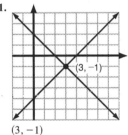

$(3, -1)$

2.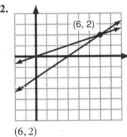

$(6, 2)$

3.
$$\begin{aligned}2x - 3y &= 0\\x + y &= 5\\x &= 5 - y\\2(5 - y) - 3y &= 0\end{aligned}$$
$$\begin{aligned}10 - 2y - 3y &= 0\\10 - 5y &= 0\\5y &= 10\\y &= 2\end{aligned}$$
$$\begin{aligned}x + 2 &= 5\\x &= 3\end{aligned}$$
Solution is $(3, 2)$.

4.
$$\begin{aligned}2x &= y - 5\\5x + 3y &= 4\end{aligned}$$
$$x = \frac{y}{2} - \frac{5}{2}$$
$$5\left(\frac{y}{2} - \frac{5}{2}\right) + 3y = 4$$
$$\frac{5y}{2} - \frac{25}{2} + 3y = 4$$
$$\frac{11y}{2} = \frac{33}{2}$$
$$\begin{aligned}11y &= 33\\y &= 3\end{aligned}$$
$$\begin{aligned}2x &= 3 - 5\\2x &= -2\\x &= -1\end{aligned}$$
Solution is $(-1, 3)$.

5.
$$\begin{aligned}x - 5y &= 6\\3x + 4y &= 18\end{aligned} \qquad \begin{aligned}-3(x - 5y) &= -3(6)\\3x + 4y &= 18\end{aligned} \qquad \begin{aligned}-3x + 15y &= -18\\3x + 4y &= 18\\\hline 19y &= 0\\y &= 0\end{aligned}$$

$$\begin{aligned}x - 5(0) &= 6\\x &= 6 \qquad \text{Solution is } (6, 0).\end{aligned}$$

6.
$$\begin{aligned}4x - 7y &= 23\\6x + 3y &= -33\end{aligned} \qquad \begin{aligned}3(4x - 7y) &= 3(23)\\7(6x + 3y) &= 7(-33)\end{aligned}$$

$$\begin{aligned}12x - 21y &= 69\\42x + 21y &= -231\\\hline 54x &= -162\\x &= -3\end{aligned} \qquad \begin{aligned}4(-3) - 7y &= 23\\-12 - 7y &= 23\\-7y &= 35\\y &= -5\end{aligned}$$
Solution is $(-3, -5)$.

7.
$l = 2w + 42$
$606 = 2w + 2(2w + 42)$
$606 = 6w + 84$
$522 = 6w$
$87 = w$
$l = 216$
The dimensions are 87 m by 216 m.

8. $x + y - 3z = 8$

$2x - 3y + z = -6 \qquad -\frac{1}{2}②+①$

$3x + 4y - 2z = 20 \qquad -\frac{1}{3}③+①$

$\begin{array}{ll} x + y - 3z = 8 & x + y - 3z = 8 \\ \frac{5}{2}y - \frac{7}{2}z = 11 \;②2 & 5y - 7z = 22 \\ & -y - 7z = 4 \qquad 5③+② \\ -\frac{1}{3}y - \frac{7}{3}z = \frac{4}{3} \;③3 & \end{array}$

$\begin{array}{ll} x + y - 3z = 8 & 5y - 7(-1) = 22 \\ 5y - 7z = 22 & 5y + 7 = 22 \\ -42z = 42 & 5y = 15 \\ z = -1 & y = 3 \end{array}$

$x + 3 - 3(-1) = 8$
$x + 3 + 3 = 8$
$x + 6 = 8$
$x = 2 \qquad$ Solution is $(2, 3, -1)$.

9. $A + B + C = 4250$
$A + B = 2900 \qquad -1②+①$
$B + C = 3050 \qquad -1③+①$
$\begin{array}{ll} A + B + C = 4250 & 1200 + B + 1350 = 4250 \\ C = 1350 & B = 1700 \\ A = 1200 & \end{array}$

10. $x = 3y + 4$
$6y = 2x - 6$
$\overline{\rule{3cm}{0.4pt}}$
$6y = 2(3y + 4) - 6$
$0 = -2 \qquad$ Inconsistent

11.
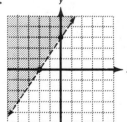

12.
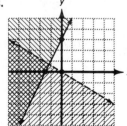

13. $r + s = 16$
$r \le 10$
$s \le 12$
$3r + 5s \le 60$
The region defined by the three inequalities is

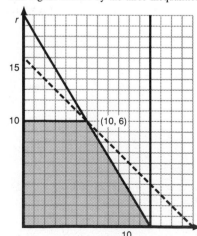

The only solution to the equation $r + s = 16$ for the region is $(6, 10)$. There should be 10 ounces of raisins and 6 ounces of sunflower seeds.

1. $-\frac{11}{13} - \frac{4}{5} = -\frac{55}{65} - \frac{52}{65} = -\frac{107}{65}$

2. $-18.9 - (-7.7) = -18.9 + 7.7 = -11.2$

3. $17 - \left(-\frac{4}{31}\right) = 17 + \frac{4}{31} = 17\frac{4}{31}$

4. $-5\left(-\frac{3}{7}\right) = \frac{15}{7}$ **5.** $-2.3(-5.5) = 12.65$

6. $-\frac{7}{8}\left(\frac{2}{3}\right) = -\frac{14}{24} = -\frac{7}{12}$

7. $-[2(-1) - 4 - 6] = -[-2 - 4 - 6] = -(-12) = 12$

8. $2|4 - 8| - |-1| = 2(4) - 1 = 7$

9. $-3|-1 + 4| = -3(3) = -9$

10. $3x - 2(5y - 4x) = 3x - 10y + 8x = 11x - 10y$

11. $8y - [2y - (5y - 7)] = 8y - [2y - 5y + 7]$
$= 8y - [-3y + 7] = 8y + 3y - 7$
$= 11y - 7$

12. $xy - (3x + xy - 5y) = xy - 3x - xy + 5y = 5y - 3x$

13. $6x - 7 = 23$ **14.** $-5y - 11 = -1$
$\quad\; 6x = 30 \qquad\qquad\qquad -5y = 10$
$\quad\;\; x = 5 \qquad\qquad\qquad\quad y = -2$

15. $120 + 4(35) = 120 + 140$ **16.** $(5y)^3 = 125y^3$
$\qquad\qquad\qquad\quad = \$260$

17. $(-3x)^4 = 81x^4$ **18.** $-\frac{1}{32}$

19. $(2x^2y)(-5x^{-5}y^6) = -10x^{-3}y^7$

20. $-\frac{28x^{-3}y^2}{4x^5y^{-3}} = -\frac{7y^5}{x^8} = -7x^{-8}y^5$

21. $(8x^3)^{-2} = \frac{1}{(8x^3)^2} = \frac{1}{64x^6} = \frac{1}{64}x^{-6}$ **22.** 6.76×10^5

23. 1.5×10^{-3} **24.** 1.009×10^1 **25.** $3x - 15 = 18x$
$\qquad\qquad\qquad\qquad\qquad\qquad\qquad\qquad -15 = 15x$
$\qquad\qquad\qquad\qquad\qquad\qquad\qquad\qquad\; -1 = x$

26. $\frac{1}{8}x + \frac{3}{2} = \frac{1}{3} - \frac{1}{6}x$ **27.** $(x - 7)(2x + 1) = 0$
$\quad 3x + 36 = 8 - 4x \qquad\qquad x - 7 = 0 \qquad 2x + 1 = 0$
$\qquad\;\; 7x = -28$
$\qquad\;\;\; x = -4 \qquad\qquad\qquad\quad x = 7 \;\; \text{or} \qquad x = -\frac{1}{2}$

28. $\qquad\quad x = $ purchases   **29.** $e = mc^2$ **30.** $f = m\dfrac{M}{g^2}$
$\quad x + .015x = 46.69$
$\qquad 1.015x = 46.69 \qquad\qquad m = \dfrac{e}{c^2} \qquad\qquad M = \dfrac{fg^2}{m}$
$\qquad\qquad\;\; x = \$46.00$

31. $3x - 8 > 2x - 1$ **32.** $-\frac{2}{3}y \le 12$
$\quad\; x - 8 > -1 \qquad\qquad\qquad y \ge -18$
$\qquad\;\; x > 7$

33. $-3 + 7x < 2x + 9$ **34.** $x + (x + 2) + (x + 4) > 30$
$\qquad\quad 7x < 2x + 12 \qquad\qquad\qquad 3x + 6 > 30$
$\qquad\quad 5x < 12 \qquad\qquad\qquad\qquad\quad 3x > 24$
$\qquad\qquad\qquad\qquad\qquad\qquad\qquad\qquad\quad x > 8$
$\qquad\qquad x < \dfrac{12}{5} \qquad\qquad\qquad 9, 11, 13$

35. $-3 < 4x + 1 < 6$
$\quad -4 < 4x < 5$

$\quad -1 < x < \dfrac{5}{4}$

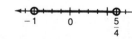

36. $2x + 1 < -1 \quad$ or $\quad x - 3 > 4$
$\qquad 2x < -2$
$\qquad\; x < -1 \quad$ or $\qquad x > 7$

37. $|x| < \dfrac{1}{2}$

$-\dfrac{1}{2} < x < \dfrac{1}{2}$

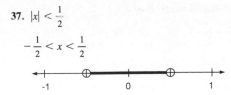

38. $|14 - y| < 10$

$\quad 14 - y < 10 \qquad -14 + y < 10$

$\qquad y > 4 \qquad\qquad y < 24$

$\qquad\quad 4 < y < 24$

39. $|-x + 7| \geq 3$

$\quad -x + 7 \geq 3 \qquad x - 7 \geq 3$

$\qquad x \leq 4 \qquad\qquad x \geq 10$

40. $\{(-3,1), (-3,2), (-2,1), (-2,2), (-1,1), (-1,2)\}$

41. $\{(-1,-1), (-1,0), (-1,1), (-1,2), (-1,3), (0,0), (0,1), (0,2),$
$(0,3), (1,1), (1,2), (1,3), (2,2), (2,3), (3,3)\}$

42. 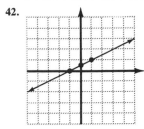 **43.**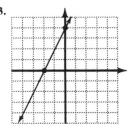

44. $\{x \mid x \neq -3\}$ **45.** R

46. 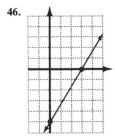 **47.**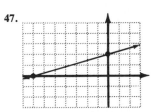

48.
$$0 = -\dfrac{1}{2}(-8) + b$$
$$b = -4$$
$$y = -\dfrac{1}{2}x - 4$$
$$x + 2y + 8 = 0$$

49.
$$m = \dfrac{-1 - 7}{-2 + 3} = -8$$
$$7 = -3(-8) + b$$
$$b = -17$$
$$y = -8x - 17$$
$$8x + y + 17 = 0$$

50. $m = 0$ **51.** $m = \dfrac{3}{5}$

$\quad\; b = -4 \qquad\qquad b = -\dfrac{8}{5}$

52. $2y + x = -4$ **53.** $2x - y = 7$

54. $(0, 39.2)$ $\quad m = \dfrac{622.3 - 39.2}{72} = \dfrac{583.1}{72} = 8.099$
$\quad\;\, (72, 622.3)$

$\qquad\qquad\qquad 39.2 = 0(8.099) + b$
$\qquad\qquad\qquad\qquad b = 39.2$
$\quad y = (102)(8.099) + 39.2 = 865.3 \text{ mi/h}$

55. $g(-3) = 2 - (-3)^2 = 2 - 9 = -7$
$\quad f(g(-3)) = 1 + 3(-7) = -20$

56.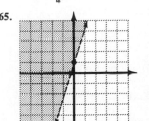

57.
$$x = -8 - 2y$$
$$4(-8 - 2y) - 3y = 1$$
$$-11y = 33$$
$$y = -3$$
$$x = -8 + 6 = -2$$
$$(-2, -3)$$

58.
$$\begin{array}{r} 12x - 16y = 28 \\ -12x + 4y = 20 \\ \hline -12y = 48 \\ y = -4 \end{array}$$
$$12x - 16(-4) = 28$$
$$12x = -36$$
$$x = -3$$
$$(-3, -4)$$

59. $3.5x + 4y = 4.90 \qquad\quad 14x + 16y = 19.6$
$\quad\;\; 2x + 0.5y = 1.05 \qquad \dfrac{-14x - 3.5y = -7.35}{12.5y = 12.25}$
$\qquad\qquad\qquad\qquad\qquad\qquad\qquad y = 0.98$

$\quad 2x + 0.5(0.98) = 1.05$
$\qquad\qquad\quad x = 0.28$

Rice 28¢/lb
Seeds 98¢/lb

60. $\quad 2x - y - z = -11$
$\qquad x + 2y - 3z = -13 \qquad -2\textcircled{2} + \textcircled{1}$
$\quad -x - y + 4z = 22 \qquad\quad 2\textcircled{3} + \textcircled{1}$
$\quad 2x - y - z = -11$

$\qquad -5y + 5z = 15 \qquad -\dfrac{1}{5}\textcircled{2} \qquad 2x - y - z = -11$
$\qquad\qquad\qquad\qquad\qquad\qquad\qquad\qquad\qquad y - z = -3$
$\qquad -3y + 7z = 33 \qquad 3\textcircled{2} + \textcircled{3} \qquad\qquad 4z = 24$
$\quad z = 6, y = 3, x = -1 \qquad (-1, 3, 6)$

61. $3x + y - 2z = 1$
$\qquad x - y - z = -6 \qquad -3\textcircled{2} + \textcircled{1}$
$\quad -x + y - 3z = 10 \qquad 3\textcircled{3} + \textcircled{1}$
$\quad 3x + y - 2z = 1 \qquad\qquad\qquad\qquad 3x + y - 2z = 1$
$\qquad\quad 4y + z = 19 \qquad\qquad\qquad\qquad\quad 4y + z = 19$
$\qquad 4y - 11z = 31 \qquad -1\textcircled{3} + \textcircled{2} \qquad\qquad 12z = -12$
$\quad z = -1, y = 5, x = -2$
$\quad (-2, 5, -1)$

62. $\quad 2c + l + v = 120$
$\qquad 1c + 2l + v = 155 \qquad -2\textcircled{2} + \textcircled{1}$
$\qquad 1c + 1l + 2v = 105 \qquad -2\textcircled{3} + \textcircled{1}$
$\quad 2c + l + v = 120$
$\qquad -3l - v = -190$
$\qquad -l - 3v = -90 \qquad -3\textcircled{3} + \textcircled{2}$
$\quad 2c + l + v = 120 \qquad\qquad\qquad$ Vinyl $10
$\qquad -3l - v = -190 \qquad\qquad\qquad$ Linen $60
$\qquad\qquad 8v = 80 \quad v = 10, l = 60, c = 25$ Cotton $25

63. $4x - 6y = 12 \qquad 24x - 36y = 72$
$\quad -6x + 9y = 18 \qquad \dfrac{-24x + 36y = 72}{0 = 144}$ Inconsistent

64. $-8x - 9y = -12 \qquad -8x - 9y = -12$
$\quad -2x - \dfrac{9}{4}y = -3 \qquad \dfrac{8x + 9y = 12}{0 = 0}$ Dependent

65. 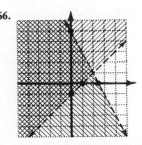 **66.**

67. $w \le 4$
$d \le 6$
$2w + 3d = 18$
$(0, 6) = \$30$
$\left(4, \dfrac{10}{3}\right) = \$27$
$(4, 0) = \$12$
Should make 0 windows and 6 doors.

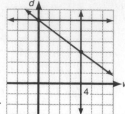

CHAPTER 5

p. 204   READY FOR POLYNOMIALS AND POLYNOMIAL EQUATIONS?

1. -2 **2.** $5(x + y)$ **3.** $5(2x + 3y - 1)$ **4.** $3y - 6$

5. $4x + 48$ **6.** $ct + cs - cf$ **7.** $5y$ **8.** $5a$ **9.** 0

10. $x - 4$ **11.** $-y + 2$ **12.** 3^3 **13.** $8a^9b$

14. $24x^{-12}y^2$ **15.** $9a^2$ **16.** $-8y^3$ **17.** 2^{-12} **18.** x^8

19. $3, -5$ **20.** $0, -5$

p. 207   5-1 TRY THIS

a. $P(x) = 2x^3 - 3x^2 + 5$
(1) $P(0) = 2 \cdot 0^3 - 3 \cdot 0^2 + 5$
$= 5$
(2) $P(4) = 2 \cdot 4^3 - 3 \cdot 4^2 + 5$
$= 128 - 48 + 5$
$= 85$
(3) $P(-2) = 2 \cdot (-2)^3 - 3 \cdot (-2)^2 + 5$
$= -16 - 12 + 5$
$= -23$

b. $5x^2 + 3x^4 - 2x^2 - x^4 = 5x^2 - 2x^2 + 3x^4 - x^4$
$= (5 - 2)x^2 + (3 - 1)x^4 = 3x^2 + 2x^4$

c. $5x^3y^2 - 2x^2y^3 + 4x^3y^2 = 5x^3y^2 + 4x^3y^2 - 2x^2y^3$
$= (5 + 4)x^3y^2 - 2x^2y^3 = 9x^3y^2 - 2x^2y^3$

d. $3xy^2 - 4x^2y + 4xy^2 + 2x^2y + 3x^2 - y^2 + 2x^2y$
$= 3xy^2 + 4xy^2 - 4x^2y + 2x^2y + 3x^2 - y^2$
$= (3 + 4)xy^2 + (-4 + 2 + 2)x^2y + 3x^2 - y^2$
$= 7xy^2 + 3x^2 - y^2$

pp. 208–209   5-1 EXERCISES

1. $54, 2$ **2.** $-84, 0$ **3.** $-45, -\dfrac{235}{27}$ **4.** $-168, -6$

5. $2x^2$ **6.** $-4y^2$ **7.** $3x + y$ **8.** $-2a - 6b$ **9.** $a + 6$

10. $7x + 14$ **11.** $-6a^2b - 2b^2$ **12.** $-8x^3 - 3x^2y^2$

13. $9x^2 + 2xy + 15y^2$ **14.** $11a^2 + 3ab - 3b^2$

15. $-x^2y + 9xy^2 + 4y$ **16.** $x^2y + 11xy - 4xy^2$

17. For $P(x) = -4x^3 + 2x^2 - 7x + 5$,
$P(a) = -4a^3 + 2a^2 - 7a + 5$.

18. $Q(-b) = 6(-b)^3 - 12(-b)^2 - 8(-b) - 3$
$= 6(-b^3) - 12(b^2) - 8(-b) - 3$
$= -6b^3 - 12b^2 + 8b - 3$

19. $P(2a) = (2a)^3 - 4(2a)^2 + 3(2a) - 7$
$= 8a^3 - 4(4a^2) + 3(2a) - 7$
$= 8a^3 - 16a^2 + 6a - 7$

20. $Q\left(\dfrac{c}{2}\right) = -7\left(\dfrac{c}{2}\right)^3 + 10\left(\dfrac{c}{2}\right)^2 + 6$
$= -7\left(\dfrac{c^3}{8}\right) + 10\left(\dfrac{c^2}{4}\right) + 6$
$= -\dfrac{7}{8}c^3 + \dfrac{10}{4}c^2 + 6$

21. $P(x + a) = -3(x + a)^2 + 6(x + a) - 4$
$= -3(x^2 + 2ax + a^2) + 6(x + a) - 4$
$= -3x^2 - 6ax - 3a^2 + 6x + 6a - 4$
$= -3x^2 - 6ax + 6x - 3a^2 + 6a - 4$

22. $Q(2x + 1) = 6(2x + 1)^2 + 8(2x + 1) - 11$
$= 6(4x^2 + 4x + 1) + 8(2x + 1) - 11$
$= 24x^2 + 24x + 6 + 16x + 8 - 11$
$= 24x^2 + 40x + 3$

23. $(13x^5 - 22x^4 - 36x^3 + 40x^2 - 16x + 75) +$
$(42x^5 - 37x^4 + 50x^3 - 28x^2 + 34x + 100)$
$= (13 + 42)x^5 + (-22 - 37)x^4 + (-36 + 50)x^3 +$
$(40 - 28)x^2 + (-16 + 34)x + (75 + 100)$
$= 55x^5 - 59x^4 + 14x^3 + 12x^2 + 18x + 175$

24. $13x^5 - 22x^4 - 36x^3 + 40x^2 - 16x + 75 - 42x^5 + 37x^4$
$- 50x^3 + 28x^2 - 34x - 100$
$= (13 - 42)x^5 + (-22 + 37)x^4 + (-36 - 50)x^3 +$
$(40 + 28)x^2 + (-16 - 34)x + (75 - 100)$
$= -29x^5 + 15x^4 - 86x^3 + 68x^2 - 50x - 25$

25. $42x^5 - 37x^4 + 50x^3 - 28x^2 + 34x + 100 - 13x^5 + 22x^4$
$+ 36x^3 - 40x^2 + 16x - 75$
$= (42 - 13)x^5 + (-37 + 22)x^4 + (50 + 36)x^3 +$
$(-28 - 40)x^2 + (34 + 16)x + (100 - 75)$
$= 29x^5 - 15x^4 + 86x^3 - 68x^2 + 50x + 25$

26. $4[P(x)] = 52x^5 - 88x^4 - 144x^3 + 160x^2 - 64x + 300$
$3[Q(x)] = 126x^5 - 111x^4 + 150x^3 - 84x^2 + 102x + 300;$
$(52 + 126)x^5 + (-88 - 111)x^4 + (-144 + 150)x^3 +$
$(160 - 84)x^2 + (-64 + 102)x + (300 + 300)$
$= 178x^5 - 199x^4 + 6x^3 + 76x^2 + 38x + 600$

27. $f(5, -2) = 3[(5)(-2)^2] - 2[(5)^2(-2)]$
$= 3[(5)(4)] - 2[(25)(-2)]$
$= 3[20] - 2[-50]$
$= 60 + 100$
$= 160$

28. $C(50) = 0.002(50)^2 - 0.21(50) + 15$
$= 5 - 10.5 + 15$
$= 9.5¢$ per km
$C(80) = 0.002(80)^2 - 0.21(80) + 15$
$= 12.8 - 16.8 + 15$
$= 11¢$ per km

29. $V \approx 0.524hD^2 + 0.262hd^2$
$\approx 0.524(48 \text{ in.})(24 \text{ in.})^2 + 0.262(48 \text{ in.})(18 \text{ in.})^2$
$\approx 14{,}487.552 \text{ in.}^3 + 4074.624 \text{ in.}^3$
$\approx 18{,}562.176 \text{ in.}^3$
$\approx 18{,}562.2 \text{ in.}^3$ or 10.7 ft^3

30. $A = \pi(R^2 - r^2)$
$= \pi[(20 \text{ cm})^2 - (15 \text{ cm})^2]$
$= \pi[400 \text{ cm}^2 - 225 \text{ cm}^2]$
$= \pi[175 \text{ cm}^2]$
$= 175\pi \text{ cm}^2$
$\approx 175(3.1416) \text{ cm}^2 \approx 549.8 \text{ cm}^2$

31. $0.49W + 0.45P - 6.36R + 8.7 = 0.49(83.9) + 0.45(6.0)$
$- 6.36(7.1) + 8.7 = 41.111 + 2.7 - 45.156 + 8.7$
$= 7.36\%$ body fat

32. $0.041h - 0.018A - 2.69 = 0.041(139.8) - 0.018(41) - 2.69$
$= 5.7318 - 0.738 - 2.69 = 2.304 \ L$

33. Answers may vary.
Example: $-2x^4y^2 - 6x^2y - 8x^2y^4$

34. x^ny^a
$n + a = n$
$n + a - n = n - n$
$a = 0$

35. $x^{(n-2)}y^a$
$(n - 2) + a = n$
$n - 2 + a = n$
$a = 2$

36. $x^ay^{n/2}$
$a + \dfrac{n}{2} = n$
$a + \dfrac{n}{2} - \dfrac{n}{2} = n - \dfrac{n}{2}$
$a = \dfrac{n}{2}$

37. $x^5y^az^a$
$5 + a + a = n$
$5 + 2a = n$
$2a = n - 5$
$a = \dfrac{n - 5}{2}$

38. 10 different terms are possible;
x^3, y^3, z^3, x^2y, x^2z, xy^2, y^2z, xz^2, yz^2, and xyz

39. Area of bottom is x^2. Area of one side is hx. Total area is $x^2 + 4hx$ square units.

40. Area of bottom is x^2. Height of a side is $\frac{1}{2}(12 - x)$. Volume is
$$x^2\left(\frac{1}{2}\right)(12 - x) = 6x^2 - \frac{1}{2}x^3.$$

41. $6m^2 + 3m = 3m(2m + 1)$ **42.** $21n - 36m = 3(7n - 12m)$

43. $17 + 51c = 17(1 + 3c)$ **44.** $2ab + 4ac = 2a(b + 2c)$

45. $m = \dfrac{-2 - 4}{1 - (-1)} = -3$

$y - y_1 = m(x - x_1)$
Substitute: $y - (-2) = -3(x - 1)$
$\qquad\qquad y + 2 = -3x + 3$
$\qquad\qquad\quad y = -3x + 1$

46. $n = \dfrac{-1 - 3}{-2 - 6} = \dfrac{1}{2}$

$y - y_1 = m(x - x_1)$

Substitute: $y - (-1) = \dfrac{1}{2}[x - (-2)]$

$\qquad\qquad y + 1 = \dfrac{1}{2}x + 1$

$\qquad\qquad\quad y = \dfrac{1}{2}x$

47. $m = \dfrac{2 - 0}{0 - (-2)} = 1$

$y - y_1 = m(x - x_1)$
$y - 2 = 1(x - 0)$
$y - 2 = x$
$\quad y = x + 2$

48. $2(m + 66) = 12$
$2m + 132 = 12$
$\quad 2m = -120$
$\quad\quad m = -60$

49. $4(1 - t) = 6$
$4 - 4t = 6$
$\quad -4t = 2$
$\quad\quad t = -0.5$

50. $\qquad 11a + 2 = 6a + 12$
$11a - 6a + 2 = 6a - 6a + 12$
$\qquad 5a + 2 = 12$
$\quad 5a + 2 - 2 = 12 - 2$
$\qquad\quad 5a = 10$

$\qquad \dfrac{1}{5} \cdot 5a = \dfrac{1}{5} \cdot 10$

$\qquad\qquad a = 2$

pp. 210–211   5-2 TRY THIS

a. $\quad 3x^3 + 4x^2 - 7x - 2$

$\quad \dfrac{-7x^3 - 2x^2 + 3x + \dfrac{1}{2}}{}$

$\quad -4x^3 + 2x^2 - 4x - \dfrac{3}{2}$

b. $5p^2q^4 - 2p^2q^2 \qquad\quad - 3q$
$\quad \dfrac{+ 3p^2q^2 - 6pq^2 \qquad\quad + 5}{5p^2q^4 + \;\; p^2q^2 - 6pq^2 - 3q + 5}$

c. $-(5x^2t^2 - 4xy^2t - 3xt + 6x - 5)$
$\quad = -5x^2t^2 + 4xy^2t + 3xt - 6x + 5$

d. $-(-3x^2y + 5xy - 7x + 4y + 2)$
$\quad = 3x^2y - 5xy + 7x - 4y - 2$

e. $\quad 5xy^4 - 7xy^2 + 4x^2 \qquad\quad - 3$
$\quad \dfrac{-(-3xy^4 + 2xy^2 \qquad\quad - 2y + 4)}{8xy^4 - 9xy^2 + 4x^2 + 2y - 7}$

f. $\quad 5x^2y - 7x^3y^2 \qquad\qquad - x^2y^2 + 4y$
$\quad \dfrac{-(-2x^2y + 2x^3y^2 - 5x^2y^3 \qquad\quad - 5y)}{7x^2y - 9x^3y^2 + 5x^2y^3 - x^2y^2 + 9y}$

pp. 212–213   5-2 EXERCISES

1. $3x^3 - x^2 + 7x$ **2.** $-9x^3 + 10x^2 - 8x - 18$

3. $3x^2y - 5xy^2 + 7xy + 2$ **4.** $2x^2y - 7xy^2 + 8xy + 5$

5. $3x + 2y - 2z - 3$ **6.** $7x^2 + 12xy - 2x - y - 9$

7. $9.46y^4 + 2.5y^3 - 11.8y - 3.1$

8. $\dfrac{1}{2}x^5 - \dfrac{3}{10}x^3 - \dfrac{1}{4}x^2 + \dfrac{2}{3}x - 19$

9. $\dfrac{3}{4}x^3 + \dfrac{1}{4}x^2 + \dfrac{1}{16}x + \dfrac{23}{24}$ **10.** $-5x^3 + 7x^2 - 3x + 6$

11. $4y^4 - 7y^2 + 2y + 1$ **12.** $6x^2y - 2xy^2 + 5y^3 - 10$

13. $-20x^4y^4 + 12x^3y^3 - 5x^2y^2 + 3xy - 19$

14. $-2x^2 + 6x - 2$ **15.** $-2x^3 - 6x^2 - x + 11$

16. $-2x^2 + 6x - 2$ **17.** $-4x^2 - 5y^2 + 3$

18. $-4a^2 + 8ab - 5b^2$ **19.** $6x^4 - 8x^2 + 9x - 4$

20. $3x^4 - 9x^3 + 7x - x^3y$

21. $0.06y^4 + 0.032y^3 - 0.94y^2 + 0.93$ **22.** $x^4 - x^2 - 1$

23. $-\dfrac{4}{9}y^3 + \dfrac{4}{9}y^2 + \dfrac{26}{27}y + \dfrac{4}{9}$

24. $(2 + 6)x^{2a} + (4 + 3)x^a + (3 + 4) = 8x^{2a} + 7x^a + 7$

25. $47x^{4a} + (3 + 37)x^{3a} + (22 + 8)x^{2a} + x^a + (1 + 3)$
$\quad = 47x^{4a} + 40x^{3a} + 30x^{2a} + x^a + 4$

26. $(3 - 2)x^{6a} + (-5x^{5a}) + (0 - 4)x^{4a} + (4 - 3)x^{3a} +$
$(0 - 2)x^{2a} + 8$
$\quad = x^{6a} - 5x^{5a} - 4x^{4a} + x^{3a} - 2x^{2a} + 8$

27. $(2 - 1)x^{5b} + 4x^{4b} + (3 - 2)x^{3b} + (0 - 6)x^{2b} + (0 - 9)x^b$
$+ (8 - 8) = x^{5b} + 4x^{4b} + x^{3b} - 6x^{2b} - 9x^b$

28. $3x^2y + (5 - 11)x^2z + 2y^2z + (-1 + 7)xyz + (-5xy^2) + z^2y$
$\quad = 3x^2y - 6x^2z + 2y^2z + 6xyz - 5xy^2 + z^2y$

29. $(12 - 7)x^3y^2z + (-4x^2y^2z^2) + (16 - 16)xy^2z^3 + 2xyz$
$+ (-12x^3yz) + 4x^2y^2z + (-xyz^2) + (-9)$
$\quad = 5x^3y^2z - 4x^2y^2z^2 + 2xyz - 12x^3yz + 4x^2y^2z - xyz^2 - 9$

30. $(8 - 11 - 1)ab^2c + (-10 + 10)ab^2 + 2ac + (15 + 9)b^2c +$
$2ab = -4ab^2c + 2ac + 24b^2c + 2ab$

31. $17 + (-24 - 6)pq^2 + (4 - 4)p^2q + (1 + 7)p^2qr +$
$(8 - 8)pq^2r + 3pqr = 17 - 30pq^2 + 8p^2qr + 3pqr$

32. Answers may vary. Example:
$10x^3y^2 - 4x^2y^2 + 9xy^2 - 4xy$ and $-x^3y^2 + x^2y^2 - xy^2 + xy$

33. $f(2) = 2 \cdot 2^2 + 3(2) + 5$
$\quad = 8 + 6 + 5 = 19,$
$g(2) = 6 \cdot 2^2 - 9 \cdot 2 - 11$
$\quad = 24 - 18 - 11 = -5,$
$f(2) + g(2) = 19 - 5 = 14;$
$h(x) = (2 + 6)x^2 + (3 - 9)x + (5 - 11)$
$\quad = 8x^2 - 6x - 6,$
$h(2) = 8 \cdot 2^2 - 6(2) - 6$
$\quad = 32 - 12 - 6$
$\quad = 14;$
thus, $h(2) = f(2) + g(2).$

34. $f(3) = 2 \cdot 3^2 + 3(3) + 5$
$\quad = 18 + 9 + 5 = 32,$
$g(3) = 6 \cdot 3^2 - 9 \cdot 3 - 11$
$\quad = 54 - 27 - 11 = 16,$
$f(3) - g(3) = 32 - 16 = 16;$
$p(x) = (2 - 6)x^2 + (3 + 9)x + (5 + 11)$
$\quad = -4x^2 + 12x + 16,$
$p(3) = -4 \cdot 3^2 + 12 \cdot 3 + 16$
$\quad = -36 + 36 + 16$
$\quad = 16;$
thus, $p(3) = f(3) - g(3).$

35. If $a = b$ and $b = 2c$, then $a = 2c$.
Then $-4ab^2c + 2ac + 24b^2c + 2ab$
$= -2ab^2(2c) + a(2c) + 12b^2(2c) + 2ab$
$= -2a^4 + a^2 + 12a^3 + 2a^2$
$= -2a^4 + 12a^3 + 3a^2$.

36. $(3 + 2)(-2 + 5) = (5)(3) = 15$

37. $[4(-2)]^{-2} = (-8)^{-2} = \left(-\frac{1}{8}\right)^2 = \frac{1}{64}$

38. $9(-2) - [3(-2)]^2$
$= -8 - (-6)^2$
$= -18 - 36 = -54$

39.
$6 - 4y = 2x$
$-2x - 4y + 6 = 0$ or
$2x + 4y - 6 = 0$

40.
$2(x - y) = 4$
$2x - 2y = 4$
$2x - 2y - 4 = 0$ or
$-2x + 2y + 4 = 0$

41. $5x + 6 = 12 + 8x$
$3x + 6 = 12$
$-3x = 6$
$x = -2$

42. $7a + 11a = 162$
$18a = 162$
$a = 9$

43. $25 = 4(m - 3) - 3$
$25 = 4m - 12 - 3$
$25 = 4m - 15$
$40 = 4m$
$10 = m$

44. Let x = price of discount coupon.
Then $89x + 183(9) = 2136.50$
$89x + 1647 = 2136.50$
$89x = 489.50$
$x = 5.50$
Coupon is worth $\$9.00 - 5.50 = \$3.50$.

45. Let x = number of senior citizens.
Then $0.75(9.88x) + (247 - x)(9.88) = 2324.27$
$7.41x + 2440.36 - 9.88x = 2324.27$
$-2.47x = -116.12$
$x = 47$

There were 47 senior citizens.

p. 213   PROBLEM FOR PROGRAMMERS

```
10  REM Chapter 5 Problem
20  FOR EQN = 1 TO 2
30  PRINT "Input the coefficients for equation
      ";EQN
40  FOR DEG = 4 TO 0 STEP -1
50  PRINT "Input the coefficient of degree
      ";DEG
60  INPUT POLY (EQN,DEG)
70  NEXT
80  NEXT
90  DM$ = "Addition"
100 IND = -1
110 FOR DMY = 1 TO 2
120 IND = ( -1) * IND
130  IF IND = -1 THEN DM$ = "Subtraction "
140  PRINT "The result for ";DM$;"is: ";
150  FOR DEG = 4 TO 0 STEP - 1
160 SUM = POLY(1,DEG) + POLY(2,DEG) * IND
170  IF SUM = 0 THEN 240
180  PRINT SUM;
190  IF DEG < 1 THEN 240
200  PRINT "x";
210  IF DEG < 2 THEN 230
220  PRINT " ^ ";DEG;
230  PRINT " + ";
240  NEXT
250  PRINT
260  NEXT
270  END

10  REM Chapter 5 Challenge Problem
20  FOR EQN = 1 TO 2
30  PRINT "Input the coefficients for
      equation ";EQN
40  FOR DEG = 4 TO 0 STEP -1
50  PRINT "Input the coefficients of
      degree ";DEG
60  INPUT POLY (EQN,DEG)
```

```
70  NEXT
80  NEXT
90  DM$ = "Addition "
100 IND = -1
110 HOME
120 FOR DMY = 1 TO 2
130 IND = ( -1) * IND
140  IF IND = -1 THEN DM$ = "Subtraction "
150  VTAB (1 + 4 * DMY)
160  PRINT "The result for ";DM$;"is: ";
170  FOR DEG = 4 TO 0 STEP -1
180  VTAB (3 + 4 * DMY)
190  SN$ = " + "
200  SUM = POLY(1,DEG) + POLY(2,DEG) * IND
210  IF SUM = 0 THEN 300
220  IF SUM < 0 THEN SN$ = " - "
230  PRINT SN$;
240  PRINT ABS (SUM) ;
250  IF DEG < 1 THEN 300
260  PRINT "x";
270  IF DEG < 2  THEN 300
280  VTAB (2 + 4 * DMY)
290  PRINT DEG;
300  NEXT
310  PRINT
320  NEXT
330  END
```

pp. 214–217   5-3 TRY THIS

a.
$$3x^2y - 2xy + 3y$$
$$\times \qquad xy + 2y$$
$$\overline{3x^3y^2 - 2x^2y^2 + 3xy^2}$$
$$\times \qquad 6x^2y^2 - 4xy^2 + 6y^2$$
$$\overline{3x^3y^2 + 4x^2y^2 - xy^2 + 6y^2}$$

b.
$$p^2q + 2pq + 2q$$
$$\times 2p^2q - pq + q$$
$$\overline{2p^4q^2 + 4p^3q^2 + 4p^2q^2}$$
$$\qquad -p^3q^2 - 2p^2q^2 - 2pq^2$$
$$\times \qquad\qquad p^2q^2 + 2pq^2 + 2q^2$$
$$\overline{2p^4q^2 + 3p^3q^2 + 3p^2q^2 \qquad + 2q^2}$$

                    F   O   I   L
c. $(2xy + 3x)(x^2 - 2) = 2x^3y - 4xy + 3x^3 - 6x$
                    F   O   I   L
d. $(3x - 2y)(5x + 3y) = 15x^2 + 9xy - 10xy - 6y^2$
$$= 15x^2 - xy - 6y^2$$
                    F   O   I   L
e. $(2x + 20)(3y - 20) = 6xy - 40x + 60y - 400$
f. $(4x - 5y)^2 = (4x)^2 - 2(4x)(5y) + (-5y)^2$
$$= 16x^2 - 40xy + 25y^2$$
g. $(2y^2 + 6x^2y) = (2y^2)^2 + 2(2y^2)(6x^2y) + (6x^2y)^2$
$$= 4y^4 + 24x^2y^3 + 36x^4y^2$$
h. $(4x + 7)(4x - 7) = (4x)^2 - 7^2 = 16x^2 - 49$
i. $(5x^2y + 2y)(5x^2y - 2y) = (5x^2y)^2 - (2y)^2$
$$= 25x^4y^2 - 4y^2$$
j. $(2x + 3 + 5y)(2x + 3 - 5y) = (2x + 3)^2 - (5y)^2$
$$= (2x)^2 + 2(2x)(3) + 3^2 - 25y^2 = 4x^2 + 12x + 9 - 25y^2$$
k. $(-2x^3y^2 + 5t)(2x^3y^2 + 5t) = (5t)^2 - (2x^3y^2)^2$
$$= 25t^2 - 4x^6y^4$$
l. $(x + 3)^3 = x^3 + 3(x)^2(1) + 3(x)(1)^2 + (1)^3$
$$= x^3 + 3x^2 + 3x + 1$$
m. $(x - 1)^3 = x^3 + 3(x)^2(-1) + 3(x)(-1)^2 + (-1)^3$
$$= x^3 - 3x^2 + 3x - 1$$
n. $(t^2 + 3b)^3 = (t^2)^3 + 3(t^2)^2(3b) + 3(t^2)(3b)^2 + (3b)^3$
$$= t^6 + 9t^4b + 27t^2b^2 + 27b^3$$
o. $(2a^3 - 5b^2)^3 = (2a^3)^3 + 3(2a^3)^2(-5b^2) + 3(2a^3)(-5b^2)^2$
$$+ (-5b^2)^3$$
$$= 8a^9 - 60a^6b^2 + 150a^3b^4 - 125b^6$$

pp. 217–218   5-3 EXERCISES

1. $6x^3 + 4x^2 + 32x - 64$ **2.** $6y^3 + 3y^2 + 9y + 27$

3. $4a^3b^2 - 10a^2b^2 + 3ab^3 + 4ab^2 - 6b^3 + 4a^2b - 2ab + 3b^2$

4. $2x^4 - x^2y^2 - 4x^3y - 2y^4 + 3xy^3$

5. $a^3 - b^3$ **6.** $t^3 + 1$ **7.** $4x^2 + 8xy + 3y^2$

8. $4a^2 - 8ab - 3b^2$ **9.** $12x^3 + x^2y - \dfrac{3}{2}xy - \dfrac{1}{8}y^2$

10. $6y^4 - \dfrac{1}{2}xy^3 + \dfrac{3}{5}xy - \dfrac{1}{20}x^2$

11. $4x^3 - 4x^2y - 2xy^2 + 2y^3$ **12.** $9y^3 - 3y^2x - 6y + 2x$

13. $4x^2 + 12xy + 9y^2$ **14.** $25x^2 + 20xy + 4y^2$

15. $4x^4 - 12x^2y + 9y^2$ **16.** $16x^4 - 40x^2y + 25y^2$

17. $4x^6 + 12x^3y^2 + 9y^4$ **18.** $25x^6 + 20x^3y^2 + 4y^4$

19. $9x^2 - 4y^2$ **20.** $9x^2 - 25y^2$ **21.** $x^4 - y^2z^2$

22. $4x^4 - 25y^2$ **23.** $9x^4 - 4$ **24.** $25x^4 - 9$

25. $y^3 + 15y^2 + 75y + 125$ **26.** $t^3 - 21t^2 + 147t - 343$

27. $m^6 - 6m^4n + 12m^2n^2 - 8n^3$

28. $8f^3 + 36f^2d + 54fd^2 + 27d^3$

29. $\left(\dfrac{1}{2}x^2 - \dfrac{3}{5}y\right)^2 = \left(\dfrac{1}{2}x^2\right)^2 - 2\left(\dfrac{1}{2}x^2\right)\left(\dfrac{3}{5}y\right) + \left(\dfrac{3}{5}y\right)^2$
$$= \dfrac{1}{4}x^4 - \dfrac{3}{5}x^2y + \dfrac{9}{25}y^2$$

30. $\left(\dfrac{1}{4}x^2 - \dfrac{2}{3}y\right)^2 = \left(\dfrac{1}{4}x^2\right)^2 - 2\left(\dfrac{1}{4}x^2\right)\left(\dfrac{2}{3}y\right) + \left(\dfrac{2}{3}y\right)^2$
$$= \dfrac{1}{16}x^4 - \dfrac{1}{3}x^2y + \dfrac{4}{9}y^2$$

31. $(0.5x + 0.7y^2)^2 = (0.5x)^2 + 2(0.5x)(0.7y^2) + (0.7y^2)^2$
$$= 0.25x^2 + 0.70xy^2 + 0.49y^4$$

32. $(0.3x + 0.8y^2)^2 = (0.3x)^2 + 2(0.3x)(0.8y^2) + (0.8y^2)^2$
$$= 0.09x^2 + 0.48xy^2 + 0.64y^4$$

33. $(2x + 3y + 4)(2x + 3y - 4) = (2x + 3y)^2 - (4)^2$
$$= 4x^2 + 12xy + 9y^2 - 16$$

34. $(x^2 + 3y + y^2)(x^2 + 3y - y^2) = (x^2 + 3y)^2 - (y^2)^2$
$$= x^4 + 6x^2y + 9y^2 - y^4$$

35. $(x + 1)(x - 1)(x^2 + 1) = [(x)^2 - (1)^2](x^2 + 1)$
$$= (x^2 - 1)(x^2 + 1)$$
$$= (x^2)^2 - (1)^2$$
$$= x^4 - 1$$

36. $(y - 2)(y + 2)(y^2 + 4) = [(y)^2 - (2)^2](y^2 + 4)$
$$= (y^2 - 4)(y^2 + 4)$$
$$= (y^2)^2 - (4)^2$$
$$= y^4 - 16$$

37. $(2x + y)(2x - y)(4x^2 + y^2)$
$$= [(2x)^2 - (y)^2](4x^2 + y^2)$$
$$= (4x^2 - y^2)(4x^2 + y^2)$$
$$= (4x^2)^2 - (y^2)^2$$
$$= 16x^4 - y^4$$

38. $(5x + y)(5x - y)(25x^2 + y^2)$
$$= [(5x)^2 - (y)^2](25x^2 + y^2)$$
$$= (25x^2 - y^2)(25x^2 + y^2)$$
$$= (25x^2)^2 - (y^2)^2$$
$$= 625x^4 - y^4$$

39. $[4x(x - 1)]^2 = (4x^2 - 4x)^2$
$$= (4x^2)^2 - 2(4x^2)(4x) + (-4x)^2$$
$$= 16x^4 - 32x^3 + 16x^2$$

40. $\left(3x^3 - \dfrac{5}{11}\right)^2 = (3x^3)^2 - 2(3x^3)\left(\dfrac{5}{11}\right) + \left(\dfrac{5}{11}\right)^2$
$$= 9x^6 - \dfrac{30}{11}x^3 + \dfrac{25}{121}$$

41. $(x^a + y^b)(x^a - y^b)(x^{2n} + y^{2b})$
$$= [(x^a)^2 - (y^b)^2](x^{2a} + y^{2b})$$
$$= (x^{2a} - y^{2b})(x^{2a} + y^{2b})$$
$$= (x^{2a})^2 - (y^{2b})^2$$
$$= x^{4a} - y^{4b}$$

42. $(x^{a-b})^{a+b} = x^{(a-b)(a+b)}$
$$= x^{(a)^2 - (b)^2}$$
$$= x^{a^2 - b^2}$$

43. a. $A(17\%) = 1000(1 + 0.17)^2 = 1000(1.17)^2$
$$= 1000(1.3689) = \$1368.90$$
  b. $A(11\%) = 1000(1 + 0.11)^3 = 1000(1.11)^3$
$$= 1000(1.367631) = \$1367.63$$
  c. $A(8\%) = 1000(1 + 0.08)^4 = 1000(1.08)^4$
$$= 1000(1.360489) = \$1360.49$$
  d. $b = 2, A(r) = 1000(1 + r)^2$
$$= 1000(r^2 + 2r + 1)$$
$$b = 3, A(r) = 1000(1 + r)^3$$
$$= 1000(r^3 + 3r^2 + 3r + 1)$$
$$b = 4, A(r) = 1000(1 + r)^4$$
$$= 1000(r^4 + 4r^3 + 6r^2 + 4r + 1)$$

44. $2y - 3$

45. $[(2x - 1)^2 - 1]^2 = [4x^2 - 4x + 1 - 1]^2$
$$= [4x^2 - 4x]^2$$
$$= (4x^2)^2 - 2(4x^2)(4x) + (-4x)^2$$
$$= 16x^4 - 32x^3 + 16x^2$$

46. $(a^2 - b^2)[5 - (a + b)][5 + (a + b)]$
$$= (a^2 - b^2)[25 - (a + b)^2]$$
$$= (a^2 - b^2)[25 - (a^2 + 2ab + b^2)]$$
$$= (a^2 - b^2)[25 - a^2 - 2ab - b^2]$$
$$= 25a^2 - a^4 - 2a^3b - a^2b^2 - 25b^2 + a^2b^2 + 2ab^3 + b^4$$
$$= -a^4 + (-2a^3b) + 25a^2 + 2ab^3 - 25b^2 + b^4$$

47. $[(x^3 + x^2 + x) - (x^2 + x + 1)](x^3 + 1)$
$$= (x^3 - 1)(x^3 + 1)$$
$$= x^6 - 1$$

48. $[x + y + 1][(x^2 - xy - x) + (y^2 + 2y + 1)]$
$$= (x + y + 1)(x^2 - xy - x + y^2 + 2y + 1)$$
$$= (x^3 - x^2y - x^2 + xy^2 + 2xy + x)$$
$$+ (x^2y - xy^2 - xy + y^3 + 2y^2 + y)$$
$$+ (x^2 - xy - x + y^2 + 2y + 1)$$
$$= x^3 + y^3 + 3y^2 + 3y + 1$$

49. $[(y - 1)(y + 1)][(y - 1)(y + 1)][(y - 1)(y + 1)]$
$$= (y^2 - 1)(y^2 - 1)(y^2 - 1)$$
$$= (y^2 - 1)^3$$
$$= (y^2)^3 + 3(y^2)^2(-1) + 3(y^2)(-1)^2 + (-1)^3$$
$$= y^6 - 3y^4 + 3y^2 - 1$$

50. $(r^4 + 2r^2s^2 + s^4)[(r^4 - 2r^3s + r^2s^2)$
$$+ (2r^3s - 4r^2s^2 + 2rs^3) + (r^2s^2 - 2rs^3 + s^4)]$$
$$= (r^4 + 2r^2s^2 + s^4)(r^4 - 2r^2s^2 + s^4)$$
$$= (r^8 - 2r^6s^2 + r^4s^4) + (2r^6s^2 - 4r^4s^4 + 2r^2s^6)$$
$$+ (r^4s^4 - 2r^2s^6 + s^8)$$
$$= r^8 - 2r^4s^4 + s^8$$

51. $[(a - b) + (c - d)][(a + b) + (c + d)]$
$$= [(a - b)(a + b)] + [(a - b)(c + d)]$$
$$+ [(a + b)(c - d)] + [(c - d)(c + d)]$$
$$= (a^2 - b^2) + (ac + ad - bc - bd)$$
$$+ (ac - ad + bc - bd) + (c^2 - d^2)$$
$$= a^2 + 2ac + c^2 - b^2 - 2bd - d^2$$

52. $[(4x^2 + 2xy) + y^2][(4x^2 - 2xy) + y^2]$
$$= [(4x^2 + 2xy)(4x^2 - 2xy)] + [y^2(4x^2 + 2xy)]$$
$$+ [y^2(4x^2 - 2xy)] + (y^2)(y^2)$$
$$= (16x^4 - 4x^2y^2) + (4x^2y^2 + 2xy^3) + (4x^2y^2 - 2xy^3) + y^4$$
$$= 16x^4 + 4x^2y^2 + y^4$$

53. $= y^3z^n(y^{3n}z^3 - 4yz^{2n})$
$$= y^3z^n \cdot y^{3n}z^3 - y^3z^n \cdot 4yz^{2n}$$
$$= y^{3+3n}z^{n+3} - 4y^4z^{3n}$$

54. $\dfrac{x^3}{y^{-2}} = x^3 \cdot \left(\dfrac{1}{y^{-2}}\right) = x^3y^2$

55. $\dfrac{1}{8c^3} = \dfrac{1}{(2c)^3} = (2c)^{-3}$

56. $\dfrac{xy^5}{a^2b^{-2}} = xy^5\left(\dfrac{1}{a^2b^{-2}}\right)$
$$= xy^5(a^{-2}b^2)$$
$$= xy^5b^2a^{-2}$$

57. $m^{-4} \cdot m^3 = m^{-4+3} = m^{-1}$ **58.** $t^2 \cdot t^{-1} = t^{2-1} = t$

59. $(4x^3y^2)(-2x^ay^6) = -8x^{3+a}y^8$

60. $(2.5 \times 10^4)(6 \times 10^{-6}) = (2.5 \cdot 6) \times (10^4 \cdot 10^{-6})$
$$= 15 \times 10^{-2} = (1.5 \times 10^1) \times 10^{-2}$$
$$= 1.5 \times 10^{-1}$$

61. $|3| \cdot |y^2| \cdot |y| = 3y^2|y|$

62. $3c + 9 + (-6c) - 12 = 3c + (-6c) + 9 - 12$
$$= -3c - 3$$
$$= -3(c + 1)$$

63. Let $(x_1, y_1) = (15,000, 4300)$,
$\quad\quad (x_2, y_2) = (5000, 2500)$.

$\text{Slope} = \dfrac{4300 - 2500}{15,000 - 5000}$

$\quad\quad = 0.18$
Then $y - 4300 = 0.18(x - 15,000)$
$\quad\quad y - 4300 = 0.18x - 2700$
$\quad\quad\quad\quad\quad y = 0.18x + 1600$
The cost of operating the car is $1600 + $0.18 per mile.

pp. 219–222　　　**5-4 TRY THIS**

a. $9x^2 - 6x = 3x \cdot 3x - 3x \cdot 2 = 3x(x - 2)$
b. $P + Prt = P(1 + rt)$
c. $9y^4 - 15y^3 + 3y^2 = 3y^2(3y^2 - 5y + 1)$
d. $6x^2y - 21x^3y^2 + 3x^2y^3 = 3x^2y(2 - 7xy + y^2)$
e. $x^2 + 14x + 49 = (x + 7)^2$
f. $9y^2 - 30y + 25 = (3y - 5)^2$
g. $81y^2 + 72xy + 16x^2 = (9y + 4x)^2$
h. $100x^2 + 10xy + y^2$
Not a trinomial square, since $2AB$ is $2 \cdot 10x \cdot y$, or $20xy$.
i. $16x^4 - 40x^2y^3 + 25y^6 = (4x^2 - 5y^3)^2$
j. $24ab - 8a^2 - 18b^2 - 2(2a^2 - 3b^2)^2$
$$= -2(4a^4 - 12a^2b^2 + 9b^4) - 2(2a^2 - 3b^2)^2$$
$$= -2(2a^2 - 3b^2)^2 - 2(2a^2 - 3b^2)^2$$
$$= (-2 - 2)(2a^2 - 3b^2)^2$$
$$= -4(2a^2 - 3b^2)^2$$
k. $-12x^4y^2 + 60x^2y^5 - 75y^8 = -3y^2(4x^4 - 20x^2y^3 + 25y^6)$
$$= -3y^2(2x^2 - 5y^3)^2$$
l. $y^2 - 4 = (y)^2 - (2)^2 = (y + 2)(y - 2)$
m. $49x^4 - 25y^{10} = (7x^2)^2 - (5y^5)^2 = (7x^2 + 5y^5)(7x^2 - 5y^5)$
n. $36x^4 - 16y^6 = (6x^2)^2 - (4y^3)^2 = (6x^2 + 4y^3)(6x^2 - 4y^3)$
o. $x^2 + 2x + 1 - p^2 = (x + 1)^2 - p^2$
$$= (x + 1 + p)(x + 1 - p)$$
p. $64 - (x^2 + 8x + 16) = 8^2 - (x + 4)^2$
$$= [8 + (x + 4)][8 - (x + 4)]$$
$$= (12 + x)(4 - x)$$
q. $x^2 + 5x + 4x + 20 = x(x + 5) + 4(x + 5)$
$$= (x + 4)(x + 5)$$
r. $5y^2 + 10y + 2y + 4 = 5y(y + 2) + 2(y + 2)$
$$= (5y + 2)(y + 2)$$
s. $px + py - qx - qy = p(x + y) - q(x + y)$
$$= (p - q)(x + y)$$

pp. 222–223　　　**5-4 EXERCISES**

1. $y(y - 5)$　　**2.** $2a(2a + 1)$　　**3.** $3y(2y + 1)$

4. $y^2(y + 9)$　　**5.** $x^2(x + 8)$　　**6.** $3(y^2 - y - 3)$

7. $5(x^2 - x + 3)$　　**8.** $3x^2(2 - x^2)$　　**9.** $4y^2(2 + y^2)$

10. $2a(2b - 3c + 6d)$　　**11.** $2x(4y + 5z - 7w)$

12. $4xy(x - 3y)$　　**13.** $5x^2y^2(y + 3x)$　　**14.** $x^2(x^4 + x^3 - x + 1)$

15. $y(y^3 - y^2 + y + 1)$　　**16.** $12x(2x^2 - 3x + 6)$

17. $5(2a^4 + 3a^2 - 5a - 6)$　　**18.** $(y - 3)^2$　　**19.** $(x - 4)^2$

20. $(x + 7)^2$　　**21.** $(x + 8)^2$　　**22.** $(x + 1)^2$　　**23.** $(x - 1)^2$

24. $(a + 2)^2$　　**25.** $(a - 2)^2$　　**26.** $(y - 6)^2$　　**27.** $(y + 6)^2$

28. $y(y - 9)^2$　　**29.** $a(a + 12)^2$　　**30.** $3(2a + 3)^2$

31. $5(2y + 5)^2$　　**32.** $2(x - 10)^2$　　**33.** $2(4x + 3)^2$

34. $(1 - 4d)^2$　　**35.** $(5y - 8)^2$　　**36.** $(x + 4)(x - 4)$

37. $(y + 3)(y - 3)$　　**38.** $(3x + 5)(3x - 5)$

39. $(2a + 7)(2a - 7)$　　**40.** $(2x + 5)(2x - 5)$

41. $(10y + 9)(10y - 9)$　　**42.** $6(x + y)(x - y)$

43. $8(x + y)(x - y)$　　**44.** $3(x^4 + y^4)(x^2 + y^2)(x + y)(x - y)$

45. $5(x^2 + y^2)(x + y)(x - y)$　　**46.** $4x(y^2 + z^2)(y + z)(y - z)$

47. $a^2(3a + b)(3a - b)$　　**48.** $(a + b + 3)(a + b - 3)$

49. $(x - y - 5)(x - y + 5)$　　**50.** $(r - 1 + 2s)(r - 1 - 2s)$

51. $(c + 2d - 3p)(c + 2d + 3p)$

52. $2(m + n - 5b)(m + n + 5b)$

53. $3(2x + 1 - y)(2x + 1 + y)$　　**54.** $(3 - a - b)(3 + a + b)$

55. $(4 - x + y)(4 + x - y)$　　**56.** $(a + b)(c + d)$

57. $(x + w)(y + z)$　　**58.** $(b^2 + 2)(b - 1)$

59. $(y^2 + 3)(y - 1)$　　**60.** $(y - 1)(y - 8)$

61. $(t - 2)(t + 6)$　　**62.** $(2y^2 + 5)(y^2 + 3)$

63. $(xy - 3)(2 - x)$

64. $\dfrac{4}{7}x^6 - \dfrac{6}{7}x^4 + \dfrac{1}{7}x^2 - \dfrac{3}{7}x = \dfrac{1}{7}x(4x^5 - 6x^3 + x - 3)$

65. $4y^{4a} + 12y^{2a} + 10y^{2a} + 30 = 2(2y^{4a} + 6y^{2a} + 5y^{2a} + 15)$
$$= 2[2y^{2a}(y^{2a} + 3) + 5(y^{2a} + 3)] = 2(2y^{2a} + 5)(y^{2a} + 3)$$

66. $(0.25 - y^2) = (0.5)^2 - (y)^2 = (0.5 + y)(0.5 - y)$

67. $(0.04x^2 - 0.09y^2) = (0.2x)^2 - (0.3y)^2$
$$= (0.2x + 0.3y)(0.2x - 0.3y)$$

68. $\dfrac{1}{25} - x^2 = \left(\dfrac{1}{5}\right)^2 - (x)^2$

$$= \left(\dfrac{1}{5} + x\right)\left(\dfrac{1}{5} - x\right)$$

69. $\dfrac{1}{36}y^4 - \dfrac{1}{81}x^2 = \left(\dfrac{1}{6}y^2\right)^2 - \left(\dfrac{1}{9}x\right)^2$

$$= \left(\dfrac{1}{6}y^2 + \dfrac{1}{9}x\right)\left(\dfrac{1}{6}y^2 - \dfrac{1}{9}x\right)$$

70. Answers may vary. Example:
$(x + y)(x - y)$
$(x + y)(x + y)$
$(x + y)(z + x)$

71. $a^{16} - 1 = (a^8 + 1)(a^8 - 1) = (a^8 + 1)(a^4 + 1)(a^4 - 1)$
$$= (a^8 + 1)(a^4 + 1)(a^2 + 1)(a^2 - 1)$$
$$= (a^8 + 1)(a^4 + 1)(a^2 + 1)(a + 1)(a - 1)$$

72. $x^{2a} - y^2 = (x^a)^2 - (y)^2$
$$= (x^a - y)(x^a + y)$$

73. $y^{32} - 1 = (y^{16} + 1)(y^{16} - 1) = (y^{16} + 1)(y^8 + 1)(y^8 - 1)$
$$= (y^{16} + 1)(y^8 + 1)(y^4 + 1)(y^4 - 1)$$
$$= (y^{16} + 1)(y^8 + 1)(y^4 + 1)(y^2 + 1)(y^2 - 1)$$
$$= (y^{16} + 1)(y^8 + 1)(y^4 + 1)(y^2 + 1)(y + 1)(y - 1)$$

74. $x^2 + ax + bx + ab = x(x + a) + b(x + a)$
$$= (x + b)(x + a)$$

75. $\dfrac{1}{4}p^2 - \dfrac{2}{5}p + \dfrac{4}{25} = \left(\dfrac{1}{2}p - \dfrac{2}{5}\right)^2$

76. $bdx^2 + adx + bcx + ac = dx(bx + a) + c(bx + a)$
$$= (bx + a)(dx + c)$$

77. $x^3 - 225x = x(x^2 - 225)$
$$= x(x + 15)(x - 15)$$

78. $\dfrac{4}{27}r^2 + \dfrac{5}{9}rs + \dfrac{1}{12}s^2 - \dfrac{1}{3}rs = \dfrac{1}{3}\left(\dfrac{4}{9}r^2 + \dfrac{5}{3}rs + \dfrac{1}{4}s^2 - rs\right)$

$$= \dfrac{1}{3}\left(\dfrac{4}{9}r^2 + \dfrac{2}{3}rs + \dfrac{1}{4}s^2\right)$$

$$= \dfrac{1}{3}\left(\dfrac{2}{3}r + \dfrac{1}{2}s\right)^2$$

79. $9^4x^8 - 16^2y^{16} = (9^2x^4)^2 - (16y^8)^2$
$$= (9^2x^4 + 16y^8)(9^2x^4 - 16y^8)$$
$$= (81x^4 + 16y^8)(9x^2 + 4y^4)(9x^2 - 4y^4)$$
$$= (81x^4 + 16y^8)(9x^2 + 4y^4)(3x + 2y^2)(3x - 2y^2)$$

80. $4x^{a+b} + 7x^{a-b} = x^{a-b}[4x^{a+b-(a-b)} + 7x^{a-b-(a-b)}] = x^{a-b}(4x^{2b} + 7)$

81. $7y^{2a+b} - 5y^{a+b} + 3y^{a+2b}$
$$= y^{a+b}[7y^{2a+b-(a+b)} - 5y^{a+b-(a+b)} + 3y^{a+2b-(a+b)}]$$
$$= y^{a+b}(7y^a - 5 + 3y^b)$$

82. $f(0) = -3(0) + 1 = 1$ **83.** $f(-2) = -3(-2) + 1 = 7$

84. $f(3) = -3(3) + 1 = -8$ **85.** $f(-9) = -3(-9) + 1 = 28$

86. $f(4) = -3(4) + 1 = -11$

87. The equation is in slope-intercept form, so the slope is -5 and the y-intercept is 6.

88. For $y = 3x - 1$; $m = 3$, $b = -1$.

89. $3y = -6x + 9$
$y = -2x + 3$; $m = -2$, $b = 3$

90. $2y = x$

$y = \frac{1}{2}x + 0$; $m = \frac{1}{2}$, $b = 0$

91. $-15 - c = 4c$
$-15 = 5c$
$-3 = c$

92. $14 + a = 3a + 2$
$14 = 2a + 2$
$12 = 2a$
$6 = a$

93. $9m + 4m + 6 = 32$
$13m + 6 = 32$
$13m = 26$
$m = 2$

pp. 224–226   **5-5 TRY THIS**

a. $1000x^3 + 1 = (10x)^3 + (1)^3$
$$= (10x + 1)(100x^2 - 10x + 1)$$
b. $y^3 + 64x^3 = (y)^3 + (4x)^3$
$$= (y + 4x)(y^2 - 4xy + 16x^2)$$
c. $x^3 - 8 = (x)^3 - (2)^3$
$$= (x - 2)(x^2 + 2x + 4)$$
d. $-8x^3 + 27y^3 = 27y^3 - 8x^3$
$$= (3y)^3 - (2x)^3$$
$$= (3y - 2x)(9y^2 + 6xy + 4x^2)$$
e. $x^2 + 5x - 14$

Pairs of Factors	Sums of Factors
$-2, 7$	5
$2, -7$	-5
$-1, 14$	13
$1, -14$	-13

The desired integers are -2 and 7: $(x - 2)(x + 7)$
Check by multiplying: $(x - 2)(x + 7) = x^2 + 5x - 14$

f. $x^2 + 21 - 10x = x^2 - 10x + 21$

Pairs of Factors	Sums of Factors
$3, 7$	10
$-3, -7$	-10
$1, 21$	22
$-1, -21$	-22

The desired integers are -3 and -7: $(x - 3)(x - 7)$
Check: $(x - 3)(x - 7) = x^2 - 10x + 21$

g. $y^2 - y - 2$

Pairs of Factors	Sums of Factors
$-2, 1$	-1
$2, -1$	1

The desired integers are $-2, 1$: $(y - 2)(y + 1)$
Check: $(y - 2)(y + 1) = y^2 - y - 2$

h. $y^2 + 18y + 32$

Pairs of Factors	Sums of Factors
$4, 8$	12
$-4, -8$	-12
$2, 16$	18
$-2, -16$	-18
$1, 32$	33
$-1, -32$	-33

The desired integers are 2, 16: $(y + 2)(y + 16)$
Check: $(y + 2)(y + 16) = y^2 + 18y + 32$

i. $3x^2 + 5x + 2 = (3x + \underline{\quad})(x + \underline{\quad})$
Try possible factors of 2: 2, 1 and $-2, -1$. By multiplying we find the answer is $(3x + 2)(x + 1)$.

j. $4x^2 + 4x - 3 = (4x + \underline{\quad})(x + \underline{\quad})$ or $(2x + \underline{\quad})(2x + \underline{\quad})$
Try factors of -3: $-3, 1$ and $3, -1$. By multiplying we find the answer is $(2x + 3)(2x - 1)$.

k. $24y^2 - 46y + 10 = 2(12y^2 - 23y + 5)$
$$= 1(12y + \underline{\quad})(y + \underline{\quad})$$
or $2(4y + \underline{\quad})(3y + \underline{\quad})$ or $2(6y + \underline{\quad})(2y + \underline{\quad})$
Try factors of 5: 5, 1 and $-5, -1$ to find the answer
$2(4y - 1)(3y - 5)$

l. $2x^4y^6 - 3x^2y^3 - 20 = (2x^2y^3 + \underline{\quad})(x^2y^3 + \underline{\quad})$
Try factors of -20: $-20, 1$; $20, -1$; $-4, 5$; $4, -5$; $-2, 10$; $2, -10$ to find the answer
$(2x^2y^3 + 5)(x^2y^3 - 4)$

pp. 227–228   **5-5 EXERCISES**

1. $(x + 2)(x^2 - 2x + 4)$ **2.** $(c + 3)(c^2 - 3c + 9)$

3. $(y - 4)(y^2 + 4y + 16)$ **4.** $(z - 1)(z^2 + z + 1)$

5. $(w + 1)(w^2 - w + 1)$ **6.** $(x + 5)(x^2 - 5x + 25)$

7. $(2a + 1)(4a^2 - 2a + 1)$ **8.** $(3x + 1)(9x^2 - 3x + 1)$

9. $(y - 2)(y^2 + 2y + 4)$ **10.** $(p - 3)(p^2 + 3p + 9)$

11. $(2 - 3b)(4 + 6b + 9b^2)$ **12.** $(4 - 5x)(16 + 20x + 25x^2)$

13. $(4y + 1)(16y^2 - 4y + 1)$ **14.** $(5x + 1)(25x^2 - 5x + 1)$

15. $(7x + 3)(49x^2 - 21x + 9)$ **16.** $(3y + 4)(9y^2 - 12y + 16)$

17. $(a - b)(a^2 + ab + b^2)$ **18.** $(x - y)(x^2 + xy + y^2)$

19. $\left(a + \frac{1}{2}b\right)\left(a^2 - \frac{1}{2}ab + \frac{1}{4}b^2\right)$

20. $\left(b + \frac{1}{3}a\right)\left(b^2 - \frac{1}{3}ab + \frac{1}{9}a^2\right)$

21. $(2x - 3y)(4x^2 + 6xy + 9y^2)$ **22.** $(x + 5)(x + 4)$

23. $(y + 5)(y + 3)$ **24.** $(y - 4)^2$ **25.** $(a - 5)^2$

26. $(x - 9)(x + 3)$ **27.** $(t - 5)(t + 3)$ **28.** $(m - 7)(m + 4)$

29. $(x - 4)(x + 2)$ **30.** $(x + 9)(x + 5)$ **31.** $(y + 8)(y + 4)$

32. $(y + 9)(y - 7)$ **33.** $(x + 8)(x - 5)$ **34.** $(t - 7)(t - 4)$

35. $(y - 5)(y - 9)$ **36.** $(x + 5)(x - 2)$ **37.** $(x + 3)(x - 2)$

38. $(x + 2)(x + 3)$ **39.** $(y + 7)(y + 1)$ **40.** $(8 - y)(4 + y)$

41. $(8 - x)(7 + x)$ **42.** $(t + 5)(t + 3)$ **43.** $(3b + 2)(b + 2)$

44. $(3x + 1)(3x + 4)$ **45.** $(3y - 2)(2y + 1)$

46. $(3a - 4)(a + 1)$ **47.** $(6a + 5)(a - 2)$

48. $(12z + 1)(z - 3)$ **49.** $(3a + 4)(3a - 2)$

50. $(2t + 5)(2t - 3)$ **51.** $(3x + 2)(x - 6)$

52. $(3x + 5)(2x - 5)$ **53.** $(3x - 5)(2x + 3)$

54. $(5y + 4)(2y - 3)$ **55.** $(3a - 4)(a - 2)$

56. $(4a - 1)(3a - 1)$ **57.** $(5y + 2)(7y + 4)$

58. $(3a + 2)(3a + 4)$ **59.** $(5t - 3)(t + 1)$

60. $(5x + 3)(3x - 1)$ **61.** $4(2x + 1)(x - 4)$

62. $6(3x - 4)(x + 1)$ **63.** $x(3x + 1)(x - 2)$

64. $y(6y - 5)(3y + 2)$ **65.** $(24x + 1)(x - 2)$

66. $(5y + 2)(3y - 5)$ **67.** $(7x + 3)(3x + 4)$

68. $(5y + 4)(2y + 3)$ **69.** $(5x + 4)(8x - 3)$

70. $(6y + 5)(4y - 3)$ **71.** $(4a - 3)(3a - 2)$

72. $(4a - 3)(5a - 2)$

73. $x^4 + 11x^2 - 80 = x^4 + (16 - 5)x^2 - (16)(-5)$
$= (x^2 + 16)(x^2 - 5)$

74. $y^4 + 5y^2 - 84 = y^4 + (12 - 7)y + (12)(-7)$
$= (y^2 + 12)(y^2 - 7)$

75. $x^2 + \dfrac{3}{5}x - \dfrac{4}{25} = x^2 + \dfrac{(4 - 1)}{5}x + \left(\dfrac{4}{5}\right)\left(\dfrac{-1}{5}\right)$
$= \left(x + \dfrac{4}{5}\right)\left(x - \dfrac{1}{5}\right)$

76. $y^2 + \dfrac{2}{7}y - \dfrac{8}{49} = y^2 + \dfrac{(4 - 2)}{7}y + \left(\dfrac{4}{7}\right)\left(\dfrac{2}{7}\right)$
$= \left(y + \dfrac{4}{7}\right)\left(y - \dfrac{2}{7}\right)$

77. $y^2 + 0.4y - 0.05 = y^2 + (0.5 - 0.1)y + (0.5)(-0.1)$
$= (y + 0.5)(y - 0.1)$

78. $t^2 + 0.6t - 0.27 = t^2 + (0.9 - 0.3t) - (0.9)(0.3)$
$= (t + 0.9)(t - 0.3)$

79. $2x^2 + xy - 6y^2 = 2x^2 + 4xy - 3xy - 6y^2$
$= 2x(x + 2y) - 3y(x + 2y)$
$= (2x - 3y)(x + 2y)$

80. $2m^2 + mn - 10n^2 = 2m^2 - 4mn + 5mn - 10n^2$
$= 2m(m - 2n) + 5n(m - 2n)$
$= (2m + 5n)(m - 2n)$

81. $-6xy + 8x^2 - 9y^2 = 8x^2 - 6xy - 9y^2$
$= 8x^2 + 6xy - 12xy - 9y^2$
$= 2x(4x + 3y) - 3y(4x + 3y)$
$= (2x - 3y)(4x + 3y)$

82. $-7ts + 2t^2 - 4s^2 = 2t^2 - 7ts - 4s^2$
$= 2t^2 - 8ts + ts - 4s^2$
$= 2t(t - 4s) + s(t - 4s)$
$= (2t + s)(t - 4s)$

83. $7a^2b^2 + 6 + 13ab = 7a^2b^2 + 7ab + 6ab + 6$
$= 7ab(ab + 1) + 6(ab + 1)$
$= (7ab + 6)(ab + 1)$

84. $9x^2y^2 - 4 + 5xy = 9x^2y^2 + 9xy - 4xy - 4$
$= 9xy(xy + 1) - 4(xy + 1)$
$= (9xy - 4)(xy + 1)$

85. $r(s^3 + 64) = r(s^3 + 4^3) = r(s + 4)(s^2 - 4s + 16)$

86. $a(b^3 + 125) = a(b^3 + 5^3) = a(b + 5)(b^2 - 5b + 25)$

87. $5(x^3 - 8z^3) = 5(x^3 - (2z)^3) = 5(x - 2z)(x^2 + 2zx + 4z^2)$

88. $2(y^3 - 27z^3) = 2(y^3 - (3z)^3) = 2(y - 3z)(y^2 + 3yz + 9z^2)$

89. $x^3 + 0.001 = x^3 + (0.1)^3 = (x + 0.1)(x^2 - 0.1x + 0.01)$

90. $y^3 + 0.125 = y^3 + (0.5)^3 = (y + 0.5)(y^2 - 0.5y - 0.25)$

91. $8(8x^6 - t^6) = 8((2x^2)^3 - (t^2)^3) = 8(2x^2 - t^2)(4x^4 + 2x^2t^2 + t^4)$

92. $(5c^2)^3 - (2d^2)^3 = (5c^2 - 2d^2)(25c^4 + 10c^2d^2 + 4d^4)$

93. The cube has volume a^3, the missing piece has volume b^3, so the figure has volume $a^3 - b^3$. The large piece has volume $(a - b)a^2$, the piece below it $(a - b)ab$, the small piece $(a - b)b^2$. Adding the three gives $(a - b)(a^2 + ab + b^2)$. Thus, $a^3 - b^3 = (a - b)(a^2 + ab + b^2)$.

94. $3(x^2 + 4x - 165) = 3(x - 11)(x + 15)$

95. $(x^{2a})^3 + (y^b)^3 = (x^{2a} + y^b)(x^{4a} - x^{2a}y^b + y^{2b})$

96. $4y(y^2 - 24y + 144) = 4y(y - 12)^2$

97. $3x(y^2 - 50y + 625) = 3x(y - 25)^2$

98. $(ax)^3 - (by)^3 = (ax - by)(a^2x^2 + abxy + b^2y^2)$

99. $12(x^2 - 6xy + 9y^2) = 12(x - 3y)^2$

100. $15t(t^2 - 4t - 21) = 15t(t - 7)(t + 3)$

101. $6x(36 + 13x + x^2) = 6x(9 + x)(4 + x)$
$= 6x(x + 9)(x + 4)$

102. $x^{2a} + 5x^a - 24 = (x^a)^2 + 8x^a - 3x^a + (8)(-3)$
$= (x^a + 8)(x^a - 3)$

103. $\dfrac{8}{27}x^3 + \dfrac{1}{64}y^3 = \left(\dfrac{2}{3}x\right)^2 + \left(\dfrac{1}{4}y\right)^3$

$= \left(\dfrac{2}{3}x + \dfrac{1}{4}y\right)\left(\dfrac{4}{9}x^2 - \dfrac{1}{6}xy + \dfrac{1}{16}y^2\right)$

104. $4x^{2a} - 4x^a - 3 = (2x^a - 3)(2x^a + 1)$

105. $\dfrac{1}{2}\left(\dfrac{1}{8}x^{3a} + y^{6a}z^{9b}\right) = \dfrac{1}{2}\left[\left(\dfrac{1}{2}x^a\right)^3 + (y^{2a}z^{3b})^3\right]$

$= \dfrac{1}{2}\left(\dfrac{1}{2}x^a + y^{2a}z^{3b}\right)\left(\dfrac{1}{4}x^{2a} - \dfrac{1}{2}x^ay^{2a}z^{3b} + y^{4a}z^{6b}\right)$

106. $8x^2 - 10x - 3 = (4x + 1)(2x - 3)$. If we include negative factors, $8x^2 - 10x - 3$ also $= (-4x - 1)(-2x + 3)$.
$(-4x - 1)(-2x + 3) = -1(4x + 1)(-2x + 3)$
$= (-1)^2(4x + 1)(2x - 3)$
$= (4x + 1)(2x - 3)$
The negative factorization is equivalent.

107.
$$x - y - z = -5 \ \textcircled{1}$$
$$3y + 2z = 22 \ \textcircled{2}$$
$$3x - 2y - 3z = -7 \ \textcircled{3}$$
Multiply $\textcircled{1}$ by 3 and subtract $\textcircled{3}$.
$$-y = -8$$
$$y = 8$$
Substitute 8 for y in $\textcircled{2}$.
$$24 + 2z = 22$$
$$2z = -2$$
$$z = -1$$
Substitute $y = 8$ and $= -1$ in $\textcircled{1}$.
$$x - 8 + 1 = -5$$
$$x = 2$$
The solution is $(2, 8, -1)$.

108. $4a = 2c - 6 \quad \longrightarrow \quad 4a - 2c = -6 \quad \textcircled{1}$
$3a + 3b + c = -1 \longrightarrow 3a + 3b + c = -1 \ \textcircled{2}$
$2(a - b) = c + 3 \quad \longrightarrow \quad 2a - 2b - c = 3 \quad \textcircled{3}$
Multiply $\textcircled{2}$ by 2 and $\textcircled{3}$ by 3.
$4a - 2c = -6 \qquad \textcircled{1}$
$6a + 6b + 2c = -2 \ \textcircled{2}$
$6a - 6b - 3c = 3 \quad \textcircled{3}$
Add $\textcircled{2}$ to $\textcircled{3}$.
$12a - c = 1 \ \textcircled{3}$
Multiply $\textcircled{1}$ by $-\dfrac{1}{2}$ and add it to $\textcircled{3}$.
$$10a = 10$$
$$a = 1$$
Substitute 1 for a in $\textcircled{1}$.
$$4 - 2c = -6$$
$$-2c = -10$$
$$c = 5$$
Substitute 1 for a and 5 for c in $\textcircled{2}$.
$$6 + 6b + 10 = -2$$
$$6b = -18$$
$$b = -3$$
The solution is $(1, -3, 5)$.

109. $2x - 4y = 12$

$y = \dfrac{1}{2}x - 3; \ m = \dfrac{1}{2}$

A line perpendicular to this line will have a slope of -2.
$$y - y_1 = m(x - x_1)$$
$$y - 3 = -2(x - 0)$$
$$y = -2x + 3$$

110.
$$y - y_1 = m(x - x_1)$$
$$y - (-2) = -1(x - 3)$$
$$y + 2 = -x + 3$$
$$y = -x + 1$$

111.
$$y - y_1 = m(x - x_1)$$
$$y - 4 = 2(x - 0)$$
$$y = 2x + 4$$

112.
$$\frac{(3.7 \times 4.1)}{7.7} \times \frac{10^{-7} \times 10^4}{10^{-2}}$$
$$\approx \frac{4 \times 4}{8} \times \frac{10^{-3}}{10^{-2}}$$
$$\approx 2 \times 10^{-1}$$

113. Let x be total dental fees.
$$0.80(x - 75) = 168$$
$$0.80x - 60 = 168$$
$$0.80x = 228$$
$$x = \$285$$

p. 230   5-6 TRY THIS

a. $2 - 32x^4 = 2(1 - 16x^4)$
$$= 2(1 + 4x^2)(1 - 4x^2)$$
$$= 2(1 + 4x^2)(1 + 2x)(1 - 2x)$$

b. $7a^6 - 7 = 7(a^6 - 1)$
$$= 7(a^3 + 1)(a^3 - 1)$$
$$= 7(a + 1)(a^2 - a + 1)(a - 1)(a^2 + a + 1)$$
$$= 7(a + 1)(a - 1)(a^2 - a + 1)(a^2 + a + 1)$$

c. $3x + 12 + 4x + x^2 = 3(x + 4) + x(4 + x)$
$$= (3 + x)(4 + x)$$

d. $(c^2 - 2cd + d^2) - (t^2 + 8t + 16) = (c - d)^2 - (t + 4)^2$
$$= (c - d + t + 4)(c - d - t - 4)$$

e. $5y^4 + 20x^6 = 5(y^4 + 4x^6)$

f. $6x^2 - 3x - 18 = 3(2x^2 - x - 6) = 3(2x + 3)(x - 2)$

g. $a^3 - ab^2 - a^2b + b^3 = a(a^2 - b^2) - b(a^2 - b^2)$
$$= (a - b)(a^2 - b^2) = (a - b)(a + b)(a - b)$$
$$= (a + b)(a - b)^2$$

h. $3x^2 - 18ax + 27a^2 = 3(x^2 + 6ax + 9) = 3(x + 3a)^2$

i. $(a^2 + 2ab + b^2) - c^2 = (a + b)^2 - c^2$
$$= (a + b - c)(a + b + c)$$

p. 231   5-6 EXERCISES

1. $(x + 12)(x - 12)$ **2.** $(2x + 3)(x + 4)$

3. $3(x^2 + 2)(x^2 - 2)$ **4.** $2x(y + 5)(y - 5)$ **5.** $(a + 5)^2$

6. $(p + 8)^2$ **7.** $2(x - 11)(x + 6)$ **8.** $3(y - 12)(y + 7)$

9. $(3x + 5y)(3x - 5y)$ **10.** $(4a + 9b)(4a - 9b)$

11. $(2c - d)^2$ **12.** $(10b + a)(7b - a)$ **13.** $(x^2 + 2)(2x - 7)$

14. $(3m^2 + 8)(m + 3)$ **15.** $(4x - 15)(x - 3)$

16. $3(y + 7)(y - 2)$ **17.** $(m^3 + 10)(m^3 - 2)$

18. $(x + 6)(x - 6)(x + 1)(x - 1)$ **19.** $(c - b)(a + d)$

20. $(w + z)(x - y)$

21. $(m + 1)(m^2 - m + 1)(m - 1)(m^2 + m + 1)$

22. $(2t + 1)(4t^2 - 2t + 1)(2t - 1)(4t^2 + 2t + 1)$

23. $(x + y + 3)(x - y + 3)$ **24.** $(t + p + 5)(t - p + 5)$

25. $(6y - 5)(6y + 7)$ **26.** $-2b(7a + 1)(2a - 1)$

27. $(a^4 + b^4)(a^2 + b^2)(a + b)(a - b)$

28. $2(x^2 + 4)(x + 2)(x - 2)$ **29.** $(2p + 3q)(4p^2 - 6pq + 9q^2)$

30. $(5x + 4y)(25x^2 - 20xy + 16y^2)$

31. $(4p - 1)(16p^2 + 4p + 1)$ **32.** $(2y - 5)(4y^2 + 10y + 25)$

33. $ab(a + 4b)(a - 4b)$ **34.** $xy(x + 5y)(x - 5y)$

35. $(4xy - 3)(5xy - 2)$ **36.** $(3ab + 4)(9ab + 2)$

37. $2(x + 2)(x - 2)(x + 3)$ **38.** $3(x + 3)(x - 3)(x + 2)$

39. $2(5x - 4y)(25x^2 + 20xy + 16y^2)$

40. $(3a - 7b)(9a^2 + 21ab + 49b^2)$

41. $2(2x + 3y)(4x^2 - 6xy + 9y^2)$

42. $(x - p)^2 - p^2 = (x - p + p)(x - p - p) = x(x - 2p)$

43. $30y^4 - 97xy^2 + 60x^2$. By trial and error we find that $-97 = 6 \cdot (-12) + 5 \cdot (-5)$, where $6 \cdot 5 = 30$ and $(-12) \cdot (-5) = 60$. Our factorization is then $(6y^2 - 5x)(5y^2 - 12x)$.

44. $5c^{100} - 80d^{100} = 5(c^{100} - 16d^{100})$
$$= 5((c^{50})^2 - (4d^{50})^2) = 5(c^{50} + 4d^{50})(c^{50} - 4d^{50})$$
$$= 5(c^{50} + 4d^{50})(c^{25} + 2d^{25})(c^{25} - 2d^{25})$$

45. $3a^2 + 3b^2 - 3c^2 - 3d^2 + 6ab - 6cd$
$$= 3(a^2 + b^2 - c^2 - d^2 + 2ab - 2cd)$$
$$= 3[(a^2 + 2ab + b^2) - (c^2 + 2cd + d^2)]$$
$$= 3[(a + b)^2 - (c + d)^2]$$
$$= 3(a + b + c + d)(a + b - c - d)$$

46. $8(a - 3)^2 - 64(a - 3) + 128$
$$= 8[(a - 3)^2 - 8(a - 3) + 16]$$
$$= 8[(a - 3) - 4][(a - 3) - 4]$$
$$= 8(a - 7)^2$$

47. $-16 + 17(5 - y^2) - (5 - y^2)^2$
$$= -(5 - y^2)^2 + 17(5 - y^2) - 16$$
$$= -(5 - y^2)^2 + (16 + 1)(5 - y^2) - 16$$
$$= [-(5 - y^2) + 1][(5 - y^2) - 16]$$
$$= (y^2 - 5 + 1)(-y^2 + 5 - 16)$$
$$= (y^2 - 4)(-y^2 - 11) = (11 + y^2)(4 - y^2)$$
$$= (11 + y^2)(2 + y)(2 - y)$$

48. $x^6 - y^6 = (x^2)^3 - (y^2)^3 = (x^2 - y^2)(x^4 + x^2y^2 + y^4)$
$$= (x - y)(x + y)(x^2 + xy + y^2)(x^2 - xy + y^2)$$

49. $x^6 - 2x^5 + x^4 - x^2 + 2x - 1$
$$= (x^6 - 2x^5 + x^4) - (x^2 - 2x + 1)$$
$$= x^4(x^2 - 2x + 1) - (x^2 - 2x + 1)$$
$$= (x^4 - 1)(x^2 - 2x + 1) = (x^4 - 1)(x - 1)^2$$
$$= (x^2 + 1)(x^2 - 1)(x - 1)^2$$
$$= (x^2 + 1)(x + 1)(x - 1)(x - 1)^2$$
$$= (x - 1)^3(x^2 + 1)(x + 1)$$

50. $(y - 1)^4 - (y - 1)^2 = (y - 1)^2[(y - 1)^2 - 1]$
$$= (y - 1)^2(y^2 - 2y)$$
$$= (y - 1)^2[(y)(y - 2)]$$
$$= y(y - 1)^2(y - 2)$$

51. $27x^{6s} + 64y^{3t} = (3x^{2s})^3 + (4y^t)^3$
$$= (3x^{2s} + 4y^t)(9x^{4s} - 12x^{2s}y^t + 16y^{2t})$$

52. $c^{2w+1} + 2c^{w+1} + c = c(c^{2w} + 2c^w + 1) = c(c^w + 1)^2$

53. $24x^{2a} - 6 = 6(4x^{2a} - 1) = 6(2x^a - 1)(2x^a + 1)$

54. $m = \dfrac{3 - 9}{1 - 4} = 2$ **55.** $m = \dfrac{1 - (-5)}{-2 - 1} = -2$

$$y - y_1 = m(x - x_1)$$
$$y - 3 = 2(x - 1)$$
$$y - 3 = 2x - 2$$
$$y = 2x + 1$$

$$y - y_1 = m(x - x_1)$$
$$y - 1 = -2[x - (-2)]$$
$$y - 1 = -2x - 4$$
$$y = -2x - 3$$

56. $m = \dfrac{11 - (-9)}{3 - (-2)} = 4$

$$y - y_1 = m(x - x_1)$$
$$y - 11 = 4(x - 3)$$
$$y - 11 = 4x - 12$$
$$y = 4x - 1$$

57. $P(1) = 3(1)^3 - 4(1)^2 + 2(1) - 1$
$$= 3 - 4 + 2 - 1$$
$$= 0$$

58. $P(-1) = 3(-1)^3 - 4(-1)^2 + 2(-1) - 1$
$$= -3 - 4 - 2 - 1$$
$$= -10$$

59. $P(0) = 3(0)^3 - 4(0)^2 + 2(0) - 1$
$$= -1$$

60. $P(m) = 3(m)^3 - 4(m)^2 + 2(m) - 1$
$$= 3m^3 - 4m^2 + 2m - 1$$

p. 232   5-7 TRY THIS

a. $x^2 + 8 - 6x = 0$
$$x^2 - 6x + 8 = 0$$
$$(x - 4)(x - 2) = 0$$
$$x - 4 = 0 \quad \text{or} \quad x - 2 = 0$$
$$x = 4 \quad \text{or} \quad x = 2$$

b.
$$12y^2 - 3y = 9$$
$$12y^2 - 3y - 9 = 0$$
$$3(4y^2 - y - 3) = 0$$
$$3(y - 1)(4y + 3) = 0$$
$$y - 1 = 0 \quad \text{or} \quad 4y + 3 = 0$$
$$y = 1 \quad \text{or} \quad y = -\frac{3}{4}$$

c.
$$25 + x^2 = -10x$$
$$x^2 + 10x + 25 = 0$$
$$(x + 5)(x + 5) = 0$$
$$x + 5 = 0 \quad \text{or} \quad x + 5 = 0$$
$$x = -5 \qquad x = -5$$

d. $8b^2 - 16b = 0$
$$8b(b - 2) = 0$$
$$8b = 0 \quad \text{or} \quad b - 2 = 0$$
$$b = 0 \quad \text{or} \quad b = 2$$

e. $9x^2 + 27x = 0$
$$9x(x + 3) = 0$$
$$9x = 0 \quad \text{or} \quad x + 3 = 0$$
$$x = 0 \quad \text{or} \quad x = -3$$

f.
$$x^3 + 3 = x + 3x^2$$
$$x^3 - 3x^2 - x + 3 = 0$$
$$x^2(x - 3) - 1(x - 3) = 0$$
$$(x^2 - 1)(x - 3) = 0$$
$$(x + 1)(x - 1)(x - 3) = 0$$
$$x + 1 = 0 \quad \text{or} \quad x - 1 = 0 \quad \text{or} \quad x - 3 = 0$$
$$x = -1 \quad \text{or} \quad x = 1 \quad \text{or} \quad x = 3$$

pp. 238–239   5-7 EXERCISES

1. $-7, 4$ **2.** $9, -5$ **3.** 4 **4.** 1 **5.** 6 **6.** -8

7. $-5, -4$ **8.** $-5, -3$ **9.** $0, -8$ **10.** $0, -9$

11. $-3, 3$ **12.** $-4, 4$ **13.** $-6, 6$ **14.** $-9, 9$

15. $-5, -9$ **16.** $-8, -4$ **17.** $-9, 7$ **18.** $-8, 5$

19. $7, 4$ **20.** $9, 5$ **21.** $8, -4$ **22.** $-9, -3$

23. $-\frac{2}{3}, -2$ **24.** $-\frac{4}{3}, -\frac{1}{3}$ **25.** $\frac{3}{4}, \frac{1}{2}$ **26.** $-\frac{3}{4}, -2$

27. $0, 6$ **28.** $0, 8$ **29.** $-\frac{3}{4}, \frac{2}{3}$ **30.** $-\frac{5}{6}, 2$ **31.** $-2, 2$

32. $-3, 3$ **33.** $\frac{1}{2}, 7$ **34.** $8, 1$ **35.** $-\frac{5}{7}, \frac{2}{3}$

36. $\frac{7}{4}, -\frac{4}{3}$ **37.** $0, \frac{1}{5}$ **38.** $0, \frac{1}{2}$ **39.** $-\frac{9}{10}, \frac{9}{10}$

40.
$$x^2 - \frac{1}{25} = 0$$
$$\left(x + \frac{1}{5}\right)\left(x - \frac{1}{5}\right) = 0$$
$$x + \frac{1}{5} = 0 \quad \text{or} \quad x - \frac{1}{5} = 0$$
$$x = -\frac{1}{5} \quad \text{or} \quad x = \frac{1}{5}$$

41.
$$y^2 - \frac{1}{64} = 0$$
$$\left(y + \frac{1}{8}\right)\left(y - \frac{1}{8}\right) = 0$$
$$y + \frac{1}{8} = 0 \quad \text{or} \quad y - \frac{1}{8} = 0$$
$$y = -\frac{1}{8} \quad \text{or} \quad y = \frac{1}{8}$$

42.
$$16x^3 - x = 0$$
$$x(16x^2 - 1) = 0$$
$$x(4x + 1)(4x - 1) = 0$$
$$x = 0 \quad \text{or} \quad 4x + 1 = 0 \quad \text{or} \quad 4x - 1 = 0$$
$$x = 0 \quad \text{or} \quad x = -\frac{1}{4} \quad \text{or} \quad x = \frac{1}{4}$$

43.
$$9x^3 = x$$
$$9x^3 - x = 0$$
$$x(9x^2 - 1) = 0$$
$$x(3x - 1)(3x + 1) = 0$$
$$x = 0 \quad \text{or} \quad 3x - 1 = 0 \quad \text{or} \quad 3x + 1 = 0$$
$$x = 0 \quad \text{or} \quad x = \frac{1}{3} \quad \text{or} \quad x = -\frac{1}{3}$$

44.
$$x(x + 8) = 16(x - 1)$$
$$x^2 + 8x = 16x - 16$$
$$x^2 - 8x + 16 = 0$$
$$(x - 4)(x - 4) = 0$$
$$x - 4 = 0$$
$$x = 4$$

45.
$$m(m + 9) = 4(2m + 5)$$
$$m^2 + 9m = 8m + 20$$
$$m^2 + m - 20 = 0$$
$$(m + 5)(m - 4) = 0$$
$$m + 5 = 0 \quad \text{or} \quad m - 4 = 0$$
$$m = -5 \quad \text{or} \quad m = 4$$

46.
$$(a - 5)^2 = 36$$
$$a^2 - 10a + 25 = 36$$
$$a^2 - 10a - 11 = 0$$
$$(a + 1)(a - 11) = 0$$
$$a + 1 = 0 \quad \text{or} \quad a - 11 = 0$$
$$a = -1 \quad \text{or} \quad a = 11$$

47.
$$(x - 6)^2 = 81$$
$$x^2 - 12x + 36 = 81$$
$$x^2 - 12x - 45 = 0$$
$$(x + 3)(x - 15) = 0$$
$$x + 3 = 0 \quad \text{or} \quad x - 15 = 0$$
$$x = -3 \quad \text{or} \quad x = 15$$

48.
$$(x + 1)^3 = (x - 1)^3 + 26$$
$$x^3 + 3x^2 + 3x + 1 = x^3 - 3x^2 + 3x - 1 + 26$$
$$6x^2 - 24 = 0$$
$$6(x^2 - 4) = 0$$
$$6(x - 2)(x + 2) = 0$$
$$x - 2 = 0 \quad \text{or} \quad x + 2 = 0$$
$$x = 2 \quad \text{or} \quad x = -2$$

49.
$$(x - 2)^3 = x^3 - 2$$
$$x^3 - 6x^2 + 12x - 8 = x^3 - 2$$
$$-6x^2 + 12x - 6 = 0$$
$$-6(x^2 - 2x + 1) = 0$$
$$-6(x - 1)(x - 1) = 0$$
$$x - 1 = 0 \quad \text{or} \quad x - 1 = 0$$
$$x = 1 \qquad x = 1$$

50. Answers may vary. Example:
$$x^2 + 3x - 40 = 0$$
$$3x^2 + 9x = 120$$

51.
$$x^2 + 2ax - 3x - 6a = 0$$
$$x(x + 2a) - 3(x + 2a) = 0$$
$$(x - 3)(x + 2a) = 0$$
$$x - 3 = 0 \quad \text{or} \quad x + 2a = 0$$
$$x = 3 \quad \text{or} \quad x = -2a$$

52.
$$2x^2 - 5bx + 4cx - 10bc = 0$$
$$x(2x - 5b) + 2c(2x - 5b) = 0$$
$$(2x - 5b)(x + 2c) = 0$$
$$2x - 5b = 0 \quad \text{or} \quad x + 2c = 0$$
$$2x = 5b$$
$$x = \frac{5b}{2} \quad \text{or} \quad x = -2c$$

53.
$$x^3 + ax^2 - a^2x - a^3 = 0$$
$$x^2(x + a) - a^2(x + a) = 0$$
$$(x^2 - a^2)(x + a) = 0$$
$$(x + a)(x - a)(x + a) = 0$$
$$x + a = 0 \quad \text{or} \quad x - a = 0 \quad \text{or} \quad x + a = 0$$
$$x = -a \quad \text{or} \quad x = a \quad \text{or} \quad x = -a$$

54.
$$x^2 + 10x + 25 - 9a^2 = 0$$
$$(x + 5)^2 - 9a^2 = 0$$
$$(x + 5 + 3a)(x + 5 - 3a) = 0$$
$$x + 5 + 3a = 0 \quad \text{or} \quad x + 5 - 3a = 0$$
$$x = -3a - 5 \quad \text{or} \quad x = 3a - 5$$

55.
$$3x + 5y = 2$$
$$x = 3y - 4$$
$$3x + 5y = 2$$
$$\underline{-3x + 9y = 12} \qquad \text{Multiplying by } -3$$
$$14y = 14 \qquad \text{Adding}$$
$$y = 1$$
$$x = 3(1) - 4 \qquad \text{Substituting}$$
The solution is $(-1, 1)$.

56.
$$6x - y = 17$$
$$\underline{2x + y = -1}$$
$$8x = 16 \qquad \text{Adding}$$
$$x = 2$$
$$6(2) - y = 17 \qquad \text{Substituting}$$
$$-y = 5$$
$$y = -5$$
The solution is $(2, -5)$.

57.
$$2x - y = 0$$
$$\underline{y + x = 0}$$
$$3x = 3 \qquad \text{Adding}$$
$$x = 1$$
$$y + 1 = 3 \qquad \text{Substituting}$$
$$y = 2$$
The solution is $(1, 2)$.

58. Find a linear function that fits this data.
Let $(x_1, y_1) = (0.20)$,
$(x_2, y_2) = (8, 51)$.

The slope m is $\dfrac{20 - 51}{0 - 8} = \dfrac{31}{8}$.

Use $y - y_1 = m(x - x_1)$.

$$y - 20 = \frac{31}{8}(x - 0)$$

$$y = \frac{31}{8}x + 20$$

Substitute 60 for x.

$$y = \frac{31}{8}(60) + 20$$

$$y = 232.5 + 20 = 252.5 \text{ in. or } 21 \text{ ft } \frac{1}{2} \text{ in.}$$

pp. 235   5-8 TRY THIS

a. Let x be the number.
$$x^2 - 2x = 48$$
$$x^2 - 2x - 48 = 0$$
$$(x - 8)(x + 6) = 0$$
$$x - 8 = 0 \quad \text{or} \quad x + 6 = 0$$
$$x = 8 \quad \text{or} \qquad x = -6$$

b. Let l be the length of the rectangle.
Then the width is $l - 5$.
$$l(l - 5) = 24$$
$$l^2 - 5l = 24$$
$$l^2 - 5l - 24 = 0$$
$$(l - 8)(l + 3) = 0$$
$$l - 8 = 0 \quad \text{or} \quad l + 3 = 0$$
$$l = 8 \quad \text{or} \qquad l = -3$$
Since the length of a side of a rectangle must be a positive length, the only acceptable answer is 8 cm. The width, therefore, is $l - 5$ cm, or 3 cm.

pp. 235–236   5-8 EXERCISES

1. $4x^2 = 8x + 21$
$\dfrac{7}{2}$ or $-\dfrac{3}{2}$

2. $4x^2 = 8x + 45$
$\dfrac{9}{2}$ or $-\dfrac{5}{2}$

3. $x^2 + x = 132$
-12 or 11

4. $x^2 + x = 156$
-13 or 12

5. $(w + 5)w = 84$
Length = 12 ft
Width = 7 ft

6. $(w + 4)w = 96$
Length = 12 ft
Width = 8 ft

7. $(w + 25)w = 7500$
Length = 100 m
Width = 75 m

8. $(w + 3)w = 108$
Length = 12 m
Width = 9 m

9. $x^2 + (x + 2)^2 = 202$
9 and 11

10. $x^2 + (x + 2)^2 = 394$
13 and 15

11. $(x + 4)^2 = 49$
$x = 3$ cm

12. $(x + 6)^2 = 144$
$x = 6$ m

13. $(h + 9)h = 56$
Height = 7 cm
Base = 16 cm

14. $(h - 5)h = 18$
Height = 9 cm
Base = 4 cm

15. $(x + 4)^2 = (x + 2)^2 + 76$
$16, 18, 20$

16. $x(x + 2) - (x + 1) = 10(x + 2) + 1$
$11, 12, 13$ or $-2, -1, 0$

17. $4(x + 2)^2 - 3x^2 - 41 = 2(x + 1)^2$
$9, 10, 11$ or $3, 4, 5$

18. If $a + b = 17$, then $a = 17 - b$.
Substitute for a.
$$(17 - b)^2 + b^2 = 205$$
$$289 - 34b + b^2 + b^2 = 205$$
$$2b^2 - 34b + 84 = 0$$
$$2(b^2 - 17b + 42) = 0$$
$$2(b - 14)(b - 3) = 0$$
$$b - 14 = 0 \qquad \text{or} \quad b - 3 = 0$$
$$b = 14 \qquad \text{or} \qquad b = 3$$
$$a = 17 - b \quad \text{or} \qquad a = 17 - b$$
$$a = 17 - 14 \quad \text{or} \qquad a = 17 - 3$$
$$a = 3 \qquad \text{or} \qquad a = 14$$
The solutions are $(3, 14)$ or $(14, 3)$.

19. When the ends are turned up to make a box, the height of the box made will be 2 cm. The box will have a length of $(2x - 4)$ cm and a width of $(x - 4)$ cm.

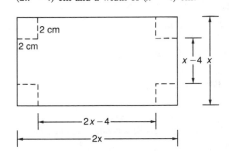

$$(2x - 4)(x - 4)(2) = 480$$
$$(2x^2 - 12x + 16)2 = 480$$
$$4x^2 - 24x + 32 = 480$$
$$4x^2 - 24x - 448 = 0$$
$$4(x^2 - 6x - 112) = 0$$
$$4(x - 14)(x + 8) = 0$$
$$x - 14 = 0 \quad \text{or} \quad x + 8 = 0$$
$$x = 14 \quad \text{or} \qquad x = -8$$
Since the width of the tin must be a positive number, the answer must be $x = 14$. Therefore, the width is 14 cm; length is 28 cm.

20.

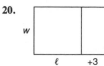

$l \cdot w = 180 \text{ m}^2$
$l + 3 = w$

$$l(l + 3) = 180$$
$$l^2 + 3l = 180$$
$$l^2 + 3l - 180 = 0$$
$$(l + 15)(l - 12) = 0$$
$$l = -15, 12$$
The dimensions are $l = 12$, $w = 15$.

21. Let x be the width of the tank.

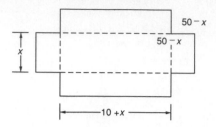

$$2[x(10 + x)] = 2[x(50 - x)] + 2[(10 + x)(50 - x)] - 400$$
$$2(10x + x^2) = 2(50x - x^2) + 2(500 + 40x - x^2) - 400$$
$$20x + 2x^2 = 100x - 2x^2 + 1000 + 80x - 2x^2 - 400$$
$$6x^2 - 160x - 600 = 0$$
$$2(3x^2 - 80x - 300) = 0$$
$$2(3x + 10)(x - 30) = 0$$
$$3x + 10 = 0 \quad \text{or} \quad x - 30 = 0$$
$$x = -\frac{10}{3} \quad \text{or} \quad x = 30$$

The width must be positive, so the dimensions of the tank are width 30 in.; length 40 in.; depth 20 in.

22. Let x be the width of the strip of yard surrounding the pool.

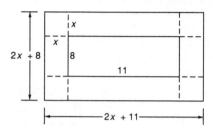

$$(2x + 8)(2x + 11) = 1120$$
$$4x^2 + 38x + 88 = 1120$$
$$4x^2 + 38x - 1032 = 0$$
$$2(2x^2 + 19x - 516) = 0$$
$$2(2x + 43)(x - 12) = 0$$
$$2x + 43 = 0 \quad \text{or} \quad x - 12 = 0$$
$$x = -\frac{43}{2} \quad \text{or} \quad x = 12$$

Since the width of the strip must be a positive number, the answer must be 12 m.

23. Let x be the hypotenuse of the right triangle. Use the Pythagorean theorem to find the hypotenuse of the triangle.

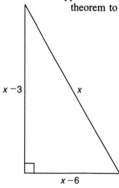

$$(x - 3)^2 + (x - 6)^2 = x^2$$
$$x^2 - 6x + 9 + x^2 - 12x + 36 = x^2$$
$$x^2 - 18x + 45 = 0$$
$$(x - 15)(x - 3) = 0$$
$$x - 15 = 0 \quad \text{or} \quad x - 3 = 0$$
$$x = 15 \quad \text{or} \quad x = 3$$

Since a hypotenuse of 3 cm would give lengths of 0 and -3 to the two legs, this answer is not acceptable. Therefore, the hypotenuse of the triangle must be 15 cm. The area is

$$\frac{1}{2}(9)(12) = 54 \text{ cm}^2.$$

24. $(5x^2y + 3xy - 6) + (4x^2y + 2xy^2 - 4xy - 9)$
$= (5 + 4)x^2y + 2xy^2 + (3 - 4)xy + (-6 - 9)$
$= 9x^2y + 2xy^2 - xy - 15$

25. $(2x^2 - 1)^3 = 8x^6 - 12x^4 + 6x^2 - 1$

26. $y^2 + 7y = y(y + 7)$

27. $x^2 - 4 = x^2 - 2^2 = (x + 2)(x - 2)$

28. $16y^2 + 4y = 4y(4y + 1)$ **29.** $4y^2 - 2y = 2y(2y - 1)$

30. $3a - 5 = 19$
$3a = 24$
$a = 8$

31. $-16 = 3x + 2$
$-18 = 3x$
$-6 = x$

32. $-6 = 0.75y + 3$
$-9 = 0.75y$
$-12 = y$

p. 238   COLLEGE ENTRANCE EXAMS

1. $r - 3 = 0 \quad \text{or} \quad \frac{1}{r} = 0$
$r = 3 \quad \text{or} \quad \text{No solution}$
(D)

2. $x^2 - y^2 = (x - y)(x + y)$
$= (7)(5)$
$= 35$
(E)

3. $0.53^2 - 0.47^2$
$= (0.53 - 0.47)(0.53 + 0.47)$
$= (0.06)(1)$
$= (0.06)$
(B)

4. $(13)^2 - 2(13)(23) + (23)^2$
$= (13 - 23)(13 - 23)$
$= (-10)(-10)$
$= 100$
(C)

5. $\qquad x^2 - 16 = (12)(20)$
$= (x - 4)(x + 4)$
Therefore, $x - 4 = 12, x = 16;$
$x + 4 = 20, x = 16.$
(C)

6. $(a - b)^2 = a^2 - 2ab + b^2 = 10$
$(a^2 + b^2) - 2ab = 10$
$(a^2 + b^2) - 2(2) = 10$
$(a^2 + b^2) - 4 = 10$
$(a^2 + b^2) = 14$
(A)

7. $\dfrac{m^2 - n^2}{m - n} = \dfrac{(m - n)(m + n)}{m - n}$
$= \dfrac{m - n}{m - n} \cdot (m + n)$
$= m + n$
$= 5 + 4 = 9$
(B)

8. $x^2 - y^2 = (x - y)(x + y)$
$= \left(\dfrac{1}{r}\right)(r)$
$= 1$
(B)

9. $(x^2 - y^2) = (x - y)(x + y)$
$60 = (x - y)(10)$
$\dfrac{60}{10} = x - y$
$6 = x - y$
(C)

1. $P(2) = -3(2)^2 + 2(2) - 1$
$= -3(4) + 4 - 1$
$= -12 + 4 - 1$
$= -9$

2. $P(-3) = 2(-3)^3 - 2(-3)^2 - (-3) - 33$
$= 2(-27) - 2(9) + 3 - 33$
$= (-54) - 18 - 30$
$= -72 - 30$
$= -102$

3. $2a + 7 - 3 + 9a + 3 - 7a = 4a + 7$

4. $-3x^2y - 2xy + 5xy - 7xy^2 = -3x^2y + 3xy - 7xy^2$

5. $5x^2 - 8x^3 + 3x - 2 + 4x^3 + 5x^2 + 9 - x$
$= -4x^3 + 10x^2 + 2x + 7$

6. $5a^4 + 7a^3 + 6a^2 - 7 + 3a^4 - 5a^2 + 2 - a^3$
$= 8a^4 + 6a^3 + a^2 - 5$

7. $p^3 - 5q^2 + 2pq + 3pq^3 - p^3 - 6 + 4pq^2 + 5p^3 - pq + 6$
$= 5p^3 + pq + 4pq^2 + 3pq^3 - 5q^2$

8. $-x^5 + x^3 + 2x^2 - 18x + 1$ 9. $4y^4 + 16x^3y^3 - 13xy^2$

10. $(8y^2 + 3y + 6) - (-5y^2 + 4y - 3)$
$= 8y^2 + 3y + 6 + 5y^2 + 4y + 3 = 13y^2 - y + 9$

11. $(8p - 5q + 7r) - (2p + 5q - 4r)$
$= 8p - 5q + 7r - 2p - 5q + 4r = 6p - 10q + 11r$

12. $(8x^2 - 3xy - 7y^2) - (4x^2 - 6xy - 8y^2)$
$= 8x^2 - 3xy - 7y^2 - 4x^2 + 6xy + 8y^2 = 4x^2 + 3xy + y^2$

13. $(15a - 5c + 4b) - (8b + 4c + 5a)$
$= 15a - 5c + 4b - 8b - 4c - 5a = 10a - 9c - 4b$

14. $(-8x^2y)(4xy^2) = -32x^3y^3$

15. $(3xy + 4y)(x^2 - 2) = 3x^3y - 6xy + 4yx^2 - 8y$

16. $(3x - 2y + 5z)(-3x + 4z)$
$= -9x^2 + 12xz + 6xy - 8yz - 15xz + 20z^2$
$= -9x^2 + 6xy - 3xz - 8yz + 20z^2$

17. $(5y^3 + 3y - 6)(6y^3 - 4y + 7)$
$= 30y^6 - 20y^4 + 35y^3 + 18y^4 - 12y^2 + 21y - 36y^3$
$+ 24y - 42 = 30y^6 - 2y^4 - y^3 - 12y^2 + 45y - 42$

18. $(a - b)(a^2 + ab + b^2) = a^3 + a^2b + ab^2 - a^2b - ab^2 - b^3$
$= a^3 - b^3$

19. $(-3x^2y^3 + 2t)(3x^2y^3 + 2t) = -9x^4y^6 - 6x^2y^3t + 6x^2y^3t + 4t^2$
$= -9x^4y^6 + 4t^2$

20. $(7x - 5y)^2 - (7x - 5y)(7x - 5y) = 49x^2 - 35xy - 35xy + 25y^2$
$= 49x^2 - 70xy + 25y^2$

21. $(2x + 1)^3 = (2x + 1)(2x + 1)(2x + 1)$
$= (4x^2 + 2x + 2x + 1)(2x + 1)$
$= (4x^2 + 4x + 1)(2x + 1)$
$= 8x^3 + 4x^2 + 8x^2 + 4x + 2x + 1$
$= 8x^3 + 12x^2 + 6x + 1$

22. $24x^2y - 40y^2 = 8y(3x^2 - 5y)$

23. $28t^4 - 35t^3 + 14t^2 = 7t^2(4t^2 - 5t + 2)$

24. $49y^2 - 81 = (7y - 9)(7y + 9)$

25. $9y^2 - 64 = (3y - 8)(3y + 8)$ 26. $4x^2y - xy^2 = xy(4x - y)$

27. $9x^2 - 9y^2 = 9(x^2 - y^2) = 9(x + y)(x - y)$

28. $x^2 - 2xy + y^2 - 9 = (x - y)^2 - 3^2 = (x - y - 3)(x - y + 3)$

29. $y^2 - 4y + 4 - 4x^2 = (y - 2)^2 - (2x)^2$
$= (y - 2 - 2x)(y - 2 + 2x)$

30. $8a^3 - 1 = (2a - 1)(4a^2 + 2a + 1)$

31. $25x^2 - 20xy + 4y^2 = (5x - 2y)^2$

32. $x^3 + y^6 = x^3 + (y^2)^3 = (x + y^2)(x^2 - xy^2 + y^4)$

33. $a^2 - 10a + 24 = (a - 4)(a - 6)$

34. $a^2b^2 + 7ab + 12 = (ab + 3)(ab + 4)$

35. $72 - x - x^2 = (9 + x)(8 - x)$

36. $2y^2 - 3y - 2 = (2y + 1)(y - 2)$

37. $8x^2 - 18x + 9 = (4x - 3)(2x - 3)$

38. $x^2 - 81 = (x + 9)(x - 9)$

39. $3x^2 - 27 = 3(x^2 - 9) = 3(x - 3)(x + 3)$

40. $8x^2 + 40x + 50 = 2(4x^2 + 20x + 25) = 2(2x + 5)^2$

41. $4y^2 + 20y - 56 = 4(y^2 + 5y - 14) = 4(y + 7)(y - 2)$

42. $x^2y - 16y^3 = y(x^2 - 16y^2) = y(x - 4y)(x + 4y)$

43. $8x^3 - 27y^3 = (2x)^3 - (3y)^3 = (2x - 3y)(4x^2 + 6xy + 9y^2)$

44. $5x^3 + 10x^2 - 45x - 90 = 5(x^3 + 2x^2 - 9x - 18)$
$= 5\{x^2(x + 2) - 9(x + 2)\}$
$= 5(x^2 - 9)(x + 2)$
$= 5(x - 3)(x + 3)(x + 2)$

45. $kw - tw + ky - ty = w(k - t) + y(k - t) = (k - t)(w + y)$

46. $x^2 - 8x = x(x - 8) = 0$
$x = 0$ or $x - 8 = 0$
$x = 8$

47. $2x^2 + 9x + 4 = (2x + 1)(x + 4) = 0$
$2x + 1 = 0$ or $x + 4 = 0$
$x = -\dfrac{1}{2}$ $x = -4$

48. $x^2 + 7x = -12$
$x^2 + 7x + 12 = (x + 3)(x + 4) = 0$
$x + 3 = 0$ or $x + 4 = 0$
$x = -3$ $x = -4$

49.
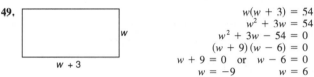

$w(w + 3) = 54$
$w^2 + 3w = 54$
$w^2 + 3w - 54 = 0$
$(w + 9)(w - 6) = 0$
$w + 9 = 0$ or $w - 6 = 0$
$w = -9$ $w = 6$

The dimensions are $w = 6$ and $l = 9$.

1. $Q(0) = 3(0)^3 - 0 + 3$ $Q(-2) = 3(-2)^3 - (-2) + 3$
$= (3 \cdot 0) - 0 + 3$ $= 3(-8) + 2 + 3$
$= 0 - 0 + 3 = 3$ $= -24 + 2 + 3$
        $= -19$

2. $H(2) = -2(2)^4 + (2)^3 + 3(2)^2 - 2 - 6$
$= -2(16) + 8 + 3(4) - 2 - 6$
$= -32 + 8 + 12 - 2 - 6$
$= -20$

   $H(-2) = -2(-2)^4 + (-2)^3 + 3(-2)^2 - (-2) - 6$
$= -2(16) + (-8) + 3(4) + 2 - 6$
$= -32 + (-8) + 12 + 2 - 6$
$= -32$

3. $3x - 5 - 3 - 3x + 5 - 1 = -4$

4. $-3xy - 2x^2 + y^2 - xy + 3x^2 = x^2 - 4xy + y^2$

5. $3x^2 - 4x^3 + 2x - 1 + 5x^3 + 4x^2 + 3 - x$
$= x^3 + 7x^2 + x + 2$

6. $4y^2 - 3xy + 4x^2 + 7x^3 + 5x^3 - 3x^2 - 2xy + 5y^2$
$= 9y^2 - 5xy + x^2 + 12x^3$

7. $-3x^2 - 2x - 6x^3 + x^3 - 7 + 2x^2 + 2x = -x^2 - 5x^3 - 7$

8. $x^2 - 3x - 2 + 3x^2 - 2x + 5 + (-2x^3) - 5x - 3$
$= -2x^3 + 4x^2 - 10x$

9. $3x^5 + x^3 - 2x^2 + 28x - 2$

10. $-4xy^4 - x^3y^3 + 23xy^2 - 16x^2$

11. $7x^2 + 2x + 4$ 12. $5r^2 - 2rs - 6s^2$
        $\underline{-(-2x^2 + 2x - 2)}$ $\underline{-(3r^2 - 4rs - 7s^2)}$
        $9x^2 + 6$ $2r^2 + 2rs + s^2$

13.
$$3x^4 - 2x^2 - 4$$
$$\underline{-(3x^3 - 2x^2 + 4)}$$
$$3x^4 - 3x^3 - 8$$

14.
$$x^3 - x^2 + x - 1$$
$$\underline{-(-x^3 - x^2 + x - 1)}$$
$$2x^3$$

15. $(14x^2y)(3xy^2) = 42x^3y^3$

16. $(-3x^2y^2)(-2xy)(-x^2y) = -6x^5y^4$

17. $(-4x + 3z)(2x - 3y + 4z)$
$$= -8x^2 + 12xy - 16xz + 6xz - 9yz + 12z^2$$
$$= -8x^2 + 12xy - 10xz - 9yz + 12z^2$$

18. $(3x - 5)(3x + 5) = 9x^2 + 15x - 15x - 25 = 9x^2 - 25$

19. $(x - 2)(x^2 + 2x + 4) = x^3 + 2x^2 + 4x - 2x^2 - 4x - 8$
$$= x^3 - 8$$

20. $(5x + 2y)^2 = (5x + 2y)(5x + 2y) = 25x^2 + 10xy + 10xy + 4y^2$
$$= 25x^2 + 20xy + 4y^2$$

21. $(7x - 2y)(3x + y) = 21x^2 + 7xy - 6xy - 2y^2$
$$= 21x^2 + xy - 2y^2$$

22. $(9x - 5y)(2x - 7y) = 18x^2 - 63xy - 10xy + 35y^2$
$$= 18x^2 - 73xy + 35y^2$$

23. $(2x^2 - 3)^2 = (2x^2 - 3)(2x^2 - 3) = 4x^4 - 6x^2 - 6x^2 + 9$
$$= 4x^4 - 12x^2 + 9$$

24. $(y^2 - 3y + 9)(y + 3) = y^3 + 3y^2 - 3y^2 - 9y + 9y + 27$
$$= y^3 + 27$$

25. $9t - 27 = 9(t - 3)$

26. $16x^2 - 81 = (4x - 9)(4x + 9)$

27. $9x^2 - 24x + 16 = (3x + 4)(3x + 4) = (3x + 4)^2$

28. $3y^3 - 27y = 3y(y^2 - 9) = 3y(y - 3)(y + 3)$

29. $x^2y^2 - 2xy - 15 = (xy - 5)(xy + 3)$

30. $6x^2 + 11x - 10 = (3x - 2)(2x + 5)$

31. $36 - 16x - x^2 = (2 - x)(18 + x)$

32. $y^6 - z^6 = (y^2)^3 - (z^2)^3$
$$= (y + z)(y - z)(y^2 - yz + z^2)(y^2 + yz + z^2)$$

33. $64p^3 - 125q^3 = (4p)^3 - (5q)^3$
$$= (4p - 5q)(16p^2 + 20pq + 25q^2)$$

34. $(x^2 - 6x + 9) - a^2 + 2a - 1 = (x - 3)^2 - (a - 1)^2$
$$= [x - 3 - (a - 1)][x - 3 + (a + 1)]$$
$$= [x - a - 2][x + a - 4]$$

35. $x^3 + 4x^2 - 8x - 32 = x^2(x + 4) - 8(x + 4)$
$$= (x^2 - 8)(x + 4)$$

36. $2a^2 + 4ab^2 - ab - 2b^3 = 2a(a + 2b^2) - b(a + 2b^2)$
$$= (2a - b)(a + 2b^2)$$

37.
$$x^2 - 21 = 4x$$
$$x^2 - 4x - 21 = 0$$
$$(x - 7)(x + 3) = 0$$
$$x - 7 = 0 \quad \text{or} \quad x + 3 = 0$$
$$x = 7 \qquad\qquad x = -3$$

38.
$$y^2 - 9y = 0$$
$$y(y - 9) = 0$$
$$y = 0 \quad \text{or} \quad y - 9 = 0$$
$$y = 9$$

39.
$$2x^2 + 75 = 25x$$
$$2x^2 - 25x + 75 = 0$$
$$(2x - 15)(x - 5) = 0$$
$$2x - 15 = 0 \quad \text{or} \quad x - 5 = 0$$
$$2x = 15 \qquad\qquad x = 5$$
$$x = \frac{15}{2}$$

40.
$$x^3 + 2x^2 = 9x + 18$$
$$x^3 + 2x^2 - 9x - 18 = 0$$
$$x^2(x + 2) - 9(x + 2) = 0$$
$$(x^2 - 9)(x + 2) = 0$$
$$(x + 3)(x - 3)(x + 2) = 0$$
$$x + 3 = 0 \quad x - 3 = 0 \quad x + 2 = 0$$
$$x = -3 \qquad x = 3 \qquad x = -2$$

41.
$$x^2 + 9x = -8$$
$$x^2 + 9x + 8 = 0$$
$$(x + 8)(x + 1) = 0$$
$$x + 8 = 0 \quad x + 1 = 0$$
$$x = -8 \qquad x = -1$$

42.
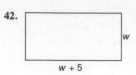

$$w(w + 5) = 84$$
$$w^2 + 5w = 84$$
$$w^2 + 5w - 84 = 0$$
$$(w + 12)(w - 7) = 0$$
$$w + 12 = 0 \quad \text{or} \quad w - 7 = 0$$
$$w = -12 \qquad\qquad w = 7$$
The dimensions are $w = 7$, $l = 12$.

CHAPTER 6

p. 242   READY FOR RATIONAL EXPRESSIONS AND EQUATIONS?

1. $-\frac{31}{63}$ **2.** $\frac{34}{15}$ **3.** $-\frac{14}{3}$ **4.** $\frac{3}{14}$ **5.** $\frac{8}{9}$ **6.** $-\frac{14}{3}$

7. -3 **8.** -18 **9.** $4(x + y)$ **10.** $3(y + 2)$

11. $c(x - r + w)$ **12.** $14xy^2$ **13.** $\frac{5x^4}{y^2}$

14. $16x^8y^{-16}z^{12}$ **15.** 3 **16.** $m = \frac{E}{c^2}$

pp. 244–247   6-1 TRY THIS

a. $\dfrac{3x + 2y}{5x + 4y} \cdot \dfrac{x}{x} = \dfrac{(3x + 2y)x}{(5x + 4y)x}$
$$= \dfrac{3x^2 + 2xy}{5x^2 + 4xy}$$

b. $\dfrac{2x^2 - y}{3x + 4} \cdot \dfrac{3x - 2}{3x - 2} = \dfrac{(2x^2 - y)(3x - 2)}{(3x + 4)(3x - 2)}$
$$= \dfrac{6x^3 + 4x^2 - 3xy - 2y}{9x^2 + 18x + 8}$$

c. $\dfrac{2a - 5}{a - b} \cdot \dfrac{-1}{-1} = \dfrac{(2a - 5) \cdot -1}{(a - b) \cdot -1}$
$$= \dfrac{-2a + 5}{-a + b}$$
$$= \dfrac{5 - 2a}{b - a}$$

d. $\dfrac{7x^2}{x} = \dfrac{7x \cdot x}{1 \cdot x}$
$$= \dfrac{7x}{1}$$
$$= 7x$$

e. $\dfrac{6a + 9}{3} = \dfrac{3 \cdot 2a + 3 \cdot 3}{3 \cdot 1}$
$$= \dfrac{3(2a + 3)}{3 \cdot 1}$$
$$= \dfrac{3}{3} \cdot \dfrac{2a + 3}{1}$$
$$= 2a + 3$$

f. $\dfrac{20y^2 + 32y}{4y} = \dfrac{4y \cdot 5y + 4y \cdot 8}{4y \cdot 1}$
$$= \dfrac{4y(5y + 8)}{4y \cdot 1}$$
$$= \dfrac{4y}{4y} \cdot \dfrac{5y + 8}{1}$$
$$= 5y + 8$$

g. $\dfrac{6x^2 + 4x}{2x^2 + 4x} = \dfrac{2x(3x + 2)}{2x(x + 2)}$
$$= \dfrac{2x}{2x} \cdot \dfrac{(3x + 2)}{(x + 2)}$$
$$= \dfrac{3x + 2}{x + 2}$$

h. $\dfrac{y^2 + 3y + 2}{y^2 - 1} = \dfrac{(y + 2)(y + 1)}{(y + 1)(y - 1)}$
$$= \dfrac{(y + 1)}{(y + 1)} \cdot \dfrac{(y + 2)}{(y - 1)}$$
$$= \dfrac{y + 2}{y - 1}$$

i. $\dfrac{10x^2 - 25xy + 15y^2}{7x^2 + 7xy - 14y^2} = \dfrac{5(x - y)(2x - 3y)}{7(x - y)(x + 2y)}$
$$= \dfrac{x - y}{x - y} \cdot \dfrac{5(2x - 3y)}{7(x + 2y)}$$
$$= \dfrac{5(2x - 3y)}{7(x + 2y)}$$

j. $\dfrac{(x-y)^2}{x+y} \cdot \dfrac{3x+3y}{x^2-y^2} = \dfrac{(x-y)^2(3x+3y)}{(x+y)(x^2-y^2)}$

$\qquad = \dfrac{(x-y)(x-y)3(x+y)}{(x+y)(x+y)(x-y)}$

$\qquad = \dfrac{(x+y)(x-y)}{(x+y)(x-y)} \cdot \dfrac{3(x-y)}{(x+y)}$

$\qquad = \dfrac{3(x-y)}{x+y}$

k. $\dfrac{a^3+b^3}{a^2-b^2} \cdot \dfrac{a^2-2ab+b^2}{a^2-ab+b^2} = \dfrac{(a^3+b^3)(a^2-2ab+b^2)}{(a^2-b^2)(a^2-ab+b^2)}$

$\qquad = \dfrac{(a+b)(a^2-ab+b^2)(a-b)(a-b)}{(a+b)(a-b)(a^2-ab+b^2)}$

$\qquad = \dfrac{(a+b)(a-b)(a^2-ab+b^2)}{(a+b)(a-b)(a^2-ab+b^2)} \cdot \dfrac{(a-b)}{1}$

$\qquad = a-b$

l. The reciprocal of $\dfrac{x+3}{x-5}$ is $\dfrac{x-5}{x+3}$.

m. The reciprocal of $x+7$ is $\dfrac{1}{x+7}$.

n. The reciprocal of $\dfrac{1}{y^3-9}$ is y^3-9.

o. $\dfrac{x^2+7x+10}{2x-4} \div \dfrac{x^2-3x-10}{x-2} = \dfrac{x^2+7x+10}{2x-4} \cdot \dfrac{x-2}{x^2-3x-10}$

$\qquad = \dfrac{(x+5)(x+2)}{2(x-2)} \cdot \dfrac{(x-2)}{(x-5)(x+2)}$

$\qquad = \dfrac{(x+2)(x-2)}{(x+2)(x-2)} \cdot \dfrac{(x+5)}{2(x-5)}$

$\qquad = \dfrac{(x+5)}{2(x-5)}$

p. $\dfrac{a^2-b^2}{ab} \div \dfrac{a^2-2ab+b^2}{2a^2b^2} = \dfrac{a^2-b^2}{ab} \cdot \dfrac{2a^2b^2}{a^2-2ab+b^2}$

$\qquad = \dfrac{(a+b)(a-b)}{ab} \cdot \dfrac{2ab(ab)}{(a-b)(a-b)}$

$\qquad = \dfrac{(a-b)(ab)}{(a-b)(ab)} \cdot \dfrac{2ab(a+b)}{(a-b)}$

$\qquad = \dfrac{2ab(a+b)}{(a-b)}$

pp. 248–249   6-1 -EXERCISES

1. $\dfrac{3x(x+1)}{3x(x+3)}$ **2.** $\dfrac{(4-y^2)\cdot(-1)}{(6-y)\cdot(-1)}$ **3.** $\dfrac{(t-3)(t+3)}{(t+2)(t+3)}$

4. $\dfrac{(p-4)(p+5)}{(p-5)(p+5)}$ **5.** $a-2$ **6.** $\dfrac{y-3}{y+3}$ **7.** $\dfrac{x+2}{x-2}$

8. $\dfrac{t+4}{t-4}$ **9.** $\dfrac{p-5}{p+5}$ **10.** $\dfrac{x+8}{4(x-1)}$ **11.** $\dfrac{y+6}{3(y-2)}$

12. $x-2$ **13.** $\dfrac{a^2+ab+b^2}{a+b}$ **14.** $\dfrac{x^2-xy+y^2}{x-y}$

15. $\dfrac{(x+4)(x-4)}{x(x+3)}$ **16.** $\dfrac{y+5}{y-3}$ **17.** $\dfrac{y+4}{2}$ **18.** $\dfrac{m+n}{4}$

19. $\dfrac{(x+5)(2x+3)}{7x}$ **20.** $\dfrac{1}{y+1}$ **21.** $\dfrac{1}{x+y}$ **22.** $\dfrac{1}{2x+3y}$

23. 3 **24.** $6x^2$ **25.** $\dfrac{(y-3)(y+2)}{y}$ **26.** $\dfrac{(x+2)(x+4)}{x}$

27. $\dfrac{2a+1}{a+2}$ **28.** $\dfrac{5x+2}{x-3}$ **29.** $\dfrac{(x+4)(x+2)}{3(x-5)}$

30. $\dfrac{(y+6)(y+3)}{3(y-4)}$ **31.** $\dfrac{x^2+4x+16}{(x+4)^2}$ **32.** $\dfrac{4y^2-6y+9}{(4y-1)(2y-3)}$

33. $\dfrac{x^2+x-2x-6}{(x+1)(x+2)(x+3)}$

$= \dfrac{x^2-x-6}{(x+1)(x+2)(x+3)}$

$= \dfrac{(x-3)(x+2)}{(x+1)(x+2)(x+3)}$

$= \dfrac{x-3}{(x+1)(x+3)}$

34. $\dfrac{2x-5x-10-x+2}{x^2-4}$

$= \dfrac{-4x-8}{x^2-4}$

$= \dfrac{-4(x+2)}{(x+2)(x-2)}$

$= \dfrac{-4}{x-2}$

35. $\dfrac{m^2-t^2}{m^2+2mt+t^2+m+t}$

$= \dfrac{m^2-t^2}{(m+t)^2+(m+t)}$

$= \dfrac{(m+t)(m-t)}{(m+t)[(m+t)+1]}$

$= \dfrac{m-t}{m+t+1}$

36. $\dfrac{a^2(a-2)+2(a-2)}{a^2(a-2)-3(a-2)}$

$= \dfrac{(a^2+2)\cdot(a-2)}{(a^2-3)\cdot(a-2)}$

$= \dfrac{a^2+2}{a^2-3}$

37. $\dfrac{x^3+x^2-y^3-y^2}{(x-y)^2} = \dfrac{(x^3-y^3)+(x^2-y^2)}{(x-y)^2}$

$= \dfrac{(x-y)(x^2+xy+y^2)+(x-y)(x+y)}{(x-y)^2}$

$= \dfrac{(x-y)(x^2+xy+y^2+x+y)}{(x-y)^2}$

$= \dfrac{x^2+xy+y^2+x+y}{x-y}$

38. $\dfrac{(u^3+v^3)^2}{(u^3-v^3)+(u^2v-uv^2)}$

$= \dfrac{[(u+v)(u^2-uv+v^2)]^2}{(u-v)(u^2+uv+v^2)+uv(u-v)}$

$= \dfrac{[(u+v)(u^2-uv+v^2)]^2}{(u-v)(u^2+uv+v^2+uv)}$

$= \dfrac{[(u+v)(u^2-uv+v^2)]^2}{(u-v)(u^2+2uv+v^2)}$

$= \dfrac{[(u+v)(u^2-uv+v^2)]^2}{(u-v)(u+v)^2}$

$= \dfrac{(u^2-uv+v^2)^2}{(u-v)}$

39. Answers may vary. Example:

$\dfrac{x^2+4x+4}{x^2-1}, \dfrac{7x+21}{7x-7}$

40. $\dfrac{x^5-x^3+x^2-1-[(x^3-1)(x^2+2x+1)]}{(x^2-1)^2}$

$= \dfrac{x^5-x^3+x^2-1-[x^5+2x^4+x^3-x^2-2x-1]}{(x^2-1)^2}$

$= \dfrac{2x^4-2x^3+2x^2+2x}{(x^2-1)^2}$

$= \dfrac{-2x^3(x+1)+2x(x+1)}{(x^2-1)^2}$

$= \dfrac{(-2x^3+2x)(x+1)}{(x^2-1)^2}$

$= \dfrac{-2x(x+1)(x^2-1)}{(x^2-1)^2}$

$= \dfrac{-2x(x+1)}{(x^2-1)}$

$= \dfrac{-2x(x+1)}{(x-1)(x+1)}$

$= \dfrac{-2x}{x-1}$

41. $\dfrac{a}{b} = a \cdot \dfrac{1}{b}$ by the definition of division. Likewise $\dfrac{c}{d} = c \cdot \dfrac{1}{d}$.

Hence $\dfrac{a}{b} \cdot \dfrac{c}{d} = a \cdot \dfrac{1}{b} \cdot c \cdot \dfrac{1}{d}$. By the commutative property of

multiplication, $a \cdot \dfrac{1}{b} \cdot c \cdot \dfrac{1}{d} = a \cdot c \cdot \dfrac{1}{b} \cdot \dfrac{1}{d}$.

$ac \cdot \dfrac{1}{bd} = \dfrac{ac}{bd}$ by the definition of division.

42. To prove: $\dfrac{a}{b} \cdot \dfrac{b}{a} = 1$. We have that $\dfrac{a}{b} = a \cdot \dfrac{1}{b}$ and $\dfrac{b}{a} = b \cdot \dfrac{1}{a}$

by the definition of division. Hence $\dfrac{a}{b} \cdot \dfrac{b}{a} = a \cdot \dfrac{1}{b} \cdot b \cdot \dfrac{1}{a}$.

By the commutativity of multiplication,

$a \cdot \dfrac{1}{b} \cdot b \cdot \dfrac{1}{a} = a \cdot \dfrac{1}{a} \cdot b \cdot \dfrac{1}{b}$.

But this is equal to $\dfrac{a}{a} \cdot \dfrac{b}{b} \cdot \dfrac{a}{a} \cdot \dfrac{b}{b} = 1 \cdot 1 = 1$.

43. $\dfrac{a}{b} \div \dfrac{c}{d} = \dfrac{\left(\dfrac{a}{b}\right)}{\left(\dfrac{c}{d}\right)}$. Multiply by 1 in the form $\dfrac{d}{d}$:

$\dfrac{\left(\dfrac{a}{b}\right) \cdot d}{\left(\dfrac{c}{d}\right) \cdot d} = \dfrac{\left(\dfrac{a}{b}\right) \cdot d}{c}$. By the definition of division, we have that

$\dfrac{\left(\dfrac{a}{b}\right) \cdot d}{c} = \left(\dfrac{a}{b}\right) \cdot d \cdot \dfrac{1}{c} = \dfrac{a}{b} \cdot \dfrac{d}{c}$.

44. $(a^{-1}b^{-1})(ab) = (a^{-1}a)(b^{-1}b)$ by the commutative property of multiplication. But $(a^{-1}a) = 1$ and $(b^{-1}b) = 1$. Hence $(a^{-1}a)(b^{-1}b) = 1$. Since $(ab)^{-1}(ab) = 1$. Since $(ab)^{-1}(ab) = 1 = (a^{-1}b^{-1})(ab)$ we can divide both sides of the equation by (ab) and we get the result $(ab)^{-1} = (a^{-1}b^{-1})$.

45. $-x^7 + x^4 + 4x^3y^3 + 2xy^2 - \dfrac{1}{2}$

46. $81x^4 - 16 = (9x^2 - 4)(9x^2 + 4)$
$\qquad\qquad\quad = (3x - 2)(3x + 2)(9x^2 + 4)$

47. $x^2 - 4x + 4 - y^2 = (x - 2)^2 - y^2$
$\qquad\qquad\qquad\quad = (x - 2 - y)(x - 2 + y)$

48. $ab - bc + 2ad - 2cd = ab + 2ad - bc - 2cd$
$\qquad\qquad\qquad\qquad\quad = a(b + d) - c(b + 2d)$
$\qquad\qquad\qquad\qquad\quad = (a - c)(b + 2d)$

p. 249   CONNECTIONS: CALCULUS

a. $3x^2$ **b.** $4x^3$ **c.** $5x^4$ **d.** $-\dfrac{1}{x^2}$

pp. 250–253   6-2 TRY THIS

a. $\dfrac{5 + y}{y} + \dfrac{7}{y} = \dfrac{5 + y + 7}{y}$

$\qquad\qquad = \dfrac{12 + y}{y}$

b. $\dfrac{2x^2 + 5x - 9}{x - 5} + \dfrac{x^2 - 19x + 4}{x - 5} = \dfrac{2x^2 + 5x - 9 + x^2 - 19x + 4}{x - 5}$

$\qquad\qquad\qquad\qquad\qquad = \dfrac{3x^2 - 14x - 5}{x - 5}$

$\qquad\qquad\qquad\qquad\qquad = \dfrac{(3x + 1)(x - 5)}{x - 5}$

$\qquad\qquad\qquad\qquad\qquad = 3x + 1$

c. $\dfrac{a}{b + 2} - \dfrac{b}{b + 2} = \dfrac{a - b}{b + 2}$

d. $\dfrac{4y + 7}{x^2 + y^2} - \dfrac{3y - 5}{x^2 + y^2} = \dfrac{4y + 7 - (3y - 5)}{x^2 + y^2}$

$\qquad\qquad\qquad\qquad = \dfrac{4y + 7 - 3y + 5}{x^2 + y^2}$

$\qquad\qquad\qquad\qquad = \dfrac{y + 12}{x^2 + y^2}$

e. $\dfrac{3x^2 + 4}{x - 5} + \dfrac{x^2 - 7}{5 - x} = \dfrac{3x^2 + 4}{x - 5} + \dfrac{-1}{-1} \cdot \dfrac{x^2 - 7}{5 - x}$

$\qquad\qquad\qquad\qquad = \dfrac{3x^2 + 4}{x - 5} + \dfrac{-x^2 + 7}{x - 5}$

$\qquad\qquad\qquad\qquad = \dfrac{3x^2 + 4 - x^2 + 7}{x - 5} = \dfrac{2x^2 + 11}{x - 5}$

f. $\dfrac{4x^2}{2x - y} - \dfrac{7x^2}{y - 2x} = \dfrac{4x^2}{2x - y} - \dfrac{-1}{-1} \cdot \dfrac{7x^2}{2x - y}$

$\qquad\qquad\qquad\qquad = \dfrac{4x^2 + 7x^2}{2x - y} = \dfrac{11x^2}{2x - y}$

g. $\dfrac{3x}{7} + \dfrac{4y}{3x} =$ The LCD is $7 \cdot 3x$, or $21x$.

$\qquad = \dfrac{3x}{7} \cdot \dfrac{3x}{3x} + \dfrac{4y}{3x} \cdot \dfrac{7}{7}$

$\qquad = \dfrac{9x^2}{21x} + \dfrac{28y}{21x}$

$\qquad = \dfrac{9x^2 + 28y}{21x}$

h. $\dfrac{4y - 5}{y^2 - 7y + 12} - \dfrac{y + 7}{y^2 + 2y - 15}$

$\qquad = \dfrac{4y - 5}{(y - 4)(y - 3)} - \dfrac{y + 7}{(y + 5)(y - 3)}$

The LCD is $(y - 4)(y - 3)(y + 5)$.

$\qquad = \dfrac{4y - 5}{(y - 4)(y - 3)} \cdot \dfrac{(y + 5)}{(y + 5)} - \dfrac{y + 7}{(y + 5)(y - 3)} \cdot \dfrac{y - 4}{y - 4}$

$\qquad = \dfrac{4y^2 + 15y - 25}{(y - 4)(y - 3)(y + 5)} - \dfrac{y^2 + 3y - 28}{(y + 5)(y - 3)(y - 4)}$

$\qquad = \dfrac{4y^2 + 15y - 25 - (y^2 + 3y - 28)}{(y - 4)(y - 3)(y + 5)}$

$\qquad = \dfrac{4y^2 + 15y - 25 - y^2 - 3y + 28}{(y - 4)(y - 3)(y + 5)}$

$\qquad = \dfrac{3y^2 + 12y + 3}{(y - 4)(y - 3)(y + 5)}$

i. $\dfrac{a}{a + 3} - \dfrac{a - 4}{a}$. The LCD is $a(a + 3)$.

$\qquad = \dfrac{a}{a + 3} \cdot \dfrac{a}{a} - \dfrac{a - 4}{a} \cdot \dfrac{(a + 3)}{(a + 3)}$

$\qquad = \dfrac{a^2}{a(a + 3)} - \dfrac{a^2 - a - 12}{a(a + 3)}$

$\qquad = \dfrac{a^2 - (a^2 - a - 12)}{a(a + 3)}$

$\qquad = \dfrac{a^2 - a^2 + a + 12}{a(a + 3)}$

$\qquad = \dfrac{a + 12}{a(a + 3)}$

j. $\dfrac{8x}{x^2 - 1} + \dfrac{2}{1 - x} - \dfrac{4}{x + 1} = \dfrac{8x}{(x + 1)(x - 1)} + \dfrac{-2}{x - 1} - \dfrac{4}{x + 1}$

The LCD is $(x + 1)(x - 1)$.

$\qquad = \dfrac{8x}{(x + 1)(x - 1)} + \dfrac{-2}{x - 1} \cdot \dfrac{x + 1}{x + 1}$

$\qquad - \dfrac{4}{x + 1} \cdot \dfrac{x - 1}{x - 1}$

$\qquad = \dfrac{8x - 2(x + 1) - 4(x - 1)}{(x + 1)(x - 1)}$

$$= \frac{8x - 2x - 1 - 4x + 1}{(x+1)(x-1)}$$

$$= \frac{2x + 2}{(x+1)(x-1)} = \frac{2(x+1)}{(x+1)(x-1)}$$

$$= \frac{2}{x-1}$$

k. $\dfrac{7y}{y^2 - y} + \dfrac{8}{2-y} - \dfrac{3}{y+2} = \dfrac{7 \cdot y}{y(y-1)} + \dfrac{8}{2-y} - \dfrac{3}{y+2}$

$$= \frac{7}{y-1} + \frac{8}{2-y} - \frac{3}{y+2}$$

The LCD is $(y-1)(2-y)(y+2)$.

$$= \frac{7}{y-1} \cdot \frac{(2-y)(y+2)}{(2-y)(y+2)} + \frac{8}{2-y} \cdot \frac{(y-1)(y+2)}{(y-1)(y+2)}$$

$$- \frac{3}{y+2} \cdot \frac{(y-1)(2-y)}{(y-1)(2-y)}$$

$$= \frac{7(2-y)(y+2) + 8(y-1)(y+2) - 3(y-1)(2-y)}{(y-1)(2-y)(y+2)}$$

$$= \frac{28 - 7y^2 + 8y^2 + 8y + 16 + 3y^2 - 9y + 6}{(y-1)(2-y)(y+2)}$$

$$= \frac{4y^2 - y + 18}{(y-1)(2-y)(y+2)}$$

pp. 253–255　　　6-2 EXERCISES

1. $\dfrac{8y}{x}$　　**2.** $\dfrac{-2x}{3y}$　　**3.** $\dfrac{7y}{x+y}$　　**4.** $\dfrac{-a^2}{a-b}$

5. $\dfrac{9xy}{x^2 + y^2}$　　**6.** $\dfrac{-5a^2b}{a^2 - b}$　　**7.** 2　　**8.** 2　　**9.** $\dfrac{3y+5}{y-2}$

10. $\dfrac{2t+6}{t-4}$　　**11.** $a + b$　　**12.** $r + s$

13. $\dfrac{11}{x}$　　**14.** $\dfrac{7}{a}$　　**15.** $\dfrac{1}{x+5}$

16. $\dfrac{-2}{y^2 - 16}$　　**17.** $\dfrac{x+y}{x-y}$　　**18.** $\dfrac{a^2 + 7ab + b^2}{a^2 - b^2}$

19. $\dfrac{3x-4}{(x-2)(x-1)}$　　**20.** $\dfrac{3y^2 + 7y + 14}{(2y-5)(y+2)(y-1)}$　　**21.** $\dfrac{8x+1}{x^2-1}$

22. $\dfrac{4y+17}{y^2-4}$　　**23.** $\dfrac{2x-14}{15x+75}$　　**24.** $\dfrac{y-34}{20y+40}$

25. $\dfrac{-a^2 + 7ab - b^2}{a^2 - b^2}$　　**26.** $\dfrac{-x^2 + 4xy - y^2}{x^2 - y^2}$

27. $\dfrac{y}{(y-2)(y-3)}$　　**28.** $\dfrac{2x^2 + 21x}{(x-2)(x-4)(x+3)}$

29. $\dfrac{3y-10}{y^2 - y - 20}$　　**30.** $\dfrac{11y-3}{(y+3)^2(y-3)}$

31. $\dfrac{3y^2 - 3y - 29}{(y-3)(y+8)(y-4)}$　　**32.** $\dfrac{5y^2 - 11y - 6}{(y-2)(y-5)(y-3)}$

33. $\dfrac{2x^2 - 13x + 7}{(x+3)(x-1)(x-3)}$　　**34.** $\dfrac{2p^2 + 7p + 10}{(p-4)(p+6)(p+4)}$　　**35.** 0

36. $\dfrac{-y}{y^2 + 2y - 3}$　　**37.** $\dfrac{-3x^2 - 3x - 4}{x^2 - 1}$　　**38.** $\dfrac{-14y^2 - 3y + 3}{4y^2 - 1}$

39. $2x^{-2} + 3x^{-2}y^{-2} - 7xy^{-1}$
LCM $= x^2y^2$

$$= \frac{2}{x^2} + \frac{3}{x^2y^2} - \frac{7x}{y}$$

$$= \frac{2}{x^2} \cdot \frac{y^2}{y^2} + \frac{3}{x^2y^2} - \frac{1x \cdot x^2y}{y \cdot x^2y}$$

$$= \frac{2y^2 + 3 - 7x^3y}{x^2y^2}$$

40. $5(x-3)^{-1} + 4(x+3)^{-1} - 2(x+3)^{-2}$
LCM $= (x-3)(x+3)^2$

$$= \frac{5}{x-3} + \frac{4}{x+3} - \frac{2}{(x+3)^2}$$

$$= \frac{5(x+3)^2}{(x-3)(x+3)^2} + \frac{4(x-3)(x+3)}{(x+3)(x+3)(x+3)}$$

$$- \frac{2}{(x+3)^2} \cdot \frac{x-3}{x-3}$$

$$= \frac{5(x^2 + 6x + 9) + 4(x^2 - 9) - 2(x-3)}{(x+3)^2(x-3)}$$

$$= \frac{9x^2 + 28x + 15}{(x-3)(x+3)^2}$$

41. $4(y-1)(2y-5)^{-1} + 5(2y+3)(5-2y)^{-1}$
$+ (y-4)(2y-5)^{-1} = \dfrac{4(y-1)}{2y-5} + \dfrac{5(2y+3)}{5-2y} + \dfrac{y-4}{2y-5}$

$$= \frac{4(y-1)}{2y-5} + \frac{5(2y+3)}{5-2y} \cdot \frac{-1}{-1} + \frac{y-4}{2y-5}$$

$$= \frac{4y - 4 - 10y - 15 + y - 4}{2y-5}$$

$$= \frac{-5y - 23}{2y-5} = \frac{5y + 23}{5 - 2y}$$

42. $\dfrac{A+B}{A-B} - \dfrac{A-B}{A+B} = \dfrac{(x+y)+(x-y)}{(x+y)-(x-y)} - \dfrac{(x+y)-(x-y)}{(x+y)+(x-y)}$

$$= \frac{2x}{2y} - \frac{2y}{2x}$$

$$= \frac{x}{y} - \frac{y}{x}$$

$$= \frac{x^2 - y^2}{xy}$$

43. $\left(\dfrac{1}{A} + \dfrac{x}{B}\right) \div \left(\dfrac{1}{B} - \dfrac{x}{A}\right) = \left(\dfrac{1}{x+y} + \dfrac{x}{x-y}\right) \div \left(\dfrac{1}{x-y} - \dfrac{x}{x+y}\right)$

$$= \left(\frac{1}{x+y} \cdot \frac{x-y}{x-y} + \frac{x}{x-y} \cdot \frac{(x+y)}{(x+y)}\right)$$

$$\div \left(\frac{1}{(x-y)} \cdot \frac{x+y}{(x+y)} - \frac{x}{(x+y)} \cdot \frac{x-y}{(x-y)}\right)$$

$$= \frac{x - y + x^2 + xy}{x^2 - y^2} \cdot \frac{x^2 - y^2}{x + y - (x^2 - xy)}$$

$$= \frac{x - y + x^2 + xy}{x + y - x^2 + xy}$$

44. Answers may vary.

Example: $\dfrac{2xy}{(x-y)^2}, \dfrac{3x^2y}{x+y}, \dfrac{1}{x^2 + xy + y^2}$

45. $R(x) = \dfrac{h(x)}{d(x)}$

$$= \frac{x^2 + x - 20}{x^2 - 25}$$

$$= \frac{(x+5)(x-4)}{(x+5)(x-5)}$$

$$= \frac{x-4}{x-5}$$

46. $R(x) = \dfrac{g(x)}{h(x)}$

$$= \frac{x^2 - 16}{x^2 + x - 20}$$

$$= \frac{(x-4)(x+4)}{(x+5)(x-4)}$$

$$= \frac{x+4}{x+5}$$

47. $R(x) = \dfrac{d(d(x))}{h(g(x))}$

$$= \dfrac{(x^2 - 25)^2 - 25}{(x^2 - 16)^2 + (x^2 - 16) - 20}$$

$$= \dfrac{x^4 - 50x + 625 - 25}{x^4 - 32x^2 + 256 + x^2 - 36}$$

$$= \dfrac{x^4 - 50x + 600}{x^4 - 31x^2 + 220}$$

$$= \dfrac{(x^2 - 30)(x^2 - 20)}{(x^2 - 11)(x^2 - 20)}$$

$$= \dfrac{x^2 - 30}{x^2 - 11}$$

48. To prove: $\dfrac{a}{c} + \dfrac{b}{c} = \dfrac{a + b}{c}$;

$\dfrac{a}{c} + \dfrac{b}{c} = a\left(\dfrac{1}{c}\right) + b\left(\dfrac{1}{c}\right)$ by the definition of division.

$a\left(\dfrac{1}{c}\right) + b\left(\dfrac{1}{c}\right) = (a + b)\dfrac{1}{c}$ by the distributive property.

$(a + b)\dfrac{1}{c} = \dfrac{a + b}{c}$ by the definition of division.

$\therefore \dfrac{a}{c} + \dfrac{b}{c} = \dfrac{a + b}{c}$

49. To prove: $\dfrac{a}{c} - \dfrac{b}{c} = \dfrac{a - b}{c}$;

$\dfrac{a}{c} = a \cdot \dfrac{1}{c}$ and $\dfrac{b}{c} = b \cdot \dfrac{1}{c}$ by the definition of division.

$\dfrac{a}{c} - \dfrac{b}{c} = (a - b)\dfrac{1}{c}$ by the distributive property.

$(a - b)\dfrac{1}{c} = \dfrac{a - b}{c}$ by the definition of division.

50. $x^8 - x^4 = x^4(x^4 - 1) = x^4(x^2 - 1)(x^2 + 1)$
$\qquad = x^4(x - 1)(x + 1)(x^2 + 1);$
$x^5 - x^2 = x^2(x^3 - 1) = x^2(x - 1)(x^2 + x + 1);$
$x^5 + x^2 = x^2(x^3 + 1) = x^2(x + 1)(x^2 - x + 1);$
$\text{LCM} = (x^2)^2(x^2 + 1)(x + 1)(x - 1)$
$\qquad (x^2 + x + 1)(x^2 - x + 1)$
$\qquad = x^4(x^2 + 1)(x^2 - 1)(x^2 + x + 1)(x^2 - x + 1)$

51. $8a^4b^7 = 2 \cdot 2 \cdot 2 \cdot a^3 \cdot a \cdot b^7;$
$2a^3b^7 = 2a^3b^7$
There must be 3 factors of 2, 4 factors of a, and 7 factors of b.
Other factors are: $8a^4$, $8a^4b$, $8a^4b^2$, $8a^4b^3$, $8a^4b^4$, $8a^4b^5$,
$8a^4b^6$, $8a^4b^7$.

52. $\quad x + \dfrac{1}{3}y = 19 \quad ①$ $\qquad 3x + y = 57 \quad 3①$
$\qquad\qquad\qquad\qquad\qquad -x - 8y = -134 \ 2②$
$-\dfrac{1}{2}x - 4y = -67 \ ②$

$\qquad\qquad 3② + ①: \qquad 3x + y = 57$
$\qquad\qquad\qquad\qquad\quad -3x - 24y = -402$
$\qquad\qquad\qquad\qquad\qquad\quad -23y = -345$
$\qquad\qquad\qquad\qquad\qquad\qquad\quad y = 15$
Substitution: $\qquad\qquad\quad 3x + 15 = 57$
$\qquad\qquad\qquad\qquad\qquad\quad 3x = 42$
$\qquad\qquad\qquad\qquad\qquad\quad x = 14$

Solution: $(14, 15)$

53. $0.25x + 1.25y = 0.84 \quad ①$
$\quad 6x + 30y = 20.16 \quad ②$
$\quad 25x + 125y = 84 \quad 100 \ ①$
$\quad 600x + 3000y = 2016 \ 100 \ ②$
$24 \ ①: 600x + 3000y = 2016$
$① = ②$ so equations are dependent

54. $\quad x - y + z = 6 \quad ① \qquad x - y + z = 6 \ ① + ②$
$\quad 2x + y - z = 0 \quad ② \qquad 2x + y - z = 0$
$\quad 3x - 2y - 4z = -2 \ ③ \qquad \overline{\quad 3x = 6}$
$\qquad\qquad\qquad\qquad\qquad\qquad\qquad x = 2$

Substitution in ② and ③: $\quad 4 + y - z = 0 \quad ④$
$\qquad\qquad\qquad\qquad\qquad 6 - 2y - 4z = -2 \ ⑤$
$2 ④ + ⑤: \qquad\qquad\qquad 2y - 2z = -8$
$\qquad\qquad\qquad\qquad\qquad \underline{-2y - 4z = -8}$
$\qquad\qquad\qquad\qquad\qquad\qquad -6z = -16$

$$z = \dfrac{8}{3}$$

Substitute x and z in ①: $\quad 2 - y + \dfrac{8}{3} = 6$

$$y = -\dfrac{4}{3}$$

Solution: $\left(2, -\dfrac{4}{3}, \dfrac{8}{3}\right)$

55. $2x^2 - 24x + 22 = 0$
$2(x^2 - 12x + 11) = 0$
$x^2 - 12x + 11 = 0$
$(x - 11)(x - 1) = 0$
$\qquad x = 11 \quad \text{or} \quad x = 1$

56. $\qquad\qquad 256x^4 = 16$
$\qquad\quad 256x^4 - 16 = 0$
$\qquad 16(16x^4 - 1) = 0$
$\qquad\qquad 16x^4 - 1 = 0$
$(4x^2 + 1)(4x^2 - 1) = 0$
$\quad 4x^2 + 1 = 0 \quad \text{or} \quad 4x^2 - 1 = 0$
$\qquad\quad 4x^2 = -1 \qquad\qquad 4x^2 = 1$

No real solutions $\qquad\qquad x^2 = \dfrac{1}{4}$

$$x = \pm\dfrac{1}{2}$$

57. $\qquad\qquad 2x^3 = 6x^2 + 8x$
$\quad 2x^3 - 6x^2 - 8x = 0$
$\quad 2x(x^2 - 3x - 4) = 0$
$\quad 2x(x - 4)(x + 1) = 0$
$\qquad 2x = 0 \quad \text{or} \quad x - 4 = 0 \quad \text{or} \quad x + 1 = 0$
$\qquad x = 0 \quad \text{or} \qquad x = 4 \quad \text{or} \qquad x = -1$

p. 255   BONUS TOPIC: GRAPHING RATIONAL FUNCTIONS

1. As x approaches 2 from the left-hand side, $f(x)$ becomes very small and is negative. As x approaches 2 from the right-hand side, $f(x)$ becomes very large and is positive.

2. No, as $f(x)$ will never be zero.

3. a. $f(x) = \dfrac{2}{x + 3}$

x	-5	-4	-3.5	-3.2	-3	-2.8	-2.5	-2	-1
$f(x)$	-1	-2	-4	-10	—	10	4	2	1

b. $f(x) = \dfrac{1}{x + 3}$

x	-5	-4	-3.5	-3	-2.8	-2.5	-2	-1
$f(x)$	$-.5$	-1	-2	—	5	2	1	$.5$

a.

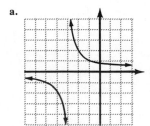

b.

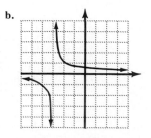

4.

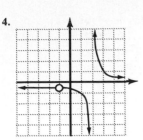

$$= \frac{(x + 2)(x - 2)(x + 2)}{(x - 2)(x - 1)(x + 2)(x - 2)}$$

$$= \frac{x + 2}{(x - 2)(x - 1)}$$

p. 258   6-3 EXERCISES

1. $\dfrac{1 + 4x}{1 - 3x}$ **2.** $\dfrac{1 + 7y}{1 - 5y}$ **3.** $\dfrac{(x + 1)(x - 1)}{x^2 + 1}$ **4.** $\dfrac{y^2 + 1}{(y + 1)(y - 1)}$

5. $\dfrac{3y + 4x}{4y - 3x}$ **6.** $\dfrac{2z + 5y}{z - 4y}$ **7.** $\dfrac{x + y}{x}$ **8.** $\dfrac{a - b}{a}$

9. $\dfrac{a^2(b - 3)}{b^2(a - 1)}$ **10.** $\dfrac{3}{3x + 2}$ **11.** $\dfrac{1}{a - b}$ **12.** $\dfrac{-1}{x + y}$

13. $\dfrac{1 + x^2}{x}$ **14.** $\dfrac{1 + y^4}{y(1 + y^2)}$ **15.** $\dfrac{y - 3}{y + 5}$ **16.** $\dfrac{(x - 4)(x - 7)}{(x - 5)(x + 6)}$

17. $\dfrac{1 + x}{1 - x}$ **18.** $\dfrac{x^3(x + y)}{y(x - y)(x^2 + xy - y^2)}$ **19.** $\dfrac{5(y - x + 2)}{6(x + 2)}$

20. $\dfrac{6x - 2}{5x + 6}$ **21.** $\dfrac{1}{x} + 1 = \dfrac{1}{x} + \dfrac{x}{x} = \dfrac{1 + x}{x}$; Reciprocal is $\dfrac{x}{1 + x}$.

22. $x^2 - \dfrac{1}{x} = x^2 \cdot \dfrac{x}{x} - \dfrac{1}{x} = \dfrac{x^3}{x} - \dfrac{1}{x}$.

$$= \frac{x^3 - 1}{x}; \text{Reciprocal is } \frac{x}{x^3 - 1}.$$

23. $\dfrac{1 - \dfrac{1}{a}}{a - 1} = \dfrac{1 \cdot \dfrac{a}{a} - \dfrac{1}{a}}{a - 1} = \dfrac{\dfrac{a - 1}{a}}{a - 1}$

$$= \frac{(a - 1)}{a} \cdot \frac{1}{(a - 1)} = \frac{1}{a}; \text{Reciprocal is } a.$$

24. $\dfrac{a^3 + b^3}{a + b} = \dfrac{(a + b)(a^2 - ab + b^2)}{a + b}$

$$= a^2 - ab + b^2; \text{Reciprocal is } \frac{1}{a^2 - ab + b^2}.$$

25. Answers may vary. Example:

$$\frac{\dfrac{1}{x}}{1 + \dfrac{1}{x}}$$

26. $1 + \dfrac{1}{1 + \dfrac{1}{1 + \dfrac{1}{1 + \dfrac{1}{x}}}} = 1 + \dfrac{1}{1 + \dfrac{1}{1 + \left(\dfrac{1}{1 + \dfrac{1}{x}} \cdot \dfrac{x}{x}\right)}}$

$$= 1 + \frac{1}{1 + \left(\dfrac{1}{1 + \dfrac{x}{x + 1} \cdot (1 + x)} \cdot \dfrac{(1 + x)}{(1 + x)}\right)}$$

$$= 1 + \left(\frac{1}{1 + \dfrac{(1 + x)}{(1 + x) + x}} \cdot \frac{1 + 2x}{1 + 2x}\right)$$

$$= 1 + \left(\frac{1 + 2x}{(1 + 2x) + (1 + x)}\right)$$

$$= 1 + \frac{1 + 2x}{2 + 3x}$$

$$= \frac{2 + 3x}{2 + 3x} + \frac{1 + 2x}{2 + 3x}$$

$$= \frac{3 + 5x}{2 + 3x}$$

---

pp. 256–257   6-3 TRY THIS

a. $\dfrac{y + \dfrac{1}{2}}{y - \dfrac{1}{7}} = \text{LCM} = 14: \dfrac{\left(y + \dfrac{1}{2}\right)}{\left(y - \dfrac{1}{7}\right)} \cdot \dfrac{14}{14}$

$$= \frac{14y + 7}{14y - 2}$$

b. $\dfrac{1 - \dfrac{1}{x}}{1 - \dfrac{1}{x^2}} = \text{LCM} = x^2: \dfrac{\left(1 - \dfrac{1}{x}\right)x^2}{\left(1 - \dfrac{1}{x^2}\right)x^2}$

$$= \frac{x^2 - x}{x^2 - 1}$$

$$= \frac{x(x - 1)}{(x - 1)(x + 1)}$$

$$= \frac{x}{x + 1}$$

c. $\dfrac{\dfrac{c^2 - 1}{4c + 4}}{\dfrac{c - 1}{c + 1}} = \dfrac{\dfrac{(c - 1)(c + 1)}{4(c + 1)}}{\dfrac{c - 1}{c + 1}} = \dfrac{(c - 1)(c + 1)}{4(c + 1)} \cdot \dfrac{c + 1}{c - 1}$

$$= \frac{(c - 1)(c + 1)(c + 1)}{4(c - 1)(c + 1)}$$

$$= \frac{c + 1}{4}$$

d. $\dfrac{\dfrac{a^3 + b^3}{a^2 - b^2}}{\dfrac{a^2 - ab + b^2}{a^2 - 2ab + b^2}} = \dfrac{\dfrac{(a + b)(a^2 - ab + b^2)}{(a + b)(a - b)}}{\dfrac{a^2 - ab + b^2}{(a - b)(a - b)}}$

$$= \frac{(a + b)(a^2 - ab + b^2)}{(a + b)(a - b)} \cdot \frac{(a - b)(a - b)}{a^2 - ab + b^2}$$

$$= \frac{(a + b)(a^2 - ab + b^2)(a - b)(a - b)}{(a + b)(a - b)(a^2 - ab + b^2)}$$

$$= a - b$$

e. $\dfrac{x^{-1} + y^{-1}}{x^{-1} + 3y^{-1}} = \dfrac{\dfrac{1}{x} + \dfrac{1}{y}}{\dfrac{1}{x} + \dfrac{3}{y}} = \dfrac{\dfrac{1}{x} \cdot \dfrac{y}{y} + \dfrac{1}{y} \cdot \dfrac{x}{x}}{\dfrac{1}{x} \cdot \dfrac{y}{y} + \dfrac{3}{y} \cdot \dfrac{x}{x}}$

$$= \frac{\dfrac{y}{xy} + \dfrac{x}{xy}}{\dfrac{y}{xy} + \dfrac{3x}{xy}} = \frac{\dfrac{x + y}{xy}}{\dfrac{y + 3x}{xy}}$$

$$= \frac{x + y}{xy} \cdot \frac{xy}{y + 3x} = \frac{x + y}{y + 3x}$$

f. $\dfrac{(x - 2)^{-2}(x + 2)}{(x^2 + x - 2)^{-1}(x^2 - 4)} = \dfrac{\left(\dfrac{1}{x - 2}\right)^2(x + 2)}{\dfrac{x^2 + x - 2}{x^2 - 4}} = \dfrac{\dfrac{x + 2}{(x - 2)(x - 2)}}{\dfrac{(x + 2)(x - 1)}{(x - 2)(x + 2)}}$

$$= \frac{x + 2}{(x - 2)(x - 2)} \cdot \frac{(x - 2)(x + 2)}{(x - 1)(x + 2)}$$

Bonus Topic–Lesson 6-3   *Algebra and Trigonometry*

27. $f(f(x)) = f\left(\dfrac{1}{1-x}\right) = \dfrac{1}{1 - \left(\dfrac{1}{1-x}\right)}$

$\qquad = \dfrac{1}{1 - \left(\dfrac{1}{1-x}\right)} \cdot \dfrac{(1-x)}{(1-x)}$

$\qquad = \dfrac{1-x}{(1-x) - 1}$

$\qquad = \dfrac{1-x}{-x}$

$\qquad = \dfrac{x-1}{x}$

$f(f(x)) = f\left(\dfrac{x-1}{x}\right) = \dfrac{1}{1 - \left(\dfrac{x-1}{x}\right)}$

$\qquad = \dfrac{1}{1 - \left(\dfrac{x-1}{x}\right)} \cdot \dfrac{x}{x}$

$\qquad = \dfrac{x}{x - (x-1)}$

$\qquad = \dfrac{x}{1}$

$\qquad = x$

28. $\dfrac{f(x+h) - f(x)}{h} = \dfrac{\dfrac{x+h}{1+x+h} - \dfrac{x}{1+x}}{h}$

$\qquad = \dfrac{\dfrac{(x+h)(1+x) - x[1 + (x+h)]}{[1 + (x+h)](1+x)}}{h}$

$\qquad = \dfrac{\dfrac{(x^2 + x + hx + h) - (x + x^2 + xh)}{[1 + (x+h)](1+x)}}{h}$

$\qquad = \dfrac{\dfrac{h}{(1+x)(1+x+h)}}{h}$

$\qquad = \dfrac{h}{(1+x)(1+x+h)} \cdot \dfrac{1}{h}$

$\qquad = \dfrac{1}{(1+x)(1+x+h)}$

29. Let x = number.

$\qquad x + x^2 = 42 + 2x$

$\qquad x^2 - x - 42 = 0$

$\qquad (x-7)(x+6) = 0$

$\qquad x = 7 \quad \text{or} \quad x = -6$

The number is 7 or -6.

30. Let x = Jeremy's salary before raise;

$\qquad x + 0.14x$ = Jeremy's salary after raise.

$\qquad x + 0.14x = 25,080$

$\qquad 1.14x = 25,080$

$\qquad x = 22,000$

Jeremy's salary was $22,000.

pp. 259–261   6-4 TRY THIS

a. $\dfrac{x^3 + 16x^2 + 6x}{2x} = \dfrac{x^3}{2x} + \dfrac{16x^2}{2x} + \dfrac{6x}{2x} = \dfrac{x^2}{2} + 8x + 3$

b. $(12x^3 + 3x^2 + 6x) \div 3x = \dfrac{12x^3}{3x} + \dfrac{3x^2}{3x} + \dfrac{6x}{3x} = 4x^2 + x + 2$

c. $(4x^7 + 3x^6 + 6x^5 + 12x^4 + 2x^3 + x^2 + 2x) \div 2x$

$\qquad = \dfrac{4x^7}{2x} + \dfrac{3x^6}{2x} + \dfrac{6x^5}{2x} + \dfrac{12x^4}{2x} + \dfrac{2x^3}{2x} + \dfrac{x^2}{2x} + \dfrac{2x}{2x}$

$\qquad = 2x^6 + \dfrac{3}{2}x^5 + 3x^4 + 6x^3 + x^2 + \dfrac{1}{2}x + 1$

d. $(15y^5 - 6y^4 + 18y^3) \div 3y^2 = \dfrac{15y^5}{3y^2} - \dfrac{6y^4}{3y^2} + \dfrac{18y^3}{3y^2}$

$\qquad = 5y^3 - 2y^2 + 6y$

e. $(x^4 + 10x^3 + 16x^2) \div 2x^2 = \dfrac{x^4}{2x^2} + \dfrac{10x^3}{2x^2} + \dfrac{16x^2}{2x^2}$

$\qquad = \dfrac{x^2}{2} + 5x + 8$

f. $\dfrac{16y^4 + 4y^3 + 2y^2}{4y} = \dfrac{16y^4}{4y} + \dfrac{4y^3}{4y} + \dfrac{2y^2}{4y} = 4y^3 + y^2 + \dfrac{1}{2}y$

g. $x - 2\overline{)x^2 + 3x - 10}$

$\qquad = x - 2\overline{\begin{array}{l} x+5 \\ x^2 + 3x - 10 \end{array}}$

$\qquad\qquad \underline{x^2 - 2x}$

$\qquad\qquad\quad 5x - 10$

$\qquad\qquad\quad \underline{5x - 10}$

Check: $(x-2)(x+5) = x^2 + 3x - 10$

h. $(9y^4 + 14y^2 - 8) \div (3y + 2)$

$\qquad\qquad\qquad\quad 3y^3 - 2y^2 + 6y - 4$

$\qquad = 3y + 2\overline{)9y^4 + 0y^3 + 14y^2 + 0y - 8}$

$\qquad\qquad\quad \underline{9y^4 + 6y^3}$

$\qquad\qquad\qquad -6y^3 + 14y^2$

$\qquad\qquad\qquad \underline{-6y^3 - 4y^2}$

$\qquad\qquad\qquad\qquad 18y^2 + 0y$

$\qquad\qquad\qquad\qquad \underline{18y^2 + 12y}$

$\qquad\qquad\qquad\qquad\quad -12y - 8$

$\qquad\qquad\qquad\qquad\quad \underline{-12y - 8}$

Check: $(3y+2)(3y^3 - 2y^2 + 6y - 4)$

$\qquad = 9y^4 - 6y^3 + 18y^2 - 12y + 6y^3 - 4y^2 + 12y - 8$

$\qquad = 9y^4 + 14y^2 - 8$

i.

$\qquad\qquad\quad y^2 - 8y - 24 \text{ R: } -66$

$\qquad y - 3\overline{)y^3 - 11y^2 + 0y + 6}$

$\qquad\qquad \underline{y^3 - 3y^2}$

$\qquad\qquad\quad -8y^2 + 0y$

$\qquad\qquad\quad \underline{-8y^2 + 24y}$

$\qquad\qquad\qquad -24y + 6$

$\qquad\qquad\qquad \underline{-24y + 72}$

$\qquad\qquad\qquad\qquad -66$

Check: $(y-3)(y^2 - 8y - 24) - 66$

$\qquad = y^3 - 8y^2 - 24y - 3y^2 + 24y + 72 - 66$

$\qquad = y^3 - 11y^2 + 72 - 66$

$\qquad = y^3 - 11y^2 + 6$

j.

$\qquad\qquad\qquad y - 11 + \dfrac{3y - 27}{y^2 - 3}$

$\qquad y^2 - 3\overline{)y^3 - 11y^2 + 0y + 6}$

$\qquad\qquad \underline{y^3 \qquad\quad - 3y}$

$\qquad\qquad\quad -11y^2 + 3y$

$\qquad\qquad\quad \underline{-11y^2 + \qquad - 33}$

$\qquad\qquad\qquad\quad 3y - 27$

Check: $(y-11)(y^2 - 3) + 3y - 27$

$\qquad = y^3 - 3y - 11y^2 + 33 + 3y - 27$

$\qquad = y^3 - 11y^2 + 6$

p. 262   6-4 EXERCISES

1. $6x^4 - 3x^2 + 8$ **2.** $4y^4 + 3y^3 - 6$ **3.** $-2a^2 + 4a - 3$

4. $-8x^3 - 6x^2 - 3x$ **5.** $y^3 - 2y^2 + 3y$

6. $12a^2 + 14a - 10$ **7.** $-6x^5 + 3x^3 + 2x$

8. $-6y^5 + 9y^2 + 1$ **9.** $1 - ab^2 - a^3b$ **10.** $x - xy - x^2$

11. $-2pq + 3p - 4q$ **12.** $4z - 2y^2z^3 + 3y^4z^2$

13. $x + 7$ **14.** $y - 4$ **15.** $a - 12$, R: 32

16. $y - 5$, R: -50 **17.** $y - 5$ **18.** $a + 9$

19. $y^2 - 2y - 1$, R: -8 **20.** $x^2 - 2x - 2$, R: -13

21. $a^2 + 4a + 15$, R: 72   **22.** $x^2 - 2x + 3$

23. $4x^2 - 6x + 9$ **24.** $16y^2 + 8y + 4$ **25.** $x^2 + 6$

26. $y^2 + 2$, R: -48 **27.** $4x^2 - 1$, R: $-2x + 1$

28. $y^3 - y^2 - 1$, R: 4   **29.** $2y^2 + 2y - 1 + \dfrac{8}{5y - 2}$

30. $3x^2 - x + 4 + \dfrac{10}{2x - 3}$

31.
$$
\begin{array}{r}
x^2 + 2y \\
x^2 - xy + y^2 \overline{)x^4 - x^3y + x^2y^2 + 2x^2y - 2xy^2 + 2y^3} \\
\underline{x^4 - x^3y + x^2y^2} \\
2x^2y - 2xy^2 + 2y^3 \\
\underline{2x^2y - 2xy^2 + 2y^3}
\end{array}
$$

32.
$$
\begin{array}{r}
a^2 + ab \\
a^2 + 3ab + 2b^2 \overline{)a^4 + 4a^3b + 5a^2b^2 + 2ab^3} \\
\underline{a^4 + 3a^3b + 2a^2b^2} \\
a^3b + 3a^2b^2 + 2ab^3 \\
\underline{a^3b + 3a^2b^2 + 2ab^3}
\end{array}
$$

33.
$$
\begin{array}{r}
x^3 + x^2y + xy^2 + y^3 \\
x - y \overline{)x^4 + 0x^3y + 0x^2y^2 + 0xy^3 - y^4} \\
\underline{x^4 - x^3y} \\
x^3y + 0x^2y^2 \\
\underline{x^3y - x^2y} \\
x^2y + 0xy^3 \\
\underline{x^2y - xy^3} \\
xy^3 - y^4 \\
\underline{xy^3 - y^4}
\end{array}
$$

34.
$$
\begin{array}{r}
a^6 - a^5b + a^4b^2 - a^3b^3 + a^2b^4 - ab^5 + b^6 \\
a + b \overline{)a^7 + 0a^6b + 0a^5b^2 + 0a^4b^3 + 0a^3b^4 + 0a^2b^5 + 0ab^6 + b^7} \\
\underline{a^7 + a^6b} \\
- a^6b + 0a^5b^2 \\
\underline{- a^6b - a^5b^2} \\
a^5b^2 + 0a^4b^3 \\
\underline{a^5b^2 + a^4b^3} \\
- a^4b^3 + 0a^3b^4 \\
\underline{- a^4b^3 - a^3b^4} \\
a^3b^4 - 0a^2b^5 \\
\underline{a^3b^4 + a^2b^5} \\
- a^2b^5 + 0ab^6 \\
\underline{- a^2b^5 - ab^6} \\
ab^6 + b^7 \\
\underline{ab^6 + b^7}
\end{array}
$$

35. Answers may vary.
Example: $5x^3 + 28x^2 + 27x + 67$, R: $x + 5$

36.
$$
\begin{array}{r}
x^2 + (-k - 2)x + (7 + 2k) \\
x + 2 \overline{)x^3 - kx^2 + 3x + 7k} \\
\underline{x^3 + 2x^2} \\
(-k - 2)x^2 + \qquad\ 3x \\
\underline{- k - 2x^2 + (-2k - 4)x} \\
(7 + 2k)x + 7k \\
\underline{7 + 2kx + (14 + 4)k} \\
3k - 14
\end{array}
$$
The remainder: $3k - 14 = 0$;
$$3k = 14;$$
$$k = \frac{14}{3}.$$

37.
$$
\begin{array}{r}
x - 5 \\
x + 2 \overline{)x^2 - 3x + 2k} \\
\underline{x^2 + 2x} \\
- 5x + 2k \\
\underline{- 5x - 10} \\
2k + 10
\end{array}
$$
The remainder: $2k + 10 = 7$;
$$2k = -3;$$
$$k = -\frac{3}{2}.$$

38. $\dfrac{-16n^5m^{-7}}{-4n^{-3}m^6} = 4n^8m^{-13}$ **39.** $\dfrac{25w^2}{(-5w)^2} = 1$

40. $\left(\dfrac{3m^2n^3}{4mn}\right)^2 = \dfrac{9m^2n^2}{16}$ **41.** $\left(\dfrac{n^3}{2m^2}\right)^3 = \dfrac{n^9}{8m^6}$

42. $1.04 \times 10^3 = 1040$ **43.** $6.34 \times 10^{-4} = 0.000634$

44. $(y + 6)^2$ **45.** $4(2x + y)^2$ **46.** $x(x - 7)$

p. 264   6-5 TRY THIS

a. $(x^3 + 5x^2 - 9x - 45) \div (x - 3)$
$$
\begin{array}{r|rrrr}
3 & 1 & 5 & -9 & -45 \\
& & 3 & 24 & 45 \\
\hline
& 1 & 8 & 15 & \!\!\!\mid\ 0
\end{array}
$$
$Q = x^2 + 8x + 15$, R: 0

b. $(8x^2 - 12x + 4) \div (x - 3)$
$$
\begin{array}{r|rrr}
3 & 8 & -12 & 4 \\
& & 24 & 36 \\
\hline
& 8 & 12 & \!\!\!\mid\ 40
\end{array}
$$
$Q = 8x + 12$, R: 40

c. $(x^3 - 2x^2 + 5x - 4) \div (x + 2)$
$$
\begin{array}{r|rrrr}
-2 & 1 & -2 & 5 & -4 \\
& & -2 & 8 & -26 \\
\hline
& 1 & -4 & 13 & \!\!\!\mid\ -30
\end{array}
$$
$Q = x^2 - 4x + 13$, R: -30

d. $(y^3 + 1) \div (y + 1)$
$$
\begin{array}{r|rrrr}
-1 & 1 & 0 & 0 & 1 \\
& & -1 & 1 & -1 \\
\hline
& 1 & -1 & 1 & \!\!\!\mid\ 0
\end{array}
$$
$Q = y^2 - y + 1$, R: 0

p. 265   6-5 EXERCISES

1. Q: $x^2 - x + 1$, R: 6

2. Q: $x^2 - 3x + 5$, R: 0

3. Q: $a + 7$, R: -47

4. Q: $a + 15$, R: 41

5. Q: $x^2 - 5x - 23$, R: -43

6. Q: $x^2 - 9x + 5$, R: 0

7. Q: $3x^2 - 2x + 2$, R: -3

8. Q: $3x^2 + 16x + 44$, R: 135

9. Q: $y^2 + 2y + 1$, R: 12   **10.** Q: $x^2 - 4x + 8$, R: -8

11. Q: $3x^3 + 9x^2 + 2x + 6$, R: 0

12. Q: $6y^3 - 3y^2 + 9y - 27$, R: 87

13. Q: $x^2 + 3x + 9$, R: 0   **14.** Q: $y^2 - 3y + 9$, R: 0

15. Q: $y^3 + y^2 + y + 1$, R: 2

16. Q: $x^4 + 2x^3 + 4x^2 + 8x + 16$, R: 0

17. Q: $5x + 8$, R: 24   **18.** Q: $9x^2 + 12x + 40$, R: 120

19. Q: $3x^3 + 21x^2 + 142x + 994$, R: 6968

20. Q: $x^3 - 5x^2 + 25x - 120$, R: 600

21. Q: $4x^2 + 12x + 52$, R: 199

22. Q: $-7x^2 + 55x - 385$, R: 2745

23. $(3x^4 - 24x^2 - 13) \div (x - 2.41)$
$$
\begin{array}{r|rrrrr}
2.41 & 3 & 0 & -24 & 0 & -13 \\
& & 7.23 & 17.42 & -15.85 & -38.19 \\
\hline
& 3 & 7.23 & -6.58 & -15.85 & \!\!\!\mid\ -51.19
\end{array}
$$
Q: $3x^3 + 7.23x^2 - 6.58x - 15.85$, R: -51.19

24. $(5x^5 + 11x^3 + 217) \div (x + 17.07)$
$$
\begin{array}{r|rrrrr}
-17.07 & 5 & 0 & 11 & & 0 \\
& & -85.35 & 1456.9245 & & -25057.471 \\
\hline
& 5 & -85.35 & 1467.9245 & & \!\!\!\mid\ -25057.471
\end{array}
$$
$$
\begin{array}{rr}
0 & 217 \\
427731.03 & -7301368.7 \\
\hline
427731.03 & -7301151.7
\end{array}
$$
Q: $5x^4 - 85.35x^3 + 1467.9245x^2 - 25057.471x + 427731.03$,
R: -7301151.7

25. $P(x) = 8x^5 - 3x^4 + 7x - 4$

$$\begin{array}{r|rrrrrr}
2 & 8 & -3 & 0 & 0 & 7 & -4 \\
  &   & 16 & 26 & 52 & 104 & 222 \\
\hline
  & 8 & 13 & 26 & 52 & 111 & | \ 218
\end{array}$$

$$\begin{array}{r|rrrrrr}
-4 & 8 & -3 & 0 & 0 & 7 & -4 \\
   &   & -32 & 140 & -560 & 2240 & -8988 \\
\hline
   & 8 & -35 & 140 & -560 & 2247 & | \ -8992
\end{array}$$

a. R: 218   R: -8992

b. $P(2) = 8 \cdot 2^5 - 3 \cdot 2^4 + 7(2) - 4$
$ = 256 - 48 + 14 - 4$
$ = 218$
$P(-4) = 8(-4)^5 - 3(-4)^4 + 7(-4) - 4$
$ = -8192 - 768 - 28 - 4$
$ = -8992$

c. The answers equal the algorithm answers.

26. Put $ax + b$ in the form $ax - (-b)$ and divide by a. Also, divide each term of the dividend by a.

$$\frac{b}{a} \Big| \ \frac{c^1}{a} + \frac{c^2}{a} + \frac{c^3}{a} \cdots$$

$ax + b = 6x + 12$
$$ = x + \frac{12}{6}$$
$$ = x - (-2) \text{ divisor}$$

$$\frac{12x^4}{6} - \frac{30x^2}{6} + \frac{30x}{6} - \frac{12}{6}$$

$2x^4 - 5x^2 + 5x - 2$ dividend
We now have:

$$\begin{array}{r|rrrr}
-2 & 2 & 0 & -5 & 5 & -2 \\
   &   & -4 & 8 & -6 & 2 \\
\hline
   & 2 & -4 & 3 & -1 & | \ 0
\end{array}$$

Q: $2x^3 - 4x^2 + 3x - 1$

27. Let $x^3 = x$.

$$\begin{array}{r|rrrr}
3 & 7 & -15 & -3 & 10 \\
  &   & 21 & 18 & 45 \\
\hline
  & 7 & 6 & 15 & | \ 55
\end{array}$$

$7x^2 + 6x + 15$, R: 55
Since $x^3 = x$, then $7(x^3)^2 + 6x^3 + 15$, R: 55
$ = 7x^6 + 6x^3 + 15$, R: 55

28. $f(x) = x^2 = $ Real numbers   **29.** $f(x) = \dfrac{7}{x + 3} = \{x \mid x \neq -3\}$

30. $f(x) = \dfrac{2}{x + 2x} = \{x \mid x \neq 0\}$

31. $f(x) = \dfrac{6}{x(x + 3)} = \{x \mid x \neq 0, x \neq -3\}$

32. $f(x) = \dfrac{1}{2 + x^2} = $ Real numbers

33. $8x^2 - 8xy + 2y^2 = 2(2x - y)^2$

34. $9y^2 - x^2 - 2x - 1 = (3y - x - 1)(3y + x + 1)$

35. $27x^3 - 1 = (3x - 1)(9x^2 + 3x + 1)$

pp. 266–268   **6-6 TRY THIS**

a.
$$\frac{2}{3} + \frac{5}{6} = \frac{1}{x}$$
$$6x\left(\frac{2}{3} + \frac{5}{6}\right) = 6x\left(\frac{1}{x}\right)$$
$$6x\left(\frac{2}{3}\right) + 6x\left(\frac{5}{6}\right) = 6x\left(\frac{1}{x}\right)$$
$$4x + 5x = 6$$
$$9x = 6$$
$$x = \frac{2}{3}$$

b.
$$\frac{1}{8} - \frac{2}{5} = \frac{3}{x}$$
$$40x\left(\frac{1}{8} - \frac{2}{5}\right) = 40x\left(\frac{3}{x}\right)$$
$$40x\left(\frac{1}{8}\right) - 40x\left(\frac{2}{5}\right) = 40x\left(\frac{3}{x}\right)$$
$$5x - 16x = 120$$
$$-11x = 120$$
$$x = -\frac{120}{11}$$

c.
$$\frac{y - 2}{5} - \frac{y - 5}{4} = -2$$
$$20\left(\frac{y - 2}{5} - \frac{y - 5}{4}\right) = 20(-2)$$
$$20\left(\frac{y - 2}{5}\right) - 20\left(\frac{y - 5}{4}\right) = 20(-2)$$
$$4y - 8 - 5y + 25 = -40$$
$$-y = -57$$
$$y = 57$$

d.
$$\frac{x - 7}{x - 9} = \frac{2}{x - 9}$$
$$(x - 9) \cdot \frac{x - 7}{x - 9} = (x - 9) \cdot \frac{2}{x - 9}$$
$$x - 7 = 2$$
$$x = 9$$
9 is not acceptable since it would cause division by 0. There is no solution.

e.
$$\frac{x^2}{x + 3} = \frac{9}{x + 3}$$
$$(x + 3) \cdot \frac{x^2}{x + 3} = (x + 3) \cdot \frac{9}{x + 3}$$
$$x^2 = 9$$
$$x^2 - 9 = 0$$
$$(x - 3)(x + 3) = 0$$
$$x - 3 = 0 \quad \text{or} \quad x + 3 = 0$$
$$x = 3 \quad \text{or} \quad x = -3$$
The only acceptable solution is 3.

f.
$$x - \frac{12}{x} = 1$$
$$x\left(x - \frac{12}{x}\right) = x(1)$$
$$x(x) - x\left(\frac{12}{x}\right) = x(1)$$
$$x^2 - 12 = x$$
$$x^2 - x - 12 = 0$$
$$(x + 3)(x - 4) = 0$$
$$x = -3 \quad \text{or} \quad x = 4$$
The solutions check.

g.
$$1 + \frac{1}{x} = 2x$$
$$x\left(1 + \frac{1}{x}\right) = x(2x)$$
$$x(1) + x\left(\frac{1}{x}\right) = x(2x)$$
$$x + 1 = 2x^2$$
$$0 = 2x^2 - x - 1$$
$$0 = (2x + 1)(x - 1)$$
$$0 = 2x + 1 \quad \text{or} \quad 0 = x - 1$$
$$-\frac{1}{2} = x \quad \text{or} \quad 1 = x$$
The solutions check.

h.
$$2 - \frac{1}{x^2} = \frac{1}{x}$$
$$x^2\left(2 - \frac{1}{x^2}\right) = x^2\left(\frac{1}{x}\right)$$

$$x^2(2) - x^2\left(\frac{1}{x^2}\right) = x^2\left(\frac{1}{x}\right)$$

$$2x^2 - 1 = x$$
$$2x^2 - x - 1 = 0$$
$$(2x + 1)(x - 1) = 0$$
$$2x + 1 = 0 \quad \text{or} \quad x - 1 = 0$$
$$x = -\frac{1}{2} \quad \text{or} \quad x = 1$$

The solutions check.

i.
$$\frac{2}{x - 1} = \frac{3}{x + 2}$$

$$(x - 1)(x + 2) \cdot \frac{2}{x - 1} = (x - 1)(x + 2) \cdot \frac{3}{x + 2}$$

$$2(x + 2) = 3(x - 1)$$
$$2x + 4 = 3x - 3$$
$$-x = -7$$
$$x = 7$$

The solution checks.

j.
$$\frac{2}{x^2 - 9} + \frac{5}{x - 3} = \frac{3}{x + 3}$$

$$\frac{2}{(x + 3)(x - 3)} + \frac{5}{x - 3} = \frac{3}{x + 3}$$

$$(x + 3)(x - 3)\left[\frac{2}{(x + 3)(x - 3)} + \frac{5}{x - 3}\right]$$

$$= (x + 3)(x - 3) \cdot \frac{3}{x + 3}$$

$$(x + 3)(x - 3) \cdot \frac{2}{(x + 3)(x - 3)} + (x + 3)(x - 3) \cdot \frac{5}{x - 3}$$

$$= (x + 3)(x - 3) \cdot \frac{3}{x + 3}$$

$$2 + 5(x + 3) = 3(x - 3)$$
$$2 + 5x + 15 = 3x - 9$$
$$2x = -26$$
$$x = -13$$

The solution checks.

p. 269   6-6 EXERCISES

1. $\frac{51}{2}$ **2.** -2 **3.** $\frac{40}{9}$ **4.** 144 **5.** $-5, -1$

6. 286 **7.** -1 **8.** $-\frac{1}{2}$ **9.** $\frac{17}{4}$ **10.** 14

11. No solution   **12.** 11 **13.** 2 **14.** 3 **15.** $\frac{3}{5}$

16. $\frac{3}{4}$ **17.** 6 **18.** -1 **19.** -145 **20.** -23

21. $-\frac{10}{3}$ **22.** No solution   **23.** -3 **24.** 4

25. $-6, 5$ **26.** 3 **27.** No solution

28.
$$\frac{x^2 + 6x - 16}{x - 2} = x + 8$$

$$(x - 2) \cdot \left(\frac{x^2 + 6x - 16}{x - 2}\right) = (x - 2) \cdot (x + 8)$$

$$x^2 + 6x - 16 = x^2 + 6x - 16$$
$$0 = 0 \quad \text{Yes}$$

29.
$$\frac{x^3 + 8}{x^2 - 4} = \frac{x^2 - 2x + 4}{x - 2}$$

$$\frac{x^3 + 8}{(x + 2)(x - 2)} = \frac{x^2 - 2x + 4}{x - 2}$$

$$(x + 2)(x - 2) \cdot \frac{(x^3 + 8)}{(x + 2)(x - 2)}$$

$$= (x + 2)(x - 2) \cdot \left(\frac{x^2 - 2x + 4}{x - 2}\right)$$

$$x^3 + 8 = (x + 2)(x^2 - 2x + 4)$$
$$x^3 + 8 = x^3 - 2x^2 + 4x + 2x^2 - 4x + 8$$
$$0 = 0 \quad \text{Yes}$$

30. Answers may vary.

Example: $\dfrac{x - 2}{x^2 + 5x - 14} = \dfrac{1}{x + 7}$

31. $\dfrac{x^3 + 8}{x + 2} = x^2 - 2x + 4$

$$= (x + 2) \cdot \left(\frac{x^3 + 8}{x + 2}\right) = (x + 2)(x^2 - 2x + 4)$$

$$x^3 + 8 = x^3 - 2x^2 + 4x + 2x^2 - 4x + 8$$
$$x^3 + 8 = x^3 + 8$$

True for all real numbers except -2.

32.
$$\frac{(x - 3)^2}{x - 3} = x - 3$$

$$(x - 3) \cdot \left[\frac{(x - 3)^2}{x - 3}\right] = (x - 3) \cdot (x - 3)$$

$$(x - 3)^2 = (x - 3)^2$$

This is true for all real numbers except 3.

33.
$$\frac{x + 3}{x + 2} - \frac{x + 4}{x + 3} = \frac{x + 5}{x + 4} - \frac{x + 6}{x + 5}$$

$$\frac{(x + 3)(x + 3) - (x + 4)(x + 2)}{(x + 2)(x + 3)}$$

$$= \frac{(x + 5)(x + 5) - (x + 6)(x + 4)}{(x + 4)(x + 5)}$$

$$\frac{(x^2 + 6x + 9) - (x^2 + 6x + 8)}{(x + 2)(x + 3)}$$

$$= \frac{(x^2 + 10x + 25) - (x^2 + 10x + 24)}{(x + 4)(x + 5)}$$

$$\frac{x^2 + 6x + 9 - x^2 - 6x - 8}{(x - 3)(x + 2)}$$

$$= \frac{x^2 + 10x + 25 - x^2 - 10x - 24}{(x + 5)(x + 4)}$$

$$\frac{1}{(x + 3)(x + 2)} = \frac{1}{(x + 5)(x + 4)}$$

$$(x + 5)(x + 4) = (x + 3)(x + 2)$$
$$x^2 + 9x + 20 = x^2 + 5x + 6$$
$$4x = -14$$

$$x = -\frac{7}{2}$$

34.
$$\left(\frac{y + 3}{y - 1}\right) - 2 = \frac{y + 3}{y - 1}$$

$$(y - 1)(y - 1) \cdot \left[\left(\frac{y + 3}{y - 1}\right)^2 - 2\right] = (y - 1)(y - 1) \cdot \frac{y + 3}{y - 1}$$

$$(y - 1)(y - 1) \cdot \left(\frac{y + 3}{y - 1}\right)^2 - 2(y - 1)(y - 1)$$

$$= (y - 1)(y - 1)\left(\frac{y + 3}{y - 1}\right)$$

$$(y + 3)^2 - 2(y^2 - 2y + 1) = (y - 1)(y + 3)$$
$$y^2 + 6y + 9 - 2y^2 + 4y - 2 = y^2 + 2y - 3$$
$$-2y^2 + 8y + 10 = 0$$
$$-2(y^2 - 4y - 5) = 0$$
$$-2(y - 5)(y + 1) = 0$$
$$y = 5 \quad \text{or} \quad y = -1$$

35. $\dfrac{25y^2}{10y} - \dfrac{5 \cdot 5y^2}{5 \cdot 2y} = \dfrac{5y}{2} = 2.5y$

36. $\dfrac{6x + 12}{6} = \dfrac{6(x + 2)}{6} = x + 2$

37. $\dfrac{3x + 9}{3x - 9} = \dfrac{3(x + 3)}{3(x - 3)} = \dfrac{x + 3}{x - 3}$

Lesson 6-6

Algebra and Trigonometry   79

38. $\dfrac{x^2 - y^2}{x^3 - y^3} = \dfrac{(x - y)(x + y)}{(x - y)(x^2 + xy + y^2)} = \dfrac{x + y}{x^2 + xy + y^2}$

39. $2(a - b) = 2(2.5 - 3) = 2(-0.5) = -1$

40. $b(b^2 - a) = 3[(3)^2 - 2.5] = 3(9 - 2.5) = 3(6.5) = 19.5$

41. $(a + b)(a - b) = (2.5 + 3)(2.5 - 3)$
$= (5.5)(-0.5) = -2.75$

pp. 271–273   6-7 TRY THIS

a. Let t represent the total number of hours it takes them working together.

$$\frac{1}{6} + \frac{1}{4} = \frac{1}{t}$$

$$24t\left(\frac{1}{6} + \frac{1}{4}\right) = 24t\left(\frac{1}{t}\right)$$

$$\frac{24t}{6} + \frac{24t}{4} = 24$$

$$4t + 6t = 24$$
$$10t = 24$$

$$t = \frac{24}{10} \quad \text{or} \quad 2\frac{2}{5} \text{ hours}$$

b. Let x represent the number of hours it takes A to fill the tank alone.

$$\frac{1}{x} + \frac{1}{3x} = \frac{1}{24}$$

$$24x\left(\frac{1}{x} + \frac{1}{3x}\right) = 24x\left(\frac{1}{24}\right)$$

$$\frac{24x}{x} + \frac{24x}{3x} = \frac{24x}{24}$$

$$24 + 8 = x$$
$$32 = x$$

We get 32 hours for pipe A, and $3x$, or 96 hours, for pipe B.

c. Let r represent the speed of the boat in still water.

$$\frac{246}{r + 5.5} = \frac{180}{r - 5.5}$$

$$(r + 5.5)(r - 5.5)\left(\frac{246}{r + 5.5}\right) = (r + 5.5)(r - 5.5)\left(\frac{180}{r - 5.5}\right)$$

$$246(r - 5.5) = 180(r + 5.5)$$
$$246r - 1353 = 180r + 990$$
$$66r = 2343$$
$$r = 35.5 \text{ mi/h}$$

pp. 273–275   6-7 EXERCISES

1. Let t represent the total number of hours it takes them working together.

$$\frac{1}{5} + \frac{1}{9} = \frac{1}{t}$$

$$45t\left(\frac{1}{5} + \frac{1}{9}\right) = 45t\left(\frac{1}{t}\right)$$

$$\frac{45t}{5} + \frac{45t}{9} = \frac{45t}{t}$$

$$9t + 5t = 45$$
$$14t = 45$$

$$t = \frac{45}{14}, \quad \text{or} \quad 3\frac{3}{14} \text{ hours}$$

2. Let t represent the total number of hours it takes them working together.

$$\frac{1}{4} + \frac{1}{3} = \frac{1}{t}$$

$$12t\left(\frac{1}{4} + \frac{1}{3}\right) = 12t\left(\frac{1}{t}\right)$$

$$\frac{12t}{4} + \frac{12t}{3} = \frac{12t}{t}$$

$$3t + 4t = 12$$
$$7t = 12$$

$$t = \frac{12}{7}, \quad \text{or} \quad 1\frac{5}{7} \text{ hours}$$

3. Let t represent the total number of hours it takes them working together.

$$\frac{1}{5} + \frac{1}{4} = \frac{1}{t}$$

$$20t\left(\frac{1}{5} + \frac{1}{4}\right) = 20t\left(\frac{1}{t}\right)$$

$$\frac{20t}{5} + \frac{20t}{4} = \frac{20t}{t}$$

$$4t + 5t = 20$$
$$9t = 20$$

$$t = \frac{20}{9}, \quad \text{or} \quad 2\frac{2}{9} \text{ hours}$$

4. Let t represent the total number of hours it takes them working together.

$$\frac{1}{6} + \frac{1}{4} = \frac{1}{t}$$

$$24t\left(\frac{1}{6} + \frac{1}{4}\right) = 24t\left(\frac{1}{t}\right)$$

$$\frac{24t}{6} + \frac{24t}{4} = \frac{24t}{t}$$

$$4t + 6t = 24$$
$$10t = 24$$

$$t = \frac{24}{10}, \quad \text{or} \quad 2\frac{2}{5} \text{ hours}$$

5. Let t represent the number of hours it takes the hose working alone.

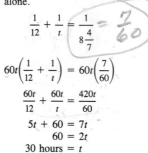

$$\frac{1}{12} + \frac{1}{t} = \frac{1}{8\frac{4}{7}}$$

$$60t\left(\frac{1}{12} + \frac{1}{t}\right) = 60t\left(\frac{7}{60}\right)$$

$$\frac{60t}{12} + \frac{60t}{t} = \frac{420t}{60}$$

$$5t + 60 = 7t$$
$$60 = 2t$$
$$30 \text{ hours} = t$$

6. Let t represent the number of hours B will take working alone.

$$\frac{1}{18} + \frac{1}{t} = \frac{1}{9.9}$$

$$178.2t\left(\frac{1}{18} + \frac{1}{t}\right) = 178.2t\left(\frac{1}{9.9}\right)$$

$$\frac{178.2t}{18} + \frac{178.2t}{t} = \frac{178.2t}{9.9}$$

$$9.9t + 178.2 = 18t$$
$$178.2 = 8.1t$$
$$22 \text{ hours} = t$$

7. Let t represent the total number of hours it will take them working together.

$$\frac{1}{5.5} + \frac{1}{7.5} = \frac{1}{t}$$

$$41.25t\left(\frac{1}{5.5} + \frac{1}{7.5}\right) = 41.25t\left(\frac{1}{t}\right)$$

$$\frac{41.25t}{5.5} + \frac{41.25t}{7.5} = 41.25$$

$$7.5t + 5.5t = 41.25$$
$$13t = 41.25$$
$$t = 3.173 \text{ hours}$$

8. Let t represent the total number of hours it will take them working together.

$$\frac{1}{4.5} + \frac{1}{5.5} = \frac{1}{t}$$

$$24.75t\left(\frac{1}{4.5} + \frac{1}{5.5}\right) = 24.75t\left(\frac{1}{t}\right)$$

$$\frac{24.75t}{4.5} + \frac{24.75t}{5.5} = \frac{24.75t}{t}$$

$$5.5t + 4.5t = 24.75$$
$$10t = 24.75$$
$$t = 2.475 \text{ hours}$$

9. Let r be the speed of the boat in still water.

$$\frac{10}{r+3} = \frac{4}{r-3}$$

	Distance	Rate	Time
Downstream	10	$r+8$	t
Upstream	4	$r-3$	t

$$(r+3)(r-3)\left(\frac{10}{r+3}\right) = (r+3)(r-3)\left(\frac{4}{r-3}\right)$$

$$10(r-3) = 4(r+3)$$
$$10r - 30 = 4r + 12$$
$$6r = 42$$
$$r = 7 \text{ km/h}$$

10. Let r be the speed of the boat in still water.

$$\frac{12}{r+4} = \frac{6}{r-4}$$

	Distance	Rate	Time
Downstream	12	$r+4$	t
Upstream	6	$r-4$	t

$$(r+4)(r-4)\left(\frac{12}{r+4}\right) = (r+4)(r-4)\left(\frac{6}{r-4}\right)$$

$$12(r-4) = 6(r+4)$$
$$12r - 48 = 6r + 24$$
$$6r = 72$$
$$r = 12 \text{ km/h}$$

11. Let r represent the speed of train B.

	Distance	Rate	Time
Train A	230	$r-12$	t
Train B	290	r	t

$$\frac{230}{r-12} = \frac{290}{r}$$

$$r(r-12)\left(\frac{230}{r-12}\right) = r(r-12)\left(\frac{290}{r}\right)$$

$$230r = 290(r-12)$$
$$230r = 290r - 3480$$
$$3480 = 60r$$
$$58 \text{ km/h} = r$$

The speed of train B is 58 km/h.
The speed of train A is $r - 12$, or 46 km/h.

12. Let r represent the speed of train Y.

	Distance	Rate	Time
Train X	400	$r+14$	t
Train Y	330	r	t

$$\frac{400}{r+14} = \frac{330}{r}$$

$$r(r+14)\left(\frac{400}{r+14}\right) = r(r+14)\left(\frac{330}{r}\right)$$

$$400r = 330(r+14)$$
$$400r = 330r + 4620$$
$$70r = 4620$$

$r = 66$ km/h, the speed of train Y.
The speed of train X is $r + 14$, or 80 km/h.

13. Let r represent the speed of the river.

	Distance	Rate	Time
Downstream	140	$15+r$	t
Upstream	35	$15-r$	t

$$\frac{140}{15+r} = \frac{35}{15-r}$$

$$(15+r)(15-r)\left(\frac{140}{15+r}\right) = (15+r)(15-r)\left(\frac{35}{15-r}\right)$$

$$140(15-r) = 35(15+r)$$
$$2100 - 140r = 525 + 35r$$
$$1575 = 175r$$
$$9 \text{ km/h} = r$$

14. Let r be the speed of the river.

	Distance	Rate	Time
Downstream	4	$2+r$	t
Upstream	1	$2-r$	t

$$\frac{4}{2+r} = \frac{1}{2-r}$$

$$(2+r)(2-r)\left(\frac{4}{2+r}\right) = (2+r)(2-r)\left(\frac{1}{2-r}\right)$$

$$4(2-r) = 2+r$$
$$8 - 4r = 2+r$$
$$-5r = -6$$

$$r = \frac{6}{5}, \quad \text{or} \quad 1\frac{1}{5} \text{ km/h}$$

15. Let t be the time she paddles out on the lake.

	Distance	Rate	Time
Out	d	2	t
Back	d	4	$1\frac{1}{2} - t$

$$2t = 4\left(1\frac{1}{2} - t\right)$$

$$2t = 6 - 4t$$
$$6t = 6$$
$$t = 1$$

The distance she travels out on the lake is $2t$, or 2 km.

16. Let t be the time she paddles out on the lake.

	Distance	Rate	Time
Out	d	3	t
Back	d	2	$2\frac{1}{2} - t$

$$3t = 2\left(2\frac{1}{2} - t\right)$$

$$3t = 5 - 2t$$
$$5t = 5$$
$$t = 1$$

The distance she travels out on the lake is $3t$, or 3 km.

17. Let r be the speed of the first car.

	Distance	Rate	Time
1st car	300	r	t
2nd car	450	$r+25$	t

$$\frac{300}{r} = \frac{450}{r+25}$$

$$r(r+25) \cdot \frac{300}{r} = r(r+25)\left(\frac{450}{r+25}\right)$$

$$300(r+25) = 450r$$
$$300r + 7500 = 450r$$
$$7500 = 150r$$
$$50 \text{ km/h} = r$$

The first car travels at a speed of 50 km/h. The second car travels at a speed of $r + 25$, or 75 km/h.

18. Let r be the speed of the first car.

	Distance	Rate	Time
1st car	450	r	t
2nd car	600	$r + 30$	t

$$\frac{450}{r} = \frac{600}{r+30}$$

$$r(r+30) \cdot \frac{450}{r} = r(r+30)\left(\frac{600}{r+30}\right)$$

$$450(r+30) = 600r$$
$$450r + 13{,}500 = 600r$$
$$13{,}500 = 150r$$
$$90 \text{ km/h} = r$$

The first car travels at a speed of 90 km/h. The second car travels at a speed of $r + 30$, or 120 km/h.

19. Let x be the number.

$$\frac{1}{5} + \frac{1}{7} = \frac{1}{x}$$

$$35x\left(\frac{1}{5} + \frac{1}{7}\right) = 35x\left(\frac{1}{x}\right)$$

$$\frac{35x}{5} + \frac{35x}{7} = \frac{35x}{x}$$

$$7x + 5x = 35$$
$$12x = 35$$

$$x = \frac{35}{12}$$

20. Let x be the number.

$$\frac{1}{3} + \frac{1}{6} = \frac{1}{x}$$

$$18x\left(\frac{1}{3} + \frac{1}{6}\right) = 18x\left(\frac{1}{x}\right)$$

$$\frac{18x}{3} + \frac{18x}{6} = \frac{18x}{x}$$

$$6x + 3x = 18$$
$$9x = 18$$
$$x = 2$$

21. Let x be the number.

$$x + 6\left(\frac{1}{x}\right) = -5$$

$$x + \frac{6}{x} = -5$$

$$x\left(x + \frac{6}{x}\right) = x \cdot -5$$

$$x^2 + 6 = -5x$$
$$x^2 + 5x + 6 = 0$$
$$(x + 2)(x + 3) = 0$$
$$x = -2 \quad \text{or} \quad x = -3$$

22. Let x be the number.

$$x + 21\left(\frac{1}{x}\right) = -10$$

$$x + \frac{21}{x} = -10$$

$$x\left(x + \frac{21}{x}\right) = x \cdot (-10)$$

$$x^2 + 21 = -10x$$
$$x^2 + 10x + 21 = 0$$
$$(x + 3)(x + 7) = 0$$
$$x = -3 \quad \text{or} \quad x = -7$$

23. Let x be the denominator of the original number. The original number is $\dfrac{x+3}{x}$.

$$\frac{(x+3)+2}{x+2} = \frac{3}{2}$$

$$2(x+2)\left(\frac{x+5}{x+2}\right) = 2(x+2) \cdot \frac{3}{2}$$

$$2(x+5) = 3(x+2)$$
$$2x + 10 = 3x + 6$$
$$4 = x$$

The original number is $\dfrac{4+3}{4}$, or $\dfrac{7}{4}$.

24. Let x be the denominator of the original number. The original number is $\dfrac{x-8}{x}$.

$$\frac{(x-8)-5}{x-5} = \frac{1}{2}$$

$$\frac{x-13}{x-5} = \frac{1}{2}$$

$$2(x-5)\left(\frac{x-13}{x-5}\right) = 2(x-5) \cdot \frac{1}{2}$$

$$2(x-13) = x - 5$$
$$x = 21$$

The original number is $\dfrac{13}{21}$.

25.
$$3 \text{ hours at 55 mph: } 3(55) = 165 \text{ mi}$$

$$10 \text{ miles at 35 mph: } \frac{10}{35} = 17.14 \text{ min}$$

Total driving time: 3 hr, 17.15 hr = 3.286 hr
Total distance: $10 + 165 = 175$ mi

$$\text{Average speed: } \frac{175 \text{ miles}}{3.286 \text{ hours}} = 53.26 \text{ mi/h}$$

26. 100 miles at 40 mi/h

$$t = \frac{d}{r} = \frac{100}{40} = 2\frac{1}{2} \text{ hr}$$

100 miles at 60 mi/h

$$t = \frac{d}{r} = \frac{100}{60} = 1\frac{2}{3} \text{ hr}$$

$$\text{Total } d = 200 \text{ mi}, \; t = 2\frac{1}{2} + 1\frac{2}{3} = 4\frac{1}{6} \text{ hr}$$

$$\text{Average speed} = \frac{200}{4\frac{1}{6}} = 48 \text{ mi/h}$$

27.
d = trip distance
t_1 = time spent driving at 40 mi/h
t_2 = time spent driving at r_2 mi/h
Then $d = 45(t_1 + t_2) = 45t_1 + 45t_2$

$$\frac{d}{2} = 40t_1, \quad \text{or} \quad d = 80t_1$$

Equating our two expressions for d,
$$80t_1 = 45(t_1 + t_2) = 45t_1 + 45t_2$$
$$35t_1 = 45t_2$$

$$\frac{7}{9}t_1 = t_2$$

$$\frac{d}{2} = r_1 t_1 = r_2 t_2$$

$$40t_1 = r_2\left(\frac{7}{9}t_1\right)$$

$$40 = \frac{7}{9}r_2$$

$$r_2 = \frac{9}{7}(40) = \frac{360}{7} = 51\frac{3}{7}$$

28. A: $\dfrac{1}{t+1}$ of the job in 1 hour.

B: $\dfrac{1}{t+6}$ of the job in 1 hour.

C: $\dfrac{1}{2t}$ of the job in 1 hour.

Together, A, B, and C do $\dfrac{1}{t}$ of the job in 1 hour.

$$\dfrac{1}{t+1} + \dfrac{1}{t+6} + \dfrac{1}{2t} = \dfrac{1}{t}$$

The LCM of the denominators is $(t+1)(t+6)(2t)$:

$$\dfrac{(2t)(t+6) + (2t)(t+1) + (t+1)(t+6)}{(2t)(t+1)(t+6)} = \dfrac{2(t+1)(t+6)}{(2t)(t+1)(t+6)}$$

$$2t^2 + 12t + 2t^2 + 2t + t^2 + 7t + 6 = 2t^2 + 14t + 12$$
$$3t^2 + 7t - 6 = 0$$
$$(3t - 2)(t + 3) = 0$$

$$t = \dfrac{2}{3}\,\text{h} \quad \text{or} \quad t = -3\,\text{h}.$$

Since time can't be negative, the solution is $t = \dfrac{2}{3}$ hour.

29. At 4:00, the hour hand has a 20-minute lead on the minute hand. The hour hand travels at $\dfrac{1}{12}$ the minute hand's rate. How far will the minute hand travel to catch the hour hand?

$$d = rt$$

$$d = 20 + \left(\dfrac{r}{12}\right)t$$

So $rt = 20 + \dfrac{rt}{12}$

$$12rt = 240 + rt$$
$$11rt = 240$$

$$rt = \dfrac{240}{11} = 21\dfrac{9}{11}$$

Since $d = rt$, $d = 21\dfrac{9}{11}$ min, $4{:}21\dfrac{9}{11}$

30. At 10:00, the hour hand has a 50-minute lead on the minute hand. When they are perpendicular after 10:30, the hour hand will be 15 min ahead. The hour hand travels at $\dfrac{1}{12}$ the rate of the minute hand.

$d - 15 = rt$, so $d = rt + 15$

$$d = 50 + \left(\dfrac{r}{12}\right)t$$

$$rt + 15 = 50 + \left(\dfrac{r}{12}\right)t$$

$$rt = 35 + \dfrac{rt}{12}$$

$$12rt = 420 + rt$$

$$11rt = 420, \ rt = \dfrac{420}{11} = 38\dfrac{2}{11}$$

$$d = rt = 38\dfrac{2}{11}, \ \text{time} = 10{:}38\dfrac{2}{11}$$

31. a. Let t represent the time in hours the employee needs to drive in order to arrive on time.

	Distance	Rate	Time
Monday	d	45	$t - \dfrac{1}{60}$
Tuesday	d	40	$t + \dfrac{1}{60}$

$$45\left(t - \dfrac{1}{60}\right) = 40\left(t + \dfrac{1}{60}\right)$$

$$45t - \dfrac{3}{4} = 40t + \dfrac{2}{3}$$

$$5t = \dfrac{17}{12}$$

$$t = \dfrac{17}{60}$$

The distance the employee lives from work is $45\left(t - \dfrac{1}{60}\right)$, or 12 miles.

b. Let r be the speed the employee needs to drive to arrive five minutes early.

$$12 = r\left(\dfrac{17}{60} - \dfrac{5}{60}\right)$$

$$12 = \dfrac{12}{60}r$$

$$60\ \text{mi/h} = r$$

32. a. Let d = the distance from Los Angeles to the point of no return. The actual rate of speed from L.A. to Honolulu is 400 mi/h + 50 mi/h and returning from Honolulu is 400 mi/h − 50 mi/h. Using $t = \dfrac{d}{r}$, we have

$$\dfrac{(2574 - d)}{400 + 50} = t = \dfrac{d}{400 - 50}$$

$$350(2574 - d) = 450d$$
$$900{,}900 = (450 + 350)d = 800d$$
$$1126.125 = d$$

The point of no return is $1126\dfrac{1}{8}$ miles from Los Angeles.

b. Since 1187 miles is past the point of no return, it would take less time to continue on to Honolulu.

33. $\dfrac{\dfrac{1}{x} + 2}{\dfrac{1}{x} - 5} = \dfrac{\left(\dfrac{1}{x} + 2\right) \cdot x}{\left(\dfrac{1}{x} - 5\right) \cdot x} = \dfrac{\dfrac{1 + 2x}{x}}{\dfrac{1 - 5x}{x}}$

$$= \dfrac{\dfrac{1 + 2x}{x} \cdot x}{\dfrac{1 - 5x}{x}} = \dfrac{1 + 2x}{1 - 5x}$$

34. $\dfrac{y - \dfrac{2}{y}}{y + \dfrac{2}{y}} = \dfrac{\left(y - \dfrac{2}{y}\right) \cdot y}{\left(y + \dfrac{2}{y}\right) \cdot y} = \dfrac{\dfrac{y^2 - 2}{y}}{\dfrac{y^2 + 2}{y}}$

$$= \dfrac{y^2 - 2}{y} \cdot \dfrac{y}{y^2 + 2} = \dfrac{y^2 - 2}{y^2 + 2}$$

35. $\dfrac{\dfrac{3}{x} + \dfrac{2}{y}}{\dfrac{2}{x} - \dfrac{3}{y}} = \dfrac{\left(\dfrac{3}{x} + \dfrac{2}{y}\right) \cdot xy}{\left(\dfrac{2}{x} - \dfrac{3}{y}\right) \cdot xy}$

$$= \dfrac{\dfrac{3y + 2x}{xy}}{\dfrac{2y - 3x}{xy}}$$

$$= \dfrac{3y + 2x}{xy} \cdot \dfrac{xy}{2y - 3x}$$

$$= \dfrac{3y + 2x}{2y - 3x}$$

36. $8x^2 + 12x - 8 = 4(2x^2 + 3x - 2) = 4(x + 2)(2x - 1)$

37. $2x^2 + x - 3 = (2x + 3)(x - 1)$

38. $x^3 + 27 = x^3 + (3)^3 = (x + 3)(x^2 - 3x + 9)$

39. $x^2 + 3x + 2 = 0$
$(x + 2)(x + 1) = 0$
$\quad x = -2 \quad \text{or} \quad x = -1$

40. $y^2 + 12y + 36 = 0$
$(y + 6)(y + 6) = 0$
$\quad y = -6$

41. $6 = 0.8m$
$$\dfrac{6}{0.8} = \dfrac{0.8m}{0.8}$$
$$7.5 = m$$

```
10   REM   Chapter 6 Problem
20   A = 0
30   INPUT "How many people to do the job? ";N
40   FOR I = 1 to N
50   PRINT "How many hours does person #";I;:
     INPUT " take? ";H
60   A = A + 1 / H
70   NEXT I
80   PRINT "Time for ";N;" people working
     together is ";1 / A;" hours"
90   END
```

```
10   REM   Chapter 6 Challenge Problem
20   INPUT "How much time does it take them
     working together? ";T
30   A = 1 / T
40   INPUT "How many people to do the job? ";N
50   FOR I = 2 TO N
60   PRINT "How many hours does person #";I;:
     INPUT " take? ";H
70   A = A - 1 / H
80   NEXT I
90   PRINT "Time for person one working alone
     is ";1 / A;" hours"
100  END
```

pp. 276–277   6-8 TRY THIS

a.
$$\frac{PV}{T} = k$$
$$T \cdot \frac{PV}{T} = T \cdot k$$
$$PV = Tk$$
$$\frac{PV}{k} = T$$
$$T = \frac{PV}{k}$$

b.
$$\frac{1}{p} + \frac{1}{q} = \frac{1}{f}$$
$$pqf\left(\frac{1}{p} + \frac{1}{q}\right) = pqf\left(\frac{1}{f}\right)$$
$$qf + pf = pq$$
$$f(q + p) = pq$$
$$f = \frac{pq}{q + p}$$

We now substitute in the formula.
$$f = \frac{(10)(15)}{15 + 10}$$
$$f = \frac{150}{25} = 6$$

The focal length of the lens is 6 cm.

p. 278   6-8 EXERCISES

1. $d_1 = \frac{d_2 W_1}{W_2}$ **2.** $W_2 = \frac{d_2 W_1}{d_1}$ **3.** $t = \frac{2S}{v_1 + v_2}$

4. $v_1 = \frac{2S - v_2 t}{t}$ **5.** $r_2 = \frac{Rr_1}{r_1 - R}$ **6.** $R = \frac{r_1 r_2}{r_2 + r_1}$

7. $s = \frac{Rg}{g - R}$ **8.** $g = \frac{Rs}{s - R}$ **9.** $r = \frac{2V - IR}{2I}$

10. $R = \frac{2V - 2Ir}{I}$ **11.** $r = \frac{nE - IR}{In}$ **12.** $n = \frac{IR}{E - Ir}$

13. $H = m(t_1 - t_2)S$ **14.** $t_1 = \frac{H + Smt_2}{Sm}$ **15.** $e = \frac{Er}{R + r}$

16. $r = \frac{eR}{E - e}$ **17.** $a = \frac{S - Sr}{1 - r^n}$ **18.** $r = \frac{S - a}{S}$

19. $\frac{120}{23}$ ohms   **20.** $\frac{10}{3}$ ohms   **21.** 12 cm   **22.** 12 runs

23. In one hour Pam does $\frac{1}{a}$ of the job. Elaine does $\frac{1}{b}$ of the job.

a. Working together Pam and Elaine can perform $\frac{1}{a} + \frac{1}{b} = \frac{1}{t}$ of the job in one hour.
$$abt\left(\frac{1}{a} + \frac{1}{b}\right) = abt\left(\frac{1}{t}\right)$$
$$bt + at = ab$$
$$t(b + a) = ab$$
$$t = \frac{ab}{b + a}$$

b. $bt + at = ab$
$$bt = ab - at$$
$$bt = a(b - t)$$
$$\frac{bt}{b - t} = a$$
$$a = \frac{bt}{b - t}$$

c. $bt + at = ab$
$$bt - ab = -at$$
$$b(t - a) = -at$$
$$b = \frac{-at}{t - a}$$
$$b = \frac{at}{a - t}$$

24. $\frac{1}{M} = \frac{\frac{1}{a} + \frac{1}{b}}{2}$
$$2 \cdot \frac{1}{M} = 2 \cdot \frac{\frac{1}{a} + \frac{1}{b}}{2}$$
$$\frac{2}{M} = \frac{1}{a} + \frac{1}{b}$$
$$\frac{2}{M} = \frac{b + a}{ab}$$
$$Mab \cdot \frac{2}{M} = Mab \cdot \frac{b + a}{ab}$$
$$2ab = M(b + a)$$
$$\frac{2ab}{b + a} = M$$

25. $F = \frac{mv^2}{r}$
$$r \cdot F = r \cdot \frac{mv^2}{r}$$
$$rF = mv^2$$
$$r = \frac{mv^2}{F}$$
$$r = \frac{5(3)}{22.5} = 2 \text{ meters}$$

26. $24xy = 2^3 \cdot 3 \cdot x \cdot y$, $6x^3 = 2 \cdot 3 \cdot x^3$, $8y^2 = 2^3 \cdot y^2$
The LCM is $2^3 \cdot 3 \cdot x^3 \cdot y^2$, or $24x^3 y^2$.

27. $3a = 3 \cdot a$, $6b = 2 \cdot 3 \cdot b$, $7a = 7 \cdot a$
The LCM is $2 \cdot 3 \cdot 7 \cdot a \cdot b$, or $42ab$.

28. $x^2 + x - 12 = 0$
$(x + 4)(x - 3) = 0$
$x = -4$ or $x = 3$

29. $x^2 + 10x + 21 = 0$
$(x + 7)(x + 3) = 0$
$x = -7$ or $x = -3$

30. $x^2 - 25 = 0$
$(x + 5)(x - 5) = 0$
$x = -5$ or $x = 5$

pp. 279–282   6-9 TRY THIS

a. y varies directly as x. $y = 8$ when $x = 20$. $(20, 8)$ is a solution of $y = kx$.
$$8 = 20k$$
$$k = \frac{8}{20} = \frac{2}{5} \text{ or } 0.4$$

The equation of variation is $y = 0.4x$.

b.
$$y = \frac{k}{x}$$
$$0.012 = \frac{k}{50}$$
$$50(0.012) = k$$
$$0.6 = k$$
$$y = \frac{0.6}{x}$$

c. $V = kc$, $V = 10$ when $c = 3$
$$10 = k(3)$$
$$\frac{10}{3} = k$$

The equation of variation is $V = \frac{10}{3}A$.

$$V = \frac{10}{3}(15) = 50 \text{ volts}$$

d. $t = \frac{k}{r}$, $t = 5$ when $r = 60$
$$5 = \frac{k}{60}$$
$$300 = k$$

The equation of variation is $t = \frac{300}{r}$.

$$t = \frac{300}{40} = 7\frac{1}{2} \text{ hours}$$

pp. 283–284   6-9 EXERCISES

1. $k = 8$, $y = 8x$ **2.** $k = \frac{5}{12}$, $y = \frac{5}{12}x$

3. $k = 16$, $y = 16x$ **4.** $k = \frac{2}{5}$, $y = \frac{2}{5}x$

5. $k = 5$, $y = 5x$ **6.** $k = \frac{1}{2}$, $y = \frac{1}{2}x$

7. $k = 1$, $y = x$ **8.** $k = \frac{3}{2}$, $y = \frac{3}{2}x$

9. $k = 60$, $y = \frac{60}{x}$ **10.** $k = 64$; $y = \frac{64}{x}$

11. $k = 36$, $y = \frac{36}{x}$ **12.** $k = 45$, $y = \frac{45}{x}$

13. $k = 9$, $y = \frac{9}{x}$ **14.** $k = 9$, $y = \frac{9}{x}$ **15.** 6 amperes

16. $66\frac{2}{3}$ cm   **17.** $\frac{2}{9}$ ampere   **18.** 27 minutes

19. 125,000   **20.** 3.5 hours   **21.** 160 cm³   **22.** 16.8 kg

23. 532,500 tons   **24.** $6\frac{2}{3}$ hours   **25.** 40 kg

26. 204,000,000   **27.** 450 m   **28.** 50 kg

29. $72 = k \cdot 244$ **30.** $60 = k \cdot 3000$
$$\frac{72}{244} = k$$
$$0.295 = k$$
$$612 = 0.295x$$
$$\frac{612}{0.295} = x$$
$$2074 = x$$

$$\frac{60}{3000} = k$$
$$0.02 = k$$
$$x = (0.02)(5000)$$
$$x = 100 \text{ oz}$$

31. **a.** Inverse variation
b. Direct variation
c. Neither

32. If P varies directly as Q, then $P = kQ$ and $Q = \frac{1}{k} \cdot P$. Since k is a constant, $\frac{1}{k}$ is also a constant. Let $c = \frac{1}{k}$. Then $Q = cP$, which is an equation of direct variation.

33. If A varies inversely as B, then $A = \frac{k}{B}$. Therefore, $AB = k$ and $B = \frac{k}{A}$. Thus B varies inversely as A. From $B = \frac{k}{A}$, $\frac{B}{k} = \frac{1}{A}$. So $\frac{1}{A} = \frac{1}{k}B$. Since k is a constant, $\frac{1}{k}$ is a constant. Let $c = \frac{1}{k}$, then $\frac{1}{A} = cB$, so $\frac{1}{A}$ and B vary directly.

34. $(-4x^2y^{-3})(2x^3y^2) = (-4 \cdot 2)(x^2 \cdot x^3 \cdot y^{-3} \cdot y^2) = -8x^5y^{-1}$

35. $(-5x^2y^5)(-8x^ay^{-3}) = (-5 \cdot -8)(x^2 \cdot x^a \cdot y^5 \cdot y^{-3}) = 40x^{2+a}y^2$

36. $(3.4 \times 10^{10})(5.5 \times 10^{-4}) = (3.4 \times 5.5)(10^{10} \times 10^{-4})$
$$= 18.7 \times 10^6 = 1.87 \times 10^7$$

37. $\frac{21a^5b^3}{3a^2b^2} = \frac{21}{3} \cdot \frac{a^5}{a^2} \cdot \frac{b^3}{b^2} = 7a^3b$

38. $\frac{64w^{-2}v^2}{8w^{-2}v} = \frac{64}{8} \cdot \frac{w^{-2}}{w^{-2}} \cdot \frac{v^2}{v} = 8v$

39. $4.6 \times \frac{10^5}{2.3} \times 10^{-7} = \left(\frac{4.6}{2.3}\right)(10^5 \times 10^{-7}) = 2 \times 10^{-2}$

40. $x^3 - 27 = (x - 3)(x^2 + 3x + 9)$

41. $16x^2 - 36 = 4(4x^2 - 9) = 4(2x + 3)(2x - 3)$

42. $6x^4 - 3x^3 + 18x^2 = 3x^2(2x^2 - x + 6)$

p. 286   6-10 PROBLEM SOLVING: STRATEGIES

1. Strategy: Make a table

Height (h)	1	2	3	4	5	6	7	8	9	10
Total of dots	1(2)	2(3)	3(4)	4(5)	5(6)	6(7)	7(8)	8(9)	9(10)	10(11)

In each array the total number of dots is $h(h + 1)$.
Therefore, in B_{10} there will be $10(10 + 1) = 10(11) = 110$ dots.

2. Strategy: Write an equation
Let x and y represent the page numbers of the facing pages.
$$y = 2x + 11$$
$$\underline{y - x = 23}$$
$$(2x + 11) - x = 23$$
$$x + 11 = 23$$
$$x = 12$$
$$y = 2(12) + 11 = 35$$
Since each sheet is made up of two pages, there will be 11 sheets missing from the book.

3. Strategy: Make a table

Number of bags	1	2	3	4	5	6	7	8	9	10	11	12	13	14	15	16
Seed in 3-lb bag	3	6	9	12	15	18	21	24	27	30	33	36	39	42	45	48
Seed in 5-lb bag	5	10	15	20	25	30	35	40	45	—	—	—	—	—	—	—

To fill the order one could buy sixteen 3-lb bags, or one 3-lb bag and nine 5-lb bags, or six of each, or eleven 3-lb bags and three 5-lb bags.

4. Strategies: Draw a diagram, make a table

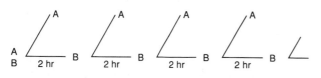

Hours	Number of cells	
0	1A	1B
2	2A	2B
4	4A	4B
6	8A	8B
8	16A	16B
...	...	
N	$2^{1/2N}$	

There would be 2^{12}, or 4096, cells of each type after 24 hours.

5. Strategy: Make a table

1st Waiter															
Days worked	1	2	3	4	5	6	7	8	9	10	11	12	13	14	15
Total earnings	$15	$30	$45	$60	$75	$90	$105	$120	$135	$150	$165	$180	$195	$210	$225

2nd Waiter															
Days worked	1	2	3	4	5	6	7	8	9	10	11	12	13	14	15
Total earnings	$10	$20	$30	$40	$50	$60	$70	$80	$90	$100	$110	$120	$130	$140	$150

One worked 10 days and the other 15 days.

6. Strategy: Make an organized list

Entry Number	Number of Stickers
1–9	1(9) = 9
10–99	90(2) = 180
100–199	100(3) = 300
200–299	100(3) = 300
300–330	31(3) = 93
	Total = 882

The total cost of the stickers is $0.25(882), or $220.50. Each of the 330 entries must pay $220.50/330, or about $0.67, for stickers.

7. Strategy: Make an organized list
They could have scored 34 points 7 different ways.

Touchdowns 6 Points	Extra Points 1 Point	Field Goals 3 Points	Total Points
5	4	0	30 + 4 = 34
5	1	1	30 + 1 + 3 = 34
4	4	2	24 + 4 + 6 = 34
4	1	3	24 + 1 + 9 = 34
3	1	5	18 + 1 + 15 = 34
2	1	7	12 + 1 + 21 = 34
1	1	9	6 + 1 + 27 = 34

1. $\dfrac{4y^2 - 3y}{2y^2 + 5y}$ **2.** $\dfrac{4x^3 - 3x^2 - 4x + 3}{x^3 + 5x^2 - x - 5}$

3. $\dfrac{3a^2 - 3b^2}{4a^2 + 8ab + 4b^2} = \dfrac{3(a^2 - b^2)}{4(a^2 + 2ab + b^2)} = \dfrac{3(a+b)(a-b)}{4(a+b)(a+b)} = \dfrac{3(a-b)}{4(a+b)}$

4. $\dfrac{3x^2 - 4x - 4}{4x^2 - 3x - 10} = \dfrac{(3x+2)(x-2)}{(4x+5)(x-2)} = \dfrac{3x+2}{4x+5}$

5. $\dfrac{x^3 - 64}{8x^3 + 1} \cdot \dfrac{4x^2 - 1}{x^2 + 4x + 16} = \dfrac{(x-4)(x^2+4x+16)(2x+1)(2x-1)}{(2x+1)(4x^2-2x+1)(x^2+4x+16)}$

$= \dfrac{(x-4)(2x-1)}{4x^2 - 2x + 1}$

6. $\dfrac{6y^2}{y^2 - 9} \div \dfrac{3y^2}{2y^2 + 7y + 3} = \dfrac{6y^2}{(y+3)(y-3)} \cdot \dfrac{(2y+1)(y+3)}{3y^2}$

$= \dfrac{2(2y+1)}{y - 3}$

7. $\dfrac{a+9}{a+3} + \dfrac{12-5a}{a+3} = \dfrac{-4a+21}{a+3}$

8. $\dfrac{y+2}{y-3} + \dfrac{y}{3-y} = \dfrac{y+2}{y-3} + \dfrac{y}{-1(-3+y)} = \dfrac{y+2}{y-3} - \dfrac{y}{y-3} = \dfrac{2}{y-3}$

9. $\dfrac{7}{x^2 - 81} - \dfrac{x-4}{3x^2 - 25x - 18} = \dfrac{7(3x+2)}{(x^2-81)(3x+2)}$

$- \dfrac{(x-4)(x+9)}{(3x^2-25x-18)(x+9)}$

$x^2 - 81 = (x+9)(x-9)$ $= \dfrac{21x + 14 - (x^2 + 5x - 36)}{(x^2-81)(3x+2)}$

$3x^2 - 25x - 18 = (3x+2)(x-9)$

$\text{LCM} = (x+9)(x-9)(3x+2)$ $= \dfrac{-x^2 + 16x + 50}{(x+9)(x-9)(3x+2)}$

10. $\dfrac{1}{3y} + \dfrac{4y}{y^2 - 1} + \dfrac{7}{y-1} = \dfrac{y^2-1}{3y(y^2-1)} + \dfrac{12y^2}{3y(y^2-1)} + \dfrac{7(y+1)3y}{3y(y^2-1)}$

$= \dfrac{34y^2 + 21y - 1}{3y(y+1)(y-1)}$

$\text{LCM} = (y+1)(y-1)3y$

11. $\dfrac{\dfrac{1}{a} + \dfrac{1}{b}}{\dfrac{1}{a} - \dfrac{1}{b}} = \dfrac{\dfrac{b+a}{ab}}{\dfrac{b-a}{ab}} = \dfrac{b+a}{b-a}$

12. $\dfrac{\dfrac{x^2 - 16}{x^2 - 6x + 9}}{\dfrac{x^2 - 3x - 4}{x^2 - 2x - 3}} = \dfrac{(x+4)(x-4)}{(x-3)(x-3)} \cdot \dfrac{(x-3)(x+1)}{(x-4)(x+1)} = \dfrac{(x+4)}{(x-3)}$

13. $\dfrac{a^{-1} - b^{-1}}{a^{-2} - b^{-2}} = \dfrac{\dfrac{1}{a} - \dfrac{1}{b}}{\dfrac{1}{a^2} - \dfrac{1}{b^2}} = \dfrac{\dfrac{b-a}{ab}}{\dfrac{b^2-a^2}{a^2b^2}} = \dfrac{(b-a)(ab)}{b^2 - a^2} = \dfrac{(ab)}{(b+a)}$

14. $\dfrac{10y^4}{2y^2} - \dfrac{8y^3}{2y^2} + \dfrac{12y^2}{2y^2} = 5y^2 - 4y + 6$

15.
$$2x - 3 \overline{\smash{\big)}\ 4x^4 + 0x^3 - 5x^2 + 2x - 10}$$
quotient: $2x^3 + 3x^2 + 2x + 4 + \dfrac{2}{2x-3}$

$\underline{-(4x^4 - 6x^3)}$
$6x^3 - 5x^2$
$\underline{-(6x^3 - 9x^2)}$
$4x^2 + 2x$
$\underline{-(4x^2 - 6x)}$
$8x - 10$
$\underline{-(8x - 12)}$
2

16.

2⌋	1	−3	0	−2	4
		2	−2	−4	−12
	1	−1	−2	−6	−8

$x^3 - x^2 - 2x - 6$, R: −8

17. $-1\rfloor \quad 3 \quad\;\; 5 \quad\;\; 0 \quad -3$

$\qquad\qquad -3 \quad -2 \quad\;\; 2$

$\qquad\quad\overline{3 \quad\;\; 2 \quad -2 \mid -1}$

$\qquad 3x^2 + 2x - 2, \text{ R: } -1$

18. $\dfrac{x^2}{x+3} = \dfrac{9}{x+3}$

$\qquad x^2 = 9$

$\qquad x = 3 \quad \text{or} \quad x = -3$

The solution is $x = 3$.

19. $\qquad \dfrac{15}{y} - \dfrac{15}{y-2} = -2$

$\qquad 15(y-2) - 15(y) = -2y(y-2)$

$\qquad\qquad\qquad -30 = -2y^2 + 4y$

$\qquad\qquad 2y^2 - 4y - 30 = 0$

$\qquad\quad 2(y^2 - 2y - 15) = 0$

$\qquad 2(y-5)(y+3) = 0 \qquad y = 5 \quad \text{or} \quad y = -3$

20. $\dfrac{2}{y+4} + \dfrac{2y-1}{y^2+2y-8} = \dfrac{1}{y-2}$

$\qquad 2(y-2) + 2y - 1 = y + 4$

$\qquad 2y - 4 + 2y - 1 = y + 4$

$\qquad\qquad\quad 4y - 5 = y + 4$

$\qquad\qquad\qquad 3y = 9$

$\qquad\qquad\qquad\;\; y = 3$

21. $d = rt$ $\qquad\qquad\qquad \dfrac{90}{x} = \dfrac{60}{x-10}$

$\quad 90 = xt$

$\quad 60 = (x-10)t \qquad 90(x-10) = 60x$

$\qquad\qquad\qquad\qquad 90x - 900 = 60x$

$\qquad\qquad\qquad\qquad\quad 30x = 900$

$\qquad\qquad\qquad\qquad\quad\;\; x = 30 \text{ km/h}$

$\qquad\qquad\qquad\quad x - 10 = 20 \text{ km/h}$

22. $d = rt \qquad\qquad d = rt$

$\quad 1 = r(3)$

$\qquad\qquad\qquad\quad 10 = \left(\dfrac{1}{3} + \dfrac{2}{5}\right)t$

$\quad 1 = r\left(\dfrac{5}{2}\right)$

$\qquad\qquad\qquad\quad 10 = \left(\dfrac{5}{15} + \dfrac{6}{15}\right)t$

$\qquad\qquad\quad 13\dfrac{7}{11} = \dfrac{150}{11} = t$

23. $\qquad\qquad R = 420$

$\qquad\qquad R = 420 + x \quad \text{with the wind}$

$\qquad\qquad R = 420 - x \quad \text{against the wind}$

$\qquad\qquad 560 = (420 - x)t$

$\qquad\qquad 840 = (420 + x)t$

$\qquad\qquad \dfrac{560}{420-x} = \dfrac{840}{420+x}$

$\qquad 560(420 + x) = 840(420 - x)$

$\quad 235,200 + 560x = 352,800 - 840x$

$\qquad\qquad 1400x = 117,600$

$\qquad\qquad\qquad x = 84 \text{ mi/h}$

24. $T = Rn + \dfrac{mn}{p}$ **25.** $\dfrac{1}{p} + \dfrac{1}{q} = \dfrac{1}{f}$

$\quad T - Rn = \dfrac{mn}{p} \qquad\qquad \dfrac{1}{q} = \dfrac{1}{f} - \dfrac{1}{p}$

$\quad p(T - Rn) = mn$

$\qquad\qquad\qquad\qquad 1 = \dfrac{q}{f} - \dfrac{q}{p} = q\left(\dfrac{1}{f} - \dfrac{1}{p}\right)$

$\qquad p = \dfrac{mn}{(T - Rn)}$

$\qquad\qquad\qquad\qquad\quad = q\left(\dfrac{p-f}{fp}\right)$

$\qquad\qquad\qquad\qquad\quad q = \dfrac{fp}{p-f}$

26. $y = kx$

$\quad 36 = k(8)$

$\quad k = \dfrac{36}{8} = \dfrac{9}{2}$

$\quad y = \dfrac{9}{2}x$

27. $\qquad M = kE$

$\qquad 12 = k(75)$

$\quad \dfrac{4}{25} = \dfrac{12}{75} = k$

$\qquad 27 = \dfrac{4}{25}E$

$\qquad E = \dfrac{27 \cdot 25}{4} = 168.75 \text{ kg}$

28. $y = \dfrac{k}{x}$ $\qquad$ **29.** $B = \dfrac{k}{W}$

$\quad 36 = \dfrac{k}{8} \qquad\qquad\quad 25 = \dfrac{k}{8}$

$\quad\;\; k = 288 \qquad\qquad\quad K = 200$

$\quad\;\; y = \dfrac{288}{x} \qquad\qquad\;\; B = \dfrac{200}{5} = 40 \text{ days}$

p. 289   CHAPTER 6 TEST

1. $\dfrac{y+1}{2y-3} \cdot \dfrac{y^2}{y^2} = \dfrac{y^3+y^2}{2y^3-3y^2}$

2. $\dfrac{5x^2+38x+21}{3x^2+22x+7} = \dfrac{(5x+3)(x+7)}{(3x+1)(x+7)} = \dfrac{5x+3}{3x+1}$

3. $\dfrac{y^3+27}{9y} \cdot \dfrac{3y}{y+3} = \dfrac{(y+3)(y^2-3y+9) \cdot 3y}{9y(y+3)} = \dfrac{y^2-3y+9}{3}$

4. $\dfrac{8t^5}{t^2-25} \div \dfrac{4t^2}{7t^2-34t-5} = \dfrac{8t^5}{(t+5)(t-5)} \cdot \dfrac{(7t+1)(t-5)}{4t^2}$

$\qquad = \dfrac{2t^3(7t+1)}{(t+5)}$

5. $\dfrac{t+9}{t-5} + \dfrac{2t}{5-t} = \dfrac{t+9}{t-5} + \dfrac{2t}{-1(t-5)} = \dfrac{t+9-2t}{t-5} = \dfrac{-t+9}{t-5}$

6. $\dfrac{4}{5(x-3)} + \dfrac{x+8}{(4x+1)(x-3)} = \dfrac{4(4x+1)+5(x+8)}{5(4x+1)(x-3)}$

$\qquad = \dfrac{21x+44}{5(4x+1)(x-3)}$

7. $\dfrac{8}{(y+8)(y-8)} - \dfrac{y-5}{(2y+1)(y-8)} = \dfrac{8(2y+1)-(y-5)(y+8)}{(2y+1)(y+8)(y-8)}$

$\qquad = \dfrac{16y+8-(y^2+3y-40)}{(2y+1)(y+8)(y-8)} = \dfrac{-y^2+13y+48}{(2y+1)(y+8)(y-8)}$

$\qquad = \dfrac{-(y-16)(y+3)}{(2y+1)(y+8)(y-8)}$

8. $\dfrac{1}{2x} + \dfrac{4x}{x^2-1} - \dfrac{2}{x+1} = \dfrac{x^2-1+8x^2-(4x^2-4x)}{2x(x^2-1)} = \dfrac{5x^2+4x-1}{2x(x^2-1)}$

$\qquad = \dfrac{(5x-1)(x+1)}{2x(x+1)(x-1)} = \dfrac{5x-1}{2x(x-1)}$

9. $\dfrac{b^2+3b-10}{b^2-5b+6} \cdot \dfrac{b^2-4b-5}{b^2-25} = \dfrac{(b+5)(b-2)(b-5)(b+1)}{(b-3)(b-2)(b+5)(b-5)}$

$\qquad = \dfrac{b+1}{b-3}$

10. $\dfrac{\dfrac{1}{3a}-4}{\dfrac{1}{2u}-1} = \dfrac{2-24a}{3-6a} = \dfrac{2(1-12a)}{3(1-2a)}$

11. $\dfrac{-6x^3}{-2x} + \dfrac{4x^2}{-2x} - \dfrac{10x}{-2x} = 3x^2 - 2x + 5$

12.
$$\begin{array}{r} 5x^3 + x - 1 + \dfrac{1}{3x-1} \\ 3x-1{\overline{\smash{)}\,15x^4 - 5x^3 + 3x^2 - 4x + 2}} \\ \underline{-(15x^4 - 5x^3)} \\ 3x^2 - 4x \\ \underline{-(3x^2 - x)} \\ -3x + 2 \\ \underline{-(-3x + 1)} \\ 1 \end{array}$$

13.
$$\begin{array}{r|rrrrr} 2 & 1 & -2 & 3 & -1 & 2 \\ & & 2 & 0 & 6 & 10 \\ \hline & 1 & 0 & 3 & 5 & | \; 12 \end{array}$$

Q: $x^3 + 3x + 5$, R: 12

14.
$$\begin{array}{r|rrrrr} -1 & 2 & -1 & -2 & -2 & -3 \\ & & -2 & 3 & -1 & 3 \\ \hline & 2 & -3 & 1 & -3 & | \; 0 \end{array}$$

Q: $2x^3 - 3x^2 + x - 3$, R: 0

15.
$$\frac{x}{x-1} = \frac{7}{1-x}$$
$$x(1-x) = 7(x-1)$$
$$x - x^2 = 7x - 7$$
$$x^2 + 6x - 7 = 0$$
$$(x+7)(x-1) = 0$$
$$x = -7 \quad \text{or} \quad x = 1$$
Solution is $x = -7$.

16.
$$\frac{12}{x-1} - \frac{8}{x} = 2$$
$$12x - 8x + 8 = 2x(x-1)$$
$$4x + 8 = 2x^2 - 2x$$
$$2x^2 - 6x - 8 = 0$$
$$2(x^2 - 3x - 4) = 0$$
$$2(x-4)(x+1) = 0$$
$$x = 4 \quad \text{or} \quad x = -1$$

17.
$$W = J + 3$$
$$\frac{60}{J+3} = \frac{48}{J}$$
$$60J = 48J + 144$$
$$12J = 144$$
$$J = 12 \text{ mi/h}$$
$$W = 15 \text{ mi/h}$$

18.
$$\frac{1}{4} + \frac{1}{r} = \frac{2}{5}$$
$$\frac{r+4}{4r} = \frac{2}{5}$$
$$5r + 20 = 8r$$
$$20 = 3r$$
$$r = \frac{20}{3} = 6\frac{2}{3} \text{ hr}$$

19.
$$\frac{E}{e} = \frac{T+r}{r}$$
$$T + r = \frac{rE}{e}$$
$$T = \frac{rE}{e} - r$$
$$\text{or } T = \frac{rE - re}{e}$$

20.
$$y = kx$$
$$5 = k16$$
$$k = \frac{5}{16}$$
$$y = \frac{5}{16}x$$

21.
$$y = \frac{k}{x}$$
$$5 = \frac{k}{16}$$
$$k = 80$$
$$y = \frac{80}{x}$$

22.
$$t = \frac{k}{p}$$
$$18 = \frac{k}{12}$$
$$k = 216$$
$$t = \frac{216}{8} = 27 \text{ hours}$$

23.
$$t = kd$$
$$8 = k380$$
$$k = \frac{8}{380}$$
$$t = \frac{8}{380}(475)$$
$$t = 10 \text{ hours}$$

CHAPTER 7

p. 290 READY FOR POWERS, ROOTS, AND COMPLEX NUMBERS?

1. 8 **2.** 0 **3.** $\sqrt{3}$ **4.** y^{10} **5.** 8 **6.** $12x^5y^{-2}$
7. 4^6 **8.** 3^2 **9.** $8x^{-1}y^6$ **10.** 4^8 **11.** a^{12}
12. $64x^3y^{-9}$ **13.** $100x^6y^{-4}z^{-8}$ **14.** 8 **15.** $-\dfrac{14}{11}$
16. $5, -3$ **17.** $-5, 7$ **18.** $2 + 5y - 12y^2$
19. $9x^2 + 48x + 64$ **20.** $4x^2 - 9$ **21.** $(x+1)(x-1)$
22. $(4x^2 - 5y^4)^2$ **23.** $-3(3x-2)^2$ **24.** $(x-4)(x-9)$

pp. 292–295 7-1 TRY THIS

a. $3, -3$ **b.** $6, -6$ **c.** $11, -11$ **d.** 1 **e.** -6
f. $\dfrac{9}{10}$ **g.** -0.08 **h.** 24 **i.** $5|y|$ **j.** $4|y|$ **k.** $|x+7|$
l. -4 **m.** $3y$ **n.** $-\dfrac{7}{4}$ **o.** $b^5 = a$ **p.** $c^{12} = 63$
q. $n^9 = 16a$ **r.** -3 **s.** -3 **t.** $-2x$ **u.** $3x + 2$
v. 3 **w.** -3 **x.** no real root **y.** $2|x-2|$ **z.** $|x+3|$

pp. 295–296 7-1 EXERCISES

1. $4, -4$ **2.** $15, -15$ **3.** $12, -12$ **4.** $3, -3$
5. $20, -20$ **6.** $9, -9$ **7.** $-\dfrac{7}{6}$ **8.** $-\dfrac{19}{3}$ **9.** 14
10. $-\dfrac{4}{9}$ **11.** $\dfrac{9}{12} = \dfrac{3}{4}$ **12.** 0.3 **13.** -0.07 **14.** 0.12
15. $4|x|$ **16.** $6|b|$ **17.** $5|t|$ **18.** $7|c|$ **19.** $|a+1|$
20. $|5 - b|$ **21.** $|x - 2|$ **22.** $|2x + 7|$ **23.** 3 **24.** -4
25. $-4x$ **26.** $-5y$ **27.** 10 **28.** $-4xy^2$ **29.** $0.7(x+1)$
30. $0.2(y-2)$ **31.** $p^4 = 10$ **32.** $k^8 = 56$ **33.** $r^{28} = 500h$
34. $a^x = y$ **35.** 5 **36.** -4 **37.** -1 **38.** 2
39. $-\dfrac{2}{3}$ **40.** $-\dfrac{1}{2}$ **41.** $|x|$ **42.** $|y|$ **43.** $5|a|$ **44.** $7|b|$
45. 6 **46.** 10 **47.** y **48.** -6 **49.** $x - 2$ **50.** $2xy$

51. **a.** $N = 2.5\sqrt{25}$ **b.** $N = 2.5\sqrt{36}$
$ = 2.5(5)$ $ = 2.5(6)$
$N = 13$ $N = 15$
c. $N = 2.5\sqrt{49}$ **d.** $N = 2.5\sqrt{64}$
$ = 2.5(7)$ $ = 2.5(8)$
$N = 18$ $N = 20$

52. $f(x) = \sqrt{x}$ **53.** $f(x) = \sqrt[3]{x}$
$\{x \mid x \geq 0\}$ $\{\text{All real numbers}\}$
54. $f(x) = \sqrt{2x + 8}$ **55.** $f(x) = \sqrt{4 - 3x}$
$2x + 8 \geq 0$ $4 - 3x \geq 0$
$x \geq -4$ $-3x \geq 4$
$\{x \mid x \geq -4\}$ $x \leq -\dfrac{4}{3}$
$\left\{ x \mid x \leq \dfrac{4}{3} \right\}$
56. $f(x) = \sqrt{-3x^2}$ **57.** $f(x) = \sqrt{x^2 + 1}$
$-3x^2 \geq 0$ $x^2 + 1 \geq 0$
$x^2 \leq 0$ $x^2 \geq -1$
$\{x \mid x = 0\}$ $\{\text{All real numbers}\}$

58. Answers may vary. Some examples are 1 and 1, 16 and 1024, 81 and 59,049. Note that $\sqrt{x^4} = \sqrt[5]{x^{10}}$

59. $f(x) = \dfrac{\sqrt{x}}{2x^2 - 3x - 5}$

$f(x) = \dfrac{\sqrt{x}}{(2x - 5)(x + 1)}$

$x \geq 0$ and $2x - 5 \neq 0$ and $x + 1 \neq 0$

$x \geq 0$ and $x \neq -\dfrac{5}{2}$ and $x \neq -1$

$x \neq -1$ is already restricted by $x \geq 0$

$\left\{ x \mid x \geq 0 \text{ and } x \neq \dfrac{5}{2} \right\}$

60. $f(x) = \dfrac{\sqrt{x + 3}}{x^2 - x - 2}$

$f(x) = \dfrac{\sqrt{x + 3}}{(x + 1)(x - 2)}$

$x + 3 \geq 0$ and $x + 1 \neq 0$ and $x - 2 \neq 0$
$x \geq -3$ and $x \neq -1$ and $x \neq 2$
$\{ x \mid x \geq -3 \text{ and } x \neq -1 \text{ and } x \neq 2 \}$

61. $f(x) = \dfrac{\sqrt{x + 1}}{x + |x|}$

$x \neq 0$
$2 = \sqrt{x + 1}$
$4 = x + 1$
$3 = x$
$\{ x \mid x > 0 \}$

62. $\dfrac{1}{3} + \dfrac{2}{5} = \dfrac{x}{6}$

$\dfrac{10}{30} + \dfrac{12}{30} = \dfrac{5x}{30}$

$22 = 5x$

$\dfrac{22}{5} = x$

63. $y \left(y - \dfrac{4}{y} = 3 \right)$

$y^2 - 4 = 3y$
$y^2 - 3y - 4 = 0$
$(y + 1)(y - 4) = 0$
$y + 1 = 0;\ y - 4 = 0$
$y = -1;\ y = 4$

64. $\dfrac{2}{x - 2} = \dfrac{5}{x + 4}$

$2x + 8 = 5x - 10$
$18 = 3x$
$6 = x$
$\{6\}$

65. Let $x =$ number
$x^2 - x = 6$
$x^2 - x - 6 = 0$
$(x + 2)(x - 3) = 0$
$x = -2;\ x = 3$
3, or -2

66.
$x =$ sophomore year
$x + 426 =$ junior year
$2x + 426 =$ senior year
$3416 = 2x + 426 + (2x + 426)$
$3416 = 4x + 852$
$2564 = 4x$
$641 = x$
Soph. 641 yd, jr. 1067 yd, sr. 1708 yd

pp. 297–298 7-2 TRY THIS

a. $\sqrt{19}\,\sqrt{7} = \sqrt{133}$
b. $\sqrt{x + 2y}\,\sqrt{x - 2y} = \sqrt{(x + 2y)(x - 2y)} = \sqrt{x^2 - 4y^2}$
c. $\sqrt[4]{403}\,\sqrt[4]{7} = \sqrt[4]{2821}$
d. $\sqrt[3]{8x}\,\sqrt[3]{x^4 + 5} = \sqrt[3]{8x(x^4 + 5)} = \sqrt[3]{8x^5 + 40x}$
e. $\sqrt{32} = \sqrt{16 \cdot 2} = 4\sqrt{2}$ **f.** $\sqrt[3]{80} = \sqrt[3]{8 \cdot 10} = 2\sqrt[3]{10}$
g. $\sqrt{300} = \sqrt{100 \cdot 3} = 10\sqrt{3}$
h. $\sqrt{3x^2 + 12x + 12} = \sqrt{3(x^2 + 4x + 4)}$
  $= \sqrt{3(x + 2)^2} = |x + 2|\sqrt{3}$
i. $\sqrt{12ab^3/c^2} = \sqrt{4 \cdot 3ab^3c^2} = 2|bc|\sqrt{3ab}$
j. $\sqrt[3]{16} = \sqrt[3]{8 \cdot 2} = 2\sqrt[3]{2}$
k. $\sqrt[4]{81x^4y^8} = 3|x|y^2$ **l.** $\sqrt[3]{(a + b)^4} = (a + b)\sqrt[3]{a + b}$
m. $\sqrt{3}\,\sqrt{6} = \sqrt{3 \cdot 6} = \sqrt{18} = \sqrt{9 \cdot 2} = 3\sqrt{2}$
n. $\sqrt{18y}\,\sqrt{14y} = \sqrt{252y^2} = \sqrt{36 \cdot 7y^2} = 6|y|\sqrt{7}$
o. $\sqrt[3]{3x^2y}\,\sqrt[3]{36x} = \sqrt[3]{108x^3y} = \sqrt[3]{27 \cdot 4x^3y} = 3x\sqrt[3]{4y}$
p. $\sqrt{7a} + \sqrt{21b} = \sqrt{147ab} = \sqrt{49 \cdot 3ab} = 7\sqrt{3ab}$

p. 299 7-2 EXERCISES

1. $\sqrt{6}$ **2.** $\sqrt{35}$ **3.** $\sqrt[3]{10}$ **4.** $\sqrt[3]{14}$ **5.** $\sqrt[4]{72}$

6. $\sqrt[4]{18}$ **7.** $\sqrt{30ab}$ **8.** $\sqrt{26xy}$ **9.** $\sqrt[3]{18t^3}$

10. $\sqrt[3]{80y^4}$ **11.** $\sqrt{x^2 - a^2}$ **12.** $\sqrt{y^2 - b^2}$ **13.** $\sqrt[3]{0.06x^2}$

14. $\sqrt[3]{0.21y^2}$ **15.** $\sqrt[4]{x^3 - 1}$ **16.** $\sqrt[3]{(x - 2)^3}$ **17.** $\sqrt{\dfrac{6y}{5x}}$

18. $2\sqrt{6}$ **19.** $2\sqrt{5}$ **20.** $6x^2\sqrt{5}$ **21.** $5|y^3|\sqrt{7}$

22. $3x^2\sqrt[3]{2x^2}$ **23.** $2y\sqrt[3]{5}$ **24.** $2x^2\sqrt[3]{10x^2}$ **25.** $3m\sqrt[3]{4m^2}$

26. $2\sqrt[4]{2}$ **27.** $2\sqrt[4]{5}$ **28.** $3|cd|\sqrt[4]{2d^2}$ **29.** $3x^2y^2\sqrt[4]{3y^2}$

30. $(x + y)\sqrt[3]{x + y}$ **31.** $2xy\sqrt[3]{2xy^4}$ **32.** $|a + b|\sqrt[6]{a + b}$

33. $2y\sqrt[9]{x^3y^3}$ **34.** $3\sqrt{2}$ **35.** $5\sqrt{2}$ **36.** 8 **37.** $4\sqrt{3}$

38. $6\sqrt{7}$ **39.** $30\sqrt{3}$ **40.** $3\sqrt[3]{2}$ **41.** $5|b|c^2\sqrt{2b}$

42. $2x^2|y|\sqrt{6}$ **43.** $2y^3\sqrt[3]{2}$ **44.** $25t^3\sqrt[3]{t}$ **45.** $(b + 3)^2$

46. $(x + y)^2\sqrt[3]{(x + y)^2}$

47. $r = 2\sqrt{5(20)}$ **48.** $r = 2\sqrt{5(70)}$ **49.** $r = 2\sqrt{5(156.8)}$
  $= 2(10)$ $= 2(18.70)$ $= 2\sqrt{784}$
  $r = 20$ mi/h $r = 37.4$ mi/h $= 2(28)$
  $r = 56$ mi/h

50. Answers may vary. Examples are $\sqrt{2} \cdot \sqrt{125}$, $\sqrt{25} \cdot \sqrt{10}$, and $\sqrt{50} \cdot \sqrt{5}$.

51. $T = 7°C$, $v = 8$ mi/sec
$T_w = 33 - (10.45 + 10\sqrt{8} - 8)(33 - 7) \div 22$
  $= 33 - (2.45 + 20\sqrt{2})(26) \div 22$
  $= 33 - (2.45 + 20(1.41))(26) \div 22$
  $= 33 - (30.73)(26) \div 22$
  $= 33 - (799.1) \div 22$
  $= 33 - 36.32$
$T_w = -3.3°C$

52. $T = 0°C$, $v = 12$ mi/sec
$T_w = 33 - (10.45 + 10\sqrt{12} - 12)(33 - 0) \div 22$
  $= 33 - (-1.55 + 20(1.73))(33) \div 22$
  $= 33 - (-1.55 + 34.60)(33) \div 22$
  $= 33 - (1090.65) \div 22$
  $= 33 - 49.6$
$T_w = -16.6°C$

53. $T = -23°C$, $v = 15$ mi/sec
$T_w = 33 - (10.45 + 10\sqrt{15} - 15)(33 + 23) \div 22$
  $= 33 - (-4.55 + 38.7)(56) \div 22$
  $= 33 - (1912.4) \div 22$
  $= 33 - 87$
$T_w = -54°C$

54. $4x^2 + 6x + 2$ **55.** $3y^2 - 14y - 5$ **56.** $9a^2 - 3a$
$2(2x^2 + 3x + 1)$ $(3y + 1)(y - 5)$ $3a(3a - 1)$
$2(2x + 1)(x + 1)$

57. $\begin{array}{r} x + 7 \\ x + 3\overline{)x^2 + 10x + 21} \\ \underline{-x^2 - 3x} \\ 7x + 21 \\ \underline{-7x - 21} \\ 0 \end{array}$ **58.** $\begin{array}{r} 3y + 2,\ R: -2 \\ y - 5\overline{)3y^2 - 13y - 12} \\ \underline{-3y^2 + 15y} \\ 2y - 12 \\ \underline{-2y + 10} \\ -2 \end{array}$

pp. 301–303 7-3 TRY THIS

a. $\dfrac{5}{6}$ **b.** $\dfrac{10}{3}$ **c.** $\dfrac{|x|}{10}$ **d.** $\dfrac{2|a|\sqrt{a}}{b^2}$

e. $\dfrac{\sqrt{75}}{\sqrt{3}} = \sqrt{\dfrac{75}{3}} = \sqrt{25} = 5$

f. $\dfrac{14\sqrt{128xy}}{2\sqrt{2}} = 7\sqrt{64xy} = 7 \cdot 8\sqrt{xy} = 56\sqrt{xy}$

g. $\dfrac{4\sqrt[3]{250}}{7\sqrt[3]{2}} = \dfrac{4\sqrt[3]{125}}{7} = \dfrac{20}{7}$ **h.** $\dfrac{\sqrt[3]{8a^3b}}{\sqrt[3]{27b^{-2}}} = \dfrac{2ab}{3}$

i. $13\sqrt{2}$ **j.** $10\sqrt[4]{5x} - \sqrt{7}$

k. $7\sqrt{45} - 2\sqrt{5} = 21\sqrt{5} - 2\sqrt{5} = 19\sqrt{5}$

l. $3\sqrt[3]{y^5} + 4\sqrt[3]{y^2} + \sqrt[3]{8y^6} = 3y\sqrt[3]{y^2} + 4\sqrt[3]{y^2} + 2y^2$

$\qquad = (3y + 4)\sqrt[3]{y^2} + 2y^2$

m. $\sqrt{25x - 25} - \sqrt{9x - 9} = 5\sqrt{x - 1} - 3\sqrt{x - 1}$

$\qquad = 2\sqrt{x - 1}$

n. $\sqrt[3]{54} - \sqrt{54} = 3\sqrt[3]{2} - 3\sqrt{6} = 3(\sqrt[3]{2} - \sqrt{6})$

pp. 303–304   7-3 EXERCISES

1. $\frac{4}{5}$ **2.** $\frac{10}{9}$ **3.** $\frac{4}{3}$ **4.** $\frac{7}{8}$ **5.** $\frac{7}{|y|}$ **6.** $\frac{11}{|x|}$

7. $\frac{5|y|\sqrt{y}}{x^2}$ **8.** $\frac{6a^2\sqrt{a}}{|b^3|}$ **9.** $\frac{2x\sqrt[3]{x^2}}{3y}$ **10.** $\frac{2x\sqrt[3]{x}}{3y^2}$

11. $\sqrt{7}$ **12.** $\sqrt{7}$ **13.** 3   **14.** 2   **15.** $|y|\sqrt{5y}$

16. $2|b|\sqrt{2b}$ **17.** $2\sqrt[3]{a^2b}$ **18.** $3xy\sqrt[3]{y^2}$ **19.** $3\sqrt{xy}$

20. $\frac{5\sqrt{ab}}{3}$ **21.** $\sqrt{x^2 + xy + y^2}$ **22.** $\sqrt{r^2 - rs + s^2}$

23. $8\sqrt{3}$ **24.** $17\sqrt{5}$ **25.** $3\sqrt[3]{5}$ **26.** $8\sqrt[5]{2}$ **27.** $13\sqrt[3]{y}$

28. $3\sqrt[4]{t}$ **29.** $7\sqrt{2}$ **30.** $7\sqrt{6}$ **31.** $6\sqrt[3]{5}$

32. $6\sqrt{7} + \sqrt[4]{11}$ **33.** $23\sqrt{2}$ **34.** $9\sqrt{3}$ **35.** $21\sqrt{3}$

36. $41\sqrt{2}$ **37.** $38\sqrt{5}$ **38.** $66\sqrt{3}$ **39.** $122\sqrt{2}$ **40.** $4\sqrt{5}$

41. $9\sqrt[3]{2}$ **42.** -7 **43.** $4\sqrt[4]{4}$ **44.** $-3\sqrt[3]{5}$ **45.** $29\sqrt{2}$

46. $55\sqrt{2}$ **47.** $(1 + 6|a|)\sqrt{5a}$ **48.** $(4|x| - 2)\sqrt{3x}$

49. $(2 - x)\sqrt[3]{3x}$ **50.** $(3 - x)\sqrt[3]{2x}$ **51.** $10(a - 1)\sqrt[3]{a}$

52. $2(9x - 4)\sqrt[3]{2x^2y}$ **53.** $3\sqrt{2y - 2}$ **54.** $3\sqrt{3t + 3}$

55. $(|x| + 3)\sqrt{x - 1}$ **56.** $(2 - |x|)\sqrt{x - 1}$

57. $T = 2(3, 14)\sqrt{\frac{65}{980}}$ **58.** $T = 2(3.14)\sqrt{\frac{98}{980}}$

$\qquad = 6.28\sqrt{0.066}$ $= 6.28\sqrt{0.01}$

$\qquad = 6.28(0.258)$ $= 6.28(0.316)$

$\qquad T = 1.62$ sec $T = 1.99$ sec

59. $T = 2(3.14)\sqrt{\frac{120}{980}}$

$\qquad = 6.28(0.35)$

$\qquad T = 2.20$ sec

60. $\sqrt{a} + \sqrt{b} = \sqrt{a + b}$

Squaring both sides

$a + 2\sqrt{a}\sqrt{b} = a + b$

$2\sqrt{a}\sqrt{b} = 0$

$\sqrt{a}\sqrt{b} = 0$

$\sqrt{a} = 0$ or $\sqrt{b} = 0$

$a = 0$ or $b = 0$

Expressions under radicals are assumed nonnegative, so

$a = 0$ and $b \geq 0$, or $b = 0$ and $a \geq 0$

61. $\sqrt[3]{a} + \sqrt[3]{b} = \sqrt[3]{a + b}$

Cubing both sides

$a + 3(\sqrt[3]{a})^2\sqrt[3]{b} + 3\sqrt[3]{a}(\sqrt[3]{b})^2 + b = a + b$

$3(\sqrt[3]{a})^2\sqrt[3]{b} + 3\sqrt[3]{a}(\sqrt[3]{b})^2 = 0$

Dividing by 3 and factoring

$\sqrt[3]{a}\sqrt[3]{b}(\sqrt[3]{a} + \sqrt[3]{b}) = 0$

$a = 0$ or $b = 0$ or $(\sqrt[3]{a} + \sqrt[3]{b}) = 0$

For $(\sqrt[3]{a} + \sqrt[3]{b})$ to be 0, $a = -b$,

$a = 0$, or $b = 0$ or $a = -b$

62. Answers may vary. Examples are:

$5\sqrt{7} - 3\sqrt{7}$ and $\sqrt{7} + \sqrt{7}$.

63. $\frac{2}{3}\sqrt{\frac{9}{2}} + \frac{3}{2}\sqrt[3]{16} + \frac{1}{4}\sqrt{72} = \frac{2}{3}(3)\sqrt{\frac{1}{2}} + \frac{3}{2}(2)\sqrt[3]{2} + \frac{1}{4}(6)\sqrt{2}$

$\qquad\qquad = 2\left(\frac{1}{2}\right)\sqrt{2} + 3\sqrt[3]{2} + \frac{3}{2}\sqrt{2}$

$\qquad\qquad = \frac{5}{2}\sqrt{2} + 3\sqrt[3]{2}$

64. $x\sqrt[3]{2y} - \sqrt[3]{16x^3y} + \frac{x}{3}\sqrt[3]{54y}$

$= x\sqrt[3]{2y} - \sqrt[3]{2 \cdot 2^3 x^3 y} + \frac{x}{3}\sqrt[3]{2 \cdot 3^3 y}$

$= x\sqrt[3]{2y} - 2x\sqrt[3]{2y} + x\sqrt[3]{2y} = 0$

65. $(5\sqrt[3]{2})^3 = 5^3 \cdot 2 = 250$

$(2\sqrt[3]{31})^3 = 2^3 \cdot 31 = 248$

If $a^3 < b^3$ then $a < b$. Thus, $2\sqrt[3]{31} < 5\sqrt[3]{2}$.

66. $\frac{y}{x} = \frac{3}{6} = \frac{1}{2}$;   **67.** $\frac{y}{x} = \frac{-2}{1}$;   **68.** $\frac{y}{x} = \frac{4}{7}$;

$y = \frac{1}{2}x$ $y = -2x$ $y = \frac{4x}{7}$

69. $\frac{5.2 \times 10^{-3}}{2.6 \times 10^4} = 2 \times 10^{-7}$ **70.** $\frac{3.78 \times 10^7}{2.7 \times 10^8} = 1.4 \times 10^{-1}$

71. $\frac{5.95 \times 10^8}{1.7 \times 10^5} = 3.5 \times 10^3$

72. $x^2 - 2x - 8 = 0$ **73.** $(y + 3)(y - 7) = 0$

$\quad (x + 2)(x - 4) = 0$ $y = -3$

$\qquad\qquad x = -2, 4$ $y = 7$

74. $\qquad 4a^2 - 25 = 0$

$\quad (2a - 5)(2a + 5) = 0$

$\qquad a = \frac{5}{2}; a = -\frac{5}{2}$

75. a. $f(x) = (2) + 1.5x$ **76.**   Let x = Juice A

    b. $f(x) = 2 + 1.5(11)$ Let y = Juice B

$\qquad\qquad = 2 + 16.50$ $x + y = 12$

$\qquad\qquad = 18.50$ $70x + 55y = 12(60)$

$\qquad\qquad\qquad\qquad\qquad\qquad\qquad \underline{-55(x + y) = 12}$

$\qquad\qquad\qquad\qquad\qquad\qquad\qquad 70x + 55y = 720$

$\qquad\qquad\qquad\qquad\qquad\qquad\qquad\qquad 15x = 60$

$\qquad\qquad\qquad\qquad\qquad\qquad\qquad\qquad\quad x = 4$

$\qquad\qquad\qquad\qquad\qquad\qquad$ 4 L of Juice A,

$\qquad\qquad\qquad\qquad\qquad\qquad$ 8 L of Juice B

p. 304   PROBLEM FOR PROGRAMMERS

```
10   REM Chapter 7 Problem 1
20   INPUT " Input the integer and the root
     ";M,K
30   FOR LOOP = M - 1 TO 2 STEP - 1
40   ROOT = INT (LOOP ^K)
50   IF M / ROOT < > INT (M / ROOT) THEN 70
60   GOTO 100
70   NEXT LOOP
80   PRINT "No simplification possible"
90   GOTO 130
100   PRINT LOOP;
110   IF M = ROOT THEN 130
120   PRINT "(";M / ROOT;")"^1/";K
130 END
```

pp. 305–307   7-4 TRY THIS

a. $\sqrt{2}(5\sqrt{3} + 3\sqrt{7}) = 5\sqrt{6} + 3\sqrt{14}$

b. $(\sqrt{a} + 2\sqrt{3})(3\sqrt{b} - 4\sqrt{3}) = 3\sqrt{ab} - 4\sqrt{3a} + 6\sqrt{3b} - 24$

c. $(2\sqrt{5} - y)^2 = (2\sqrt{5} - y)(2\sqrt{5} - y) = 20 - 4y\sqrt{5} + y^2$

d. $(8 - 5\sqrt{x})(8 + 5\sqrt{x}) = 64 - 40\sqrt{x} + 40\sqrt{x} - 25x$

$\qquad\qquad\qquad\qquad\qquad\qquad = 64 - 25|x|$

e. $\sqrt{\frac{2}{3}} = \frac{\sqrt{2}}{\sqrt{3}}\left(\frac{\sqrt{3}}{\sqrt{3}}\right) = \frac{\sqrt{6}}{3}$ **f.** $\sqrt{\frac{10}{7}} = \frac{\sqrt{10}}{\sqrt{7}}\left(\frac{\sqrt{7}}{\sqrt{7}}\right) = \frac{\sqrt{70}}{7}$

g. $\sqrt[3]{\frac{3}{6}} = \frac{\sqrt[3]{3}}{\sqrt[3]{6}}\left(\frac{\sqrt[3]{6^2}}{\sqrt[3]{6^2}}\right) = \frac{\sqrt[3]{108}}{\sqrt[3]{6}} = \frac{3\sqrt[3]{4}}{6} = \frac{\sqrt[3]{4}}{2}$

h. $\sqrt{\frac{4a}{3b}} = \frac{2\sqrt{a}}{\sqrt{3b}}\left(\frac{\sqrt{3b}}{\sqrt{3b}}\right) = \frac{2\sqrt{3ab}}{3|b|}$

i. $\frac{\sqrt{4x^5}}{\sqrt{3y^3}} = \frac{2x^2\sqrt{x}}{y\sqrt{3y}}\left(\frac{\sqrt{3y}}{\sqrt{3y}}\right) = \frac{2x^2\sqrt{3xy}}{3y^2}$ **j.** $\frac{\sqrt[3]{7}}{\sqrt[3]{2}}\left(\frac{\sqrt[3]{2^2}}{\sqrt[3]{2^2}}\right) = \frac{\sqrt[3]{28}}{2}$

k. $\sqrt[7]{\dfrac{3x^5}{2y}} = \dfrac{\sqrt[7]{3x^5}}{\sqrt[7]{2y}}\left(\dfrac{\sqrt[7]{(2y)^6}}{\sqrt[7]{(2y)^6}}\right) = \dfrac{\sqrt[7]{192x^5y^6}}{2|y|}$

l. $\dfrac{5}{1-\sqrt{2}}\left(\dfrac{1+\sqrt{2}}{1+\sqrt{2}}\right)\dfrac{5+5\sqrt{2}}{-1} = -5(1+\sqrt{2})$

m. $\dfrac{1}{\sqrt{2}+\sqrt{3}}\left(\dfrac{\sqrt{2}-\sqrt{3}}{\sqrt{2}-\sqrt{3}}\right) = \dfrac{\sqrt{2}-\sqrt{3}}{-1} = -\sqrt{2}+\sqrt{3}$

n. $\dfrac{\sqrt{5}+1}{\sqrt{3}-1}\left(\dfrac{\sqrt{3}+1}{\sqrt{3}+1}\right) = \dfrac{\sqrt{15}+\sqrt{3}+\sqrt{5}+1}{2}$

o. $\dfrac{2\sqrt{3}-3}{3\sqrt{3}-3}\left(\dfrac{3\sqrt{3}+3}{3\sqrt{3}+3}\right) = \dfrac{18-3\sqrt{3}-9}{18} = \dfrac{9-3\sqrt{3}}{18} = \dfrac{3-\sqrt{3}}{6}$

p. 308   7-4 EXERCISES

1. $2\sqrt{6}-18$ **2.** $4\sqrt{3}+3$ **3.** $\sqrt{6}-\sqrt{10}$ **4.** $5-\sqrt{10}$

5. $2\sqrt{15}-6\sqrt{3}$ **6.** $6\sqrt{5}-4$ **7.** -6 **8.** $3-4\sqrt[3]{63}$

9. $3a\sqrt[3]{2}$ **10.** $-2x\sqrt[3]{3}$ **11.** 1 **12.** -1 **13.** -12

14. -45 **15.** $|a|-|b|$ **16.** $|x|-|y|$ **17.** $1+\sqrt{5}$

18. $2+2\sqrt{6}$ **19.** $7+3\sqrt{3}$ **20.** $2-3\sqrt{3}$ **21.** -6

22. $24-7\sqrt{15}$ **23.** $|a|+\sqrt{3a}+\sqrt{2a}+\sqrt{6}$

24. $2-3\sqrt{x}+|x|$ **25.** $2\sqrt[3]{9}-3\sqrt[3]{6}-2\sqrt[3]{4}$

26. $6\sqrt[4]{63}-9\sqrt[4]{42}+2\sqrt[4]{54}-3\sqrt[4]{36}$ **27.** $7+4\sqrt{3}$

28. $6+2\sqrt{5}$ **29.** $21-6\sqrt{6}$ **30.** $120+30\sqrt{15}$

31. $\dfrac{\sqrt{30}}{5}$ **32.** $\dfrac{\sqrt{66}}{6}$ **33.** $\dfrac{\sqrt{70}}{7}$ **34.** $\dfrac{\sqrt{66}}{3}$ **35.** $\dfrac{2\sqrt{15}}{5}$

36. $\dfrac{\sqrt{6}}{5}$ **37.** $\dfrac{2\sqrt[3]{6}}{3}$ **38.** $\dfrac{\sqrt[3]{9}}{3}$ **39.** $\dfrac{\sqrt[3]{75ac^2}}{5c}$ **40.** $\dfrac{\sqrt[3]{63xy^2}}{3y}$

41. $\dfrac{y\sqrt[3]{9yx^2}}{3x^2}$ **42.** $\dfrac{a\sqrt[3]{147ab}}{7b}$ **43.** $\dfrac{\sqrt[3]{x^2y^2}}{xy}$ **44.** $\dfrac{\sqrt[3]{a^2b^2}}{ab}$

45. $\dfrac{5(8+\sqrt{6})}{58}$ **46.** $\dfrac{7(9-\sqrt{10})}{71}$ **47.** $-2\sqrt{7}(\sqrt{5}+\sqrt{3})$

48. $\dfrac{3\sqrt{2}(\sqrt{3}+\sqrt{5})}{2}$ **49.** $-\dfrac{\sqrt{15}+20-6\sqrt{2}-8\sqrt{30}}{77}$

50. $-\dfrac{3\sqrt{2}+2\sqrt{42}-3\sqrt{15}-6\sqrt{35}}{25}$ **51.** $\dfrac{|x|-2\sqrt{xy}+|y|}{|x|-|y|}$

52. $\dfrac{|a|+2\sqrt{ab}+|b|}{|a|-|b|}$ **53.** $\dfrac{3\sqrt{6}+4}{2}$ **54.** $\dfrac{4\sqrt{6}+9}{3}$

55. $\dfrac{4\sqrt{ab}-12|b|}{a-9|b|}$ **56.** $\dfrac{3\sqrt{c}+2\sqrt{cd}+12\sqrt{d}+8|d|}{|c|-16|d|}$

57. $\dfrac{|x|+8\sqrt{xy}+15|y|}{|x|-25|y|}$ **58.** $\dfrac{\sqrt{7}}{\sqrt{3}}\cdot\dfrac{\sqrt{7}}{\sqrt{7}} = \dfrac{7}{\sqrt{21}}$

59. $\sqrt{\dfrac{2}{3}}\cdot\dfrac{\sqrt{2}}{\sqrt{2}} = \dfrac{2}{\sqrt{6}}$ **60.** $\dfrac{4\sqrt{13}}{3\sqrt{7}}\cdot\dfrac{\sqrt{13}}{\sqrt{13}} = \dfrac{52}{3\sqrt{91}}$

61. $\dfrac{\sqrt[3]{7}}{\sqrt[3]{2}}\cdot\dfrac{\sqrt[3]{49}}{\sqrt[3]{49}} = \dfrac{7}{\sqrt[3]{98}}$ **62.** $\sqrt{\dfrac{7x}{3y}}\cdot\sqrt{\dfrac{7x}{7x}} = \dfrac{7|x|}{\sqrt{21xy}}$

63. $\sqrt[3]{\dfrac{5y^4}{6x^5}}\cdot\sqrt[3]{\dfrac{25y^2}{25y^2}} = \dfrac{5y^2}{x\sqrt[3]{150x^2y^2}}$

64. $\dfrac{\sqrt{3}+5}{8}\cdot\dfrac{\sqrt{3}-5}{\sqrt{3}-5} = \dfrac{-22}{8(\sqrt{3}-\sqrt{5})} = \dfrac{-11}{4(\sqrt{3}-5)}$

65. $\dfrac{\sqrt{3}-5}{\sqrt{2}+5}\cdot\dfrac{\sqrt{3}+\sqrt{5}}{\sqrt{3}+\sqrt{5}} = \dfrac{-22}{\sqrt{6}+5\sqrt{2}+5\sqrt{3}+25}$

66. $\dfrac{\sqrt{5}-\sqrt{2}}{\sqrt{2}+\sqrt{3}}\cdot\dfrac{\sqrt{5}+\sqrt{2}}{\sqrt{5}+\sqrt{2}} = \dfrac{3}{\sqrt{10}+2+\sqrt{15}+\sqrt{6}}$

67. $(\sqrt{x+3}-3)(\sqrt{x+3}+3) = |x+3|-9$

68. $(\sqrt{x+h}-\sqrt{x})(\sqrt{x+h}+\sqrt{x}) = |x+h|-|x|$

69. Answers may vary. Examples are:
$(\sqrt{15}+7)(\sqrt{15}-7)$ and $(\sqrt{10}+\sqrt{2})(\sqrt{10}-\sqrt{2})$.

70. $\dfrac{\sqrt[3]{c^3+3c^2d+3cd^2+d^3}}{\sqrt{c^2-d^2}\cdot\sqrt{c^2-d^2}} = \dfrac{\sqrt[3]{c^3+d^3+3cd(c+d)}}{c^2-d^2}$

$= \dfrac{\sqrt[3]{(c+d)(c^2-cd+d^2)+3cd(c+d)}}{c^2-d^2}$

$= \dfrac{\sqrt[3]{(c+d)[c^2-cd+d^2+3cd]}}{c^2-d^2}$

$= \dfrac{\sqrt[3]{(c+d)(c^2+2cd+d^2)}}{c^2-d^2}$

$= \dfrac{\sqrt[3]{(c+d)^3}}{c^2-d^2}$

$= \dfrac{c+d}{(c+d)(c-d)}$

$= \dfrac{1}{c-d}$

71. $\dfrac{1+\sqrt{y}}{\sqrt{x}(1+\sqrt{y})}\cdot\dfrac{1-\sqrt{y}}{1-y}\cdot\dfrac{x(1-y)}{\sqrt{x}(1-\sqrt{y})}$

$= \dfrac{x(1-y)(1+\sqrt{y})(1-\sqrt{y})}{x(1+\sqrt{y})(1-y)(1-\sqrt{y})} = 1$

72. $\dfrac{\sqrt{x}}{\sqrt{x}-\sqrt{x+1}}\cdot\dfrac{\sqrt{x}+\sqrt{x+1}}{\sqrt{x}+\sqrt{x+1}} = \dfrac{\sqrt{x}(\sqrt{x}+\sqrt{x+1})}{x-(\sqrt{x+1})(\sqrt{x+1})}$

$= \dfrac{x+\sqrt{x(x+1)}}{x-(x+1)}$

$= \dfrac{x+\sqrt{x^2+x}}{x-x-1}$

$= -x-\sqrt{x^2+x}$

73. $\dfrac{\sqrt{p-4q}}{\sqrt{3q^2+4pq+p^2}}\cdot\dfrac{\sqrt{p+3q}}{\sqrt{p^2+6pq+8q^2}}\cdot\sqrt{p^2+3pq+2q^2}$

$= \dfrac{\sqrt{(p-4q)(p+3q)(p+q)(p+2q)}}{\sqrt{(3q+p)(q+p)(p+2q)(p+4q)}}$

$= \dfrac{\sqrt{p-4q}}{\sqrt{p+4q}}\cdot\dfrac{\sqrt{p+4q}}{\sqrt{p+4q}}$

$= \dfrac{\sqrt{p^2-16q^2}}{|p+4q|}$

74. $(2)(-4) = k$ **75.** $(7)(4) = k$
$\quad -8 = k$ $\qquad 28 = k$
Then $xy = -8$ Then $xy = 28$
$\quad y = \dfrac{-8}{x}$ $\qquad y = \dfrac{28}{x}$

76. $2x^2+4x+2 = 2(x^2+2x+1) = 2(x+1)(x+1)$

77. $9y^2-x^2-2x-1 = 9y^2+(-x-1)(x+1)$
$\qquad\qquad = (3y-x-1)(3y+x+1)$

78. $8y^3-27 = (2y-3)(4y^2+6y+9)$

79. 5 **80.** 47.5 **81.** $\dfrac{1}{4}x^2-3x+10$ **82.** $\dfrac{1}{2}x^2-\dfrac{5}{2}$

83. $\qquad\qquad x = $ 1st integer
$\qquad\qquad x+2 = $ 2nd integer
$\quad x^2+(x+2)^2 = 52$
$\quad 2x^2+4x-48 = 0$
$\quad 2(x-4)(x+6) = 0$
$\qquad\qquad x = 4;\ x = -6$
$\qquad x+2 = 6;\ x+2 = -4$
$\quad 4, 6$ and $-6, -4$

84. $\$125+6(\$85) = \$635$ **85.** $\dfrac{\$1250}{0.025} = \$50,000$

pp. 310–314   7-5 TRY THIS

a. $\sqrt[3]{8^2} = \sqrt[3]{64} = 4$ or $(\sqrt[3]{8})^2 = (2)^2 = 4$

b. $(\sqrt{6y})^3 = \sqrt{216y^3} = 6y\sqrt{6y}$
or $(\sqrt{6y})^3 = \sqrt{6y}\cdot\sqrt{6y}\cdot\sqrt{6y}$
$\qquad\qquad = \sqrt{6^3y^3}$
$\qquad\qquad = \sqrt{6^2y^2}\sqrt{6y}$
$\qquad\qquad = 6|y|\sqrt{6y}$

c. $y^{1/4} = \sqrt[4]{y}$ **d.** $(3a)^{1/2} = \sqrt{3a}$ **e.** $16^{1/4} = \sqrt[4]{16}$, or 2
f. $\sqrt[4]{a^3b^2c} = a^{3/4}b^{1/2}c^{1/4} = (a^3b^2c)^{1/4}$

g. $\sqrt[5]{\dfrac{x^2y}{16}} = \left(\dfrac{x^2y}{16}\right)^{1/5}$ **h.** $x^{3/2} = x\sqrt{x}$

i. $8^{2/3} = \sqrt[3]{8^2} = \sqrt[3]{64} = 4$ **j.** $(7abc)^{4/3}$ **k.** $6^{7/5}$

l. $\sqrt[4]{x^2y^3} = (x^2y^3)^{1/4}$, or $x^{1/2}y^{3/4}$ **m.** $5^{-1/4} = \dfrac{1}{5^{1/4}}$

n. $(3xy)^{-7/8} = \dfrac{1}{(3xy)^{7/8}}$ **o.** $7^{1/3} \cdot 7^{3/5} = 7^{5/15} \cdot 7^{9/15} = 7^{14/15}$

p. $\dfrac{5^{7/6}}{5^{5/6}} = 5^{2/6} = 5^{1/3}$ **q.** $(9^{3/5})^{2/3} = 9^{6/15} = 9^{2/5}$

r. $\sqrt[4]{a^2} = a^{2/4} = a^{1/2} = \sqrt{a}$ **s.** $\sqrt[4]{x^4} = x^{4/4} = x$
t. $\sqrt[6]{8} = 2^{3/6} = 2^{1/2} = \sqrt{2}$ **u.** $\sqrt[4]{x^4y^{12}} = x^{4/4}y^{12/4} = xy^3$
v. $\sqrt[12]{x^3y^6} = x^{3/12}y^{6/12} = x^{1/4}y^{2/4} = \sqrt[4]{xy^2}$
w. $\sqrt[4]{7} \cdot \sqrt{3} = 7^{1/4} \cdot 3^{1/2} = 7^{1/4} \cdot 3^{2/4} = \sqrt[4]{63}$

x. $\dfrac{\sqrt[4]{(a-b)^5}}{a-b} = \sqrt[4]{(a-b)}$

y. $x^{-2/3}y^{1/2}z^{5/6} = x^{-4/6}y^{3/6}z^{5/6} = \sqrt[6]{x^{-4}y^3z^5}$

z. $\dfrac{a^{1/2}b^{3/8}}{a^{1/4}b^{1/8}} = \dfrac{\sqrt[4]{a^4b^3}}{\sqrt[8]{a^2b}} = \sqrt[8]{a^2b^2} = \sqrt[4]{ab}$

pp. 315–316   **7-5 EXERCISES**

1. $6a\sqrt{6a}$ **2.** $7y\sqrt{7y}$ **3.** $4b\sqrt[3]{4b}$ **4.** $5r\sqrt[3]{5r}$
5. $54a^3b\sqrt{2b}$ **6.** $24x^3y\sqrt{3y}$ **7.** $2c\sqrt[3]{18cd^2}$
8. $3x\sqrt[3]{3xy^2}$ **9.** $\sqrt[4]{x}$ **10.** $\sqrt[5]{y}$ **11.** 2 **12.** 4
13. $\sqrt[5]{a^2b^2}$ **14.** $\sqrt[4]{x^3y^3}$ **15.** $\sqrt[3]{a^2}$ **16.** $b\sqrt{b}$
17. 8 **18.** 128 **19.** $\sqrt{a^5t^3}$ **20.** $\sqrt[6]{m^5}$ **21.** $\sqrt{y^7}$
22. 8 **23.** $\sqrt[4]{m^3n^5}$ **24.** $20^{1/3}$ **25.** $19^{1/3}$ **26.** $17^{1/2}$
27. $6^{1/2}$ **28.** $(cd)^{1/4}$ **29.** $(xy)^{1/5}$ **30.** $(xy^2z)^{1/5}$
31. $(x^3y^2z^2)^{1/7}$ **32.** $(3mn)^{3/2}$ **33.** $(7xy)^{4/3}$ **34.** $(8x^2y)^{5/7}$
35. $(2a^5b)^{7/6}$ **36.** $(16xy)^{5/4}$ or $32(xy)^{5/4}$
37. $(12ab)^{1/2}$ or $2(3ab)^{1/2}$ **38.** $(2x^4y^6)^{3/8}$ **39.** $(3a^4b^3)^{4/7}$
40. $\dfrac{1}{x^{1/3}}$ **41.** $\dfrac{1}{y^{1/4}}$ **42.** $\dfrac{1}{(2rs)^{3/4}}$ **43.** $\dfrac{1}{(5xy)^{5/6}}$ **44.** $10^{2/3}$
45. $8^{3/4}$ **46.** $x^{2/3}$ **47.** $x^{5/6}$ **48.** $5^{7/8}$ **49.** $11^{7/6}$
50. $7^{1/4}$ **51.** $9^{2/11}$ **52.** $8.3^{7/20}$ **53.** $3.9^{7/20}$ **54.** $10^{6/25}$
55. $5^{15/28}$ **56.** $\sqrt[3]{a^2}$ **57.** $\sqrt[3]{y}$ **58.** $2y^2$ **59.** x^2y^3
60. $2c^2d^3$ **61.** $2x^3y^4$ **62.** $\dfrac{m^2n^4}{2}$ **63.** $\dfrac{x^3y^4}{2}$ **64.** $\sqrt[4]{r^2s}$
65. $3ab^3$ **66.** $\sqrt{2ts}$ **67.** $3x^2y^2$ **68.** $\sqrt[6]{x^5 - 4x^4 + 4x^3}$
69. $\sqrt[6]{3xy^2 + 24xy + 48x}$ **70.** $\sqrt[6]{a+b}$ **71.** $\sqrt[12]{(x+y)^{-1}}$
72. $\sqrt[12]{a^8b^9}$ **73.** $\sqrt[12]{x^4y^3z^2}$ **74.** $\sqrt[4]{st^4}$ **75.** $\sqrt[5]{xy^5}$

76. $\dfrac{1}{\sqrt{xy}} \cdot \sqrt{\dfrac{xy}{xy}} = \dfrac{\sqrt{xy}}{xy}$ **77.** $\sqrt{a+b} \cdot \sqrt{a-b} = \sqrt{a^2 - b^2}$

78. $\sqrt[3]{x^2 + 2xy + y^2} \cdot \sqrt[3]{x+y} = \sqrt[3]{(x+y)^3} = x+y$

79. $\dfrac{1}{\sqrt{a^3 - 3a^2b + 3ab^2 - b^3}} = \dfrac{1}{\sqrt{a^3 - b^3 - 3a^2b + 3ab^2}}$

$$= \dfrac{1}{\sqrt{(a-b)(a^2 + ab + b^2) - 3ab(a-b)}}$$

$$= \dfrac{1}{\sqrt{(a-b)(a^2 + ab + b^2 - 3ab)}}$$

$$= \dfrac{1}{\sqrt{(a-b)^3}}$$

$$= \dfrac{1}{(a-b)\sqrt{a-b}} \cdot \sqrt{\dfrac{a-b}{a-b}}$$

$$= \dfrac{\sqrt{a-b}}{(a-b)^2}$$

80. $\sqrt{(x+y)} \cdot \sqrt{x-y} = \sqrt{x^2 - y^2}$
81. $(a^2 + 4ab + 4b^2)^{-1/2} = [(a+2b)^2]^{-1/2}$
$$= (a+2b)^{-1}$$
$$= \dfrac{1}{a+2b}$$

82. $\sqrt[20]{x} = x^{1/20}$ **83.** $\sqrt[15]{a^2} = a^{2/15}$ **84.** $\sqrt[3]{(c+1)^2} = (c+1)^{2/3}$

85. $\dfrac{\sqrt{(x+1)(x+6)}}{\sqrt{x+1}} = \sqrt{x+6} = (x+6)^{1/2}$

86. $\dfrac{1}{\sqrt{x+y}} + \dfrac{1}{\sqrt{x-y}} = \dfrac{\sqrt{x-y} + \sqrt{x+y}}{\sqrt{(x+y)(x-y)}}$
$$= [(x-y)^{1/2} + (x+y)^{1/2}](x^2 - y^2)^{-1/2}$$

87. Answers may vary.
Notice $a^{m/n} \cdot a^{-m/n} = a^{m/n + (-m/n)} = a^0 = 1$

88. $L = \dfrac{(0.00252)(60)^{2.27}}{1 \text{ m}} = \dfrac{(0.00252)(10874.35)}{1 \text{ m}} = 27.4 \text{ m}$

89. $L = \dfrac{(0.00252)(75)^{2.27}}{0.9906 \text{ m}} = \dfrac{(0.00252)(18046)}{0.9906 \text{ m}} = 45.9 \text{ m}$

90. $L = \dfrac{(0.00252)(80)^{2.27}}{2.4 \text{ m}} = \dfrac{(0.00252)(20894)}{2.4 \text{ m}} = 21.9 \text{ m}$

91. $L = \dfrac{(0.00252)(100)^{2.27}}{1.1 \text{ m}} = \dfrac{(0.00252)(34673.7)}{1.1 \text{ m}} = 79.4 \text{ m}$

92. $3x + y = 5$ and $6x + 2y = 10$ are the same line, so they are dependent.

93. $y = \dfrac{x}{2} - \dfrac{3}{2}$ and $y = \dfrac{x}{2} + \dfrac{3}{2}$ are parallel lines, so they are not dependent.

94. $y = -\dfrac{1}{2}x + \dfrac{3}{2}$ and $y = \dfrac{1}{2}x - \dfrac{3}{2}$ are intersecting lines, so they are not dependent.

95. $x^2 + 2x^2 + x^3 + 3x^3 = 3x^2 + 4x^3$ **96.** $x^5 \cdot 6x^5 = 6x^{10}$

pp. 317–318   **7-6 TRY THIS**

a. $\sqrt{x} - 7 = 3$
  $\sqrt{x} = 10$
  $x = 10^2$ or 100;
  Check: $\sqrt{x} - 7 = 3$
  $\overline{\sqrt{100} - 7 = 3}$
  $10 - 7 = 3$
  $3 = 3$

b. $3 - \sqrt{x} = 12$
  $-9 = \sqrt{x}$
  $81 = (-9)^2 = x$; does not check—no solution
  Check: $\dfrac{3 - \sqrt{x} = 12}{3 - \sqrt{81} = 12}$
  $-6 \neq 12$

c. $\sqrt{x} - \sqrt{x-5} = 1$
  $\sqrt{x} = \sqrt{x-5} + 1$
  $(\sqrt{x})^2 = (\sqrt{x-5} + 1)^2$
  $x = x - 5 + 2\sqrt{x-5} + 1$
  $4 = 2\sqrt{x-5}$
  $(4)^2 = (2\sqrt{x-5})^2$
  $16 = 4(x-5)$
  $16 = 4x - 20$
  $4x = 36$
  $x = 9$ This checks

d. $\sqrt{3x+1} = 1 + \sqrt{x+4}$
  $(\sqrt{3x+1})^2 = (1 + \sqrt{x+4})^2$
  $3x + 1 = 1 + 2\sqrt{x+4} + x + 4$
  $3x + 1 = x + 5 + 2\sqrt{x+4}$
  $2x - 4 = 2\sqrt{x+4}$
  $(2x-4)^2 = (2\sqrt{x+4})^2$
  $4x^2 - 16x + 16 = 4(x+4)$
  $4x^2 - 16x + 16 = 4x + 16$
  $4x^2 - 20x = 0$
  $4x(x-5) = 0$
  $x = 0$ or $x = 5$; only $x = 5$ checks

e.
$$s = \pi r \sqrt{r^2 + h^2}$$
$$s^2 = \pi^2 r^2 (r^2 + h^2)$$
$$(r^2 + h^2) = \frac{s^2}{\pi^2 r^2}$$
$$h^2 = \frac{s^2}{\pi^2 r^2} - r^2$$
$$= \frac{s^2}{\pi^2 r^2} - \frac{r^4 \pi^2}{\pi^2 r^2}$$
$$= \frac{s^2 - r^4 \pi^2}{\pi^2 r^2}$$
$$h = \frac{\sqrt{s^2 - r^4 \pi^2}}{\pi r}$$
$$h = \frac{\sqrt{225\pi^2 - 81\pi^2}}{3\pi} = \frac{\sqrt{144\pi^2}}{3\pi} = \frac{12\pi}{3\pi} = 4$$

pp. 319–320   7-6 EXERCISES

1. 2   **2.** 33   **3.** 168   **4.** 11   **5.** 3   **6.** 29   **7.** 19

8. 78   **9.** $\frac{80}{3}$ **10.** 84   **11.** 4   **12.** $\frac{1}{16}$ **13.** -27

14. -64 **15.** 397   **16.** 117   **17.** No solution

18. No solution   **19.** $\frac{1}{64}$ **20.** $\frac{1}{9}$ **21.** -6 **22.** $-\frac{5}{3}$

23. 5   **24.** 2   **25.** $-\frac{1}{4}$ **26.** 3   **27.** 3   **28.** -1

29. 9   **30.** No solution   **31.** 7   **32.** 7, 3   **33.** $\frac{80}{9}$

34. $\frac{15}{4}$ **35.** -1 **36.** $\frac{1}{3}, -1$ **37.** 6, 2   **38.** 1

39. No solution   **40.** 2

41. $v = \sqrt{2gs}$
$$v^2 = 2gs$$
$$s = \frac{v^2}{2g}$$
$$s = \frac{(32)^2}{2g} = 512g$$

42. $R = 1.826 \times 10^{-2} \sqrt{Q}$
$$\sqrt{Q} = \frac{R}{1.826 \times 10^{-2}}$$
$$Q = \frac{R^2}{(1.826 \times 10^{-2})^2}$$
$$Q = \frac{(1.5)^2}{(1.826 \times 10^{-2})^2} = 6,748.09 \, C$$

43. $x^{1/3} + 5 = 7$
$$x^{\frac{1}{3}} = 2$$
$$x = 2^3$$
$$x = 8$$

44. $(x - 5)^{1/5} - 3 = 7$
$$(x - 5)^{1/5} = 10$$
$$x - 5 = 10^5$$
$$x = 5 + 10^5$$

45. $(x - 5)^{2/3} = 2$
$$[(x - 5)^{2/3}]^{3/2} = 2^{3/2}$$
$$x - 5 = \sqrt{2^3}$$
$$x - 5 = \pm 2\sqrt{2}$$
$$x = 5 \pm 2\sqrt{2}$$

46.
$$\frac{x + \sqrt{x + 1}}{x - \sqrt{x + 1}} = \frac{5}{11}$$
$$11(x + \sqrt{x + 1}) = 5(x - \sqrt{x + 1})$$
$$11x + 11\sqrt{x + 1} = 5x - 5\sqrt{x + 1}$$
$$3x = -8\sqrt{x + 1}$$
$$9x^2 = 64(x + 1)$$
$$9x^2 - 64x - 64 = 0$$
$$x = \frac{64 \pm \sqrt{(64)^2 - 4(9)(-64)}}{18}$$
$$= \frac{64 \pm \sqrt{6400}}{18}$$
$$= \frac{64 \pm 80}{18}$$
$$x = 8; x = -\frac{8}{9}$$

47.
$$\sqrt{x + 2} - \sqrt{x - 2} = \sqrt{2x}$$
$$(\sqrt{x + 2} - \sqrt{x - 2})^2 = (\sqrt{2x})^2$$
$$x + 2 - 2\sqrt{x^2 - 4} + x - 2 = 2x$$
$$-2\sqrt{x^2 - 4} = 0$$
$$x^2 - 4 = 0$$
$$x = 2$$

48.
$$2\sqrt{x + 3} = \sqrt{x} + \sqrt{x + 8}$$
$$(2\sqrt{x + 3})^2 = (\sqrt{x} + \sqrt{x + 8})^2$$
$$x + 2 = \sqrt{x^2 + 8x}$$
$$x^2 + 4x + 4 = x^2 + 8x$$
$$4 = 4x$$
$$1 = x$$

49.
$$\sqrt[3]{2x - 1} = \sqrt[6]{x + 1}$$
$$(\sqrt[3]{2x - 1})^6 = (\sqrt[6]{x + 1})^6$$
$$(2x - 1)^2 = x + 1$$
$$4x^2 - 5x = 0$$
$$x(4x - 5) = 0$$
$$x = 0; x = \frac{5}{4}$$
$$\left\{\frac{5}{4}\right\}$$

50. Use a calculator to estimate, or solve the equation $x = \sqrt{6 + x}$. The solution is 3.

51. Prove: If $a = b$, then $a^n = b^n$
Let $a = b$.
$$a^n = a \cdot a^{n-1}$$
Substitute b for a.
$$a^n = b \cdot a^{n-1}$$
$$= b \cdot b \cdot a^{n-2}$$
$$= b \cdot b \cdot b \cdot a^{n-3}$$

52.
$$\sqrt{y + \sqrt{2y}} = 2$$
$$(\sqrt{y + \sqrt{2y}})^2 = 2^2$$
$$y + \sqrt{2y} = 4$$
$$(\sqrt{2y})^2 = (4 - y)^2$$
$$0 = y^2 - 10y + 16$$
$$0 = (y - 2)(y - 8)$$
$$2 = y; 8 = y$$
$$\{2\}$$

53. $\sqrt{\sqrt{x + 25}} - \sqrt{x} = 5$
$$(\sqrt{\sqrt{x + 25}})^2 = (5 + \sqrt{x})^2$$
$$\sqrt{x + 25} = x + 10\sqrt{x} + 25$$
$$x + 25 = x^2 + 20x\sqrt{x} + 150x + 500\sqrt{x} + 625$$
$$0 = x^2 + 20x\sqrt{x} + 149 + 500\sqrt{x} + 600$$
Cannot be factored. No solution

54. $\sqrt[3]{216} = \sqrt[3]{8 \cdot 27} = 2 \cdot 3 = 6$

55. $\sqrt{12y^2} = \sqrt{4 \cdot 3y^2} = 2|y|\sqrt{3}$

56. $\sqrt[3]{(y - 5)^4} = \sqrt[3]{(y - 5)^3(y - 5)} = (y - 5)\sqrt[3]{y - 5}$

57. $\sqrt{2} \cdot \sqrt{8} = \sqrt{16} = 4$

pp. 321–322   7-7 TRY THIS

a. $\sqrt{-7} = \sqrt{-1 \cdot 7} = \sqrt{-1}\sqrt{7} = i\sqrt{7}$
b. $-\sqrt{-36} = -\sqrt{-1 \cdot 36} = -\sqrt{-1}\sqrt{36} = -6i$
c. $\sqrt{-160} = \sqrt{-1 \cdot 16 \cdot 10} = i\sqrt{16}\sqrt{10} = 4i\sqrt{10}$
d. $6i \cdot 3i = 18i^2 = -18$
e. $\sqrt{-3} \cdot 3i = i\sqrt{3} \cdot 3i = 3i^2\sqrt{3} = -3\sqrt{3}$
f. $\sqrt{-3} \cdot \sqrt{-6} = i\sqrt{3} \cdot i\sqrt{6} = i^2\sqrt{18}$
$$= i^2\sqrt{9 \cdot 2} = 3i^2\sqrt{2} = -3\sqrt{2}$$
g. $(-2 + 3i) + (2 - 3i) = -2 + 3i + 2 - 3i = 0$
h. $3i - 4i = -1i = -i$
i. $(-4 + 10i) - (-2 + 3i) = -4 + 10i + 2 - 3i = -2 + 7i$

p. 323   7-7 EXERCISES

1. $i\sqrt{2}$ **2.** $i\sqrt{3}$ **3.** $6i$ **4.** $5i$ **5.** $-3i$ **6.** $-4i$

7. $8i\sqrt{2}$ **8.** $2i\sqrt{3}$ **9.** $\frac{3}{4}i$ **10.** $\frac{5}{2}i$ **11.** $-4i\sqrt{5}$

12. $-5i\sqrt{3}$ **13.** $92i$ **14.** $36i$ **15.** $-4\sqrt{3}$ **16.** $-6\sqrt{5}$

17. $-\sqrt{6}$ **18.** $-\sqrt{15}$ **19.** 6 **20.** $3\sqrt{5}$ **21.** $-3\sqrt{5}$

22. $-2\sqrt{5}$ **23.** -10 **24.** -7 **25.** $3i$ **26.** $-6i$

27. $8 + i$ **28.** $5 + 11i$ **29.** $9 - 5i$ **30.** $-4 + 5i$

31. $-5 + 5i$ **32.** $-2 - 3i$ **33.** $-9 + 5i$ **34.** $-1 + i$

35. $i^{13} = (i^4)^3 \cdot i = 1 \cdot i = i$ **36.** $i^{20} = (i^4)^5 = (1)^5 = 1$

37. $i^{18} = (i^4)^4 \cdot i^2 = 1 \cdot -1 = -1$

38. $i^{27} = (i^4)^6 \cdot i^3 = 1(-i) = -i$

39. $i^{99} = (i^4)^{24} \cdot i^3 = 1(-i) = -i$

40. $i^{71} - i^{49} = ((i^4)^{17} \cdot i^3) - ((i^4)^{12} \cdot i) = -i - i = -2i$

41. $i^{68} - i^{72} - i^{80} = (i^4)^{17} - (i^4)^{18} + (i^4)^{19} - (i^4)^{20}$
$$= 1 - 1 + 1 - 1 = 0$$

42. $i^{4k} = 1$ and $i^{4k-2} = -1$ for $k = 1, 2, 3, \ldots$

43. $i^{-1} = \dfrac{1}{i} \cdot \dfrac{i}{i} = -i$ **44.** $\dfrac{1}{i^2} = \dfrac{1}{-1} = -1$

45. $\dfrac{1}{i^3} = \dfrac{1}{-i} \cdot \dfrac{i}{i} = i$ **46.** $\dfrac{1}{i^4} = \dfrac{1}{1} = 1$

47. $\dfrac{1}{i^{99}} = \dfrac{1}{i^{96}i^3} = \dfrac{1}{-i} \cdot \dfrac{i}{i} = i$ **48.** $\dfrac{1}{i^{27}} = \dfrac{1}{i^{24}i^3} = \dfrac{1}{-i} \cdot \dfrac{i}{i} = i$

49. $i^{4n} \cdot i^3 = 1(-i) = -i$ **50.** $(i^{4n})(i^2) = 1(-1) = -1$

51. $(i^{4n})(i) = (1)(i) = i$ **52.** $(i^{4n})(i^0) = 1 \cdot 1 = 1$

53. $(i^{4n})(i^{-1}) = \dfrac{1}{i} \cdot \dfrac{i}{i} = -i$

54. $(i^{4n})(i^{-2}) = 1\left(\dfrac{1}{i^2}\right)$ **55.** $(i^{4n})(i^{-3}) = 1 \cdot \dfrac{1}{i^3}$
$$\qquad\qquad\quad = 1(-1) \qquad\qquad\qquad\qquad = 1 \cdot \dfrac{1}{-i}$$
$$\qquad\qquad\quad = -1 \qquad\qquad\qquad\qquad\quad = -\dfrac{1}{i} \cdot \dfrac{i}{i}$$
$$\qquad\qquad\qquad\qquad\qquad\qquad\qquad\qquad\quad = \dfrac{-i}{-1}$$
$$\qquad\qquad\qquad\qquad\qquad\qquad\qquad\qquad\quad = i$$

56. $\sqrt[3]{7} \cdot \sqrt[3]{5} = \sqrt[3]{35}$ **57.** $\sqrt{(m+n)(m-n)} = \sqrt{m^2 - n^2}$

58. $\sqrt[4]{112m^5n^2} = \sqrt[4]{16 \cdot 7m^5n^2} = 2|m|\sqrt[4]{7mn^2}$

59. $\dfrac{(x-2)(x+3)}{(x-2)(x+5)} = \dfrac{(x+3)}{(x+5)}$ **60.** $\dfrac{(y-4)(y-1)}{(y-4)} = y - 1$

61. $\dfrac{(x+2)(x-2)}{(4x+1)(x+3)} \cdot \dfrac{(x+3)}{(x+2)} = \dfrac{x-2}{4x+1}$

62.
$$\dfrac{x^2}{x} + \dfrac{8}{x} = 6$$
$$\dfrac{x^2+8}{x} = \dfrac{6}{1}$$
$$x^2 + 8 = 6x$$
$$x^2 - 6x + 8 = 0$$
$$(x-2)(x-4) = 0$$
$$x - 2 = 0 \qquad x - 4 = 0$$
$$x = 2 \qquad\quad x = 4$$

63.
$$\dfrac{x+2}{3x+1} = \dfrac{2x-3}{2x}$$
$$\dfrac{(x+2)(2x)}{2x(3x+1)} = \dfrac{(2x-3)(3x+1)}{2x(3x+1)}$$
$$(x+2)(2x) = (2x-3)(3x+1)$$
$$2x^2 + 4x = 6x^2 + 2x - 9x - 3$$
$$0 = 4x^2 - 11x - 3$$
$$0 = (4x+1)(x-3)$$
$$4x + 1 = 0 \qquad x - 3 = 0$$
$$x = -\dfrac{1}{4} \qquad\quad x = 3$$

64.

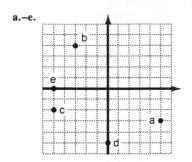
$$\dfrac{3x^2}{x} - \dfrac{2}{x} = 1$$
$$\dfrac{3x^2 - 2}{x} = 1$$
$$3x^2 - 2 = x$$
$$3x^2 - x - 2 = 0$$
$$(3x+2)(x-1) = 0$$
$$3x + 2 = 0 \qquad x - 1 = 0$$
$$3x = -2 \qquad\quad x = 1$$
$$x = -\dfrac{2}{3}$$

pp. 324–325   **7-8 TRY THIS**

a.–e.

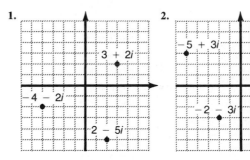

f. $|4 - 3i| = \sqrt{(4)^2 + (3)^2} = \sqrt{16 + 9} = \sqrt{25} = 5$

g. $|-12 - 5i| = \sqrt{(-12)^2 + (-5)^2}$
$$= \sqrt{144 + 25} = \sqrt{169} = 13$$

h. $|1 + i| = \sqrt{(1)^2 + (1)^2} = \sqrt{2}$

p. 325   **7-8 EXERCISES**

1.   **2.**

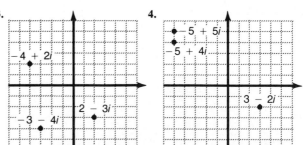

3.   **4.**

5.   **6.**

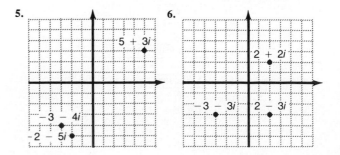

7. 5   **8.** 5   **9.** 17   **10.** 25   **11.** $\sqrt{10}$ **12.** $\sqrt{5}$

13. 3   **14.** 2   **15.** $\sqrt{c^2 + d^2}$ **16.** $\sqrt{c^2 + d^2}$

17. $2\sqrt{4c^2 + 1}$ **18.** $\sqrt{16p^2 + 9q^2}$

19. a. 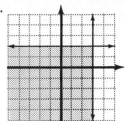   **b.**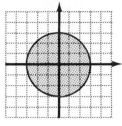

c.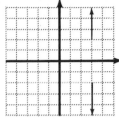

20. $G = \{a + bi \mid |a + bi| \leq 4\}$

a. $|a + bi| \leq 4$ **b.** $|a + bi| \leq 4$
$|3 + 2i| \leq 4$ $|0 + 3i| \leq 4$
$\sqrt{3^2 + 3^2} \leq 4$ $\sqrt{0^2 + 3^2} \leq 4$
$\sqrt{9 + 9} \leq 4$ $\sqrt{9} \leq 4$
$\sqrt{18} > 4$ $3 \leq 4$
no   yes

c. $|a + bi| \leq 4$ **d.** $|a + bi| \leq 4$
$|-4 + 3i| \leq 4$ $|0 + i^5| \leq 4$
$\sqrt{(-4)^2 + 3^2} \leq 4$ $\sqrt{0 + i^{10}} \leq 4$
$\sqrt{16 + 9} \leq 4$ $\sqrt{0 + i^4 \cdot i^4 \cdot i^2} \leq 4$
$\sqrt{25} \leq 4$ $1\sqrt{i^2} \leq 4$
$5 > 4$ $i \leq 4$
no   yes

e. $|a + bi| \leq 4$ **f.** $|a + bi| \leq 4$
$|2 + (-4i)| \leq 4$ $|6 + 2i| \leq 4$
$\sqrt{2^2 + (-4)^2} \leq 4$ $\sqrt{6^2 + 2^2} \leq 4$
$\sqrt{4 + 16} \leq 4$ $\sqrt{36 + 4} \leq 4$
$\sqrt{20} > 4$ $\sqrt{40} > 4$
no   no

21. The absolute value does not change. The coordinates of the graph change from (a, b) to $(-b, a)$. (The point is rotated 90°.)

22.   Let $z = a + bi$
$|z| = |a + bi| = \sqrt{a^2 + b^2}$
$|-z| = |-(a + bi)| = |-a - bi|$
$= \sqrt{(-a)^2 + (-b)^2}$
$= \sqrt{a^2 + b^2}$
Therefore $|z| = |-z|$

23. $\sqrt{27} = \sqrt{9 \cdot 3} = 3\sqrt{3}$

24. $\sqrt{45m^2} = \sqrt{9 \cdot 5 \cdot m^2} = 3m\sqrt{5}$

25. $\sqrt[3]{16a^3} = \sqrt[3]{8 \cdot 2 \cdot a^3} = 2a\sqrt[3]{2}$

26. $\sqrt[8]{(-2)^8} = \sqrt[8]{256} = \sqrt[8]{2^8} = 2$

27. $a^3 + 27 = (a + 3)(a^2 - 3a + 9)$

28. $m^3 - 8 = (m - 2)(m^2 + 2m + 4)$

29. $x^3 - 12x^2 + 48x - 64 = (x^3 - 64) - 12x^2 + 48$
$= (x - 4)(x^2 + 4x + 16) - 12x(x - 4)$
$= (x - 4)(x^2 + 4x - 12x + 16)$
$= (x - 4)(x^2 - 8x + 16)$
$= (x - 4)(x - 4)(x - 4)$
$= (x - 4)^3$

pp. 326–328   7-9 TRY THIS

a. $3x + 1 + (y + 2)i = 2x + 2yi$
$3x + 1 + yi + 2i = 2x + 2yi$
$3x + 1 = 2x \qquad yi + 2i = 2yi$
$x = -1 \qquad -yi = -2i$
$y = 2$

b. $5i \cdot 6i = (5 \cdot 6)i^2 = 30(-1) = -30$
c. $(10i)^2 = (10 \cdot 10)i^2 = 100(-1) = -100$
d. $(-2 - 3i)(6 + 5i) = -12 - 10i - 18i + 15 = 3 - 28i$
e. The conjugate of $6 + 3i$ is $6 - 3i$.
f. The conjugate of $-9 - 5i$ is $-9 + 5i$.
g. The conjugate of $-7i$ is $7i$.
h. The conjugate of -8 is -8.
i. $(7 - 2i)(7 + 2i) = 49 + 4 = 53$
j. $(-3 + i)(-3 - i) = 9 + 1 = 10$
k. $(3p - 2qi)(3p + 2qi) = (3p)^2 - (2qi)^2 = 9p^2 - (4q^2i^2)$
$= 9p^2 + 4q^2$

l. $\dfrac{6 + 2i}{1 - 3i} \cdot \dfrac{1 + 3i}{1 + 3i} = \dfrac{6 + 2i + 18i - 6}{1 + 9} = \dfrac{20i}{10} = 2i$

m. $\dfrac{2 + 3i}{-1 + 4i} \cdot \dfrac{-1 - 4i}{-1 - 4i} = \dfrac{-2 - 11i + 12}{1 + 16} = \dfrac{10 - 11i}{17}$, or $\dfrac{10}{17} - \dfrac{11i}{17}$

n. The reciprocal of $3 + 4i$ is $\dfrac{1}{3 + 4i}$.

$\dfrac{1}{3 + 4i} \cdot \dfrac{3 - 4i}{3 - 4i} = \dfrac{3 - 4i}{9 + 16} = \dfrac{3 - 4i}{25}$, or $\dfrac{3}{25} - \dfrac{4i}{25}$

p. 329   7-9 EXERCISES

1. $x = -\dfrac{3}{2}, y = 7$ **2.** $x = 2, y = -\dfrac{1}{4}$

3. $x = -2, y = -8$ **4.** -63 **5.** -3 **6.** -81 **7.** -25

8. $1 + 5i$ **9.** $5 + 10i$ **10.** $21 - 20i$ **11.** $-8i$

12. $-4 - 8i$ **13.** $7 + i$ **14.** $\sqrt{2} + \dfrac{1}{2}i$ **15.** $-m - ni$

16. 2   **17.** 45   **18.** 11   **19.** $\dfrac{8}{5} + \dfrac{1}{5}i$ **20.** $-\dfrac{37}{53} - \dfrac{50}{53}i$

21. $-\dfrac{11}{5} + \dfrac{2}{5}i$ **22.** $\dfrac{1}{3} + \dfrac{2}{3}i\sqrt{2}$ **23.** $-i$ **24.** i

25. $\dfrac{1}{10} + \dfrac{1}{5}i$ **26.** $-\dfrac{3}{34} + \dfrac{5i}{34}$ **27.** $-\dfrac{4}{65} - \dfrac{7i}{65}$

28. $i^{-3} = \dfrac{1}{i^3} = \dfrac{1}{-i} \cdot \dfrac{i}{i} = \dfrac{-i}{i^2} = \dfrac{-i}{-1} = i$ **29.** $i^2 = -1$

30. $\dfrac{1 - i}{(1 + i)(1 + i)} = \dfrac{1 - i}{1 + 2i + i^2} = \dfrac{1 - i}{2i} \cdot \dfrac{2i}{2i} = \dfrac{2i - 2i^2}{4i^2} = \dfrac{2i + 2}{-4}$
$= -\dfrac{1}{2} - \dfrac{1}{2}i$

31. $\dfrac{1 + i}{(1 - i)(1 - i)} = \dfrac{1 + i}{1 - 2i + i^2} = \dfrac{1 + i}{1 - 2i - 1} = \dfrac{1 + i}{-2i} \cdot \dfrac{i}{i} = \dfrac{i + i^2}{-2i^2}$
$= \dfrac{i - 1}{-2(-1)} = -\dfrac{1}{2} + \dfrac{1}{2}i$

32. $\dfrac{1}{z} = \dfrac{1}{a + bi} \cdot \dfrac{a - bi}{a - bi} = \dfrac{a - bi}{a^2 - b^2i^2} = \dfrac{a - bi}{a^2 - b^2(-1)} = \dfrac{a - bi}{a^2 + b^2}$
$= \dfrac{a}{a^2 + b^2} - \dfrac{b}{a^2 + b^2}i$

33. For example, $\sqrt{-1}\sqrt{-1} - i^2 = -1$
but $\sqrt{(-1)(-1)} = \sqrt{1} = 1$

34. $\dfrac{5}{61} - \dfrac{6i}{61}$

35. $(1 + \sqrt{-3})^{-2} = \dfrac{1}{(1 + \sqrt{-3})^2} = \dfrac{1}{(1 + i\sqrt{3})(1 + i\sqrt{3})}$
$= \dfrac{1}{1 + 2i\sqrt{3} + 3i^2} = \dfrac{1}{1 + 2i\sqrt{3} - 3}$

$$= \frac{1}{-2 + 2i\sqrt{3}} \cdot \frac{-2 - 2i\sqrt{3}}{-2 - 2i\sqrt{3}} = \frac{-2 - 2i\sqrt{3}}{4 - 4i^2(3)}$$

$$= \frac{-2 - 2i\sqrt{3}}{4 + 12} = \frac{-2 - 2i\sqrt{3}}{16} = -\frac{1}{8} - \frac{\sqrt{3}}{8}i$$

36. $(\sqrt{-2} + 2\sqrt{-6})^2$
$$= (i\sqrt{2} + 2i\sqrt{6})(i\sqrt{2} + 2i\sqrt{6})$$
$$= 2i^2 + 2i^2\sqrt{(2)(2)(3)} + 2i^2\sqrt{(2)(2)(3)} + 4i^2\sqrt{(6)(6)}$$
$$= -2 - 2(2)\sqrt{3} - 2(2)\sqrt{3} - 4(6)$$
$$= -2 - 4\sqrt{3} - 4\sqrt{3} - 24 = -26 - 8\sqrt{3}$$

37. $(1 + i)^{-3}(2 - i)^{-2} = \frac{1}{(1 + i)(1 + i)(1 + i)} \cdot \frac{1}{(2 - i)(2 - i)}$

$$= \frac{1}{(1 + 2i + i^2)(1 + i)} \cdot \frac{1}{4 - 4i + i^2}$$

$$= \frac{1}{2i(1 + i)} \cdot \frac{1}{4 - 4i - 1} = \frac{1}{2i + 2i^2} \cdot \frac{1}{3 - 4i}$$

$$= \frac{1}{(-2 + 2i)(3 - 4i)} = \frac{1}{-6 + 8i + 6i - 8i^2}$$

$$= \frac{1}{-6 + 14i + 8} = \frac{1}{2 + 14i} \cdot \frac{2 - 14i}{2 - 14i}$$

$$= \frac{2 - 14i}{4 - 196i^2} = \frac{2 - 14i}{4 + 196}$$

$$= \frac{2 - 14i}{200} = \frac{1}{100} - \frac{7}{100}i$$

38. $\sqrt{\frac{9}{2}} \cdot \frac{\sqrt{2}}{\sqrt{2}} = \frac{\sqrt{(3)(3)(2)}}{2} = \frac{3\sqrt{2}}{2}$

39. $\frac{3\sqrt{3}}{2\sqrt{5}} \cdot \frac{\sqrt{5}}{\sqrt{5}} = \frac{3\sqrt{15}}{2(5)} = \frac{3\sqrt{15}}{10}$

40. $\frac{\sqrt{m} - \sqrt{n}}{\sqrt{m} + \sqrt{n}} \cdot \frac{\sqrt{m} - \sqrt{n}}{\sqrt{m} - \sqrt{n}} = \frac{\sqrt{(m)(m)} - \sqrt{mn} - \sqrt{mn} + \sqrt{(n)(n)}}{m - n}$

$$= \frac{m + n - 2\sqrt{mn}}{m - n}$$

41. $m = \frac{y_2 - y_1}{x_2 - x_1} = \frac{-6 - 3}{-1 - 2} = \frac{-9}{-3} = 3$, $y = mx + b$, so use either set

of points to find y-intercept. $3 = 3(2) + b$
$3 = 6 + b$, $b = -3$; $y = 3x - 3$

pp. 330–332   7-10 TRY THIS

a. $x^2 + 2x + 1 = 0$
$(1 - i)^2 + 2(1 - i) + 1 = (1 - 2i - 1) + (2 - 2i) + 1$
$$= 3 - 4i \neq 0$$
Therefore, $1 - i$ is not a solution of $x^2 + 2x + 1 = 0$.
b. $x = 1 + i$ or $x = 1 - i$
$[x - (1 + i)][x - (1 - i)] = 0$
$[x - 1 - i][x - 1 - i] = 0$
$(x - 1)^2 - i^2 = 0$
$x^2 - 2x + 1 + 1 = 0$
$x^2 - 2x + 2 = 0$
c. $x = 2 - 3i$ or $x = 2 + 3i$
$[x - (2 - 3i)][x - (2 + 3i)] = 0$
$[x - 2 + 3i][x - 2 - 3i] = 0$
$(x - 2)^2 - (3i)^2 = 0$
$x^2 - 4x + 4 + 9 = 0$
$x^2 - 4x + 13 = 0$
d. $3 - 4i + 2ix = 3i - (1 - i)x$
$2ix + (1 - i)x = 7i - 3$
$(1 + i)x = -3 + 7i$

$$x = \frac{-3 + 7i}{1 + i} \cdot \frac{(1 - i)}{(1 - i)}$$

$$x = \frac{4 + 10i}{2}$$

$$x = 2 + 5i$$

e. $(x + 2i)(x - 2i) = x^2 + 2ix - 2ix - 4i^2$
$$= x^2 + 4$$
f. $(-1 + i)^2 = 1 - 2i + i^2 = 1 - 2i - 1 = -2i$
The other root is the additive inverse of $(-1 + i)$, $1 - i$.

1. Yes, yes   **2.** Yes, yes   **3.** No, yes   **4.** No, yes
5. Yes, yes   **6.** Yes, yes   **7.** $x^2 + 25 = 0$
8. $x^2 + 49 = 0$ **9.** $x^2 - 4x + 13 = 0$
10. $x^2 - 8x + 25 = 0$ **11.** $x^2 + 3 = 0$
12. $x^2 - 4x + 6 = 0$ **13.** $x^2 - 12x + 42 = 0$
14. $x^2 - 2x + 9 = 0$ **15.** $x^2 - 6x + 26 = 0$ **16.** $\frac{2}{5} + \frac{6}{5}i$

17. $\frac{12}{5} - \frac{1}{5}i$ **18.** $\frac{8}{5} - \frac{9}{5}i$ **19.** $\frac{8}{29} + \frac{9}{29}i$ **20.** $2 - i$

21. $\frac{11}{25} + \frac{2}{25}i$ **22.** $\frac{4}{5} + \frac{3}{5}i$

23. $(2x + i)(2x - i) = 4x^2 - 2ix + 2ix - i^2 = 4x^2 + 1$
24. $(2x + 2i)(2x - 2i) = 4x^2 - 4ix + 4ix - 4i^2 = 4x^2 + 4$
25. $(2 + i)(2 + i) = 4 + 4i + i^2 = 3 + 4i$, $-2 - i$
26. $(2 - i)(2 - i) = 4 - 4i + i^2 = 3 - 4i$, $-2 + i$
27. $x = 5$ or $x = i$
$(x - 5)(x - i) = 0$
$x^2 - ix - 5x + 5i = 0$
28. $x = 1$ or $x = 3i$ or $x = -3i$
$(x - 1)(x - 3i)(x + 3i) = 0$
$(x - 1)(x^2 - 9i^2) = 0$
$(x - 1)(x^2 + 9) = 0$
$x^3 - x^2 + 9x - 9 = 0$
29. $x = 2$ or $x = i$ or $x = 1 + i$
$(x - 2)(x - i)(x - 1 - i) = 0$
$(x^2 - xi - 2x + 2i)(x - 1 - i) = 0$
$x^3 - x^2 - ix^2 - ix^2 + ix + i^2x$
$- 2x^2 + 2x + 2ix - 2i - 2i^2 = 0$
$x^3 - 2ix^2 - 3x^2 + 5ix + x - 2i + 2 = 0$
30. $x = 2i$ or $x = i$ or $x = -i$
$(x - 2i)(x - i)(x + i) = 0$
$(x - 2i)(x^2 - i^2) = 0$
$(x - 2i)(x^2 + 1) = 0$
$x^3 - 2ix^2 + x - 2i = 0$
31. $3 + 5i = \sqrt{a + bi}$
$a + bi = 9 + 30i - 25 = 30i - 16$
$b = 30 \qquad a = -16$
$-16 + 30i$
32. $(a + bi)^2 = a^2 + 2abi - b^2$
$$= (a^2 - b^2) + 2abi$$
$$= (a + b)(a - b) + 2abi$$
33. $(a + bi)^2 = 3 - 4i$ but $(a + bi)^2 = a^2 - b^2 + 2abi$
equating the real and imaginary parts,
$a^2 - b^2 = 3$
$2ab = -4$
We have a system of equations. Solving the second equation for

$b, b = -\frac{2}{a}$

Substituting in the first equation,

$a^2\left(-\frac{2}{a}\right)^2 = 3$

$a^2 - \frac{4}{a^2} = 3$

$0 = a^4 - 3a^2 - 4$
$0 = (a^2 - 4)(a^2 + 1)$
$0 = a^2 - 4, 0 = a^2 + 1$
$\pm 2 = a, \qquad \pm i = a$
So, $1 = b, \qquad \pm 2i = b$
$\{(-2 + i), (2 - i)\}$

34. $5.023 \times 10^{-5} = 0.00005023$

35. $4.441 \times 10^6 = 4,441,000$

36. $\dfrac{\dfrac{2}{x} + 3}{\dfrac{2}{x} - 5} = \dfrac{\dfrac{2 + 3x}{x}}{\dfrac{2 - 5x}{x}} = \dfrac{2 + 3x}{2 - 5x}$

37. $\dfrac{m - \dfrac{3}{m}}{m + \dfrac{3}{m}} = \dfrac{\dfrac{m^2 - 3}{m}}{\dfrac{m^2 + 3}{m}} = \dfrac{m^2 - 3}{m^2 + 3}$

38. $\dfrac{\dfrac{2}{x} + \dfrac{5}{y}}{\dfrac{5}{x} - \dfrac{2}{y}} = \dfrac{\dfrac{2y + 5x}{xy}}{\dfrac{5y - 2x}{xy}} = \dfrac{2y + 5x}{5y - 2x}$

39. $\dfrac{3c + \dfrac{2}{c}}{3c - \dfrac{2}{c}} = \dfrac{\dfrac{3c^2 + 2}{c}}{\dfrac{3c^2 - 2}{c}} = \dfrac{3c^2 + 2}{3c^2 - 2}$

1. $\dfrac{79 + 85 + 90 + x}{4} = \dfrac{85}{1}$

$\dfrac{254 + x}{4} = \dfrac{85}{1}$

$85(4) = 254 + x$
$340 - 254 = x$
$86 = x$
(B)

2. $\dfrac{80 + 71 + x}{3} = \dfrac{70}{1}$

$\dfrac{151 + x}{3} = \dfrac{70}{1}$

$70(3) = 151 + x$
$210 - 151 = x$
$59 = x$
(A)

3. $\dfrac{47 + 48 + x}{3} > \dfrac{50}{1}$

$95 + x > 150$
$x > 55$
(A)

4. 20 boys average 50 = 1000
15 girls average 57 = 855
Total average = 1855
Total students = 35

$\dfrac{1855}{35} = 53$
(C)

5. $8 < \dfrac{x}{3} < 12$

$24 < x < 36$
(A)

6. $N + x = 2A$
$x = 2A - N$
(E)

7. $\dfrac{75 + 75 + 90 + 90 + 90}{5}$

$\dfrac{420}{5} = 84$
(B)

8. Example:

$\dfrac{60 + 90 + 100 + 70 + 80}{5} = \dfrac{400}{5} = 80$

$\dfrac{60 + 90 + 100 + 70}{4} = 80$
(A)

9. $\dfrac{25 + 28 + 22 + x + y}{5} = 26$

$75 + x + y = 26(5)$
$x + y = 130 - 75$
$x + y = 55$
(E)

10. If 10 students ≤ 30,
then 20 students ≥ 30.
(10)(30) = 300 maximum points
(20)(60) = 1200 maximum points
Total = 1500
Average = 1500 ÷ 30
Average = 50 (D)

11. Let $m = 25, 100, 75, 50, 55$.
Let $n = 50, 100$.

Then $A = \dfrac{305}{5} = 61$.

Then $B = \dfrac{150}{2} = 75$.

So, $\dfrac{(61)(305) + 75(150)}{305 + 150} = 65.6$

and $\dfrac{m + n}{7} = \dfrac{455}{7} = 65$
(D)

1. 36   **2.** $4|x|$ **3.** $\dfrac{-2x}{3}$ **4.** -3 **5.** $2|x|$

6. $\sqrt{18x} \cdot \sqrt{12x} = \sqrt{18 \cdot 12x^2} = \sqrt{216x^2} = \sqrt{36 \cdot 6x^2} = 6|x|\sqrt{6}$

7. $\sqrt[3]{a^2b}\,\sqrt[3]{a^4b^6} = \sqrt[3]{a^6b^7} = a^2b^2\sqrt[3]{b}$

8. $\sqrt[3]{3c^2d^5}\,\sqrt[3]{16c^2d^2} = \sqrt[3]{48c^4d^7} = \sqrt[3]{(2cd^2)^3 \cdot 6cd} = 2cd^2\sqrt[3]{6cd}$

9. $\dfrac{\sqrt[3]{32}}{\sqrt[3]{2}} = \sqrt[3]{\dfrac{32}{2}} = \sqrt[3]{16} = \sqrt[3]{8 \cdot 2} = 2\sqrt[3]{2}$

10. $\sqrt{\dfrac{12a^3}{b^7}} = \dfrac{\sqrt{12a^3}}{\sqrt{b^7}} = \dfrac{\sqrt{(4a^2) \cdot 3a}}{\sqrt{b^6 \cdot b}} = \dfrac{2|a|\sqrt{3a}}{|b^3|\sqrt{b}} = \dfrac{2|a|\sqrt{3ab}}{b^4}$

11. $\dfrac{\sqrt{40x^7}}{\sqrt{32x^3}} = \sqrt{\dfrac{40x^7}{32x^3}} = \sqrt{\dfrac{5x^4}{4}} = \dfrac{x^2\sqrt{5}}{2}$

12. $2\sqrt{32} - \sqrt{50} + \sqrt{162} = 2\sqrt{16 \cdot 2} - \sqrt{25 \cdot 2} + \sqrt{81 \cdot 2}$
$= 8\sqrt{2} - 5\sqrt{2} + 9\sqrt{2} = 12\sqrt{2}$

13. $\sqrt[3]{24} - \sqrt[3]{81} = \sqrt[3]{8 \cdot 3} - \sqrt[3]{27 \cdot 3} = 2\sqrt[3]{3} - 3\sqrt[3]{3} = -\sqrt[3]{3}$

14. $5\sqrt{3y^3} - \sqrt{12y} = 5|y|\sqrt{3y} - 2\sqrt{3y} = (5|y| - 2)\sqrt{3y}$

15. $(7 - 4\sqrt{3})(7 + 4\sqrt{3}) = 49 + 28\sqrt{3} - 28\sqrt{3} - 16 \cdot 3$
$= 49 - 48 = 1$

16. $(3\sqrt{6} + 2)(3\sqrt{6} + 2) = 9 \cdot 6 + 6\sqrt{6} + 6\sqrt{6} + 4$
$= 58 + 12\sqrt{6}$

17. $(2\sqrt[3]{2} + \sqrt[3]{3})(\sqrt[3]{2} + 3\sqrt[3]{3}) = 2\sqrt[3]{4} + 6\sqrt[3]{6} + \sqrt[3]{6} + 3\sqrt[3]{9}$
$= 2\sqrt[3]{4} + 7\sqrt[3]{6} + 3\sqrt[3]{9}$

18. $\dfrac{\sqrt{8}}{\sqrt{3}} \cdot \dfrac{\sqrt{3}}{\sqrt{3}} = \dfrac{\sqrt{24}}{3} = \dfrac{\sqrt{4 \cdot 6}}{3} = \dfrac{2\sqrt{6}}{3}$

19. $\dfrac{6}{3 - \sqrt{17}} \cdot \dfrac{3 + \sqrt{17}}{3 + \sqrt{17}} = \dfrac{18 + 6\sqrt{17}}{9 - 17} = \dfrac{18 + 6\sqrt{17}}{-8} = \dfrac{9 + 3\sqrt{17}}{-4}$

20. $\dfrac{\sqrt{3} + 5}{7 + \sqrt{3}} \cdot \dfrac{7 - \sqrt{3}}{7 - \sqrt{3}} = \dfrac{7\sqrt{3} - 3 + 35 - 5\sqrt{3}}{49 - 3} = \dfrac{2\sqrt{3} + 32}{46}$
$= \dfrac{\sqrt{3} + 16}{23}$

21. $(\sqrt[3]{16})^2 = (\sqrt[3]{16})(\sqrt[3]{16}) = \sqrt[3]{16 \cdot 16} = \sqrt[3]{4^4} = 4\sqrt[3]{4}$

22. $(\sqrt{3x})^3 = (\sqrt{3x})(\sqrt{3x})(\sqrt{3x}) = \sqrt{27x^3} = 3|x|\sqrt{3x}$

23. $\sqrt{a^6b^4} = |a^3|b^2$ **24.** $\sqrt[3]{\dfrac{27}{a^6}} = \sqrt[3]{\dfrac{3^3}{(a^2)^3}} = \dfrac{3}{a^2}$

25. $x^{2/3} = \sqrt[3]{x^2}$ **26.** $27^{1/3} = \sqrt[3]{27} = 3$ **27.** $32^{2/5} = \sqrt[5]{32^2} = 4$

28. $(8x)^{5/2} = \sqrt{(8x)^5} = \sqrt{(8x)^4 \cdot (8x)} = (8x)^2\sqrt{8x} = 2 \cdot (8x)^2\sqrt{2x}$
$= 128x^2\sqrt{2x}$

29. $\sqrt[3]{15} = 15^{1/3}$ **30.** $\sqrt[2]{32} = \sqrt[2]{2^5} = 2^{5/2}$

31. $\sqrt[3]{x^3y^4z^5} = x^1y^{4/3}z^{5/3}$ **32.** $\sqrt[4]{8x^3y^2} = \sqrt[4]{2^3x^3y^2} = 2^{3/4}x^{3/4}y^{1/2}$

33. $x^{-1/2} = \dfrac{1}{x^{1/2}}$ **34.** $\dfrac{1}{x^{-4}} = x^4$

35. $\left(\dfrac{1}{16}\right)^{-1/2} = \dfrac{1}{\left(\dfrac{1}{16}\right)^{1/2}} = 16^{1/2} = 4$

36. $\dfrac{1}{8^{-2/3}} = 8^{2/3} - \sqrt[3]{8^2} = \sqrt[3]{64} = 4$

37. $\sqrt[4]{x^2} = x^{2/4} = x^{1/2} = \sqrt{x}$

38. $\sqrt[3]{16y^6} = \sqrt[3]{2^4 y^6} = 2^{4/3} y^2 = 2y^2 \sqrt[3]{2}$

39. $\sqrt[4]{\dfrac{x^{-8}y^{12}}{16}} = \sqrt[4]{\dfrac{y^{12}}{x^8 16}} = \dfrac{y^3}{x^2 16^{1/4}} = \dfrac{y^3}{x^2 2}$

40. $\sqrt[10]{\dfrac{64x^6}{y^8 z^{-4}}} = \sqrt[10]{\dfrac{2^6 x^6 z^4}{y^8}} = \dfrac{2^{3/5} x^{3/5} z^{2/5}}{y^{4/5}}$

$= \sqrt[5]{\dfrac{2^3 x^3 z^2}{y^4}} = \sqrt[5]{\dfrac{8x^3 z^2}{y^4}} = \dfrac{\sqrt[5]{8x^3 z^2 y}}{y}$

41. $\sqrt{5 - 3x} - 6 = 0$
$\sqrt{5 - 3x} = 6$
$5 - 3x = 36$
$-3x = 31$
$x = -\dfrac{31}{3}$

42. $\sqrt{7 - 4x} - \sqrt{3 - 2x} = 1$
$\sqrt{7 - 4x} = 1 + \sqrt{3 - 2x}$
$7 - 4x = 1 + 2\sqrt{3 - 2x} + 3 - 2x$
$7 - 4x = 4 - 2x + 2\sqrt{3 - 2x}$
$3 - 2x = 2\sqrt{3 - 2x}$
$9 - 12x + 4x^2 = 4(3 - 2x)$
$4x^2 - 12x + 9 = 12 - 8x$
$4x^2 - 4x - 3 = 0$
$(2x + 1)(2x - 3) = 0$
$2x + 1 = 0$ or $2x - 3 = 0$
$2x = -1 \qquad\qquad 2x = 3$
$x = -\dfrac{1}{2} \qquad\qquad x = \dfrac{3}{2}$

43. $T = 4\pi\sqrt{\dfrac{L}{g}}$

$\dfrac{T}{4\pi} = \sqrt{\dfrac{L}{g}}$

$\dfrac{L}{g} = \dfrac{T^2}{16\pi^2}$

$L = \dfrac{gT^2}{16\pi^2}$

44. $\sqrt{\dfrac{E}{m}} = C$

$\dfrac{E}{m} = C^2$

$E = C^2 m$

45. $A = \sqrt{\dfrac{w_1}{w_2}}$

$A^2 = \dfrac{w_1}{w_2}$

$w_2 A^2 = w_1$

$w_2 = \dfrac{w_1}{A^2}$

46. $\sqrt{-49} = \sqrt{49i^2}$
$= 7i$

47. $-\sqrt{-25} = -\sqrt{25i^2}$
$= -5i$

48. $\sqrt{-6} \cdot 6i = \sqrt{6i^2} \cdot 6i$
$= i\sqrt{6} \cdot 6i$
$= 6i^2\sqrt{6} = -6\sqrt{6}$

49. $(6 + 2i) + (-4 - 3i) = 2 - i$

50. $(3 - 5i) - (2 - i) = (3 - 5i) + (-2 + i)$
$= 1 - 4i$

51.

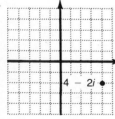

52.

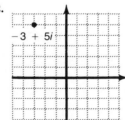

53. $|5 - 3i| = \sqrt{25 + 9} = \sqrt{34}$

54. $|-4 + 3i| = \sqrt{16 + 9} = \sqrt{25} = 5$

55. $(2 - 2i)(3 + 4i) = 6 + 8i - 6i - 8i^2$
$= 6 + 2i + 8$
$= 14 + 2i$

56. $(2 - 3i)(3 + 2i) = 6 + 4i - 9i - 6i^2$
$= 6 - 5i + 6$
$= 12 - 5i$

57. $(3 - 2i)(3 + 2i) = 9 + 6i - 6i - 4i^2$
$= 9 + 4$
$= 13$

58. $(2 + 6i)(2 - 6i) = 4 - 12i + 12i - 36i^2$
$= 4 + 36 = 40$

59. $\dfrac{3 - 2i}{2 - i} \cdot \dfrac{2 + i}{2 + i} = \dfrac{6 + 3i - 4i + 2}{4 + 1} = \dfrac{8 - i}{5}$

60. $\dfrac{4 - 2i}{4 + 2i} \cdot \dfrac{4 - 2i}{4 - 2i} = \dfrac{16 - 8i - 8i - 4}{16 + 4} = \dfrac{12 - 16i}{20} = \dfrac{3 - 4i}{5}$

61. $\dfrac{1}{2 + 4i} \cdot \dfrac{2 - 4i}{2 - 4i} = \dfrac{2 - 4i}{4 + 16} = \dfrac{2 - 4i}{20} = \dfrac{1 - 2i}{10} = \dfrac{1}{10} - \dfrac{1i}{5}$

62. $\dfrac{1}{1 - i} \cdot \dfrac{1 + i}{1 + i} = \dfrac{1 + i}{1 + 1} = \dfrac{1 + i}{2} = \dfrac{1}{2} + \dfrac{1}{2}i$

63. $2ix - 5 + 3i = (2 - i)x + i$
$2ix - 5 + 3i = 2x - ix + i$
$-5 + 2i = 2x - ix - 2ix$
$-5 + 2i = x(2 - 3i)$
$x = \dfrac{-5 + 2i}{2 - 3i} \cdot \dfrac{2 + 3i}{2 + 3i}$

$= \dfrac{-10 - 15i + 4i - 6}{4 + 9} = \dfrac{-16 - 11i}{13}$

$x = -\dfrac{16}{13} - \dfrac{11}{13}i$

p. 339   CHAPTER 7 TEST

1. $-\sqrt{121} = -11$ **2.** $\sqrt[3]{-0.027} = -0.3$

3. $\sqrt{x^2 - 10x + 25} = \sqrt{(x - 5)^2} = |x - 5|$ **4.** $\sqrt{49y^2} = 7|y|$

5. $\sqrt[3]{-y^3} = -y$ **6.** $\sqrt[8]{x^8} = |x|$

7. $\sqrt{20}\sqrt{18} = \sqrt{360} = \sqrt{36 \cdot 10} = 6\sqrt{10}$

8. $\sqrt[3]{x^2 y^4}\sqrt[3]{x^5 y^2} = \sqrt[3]{x^7 y^6} = y^2 x^2 \sqrt[3]{x}$

9. $\sqrt{12x^5}\sqrt{6x^2 y} = \sqrt{72x^7 y} = 6|x^3|\sqrt{2xy}$

10. $\dfrac{\sqrt{8x^2}}{\sqrt{2x}} = \sqrt{\dfrac{8x^2}{2x}} = \sqrt{4x} = 2\sqrt{x}$

11. $\dfrac{\sqrt[3]{750}}{\sqrt[3]{3}} = \sqrt[3]{\dfrac{750}{3}} = \sqrt[3]{250} = 5\sqrt[3]{2}$

12. $\sqrt[4]{\dfrac{64x^5 y^7}{36xy^2}} = \sqrt[4]{\dfrac{16x^4 y^5}{9}} = 2|xy|\sqrt[4]{\dfrac{y}{9}} = 2|xy|\dfrac{\sqrt[4]{9y}}{3}$

13. $\sqrt{27} + \sqrt{108} = 3\sqrt{3} + 6\sqrt{3} = 9\sqrt{3}$

14. $\sqrt[3]{40} - \sqrt[3]{135} = 2\sqrt[3]{5} - 3\sqrt[3]{5} = -\sqrt[3]{5}$

15. $(8 + 5\sqrt{6})(8 - 5\sqrt{6}) = 64 - 40\sqrt{6} + 40\sqrt{6} - 25(6)$
$= 64 - 150 = -86$

16. $(2\sqrt{7} - 3\sqrt{5})(\sqrt{7} - \sqrt{5}) = 2 \cdot 7 - 2\sqrt{35} - 3\sqrt{35} + 3 \cdot 5$
$= 14 - 5\sqrt{35} + 15$
$= 29 - 5\sqrt{35}$

17. $\dfrac{\sqrt{5}}{\sqrt{7}} \cdot \dfrac{\sqrt{7}}{\sqrt{7}} = \dfrac{\sqrt{35}}{7}$

18. $\dfrac{\sqrt{3} + 7}{8 - \sqrt{5}} \cdot \dfrac{8 + \sqrt{5}}{8 + \sqrt{5}} = \dfrac{8\sqrt{3} + 56 + \sqrt{15} + 7\sqrt{5}}{64 - 5}$

$= \dfrac{8\sqrt{3} + \sqrt{15} + 56 + 7\sqrt{5}}{59}$

19. $\sqrt[3]{9a^2 b^4} = b\sqrt[3]{9a^2 b}$ **20.** $\sqrt[3]{\dfrac{n^{24}}{a^8}} = \dfrac{n^8}{a^2}\sqrt[3]{\dfrac{1}{a^2}} = \dfrac{n^8\sqrt[3]{a}}{|a^3|}$

21. $\sqrt[4]{81x^8 y^8} = 3x^2 y^2$ **22.** $x^{-2/3} = \dfrac{1}{x^{2/3}} = \dfrac{1}{\sqrt[3]{x^2}} = \dfrac{\sqrt[3]{x}}{x}$

23. $\sqrt[3]{\dfrac{81x^8 y^{-3}}{z^2}} = \sqrt[3]{\dfrac{81x^8}{y^3 z^2}} = \dfrac{3x^2}{y}\sqrt[3]{\dfrac{3x^2}{z^2}} = \dfrac{3x^2}{zy}\sqrt[3]{3x^2 z}$

24. $\sqrt[4]{9x^6} = \sqrt[4]{3^2 x^6} = 3^{1/2} x^{3/2} = |x|\sqrt{3x}$

25.
$$x - 5 = \sqrt{x + 7}$$
$$x^2 - 10x + 25 = x + 7$$
$$x^2 - 11x + 18 = 0$$
$$(x - 9)(x - 2) = 0$$
$$x - 9 = 0 \quad \text{or} \quad x - 2 = 0$$
$$x = 9 \qquad\qquad x = 2$$
2 is not a solution.
$$x = 9$$

26.
$$\sqrt{2x - 5} = 1 + \sqrt{x - 3}$$
$$2x - 5 = 1 + 2\sqrt{x - 3} + x - 3$$
$$2x - 5 = x - 2 + 2\sqrt{x - 3}$$
$$x - 3 = 2\sqrt{x - 3}$$
$$x^2 - 6x + 9 = 4(x - 3)$$
$$x^2 - 6x + 9 = 4x - 12$$
$$x^2 - 10x + 21 = 0$$
$$(x - 7)(x - 3) = 0$$
$$x - 7 = 0 \quad \text{or} \quad x - 3 = 0$$
$$x = 7 \qquad\qquad x = 3$$

27.
$$c = \sqrt{a^2 + b^2}$$
$$c^2 = a^2 + b^2$$
$$b^2 = c^2 - a^2$$
$$b = \sqrt{c^2 - a^2}$$
$$b = \sqrt{169 - 25}$$
$$b = \sqrt{144} = 12$$

28. $(3 + 2i) + (2 - 3i) = 5 - i$

29. $(9 - 4i) - (3 + 2i) = (9 - 4i) + (-3 - 2i) = 6 - 6i$

30.

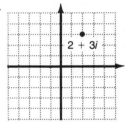

2 + 3i

31. $|4 + 2i| = \sqrt{16 + 4} = \sqrt{20} = 2\sqrt{5}$

32. $(1 + 2i)(2i - 1) = 2i - 1 - 4 - 2i = -5$

33. $(2 + 5i)(2 - 5i) = 4 - 10i + 10i + 25 = 29$

34. $\dfrac{1 - 3i}{2 + i} \cdot \dfrac{2 - i}{2 - i} = \dfrac{2 - i - 6i - 3}{4 + 1} = \dfrac{-1 - 7i}{5} = -\dfrac{1}{5} - \dfrac{7}{5}i$

35. $\dfrac{1}{1 + 2i} \cdot \dfrac{1 - 2i}{1 - 2i} = \dfrac{1 - 2i}{1 + 4} = \dfrac{1 - 2i}{5} = \dfrac{1}{5} - \dfrac{2}{5}i$

36.
$$-5ix + 8i - 4 = (7 + i)x + 10i$$
$$-2i - 4 = (7 + i)x + 5ix$$
$$-2i - 4 = (7 + 6i)x$$

$$x = \dfrac{-2i - 4}{7 + 6i} \cdot \dfrac{7 - 6i}{7 - 6i}$$

$$= \dfrac{-14i - 12 - 28 + 24i}{49 + 36}$$

$$= \dfrac{10i - 40}{85} = \dfrac{2i - 8}{17} = \dfrac{-8}{17} + \dfrac{2}{17}i$$

CHAPTER 8

p. 340   READY FOR QUADRATIC EQUATIONS?

1. $7, -2$ **2.** $0, 2$ **3.** -5 **4.** $3, -3$ **5.** $\dfrac{2}{5}, y = \dfrac{2}{5}x$

6. $160, y = \dfrac{160}{x}$ **7.** $\dfrac{2\sqrt{14}}{7}$ **8.** $\dfrac{\sqrt{2}}{4}$ **9.** $\dfrac{3 + \sqrt{3}}{6}$

10. $i\sqrt{7}$ **11.** $2i\sqrt{5}$

a.
$$5x^2 + 8x = 0$$
$$x(5x + 8) = 0$$
$$x = 0 \quad \text{or} \quad 5x + 8 = 0$$
$$x = 0 \quad \text{or} \qquad 5x = -8$$
$$x = 0 \quad \text{or} \qquad x = -\dfrac{8}{5}$$

b.
$$14x^2 + 2 = 11x$$
$$14x^2 - 11x + 2 = 0$$
$$(7x - 2)(2x - 1) = 0$$
$$7x - 2 = 0 \quad \text{or} \quad 2x - 1 = 0$$
$$7x = 2 \quad \text{or} \qquad 2x = 1$$
$$x = \dfrac{2}{7} \quad \text{or} \qquad x = \dfrac{1}{2}$$

c.
$$(x + 2)(x - 2) = 2 - x$$
$$x^2 - 4 = 2 - x$$
$$x^2 + x - 6 = 0$$
$$(x + 3)(x - 2) = 0$$
$$x + 3 = 0 \quad \text{or} \quad x - 2 = 0$$
$$x = -3 \quad \text{or} \qquad x = 2$$

d.
$$7x^2 - 5 = 0$$
$$7x^2 = 5$$
$$x^2 = \dfrac{5}{7}$$
$$x = \pm\sqrt{\dfrac{5}{7}} = \pm\dfrac{\sqrt{5}\sqrt{7}}{\sqrt{7}\sqrt{7}} = \pm\dfrac{\sqrt{35}}{7}$$

e.
$$2x^2 + 1 = 0$$
$$2x^2 = -1$$
$$x^2 = -\dfrac{1}{2}$$
$$x = \pm\sqrt{-\dfrac{1}{2}}$$
$$= \pm\sqrt{\dfrac{1}{2}}i$$
$$= \pm\dfrac{\sqrt{1}\cdot\sqrt{2}}{\sqrt{2}\cdot\sqrt{2}}i$$
$$= \pm\dfrac{\sqrt{2}}{2}i$$

f.
$$49x^2 + 4 = 0$$
$$49x^2 = -4$$
$$x^2 = -\dfrac{4}{49}$$
$$x = \pm\sqrt{\dfrac{-4}{49}}$$
$$= \pm\dfrac{2}{7}i$$

g.
$$x^2 + 14x$$
$$x^2 + 14x + \left(\dfrac{14}{2}\right)^2$$
$$= x^2 + 14x + (7)^2$$
$$= x^2 + 14x + 49$$

h.
$$y^2 - 11y$$
$$y^2 - 11y + \left(-\dfrac{11}{12}\right)^2$$
$$= y^2 - 11y + \dfrac{121}{4}$$

i.
$$x^2 - \dfrac{2}{5}x$$
$$x^2 - \dfrac{2}{5}x + \left(\dfrac{\left(-\dfrac{2}{5}\right)}{2}\right)^2$$
$$= x_2 - \dfrac{2}{5}x + \left(\dfrac{4}{25}\right)\left(\dfrac{1}{4}\right)$$
$$= x^2 - \dfrac{2}{5}x + \dfrac{1}{25}$$

j.
$$x^2 + 2ax$$
$$x^2 + 2ax + \left(\dfrac{2a}{2}\right)^2$$
$$x^2 + 2ax + a^2$$

k.
$$x^2 + x - 1 = 0$$
$$x^2 + x = 1$$
$$x^2 + x + \left(\dfrac{1}{2}\right)^2 = 1 + \left(\dfrac{1}{2}\right)^2$$
$$\left(x + \dfrac{1}{2}\right)^2 = 1 + \dfrac{1}{4}$$
$$\left(x + \dfrac{1}{2}\right)^2 = \dfrac{5}{4}$$

$$x + \frac{1}{2} = \pm\sqrt{\frac{5}{4}}$$

$$x + \frac{1}{2} = \pm\frac{\sqrt{5}}{2}$$

$$x = \frac{\pm\sqrt{5} - 1}{2}$$

$$x = \frac{-1 \pm \sqrt{5}}{2}$$

l. $x^2 - \frac{1}{2}x - \frac{1}{2} = 0$

$$x^2 - \frac{1}{2}x = \frac{1}{2}$$

$$x^2 - \frac{1}{2}x + \left(-\frac{1}{4}\right)^2 = \frac{1}{2} + \left(-\frac{1}{4}\right)^2$$

$$\left(x - \frac{1}{4}\right)^2 = \frac{8}{16} + \frac{1}{16}$$

$$\left(x - \frac{1}{4}\right)^2 = \frac{9}{16}$$

$$x - \frac{1}{4} = \pm\sqrt{\frac{9}{16}}$$

$$x - \frac{1}{4} = \pm\frac{3}{4}$$

$$x - \frac{1}{4} = \frac{3}{4} \quad \text{or} \quad x - \frac{1}{4} = -\frac{3}{4}$$

$$x = 1 \quad \text{or} \quad x = -\frac{2}{4} = -\frac{1}{2}$$

m. $8x^2 - x - 1 = 0$
$8x^2 - x = 1$

$$x^2 - \frac{1}{8}x = \frac{1}{8}$$

$$x^2 - \frac{1}{8}x + \left(-\frac{1}{8}\left(\frac{1}{2}\right)\right)^2 = \frac{1}{8} + \left(-\frac{1}{8}\left(\frac{1}{2}\right)\right)^2$$

$$x^2 - \frac{1}{8}x + \left(-\frac{1}{16}\right)^2 = \frac{1}{8} + \frac{1}{256}$$

$$\left(x - \frac{1}{16}\right)^2 = \frac{32}{256} + \frac{1}{256}$$

$$\left(x - \frac{1}{16}\right)^2 = \frac{33}{256}$$

$$x - \frac{1}{16} = \pm\frac{\sqrt{33}}{16}$$

$$x = \frac{1}{16} \pm \frac{\sqrt{33}}{16}$$

$$x = \frac{1 \pm \sqrt{33}}{16}$$

n. $9x^2 + 9x - 10 = 0$

$$x^2 + x - \frac{10}{9} = 0$$

$$x^2 + x + \left(\frac{1}{2}\right)^2 = \frac{10}{9} + \left(\frac{1}{2}\right)^2$$

$$\left(x + \frac{1}{2}\right)^2 = \frac{10}{9} + \frac{1}{4}$$

$$\left(x + \frac{1}{2}\right)^2 = \frac{40}{36} + \frac{9}{36} = \frac{49}{36}$$

$$x + \frac{1}{2} = \pm\sqrt{\frac{49}{36}}$$

$$x + \frac{1}{2} = \pm\frac{7}{6}$$

$$x = -\frac{1}{2} \pm \frac{7}{6}$$

$$x = -\frac{3}{6} \pm \frac{7}{6}$$

$$x = \frac{-3 \pm 7}{6}$$

$$x = \frac{-3 + 7}{6} \quad \text{or} \quad x = \frac{-3 - 7}{6}$$

$$= \frac{4}{6} \quad \text{or} \quad = -\frac{10}{6}$$

$$= \frac{2}{3} \quad \text{or} \quad = -\frac{5}{3}$$

pp. 345–346 **8-1 EXERCISES**

1. $0, \frac{3}{7}$ **2.** $0, -\frac{9}{14}$ **3.** $0, -\frac{8}{19}$ **4.** $-5, -3$ **5.** $-7, -2$

6. $\frac{2}{3}, -\frac{1}{2}$ **7.** $-\frac{3}{2}, -5$ **8.** $-\frac{4}{3}, -\frac{1}{3}$ **9.** $\frac{2}{3}, -4$

10. $-\frac{5}{3}, 1$ **11.** $\frac{5}{3}, -4$ **12.** $-\frac{1}{4}, \frac{3}{2}$ **13.** $-\frac{7}{2}, -1$

14. $10, -3$ **15.** 4 **16.** $-2, -1$ **17.** $10, 5$ **18.** $\pm\sqrt{5}$

19. $\pm\sqrt{7}$ **20.** 0 **21.** 0 **22.** $\pm\frac{\sqrt{6}}{2}$ **23.** $\pm\frac{\sqrt{21}}{3}$

24. $\pm\frac{\sqrt{15}}{3}$ **25.** $\pm\frac{\sqrt{2}}{2}$ **26.** $\pm\frac{2}{5}i$ **27.** $\pm\frac{4}{3}i$

28. $\pm\frac{i\sqrt{3}}{3}$ **29.** $\pm\frac{i\sqrt{5}}{5}$ **30.** $\pm i\sqrt{5}$ **31.** $\pm i\sqrt{6}$

32. $\pm i\sqrt{7}$ **33.** $\pm i\sqrt{5}$ **34.** $\pm\frac{3}{2}$ **35.** $\pm\frac{5}{4}$

36. $x^2 + 8x + 16$ **37.** $y^2 - 20y + 100$ **38.** $a^2 - 7a + \frac{49}{4}$

39. $y^2 - \frac{1}{5}y + \frac{1}{100}$ **40.** $x^2 + \frac{1}{2}x + \frac{1}{16}$

41. $x^2 - 2.6kx + 1.69k^2$ **42.** $1, 2$ **43.** $-3, -4$

44. $\frac{-1 \pm i\sqrt{3}}{2}$ **45.** $2 \pm \sqrt{3}$ **46.** $-3 \pm 2\sqrt{3}$

47. $\frac{-1 \pm \sqrt{69}}{2}$ **48.** $\frac{5 \pm \sqrt{77}}{2}$ **49.** $\frac{5 \pm \sqrt{145}}{6}$ **50.** $1, -\frac{9}{2}$

51. $3 \pm 3i$ **52.** $-\frac{1}{2} \pm \frac{\sqrt{7}}{2}i$

53. $(3x^2 - 7x - 20)(2x - 5) = 0$
$(3x + 5)(x - 4)(2x - 5) = 0$
$3x + 5 = 0 \quad \text{or} \quad x - 4 = 0 \quad \text{or} \quad 2x - 5 = 0$

$$x = -\frac{5}{3} \quad \text{or} \quad x = 4 \quad \text{or} \quad x = \frac{5}{2}$$

$$\left\{-\frac{5}{3}, 4, \frac{5}{2}\right\}$$

54. $x(2x^2 + 9x - 56)(3x + 10) = 0$
$x(2x - 7)(x + 8)(3x + 10) = 0$
$x = 0 \quad \text{or} \quad 2x - 7 = 0 \quad \text{or} \quad x + 8 = 0 \quad \text{or} \quad 3x + 10 = 0$

$$x = 0 \quad \text{or} \quad x = \frac{7}{2} \quad \text{or} \quad x = -8 \quad \text{or} \quad x = -\frac{10}{3}$$

$$\left\{-8, -\frac{10}{3}, 0, \frac{7}{2}\right\}$$

55. $ax^2 - b = 0$
$ax^2 = b$

$$x^2 = \frac{b}{a}$$

$$\sqrt{x^2} = \pm\sqrt{\frac{b}{a}}$$

$$x = \pm\frac{\sqrt{ab}}{a}$$

56. $ax^2 - bx = 0$
$x(ax - b) = 0$
$x = 0 \quad \text{or} \quad ax - b = 0$
$x = 0 \quad \text{or} \quad ax = b$

$$x = \frac{b}{a}$$

57. $\left(x - \frac{1}{3}\right)\left(x - \frac{1}{3}\right) + \left(x - \frac{1}{3}\right)\left(x + \frac{2}{9}\right) = 0$

$$\left(x - \frac{1}{3}\right)\left(x - \frac{1}{3} + x + \frac{2}{9}\right) = 0$$

$$\left(x - \frac{1}{3}\right)\left(2x - \frac{1}{9}\right) = 0$$

$$x - \frac{1}{3} = 0 \quad \text{or} \quad 2x - \frac{1}{9} = 0$$

$$x = \frac{1}{3} \quad \text{or} \quad 2x = \frac{1}{9}$$

$$x = \frac{1}{18}$$

58. $\frac{1}{2}(1 + m)(1 - m) = 10m$

$$\frac{1}{2}(1 - m^2) = 10m$$

$$1 - m^2 = 20m$$

$$1 = m^2 + 20m$$

$$m^2 + 20m + 100 = 1 + 100$$

$$(m + 10)^2 = 101$$

$$\sqrt{(m + 10)^2} = \pm\sqrt{101}$$

$$m + 10 = \pm\sqrt{101}$$

$$m = -10 \pm \sqrt{101}$$

59. $a^2 - 2\sqrt{3}\,a + 2 = 0$

$$a^2 - 2\sqrt{3}\,a = -2$$

$$a^2 - 2\sqrt{3}\,a + 3 = -2 + 3$$

$$(a - \sqrt{3})^2 = 1$$

$$\sqrt{(a - \sqrt{3})^2} = \pm\sqrt{1}$$

$$a - \sqrt{3} = \pm 1$$

$$a = \sqrt{3} \pm 1$$

60.

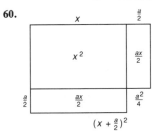

$$(x + \tfrac{a}{2})^2$$

61. $ax^n + bx^{n-1} = 0$

$x^{n-1}(ax + b) = 0$

$x^{n-1} = 0 \quad \text{or} \quad ax + b = 0$

$$x = 0 \quad \text{or} \quad x = -\frac{b}{a}$$

62. $ax^n + b = 0$

$ax^n = -b$

$$x^n = -\frac{b}{a}$$

$$\sqrt[n]{x^n} = \sqrt[n]{-\frac{b}{a}}$$

$$x = \sqrt[n]{-\frac{b}{a}}, \quad \text{or} \quad \frac{\sqrt[n]{-a^{n-1}b}}{a}$$

63. The solutions to $ax^2 = h$ are $\pm\sqrt{\dfrac{h}{a}}$; the solutions to

$ax^2 + h = 0$ are $\pm i\sqrt{\dfrac{h}{a}}$.

64. $\sqrt[5]{(m + 4)^{6+4}} = \sqrt[5]{(m + 4)^{10}} = (m + 4)^2$

65. $\sqrt{(2)(3)(2)(5)a^6} = 2a^3\sqrt{15}$

66. $\sqrt{(3)(2)(2)(2)(2)m^3n^8} = 4m^2n^4\sqrt{3m}$

67. $\sqrt{2}(1 - 4\sqrt{5}) = \sqrt{2} - 4\sqrt{10}$

68. $(\sqrt{m} + \sqrt{n})(\sqrt{m} - \sqrt{n}) = (\sqrt{m \cdot m} - \sqrt{n \cdot n}) = m - n$

69. $(\sqrt{7} + \sqrt{2})(\sqrt{7} - \sqrt{3})$

$= \sqrt{7(7)} - \sqrt{7(3)} + \sqrt{2(7)} - \sqrt{2(3)}$

$= 7 - \sqrt{21} + \sqrt{14} - \sqrt{6}$

70.

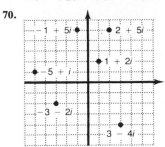

71. $|12 + 5i| = \sqrt{(12)^2 + (5)^2} = \sqrt{144 + 25} = \sqrt{169} = 13$

72. $|4 - 3i| = \sqrt{(4)^2 + (3)^2} = \sqrt{16 + 9} = \sqrt{25} = 5$

73. $|4i| = \sqrt{0^2 + (4)^2} = \sqrt{16} = 4$

74. $\$400 \times 0.015 = \$6.00$

$\$406 \times 0.015 = \$6.09$

$\$400 + \$6.00 + \$6.09 = \$412.09$

p. 348   8-2 TRY THIS

a.

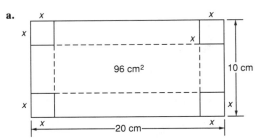

Total area $= (20 \text{ cm}) \cdot (10 \text{ cm})$

(with corners) $= 200 \text{ cm}^2$

Total area $-$ top strips $-$ side strips $= 96 \text{ cm}^2$

$200 - 2(20 - 2x)x - 2(10x) = 96$

$200 - (40 - 4x)x - 20x = 96$

$200 - 40x + 4x^2 - 20x - 96 = 0$

$4x^2 - 60x + 104 - 0$

$x^2 - 15x + 26 = 0$

$(x - 2)(x - 13)$

$x - 2 = 0 \quad \text{or} \quad x - 13 = 0$

$x = 2 \quad \text{or} \quad x = 13$

$x = 13$ would mean that the corners were larger than the side $= 10 \text{ cm}$. So, $x = 2 \text{ cm}$ is the only acceptable solution.

b.

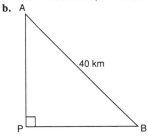

Speed of B $= x$

Speed of A $= x + 4$

$40^2 = (2x)^2 + (2(x + 4))^2$

$1600 = 4(x^2) + 4(x + 4)^2$

$1600 = 4x^2 + 4(x^2 + 8x + 16)$

$1600 = 4x^2 + 4x^2 + 32x + 64$

$8x^2 + 32x - 1536 = 0$

$x^2 + 4x - 192 = 0$

$(x - 12)(x + 16) = 0$

$x - 12 = 0 \quad \text{or} \quad x + 16 = 0$

$x = 12 \quad \text{or} \quad x = -16$

Speed cannot be negative. So, $x = 12$ is the solution.

Speed of B $= 12 \text{ km/h}$

Speed of A $= 16 \text{ km/h}$

1. 2 cm   **2.** 3 cm   **3.** Length 6 m; width 2 m

4. Length 8 cm; width 3 cm   **5.** Length 24 m; width 12 m

6. Length 26 km; width 13 km   **7.** 24 m and 10 m

8. 24 km and 7 km   **9.** A: 15 km/h; B: 8 km/h

10. Let x, $x + 1$, and $x + 2$ be the three integers.
$$x^2 + (x + 1)(x + 2) = 46$$
$$x^2 + x^2 + 2x + x + 2 = 46$$
$$2x^2 + 3x - 44 = 0$$
$$(2x + 11)(x - 4)$$

$x = 4, \dfrac{-11}{2}$. Since the problem calls for an integer solution,

$x = 4$. The consecutive integers are $4, 5, 6$.

11. Using $rt = d$, we have a system of equations
$rt = 280$
$(r + 5)(t - 1) = 280$, or $rt - r + 5t - 5 = 280$
so $rt = rt - r + 5t - 5$
$0 = -r + 5t - 5$
$r = 5t - 5$
Substitute into the first equation: $(5t - 5) \cdot t = 280$
$5t^2 - 5t - 280 = 0$
$t^2 - t - 56 = 0$
$(t - 8)(t + 7) = 0$
$t = 8$ or -7
Since time is nonnegative, $t = 8$. Solving for r:

$r = \dfrac{280}{t} = \dfrac{280}{8} = 35$ km/h

12. B: $(r + 50)(t - 3) = 2000$, or $rt - 3r + 50t - 150 = 2000$
A: $rt = 2800$
Subtracting the second equation: $3r - 50t + 150 = 800$
Solve for r: $3r = 650 + 50t$

$r = \dfrac{650 + 50t}{3}$

Substitute into equation A: $\dfrac{650 + 50t}{3} \cdot t = 2800$

$650t + 50t^2 = 8400$
$t^2 + 13t - 168 = 0$
$(t + 21)(t - 8) = 0$
$t = -21$ or $t = 8$. Choose $t = 8$.

Solving for r, $r = \dfrac{2800}{t} = 350$ km/h for plane A.

For plane B, $(r + 50) = (350 + 50) = 400$ km/h.

13. Answers may vary. Find two consecutive integers such that thirteen less than the square of the smaller one equals negative one times the larger one.

14. Let x, $x + 1$, and $x + 2$ be the three integers.
$$x^2 + (x + 1)^2 + (x + 2)^2 = 149$$
$$x^2 + x^2 + 2x + 1 + x^2 + 4x + 4 = 149$$
$$3x^2 + 6x + 5 = 149$$
$$3x^2 + 6x - 144 = 0$$
$$3(x^2 + 2x - 48) = 0$$
$$3(x - 6)(x + 8) = 0$$
$x - 6 = 0$ or $x + 8 = 0$
$\quad x = 6$ or $\quad x = -8$
$x + 1 = 7$ $\quad x + 1 = -7$
$x + 2 = 8$ $\quad x + 2 = -6$

15. $(20 - 2x)(15 - 2x)(x) = (18 - 2x)^2(x)$
$x(300 - 30x - 40x + 4x^2) = (324 - 72x + 4x^2)x$
$300x - 70x^2 + 4x^3 = 324x - 72x^2 + 4x^3$
$-24x + 2x^2 = 0$
$2x(x - 12) = 0$
$2x = 0$ or $x - 12 = 0$
$x = 0$ or $x = 12$
If $x = 0$, no box can be made.
If $x = 12$, all side lengths would be negative. Therefore it is not possible for the boxes to have equal volume.

16. $\sqrt[3]{x + 3} = 2$
$(\sqrt[3]{x + 3})^3 = 2^3$
$x + 3 = 8$
$x = 5$

17. $\sqrt{2x - 1} - 3 = 0$
$(\sqrt{2x - 1})^2 = 3^2$
$2x - 1 = 9$
$2x = 10$
$x = 5$

18. $\sqrt[4]{x} - 2 = 0$
$(\sqrt[4]{x})^4 = 2^4$
$x = 16$

19. $\dfrac{x}{4} - \dfrac{x}{5} = 5$

$\dfrac{5x - 4x}{20} = \dfrac{100}{20}$

$5x - 4x = 100$
$x = 100$

20. $\dfrac{(x + 2)}{2} - \dfrac{(x - 2)}{4} = 3$

$\dfrac{2(x + 2) - (x - 2)}{4} = \dfrac{12}{4}$

$\dfrac{2x + 4 - x + 2}{4} = \dfrac{12}{4}$

$x + 6 = 12$
$x = 6$

21. $\dfrac{5x}{8} - \dfrac{15}{6} = \dfrac{x}{2}$

$\dfrac{15x - 60}{24} = \dfrac{12x}{24}$

$15x - 60 = 12x$
$-60 = -3x$
$20 = x$

a. $3x^2 + 2x = 7$
$3x^2 + 2x - 7 = 0$
$a = 3, b = 2, c = -7$

$x = \dfrac{-2 \pm \sqrt{2^2 - 4(3)(-7)}}{2(3)}$

$= \dfrac{-2 \pm \sqrt{4 + 84}}{6}$

$= \dfrac{-2 \pm \sqrt{88}}{6}$

$= \dfrac{-2 \pm \sqrt{4} \cdot \sqrt{22}}{6}$

$= \dfrac{-2 \pm 2\sqrt{22}}{6}$

$= \dfrac{-1 \pm \sqrt{22}}{3}$

b. $5x^2 + 3x = 9$
$5x^2 + 3x - 9 = 0$
$a = 5, b = 3, c = -9$

$x = \dfrac{-3 \pm \sqrt{3^2 - 4(5)(-9)}}{2(5)} = \dfrac{-3 \pm \sqrt{9 + 180}}{10}$

$= \dfrac{-3 \pm \sqrt{189}}{10} = \dfrac{-3 \pm \sqrt{9} \cdot \sqrt{21}}{10}$

$= \dfrac{-3 \pm 3\sqrt{21}}{10}$

c. $x^2 - x + 2$
$a = 1, b = -1, c = 2$

$x = \dfrac{-(-1) \pm \sqrt{(-1)^2 - 4(1)(2)}}{2(1)} = \dfrac{1 \pm \sqrt{1 - 8}}{2} = \dfrac{1 \pm \sqrt{-7}}{2}$

$= \dfrac{1 \pm \sqrt{-1} \cdot \sqrt{7}}{2} = \dfrac{1 \pm i\sqrt{7}}{2}$

d. $3x^2 + 2x + 2 = 0$
$a = 3, b = 2, c = 2$

$x = \dfrac{-2 \pm \sqrt{2^2 - 4(3)(2)}}{2(3)} = \dfrac{-2 \pm \sqrt{4 - 24}}{6} = \dfrac{-2 \pm \sqrt{-20}}{6}$

$= \dfrac{-2 \pm \sqrt{5} \cdot \sqrt{4} \cdot \sqrt{-1}}{6} = \dfrac{-2 \pm i2\sqrt{5}}{6}$

$= \dfrac{-1 \pm i\sqrt{5}}{3}$

e. $3x^2 + 2x = 7$
$3x^2 + 2x - 7 = 0$
$a = 3, b = 2, c = -7$

$$x = \frac{-2 \pm \sqrt{2^2 - 4(3)(-7)}}{2(3)} = \frac{-2 \pm \sqrt{4 + 84}}{6} = \frac{-2 \pm \sqrt{88}}{6}$$

$$\frac{-2 + 9.381}{6} \approx \frac{7.381}{6} \approx 1.23$$

$$\frac{-2 - 9.381}{6} \approx \frac{-11.381}{6} \approx -1.90$$

pp. 352–353   **8-3 EXERCISES**

1. $-3 \pm \sqrt{5}$ **2.** $3 \pm \sqrt{13}$ **3.** $1, -5$ **4.** $5, -3$

5. $3, -10$ **6.** $10, -3$ **7.** $2, -\dfrac{1}{2}$ **8.** $\dfrac{2}{5}, -1$

9. $-1, -\dfrac{5}{3}$ **10.** $3 \pm \sqrt{7}$ **11.** $\dfrac{1 \pm i\sqrt{3}}{2}$ **12.** $\dfrac{-1 \pm i\sqrt{7}}{2}$

13. $-1 \pm 2i$ **14.** $1 \pm 2i$ **15.** $1 \pm 2i$ **16.** $2 \pm i$

17. $2 \pm 3i$ **18.** $3 \pm 2i$ **19.** $\pm i\sqrt{5}$ **20.** $\pm i\sqrt{3}$

21. $\dfrac{-3 \pm \sqrt{41}}{2}$ **22.** $3 \pm \sqrt{5}$ **23.** $\pm \dfrac{\sqrt{10}}{2}$ **24.** $\pm \dfrac{\sqrt{6}}{3}$

25. $0, -1$ **26.** $0, -1$ **27.** $\dfrac{-1 \pm 2i}{5}$ **28.** $\dfrac{-1 \pm i\sqrt{23}}{6}$

29. $\dfrac{3}{4}, -2$ **30.** $2, -3$ **31.** $\dfrac{1 \pm 3i}{2}$ **32.** $-1 \pm 2i$

33. $\dfrac{3}{2}, \dfrac{2}{3}$ **34.** $6, \dfrac{3}{2}$ **35.** $1.32, -5.32$ **36.** $-0.76, -5.24$

37. $5.24, 0.76$ **38.** $3.73, 0.27$ **39.** $2.77, -1.27$

40. $1.46 - 0.46$

41. $x^2 + x - \sqrt{2} = 0$
$$x = \frac{-1 \pm \sqrt{(1)^2 + 4(1)(\sqrt{2})}}{2(1)} = \frac{-1 \pm \sqrt{1 + 4\sqrt{2}}}{2}$$

42. $x^2 - x - \sqrt{3} = 0$
$$x = \frac{1 \pm \sqrt{(-1)^2 + 4(1)(\sqrt{3})}}{2(1)} = \frac{1 \pm \sqrt{1 + 4\sqrt{3}}}{2}$$

43. $\sqrt{2}x^2 + 5x + \sqrt{2} = 0$
$$x = \frac{-5 \pm \sqrt{(5)^2 - 4(\sqrt{2})(\sqrt{2})}}{2\sqrt{2}} = \frac{-5 \pm \sqrt{25 - 8}}{2\sqrt{2}}$$
$$= \frac{-5 \pm \sqrt{17}}{2\sqrt{2}} = \frac{-5\sqrt{2} \pm \sqrt{17} \cdot \sqrt{2}}{4} = \frac{-5\sqrt{2} \pm \sqrt{34}}{4}$$

44. $x^2 + \sqrt{5}x - \sqrt{3} = 0$
$$x = \frac{-\sqrt{5} \pm \sqrt{(\sqrt{5})^2 + 4(\sqrt{3})(1)}}{2(1)} = \frac{-\sqrt{5} \pm \sqrt{5 + 4\sqrt{3}}}{2}$$

45. $x^2 + 3x + i = 0$
$$x = \frac{-3 \pm \sqrt{(3)^2 - 4(1)(i)}}{2(1)} = \frac{-3 \pm \sqrt{9 - 4i}}{2}$$

46. $ix^2 - 2x + 1 = 0$
$$x = \frac{2 \pm \sqrt{(-2)^2 - 4(i)(1)}}{2(i)} = \frac{2 \pm \sqrt{4 - 4i}}{2i}$$
$$= \frac{2 \pm \sqrt{4} \cdot \sqrt{1 - i}}{2i} = \frac{2 \pm 2\sqrt{1 - i}}{2i} = \frac{1 \pm \sqrt{1 - i}}{i}$$

47. Upstream: $(r - 2) \cdot t = 2$
Downstream: $(r + 2)(1 - t) = 2$

Using the first equation: $t = \dfrac{2}{r - 2}$

Substituting: $(r + 2)\left(1 - \dfrac{2}{r - 2}\right) = 2$

$$r - \frac{2r}{r - 2} + 2 - \frac{4}{r - 2} = 2$$
$$r(r - 2) - 2r + 2(r - 2) - 4 = 2(r - 2)$$
$$r^2 - 2r - 2r + 2r - 4 - 4 - 2r + 4 = 0$$

$$r^2 - 4r - 4 = 0$$
$$r = \frac{4 \pm \sqrt{16 + 16}}{2} = \frac{4 \pm \sqrt{32}}{2} = \frac{4 \pm 4\sqrt{2}}{2}$$
$$= 2 \pm 2\sqrt{2}$$
$$r \approx 4.8 \text{ km/h or } -0.8 \text{ km/h}$$
r is positive, so $r = 4.8$ km/h, and this checks.

48. Answers may vary. Example: $x^2 + 1 = 0$

49. $3x^2 + xy + 4y^2 - 9 = 0$
Let $a = 3$, $b = y$, $c = 4y^2 - 9$.
$$x = \frac{-y \pm \sqrt{y^2 - 4(3)(4y^2 - 9)}}{2(3)}$$
$$x = \frac{-y \pm \sqrt{y^2 - 12(4y^2 - 9)}}{6}$$
$$x = \frac{-y \pm \sqrt{-47y^2 + 108}}{6}$$

50. $kx^2 + 3x - k = 0$
Since $x = -2$,
then $4k - 6 - k = 0$.
$$k = 2$$
To get the other solution, substitute 2 for k.
$$2x^2 + 3x - 2 = 0$$
$$(2x - 1)(x + 2) = 0$$
$$x = \frac{1}{2} \quad \text{or} \quad x = -2$$
$\dfrac{1}{2}$ is the other solution.

51. The solutions for $cx^2 + bx + a = 0$ are $\dfrac{-b \pm \sqrt{b^2 - 4ac}}{2c}$.

The reciprocals of these are $\dfrac{2c}{-b \pm \sqrt{b^2 - 4ac}}$. Multiply

$\dfrac{2c}{-b + \sqrt{b^2 - 4ac}}$ by $\dfrac{-b - \sqrt{b^2 - 4ac}}{-b - \sqrt{b^2 - 4ac}}$ and multiply

$\dfrac{2c}{-b - \sqrt{b^2 - 4ac}}$ by $\dfrac{-b + \sqrt{b^2 - 4ac}}{-b + \sqrt{b^2 - 4ac}}$. The results are

$\dfrac{-b - \sqrt{b^2 - 4ac}}{2a}$ and $\dfrac{-b + \sqrt{b^2 - 4ac}}{2a}$ which are the solutions

to $ax^2 + bx + c = 0$.

52. $\sqrt{\dfrac{35x}{7x}} = \sqrt{5}$ **53.** $\sqrt[3]{\dfrac{216}{8}} = \sqrt[3]{27} = 3$

54. $\sqrt{\dfrac{42x^2y^2}{7x}} = |y|\sqrt{6x}$ **55.** $-i$

56. $\dfrac{1}{1 - 3i} \cdot \dfrac{1 + 3i}{1 + 3i} = \dfrac{1 + 3i}{1 - 9i^2} = \dfrac{1 + 3i}{1 + 9} = \dfrac{1 + 3i}{10}$

57. $\dfrac{1}{3 + i} \cdot \dfrac{3 - i}{3 - i} = \dfrac{3 - i}{9 - i^2} = \dfrac{3 - i}{10}$

58. $\dfrac{1}{3 - 4i} \cdot \dfrac{3 + 4i}{3 + 4i} = \dfrac{3 + 4i}{9 - 16i^2} = \dfrac{3 + 4i}{25}$

59. $x(2 - 5i) = 19 - 4i$
$$x = \frac{19 - 4i}{2 - 5i} \cdot \frac{2 + 5i}{2 + 5i} = \frac{38 + 87i + 20}{4 + 25}$$
$$x = \frac{58 + 87i}{29} = 2 + 3i$$

60. $x^2 = -9$
$$\sqrt{x^2} = \pm\sqrt{9i^2}$$
$$x = \pm 3i$$

61. $x^2 = 9$
$$\sqrt{x^2} = \pm\sqrt{9}$$
$$x = \pm 3$$

```
10   REM Chapter 8 Problem
20   INPUT "For ax^2 + bx + c = 0:
     Enter a, b, c ";A,B,C
30   DISC =  SQR (B ^ 2 - 4 * A * C)
40   PRINT "x1 = ";( - B + DISC) / 2 * A
50   PRINT "x2 = ";( - B - DISC) / 2 * A
60   END
```

```
10   REM  Chapter 8 Challenge Problem
20   INPUT "For ax^2 + bx + c = 0:
     Enter a, b, c ";A,B,C
30   R = (B / (2 * A)) ^ 2 - C / A
40   RT =  - B / (2 * A)
50   IF R < 0 THEN 90
60   PRINT "x1 =";RT + SQR (R)
70   PRINT "x2 =";RT - SQR (R)
80   GOTO 130
90   R =  - R
100    PRINT "x1 = ";RT;" + "; SQR (R);"i"
110    PRINT "x2 = ";RT;" - "; SQR (R);"i"
120    PRINT
130    END
```

pp. 355–356   8-4 TRY THIS

a. $x^2 + 5x - 3 = 0$
$a = 1, b = 5, c = -3$
$b^2 - 4ac = 25 - 4(1)(-3) = 25 + 12 = 37 > 0$
two real roots

b. $9x^2 - 6x + 1 = 0$
$a = 9, b = -6, c = 1$
$b^2 - 4ac = 36 - 4(9)(1) = 36 - 36 = 0$
one real root

c. $3x^2 - 2x + 1 = 0$
$a = 3, b = -2, c = 1$
$b^2 - 4ac = 4 - 4(3)(1) = 4 - 12 = -8 < 0$
two nonreal roots

d. $3x^2 + 4 = 12x$
$3x^2 - 12x + 4 = 0$
$a = 3, b = -12, c = 4$

$$x_1 + x_2 = -\frac{b}{a} = \frac{12}{3} = 4$$

$$x_1 \cdot x_2 = \frac{c}{a} = \frac{4}{3}$$

e. $x^2 + \sqrt{2}x - 4 = 0$
$a = 1, b = \sqrt{2}, c = -4$

$$x_1 + x_2 = -\frac{b}{a} = -\frac{\sqrt{2}}{1} = -\sqrt{2}$$

$$x_1 \cdot x_2 = \frac{c}{a} = -4$$

f. $x_1 + x_2 = 3$ and $x_1 \cdot x_2 = -\frac{1}{4}$

$$-\frac{b}{a} = 3, \frac{c}{a} = -\frac{1}{4}$$

$$x^2 - \left(-\frac{b}{a}\right)x + \left(\frac{c}{a}\right) = 0$$

$$x^2 - 3x - \frac{1}{4} = 0$$

$$4x^2 - 12x - 1 = 0$$

g. $x = -4$ or $x = \frac{5}{3}$

$$x + 4 = 0 \quad \text{or} \quad x - \frac{5}{3} = 0$$

$$(x + 4)\left(x - \frac{5}{3}\right) = 0$$

$$x^2 + 4x - \frac{5}{3}x - \frac{20}{3} = 0$$

$$3x^2 + 12x - 5x - 20 = 0$$
$$3x^2 + 7x - 20 = 0$$

h. $x = -7$ or $x = 8$
$x + 7 = 0$ or $x - 8 = 0$
$(x + 7)(x - 8) = 0$
$x^2 - 8x + 7x - 56 = 0$
$x^2 - x - 56 = 0$

i. $x = m$ or $x = n$
$x - m = 0$ or $x - n = 0$
$(x - m)(x - n) = 0$
$x^2 - nx - mx + mn = 0$
$x^2 - (m + n)x + mn = 0$

j. $x = 8$ or $x = -9$
$x - 8 = 0$ or $x + 9 = 0$
$(x - 8)(x + 9) = 0$
$x^2 + 9x - 8x - 72 = 0$
$x^2 + x - 72 = 0$

k. $x = 3 + \sqrt{2}$ or $x = 3 - \sqrt{2}$
$x - 3 - \sqrt{2} = 0$ or $x - 3 + \sqrt{2} = 0$
$(x - 3 - \sqrt{2})(x - 3 + \sqrt{2}) = 0$
$x^2 - 3x + \sqrt{2}x - 3x - \sqrt{2}x + 9$
$-3\sqrt{2} + 3\sqrt{2} - 2 = 0$
$x^2 - 6x + 7 = 0$

l.
$$x = \frac{2 + \sqrt{5}}{2} \quad \text{or} \quad x = \frac{2 - \sqrt{5}}{2}$$

$$x - \left(\frac{2 + \sqrt{5}}{2}\right) = 0 \quad \text{or} \quad x - \left(\frac{2 - \sqrt{5}}{2}\right) = 0$$

$$\left(x - \left(\frac{2 + \sqrt{5}}{2}\right)\right)\left(x - \left(\frac{2 - \sqrt{5}}{2}\right)\right) = 0$$

$$x^2 - x\left(\frac{2 - \sqrt{5}}{2}\right) - x\left(\frac{2 + \sqrt{5}}{2}\right) + \left(\frac{2 + \sqrt{5}}{2}\right)\left(\frac{2 - \sqrt{5}}{2}\right) = 0$$

$$x^2 - x + \frac{\sqrt{5}}{2}x - x - \frac{\sqrt{5}}{2}x + 1 - \frac{\sqrt{5}}{2} + \frac{\sqrt{5}}{2} - \frac{5}{4} = 0$$

$$x^2 - 2x + 1 - \frac{5}{4} = 0$$

$$x^2 - 2x - \frac{1}{4} = 0$$

$$4x^2 - 8x - 1 = 0$$

pp. 357–358   8-4 EXERCISES

1. One real   **2.** One real   **3.** Two nonreal   **4.** Two nonreal

5. Two real   **6.** Two real   **7.** One real   **8.** Two real

9. Two nonreal   **10.** Two nonreal   **11.** Two real

12. Two real   **13.** Two real   **14.** Two real   **15.** One real

16. Sum $= -7$; product $= 8$ **17.** Sum $= 2$; product $= 10$

18. Sum $= 1$; product $= 1$ **19.** Sum $= -1$; product $= -1$

20. Sum $= 2$; product $= -4$ **21.** Sum $= -\frac{1}{2}$; product $= 2$

22. Sum $= 0$; product $= -25$ **23.** Sum $= 0$; product $= -49$

24. Sum $= -\frac{5}{9}$; product $= \frac{4}{9}$ **25.** Sum $= \frac{12}{25}$; product $= \frac{2}{25}$

26. Sum $= 54$; product $= 9$ **27.** Sum $= -4$; product $= -2$

28. $2x^2 + 10x + 1 = 0$ **29.** $4x^2 + 4\pi x + 1 = 0$

30. $x^2 - \sqrt{3}x + 8 = 0$ **31.** $x^2 - 5x - \sqrt{2} = 0$

32. $x^2 + 2x - 99 = 0$ **33.** $x^2 - 16 = 0$

34. $x^2 - 14x + 49 = 0$ **35.** $x^2 + 10x + 25 = 0$

36. $25x^2 - 20x - 12 = 0$ **37.** $8x^2 + 6x + 1 = 0$

38. $4x^2 - 2(c + d)x + cd = 0$

39. $12x^2 - (4k + 3m)x + km = 0$

40. $x^2 - 4\sqrt{2}x + 6 = 0$ **41.** $x^2 - \sqrt{3}x - 6 = 0$

42. $x^2 + \pi x - 2\pi^2 = 0$ **43.** $x^2 - \pi x - 12\pi^2 = 0$

44. $x^2 - 7x + 12 = 0$ **45.** $x^2 - 11x + 30 = 0$

46. $4x^2 + 3x - 10 = 0$ **47.** $4x^2 + 23x - 6 = 0$

48. $x^2 - 2x - 1 = 0$ **49.** $x^2 - 4x + 1 = 0$

50. $4x^2 - 8x + 1 = 0$ **51.** $x^2 - x - 3 = 0$

52. $mnx^2 - (m^2 - n^2)x - mn = 0$

53. $ghx^2 - (g^2 - h^2)x - gh = 0$ **54.** $x^2 - 4x + 29 = 0$

55. $x^2 - 8x + 25 = 0$

56. $x^2 + 3x + k = 0$ $a = 1, b = 3, c = k$ Substitute into $\sqrt{b^2 - 4ac}$. **a.** $k < \dfrac{9}{4}$ **b.** $k = \dfrac{9}{4}$ **c.** $k > \dfrac{9}{4}$

57. $x^2 + x + k = 0$ $a = 1, b = 1, c = k$ Substitute into $\sqrt{b^2 - 4ac}$. **a.** $k < \dfrac{1}{4}$ **b.** $k = \dfrac{1}{4}$ **c.** $k > \dfrac{1}{4}$

58. $kx^2 - 4x + 1 = 0$ $a = k, b = -4, c = 1$ Substitute into $\sqrt{b^2 - 4ac}$. **a.** $k < 4$ **b.** $k = 4$ **c.** $k > 4$

59. $x^2 - x + 3x + k = 0$ $a = 1, b = -1 + 3 = 2, c = k$ Substitute into $\sqrt{b^2 - 4ac}$. **a.** $k < 1$ **b.** $k = 1$ **c.** $k > 1$

60. $x^2 + x = 1 - k$ $a = 1, b = 1, c = -1 + k$ Substitute into $\sqrt{b^2 - 4ac}$. **a.** $k < \dfrac{5}{4}$ **b.** $k = \dfrac{5}{4}$ **c.** $k > \dfrac{5}{4}$

61. $3x^2 + 4x = k - 5$ $a = 3, b = 4, c = -k + 5$. Substitute into $\sqrt{b^2 - 4ac}$. **a.** $k > \dfrac{11}{3}$ **b.** $k = \dfrac{11}{3}$ **c.** $k < \dfrac{11}{3}$

62. $\quad kx^2 - 17x + 33 = 0$
$k(3)^2 - 17(3) + 33 = 0$
$9k = 18$
$k = 2$
So, $2x^2 - 17x + 33 = 0$
$(2x - 11)(x - 3) = 0$
$x = \dfrac{11}{2}, x = 3$

63. $\quad kx^2 - 2x + k = 0$
$k(-3) - 2(-3) + k = 0$
$10k = -6$
$k = -\dfrac{3}{5}$

So, $-\dfrac{3}{5}x^2 - 2x - \dfrac{3}{5} = 0$
$3x^2 + 10x + 3 = 0$
$(3x + 1)(x + 3) = 0$
$x = -\dfrac{1}{3}, x = -3$

64. $\quad x^2 - kx - 25 = 0$
$25 + 5k - 25 = 0$
$5k = 0$
$k = 0$
So, $x^2 - 25 = 0$
$(x + 5)(x - 5) = 0$
$x = -5, x = 5$

65. $kx^2 - 4x + (2k - 1) = 0$ Product of solutions $= \dfrac{c}{a}$, $a = k$

and $c = 2k - 1$. So $\dfrac{2k - 1}{k} = \dfrac{3}{1}$, then $k = -1$.

66. Solving for x yields $x = \dfrac{-b \pm \sqrt{b^2 + 4c}}{2}$. This is equivalent to the quadratic formula $x^2 + bx - c = 0$.

67. Given $a^2x + bx + c = 0$, $a \neq 0$, $a, b, c \in$ rationals, $b^2 - 4ac > 0$ and $b^2 - 4ac = d^2$ where d is rational.
$x = \dfrac{-b \pm \sqrt{b^2 - 4ac}}{2a} = \dfrac{-b \pm d}{2a}$ then $\dfrac{-b + d}{2a}$ and $\dfrac{-b - d}{2a}$ are rational by closure properties in rationals.

68. a. $\qquad 6x^2 + 5x + 1 = 0$
$(3x + 1)(2x + 1) = 0$
$3x + 1 = 0$ or $2x + 1 = 0$
$x = -\dfrac{1}{3} \qquad x = -\dfrac{1}{2}$

Two rational solutions

b. $x^2 + 4x - 2 = 0$
$x = \dfrac{-4 \pm \sqrt{16 - 4(1)(-2)}}{2}$
$x = \dfrac{-4 \pm \sqrt{16 + 8}}{2}$

$x = \dfrac{-4 \pm \sqrt{24}}{2}$

$x = \dfrac{-4 \pm 2\sqrt{6}}{2}$

$x = -2 \pm \sqrt{6}$ Two real (nonrational) solutions

69. The solutions of $ax^2 + bx + c = 0$ can be written as $-\dfrac{b}{2a} + \dfrac{\sqrt{b^2 - 4ac}}{2a}$ or $-\dfrac{b}{2a} - \dfrac{\sqrt{b^2 - 4ac}}{2a}$. The solutions of $ax^2 - bx + c = 0$ are $\dfrac{b \pm \sqrt{(-b)^2 - 4ac}}{2a}$ or $\dfrac{b}{2a} \pm \dfrac{\sqrt{b^2 - 4ac}}{2a}$.
$\left(\dfrac{b}{2a} - \dfrac{\sqrt{b^2 - 4ac}}{2a}\right) + \left(-\dfrac{b}{2a} + \dfrac{\sqrt{b^2 - 4ac}}{2a}\right) = 0$,
$\left(\dfrac{b}{2a} + \dfrac{\sqrt{b^2 - 4ac}}{2a}\right) + \left(-\dfrac{b}{2a} - \dfrac{\sqrt{b^2 - 4ac}}{2a}\right) = 0$ Thus the solutions are additive inverses.

70. (1) If $b^2 - 4ac = 0$, then $x = \dfrac{-b \pm \sqrt{b^2 - 4ac}}{2a} = -\dfrac{b}{2a}$. Since a and b are real, then $-\dfrac{b}{2a}$ is real and $ax^2 + bx + c = 0$ has one real solution. (2) If a, b, and c are real and $b^2 - 4ac > 0$, then $\sqrt{b^2 - 4ac}$ represents a positive real number (let $d = \sqrt{b^2 - 4ac}$). Thus, $x = \dfrac{-b \pm \sqrt{b^2 - 4ac}}{2a} = \dfrac{-b \pm d}{2a}$.
Then $\dfrac{-b - d}{2a}$ and $\dfrac{-b + d}{2a}$ are real. Since $\dfrac{-b + d}{2a} \neq \dfrac{-b - d}{2a}$, there exist two real solutions. (3) If $b^2 - 4ac < 0$ then $\sqrt{b^2 - 4ac}$ represents an imaginary number. The two solutions $x = \dfrac{-b \pm \sqrt{b^2 - 4ac}}{2a}$ are complex and can be written as $-\dfrac{b}{2a} + \dfrac{1}{2a}\sqrt{b^2 - 4ac}$ and $-\dfrac{b}{2a} - \dfrac{1}{2a}\sqrt{b^2 - 4ac}$. They are complex conjugates of each other.

71. Sum $= -\dfrac{b}{a} = -\dfrac{12}{1}$, Product $= \dfrac{c}{a} = \dfrac{20}{1}$
So $x^2 + 12x + 20 = 0$
Given $3x^2 - hx + 4k = 0$ then
$x^2 - \dfrac{h}{3}x + \dfrac{4}{3}k = 0$. $x^2 + 12x + 20 = x^2 - \dfrac{h}{3}x + \dfrac{4}{3}k$,
therefore $-\dfrac{h}{3} = 12$ and $\dfrac{4}{3}k = 20$. So, $h = -36$ and $k = 15$.

72. $b^2 \geq 0$; $4ac$ must be negative since a and c have opposite signs. So $b^2 - 4ac$ must be positive. Thus $\sqrt{b^2 - 4ac}$ is real and nonzero; and the solutions are real and unequal.

73. $15x^2 + 11x + 2 = (5x + 2)(3x + 1)$

74. $2y^2 + y - 3 = (2y + 3)(y - 1)$

75. $a^3 - a = a(a^2 - 1) = a(a + 1)(a - 1)$

76. $4y^2 - 1 = 7$
$4y^2 = 8$
$y^2 = 2$
$y = \pm\sqrt{2}$

77. $9c^2 - 18c = 0$
$9c(c - 2) = 0$
$9c = 0$ or $c - 2 = 0$
$c = 0$ or $c = 2$

78. $\dfrac{1}{2}x^3 - \dfrac{1}{18}x = 0$
$\dfrac{1}{2}x\left(x^2 - \dfrac{1}{9}\right) = 0$
$\dfrac{1}{2}x = 0$ or $x^2 - \dfrac{1}{9} = 0$
$x = 0$ or $x^2 = \dfrac{1}{9}$
$x = \sqrt{\dfrac{1}{9}}$
$x = \pm\dfrac{1}{3}$

Lesson 8-4

79.
$$(a - 8)(a - 2) = -8$$
$$a^2 - 10a + 16 + 8 = 0$$
$$a^2 - 10a + 24 = 0$$
$$(a - 4)(a - 6) = 0$$
$$a = 4, a = 6$$

80.
$$m(m - 5) = 2(m - 6)$$
$$m^2 - 5m = 2m - 12$$
$$m^2 - 5m - 2m + 12 = 0$$
$$m^2 - 7m + 12 = 0$$
$$(m - 4)(m - 3) = 0$$
$$m = 4, m = 3$$

81.
$$3x^2 = 75$$
$$x^2 = 25$$
$$x = \sqrt{25}$$
$$x = \pm 5$$

p. 360   8-5 TRY THIS

a. $x^4 - 10x^2 + 9 = 0$
Let $u = x^2$.
$$u^2 - 10u + 9 = 0$$
$$(u - 9)(u - 1) = 0$$
$$u - 9 = 0 \quad \text{or} \quad u - 1 = 0$$
$$u = 9 \quad \text{or} \quad u = 1$$
$$x^2 = 9 \quad \text{or} \quad x^2 = 1$$
$$x = \pm 3 \quad \text{or} \quad x = \pm 1$$

b. $x^4 - 4 = 0$
Let $u = x^2$.
$$u^2 - 4 = 0$$
$$u^2 = 4$$
$$u = \pm 2$$
$$x^2 = 2 \quad \text{or} \quad x^2 = -2$$
$$x = \pm\sqrt{2} \quad \text{or} \quad x = \pm i\sqrt{2}$$

c. $x + 3\sqrt{x} - 10 = 0$
Let $u = \sqrt{x}$.
$$u^2 + 3u - 10 = 0$$
$$(u + 5)(u - 2) = 0$$
$$u + 5 = 0 \quad \text{or} \quad u - 2 = 0$$
$$u = -5 \quad \text{or} \quad u = 2$$
$$\sqrt{x} = -5 \quad \text{or} \quad \sqrt{x} = 2$$
no solution $\qquad x = 4$

d. $(x^2 - x)^2 - 14(x^2 - x) + 24 = 0$
Let $u = x^2 - x$.
$$u^2 - 14u + 24 = 0$$
$$(u - 12)(u - 2) = 0$$
$$u - 12 = 0 \quad \text{or} \quad u - 2 = 0$$
$$u = 12 \quad \text{or} \quad u = 2$$

$$x^2 - x = 12 \qquad\qquad x^2 - x = 2$$
$$x^2 - x - 12 = 0 \qquad x^2 - x - 2 = 0$$
$$(x - 4)(x + 3) = 0 \qquad (x - 2)(x + 1) = 0$$
$$x - 4 = 0 \ \text{or} \ x + 3 = 0 \qquad x - 2 = 0 \ \text{or} \ x + 1 = 0$$
$$x = 4 \ \text{or} \ x = -3 \qquad x = 2 \ \text{or} \ x = -1$$

e. $t^{2/3} - 3t^{1/3} - 10 = 0$
Let $u = t^{1/3}$.
$$u^2 - 3u - 10 = 0$$
$$(u - 5)(u + 2) = 0$$
$$u - 5 = 0 \qquad u + 2 = 0$$
$$u = 5 \qquad u = -2$$
$$t^{1/3} = 5 \qquad t^{1/3} = -2$$
$$t = 125 \qquad t = -8$$

f. $\sqrt[7]{y^2} + 4\sqrt[7]{y} + 4 = 0$
Let $u = y^{1/7}$.
$$u^2 + 4u + 4 = 0$$
$$(u + 2)^2 = 0$$
$$u + 2 = 0$$
$$u = -2$$
$$y^{1/7} = -2$$
$$y = -2^7$$
$$= -128$$

p. 361   8-5 EXERCISES

1. $81, 1$ **2.** $\frac{1}{4}, 16$ **3.** $\pm\sqrt{5}$ **4.** $\pm\sqrt{2}, \pm 1$

5. $7, -1, 5, 1$ **6.** 1 **7.** $4, 1, 6, -1$ **8.** $-\frac{3}{2}, 1, \frac{1}{2}, -1$

9. $\pm\sqrt{6}, \pm i\sqrt{2}$ **10.** $\pm 3, \pm 2i$ **11.** $\frac{1}{3}, -\frac{1}{2}$ **12.** $\frac{4}{5}, -1$

13. $2, -1$ **14.** $-\frac{1}{10}, 1$ **15.** $-27, 8$ **16.** $64, -8$ **17.** 16

18. 729 **19.** $x = 16$ **20.** $t = -32$ or $t = -243$

21. $\left(\dfrac{x^2 - 1}{x}\right) - \left(\dfrac{x^2 - 1}{x}\right) - 2 = 0$

Let $u = \dfrac{x^2 - 1}{x}$.

$$u^2 - u - 2 = 0$$
$$(u - 2)(u + 1) = 0$$
$$u = 2, -1$$

$$\frac{x^2 - 1}{x} = 2 \qquad \frac{x^2 - 1}{x} = -1$$
$$x^2 - 1 = 2x \qquad\qquad x^2 - 1 = -x$$
$$x^2 - 2x - 1 = 0 \qquad\qquad x^2 + x - 1 = 0$$
$$x = \frac{2 \pm \sqrt{4 + 4}}{2} \qquad x = \frac{-1 \pm \sqrt{1 + 4}}{2}$$
$$x = \frac{2 \pm \sqrt{8}}{2} \qquad\qquad x = \frac{-1 \pm \sqrt{5}}{2}$$
$$x = \frac{2 \pm 2\sqrt{2}}{2}$$
$$x = 1 \pm \sqrt{2}$$

22. $\left(\dfrac{x^2 - 2}{x}\right)^2 - 7\left(\dfrac{x^2 - 2}{x}\right) - 18 = 0$

Let $u = \dfrac{x^2 - 2}{x}$.

$$u^2 - 7u - 18 = 0$$
$$(u - 9)(u + 2) = 0$$
$$u = 9, -2$$

$$\frac{x^2 - 2}{x} = 9 \qquad \text{or} \qquad \frac{x^2 - 2}{x} = -2$$
$$x^2 - 9x - 2 = 0 \qquad\qquad x^2 + 2x - 2 = 0$$
$$x = \frac{9 \pm \sqrt{81 - 4(-2)}}{2} \qquad x = \frac{-2 \pm \sqrt{4 - 4(-2)}}{2}$$
$$x = \frac{9 \pm \sqrt{89}}{2} \qquad\qquad x = \frac{-2 \pm \sqrt{12}}{2}$$
$$x = \frac{9 \pm \sqrt{89}}{2} \qquad \text{or} \qquad x = -1 \pm \sqrt{3}$$

23. $\left(\dfrac{x^2 + 1}{x}\right)^2 - 8\left(\dfrac{x^2 + 1}{x}\right) + 15 = 0$

Let $u = \dfrac{x^2 + 1}{x}$.

$$u^2 - 8u + 15 = 0$$
$$(u - 5)(u - 3) = 0$$
$$u = 5, 3$$

$$\frac{x^2 + 1}{x} = 5 \qquad\qquad \frac{x^2 + 1}{x} = 3$$
$$x^2 - 5x + 1 = 0 \qquad x^2 - 3x + 1 = 0$$
$$x = \frac{5 \pm \sqrt{25 - 4}}{2} \qquad\qquad x = \frac{3 \pm \sqrt{9 - 4}}{2}$$
$$x = \frac{5 \pm \sqrt{21}}{2} \quad \text{or} \quad x = \frac{3 \pm \sqrt{5}}{2}$$

24. $\dfrac{x}{x - 1} - 6\sqrt{\dfrac{x}{x - 1}} - 40 = 0$

Let $u = \sqrt{\dfrac{x}{x - 1}}$.

$$u^2 - 6u - 40 = 0$$
$$(u - 10)(u + 4) = 0$$
$$u = 10 \quad \text{or} \quad -4 \qquad \text{Since } u > 0, u = 10.$$

$$10 = \sqrt{\frac{x}{x - 1}}$$

$$10 = \frac{x}{x - 1}; \qquad 100x - 100 = x$$
$$99x - 100 = 0$$
$$99x = 100$$
$$x = \frac{100}{99}$$

25. $\left(\dfrac{x+1}{x-1}\right)^2 + \left(\dfrac{x+1}{x-1}\right) - 2 = 0$

Let $u = \dfrac{x+1}{x-1}$.

$u^2 + u - 2 = 0$
$(u+2)(u-1) = 0$
$u = -2, 1$

$-2 = \dfrac{x+1}{x-1}$ or $1 = \dfrac{x+1}{x-1}$

$x+1 = -2(x-1)$ or $x+1 = x-1$
$3x + 1 - 2 = 0$ $\qquad\qquad 0 = -2$
$3x = 1$

$x = \dfrac{1}{3}$

26. $5\left(\dfrac{x+2}{x-2}\right)^2 - 3\left(\dfrac{x+2}{x-2}\right) - 2 = 0$

Let $u = \dfrac{x+2}{x-2}$.

$5u^2 - 3u - 2 = 0$
$(5u+2)(u-1) = 0$

$u = -\dfrac{2}{5}, 1$

$\dfrac{x+2}{x-2} = -\dfrac{2}{5}$ or $\dfrac{x+2}{x-2} = 1$

$5(x+2) = -2(x-2)$ or $x+2 = x-2$
$5x + 10 = -2x + 4$ or $\qquad 0 = -4$
$7x = -6$

$x = -\dfrac{6}{7}$

The only solution is $-\dfrac{6}{7}$.

27. $\dfrac{1}{4}x + 2\sqrt{x} + 15 = x \qquad$ Let $u^2 = x$, then

$\dfrac{1}{4}u^2 + 2x + 15 = u^2$.

$u^2 + 8x + 60 = 4u^2$
$3u^2 - 8x - 60 = 0$
$(3u + 10)(u - 6) = 0$
$3u + 10 = 0$ or $u - 6 = 0$
$3u = -10$ $\qquad\quad u = 6$

$u = -\dfrac{10}{3}$

If $u = 6$, then $x = 36$.
There were 36 camels in the herd.

28. $9x^{3/2} - 8 = x^3$
Let $u = x^{3/2}$.
$9u - 8 = u^2$
$u^2 - 9u + 8 = 0$
$(u - 8)(u - 1) = 0$
$u = 1, 8$
$x^{3/2} = 1$ or $x^{3/2} = 8$
$(x^{3/2})^2 = 1^2$ $\quad (x^{3/2})^2 = 8^2$
$x^3 = 1$ $\qquad\quad x^3 = 64$
$x = 1$ $\qquad\qquad x = 4$
Solution: $x = 1, 4$

29. $\sqrt[3]{2x+3} = \sqrt[6]{2x+3}$
Let $u = \sqrt[6]{2x+3}$.
$u^2 = u$
$u^2 - u = 0;\ u(u-1) = 0$
$u = 0$ or 1
$\sqrt[6]{2x+3} = 1 \qquad \sqrt[6]{2x+3} = 0$
$2x + 3 = 1^6 = 1 \qquad 2x + 3 = 0$
$\qquad\qquad\qquad\qquad 2x = -3$

$2x = -2 \qquad\qquad x = \dfrac{-3}{2}$

$x = -1$

$x = -1$ or $x = -\dfrac{3}{2}$

30. $\sqrt{x-3} - \sqrt[4]{x-3} = 2$
Let $u = \sqrt[4]{x-3}$.
$u^2 - u = 2$
$u^2 - u - 2 = 0$
$(u-2)(u+1) = 0$
$u = 2, -1$. Since $u > 0$, $u = 2$.
$2 = \sqrt[4]{x-3}$
$16 = x - 3$
$x = 19$

31. $a^3 - 26a^{3/2} - 27 = 0$
Let $u = a^{3/2}$.
$u^2 - 26u - 27 = 0$
$(u-27)(u+1) = 0$
$u = 27, -1$. But $u = a^{3/2} = (a^3)^{1/2} > 0$.
Hence $u = 27$.
$27 = a^{3/2}$
$27^2 = (a^{3/2})^2$
$729 = a^3$
$a = 9$

32. $x^8 - 20x^4 + 64 = 0$
Let $u = x^4$.
$u^2 - 20u + 64 = 0$
$(u - 16)(u - 4) = 0$
$\qquad\quad u = 16$ or $\qquad u = 4$
So $x^4 = 16$ or $\qquad x^4 = 4$
$x^4 - 16 = 0$ or $x^4 - 4 = 0$
$(x^2 + 4)(x+2)(x-2) = 0$ or $(x^2 + 2)(x^2 - 2) = 0$
$x^2 = -4,\ x = -2,\ x = 2$ or $\quad x^2 = -2,\ x^2 = 2$
$x = \pm 2i, -2, 2, \pm i\sqrt{2}, \pm\sqrt{2}$

33. $x^8 + 20x^4 + 64 = 0$
Let $u = x^4$.
$u^2 + 20u + 64 = 0$
$(u + 16)(u + 4) = 0$
$u = -16$ or $\quad u = -4$
$x^4 = -16$ or $\quad x^4 = -4$
$x^2 = \pm 4i$ or $\quad x^2 = \pm 2i$
$x = \sqrt{4i}, -\sqrt{4i}, \sqrt{-4i}, -\sqrt{-4i}, \sqrt{2i}, -\sqrt{2i}, \sqrt{-2i}$
or $-\sqrt{-2i}$
$x = 2\sqrt{i}, -2\sqrt{i}, 2i\sqrt{i}, -2i\sqrt{i}, \sqrt{2}\sqrt{i}, -\sqrt{2}\sqrt{i}, i\sqrt{2}\sqrt{i}$
or $-i\sqrt{2}\sqrt{i}$
To find $\sqrt{i}$, $\qquad\qquad (a+bi)^2 = 0 + 1i$
$\qquad\qquad (a^2 - b^2) + 2abi = 0 + 1i$
$\qquad\qquad\qquad a^2 + b^2 = 0 \quad$ and $\quad 2ab = 1$

$\qquad\qquad\qquad a = \pm b \quad$ and $\quad a = \dfrac{1}{2b}$

a and b must be the same sign, so $a = b$. Substituting b for a in $2ab = 1$,
$2a^2 = 1$

$a^2 = \dfrac{1}{2}$

$a = \dfrac{\sqrt{2}}{2}$

Since $b = a$, $b - \dfrac{\sqrt{2}}{2}$. Thus $\sqrt{i} = \dfrac{\sqrt{2}}{2} + i\dfrac{\sqrt{2}}{2}$.

$x = 2\left(\dfrac{\sqrt{2}}{2} + i\dfrac{\sqrt{2}}{2}\right), -2\left(\dfrac{\sqrt{2}}{2} + i\dfrac{\sqrt{2}}{2}\right), 2i\left(\dfrac{\sqrt{2}}{2} + i\dfrac{\sqrt{2}}{2}\right),$

$\qquad -2i\left(\dfrac{\sqrt{2}}{2} + i\dfrac{\sqrt{2}}{2}\right), \sqrt{2}\left(\dfrac{\sqrt{2}}{2} + i\dfrac{\sqrt{2}}{2}\right), -\sqrt{2}\left(\dfrac{\sqrt{2}}{2} + i\dfrac{\sqrt{2}}{2}\right),$

$\qquad i\sqrt{2}\left(\dfrac{\sqrt{2}}{2} + i\dfrac{\sqrt{2}}{2}\right)$ or $-i\sqrt{2}\left(\dfrac{\sqrt{2}}{2} + i\dfrac{\sqrt{2}}{2}\right)$

$= \sqrt{2} + i\sqrt{2}, -\sqrt{2} - i\sqrt{2}, i\sqrt{2} - \sqrt{2}, -i\sqrt{2} + \sqrt{2},$
$\quad 1 + i, -1 - i, i - \sqrt{2}, -i + \sqrt{2}$
$x = \sqrt{2} \pm i\sqrt{2}, -\sqrt{2} \pm i\sqrt{2}, 1 \pm i, -1 \pm i$

34. $\sqrt{\dfrac{15}{7}} \cdot \dfrac{\sqrt{7}}{\sqrt{7}} = \dfrac{\sqrt{105}}{7}$ $\qquad$ **35.** $\dfrac{1}{\sqrt{ab}} \cdot \dfrac{\sqrt{ab}}{\sqrt{ab}} = \dfrac{\sqrt{ab}}{ab}$

36. $\dfrac{2\sqrt{5} - 3\sqrt{2}}{3\sqrt{2} - 2\sqrt{5}} \cdot \dfrac{3\sqrt{2} + 2\sqrt{5}}{3\sqrt{2} + 2\sqrt{5}} = \dfrac{6\sqrt{10} + 20 - 18 - 6\sqrt{10}}{18 - 20}$

$= \dfrac{2}{-2} = -1$

37. $(x - 4i)(x + 4i) = 0$
$x^2 - 16i^2 = 0$
$x^2 + 16 = 0$

38. $(x - 7i)(x + 7i) = 0$
$x^2 - 49i^2 = 0$
$x^2 + 49 = 0$

39.
$(x - 2 + 5i)(x - 2 - 5i) = 0$
$x^2 - 2x - 5ix - 2x + 4 + 10i + 5ix - 10i - 25i^2 = 0$
$x^2 - 4x + 29 = 0$

40. $x^2 - 5x - 6 = 0$
$(x + 1)(x - 6) = 0$
$x + 1 = 0 \quad \text{or} \quad x - 6 = 0$
$x = -1 \quad \text{or} \qquad x = 6$

41. $2y^2 - y - 15 = 0$
$(2y + 5)(y - 3) = 0$
$2y + 5 = 0 \quad \text{or} \quad y - 3 = 0$
$y = -\dfrac{5}{2} \quad \text{or} \qquad y = 3$

42. $(a - 1)(a - 3) = 15$
$a^2 - 4a + 3 = 15$
$a^2 - 4a - 12 = 0$
$(a + 2)(a - 6) = 0$
$a + 2 = 0 \quad \text{or} \quad a - 6 = 0$
$a = -2 \quad \text{or} \qquad a = 6$

43. $c(c - 2) = 3(c + 8)$
$c^2 - 2c - 3c - 24 = 0$
$c^2 - 5c - 24 = 0$
$(c + 3)(c - 8) = 0$
$c + 3 = 0, \ c - 8 = 0$
$c = -3, \ c = 8$

44. $4m^2 = 9$
$m^2 = \dfrac{9}{4}$
$\sqrt{m^2} = \pm\sqrt{\dfrac{9}{4}}$
$m = \pm\dfrac{3}{2}$

pp. 362–363   8-6 TRY THIS

a. $V = \pi r^2 h$
$\dfrac{V}{\pi \cdot h} = r^2$
$\dfrac{\sqrt{V\pi h}}{\pi h} = \sqrt{\dfrac{V}{\pi h}} = r$

b. $2\pi r^2 + 2\pi rh = 1$
$2\pi r^2 + 2\pi rh - 1 = 0$
$r = \dfrac{-2\pi h \pm \sqrt{4\pi^2 h^2 - 4(2\pi)(-1)}}{4\pi}$
$= \dfrac{-2\pi h \pm \sqrt{4\pi^2 h^2 + 8\pi}}{4\pi}$
$= \dfrac{-2\pi h \pm \sqrt{4\pi^2(h^2 + 2)}}{4\pi}$
$= \dfrac{-2\pi h \pm 2\pi^2 h^2 + 2\pi}{4\pi}$
$= \dfrac{-\pi h \pm \sqrt{\pi^2 h^2 + 2\pi}}{2\pi}$

r cannot be negative
$r = \dfrac{-\pi h + \sqrt{\pi^2 h^2 + 2\pi}}{2\pi}$

c. (1) $s = 92$ m, $v_0 = 0$
$92 = 4.9t^2 + 0 \cdot t$
$92 = 4.9t^2$
$t^2 \approx 18.88$
$t \approx 4.33$ sec

(2) $s = 92$ m, $v_0 = 40$ m/sec
$92 = 4.9t^2 + 40 \cdot t$
$4.9t^2 + 40t - 92 = 0$
$a = 4.9, \ b = 40 \text{ and } c = -92$
$t = \dfrac{-40 \pm \sqrt{40^2 - 4(4.9) \cdot (-92)}}{2 \cdot (4.9)}$
$t = \dfrac{-40 \pm \sqrt{3403.2}}{9.8} \approx \dfrac{-40 \pm 58.337}{9.8}$

t cannot be negative, so $t \approx \dfrac{18.337}{9.8} \approx 1.87$ sec

(3) $t = 1$, $v_0 = 40$ m/sec and solve for s
$s = 4.9(1)^2 + 40 \cdot 1$
$s = 4.9 + 40$
$s = 44.9$ m

pp. 364–365   8-6 EXERCISES

1. $s = \dfrac{\sqrt{P}}{2}$ **2.** $r = \sqrt{\dfrac{A}{\pi}}$ **3.** $r = \sqrt{\dfrac{Gm_1 m_2}{F}}$

4. $t = \sqrt{\dfrac{Qab}{k}}$ **5.** $r = \sqrt{x^2 + y^2}$ **6.** $h = \sqrt{a^2 + b^2}$

7. $z = \sqrt{d^2 - x^2 - y^2}$ **8.** $b = \sqrt{t^2 - a^2 - c^2}$

9. $t = \dfrac{v_0 \pm \sqrt{v_0^2 - 19.6h}}{9.8}$ **10.** $r = \dfrac{-\pi s \pm \sqrt{\pi^2 s^2 + 4\pi A}}{2\pi}$

11. $t = \sqrt{\dfrac{2S}{g}}$ **12.** $V = \sqrt{2gh}$ **13.** $r = \dfrac{-\pi h \pm \sqrt{\pi^2 h^2 + 2\pi A}}{2\pi}$

14. $t = \sqrt{\dfrac{h - 2v_0}{10}}$ **15.** $t = \dfrac{\pi \pm \sqrt{\pi^2 - 12k\sqrt{2}}}{2\sqrt{2}}$

16. $t = \dfrac{0.2 \pm \sqrt{0.04 + 16\pi\sqrt{3}}}{2\sqrt{3}}$

17. a. 3.91 sec   **b.** 1.91 sec; 79.6 m

18. a. 10.10 sec   **b.** 8.95 sec; 182.5 m

19. a. 18.75%   **b.** 10%   **c.** 11%   **d.** 12.75%

20. 2 ft   **21.** 7 ft

22. A: 15 mi/h; B: 20 mi/h   **23.** A: 24 km/h; B: 10 km/h

24.

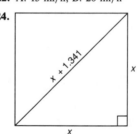

$x^2 + x^2 = (x + 1.341)^2$
$2x^2 = x^2 + 2.682x + 1.798281$
$x^2 - 2.682x - 1.798281 = 0$
$x = \dfrac{2.682 \pm \sqrt{(2.682)^2 - 4(-1.798281)}}{2}$
$= \dfrac{2.682 \pm \sqrt{14.386248}}{2} \approx \dfrac{2.682 \pm 3.79292}{2}$
$x \approx 3.23746 \quad \text{or} \quad x \approx -0.55546$
Since x is nonnegative, the length of a side is about 3.237 cm.

25.

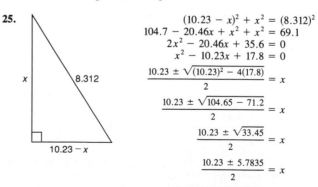

$(10.23 - x)^2 + x^2 = (8.312)^2$
$104.7 - 20.46x + x^2 + x^2 = 69.1$
$2x^2 - 20.46x + 35.6 = 0$
$x^2 - 10.23x + 17.8 = 0$
$\dfrac{10.23 \pm \sqrt{(10.23)^2 - 4(17.8)}}{2} = x$
$\dfrac{10.23 \pm \sqrt{104.65 - 71.2}}{2} = x$
$\dfrac{10.23 \pm \sqrt{33.45}}{2} = x$
$\dfrac{10.23 \pm 5.7835}{2} = x$
$8.0101 \quad \text{or} \quad 2.2199 = x$
The lengths of the legs are 8.0101 cm and 2.2199 cm.

26.

$$m = \frac{m_0}{\sqrt{1 - \frac{v^2}{c^2}}}$$

$$\left(m\sqrt{1 - \frac{v^2}{c^2}}\right)^2 = (m_0)^2$$

$$m^2\left(1 - \frac{v^2}{c^2}\right) = m_0^2$$

$$m^2 - \frac{v^2 m^2}{c^2} = m_0^2$$

$$-\frac{v^2 m^2}{c^2} = m_0^2 - m^2$$

$$-v^2 m^2 = c^2(m_0^2 - m^2)$$

$$v^2 = \frac{c^2(m_0^2 - m^2)}{-m^2}$$

$$\sqrt{v^2} = \sqrt{\frac{-c^2(m_0^2 - m^2)}{m^2}}$$

$$v = \frac{c\sqrt{m^2 - m_0^2}}{m}$$

27.

$$T = \sqrt{\frac{a^2 + b^2}{a^2}}$$

$$T = \sqrt{1 + \frac{b^2}{a^2}}$$

$$T^2 = 1 + \frac{b^2}{a^2}$$

$$T^2 - 1 = \frac{b^2}{a^2}$$

$$a^2(T^2 - 1) = b^2$$

$$a^2 = \frac{b^2}{T^2 - 1}$$

$$a = \sqrt{\frac{b^2}{T^2 - 1}} \quad \text{or}$$

$$a = \frac{b}{\sqrt{T^2 - 1}}$$

28. $140 = cN$
$140 = (c + 15)(N - 3)$

$$140 = \left(\frac{140}{N} + 15\right)(N - 3)$$

$0 = 15N^2 - 45N - 420$
$0 = N^2 - 3N - 28$
$0 = (N - 7)(N + 4)$
$7 = N \quad \text{or} \quad N = -4$

Since there could not be a negative number of students, 7 students were in the group.

29. $cN = 8400$
$8400 = (c + 350)(N - 4)$

Substituting, $8400 = \left(\frac{8400}{N} + 350\right)(N - 4)$

$0 = 350N^2 - 1400N - 33{,}600$
$0 = N^2 - 4N - 96$
$0 = (N - 12)(N + 8)$
$0 = N - 12 \quad \text{or} \quad N + 8 = 0$
$12 = N \qquad \text{or} \qquad N = -8$

Since the number of lots purchased was nonnegative, 12 lots were purchased.

30. $s = 4.9t^2 + v_0 t$
$4.9t^2 + v_0 t - s = 0$

$$t = \frac{-v_0 \pm \sqrt{v_0^2 + 4(4.9)s}}{2(4.9)} = \frac{-v_0 \pm \sqrt{v_0^2 + 19.6s}}{9.8}$$

There is only one solution because the negative square root would give a negative answer for time.

31. $xy = 12$

By similar triangles, $\frac{6}{8} = \frac{6 - y}{x}$, where $6 - y$ is the vertical side

of the small triangle above the inscribed rectangle.

Since $x = \frac{12}{y}$,

$$\frac{6}{8} = \frac{6 - y}{\left(\frac{12}{y}\right)} = \frac{6y - y^2}{12}$$

Therefore, $72 = 48y - 8y^2$.
$y^2 - 6y + 9 = 0$
$(y - 3)^2 = 0$

$$y = 3, \quad x = \frac{12}{3} = 4$$

3 cm × 4 cm

32. $s = 16t^2 + v_0 t$
$175 = 16t^2 + 0t$
$10.938 = t^2$
$3.3 = t$
3.3 sec

33. $i^3 = (i^2)i = -1(i) = -i$

34. $(5i)^2 = 25i^2 = 25(-1) = -25$

35. $(-6i)^2 = 36i^2 = 36(-1) = -36$

36. $(1 + i)^2 = 1 + 2i + i^2 = 1 + 2i + (-1) = 2i$

37. $(1 + i)^3 = 1^3 + 3(1)(i) + 3(1)(i^2) + i^3$
$= 1 + 3i - 3 - i = -2 + 2i$

38. $8x^2 - 6x + 1 = 0$
$(4x - 1)(2x - 1) = 0$

$$x = \frac{1}{4} \quad \text{or} \quad x = \frac{1}{2}$$

$$\frac{1}{4}, \frac{1}{2}$$

39. $y(y - 7) = 12(y - 5)$
$y^2 - 7y = 12y - 60$
$y^2 - 19y + 60 = 0$
$(y - 4)(y - 15) = 0$
$y = 4 \quad \text{or} \quad y = 15$

40. $5m^2 = 0$
$m^2 = 0$
$m = 0$

41. $3a^2 + 12a = 0$
$3a(a + 4) = 0$
$a = 0 \quad \text{or} \quad a = -4$

42. $2c^2 = 4$
$c^2 = 2$
$c = \pm\sqrt{2}$
$\{\sqrt{2}, -\sqrt{2}\}$

43. $6x^2 = 25$

$$x^2 = \frac{25}{6}$$

$$x = \pm\frac{5\sqrt{6}}{6}$$

$$\left\{\frac{5\sqrt{6}}{6}, -\frac{5\sqrt{6}}{6}\right\}$$

44. $x^2 - 4x + 7 = 0$

$$x = \frac{4 \pm \sqrt{16 - 4(1)(7)}}{2}$$

$$= \frac{4 \pm \sqrt{-12}}{2} = \frac{4 \pm 2\sqrt{-3}}{2}$$

$$= 2 \pm i\sqrt{3} \quad \{2 \pm i\sqrt{3}\}$$

45. $y^2 + 4y + 8 = 0$

$$y = \frac{-4 \pm \sqrt{16 - 32}}{2}$$

$$= \frac{-4 \pm \sqrt{16i^2}}{2}$$

$$= \frac{-4 \pm 4i}{2}$$

$$y = -2 \pm 2i$$

$$\{-2 + 2i, -2 - 2i\}$$

46. $6a^2 - a - 15 = 0$
$(3a - 5)(2a + 3) = 0$

$$a = \frac{5}{3} \quad \text{or} \quad a = -\frac{3}{2}$$

47.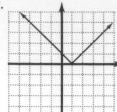

48.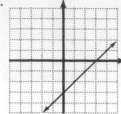

16. $22.5 \ w/m^2$

17. If p varies directly as q, then $p = kq$. Thus $q = \frac{1}{k}p$. Since k is a constant, $\frac{1}{k}$ is also a constant. Let $k_1 = \frac{1}{k}$. Then $q = k_1 p$, so q varies directly as p.

18. Let $u = 2$, $v = 4$, $k = 8$.

If $u = \frac{k}{v}$, then $v = \frac{k}{u}$ and $\frac{1}{u} = \frac{1}{k}(v)$.

If $2 = \frac{8}{4}$, then $4 = \frac{8}{2}$ and $\frac{1}{2} = \frac{1}{8}(4)$.

19. $\pi r^2 = k(2r)^2$

$\pi = \frac{4r^2 k}{r^2}$

$\pi = 4k$

$\frac{\pi}{4} = k$

20. $p = t^2$

$\sqrt{p} = t$

t varies directly as $\sqrt{p}$.

21. Division by zero is undefined.

22. a. $y = kx^2$, $y = k(2x)^2$

$y = 4kx^2$

y is multiplied by 4.

$y = k(nx)^2$

$y = n^2 kx^2$

y is multiplied by n^2.

b. $y = \frac{k}{x^2}$

$y = \frac{k}{(3x)^2} = \frac{k}{9x^2}$

y is divided by 9.

$y = \frac{k}{(nx)^2} = \frac{k}{n^2 x^2}$

y is divided by n^2.

23. a. $8205 = \frac{k(690{,}000)(360{,}000)}{(174)^2}$

$(8205)(30{,}276) = 1{,}000{,}000k(690)(360)$

$1{,}000{,}000k = \frac{(8205)(30{,}276)}{(690)(360)}$

$1{,}000{,}000k = \frac{248{,}414{,}580}{248{,}400}$

$1{,}000{,}000k = 1000$

$k = \frac{1}{1000}$ or 0.001

$N = \frac{P_1 P_2}{1000d^2}$

b. $N = \frac{(1{,}100{,}000)(690{,}000)}{1000(446 \ km)^2}$

$= \frac{(1{,}100{,}000)(690{,}000)}{198{,}916{,}000}$

$= 3815.68$

$N = 3816$ calls

c. $N = \frac{P_1 P_2}{1000d^2}$

$d^2 = \frac{P_1 P_2}{1000N}$

$d = \sqrt{\frac{(690{,}000)(6{,}700{,}000)}{100(3514)}}$

$= \sqrt{1{,}315{,}594.5}$

$d = 1147 \ km$

---

pp. 366–370   8-7 TRY THIS

a. $y = kx^2$

$175 = k(25)$

$7 = k$

$y = 7x^2$

b. $y = \frac{k}{x^2}$

$\frac{1}{4} = \frac{k}{36}$

$\frac{36}{4} = k$

$9 = k$

$y = \frac{9}{x^2}$

c. $y = kxz$

$65 = k(10)(13)$

$65 = 130k$

$\frac{65}{130} = k$

$\frac{1}{2} = k$

$y = \frac{1}{2}xz$

d. $y = \frac{kxz^2}{w}$

$80 = \frac{k(4)(10)^2}{25}$

$80(25) = 400k$

$\frac{2000}{400} = k$

$5 = k$

$y = \frac{5xz^2}{w}$

e. When $D_1 = 19.6$ m, $t_1 = 2$ sec, and $t_2 = 10$ sec,

$D_1 = kt_1^2$ and $D_2 = kt_2^2$

$\frac{D_1}{D_2} = \frac{kt_1^2}{kt_2^2} = \frac{t_1^2}{t_2^2}$

$D_2 t_1^2 = D_1 t_2^2$

$D_2 = \frac{(19.6)(10)^2}{2^2}$

$= 490$ m

---

pp. 370–371   8-7 EXERCISES

1. $y = \frac{54}{x^2}$ **2.** $y = 3.75x^2$ **3.** $y = \frac{0.256}{x^2}$ **4.** $y = 15x^2$

5. $y = \frac{2}{3}x^2$ **6.** $y = \frac{0.0015}{x^2}$ **7.** $y = xz$ **8.** $y = \frac{5x}{z}$

9. $y = 187.5\frac{x}{z^2}$ **10.** $y = \frac{xz}{w}$ **11.** $y = \frac{xz}{5wp}$

12. $y = \frac{5xz}{4w^2}$ **13.** 180 m   **14.** 624.24 m²   **15.** 94.03 kg

---

110   *Algebra and Trigonometry*

Lessons 8-6–8-7

d. Adjoining cities have $d = 0$;

$N = \dfrac{P_1 P_2}{1000(0)^2}$ is undefined.

24. $x^2 - 10x + 25 = 0$; $\sqrt{100 - 4(25)} = 0$, so 1 real.

25. $y^2 + y + 1 = 0$; $\sqrt{1 - 4(1)} = \sqrt{-3} < 0$, so 2 nonreal.

26. $a^2 - 121 = 0$; $\sqrt{-4(1)(-121)} = \sqrt{484} > 0$, so 2 real.

27. $m^2 + 5m - 2 = 0$; sum $= \dfrac{-b}{a} = \dfrac{-5}{1} = -5$;

product $= \dfrac{c}{a} = \dfrac{-2}{1} = -2$

28. $2x^2 + 6x = 0$; sum $= \dfrac{-6}{2} = -3$; product $= \dfrac{c}{a} = 0$

29. $2y^2 + 8y - 3 = 0$; sum $= \dfrac{-8}{2} = -4$; product $= \dfrac{-3}{2}$

30. $c^2 + 6c - 5 = 0$

$$c = \frac{-6 \pm \sqrt{36 - 4(-5)}}{2}$$

$$= \frac{-6 \pm \sqrt{56}}{2}$$

$$= \frac{-6 \pm 2\sqrt{14}}{2}$$

$$c = -3 \pm \sqrt{14}$$
$$\{-3 + \sqrt{14}, -3 - \sqrt{14}\}$$

31. $3m^2 - 10m + 3 = 0$
$(3m - 1)(m - 3) = 0$
$3m - 1 = 0$ or $m - 3 = 0$
$m = \dfrac{1}{3}$ or $m = 3$

32. The conjugate of $a - bi$ is $a + bi$.

33. The conjugate of $-x + yi$ is $-x - yi$.

p. 373   8-8 PROBLEM SOLVING: STRATEGIES

1. Strategy: Draw a diagram

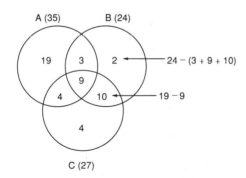

A (35)   B (24)

19   3   2 ← 24 − (3 + 9 + 10)

9

4   10 ← 19 − 9

4

C (27)

$19 + 3 + 9 + 4 + 2 + 10 + 4 = 51$
There were 51 companies contacted.

2. Strategy: Guess, check, revise or make a table
For a 7-minute interval:

Time	7:00	7:07	7:14	7:21	7:28	7:35	7:42	7:49	7:56
On	✓		✓		✓		✓		✓
Off		✓		✓		✓		✓	

Time	8:03	8:10	8:17	8:24	8:31	8:38	8:45	8:52	8:59	9:06
On		✓		✓		✓		✓		✓
Off	✓		✓		✓		✓		✓	

The buzzer was off at 9:00 a.m.

3. Strategy: Make a table

	IN	IL	FL	HA	CA	NY
Tracy	NO	YES	NO	NO	NO	NO
Sally	NO	NO	NO	YES	NO	NO
Juan	NO	NO	NO	NO	YES	NO
Herb	NO	NO	NO	NO	NO	YES
Rick	YES	NO	NO	NO	NO	NO
Terry	NO	NO	YES	NO	NO	NO

Tracy—Illinois; Sally—Hawaii; Juan—California;
Herb—New York; Rick—Indiana; Terry—Florida.

4. Strategy: Make a table

January	= 1
February	= 1 + 4
March	= 5 + 4
April	= 9 + 4
May	= 13 + 4
June	= 17 + 4
July	= 21 + 4
August	= 25 + 4

It took 8 months to hire the needed number of employees.

$$\begin{array}{r} 120 \\ \text{starting} \rightarrow + \underline{220} \\ 340 \end{array}$$

5. Strategy: Draw a picture; make a table

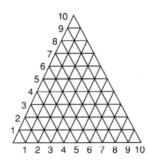

100 regular △ with side length 1 make one regular △ with side length 10.

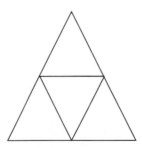

4 regular △ with side length 1 make one regular △ with side length 2.
Make a table.

length of side	number of △
2	4
3	9
10	100
⋮	⋮

The picture and table suggest that (length of side)^2 = number of △ $10^2 = 100$.

1. $7x^2 + 6x = 0$
$x(7x + 6) = 0$
$x = 0$ or $7x + 6 = 0$
$\phantom{x = 0 \text{ or } 7x} 7x = -6$
$$x = -\frac{6}{7}$$

2. $7x^2 - 21x = 0$
$7x(x - 3) = 0$
$7x = 0$ or $x - 3 = 0$
$x = 0$ $ x = 3$

3. $3x^2 + 10x - 8 = 0$
$(3x - 2)(x + 4) = 0$
$3x - 2 = 0$ or $x + 4 = 0$
$3x = 2$ $ x = -4$
$$x = \frac{2}{3}$$

4. $4x^2 - 27x + 18 = 0$
$(4x - 3)(x - 6) = 0$
$4x - 3 = 0$ or $x - 6 = 0$
$4x = 3$ $ x = 6$
$$x = \frac{3}{4}$$

5. $4x^2 + 2 = 0$
$4x^2 = -2$
$$x^2 = -\frac{1}{2}$$
$$x = \pm i\sqrt{\frac{1}{2}} = \pm i\frac{\sqrt{2}}{2}$$

6. $9x^2 - 4 = 0$
$9x^2 = 4$
$$x^2 = \frac{4}{9}$$
$$x = \pm\frac{2}{3}$$

7. $x^2 + 16x$
$x^2 + 16x + 64 = (x + 8)^2$

8. $x^2 - 9x$
$$x^2 - 9x + \frac{81}{4} = \left(x - \frac{9}{2}\right)^2$$

9. $x^2 + 4x - 6 = 0$
$x^2 + 4x + 4 = 6 + 4$
$(x + 2)^2 = 10$
$x + 2 = \pm\sqrt{10}$
$x = -2 \pm \sqrt{10}$

10. $4x^2 - 4x - 15 = 0$
$$x^2 - x - \frac{15}{4} = 0$$
$$x^2 - x + \frac{1}{4} = \frac{15}{4} + \frac{1}{4}$$
$$\left(x - \frac{1}{2}\right)^2 = 4$$
$$x - \frac{1}{2} = \pm 2$$
$$x = \frac{1}{2} \pm 2$$
$$x = \frac{5}{2}, -\frac{3}{2}$$

11.

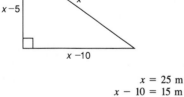

$(x - 5)^2 + (x - 10)^2 = x^2$
$x^2 - 10x + 25 + x^2 - 20x + 100 = x^2$
$2x^2 - 30x + 125 = x^2$
$x^2 - 30x + 125 = 0$
$(x - 25)(x - 5) = 0$
$x - 25 = 0$ or $x - 5 = 0$
$x = 25$ $ x = 5$

$x = 25$ m
$x - 10 = 15$ m
$x - 5 = 20$ m

12. $x^2 + 4x - 7 = 0$
$$x = \frac{-4 \pm \sqrt{16 - 4(1)(-7)}}{2} = \frac{-4 \pm \sqrt{44}}{2}$$
$$= \frac{-4 \pm 2\sqrt{11}}{2} = -2 \pm \sqrt{11}$$

13. $x^2 + 3x - 5 = 0$
$$x = \frac{-3 \pm \sqrt{9 - 4(1)(-5)}}{2} = \frac{-3 \pm \sqrt{29}}{2}$$

14. $x^2 + 2x + 4 = 0$
$$x = \frac{-2 \pm \sqrt{4 - 4(1)(4)}}{2} = \frac{-2 \pm \sqrt{-12}}{2}$$
$$= \frac{-2 \pm i2\sqrt{3}}{2} = -1 \pm i\sqrt{3}$$

15. $x^2 + x + 4 = 0$
$$x = \frac{-1 \pm \sqrt{1 - 4(1)(4)}}{2} = \frac{-1 \pm \sqrt{-15}}{2} = \frac{-1 \pm i\sqrt{15}}{2}$$

16. $x^2 - 8x + 5 = 0$
$$x = \frac{8 \pm \sqrt{64 - 4(1)(5)}}{2} = \frac{8 \pm \sqrt{44}}{2} \approx 7.3, 0.7$$

17. $25 - 16 = 9 > 0$ There are two real roots.

18. Sum $= \frac{4}{5}$; product $= \frac{2}{5}$

19. $10x^2 + 5x + 6 = 0$

20. $2x^2 + 7x + 3 = 0$

21. $y^2 = x, y = \pm\sqrt{x}$
$x^2 - 2x + 1 = 0$
$(x - 1)(x - 1) = 0$
$x - 1 = 0$
$x = 1, y = \pm 1$

22. Let $y = (x^2 + 1)$.
$y^2 - 15y + 50 = 0$
$(y - 5)(y - 10) = 0$
$y - 5 = 0$ $y - 10 = 0$
$y = 5$ $y = 10$
$5 = x^2 + 1$ $10 = x^2 + 1$
$x^2 = 4$ $x^2 = 9$
$x = \pm 2$ $x = \pm 3$

23. $A^2 + a^2 = 1$
$A^2 = 1 - a^2$
$A = \sqrt{1 - a^2}$

24. $s = at + \frac{1}{2}gt^2$
$$\frac{1}{2}gt^2 + at - s = 0$$
$$t = \frac{-a \pm \sqrt{a^2 - 4\left(\frac{1}{2}g\right)(-s)}}{2 \cdot \frac{1}{2}g} = \frac{-a \pm \sqrt{a^2 + 2gs}}{g}$$

25.
$s = 4.9t^2 + v_0 t$
$200 = 4.9t^2 + 20t$
$4.9t^2 + 20t - 200 = 0$
$$t = \frac{-20 + \sqrt{400 + 4(4.9)(200)}}{9.8}$$
$$t = \frac{-20 + \sqrt{4320}}{9.8} = 4.67 \text{ s}$$

26. $y = kx^2$
$2 = k3^2$
$$k = \frac{2}{9}$$
$$y = \frac{2}{9}x^2$$

27. $y = kx^2$
$0.1 = k(0.2)^2$
$k = 2.5$
$y = 2.5x^2$

28. $y = \frac{k}{x^2}$
$$0.5 = \frac{k}{4}$$
$k = 2$
$$y = \frac{2}{x^2}$$

29. $y = \frac{k}{x^2}$
$$-0.1 = \frac{k}{100}$$
$k = -10$
$$y = -\frac{10}{x^2}$$

30. $s = kr^2$
$1257 = k100$
$k = 12.57$
$s = (12.57)(9)$
$s = 113.13 \ m^2$

1. $3x^2 - 15x = 0$
$3x(x - 5) = 0$
$3x = 0$ or $x - 5 = 0$
$x = 0$ $ x = 5$

2. $5x^2 - 6x = 0$
$x(5x - 6) = 0$
$x = 0$ or $5x - 6 = 0$
$5x = 6$
$x = \dfrac{6}{5}$

3. $x^2 - 6x + 5 = 0$
$(x - 5)(x - 1) = 0$
$x - 5 = 0$ or $x - 1 = 0$
$x = 5$ $x = 1$

4. $16x^2 - 9 = 0$
$16x^2 = 9$
$x^2 = \dfrac{9}{16}$
$x = \pm\dfrac{3}{4}$

5. $5x^2 + 13x - 6 = 0$
$(5x - 2)(x + 3) = 0$
$5x - 2 = 0$ or $x + 3 = 0$
$5x = 2$ $x = -3$
$x = \dfrac{2}{5}$

6. $3x^2 + 15 = 0$
$3x^2 = -15$
$x^2 = -5$
$x = \pm i\sqrt{5}$

7. $x^2 - \dfrac{1}{4}x$
$x^2 - \dfrac{1}{4}x + \dfrac{1}{64}$

8. $y^2 + 2.5y$
$y^2 + 2.5y + 1.5625$

9. $x^2 + 4x - 11 = 0$
$x^2 + 4x + 4 = 11 + 4$
$(x + 2)^2 = 15$
$x + 2 = \pm\sqrt{15}$
$x = -2 \pm \sqrt{15}$

10. $2x^2 + 4x - 11 = 0$
$x^2 + 2x - \dfrac{11}{2} = 0$
$x^2 + 2x + 1 = \dfrac{11}{2} + 1$
$(x + 1)^2 = \dfrac{13}{2}$
$x + 1 = \pm\sqrt{\dfrac{13}{2}}$
$x = -1 \pm \dfrac{\sqrt{26}}{2}$

11.
$d = rt$
$4x = x \cdot 4$
$4x + 16 = (x + 4)4$

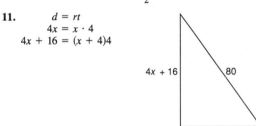

$(4x + 16)^2 + (4x)^2 = 80^2$
$16x^2 + 128x + 256 + 16x^2 = 6400$
$32x^2 + 128x - 6144 = 0$
$32(x^2 + 4x - 192) = 0$
$32(x + 16)(x - 12) = 0$
$x + 16 = 0$ or $x - 12 = 0$
$x = -16$ $x = 12$
Eric travels 12 mi/h;
Hilary travels 16 mi/h.

12. $4x^2 + 8x + 1 = 0$
$x = \dfrac{-8 \pm \sqrt{64 - 4(4)(1)}}{8}$
$= \dfrac{-8 \pm \sqrt{48}}{8}$
$= \dfrac{-8 \pm 4\sqrt{3}}{8}$
$= \dfrac{-2 \pm \sqrt{3}}{2}$

13. $2x^2 - 3x - 1 = 0$
$x = \dfrac{3 \pm \sqrt{9 - 4(2)(-1)}}{4}$
$= \dfrac{3 \pm \sqrt{17}}{4}$

14. $x^2 + x - 1 = 0$
$x = \dfrac{-1 \pm \sqrt{1 - 4(1)(-1)}}{2}$
$= \dfrac{-1 \pm \sqrt{5}}{2}$

15. $2x^2 + 2x + 9 = 0$
$x = \dfrac{-2 \pm \sqrt{4 - 4(2)(9)}}{4}$
$= \dfrac{-2 \pm \sqrt{-68}}{4}$
$= \dfrac{-2 \pm i2\sqrt{17}}{4}$
$= \dfrac{-1 \pm i\sqrt{17}}{2}$

16. $2x^2 - 5x + 1 = 0$
$x = \dfrac{5 \pm \sqrt{25 - 4(2)(1)}}{4}$
$= \dfrac{5 \pm \sqrt{17}}{4}$
$= 2.3, 0.2$

17. $2x^2 - 5x + 3 = 0$
$25 - 4(2)(3) = 1 > 0$
There are two real, unequal solutions.

18. $-\dfrac{4}{3}, -\dfrac{7}{6}$ **19.** $6x^2 - 4x + 5 = 0$

20. $x^2 - 6x + 7 = 0$

21. $x^4 - 5x^2 + 4 = 0$
Let $u = x^2$.
$u^2 - 5u + 4 = 0$
$(u - 4)(u - 1) = 0$
$u - 4 = 0$ or $u - 1 = 0$
$u = 4$ $u = 1$
$x^2 = 4$ $x^2 = 1$
$x = \pm2$ $x = \pm1$

22. $y^4 - 13y^2 + 36 = 0$
Let $u = y^2$.
$u^2 - 13u + 36 = 0$
$(u - 9)(u - 4) = 0$
$u - 9 = 0$ or $u - 4 = 0$
$u = 9$ $u = 4$
$y^2 = 9$ $y^2 = 4$
$y = \pm3$ $y = \pm2$

23. $x^2 + x + 6 = 0$
$x = \dfrac{-1 \pm \sqrt{1 - 4(1)(6)}}{2}$
$= \dfrac{-1 \pm \sqrt{-23}}{2}$
$= \dfrac{-1 \pm i\sqrt{23}}{2}$

24. $x - 2x^{1/2} + 1 = 0$
Let $u = \sqrt{x}$.
$u^2 - 2u + 1 = 0$
$(u - 1)(u - 1) = 0$
$u - 1 = 0$
$u = 1$
$\sqrt{x} = 1$
$x = 1$

25. $A^2 + a^2 = 4$
$A^2 = 4 - a^2$
$A = \sqrt{4 - a^2}$

26. $s = 4.9(4)^2 + 20(4)$
$s = 78.4 + 80$
$s = 158.4$ m

27. $y = kx^2$
$7 = k4$
$k = \dfrac{7}{4}$
$y = \dfrac{7}{4}x^2$

28. $y = \dfrac{k}{x^2}$
$\dfrac{1}{3} = \dfrac{k}{3^2}$
$k = 3$
$y = \dfrac{3}{x^2}$

29. $y = \dfrac{kt^r}{w^2}$
$2 = \dfrac{k \cdot 4 \cdot 9}{36}$
$k = 2$
$y = \dfrac{2tr}{w^2}$

30.
$s = kt^2$
$44 \cdot 1 = k \cdot 3^2$
$k = 4.9$
$s = 4.9(25)$
$s = 122.5$ m

pp. 377–381 CHAPTERS 1–8 CUMULATIVE REVIEW

1. $5x - 3 - 2 + 3x = 8x - 5$

2. $-3[y - 12y + 6 - 5 + y] = -3[-10y + 1]$
$= 30y - 3$

3. $5x - 3 = 7 - x$
$6x = 10$
$x = \dfrac{5}{3}$

4. $3y - 20 - y = 6 - 3y - 6$
$5y = 20$
$y = 4$

5. $4(1.00) + 3(1.75) = 4.00 + 5.25 = \$9.25$

6. $\dfrac{1}{9^2} = \dfrac{1}{81}$ **7.** $\dfrac{-3y^3z^4}{x^2}$ **8.** 9×10^8

9. $32.4 \times 10^{-3} = 3.24 \times 10^{-2}$

10. $x + (x + 2) + (x + 4) = x + 4 + 240$
$3x + 6 = x + 224$
$2x = 238$
$x = 119, 121, 123$

11. $x \leq 5$

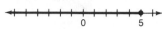

12. $-15 < 3y$
$-5 < y$

13. $18.75(7) + x(.25) < 200$
$.25x < 68.75$
$x < 275$
Less than 275 miles

14. $-x + 3 \leq 6$ $x - 3 \leq 6$
$x \geq -3$ $x \leq 9$
$-3 \leq x \leq 9$

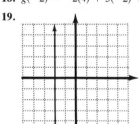

15. $-2x + 5 \geq 7$ $2x - 5 \geq 7$
$x \leq -1$ $x \geq 6$

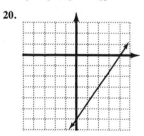

16. Domain: $\{0, 3\}$, Range: $\{-2, 0, 2\}$

17. $g(0) = -2(0) + 3(0) + 1 = 1$

18. $g(-2) = -2(4) + 3(-2) + 1 = -8 - 6 + 1 = -13$

19.

20.

21. $-5 = 2\left(-\dfrac{5}{4}\right) + b$
$b = -5 + \dfrac{5}{2} = -\dfrac{5}{2}$
$y = -\dfrac{5}{4}x - \dfrac{5}{2}$

22. $m = \dfrac{-5 + 1}{-4 + 2} = 2$
$-5 = (-4)(2) + b$
$b = 3$
$y = 2x + 3$

23. $m = \dfrac{3}{4}, b = -3$ **24.** $2x - 3y + 9 = 0$

25. Slope $= -\dfrac{4}{5}$
$-5 = 2\left(-\dfrac{4}{5}\right) + b$
$b = -5 + \dfrac{8}{5} = -\dfrac{17}{5}$
$y = -\dfrac{4}{5}x - \dfrac{17}{5}$

26. Slope $= \dfrac{5}{4}$
$-5 = 2\left(\dfrac{5}{4}\right) + b$
$b = -5 - \dfrac{5}{2} = -\dfrac{15}{2}$
$y = \dfrac{5}{4}x - \dfrac{15}{2}$

27. $(8, 30)(15, 55)$
$m = \dfrac{55 - 30}{15 - 8} = \dfrac{25}{7}$
$30 = \dfrac{25}{7}(8) + b$
$b = 30 - \dfrac{200}{7} = \dfrac{10}{7}$
$y = \dfrac{25}{7}x + \dfrac{10}{7}$

28. $y = \dfrac{25}{7}(25) + \dfrac{10}{7}$
$= \dfrac{635}{7} = 90\dfrac{5}{7}$
approximately 91¢

29. $g(-3) = 2(9) = 18$
$f(g(-3)) = 3(18) - 2 = 52$

30. $g(x) = 2x^2$
$f(g(x)) = 3(2x^2) - 2 = 6x^2 - 2$
$h(f(g(x))) = -2[6x^2 - 2] = -12x^2 + 4$

31. $-3x + 3y = -18$
$\underline{12x - 3y = 15}$
$9x = -3$
$x = -\dfrac{1}{3}$
$-3\left(-\dfrac{1}{3}\right) + 3y = -18$
$3y = -19$
$y = -\dfrac{19}{3}$ $\left(-\dfrac{1}{3}, -\dfrac{19}{3}\right)$

32. $4x - 6y = 16$
$\underline{15x + 6y = 3}$
$19x = 19$
$x = 1$
$2(1) - 3y = 8$
$-3y = 6$
$y = -2$ $(1, -2)$

33. $x, x - 10$
$8(x - 10) + 40 = 3x - 10$
$5x = 30$
$x = 6$
$x - 10 = -4$

34. $2x + y - z = 5$
$y - 2z = 7$
$2y + 3z = 0$ $-2\text{②} + \text{③}$
$z = -2, y = 3, x = 0$
$2x + y - z = 5$
$y - 2z = 7$
$7z = -14$
$(0, 3, -2)$

35. $5x + 3y + 2z = 1$
$2x - y + z = -1$
$-2x + 2y - z = 2$ ② + ③
$5x + 3y + 2z = 1$
$2x - y + z = -1$ $2\text{①} - 5\text{②}$
$y = 1$
$y = 1, z = 4, x = -2$ $(-2, 1, 4)$
$5x + 3y + 2z = 1$
$11y - z = 7$
$y = 1$

36.

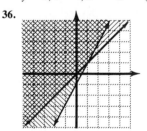

37. $-7y$ **38.** $7x^2 - 6x$ **39.** $4x - 2$

40. $(-2x^2 + x - 3) + (-5x^2 + 3x + 3) = -7x^2 + 4x$

41. $(x^2 - 3y)(x^2 - 3y) = x^4 - 3x^2y - 3x^2y + 9y^2$
$= x^4 - 6x^2y + 9y^2$

42. $(3x - 2y - 1)(3x + 2y + 1)$
$= 9x^2 - 6xy - 3x + 6xy - 4y^2 - 2y + 3x - 2y - 1$
$= 9x^2 - 4y^2 - 4y - 1$

43. $12x(2x^2 - 7x + 6) = 12x(2x - 3)(x - 2)$

44. $4(9y^2 - 25) = 4(3y - 5)(3y + 5)$

45. $x(x - y)^2 - 36 = (x - y - 6)(x - y + 6)$

46. $(z - 3)(z^2 + 3z + 9)$

47. $-3y(1 - 4y^2 + 4y^4) = -3y(1 - 2y^2)(1 - 2y^2)$,
or $-3y(2y^2 - 1)^2$

48. $(x - 2)(5x + 1)$

49. $2(x^2 - 2xy + y^2 - 9t^2) = 2[(x - y)^2 - 9t^2]$
$$= 2(x - y - 3t)(x - y + 3t)$$

50. $(x - y)^2 - (r - 4)^2 = (x - y - r + 4)(x - y + r - 4)$

51. $4x^2 + 11x + 6 = 0$
$(x + 2)(4x + 3) = 0$

$x = -2 \qquad x = -\dfrac{3}{4}$

52. $3x(x + 12) = 0$
$x = 0, -12$

53. $w, 2w + 1$
$w(2w + 1) = 15$
$2w^2 + w - 15 = 0$
$(2w - 5)(w + 3) = 0$

$w = \dfrac{5}{2} \qquad l = 6$

54. $\dfrac{(3x - 2y)(x + y)}{(x - y)(x + y)} = \dfrac{3x - 2y}{x - y}$

55. $\dfrac{(2x - 3)(4x^2 + 6x + 9)}{(4x + 1)(16x^2 - 4x + 1)} \cdot \dfrac{(4x + 1)(4x + 1)}{(2x - 3)(2x - 3)}$

$= \dfrac{(4x + 1)(4x^2 + 6x + 9)}{(2x - 3)(16x^2 - 4x + 1)}$

56. $\dfrac{(x - 1)(x + 2)}{x^2 - 4} - \dfrac{(x + 1)(x - 2)}{x^2 - 4} + \dfrac{x - 6}{x^2 - 4}$

$= \dfrac{x^2 + x - 2 - x^2 + x + 2 + x - 6}{x^2 - 4} = \dfrac{3x - 6}{x^2 - 4} = \dfrac{3}{x + 2}$

57. $\dfrac{y + x}{xy} \div \dfrac{(x - y)(x + y)}{xy} = \dfrac{x + y}{xy} \cdot \dfrac{xy}{(x + y)(x - y)} = \dfrac{1}{(x - y)}$

58. $\dfrac{18xy^2}{3x^2y} - \dfrac{6x^2y}{3x^2y} + \dfrac{9x^3y^3}{3x^2y} = \dfrac{6y}{x} - 2 + 3xy^2$

59. $\begin{array}{r} 16x^2 + 12x + 9 \\ 4x - 3 \overline{)64x^3 - 27} \\ \underline{64x^3 - 48x^2} \\ 48x^2 \\ \underline{48x^2 - 36x} \\ 36x - 27 \\ \underline{36x - 27} \\ 0 \end{array}$

60. $\begin{array}{r} y^2 - 2y + 3 \\ y + 2 \overline{)y^3 + 0y^2 - y + 6} \\ \underline{y^3 + 2y^2} \\ -2y^2 - y \\ \underline{-2y^2 - 4y} \\ 3y + 6 \\ \underline{3y + 6} \\ 0 \end{array}$

61. $\begin{array}{r|rrrr} 2 & 1 & -2 & -4 & -6 \\ & & 2 & 0 & -8 \\ \hline & 1 & 0 & -4 & -14 \end{array}$

$x^2 - 4$, R: -14

62. $\begin{array}{r|rrrrr} -1 & 1 & 0 & 0 & 0 & -1 \\ & & -1 & 1 & -1 & 1 \\ \hline & 1 & -1 & 1 & -1 & 0 \end{array}$

Q: $y^3 - y^2 + y - 1$, R: 0

63. $-\dfrac{1}{3} - \dfrac{5}{4x} = \dfrac{3}{4} - \dfrac{1}{6x}$

$-8x - 30 = 18x - 4$
$-26 = 26x$
$-1 = x$

64. $\dfrac{x}{2x - 6} - \dfrac{3}{(x - 3)^2} = \dfrac{x - 2}{3(x - 3)}$

$3(x - 3)x - 18 = 2(x - 3)(x - 2)$
$3x^2 - 9x - 18 = 2x^2 - 10x + 12$
$x^2 + x - 30 = 0$
$(x + 6)(x - 5) = 0$
$x = -6, 5$

65. $4 = \left(\dfrac{1}{8} + \dfrac{1}{6}\right)t$

$t = \dfrac{96}{7} = 13\dfrac{5}{7}\,h$

66. $r = $ rate B
$r - 10 = $ rate A

$\dfrac{400}{r - 10} = \dfrac{500}{r}$

$400r = 500r - 5000$
$5000 = 100r$
$50 = r$
Train B: 50 mi/h
Train A: 40 mi/h

67. $\dfrac{x_1}{y_1} = \dfrac{x_2}{y_2}$

$x_1 y_2 = x_2 y_1$

$y_2 = \dfrac{x_2 y_1}{x_1}$

68. $3T = (k_1 + k_2)t$

$k_1 + k_2 = \dfrac{3T}{t}$

$k_1 = \dfrac{3T}{t} - k_2$

69. $N = kt$
$350 = 15k$

$k = \dfrac{70}{3}$

$N = \dfrac{70}{3}(50) = \dfrac{3500}{3} = 1166$

70. $25|t|$ **71.** $-(-2) = 2$ **72.** $2x^2|y|$

73. $\sqrt[3]{24x^7} = 2x^2\sqrt[3]{3x}$

74. $\dfrac{\sqrt{60a^8}}{\sqrt{72a^5}} = \sqrt{\dfrac{60a^8}{72a^5}} = \sqrt{\dfrac{5}{6}a^3} = \dfrac{|a|\sqrt{30a}}{6}$

75. $\dfrac{\sqrt{y^3 + x^3}}{\sqrt{y + x}} = \sqrt{\dfrac{(y + x)(y^2 - xy + x^2)}{(y + x)}} = \sqrt{y^2 - xy + x^2}$

76. $\sqrt[3]{108} - 2\sqrt{75} + \sqrt{147}$
$= 3\sqrt[3]{4} - 10\sqrt{3} + 7\sqrt{3}$
$= 3\sqrt[3]{4} - 3\sqrt{3}$

77. $\sqrt[3]{x}(\sqrt[3]{3x^2} + \sqrt[3]{12x})$
$= \sqrt[3]{3x^3} + \sqrt[3]{12x^2}$
$= x\sqrt[3]{3} + \sqrt[3]{12x^2}$

78. $\left(\dfrac{1}{8}\right)^{-\frac{2}{3}} = 8^{\frac{2}{3}} = 4$ **79.** $2x(y)^{-\frac{1}{4}} = \dfrac{2x}{y^{\frac{1}{4}}}$

80. $(5x + 4) = 144$
$5x = 140$
$x = 28$

81. $(4x + 1) = (3 + \sqrt{x - 2})^2$
$= 9 + 6\sqrt{x - 2} + x - 2$
$3x - 6 = 6\sqrt{x - 2}$
$9x^2 - 36x + 36 = 36(x - 2)$
$9x^2 - 72x + 108 = 0$
$9(x^2 - 8x - 12) = 0$
$9(x - 6)(x - 2) = 0 \qquad x = 6, 2$

82. $\sqrt{3} \cdot 5i = i\sqrt{3} \cdot 5i = -5\sqrt{3}$

83. $(8 - 5i) + (1 - 3i) = 9 - 8i$

84.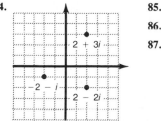

85. $\sqrt{9 - 4i^2} = \sqrt{13}$

86. $\sqrt{9 - 16i^2} = \sqrt{25} - 5$

87. $(8 - 5i)(8 + 5i)$
$= 64 + 40i - 40i - 25i^2$
$= 64 + 25$
$= 89$

88. $(2 - i\sqrt{3})(2 + i\sqrt{3}) = 4 + 2i\sqrt{3} - 2i\sqrt{3} - i^2\sqrt{9}$
$= 4 + 3 = 7$

89. $\dfrac{2}{4i} \cdot \dfrac{i}{i} = \dfrac{2i}{-4} = -\dfrac{i}{2}$

90. $\dfrac{\sqrt{2 + i}}{\sqrt{2 - i}} \cdot \dfrac{\sqrt{2 - i}}{\sqrt{2 - i}} = \dfrac{\sqrt{4 - i^2}}{2 - i} = \dfrac{\sqrt{5}}{2 - i}$

$\dfrac{\sqrt{5}}{2 - i} \cdot \dfrac{2 + i}{2 + i} = \dfrac{(2 + i)\sqrt{5}}{5}$

91. $x^2 + 4 = 0$

92. $x^2 - 6x + 25 = 0$

93. $x + 2ix - 1 = 2i + 3ix - 5i$
$x - ix = -3i + 1$
$x(1 - i) = -3i + 1$

$x = \dfrac{-3i + 1}{1 - i} \cdot \dfrac{1 + i}{1 + i}$

$= \dfrac{-3i + 3 + 1 + i}{2} = \dfrac{-2i + 4}{2} = -i + 2$

94. $9x^2 - 15x + 4 = 0$
$(3x - 4)(3x - 1) = 0$
$3x - 4 = 0$ or $3x - 1 = 0$

$x = \dfrac{4}{3}$ or $x = \dfrac{1}{3}$

95. $x^2 = 5$
$x = \pm\sqrt{5}$

96. $x^2 + 14x + 49$

97. $y^2 - \dfrac{1}{3}y + \dfrac{1}{36}$

98.
$2x^2 - 7x = 15$

$x^2 - \dfrac{7}{2}x = \dfrac{15}{2}$

$x^2 - \dfrac{7}{2}x + \dfrac{49}{16} = \dfrac{169}{16}$

$\left(x - \dfrac{7}{4}\right)^2 = \dfrac{169}{16}$

$x - \dfrac{7}{4} = \dfrac{13}{4} \qquad x - \dfrac{7}{4} = -\dfrac{13}{4}$

$x = 5 \qquad x = -\dfrac{6}{4} = -\dfrac{3}{2}$

99. $w, 2w - 10$
$w(2w - 10) = 1000$
$2w^2 - 10w - 1000 = 0$
$2(w^2 - 5w - 500) = 0$
$2(w - 25)(w + 20) = 0$
$w = 25 \quad l = 40$

100. $x^2 - 3x + 5 = 0$
$x = \dfrac{3 \pm \sqrt{9 - 4(5)}}{2}$

$= \dfrac{3 \pm i\sqrt{11}}{2}$

101. $4x^2 - 2x + 5 = 0$
$x = \dfrac{2 \pm \sqrt{4 - 4(4)(5)}}{8} = \dfrac{2 \pm i\sqrt{76}}{8}$

$= \dfrac{2 \pm 2i\sqrt{19}}{8} = \dfrac{1 \pm i\sqrt{19}}{4}$

102. $9 - 4(5) = -11$
Two complex roots.

103. $36 - 4(-2)(10) = 116$
There are 2 irrational roots.

104. $4x^2 + 16x + 1 = 0$

105. $x^2 = y \qquad x^2 - 5x + 4 = 0 \qquad (x - 4)(x - 1) = 0$
$x = 4 \qquad y = 16$
$x = 1 \qquad y = 1$

106. $y = x^2 \qquad y^2 - 3y - 18 = 0 \qquad (y - 6)(y + 3) = 0$
$y = 6 \qquad x = \pm\sqrt{6}$
$y = -3 \qquad x = \pm i\sqrt{3}$

107. $y = x^{-1} \qquad y^2 - y - 6 = 0 \qquad (y - 3)(y + 2) = 0$

$y = 3 \qquad x = \dfrac{1}{3}$

$y = -2 \qquad x = -\dfrac{1}{2}$

108. $3T = gt^2$

$t^2 = \dfrac{3T}{g}$

$t = \pm\sqrt{\dfrac{3T}{g}}$

109. $k^2 = \dfrac{x + 2}{y^2}$

$y^2 = \dfrac{x + 2}{k^2}$

$y = \pm\sqrt{\dfrac{x + 2}{k^2}} = \pm\dfrac{\sqrt{x + 2}}{|k|}$

110. $s = 4.9(25) + 30(5)$
$s = 272.5$ m

111. $x = \dfrac{ky}{z^2}$

$20 = \dfrac{k50}{3600}$

$k = 1440$

$x = \dfrac{1440y}{z^2}$

$xz^2 = 1440y$

112. $l = \dfrac{k}{d^2}$

$160 = \dfrac{k}{16}$

$k = 2560$

$l = \dfrac{2560}{144} = \dfrac{160}{9}$ w/m^2

CHAPTER 9

p. 382
READY FOR QUADRATIC FUNCTIONS AND TRANSFORMATIONS?

1. 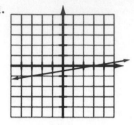   **2.**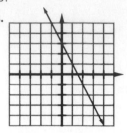

3. No   **4.** Yes   **5.** $5, -2$ **6.** $2, 6$ **7.** $-3, 4$

8. $-4, 2$ **9.** $\dfrac{10}{3}, 2$ **10.** $4, -\dfrac{4}{7}$ **11.** $-\dfrac{1}{3}, 1$

12. $-1 \pm \sqrt{7}$

pp. 386–388
     9-1 TRY THIS

a. $y = x^2 + 3$
$y = (-x)^2 + 3$ is equivalent to $y = x^2 + 3$. Symmetric with respect to the y-axis. $-y = x^2 + 3$ is not equivalent to $y = x^2 + 3$. Therefore the graph is not symmetric with respect to the x-axis.

b. $x^2 + y^2 = 2$
$(-x)^2 + y^2 = 2$ is equivalent to $x^2 + y^2 = 2$.
$x^2 + (-y)^2 = 2$ is equivalent to $x^2 + y^2 = 2$.
Symmetric with respect to both axes

c. $y^2 + x^2 = 16$
$(-y)^2 + (-x)^2 = 16$ is equivalent to $y^2 + x^2 = 16$.
Symmetric with respect to the origin

d. $y = x^3$
$-y = (-x)^3$ is equivalent to $y = x^3$.
Symmetric with respect to the origin

e. $y = x^2$
$-y = (-x)^2$ is not equivalent to $y = x^2$.
No symmetry with respect to the origin

f. $\dfrac{1}{2}y^2 + x = \dfrac{3}{4}$

$\dfrac{1}{2}(-y)^2 - x = \dfrac{3}{4}$ is not equivalent to $\dfrac{1}{2}y^2 + x = \dfrac{3}{4}$

No symmetry with respect to the origin

g. $f(x) = x^4 - x^6$
$f(-x) = (-x)^4 - (-x)^6 = x^4 - x^6$
$-f(x) = -(x^4 - x^6) = x^4 + x^6$
Comparing $f(-x)$ and $-f(x)$, they are not the same for all x, so f is not odd. Comparing $f(x)$ and $f(-x)$, they are the same for all x, so f is an even function.

h. $f(x) = 3x^2 + 3x^5$
$f(-x) = 3(-x)^2 + 3(-x)^5 = 3x^2 - 3x^5$
$-f(x) = -(3x^2 + 3x^5) = -3x^2 - 3x^5$
Comparing $f(-x)$ and $-f(x)$ as well as $f(x)$ and $f(-x)$, neither is the same for all x, so f is neither even nor odd.

i. $f(x) = x^3 + x$
$f(-x) = (-x)^3 + (-x) = -x^3 - x$
$-f(x) = -(x^3 + x) = -x^3 - x$
Comparing $f(-x)$ and $-f(x)$, they are the same for all x, so f is an odd function. Comparing $f(x)$ and $f(-x)$, they are not the same for all x, so f is not even.

pp. 389–390
     9-1 EXERCISES

1. y-axis   **2.** y-axis   **3.** Both axes   **4.** Both axes

5. Neither axis   **6.** Neither axis   **7.** y-axis

8. y-axis   **9.** Both axis   **10.** Both axes

11. Neither axis   **12.** Neither axis

13. Yes   **14.** Yes   **15.** Yes

16. Yes   **17.** Yes   **18.** Yes

19. Yes   **20.** Yes

21. No   **22.** No   **23.** No

24. No   **25.** Neither

26. Odd   **27.** Even   **28.** Odd

29. Even   **30.** Even

31. Odd   **32.** Neither   **33.** Neither   **34.** Odd

35. Even   **36.** Even and odd   **37.** Even   **38.** Even

39. Even   **40.** Even   **41.** Odd   **42.** Neither

43. Odd   **44.** Neither

45. 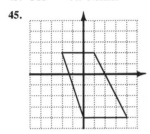   **46.**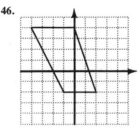

47. 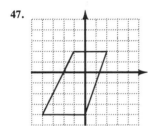   **48.** $f(x) = 0$

49. $y = |x|$
Replace x by $-x$.
$y = |-x| = |x|$ y-axis symmetry exists.
Replace y by $-y$.
$-y = |x|$ $y = -|x| \neq |x|$ x-axis symmetry does not exist.

50. $|x| = |y|$
Replace x by $-x$.
$|-x| = |x| = |y|$ y-axis symmetry exists.
Replace y by $-y$.
$|x| = |-y| = |y|$ x-axis symmetry exists.

51. $|y| = |x| + 1$
Replace x by $-x$.
$|y| = |-x| + 1 = |x| + 1$ y-axis symmetry exists.
Replace y by $-y$.
$|-y| = |y| = |x| + 1$ x-axis symmetry exists.

52. $y = |x| - 3$
Replace x by $-x$.
$y = |-x| - 3 = |x| - 3$ y-axis symmetry exists.
Replace y by $-y$.
$-y = |x| - 3 \Rightarrow y = -|x| + 3 \neq |x| - 3$ x-axis symmetry does not exist.

53. $|x| + |y| = 3$
Replace x by $-x$.
$|-x| + |y| = |x| + |y| = 3$ y-axis symmetry exists.
Replace y by $-y$.
$|x| + |-y| = |x| + |y| = 3$ x-axis symmetry exists.

54. $|x| - |y| = 5$
Replace x by $-x$.
$|-x| - |y| = |x| - |y| = 5$ y-axis symmetry exists.
Replace y by $-y$.
$|x| - |-y| = |x| - |y| = 5$ x-axis symmetry exists.

55. $\sqrt{12}\sqrt{20} = \sqrt{3 \cdot 4 \cdot 4 \cdot 5} = 4\sqrt{15}$

56. $\sqrt[3]{512} = 8$

57. $\sqrt{80} = \sqrt{16 \cdot 5} = 4\sqrt{5}$

58. $\sqrt{3}\sqrt{12} = \sqrt{3^2 \cdot 4} = 3\sqrt{4} = 3 \cdot 2 = 6$

59. sum $= \dfrac{-b}{a} = \dfrac{-8}{2} = -4$; product $= \dfrac{c}{a} = \dfrac{-3}{2} = -\dfrac{3}{2}$

60. sum $= \dfrac{5}{3}$; product $= \dfrac{2}{3}$

61. sum $= -5$, product $= 6$

62. $(x - 6)(x - 4) = 0$ so, $x^2 - 10x + 24 = 0$.

63. $(x)(x + 4) = 0$ so, $x^2 + 4x = 0$.

64. $(x - 3 - \sqrt{3})(x - 3 + \sqrt{3}) = 0$ so, $x^2 - 6x + 6 = 0$.

65. $(x - 3 - 2i)(x - 3 + 2i) = 0$ so, $x^2 - 6x + 13 = 0$.

pp. 392–393   9-2 TRY THIS

a. 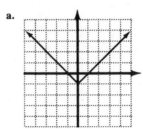   **b.**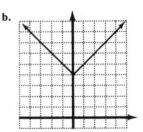

c. 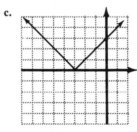   **d.**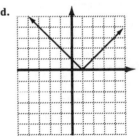

pp. 393–394   9-2 EXERCISES

1. 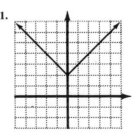   **2.**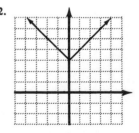

3. 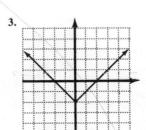   **4.**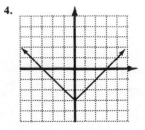

5.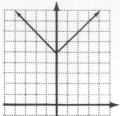

6.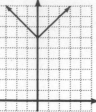

19.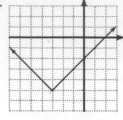

20.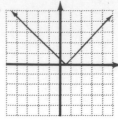

7.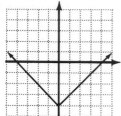

8.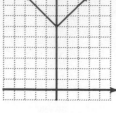

21.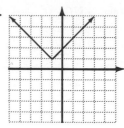

22.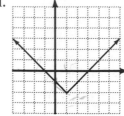

9.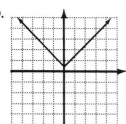

10.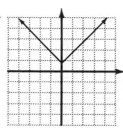

23.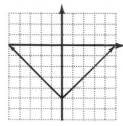

24.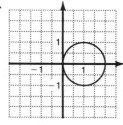

11.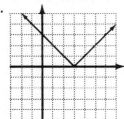

12.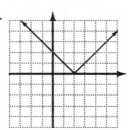

25.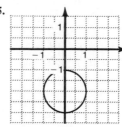

26.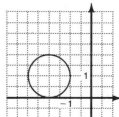

27.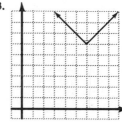

13.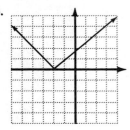

14.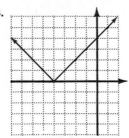

28. $x - h = x - 2 \Rightarrow h = 2$ ∴ Center of circle translates by $+2$ along x-axis.
$y - h = y + 3 = y - (-3)$ ∴ Center of circle translates by -3 along y-axis.
This yields center of circle at point $(2, -3)$.

29. Circle at center $(2, 4) \Rightarrow (x - 2)^2 + (y - 4)^2 = 1$
Replace x with $x - 3$ and y with $y + 5$.
$[(x - 3) - 2]^2 + [(y + 5) - 4]^2 = 1$
$(x - 5)^2 + (y + 1)^2 = (x - h)^2 + (y - k)^2 = 1$
∴ $h = 5$, $k = -1$ and center of circle is at $(5, -1)$.

30. The graph of the relation is translated upward 6 units and 4 units to the left.

15.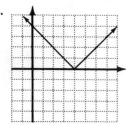

16.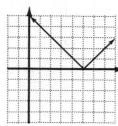

31.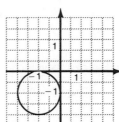

32.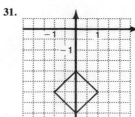

17.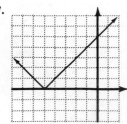

18.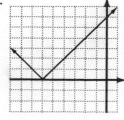

33.

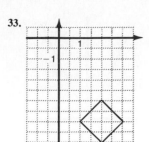

34. Sum $= \dfrac{1}{3}$; product $-\dfrac{9}{3}$. Therefore, $3x^2 - x + 9 = 0$.

35. Sum $= -3$; product $= 2$. Therefore, $x^2 + 3x + 2 = 0$.

36. $(-7i)(-7i) = 49i^2 = 49(-1) = -49$

37. $(5 + i)(5 - i) = 25 - i^2 = 25 + 1 = 26$

38. $(\sqrt{5} + i)(\sqrt{5} - i) = 5 - i^2 = 5 + 1 = 6$

39. $|m - ni| = \sqrt{m^2 + n^2}$ **40.** $|n + mi| = \sqrt{n^2 + m^2}$

41. $|3i| = \sqrt{3^2} = 3$

42. $x^2 = \dfrac{20 \pm \sqrt{400 - 4(1)(64)}}{2}$

$= \dfrac{20 \pm \sqrt{144}}{2}$

$= \dfrac{20 \pm 12}{2}$

$x^2 = 16;\ 4$

$x = \pm 4;\ \pm 2$

43.
$$\text{Let } y = x^2.$$
$$y^2 - 9y = 0$$
$$y(y - 9) = 0$$
$$y = 0;\qquad y - 9 = 0$$
$$y = 9$$
$$\text{Then } x^2 = 0;\qquad x^2 = 9$$
$$x = 0;\qquad x = \pm 3$$

44. $\dfrac{y}{x^2} = \dfrac{18}{9}$

$\dfrac{y}{x^2} = \dfrac{2}{1}$

$y = 2x^2$

pp. 396–398   9-3 TRY THIS

a.

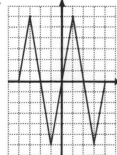

b.

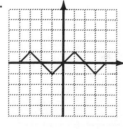

c.

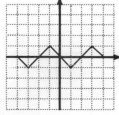

d.

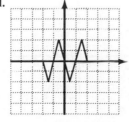

e.

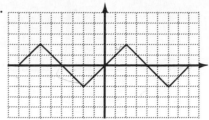

f.

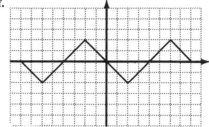

pp. 398–399   9-3 EXERCISES

1.

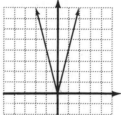

2.

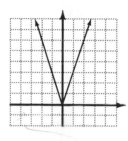

3.

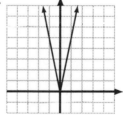

4.

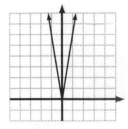

5.

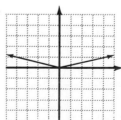

6.

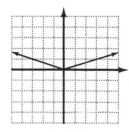

7.

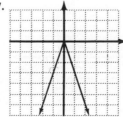

8.

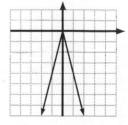

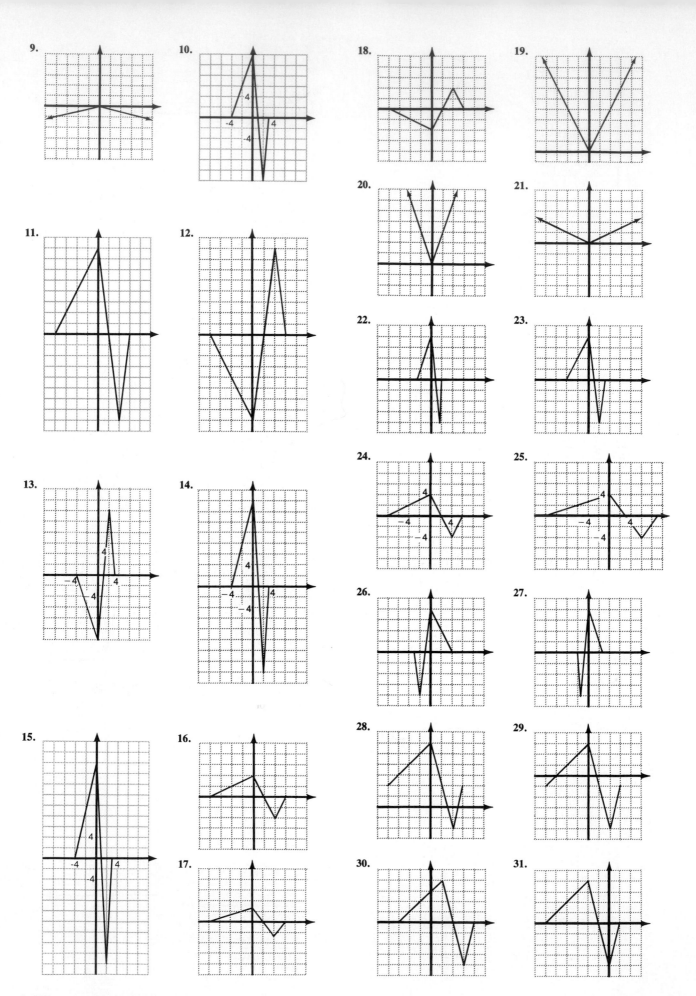

32.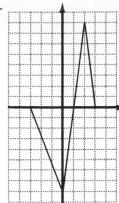

33.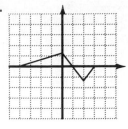

41.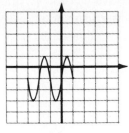

42.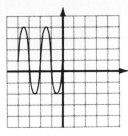

43.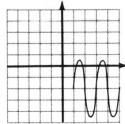

44.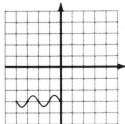

45. $x^2 + 9 = 0$
$x^2 = -9$
$x = \pm 3i$
Yes; yes

46. $x^2 + 5 = 0$
$x^2 = -5$
$x = \pm i\sqrt{5}$
No, yes

47. $\left(x - \dfrac{1}{3}\right)\left(x - \dfrac{1}{2}\right) = 0$
$(3x - 1)(2x - 1) = 0$
$6x^2 - 5x + 1 = 0$

48. $(x - 4)\left(x - \dfrac{1}{3}\right) = 0$
$(x - 4)(3x - 1) = 0$
$3x^2 - 13x + 4 = 0$

49. $-4x - 10i = 2ix$
$-4x - 2ix = 10i$
$-2x(2 + i) = 10i$

$$x = \frac{10i}{-2(2 + i)} \cdot \frac{2 - i}{2 - i}$$

$$= \frac{20i - 10i^2}{-8 + 2i^2}$$

$$= \frac{10 + 20i}{-10}$$

$$x = -1 - 2i$$

34.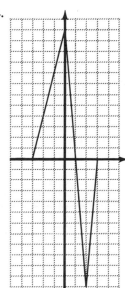

35.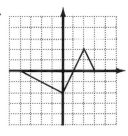

36.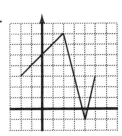

50. $x^4 - 10x^2 + 9 = 0$
$(x^2 - 1)(x^2 - 9) = 0$
$x^2 - 1 = 0, x^2 - 9 = 0$
$x = \pm 1, x = \pm 3$

51. $x - 2x^{1/2} + 1 = 0$
Let $x^{1/2} = x$.
$x^2 - 2x + 1 = 0$
$(x - 1)(x - 1) = 0$
$x^{1/2} - 1 = 0$
$x^{1/2} = 1$
$x = 1$

37.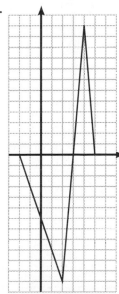

38. The graph is stretched horizontally, shrunk vertically, and reflected across both the x-axis and the y-axis.

52. $x^2 - 7x + 12 = 0$
$(x - 3)(x - 4) = 0$
$x - 3 = 0$ or $x - 4 = 0$
$x = 3$ or $x = 4$

53. $(x + 6)(x - 1) = 18$
$x^2 + 5x - 6 - 18 = 0$
$x^2 + 5x - 24 = 0$
$(x - 3)(x + 8) = 0$
$x - 3 = 0$ or $x + 8 = 0$
$x = 3$ or $x = -8$

54. $x(x - 8) = 0$
$x = 0$ or $x - 8 = 0$
$x = 0$ or $x = 8$

39.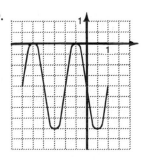

40.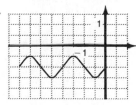

pp. 401–402   9-4 TRY THIS

a. (1) 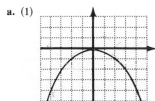   (2) y-axis ($x = 0$)   (3) $(0, 0)$

b. (1)

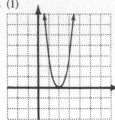

(2) $x = 2$ (3) $(2, 0)$

9. Vertex: $(7, 0)$
Line of symmetry: $x = 7$

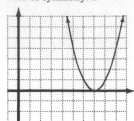

10. Vertex: $(-4, 0)$
Line of symmetry: $x = -4$

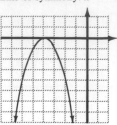

p. 402   9-4 EXERCISES

11. Vertex: $(2, 0)$
Line of symmetry: $x = 2$

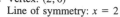
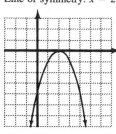

12. Vertex: $(3, 0)$
Line of symmetry: $x = 3$

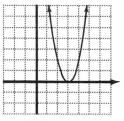

1. Vertex: $(0, 0)$
Line of symmetry: $x = 0$

$1^2 = 1$
$2^2 = 4$

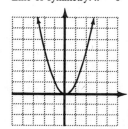

2. Vertex: $(0, 0)$
Line of symmetry: $x = 0$

$-\frac{1}{4}$

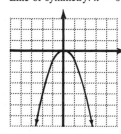

13. Vertex: $(7, 0)$
Line of symmetry: $x = 7$

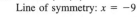
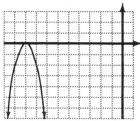

14. Vertex: $(-9, 0)$
Line of symmetry: $x = -9$

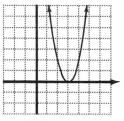

3. Vertex: $(0, 0)$
Line of symmetry: $x = 0$

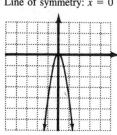

4. Vertex: $(0, 0)$
Line of symmetry: $x = 0$

$2(1)^2 = 2$
$2(2)^2 = 8$

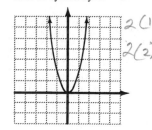

15. Vertex: $(-7, 0)$
Line of symmetry: $x = -7$

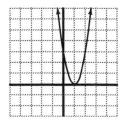

16. Vertex: $(1, 0)$
Line of symmetry: $x = 1$

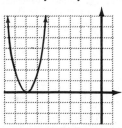

5. Vertex: $(0, 0)$
Line of symmetry: $x = 0$

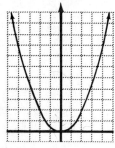

6. Vertex: $(0, 0)$
Line of symmetry: $x = 0$

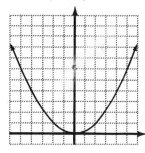

shrink

17. Vertex: $(2, 0)$
Line of symmetry: $x = 2$

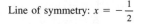
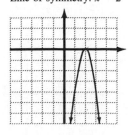

18. Vertex: $\left(-\frac{1}{2}, 0\right)$

Line of symmetry: $x = -\frac{1}{2}$

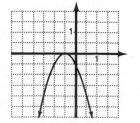

7. Vertex: $(0, 0)$
Line of symmetry: $x = 0$

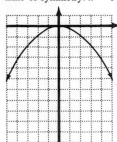

8. Vertex: $(0, 0)$
Line of symmetry: $x = 0$

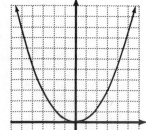

19. Vertex: $(-1, 0)$
Line of symmetry: $x = -1$

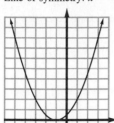

20. Vertex: $(2, 0)$
Line of symmetry: $x = 2$

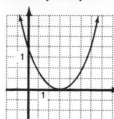

21.

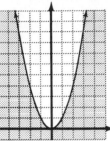

22.

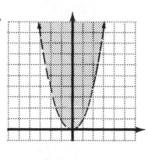

23.

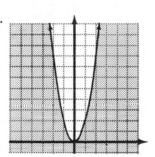

24.

25.

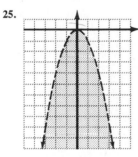

26.

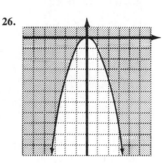

27.

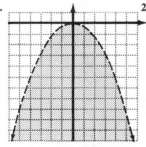

28.

29. Both go through the origin.

30. If the graph opens upward and vertex is (h, k), then the range will be equal to or greater than k. $\{y \mid y \geq k\}$

31. **a.** $|n| > |m|$ **b.** m is negative and n is positive, or n is negative and m is positive.

32. **a.** Yes $(1, 0)$ **33.** **a.** No
   b. Yes $x = 1$ **b.** No
   c. No   **c.** Yes $(1, 0)$

34. $\sqrt{36 - 4(9)} = 0$, one real root

35. $\sqrt{9 - 4(9)} < 0$, two imaginary roots or 2 nonreal

36. $\sqrt{-4(-81)} > 0$, two real roots

37. $x = \dfrac{-6 \pm \sqrt{36 - 16}}{2}$
$= \dfrac{-6 \pm 2\sqrt{5}}{2}$
$x = -3 \pm \sqrt{5}$

38. $x^2(x^2 - 25) = 0$
$x^2 = 0$ or $x^2 - 25 = 0$
$x = 0$ or $x = \pm 5$

39. $2x^2 + 3x - 2 = 0$
$\sqrt{x} = \dfrac{-3 \pm \sqrt{9 - 4(2)(-2)}}{4}$
$= \dfrac{-3 \pm 5}{4}$
$\sqrt{x} = \dfrac{1}{2}, -2$
$x = \dfrac{1}{4}, 4\left\{\dfrac{1}{4}\right\}$

p. 405–406   9-5 TRY THIS

a. Vertex: $(2, 4)$
Line of symmetry: $x = 2$
Minimum: 4

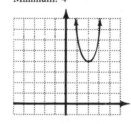

b. Vertex: $(-2, -1)$
Line of symmetry: $x = -2$
Maximum: -1

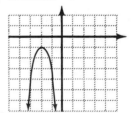

c. $h = 5$, $k = 40$, vertex at $(5, 40)$
Line of symmetry: $x = h$ or $x = 5$
Minimum: 40

d. $h = 5$, $k = 0$, vertex at $(5, 0)$
Line of symmetry: $x = h$ or $x = 5$
Maximum: 0

e. Vertex: $\left(-\dfrac{3}{4}, -6\right)$
Line of symmetry: $x = -\dfrac{3}{4}$
Minimum: -6

f. Vertex: $(-9, 3)$
Line of symmetry: $x = -9$
Maximum: 3

p. 406–407   9-5 EXERCISES

1. Vertex: $(3, 1)$
Line of symmetry: $x = 3$
Minimum: 1

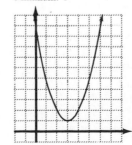

2. Vertex: $(-2, -3)$
Line of symmetry: $x = -2$
Minimum: -3

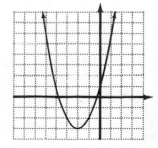

3. Vertex: $(-1, -2)$
Line of symmetry: $x = -1$
Minimum: -2

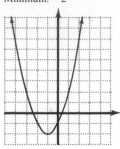

4. Vertex: $(1, 2)$
Line of symmetry: $x = 1$
Minimum: 2

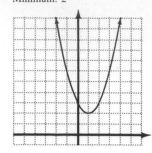

5. Vertex: $(1, -3)$
Line of symmetry: $x = 1$
Minimum: -3

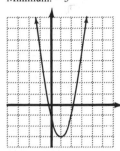

6. Vertex: $(-1, 4)$
Line of symmetry: $x = -1$
Minimum: 4

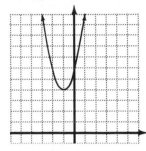

7. Vertex: $(-4, 1)$
Line of symmetry: $x = -4$
Maximum: 1

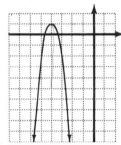

8. Vertex: $(5, -3)$
Line of symmetry: $x = 5$
Maximum: -3

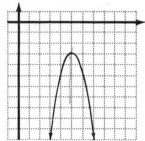

9. $(9, 5)$; $x = 9$; min. $= 5$ **10.** $(-5, -8)$; $x = -5$; min. $= -8$

11. $\left(-\dfrac{1}{4}, -13\right)$; $x = -\dfrac{1}{4}$; min. $= -13$

12. $\left(\dfrac{1}{4}, 19\right)$; $x = \dfrac{1}{4}$; min. $= 19$

13. $(10, -20)$; $x = 10$; max. $= -20$

14. $(-12, 23)$; $x = -12$; max. $= 23$

15. $(-4.58, 65\pi)$; $x = -4.58$; min. $= 65\pi$

16. $(38.2, -\sqrt{34})$; $x = 38.2$; min. $= -\sqrt{34}$

17. $h = 0, k = 4$, maximum so graph extends downward
$f(x) = -2(x - 0)^2 + 4 = -2x^2 + 4$

18. $h = 2, k = 0$, minimum so graph extends upward
$f(x) = 2(x - 2)^2$

19. $h = 6, k = 0$, minimum so graph extends upward
$f(x) = 2(x - 6)^2$

20. $h = 0, k = 3$, maximum so graph extends downward
$f(x) = -2(x - 0)^2 + 3 = -2x^2 + 3$

21. $h = 3, k = 8$, maximum so graph extends downward
$f(x) = -2(x - 3)^2 + 8$

22. $h = -2, k = 3$, minimum so graph extends upward
$f(x) = 2(x + 2)^2 + 3$

23. $h = -3, k = 5$, minimum so graph extends upward
$f(x) = 2(x + 3)^2 + 5$

24. $h = -4, k = -3$, maximum so graph extends downward
$f(x) = -2(x + 4)^2 - 3$

25. $h = 2, k = -3$, minimum so graph extends upward
$f(x) = 2(x - 2)^2 - 3$

26. $x = a(y - h)^2 + k$
The graph is a parabola with a line of symmetry $y = h$ and vertex (k, h).

27. $f(x) = 3(x - 4)^2$. To double values, multiply by 2.
$g(x) = 6(x - 4)^2$

28. $g(x) = -2(x - 1)^2 - 6$. Maximum point is $(1, -6)$.

Translate $f(x) = -\dfrac{1}{2}(x - 2)^2 + 4$

$h(x) = -\dfrac{1}{2}(x - 1)^2 - 6$

29. $h = 2, k = 5$,
$f(x) = a(x - 2)^2 + 5$
$f(1) = 2$ so $2 = a(1 - 2)^2 + 5$
$2 = a + 5$
$-3 = a$
so $f(x) = -3(x - 2)^2 + 5$

30. $h = -2, k = -6$
$f(x) = a(x + 2)^2 - 6$
$f(1) = 0$ so $0 = a(1 + 2)^2 - 6$
$0 = 9a - 6$
$a = \dfrac{2}{3}$
so $f(x) = \dfrac{2}{3}(x + 2)^2 - 6$

31. $f(x) = 2(x - 5)^2 + 3$
Reflect across $y = -4$. Graph will extend downward and $k = 3$ will be translated to $k = -11$.
$g(x) = -2(x - 5)^2 = 11$

32. **a.** $f(x) = 10x + 140$
$g(y) = -5y + 80$
b. $(120, 60), (140, 80),$ and $(160, 60)$

33. $a^2 + b^2 = c^2$
$\pm\sqrt{a^2 + b^2} = c$

34. $\dfrac{A}{\pi} = r^2$

$\pm\sqrt{\dfrac{A}{\pi}} = r$

$\pm\dfrac{\sqrt{A\pi}}{\pi} = r$

35. $\dfrac{E}{m} = c^2$

$\pm\sqrt{\dfrac{E}{m}} = c$

$\pm\dfrac{\sqrt{Em}}{m} = c$

36. $R_2 t + R_1 t = R_1 R_2$
$t(R_2 + R_1) = R_1 R_2$

$t = \dfrac{R_1 R_2}{R_2 + R_1}$

37. $\dfrac{y}{xz} = \dfrac{24}{12}$

$\dfrac{y}{xz} = 2$

$y = 2xz$

pp. 408–410   **9-6 TRY THIS**

a. (1) $f(x) = x^2 - 4x + 7$
$= (x^2 - 4x + 4) - 4 + 7$
$= (x - 2)^2 + 3$
(2) Vertex: $(2, 3)$
Line of symmetry: $x = 2$
Minimum value: 3

b. (1) $f(x) = -4x^2 + 12x - 5$
$= -4(x^2 - 3x) - 5$

$= -4\left(x^2 - 3x - \dfrac{3}{4}\right) + 4\left(\dfrac{9}{4}\right) - 5$

$= -4\left(x - \dfrac{3}{2}\right)^2 + 4$

(2) Vertex: $\left(\dfrac{3}{2}, 4\right)$

Line of symmetry: $x = \dfrac{3}{2}$

Maximum value: 4

c. $x + y = 30$ or $y = 30 - x$
$p = x \cdot y$
$p = x(30 - x)$
$p = -x^2 + 30x = -1(x^2 - 30x)$
$p = -1(x^2 - 30x + 225 - 225)$
$\quad = -1(x - 15)^2 + 225$
Thus, the maximum function value is 225.

d. $2w + 2l = 100$ so $w + l = 50$ or $w = 50 - l$
$A = w \cdot l$
$A = (50 - l)l$
$A = 50l - l^2 = -l^2 + 50l$
$A = -(l - 25)^2 + 625$
Thus, the maximum function value is 625. It occurs when
$l = 25$ and $w = 50 - l = 25$. Therefore, the dimensions are
25 m by 25 m.

p. 410 **9-6 EXERCISES**

1. $f(x) = (x - 1)^2 - 4$
Vertex: $(1, -4)$
Line of symmetry: $x = 1$
Minimum: -4

2. $f(x) = (x + 1)^2 - 6$
Vertex: $(-1, -6)$
Line of symmetry: $x = -1$
Minimum: -6

3. $f(x) = -(x - 2)^2 + 10$
Vertex: $(2, 10)$
Line of symmetry: $x = 2$
Maximum: 10

4. $f(x) = -(x + 2)^2 + 7$
Vertex: $(-2, 7)$
Line of symmetry: $x = -2$
Maximum: 7

5. $f(x) = \left(x + \dfrac{3}{2}\right)^2 - \dfrac{49}{4}$

Vertex: $\left(-\dfrac{3}{2}, -\dfrac{49}{4}\right)$

Line of symmetry: $x = -\dfrac{3}{2}$

Minimum: $-\dfrac{49}{4}$

6. $f(x) = \left(x + \dfrac{5}{2}\right)^2 - \dfrac{9}{4}$

Vertex: $\left(-\dfrac{5}{2}, -\dfrac{9}{4}\right)$

Line of symmetry: $x = -\dfrac{5}{2}$

Minimum: $-\dfrac{9}{4}$

7. $f(x) = \left(x - \dfrac{9}{2}\right)^2 - \dfrac{81}{4}$

Vertex: $\left(\dfrac{9}{2}, -\dfrac{81}{4}\right)$

Line of symmetry: $x = \dfrac{9}{2}$

Minimum: $-\dfrac{81}{4}$

8. $f(x) = \left(x + \dfrac{1}{2}\right)^2 - \dfrac{1}{4}$

Vertex: $\left(-\dfrac{1}{2}, -\dfrac{1}{4}\right)$

Line of symmetry: $x = -\dfrac{1}{2}$

Minimum: $-\dfrac{1}{4}$

9. $f(x) = 3(x - 4)^2 + 2$
Vertex: $(4, 2)$
Line of symmetry: $x = 4$
Minimum: 2

10. $f(x) = 4(x + 1)^2 - 7$
Vertex: $(-1, -7)$
Line of symmetry: $x = -1$
Minimum: -7

11. $f(x) = \dfrac{3}{4}(x + 6)^2 - 27$

Vertex: $(-6, -27)$
Line of symmetry: $x = -6$
Minimum: -27

12. $f(x) = -2\left(x - \dfrac{1}{2}\right)^2 + \dfrac{3}{2}$

Vertex: $\left(\dfrac{1}{2}, \dfrac{3}{2}\right)$

Line of symmetry: $x = \dfrac{1}{2}$

Maximum: $\dfrac{3}{2}$

13. 19 m by 19 m; 361 m²   **14.** 17 m by 17 m; 289 m²

15. 121; 11 and 11   **16.** 506.25; 22.5 and 22.5

17. -4; 2 and -2 **18.** -9; 3 and -3

19. $-\dfrac{25}{4}; \dfrac{5}{2}$ and $-\dfrac{5}{2}$ **20.** $-\dfrac{49}{4}; \dfrac{7}{2}$ and $-\dfrac{7}{2}$

21. $f(x) = 3x^2 + mx + m^2$

$\quad = 3\left(x^2 + \dfrac{m}{3}x\right) + m^2$

$= 3\left(x^2 + \dfrac{m}{3}x + \dfrac{m^2}{36}\right) + m^2 - \dfrac{m^2}{12}$

$= 3\left(x + \dfrac{m}{6}\right)^2 + \dfrac{12m^2 - m^2}{12}$

$= 3\left[\left(x - \left(-\dfrac{m}{6}\right)\right)\right]^2 + \dfrac{11m^2}{12}$

22.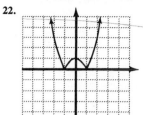

23.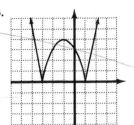

24. $f(x) = 2.31x^2 - 3.135x - 5.89$

$= 2.31\left(x^2 - \dfrac{3.135}{2.31}x\right) - 5.89$

$= 2.31\left[x - \left(\dfrac{1}{2}\right)\left(\dfrac{3.135}{2.31}\right)\right]^2 - 5.89 - 2.31\left[\dfrac{1}{2}\left(\dfrac{3.135}{2.31}\right)\right]^2$

Minimum is $-5.89 - 2.31\left[\dfrac{1}{2}\left(\dfrac{3.135}{2.31}\right)\right]^2 \approx -6.95$

25. $f(x) = -18.8x^2 + 7.92x + 6.18$

$= -18.8\left(x^2 - \dfrac{7.92}{18.8}x\right) + 6.18$

$= -18.8\left[x - \left(\dfrac{1}{2}\right)\left(\dfrac{7.92}{18.8}\right)\right]^2 + 6.18 + 18.8\left[\dfrac{1}{2}\left(\dfrac{7.92}{18.8}\right)\right]^2$

Maximum is $6.18 + 18.8\left[\dfrac{1}{2}\left(\dfrac{7.92}{18.8}\right)\right]^2 \approx 7.014$

26. Let $P = xy$
$x - y = 4.932$
$\quad x = y + 4.932$
$P = (y + 4.932)y = y^2 + 4.932y$
$\quad = (y + 2.466)^2 - 6.081$
Minimum is -6.081 when $y = -2.466$ and
$x = -2.446 + 4.932 = 2.466$, or when $y = 2.466$ and
$x = -2.466$.

27. Let $P = xy$
$x + y = 21.355$
$\quad x = -y + 21.355$
$P = y(-y + 21.355) = -y^2 + 21.355$
$\quad = -(y - 10.678)^2 + 114.009$
Maximum is 114.009 when $y = 10.678$ and
$x = -10.678 + 21.355 = 10.678$, or when $y = -10.678$ and
$x = -10.678$.

28. $f(x) = ax^2 + bx + c$

$= a\left(x^2 + \dfrac{b}{a}x\right) + c$

$= a\left(x + \dfrac{b}{2a}\right)^2 + c - a\left(\dfrac{b}{2a}\right)^2$

$= a\left(x - \dfrac{b}{2a}\right)^2 + c - \dfrac{b^2}{4a}$

Vertex: $\left(-\dfrac{b}{2a}, c - \dfrac{b^2}{4a}\right)$

Line of symmetry: $x = -\dfrac{b}{2a}$

29. $f(x) = ax^2 + bx + c$ if $a \neq 0$

$\dfrac{f(x)}{a} = x^2 + \dfrac{b}{a}x + \dfrac{c}{a}$

$\dfrac{f(x)}{a} = x^2 + \dfrac{b}{a}x + \dfrac{b^2}{4a^2} + \dfrac{c}{a} - \dfrac{b^2}{4a^2}$

$\dfrac{f(x)}{a} = \left(x + \dfrac{b}{2a}\right)^2 + \dfrac{4ac - b^2}{4a^2}$

$f(x) = a\left(x + \dfrac{b}{2a}\right)^2 + \dfrac{4ac - b^2}{4a^2}$

$h = -\dfrac{b}{2a}; k = \dfrac{4ac - b^2}{4a^2}$

30. Let $x + 20$ = number of trees;
$40 - x$ = bushels per tree.
$$\text{Total yield} = (x + 20)(40 - x)$$
$$= -x^2 + 20x + 800$$
$$= -(x^2 - 20x) + 800$$
$$= -(x - 10)^2 + 800 + 100$$
$$= -(x - 10)^2 + 900$$
Maximum yield is 900 bushels when $x = 10$ and there are 30 trees.

31. Let $2 + 0.1x$ = price;
$100 - x$ = number of people.
$$\text{Money} = (2 + 0.1x)(100 - x)$$
$$= -0.1x^2 + 8x + 200$$
$$= -0.1(x^2 - 80x) + 200$$
$$= -0.1(x - 40)^2 + 200 + 0.1(40)^2$$
$$= -0.1(x - 40)^2 + 360$$
Maximum profit is \$360 when $x = 40$ and price $= 2 + 0.1(40) = \$6$.

32.
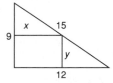

Let x and y be the sides of the rectangle. The large triangle is similar to the smaller triangles, so
$$\frac{9}{9 - y} = \frac{12}{x}$$
$$9x = 12(9 - y)$$
$$x = \frac{4}{3}(9 - y) = 12 - \frac{4}{3}y$$
Area of rectangle $= xy = \left(12 - \frac{4}{3}y\right)y$
$$= 12y - \frac{4}{3}y^2$$
$$= -\frac{4}{3}(y^2 - 9)$$
$$= -\frac{4}{3}\left(y - \frac{9}{2}\right) - \left(-\frac{4}{3}\right)\left(-\frac{9}{2}\right)^2$$
$$= -\frac{4}{3}\left(y - \frac{9}{2}\right) + 27$$
Maximum area is 27 cm^2 when $y = 4.5$ cm and
$$x = 12 - \left(\frac{4}{3}\right)\left(\frac{9}{2}\right) = 6 \text{ cm.}$$

33. The dimensions of the region are x and $120 - 2x$.
$$\text{Area} = x(120 - 2x)$$
$$= 120x - 2x^2$$
$$= -2(x^2 - 60x)$$
$$= -2(x - 30)^2 + 1800$$
The maximum area is 1800 ft^2 when the sides of the fence are 30 ft and 60 ft.

34. $b + h = 38$
$h = 38 - b$
$$A = \frac{1}{2}bh = \frac{1}{2}b(38 - b)$$
$$= 19b - \frac{1}{2}b^2$$
$$= -\frac{1}{2}(b^2 - 38)$$
$$= -\frac{1}{2}(b - 19)^2 - \left(-\frac{1}{2}\right)(381)$$
$$= -\frac{1}{2}(b - 19)^2 + 180.5$$
The maximum area is 180.5 cm^2 when $b = 19$ and $h = 38 - 19 = 19$.

35. Let x and y be the sides of the rectangle.
$2x + 2y = 44$; $2y = 44 - 2x$; $y = 22 - x$.
Diagonal is $\sqrt{x^2 + y^2}$. To minimize the diagonal, minimize $x^2 + y^2$.
$$x^2 + y^2 = x^2 + (22 - x)^2 = x^2 + x^2 - 44x + 484$$
$$= 2x^2 - 44x + 484$$
Complete the square:
$$2(x^2 - 22x) + 484 = 2(x^2 - 22x + (-11)^2 - (-11)^2) + 484$$
$$= 2(x - 11)^2 - 2(11)^2 + 484$$
$$= 2(x - 11)^2 + 363$$
This function is at a minimum when $x = 11$. Here $y = 22 - 11 = 11$.
The diagonal is at a minimum when $x, y = 11$:
$$d = \sqrt{(11)^2 + (11)^2} = \sqrt{2(11)^2} = 11\sqrt{2} \text{ ft.}$$

36. y-axis   **37.** Both   **38.** Neither   **39.** x-axis

40. $x + 2 = x^2$
$0 = x^2 - x - 2$
$0 = (x + 1)(x - 2)$
$0 = x + 1$ or $0 = x - 2$
$-1 = x$ or $2 = x$

41. $x^5 = 32^2$
$x^5 = 32 \cdot 32$
$\sqrt[5]{x^5} = \sqrt[5]{2^5 \cdot 2^5}$
$x = 4$

42. $r - 2 = 1$
$r = 3$

43. $16i$

44. $(\sqrt{3i^2})(\sqrt{7i^2})$
$(i\sqrt{3})(i\sqrt{7})$
$i^2\sqrt{21}$
$-\sqrt{21}$

45. $(-\sqrt{50i^2})(\sqrt{2i^2})$
$(-5i\sqrt{2})(i\sqrt{2})$
$-5i^2(2)$
10

46. 7.112×10^{-2} **47.** 3.40956×10^7

p. 412   9-7 TRY THIS

a. $f(x) = x^2 - 2x - 5$
$$x = \frac{2 \pm \sqrt{4 + 20}}{2}$$
$$x = \frac{2 \pm 2\sqrt{6}}{2} = 1 \pm \sqrt{6}$$

b. $f(x) = x^2 + 8x + 16$
$= (x + 4)^2$
$x = -4$

c. $f(x) = -2x^2 - 4x - 3$
$$x = \frac{4 \pm \sqrt{16 - 24}}{-4}$$
$$x = \frac{4 \pm i\sqrt{8}}{-4}$$
None

p. 413   9-7 EXERCISES

1. $2 + \sqrt{3}, 2 - \sqrt{3}$ **2.** None   **3.** $3, -1$

4. $-1 - \sqrt{6}, -1 + \sqrt{6}$ **5.** $4, -1$ **6.** $4 + \sqrt{11}, 4 - \sqrt{11}$

7. $4, -1$ **8.** None   **9.** $\frac{-2 \pm \sqrt{6}}{2}$ **10.** None   **11.** None

12. $-\frac{3}{2}$ **13.** None   **14.** None   **15.** $\frac{3 \pm \sqrt{6}}{3}$ **16.** 2

17. a. $3.4, -2.4$
b. $2.3, -1.3$

18. a. $1, -3$
b. $2.5, -4.5$
c. $3.5, -5.5$

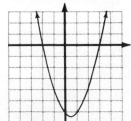

19. $f(x) = (x - 1)^2 - 16$
$= x^2 - 2x + 1 - 16$
$= x^2 - 2x - 15$

20. $0 = x^4 - 10$

$x^2 = \dfrac{\pm\sqrt{-4(-10)}}{2}, x^2 \geq 0$ so

$x^2 = \dfrac{\sqrt{40}}{2}$

$= \dfrac{2\sqrt{10}}{2}$

$x^2 = \sqrt{10}$

$x = \pm\sqrt[4]{10}\{\sqrt[4]{10}, -\sqrt[4]{10}\}$

21. $0 = x^4 - 3x^2 + 9$

$x^2 = \dfrac{3 \pm \sqrt{9 - 4(1)(9)}}{2}$

$= \dfrac{3 \pm \sqrt{9 - 36}}{2}$

$x^2 = \dfrac{3 \pm 3i\sqrt{3}}{2}$

$x = \sqrt{\dfrac{3 \pm 3i\sqrt{3}}{2}}$

No real solutions

22. $y + x = 1 \qquad -y + (-x) = 1$
No $\qquad\qquad -y - x = 1$

23. $y - x^2 = 4 \qquad y - (-x)^2 = 4$
No $\qquad\qquad -y - x^2 = 4$

24. $4y = 3x - 7 \qquad 4(-y) = 3(-x) - 7$
$\qquad\qquad\qquad -4y = -3x - 7$
No $\qquad\qquad\qquad 4y = 3x + 7$

25. $x^2 + y^2 = 3 \qquad (-x)^2 + (-y)^2 = 3$
Yes $\qquad\qquad\qquad x^2 + y^2 = 3$

26. Vertex: $(0,0)$
Line of symmetry: y-axis

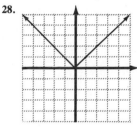

27. Vertex: $(-3, 0)$
Line of symmetry: $x = -3$

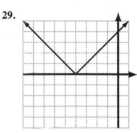

28.

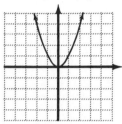

29.

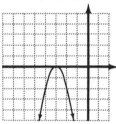

30. a. $19.6 = k(2)^2$
$\quad 19.6 = 4k$
$\quad 4.9 = k$
$\quad s = 4.9t^2$

b. $4.9(15)^2 = s$
$\quad s = 1102.5$ m

c. $122.5 = 4.9t^2$
$\quad 25 = t^2$
$\quad t = 5$ sec

pp. 414–417 9-8 TRY THIS

a. $0 = a \cdot 1^2 + b \cdot 1 + c = a + b + c$
$4 = a(-1)^2 + b(-1) + c = a - b + c$
$1 = a \cdot 2^2 + b \cdot 2 + c = 4a + 2a + c$
Solve this system, obtaining $a = 1$, $b = -2$, and $c = 1$
$f(x) = x^2 - 2x + 1$

b. $a = 1$, $b = 2$, $c = 3$; $f(x) = x^2 + 2x + 3$

c. (1) $250 = a \cdot 20^2 + b \cdot 20 + c = 400a + 20b + c$
$150 = a \cdot 40^2 + b \cdot 40 + c = 1600a + 40b + c$
$200 = a \cdot 60^2 + b \cdot 60 + c = 3600a + 60b + c$
Solve this system, obtaining $a = 0.1875$, $b = -16.25$,
and $c = 500$
$f(x) = 0.1875x^2 - 16.25x + 500$
(2) $f(16) = 0.1875(16)^2 - 16.25(16) + 500 = 288$

d. (1) $s = -4.9t^2 + 2.8t + 12$

$s = -4.9\left(t^2 - \dfrac{2.8}{4.9}t\right) + 12$

$s = -4.9(t^2 - 0.57t + 0.082 - 0.082) + 12$
$s = -4.9(t - 0.286)^2 + (-4.9)(-0.082) + 12$
$s = -4.9(t - 0.286)^2 + 12.4$
Maximum height = 12.4 m, attained in 0.286 s.
(2) $0 = -4.9(t - 0.286)^2 + 12.4$

$\dfrac{-12.4}{-4.9} = (t - 0.286)^2$

$\sqrt{2.53} = t - 0.286$
$1.59 \approx t - 0.286$
$1.876s \approx t$

pp. 418–419 9-8 EXERCISES

1. $f(x) = 2x^2 + 3x - 1$ **2.** $f(x) = 3x^2 - x + 2$

3. $f(x) = -3x^2 + 13x - 5$ **4.** $f(x) = x^2 - 5x$

5. a. $-4x^2 + 40x + 2$ **b.** \$98

6. a. $2500x^2 - 6500x + 5000$ **b.** \$19,000

7. a. $0.0875r^2 - 10.5r + 436.25$ **b.** 121.25

8. a. $0.1875r^2 - 18r + 670$ **b.** 568.75

9. a. 3077 m at 25 sec **b.** 50.1 sec

10. a. 1176 m at 15 sec **b.** 30.5 sec

11. Let x = the number of daytime accidents at 80 km/h
$\quad x = 0.0875(80)^2 - 10.5(80) + 436.25$
$\quad\quad = 560 - 840 + 436.25$
$\quad\quad = 156.25$
There are about 156.25 daytime accidents at 80 km/h.
$156.25 = 0.0875x^2 - 10.5x + 436.25$
$\quad\quad 0 = 0.0875x^2 - 10.5x + 280$

$\quad x = \dfrac{10.5 \pm \sqrt{(10.5)^2 - 4(0.0875)(280)}}{2(0.0875)}$

$\quad\quad = \dfrac{10.5 \pm \sqrt{12.25}}{0.175}$

$\quad\quad = \dfrac{10.5 \pm 3.5}{0.175}$

$x = 80$ or $x = 40$
40 km/h has the same number of daytime accidents.

12. Let x = the number of nighttime accidents at 70 km/h
$\quad x = 0.1875(70)^2 - 18(70) + 670$
$\quad\quad = 918.75 - 1260 + 670$
$\quad\quad = 328.75$
There are about 328.75 nighttime accidents at 70 km/h.
$328.75 = 0.1875x^2 - 18x + 670$
$\quad\quad 0 = 0.1875x^2 - 18x + 341.25$

$\quad x = \dfrac{18 \pm \sqrt{(18)^2 - 4(0.1875)(341.25)}}{2(0.1875)}$

$\quad\quad = \dfrac{18 \pm 8.25}{0.375}$

$x = 70$ or $x = 26$
26 km/h has the same number of nighttime accidents.

13. $W = VI - R^2$
Find I, W = max, $V = 120$, $R = 12$
a. $W = 120I - 12I^2$
$W = -12(I^2 - 10I + (-5)^2) + 12(25)$
$\quad = -12(I - 5)^2 + 300$
The wattage has a maximum at $I = 5$ amperes.
b. The maximum, $W = 300$ watts

14. $s = -4.9t^2 + 196t - 29.4$
a. $s = -4.9(t^2 - 40t + 20^2) - 29.4 + 4.9(20^2)$
$\quad = -4.9(t - 20)^2 + 1930.6$
s is a maximum at $t = 20$ sec;
$s = 1931$ m.
b. $a = -4.9$, $b = 196$, $c = -29.4$

$s = \dfrac{-196 \pm \sqrt{196^2 - 4(-4.9)(-29.4)}}{-2(4.9)}$

$\quad = \dfrac{-196 \pm 194.5}{-9.8} = 0.15$ or 39.9

Since the maximum height occurs at $t = 20$ sec, then the first
level point is at $t = 0.15$ sec.
c. 39.9 sec from b. above

15. Answers may vary. The points lie on a straight line and the
function is $f(x) = 5$, which has no equivalent quadratic function.

16. $y = (x - p)^2 + (x - q)^2$
$= x^2 - 2px + p^2 + x^2 - 2qx + q^2$
$= 2x^2 - 2x(p + q) + (p^2 + q^2)$
$= 2(x^2 - (p + q)x) + (p^2 + q^2)$
$= 2\left[x^2 - (p + q)x + \left(-\frac{p + q}{2} \right)^2 - \left(-\frac{p + q}{2} \right)^2 \right]$
$\quad + (p^2 + q^2)$
$= 2\left(x - \left(\frac{p + q}{2} \right) \right)^2 + \frac{2(p + q)^2}{4} + (p^2 + q^2)$

Since the last two terms of this expression are constant, the way to minimize y is to minimize the first term. Setting $x = \frac{p + q}{2}$ makes the first term zero, its minimal value. Hence, y is a minimum when $x = \frac{p + q}{2}$.

17. Let x = length of fence on short side of rectangle. Then the length of the long side is $60 - 3x$, and the area of the rectangle is $x(60 - 3x)$.
$-3x^2 + 60x = -3(x^2 - 20x + (-10)^2 - (-10)^2)$
$\qquad = -3(x - 10)^2 + 3(+100)$
$\qquad = -3(x - 10)^2 + 300$
At $x = 10$, area is a maximum: 300 m^2.

18.

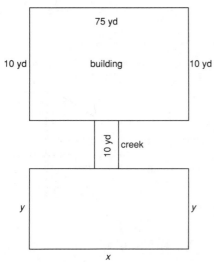

The exercise yard adjacent to the building is at most 10 yd $\times$ 75 yd = 750 yd^2. Since no fencing is required next to the building or the creek, and $2 \cdot 10$ yd are required for the other two sides, no matter the length of the sides next to the building and creek, the problem reduces to that of maximizing the area of the yard across the creek. This yard has dimensions x by $[(200 - 2(10)) - 2x = 180 - 2x]$, where x is the length of the side perpendicular to the creek. Area = $x(180 - 2x)$. To maximize, complete the square.

$-2x^2 + 180x = -2\left(x^2 - 90x + \left(-\frac{90}{2} \right)^2 - \left(-\frac{90}{2} \right)^2 \right)$
$\qquad = -2(x - 45)^2 + 2(45)^2$
$\qquad = -2(x - 45)^2 + 2(2025)$

The maximum occurs when $x = 45$ yd. The maximum area = $2(2025) + 750 = 4800 \text{ yd}^2$.

19. Neither   **20.** x-axis   **21.** y-axis   **22.** Both

23. Vertex: $(0, 0)$
Line of symmetry: y-axis

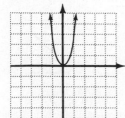

24. Vertex: $(2, 0)$
Line of symmetry: $x = 2$

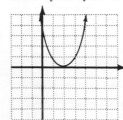

25. Vertex: $(-1, 0)$
Line of symmetry: $x = -1$

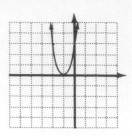

26. $\quad x - 16x^{1/2} + 64 = 0$
$(x^{1/2} - 8)(x^{1/2} - 8) = 0$
$\qquad\qquad x^{1/2} = 8$
$\qquad\qquad\quad x = 64$

27. $(x^2 + 4)(x^2 - 9) = 0$
$x^2 + 4 = 0 \quad$ or $\quad x^2 - 9 = 0$
$\quad x^2 = -4 \quad$ or $\qquad x^2 = 9$
$\quad x = \pm 2i \quad$ or $\qquad x = \pm 3$

28. $y = \frac{kx}{z}$

$6 = \frac{16k}{8}$

$48 = 16k$

$3 = k \quad$ so $\quad y = \frac{3x}{z}$

p. 421   COLLEGE ENTRANCE EXAMS

1. Let $a = 3$ and $b = 2$, then $2(3) + 2 = 8$ which is even;
$\qquad\qquad\qquad\qquad\qquad 4(3) - 2 = 10$ which is even;
$\qquad\qquad\qquad\qquad\qquad 3 + 3(2) = 9$ which is odd;
$\qquad\qquad\qquad\qquad\qquad 2(2) = 4$ which is even;
$\qquad\qquad\qquad\qquad\qquad \frac{3}{2} + \frac{2}{2} = \frac{5}{2}$ which is even. (C)

2. Let $a = 1$ and $b = 1$, then $\frac{1 + 1}{2} = \frac{2}{2}$ is not even,
$\qquad\qquad\qquad 1 + 1$ is a multiple of 2,
$\qquad\qquad\qquad 1 - 1$ is even. (B)

3. Consecutive odd integers add two to any integer n or add an odd integer to any even multiple of n. (E)

4. $w + w + 1 + w + 2 = $ even
$\qquad\qquad\quad 3w + 3 = $ even
If $w = 1$, then $3w + 3 = 6$
If $w = 2$, then $3w + 3 = 9$. (A)

5. If $3(2) + y = 18$, then $y = 12$.
If $3(4) + y = 18$, then $y = 6$.
If $3(6) + y = 18$, then $y = 0$. (E)

6. $\qquad 5x - 1 = $ even integer
$\quad 5x - 1 + 2 = $ even integer
$\qquad 5x + 1 = $ even integer (D)

p. 423   PROBLEM SOLVING: APPLICATION

1. $d = -10s + 8000$
$P = d(s - 40)$
$\quad = (-10s + 8000)(s - 40)$
$\quad = -10s^2 + 8000s + 400s - 320,000$
$\quad = -10(s^2 + 840s) - 320,000$
$\quad = -10[(s^2 - 840s + (420)^2] - 320,000 + 10(420)^2$
$\quad = -10(s - 420)^2 - 320,000 + 1,764,000$
$\quad = -10(s - 420)^2 + 1,444,000; \ s = 420$
The selling price should be \$420.
$d = -10(420) + 8000$
$\quad = 3800$
There is a demand of 3800 printers at this price.
$P = s \cdot d - 40d$
$\quad = 420(3800) - 40(3800)$
$\quad = 1,444,000$
The profit maximizes at \$1,444,000.

Lesson 9-8–Application: Merchandising

2. $d = -10s + 8000$
$P = d(s - 60)$
$\quad = (-10s + 8000)(s - 60)$
$\quad = -10s^2 + 8000s + 600s - 480,000$
$\quad = -10s^2 + 8600s - 480,000$
$\quad = -10(s^2 - 860s) - 480,000$
$\quad = -10[s^2 - 860s + (430)^2] - 480,000 + 10(430)^2$
$\quad = -10(s - 430)^2 - 480,000 + 1,849,000$
$\quad = -10(s - 430)^2 + 1,369,000;\ s = 430$
The selling price should be $430.
$d = -10(430) + 8000$
$\quad = 3700$
The demand will be 3700 printers.
$P = s \cdot d - 60d$
$\quad = 430(3700) - 60(3700)$
$\quad = 1,369,000$
The maximum profit is $1,369,000.

3. The selling price is $75. At this price, demand is 0, so the expected profit is 0. The product should not be marketed unless demand rises or costs are reduced.

p. 424–426   CHAPTER 9 SUMMARY AND REVIEW

1. Both   **2.** x-axis   **3.** Neither   **4.** y-axis

5. Neither   **6.** y-axis   **7.** No   **8.** Yes   **9.** No

10. No   **11.** Yes   **12.** No

13.
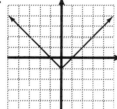

14.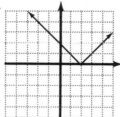

15.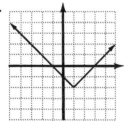

16.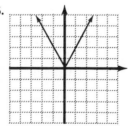

17.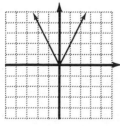

18.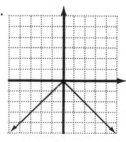

19.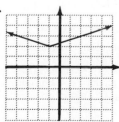

20. Vertex: $(0, 0)$
Line of symmetry: $x = 0$
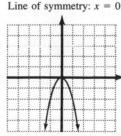

21. Vertex: $(0,0)$
Line of symmetry: $x = 0$
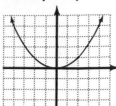

22. Vertex: $(-1, 0)$
Line of symmetry: $x = -1$
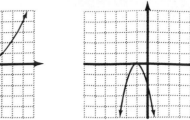

23. Vertex: $(2, 0)$
Line of symmetry: $x = 2$
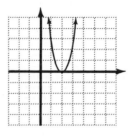

24. Vertex: $(-1, -2)$
Line of symmetry: $x = -1$
Maximum: -2
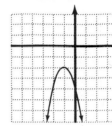

25. Vertex: $(1, 5)$
Line of symmetry: $x = 1$
Minimum: 5
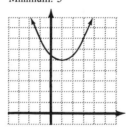

26. Vertex: $(-2, 1)$
Line of symmetry: $x = -2$
Maximum: 1
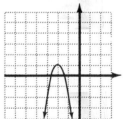

27. $(x - 4)^2 - 11$ **28.** $-\dfrac{1}{2}(x - 6)^2 + 2$

29. $-2(x + 1)^2 + 5$ **30.** 256; 16 and 16   **31.** -16; 4 and -4

32. $\dfrac{-2 \pm \sqrt{10}}{2}$ **33.** $-1 \pm \sqrt{5}$ **34.** 3, 1

35. $f(x) = -2x^2 - 4x + 3$ **36.** $f(x) = 3x^2 - 6x + 5$

37. $f(x) = -x^2 + 8x - 8$

38. **a.** $f(x) = -0.005x^2 + 0.2x + 7$
    b. 1 ft

p. 426–427   CHAPTER 9 TEST

1. y-axis   **2.** Both   **3.** Both   **4.** x-axis   **5.** Neither

6. x-axis   **7.** No   **8.** Yes   **9.** No

10.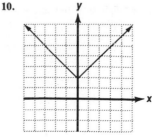

11.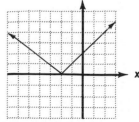

12. Vertex: $(0, 0)$
Line of symmetry: $x = 0$

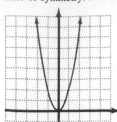

13. Vertex: $(5, 0)$
Line of symmetry: $x = 5$

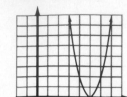

Vertex $(12, 72)$
The maximum area is 72.
The base is 12 and the height is 12.

CHAPTER 10

p. 428   READY FOR EQUATIONS OF SECOND DEGREE?

1. 13   **2.** $4\sqrt{3}$ **3.** $x^2 - 4x + 4$ **4.** $x^2 + 3x + \dfrac{9}{4}$

5.

6.

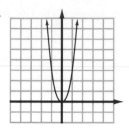

7. $\left(\dfrac{1}{2}, -5\right)$ **8.** $(-2, -10)$ **9.** $2, 7$ **10.** $\sqrt{5}, -\sqrt{5}$

14. Vertex: $(5, -4)$
Line of symmetry: $x = 5$
Minimum: -4

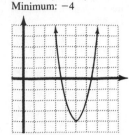

15. Vertex: $(-1, -2)$
Line of symmetry: $x = -1$
Maximum: -2

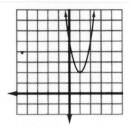

p. 431   10-1 TRY THIS

a. $\sqrt{(-5 - 2)^2 + (3 + 7)^2} = \sqrt{49 + 100} = \sqrt{149}$
b. $\sqrt{(3 + 3)^2 + (3 + 3)^2} = \sqrt{36 + 36} + \sqrt{72} = 6\sqrt{2}$
c. $\left(\dfrac{-2 + 5}{2}, \dfrac{1 + (-6)}{2}\right) = \left(\dfrac{3}{2}, -\dfrac{5}{2}\right)$
d. $\left(\dfrac{9 + 9}{2}, \dfrac{-6 + (-4)}{2}\right) = (9, -5)$

16. $f(x) = -(x + 3)^2 + 16$
Vertex: $(-3, 16)$
Line of symmetry: $x = -3$
Maximum: 16

17. $f(x) = 2\left(x - \dfrac{5}{2}\right)^2 - \dfrac{39}{2}$

Vertex: $\left(\dfrac{5}{2}, -\dfrac{39}{2}\right)$

Line of symmetry: $x = \dfrac{5}{2}$

Minimum: $-\dfrac{39}{2}$

pp. 431–432   10-1 EXERCISES

1. 5   **2.** $3\sqrt{5}$ **3.** $3\sqrt{2}$ **4.** $4\sqrt{2}$ **5.** 5   **6.** 10
7. 8   **8.** 5   **9.** $\sqrt{a^2 + 64}$ **10.** $\sqrt{64 + k^2}$
11. $\sqrt{a^2 + b^2}$ **12.** $\sqrt{5}$ **13.** $2\sqrt{a}$ **14.** $2\sqrt{d^2 + c^2}$
15. $\left(-\dfrac{1}{2}, -1\right)$ **16.** $(5, -1)$ **17.** $\left(-\dfrac{7}{2}, -\dfrac{15}{2}\right)$
18. $\left(\dfrac{5}{2}, \dfrac{5}{2}\right)$ **19.** $(4, 4)$ **20.** $\left(\dfrac{1}{2}, 0\right)$

18. $x, 40 - x$
$f(x) = x(40 - x)$
$= 40x - x^2$
$= -(x - 20)^2 + 400$
Vertex $(20, 400)$
The maximum product is 400.
The numbers are 20 and 20.

19. $f(x) = 2x^2 - 5x + 8$
$0 = 2x^2 - 5x + 8$

$x = \dfrac{5 \pm \sqrt{25 - 4(2)(8)}}{4}$

The x values are not real numbers, so there are no x intercepts.

20. $f(x) = -x^2 - 2x + 2$
$0 = -x^2 - 2x + 2$

$x = \dfrac{2 \pm \sqrt{4 - 4(-1)(2)}}{-2}$

$= \dfrac{2 \pm \sqrt{12}}{-2}$

$= -1 \pm \sqrt{3}$

21. a. $f(t) = -30t^2 + 285t - 495$
b. $f(4) = -30(16) + 285(4) - 495$
$= 165$

22. a. $s = -4.9t^2 + 9.8t + 27$
$= -4.9(t^2 - 2t + 1) + 31.9$
$= -4.9(t - 1)^2 + 31.9$
Vertex is $(1, 31.9)$. The maximum height is 31.9 m at 1 sec.
b. $0 = -4.9t^2 + 9.8t + 27$
$t = 3.55$ sec

23. $b =$ base, $24 - b =$ height

Area $= \dfrac{1}{2}b(24 - b) = 12b - \dfrac{1}{2}b^2$

$2 \cdot$ Area $= -(b^2 - 24b) = -(b - 12)^2 + 144$

Area $= \dfrac{-(b - 12)^2}{2} + 72$

21. $(a, 0)$ **22.** $(0, d)$

23. The distance between $(9, 6)$ and $(-1, 2)$ is
$\sqrt{(9 + 1)^2 + (6 - 2)^2} = \sqrt{10^2 + 4^2} = \sqrt{116} = 2\sqrt{29}$.
The distance between $(9, 6)$ and $(1, -3)$ is
$\sqrt{(9 - 1)^2 + (6 + 3)^2} = \sqrt{8^2 + 9^2} = \sqrt{145}$.
The distance between $(-1, 2)$ and $(1, -3)$ is
$\sqrt{(-1 - 1)^2 + (2 + 3)^2} = \sqrt{2^2 + 5^2} = \sqrt{29}$.
Since $(2\sqrt{29})^2 + (\sqrt{29})^2 = (\sqrt{145})^2$, the points whose coordinates are given are vertices of a right triangle.

24. The distance between $(-8, -5)$ and $(6, 1)$ is
$\sqrt{(-8 - 6)^2 + (-5 - 1)^2} = \sqrt{14^2 + 6^2} = \sqrt{232} = 2\sqrt{58}$.
The distance between $(-8, -5)$ and $(-4, 5)$ is
$\sqrt{(-8 + 4)^2 + (-5 - 5)^2} = \sqrt{4^2 + 10^2} = \sqrt{116} = 2\sqrt{29}$.
The distance between $(6, 1)$ and $(-4, 5)$ is
$\sqrt{(6 + 4)^2 + (1 - 5)^2} = \sqrt{10^2 + 4^2} = \sqrt{116} = 2\sqrt{29}$.
Since $(2\sqrt{29})^2 + (2\sqrt{29})^2 = (2\sqrt{58})^2$, the points whose coordinates are given are vertices of a right triangle.

25. If two points lie along a horizontal line, their y-coordinates are constant. If two points lie along a vertical line, their x-coordinates are constant. Assume the two points lie along the horizontal line whose equation is given by $y = k$ and the points have coordinates (x_1, k) and (x_2, k). Then
$d = \sqrt{(x_2 - x_1)^2 + (k - k)^2} = \sqrt{(x_2 - x_1)^2 + 0} = |x_2 - x_1|$
and the distance formula given in Theorem 10-1 holds. Similarly, if the points lie along a vertical line, their coordinates can be written (k, y_1) and (k, y_2) and the distance formula holds.

130   *Algebra and Trigonometry*

Chapter 9 Test–Lesson 10-1

26. To show that $\left(\dfrac{x_1 + x_2}{2}, \dfrac{y_1 + y_2}{2}\right)$ is the midpoint of the line

segment between two points whose coordinates are given by (x_1, y_1) and (x_2, y_2), we must show the distances of the two line segments between it (the midpoint) and each of the two points equal exactly half the distance of the line segment between those two points. The distance between the midpoint and (x_1, y_1) is

$$\sqrt{\left(\dfrac{x_1 + x_2}{2} - x_1\right)^2 + \left(\dfrac{y_1 + y_2}{2} - y_1\right)^2}$$

$$= \sqrt{\left(\dfrac{x_1 + x_2 - 2x_1}{2}\right)^2 + \left(\dfrac{y_1 + y_2 - 2y_1}{2}\right)^2}$$

$$= \sqrt{\dfrac{(x_2 - x_1)^2 + (y_2 - y_1)^2}{4}}$$

$$= \dfrac{1}{2}\sqrt{(x_2 - x_1)^2 - (y_2 + y_1)^2}$$

which is half the distance of the line segment between (x_1, y_1) and (x_2, y_2). Similarly, the distance between the midpoint and (x_2, y_2) can be shown to be the same.

27. The diagonals between $(0, b)$ and $(a, 0)$ and $(0, 0)$ and (a, b) both

have the same midpoint $\left(\dfrac{a}{2}, \dfrac{b}{2}\right)$, proving that the diagonals bisect

each other.

28. Let $(x, 0)$ be the coordinates of the point along the x-axis.
$$\sqrt{(x - 1)^2 + (3 - 0)^2} = \sqrt{(x - 8)^2 + (4 - 0)^2}$$
$$\sqrt{x^2 - 2x + 10} = \sqrt{x^2 - 16x + 80}$$
$$x^2 - 2x + 10 = x^2 - 16x + 80$$
$$14x = 70$$
$$x = 5$$
$(5, 0)$ are the coordinates of the point.

29. Let $(0, y)$ be the coordinates of the point along the y-axis.
$$\sqrt{(0 + 2)^2 + (y - 0)^2} = \sqrt{(4 - 0)^2 + (y - 6)^2}$$
$$\sqrt{y^2 + 4} = \sqrt{y^2 - 12y + 52}$$
$$y^2 + 4 = y^2 - 12y + 52$$
$$12y = 48$$
$$y = 4$$
$(0, 4)$ are the coordinates of the point.

30. a. $x_m + (x_m - x_1) = 2x_m - x_1$
$y_m + (y_m - y_1) = 2y_m - y_1$
b. $(-17, 13)$

31. The vertices are $O(0, 0)$, $H(0, h)$, and $B(b, 0)$. Then

$P = \left(\dfrac{b}{2}, \dfrac{h}{2}\right)$. Use the distance formula to find the distances

between P and H, P and B, and P and O.

32. The vertices are $O(0, 0)$, $A(a, b)$, $B(c, d)$, and $C(k, 0)$. The

midpoints are $M_1\left(\dfrac{a}{2}, \dfrac{b}{2}\right)$, $M_2\left(\dfrac{a + c}{2}, \dfrac{b + d}{2}\right)$, $M_3\left(\dfrac{c + k}{2}, \dfrac{d}{2}\right)$,

and $M_4\left(\dfrac{k}{2}, 0\right)$. $M_1M_2 = M_4M_3 = \sqrt{\left(\dfrac{c}{2}\right)^2 + \left(\dfrac{d}{2}\right)^2}$, slopes $= \dfrac{d}{c}$.

$M_1M_4 = M_2M_3 = \sqrt{\left(\dfrac{a}{2} - \dfrac{k}{2}\right)^2 + \left(\dfrac{b}{2}\right)^2}$, slopes $= \dfrac{b}{a - k}$. The

opposite sides of a parallelogram are parallel and have equal lengths.

33. The distance between (a, b) and (c, d) is $\sqrt{(a - c)^2 + (b - d)^2}$.
a. The distance between (a, d) and (c, b) is
$$\sqrt{(a - c)^2 + (d - b)^2}.$$
b. The distance between (b, a) and (d, c) is
$$\sqrt{(b - d)^2 + (a - c)^2}.$$
c. The distance between (b, c) and (d, a) is
$$\sqrt{(b - d)^2 + (c - a)^2}.$$ Since $(a - c)^2 = (c - a)^2$ and
$(b - d)^2 = (d - b)^2$, the distances are all the same.

34.
$$x(x + 7) = 4(x + 10)$$
$$x^2 + 7x = 4x + 40$$
$$x^2 + 3x - 40 = 0$$
$$(x - 5)(x + 8) = 0$$
Solutions are 5 and -8.

35. $4y^2 + 24y = 0$
$4y(y + 6) = 0$.
Solutions are 0 and -6.

36. $m^2 + 5m + 6 = 0$
$(m + 3)(m + 2) = 0$
Solutions are -3 and -2.

37. The graph of $y = |x| + 1$ is not symmetric with respect to the origin. Substituting $-x$ and $-y$ into the equation for x and y produces a different result: $-y = |x| + 1$.

38. The graph of $5y^4 - 2x^2 = 1$ is symmetric with respect to the origin. Substituting $-x$ and $-y$ into the equation $5(-y)^4 - 2(-x)^2 = 1$ produces the same result as the original: $5y^4 - 2x^2 = 1$.

39. $x - y = 9$ does not define a graph which is symmetric with respect to the origin. The point $A(1, -8)$ is a point on the graph but the point $B(-1, 8)$ is not. Substituting $-x$ and $-y$ into the equation produces a different result: $-x + y = 9$.

40. $3n^2 - 4m = n$ does not define a graph which is symmetric with respect to the origin. Substituting $-m$ and $-n$ into the equation produces a different result: $3(-n)^2 - 4(-m) = -n$
$$3n^2 + 4m = -n.$$

41. $x^2 - 6x + \left(-\dfrac{6}{2}\right)^2 = x^2 - 6x + 9$

42. $y^2 + 14y + \left(\dfrac{14}{2}\right)^2 = y^2 + 14y + 49$

43. $x^2 + 3x + \left(\dfrac{3}{2}\right)^2 = x^2 + 3x + \dfrac{9}{4}$

44. $y^2 - 9y + \left(\dfrac{9}{2}\right)^2 = y^2 - 9y + \dfrac{81}{4}$

45. $m^2 + 7.4m + \left(\dfrac{7.4}{2}\right)^2 = m^2 + 7.4m + 13.69$

46. $a^2 - 3.2a + \left(\dfrac{3.2}{2}\right)^2 = a^2 - 3.2a + 2.56$

47. $c^2 - c + \left(-\dfrac{1}{2}\right)^2 = c^2 - c + \dfrac{1}{4}$

pp. 435–436   **10-2 TRY THIS**

a. $x^2 + y^2 = 6$ **b.** $(x + 3)^2 + (y - 7)^2 = 25$
c. $(x - 5)^2 + (y + 2)^2 = 3$ **d.** $(x + 2)^2 + (y + 6)^2 = 28$
e. center $(-1, 3)$; radius 2

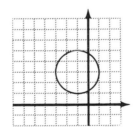

f.
$$x^2 + y^2 - 14x + 4y - 11 = 0$$
$$(x^2 - 14x + 49) + (y^2 + 4y + 4) - 11 - 49 - 4 = 0$$
$$(x - 7)^2 + (y + 2)^2 = 64 = 8^2$$
center $(7, -2)$, $r = 8$
g.
$$x^2 + y^2 - 12x - 8y + 27 = 0$$
$$(x^2 - 12x + 36) + (y^2 - 8y + 16) + 27 - 36 - 16 = 0$$
$$(x - 6)^2 + (y - 4)^2 = 25 = 5^2$$
center $(6, 4)$, $r = 5$

pp. 436–437   **10-2 EXERCISES**

1. $x^2 + y^2 = 49$ **2.** $x^2 + y^2 = \pi^2$

3. $(x + 2)^2 + (y - 7)^2 = 5$ **4.** $(x - 5)^2 + (y - 6)^2 = 12$

5. $(-1, -3)$; radius 2   **6.** $(2, -3)$; radius 1

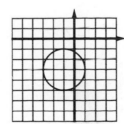

7. $(8, -3)$; radius $2\sqrt{10} \approx 6.3$

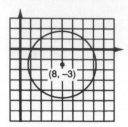

8. $(-5, 1)$; radius $5\sqrt{3}$

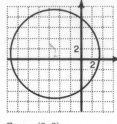

9. Center $(0, 0)$;
radius $\sqrt{2} \approx 1.4$

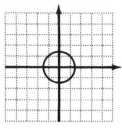

10. Center $(0, 0)$;
radius $\sqrt{3} \approx 1.7$

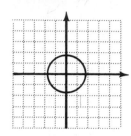

11. Center $(5, 0)$; radius $\dfrac{1}{2}$

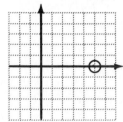

12. Center $(0, 1)$; radius $\dfrac{1}{5}$

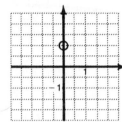

13. $(-4, 3)$, $2\sqrt{10}$ **14.** $(-3, 2)$, $2\sqrt{7}$ **15.** $(4, -1)$, 2

16. $(-3, -2)$, 1   **17.** $(2, 0)$, 2   **18.** $(0, -5)$, 10

19. $(x - 0)^2 + (y - 0)^2 = r^2$ has center $(0, 0)$.
$$x^2 + y^2 = r^2$$
$$(-3)^2 + (4)^2 = r^2$$
$$9 + 16 = r^2$$
$$25 = r^2$$
So, $x^2 + y^2 = 25$ is the equation.

20. $(x - 3)^2 + (y + 2)^2 = r^2$ has center $(3, -2)$.
$$(11 - 3)^2 + (-2 + 2)^2 = r^2$$
$$8^2 + 0 = r^2$$
$$64 = r^2$$
So, $(x - 3)^2 + (y + 2)^2 = 64$ is the equation.

21.

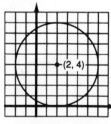

The circle would be tangent to the x-axis at the point $(2, 0)$, and the radius would be 4 units.
$(x - 2)^2 + (y - 4)^2 = 16$

22.

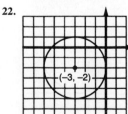

The circle would be tangent to the y-axis at the point $(0, -2)$ and have radius 3 units. $(x + 3)^2 + (y + 2)^2 = 9$

23. $(x - 1)^2 + (y - 2)^2 = 81$
For the x-intercepts, let $y = 0$.
$$(x - 1)^2 + (0 - 2)^2 = 81$$
$$x^2 - 2x + 1 + 4 = 81$$
$$x^2 - 2x - 76 = 0$$
Solutions: $\dfrac{2 \pm \sqrt{4 + 4(76)}}{2} = 1 \pm \sqrt{77}$

For the y-intercepts, let $x = 0$.
$$(0 - 1)^2 + (y - 2)^2 = 81$$
$$1 + y^2 - 4y + 4 = 81$$
$$y^2 - 4y - 76 = 0$$
Solutions: $\dfrac{4 \pm \sqrt{16 + 4(76)}}{2} = 2 \pm 4\sqrt{5}$

24. The center is the midpoint and the radius is half the length of the diameter.

Center $\left(\dfrac{5 - 3}{2}, \dfrac{-3 + 7}{2}\right) = (1, 2)$

$r = \dfrac{1}{2}\sqrt{(5 + 3)^2 + (-3 - 7)^2} = \dfrac{1}{2}\sqrt{64 + 100} = \sqrt{41}$

$(x - 1)^2 + (y - 2)^2 = 41$ is the equation.

25. $(x - 2)^2 + (y + 3)^2 = 9$
For the x-intercepts, let $y = 0$.
$$(x - 2)^2 + (0 + 3)^2 = 9$$
$$(x - 2)^2 + 9 = 9$$
$$(x - 2)^2 = 0$$
$$x = 2$$
(so the circle is tangent to the x-axis at $x = 2$).
For the y-intercepts, let $x = 0$.
$$(0 - 2)^2 + (y + 3)^2 = 9$$
$$4 + y^2 + 6y + 9 = 9$$
$$y^2 + 6y + 4 = 0$$
Solutions: $\dfrac{-6 \pm \sqrt{36 - 4(4)}}{2} = -3 \pm \sqrt{5}$

26. a. $(0)^2 + (-1)^2 = 1$
$1 = 1$ yes

b. $\left(\dfrac{\sqrt{3}}{2}\right)^2 + \left(\dfrac{-1}{2}\right)^2 = 1$
$\dfrac{3}{4} + \dfrac{1}{4} = 1$
$1 = 1$ yes

c. $(\sqrt{2} + \sqrt{3})^2 + 0^2 = 1$
$2 + 2\sqrt{6} + 3 = 1$
$5 + 2\sqrt{6} \neq 1$ No

d. $\left(\dfrac{\pi}{4}\right)^2 + \left(\dfrac{4}{\pi}\right)^2 = 1$
$\dfrac{\pi^2}{16} + \dfrac{16}{\pi^2} \neq 1$ No

27. $x^2 + y^2 = 0$ This is one point at the origin.

28. a.

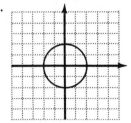

No, it is not a function because it does not pass the vertical line test. For example, on the y-axis, there are two points $(0, 2)$ and $(0, -2)$ for which the same x-coordinate, 0, has different y-coordinates, 2 and -2.

b.

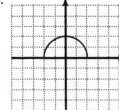

Yes, it is a function because it passes the vertical line test.
Domain $\{x \mid -2 \leq x \leq 2\}$;
range $\{y \mid 0 \leq y \leq 2\}$

c.

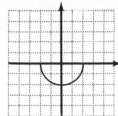

Yes, it is a function because it passes the vertical line test. Domain $\{x \mid -2 \le x \le 2\}$; range $\{y \mid -2 \le y \le 0\}$

d. $x^2 + y^2 = r^2$
$y^2 = r^2 - x^2$
$y = \pm\sqrt{r^2 - x^2}$; no

e. It should graph $y = +\sqrt{r^2 - x^2}$ then $y = -\sqrt{r^2 - x^2}$.

29. From the equation of a circle we have $b^2 + c^2 = a^2$;

$c^2 = a^2 - b^2$; the slope of $\overline{AB}$ is $\dfrac{c}{b+a}$ and the slope of $\overline{BC}$ is

$\dfrac{c}{b-a}$; since $\dfrac{c}{b+a} \cdot \dfrac{c}{b-a} = \dfrac{c^2}{b^2-a^2} = \dfrac{a^2-b^2}{b^2-a^2} = -1$, $\overline{AB}$

and $\overline{BC}$ are perpendicular and angle ABC is a right angle.

30. $\pi r^2 = 25\pi$ center (h, k);
$r^2 = 25$ points $(2, 2)$ and $(2, 10)$
$r = 5$
The distance from each point to the center is 5.
$$\sqrt{(h-2)^2 + (k-2)^2} = 5$$
$$(h-2)^2 + (k-2)^2 = 25$$
$$(h-2)^2 = 25 - (k-2)^2$$
$$\sqrt{(h-2)^2 + (k-10)^2} = 5$$
$$(h-2)^2 + (k-10)^2 = 25$$
$$(25 - (k-2)^2) + (k-10)^2 = 25$$
$$-k^2 + 4k - 4 + k^2 - 20k + 100 = 0$$
$$96 = 16k$$
$$6 = k$$
$$(h-2)^2 = 25 - (k-2)^2$$
$$(h-2)^2 = 25 - (6-2)^2$$
$$(h-2)^2 = 9$$
$$h - 2 = \pm3$$
$$h = 2 \pm 3$$
$$h = 5 \quad \text{or} \quad h = -1$$
$(x-5)^2 + (y-6)^2 = 25$ is one circle.
$(x+1)^2 + (y-6)^2 = 25$ is the other circle.

31.

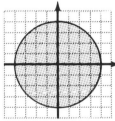

32.

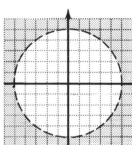

33.

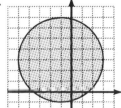

34. If (x, y) is any point on the circle, its distance to the center, (h, k), is $\sqrt{(x-h)^2 + (y-k)^2}$, which must equal r. Thus, $\sqrt{(x-h)^2 + (y-k)^2} = r$, so $(x-h)^2 + (y-k)^2 = r^2$. Now assume that $(x-h)^2 + (y-k)^2 = r^2$ is true for (x, y). The principal square root $\sqrt{(x-h)^2 + (y-k)^2} = r$, so the distance from (x, y) to (h, k) is r. Thus, (x, y) is on the circle.

35. Substituting $(-y)$ for y in the equation $3(-y)^2 = 5x + 1$ and simplifying $3y^2 = 5x + 1$ produces the same result. Therefore, the graph is symmetric with respect to the x-axis. Substituting $(-x)$ for x produces a different equation: $3y^2 = -5x + 1$. No symmetry about y-axis.

36. Substituting $(-x)$ for x in the equation and simplifying $y^2 - (-x)^2 - 1$ to $y^2 - x^2 - 1$ produces the same equation. Therefore, the graph is symmetric with respect to the y-axis. Substituting $(-y)$ for y in the equation and simplifying $(-y)^2 - x^2 = 1$ to $y^2 - x^2 = 1$ produces the same equation. Therefore, the graph is symmetric with respect to the x-axis also.

37. Substituting $(-x)$ for x in the equation and simplifying $y^3 = 5(-x)^2 - 7$ to $y^3 = 5x^2 - 7$ produces the same equation. Therefore, the graph is symmetric with respect to the y-axis. Substituting $(-y)$ for y in the equation and simplifying $(-y)^3 = 5x^2 - 7$ to $-y^3 = 5x^2 - 7$ produces a different result. Therefore, the graph is not symmetric with respect to the x-axis.

38. To find the x-intercepts, let $f(x) = 0$. $4x^2 - 2x + 1 = 0$. Since $b^2 - 4ac = 4 - 4(4)(1) = -12 < 0$, there are no solutions. The graph in this case lies strictly above the x-axis.

39.
$$f(x) = 0$$
$$x^2 - 6x + 5 = 0$$
$$(x-5)(x-1) = 0$$
$$x = 5 \quad \text{or} \quad x = 1$$
$$(5, 0)(1, 0)$$

40. $y = ax^2 + bx + c$
$-2 = a(1)^2 + b(1) + c$ or $a + b + c = -2$
$8 = a(-1)^2 + b(-1) + c$ or $a - b + c = 8$
$-1 = a(2)^2 + b(2) + c$ or $4a + 2b + c = -1$
Equations ① $-$ ②: $a + b + c = -2$
$$\underline{-a + b - c = -8}$$
$$2b = -10$$
$$b = -5$$
Equations ③ $-$ ①: $4a + 2b + c = -1$
$$\underline{-a - b - c = 2}$$
$$3a + b = 1$$
$$3a + (-5) = 1$$
$$3a = 6$$
$$a = 2$$
$$a + b + c = -2$$
$$2 + (-5) + c = -2$$
$$c = 1$$
$$y = 2x^2 - 5x + 1$$

41. $y = ax^2 + bx + c$
$-4 = a(1)^2 + b(1) + c$ or $a + b + c = -4$
$-4 = a(2)^2 + b(2) + c$ or $4a + 2b + c = -4$
$8 = a(-1)^2 + b(-1) + c$ $a - b + c = 8$
Equations ① $-$ ③ $a + b + c = -4$
$$\underline{-a + b - c = -8}$$
$$2b = -12$$
$$b = -6$$
Equations ② $-$ ① $4a + 2b + c = -4$
$$\underline{-a - b - c = 4}$$
$$3a + b = 0$$
$$3a - 6 = 0$$
$$3a = 6$$
$$a = 2$$
$$a + b + c = -4$$
$$2 - 6 + c = -4$$
$$c = 0$$
$$y = 2x^2 - 6x$$

42. $x(2x - 7) + 30 = (x + 9)(x - 2)$
$$2x^2 - 7x + 30 = x^2 + 7x - 18$$
$$x^2 - 14x + 48 = 0$$
$$(x - 6)(x - 8) = 0$$
$$x = 6 \quad \text{or} \quad x = 8$$

43. $\quad 8x^2 - 14x - 15 = 0$
$$(2x - 5)(4x + 3) = 0$$
$$2x - 5 = 0 \text{ or } 4x + 3 = 0$$
$$x = \frac{5}{2} \text{ or } x = -\frac{3}{4}$$

44. $2 + \sqrt{x} = x$ Notice $\sqrt{x}$ restrictions: $x \geq 0$ and $\sqrt{x} \geq 0$.
$\sqrt{x} = x - 2$ Squaring both sides
$x = x^2 - 4x + 4$
$0 = x^2 - 5x + 4$
$0 = (x - 1)(x - 4)$
$x = 1$ or $x = 4$
4 is the only solution

45. $2\sqrt{x} = x - 3$ Notice $\sqrt{x}$ restrictions: $x \geq 0$ and $\sqrt{x} \geq 0$
$4x = x^2 - 6x + 9$ Squaring both sides
$0 = x^2 - 10x + 9$
$0 = (x - 9)(x - 1)$
$x = 9$ or $x = 1$
9 is the only solution

46. $4\sqrt{x} = x - 12$ Notice $\sqrt{x}$ restrictions: $x \geq 0$ and $\sqrt{x} \geq 0$.
$16x = x^2 - 24x + 144$
$0 = x^2 - 40x + 144$
$0 = (x - 36)(x - 4)$
$x = 36$ or $x = 4$
36 is the only solution

47. $x^4 - 8x^2 = 0$
$x^2(x^2 - 8) = 0$
$x = 0$ or $x^2 = 8$
$x = 0$ or $x = \pm\sqrt{8} = \pm 2\sqrt{2}$

48. Let x = number of cars initially in the garage;
y = maximum number of cars for the garage.

$$\frac{x}{y} = 0.84 \quad \text{and} \quad \frac{x + 37 - 23}{y} = 0.91$$

$x = 0.84y$ and $x = 0.91y - 14$
$0.84y = 0.91y - 14$
$14 = 0.07y$
$200 = y$
The garage holds 200 cars.

pp. 440–442   **10-3 TRY THIS**

a. $x^2 + 9y^2 = 9$
$\dfrac{x^2}{9} + \dfrac{y^2}{1} = 1$
$\dfrac{x^2}{3^2} + \dfrac{y^2}{1^2} = 1$
$a = 3, b = 1$
Vertices: $(-3, 0), (3, 0),$
$(0, -1), (0, 1)$
$c^2 = 9 - 1$
$c = \sqrt{8} = \pm 2\sqrt{2}$
Foci: $(-2\sqrt{2}, 0), (2\sqrt{2}, 0)$

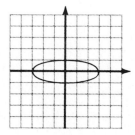

b. $9x^2 + 25y^2 = 225$
$\dfrac{x^2}{25} + \dfrac{y^2}{9} = 1$
$\dfrac{x^2}{5^2} + \dfrac{y^2}{3^2} = 1$
$a = 5, b = 3$
Vertices: $(-5, 0), (5, 0),$
$(0, -3), (0, 3)$
$c^2 = 25 - 9$
$c = \sqrt{16} = 4$
Foci: $(-4, 0), (4, 0)$

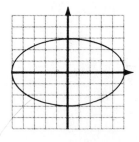

c. $2x^2 + 4y^2 = 8$
$\dfrac{x^2}{4} + \dfrac{y^2}{2} = 1$
$\dfrac{x^2}{2^2} + \dfrac{y^2}{(\sqrt{2})^2} = 1$
$a = 2, b = \sqrt{2}$
Vertices: $(-2, 0), (2, 0),$
$(0, -\sqrt{2}), (0, \sqrt{2})$
$c^2 = 4 - 2$
$c = \sqrt{2}$
Foci: $(-\sqrt{2}, 0), (\sqrt{2}, 0)$

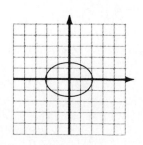

d. $9x^2 + y^2 = 9$
$\dfrac{x^2}{1} + \dfrac{y^2}{9} = 1$
$\dfrac{x^2}{1^2} + \dfrac{y^2}{3^2} = 1$
Center $(0, 0)$
$a = 1, b = 3$
Vertices: $(-1, 0), (1, 0),$
$(0, -3), (0, 3)$
$c^2 = 9 - 1$
$c = \sqrt{8} = 2\sqrt{2}$
Foci: $(0, -2\sqrt{2}), (0, 2\sqrt{2})$

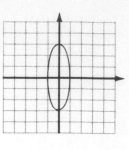

e. $25x^2 + 9y^2 = 225$
$\dfrac{x^2}{9} + \dfrac{y^2}{25} = 1$
$\dfrac{x^2}{3^2} + \dfrac{y^2}{5^2} = 1$
Center: $(0, 0)$
$a = 3, b = 5$
Vertices: $(-3, 0), (3, 0),$
$(0, -5), (0, 5)$
$c^2 = 25 - 9$
$c = \sqrt{16} = 4$
Foci: $(0, -4), (0, 4)$

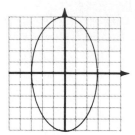

f. $4x^2 + 2y^2 = 8$
$\dfrac{x^2}{2} + \dfrac{y^2}{4} = 1$
$\dfrac{x^2}{(\sqrt{2})^2} + \dfrac{y^2}{2^2} = 1$
Center: $(0, 0)$
$a = \sqrt{2}, b = 2$
Vertices: $(-\sqrt{2}, 0), (\sqrt{2}, 0),$
$(0, -2), (0, 2)$
$c^2 = 4 - 2$
$c = \sqrt{2}$
Foci: $(0, -\sqrt{2}), (0, \sqrt{2})$

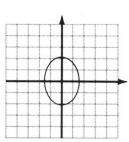

g. $x^2 + 3y^2 = 48$
$\dfrac{x^2}{48} + \dfrac{y^2}{16} = 1$
$\dfrac{x^2}{(4\sqrt{3})^2} + \dfrac{y^2}{4^2} = 1$
Center: $(0, 0)$
$a = 4\sqrt{3}, b = 4$

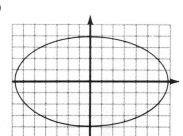

Vertices: $(-4\sqrt{3}, 0), (4\sqrt{3}, 0), (0, -4), (0, 4)$
$c^2 = 48 - 16$
$c = \sqrt{32} = 4\sqrt{2}$
Foci: $(-4\sqrt{2}, 0), (4\sqrt{2}, 0)$

h.

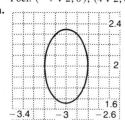

$25x^2 + 9y^2 + 150x - 36y + 260 = 0$
$25(x^2 + 6x +) + 9(y^2 - 4y +) = -260$
$25(x^2 + 6x + 9 - 9)$
$\qquad + 9(y^2 - 4y + 4 - 4) = -260$
$25(x^2 + 6x + 9) + 9(y^2 - 4y + 4) = -260 + 25 \cdot 9 + 9 \cdot 4$
$25(x^2 + 6x + 9) + 9(y^2 - 4y + 4) = -260 + 225 + 36$
$25(x + 3)^2 + 9(y - 2)^2 = 1$

$$\frac{(x + 3)^2}{\left(\frac{1}{5}\right)^2} + \frac{(y - 2)^2}{\left(\frac{1}{3}\right)^2} = 1$$

Center: $(-3, 2)$, $a = \frac{1}{5}$, $b = \frac{1}{3}$

The equation $\dfrac{x^2}{\left(\frac{1}{5}\right)^2} + \dfrac{y^2}{\left(\frac{1}{3}\right)^2} = 1$: has

Vertices: $\left(\frac{-1}{5}, 0\right), \left(\frac{1}{5}, 0\right), \left(0, \frac{-1}{3}\right), \left(0, \frac{1}{3}\right)$

Foci: $\left(0, -\frac{4}{15}\right), \left(0, \frac{4}{15}\right)$

$c^2 = \dfrac{1}{9} - \dfrac{1}{25} = \dfrac{25}{225} - \dfrac{9}{225} = \dfrac{16}{225}$

$c = \sqrt{\dfrac{16}{225}} = \dfrac{4}{15}$

Vertices: $\left(-3 - \frac{1}{5}, 2\right), \left(-3 + \frac{1}{5}, 2\right),$

$\qquad\qquad \left(-3, 2 - \frac{1}{3}\right), \left(-3, 2 + \frac{1}{3}\right)$

or $\quad \left(-3\frac{1}{5}, 2\right), \left(-2\frac{4}{5}, 2\right),$

$\qquad\qquad \left(-3, 1\frac{2}{3}\right), \left(-3, 2\frac{1}{3}\right)$

Foci: $\left(-3, 2 - \frac{4}{15}\right), \left(-3, 2 + \frac{4}{15}\right)$

or $\quad \left(-3, 1\frac{11}{15}\right), \left(-3, 2\frac{4}{15}\right)$

i.

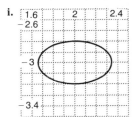

$9x^2 + 25y^2 - 36x + 150y + 260 = 0$
$9(x^2 - 4x + \ ) + 25(y^2 + 6y + \ ) = -260$
$9(x^2 - 4x + 4 - 4) + 25(y^2 + 6y + 9 - 9)$
$\qquad\qquad\qquad\qquad\qquad = -260$
$9(x^2 - 4x + 4) + 25(y^2 + 6y + 9) = -260 + 9 \cdot 4 + 25 \cdot 9$
$9(x^2 - 4x + 4) + 25(y^2 + 6y + 9) = -260 + 36 + 225$
$\qquad\qquad 9(x - 2)^2 + 25(y + 3)^2 = 1$

$$\dfrac{(x - 2)^2}{\left(\frac{1}{3}\right)^2} + \dfrac{(y + 3)^2}{\left(\frac{1}{5}\right)^2} = 1$$

Center: $(2, -3)$, $a = \frac{1}{3}$, $b = \frac{1}{5}$

The equation $\dfrac{x^2}{\left(\frac{1}{3}\right)^2} + \dfrac{y^2}{\left(\frac{1}{5}\right)^2} = 1$ has

Vertices: $\left(\frac{-1}{3}, 0\right), \left(\frac{1}{3}, 0\right), \left(0, \frac{-1}{5}\right), \left(0, \frac{1}{5}\right)$

Foci: $\left(-\frac{4}{15}, 0\right), \left(\frac{4}{15}, 0\right)$

$c^2 = \dfrac{1}{9} - \dfrac{1}{25} = \dfrac{25}{225} - \dfrac{9}{225} = \dfrac{16}{225}$

$c = \sqrt{\dfrac{16}{225}} = \dfrac{4}{15}$

Vertices: $\left(2 - \frac{1}{3}, -3\right), \left(2 + \frac{1}{3}, -3\right),$

$\qquad\qquad \left(2, -3 - \frac{1}{5}\right), \left(2, -3 + \frac{1}{5}\right)$

or $\quad \left(1\frac{2}{3}, -3\right), \left(2\frac{1}{3}, -3\right), \left(2, -3\frac{1}{5}\right), \left(2, -2\frac{4}{5}\right)$

Foci: $\left(2 - \frac{4}{15}, -3\right), \left(2 + \frac{4}{15}, -3\right)$ or $\left(1\frac{11}{15}, -3\right), \left(2\frac{4}{15}, -3\right)$

1. Vertices: $(\pm 2, 0), (0, \pm 1)$;
foci: $(\pm \sqrt{3}, 0)$

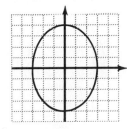

2. Vertices: $(\pm 1, 0), (0, \pm 2)$;
foci: $(0, \pm \sqrt{3})$

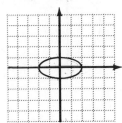

3. Vertices: $(\pm 3, 0), (0, \pm 4)$;
foci: $(0, \pm \sqrt{7})$

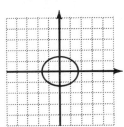

4. Vertices: $(\pm 4, 0), (0, \pm 3)$;
foci: $(\pm \sqrt{7}, 0)$

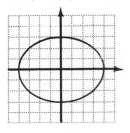

5. Vertices: $(\pm \sqrt{3}, 0), (0, \pm \sqrt{2})$;
foci: $(\pm 1, 0)$

6. Vertices: $(\pm \sqrt{7}, 0), (0, \pm \sqrt{5})$;
foci: $(\pm \sqrt{2}, 0)$

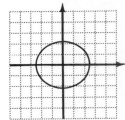

7. Vertices: $\left(\pm \frac{1}{2}, 0\right), \left(0, \pm \frac{1}{3}\right)$;

foci: $\left(\pm \frac{\sqrt{5}}{6}, 0\right)$

8. Vertices: $\left(\pm \frac{1}{5}, 0\right), \left(0, \pm \frac{1}{4}\right)$;

foci: $\left(0, \pm \frac{3}{20}\right)$

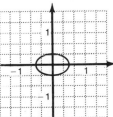
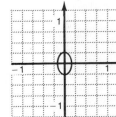

9. Center: $(1, 2)$;
Vertices: $(-1, 2), (3, 2),$
$(1, 1), (1, 3)$;
Foci: $(1 \pm \sqrt{3}, 2)$

10. Center: $(1, 2)$
Vertices: $(0, 2), (2, 2),$
$(1, 0), (1, 4)$;
Foci: $(1, 2 \pm \sqrt{3})$

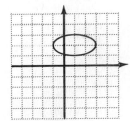
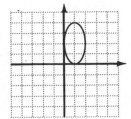

11. Center: $(-3, 2)$;
Vertices: $(-8, 2)$, $(2, 2)$,
$(-3, -2)$, $(-3, 6)$;
Foci: $(-6, 2)$, $(0, 2)$

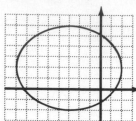

12. Center: $(2, -3)$;
Vertices: $(-3, -3)$, $(7, -3)$,
$(2, -7)$, $(2, 1)$;
Foci: $(-1, -3)$, $(5, -3)$

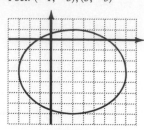

13. Center: $(-2, 1)$;
Vertices: $(-10, 1)$, $(6, 1)$,
$(-2, 1 \pm 4\sqrt{3})$;
Foci: $(-6, 1)$, $(2, 1)$

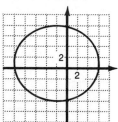

14. Center: $(5, 5)$;
Vertices: $(5 \pm 4\sqrt{3}, 5)$,
$(5, 13)$, $(5, -3)$;
Foci: $(5, 9)$, $(5, 1)$

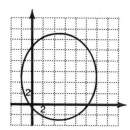

15. Center: $(2, -1)$;
Vertices: $(-1, -1)$, $(5, -1)$,
$(2, -3)$, $(2, 1)$;
Foci: $(2 \pm \sqrt{5}, -1)$

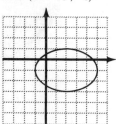

16. Center: $(5, -2)$;
Vertices: $(3, -2)$, $(7, -2)$,
$(5, -2 \pm \sqrt{2})$;
Foci: $(5 \pm \sqrt{2}, -2)$

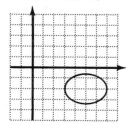

17. Center: $(1, 1)$;
Vertices: $(0, 1)$, $(2, 1)$,
$(1, -1)$, $(1, 3)$;
Foci: $(1, 1 \pm \sqrt{3})$

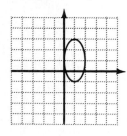

18. Center: $(-3, 1)$;
Vertices: $(-5, 1)$, $(-1, 1)$,
$(-3, -2)$, $(-3, 4)$;
Foci: $(-3, 1 \pm \sqrt{5})$

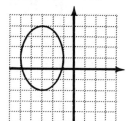

19. $\pi x^2 + \pi^2 y^2 - 5\pi x + 6\pi y - \pi^2 = 0$
Divide by π.
$$x^2 + \pi y^2 - 5x + 6y - \pi = 0$$
Group x and y terms.
$$x^2 - 5x + \pi y^2 + 6y = \pi$$
Complete the square for x and y.
$$\left(x^2 - 5x + \frac{25}{4}\right) + \pi\left(y^2 + \frac{6}{\pi}y + \frac{9}{\pi^2}\right) = \pi + \frac{25}{4} + \pi\left(\frac{9}{\pi^2}\right)$$
$$\left(x - \frac{5}{2}\right)^2 + \pi\left(y + \frac{3}{\pi}\right)^2 = \frac{4\pi^2 + 25\pi + 36}{4\pi}$$
$$= \pi^2 + \frac{25}{4}\pi + 9$$

$$= (\pi + 4)\left(\pi + \frac{9}{2}\right)$$

$$\frac{\left(x - \frac{5}{2}\right)^2}{\left(\frac{4\pi^2 + 25\pi + 36}{4\pi}\right)} + \frac{\left(y + \frac{3}{\pi}\right)^2}{\left(\frac{4\pi^2 + 25\pi + 36}{4\pi^2}\right)} = 1$$

Center $\left(2\frac{1}{2}, \frac{3}{\pi}\right) \approx (2.5, -1.0)$ rounded to the nearest tenth.

Distance from center to vertices along the major axis is

$$\sqrt{\frac{4\pi^2 + 25\pi + 36}{4\pi}} \approx 3.5 \text{ rounded to the nearest tenth.}$$

Distance from center to vertices along the minor axis is

$$\sqrt{\frac{4\pi^2 + 25\pi + 36}{4\pi^2}} \approx 2.0 \text{ rounded to nearest tenth.}$$

Vertices:

$$\left(2.5, -\frac{3}{\pi} \pm \sqrt{\frac{4\pi^2 + 25\pi + 36}{4\pi^2}}\right)$$
$$\approx (2.5, 1.0) \text{ and } (2.5, -2.9)$$

$$\left(2.5 \pm \sqrt{\frac{4\pi^2 + 25\pi + 36}{4\pi}}, -\frac{3}{\pi}\right)$$
$$\approx (6.0, -1.0) \text{ and } (-1.0, -1.0)$$

20. $\pi^2 x^2 + \pi y^2 + \pi^3 x - \pi^2 y + \frac{5}{4}\pi = 0$

Divide by π.

$$\pi x^2 + y^2 + \pi^2 x - \pi y + \frac{5}{4} = 0$$

Group x and y terms.

$$\pi(x^2 + \pi x) + y^2 - \pi y = -\frac{5}{4}$$

Complete the square for x and y.

$$\pi\left(x^2 + \pi x + \frac{\pi^2}{4}\right) + \left(y^2 - \pi y + \frac{\pi^2}{4}\right)$$
$$= -\frac{5}{4} + \pi\left(\frac{\pi^2}{4}\right) + \frac{\pi^2}{4}$$
$$\pi\left(x + \frac{\pi}{2}\right)^2 + \left(y - \frac{\pi}{2}\right)^2 = \frac{\pi^3 + \pi^2 - 5}{4}$$

$$\frac{\left(x + \frac{\pi}{2}\right)^2}{\left(\frac{\pi^3 + \pi^2 - 5}{4\pi}\right)} + \frac{\left(y - \frac{\pi}{2}\right)^2}{\left(\frac{\pi^3 + \pi^2 - 5}{4}\right)} = 1$$

Center $\left(-\frac{\pi}{2}, \frac{\pi}{2}\right) \approx (-1.6, 1.6)$ rounded to nearest tenth.

Distance from center to vertices along major axis is

$$\frac{\sqrt{\pi^3 + \pi^2 - 5}}{2} \approx 3.0 \text{ rounded to nearest tenth. Distance from}$$

center to vertices along the minor axis is $\sqrt{\frac{\pi^3 + \pi^2 - 5}{4\pi}} \approx 1.7$

rounded to nearest tenth.

Vertices:

$$\left(-\frac{\pi}{2}, \frac{\pi}{2} \pm \frac{\sqrt{\pi^3 + \pi^2 - 5}}{2}\right) \approx (-1.6, 4.6) \text{ and}$$

$(-1.6, -1.4)$ rounded to nearest tenth.

$$\left(-\frac{\pi}{2} \pm \sqrt{\frac{\pi^3 + \pi^2 - 5}{4\pi}}, \frac{\pi}{2}\right) \approx (0.1, -1.6) \text{ and } (-3.3, -1.6)$$

rounded to nearest tenth.

21.

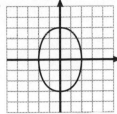

Center = midpoint of line
Segment connecting vertices = $(0, 0)$
Length of major axis = 6 (vertical)
Length of minor axis = 4

$$\frac{x^2}{\left[\left(\frac{1}{2}\right)(4)\right]^2} + \frac{y^2}{\left[\left(\frac{1}{2}\right)(6)\right]^2} = 1 \quad \text{or} \quad \frac{x^2}{4} + \frac{y^2}{9} = 1$$

22.

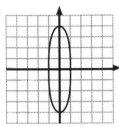

Center: $(0, 0)$
Length of major axis = 8 (vertical)
Length of minor axis = 2

$$x^2 + \frac{y^2}{16} = 1$$

23.

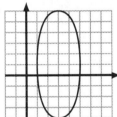

Center: $(3, 1)$
Length of major axis = 10 (vertical)
Length of minor axis = 4

$$\frac{(x - 3)^2}{4} + \frac{(y - 1)^2}{25} = 1$$

24.

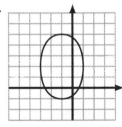

Center: $(-1, 2)$
Length of major axis = 6 (vertical)
Length of minor axis = 4

$$\frac{(x + 1)^2}{4} + \frac{(y - 2)^2}{9} = 1$$

25. Center: $(-2, 3)$ Major axis of length 8 (vertical)
Minor axis of length 2
vertices: $(-2, 7)$ and $(-2, -1)$ along major axis
vertices: $(-3, 3)$ and $(-1, 3)$ along minor axis

$$(x + 2)^2 + \frac{(y - 3)^2}{16} = 1$$

26. Center: $(0, 0)$ midpoint of vertices
Horizontal axis has length 6.

$$\frac{x^2}{9} + \frac{y^2}{b^2} = 1 \quad \text{Substitute } \left(2, \frac{22}{3}\right)$$

$$\frac{4}{9} + \frac{484}{9b^2} = 1$$

Multiplying by $9b^2$
$$4b^2 + 484 = 9b^2$$
$$484 = 5b^2$$

$$\frac{484}{5} = b^2$$

$$\frac{x^2}{9} + \frac{y^2}{\frac{484}{5}} = 1$$

27. a.

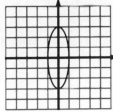

$x^2 + \frac{y^2}{9} = 1$ Ellipse with
center $(0, 0)$; vertices: $(-1, 0)$,
$(1, 0)$, $(0, 3)$, and $(0, -3)$
Does not pass the vertical line
test for functions.

b. $9x^2 + y^2 = 9$
$$y^2 = 9 - 9x^2$$
$$y^2 = 9(1 - x^2)$$
$$y = \pm 3\sqrt{1 - x^2}$$

c.

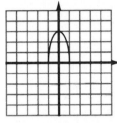

$y = 3\sqrt{1 - x^2}$ is the upper half
of the ellipse. The equation
describes a function with
domain $-1 \le x \le 1$ and range
$0 \le y \le 3$.

d.

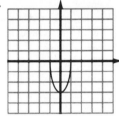

$y = -3\sqrt{1 - x^2}$ is the lower
half of the ellipse. The equation
describes a function with
domain $-1 \le x \le 1$ and range
$-3 \le y \le 0$.

28. Plot these points:

x	$y = \pm \frac{4}{5}\sqrt{25 - x^2}$
0	4
0	-4
1	$\frac{\pm 8\sqrt{6}}{5} \approx \pm 3.9$ rounded
-1	$\frac{\pm 8\sqrt{6}}{5} \approx \pm 3.9$ rounded
2	$\pm\left(\frac{4}{5}\right)(\sqrt{21}) \approx \pm 3.7$ rounded
-2	$\pm\left(\frac{4}{5}\right)(\sqrt{21}) \approx \pm 3.7$ rounded
3	$\pm 3\frac{1}{5} = \pm 3.2$
-3	$\pm 3\frac{1}{5} = \pm 3.2$
4	$\pm 2\frac{2}{5} = \pm 2.4$
-4	$\pm 2\frac{2}{5} = \pm 2.4$
5	0
-5	0

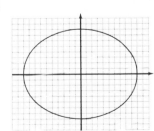

29. Distance to the other focus
$d = \text{max} - \text{min} = 9.3 \times 10^7 - 9.1 \times 10^7 = 0.2 \times 10^7$ or
2.0×10^6 miles

30. Find $F_1P = \sqrt{(7 + 25)^2 + (24)^2} = \sqrt{1600} = 40$
$F_2P = \sqrt{(7 - 25) + (24)^2} = \sqrt{900} = 30$
Since the ellipse is the locus of points such that the sum of the distances from foci to each point is a constant, the sum of the distance between F_1 and $(a, 0)$ and F_2 and $(a, 0)$ must equal $F_1P + F_2P = 70$. [Since it also equals F_1F_2 + twice the distance from F_2 to $(a, 0)$]
$F_1F_2 + 2(a - 25)$
$50 + 2a - 50 = 70$
$\qquad 2a = 70$
$\qquad a = 35$
Center $(0, 0)$; length of horizontal axis $= 70$.

$\dfrac{x^2}{35^2} + \dfrac{y^2}{b^2} = 1$ Substitute $(7, 24)$.

$\dfrac{7^2}{1225} + \dfrac{24^2}{b^2} = 1$

$\dfrac{49}{1225} + \dfrac{576}{b^2} = 1$ Multiply by $1225b^2$.

$49b^2 + 705{,}600 = 1225b^2$
$\qquad 705{,}600 = 1176b^2$
$\qquad\quad 600 = b^2$
$\qquad$ So, $b = \sqrt{600} = 10\sqrt{6}$.

31. A circle with radius a (or b) centered at the origin.

32. $F_1P + F_2P = 2a$; by the distance formula
$\sqrt{(x + c)^2 + y^2} + \sqrt{(x - c)^2 + y^2} = 2a$;
$\sqrt{(x + c)^2 + y^2} = 2a - \sqrt{(x - c)^2 + y^2}$;
$x^2 + 2cx + c^2 + y^2 = 4a^2 - 4a\sqrt{(x - c)^2 + y^2}$
$\qquad\qquad\qquad + x^2 - 2cx + c^2 + y^2$;
$-4a^2 + 4cx = -4a\sqrt{(x - c)^2 + y^2}$;
$-a^2 + cx = -a\sqrt{(x - c)^2 + y^2}$;
$a^4 - 2a^2cx + c^2x^2 = a^2x^2 - 2a^2cx + a^2c^2 + a^2y^2$;
$x^2(a^2 - c^2) + a^2y^2 = a^2(a^2 - c^2)$; with P at $(0, b)$, it follows that $b^2 = a^2 - c^2$. Substituting b^2 for $a^2 - c^2$ in the last equation, we have the equation of the ellipse
$b^2x^2 + a^2y^2 = a^2b^2$, or $\dfrac{x^2}{a^2} + \dfrac{y^2}{b^2} = 1$.

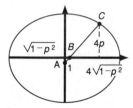

33. Suppose $0 < b < a$ so $\begin{cases} c^2 = a^2 - b^2 \\ b^2 = a^2 - c^2 \end{cases}$ and
$\quad 0 < b^2 < a^2$
$\quad 0 < a^2 - c^2 < a^2$
$\quad -a^2 < -c^2 < 0$
$\quad a^2 > c^2 > 0$
$\quad 0 < c^2 < a^2$

$\quad 0 < \dfrac{c^2}{a^2} < 1$

But if $0 < x < 1$, then $0 < \sqrt{x} < 1$.

$\quad 0 < \dfrac{c}{a} < 1$
$\quad 0 < e < 1$

34. Assume $0 < b < a$.

Then $e = \dfrac{c}{a}$

If $e = 1$

then $\dfrac{c}{a} = 1$

$\quad c = a$
$\quad b^2 = a^2 - c^2 = a^2 - a^2 = 0$
$\quad b = 0$, the distance along minor axis.
As e approaches 1, the ellipse would collapse to a line.

35. a.

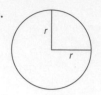

Area $= \pi r^2$

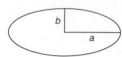

Area $= \pi ab$

b. Area $= \pi(4)(5) = 20\pi$
c. Area $= \pi(2)(\sqrt{3}) = 2\pi\sqrt{3}$

36. $\dfrac{x^2}{10^2} + \dfrac{y^2}{6^2} = 1$

$c^2 = 10^2 - 6^2 = 64$
$c = 8$
Distance from center to one focus is 8. Thus, the distance from focus to focus is 16 cm.

37.

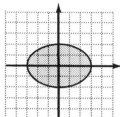

38.

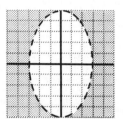

39.

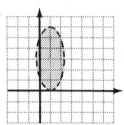

40. $f(x) = x^2 - 3x + 4$

$f(x) = \left(x^2 - 3x + \dfrac{9}{4}\right) - \dfrac{9}{4} + 4$

$f(x) = \left(x - \dfrac{3}{2}\right)^2 + 1\dfrac{3}{4}$

Vertex: $\left(1\dfrac{1}{2}, 1\dfrac{3}{4}\right)$

Line of symmetry: $x = 1\dfrac{1}{2}$

Parabola opens up so minimum value of $f(x) = 1.75$.

41. $f(x) = x^2 + 5x - 1$

$f(x) = \left(x^2 + 5x + \dfrac{25}{4}\right) - \dfrac{25}{4} - 1$

$f(x) = \left(x + \dfrac{5}{2}\right)^2 - 7\dfrac{1}{4}$

Vertex: $\left(-2\dfrac{1}{2}, -7\dfrac{1}{4}\right)$

Line of symmetry: $x = -2\dfrac{1}{2}$

Parabola opens up so minimum value of $f(x) = -7.25$.

42. $f(x) = -x^2 + 2x - 5$
$f(x) = -(x^2 - 2x + 1) - 5 + 1$
$f(x) = -(x - 1)^2 - 4$
Vertex: $(1, -4)$
Line of symmetry: $x = 1$
Parabola opens down so maximum value of $f(x) = -4$.

43. To find x-intercepts, let $f(x) = 0$.
$$0 = 2x^2 + 4x - 1$$
quadratic formula:
$$x = \frac{-4 \pm \sqrt{16 - 4(2)(-1)}}{2(2)} = \frac{-4 \pm \sqrt{24}}{4} = \frac{-4 \pm 2\sqrt{6}}{4}$$
x-intercepts: $\left(-1 + \dfrac{\sqrt{6}}{2}, 0\right)$ and $\left(-1 - \dfrac{\sqrt{6}}{2}, 0\right)$

44. To find x-intercepts, let $f(x) = 0$.
$$0 = 2x^2 - 2x - 24$$
$$0 = x^2 - x - 12$$
$$0 = (x - 4)(x + 3)$$
$$x = 4 \quad \text{or} \quad x = -3$$
x-intercepts: $(4, 0)$ and $(-3, 0)$

45. $d = \sqrt{(7 - 4)^2 + (10 - 5)^2} = \sqrt{9 + 25} = \sqrt{34}$

46. $d = \sqrt{(-5 + 2)^2 + (-2 - 1)^2} = \sqrt{9 + 9} = \sqrt{18} = 3\sqrt{2}$

47. General quadratic $ax^2 + bx + c = y$
Use $(1, 1)$, $(-1, -3)$, and $(2, 12)$.
① $a + b + c = 1$ using $(1, 1)$
② $a - b + c = -3$ using $(-1, -3)$
③ $4a + 2b + c = 12$ using $(2, 12)$
Eliminating a and c by subtracting ② from ①
$$\begin{aligned} a + b + c &= 1 \\ -a + b - c &= 3 \\ \hline 2b &= 4 \\ b &= 2 \end{aligned}$$
Substituting $b = 2$ into ① and ③
$a + 2 + c = 1$ or $a + c = -1$
$4a + 4 + c = 12$ $4a + c = 8$
By subtracting the top equation from the bottom one we get
$3a = 9$ so $a = 3$.
Since $a + b = 1$
$3 + 2 + c = 1$
$c = -4$
Hence, the equation is $y = 3x^2 + 2x - 4$.

48. Substituting $(1, -22)$, $(-2, 14)$, and $(-1, -4)$ into the general form of the equation:
① $a(1)^2 + b(1) + c = -22$ so $a + b + c = -22$
② $a(-2)^2 + b(-2) + c = 14$ so $4a - 2b + c = 14$
③ $a(-1)^2 + b(-1) + c = -4$ so $a - b + c = -4$
①$-$③ $a + b + c = -22$
$$\begin{aligned} -a + b - c &= 4 \\ \hline 2b &= -18 \\ b &= -9 \end{aligned}$$
Substituting $b = -9$ into ① and ②
$a - 9 + c = -22$ so $a + c = -13$
$4a - 2(-9) + c = 14$ so $4a + c = -4$
Subtracting the new top equation from the new bottom equation
$$\begin{aligned} 4a + c &= -4 \\ -a - c &= 13 \\ \hline 3a &= 9 \\ a &= 3 \end{aligned}$$
Since $a + c = -13$
$3 + c = -13$
$c = -16$
Hence, the solution is $y = 3x^2 - 9x - 16$.

49. $315 + 28n > 32.5n$; $70 > n$, < 70 hours

pp. 446–450   **10-4 TRY THIS**

a. $4x^2 - 9y^2 = 36$
$$\frac{x^2}{9} - \frac{y^2}{4} = 1$$
$a = 3$, $b = 2$
Vertices: $(-3, 0)$, $(3, 0)$
$c = \sqrt{3^2 + 2^2} = \sqrt{13}$
Foci: $(-\sqrt{13}, 0)$, $(\sqrt{13}, 0)$
Asymptotes: $y = -\dfrac{2}{3}x$, $y = \dfrac{2}{3}x$

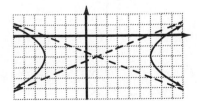

b. $x^2 - y^2 = 16$
$$\frac{x^2}{16} - \frac{y^2}{16} = 1$$
$a = 4$, $b = 4$
Vertices: $(-4, 0)$, $(4, 0)$
$c = \sqrt{4^2 + 4^2} = \sqrt{32} = 4\sqrt{2}$
Foci: $(-4\sqrt{2}, 0)$, $(4, \sqrt{2}, 0)$
Asymptotes: $y = -x$, $y = x$

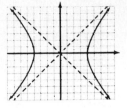

c. $9y^2 - 25x^2 = 225$
$$\frac{y^2}{25} - \frac{x^2}{9} = 1$$
$a = 3$, $b = 5$
Vertices: $(0, -5)$, $(0, 5)$
$c = \sqrt{3^2 + 5^2} = \sqrt{34}$
Foci: $(0, -\sqrt{34})$, $(0, \sqrt{34})$
Asymptotes: $y = -\dfrac{5}{3}x$, $y = \dfrac{5}{3}x$

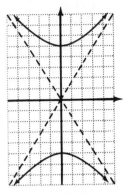

d. $y^2 - x^2 = 25$
$$\frac{y^2}{25} - \frac{x^2}{25} = 1$$
$a = 5$, $b = 5$
Vertices: $(0, -5)$, $(0, 5)$
$c = \sqrt{5^2 + 5^2} = \sqrt{50} = 5\sqrt{2}$
Foci: $(0, -5\sqrt{2})$, $(0, 5\sqrt{2})$
Asymptotes: $y = -x$, $y = x$

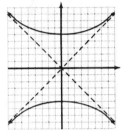

e.
$$4x^2 - 25y^2 - 8x - 100y - 196 = 0$$
$$4(x^2 - 2x + \quad) - 25(y^2 + 4y + \quad) = 196$$
$$4(x^2 - 2x + 1 - 1) - 25(y^2 + 4y + 4 - 4) = 196$$
$$4(x^2 - 2x + 1) - 25(y^2 + 4y + 4) = 196 + 4 - 100$$
$$4(x - 1)^2 - 25(y + 2)^2 = 100$$
$$\frac{(x - 1)^2}{25} - \frac{(y + 2)^2}{4} = 1$$

Center: $(1, -2)$
$a = 5$, $b = 2$
Vertices of $\dfrac{x^2}{25} - \dfrac{y^2}{4} = 1$: $(-5, 0)$, $(5, 0)$
$c = \sqrt{5^2 + 2^2} = \sqrt{29}$
Foci of $\dfrac{x^2}{25} - \dfrac{y^2}{4} = 1$: $(-\sqrt{29}, 0)$, $(\sqrt{29}, 0)$
Asymptotes of $\dfrac{x^2}{25} - \dfrac{y^2}{4} = 1$: $y = -\dfrac{2}{5}$, $y = \dfrac{2}{5}$
Vertices: $(1 - 5, -2)$, $(1 + 5, -2)$, or $(-4, -2)$, $(6, -2)$
Foci: $(1 - \sqrt{29}, -2)$, $(1 + \sqrt{29}, -2)$
Asymptotes: $y + 2 = -\dfrac{2}{5}(x - 1)$, $y + 2 = \dfrac{2}{5}(x - 1)$

f. $\frac{(y-2)^2}{9} - \frac{(x+1)^2}{16} = 1$

Center: $(-1, 2)$
$a = 4, b = 3$

Vertices of $\frac{y^2}{9} - \frac{x^2}{16} = 1$;

$\quad\quad (0, -3), (0, 3)$
$c = \sqrt{4^2 + 3^2} = \sqrt{25} = 5$

Foci of $\frac{y^2}{9} - \frac{x^2}{16} = 1$;

$\quad\quad (0, -5), (0, 5)$

Asymptotes of $\frac{y^2}{9} - \frac{x^2}{16} = 1$;

$y = -\frac{3}{4}x, \; y = \frac{3}{4}x$

Vertices: $(0 - 1, -3 + 2), (0 - 1, 3 + 2)$
or $\quad\quad (-1, -1), (-1, 5)$
Foci: $(0 - 1, -5 + 2), (0 - 1, 5 + 2)$
or $\quad\quad (-1, -3), (-1, 7)$

Asymptotes: $y - 2 = \pm\frac{3}{4}(x + 1), \; y - 2 = \pm\frac{3}{4}(x + 1)$

g.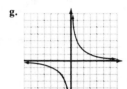

h.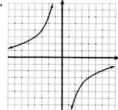

pp. 450–451   10-4 EXERCISES

1. Center: $(0, 0)$;
foci: $(\pm\sqrt{10}, 0)$;
vertices: $(\pm 3, 0)$;

asymptotes: $y = \pm\frac{1}{3}x$

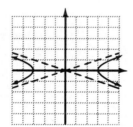

2. Center: $(0, 0)$;
foci: $(\pm\sqrt{10}, 0)$;
vertices: $(\pm 1, 0)$;
asymptotes: $y = \pm 3x$

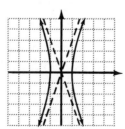

3. Center: $(0, 0)$;
foci: $(0, \pm 2\sqrt{5})$;
vertices: $(0, \pm 4)$;
asymptotes: $y = \pm 2x$

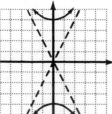

4. Center: $(0, 0)$;
foci: $(\pm\sqrt{5}, 0)$;
vertices: $(\pm 2, 0)$;

asymptotes: $y = \pm\frac{1}{2}x$

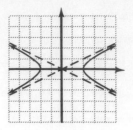

5. Center: $(0, 0)$;
foci: $(\pm\sqrt{5}, 0)$;
vertices: $(\pm 1, 0)$;
asymptotes: $y = \pm 2x$

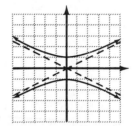

6. Center: $(0, 0)$;
foci: $(0, \pm\sqrt{5})$;
vertices: $(0, \pm 1)$;

asymptotes: $y = \pm\frac{1}{2}x$

7. Center: $(0, 0)$;
foci: $(0, \pm\sqrt{5})$;
vertices: $(0, \pm 2)$;
asymptotes: $y = \pm 2x$

8. Center: $(0, 0)$;
foci: $(\pm 2, 0)$;
vertices: $(\pm\sqrt{2}, 0)$;
asymptotes: $y = \pm x$

9. Center: $(0, 0)$;
foci: $(\pm\sqrt{6}, 0)$;
vertices: $(\pm\sqrt{3}, 0)$;
asymptotes: $y = \pm x$

10. Center: $(2, -5)$;
foci: $(2 \pm \sqrt{10}, -5)$;
vertices: $(3, -5), (1, -5)$;
asymptotes: $y = 3x - 11$,
$\quad\quad\quad\quad y = -3x + 1$

11. Center: $(-1, -3)$;
foci: $(-1, -3 \pm 2\sqrt{5})$;
vertices: $(-1, -1)$, $(-1, -5)$;

asymptotes: $y = \frac{1}{2}x - \frac{5}{2}$,

$y = -\frac{1}{2}x - \frac{7}{2}$

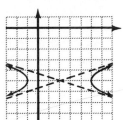

12. Center: $(2, -5)$;
foci: $(2 \pm \sqrt{10}, -5)$;
vertices: $(5, -5)$, $(-1, -5)$;

asymptotes: $y = \frac{1}{3}x - \frac{17}{3}$,

$y = -\frac{1}{3}x - \frac{13}{3}$

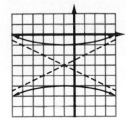

13. Center: $(-1, -3)$;
foci: $(-1, -3 \pm \sqrt{41})$;
vertices: $(-1, -8)$, $(-1, 2)$;

asymptotes: $y = \frac{5}{4}x - \frac{7}{4}$,

$y = -\frac{5}{4}x - \frac{17}{4}$

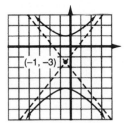
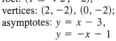

14. Center: $(1, -2)$;
foci: $(1 \pm \sqrt{2}, -2)$;
vertices: $(2, -2)$, $(0, -2)$;
asymptotes: $y = x - 3$,
$y = -x - 1$

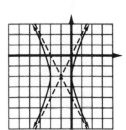

15. Center: $(-1, -2)$;
foci: $(-1 \pm \sqrt{5}, -2)$;
vertices: $(-2, -2)$, $(0, -2)$;
asymptotes: $y = 2x$,
$y = -2x - 4$

16. Center: $\left(\frac{1}{3}, 3\right)$;

foci: $\left(\frac{1}{3} \pm \sqrt{37}, 3\right)$;

vertices: $\left(-\frac{2}{3}, 3\right)$, $\left(\frac{4}{3}, 3\right)$;

asymptotes: $y = 6x + 1$,
$y = -6x + 5$

17. Center: $(-3, 1)$;
foci: $(-3 \pm \sqrt{13}, 1)$;
vertices: $(-1, 1)$, $(-5, 1)$;

asymptotes: $y = -\frac{3}{2}x - \frac{7}{2}$,

$y = \frac{3}{2}x + \frac{11}{2}$

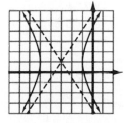

18.
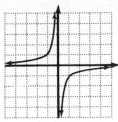

19.
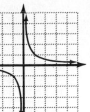

20.
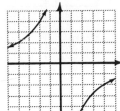

21.
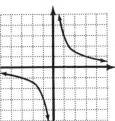

22. Vertices are along the x-axis: $(-1, 0)$ and $(1, 0)$. So, $a = 1$.
Foci: $(-2, 0)$, $(2, 0)$. So, $c = 2$. Since $c^2 = a^2 + b^2$
$$2^2 = 1^2 + b^2$$
$$3 = b^2$$
$$\pm\sqrt{3} = b$$

Hence the equation: $x^2 - \frac{y^2}{3} = 1$

23. $y = \pm\frac{b}{a}x$. Since $y = \pm\frac{3}{2}x$, $b = 3k$ and $a = 2k$ for some

constant k. Vertex at $(2, 0)$ implies $a = 2$ since it is centered
at the origin. Therefore, $k = 1$ and hence, $b = 3$. The equation

is $\frac{x^2}{4} - \frac{y^2}{9} = 1$.

24. The graph of $\frac{x^2}{9} - \frac{y^2}{4} = 1$ has vertices $(3, 0)$ and $(-3, 0)$. The

asymptotes are $y = \pm\frac{2}{3}x$. The graph of $\frac{x^2}{4} - \frac{y^2}{9} = 1$ has

vertices $(2, 0)$ and $(-2, 0)$. The asymptotes are $y = \pm\frac{3}{2}x$. The

graph of $\frac{x^2}{a^2} - \frac{y^2}{b^2} = 1$ is the graph of $\frac{x^2}{b^2} - \frac{y^2}{a^2}$, rotated 90°.

25. $PF_2 = \sqrt{(x - (-c))^2 + (y - 0)^2} = \sqrt{(x + c)^2 + y^2}$
$PF_1 = \sqrt{(x - c)^2 + (y - 0)^2} = \sqrt{(x - c)^2 + y^2}$
$PF_2 - PF_1 = 2a$
$\sqrt{(x + c)^2 + y^2} - \sqrt{(x - c)^2 + y^2} = 2a$
$\sqrt{(x + c)^2 + y^2} = 2a + \sqrt{(x - c)^2 + y^2}$
Squaring both sides:
$(x + c)^2 + y^2 = 4a^2 + 4a\sqrt{(x - c)^2 + y^2} + (x - c)^2 + y^2$
$x^2 + 2cx + c^2 + y^2 =$
$\qquad 4a^2 + 4a\sqrt{(x - c)^2 + y^2} + x^2 - 2cx + c^2 + y^2$
$4cx - 4a^2 = 4a\sqrt{(x - c)^2 + y^2}$
$cx - a^2 = a\sqrt{(x - c)^2 + y^2}$
Squaring both sides:
$c^2x^2 - 2xca^2 + a^4 = a^2(x - c)^2 + a^2y^2$
$c^2x^2 - 2a^2cx + a^4 = a^2x^2 - 2a^2cx + a^2c^2 + a^2y^2$
$c^2x^2 - a^2x^2 - a^2y^2 = a^2c^2 - a^4$ (Divide by a^2.)

$\qquad x^2\frac{(c^2 - a^2)}{a^2} - y^2 = c^2 - a^2$ (Divide by $c^2 - a^2$.)

$\qquad \frac{x^2}{a^2} - \frac{y^2}{c^2 - a^2} = 1$, $\frac{x^2}{a^2} - \frac{y^2}{b^2} = 1$

26. $\frac{x^2}{16} - \frac{y^2}{9} = 1$; $-\frac{y^2}{9} = 1 - \frac{x^2}{16}$

$\qquad y^2 = \frac{9x^2}{16} - 9$; $y^2 = \frac{9x^2 - 144}{16}$

$\qquad y = \pm\frac{\sqrt{9x^2 - 144}}{4} = \pm\frac{3\sqrt{x^2 - 16}}{4}$

As $|x|$ gets large, x^2 gets large and $\sqrt{x^2 - 16}$ gets large.
Therefore, $|y|$ gets large as $|x|$ gets large.

Asymptotes: $y = \frac{3}{4}x$ and $y = -\frac{3}{4}x$.

27. Since $c^2 = a^2 + b^2$, $c > a$ and $c > b$ for the same reason that the hypotenuse of a right triangle is longer than each of its legs.

Therefore, $\frac{c}{a} > 1$.

28. Let $a = 2$ and $b = 4$.

$\frac{x^2}{4} - \frac{y^2}{16} = 1$

Vertices: $(2, 0)$ and $(-2, 0)$
Asymptotes: $y = \pm 2x$

$\frac{y^2}{16} - \frac{x^2}{4} = 1$

Vertices: $(0, 4)$ and $(0, -4)$
Asymptotes: also $y = \pm 2x$

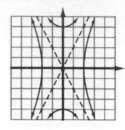

29. $y = \frac{k}{x}$

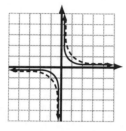

Compare $y = \frac{1}{x}$ with $y = \frac{0.5}{x}$.

The y-coordinates for the curve $y = \frac{0.5}{x}$ would be half those of

the curve $y = \frac{1}{x}$ for the same value of x, causing the curve to

bow in towards the x- and y-axes.

30. $\frac{x^2}{25} - \frac{y^2}{16} < 1$ **31.** $\frac{y^2}{36} - \frac{x^2}{25} \geq 1$

$\frac{y^2}{16} > \frac{x^2}{25} - 1$ $\frac{y^2}{36} \geq 1 + \frac{x^2}{25}$

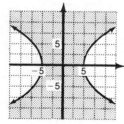

32.

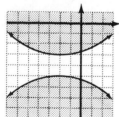

33. $\left(\frac{2 + 4}{2}, \frac{7 + 5}{2}\right) = (3, 6)$ **34.** $\left(\frac{-1 + 4}{2}, \frac{6 - 2}{2}\right) = \left(\frac{3}{2}, 2\right)$

35. $\left(\frac{3 + 9}{2}, \frac{0 + 0}{2}\right) = (6, 0)$

36. $\sqrt{(13 - 1)^2 + (-7 + 2)^2} = \sqrt{12^2 + 5^2} = \sqrt{169} = 13$

37. $\sqrt{(2 + 4)^2 + (6 - 14)^2} = \sqrt{6^2 + 8^2} = \sqrt{100} = 10$

38. $\sqrt{(-1 + 4)^2 + (6 - 10)^2} = \sqrt{3^2 + 4^2} = \sqrt{25} = 5$

39. $\sqrt{(-7 + 2)^2 + (2 - 2)^2} = \sqrt{5^2 + 0^2} = 5$

40. Substituting $(-x)$ for x in the equation produces the same equation. Substituting $(-y)$ for y produces the same equation. There is symmetry with respect to both axes.

41. Substituting $(-x)$ for x in the equation $y = (-x)^3 + 2 = -x^3 + 2$ produces a result different from the one using x. Hence, there is no symmetry with respect to the y-axis. Substituting $(-y)$ for y in the equation $(-y) = x^3 + 2$, $y = -x^3 - 2$ produces a result different from the one using y. Hence, there is no symmetry with respect to the x-axis.

42. $y = 2x - 3$ has slope 2.

$x = 2y - 3$ (the inverse function for $y = 2x - 3$) has slope $\frac{1}{2}$.

Not perpendicular.

43. $y = -\frac{1}{3}x + 2$ has slope $-\frac{1}{3}$.

$y = 3x + 2$ has slope 3, the negative reciprocal of $-\frac{1}{3}$. Yes

44. $x = y - 10$ has slope 1.
$y - x = 5$ has slope 1 and is parallel to the first line. Not perpendicular.

45. $x = kx^2$ where x is the length of a side.
$168.54 = k(5.3)^2$
$168.54 = 28.09k$
$\quad\quad 6 = k$ (6 sides for a cube)
$\quad\quad s = 6x^2$
$\quad\quad s = 6(4.8 \text{ m})^2 = 138.24 \text{ m}^2$

pp. 453–456   10-5 TRY THIS

a.

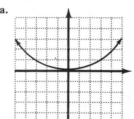

Vertex: $(0, 0)$;
focus: $(0, 2)$
directrix: $y = -2$

b.

Vertex: $(0, 0)$;

focus: $\left(0, -\frac{1}{2}\right)$;

directrix: $y = \frac{1}{2}$

c.

Vertex: $(0, 0)$;

focus: $\left(\frac{1}{2}, 0\right)$;

directrix: $x = -\frac{1}{2}$

d.

Vertex: $(0, 0)$;
focus: $(-1, 0)$;
directrix: $x = 1$

e.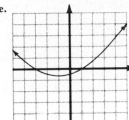

Vertex: $\left(-1, -\frac{1}{2}\right)$;

focus: $\left(-1, \frac{3}{2}\right)$;

directrix: $y = -\frac{5}{2}$

5.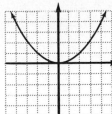

Vertex: $(0, 0)$;
focus: $(0, 1)$;
directrix: $y = -1$

f.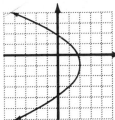

Vertex: $(2, -1)$;
focus: $(1, -1)$;
directrix: $x = 3$

6.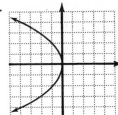

Vertex: $(0, 0)$;
focus: $(-1, 0)$;
directrix: $x = 1$

g. $x^2 = -12y$ **h.** $(y + 2)^2 = 4(x + 5)$
i. $(x + 4)^2 = -12(y + 5)$

7.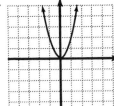

Vertex: $(0, 0)$;

focus: $\left(0, \frac{1}{8}\right)$;

directrix: $y = -\frac{1}{8}$

pp. 456–457   10-5 EXERCISES

1.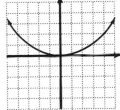

Vertex: $(0, 0)$;
focus: $(0, 2)$;
directrix: $y = -2$

8.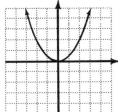

Vertex: $(0, 0)$;

focus: $\left(0, \frac{1}{2}\right)$;

directrix: $y = -\frac{1}{2}$

2.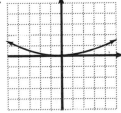

Vertex: $(0, 0)$;
focus: $(0, 4)$;
directrix: $y = -4$

9.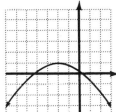

Vertex: $(-2, 1)$;

focus: $\left(-2, -\frac{1}{2}\right)$;

directrix: $y = \frac{5}{2}$

3.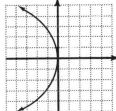

Vertex: $(0, 0)$;

focus: $\left(-\frac{3}{2}, 0\right)$;

directrix: $x = \frac{3}{2}$

10.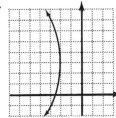

Vertex: $(-2, 3)$;
focus: $(-7, 3)$;
directrix: $x = 3$

4.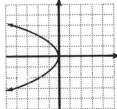

Vertex: $(0, 0)$;

focus: $\left(-\frac{1}{2}, 0\right)$;

directrix: $x = \frac{1}{2}$

11.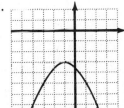

Vertex: $(-1, -3)$;

focus: $\left(-1, -3\frac{1}{2}\right)$;

directrix: $y = -2\frac{1}{2}$

12.

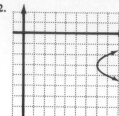

Vertex: $(7, -3)$;

focus: $\left(7\frac{1}{4}, -3\right)$;

directrix: $x = 6\frac{3}{4}$

13.

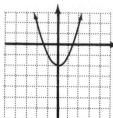

Vertex: $(0, -2)$;

focus: $\left(0, -1\frac{3}{4}\right)$;

directrix: $y = -2\frac{1}{4}$

14.

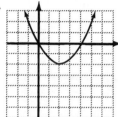

Vertex: $(2, -2)$;

focus: $\left(2, -1\frac{1}{2}\right)$;

directrix: $y = -2\frac{1}{2}$

15.

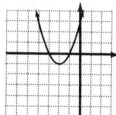

Vertex: $(-2, -1)$;

focus: $\left(-2, -\frac{3}{4}\right)$;

directrix: $y = -1\frac{1}{4}$

16.

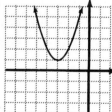

Vertex: $(-3, 1)$;

focus: $\left(-3, 1\frac{1}{4}\right)$;

directrix: $y = \frac{3}{4}$

17.

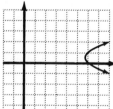

Vertex: $\left(5\frac{3}{4}, \frac{1}{2}\right)$;

focus: $\left(6, \frac{1}{2}\right)$;

directrix: $x = 5\frac{1}{2}$

18.

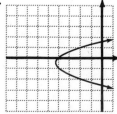

Vertex: $\left(-4\frac{1}{4}, -\frac{1}{2}\right)$;

focus: $\left(-4, -\frac{1}{2}\right)$;

directrix: $x = -4\frac{1}{2}$

19. $y^2 = 16x$ **20.** $x^2 = y$ **21.** $y^2 = -4\sqrt{2}\,x$

22. $x^2 = -4\pi y$ **23.** $x^2 = 12\sqrt{3}\,y$

24. $y^2 = (2\sqrt{2} - 4)(x + 2 - \sqrt{2})$

25. Line of symmetry: $y = 2$
Vertex is the midpoint between $(3, 2)$ and $(-4, 2)$, which is
$$\left(-\frac{1}{2}, 2\right).$$

The distance from the focus to the vertex is $p = 3\frac{1}{2}$.

Substituting into $(y - k)^2 = 4p(x - h)$ we get

$$(y - 2)^2 = 14\left(x + \frac{1}{2}\right).$$

26. Line of symmetry: $x = -2$
Vertex is the midpoint between $(-2, 3)$ and $(-2, -3)$, which is
$(-2, 0)$. The distance from the focus to the vertex is $p = 3$.
Substituting into $(x - h)^2 = 4p(y - k)$ we get $(x + 2)^2 = 12y$.

27. Since vertex $(3, 7)$ is 3 units above the focus $(3, 4)$, $p = -3$.
Substituting into $(x - h)^2 = 4p(y - k)$ we get
$(x - 3)^2 = -12(y - 7)$.

28. Since vertex $(0, -1)$ is 2 units to the right of focus $(-2, -1)$,
$p = -2$. Substituting into $(y - k)^2 = 4p(x - h)$ we get
$(y + 1)^2 = -8x$.

29. Vertex: $(0, 0)$
$4p = 8056.25$
$p = 2014.0625$ focus: $(h, k + p)$; directrix: $y = k - p$;
focus: $(0, 2014.0625)$; directrix: $y = -2014.0625$

30. Vertex: $(0, 0)$
$4p = -7645.88$
$p = -1911.47$ focus: $(h + p, k)$; directrix: $x = h - p$;
focus: $(-1911.47, 0)$; directrix $x = 1911.47$

31. $x^2 - y^2 = 0$
$\quad y^2 = x^2$
$\quad y = \pm\sqrt{x^2} = \pm|x|$; The lines $y = x$ and $y = -x$.
$x^2 - y^2 = 1$; Hyperbola with asymptotes: $y = x$ and
$y = -x$; vertices: $(1, 0)$ and $(-1, 0)$.
$x^2 + y^2 = 1$; circle with radius 1; center $(0, 0)$, the unit circle
$y = x^2$; the parabola in x with vertex $(0, 0)$ opening up with focus
$\left(0, \frac{1}{4}\right)$ and directrix $y = -\frac{1}{4}$.

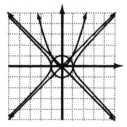

32.

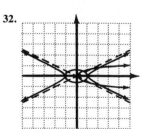

33. $\quad (x + 1)^2 = a(y - 2)$
$(-3 + 1)^2 = a(1 - 2)$
$\qquad\qquad 4 = -a$
$\qquad\quad -4 = a$
$\quad (x + 1)^2 = -4(y - 2)$

34. a.

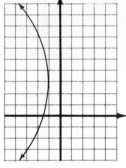

Not a function. Doesn't pass the vertical line test.

b. If $p \neq 0$, $x = \dfrac{(y - k)^2}{4p} + h$.

For most values of x, there will be 2 values of y; e.g., $y = k + 2$ and $y = k - 2$ have the same value of x. If $p = 0$, the graph is a horizontal line $y = k$.

35. A parabola with vertex $(0, 10)$ through the point $(100, 50)$ has equation $x^2 = 250(y - 10)$ or $y = \dfrac{1}{250}x^2 + 10$ where y is the length of the cable at x.

x	$y = \dfrac{x^2}{250} + 10$	
0	10 ft	the middle cable
20	11.6 ft	two cables closest to the middle cable
40	16.4 ft	two cables 40 feet from the middle
60	24.4 ft	two cables 60 feet from the middle
80	35.6 ft	two cables next to the outside cables
100	50 ft	the outside two cables

36. Answers may vary
  a. $(x + 3)^2 = 4(x - 1)$ **b.** $(y - 1)^2 = -4(x + 3)$
  c. $(x + 3)^2 = -4(y - 1)$ **d.** $(y - 1)^2 = 4(x + 3)$

37. a. The length of OF is the distance of P to the directrix. By the definition of a parabola this equals PF, the distance of P to the focus. Hence, PF and OF are of equal length, so $\angle POF$ measures 45°.
  b. In this case $\angle PFO$ measures 45°, so the segment of PP' intersects the axis of symmetry at the focus. The vertex will be the midpoint of the segment OF. If the vertex is 3 units from the segment, the segment has length 12.

38.

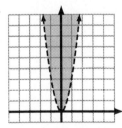

39.

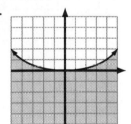

40.

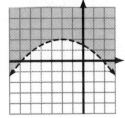

41. $f(x) = 5(x - 3)^2 + 11$
  $y - 11 = 5(x - 3)^2$
  vertex: $(3, 11)$; line of symmetry: $x = 3$; opens up, so the minimum value of f is 11, which occurs when $x = 3$.

42. $f(x) = -2(x - 13.5)^2 + 1.6$
  $y - 1.6 = -2(x - 13.5)^2$
  vertex: $(13.5, 1.6)$; line of symmetry: $x = 13.5$; opens down, so the maximum value of f is 1.6, which occurs when $x = 13.5$.

43. $y^2 - 8y$

$y^2 - 8y + \left(-\dfrac{8}{2}\right)^2$

$y^2 - 8y + 16$
$(y - 4)^2$

44. $m^2 + 5m$

$m^2 + 5m + \left(\dfrac{5}{2}\right)^2$

$m^2 + 5m + \dfrac{25}{4}$

$\left(m + \dfrac{5}{2}\right)^2$

45. $a^2 - 0.2a$

$a^2 - 0.2a + \left(-\dfrac{0.2}{2}\right)^2$

$a^2 - 0.2a + 0.01$
$(a - 0.1)^2$

46. $\sqrt{(\sqrt{m} - \sqrt{m})^2 + (\sqrt{n} + \sqrt{n})^2} = \sqrt{0 + (2\sqrt{n})^2}$
$\qquad\qquad = \sqrt{4n} = 2\sqrt{n}$

47. $3x^2 + 13x + 12 = 0$
  $(3x + 4)(x + 3) = 0$

$\qquad x = -\dfrac{4}{3}$ or $x = -3$

48. $2x^2 - 3x - 9 = 0$
  $(2x + 3)(x - 3) = 0$

$\qquad x = -\dfrac{3}{2}$ or $x = 3$

49. $\qquad 10x^2 + x = 2$
  $\qquad 10x^2 + x - 2 = 0$
  $\qquad (5x - 2)(2x + 1) = 0$

$\qquad x = \dfrac{2}{5}$ or $x = -\dfrac{1}{2}$

50. $\dfrac{3}{5}x^2 + x + \dfrac{2}{5} = 0$

$3x^2 + 5x + 2 = 0$
$(3x + 2)(x + 1) = 0$

$\qquad x = -\dfrac{2}{3}$ or $x = -1$

51. $\qquad \dfrac{6}{13}x^2 + x = \dfrac{5}{13}$

$6x^2 + 13x - 5$
$6x^2 + 13x - 5 = 0$
$(2x + 5)(3x - 1) = 0$

$\qquad x = -\dfrac{5}{2}$ or $x = \dfrac{1}{3}$

pp. 459–461   10-6 TRY THIS

  a. Ellipse   **b.** Circle   **c.** Parabola   **d.** Hyperbola
  e. $(x - 3)^2 + (y + 1)^2 = 16$

  f. $x^2 = -\dfrac{2}{3}y$ **g.** $\dfrac{(y + 3)^2}{4} - \dfrac{(x + 1)^2}{1} = 1$

  h.

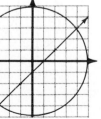

  i.

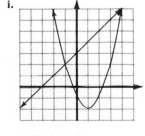

$(4, 3), (-3, -4)$ $(4, 7), (-1, 2)$

j.

$(\pm 2, 0)$

k.

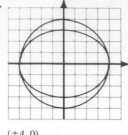

$(\pm 4, 0)$

26.

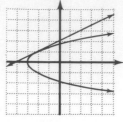

$(-2, 1)$

27.

$(1, 1)$
$(2, 4)$

pp. 462–463   10-6 EXERCISES

1. Hyperbola   **2.** Circle   **3.** Parabola   **4.** Ellipse

5. Hyperbola   **6.** Circle   **7.** Hyperbola   **8.** Ellipse

9. Does not exist   **10.** Circle   **11.** $x^2 + y^2 = 9$

12. $\dfrac{x^2}{16} + \dfrac{y^2}{9} = 1$ **13.** $x = 2y^2$ **14.** $\dfrac{x^2}{4} - \dfrac{y^2}{9} = 1$

15. $\dfrac{x^2}{4} + \dfrac{(y + 1)^2}{9} = 1$ **16.** $(x + 3)^2 + (y + 4)^2 = 16$

17. $\dfrac{(y - 4)^2}{9} - \dfrac{(x - 2)^2}{36} = 1$ **18.** $(x - 1)^2 = 2(y - 1)$

19. $\dfrac{(x + 1)^2}{4} + \dfrac{(y + 3)^2}{9} = 1$

20.

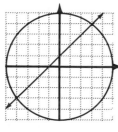

$(-4, -3)$
$(3, 4)$

21.

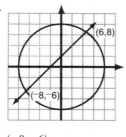

$(-8, -6)$
$(6, 8)$

22.

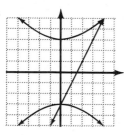

$(4, 5), (0, -3)$

23.

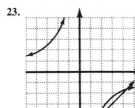

$(-7, 1)\ (1, -7)$

24.

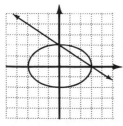

$(0, 2)$
$(3, 0)$

25.

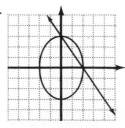

$(0, 3)$
$(2, 0)$

28.

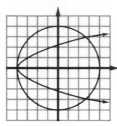

$(4, -3), (4, 3), (-5, 0)$

29.

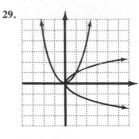

$(1, 1), (0, 0)$

30.

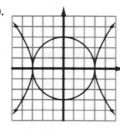

$(\pm 3, 0)$

31.

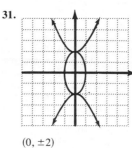

$(0, \pm 2)$

32.

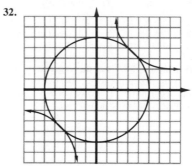

$(-4, -3), (-3, -4),$
$(3, 4), (4, 3)$

33.

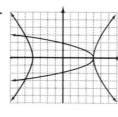

$(-5, \pm 3), (4, 0)$

34.

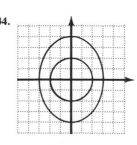

No solution

$(0, \pm 5)$

35.

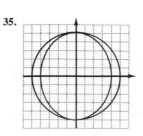

146 *Algebra and Trigonometry*

Lesson 10-6

36.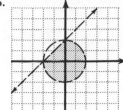

37.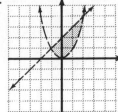

38.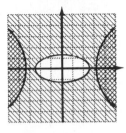

39.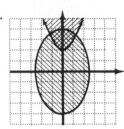

40.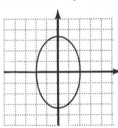

41. Answers may vary.
Circle $x^2 + y^2 + 2x + 2y - 9 = 0$
Ellipse $x^2 + 2y^2 + 2x + 2y - 9 = 0$
Hyperbola $x^2 - 2y^2 + 2x + 2y - 9 = 0$
Parabola $x^2 + 0y^2 + 2x + 2y - 9 = 0$

42. 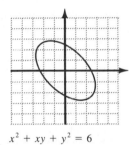

$3x^2 + y^2 = 12$ $\qquad\qquad$ $x^2 + xy + y^2 = 6$

43. $\quad x^2 + 4x + y^2 + 6y + 13 = 0$
$\qquad (x + 2)^2 + (y + 3)^2 = 0$
a. a circle
b. The point $(-2, -3)$
c. $A = 1, B = 1, C = 4, D = 6, E = -B$
$\quad C^2 + D^2 - 4AE = 0$
If $C^2 + D^2 - 4AE = 0$, the equation represents a single point.

44. $\quad x^2 - 7x + 10 = 0$
$\quad (x - 5)(x - 2) = 0$
$\qquad\qquad x = 5 \quad$ or $\quad x = 2$

45. $\qquad x^4 - 16x^2 = 0$
$\qquad x^2(x^2 - 16) = 0$
$x^2(x - 4)(x + 4) = 0$
$\qquad x = 0, \quad$ or $\quad x = 4, \quad$ or $\quad x = -4$

46. $\qquad\qquad x^4 - 16x^2 + 63 = 0$
$\qquad\qquad (x^2 - 9)(x^2 - 7) = 0$
$(x - 3)(x + 3)(x - \sqrt{7})(x + \sqrt{7}) = 0$
$\qquad\qquad x = \pm 3 \quad$ or $\quad x = \pm\sqrt{7}$

47. $|y| = 2x + 6$ does not define a graph which is symmetric with respect to the origin. $(2,10)$ is a point on the graph but $(-2, -10)$ is not. Substituting $-x$ and $-y$ into the equation
$|-y| = 2(-x) + 6$
$|y| = -2x + 6$ produces a different result.

48. $\sqrt{(-4 - 1)^2 + (-6 - 7)^2} = \sqrt{5^2 + 13^2}$
$\qquad\qquad\qquad\qquad = \sqrt{194} \approx 13.92839$
49. $\sqrt{(-1 + 1)^2 + (6 - 3)^2} = \sqrt{0^2 + 3^2} = 3$
50. $\sqrt{(2 + 4)^2 + (-4 - 4)^2} = \sqrt{6^2 + 8^2} = \sqrt{100} = 10$
51. $\sqrt{(0 - \sqrt{m})^2 + (0 - \sqrt{n})^2} = \sqrt{m + n}$
52. $\left(\dfrac{-2 - 7}{2}, \dfrac{3 - 1}{2}\right) = \left(-\dfrac{9}{2}, 1\right)$
53. $\left(\dfrac{3 + 2}{2}, \dfrac{11 + 14}{2}\right) = \left(\dfrac{5}{2}, \dfrac{25}{2}\right)$
54. $\left(\dfrac{6 - 11}{2}, \dfrac{0 + 4}{2}\right) = \left(-\dfrac{5}{2}, 2\right)$

pp. 464–465 $\qquad$ **10-7 TRY THIS**

a. $\qquad\qquad x^2 + y^2 = 25$
$\qquad\qquad\quad y - x = -1$
$\qquad\qquad\qquad -x = -1 - y$
$\qquad\qquad\qquad\quad x = 1 + y$
$\qquad\quad (1 + y)^2 + y^2 = 25$
$\qquad 1 + 2y + y^2 + y^2 = 25$
$\qquad\quad 2y^2 + 2y + 1 - 25 = 0$
$\qquad\qquad 2y^2 + 2y - 24 = 0$
$\qquad\quad (2y - 6)(y + 4) = 0$
$\qquad\qquad\qquad\qquad y = 3, -4$
$\qquad\qquad\qquad x = 1 + 3 = 4$
$\qquad\qquad\qquad x = 1 - 4 = -3$
$\qquad\qquad\qquad (4, 3), (-3, -4);$ these check

b. $\qquad y = x^2 - 2x - 1$
$\qquad\qquad y = x + 3$
$\quad y - 3 = x$
$\qquad y = (y - 3)^2 - 2(y - 3) - 1$
$\qquad y = y^2 - 6y + 9 - 2y + 6 - 1$
$\qquad 0 = y^2 - 9y + 14$
$\qquad 0 = (y - 2)(y - 7)$
$\qquad y = 2, 7$
$\qquad x = 2 - 3 = -1$
$\qquad x = 7 - 3 = 4$
$\qquad (-1, 2), (4, 7);$ these check

c. $\qquad y = \dfrac{x^2}{4}$
$\quad x + 2y = 4$
$\qquad\quad x = 4 - 2y$
$\qquad\quad y = \dfrac{(4 - 2y)^2}{4}$
$\qquad\quad y = \dfrac{16 - 16y + 4y^2}{4}$
$\qquad\quad y = \dfrac{4(4 - 4y + y^2)}{4}$
$\qquad\quad y = y^2 - 4y + 4$
$\qquad\quad 0 = y^2 - 5y + 4$
$\qquad\quad 0 = (y - 1)(y - 4)$
$\qquad\quad y = 1, 4$
$\qquad x = 4 - 2(1) = 2$
$\qquad x = 4 - 2(4) = -4$
$\qquad (2, 1), (-4, 4);$ these check

d. $\quad x^2 + y^2 = 4$
$\quad \dfrac{x^2}{25} + \dfrac{y^2}{4} = 1$
$\quad x^2 + y^2 = 4$
$\quad -\dfrac{4x^2}{25} - y^2 = -4$
$\overline{\qquad\qquad\qquad\qquad}$
$\quad \dfrac{21x^2}{25} = 0$
$\qquad\qquad x = 0$
$\quad 0 + y^2 = 4$
$\qquad\qquad y = \pm 2$
$\qquad (0, 2), (0, -2)$

e.
$$2y^2 - 3x^2 = 6$$
$$5y^2 + 2x^2 = 53$$
$$4y^2 - 6x^2 = 12$$
$$\underline{15y^2 + 6x^2 = 159}$$
$$19y^2 = 171$$
$$y^2 = 9$$
$$y = \pm 3$$
$$2 \cdot 3^2 - 3x^2 = 6$$
$$18 - 3x^2 = 6$$
$$x^2 = 4$$
$$x = \pm 2$$
$$(-2, -3), (-2, 3), (2, -3), (2, 3)$$

f.
$$y^2 + 2xy + 5 = 2$$
$$2y + x = -4$$
$$2y = -4 - x$$
$$y = \frac{-4 - x}{2}$$
$$\left(\frac{-4 - x}{2}\right)^2 + 2x\left(\frac{-4 - x}{2}\right) + 5 = 2$$
$$\frac{16 + 8x + x^2}{4} + \frac{-8x - 2x^2}{2} + 5 = 2$$
$$16 + 8x + x^2 - 16x - 4x^2 = -12$$
$$-3x^2 - 8x + 28 = 0$$
$$-(3x^2 + 8x - 28) = 0$$
$$-(3x + 14)(x - 2) = 0$$
$$x = 2, -\frac{14}{3}$$
$$y = \frac{-4 - 2}{2}, \frac{-4 - \left(-\frac{14}{3}\right)}{2}$$
$$y = -3, \frac{1}{3}$$
$$(2, -3), \left(-\frac{14}{3}, \frac{1}{3}\right)$$

g.
$$x^2 + xy + y^2 = 19$$
$$xy = 6$$
$$y = \frac{6}{x}$$
$$x^2 + x \cdot \frac{6}{x} + \left(\frac{6}{x}\right)^2 = 19$$
$$x^2 + 6 + \frac{36}{2} = 19$$
$$x^4 + 6x^2 + 36 = 19x^2$$
$$x^4 - 13x^2 + 36 = 0$$
$$u^2 - 13u + 36 = 0 \quad \text{Let } u = x^2$$
$$(u - 9)(u - 4) = 0$$
$$x = \pm 3, \text{ or } \pm 2$$

Since $y = \frac{6}{x}$, if $x = -3$, $y = -2$; if $x = 3$, $y = 2$; if

$x = -2$, $y = -3$; if $x = 2$, $y = 3$. The solutions are
$(-3, -2), (3, 2), (-2, -3), (2, 3)$.

h.
$$xy = 8 \Rightarrow y = \frac{8}{x}$$
$$8x^2 - y^2 = 16$$
$$8x^2 - \left(\frac{8}{x}\right)^2 = 16$$
$$8x^2 - \frac{64}{x^2} = 16$$
$$8x^4 - 64 = 16x^2$$
$$8x^4 - 16x^2 - 64 = 0$$
$$8(x^4 - 2x^2 - 8) = 0$$
$$u^2 - 2u - 8 = 0 \quad \text{Let } u = x^2.$$
$$(u - 4)(u + 2) = 0$$
$$u = 4 \quad \text{or} \quad u = -2$$
$$x = \pm 2 \quad \text{or} \quad x = \pm\sqrt{-2}$$

Since $y = \frac{8}{x}$, if $x = \pm 2$, $y = 4$; if $x = -2$, $y = -4$.

$(2, 4), (-2, -4)$

1. $(3, 2)$ $\left(4, \frac{3}{2}\right)$ **2.** $(3, 5)$ $\left(-\frac{5}{3}, -\frac{13}{3}\right)$ **3.** $\left(\frac{7}{3}, \frac{1}{3}\right)(1, -1)$

4. $(1, -2)$ $\left(\frac{11}{4}, -\frac{9}{8}\right)$ **5.** $(1, 4)$ $\left(\frac{11}{4}, -\frac{5}{4}\right)$

6. $\left(-3, \frac{5}{2}\right)(3, 1)$ **7.** $(0, 2)$ $(3, 1)$ **8.** $\left(\frac{9}{22}, \frac{13}{23}\right)$; $\left(\frac{1}{2}, \frac{1}{3}\right)$

9. $(2, -8)$; $\left(-\frac{40}{3}, -\frac{6}{5}\right)$

10. $(-\sqrt{2}, -\sqrt{14})(-\sqrt{2}, \sqrt{14})(\sqrt{2}, -\sqrt{14})(\sqrt{2}, \sqrt{14})$

11. $(-3, -\sqrt{5}), (-3, \sqrt{5})$ $(3, -\sqrt{5})$ $(3, \sqrt{5})$

12. $(-2, -1)$ $(-1, -2)$, $(1, 2)$ $(2, 1)$

13. $(-4, -2), (-2, -4), (2, 4), (4, 2)$

14. $(-3, -2)$ $(-2, -3)$ $(2, 3)$ $(3, 2)$

15. $(-2, -2)$ $(2, 2)$ $(4, 1)$ $(-4, -1)$ **16.** No solution

17. $(-2, -1)$ $(2, 1)$ **18.** $(2, 4), (-2, 4)$ **19.** No solution

20.
$$x + y = 4$$
$$y = 4 - x$$
$$xy = 1$$
$$x(4 - x) = 1$$
$$4x - x^2 = 1$$
$$0 = x^2 - 4x + 1$$
$$x = \frac{4 \pm \sqrt{16 - 4}}{2} = \frac{4 \pm 2\sqrt{3}}{2} = 2 \pm \sqrt{3}$$

$y = 4 - x$	$y = 4 - x$
$y = 4 - (2 + \sqrt{3})$	$y = 4 - (2 - \sqrt{3})$
$y = 2 - \sqrt{3}$	$y = 2 + \sqrt{3}$
$(2 + \sqrt{3}, 2 - \sqrt{3})$	$(2 - \sqrt{3}, 2 + \sqrt{3})$

21. Consider all $x \geq 0$.
$y = |x| = x$
Substituting into the equation $y = 3x^2$
$$x = 3x^2$$
$$0 = 3x^2 - x$$
$$x = 0 \text{ or } x = \frac{1}{3}$$

Since $y = x$, $y = 0$ or $y = \frac{1}{3}$

Consider all $x < 0$.
$y = |x| = -x$
Substituting into the equation $y = 3x^2$
$$-x = 3x^2$$
$$0 = 3x^2 + x$$
$$x = 0 \text{ or } x = -\frac{1}{3}. \text{ but, since } x < 0, x = -\frac{1}{3}.$$

Since $y = -x$, $y = \frac{1}{3}$.

So the solutions are $\left(\frac{1}{3}, \frac{1}{3}\right)$, $\left(-\frac{1}{3}, \frac{1}{3}\right)$, and $(0, 0)$

22.
$$x^2 + y^2 + 6y + 5 = 0$$
$$x^2 + y^2 - 2x - 8 = 0$$
Eq. ① − Eq. ②
$$x^2 + y^2 + 6y + 5 = 0$$
$$\underline{-x^2 - y^2 + 2x + 8 = 0}$$
$$6y + 2x + 13 = 0$$
$$2x = -6y - 13$$
$$x = -3y - \frac{13}{2}$$

Substituting back in equation ①
$$\left(-3y - \frac{13}{2}\right)^2 + y^2 + 6y + 5 = 0$$
$$9y^2 + 39y + \frac{169}{4} + y^2 + 6y + 5 = 0$$
$$10y^2 + 45y + \frac{189}{4} = 0$$

$$y = \frac{-45 \pm \sqrt{2025 - 4(10)\left(\frac{189}{4}\right)}}{2(10)} = \frac{-45 \pm \sqrt{135}}{20}$$

$$= \frac{-45 \pm 3\sqrt{15}}{20}$$

$$x = -3y - \frac{13}{2}$$

$$x = -3\left(\frac{-45 + 3\sqrt{15}}{20}\right) - \frac{13}{2} = \frac{135 - 9\sqrt{15} - 130}{20}$$

$$= \frac{5 - 9\sqrt{15}}{20} \quad \text{so} \quad \left(\frac{5 - 9\sqrt{15}}{20}, \frac{-45 + 3\sqrt{15}}{20}\right)$$

is one point $\approx (-1.5, -1.67)$.

$$x = -3y - \frac{13}{2}$$

$$x = -3\left(\frac{-45 - 3\sqrt{15}}{20}\right) - \frac{13}{2} = \frac{135 + 9\sqrt{15} - 130}{20}$$

$$= \frac{5 + 9\sqrt{15}}{20}$$

so $\left(\frac{5 + 9\sqrt{15}}{20}, \frac{-45 - 3\sqrt{15}}{20}\right)$ is another point

$\approx (2, -2.83)$.

23. Answers may vary. Examples are:
a. $y = x;\ x^2 + y^2 = 4$
b. $x^2 - 2y^2 = 4;\ x^2 + 2y^2 = 9$
c. $x^2 + y^2 = 9;\ x^2 - y^2 = 9$
d. $y = x^2 + 2x + 3;\ 3x^2 + y^2 = 16$

24.
$$A = \ell w \text{ so } \ell = \frac{A}{w} \text{ and } w = \frac{A}{\ell}$$

$$P = 2\ell + 2w$$

$$P = 2\left(\frac{A}{w}\right) + 2w$$

$$Pw = 2A + 2w^2$$
$$Pw - 2w^2 = 2A$$
$$2w^2 - Pw = -2A$$
$$2w^2 - Pw + 2A = 0$$

$$w^2 - \frac{P}{2}w + A = 0$$

$$w = \frac{\frac{P}{2} \pm \sqrt{\left(\frac{P}{2}\right)^2 - 4A}}{2}$$

$$= \frac{P}{4} \pm \frac{\sqrt{P^2 - 16A}}{4}$$

$$= \frac{1}{4}(P \pm \sqrt{P^2 - 16A}).$$

Assuming $w \le \ell$,

$$\ell = \frac{1}{4}(P + \sqrt{P^2 - 16A}) \text{ and}$$

$$w = \frac{1}{4}(P - \sqrt{P^2 - 16A}).$$

25.
$$\frac{x^2}{a^2} - \frac{y^2}{b^2} = 1$$

Let $y = \pm\frac{b}{a}x$.

$$\frac{x^2}{a^2} - \frac{\left(\pm\frac{b}{a}x\right)^2}{b^2} = 1$$

$$\frac{x^2}{a^2} - \frac{b^2x^2}{a^2b^2} = 1$$

$$\frac{b^2x^2}{a^2b^2} - \frac{b^2x^2}{a^2b^2} = 1$$

$$0 \ne 1$$

There is no number x because the left side simplifies to 0.

26. The distance from $(2, 4)$ to the center must equal the distance from $(3, 3)$ to the center.
$\sqrt{(h - 2)^2 + (k - 4)^2} = \sqrt{(h - 3)^2 + (k - 3)^2}$ but, since (h, k) is a point on the line $y = 3x - 3$, then $k = 3h - 3$.
Substituting in
$\sqrt{(h - 2)^2 + (3h - 7)^2} = \sqrt{(h - 3)^2 + (3h - 6)^2}$
Squaring both sides
$(h - 2)^2 + (3h - 7)^2 = (h - 3)^2 + (3h - 6)^2$
$h^2 - 4h + 4 + 9h^2 - 42h + 49$
$\quad = h^2 - 6h + 9 + 9h^2 - 36h + 36 - 46h + 53$
$\quad = -42h + 45$
$\quad 8 = 4h$
$\quad 2 = h$
So, $k = 3(2) - 3 = 3$.
Center: $(2, 3)$
$r = \sqrt{(2 - 2)^2 + (4 - 3)^2} = \sqrt{0 + 1} = 1$
So, the equation is
$(x - 2)^2 + (y - 3)^2 = 1$

27. $\sqrt{(h - 7)^2 + (k - 3)^2} = \sqrt{(h - 5)^2 + (k - 5)^2}$ Since (h, k) is a point on the line $y = 4x + 1$ then $k = 4h + 1$
$\sqrt{(h - 7)^2 + (4h - 2)^2} = \sqrt{(h - 5)^2 + (4h - 4)^2}$
$(h - 7)^2 + (4h - 2)^2 = (h - 5)^2 + (4h - 4)^2$
$h^2 - 14h + 49 + 16h^2 - 16h + 4$
$\quad = h^2 - 10h + 25 + 16h^2 - 32h + 16 - 30h + 53$
$\quad = -42h + 41$
$\quad 12 = -12h$
$\quad -1 = h$
So, $k = 4(-1) + 1 = -3$.
$r = \sqrt{(5 + 1)^2 + (5 + 3)^2} = \sqrt{6^2 + 8^2} = \sqrt{100} = 10$
$(x + 1)^2 + (y + 3)^2 = 100$

28.

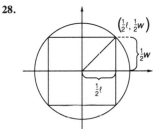

$$x^2 + y^2 = 1$$

$$\left(\frac{1}{2}\ell\right)^2 + \left(\frac{1}{2}w\right)^2 = 1$$

$$\ell^2 + w^2 = 4$$

Since area of rectangle $= 1$, $\ell w = 1$,

$$w = \frac{1}{\ell}.$$

$$\ell^2 + \left(\frac{1}{\ell}\right)^2 = 4$$

$$\ell^2 + \frac{1}{\ell^2} = 4$$

$$\ell^4 + 1 = 4\ell^2$$
$$\ell^4 - 4\ell^2 + 1 = 0$$
$$\ell^2 = \frac{4 \pm \sqrt{16 - 4}}{2} = \frac{4 \pm \sqrt{12}}{2} = \frac{4 \pm 2\sqrt{3}}{2} = 2 \pm \sqrt{3}$$

If $\ell > w$ as shown
$\ell^2 = 2 + \sqrt{3}$
$\ell = \sqrt{2 + \sqrt{3}} \approx 1.93$
Since $(1 + \sqrt{3})^2 = 1 + 2\sqrt{3} + 3 = 4 + 2\sqrt{3}$,

$$\ell = \sqrt{\frac{4 + 2\sqrt{3}}{2}} = \sqrt{\frac{(1 + \sqrt{3})^2}{2}} = \frac{1 + \sqrt{3}}{\sqrt{2}} = \frac{\sqrt{2} + \sqrt{6}}{2}.$$

Since $w = \frac{1}{\ell} = \frac{2}{\sqrt{2} + \sqrt{6}} = \frac{2(\sqrt{2} - \sqrt{6})}{2 - 6}$

$$= \frac{\sqrt{6} - \sqrt{2}}{2} \approx 0.52$$

29. $\sqrt{(2 - 2)^2 + (5 - 7)^2} = \sqrt{0 + 2^2} = 2$

30. $\sqrt{(1 - 6)^2 + (-3 + 8)^2} = \sqrt{5^2 + 5^2} = \sqrt{50} = 5\sqrt{2}$

31. Center: $(0,0)$; radius 7

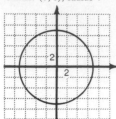

32. a. y-intercept: $(0, 273)$; $(2640, 603)$ **b.** $f(d)\dfrac{1}{8}d + 273$

slope $= \dfrac{603 - 273}{2640} = \dfrac{330}{2640} = \dfrac{1}{8}$

$f(d) = 0.125d + 273$

$500 = \dfrac{1}{8}d + 273$

$227 = \dfrac{1}{8}d$

$1816 = d$; 1816 ft

33. The distance along the old road $= 3 + 4 = 7$. The distance along the new road $= \sqrt{3^2 + 4^2} = 5$. $7 - 5 = 2$ km saved.

34. Yes **35.** No **36.** Yes **37.** No **38.** No **39.** Yes

p. 468   PROBLEM FOR PROGRAMMERS

```
10   REM Chapter 10 Problem
20   INPUT "For Ax^2 + By^2 + Cx + Dy + E = 0;
     Enter A, B, C, D, E   ";A,B,C,D,E
30   IF A = 0 and B = 0   THEN PRINT "Not a
     conic": GOTO 100
40   IF A * B = 0 THEN PRINT "Parabola":
     GOTO 100
50   IF A * B < 0 THEN PRINT "Hyperbola":
     GOTO 100
60 RHT = (H ^ 2 / B + K ^ 2 / A - E / (A * B))
70   IF RHT < 0 THEN PRINT "No real roots":
     GOTO 100
80   IF A = B THEN PRINT "Circle": GOTO 100
90   PRINT "Ellipse"
100  END


10   REM Chapter 10 Challenge Problem
20   INPUT "For Ax^2 + By^2 + Cx + Dy + E = 0;
     Enter A, B, C, D, E   ";A,B,C,D,E
30   IF A = 0 AND B = 0 THEN PRINT "Not a
     conic"; GOTO 750
40   IF A * B = 0 THEN GOSUB 160: GOTO 750
50 H = - (C / (2 * A))
60 K = - (D / (2 * B))
70   PRINT "The center is (";H;", ";K;")"
80 RHT = (H ^ 2) * A + (K ^ 2) * B - E
90 BSQ = RHT / B
100 ASQ = RHT / A
110  IF A * B < 0 THEN GOSUB 360: GOTO 750
120  IF RHT < 0 THEN PRINT "No real roots":
     GOTO 750
130  IF A = B THEN GOSUB 550: GOTO 750
140  GOSUB 600
150  GOTO 750
160  PRINT "The conic is a parabola"
170  IF A = 0 THEN 270
180 H = - (C / (2 * A))
190 K = (C * C - 4 * E * A) / (4 * A * D)
200 P = - (D / (4 * A))
210  PRINT "Standard form: (x - ";H;")^2
     = 4*";P;"(y - ";K;")"
220  PRINT "Vertex: (";H;", ";K;")"
230  PRINT "Focus: (";H;", ";K + P;")"
240  PRINT "Directrix: Y = ";K - P
250  PRINT "Line of symmetry: x = ";H
260  GOTO 350
270 H = (D * D - 4 * E * B) / (4 * B * C)
280 K = - (D / (2 * B))
290 P = - (C / (4* B))
300  PRINT "Standard form: (y - ";K;")^2
     = 4*";P;"(x - ";H;")"
```

```
310  PRINT "Vertex: (";H;", ";K;")"
320  PRINT "Focus: (";H + P;", ";K;")"
330  PRINT "Directrix: x = ";H - P
340  PRINT "Line of symmetry: y = ";K
350  RETURN
360  PRINT "The conic is a hyperbola"
370 ASQ = ABS (ASQ)
380 BSQ = ABS (BSQ)
390 C =  SQR (ASQ + BSQ)
400  IF A < 0 THEN 470
410  PRINT "Standard form: (x - ";H;")^2/";
     ASQ;" - (y - ";K;")^2/";BSQ;" = 1"
420  PRINT "Vertices: (";H + SQR (ASQ);", ";
     K;")"
430  PRINT "             (";H - SQR (ASQ);", ";
     K;")"
440  PRINT "Foci: (";H + C;", ";K;")"
450  PRINT "       (";H - C;", ";K;")"
460  GOTO 520
470  PRINT "Standard form: (y - ";K;")^2/";
     BSQ;"^2 - (x - ";H;")^2/";ASQ;" = 1"
480  PRINT "Vertices: (";H;", ";K + SQR (BSQ);
     ")"
490  PRINT "             (";H;",";K - SQR (BSQ);
     ")"
500  PRINT "Foci: (";H;", ";K + C;")"
510  PRINT "       (";H;", ";K - C;")"
520  PRINT "Asymptotes: y - ";K;" = ";
     SQR (BSQ / ASQ);"(X - ";H;")"
530  PRINT "            Y - ";K;" = ";
     - SQR (BSQ / ASQ);"(X - ";H;")"
540  RETURN
550  PRINT "The conic is a circle"
560 R = SQR ((C * C + D * D - 4 * A * E) /
     (4 * A * A))
570  PRINT "Standard form: (x - ";H;")^2
     + (y - ";K;")^2 = ";R ^ 2
580  PRINT "Radius = ";R
590  RETURN
600  PRINT "The conic is an ellipse"
610  PRINT "Standard form: (x - ";H;")^2/";
     ASQ;" + (y - ";K;")^2/";BSQ;" = 1"
620  PRINT "Vertices: (";H + SQR (ASQ);", ";
     K;")"
630  PRINT "         (";H - SQR (ASQ);", "; K;")"
640  PRINT "         (";H;", ";"K + SQR (BSQ); ")"
650  PRINT "         (";H;", ";"K - SQR (BSQ); ")"
660  IF A < B THEN 710
670 C = SQR ( ABS (BSQ) - ABS (ASQ))
680  PRINT "Foci: (";H;", ";K + C;")"
690  PRINT "         (";H;", ";K - C;")"
700  GOTO 740
710 C = SQR ( ABS (ASQ) - ABS (BSQ))
720  PRINT "Foci: (";H + C;", ";K;")"
730  PRINT "         (";H - C;", ";K;")"
740  RETURN
750  END
```

p. 469   10-8 TRY THIS

a.
$$\ell^2 + (23 - \ell)^2 = 277$$
$$\ell^2 + 529 - 46\ell + \ell^2 = 277$$
$$\ell^2 - 23\ell + 126 = 0$$
$$(\ell - 9)(\ell - 14) = 0$$
14 m, 9 m

b.
$$\ell^2 + (17 - \ell)^2 = 13^2$$
$$\ell^2 + 289 - 34\ell + \ell^2 = 169$$
$$\ell^2 - 17\ell + 60 = 0$$
$$(\ell - 5)(\ell - 12) = 0$$
$$\ell = 12;$$
$$w = 5$$

c. $\ell w = 2$; $w = \dfrac{2}{\ell}$

$$\ell^2 + w^2 = 5$$

$$\ell^2 + \dfrac{4}{\ell^2} = 5$$

$$\ell^4 - 5\ell^2 + 4 = 0$$
$$(\ell^2 - 1)(\ell^2 - 4) = 0$$
$$\ell = \pm 1 \text{ or } \pm 2$$
$\ell = 2$ ft, $w = 1$ ft is the only solution that makes sense.

pp. 470–471   10-8 EXERCISES

1. 6 cm, 8 cm   **2.** 1 m, 2 m   **3.** 4 in., 5 in.

4. 1 yd, 2 yd   **5.** 12, 13 and $-12, -13$

6. 6, 10 and $-6, -10$ **7.** $\ell = \sqrt{3}$ m, $w = 1$ m

8. $\ell = \sqrt{2}$ m, $w = 1$ m   **9.** 16 ft, 24 ft

10. Principal = \$125, $r = 6\%$ **11.** 9, 7   **12.** 8, 7

13. $b^2 + h^2 = 2500$

$$\frac{1}{2}bh = 600$$

$$h = \frac{1200}{b}$$

Substituting into the equation

$$b^2 + \left(\frac{1200}{b}\right)^2 = 2500$$

$$b^2 + \frac{1,440,000}{b^2} = 2500$$

$$b^4 + 1,440,000 = 2500b^2$$
$$b^4 - 2500b^2 + 1,440,000 = 0$$
$$(b^2 - 1600)(b^2 - 900) = 0$$
$$b^2 = 1600 \qquad b^2 = 900$$
$$b = 40 \qquad b = 30$$

$$h = \frac{1200}{b} = 30 \qquad h = \frac{1200}{b} = 40$$

Legs are 30 cm and 40 cm.

14.
$$\ell w = 60$$
$$\ell = \frac{60}{w}$$
$$\ell^2 + w^2 = 13^2$$
$$\left(\frac{60}{w}\right) + w^2 = 169$$
$$\frac{3600}{w^2} + w^2 = 169$$
$$3600 + w^4 = 169w^2$$
$$w^4 - 169w^2 + 3600 = 0$$
$$(w^2 - 144)(w^2 - 25) = 0$$
$$w^2 = 144 \qquad w^2 = 25$$
$$w = 12 \qquad w = 5$$

$$\ell = \frac{60}{w} = 5 \qquad \ell = \frac{60}{w} = 12$$

Length is 12 m, width is 5 m.

15. $x^2 + \frac{1}{2}x(16 - x) = 130$

$$x^2 - 16x - 260 = 0$$
$$(x - 10)(x + 26) = 0$$
$$x = 10$$
10 by 10 and 5 by 6

16.

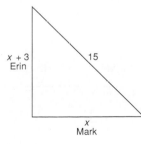

$$(x + 3)^2 + x^2 = 15^2$$
$$x^2 + 6x + 9 + x^2 = 225$$
$$2x^2 + 6x - 216 = 0$$
$$x^2 + 3x - 108 = 0$$
$$(x + 12)(x - 9) = 0$$
$x = 9$ miles Mark walked
$x + 3 = 12$ miles Erin walked
Rate is equal to distance divided by time (3h).
Erin 4 mi/h, Mark 3 mi/h

17. Let x = the number of days the carpenter would take to do the entire job alone. Then $x + 4$ = the number of days the helper would take to do the entire job alone.

	rate	time spent	Amount = (rate)(time)
carpenter	$\dfrac{1 \text{ job}}{x \text{ days}}$	$5\dfrac{5}{7}$	$\left(\dfrac{1}{x}\right)\left(5\dfrac{5}{7}\right)$
helper	$\dfrac{1 \text{ job}}{(x + 4) \text{ days}}$	$3\dfrac{5}{7}$	$\left(\dfrac{1}{x} + 4\right)\left(3\dfrac{5}{7}\right)$

Total amount completed = $\left(\dfrac{1}{x}\right)\left(5\dfrac{5}{7}\right) + \left(\dfrac{1}{x + 4}\right)\left(3\dfrac{5}{7}\right)$

$$\left(\frac{1}{x}\right)\left(5\frac{5}{7}\right) + \left(\frac{1}{x} + 4\right)\left(3\frac{5}{7}\right) = 1 \text{ job finished}$$

$$\left(\frac{1}{x}\right)\left(\frac{40}{7}\right) + \left(\frac{1}{x + 4}\right)\left(\frac{26}{7}\right) = 1$$

$$\frac{40}{x} + \frac{26}{x + 4} = 7 \qquad \text{multiply by } (x)(x + 4)$$

$$40(x + 4) + 26(x) = 7x(x + 4)$$
$$40x + 160 + 26x = 7x^2 + 28x$$
$$0 = 7x^2 - 38x - 160$$

$$x = \frac{38 \pm \sqrt{5924}}{14} = \frac{19 \pm \sqrt{1481}}{7}$$

Since $x > 0$, $x = \dfrac{19 + \sqrt{1481}}{7} \approx 8.21$ days (carpenter)

helper = $x + 4 = \dfrac{47 + \sqrt{1481}}{7} = 12.21$ days

18. a.

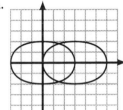

The second ellipse is simply the first ellipse shifted $a = 3$ units to the right. To do that, simply substitute $x - 3$ for x in the first equation to get $4(x - 3)^2 + 9y^2 = 36$ or

$$\frac{(x - 3)^2}{9} + \frac{y^2}{4} = 1$$

b. $4(x - 3)^2 + 9y^2 = 36$
$\underline{-(4x^2 + 9y^2) = -36}$
$4(x - 3)^2 - 4x^2 = 0$
$(x - 3)^2 - x^2 = 0$
$x^2 - 6x + 9 - x^2 = 0$
$9 = 6x$

$$\frac{3}{2} = x$$

$$4x^2 + 9y^2 = 36$$

$$4\left(\frac{3}{2}\right)^2 + 9y^2 = 36$$

$$9y^2 = 36 - 9 = 27$$
$$y^2 = 3$$
$$y = \pm\sqrt{3}$$

points of intersection: $\left(\dfrac{3}{2}, +\sqrt{3}\right)$ and $\left(\dfrac{3}{2}, -\sqrt{3}\right)$

19. $\left(\dfrac{3 + 3}{2}, \dfrac{11 + 9}{2}\right) = (3, 10)$

20. $\left(\dfrac{6 + 11}{2}, \dfrac{-7 + 4}{2}\right) = \left(\dfrac{17}{2}, \dfrac{3}{2}\right)$

Algebra and Trigonometry **151**

21. $y = ax^2 + bx + c$

    ① $5 = a(1)^2 + b(1) + c$ or $a + b + c = 5$
    ② $-7 = a(-1)^2 + b(-1) + c$ or $a - b + c = -7$
    ③ $-7 = a(-2)^2 + b(-2) + c$ or $4a - 2b + c = -7$

Eq. ① − Eq. ② $a + b + c = 5$
$$\frac{-a + b - c = 7}{2b = 12}$$
$$b = 6$$

Eq. ① − Eq. ③ $a + b + c = 5$
$$\frac{-4a + 2b - c = 7}{-3a + 3b = 12}$$
$$-3a + 3(6) = 12$$
$$-3a = -6$$
$$a = 2$$

$a + b + c = 5$
$2 + 6 + c = 5$
$ c = -3$
$y = 2x^2 + 6x - 3$

22. $y = ax^2 + bx + c$

    ① $3 = a(1)^2 + b(1) + c$ or $a + b + c = 3$
    ② $11 = a(2)^2 + b(2) + c$ or $4a + 2b + c = 11$
    ③ $5 = a(-1)^2 + b(-1) + c$ or $a - b + c = 5$

Eq. ① − Eq. ③ $a + b + c = 3$
$$\frac{-a + b - c = -5}{2b = -2}$$
$$b = -1$$

Eq. ② − Eq. ③ $4a + 2b + c = 11$
$$\frac{-a + b - c = -5}{3a + 3b = 6}$$
$$3a + 3(-1) = 6$$
$$3a = 9$$
$$a = 3$$

$a + b + c = 3$
$3 - 1 + c = 1$
$ c = 1$
$y = 3x^2 - x + 1$

---

p. 473   10-9 PROBLEM SOLVING: STRATEGIES

1. Strategy: Draw a diagram; make an organized list

Number of lines	Maximum number of Regions
1	$2 = 1 + 1$
2	$4 = 1 + 2 + 1$
3	$7 = 1 + 2 + 3 + 1$
4	$11 = 1 + 2 + 3 + 4 + 1$
5	Should be $16 = 1 + 2 + 3 + 4 + 5 + 1$
6	Should be $22 = 1 + 2 + 3 + 4 + 5 + 6 + 1$

There would be 22 sections with 6 paths.

2. Strategy: Write equations
  Let c = volume of a carton
     b = volume of a box
  $24c + 20b = 1$ (1 truckload)
   $6c + 13b = 0.5$

Eq. ① − 4Eq. ② $24c + 20b = 1$
$$\frac{-24c - 52b = -2}{-32b = -1}$$
$$b = \frac{1}{32}$$

1 box is $\frac{1}{32}$ of a truckload, so the trailer can carry 32 boxes.

Substituting
$$24c + 20\left(\frac{1}{32}\right) = 1$$
$$24c = 1 - \frac{20}{32} = \frac{32}{32} - \frac{20}{32} = \frac{3}{8}$$

$$c = \frac{1}{24}\left(\frac{3}{8}\right) = \frac{1}{64}$$

64 cartons will fill the trailer.

3. Strategy: Simplify the problem
  Suppose 4 teams play (teams A, B, C, D).
  A vs. B   winner 1 vs. winner 2
  C vs. D
  2 games +   1 game = 3 games played.
  Suppose 8 teams play (teams A, B, C, D, E, F, G, H).

  A vs. B   winner 1
  C vs. D   winner 2   vs   winner 1
                       vs.
  E vs. F   winner 3
  G vs. H   winner 4   vs   winner 2

  4 games + 2 games   + 1 game = 7 games
  generalize:
  16 teams   means   15 games.
  32 teams   means   31 games.
  64 teams   means   63 games.
  A total of 63 games (1 less than the number of teams) were needed to determine the championship.

4. Strategy: Make a table

Number of rows	Number of blocks
1	1
2	$5 = 1^2 + 2^2$
3	$14 = 1^2 + 2^2 + 3^2$
4	$30 = 1^2 + 2^2 + 3^2 + 4^2$
5	$55 = 1^2 + 2^2 + 3^2 + 4^2 + 5^2$
6	$91 = 1^2 + 2^2 + 3^2 + 4^2 + 5^2$

You will have 9 blocks left over. The bottom row should be 6 by 6 to use the most blocks.

5. Strategy: Write an equation
  Let x = number in Roosevelt band;
        y = number in Central High band;
        z = number in Riverside band.
  $x + y = 385$ ①
  $x + z = 320$ ②
      $y = 65 + z$ ③
      $x = 70 + z$ or $x - z = 70$ ④

Eq. ② + Eq. ④ $x + z = 320$
$$\frac{x - z = 70}{2x = 390}$$
$$x = 195$$

$x + z = 320$ $x + y = 385$
$195 + z = 320$ $195 + y = 385$
$ z = 125$ $ y = 190$

Roosevelt 195, Central High 190, Riverside 125

---

p. 474   PROBLEM SOLVING: APPLICATION

1. **a.** 1,800,000,000 mi (1.8 billion)
    b. $1{,}800{,}000{,}000 \div 93{,}000{,}000 \approx 19$ AU
    c. $1{,}800{,}000{,}000 \div 6{,}000{,}000{,}000{,}000 \approx 3 \times 10^{-4}$ light-years

2. **a.** January 24, 1986–September 5, 1977 = 3063 days
    b. $24 \times 3063 = 73{,}512$ hours

3. $1{,}800{,}000{,}000 \div 73{,}512 \approx 24{,}000$ miles per hour

4. $186{,}000 \times 3600 \approx 670{,}000{,}000$ or 6.7×10^8 mi/h

5. $\dfrac{6.7 \times 10^8}{2.2 \times 10^4} \approx 30{,}400 : 1$ **6.** $234{,}000 \div 186{,}000 \approx 1.26$ s

7. $22{,}013 \times 73{,}512 \approx 1.62 \times 10^9$

---

pp. 475–477   CHAPTER 10 SUMMARY AND REVIEW

1. $\sqrt{(7 - (-3))^2 + (0 - 4)^2}$ **2.** $\sqrt{(4 - 0)^2 + (0 - 3)^2}$
   $= \sqrt{100 + 16}$ $= \sqrt{16 + 9}$
   $= \sqrt{116}$ $= \sqrt{25}$
   $= 2\sqrt{29}$ $= 5$

3. $\sqrt{(-9-2)^2 + (6+4)^2}$
$= \sqrt{121 + 100}$
$= \sqrt{221}$

4. $\left(-\dfrac{3+7}{2}, \dfrac{4+0}{2}\right) = (2,2)$

5. $\left(-\dfrac{2+6}{2}, \dfrac{4+8}{2}\right) = (2,6)$

6. $\left(-\dfrac{8+4}{2}, -\dfrac{1+5}{2}\right) = (-2,2)$

7. $\left(\dfrac{0+10}{2}, \dfrac{3+7}{2}\right) = (5,5)$

8. $(x+2)^2 + (y-6)^2 = 13$

9. $(x-3)^2 + (y+1)^2 = 4$

10. $(4,-3);\ 2\sqrt{3}$

11. $(0,0);\ 6$

12. $x^2 - 6x + y^2 + 10y + 24 = 0$
$(x-3)^2 + (y+5)^2 = 10$
$(3,-5);\ \sqrt{10}$

13. $x^2 - \dfrac{3}{2}x + y^2 - \dfrac{5}{2}y + \dfrac{3}{2} = 0$
$\left(x - \dfrac{3}{4}\right)^2 + \left(y - \dfrac{5}{4}\right)^2 = \dfrac{10}{16}$
$\left(\dfrac{3}{4}, \dfrac{5}{4}\right);\ \dfrac{\sqrt{10}}{4}$

14. $16x^2 - 64x + 25y^2 + 50y - 311 = 0$
$16(x^2 - 4x) + 25(y^2 + 2y) = 311$
$16(x-2)^2 + 25(y+1)^2 = 400$
$$\dfrac{(x-2)^2}{25} + \dfrac{(y+1)^2}{16} = 1$$

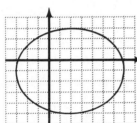

Center: $(2,-1)$; vertices:
$(7,-1)$, $(-3,-1)$,
$(2,3)$, $(2,-5)$;
foci: $(5,-1)$, $(-1,-1)$

15. $9x^2 + 36x + 16y^2 - 32y = 92$
$9(x^2 + 4x) + 16(y^2 - 2y) = 92$
$9(x+2)^2 + 16(y-1)^2 = 144$
$$\dfrac{(x+2)^2}{16} + \dfrac{(y-1)^2}{9} = 1$$
Center: $(-2,1)$; vertices: $(-6,1)$, $(2,1)$, $(-2,4)$, $(-2,-2)$;
foci: $(-2+\sqrt{7},1)$, $(-2-\sqrt{7},1)$

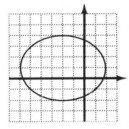

16. $x^2 + 4x - 2y^2 + y - \dfrac{1}{8} = 0$
$(x+2)^2 - 2\left(y^2 - \dfrac{1}{2}y\right) = \dfrac{33}{8}$
$(x+2)^2 - 2\left(y - \dfrac{1}{4}\right)^2 = 4$
$$\dfrac{(x+2)^2}{4} - \dfrac{\left(y - \dfrac{1}{4}\right)^2}{2} = 1$$

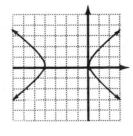

Center: $\left(-2, \dfrac{1}{4}\right)$; vertices: $\left(0, \dfrac{1}{4}\right)$, $\left(-4, \dfrac{1}{4}\right)$;
foci: $\left(-2+\sqrt{6}, \dfrac{1}{4}\right)$, $\left(-2-\sqrt{6}, \dfrac{1}{4}\right)$;
asymptotes: $y - \dfrac{1}{4} = \pm\dfrac{\sqrt{2}}{2}(x+2)$

17. $\dfrac{x^2}{6} - \dfrac{y^2}{16} = 1$

Center: $(0,0)$; vertices: $(\sqrt{6},0)$, $(-\sqrt{6},0)$;
foci: $(\sqrt{22},0)$, $(-\sqrt{22},0)$; asymptotes: $y = \pm\dfrac{2\sqrt{6}}{3}x$

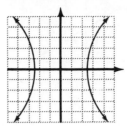

18. $y^2 = 4(-3x)$

Vertex: $(0,0)$; focus: $(-3,0)$; directrix: $x = 3$

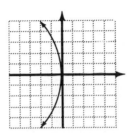

19. $(x-1)^2 = 2(y+1)$
$(x-1)^2 = 4\left[\dfrac{1}{2}(y+1)\right]$
Vertex: $(1,-1)$; focus: $\left(1, -\dfrac{1}{2}\right)$;
directrix: $y = -\dfrac{3}{2}$

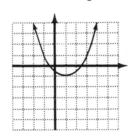

20. $y^2 + 2y = -4(x-2)$
$(y+1)^2 = -4x + 9$
$(y+1)^2 = -4\left(x + \dfrac{9}{4}\right)$
Vertex: $\left(\dfrac{9}{4}, -1\right)$; focus: $\left(\dfrac{5}{4}, -1\right)$;
directrix: $x = \dfrac{13}{4}$

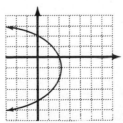

21. Hyperbola   **22.** Parabola   **23.** Circle
24. Ellipse   **25.** no conic

26. $(6, 8)$; $(-8, -6)$ **27.** $(1, 2)$; $\left(-\frac{3}{2}, \frac{13}{4}\right)$

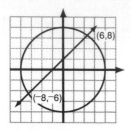 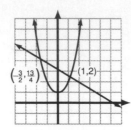

28. $(4, 0)$, $(-4, 0)$

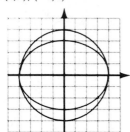

29.
$$3x = 12 - 4y$$
$$x = 4 - \frac{4}{3}y$$
$$\frac{\left(4 - \frac{4}{3}y\right)^2}{16} + \frac{y^2}{9} = 1$$
$$1 - \frac{2}{3}y + \frac{1}{9}y^2 + \frac{1}{9}y^2 = 1$$
$$\frac{2}{9}y^2 - \frac{2}{3}y = 0$$
$$2y^2 - 6y = 0$$
$$2y(y - 3) = 0$$
$$y = 0 \quad \text{or} \quad y = 3$$
$$3x + 4(0) = 12 \qquad 3x + 4(3) = 12$$
$$3x = 12 \qquad\qquad 3x = 0$$
$$x = 4 \qquad\qquad\quad x = 0$$
$$(4, 0) \qquad\qquad\quad (0, 3)$$

30.
$$y^2 = 13 + 3x^2$$
$$x^2 + (13 + 3x^2) = 29$$
$$4x^2 = 16$$
$$x^2 = 4$$
$$x = \pm 2$$
$$y^2 = 25$$
$$y = \pm 5$$
$$(2, 5) \ (2, -5)$$
$$(-2, 5) \ (-2, -5)$$

31. $x = -\frac{12}{y}$
$$4\left(\frac{144}{y^2}\right) - 9y^2 = 108$$
$$576 - 9y^4 = 108y^2$$
$$9y^4 + 108y^2 - 576 = 0$$
$$y^4 + 12y^2 - 64 = 0$$
$$(y^2 - 4)(y^2 + 16) = 0$$
$$y^2 = 4$$
$$y = \pm 2$$
$$x = -\frac{12}{2} = -6$$
$$x = \frac{-12}{2} = 6 \qquad (6, -2) \ (-6, 2)$$

32. $LW = 240$
$$L^2 + W^2 = 26^2$$
$$L^2 = 676 - W^2$$
$$L = \sqrt{676 - W^2} = 26 - W$$

$$(26 - W) \cdot W = 240$$
$$26W - W^2 = 240$$
$$W^2 - 26W + 240 = 0$$
$$(W - 24)(W - 10) = 0$$
$$W = 24 \quad \text{or} \quad W = 10$$
$$\text{dimensions } 24 \times 10$$

33. $xy = -48$
$$x^2 + y^2 = 265$$
$$x^2 = 265 - y^2$$
$$x = \sqrt{265 - y^2}$$
$$(\sqrt{265 - y^2})y = -48$$
$$(265 - y^2)y^2 = 2304$$
$$y^4 - 265y^2 + 2304 = 0$$
$$(y^2 - 9)(y^2 - 256) = 0$$
$$y^2 = 9 \qquad y = \pm 3$$
$$y^2 = 256 \qquad y = \pm 16$$
Solutions are 3 and -16; -3 and 16.

p. 477   **CHAPTER 10 TEST**

1. $\sqrt{(-3 - 7)^2 + (4 - 6)^2}$ **2.** $\sqrt{(42)^2 + (-1 - 0)^2}$
$$= \sqrt{100 + 4} \qquad\qquad\quad = \sqrt{36 + 1}$$
$$= \sqrt{104} \qquad\qquad\qquad\quad = \sqrt{37}$$
$$= 2\sqrt{26}$$

3. $\left(-\frac{3 + 7}{2}, \frac{4 + 6}{2}\right) = (2, 5)$ **4.** $\left(-\frac{2 + 0}{2}, -\frac{3 + 1}{2}\right) = (-1, -1)$

5. $(x - 4)^2 + (y + 1)^2 = 25$ **6.** $x^2 - 8x + y^2 + 12y = -49$
$$(x - 4)^2 + (y + 6)^2 = 3$$
$$\text{Center } (4, -6); \text{ radius } \sqrt{3}$$

7. $x^2 - 6x + 4y^2 + 24y + 41 = 0$
$$(x - 3)^2 + 4(y^2 + 6y) = -32$$
$$(x - 3)^2 + 4(y + 3)^2 = 4$$
$$\frac{(x - 3)^2}{4} + (y + 3)^2 = 1$$

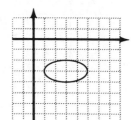

Center: $(3, -3)$
Vertices: $(1, -3)$, $(3, -2)$, $(5, -3)$, $(3, -4)$
Foci: $(3 + \sqrt{3}, -3)$, $(3 - \sqrt{3}, -3)$

8. $\frac{x^2}{9} - \frac{y^2}{25} = 1$

Center: $(0, 0)$
Vertices: $(3, 0)$, $(-3, 0)$
Foci: $(\sqrt{34}, 0)$, $(-\sqrt{34}, 0)$

Asymptotes: $y = \frac{5}{3}x$, $y = -\frac{5}{3}x$

9. $x^2 + 2x + 6y - 11 = 0$
$$(x + 1)^2 + 6y - 12 = 0$$
$$(x + 1)^2 = -6y + 12$$
$$(x + 1)^2 = 4\left(-\frac{3}{2}y + 3\right)$$

Vertex: $(-1, 2)$; Focus: $\left(-1, \frac{1}{2}\right)$;

Directrix: $y = \frac{7}{2}$

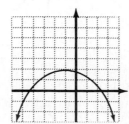

10. $2x^2 + 2x - 5y^2 - 3y - 6 = 0$

$$2(x^2 + x) - 5\left(y^2 + \frac{3}{5}y\right) = 6$$

$$2\left(x + \frac{1}{2}\right)^2 - 5\left(y + \frac{3}{10}\right)^2 = \frac{121}{20}$$

Hyperbola

11.

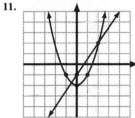

$(2, 2)$

$\left(-\frac{1}{2}, -\frac{7}{4}\right)$

12.

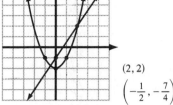

$(7, 5)$

$(-5, -7)$

13.

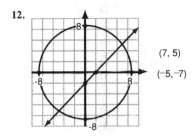

$(5, 0)$

$(0, 5)$

14.
$y^2 = x + 4$
$3x^2 - 8(x + 4) = 3$
$3x^2 - 8x - 35 = 0$
$(3x + 7)(x - 5) = 0$
$x = 5 \quad \text{or} \quad x = -\frac{7}{3}$

$(5, 3) \ (5, -3)$

$\left(-\frac{7}{3}, \sqrt{\frac{5}{3}}\right)\left(-\frac{7}{3}, -\sqrt{\frac{5}{3}}\right)$

15.
$x^2 - (x - 9)^2 = 153$
$x^2 - x^2 + 18x - 81 = 153$
$18x = 234$
$x = 13$

13 and 4

16. Since it is a circle, the distance from the center to $(0, -2)$ should equal the distance from the center to $(6, 6)$.

$$\sqrt{(x - 0)^2 + (x - 1 + 2)^2} = \sqrt{(x - 6)^2 + (x - 1 - 6)^2}$$
$$x^2 + (x + 1)^2 = (x - 6)^2 + (x - 7)^2$$
$$28x = 84$$
$$x = 3$$
$$x - 1 = 2$$

Center $(3, 2)$
$(x - 3)^2 + (y - 2)^2 = 25$

CHAPTER 11

p. 478   READY FOR POLYNOMIAL FUNCTIONS?

1. $(x + 3)(x - 2)$ **2.** $(x - 4)(x - 1)$ **3.** $(3x - 1)(x + 1)$

4. $(x + 2)(2x + 3)$ **5.** $(x - 1)(4x + 5)$ **6.** $(x - 3)(x - 8)$

7. $-3 - 8i$ **8.** $2 + 4i$ **9.** 26   **10.** 13   **11.** 37

12. Yes   **13.** No   **14.** No

15. $x^3 - 4ix^2 + 2x^2 - 8ix - 3x - 6 = 0$

16. $(-1 - i)^2 = 1 + 2i + i^2$ **17.** $3x^2 + 13x - 10 = 0$
$= 1 + 2i - 1$
$= 2i, 1 + i$

18. $4x^2 + 4x - 3 = 0$ **19.** $x^2 - 2 = 0$

pp. 481–483   11-1 TRY THIS

a. (1) $P(0) = 0^3 + 0^2 - 2(0) = 0$; Yes
(2) $P(i) = i^3 + i^2 - 2i = i - 1 - 2i = -3i$; No

b. (1) $P(2i) = (2i)^4 - 2(2i)^3 + 4(2i)^2 - 8(2i)$
$= 16 + 16i - 16 - 16i$
$= 0$; Yes
(2) $P(-2) = (-2)^4 - 2(-2)^3 + 4(-2) - 8(-2)$
$= 16 + 16 + 16 + 16$
$= 64$; No

c. (1)
$$\begin{array}{r|rrrr} 3 & 1 & 2 & -5 & -6 \\ & & 3 & 15 & 30 \\ \hline & 1 & 5 & 10 & 24 \end{array}$$
No
(2)
$$\begin{array}{r|rrrr} -1 & 1 & 2 & -5 & -6 \\ & & -1 & -1 & 6 \\ \hline & 1 & 1 & -6 & 0 \end{array}$$
Yes

d. (1)
$$x^2 + 3x + 1 \overline{\smash{\big)}\, x^4 + 3x^3 + 0x^2 - 3x - 1} \quad \underline{x^2 - 1}$$
$$\underline{x^4 + 3x^3 + x^2}$$
$$-x^2$$
$$\underline{-x^2 - 3x - 1}$$
$$0$$
Yes

(2)
$$x^3 + 2x^2 - 2x + 1 \overline{\smash{\big)}\, x^4 + 3x^3 + 0x^2 - 3x - 1} \quad \underline{x + 1}$$
$$\underline{x^4 + 2x^3 - 2x^2 + x}$$
$$x^3 + 2x^2 - 4x - 1$$
$$\underline{x^3 + 2x^2 - 2x + 1}$$
$$-2x - 2$$
No

e.
$$\begin{array}{r|rrrr} 3 & 1 & 2 & -5 & -6 \\ & & 3 & 15 & 30 \\ \hline & 1 & 5 & 10 & 24 \end{array}$$
$$x^3 + 2x^2 - 5x - 6 = (x - 3)(x^2 + 5x + 10) + 24$$

pp. 483–484   11-1 EXERCISES

1. Yes, no, no   **2.** No, no, no   **3.** Yes, no, yes, yes

4. Yes, no, yes, yes   **5. a.** Yes   **b.** No   **c.** No

6. a. No   **b.** No   **c.** No   **7. a.** Yes   **b.** Yes   **c.** No

8. a. No   **b.** Yes   **c.** No

9. a. Yes   **b.** Yes   **c.** Yes

10. a. No   **b.** Yes   **c.** No

11. a. $x^3 + 6x^2 - x - 30 = (x - 2)(x^2 + 8x + 15) + 0$
b. $x^3 + 6x^2 - x - 30 = (x - 3)(x^2 + 9x + 26) + 48$

12. a. $2x^3 - 3x^2 + x - 1 = (x - 2)(2x^2 + x + 3) + 5$
b. $2x^3 - 3x^2 + x - 1 = (x - 3)(2x^2 + 3x + 10) + 29$

13. $x^3 - 8 = (x + 2)(x^2 - 2x + 4) + (-16)$

14. $x^3 + 27 = (x + 1)(x^2 - x + 1) + 26$

15. $x^4 + 9x^2 + 20 = (x^2 + 4)(x^2 + 5) + 0$

16. $x^4 + x^2 + 2 = (x^2 + x + 1)(x^2 - x + 1) + 1$

17. $5x^5 - 3x^4 + 2x^2 - 3 =$

$$(2x^2 - x + 1)\left(\frac{5}{2}x^3 - \frac{1}{4}x^2 - \frac{11}{8}x + \frac{17}{16}\right) + \frac{29x - 55}{16}$$

18. $6x^5 + 4x^4 - 3x^2 + x - 2 =$

$$(3x^2 + 2x - 1)\left(2x^3 + \frac{2}{3}x - \frac{13}{9}\right) + \frac{41x - 31}{9}$$

Chapter 10 Test–Lesson 11-1

Algebra and Trigonometry   **155**

19.
$$D(x) \cdot Q(x) = (x + 3)(2x^2 + x - 3)$$
$$= 2x^3 + x^2 - 3x + 6x^2 + 3x - 9$$
$$= 2x^3 + 7x^2 - 9$$
$$D(x) \cdot Q(x) + R(x) = (2x^3 + 7x^2 - 9) + 4 = 2x^3 + 7x^2 - 5$$

20.
$$D(x) \cdot Q(x) = (4x - 3)(x^2 + x + 2)$$
$$= 4x^3 + 4x^2 + 8x - 3x^2 - 3x - 6$$
$$= 4x^3 + x^2 + 5x - 6$$
$$D(x) \cdot Q(x) + R(x) = (4x^3 + x^2 + 5x - 6) + (2x + 1)$$
$$= 4x^3 + x^2 + 7x - 5$$

21.
$$D(x) \cdot Q(x) = (x^2 - x + 3)(6x - 2)$$
$$= 6x^3 - 6x^2 + 18x - 2x^2 + 2x - 6$$
$$= 6x^3 - 8x^2 + 20x - 6$$
$$D(x) \cdot Q(x) + R(x) = (6x^3 - 8x^2 + 20x - 6) + (3x + 2)$$
$$= 6x^3 - 8x^2 + 23x - 4$$

22. When the graph is translated 3 units left, then the zeroes are translated 3 units left. So, if 2 is a zero of the new graph, 5 is a zero of the old graph. Thus, the original function has zeroes of 2 and 5.

23. a. $P(-i) = 2(-i)^2 - i(-i) + 1$
$$= 2(-1) - 1 + 1$$
$$= -2$$

b.
$$\begin{array}{r|rrr} -i & 2 & -i & 1 \\ & & -2i & -3 \\ \hline & 2 & -3i & -2 \text{ Remainder} \end{array}$$

24. a. $P(i) = 2(i)^2 + i(i) - 1$
$$= -2 - 1 - 1$$
$$= -4$$

b.
$$\begin{array}{r|rrr} i & 2 & i & -1 \\ & & 2i & -3 \\ \hline & 2 & 3i & -4 \text{ Remainder} \end{array}$$

25. All exponents even; Yes   **26.** All exponents odd; Yes

27. Even   **28.** Odd   **29.** Neither   **30.** Odd

31.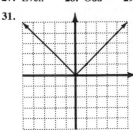

32.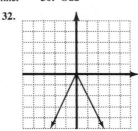

33.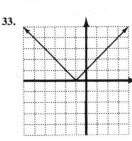

34. $x^2 + \dfrac{1}{2}x + \dfrac{1}{16} = 0 + \dfrac{1}{16}$
$$\left(x + \dfrac{1}{4}\right)^2 = \dfrac{1}{16}$$
$$x + \dfrac{1}{4} = \pm\dfrac{1}{4}$$
$$x = -\dfrac{1}{4} \pm \dfrac{1}{4}$$
$$x = 0 \quad \text{or} \quad -\dfrac{1}{2}$$

35. $y^2 - \dfrac{2}{3}y + \dfrac{1}{9} = 1 + \dfrac{1}{9}$
$$\left(y - \dfrac{1}{3}\right)^2 = \dfrac{10}{9}$$
$$y - \dfrac{1}{3} = \dfrac{\pm\sqrt{10}}{3}$$
$$y = \dfrac{1 \pm \sqrt{10}}{3}$$

36. $a^2 - \dfrac{m}{n}a + \dfrac{m^2}{4n^2} = 0 + \dfrac{m^2}{4n^2}$
$$\left(a - \dfrac{m}{2n}\right)^2 = \dfrac{m^2}{4n^2}$$
$$a - \dfrac{m}{2n} = \pm\dfrac{m}{2n}$$
$$a = \dfrac{m}{2n} \pm \dfrac{m}{2n}$$
$$a = \dfrac{m}{n} \quad \text{or} \quad 0$$

37.   7 math at 4 pts = 28
      10 chemistry at 6 pts = 60
      7 math and 10 chemistry = 88
a. 7 math, 10 chemistry
b. 88 points

p. 484   WRITING TO LEARN

The equation $P(x) = 0$ is true when the function $P(x)$ crosses the x-axis. The solution of an equation makes the equation true, a zero of a function is the value that makes the function true.

pp. 485–488   11-2 TRY THIS

a.
$$\begin{array}{r|rrrrr} 10 & 1 & -2 & -7 & 1 & 0 & 20 \\ & & 10 & 80 & 730 & 7310 & 73{,}100 \\ \hline & 1 & 8 & 73 & 731 & 7310 & 73{,}120 \end{array}$$
$$\begin{array}{r|rrrrr} -8 & 1 & -2 & -7 & 1 & 0 & 20 \\ & & -8 & 80 & -584 & 4664 & -37{,}312 \\ \hline & 1 & -10 & 73 & -583 & 4664 & -37{,}292 \end{array}$$
$$P(10) = 73{,}120$$
$$P(-8) = -37{,}292$$

b.
$$\begin{array}{r|rrrr} 2 & 1 & 6 & -1 & -30 \\ & & 2 & 16 & 30 \\ \hline & 1 & 8 & 15 & 0 \end{array}$$
Yes

c.
$$\begin{array}{r|rrrr} 5 & 1 & 6 & -1 & -30 \\ & & 5 & 55 & 270 \\ \hline & 1 & 11 & 54 & 240 \end{array}$$
No

d.
$$\begin{array}{r|rrrr} -3 & 1 & 6 & -1 & -30 \\ & & -3 & -9 & 30 \\ \hline & 1 & 3 & -10 & 0 \end{array}$$
Yes

e.
$$\begin{array}{r|rrrrr} \frac{1}{2} & 4 & 2 & 0 & 8 & -1 \\ & & 2 & 2 & 1 & \frac{9}{2} \\ \hline & 4 & 4 & 2 & 9 & \frac{7}{2} \end{array}$$
No

f.
$$\begin{array}{r|rrrr} -5 & 1 & 0 & 0 & 0 & -625 \\ & & -5 & 25 & -125 & 625 \\ \hline & 1 & -5 & 25 & -125 & 0 \end{array}$$
Yes

g.
$$\begin{array}{r|rrrr} 2 & 1 & 6 & -1 & -30 \\ & & 2 & 16 & 30 \\ \hline & 1 & 8 & 15 & 0 \end{array}$$
$$x^3 + 6x^2 - x - 30 = (x - 2)(x^2 + 8x + 15)$$
$$= (x - 2)(x + 3)(x + 5)$$
$$P(x) = (x - 2)(x + 3)(x + 5); \ 2, \ -3, \ -5$$

pp. 488–489   11-2 EXERCISES

1. $P(1) = 0; P(-2) = -60; P(3) = 0$

2. $P(-3) = 69; P(-2) = 41; P(1) = -7$

3. $P(20) = 5{,}935{,}988; P(-3) = -772$

4. $P(-10) = -220{,}050; P(5) = -750$

5. Yes, no   **6.** Yes, no   **7.** No, no   **8.** Yes, yes, yes

9. No   **10.** Yes   **11.** Yes   **12.** Yes   **13.** Yes   **14.** No

15. a. Yes   **b.** $x^2 + 3x + 2$
c. $(x - 1)(x + 2)(x + 1)$ **d.** $1, -2, -1$

16. a. Yes   **b.** $x^2 + 3x - 4$
c. $(x + 1)(x + 4)(x - 1)$ **d.** $-1, -4, 1$

17. $P(x) = (x - 1)(x + 2)(x + 3); 1, 2, -3$

18. $P(x) = (x - 2)(x + 3)(x + 4); 2, -3, -4$

19. $P(x) = (x - 2)(x - 5)(x + 1); 2, 5, -1$

20. $P(x) = (x - 1)(x - 2)(x + 5); 1, 2, -5$

21. $P(x) = (x - 2)(x - 3)(x + 4); 2, 3, -4$

156 *Algebra and Trigonometry*

22. $P(x) = (x - 2)(x - 4)(x + 3)$; $2, 4, -3$

23. $P(x) = (x - 1)(x - 2)(x - 3)(x + 5)$; $1, 2, 3, -5$

24. $P(x) = (x + 1)(x + 2)(x + 3)(x + 5)$; $-1, -2, -3, -5$

25.
$$(x - 2)(x^2 + 4x - 5) > 0$$
$$(x - 2)(x - 1)(x + 5) > 0$$
$$x - 2 > 0 \text{ or } x - 1 > 0 \text{ or } x + 5 > 0$$
$$x > 2 \text{ or } x > 1 \text{ or } x > -5$$
$$\{-5 < x < 1 \text{ or } x > 2\}$$

26.
$$(x - 3)(x^3 + 2x^2 - 13x + 10) < 0$$
$$(x - 3)(x + 5)(x^2 - 3x + 2) < 0$$
$$(x - 3)(x + 5)(x - 1)(x - 2) < 0$$
$$x - 3 < 0 \text{ or } x + 5 < 0 \text{ or } x - 1 < 0 \text{ or } x - 2 < 0$$
$$x < 3 \text{ or } x < -5 \text{ or } x < 1 \text{ or } x < 2$$
$$\{-5 < x < 1 \text{ or } 2 < x < 3\}$$

27.
$$\underline{-2|} \quad 1 \quad -k \quad\quad 2 \quad\quad 7k$$
$$\quad\quad\quad\quad -2 \quad 2k + 4 \quad -4k - 12$$
$$\overline{\quad 1 \quad -k - 2 \quad 2k + 6 \,|\, 3k - 12}$$
Since $3k - 12 = 0$, $k = 4$.

28.
$$\underline{1|} \quad 1 \quad -3 \quad\quad k \quad\quad -1$$
$$\quad\quad\quad\quad 1 \quad -2 \quad k - 2$$
$$\overline{\quad 1 \quad -2 \quad k - 2 \,|\, k - 3}$$ Since $k - 3 = 0$, $k = 3$.

29.
$$\underline{1|} \quad 1 \quad k \quad\quad 4$$
$$\quad\quad\quad\quad 1 \quad k + 1$$
$$\overline{\quad 1 \quad k + 1 \,|\, k + 5};$$

$$\underline{-1|} \quad 1 \quad k \quad\quad 4$$
$$\quad\quad\quad\quad -1 \quad -k + 1$$
$$\overline{\quad 1 \quad k - 1 \,|\, -k + 5};\ k + 5 = -k + 5,\ k = 0$$

30.
$$\underline{-2|} \quad 1 \quad -3 \quad 2k$$
$$\quad\quad\quad\quad -2 \quad 10$$
$$\overline{\quad 1 \quad -5 \,|\, 2k + 10};\ 2k + 10 = 7 \text{ then } k = -\frac{3}{2}$$

31. If $A(x)$ is a factor of $B(x)$, then $A(x) \cdot D(x) = B(x)$.
If $B(x)$ is a factor of $C(x)$, then $B(x) \cdot E(x) = C(x)$.
Thus, $A(x) \cdot D(x) \cdot E(x) = C(x)$. So, $A(x)$ is a factor of $C(x)$.

32. $P(a) = a^n - a^n = 0$; Since $P(a) = 0$, $x - a$ is a factor of $x^n - a^n$.

33. $P(r)$ is the remainder of $P(x) \div (x - r)$ by the remainder theorem. If $P(r) = 0$, then $P(x) \div (x - r)$ has a remainder of 0. Thus $(x - r)$ must be a factor of $P(x)$.

34.
$$f(x) = x^2 - 4x$$
$$f(x) + 4 = x^2 - 4x + 4$$
$$f(x) = (x^2 - 2)^2 - 4$$
Vertex: $(2, -4)$
Line of symmetry: $x = 2$
Minimum: -4

35. $f(x) = 2x^2 - 10x - 8$
$$= 2(x^2 - 5x) - 8$$
$$= 2\left(x^2 - 5x + \frac{25}{4}\right) - 8 - \frac{25}{2}$$
$$f(x) = 2\left(x - \frac{5}{2}\right)^2 - \frac{41}{2}$$
Vertex: $\left(\frac{5}{2}, -\frac{41}{2}\right)$
Line of symmetry: $x = \frac{5}{2}$
Minimum: $-\frac{41}{2}$

36. $f(x) = x^2 + c$
$f(x) = (x - 0)^2 + c$
Vertex: $(0, c)$
Line of symmetry: $x = 0$
Minimum: c

37. $(x + 1)^2 + (y + 0)^2 = 8^2$
Center: $(-1, 0)$; radius: 8

38. $x^2 - 6x + 9 + y^2 - 2y + 1 = 15 + 9 + 1$
$(x - 3)^2 + (y - 1)^2 = 5^2$
Center: $(3, 1)$; radius: 5

39. $(x + 1)^2 + (y - 1)^2 = (\sqrt{45})^2$ then center: $(-1, 1)$;
radius: $3\sqrt{5}$

pp. 491–493   **11-3 TRY THIS**

a. $P(x) = 4(x + 7)^2(x - 3)$
-7(Multiplicity 2);
3(Multiplicity 1)

b. $P(x) = (x^2 - 7x + 12)^2$
$= (x - 3)^2(x - 4)^2$
4(Multiplicity 2);
3(Multiplicity 2)

c. $P(x) = 5x^2 - 5 = 5(x^2 - 1) = 5(x + 1)(x - 1)$
1(Multiplicity 1);
-1(Multiplicity 1)

d. Given the three roots: 4, $7 - 2i$ and $3 + 7\sqrt{5}$, the remaining two roots are: $7 + 2i$ and $3 - 7\sqrt{5}$.

e. Given: $x^4 + x^3 - x^2 + x - 2 = (x - i)(x + i) \cdot Q(x)$

$(x^2 + 1) \cdot Q(x)$
$= (x^2 + 1)(x^2 + x - 2)$
$= (x^2 + 1)(x + 2)(x - 1)$

$$\begin{array}{r} x^2 + x - 2 \\ x^2 + 1 \overline{)x^4 + x^3 - x^2 + x - 2} \\ x^4 + x^2 \\ \hline x^3 - 2x^2 \\ x^3 \\ \hline -2x^2 - 2 \\ -2x^2 - 2 \end{array}$$

Roots: $i, -i, -2, 1$

f. $(x + 1)(x - 2)(x - 5) = (x + 1)(x^2 - 7x + 10)$
$= x^3 - 7x^2 + 10x + x^2 - 7x + 10$
$= x^3 - 6x^2 + 3x + 10$

g. $x^2(x + 2)^3 = x^2(x^3 + 6x^2 + 12x + 8)$
$= x^5 + 6x^4 + 12x^3 + 8x^2$

h. $(x - (1 - i))(x - (1 + i))(x - (2 + \sqrt{3}))(x - (2 - \sqrt{3}))$
$((x - 1)^2 - i^2)((x - 2)^2 - (\sqrt{3})^2)$
$= (x^2 - 2x + 1 + 1)(x^2 - 4x + 4 - 3)$
$= (x^2 - 2x + 2)(x^2 - 4x + 1)$
$= x^4 - 4x^3 + x^2 - 2x^3 + 8x^2 - 2x + 2x^2 - 8x + 2$
$= x^4 - 6x^3 + 11x^2 - 10x + 2$

i. $(x - 2)(x - 2i)(x + 2i) = (x - 2)(x^2 + 4)$
$= x^3 + 4x - 2x^2 - 8$
$= x^3 - 2x^2 + 4x - 8$

pp. 494–495   **11-3 EXERCISES**

1. -3(multiplicity 2), 1(multiplicity 1)

2. -2(multiplicity 1), π(multiplicity 5)

3. 3(multiplicity 2), -4(multiplicity 3), 0(multiplicity 4)

4. 0(multiplicity 3), 1(multiplicity 2), -4(multiplicity 1)

5. 2(multiplicity 2), 3(multiplicity 2)

6. 2(multiplicity 2), -1(multiplicity 2)

7. $5 - i$, $2i$ are the other roots

8. $-3 + 2i$, $-4i$ are the other roots   **9.** $-3 - 4i$, $4 + \sqrt{5}$

10. $6 + 7i$, $\frac{1}{2} - \sqrt{11}$ **11.** $1 + i$ **12.** $7 - i$ **13.** $i, 3, 2$

14. $i, 4$ **15.** $-2i, 2, -2$ **16.** $-i, 1, -1$ **17.** $2 + i, 2 - i$

18. $1 + 2i, 1 - 2i$ **19.** $-1 + i\sqrt{3}, -1 - i\sqrt{3}$

20. $1 + i\sqrt{3}, 1 - i\sqrt{3}$ **21.** $\sqrt{3}, 1 + 3i, 1 - 3i$

22. $-\sqrt{7}, -2 + i\sqrt{5}, -2 - i\sqrt{5}$

23. $P(x) = x^3 - 6x^2 - x + 30$ **24.** $P(x) = x^3 - 4x^2 + x + 6$

25. $P(x) = x^3 - 2x^2 + x - 2$ **26.** $P(x) = x^3 + 3x^2 + 4x + 12$

27. $P(x) = x^3 - 7x^2 + 17x - 15$

28. $P(x) = x^3 - x^2 + 15x + 17$

29. $P(x) = x^3 - \sqrt{3}x^2 - 2x + 2\sqrt{3}$, no

30. $P(x) = x^3 - \sqrt{2}x^2 - 3x + 3\sqrt{2}$, no

31. $P(x) = x^4 - 10x^3 + 25x^2$ **32.** $P(x) = x^4$

33. $P(x) = x^4 - 3x^3 - 7x^2 + 15x + 18$

34. $P(x) = x^5 - 8x^4 + 4x^3 + 80x^2 - 64x - 256$

35. $P(x) = x^3 - 4x^2 + 6x - 4$ **36.** $P(x) = x^3 - 3x^2 + x + 5$

37. $P(x) = x^3 + 2x^2 + 9x + 18$

38. $P(x) = x^3 - 5x^2 + 16x - 80$

39. $P(x) = x^4 - 6x^3 + 11x^2 - 10x + 2$

40. $P(x) = x^4 - 10x^3 + 36x^2 - 58x + 35$

41. $P(x) = x^4 + 4x^2 - 45$ **42.** $P(x) = x^4 + 14x^2 - 32$

43. $P(x) = x^4 - 4x^3 + 9x^2 + 8x - 22$

44. $P(x) = x^4 + 6x^3 + 23x^2 + 54x + 126$

45. $ax(x^2 + 1) + b(x^2 + 1) = 0$
$$(x^2 + 1)(ax + b) = 0$$
$$x^2 + 1 = 0; \quad ax + b = 0$$
$$x^2 = -1; \quad ax = -b$$
$$x = \pm i; \quad x = -\frac{b}{a}$$

46. $ax^2(x + 1) + b(x + 1) = 0$
$$(ax^2 + b)(x + 1) = 0$$
$$ax^2 + b = 0; \quad x + 1 = 0$$
$$ax^2 = -b; \quad x = -1$$
$$x^2 = -\frac{b}{a}$$
$$x = \pm\sqrt{-\frac{b}{a}}$$

47.
$$x^4 - 1 - 2x^3 - 2x = 0$$
$$(x^4 - 1) - 2x(x^2 + 1) = 0$$
$$(x^2 + 1)(x^2 - 1) - 2x(x^2 + 1) = 0$$
$$(x^2 + 1)(x^2 - 2x - 1) = 0$$

$$x^2 + 1 = 0 \qquad x = \frac{2 \pm \sqrt{4 - 4(-1)}}{2}$$
$$x^2 = -1 \qquad = \frac{2 \pm 2\sqrt{2}}{2}$$
$$x = \pm i \qquad x = 1 \pm \sqrt{2}$$

48. $x^2 + 2ax + b = 0$
$$(x + a)^2 = 0$$
$$x + a = 0$$
$$x = -a$$

49. Answers may vary. Ex: $P(x) = x - 2$

50. For $P(x) = a_n x^n + a_{n-1} x^{n-1} + \cdots + a_0$ with a, positive, consider any positive x. Every term will be positive, hence $P(x) > 0$.

51. By Theorem 11-3, $P(x)$ can be factored into n linear factors, where n is the degree of $P(x)$. By Theorem 11-5 the nonreal roots occur in conjugate pairs. There is at least one factor $(x - a)$ with a real.

52. Let $P(x) = a_n x^n + a_{n-1} x^{n-1} + \cdots + a_1 x + a_0$, where the coefficients are real numbers. Let $z = a + bi$ be a complex root of $P(x)$. Then $P(z) = 0$, or $a_n z^n + a_{n-1} z^{n-1} + \cdots + a_1 z + a_0 = 0$. Now let us find the conjugate of each side of the equation. We can represent the conjugate using a bar. First note that $\overline{0} = 0$, since 0 is a real number. Then we have the following:
$$0 = \overline{0}$$
$$= \overline{a_n z^n + a_{n-1} z^{n-1} + \cdots + a_1 z + a_0}$$
$$= \overline{a_n z^n} + \overline{a_{n-1} z^{n-1}} + \cdots + \overline{a_1 z} + \overline{a_0}$$
$$= \overline{a_n} \cdot \overline{z^n} + \overline{a_{n-1}} \cdot \overline{z^{n-1}} + \cdots + \overline{a_1} \cdot \overline{z} + \overline{a_0}$$
$$= a_n \overline{z}^n + a_{n-1} \overline{z}^{n-1} + \cdots + a_1 \overline{z} + a_0$$
$$= a_n \overline{z}^n + a_{n-1} \overline{z}^{n-1} + \cdots + a_1 \overline{z} + a_0$$
Since $P(\overline{z}) = 0$, $\overline{z} = a - bi$ is also a root.

53. Let $P(x) = s_n x^n + s_{n-1} x^{n-1} + \cdots + s_1 x + s_0$, where the coefficients are rational numbers. Suppose $a + c\sqrt{b}$ is a root of $P(x)$. Then $P(a + c\sqrt{b}) = 0$, or $s_n(a + c\sqrt{b})^n + s_{n-1}(a + c\sqrt{b})^{n-1} + \cdots + s_1(a + c\sqrt{b}) + s_0 = 0$. We take the conjugate of each side:
$$0 = \overline{0} = \overline{s_n(a + c\sqrt{b})^n} + \overline{s_{n-1}(a + c\sqrt{b})^{n-1}} + \cdots$$
$$+ \overline{s_1(a + c\sqrt{b})} + \overline{s_0}$$
$$= \overline{s_n(a + c\sqrt{b})^n} + \overline{s_{n-1}(a + c\sqrt{b})^{n-1}} + \cdots$$
$$+ \overline{s_1(a + c\sqrt{b})} + \overline{s_0}$$
$$= \overline{s_n} \cdot \overline{(a + c\sqrt{b})^n} + \overline{s_{n-1}} \cdot \overline{(a + c\sqrt{b})^{n-1}} + \cdots$$
$$+ \overline{s_1} \cdot \overline{(a + c\sqrt{b})} + \overline{s_0}$$
$$= s_n \overline{(a + c\sqrt{b})}^n + s_{n-1} \overline{(a + c\sqrt{b})}^{n-1} + \cdots$$
$$+ s_1 \overline{(a + c\sqrt{b})} + s_0$$
$$= s_n(a - c\sqrt{b})^n + s_{n-1}(a - c\sqrt{b})^{n-1} + \cdots$$
$$+ s_1(a - c\sqrt{b}) + s_0$$
Thus $P(a + c\sqrt{b}) = 0$ implies $P(a - c\sqrt{b}) = 0$. The converse is proved in the same fashion.

54. Vertex: $(2, 3)$
Line of symmetry: $x = 2$
Minimum: 3

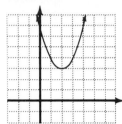

55. Vertex: $(-1, -1)$
Line of symmetry: $x = -1$
Maximum: -1

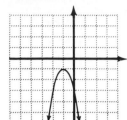

56. $(x - h)^2 = 4p(y - k)$
$$(x - 0)^2 = 4p(y - 0)$$
$$x^2 = 4py$$
$$x^2 = 2y$$
$$2y = 4py$$
$$\frac{1}{2} = p$$
Vertex: $(0, 0)$
Directrix: $y = -\frac{1}{2}$
Focus: $\left(0, \frac{1}{2}\right)$

57. $x^2 - 8y + 8 = 0$
$$x^2 = 8y - 8$$
$$(x - 0)^2 = 8(y - 1)$$
$$(x - h)^2 = 4p(y - k)$$
$$8 = 4p$$
$$2 = p$$
Vertex: $(0, 1)$
Directrix: $y = -1$
Focus: $(0, 3)$

58. $y^2 - 4y - 12x + 28 = 0$
$$y^2 - 4y = 12x - 28$$
$$y^2 - 4y + 4 = 12x - 28 + 4$$
$$(y - 2)^2 = 12(x - 2)$$
Vertex: $(2, 2)$
Directrix: $x = -1$
Focus: $(5, 2)$

59. $x(0.36) + (20 - x)0.68 = (0.5)(20)$
$$0.36x + 13.6 - 0.68x = 10$$
$$-0.32x = -3.6$$
$$x = \frac{3.6}{0.32}$$
$$x = 11.25$$
$$20 - 11.25 = 8.75$$
11.25 lb of Mocha-Java; 8.75 lb of Manager's Blend

60.
Let $x =$ one number
$y =$ other number
$y = x + 27$
when $y - x = 27$
$$2x + 27 = 0$$
$$2x = -27$$
$$x = -13.5$$
Therefore $y + 13.5 = 27$
$$y = 13.5$$
product $= -182.25$

61. a. $\dfrac{70}{5.48} = 12.77$

b. $p^3 = \dfrac{h^3}{w}$
$$p^3 w = h^3$$

$$w = \frac{h^3}{p^3}$$

c. $(12.5)^3 = \left(\dfrac{62}{\sqrt[3]{w}}\right)$

$$1953\, w = 238{,}328$$
$$w = 122$$

a. Find the rational roots of $f(x) = 2x^4 + 3x^3 - 8x^2 - 9x + 6$
c: 1, −1, 2, −2, 3, −3
d: 1, −1, 2, −2

Possibilities: $1, -1, 2, -2, 3, -3, \dfrac{1}{2}, -\dfrac{1}{2}, \dfrac{3}{2}, -\dfrac{3}{2}$

$$\begin{array}{r|rrrrr}
-2 & 2 & 3 & -8 & -9 & 6 \\
   &   & -4 & 2 & 12 & -6 \\ \hline
   & 2 & -1 & -6 & 3 & 0
\end{array}$$

−2 is a root, so $f(x) = (x + 2)(2x^3 - x^2 - 6x + 3)$

$$\begin{array}{r|rrrr}
\frac{1}{2} & 2 & -1 & -6 & 3 \\
            &   & 1 & 0 & -3 \\ \hline
            & 2 & 0 & -6 & 0
\end{array}$$

$\dfrac{1}{2}$ is a root, so $f(x) = (x + 2)\left(x - \dfrac{1}{2}\right)(2x^2 - 6)$

For $2x^2 - 6 = 0$,
$$x^2 = 3$$
$$x = \pm\sqrt{3}$$

The rational roots are -2 and $\dfrac{1}{2}$, the other roots are $\pm\sqrt{3}$.

b. $P(x) = x^3 + 7x^2 + 4x + 28$
c: 1, −1, 2, −2, 14, −14, 4, −4, 7, −7
d: 1, −1
Since the leading coefficient is 1 and all coefficients are positive, the possible rational roots are: −1, −2, −14, −4, −7.

$$\begin{array}{r|rrrr}
-7 & 1 & 7 & 4 & 28 \\
   &   & -7 & 0 & -28 \\ \hline
   & 1 & 0 & 4 & 0
\end{array}$$

−7 is a root, so $f(x) = (x + 7)(x^2 + 4)$
For $x^2 + 4 = 0$
$$x^2 = -4$$
$$x = \pm 2i$$
The only rational root is −7, the other roots are $2i$ and $-2i$.

c. $x^4 + x^2 + 2x + 6$
Possible roots: −1, −2, −3, −6

$$\begin{array}{r|rrrrr}
-1 & 1 & 0 & 1 & 2 & 6 \\
   &   & -1 & 1 & -2 & 0 \\ \hline
   & 1 & -1 & 2 & 0 & 6
\end{array}$$

$$\begin{array}{r|rrrrr}
-2 & 1 & 0 & 1 & 2 & 6 \\
   &   & -2 & 4 & -10 & 16 \\ \hline
   & 1 & -2 & 5 & -8 & 22
\end{array}$$

$$\begin{array}{r|rrrrr}
-3 & 1 & 0 & 1 & 2 & 6 \\
   &   & -3 & 9 & -30 & 84 \\ \hline
   & 1 & -3 & 10 & -28 & 90
\end{array}$$

$$\begin{array}{r|rrrrr}
-6 & 1 & 0 & 1 & 2 & 6 \\
   &   & -6 & 36 & 222 & 1320 \\ \hline
   & 1 & -6 & 37 & 224 & 1326
\end{array}$$

$P(-1) = 6$, $P(-2) = 22$, $P(-3) = 90$, $P(-6) = 1326$;
No rational roots
d. $x^5 - 2x^4 + 4x - 8$
Possible roots: −1, 1, −2, 2, 4, −4, 8, −8

$$\begin{array}{r|rrrrrr}
2 & 1 & -2 & 0 & 0 & 4 & -8 \\
  &   & 2 & 0 & 0 & 0 & 8 \\ \hline
  & 1 & 0 & 0 & 0 & 4 & 0
\end{array}$$

$x^5 - 2x^4 + 4x - 8 = (x - 2)(x^4 + 4)$

For $x^4 + 4 = 0$
$\quad x^4 = -4$ has no real solutions
The only rational root is 2.

1. $-3; \sqrt{2}, -\sqrt{2}$ **2.** $1; \sqrt{3}, -\sqrt{3}$ **3.** $1, -\dfrac{1}{5}; 2i, -2i$

4. $-1, \dfrac{1}{3}; 1 + i, 1 - i$ **5.** $-1, -2; 3 + \sqrt{13}, 3 - \sqrt{13}$

6. $1, -1, -3$ **7.** $1, 2; -4 + \sqrt{21}, -4 - \sqrt{21}$

8. $1, -1, -5$ **9.** $-2; 1 + i\sqrt{3}, 1 - i\sqrt{3}$

10. $2; -1 + i\sqrt{3}, -1 - i\sqrt{3}$ **11.** $\dfrac{3}{4}; i, -i$

12. $\dfrac{1}{2}, \dfrac{1 + \sqrt{5}}{2}, \dfrac{1 - \sqrt{5}}{2}$ **13.** $1, 2, -2$ **14.** $2, -2, 3$

15. No rational   **16.** No rational   **17.** No rational

18. $-\dfrac{3}{2}$ **19.** No rational   **20.** No rational

21. a.
$$\begin{array}{r|rrrr}
-3 & 1 & -1 & -8 & 12 \\
   &   & -3 & 12 & -12 \\ \hline
   & 1 & -4 & 4 & 0
\end{array}$$

$(x + 3)(x^2 - 4x + 4) = 0$
$(x + 3)(x - 2)(x - 2) = 0$
$\{-3, 2\}$
2(multiplicity 2),
−3(multiplicity 1)

b.
$$\begin{array}{r|rrrrr}
1 & 6 & -1 & -8 & 1 & 2 \\
  &   & 6 & 5 & -3 & -2 \\ \hline
  & 6 & 5 & -3 & -2 & 0
\end{array}$$

$(x - 1)(6x^3 + 5x^2 - 3x - 2) = 0$
$$\begin{array}{r|rrrr}
-1 & 6 & 5 & -3 & -2 \\
   &   & -6 & 1 & 2 \\ \hline
   & 6 & -1 & -2 & 0
\end{array}$$

$(x - 1)(x + 1)(6x^2 - x - 2) = 0$
$(x - 1)(x + 1)(3x - 2)(2x + 1) = 0$
$\left\{1, -1, \dfrac{2}{3}, -\dfrac{1}{2}\right\}$

c.
$$\begin{array}{r|rrrr}
\frac{1}{2} & 2 & -3 & -1 & 1 \\
            &   & 1 & -1 & -1 \\ \hline
            & 2 & -2 & -2 & 0
\end{array}$$

$\left(x + \dfrac{1}{2}\right)(2x^2 - 2x - 2) = 0$

$2\left(x - \dfrac{1}{2}\right)(x^2 - x - 1) = 0$

$\left\{\dfrac{1}{2}\right\}$

d.
$$\begin{array}{r|rrrr}
\frac{3}{4} & 4 & -3 & 4 & -3 \\
            &   & 3 & 0 & 3 \\ \hline
            & 4 & 0 & 4 & 0
\end{array}$$

$\left(x - \dfrac{3}{4}\right)(4x^2 + 4) = 0$

$4\left(x - \dfrac{3}{4}\right)(x^2 + 1) = 0$

$\left\{\dfrac{3}{4}\right\}$

22.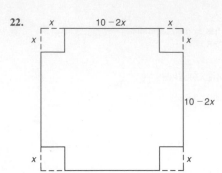

$$lwh = 48 \text{ ft}^3$$
$$(10 - 2x)^2(x) = 48$$
$$100x - 40x^2 + 4x^3 = 48$$
$$4x^3 - 40x^2 + 100x - 48 = 0$$
$$x^3 - 10x^2 + 25x - 12 = 0$$
$$(x - 3)(x^2 - 7x + 4) = 0$$
$$x - 3 = 0 \quad \text{or} \quad x^2 - 7x + 4 = 0$$
$$x = 3 \quad \text{or} \quad x = \frac{7 \pm \sqrt{49 - 4(4)}}{2}$$
$$x = \frac{7 \pm \sqrt{33}}{2}$$
$$\frac{7 + \sqrt{33}}{2} > 5$$

so not a solution

$$\left\{ 3 \text{ ft}, \frac{7 - \sqrt{33}}{2} \text{ ft} \right\}$$

23.
$$lwh = 500 \text{ cm}^3$$
$$(20 - 2x)^2(x) = 500$$
$$4x^3 - 80x^2 + 400x = 500$$
$$4x^3 - 80x^2 + 400x - 500 = 0$$
$$x^3 - 20x^2 + 100x - 125 = 0$$
$$(x - 5)(x^2 - 15x + 25) = 0$$
$$x - 5 = 0 \quad \text{or} \quad x^2 - 15x + 25 = 0$$
$$x = 5 \quad \text{or} \quad x = \frac{15 \pm \sqrt{225 - 100}}{2}$$
$$x = \frac{15 \pm \sqrt{125}}{2}$$
$$= \frac{15 \pm 5\sqrt{3}}{2}$$

Since $\dfrac{15 + 5\sqrt{3}}{2} > 10$, it is not a solution.

$$\left\{ 5 \text{ cm}, \frac{15 - 5\sqrt{5}}{2} \text{ cm} \right\}$$

24. $a_n = 5, a_0 = 12$

25. The possible rational roots of $x^2 - 5 = 0$ are $\pm 1, \pm 5$. None of these are roots.

26. The only possible rational roots of $x^3 - 3 = 0$ are $\pm 1, \pm 3$. None of these are roots.

27.
$$(38 - 2x)(32 - 2x)(x) = 2160$$
$$4x^3 - 140x^2 + 1216x - 2160 = 0$$
$$x^3 - 35x^2 + 304x - 540 = 0$$
$$(x - 10)(x^2 - 25x + 54) = 0$$
$$x = 10 \text{ in.} \quad \text{or} \quad \frac{25 + \sqrt{409}}{2} \text{ in.}$$

28. $\sqrt{(x_2 - x_1)^2 + (y_2 - y_1)^2} = \sqrt{(6 - 3)^2 + (-6 + 2)^2}$
$= \sqrt{9 + 16} = \sqrt{25} = 5$

29. $\sqrt{(0 - 4)^2 + (4 - 0)^2} = \sqrt{16 + 16} = \sqrt{32} = 4\sqrt{2}$

30. $\sqrt{(15 - 9)^2 + (-7 - 1)^2} = \sqrt{36 + 64} = \sqrt{100} = 10$

31. $\sqrt{(5 - 5)^2 + (-9 - 3)^2} = \sqrt{144} = 12$

32. $(x^2 + 14x + 49) + (y^2 + 2y + 1) = -1 + 49 + 1$
$$(x + 7)^2 + (y + 1)^2 = 7^2$$
Center: $(-7, -1)$; radius: 7

33. $(0, -4), (1, -3)$ **34.** $(2, 2)$

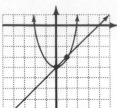 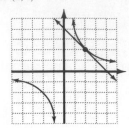

35.

$$\begin{array}{r|rrrr} 5 & 1 & -6 & 3 & 10 \\ & & 5 & -5 & -10 \\ \hline & 1 & -1 & -2 & 0 \end{array}$$

5 is a root.
$$P(x) = (x - 5)(x^2 - x - 2)$$
$$P(x) = (x - 5)(x + 1)(x - 2)$$
So 2 is a root, -2 is not.

36. 63 km

p. 502   **11-5 TRY THIS**

a. There is one variation of sign. Therefore, there is 1 positive real root.

b. There are 5 variations of sign; 5, 3, or 1 positive real roots.

c. There are 2 variations of sign; 2 or 0 positive real roots.

d. $P(x) = 5x^3 - 4x - 5$
$P(-x) = -5x^3 + 4x - 5$
There are 2 variations of sign; 2 or 0 negative real roots.

e. $P(p) = 6p^6 - 5p^4 + 3p^3 - 7p^2 + p - 2$
$P(-p) = 6p^6 - 5p^4 - 3p^3 - 7p^2 - p - 2$
There is 1 variation of sign; 1 negative real root.

f. $P(x) = 3x^2 - 2x + 4$
$P(-x) = 3x^2 + 2x + 4$
There are no variations of sign; there are 0 negative real roots.

p. 505   **11-5 EXERCISES**

1. 3 or 1   **2.** 3 or 1   **3.** 0   **4.** 0   **5.** 2 or 0

6. 2 or 0   **7.** 3 or 1   **8.** 3 or 1   **9.** 2 or 0   **10.** 3 or 1

11. 0   **12.** 0   **13.** 3 or 1   **14.** 1   **15.** 2 or 0

16. 4, 2 or 0   **17.** 0   **18.** 1   **19.** 1   **20.** 3 or 1

21. $P(x) = x^4 - 2x^2 - 8$
There is 1 variation of sign, so there is 1 positive real root.
$P(-x) = (-x)^4 - 2(-x)^2 - 8$
$= x^4 - 2x^2 - 8$
There is 1 variation of sign, so there is 1 negative real root.
There are 2 remaining complex roots.

22. $P(x) = x^3 - 7x^2 + 12$
There are 2 variations of sign, so there are 2 or 0 positive real roots.
$P(-x) = (-x)^3 - 7(-x)^2 + 12$
$= -x^3 - 7x^2 + 12$
There is 1 variation of sign, so there is 1 negative real root.
There are 3 or 1 real roots, so there are 0 or 2 complex roots.

23. $P(x) = x^4 + 5x^2 + 6$
No sign variations, so there are no positive real roots.
$P(-x) = (-x)^4 + 5(-x)^2 + 6$
$= x^4 + 5x^2 + 6$
No sign variations, so there are no negative real roots. All 4 roots are complex.

24. $P(x) = 2x^3 - 2x^2 + 6x - 1$
There are 3 variations of sign; 3 or 1 positive real roots
$P(-x) = -2x^3 - 2x^2 - 6x - 1$
No variations; no negative real roots
There are 2 or 0 complex roots (3 − 1 or 3 − 3).

25. $P(x) = x^{2n} - 1$

There is 1 sign variation, 1 positive real root
$$P(-x) = (-x)^{2n} - 1$$
$$= x^{2n} - 1$$
1 sign variation; 1 negative real root
$2n - 2$ complex roots

26. $P(x) = x^{2n} + 1$

There are no sign variations; no positive real roots
$$P(-x) = (-x)^{2n+1} + 1$$
$$= (-x)^{2n}(-x) + 1$$
$$= (x^{2n})(-x) + 1$$
$$= -x^{2n+1} + 1$$
There is 1 sign variation; 1 negative real root
There are $(2n + 1) - 1$, or $2n$ complex roots.

27. The only real root is negative.

28. Let $P(x) = x^{n-1}$. There is one variation of sign, so there is just one positive root. Since n is even, $P(-x) = P(x)$. Hence $P(-x)$ has just one variation of sign, and there is just one negative root. Zero is not a root, so the total number of real roots is 2.

29. Let $P(x) = a_n x^n + a_{n-2} x^{n-2} + a_{n-4} x^{n-4} + \cdots + a_3 x^3 + a_1 x^1$ where n is odd. By Theorem 11-7 there are no positive roots. If we replace x with $(-x)$, every term changes sign. Therefore, there are no negative roots, by Theorem 11-8. We can factor an x from every term; thus $x = 0$ is a root.

30. $x^2 - 4 + 2x + 1 = 0$
$$x^2 + 2x - 3 = 0$$
$$(x - 1)(x + 3) = 0$$
$$x - 1 = 0 \quad \text{or} \quad x + 3 = 0$$
$$x = 1 \quad \text{or} \quad x = -3$$
$$\text{so } y = -3, \quad \text{or} \quad y = 5$$
$(1, -3), (-3, 5)$

31. $y = 25 - y^2 - 13$
$$0 = y^2 + y - 12$$
$$0 = (y - 3)(y + 4)$$
$$0 = y - 3 \quad \text{or} \quad 0 = y + 4$$
$$3 = y \quad \text{or} \quad -4 = y$$
$$\text{so } \pm 4 = x \quad \text{or} \quad \pm 3 = x$$
$(4, 3), (-4, 3), (3, -4), (-3, -4)$

32. $\dfrac{x^2}{9} - y^2 = 1$

Center: $(0, 0)$
Vertices: $(h + a, k), (h - a, k)$ so vertices: $(3, 0)$ and $(-3, 0)$;
foci: $(h + c, k), (h - c, k)$ so foci: $(\sqrt{10}, 0)$ and $(-\sqrt{10}, 0)$:
because $b^2 = c^2 - a^2$ then $1^2 = c^2 - (3)^2$, therefore, $c = \pm\sqrt{10}$

asymptotes: $y = \dfrac{1}{3}x$, $y = -\dfrac{1}{3}x$ because $y - k = \pm\dfrac{b}{a}(x - h)$

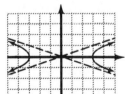

p. 503   PROBLEM FOR PROGRAMMERS

```
10   REM Chapter 11 Problem
20   DIM C(100)
30   INPUT "Enter n, the degree of the
     polynomial";N
40   FOR J = 0 TO N
50   PRINT "x^-"      ;N - J;:INPUT " coefficient
60   IF C(0) = 0 THEN N = N - 1: GOTO 40
70   NEXT J
80   PO = 0:L = C(0)
90   FOR J = 0 TO N
100   IF J = 0 GOTO 130
110   IF L * C(J) < 0 THEN PO = PO + 1
120   IF C(J) < > 0 THEN L = C(J)
130   NEXT J
```

```
140   PRINT : PRINT "Positive roots = ";PO;
150   IF PO > 1 THEN PO = PO - 2: PRINT " or ";
      PO;: GOTO 150
160   END
```

```
10   REM Chapter 11 Challenge Problem
20   DIM C(100)
30   INPUT "Enter n, the degree of the
     polynomial";N
40   FOR J = 0 TO N
50   PRINT"x^";N - J;:INPUT"coefficient = ";C(J)
60   IF C(0) = 0 THEN N = N - 1: GOTO 40
70   NEXT J
80   PO = 0:NE = 0:L = C(0)
90   FOR J = 0 TO N
100   IF J = 0 GOTO 140
110   IF L * C(J) < 0 THEN PO = PO + 1
120   IF L * C(J) > 0 THEN NE = NE + 1
130   IF C(J) < > 0 THEN L = C(J)
140   NEXT J
150   PRINT : PRINT "Positive roots = ";PO;
160   IF PO > 1 THEN PO = PO - 2: PRINT " or ";
      PO;: GOTO 160
170   PRINT : PRINT "Negative roots = ";NE;
180   IF NE > 1 THEN NE = NE - 2: PRINT " or ";
      NE;: GOTO 180
190   END
```

pp. 506   11-6 TRY THIS

a.

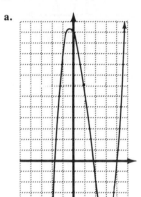

b. 0.7, −0.5, 2.9

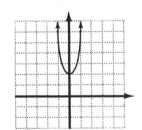

c. No real solution

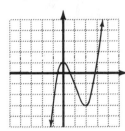

pp. 507–508   11-6 EXERCISES

1.

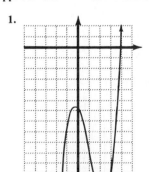

2.

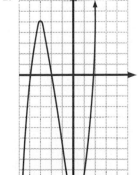

3.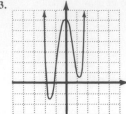

4.

15. No real solution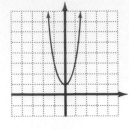

16. No real solution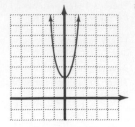

5.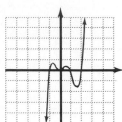

6.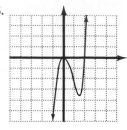

17. 0.79   **18.** 1.41   **19.** -1.27

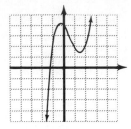

7. $-1, 2$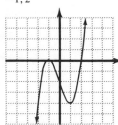

8. $-0.9, 1.3, 2.6$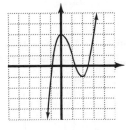

20. $-0.7, 1.24, 3.46$

21. Answers may vary.
See page 504.

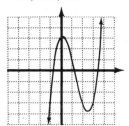

9. 2.2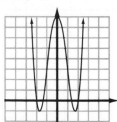

10. -1.1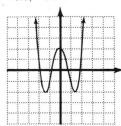

22.

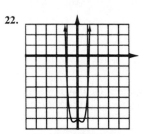

11. $\pm1.4, \pm2$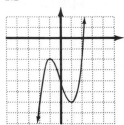

12. $\pm0.8, \pm1.8$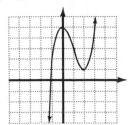

23. $P(x) = 3x^4 - 5x^3 + 4x^2 - 5$
Using synthetic division and a as the divisor and 3, -5, 4, 0, -5 as coefficients, you get $P(a) = a[a(a(3a - 5) + 4)] - 5$.

24. $4 = -\dfrac{2}{3}(6) + b$ **25.** $1 = -\dfrac{1}{2}(4) + b$

$\quad\ \ 4 = -4 + b$ $\qquad\qquad 1 = -2 + b$

$\quad\ \ 8 = b$ $\qquad\qquad\quad\ \ 3 = b$

$\quad\ \ y = -\dfrac{2}{3}x + 8$ $\qquad\ \ y = -\dfrac{1}{2}x + 3$

13. $-1, \pm1.4$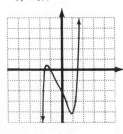

14. $\pm1.7, 2$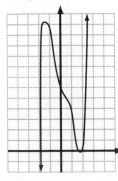

26. $2x - 3 \le 4$ and $-2x + 3 \le 4$
$\qquad 2x \le 7$ $\qquad\qquad -2x \le 1$

$\qquad\ \ x \le \dfrac{7}{2}$ and $\qquad x \ge -\dfrac{1}{2}$

$\left\{ -\dfrac{1}{2} \le x \quad \text{and} \qquad x \le \dfrac{7}{2} \right\}$

27. $3x + 2 \ge 5$ or $-3x - 2 \ge 5$
$\qquad 3x \ge 3$ $\qquad\qquad -3x \ge 7$

$\qquad\ \ x \ge 1$ or $\qquad x \le -\dfrac{7}{3}$

$\left\{ x \le -\dfrac{7}{3} \quad \text{or} \qquad x \ge 1 \right\}$

28.
$$\sqrt{y-5} = 5 - \sqrt{y}$$
$$(\sqrt{y-5})^2 = (5 - \sqrt{y})^2$$
$$y - 5 = 25 - 10\sqrt{y} + 4$$
$$-30 = -10\sqrt{y}$$
$$3 = \sqrt{y}$$
$$9 = y$$

29.
$$\sqrt{x+3} = -3 - \sqrt{x}$$
$$x + 3 = 9 + 6\sqrt{x} + x$$
$$-6 = 6\sqrt{x}$$
$$-1 = \sqrt{x}$$
$$1 = x$$
No solution

30. $P(2) = (2)^3 - 7(2)^2 + 5(2) - 4 = -14;$
$P(4) = (4)^3 - 7(4)^2 + 5(4) - 4 = -32;$
$P(-1) = (-1)^3 - 7(-1)^2 + 5(-1) - 4 = -17;$
$P(-2) = (-2)^3 - 7(-2)^2 + 5(-2) - 4 = -50$

31.
$$0 = (x - 2)(x^2 - 5x - 6)$$
$$= (x - 2)(x + 1)(x - 6)$$
$$0 = x - 2 \quad \text{or} \quad 0 = x + 1 \quad \text{or} \quad 0 = x - 6$$
$$2 = x \quad \text{or} \quad -1 = x \quad \text{or} \quad 6 = x$$

32.
$$(x - 2)(x^2 + 4x + 3) = 0$$
$$(x - 2)(x + 1)(x + 3) = 0$$
$$x - 2 = 0 \quad \text{or} \quad x + 1 = 0 \quad \text{or} \quad x + 3 = 0$$
$$x = 2 \quad \text{or} \quad x = -1 \quad \text{or} \quad x = -3$$

33. $y = 4x - 6$ then
$$2x^2 - 3(4x - 6) = 0$$
$$2x^2 - 12x + 18 = 0$$
$$2(x^2 - 6x + 9) = 0$$
$$2(x - 3)^2 = 0$$
$$x - 3 = 0$$
$$x = 3$$
$$y = 6 \quad (3, 6)$$

34.
$$2x = 8x - x^2$$
$$x^2 - 6x = 0$$
$$x(x - 6) = 0$$
$$x = 0 \quad \text{or} \quad x - 6 = 0$$
$$y = 0 \quad \text{or} \quad x = 6$$
$$y = 12$$
$$(0, 0), (6, 12)$$

p. 510 11-7 PROBLEM SOLVING: STRATEGIES

1. Strategy: Work backward
Start with the 40 points each player had at the end and work backward.

	After last round ←	Next to last round ←	Second to last round	Before last 3 rounds
Player 1	40	20	10 (lost)	65
Player 2	40	20 (lost)	70	35
Player 3	40 (lost)	80	40	20

Once a solution for the third game is found, the other columns are easily calculated because the loser of the third game did not lose in the previous two games.
They started with 65, 35, and 20 points.

2. Strategy: Simplify the problem

Number of sides of polygon	Sum of interior angles
3	180°
4	2(180°) = 360°
5	3(180°) = 540°
⋮	
8	6(180°) = 1080°

The sum of the interior angles of an octagon is 1080°.

3. Strategy: Make a table

Number of generations	Number of people	Total number
1	$2 = 2^1$	$2 = 2^2 - 2$
2	$4 = 2^2$	$6 = 2^3 - 2$
3	$8 = 2^3$	$14 = 2^4 - 2$
⋮	⋮	⋮
11	$2048 = 2^{11}$	$4094 = 2^{12} - 2$

There would be a total of 4094 people in 11 generations.

4. Strategy: Draw a diagram

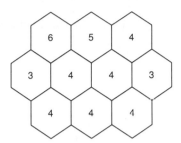

41 toothpicks are needed for 10 regular hexagons.

5. Strategy: Make an organized list; use logical reasoning
Let a, b, c, d, e be the 5 boxes from lightest to heaviest.
$a + b = 52$ (two lightest)
$a + c = 56$ (next heaviest, $a + c < b + c$)
$c + e = 73$ ($c + e < d + e$ so $c + e$ is next to greatest sum)
$d + e = 77$ (two heaviest)
For all possible pairs of weights, each box is included 4 times.
Therefore,
$$4a + 4b + 4c + 4d + 4e = 644$$
$$a + b + c + d + e = 161$$
But we have $a + b = 52$ and $d + e = 77$
$$52 + c + 77 = 161$$
$$c = 32$$

		$c = 32$
$c + e = 73,$	$32 + e = 73,$	$e = 41$
$d + e = 77,$	$d + 41 = 77,$	$d = 36$
$a + c = 56,$	$a + 32 = 56,$	$a = 24$
$a + b = 52,$	$24 + b = 52,$	$b = 28$

The boxes weigh 24, 28, 32, 36, and 41 pounds.

6. Strategy: Draw a diagram

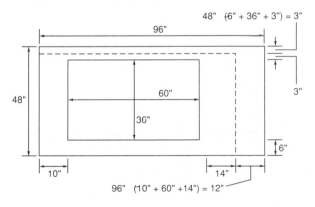

The dotted portion will be cut away.
$3 \times 96 + 12 \times 45 = 288 + 540 = 828$ in.^{2} will be wasted.
828 in.$^2 = 5.75$ ft^2 of wall board will remain.

7. Strategy: Make a table; look for a pattern
Consider the situation where there are few cabinets.

3 cabinets	4 cabinets	5 cabinets
branch 1 2 3	1 2 3	
1 1 1	1 1 2	1 1 3 1 2 2
	1 2 1	1 3 1 2 1 2
	2 1 1	3 1 1 2 2 1

6 cabinets			7 cabinets				
1 1 4	1 2 3	2 3 1	1 1 5	2 1 4	4 2 1	1 3 3	2 2 3
1 4 1	1 3 2	3 1 2	1 5 1	2 4 1	1 2 4	3 1 3	2 3 2
4 1 1	2 1 3	3 2 1	5 1 1	4 1 2	1 4 2	3 3 1	3 2 2

In general, number of cabinets	Number of ways to divide them
3	1
4	$3 = 1 + 2$
5	$6 = 1 + 2 + 3$
6	$10 = 1 + 2 + 3 + 4$
7	$15 = 1 + 2 + 3 + 4 + 5$
⋮	⋮
16	$105 = 1 + 2 + 3 + \cdots + 13 + 14$

The pattern is $1 + 2 + 3 + \cdots + (n - 2)$.

$\text{Sum} = 1 + 2 + 3 + \cdots + (n - 2)$
$\text{Sum} = n - 2 + n - 3 + n - 4 + \cdots + 1$

Adding these equations we get
$\qquad\qquad n - 2$ times

$2 \cdot \text{Sum} = n - 1 + n - 1 + n - 1 + n - 1 + \cdots + n - 1$

$\qquad \text{Sum} = \dfrac{(n - 1)(n - 2)}{2}$

$\dfrac{(16 - 1)(16 - 2)}{2} = 105$

There are 105 ways to divide the 16 filing cabinets among the three stores.

8. Strategy: Make a table.
Circled scores are possible.

1 2 ③ 4 5 ⑥ 7 ⑧ ⑨ 10 ⑪ ⑫ 13 ⑭ ⑮ ⑯ ⑰ ⑱ ...

Note: Since 14, 15, and 16 are possible scores, all subsequent scores are possible because any number greater than 16 minus one of these numbers will yield a multiple of 3.
1, 2, 4, 5, 7, 10 and 13 are impossible scores. Therefore, there are 7 impossible scores.

pp. 511–512   CHAPTER 11 SUMMARY AND REVIEW

1. No, yes   **2.** Yes, no   **3.** Yes, no   **4.** Yes, yes

5.
$$x - 2 \overline{\smash{\big)}\, x^4 + 0x^3 + 0x^2 + 0x - 16} \quad \begin{array}{l} x^3 + 2x^2 + 4x + 8 \quad \text{yes} \end{array}$$
$$\begin{array}{r} \underline{x^4 - 2x^3} \\ 2x^3 + 0x^2 \\ \underline{2x^3 - 4x^2} \\ 4x^2 + 0x \\ \underline{4x^2 - 8x} \\ 8x - 16 \\ \underline{8x - 16} \end{array}$$

6.
$$x^2 + 3x - 1 \overline{\smash{\big)}\, x^4 + 0x^3 + 0x^2 + 0x - 16} \quad \begin{array}{l} x^2 - 3x + 10 \quad \text{No} \end{array}$$
$$\begin{array}{r} \underline{x^4 + 3x^3 - x^2} \\ -3x^3 + x^2 + 0x \\ \underline{-3x^3 - 9x^2 + 3x} \\ 10x^2 - 3x - 16 \\ \underline{10x^2 + 30x - 10} \\ -33x - 6 \end{array}$$

7.
$$x - 1 \overline{\smash{\big)}\, x^3 - 2x^2 + 0x + 4} \quad \begin{array}{l} x^2 - x - 1 \end{array} \quad P(x) = (x - 1)(x^2 - x - 1) + 3$$
$$\begin{array}{r} \underline{x^3 - x^2} \\ -x^2 + 0x \\ \underline{-x^2 + x} \\ -x + 4 \\ \underline{-x + 1} \\ 3 \end{array}$$

8.
$$x^2 + 2x + 1 \overline{\smash{\big)}\, x^5 + 2x^4 + 2x^3 + 3x^2 + 3x + 3} \quad \begin{array}{l} x^3 + x + 1 \end{array}$$
$$\begin{array}{r} \underline{x^5 + 2x^4 + x^3} \\ x^3 + 3x^2 + 3x \\ \underline{x^3 + 2x^2 + x} \\ x^2 + 2x + 3 \\ \underline{x^2 + 2x + 1} \\ 2 \end{array}$$

$P(x) = (x^2 + 2x + 1)(x^3 + x + 1) + 2$

9. $P(0) = -2(0) - 8(0) + 4(0) - 2(0) + 1 = 1$
$P(1) = -2(1) - 8(1) + 4(1) - 2(1) + 1$
$\qquad = -2 - 8 + 4 - 2 + 1 = -7$
$P(-2) = -2(16) - 8(-8) + 4(4) - 2(-2) + 1$
$\qquad = -32 + 64 + 16 + 4 + 1 = 53$
$P(-4) = -2(256) - 8(-64) + 4(16) - 2(-4) + 1$
$\qquad = -512 + 512 + 64 + 8 + 1 = 73$

10. $P(x) = x^3 - x^2 - 14x + 24$
$\qquad = (x - 2)(x - 3)(x + 4)$
$\qquad x = 2, 3, -4$

11. $P(x) = x^3 - 18x^2 - x + 18$
$\qquad = (x - 1)(x + 1)(x - 18)$
$\qquad x = 1, -1, 18$

12. $P(x) = x^2(x - 2)^3(x + 1)$
0 (multiplicity 2)
2 (multiplicity 3)
−1 (multiplicity 1)

13. $P(x) = (x^2 - 12x + 11)^2$
$\qquad = [(x - 1)(x - 11)]^2$
1 (multiplicity 2)
11 (multiplicity 2)

14. $P(x) = (x + 1)(x + 3)(x - 4)$
$\qquad = x^3 - 13x - 12$

15. $P(x) = (1 - i)(1 + i)(x - 2 + \sqrt{3})(x - 2 - \sqrt{3})$
$\qquad = x^4 - 6x^3 + 11x^2 - 10x + 2$

16. $P(x) = (x - 2 - 3i)(x - 2 + 3i)(x - \sqrt{2})(x + \sqrt{2})$
$\qquad = x^4 - 4x^3 + 11x^2 + 8x - 26$

17. $P(x) = (2x - 1)(20x^2 - 20x + 2)$
$\qquad x = \dfrac{1}{2}, \dfrac{5 + \sqrt{15}}{10}, \dfrac{5 - \sqrt{15}}{10}$

18. $P(x) = (x - 2)(2x^3 + 3x^2 + 6x + 9)$
$\qquad = (x - 2)(2x + 3)(2x^2 + 6)$
$\qquad x = 2, -\dfrac{3}{2}, i\sqrt{3}, -i\sqrt{3}$

19. $P(x) = 4x^5 - 3x^2 + x - 3$
3 changes of signs
Positive roots 3 or 1.
There are no negative roots.

20. $P(x) = 3x^7 - 2x^5 + 3x^2 + x - 1$
3 changes of signs.
Positive roots 3 or 1.
Negative roots 2 or 0.

21. −3, 1.4, −1.4   **22.** −0.4, 0, 2.4

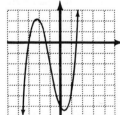   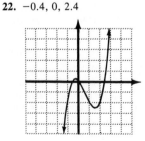

p. 513   CHAPTER 11 TEST

1.
−1⌋	1	6	1	30
		−1	−5	4
	1	5	−4	34 No

2.
4⌋	1	0	0	64
		4	16	64
	1	4	16	128 No

3.

$$x + 2 \overline{\smash{\big)}\ 4x^3 + 0x^2 - 10x + 9} \quad \overset{4x^2 - 8x + 6}{}$$
$$\underline{4x^3 + 8x^2}$$
$$-8x^2 - 10x$$
$$\underline{-8x^2 - 16x}$$
$$6x + 9$$
$$\underline{6x + 12}$$
$$-3$$

$P(x) = (x + 2)(4x^2 - 8x + 6) - 3$

4. $P(-2) = 2(16) - 3(-8) + (4) - 3(-2) + 7$
   $= 32 + 24 + 4 + 6 + 7 = 73$
   $P(3) = 2(81) - 3(27) + (9) - 3(3) + 7$
   $= 162 - 81 + 9 - 9 + 7 = 88$
   $P(-4) = 2(256) - 3(\ 64) + (16) - 3(-4) + 7$
   $= 512 + 192 + 16 + 12 + 7 = 739$

5. $P(x) = (x - 2)^2(x + 2)(x + 1)$ 2(multiplicity 2), $-2, -1$

6. $P(x) = (x - 3 + 2i)(x - 3 - 2i)(x - 1 + \sqrt{5})(x - 1 - \sqrt{5})$
   $= x^4 - 8x^3 + 21x^2 - 2x - 52$

7. The roots are $-1, 3 + \sqrt{3}, 3 - \sqrt{3}, 1 + 2i,$ and $1 - 2i$.

8. Since i is a root, then $-i$ is a root. So, $x^2 + 1$ is a factor. Through division we find $x^2 - 2x + 2$ is another factor. Thus, the roots are $i, -i, 1 + i, 1 - i$.

9. Since i has multiplicity two, then $-i$ has multiplicity two. Thus, $P(x) = (x - i)^2(x + i)^2(x - \sqrt{5})$
   $= x^5 - \sqrt{5}x^4 + 2x^3 - 2\sqrt{5}x^2 + x - \sqrt{5}$

10. By the rule of signs, there are 3 or 1 real roots.
   $P(x) = (x - 2)^2(x - 3)$, so the roots are 2, 2, 3.

11. $\frac{1}{2}, -\frac{1}{2}, -3$

12. a. One change of sign, so one positive real root.
   b. Four changes of sign, so 4, 2, or 0 negative real roots.

13. a. 3 or 1   **b.** 2 or 0

14.

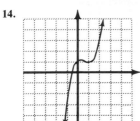

15. -0.5

16. Let $z = x^2$
   $z^3 + z^2 - 4z - 4$
   $= z^2(z + 1) - 4(z + 1)$
   $= (z^2 - 4)(z + 1)$
   $= (z - 2)(z + 2)(z + 1)$
   $= (x^2 - 2)(x^2 + 2)(x^2 + 1)$
   $= (x - \sqrt{2})(x + \sqrt{2})(x + i\sqrt{2})(x - i\sqrt{2})$
   $(x - i)(x + i)$

CHAPTER 12

p. 514   READY FOR EXPONENTIAL AND LOGARITHMIC FUNCTIONS?

1. 5   **2.** 1   **3.** $\frac{1}{8}$ **4.** x^{-2} or $\frac{1}{x^2}$ **5.** x^{-7} or $\frac{1}{x^7}$

6. x^{-12} or $\frac{1}{x^{12}}$ **7.** $-\frac{3y}{2}$ **8.** $\frac{8x^9}{3y^3}$ **9.** 8.45×10^{-2}

10. 433,500   **11.** No   **12.** No

---

a. The inverse of $y = x^2 + 4$ is $x = y^2 + 4$
b. $4x + 4y = 6$ is the same as $4y + 4x = 6$; Yes.
c. $y = 2x^2$ is not the same as $x = 2y^2$; No.
d. $g(x) = x + 2$
   $y = x + 2$
   Interchange x and y.
   $x = y + 2$
   $y = x - 2$. Thus, $g^{-1}(x) = x - 2$
e. $g(x) = 5x + 2$
   $y = 5x + 2$
   Interchange x and y.
   $x = 5y + 2$
   $y = \frac{x - 2}{5}$; Thus, $y^{-1}(x) = \frac{1}{5}(x - 2)$
f. $f(x) = \sqrt{x + 1}$
   $y = \sqrt{x + 1}$
   Interchange x and y
   $x = \sqrt{y + 1}$
   $y = x^2 - 1$; Thus, $f^{-1}(x) = x^2 - 1, x \geq 0$
g. $f^{-1}(f(579)) = 579$ $f(f^{-1}(-83,479)) = -83,479$

pp. 519–520   12-1 EXERCISES

1. $x = 4y - 5$ **2.** $x = 3y + 5$ **3.** $x = 3y^2 + 2$

4. $x = 5y^2 - 4$ **5.** $y^2 - 3x^2 = 3$ **6.** $2y^2 + 5x^2 = 4$

7. $yx = 7$ **8.** $yx = -5$ **9.** $yx^2 = 1$ **10.** $\frac{y^2}{4} + \frac{x^2}{9} = 1$

11. $x = \frac{5}{y}$ **12.** $x = \sqrt{y + 1}$ **13.** No   **14.** No   **15.** Yes

16. Yes   **17.** Yes   **18.** Yes   **19.** Yes   **20.** Yes

21. Yes   **22.** Yes   **23.** No   **24.** No

25. $f^{-1}(x) = x + 1$ **26.** $f^{-1}(x) = x + 2$ **27.** $f^{-1}(x) = x - 4$

28. $f^{-1}(x) = x - 3$ **29.** $f^{-1}(x) = x - 8$ **30.** $f^{-1}(x) = x - 7$

31. $f^{-1}(x) = \frac{1}{2}(x - 5)$ **32.** $f^{-1}(x) = \frac{1}{3}(x - 2)$

33. $f^{-1}(x) = \frac{1}{3}(x + 1)$ **34.** $f^{-1}(x) = \frac{1}{4}(x + 3)$

35. $f^{-1}(x) = 2(x - 2)$ **36.** $f^{-1}(x) = \frac{10}{7}(x - 4)$

37. $f^{-1}(x) = x^2 + 1; x \geq 0$

38. $f^{-1}(x) = x^2 + 2; x \geq 0$

39. $f^{-1}(x) = x^2 - 2; x \geq 0$

40. $f^{-1}(f(3)) = 3$
   $f(f^{-1}(-125)) = -125$

41. $g^{-1}(g(5)) = 5$
   $g(g^{-1}(-12)) = -12$

42. $f^{-1}(f(12,053)) = 12,053$
   $f(f^{-1}(-17,243)) = -17,243$

43. $g^{-1}(g(489)) = 489$
   $g(g^{-1}(-17,422)) = -17,422$

44.

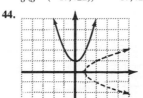

45.

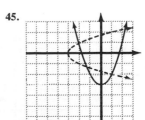

46.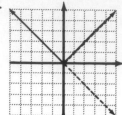

47.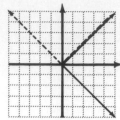

x	y
$\frac{1}{4}$	-2
1	-1
1	1
$\frac{1}{4}$	2

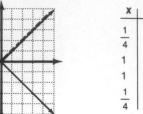

inverse: $x = \dfrac{1}{y^2}$

symmetric to x-axis

48. $f(g(x)) = f\left(\dfrac{x-1}{3}\right)$ 　　$g(f(x)) = g(3x+1)$

$\quad = 3\left(\dfrac{x-1}{3}\right) + 1$ 　　　$= \dfrac{3x+1-1}{3}$

$\quad = \dfrac{3(x-1)}{3} + 1$ 　　　　$= \dfrac{3x}{3}$

$\quad = x - 1 + 1$ 　　　　　　$= x$

$\quad = x$

49. $f(g(x)) = f(\sqrt[3]{x+5})$ 　　$g(f(x)) = g(x^3 - 5)$

$\quad = (\sqrt[3]{x+5})^3 - 5$ 　　　$= \sqrt[3]{x^3 - 5 + 5}$

$\quad = x + 5 - 5$ 　　　　　　$= \sqrt[3]{x^3}$

$\quad = x$ 　　　　　　　　$= x$

50. $f(x^2 + 1) = 2(x^2 + 1)$ 　　$g(f(x)) = g(2x)$

$\quad = 2x^2 + 2$ 　　　　　$= (2x)^2 + 1$

$\quad$ 　　　　　　　　　$= 4x^2 + 1$

51. $f(g(x)) = f(x+3)$ 　　$g(f(x)) = g(x^2)$

$\quad = (x+3)^2$ 　　　　$= x^2 + 3$

$\quad = x^2 + 6x + 9$

52. $f(g(x)) = f(x-4)$ 　　$g(f(x)) = g(2x+3)$

$\quad = 2(x-4) + 3$ 　　　$= (2x+3) - 4$

$\quad = 2x - 5$ 　　　　　$= 2x - 1$

53. $f(g(x)) = f(2x-1)$ 　　$g(f(x)) = g(3x^2 + 2)$

$\quad = 3(2x-1)^2 + 2$ 　　$= 2(3x^2 + 2) - 1$

$\quad = 12x^2 - 12x + 5$ 　　$= 6x^2 + 3$

54. $f(g(x)) = f\left(\dfrac{2}{x}\right)$ 　　$g(f(x)) = g(4x^2 - 1)$

$\quad = 4\left(\dfrac{2}{x}\right)^2 - 1$ 　　　$= \dfrac{2}{4x^2 - 1}$

$\quad = \dfrac{16}{x^2} - 1$

55. $f(g(x)) = f(x^2 - 1)$ 　　$g(f(x)) = g(x^2 - 1)$

$\quad = (x^2 - 1)^2 - 1$ 　　$= (x^2 - 1)^2 - 1$

$\quad = x^4 - 2x^2$ 　　　　$= x^4 - 2x^2$

56. a. $\{x \mid x \neq -1\}$

b. 　　$x = \dfrac{1}{y+1} + 4$

$\quad x - 4 = \dfrac{1}{y+1}$

$\quad (y+1) = \dfrac{1}{x-4}$

$\quad y = \dfrac{1}{x-4} - 1 = \dfrac{1}{x-4} - \dfrac{x-4}{x-4} = \dfrac{5-x}{x-4}; \{x \mid x \neq 4\}$

c. $\{x \mid x \neq -1, x \neq 4\}$

57. $y = \dfrac{1}{x^2}$

x	y
-2	$\frac{1}{4}$
-1	1
1	1
2	$\frac{1}{4}$

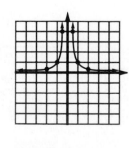

vertical asymptote at $x = 0$

symmetric to y-axis

58. $|x| - |y| = 1$
symmetric to x-axis, y-axis, and origin

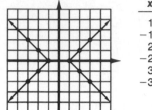

x	y
1	0
-1	0
2	±1
-2	±1
3	±2
-3	±2

$|y| - |x| = 1$
inverse
symmetric to y-axis, x-axis, and origin

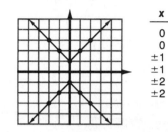

x	y
0	1
0	-1
±1	2
±1	-2
±2	3
±2	-3

59. $y = x^3$
symmetric to origin

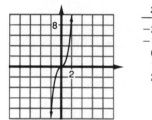

x	y
-2	-8
-1	-1
0	0
1	1
2	8

inverse:
$x = y^3$
symmetric to origin

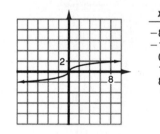

x	y
-8	-2
-1	-1
0	0
1	1
8	2

60. $y = \dfrac{|x|}{x}$

symmetric to origin

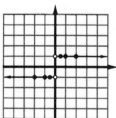

inverse:
$x = \dfrac{|y|}{y}$

symmetric to origin

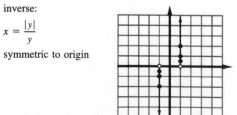

x	y
-1	-2
-1	-1
-1	$-\frac{1}{2}$
1	$\frac{1}{2}$
1	1
1	2

61. $3^5 \cdot 3^3$
3^8 or 6561

62. $(2a)^2(2a)^4$
$(2a)^6$ or $64a^6$

63. $(-3)^{-5}(-3)^7$
-3^{-5+7}
$(-3)^2$ or 9

64. $(3x^4y^3)(7xy^5)$
$(3)(7)x^{4+1}y^{3+5}$
$21x^5y^8$

65. $(m^5)^3$
$m^{(3 \cdot 5)}$
m^{15}

66. $(2x^3y^2)^5$
$2^5x^{3 \cdot 5}y^{2 \cdot 5}$
$32x^{15}y^{10}$

67. $(4m^{-3}n^7)^{-2}$
$4^{-2}m^{-3 \cdot -2}n^{7 \cdot -2}$
$\dfrac{1}{16}m^6n^{-14} = \dfrac{m^6}{16n^{14}}$

68. Center: $(-7, -1) \cdot$ radius $= 7$
$x^2 + 14x + \quad + y^2 + 2y + \quad = -1$
$x^2 + 14x + 7^2 + y^2 + 2y + 1^2 = -1 + 7^2 + 1^2$
$(x + 7)^2 + (y + 1)^2 = 49$

pp. 522–524   12-2 TRY THIS

a. $3^{1/2} \approx 1.7$

b.
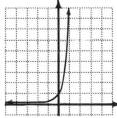

c.
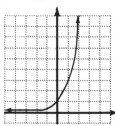

d.
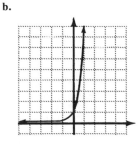

e. Domain: positive real numbers; range: all real numbers
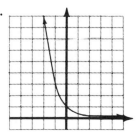

f. Domain: positive real numbers; range: all real numbers
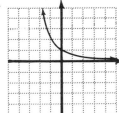

p. 525   12-2 EXERCISES

1.
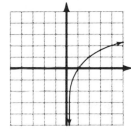

2.
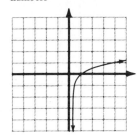

3.
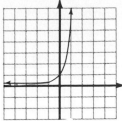

4.
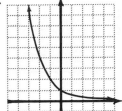

5.
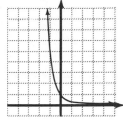

6.
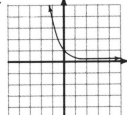

7.
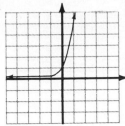

8.
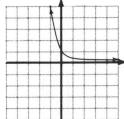

9.
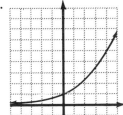

10.
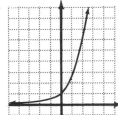

11.
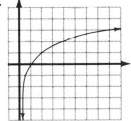

12.
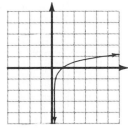

13.
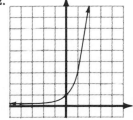

14.
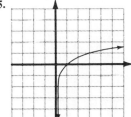

15.
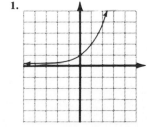

16.
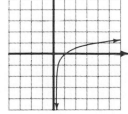

17.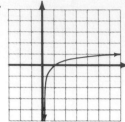

18.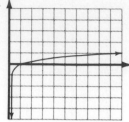

33.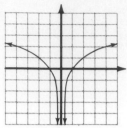

19.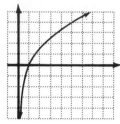

20.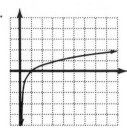

34. All real numbers   **35.** $\{x \mid x > 0\}$ **36.** $\{x \mid x \neq 0\}$

37. $\{x \mid x > 0\}$ **38.** $\left\{x \mid x > \dfrac{4}{3}\right\}$ **39.** $\{x \mid x \neq 0\}$

40. a. 8
 b. 8.574188
 c. 8.815241
 d. 8.821353
 e. 8.824411
 f. 8.824962

41. π^5 is larger.
 $5^\pi \approx 156.99$,
 $\pi^5 \approx 306.11$

42. $8^{\sqrt{3}}$ is larger.
 $\sqrt{8^3} = \sqrt{512} \approx 22.63$,
 $8^{\sqrt{3}} \approx 36.66$

21. Set of all real numbers   **22.** Set of all positive numbers

23. 1   **24.** 2.6

43.
$$3^{2x^2+5x-3} = 1$$
$$\log_3 3^{2x^2+5x-3} = \log_3 1$$
$$2x^2 + 5x - 3 = 0$$
$$(2x - 1)(x + 3) = 0$$
$$2x - 1 = 0 \quad \text{or} \quad x + 3 = 0$$
$$x = \frac{1}{2} \qquad x = -3$$

25.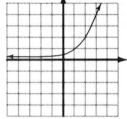

26.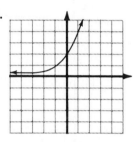

44. 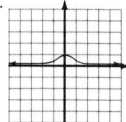   **45.**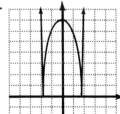

27.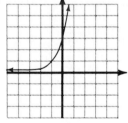

28.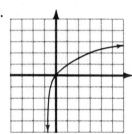

46.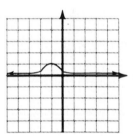

29.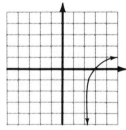

30.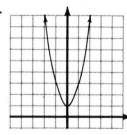

47. $3{,}007{,}114 = 3.007114 \times 10^6$ **48.** $0.002385 = 2.385 \times 10^{-3}$

49. $5.709 \times 10^{-5} = 0.00005709$

50. $6.03791 \times 10^8 = 603{,}791{,}000$

51. The focus is on the x-axis.
 $y = -6$ is the directrix.
 The equation is of the form $y^2 = 4px$.
 $p = 6$, so $y^2 = 4(6)x$ or $y^2 = 24x$.

52. $(x - 6)(x - 2)(x - (-1))$
 $= (x^2 - 8x + 12)(x + 1)$
 $= x^3 - 7x^2 + 4x + 12$

31.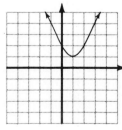

32.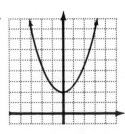

pp. 520–527   12-3 TRY THIS

 a. $\log_6 1 = 0$ **b.** $\log_{10} 0.001 = -3$ **c.** $\log_{16} 2 = \dfrac{1}{4}$

d. $\log_{6/5} \frac{25}{36} = -2$ **e.** $2^5 = 32$ **f.** $10^3 = 1000$

g. $10^{-2} = 0.01$ **h.** $(\sqrt{5})^2 = 5$

i. $\log_{10} x = 4$ **j.** $\log_x 81 = 4$ **k.** $\log_2 16 = x$
$10^4 = x$ $x^4 = 81$ $2^x = 16$
$10{,}000 = x$ $x = \sqrt[4]{81}$ $2^x = 2^4$
            $x = 3$ $x = 4$

l. $\log_5 \frac{1}{25} = x$ **m.** 3   **n.** 42   **o.** 37   **p.** 3.2

$$5^x = \frac{1}{25}$$
$$5^x = 5^{-2}$$
$$x = -2$$

p. 528   12-3 EXERCISES

1. $\log_{10} 100{,}000 = 5$ **2.** $\log_{10} 100 = 2$ **3.** $\log_8 2 = \frac{1}{3}$

4. $\log_{16} 2 = \frac{1}{4}$ **5.** $\log_5 \frac{1}{125} = -3$ **6.** $\log_4 \frac{1}{1024} = -5$

7. $\log_{10} 2 = 0.3010$ **8.** $\log_a c = -b$ **9.** $3^t = 8$

10. $7^h = 10$ **11.** $5^2 = 25$ **12.** $6^1 = 6$ **13.** $10^{-1} = 0.1$

14. $10^{-2} = 0.01$ **15.** $10^{0.845} = 7$ **16.** $10^{0.4771} = 3$

17. $k^c = A$ **18.** 9   **19.** 64   **20.** 4   **21.** 4   **22.** $\frac{1}{2}$

23. $\frac{1}{9}$ **24.** 2   **25.** 2   **26.** 3   **27.** 4   **28.** 10

29. 9   **30.** a

31.   Let $x = \log_2 64$.   **32.**   Let $x = \log_4 64$.
    Then $2^x = 64$.   Then $4^x = 64$.
       $2^x = 2^6$ $4^x = 4^3$
        $x = 6$ $x = 3$

33.   Let $x = \log_{10} 10^2$.   **34.**   Let $x = \log_3 3^4$.
    Then $10^x = 10^2$.   Then $3^x = 3^4$.
        $x = 2$ $x = 4$

35.   Let $x = \log_{10} 0.1$.   **36.**   Let $x = \log_{10} 10{,}000$.
    Then $10^x = 0.1$.   Then $10^x = 10{,}000$.
      $10^x = 10^{-1}$ $10^x = 10^4$
        $x = -1$ $x = 4$

37.   Let $x = \log_{10} 1$.   **38.**   Let $x = \log_{10} 10$.
    Then $10^x = 1$.   Then $10^x = 10$.
      $10^x = 10^0$ $x = 1$
        $x = 0$

39. $\{x \mid x > 0\}$ on graph x is always positive.
Graph $y = 2^x$ for $y > 1$.

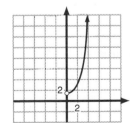

40. $3^x \leq 1$
Graph $y = 3^x$ for $y \leq 1$.
On graph $x \leq 0$.

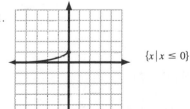

$\{x \mid x \leq 0\}$

41. $\log_2 x < 0$
Graph $y = \log_2 x$ for $y < 0$.
$y^x = x$ for $y < 0$

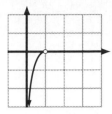

$\{x \mid 0 < x < 1\}$

42. $\log_2 x \geq 4$
Graph $y = \log_2 x$ for $y \geq 4$.

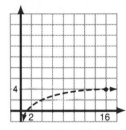

$\{x \mid x \geq 16\}$

43. $\log_{\sqrt{2}} 16 = y$ **44.** $3^{(2x)} = 6561$
     $\sqrt{2}^y = 16$ $3^{2x} = 3^8$
       $y = 8$ $2^x = 8$
                     $2^x = 2^3$
                      $x = 3$

45. $81^{(4x)} = 9$
    $81^{(4x)} = 81^{1/2}$

$$4^x = \frac{1}{2}$$
$$(2^2)^x = 2^{-1}$$
$$2x = -1$$
$$x = -\frac{1}{2}$$

46. No solution
$3^{(3x)} = 1$
To be true, $3^{(3x)} = 3^0$
$3^x = 0$
This is never true; 3^x is always positive, never 0.

47. Factors: $(x - 1)^3 (x + 1)^2$
        $(x^3 - 3x^2 + 3x + 1)(x^2 + 2x + 1)$
        $x^5 - x^4 - 2x^3 + 2x^2 + x - 1$

48. Factors: $(x - \sqrt{3})(x + \sqrt{3})(x - 2)(x + 5i)(x - 5i)$
        $(x^2 - 3)(x - 2)(x^2 + 25)$
        $(x^3 - 2x - 3x + 6)(x^2 + 25)$
        $x^5 - 2x^4 + 22x^3 - 44x^2 - 75x + 150$

49. $f(x) = Ax^2 + Bx + C$
$(1, -8)$: $-8 = A(1)^2 + B(1) + C \Rightarrow -8 = A + B + C$
$(2, -5)$: $-5 = A(2)^2 + B(2) + C \Rightarrow -5 = 4A + 2B + C$
$(-1, 4)$: $4 = A(-1)^2 + B(-1) + C \Rightarrow 4 = A - B + C$
$-8 = A + B + C$
$\underline{4 = A - B + C}$
$-4 = 2A + 2C$
$-2 = A + C$
$-5 = 4A + 2B + C \Rightarrow -5 = 4A + 2B + C$
$2(4 = A - B + C) \Rightarrow \underline{8 = 2A - 2B + 2C}$
                        $3 = 6A + 3C$
                        $1 = 2A + C$
$-1(-2 = A + C) \Rightarrow +2 = -A - C$
$1 = 2A + C \Rightarrow \underline{1 = 2A + C}$
                   $3 = A$
$-2 = A + C$ $-8 = A + B + C$
$-2 = 3 + C$ $-8 = 3 + B - 5$
$-5 = C$ $-6 = B$
$f(x) = 3x^2 - 6x - 5$

50. $f(x) = Ax^2 + Bx + C$

$(2, -4): -4 = A(2)^2 + B(2) + C \Rightarrow -4 = 4A + 2B + C$

$(-3, 26): 26 = A(-3)^2 + B(-3) + C \Rightarrow$

$\qquad\qquad\qquad\qquad\qquad 26 = 9A - 3B + C$

$(5, 2): 2 = A(5)^2 + B(5) + C \Rightarrow 2 = 25A + 5B + C$

$-1(-4 = 4A + 2B + C) \Rightarrow \quad 4 = -4A - 2B - C$

$\quad 26 = 9A - 3B + C \Rightarrow \quad \underline{26 = 9A - 3B + C}$

$\qquad\qquad\qquad\qquad\qquad 30 = 5A - 5B$

$\qquad\qquad\qquad\qquad\qquad6 = A - B$

$2 = 25A + 5B + C \Rightarrow \quad 2 = 25A + 5B + C$

$-1(26 = 9A - 3B + C) \Rightarrow \underline{-26 = -9A + 3B - C}$

$\qquad\qquad\qquad\qquad\qquad -24 = 16A + 8B$

$\qquad\qquad\qquad\qquad\qquad-3 = 2A + B$

$\begin{array}{lll} 6 = A - B & 6 = A - B & -4 = 4A + 2B + C \\ \underline{-3 = 2A + B} & \underline{6 = 1 - B} & -4 = 4 + 2(-5) + C \\ 3 = 3A & 5 = -B & -4 = 4 - 10 + C \\ 1 = A & -5 = B & 2 = C \end{array}$

$f(x) = x^2 - 5x + 2$

pp. 530–532   12-4 TRY THIS

a. **(1)** $\log_a M + \log_a N$ **b.** **(1)** $\log_3(7 \cdot 5)$
    (2) $\log_5 25 + \log_5 5$ $\log_3 35$
          $2 + 1$ **(2)** $\log_a C \cdot A \cdot B \cdot I \cdot N$
           3 $\log_a$ CABIN

c. $5 \log_7 4$ **d.** $\dfrac{1}{2} \log_a 5$

e. **(1)** $\log_a M - \log_a N$
    (2) $\log_c 1 - \log_c 4$

f. $\log_{10} 4\pi - \log_{10} \sqrt{23}$
    $\log_{10} 4 + \log_{10} \pi - [\log_{10}(23)^{1/2}]$

    $\log_{10} 4 + \log_{10} \pi - \dfrac{1}{2} \log_{10} 23$

g. $\log_a \sqrt{\dfrac{z^3}{xy}}$

    $\log_a \dfrac{(z^3)^{1/2}}{(xy)^{1/2}}$

    $\dfrac{1}{2}[3 \log_a z - \log_a x - \log_a y] = \dfrac{3}{2} \log_a z - \dfrac{1}{2} \log_a x - \dfrac{1}{2} \log_a y$

h. $5 \log_a x - \log_a y + \dfrac{1}{4} \log_a z = \log_a \dfrac{x^5 \cdot z^{1/4}}{y} = \log_a \dfrac{x^5 \sqrt[4]{z}}{y}$

i. **(1)** $\log_a 9 = 2 \log_a 3$
              $\approx 2(0.477)$
              ≈ 0.954

    (2) $\log_a \sqrt{2} = \dfrac{1}{2} \log_a 2$

                $\approx \dfrac{1}{2}(0.301)$

                ≈ 0.1505

    (3) $\log_a \sqrt[3]{2} = \dfrac{1}{3} \log_a 2$

                $\approx \dfrac{1}{3}(0.301)$

                ≈ 0.1003

    (4) $\log_a \dfrac{3}{2} = \log_a 3 - \log_a 2$

                $\approx 0.477 - 0.301$
                ≈ 0.176

    (5) $\dfrac{\log_a 3}{\log_a 2} \approx \dfrac{0.477}{0.301}$

                ≈ 1.585

pp. 532–533   12-4 EXERCISES

1. $\log_2 32 + \log_2 8 = 5 + 3 = 8$

2. $\log_3 27 + \log_3 81 = 3 + 4 = 7$

---

3. $\log_4 64 + \log_4 16 = 3 + 2 = 5$

4. $\log_5 25 + \log_5 125 \quad 2 + 3 = 5$

5. $\log_c B + \log_c x$ **6.** $\log_t 5 + \log_t Y$

7. $\log_a(6 \cdot 70) = \log_a 420$

8. $\log_b(65 \cdot 2) = \log_b 130$

9. $\log_c(Ky)$ **10.** $3 \log_a x$ **11.** $5 \log_b t$ **12.** $6 \log_c y$

13. $\log_a 67 - \log_a 5$ **14.** $\log_t T - \log_t 7$

15. $\log_b 3 - \log_b 4$ **16.** $2 \log_a x + 3 \log_a y + \log_a z$

17. $\log_a 5 + \log_a x + 4 \log_a y + 3 \log_a z$

18. $\log_b x + 2 \log_b y - 3 \log_b z$

19. $\log_a \dfrac{\sqrt[3]{x^2}\sqrt{y}}{y}$ **20.** $\log_a \dfrac{\sqrt{x}\, y^3}{x^2}$ **21.** $\log_a \dfrac{2x^4}{y^3}$

22. $\log_a x$ **23.** $\log_a \dfrac{\sqrt{a}}{x}$ **24.** $\log_a(x + 2)$

25. 0.602   **26.** 0.699   **27.** 1.699   **28.** 1.079

29. 1.778   **30.** −0.477   **31.** −0.088   **32.** 0.2158

33. 1.954   **34.** 0.051   **35.** −0.602   **36.** −0.046

37. $\dfrac{\log_a M}{\log_a N} = \log_a M - \log_a N$ **38.** $\dfrac{\log_a M}{\log_a N} = \log_a \dfrac{M}{N}$

    $\dfrac{\log_a M}{\log_a N} \neq \log_a \dfrac{M}{N}$ $\dfrac{\log_a M}{\log_a N} \neq \log_a M - \log_a N$

    False   False

39. $\log_a 2x = 2 \log_2 x$ **40.** True
    $\log_a 2x \neq \log_2 x^2$
    False

41. $\log_a(M + N) = \log_a M + \log_a N$ **42.** True
    $\log_a MN \neq \log_a M + \log_a N$
    False

43. $\log_\pi \pi^{2x+3} = 4$ **44.** $3^{\log_3(8x-4)} = 5$
      $\pi^4 = \pi^{2x+3}$ $8x - 4 = 5$
      $4 = 2x + 3$ $8x = 9$
      $1 = 2x$
      $\dfrac{1}{2} = x$ $x = \dfrac{9}{8}$

45. $4^{2\log_4 x} = 7$ **46.** $8^{2\log_8 x + \log_8 x} = 27$
     $4^{\log_4 x^2} = 7$ $8^{\log_8 x^2 + \log_8 x} = 27$
       $x^2 = 7$ $8^{\log_8 x^3} = 27$
       $x = \sqrt{7}$ $x^3 = 27$
                        $x = 3$

47. $(x + 3) \log_a a^x = x$
      $\log_a a^{x(x+3)} = x$
       $x(x + 3) = x$
       $x^2 + 2x = 0$
       $x(x + 2) = 0$
           $x = 0$ or -2

48. $\log_a 5x = \log_a 5 + \log_a x$
Identity as long as $5x$ is positive from definition of logarithm. Thus, x must be positive.
$\{x \mid x > 0\}$

49. $\log x^2 y^3 = \log x^2 + \log y^3 = 2 \log x + 3 \log y = a$

    $\log\left(\dfrac{x}{y}\right) = \log x - \log y = b$ Thus, $\log x = b + \log y$.

    So, $2(b + \log y) + 3 \log y = 2b + 5 \log y = a$.

    $\log y = \dfrac{a - 2b}{5}$ and $\log x = b + \left(\dfrac{a - 2b}{5}\right) = \dfrac{a + 3b}{5}$

50. $\log_a\left(\dfrac{1}{x}\right)$

    $= \log_a x^{-1}$
    $= -1(\log_a x)$
    $= -1(2) = -2$

51. $\log_{1/a} x$
$a^2 = x$
So $a = \sqrt{x}$
$\dfrac{1}{a} = \dfrac{1}{\sqrt{x}} \Rightarrow \log_{1/a} x = \log_{1/\sqrt{x}} x$
If $\log_{1/\sqrt{x}} x = y$
then $\left(\dfrac{1}{\sqrt{x}}\right)^y = x^1$.
$y = -2$

52. $\log_a\left(\dfrac{1}{x}\right) = \log_a 1 - \log_a x = 0 - \log_a x = -\log_a x$

53. Let $\log_a\left(\dfrac{1}{x}\right) = M$. Then $a^M = \dfrac{1}{x}$, so $a^{-M} = x$ or $\left(\dfrac{1}{a}\right)^M = x$.

Thus, $\log_{1/a} x = \log_a\left(\dfrac{1}{x}\right)$.

54. $\log_a\left(\dfrac{x + \sqrt{x^2 - 5}}{5} \cdot \dfrac{x - \sqrt{x^2 - 5}}{x - \sqrt{x^2 - 5}}\right)$

$= \log_a\left(\dfrac{x^2 - (x^2 - 5)}{5(x - \sqrt{x^2 - 5})}\right)$

$= \log_a\left(\dfrac{1}{x - \sqrt{x^2 - 5}}\right)$

$= -\log_a(x - \sqrt{x^2 - 5})$

55. Since i is a root of $x^3 - 2x^2 + x - 2$,
$-i$ is also a root.
$(x - i)(x + i) = x^2 + 1$

$$
\begin{array}{r}
x - 2 \\
x^2 + 1 \overline{)\,x^3 - 2x^2 + x - 2} \\
\underline{x^3 + x} \\
-2x^2 - 2 \\
\underline{-2x^2 - 2} \\
\end{array}
$$

The roots are i, $-i$, and 2.

56. Since $-2i$ is a root of $x^4 - 3x^2 - 28$, $2i$ is also a root.
$(x - 2i)(x + 2i) = x^2 + 4$

$$
\begin{array}{r}
x^2 - 7 \\
x^2 + 4 \overline{)\,x^4 - 3x^2 - 28} \\
\underline{x^4 + 4x^2} \\
-7x^2 - 28 \\
\underline{-7x^2 - 28} \\
\end{array}
$$

Solving $x^2 - 7 = 0$
$x = \pm\sqrt{7}$
The roots are $-2i$, $2i$, $\sqrt{7}$, and $-\sqrt{7}$.

57. The possible rational roots of $x^4 - 6x^3 + 30x - 25$ are ± 1, ± 5, ± 25.

$$
\begin{array}{r|rrrrr}
1 & 1 & -6 & 0 & 30 & -25 \\
& & 1 & -5 & -5 & 25 \\
\hline
& 1 & -5 & -5 & 25 & 0 \\
\end{array}
$$

1 is a root.
$x^4 - 6x^3 + 30x - 25 = (x - 1)(x^3 - 5x^2 - 5x + 25)$
factoring by grouping: $= (x - 1)(x^2(x - 5) - 5(x - 5))$
$= (x - 1)(x^2 - 5)(x - 5)$
The roots are 1, 5, $\sqrt{5}$, and $-\sqrt{5}$.

58. The possible rational roots of $x^3 - 6x^2 + 3x + 10$ are ± 1, ± 2, ± 5, ± 10.

$$
\begin{array}{r|rrrr}
-1 & 1 & -6 & 3 & 10 \\
& & -1 & 7 & -10 \\
\hline
& 1 & -7 & 10 & 0 \\
\end{array}
$$

-1 is a root.
$x^3 - 6x^2 + 3x + 10 = (x + 1)(x^2 - 7x + 10)$
$= (x + 1)(x - 2)(x - 5)$
The roots are -1, 2, and 5.

pp. 534–537   12-5 TRY THIS

a. 2.3238   **b.** 5.8186   **c.** 0.4625   **d.** -4.3665
e. 0.8506   **f.** 0.6021   **g.** 0.9996   **h.** $0.4609 + 2$

i. $0.4609 + (-4)$ **j.** $8.6646 - 10$ **k.** $9.7832 - 10$
l. $6.8055 - 10$ **m.** 22,003.92   **n.** 1022.8219
o. 0.00098469   **p.** 0.00000017   **q.** 64,106.2
r. 4.25×10^{-4} **s.** 0.0105

p. 538   12-5 EXERCISES

1. 0.3909   **2.** 0.8837   **3.** 0.7251   **4.** 0.9330
5. 0.5705   **6.** 0.9562   **7.** 0.0294   **8.** 0.6628
9. 0.8007   **10.** 2.5403   **11.** 3.9405   **12.** 1.7202
13. 1.3139   **14.** 2.9212   **15.** 1.9657   **16.** 3.5877
17. 5.7952   **18.** $7.1271 - 10$, or -2.8729
19. $8.8463 - 10$, or -1.1537 **20.** $9.8062 - 10$, or -0.1938
21. $6.3345 - 10$, or -3.6655 **22.** $9.2380 - 10$, or -0.7620
23. $7.5403 - 10$, or -2.4597 **24.** $5.6064 - 10$, or -4.3936
25. 7.34   **26.** 2.24   **27.** 4.79   **28.** 1.38   **29.** 5.72
30. 8.30   **31.** 2330   **32.** 83,600   **33.** 18   **34.** 0.613
35. 0.0973   **36.** 0.00973   **37.** 0.0346   **38.** 0.000613
39. 0.00000426

40. $\log x = 0.8021$ **41.** $\log x = 4.1903$
$10^{0.8021} = x$ $10^{4.1903} = x$
$6.34 \approx x$ $15,500 \approx x$

42. $\log x = 9.7875 - 10$ **43.** $\log x = -1.0218$
$10^{-0.2125} = x$ $x \approx 0.0951$
$0.613 \approx x$

44. $10^x = 345 \Rightarrow \log_{10} 345 = x$ **45.** $10^x = 5670$
$2.5378 = x$ $\log_{10} 5670 = x$
                                                         $3.7536 = x$

46. a. $8^{1000} = y$ **b.** $8^x = 10^{1000}$
$1000 \log 8 = \log y$ $x \log 8 = 1000$
$903.1 = \log y$
$10^{903.1} = y$ $x = \dfrac{1000}{\log 8}$
$903 + 1 = 904$ digits
                                  $x = 1107$

c. $y^{1000} = 10^{500}$
$1000 \log y = 500$

$\log y = \dfrac{5}{10}$

$10^{1/2} = y$
$y \approx 3.16$

47. $\sqrt[3]{8} = \log_{10} 8^{1/3}$ **48.** $2^3 = 3 \log_{10} 2$
$= \dfrac{1}{3} \log_{10} 8$ $= 3(0.3010)$
                                                        $= 0.9030$
$= \dfrac{1}{3}(0.9031)$ antilog 0.9030
                                                        $= 8$
$= 0.3010$ $10^{3 \log 2} = 8$
antilog 0.3010
$= 1.9999$
$= 2$
$10^{(1/3) \log 8} = 2$

49. $\log_{10} \dfrac{14}{2} = \log 14 - \log 2$
$= 1.1461 - 0.3010$
$= 0.8451$
antilog 0.8451
$= 7$
$10^{\log 14 - \log 2} = 7$

50. $\log_{10} 4 \cdot 2 = \log_{10} 4 + \log_{10} 2$
$= 0.6021 + 0.3010$
$= 0.9031$
antilog 0.9031
$= 8$
$10^{\log 4 + \log 2} = 8$

51. Parabola

52.

$$x^2 + 5x + 6 \overline{)\begin{array}{c} x - 1 \\ x^3 + 4x^2 + x - 6 \end{array}}$$
$$\underline{x^3 + 5x^2 + 6x}$$
$$-x^2 - 5x - 6$$
$$\underline{-x^2 - 5x - 6}$$

$P(x) = (x^2 + 5x + 6)(x - 1) + 0$

pp. 540–541   12-6 TRY THIS

a. 3.6592   **b.** $8.3779 - 10$, or -1.6221 **c.** 2856
d. 0.0005956

p. 541–542   12-6 EXERCISES

1. 1.6194   **2.** 2.6740   **3.** 0.4689   **4.** 1.3377

5. 2.8130   **6.** 1.5725   **7.** $9.1538 - 10$ **8.** $8.9564 - 10$

9. $7.6291 - 10$ **10.** 3.6549   **11.** $9.2494 - 10$

12. $8.9220 - 10$ **13.** 2.7786   **14.** 2.6991   **15.** 2.9031

16. 43.15   **17.** 224.5   **18.** 4.444   **19.** 14.53   **20.** 1.082

21. 70,030   **22.** 0.7185   **23.** 0.09245   **24.** 0.002587

25. 0.5343   **26.** 0.01589   **27.** 0.007295

28. Let $x = \log(\log 3)$.
$10^x = \log 3$
$10^x = 0.4771$
$x = \log 0.4771$
$x = -0.3214$
$x = 9.6786 - 10$

29. Let $x = \log(\log 5)$.
$10^x = \log 5$
$10^x = 0.6990$
$x = \log 0.6990$
$x = -0.1555$
$x = 9.8445 - 10$

30. Let $x = \log(\log 7)$.
$10^x = \log 7$
$10^x = 0.8451$
$x = \log 0.8451$
$x = -0.0731$
$x = 9.9269 - 10$

31. Since the logarithmic graph is always curving downward, connecting any two points on the curve with a segment will result in the segment being below the curve. So the linear approximation will be slightly less than the actual value.

32. $\log \left[\dfrac{35.24 \cdot (16.77)^3}{12.93 \cdot \sqrt{276.2}} \right]$

$= \log 35.24 + 3 \log 16.77 - \log 12.93 - \dfrac{1}{2} \log 276.2$

$= 1.5470 + 3(1.2245) - 1.1116 - \dfrac{1}{2}(2.4412)$

$= 2.8883$
$= $ antilog 2.8883
$= 773.2$

33. 0.8269

$\log \sqrt[5]{\dfrac{16.79 \cdot (4.234)^2}{18.81 \cdot 175.3}}$

$= \dfrac{1}{5}[\log 16.79 + 3 \log 4.234 - \log 18.81 - \log 175.3]$

$= \dfrac{1}{5}(1.2251 + 3(0.6268) - 1.2744 - 2.2438)$

$= \dfrac{1}{5}(-0.4127)$

$= -0.08254$
$= $ antilog $- 0.08254 = 0.8269$

34. There are 2 variations in sign: 2 positive real or 0 positive real

35. There are 3 variations in sign: 3 positive real or 1 positive real

36. $5(-x)^4 + 2(-x)^3 - 6(-x)^2 + 11(-x) + 6$
$= 5x^4 - 2x^3 - 6x^2 - 11x + 6$
There are 2 variations in sign: 2 negative real or 0 negative real

37. $-4(-x)^3 + 5(-x)^2 - 8(-x) + 10 = 4x^3 + 5x^2 + 8x + 10$
No variations in sign, so there are no negative real roots

38. $2x + 3y = 5 \Leftrightarrow 2y + 3x = 5$, interchange x and y; No

39. $xy = 2 \Leftrightarrow yx = 2$; Yes

40. $7x - 7y = 1 \Leftrightarrow 7y - 7x = 1$; No

41. $3x^2 + 3y^2 = 7 \Leftrightarrow 3y^2 + 3x^2 = 7$; Yes

42. $f(x) = x + 2$
$x = f^{-1}(x) + 2$
$x - 2 = f^{-1}(x)$

43. $f(x) = \sqrt{x + 3}$
$x = \sqrt{f^{-1}(x) + 3}$
$x^2 = f^{-1}(x) + 3$
$x^2 - 3 = f^{-1}(x)$

44. $c^2 = \left(53\dfrac{1}{3}\right)^2 + (100)^2$

$c^2 = \left(\dfrac{160}{3}\right)^2 + 10,000$

$c^2 = \dfrac{25,600}{9} + \dfrac{90,000}{9}$

$c^2 = \dfrac{115,600}{9} \qquad c = \dfrac{340}{3}$

$c = \dfrac{\sqrt{115,600}}{3} \qquad c = 113\dfrac{1}{3}$ yd

pp. 544–547   12-7 TRY THIS

a. $2^x = 7$
$x \log 2 = \log 7$

$x = \dfrac{\log 7}{\log 2}$

$x \approx \dfrac{0.8451}{0.3010}$

$x \approx 2.8076$ Using a calculator, we find $x \approx 2.8074$.

b. $4^x = 6$
$x \log 4 = \log 6$

$x = \dfrac{\log 6}{\log 4}$

$x \approx \dfrac{0.7782}{0.6021}$

$x \approx 1.2925$

c. $4^{2x-3} = 64$
$4^{2x-3} = 4^3$
$2x - 3 = 3$
$2x = 6$
$x = 3$

d. $\log_5 x = 3$
$5^3 = x$
$125 = x$

e. $\log_4(8x - 6) = 3$
$4^3 = 8x - 6$
$64 = 8x - 6$
$70 = 8x$
$\dfrac{70}{8} = x$
$8.75 = x$

f. $\log x + \log(x + 3) = 1$
$\log x(x + 3) = 1$
$x^2 + 3x = 10^1$
$x^2 + 3x - 10 = 0$
$(x + 5)(x - 2) = 0$
$ x = -5 \quad$ or $\quad x = 2$
x cannot be negative.
$ x = 2$

g. $18,540 = 500(1.14)^t$
$1.14^t = 3.708$
$t \log 1.14 = \log 3.708$

$t = \dfrac{\log 3.708}{\log 1.14}$

$t \approx \dfrac{0.5691}{0.0569}$

$t \approx 10.002 \approx 10$ years

h. $10 \log 2510 = L$
$10 \cdot 3.3997 \approx L$
$10 \cdot 3.4 \approx L$
34 decibels $\approx L$

i. $10 \log 10^6 = L$
$10 \cdot 6 = L$
60 decibels $= L$

j. $R = \log \dfrac{2.5 \times 10^8 I_0}{I_0}$

$= (\log 2.5) + 8$
$\approx 0.3980 + 8$
≈ 8.398
≈ 8.4 magnitude

12-7 EXERCISES

1. 3   **2.** 5   **3.** 3.3219   **4.** 5.0444   **5.** $\dfrac{5}{2}$ **6.** -1

7. $-3, -1$ **8.** $-3, \dfrac{1}{2}$ **9.** 1.4036   **10.** 1.1073

11. 2.7093   **12.** 7.4520   **13.** 3.6064   **14.** 3.5806

15. 5.6467   **16.** 10   **17.** 1   **18.** $\dfrac{1}{3}$ **19.** 1   **20.** 5

21. $\sqrt{41}$ **22.** 1, or 10^9 **23.** 1, or 10^{16} **24.** $\pm 2\sqrt{6}$

25. $\pm\dfrac{\sqrt{2}}{4}$ **26.** 11.9   **27.** 22.5   **28.** 65 decibels

29. 64 decibels   **30.** 140 decibels   **31.** 120 decibels

32. 6.7   **33.** 8.25   **34.** 10^5 times I_0 **35.** $6.3 \times 10^7 I_0$

36. 4.2   **37.** 7.8

38.
$\log \sqrt{x} = \sqrt{\log x}$

$\dfrac{1}{2}\log x = (\log x)^{1/2}$

$\dfrac{1}{4}\log x = \log x$

$(\log x)^2 = 4 \log x$
$(\log x)^2 - 4 \log x = 0$
$\log x(\log x - 4) = 0$
$\log x = 0$ or $\log x = 4$
$x = 1$ or $x = 10^4$

1; 10,000

39. $\log_5 \sqrt{x^2 + 1} = 2$

$\dfrac{1}{2}\log_5(x^2 + 1) = 2$

$\log_5(x^2 + 1) = 4$
$5^4 = x^2 + 1$
$625 = x^2 + 1$
$624 = x^2$
$\pm\sqrt{624} = x$
$\pm 4\sqrt{39} = x$

40. $(\log_a x)^{-1} = \log_a x^{-1}$
$(\log_a x)^{-1} = -1 \log_a x$
Let $y = \log_a x$
$y^{-1} = -y$
$1 = -y^2$
$y^2 = -1$
No solution.

41. $\log_5 x = 2$ or -2
$5^2 = x$ or $5^{-2} = x$

$25 = x$ or $\dfrac{1}{25} = x$

42. $3^2 = |x|$
$9 = |x|$
$x = \pm 9$

43. $\log(x^{\log x}) = 4$
$(\log x)(\log x) = 4$
$\log x = \pm\sqrt{4} = \pm 2$
$x = 10^2$ or $x = 10^{-2}$

$x = 100, \dfrac{1}{100}$

44. $\log\left(\dfrac{\sqrt{(a^{2x} \cdot a^{-5x-4})}}{a^x \div a^{-x}}\right) = \log a^7$

$\dfrac{1}{2}[-4(2x \log a + (-5x \log a))] - (x \log a - (-x \log a))$

$= 7 \log a$

$\dfrac{1}{2}[-4(-3x \log a)] - (2x \log a) = 7 \log a$

$6x \log a - 2x \log a = 7 \log a$
$4x \log a = 7 \log a$
$4x = 7$

$x = \dfrac{7}{4}$

45.
$\log \dfrac{(a^{3x+1})^2}{a^4} = \log a^{10x}$

$2(3x + 1) \log a - 4 \log a = 10x \log a$
$(6x + 2 - 4) \log a = 10x \log a$
$-4x - 2 = 0$

$x = -\dfrac{1}{2}$

46.
$y = ax^n$
$\log_x y = \log_x ax^n = \log_x a + \log_x x^n$
$\log_x y - \log_x a = n \log_x x$
$\log_x y - \log_x a = x$

47.
$y = kb^{at}$
$\log_b y = \log_b kb^{at} = \log_b k + \log_b b^{at}$
$\log_b y - \log_b k = at \log_b b$
$\log_b y - \log_b k = at$

$t = \dfrac{\log_b y - \log_b k}{a}$

48.
$T - T_0 = (T_1 - T_0)10^{-kt}$
$\log(T - T_0) = \log[(T_1 - T_0)10^{-kt}]$
$= \log(T_1 - T_0) + \log 10^{-kt}$
$\log(T - T_0) - \log(T_1 - T_0) = -kt \log 10$

$\log\left(\dfrac{T - T_0}{T_1 - T_0}\right) = -kt$

$t = -\dfrac{1}{k}\log\left(\dfrac{T - T_0}{T_1 - T_0}\right)$

49.
$PV^n = c$
$\log_v(PV^n) = \log_v c$
$\log_v P + \log_v V^n = \log_v c$
$n \log_v V = \log_v c - \log_v P$
$n = \log_v c - \log_v P$

$= \log_v\left(\dfrac{c}{P}\right)$

50. $\log_a Q = \dfrac{1}{3}\log_a y + b$

$a^{\log_a Q} = a^{(1/3 \log_a y + b)}$
$Q = a^{(1/3 \log_a y)} \cdot a^b$
$Q = y^{1/3} \cdot a^b = a^b\sqrt[3]{y}$

51. $\log_a y = 2x + \log_a x$
$y = a^{(2x + \log_a x)}$
$y = a^{2x} \cdot a^{\log_a x}$
$y = xa^{2x}$

52. a. $\log_2 8 = 3$ $\log_8 2 = \dfrac{1}{3}$

b. $\log_3 9 = 2$ $\log_9 3 = \dfrac{1}{2}$

c. $\log_4 16 = 2$ $\log_{16} 4 = \dfrac{1}{2}$

In general, $\log_a b = \dfrac{1}{\log_b a}$

53.
$x^{\log x} = \dfrac{x^3}{100}$

$100x^{\log x} = x^3$
$\log(100x^{\log x}) = \log x^3$
$\log 100 + \log x^{\log x} = \log x^3$
$2 + (\log x) \log x = 3 \log x$
$(\log x)^2 - 3 \log x + 2 = 0$
$(\log x - 2)(\log x - 1) = 0$
$\log x = 2$ or $\log x = 1$
$x = 100$ or $x = 10$

54.
$x^{\log x} = 100x$
$\log(x^{\log x}) = \log 100x$
$(\log x) \log x = \log 100 + \log x$
$(\log x)^2 - \log x - 2 = 0$
$(\log x - 2)(\log x + 1) = 0$
$\log x = 2$ or $\log x = -1$

$x = 100$ or $x = \dfrac{1}{10}$

55. $|\log_5 x| + 3 \log_5 |x| = 4$

The first term forces $x > 0$, hence, $3 \log_5 |x| = 3 \log_5 x$. Our equation becomes $|\log_5 x| + 3 \log_5 x = 4$. There are two cases: $\log_5 x > 0$ or $\log_5 x < 0$. For $\log_5 x > 0$,

$$\log_5 x + 3 \log_5 x = 4$$
$$4 \log_5 x = 4$$
$$\log_5 x = 1$$
$$x = 5$$

For $\log_5 x < 0$, $\log_5 x = -|\log_5 x|$ and $|\log_5 x| + 3 \log_5 x = |\log_5 x| - 3|\log_5 x| = -2|\log_5 x| = 4$
$|\log_5 x| = -2$, not possible. The solution is $x = 5$.

56. $|\log_a x| = \log_a |x|$
$x > 0$ because $\log_a x$ for $x < 0$ is not possible. Then $|\log_a x| = \log_a x$. This implies that $\log_a x \geq 0$, or $x \geq 1$. The solution set is then $\{x \mid x \geq 1\}$ for $a > 1$. For $a < 1$ we would have $\{x \mid 0 < x < 1\}$.

57. $\log(0.5)^x < \log\left(\frac{4}{5}\right)$

$$x \log(0.5) < \log(0.8)$$

$$x < \frac{\log 0.8}{\log 0.5} \approx 0.3219$$

58. $8x^{0.3} - 8x^{-0.3} = 63$
$8x^{0.6} - 63x^{0.3} - 8$
$(8x^{0.3} + 1)(x^{0.3} - 8) = 0$
$$8x^{0.3} = -1$$

$$x^{0.3} = -\frac{1}{8}$$

$$x = \left(\sqrt[3]{-\frac{1}{8}}\right)^{10}$$

$$x = \left(-\frac{1}{2}\right)^{10}$$

$$x = \left(-\frac{1}{2}\right)^{10} = 2^{10}$$

59.
$$5^{x+y} = 100$$
$$3^{2x-y} = 1000$$
$$\log 5^{x+y} = 2$$
$$\log 3^{2x-y} = 3$$
$$(x + y) \log 5 = 2$$
$$(2x - y) \log 3 = 3$$

$$x + y = \frac{2}{\log 5} \approx \frac{2}{0.6990} \approx 2.8612$$

$$2x - y = \frac{3}{\log 3} \approx \frac{3}{0.4771} \approx 6.2877$$

Adding, $3x \approx 9.1489$
$\quad\quad\quad x \approx 3.0497$
Substituting for x in the first equation,
$3.0497 + y \approx 2.8612$
$\quad\quad y \approx 2.8612 - 3.0497 = -0.1885$
The solution is approximately $(3.05, -0.19)$.

60. $\log_2[\log_3(\log_4 x)] = 0$
$$2^0 = \log_3(\log_4 x)$$
$$1 = \log_3(\log_4 x)$$
$$3^1 = \log_4 x$$
$$x = 4^3$$
$$x = 64$$
$\log_3[\log_2(\log_4 y)] = 0$
$$3^0 = \log_2(\log_4 y)$$
$$1 = \log_2(\log_4 y)$$
$$2^1 = \log_4 y$$
$$y = 4^2$$
$$y = 16$$
$\log_4[\log_3(\log_2 z)] = 0$
$$4^0 = \log_3(\log_2 z)$$
$$1 = \log_3(\log_2 z)$$
$$3^1 = \log_2 z$$
$$2^3 = z$$
$$8 = z$$
$$x = 64$$
$$y = 16$$
$$z = 8$$
$$x + y + z = 88$$

61.
$$2 \log_3(x - 2y) = \log_3 x + \log_3 y$$
$$\log_3(x - 2y)^2 = \log_3(xy)$$
$$\log_3(x - 2y)^2 = \log_3(xy)$$
$$(x - 2y)^2 = xy$$
$$x^2 - 4xy + 4y^2 - xy = 0$$
$$(x - 4y)(x - y) = 0$$
$$x = 4y \quad \text{or} \quad x = y$$

$$\frac{x}{y} = 4 \quad \text{or} \quad \frac{x}{y} = 1$$

If $\frac{x}{y} = 1$, then $x = y$.

Checking by substituting,
$2 \log_3(x - 2x) = \log_3 x + \log_3 x \Rightarrow 2 \log_3(-x) = \log_3 x + \log_3 x$
x would have to be positive for $\log_3 x$ to exist, but then $2 \log_3(-x)$ would not exist.

$\frac{x}{y} = 4$ is the only solution.

62.
$$4^{\log_{16} 27} = 2^x 3^y$$
$$(16^{1/2})^{\log_{16} 27} = 2^x 3^y$$
$$16^{\log_{16}(27)^{1/2}} = 2^x 3^y$$
$$27^{1/2} = 2^x 3^y$$
$$(3^3)^{1/2} = 2^x 3^y$$
$$3^{3/2} = 1 \cdot 3^{3/2}$$
$$= 2^0 3^{3/2}$$

So $x = 0$ and $y = \frac{3}{2}$.

Solution: $\left(0, \frac{3}{2}\right)$

63. $f^{-1}((f4))$
$$f(4) = 2(4) + 5$$
$$= 8 + 5$$
$$= 13$$

$$f^{-1}(x) = \frac{1}{2}(x - 5)$$

$$f^{-1}(13) = \frac{1}{2}(13 - 5)$$
$$= \frac{1}{2}(8)$$
$$= 4$$

64. $f(f^{-1}(-7)) = \frac{1}{2}(-7 - 5)$
$$= \frac{1}{2}(-12)$$
$$= -6$$
$$f(-6) = 2(-6) + 5$$
$$= -12 + 5$$
$$= -7$$

65. $f(x) = 0.2x - 1$
$$x = 0.2f^{-1}(x) - 1$$
$$x + 1 = 0.2f^{-1}(x)$$
$$\frac{x + 1}{0.2} = f^{-1}(x)$$
$$5x + 5 = f^{-1}(x)$$

66. $f(x) = (x - 5)^{1/2}$
$$x = (f^{-1}(x) - 5)^{1/2}$$
$$x^2 = f^{-1}(x) - 5$$
$$f^{-1}(x) = x^2 + 5 \quad x \geq 0$$

67. $10^3 = 1000$
$\log_{10} 1000 = 3$

68. $2^{-4} = \frac{1}{16}$

$$\log_2 \frac{1}{16} = -4$$

69. $81^{1/2} = 9$

$$\log_{81} 9 = \frac{1}{2}$$

70. $r^s = t$
$\log_r t = s$

71. $8^1 = 8$ **72.** $3^2 = 9$

73. $2^6 = 64$ **74.** $5^4 = 625$

75. $x^4 - 12x^2 + 35$
Possible: $\pm 35, \pm 7, \pm 5, \pm 1$
$(x^2 - 7)(x^2 - 5)$
$x = \pm\sqrt{7} \quad \text{or} \quad \pm\sqrt{5}$
None are rational.

76. $x^4 - 28x^2 + 75$
$(x^2 - 25)(x^2 - 3)$
$x = \pm 5 \quad \text{or} \quad \pm\sqrt{3}$; $x = \pm 5$ are the rational roots

77. $x^3 - x^2 - 4x + 4$
$= x^2(x - 1) - 4(x - 1)$
$= (x^2 - 4)(x - 1)$
$= (x + 2)(x - 2)(x - 1)$
The roots are -2, 2, and 1.

a.

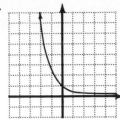

b.

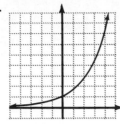

m. $\log_e 0.457 = \dfrac{\log_{10} 0.457}{\log_{10} e}$

$\approx \dfrac{9.6599 - 10}{0.4343}$

$\approx \dfrac{-0.3401}{0.4343}$

≈ -0.783

n.
$$2^x = 7$$
$$\log_2 2^x = \log_2 7$$
$$x = \log_2 7$$
$$x = \dfrac{\log_{10} 7}{\log_{10} 2}$$
$$x \approx \dfrac{0.8451}{0.3010}$$
$$x \approx 2.8076$$

c. 0.693147

d. $\ln 100 = \ln(5^2 \cdot 2^2)$
$= \ln 5^2 + \ln 2^2$
$= 2 \ln 5 + 2 \ln 2$
$= 2(\ln 5 + \ln 2)$
$\approx 2(1.6094 + 0.6931)$
$\approx 2(2.3025)$
≈ 4.605

If a calculator is used, the answer will be more precise.

e. $\ln 0.07432 = \ln(7.432 \times 10^{-7})$
$= \ln(7.432 \times 5^{-2} \times 2^{-2})$
$= \ln 7.432 + \ln 5^{-2} + \ln 2^{-2}$
$= \ln 7.432 - 2 \ln 5 - 2 \ln 2$
$= \ln 7.432 - 2(\ln 5 + \ln 2)$
$\approx 2.0058 - 4.605$
≈ -2.599

If a calculator is used, the answer will be more precise.

f. -0.000100

g. (1)
$$P = P_0 e^{kt}$$
$$107{,}000 = 64{,}000 e^{k \cdot 10}$$
$$107 = 64 e^{10k}$$
$$\ln 107 = \ln 64 + \ln e^{10k}$$
$$\ln 107 = \ln 64 + 10k$$

$$\dfrac{\ln 107 - \ln 64}{10} = k$$

$$0.0514 = k$$

(2) $P = 107{,}000 e^{0.0514 \cdot 15}$
$P = 107{,}000 e^{0.771}$
$P = 231{,}326$ people

h. $\dfrac{1}{2} N_0 = N_0 e^{-5k}$

$\dfrac{1}{2} = e^{-5k}$

$\ln \dfrac{1}{2} = \ln e^{-5k}$

$\ln \dfrac{1}{2} = -5k$

$k = -\dfrac{\ln 0.5}{5}$

$k \approx 0.1386$
$N = 224 e^{-0.1386 \cdot 30}$
$= 224 e^{-4.158}$
$\approx 224 \times 0.0156$
$N \approx 3.5$ grams

i. $\log_5 125 = \dfrac{\log_{10} 125}{\log_{10} 5}$

$\approx \dfrac{2.0969}{0.6990}$

≈ 3

j. $\log_6 4870 = \dfrac{\log_{10} 4870}{\log_{10} 6}$

$\approx \dfrac{3.6875}{0.7782}$

≈ 4.7385

k. Using 2.718 for e, $\log_{10} e = \log 2.718$
≈ 0.4342

l. $\log_e 1030 = \dfrac{\log_{10} 1030}{\log_{10} e}$

$\approx \dfrac{3.0128}{0.4343}$

≈ 6.937

1.

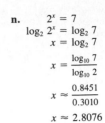

2.

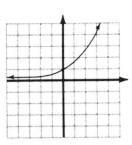

3.

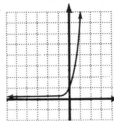

4.

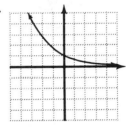

5.

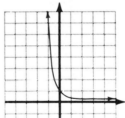

6.

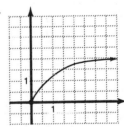

7. 0.6313   **8.** 2.9339   **9.** -3.9739 **10.** -1.6713

11. 0.7561   **12.** 5.3613   **13.** -1.5465 **14.** -6.1517

15. 8.4119   **16.** 11.3022   **17.** -7.4872 **18.** -0.001

19. -2.5256 **20.** -3.0555 **21.** 13.7953

22. $k \approx 0.01426$; $P \approx 1{,}204{,}000$

23. $k \approx 0.03148$; $P \approx 1{,}182{,}000$ **24.** 0.4 gram

25. 125 grams   **26.** 1.2 days   **27.** 248,000 years

28. a. 2948 years
   b. 5093 years

29. a. 7997

30. a. $k \approx 0.062$; $P = \$100 e^{0.062t}$
   b. \$773.69 or \$774.69 if unrounded calculator value for k is used.
   c. 1993

31. 2.1610   **32.** -0.0048 **33.** -0.1544 **34.** 3.8697

35. 2.4849   **36.** -0.2614

37.
$$P = P_0 e^{kt}$$
$$\frac{P}{P_0} = e^{kt}$$
$$\ln\left(\frac{P}{P_0}\right) = \ln e^{kt}$$
$$\ln\left(\frac{P}{P_0}\right) = kt$$
$$\frac{\ln P - \ln P_0}{k} = t$$

38.
$$P = P_0 e^{-kt}$$
$$\frac{P}{P_0} = e^{-kt}$$
$$\ln P - \ln P_0 = \ln e^{-kt}$$
$$\ln P - \ln P_0 = -kt$$
$$\frac{\ln P - \ln P_0}{-k} = t$$
$$\frac{\ln P_0 - \ln P}{k} = t$$

39. a. $\left(1 + \dfrac{0.12}{4}\right)^4 = (1 + .03)^4 = (1.03)^4$
$$\approx 1.12550881$$

b. $\left(1 + \dfrac{0.12}{12}\right)^{12} = (1 + .01)^{12} = (1.01)^{12}$
$$\approx 1.12682503$$

c. $\left(1 + \dfrac{0.12}{365}\right)^{365} = (1 + .000328767) = 1.127464614$

d. $e^{0.12} = 1.127496852$. This is the maximum for continuous compounding.

40.

x	1	2	3	4	5	6	7	8	9	10
$\sqrt[x]{x}$	1	1.42	1.44	1.42	1.38	1.35	1.32	1.30	1.28	1.26

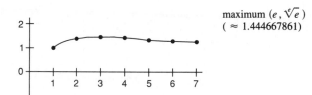

maximum $(e, \sqrt[e]{e})$
(≈ 1.444667861)

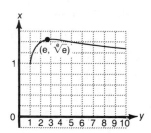

41. The model for radioactive decay is $N = N_0 e^{-kt}$, where N_0 is the amount of radioactive substance at time 0, N is the amount at time t, and k a positive constant expressing the relative rate at which a particular element decays. We solve this formula for k and set $N = \frac{1}{2}N_0$ to find k in terms of H.

$$\left(H = t \text{ for } N = \frac{1}{2}N_0\right)$$
$$N = N_0 e^{-kt}$$
$$\frac{1}{2}N_0 = N_0 e^{-kH}$$
$$\frac{1}{2} = e^{-kH}$$
$$\ln \frac{1}{2} = \ln e^{-kH} = -kH$$
$$k = \frac{-\ln \frac{1}{2}}{H} = \frac{\ln\left(\frac{1}{2}\right)^{-1}}{H} = \frac{\ln 2}{H} = \frac{1}{H}\ln 2 = \ln 2^{1/H}$$

We have found k
$$N = N_0 e^{-\ln 2^{1/H} \cdot t}$$
$$= N_0 e^{-t\ln 2^{1/H}}$$
$$= N_0 e^{\ln 2^{-t/H}}$$
$$N = N_0 2^{-t/H}$$

42. $\log_a b = \dfrac{\log_b b}{\log_b a}$
$$= \frac{1}{\log_b a}$$

43. $a^{(\log_b M) \div (\log_b a)} = a^{(\log_b M) \div (1/\log_a b)}$
$$= a^{(\log_a b) \cdot (\log_b M)}$$
$$= b^{\log_b M}$$
$$= M$$

44. $a^{(\log_b M)(\log_b a)} = a^{(\log_a M / \log_a b) \cdot \log_b a}$
$$= a^{(\log_a M \cdot \log_b a) \cdot \log_b a} \text{ by Problem 43}$$
$$= a^{\log_a M (\log_b a)^2}$$
$$= M^{(\log_b a)^2}$$

45. $\log_a(\log_a x) = \log_a \dfrac{\log_b x}{\log_b a}$ by Theorem 12-7
$$= \log_a(\log_b x) - \log_a(\log_b a) \text{ by Theorem 12-6}$$

46. $P(x) = x^3 - 3x^2 - 6x + 8$

$$
\begin{array}{r|rrrr}
1 & 1 & -3 & -6 & 8 \\
  &   & 1 & -2 & -8 \\
\hline
  & 1 & -2 & -8 & 0 \\
\end{array}
$$

$x - 1$ is a factor $\quad P(x) = (x - 1)(x^2 - 2x - 8)$
$$= (x - 1)(x - 4)(x + 2)$$
$x + 4$ and $x - 3$ are not factors

47. $P(x) = x^3 - 10x^2 - 11x + 70$

$$
\begin{array}{r|rrrr}
1 & 1 & -10 & 11 & 70 \\
  &   & 1 & -9 & 2 \\
\hline
  & 1 & -9 & 2 & 72 \\
\end{array}
$$
$x - 1$ is not a factor

$$
\begin{array}{r|rrrr}
-2 & 1 & -10 & 11 & 70 \\
   &   & -2 & 24 & -70 \\
\hline
   & 1 & -12 & 35 & 0 \\
\end{array}
$$

$x + 2$ is a factor $\quad P(x) = (x + 2)(x^2 - 12x + 35)$
$$= (x + 2)(x - 7)(x - 5)$$
$x + 5$ is not a factor

48. $f^{-1}(t(26)) = 26$ **49.** $f(f^{-1}(-9)) = -9$

p. 556   PROBLEM FOR PROGRAMMERS

```
10  REM    Chapter 12
20  INPUT "Input X1, Y1 ";X1,Y1
30  INPUT "Input X2, Y2 ";X2,Y2
40  R = LOG (Y2 / Y1) / (X2 - X1)
50  P = Y1 * EXP ( - X1 * R)
60  PRINT "Y=Pe^RX  is    Y = ";P;"e^";R;"X"
70  INPUT "Input a value of x  ";X
80  PRINT "y = ";P * (2.718281828 ^ (R * X))
90  INPUT "Continue? (Y)es or (N)o ";QUEST$
100   IF QUEST$ = "Y" THEN 70
110   END
```

p. 559   COLLEGE ENTRANCE EXAMS

1. $180° = 25° + 115° + z$
$180° = 140° + z$
$40° = z \qquad$ (D)

2. The angle directly below is 40° since $70 + 70 + 40 = 180$. y must also be 40° since these are vertical angles. (E)

3. $a + b = 180 - 80$
$a + b = 100$
$$\frac{a + b}{2} = \frac{100}{2} = 50 \quad \text{(B)}$$

4. $a + b = 60°$
$c = 120°$
$\therefore a + b + c = 180° \qquad$ (C)

5. Total interior angle size: $3(180) = 540$
$540 \div 5 = 108°$ each (B)

6. Since $AB < BC < AC$
$z < x < y$
if $z > 60°$, then $x + y < 180° - 60°$
$x + y < 120°$
so either x or y must be $\leq 60°$, which is not possible. (D)

Lesson 12-8–College Entrance Exams

1. $x = 3y - 1$
$3y = x + 1$
$y = \dfrac{x + 1}{3}$
$y = \dfrac{1}{3}x + \dfrac{1}{3}$

2. $x = 3y^2 + 2y - 1$

3. $(1, 4) (8, -3) (-5, -1)$　　**4.** $(3, 2) (7, 5) (-4, 6)$

5. $f(x) = \dfrac{7 - 6x}{6}$
$f^{-1}(x) = \dfrac{7 - 6x}{6}$
Yes

6. $y = 2x - 1$
$2y - x = 1$
$2y = 1 + x$
$y = \dfrac{1 + x}{2}$
No

7. $x = \sqrt{y} + 2$
$\sqrt{y} = x - 2$
$y = (x - 2)^2$
$y = x^2 - 4x + 4$
$g^{-1}(x) = x^2 - 4x + 4$　　$x \geq 2$

8. $x = 0.5y - 1$
$0.5y = x + 1$
$y = \dfrac{x + 1}{0.5}$
$h^{-1}(x) = 2x + 2$

9.

x	-2	-1	0	1
y	$\frac{1}{25}$	$\frac{1}{5}$	1	5

domain: all real numbers
range: all positive numbers
y-intercept: $(0, 1)$

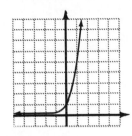

10.

x	-1	1	2
y	$\frac{1}{5}$	0	25

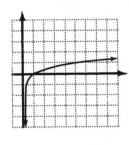

11. $\log_7 x = 2.3$　　**12.** $\log_8 2 = \dfrac{1}{3}$　　**13.** $3^4 = 81$　　**14.** $8^t = M$

15. $x^3 = 64$
$x = 4$

16. $16^x = 4$
$x = \dfrac{1}{2}$

17. $\log_h h^3 = 3$　　**18.** $3^{\log_3 t} = t$

19. $\dfrac{1}{2} \log_b a + \dfrac{3}{2} \log_b c - 4 \log_b d$
$= \log_b a^{1/2} + \log_b c^{3/2} - \log_b d^4$
$= \log_b(a^{1/2}c^{3/2}) - \log_b d^4$
$= \log_b\left[\dfrac{a^{1/2}c^{3/2}}{d^4}\right]$
$= \log_b\left[\dfrac{(ac^3)^{1/2}}{d^4}\right]$

20. $\log \sqrt[3]{\dfrac{M^2}{N}}$
$= \log \dfrac{M^{2/3}}{N^{1/3}}$
$= \log M^{2/3} - \log N^{1/3}$
$= \dfrac{2}{3} \log M - \dfrac{1}{3} \log N$
$= \dfrac{1}{3}(2 \log M - \log N)$

21. $\log_a 18$
$= \log_a 3 + \log_a 3 + \log_a 2$
$= 0.477 + 0.477 + 0.301$
$= 1.255$

22. $\log_a \dfrac{7}{2}$
$= \log_a 7 - \log_a 2$
$= 0.845 - 0.301$
$= 0.544$

23. $\log_a \dfrac{1}{4} = \log_a \dfrac{2}{8}$
$= \log_a 2 - \log_a 8$
$= \log_a 2 - (\log_a 2 + \log_a 2 + \log_a 2)$
$= 0.301 - (0.301 + 0.301 + 0.301)$
$= -0.602$

24. $\log_a \sqrt{3}$
$= \log_a 3^{1/2}$
$= \dfrac{1}{2} \log_a 3$
$= \dfrac{1}{2}(.477)$
$= 0.2385$

25. $\log 26.2$
$= 1.4183$

26. $\log_{10} 0.00806$
$= 7.9063 - 10$
$= -2.094$

27. $10^x = 5.82$
$\log 10^x = \log 5.82$
$x = \log 5.82$
$x = 0.7649$

28. antilog 0.7686
$= 5.869$

29. antilog $(7.3617 - 10)$
$= 0.0023$

30. antilog 2.3304
$= 214$

31. $\log 18.75$
$18.75 = 1.875 \times 10^1$
Characteristic 1
$\log 1.875 = 0.2730$
$1 + 0.2730 = 1.2730$

32. antilog 1.1629
Characteristic 1
$\log 1.455 = .1629$
antilog $1.1629 = 1.455 \times 10$
$= 1.629$
$= 14.55$

33. $\log_3 3^{-1-x} = \log_3(3^7)^{2x}$
$-1 - x = 4x$
$-1 = 5x$
$x = -\dfrac{1}{5}$

34. $\log_2(2^2)^{2x} = \log_2(2^3)^{x-1}$
$4x = 3x - 3$
$x = -3$

35. $\log(x^2 - 1) - \log(x - 1) = 1$
$\log \dfrac{x^2 - 1}{x - 1} = 1$
$\log(x + 1) = 1$
$10^1 = x + 1$
$9 = x$

36. $\log_4(x - 2)^{1/2} = 2$
$4^2 = (x - 2)^{1/2}$
$16 = (x - 2)^{1/2}$
$256 = x - 2$
$258 = x$

37. $2000 = 1000(1 + 0.05)^t$
$2 = (1.05)^t$
$\log 2 = t \log 1.05$
$t = \dfrac{\log 2}{\log 1.05} = 14.2$ years

38. $\ln 1.6 = .4700$　　**39.** $\ln 1600 = 7.3778$

40. $\log_4 80 = \dfrac{\log_{10} 80}{\log_{10} 4} = 3.1610$

1. $x = 2y^2 - 3y + 1$　　**2.** $f^{-1}(x) = 7 - x$
　　　　　　　　　　　　　　Yes

3. $x = \dfrac{\sqrt{y}}{3} + 1$
$\dfrac{\sqrt{y}}{3} = x - 1$
$\sqrt{y} = 3x - 3$
$y = (3x - 3)^2$
$f^{-1}(x) = 9x^2 - 18x + 9$

4.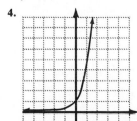

5.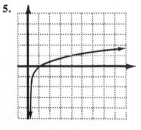

6. $\log_3 25 = x$　　**7.** $\log_{25} 5 = \dfrac{1}{2}$　　**8.** $3^2 = 9$　　**9.** $6^y = x$

Chapter 12 Summary and Review–Chapter 12 Test

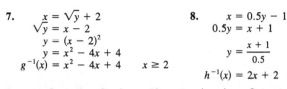
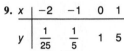

10. $x^3 = 125$ **11.** $25^x = 5$ **12.** $7t$
$x = 5$
$x = \dfrac{1}{2}$

13. $\log_2 8^{2/3} + \log_2 3^{1/3} - \log_2 4^2$
$\log_2(8^{2/3} \cdot 3^{1/3}) - \log_2 4^2$
$\log_2 \dfrac{8^{2/3} \cdot 3^{1/3}}{4^2}$
$\log_2 \dfrac{4 \cdot 3^{1/3}}{4^2} = \log_2\left(\dfrac{3^{1/3}}{4}\right)$

14. $\log_a 9 = \log_a 3 + \log_a 3$
$= 0.451 + 0.451$
$= 0.902$

15. $\log_a \dfrac{4}{3} = \log_a 4 - \log_a 3$
$= 0.569 - 0.451$
$= 0.118$

16. $\log 14.3$
$14.3 = 1.43 \times 10^1$
$\log 1.43 = 0.155$
$\log 14.3 = 1.155$

17. antilog $(7.5340 - 10)$
Characteristic -3
$10^{0.5340} = 3.420$
3.420×10^{-3}
0.003420

18. $\log_2 2^{x-1} = \log_2(2^5)$
$x - 1 = 5$
$x = 6$

19. $\log 4x + \log x = 2$
$\log 4x^2 = 2$
$10^2 = 4x^2$
$25 = x^2$
$5 = x$

20. $19{,}487 = 10{,}000(1 + .1)^t$
$1.9487 = (1.1)^t$
$\log 1.9487 = t \log 1.1$
$t = \dfrac{\log 1.9487}{\log 1.1}$
$t = 7$ years

21. $\ln 1.7 = 0.5306$

22. $1400 = 300e^{3k}$ $x = 300e^{18(0.5135)}$
$\dfrac{14}{3} = e^{3k}$ $x = 300e^{9.2430}$
  $x \approx 3{,}099{,}000$
$\ln \dfrac{14}{3} = 3k$
$\dfrac{1}{3} \ln \dfrac{14}{3} = k$
$0.5135 = k$

23. $\log_9 100 = \dfrac{\log 100}{\log 9} = 2.096$ **24.** $\log_{16} 512 = \dfrac{\log 512}{\log 16} = 2.25$

25. $\log_a\left(\dfrac{1}{x}\right) = \log_a x^{-1} = -\log_a x = -1$

---

10. $4x - 2y = 10$ $4x - 2(-3) = 10$
  $\underline{-4x + 8y = -28}$ $4x + 6 = 10$
  $6y = -18$ $4x = 4$
  $y = -3$ $x = 1$ $(1, -3)$

11. $-48x - 18y = 33$ $16\left(-\dfrac{1}{2}\right) + 6y = -11$
  $\underline{-14x + 18y = -2}$ $-8 + 6y = -11$
  $-62x = 31$ $6y = -3$
  $x = -\dfrac{31}{62} = -\dfrac{1}{2}$ $y = -\dfrac{-3}{6} = -\dfrac{1}{2}$
    $\left(-\dfrac{1}{2}, -\dfrac{1}{2}\right)$

12. $19x + 18y = -12$ $19(0) + 18y = -12$
  $\underline{-28x - 18y = 12}$ $y = -\dfrac{12}{18} = -\dfrac{2}{3}$
  $-9x = 0$
  $x = 0$ $\left(0, -\dfrac{2}{3}\right)$

13. $0.12x + (24 - x)0.60 = 24(0.50)$
$14.4 - 0.48x = 12$
$-0.48x = -2.4$
$x = 5$
5 liters of A
19 liters of B

14.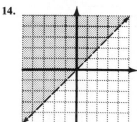

15.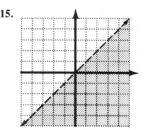

16.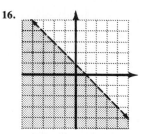

1. $-|5 + (-2)| + (15 + (-2))$ **2.** $-10 + 4 + |-12|$
$= -3 + 13 = 10$ $-6 + 12 = 6$

3. $|3| - |5| - |-2|$ **4.** $|5 + 2| + |-2 - 5|$
$= 3 - 5 - 2 = -4$ $= 7 + |-7|$
  $= 7 + 7 = 14$

5. $4x - 3 \le 5x + 2$ **6.** $-2x \le 2x + 6 - 1$
$-3 \le x + 2$ $-2x \le 2x + 5$
$-5 \le x$ $-4x \le 5$
  $x \ge -\dfrac{5}{4}$

7. $-\dfrac{2}{5}x < -24$ **8.** $m = \dfrac{1 - 1}{-1 - (-2)} = 0$
$x > 60$ $1 = 0(-1) + b$
  $b = 1$
  $y = 0(x) + 1$
  $y - 1 = 0$

9. $m = -\dfrac{3 - 3}{6 - 6}$
slope undefined
$x = 6$
$x - 6 = 0$

17. $(2z + 4y)^2 = (2z + 4y)(2z + 4y)$
$= 4z^2 + 8zy + 8yz + 16y^2$
$= 4z^2 + 16yz + 16y^2$

18. $(x - 5)^3 = (x - 5)(x - 5)(x - 5)$
$= (x^2 - 10x + 25)(x - 5)$
$= x^3 - 15x^2 + 75x - 125$

19. $(a^2 + 2b)^3 = (a^2 + 2b)(a^2 + 2b)(a^2 + 2b)$
$= (a^4 + 4a^2b + 4b^2)(a^2 + 2b)$
$= a^6 + 6a^4b + 12a^2b^2 + 8b^3$

20. $400x^2 - 441y^2 = (20x - 21y)(20x + 21y)$

21. $a^{16} - 1 = (a^8 + 1)(a^8 - 1)$
$= (a^8 + 1)(a^4 + 1)(a^4 - 1)$
$= (a^8 + 1)(a^4 + 1)(a^2 + 1)(a^2 - 1)$
$= (a^8 + 1)(a^4 + 1)(a^2 + 1)(a + 1)(a - 1)$

22. $x^4y^2 - x^2 = x^2(x^2y^2 - 1) = x^2(xy - 1)(xy + 1)$

23. $y^3 + 125 = (y^3 + 5^3) = (y + 5)(y^2 - 5y + 25)$

24. $y^3 + 2y^2 - 4y - 8 = y^2(y + 2) - 4(y + 2)$
$= (y^2 - 4)(y + 2)$
$= (y + 2)^2(y - 2)$

25. $4x^3 - 16x^2 - 9x + 36 = 4x^2(x - 4) - 9(x - 4)$
$= (4x^2 - 9)(x - 4)$
$= (2x - 3)(2x + 3)(x - 4)$

26.
$$2x^2 = 15 + x$$
$$2x^2 - x - 15 = 0$$
$$(2x + 5)(x - 3) = 0$$
$$2x + 5 = 0 \quad \text{or} \quad x - 3 = 0$$
$$x = -\frac{5}{2} \qquad x = 3$$

27.
$$3x^2 + 6 = 19x$$
$$3x^2 - 19x + 6 = 0$$
$$(3x - 1)(x - 6) = 0$$
$$3x - 1 = 0 \quad \text{or} \quad x - 6 = 0$$
$$x = \frac{1}{3} \qquad x = 6$$

28.
$$20x^2 - 3 = -28x$$
$$20x^2 + 28x - 3 = 0$$
$$(2x + 3)(10x - 1) = 0$$
$$2x + 3 = 0 \quad \text{or} \quad 10x - 1 = 0$$
$$x = -\frac{3}{2} \qquad x = \frac{1}{10}$$

29. $\left(\dfrac{3x}{y} - x\right) \div \left(\dfrac{y}{x} - y\right)$

$\left(\dfrac{3x - xy}{y}\right) \div \left(\dfrac{y - xy}{x}\right)$

$\left(\dfrac{3x - xy}{y}\right) \cdot \left(\dfrac{x}{y - xy}\right)$

$\dfrac{x^2(3 - y)}{y^2(1 - x)} = \dfrac{x^2(y - 3)}{y^2(x - 1)}$

30. $\left(\dfrac{x - 1}{x} + \dfrac{x}{1 + x}\right) \div \left(\dfrac{x}{1 - x} + \dfrac{1 + x}{x}\right)$

$\left[\dfrac{(x - 1)(x + 1) + x^2}{x(x + 1)} \div \dfrac{x^2 + (1 + x)(1 - x)}{(1 - x)x}\right]$

$\left[\dfrac{2x^2 - 1}{x(x + 1)} \div \dfrac{1}{(1 - x)(x)}\right]$

$\left[\dfrac{2x^2 - 1}{x(x + 1)} \cdot \dfrac{(1 - x)(x)}{1}\right]$

$\dfrac{(2x^2 - 1)(1 - x)}{x + 1}$

31.
$$\begin{array}{r} x^3 + 3x^2 + x - 9 \\ 2x + 1 \overline{\smash{\big)}\ 2x^4 + 7x^3 + 5x^2 - 17x - 9} \\ \underline{2x^4 + x^3} \\ 6x^3 + 5x^2 \\ \underline{6x^3 + 3x^2} \\ 2x^2 - 17x \\ \underline{2x^2 + x} \\ -18x - 9 \\ \underline{-18x - 9} \end{array}$$

32. $\dfrac{7}{5x - 2} = \dfrac{5}{4x}$

$28x = 25x - 10$
$3x = -10$
$x = -\dfrac{10}{3}$

33.
$$\dfrac{1}{x} + \dfrac{2x + 3}{2} = 8x$$
$$2 + 2x^2 + 3x = 16x^2$$
$$14x^2 - 3x - 2 = 0$$
$$(7x + 2)(2x - 1) = 0$$
$$7x + 2 = 0 \qquad 2x - 1 = 0$$
$$x = -\dfrac{2}{7} \qquad x = \dfrac{1}{2}$$

34. $\sqrt{36x^2} = 6|x|$ **35.** $\sqrt[3]{-125} = -5$ **36.** $\sqrt[4]{16x^4y^8} = 2|x|y^2$

37. $\sqrt{(-3)^2} = 3$ **38.** $\sqrt{45x} = 3\sqrt{5x}$ **39.** $\sqrt{48y^3} = 4y\sqrt{3y}$

40. $\sqrt{18} - \sqrt{50} + 2\sqrt{8} + \sqrt{8}$
$3\sqrt{2} - 5\sqrt{2} + 3\sqrt{8}$
$-2\sqrt{2} + 6\sqrt{2}$
$4\sqrt{2}$

41. $\dfrac{\sqrt{7} + \sqrt{5}}{\sqrt{7} - \sqrt{5}} \cdot \dfrac{\sqrt{7} + \sqrt{5}}{\sqrt{7} + \sqrt{5}} = \dfrac{7 + \sqrt{35} + \sqrt{35} + 5}{7 - 5}$

$= \dfrac{12 + 2\sqrt{35}}{2}$

$= 6 + \sqrt{35}$

42. $\dfrac{\sqrt{10}}{\sqrt{15}} \cdot \dfrac{\sqrt{15}}{\sqrt{15}} = \dfrac{\sqrt{150}}{15} = \dfrac{5\sqrt{6}}{15} = \dfrac{\sqrt{6}}{3}$

43. $\dfrac{\sqrt{48a^5}}{\sqrt{36a^3}} = \dfrac{4a^2\sqrt{3a}}{6|a|\sqrt{a}} = \dfrac{2a\sqrt{3}}{3}$

44. $\dfrac{\sqrt[3]{96x^6}}{\sqrt{72x^2}} = \dfrac{2x^2\sqrt[3]{12}}{6|x|\sqrt{2}} = \dfrac{x\sqrt[3]{12}}{3\sqrt{2}} = \dfrac{x\sqrt{2}(\sqrt[3]{12})}{6}$

45.
$$\sqrt{5x + 39} = x - 9$$
$$5x + 39 = (x - 9)^2$$
$$5x + 39 = x^2 - 18x + 81$$
$$x^2 - 23x + 42 = 0$$
$$(x - 2)(x - 21) = 0$$
$$x - 2 = 0 \quad \text{or} \quad x - 21 = 0$$
$$x = 2 \qquad \qquad x = 21$$
$x = 2$ is not a solution.
$x = 21$

46. $\sqrt[3]{4x + 7} + 2 = 5$
$\sqrt[3]{4x + 7} = 3$
$4x + 7 = 27$
$4x = 20$
$x = 5$

47. $(5 + 2i)^2 = (5 + 2i)(5 + 2i)$
$= 25 + 10i + 10i - 4$
$= 21 + 20i$

48. $\dfrac{1 + i}{2 - 3i} \cdot \dfrac{2 + 3i}{2 + 3i} = \dfrac{2 + 2i + 3i - 3}{4 + 9}$

$= \dfrac{-1 + 5i}{13}$

49. $-(-i^9)(i^4)$
$= -(-i)$
$= i$

50.
$$4x^2 - 5x - 6 = 0$$
$$(4x + 3)(x - 2) = 0$$
$$4x + 3 = 0 \qquad \text{or} \quad x - 2 = 0$$
$$x = -\dfrac{3}{4} \quad \text{or} \qquad x = 2$$

51.
$$5x^2 - 4x = 0$$
$$x(5x - 4) = 0$$
$$x = 0 \quad \text{or} \quad 5x - 4 = 0$$
$$x = \dfrac{4}{5}$$

52. $2x^2 + 2x + 3 = 0$

$x = \dfrac{-2 \pm \sqrt{4 - 4(2)(3)}}{4}$

$x = \dfrac{-2 \pm \sqrt{-20}}{4}$

$x = \dfrac{-2 \pm 2i\sqrt{5}}{4}$

$x = \dfrac{-1 \pm i\sqrt{5}}{2}$

53. $12x^2 + 11x - 15 = 0$ **54.** $x^2 - 2x - 2 = 0$

55.
$4y = 3(-x)^2 - 1$
$4y = 3x^2 - 1 \quad$ y-axis
$4(-y) = 3x^2 - 1$
$-4y = 3x^2 - 1$
Not symmetric to x-axis

56.
$2(-x)^2 - 3y^2 = 5$
$2x^2 - 3y^2 = 5 \quad$ y-axis
$2x^2 - 3(-y)^2 = 5$
$2x^2 - 3y^2 = 5 \quad$ x-axis

57. $(-x)^3 + 3y^3 = 10$
$-x^3 + 3y^3 = 10$
Not symmetric to y-axis
$x^3 + 3(-y)^3 = 10$
$x^3 - 3y^3 = 10$
Not symmetric to x-axis

58. $f(x) = 5$
$f(-x) = 5 \quad$ Even

59. $f(x) = x^{23}$
$f(-x) = (-x)^{23} = -x^{23} = -f(x)$
$\qquad\qquad\qquad$ Odd

60. $f(x) = \sqrt{x} + 1$
$f(-x) = \sqrt{-x} + 1$
$\qquad$ Neither

61. a. $f(x) = -3(x^2 - 4x) - 5$
$f(x) = -3(x^2 - 4x + 4) + 7$
$f(x) = -3(x - 2)^2 + 7$
 b. Vertex: $(2, 7)$;
line of symmetry: $x = 2$;
max: $= 7$

62. a. $f(x) = 4x^2 + 12x + 9$
$f(x) = (2x + 3)^2$

x intercepts $-\dfrac{3}{2}$

b. $f(x) = 9x^2 - 12x - 1$

$x = \dfrac{12 \pm \sqrt{144 - 4(9)(-1)}}{18}$

$x = \dfrac{12 \pm \sqrt{180}}{18}$

$= \dfrac{12 \pm 6\sqrt{5}}{18} = \dfrac{2 \pm \sqrt{5}}{3}$

63. $\sqrt{(-2 - 3)^2 + (5 + 4)^2}$
$\sqrt{25 + 81} = \sqrt{106}$

64. Center: $(0, 0)$;
vertices: $(\sqrt{6}, 0), (-\sqrt{6}, 0)$;
foci: $(\sqrt{22}, 0), (-\sqrt{22}, 0)$

asymptotes: $y = \pm\dfrac{2\sqrt{6}}{3}x$

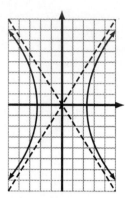

65. Vertex: $(-1, 2)$;

focus: $\left(-1, \dfrac{1}{2}\right)$

directrix: $y = \dfrac{7}{2}$

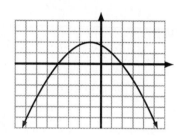

66. $x = 1 + 2y$
$y^2 + (1 + 2y)^2 = 13$
$5y^2 + 4y + 1 = 13$
$5y^2 + 4y - 12 = 0$
$(5y - 6)(y + 2) = 0$
$5y - 6 = 0 \quad\text{or}\quad y + 2 = 0$

$y = \dfrac{6}{5} \qquad\qquad y = -2$

$x = 1 + 2\left(\dfrac{6}{5}\right) \qquad x = 1 + 2(-2)$

$x = 1 + \dfrac{12}{5} \qquad\qquad x = 1 - 4$

$x = \dfrac{17}{5} \qquad\qquad x = -3$

$\left(\dfrac{17}{5}, \dfrac{6}{5}\right) \qquad\qquad (-3, -2)$

67. $x = \dfrac{8}{y}$

$\left(\dfrac{8}{y}\right)^2 + y^2 = 20$

$\dfrac{64}{y^2} + y^2 = 20$

$64 + y^4 = 20y^2$
$y^4 - 20y^2 + 64 = 0$
$(y^2 - 16)(y^2 - 4) = 0$
$y^2 - 16 = 0 \qquad y^2 - 4 = 0$
$y = \pm 4 \qquad\qquad y = \pm 2$

$x = \dfrac{8}{4}, -\dfrac{8}{4} \qquad x = \dfrac{8}{2}, -\dfrac{8}{2}$

$x = 2, -2 \qquad x = 4, -4$
$(2, 4)(-2, -4)(4, 2)(-4, -2)$

68. $-3 \big|\ \begin{array}{cccc} -2 & 1 & 0 & -1 \\ & 6 & -21 & 63 \end{array}$
$\overline{\qquad -2 \quad 7 \quad -21 \ \big|\ 62}$
$P(-3) = 62$

69. $(x - 3)(x - i)(x + i) = x^3 - 3x^2 + x - 3 = 0$

70. $2x^4 - 7x^3 + 5x^2 + 9x - 5 = (2x - 1)(x + 1)(x^2 - 4x + 5)$
$(2x - 1)(x + 1)(x - 2 - i)(x - 2 + i)$

$x = \dfrac{1}{2}, -1, 2 + i, 2 - i$

71. There are 3 changes of signs. Thus, there are 3 or 1 positive roots. Also, $-4x^5 + 3x^4 + 2x^3 + 2x^2 - 3x - 1$ has 2 changes of signs. So, there are 2 or 0 negative roots.

72. $y = 2x - 3$ **73.** $4^x = 16$ **74.** $4^3 = x$
$x = 2y - 3$ $x = 2$ $x = 64$

$y = \dfrac{x + 3}{2}$

$f^{-1}(x) = \dfrac{x + 3}{2}$

75. $\log_5 x^{1/2} - \log_5 y^3$

$\log_5 \dfrac{x^{1/2}}{y^3}$

$\log_5 \dfrac{\sqrt{x}}{y^3}$

76. $\log_a 3x + 2\left(\log_a \dfrac{2x}{x}\right)$

$\log_a 3x + 2 \log_a 2$
$\log_a 3x + \log_a 2^2$
$\log_a(3x)(4)$
$\log_a 12x$

77. $\log 0.00332 = 7.5211 - 10$ **78.** antilog $(8.3215 - 10) = 0.021$

79. $3^{3x-2} = 3^3$
$3x - 2 = 3$
$3x = 5$

$x = \dfrac{5}{3}$

80. $\log(x + 19) - \log 2x = 1$

$\log \dfrac{(x + 19)}{2x} = 1$

$10^1 = \dfrac{x + 19}{2x}$

$20x = x + 19$
$19x = 19$
$x = 1$

81. $\ln 73.2 = 4.2932$ **82.** $\log_3 45 = 3.465$

CHAPTER 13

p. 566   READY FOR MATRICES AND DETERMINANTS?

1. -10 **2.** -48 **3.** $-1, 4$ **4.** $3, 7, -\dfrac{1}{2}$
5. $-2, 5, -3$

pp. 569–571   13-1 TRY THIS

a. 3×2 **b.** 2×2 **c.** 3×3 **d.** 1×2 **e.** 2×1
f. 1×1
g. Solve $5x - 2y = 44$
$\qquad\qquad x + 5y = 2$

$\begin{bmatrix} 5 & -2 & -44 \\ 1 & 5 & 2 \end{bmatrix} \begin{array}{l} ① \\ ② \end{array}$

$\begin{bmatrix} 1 & 5 & 2 \\ 5 & -2 & 44 \end{bmatrix}$ Interchanging ① and ②

$\begin{bmatrix} 1 & 5 & 2 \\ 0 & -27 & -54 \end{bmatrix} -5① + ②$

Replacing the variables
$x + 5y = 2 \quad ①$
$\quad -27y = -54 \; ②$
Solving ②, $y = 2$
Substituting in ①
$x + 5(2) = 2$
$x + 10 = 2$
$\qquad x = -8$
$(-8, 2)$ is the solution

h. Solve $x - 2y + 3z = 4$
$$2x - y + z = -1$$
$$4x + y + z = 1$$

$$\begin{bmatrix} 1 & -2 & 3 & 4 \\ 2 & -1 & 1 & -1 \\ 4 & 1 & 1 & 1 \end{bmatrix}$$

$$\begin{bmatrix} 1 & -2 & 3 & 4 \\ 0 & 3 & -5 & -9 \\ 0 & 9 & -11 & -15 \end{bmatrix} \quad \begin{array}{l} -2①+② \\ -4①+③ \end{array}$$

$$\begin{bmatrix} 1 & -2 & 3 & 4 \\ 0 & 3 & -5 & -9 \\ 0 & 0 & 4 & 12 \end{bmatrix} \quad -3②+③$$

Replacing the variables, from row 3, $4z = 12$, so $z = 3$
Substituting in row 2,
$$3y - 5(3) = -9$$
$$3y - 15 = -9$$
$$3y = 6, \quad \text{so } y = 2$$
Substituting in row 1,
$$x - 2(2) + 3(3) = 4$$
$$x - 4 + 9 = 4$$
$$x = -1$$
The solution is $(-1, 2, 3)$.

13-1 EXERCISES

1. 2×3 **2.** 3×4 **3.** 5×2 **4.** 3×1 **5.** $\left(\dfrac{3}{2}, \dfrac{5}{2}\right)$

6. $(1, 3)$ **7.** $\left(\dfrac{1}{2}, \dfrac{3}{2}\right)$ **8.** $\left(\dfrac{1}{3}, \dfrac{1}{3}\right)$ **9.** $(-1, 2, -2)$

10. $\left(\dfrac{1}{2}, 2, 1\right)$ **11.** $\left(2, \dfrac{1}{2}, -2\right)$

12.
$$\begin{bmatrix} 2 & -2 & -2 & 2 & 10 \\ 1 & 1 & 1 & 1 & -5 \\ 3 & 1 & -1 & 4 & -2 \\ 1 & 3 & -2 & 2 & -6 \end{bmatrix}$$

$$\begin{bmatrix} 1 & -1 & -1 & 1 & 5 \\ 1 & 1 & 1 & 1 & -5 \\ 3 & 1 & -1 & 4 & -2 \\ 1 & 3 & -2 & 2 & -6 \end{bmatrix} \quad 1/2 ①$$

$$\begin{bmatrix} 1 & -1 & -1 & 1 & 5 \\ 0 & 2 & 2 & 0 & -10 \\ 0 & 4 & 2 & 1 & -17 \\ 0 & 4 & -1 & 1 & -11 \end{bmatrix} \quad \begin{array}{l} -1①+② \\ -3①+③ \\ -1①+④ \end{array}$$

$$\begin{bmatrix} 1 & -1 & -1 & 1 & 5 \\ 0 & 2 & 2 & 0 & -10 \\ 0 & 0 & -2 & 1 & 3 \\ 0 & 0 & -5 & 1 & 9 \end{bmatrix} \quad \begin{array}{l} -2②+③ \\ -2②+④ \end{array}$$

$$\begin{bmatrix} 1 & -1 & -1 & 1 & 5 \\ 0 & 2 & 2 & 0 & -10 \\ 0 & 0 & -2 & 1 & 3 \\ 0 & 0 & 0 & 3 & -3 \end{bmatrix} \quad 5③-2④$$

Replacing the variables, from row 4, $3z = -3$, $z = -1$
from row 3, $-2y + z = 3$, so
$$-2y + (-1) = 3, -2y = 4, y = -2$$
from row 2, $2x + 2y = -10$, so
$$2x + 2(-2) = -10, 2x = -6, x = -3$$
from row 1, $w - x - y + z = 5$, so
$$w - (-3) - (-2) + (-1) = 5, w + 4 = 5, w = 1$$
The solution is $(1, -3, -2, -1)$.

13.
$$\begin{bmatrix} 1 & -2 & 3 & -1 & 8 \\ 1 & -1 & -1 & 1 & 4 \\ 1 & 2 & 1 & 1 & 26 \\ 1 & -1 & 1 & 1 & 14 \end{bmatrix}$$

$$\begin{bmatrix} 1 & -2 & 3 & -1 & 8 \\ 0 & 1 & -4 & 2 & -4 \\ 0 & 4 & -2 & 2 & 18 \\ 0 & 1 & -2 & 2 & 6 \end{bmatrix} \quad \begin{array}{l} -1①+② \\ -1①+③ \\ -1①+④ \end{array}$$

$$\begin{bmatrix} 1 & -2 & 3 & -1 & 8 \\ 0 & 1 & -4 & 2 & -4 \\ 0 & 0 & 14 & -6 & 34 \\ 0 & 0 & 2 & 0 & 10 \end{bmatrix} \quad \begin{array}{l} -4②+③ \\ -1②+④ \end{array}$$

$$\begin{bmatrix} 1 & -2 & 3 & -1 & 8 \\ 0 & 1 & -4 & 2 & -4 \\ 0 & 0 & 14 & -6 & 34 \\ 0 & 0 & 0 & 6 & 36 \end{bmatrix} \quad -1③+7④$$

Replacing the variables,
from row 4, $6z = 36$, $z = 6$
from row 3, $14y - 6z = 34$,
$$14y - 6(6) = 34, 14y = 70, y = 5$$
from row 2, $x - 4y + 2z = -4$,
$$x - 4(5) + 2(6) = -4, x = 4$$
from row 1, $w - 2x + 3y - z = 8$,
$$w - 2(4) + 3(5) - 6 = 8, w + 1 = 8, w = 7$$
The solution is $(7, 4, 5, 6)$.

14. Answers may vary. Since both multiplication and subtraction (addition with inverses) are row equivalent operations, the result is a row equivalent matrix.

15.
$$\begin{bmatrix} 1 & 1 & -2 & 3 & 2 & 9 \\ 8 & 5 & -2 & -1 & 2 & 3 \\ 2 & 2 & -1 & 1 & -2 & 1 \\ 3 & 3 & -1 & 1 & 1 & 5 \\ 4 & 4 & 1 & 0 & -3 & 4 \end{bmatrix}$$

$$\begin{bmatrix} 1 & 1 & -2 & 3 & 2 & 9 \\ 0 & -3 & 14 & -25 & -14 & -69 \\ 0 & 0 & 3 & -5 & -6 & -17 \\ 0 & 0 & 5 & -8 & -5 & -22 \\ 0 & 0 & 9 & -12 & -11 & -32 \end{bmatrix} \quad \begin{array}{l} -8①+② \\ -2①+③ \\ -3①+④ \\ -4①+⑤ \end{array}$$

$$\begin{bmatrix} 1 & 1 & -2 & 3 & 2 & 9 \\ 0 & -3 & 14 & -25 & -14 & -69 \\ 0 & 0 & 3 & -5 & -6 & -17 \\ 0 & 0 & 0 & 1 & 15 & 19 \\ 0 & 0 & 0 & 3 & 7 & 19 \end{bmatrix} \quad \begin{array}{l} -5③+3④ \\ -3③+⑤ \end{array}$$

$$\begin{bmatrix} 1 & 1 & -2 & 3 & 2 & 9 \\ 0 & -3 & 14 & -25 & -14 & -69 \\ 0 & 0 & 3 & -5 & -6 & -17 \\ 0 & 0 & 0 & 1 & 15 & 19 \\ 0 & 0 & 0 & 0 & -38 & -38 \end{bmatrix} \quad -3④+⑤$$

Replacing the variables, from row 5, $-38n = -38$, $n = 1$
from row 4, $w + 15n = 19$, $w + 15 = 19$, $w = 4$
from row 3, $3z - 5w - 6n = -17$,
$$3z - 5(4) - 6 = -17, 3z = 9, z = 3$$
from row 2, $-3y + 14z - 25w - 14n = -69$,
$$-3y + 14(3) - 25(4) - 14 = -69, -3y = 3, y = -1$$
from row 1, $x + y - 2z + 3w + 2n = 9$,
$$x + (-1) - 2(3) + 3(4) + 2 = 9, x = 2$$
Using (x, y, z, w, n), the solution is $(2, -1, 3, 4, 1)$.

16.
$$\begin{bmatrix} 2 & 2 & 4 & 4 & 13 & 13 \\ 1 & -1 & 2 & 2 & 6 & 6 \\ 0 & 1 & -1 & -1 & -3 & -3 \\ 3 & -2 & 4 & 4 & 12 & 14 \\ 2 & -2 & 4 & 5 & 15 & 10 \end{bmatrix}$$

$$\begin{bmatrix} 1 & -1 & 2 & 2 & 6 & 6 \\ 2 & 2 & 4 & 4 & 13 & 13 \\ 0 & 1 & -1 & -1 & -3 & -3 \\ 3 & -2 & 4 & 4 & 12 & 14 \\ 2 & -2 & 4 & 5 & 15 & 10 \end{bmatrix} \quad \begin{array}{l} \text{Interchanging} \\ ① \text{ and } ② \end{array}$$

$$\begin{bmatrix} 1 & -1 & 2 & 2 & 6 & 6 \\ 0 & 4 & 0 & 0 & 1 & 1 \\ 0 & 1 & -1 & -1 & -3 & -3 \\ 0 & 1 & -2 & -2 & -6 & -4 \\ 0 & 0 & 0 & 1 & 3 & -2 \end{bmatrix} \quad \begin{array}{l} -2①+② \\ -3①+④ \\ -2①+⑤ \end{array}$$

$$\begin{bmatrix} 1 & -1 & 2 & 2 & 6 & 6 \\ 0 & 4 & 0 & 0 & 1 & 1 \\ 0 & 0 & 4 & 4 & 13 & 13 \\ 0 & 8 & 8 & 25 & 17 & \\ 0 & 0 & 0 & 1 & 3 & -2 \end{bmatrix} \quad \begin{array}{l} ②-4③ \\ ②-4④ \end{array}$$

$$\begin{bmatrix} 1 & -1 & 2 & 2 & 6 & 6 \\ 0 & 4 & 0 & 0 & 1 & 1 \\ 0 & 0 & 4 & 4 & 13 & 13 \\ 0 & 0 & 0 & 0 & -1 & -9 \\ 0 & 0 & 0 & 1 & 3 & -2 \end{bmatrix} \quad -2\,\text{③} + \text{④}$$

$$\begin{bmatrix} 1 & -1 & 2 & 2 & 6 & 6 \\ 0 & 4 & 0 & 0 & 1 & 1 \\ 0 & 0 & 4 & 4 & 13 & 13 \\ 0 & 0 & 0 & 1 & 3 & -2 \\ 0 & 0 & 0 & 0 & -1 & -9 \end{bmatrix} \quad \begin{array}{l}\text{Interchanging}\\ \text{④ and ⑤}\end{array}$$

Replacing the variables, from row 5, $-n = -9$, $n = 9$
from row 4, $w + 3(9) = -2$, $w = -29$
from row 3, $4z + 4(-29) + 13(9) = 13$, $4z = 12$, $z = 3$
from row 2, $4y + n = 1$, $4y + 9 = 1$, $y = -2$
from row 1, $x - (-2) + 2(3) + 2(-29) + 6(9) = 6$,
$x + 4 = 6$, $x = 2$
Using (x, y, z, w, n), the solution is $(2, -2, 3, -29, 9)$.

17. $\dfrac{4x(x-3)}{(x+3)(x-3)} - \dfrac{3x(x+3)}{(x-3)(x+3)} = \dfrac{4x^2 - 12x - 3x^2 - 9x}{(x+3)(x-3)}$

$= \dfrac{x^2 - 21x}{(x+3)(x-3)} = \dfrac{x(x-21)}{(x+3)(x-3)}$

18. $\dfrac{5a^2 + 4ab + 3b^2}{(a-b)(a^2+ab+b^2)} - \dfrac{4(a^2+ab+b^2)}{(a-b)(a^2+ab+b^2)}$

$= \dfrac{5a^2 + 4ab + 3b^2 - 4a^2 - 4ab - 4b^2}{(a-b)(a^2+ab+b^2)}$

$= \dfrac{a^2 - b^2}{(a-b)(a^2+ab+b^2)}$

$= \dfrac{(a-b)(a+b)}{(a-b)(a^2+ab+b^2)} = \dfrac{a+b}{a^2+ab+b^2}$

19. -0.3036 **20.** 3.141 **21.** 0.9562

22. $\log 9.04 + 5$ **23.** Let x = the number.
5.9562
$x^2 + 4 = 148$
$x^2 = 144$
$x = \pm\sqrt{144}$
$x = 12, -12$

pp. 573–574   13-2 TRY THIS

a. (1) $\begin{bmatrix} 4 + (-6) & -1 + (-5) \\ 6 + 7 & -3 + 3 \end{bmatrix} = \begin{bmatrix} -2 & -6 \\ 13 & 0 \end{bmatrix}$

(2) $\begin{bmatrix} -6 + 4 & -5 + (-1) \\ 7 + 6 & 3 + (-3) \end{bmatrix} = \begin{bmatrix} -2 & -6 \\ 13 & 0 \end{bmatrix}$

(3) $\begin{bmatrix} 0 + 4 & 0 + (-1) \\ 0 + 6 & 0 + (-3) \end{bmatrix} = \begin{bmatrix} 4 & -1 \\ 6 & -3 \end{bmatrix}$

b. $\begin{bmatrix} 1-2 & 3-(-1) & -2-5 \\ 4-6 & 0-4 & 5-(-3) \end{bmatrix} = \begin{bmatrix} -1 & 4 & -7 \\ -2 & -4 & 8 \end{bmatrix}$

c. $\begin{bmatrix} 1-7 & 2-(-4) \\ 4-3 & 1-5 \\ -5-2 & 4-(-1) \end{bmatrix} = \begin{bmatrix} -6 & 6 \\ 1 & -4 \\ -7 & 5 \end{bmatrix}$

d. $\begin{bmatrix} -2 & 1 & -5 \\ -6 & -4 & 3 \end{bmatrix}$

e. $\begin{bmatrix} -1 & -3 & 5 \\ 2 & 0 & 0 \\ -6 & 10 & -7 \end{bmatrix}$

f. $\begin{bmatrix} 1 & 3 & -2 \\ 4 & 0 & 5 \end{bmatrix} + \begin{bmatrix} 2 & -1 & 5 \\ 6 & 4 & -3 \end{bmatrix} = \begin{bmatrix} 3 & 2 & 3 \\ 10 & 4 & 2 \end{bmatrix}$

g. $\begin{bmatrix} 9 & 3 & 7 \\ -1 & 5 & -3 \\ 0 & -4 & -6 \end{bmatrix} + \begin{bmatrix} 2 & -5 & -14 \\ -2 & 8 & -2 \\ 7 & 6 & 0 \end{bmatrix} = \begin{bmatrix} 11 & -2 & -7 \\ -3 & 13 & -5 \\ 7 & 2 & -6 \end{bmatrix}$

p. 575   13-2 EXERCISES

1. 2×2 **2.** 3×3 **3.** 2×3 **4.** 2×2

5. $\begin{bmatrix} -2 & -3 \\ 6 & -4 \end{bmatrix}$ **6.** $\begin{bmatrix} -2 & -6 \\ 1 & 0 \end{bmatrix}$ **7.** $\begin{bmatrix} -5 & 0 & 11 \\ 3 & 2 & 0 \end{bmatrix}$

8. $\begin{bmatrix} -3 & 3 & 4 \\ 8 & 2 & -1 \end{bmatrix}$ **9.** $\begin{bmatrix} 0 & -2 & 3 \\ 1 & -1 & 2 \\ 1 & -5 & 5 \end{bmatrix}$ **10.** $\begin{bmatrix} -5 & 3 & 3 \\ 2 & 0 & -5 \\ -4 & -6 & -4 \end{bmatrix}$

11. Cannot be added   **12.** Cannot be added

13. $\begin{bmatrix} 4 & 7 \\ 2 & -2 \end{bmatrix}$ **14.** $\begin{bmatrix} 4 & 4 \\ -3 & 2 \end{bmatrix}$ **15.** Cannot be added

16. $\begin{bmatrix} 3 & -7 & 7 \\ 0 & 0 & 3 \\ 0 & 0 & 6 \end{bmatrix}$ **17.** $\begin{bmatrix} 2 & 2 & -7 \\ -1 & -1 & 4 \\ 5 & 1 & 3 \end{bmatrix}$ **18.** $\begin{bmatrix} -1 & -6 & 3 \\ -13 & 2 & 2 \end{bmatrix}$

19. Cannot be added   **20.** $\begin{bmatrix} -1 & -1 \\ -1 & -1 \end{bmatrix}$ **21.** $\begin{bmatrix} 3 & 3 & -7 \\ 5 & -2 & -1 \end{bmatrix}$

22. $\begin{bmatrix} -1 & -3 \\ -2 & -6 \end{bmatrix}$ **23.** $\begin{bmatrix} 4 & -5 & 2 \\ -1 & 0 & 4 \\ 2 & 3 & 5 \end{bmatrix}$ **24.** $\begin{bmatrix} 0 & 2 \\ 2 & 0 \end{bmatrix}$

25. $\begin{bmatrix} -3 & 7 & -7 \\ 0 & 0 & -3 \\ 0 & 0 & -6 \end{bmatrix}$ **26.** $\begin{bmatrix} 1 & 6 & -3 \\ 13 & -2 & -2 \end{bmatrix}$ **27.** Cannot be subtracted

28. $(A + B) + C = \left(\begin{bmatrix} 1 & 2 \\ 4 & -3 \end{bmatrix} + \begin{bmatrix} -3 & -5 \\ 2 & -1 \end{bmatrix} \right) + \begin{bmatrix} 1 & -1 \\ -1 & 1 \end{bmatrix}$

$= \begin{bmatrix} -2 & -3 \\ 6 & -4 \end{bmatrix} + \begin{bmatrix} 1 & -1 \\ -1 & 1 \end{bmatrix} = \begin{bmatrix} -1 & -4 \\ 5 & -3 \end{bmatrix}$

$A + (B + C) = \begin{bmatrix} 1 & 2 \\ 4 & -3 \end{bmatrix} + \left(\begin{bmatrix} -3 & -5 \\ 2 & -1 \end{bmatrix} + \begin{bmatrix} 1 & -1 \\ -1 & 1 \end{bmatrix} \right)$

$= \begin{bmatrix} 1 & 2 \\ 4 & -3 \end{bmatrix} + \begin{bmatrix} -2 & -6 \\ 1 & 0 \end{bmatrix} = \begin{bmatrix} -1 & -4 \\ 5 & -3 \end{bmatrix}$

29. $(G + H) + M$

$= \left(\begin{bmatrix} 1 & 0 & -2 \\ 0 & -1 & 3 \\ 3 & -2 & 4 \end{bmatrix} + \begin{bmatrix} -1 & -2 & 5 \\ 1 & 0 & -1 \\ -2 & -3 & 1 \end{bmatrix} \right) + \begin{bmatrix} -4 & 5 & -2 \\ 1 & 0 & -4 \\ -2 & -3 & -5 \end{bmatrix}$

$= \begin{bmatrix} 0 & -2 & 3 \\ 1 & -1 & 2 \\ 1 & -5 & 5 \end{bmatrix} + \begin{bmatrix} -4 & 5 & -2 \\ 1 & 0 & -4 \\ -2 & -3 & -5 \end{bmatrix}$

$= \begin{bmatrix} -4 & 3 & 1 \\ 2 & -1 & -2 \\ -1 & -8 & 0 \end{bmatrix}$

$(M + H) + G$

$= \left(\begin{bmatrix} -4 & 5 & -2 \\ 1 & 0 & -4 \\ -2 & -3 & -5 \end{bmatrix} + \begin{bmatrix} -1 & -2 & 5 \\ 1 & 0 & -1 \\ -2 & -3 & 1 \end{bmatrix} \right) + \begin{bmatrix} 1 & 0 & -2 \\ 0 & -1 & 3 \\ 3 & -2 & 4 \end{bmatrix}$

$= \begin{bmatrix} -5 & 3 & 3 \\ 2 & 0 & -5 \\ -4 & -6 & -4 \end{bmatrix} + \begin{bmatrix} 1 & 0 & -2 \\ 0 & -1 & 3 \\ 3 & -2 & 4 \end{bmatrix}$

$= \begin{bmatrix} -4 & 3 & 1 \\ 2 & -1 & -2 \\ -1 & -8 & 0 \end{bmatrix}$

30. Let $A = \begin{bmatrix} a & b \\ c & d \end{bmatrix}$ and $B = \begin{bmatrix} e & f \\ g & h \end{bmatrix}$.

Then $A^t = \begin{bmatrix} a & c \\ b & d \end{bmatrix}$ and $B^t = \begin{bmatrix} e & g \\ f & h \end{bmatrix}$.

$A^t + B^t = \begin{bmatrix} a+e & c+g \\ b+f & d+h \end{bmatrix}$

$(A + B) = \begin{bmatrix} a+e & b+f \\ c+g & d+h \end{bmatrix}, (A + B)^t = \begin{bmatrix} a+e & c+g \\ b+f & d+h \end{bmatrix}$

31. $A - B = [a_{ij}] - [b_{ij}]$
$= [a_{ij} - b_{ij}]$ for each element in matrix A and matrix B
$A + (-B) = [a_{ij}] + (-[b_{ij}])$
$= [a_{ij}] + [-b_{ij}]$
$= [a_{ij} + (-b_{ij})]$
$= [a_{ij} - b_{ij}]$
Thus, if A and B are the same dimensions,
$A - B = A + (-B)$.

32. Let $A = \begin{bmatrix} a_{11} & a_{12} & a_{13} \cdots \cdots & a_{1n} \\ a_{21} & a_{22} & \cdots & a_{2n} \\ a_{31} & a_{32} & \cdots & \\ \vdots & \vdots & & \vdots \\ a_{m1} & a_{m2} & \cdots & a_{mn} \end{bmatrix}$ and $B = \begin{bmatrix} b_{11} & b_{12} & \cdots & b_{1n} \\ b_{21} & b_{22} & \cdots & b_{2n} \\ \vdots & & & \vdots \\ b_{m1} & b_{m2} & \cdots & b_{mn} \end{bmatrix}$

$A + B = \begin{bmatrix} a_{11} + b_{11} & a_{12} + b_{12} \cdots & a_{1n} + b_{1n} \\ a_{21} + b_{21} & a_{22} + b_{22} & a_{2n} + b_{2n} \\ \vdots & \vdots & \vdots \\ a_{m1} + b_{m1} & \cdots & a_{mn} + b_{mn} \end{bmatrix}$

$= \begin{bmatrix} b_{11} + a_{11} & b_{12} + a_{12} \cdots & b_{1n} + a_{1n} \\ b_{21} + a_{21} & b_{22} + a_{22} \cdots & \\ \vdots & & \\ b_{m} + a_{m1} & \cdots & b_{mn} + a_{mn} \end{bmatrix}$

$= B + A$

33.
$$7^x = 10$$
$$\log_7 10 = x$$
$$x = 1.183$$

34.
$$\log x + \log(x + 8) = 1$$
$$\log x(x + 8) = 1$$
$$\log x^2 + 8x = 1$$
$$10^{\log x^2 + 8x} = 10^1$$
$$x^2 + 8x - 10 = 0$$
$$x = \frac{-8 \pm \sqrt{64 + 40}}{2} = \frac{-8 \pm 2\sqrt{26}}{2}$$
$$= -4 \pm \sqrt{26}$$
Since $\log x$ must be positive, $x = -4 + \sqrt{26}$.

35. $2x^2 = 5$
$$x^2 = \frac{5}{2}$$
$$x = \pm\sqrt{\frac{5}{2}}$$
$$x = \pm\frac{\sqrt{5}}{\sqrt{2}} \cdot \frac{\sqrt{2}}{\sqrt{2}}$$
$$x = \pm\frac{\sqrt{10}}{2}$$

36.
$$2x^2 - 9x = 5$$
$$2x^2 - 9x - 5 = 0$$
$$(2x + 1)(x - 5) = 0$$
$$2x + 1 = 0 \quad \text{or} \quad x - 5 = 0$$
$$2x = -1 \qquad x = 5$$
$$x = -\frac{1}{2}$$
$$\left\{-\frac{1}{2}, 5\right\}$$

37. $x^2 + 2x - 15 = 0$
$$(x - 3)(x + 5) = 0$$
$$x - 3 = 0 \quad \text{or} \quad x + 5 = 0$$
$$x = 3 \qquad x = -5$$
$$\{3, -5\}$$

38.
$$n^2 - 24 = 5n$$
$$n^2 - 5n - 24 = 0$$
$$(n + 3)(n - 8) = 0$$
$$n + 3 = 0 \quad \text{or} \quad n - 8 = 0$$
$$n = -3 \quad \text{or} \quad n = 8$$
$$\{-3, 8\}$$

pp. 576–580   13-3 TRY THIS

a. 24   10 = 14

b. $4 - 6 = -2$

c. $-2x + 12$

d. $x = \dfrac{\begin{vmatrix} 5 & -1 \\ 1 & -2 \end{vmatrix}}{\begin{vmatrix} 2 & -1 \\ 1 & -2 \end{vmatrix}}$ $y = \dfrac{\begin{vmatrix} 2 & 5 \\ 1 & 1 \end{vmatrix}}{\begin{vmatrix} 2 & -1 \\ 1 & -2 \end{vmatrix}}$

$\quad = \dfrac{-10 - (-1)}{-4 - (-1)}$ $= \dfrac{2 - 5}{-4 - (-1)}$

$\quad = \dfrac{-10 + 1}{-4 + 1}$ $= \dfrac{-3}{-4 + 1}$

$\quad = \dfrac{-9}{-3}$ $= \dfrac{-3}{-3}$

$\quad = 3$ $= 1$

$\qquad (3, 1)$

e. $x = \dfrac{\begin{vmatrix} -2 & 4 \\ 1 & -7 \end{vmatrix}}{\begin{vmatrix} 3 & 4 \\ 5 & -7 \end{vmatrix}}$ $y = \dfrac{\begin{vmatrix} 3 & -2 \\ 5 & 1 \end{vmatrix}}{\begin{vmatrix} 3 & 4 \\ 5 & -7 \end{vmatrix}}$

$\quad = \dfrac{14 - 4}{-21 - 20}$ $= \dfrac{3 - (-10)}{-21 - 20}$

$\quad = \dfrac{10}{-41}$ $= \dfrac{13}{-41}$

$\qquad \left(-\dfrac{10}{41}, -\dfrac{13}{41}\right)$

f. $3\begin{vmatrix} 1 & 4 \\ -3 & 3 \end{vmatrix} - 2\begin{vmatrix} -2 & 4 \\ 4 & 3 \end{vmatrix} + 2\begin{vmatrix} -2 & 1 \\ 4 & -3 \end{vmatrix}$
$= 3(3 - (-12)) - 2(-6 - 16) + 2(6 - 4)$
$= 3(15) - 2(-22) + 2(2)$
$= 45 + 44 + 4 = 93$

g. $-5\begin{vmatrix} 2 & 0 \\ 5 & -6 \end{vmatrix} - 0\begin{vmatrix} 4 & 0 \\ -3 & -6 \end{vmatrix} + 0\begin{vmatrix} 4 & 2 \\ -3 & 5 \end{vmatrix}$
$= -5(-12 - 5 \cdot 0) - 0 + 0 = -5(-12) = 60$

h. $5\begin{vmatrix} 5 & 0 \\ 0 & 5 \end{vmatrix} - 0\begin{vmatrix} 0 & 0 \\ 1 & 5 \end{vmatrix} + 5\begin{vmatrix} 0 & 5 \\ 1 & 0 \end{vmatrix}$
$= 5(25 - 0) - 0 + 5(0 - 5)$
$= 125 - 0 - 25 = 100$

i. $x = \dfrac{\begin{vmatrix} 6 & -3 & -7 \\ 9 & 3 & 1 \\ 7 & 1 & 0 \end{vmatrix}}{\begin{vmatrix} 1 & -3 & -7 \\ 2 & 3 & 1 \\ 4 & 1 & 0 \end{vmatrix}} = \dfrac{6\begin{vmatrix} 3 & 1 \\ 1 & 0 \end{vmatrix} - (-3)\begin{vmatrix} 9 & 1 \\ 7 & 0 \end{vmatrix} + (-7)\begin{vmatrix} 9 & 3 \\ 7 & 1 \end{vmatrix}}{1\begin{vmatrix} 3 & 1 \\ 1 & 0 \end{vmatrix} - (-3)\begin{vmatrix} 2 & 1 \\ 4 & 0 \end{vmatrix} + (-7)\begin{vmatrix} 2 & 3 \\ 4 & 1 \end{vmatrix}}$

$= \dfrac{6(0 - 1) + 3(0 - 7) - 7(9 - 21)}{1(0 - 1) + 3(0 - 4) - 7(2 - 12)} = \dfrac{-6 - 21 + 84}{-1 - 12 + 70} = \dfrac{57}{57} = 1$

$y = \dfrac{\begin{vmatrix} 1 & 6 & -7 \\ 2 & 9 & 1 \\ 4 & 7 & 0 \end{vmatrix}}{\begin{vmatrix} 1 & -3 & -7 \\ 2 & 3 & 1 \\ 4 & 1 & 0 \end{vmatrix}} = \dfrac{1\begin{vmatrix} 9 & 1 \\ 7 & 0 \end{vmatrix} - 6\begin{vmatrix} 2 & 1 \\ 4 & 0 \end{vmatrix} + (-7)\begin{vmatrix} 2 & 9 \\ 4 & 7 \end{vmatrix}}{1\begin{vmatrix} 3 & 1 \\ 1 & 0 \end{vmatrix} - (-3)\begin{vmatrix} 2 & 1 \\ 4 & 0 \end{vmatrix} + (-7)\begin{vmatrix} 2 & 3 \\ 4 & 1 \end{vmatrix}}$

$= \dfrac{1(0 - 7) - 6(0 - 4) - 7(14 - 36)}{1(0 - 1) + 3(0 - 4) - 7(2 - 12)}$

$= \dfrac{-7 + 24 + 154}{-1 - 12 + 70} = \dfrac{171}{57} = 3$

$z = \dfrac{\begin{vmatrix} 1 & -3 & 6 \\ 2 & 3 & 9 \\ 4 & 1 & 7 \end{vmatrix}}{\begin{vmatrix} 1 & -3 & -7 \\ 2 & 3 & 1 \\ 4 & 1 & 0 \end{vmatrix}} = \dfrac{1\begin{vmatrix} 3 & 9 \\ 1 & 7 \end{vmatrix} - (-3)\begin{vmatrix} 2 & 9 \\ 4 & 7 \end{vmatrix} + 6\begin{vmatrix} 2 & 3 \\ 4 & 1 \end{vmatrix}}{1\begin{vmatrix} 3 & 1 \\ 1 & 0 \end{vmatrix} - (-3)\begin{vmatrix} 2 & 1 \\ 4 & 0 \end{vmatrix} + (-7)\begin{vmatrix} 2 & 3 \\ 4 & 1 \end{vmatrix}}$

$= \dfrac{1(21 - 9) + 3(14 - 36) + 6(2 - 12)}{1(0 - 1) + 3(0 - 4) - 7(2 - 12)}$

$= \dfrac{12 - 66 - 60}{-1 - 12 + 70} = \dfrac{-114}{57} = -2$

$(1, 3, -2)$ is the solution.

j. $x = \dfrac{\begin{vmatrix} 2 & 2 & -1 \\ -1 & -2 & 1 \\ 5 & 4 & 3 \end{vmatrix}}{\begin{vmatrix} 1 & 2 & -1 \\ 2 & -2 & 1 \\ 6 & 4 & 3 \end{vmatrix}} = \dfrac{2\begin{vmatrix} -2 & 1 \\ 4 & 3 \end{vmatrix} - 2\begin{vmatrix} -1 & 1 \\ 5 & 3 \end{vmatrix} + (-1)\begin{vmatrix} -1 & -2 \\ 5 & 4 \end{vmatrix}}{1\begin{vmatrix} -2 & 1 \\ 4 & 3 \end{vmatrix} - 2\begin{vmatrix} 2 & 1 \\ 6 & 3 \end{vmatrix} + (-1)\begin{vmatrix} 2 & -2 \\ 6 & 4 \end{vmatrix}}$

$= \dfrac{2(-6-4) - 2(-3-5) - 1(-4+10)}{1(-6-4) - 2(6-6) - 1(8+12)}$

$= \dfrac{-20 + 16 - 6}{-10 - 0 - 20} = \dfrac{-10}{-30} = \dfrac{1}{3}$

$y = \dfrac{\begin{vmatrix} 1 & 2 & -1 \\ 2 & -1 & 1 \\ 6 & 5 & 3 \end{vmatrix}}{\begin{vmatrix} 1 & 2 & -1 \\ 2 & -2 & 1 \\ 6 & 4 & 3 \end{vmatrix}} = \dfrac{1\begin{vmatrix} -1 & 1 \\ 5 & 3 \end{vmatrix} - 2\begin{vmatrix} 2 & 1 \\ 6 & 3 \end{vmatrix} + (-1)\begin{vmatrix} 2 & -1 \\ 6 & 5 \end{vmatrix}}{1\begin{vmatrix} -2 & 1 \\ 4 & 3 \end{vmatrix} - 2\begin{vmatrix} 2 & 1 \\ 6 & 3 \end{vmatrix} + (-1)\begin{vmatrix} 2 & -2 \\ 6 & 4 \end{vmatrix}}$

$= \dfrac{1(-3-5) - 2(6-6) - 1(10-(-6))}{1(-6-4) - 2(6-6) - 1(8+12)}$

$= \dfrac{1(-8) - 2(0) - 1(16)}{-10 - 0 - 20} = \dfrac{-8 - 0 - 16}{-30} = \dfrac{-24}{-30} = \dfrac{-24}{-30} = \dfrac{4}{5}$

$z = \dfrac{\begin{vmatrix} 1 & 2 & 2 \\ 2 & -2 & -1 \\ 6 & 4 & 5 \end{vmatrix}}{\begin{vmatrix} 1 & 2 & -1 \\ 2 & -2 & 1 \\ 6 & 4 & 3 \end{vmatrix}} = \dfrac{1\begin{vmatrix} -2 & -1 \\ 4 & 5 \end{vmatrix} - 2\begin{vmatrix} 2 & -1 \\ 6 & 5 \end{vmatrix} + 2\begin{vmatrix} 2 & -2 \\ 6 & 4 \end{vmatrix}}{1\begin{vmatrix} -2 & 1 \\ 4 & 3 \end{vmatrix} - 2\begin{vmatrix} 2 & 1 \\ 6 & 3 \end{vmatrix} + (-1)\begin{vmatrix} 2 & -2 \\ 6 & 4 \end{vmatrix}}$

$= \dfrac{1(-10-(-4)) - 2(10-(-6)) + 2(8-(-12))}{1(-6-4) - 2(6-6) - 1(8+12)}$

$= \dfrac{1(-6) - 2(16) + 2(20)}{-10 - 0 - 20} = \dfrac{-6 - 32 + 40}{-30} = \dfrac{2}{-30} = -\dfrac{1}{15}$

$\left(\dfrac{1}{3}, \dfrac{4}{5}, -\dfrac{1}{15} \right)$

pp. 580–581   13-3 EXERCISES

1. 3   **2.** −13   **3.** 36   **4.** 29   **5.** −10.3   **6.** 2.88

7. 0   **8.** 0   **9.** (2, 0)   **10.** (−3, 2)   **11.** (−4, −5)

12. (4, 2)   **13.** $\left(\dfrac{1}{3}, -\dfrac{2}{3} \right)$ **14.** $\left(-\dfrac{25}{2}, -\dfrac{11}{2} \right)$ **15.** −10

16. 1   **17.** −3   **18.** 3   **19.** −11   **20.** −6

21. (2, −1, 4)   **22.** (−3, 2, 1)   **23.** (1, 2, 3)

24. (3, 4, −1)   **25.** $\left(\dfrac{3}{2}, \dfrac{13}{14}, \dfrac{33}{14} \right)$ **26.** $\left(-1, -\dfrac{6}{7}, \dfrac{11}{7} \right)$

27. $x \cdot x^2 - x \cdot 4 = x^3 - 4x$ **28.** $y^2 \cdot 3 - y \cdot (-2) = 3y^2 + 2y$

29. $z \cdot 1 - (-z^2) \cdot 3 = z + 3z^2$ **30.** $4x - 6 = x$
$\ 3x = 6$
$\ x = 2$

31. $x^2 - (-20) = 24$ **32.** $(x + 3)5 - (x - 3)4 = -7$
$\ x^2 + 20 = 24$ $\ 5x + 15 - 4x + 12 = -7$
$\ x^2 = 4$ $\ x + 27 = -7$
$\ x = \pm 2$ $\ x = -34$

33. $x = \dfrac{\begin{vmatrix} -5 & \pi \\ 4 & -3 \end{vmatrix}}{\begin{vmatrix} \sqrt{3} & \pi \\ \pi & -3 \end{vmatrix}} = \dfrac{15 - 4\pi}{-3\sqrt{3} - \pi^2}$

$y = \dfrac{\begin{vmatrix} \sqrt{3} & -5 \\ \pi & 4 \end{vmatrix}}{\begin{vmatrix} \sqrt{3} & \pi \\ \pi & -3 \end{vmatrix}} = \dfrac{4\sqrt{3} + 5\pi}{-3\sqrt{3} - \pi^2}$

$\left(\dfrac{15 - 4\pi}{-3\sqrt{3} - \pi^2}, \dfrac{4\sqrt{3} + 5\pi}{-3\sqrt{3} - \pi^2} \right)$

34. Since a given $n \times n$ matrix can only have one value for its determinant, the determinant is a function. Its domain is the set of $n \times n$ matrices and its range is the set of real numbers.

35. $1\begin{vmatrix} x & y \\ 1 & 1 \end{vmatrix} - x\begin{vmatrix} 1 & y \\ 1 & 1 \end{vmatrix} + y\begin{vmatrix} 1 & x \\ 1 & 1 \end{vmatrix}$
$= 1(x - y) - x(1 - y) + y(1 - x)$
$= x - y - x + xy + y - xy = 0$

36. $1\begin{vmatrix} y & y^2 \\ z & z^2 \end{vmatrix} - x\begin{vmatrix} 1 & y^2 \\ 1 & z^2 \end{vmatrix} + x^2\begin{vmatrix} 1 & y \\ 1 & z \end{vmatrix}$
$= yz^2 - y^2z - x(z^2 - y^2) + x^2(z - y)$
$= yz^2 - y^2z - xz^2 + xy^2 + x^2z - x^2y$
$= xyz - xz^2 - zy^2 + yz^2 - x^2y + x^2z + xy^2 - xyz$
$= (xy - xz - y^2 + yz)(zx)$
$= (x - y)(y - z)(z - x)$

37. To solve for x, multiply ① by b_2 and ② by $-b_1$.
$\ a_1 b_2 x + b_1 b_2 y = b_2 c_1$
$+\ \dfrac{-a_2 b_1 x - b_1 b_2 y = -b_1 c_2}{(a_1 b_2 - a_2 b_1)x = c_1 b_2 - c_2 b_1}$

$x = \dfrac{c_1 b_2 - c_2 b_1}{a_1 b_2 - a_2 b_1}$

Solve for y similarly.
$\ -a_1 a_2 x - a_2 b_1 y = -a_2 c_1$
$+\ \dfrac{a_1 a_2 x + a_1 b_2 y = a_1 c_2}{(a_1 b_2 - a_2 b_1)y = a_1 c_2 - a_2 c_1}$

$y = \dfrac{a_1 c_2 - a_2 c_1}{a_1 b_2 - a_2 b_1}$

38. Answers may vary.

a. $\begin{vmatrix} 2 & w \\ -1 & \ell \end{vmatrix}$ or $\begin{vmatrix} 2\ell & -w \\ 1 & 1 \end{vmatrix}$

b. $\begin{vmatrix} a^2 & b \\ -b & 1 \end{vmatrix}$ or $\begin{vmatrix} a & -1 \\ b^2 & a \end{vmatrix}$

39. $A' = \begin{vmatrix} a_1 & a_2 & a_3 \\ b_1 & b_2 & b_3 \\ c_1 & c_2 & c_3 \end{vmatrix}$
$\det(A') = a_1 b_2 c_3 + a_2 b_3 c_1 + a_3 b_1 c_2 - a_3 b_2 c_1 - a_2 b_1 c_3$
$\ - a_1 b_3 c_2$
The $\det(A') = \det A$.

40.
$\ x + 2 = 3x^2$
$\ 3x^2 - x - 2 = 0$
$\ (3x + 2)(x - 1) = 0$
$\ 3x + 2 = 0$ or $x - 1 = 0$

$\ x = -\dfrac{2}{3}$ or $x = 1$

$\left\{ 1, -\dfrac{2}{3} \right\}$

41.
$v^{4/3} = 16$
$(v^{4/3})^{3/4} = 16^{3/4}$
$v = \pm\sqrt[4]{16^3}$
$\{v = \pm 8\}$

42.
$\dfrac{6}{y} + \dfrac{2y}{3} = 5$
$18 + 2y^2 = 15y$
$2y^2 - 15y + 18 = 0$
$(2y - 3)(y - 6) = 0$
$2y - 3 = 0$ or $y - 6 = 0$

$y = \dfrac{3}{2}$ or $y = 6$

$\left\{ \dfrac{3}{2}, 6 \right\}$

43.
$z^{2/3} - 2z^{1/3} - 48 = 0$
$(z^{1/3})^2 - 2(z^{1/3}) - 48 = 0$
$((z^{1/3}) + 6)((z^{1/3}) - 8) = 0$
$z^{1/3} + 6 = 0$ or $z^{1/3} - 8 = 0$
$z^{1/3} = -6$ or $z^{1/3} = 8$
$z = -6^3$ or $z = 8^3$
$z = -216$ or $z = 512$
$\{-216, 512\}$

44. $3(x^2 - 2x + 5) - 2(3x - 5) = 4(x^2 - x - 5) - (x^2 + 3)$
$3x^2 - 6x + 15 - 6x + 10 = 4x^2 - 4x - 20 - x^2 - 3$
$3x^2 - 12x + 25 = 3x^2 - 4x - 23$
$-12x + 25 = -4x - 23$
$-8x = -48$
$x = 6$

45.
$$y^2 + 0y - 2 \overline{)y^5 - 2y^4 - 2y^3 + 9y^2 + 0y - 10}$$

quotient: $y^3 - 2y^2 + 0y + 5$

$\underline{-y^5 + 0y^4 + 2y^3}$
$-2y^4 - 0y^3 + 9y^2$
$\underline{-2y^4 + 0y^3 - 4y^2}$
$+5y^2 + 0y$
$\underline{+0y^2 + 0y}$
$5y^2 + 0y - 10$
$\underline{-5y^2 - 0y + 10}$
0

so $y^5 - 2y^4 - 2y^3 + 9y^2 - 10 \div y^2 - 2 = y^3 - 2y^2 + 5$

46. $\dfrac{1}{90} + \dfrac{1}{75} = \dfrac{1}{t}$

$\dfrac{5}{450} + \dfrac{6}{450} = \dfrac{1}{t}$

$\dfrac{11}{450} = \dfrac{1}{t}$

$11t = 450$

$t = \dfrac{450}{11} \approx 40.9$

They will finish the job together in approximately 40.9 min.

pp. 582–586   13-4 TRY THIS

a.
$$\begin{bmatrix} 1 \cdot 5 & -2 \cdot 5 & x \cdot 5 \\ 4 \cdot 5 & y \cdot 5 & 1 \cdot 5 \\ 0 \cdot 5 & -5 \cdot 5 & x^2 \cdot 5 \end{bmatrix} = \begin{bmatrix} 5 & -10 & 5x \\ 20 & 5y & 5 \\ 0 & -25 & 5x^2 \end{bmatrix}$$

b.
$$\begin{bmatrix} 1 \cdot -3t & -1 \cdot -3t & 4 \cdot -3t & x \cdot -3t \\ y \cdot -3t & 3 \cdot -3t & -2 \cdot -3t & y \cdot -3t \\ 1 \cdot -3t & 4 \cdot -3t & -5 \cdot -3t & y \cdot -3t \end{bmatrix}$$
$$= \begin{bmatrix} -3t & 3t & -12t & -3xt \\ -3yt & -9t & 6t & -3yt \\ -3t & -12t & 15t & -3yt \end{bmatrix}$$

c.
$$\begin{bmatrix} 1 \cdot 2 + 4 \cdot 1 + 2 \cdot 3 \\ -1 \cdot 2 + 6 \cdot 1 + 3 \cdot 3 \\ 3 \cdot 2 + 2 \cdot 1 - 1 \cdot 3 \\ 5 \cdot 2 + 0 \cdot 1 + 2 \cdot 3 \end{bmatrix} = \begin{bmatrix} 2 + 4 + 6 \\ -2 + 6 + 9 \\ 6 + 2 - 3 \\ 10 + 0 + 6 \end{bmatrix} = \begin{bmatrix} 12 \\ 13 \\ 5 \\ 16 \end{bmatrix}$$

d.
$$\begin{bmatrix} 4 \cdot 1 + 1 \cdot 2 + 2 \cdot -3 & 4 \cdot 4 + 1 \cdot 0 + 2 \cdot 5 \\ -3 \cdot 1 + 2 \cdot 2 + 3 \cdot -3 & -3 \cdot 4 + 2 \cdot 0 + 3 \cdot 5 \\ 2 \cdot 1 + 0 \cdot 2 + 5 \cdot -3 & 2 \cdot 4 + 0 \cdot 0 + 5 \cdot 5 \\ 3 \cdot 1 + 1 \cdot 2 + 4 \cdot -3 & 3 \cdot 4 + 1 \cdot 0 + 4 \cdot 5 \end{bmatrix}$$
$$= \begin{bmatrix} 4 + 2 - 6 & 16 + 0 + 10 \\ -3 + 4 - 9 & -12 + 0 + 15 \\ 2 + 0 - 15 & 8 + 0 + 25 \\ 3 + 2 - 12 & 12 + 0 + 20 \end{bmatrix} = \begin{bmatrix} 0 & 26 \\ -8 & 3 \\ -13 & 33 \\ -7 & 32 \end{bmatrix}$$

e. $[4 \cdot 1 + 1 \cdot 2 + 0 \cdot 3 + 2 \cdot 1 \quad 4 \cdot 0 + 1 \cdot -1 + 0 \cdot 5 + 2 \cdot 3 \quad 4 \cdot 1 + 1 \cdot 0 + 0 \cdot 1 + 2 \cdot 0]$
$= [4 + 2 + 0 + 2 \quad 0 - 1 + 0 + 6 \quad 4 + 0 + 0 + 0]$
$= [8 \quad 5 \quad 4]$

f.
$$\begin{bmatrix} -2 \cdot -1 + 4 \cdot 0 + & 0 \cdot 4 & -2 \cdot -2 + 4 \cdot 1 + & 0 \cdot 5 & -2 \cdot -3 + 4 \cdot 0 + & 0 \cdot 2 \\ -3 \cdot -1 + 0 \cdot 0 + & -8 \cdot 4 & -3 \cdot -2 + 0 \cdot 1 + & -8 \cdot 4 & -3 \cdot -3 + 0 \cdot 0 + & -8 \cdot 2 \end{bmatrix}$$
$$= \begin{bmatrix} 2 + 0 + & 0 & 4 + 4 + & 0 & 6 + 0 + & 0 \\ 3 + 0 - & 32 & 6 + 0 - & 40 & 9 + 0 - & 16 \end{bmatrix}$$
$$= \begin{bmatrix} 2 & 8 & 6 \\ -29 & -34 & -7 \end{bmatrix}$$

g. Undefined since the number of columns in A does not equal the number of rows in C.

h.
$$\begin{bmatrix} 1 \cdot -2 + (-1) \cdot -3 & 1 \cdot 4 + (-1) \cdot 0 & 1 \cdot 0 + (-1) \cdot -8 \\ 2 \cdot -2 + (-1) \cdot -1 & 2 \cdot 4 + (-1) \cdot 0 & 2 \cdot 0 + (-1) \cdot -8 \end{bmatrix}$$
$$= \begin{bmatrix} -2 + 3 & 4 - 0 & 0 + 8 \\ -2 + 1 & 8 - 0 & 0 + 8 \end{bmatrix} = \begin{bmatrix} 1 & 4 & 8 \\ -1 & 8 & 8 \end{bmatrix}$$

i.
$$\begin{bmatrix} 3 & 4 & -2 \\ 2 & -2 & 5 \\ 6 & 7 & -1 \end{bmatrix} \begin{bmatrix} x \\ y \\ z \end{bmatrix} = \begin{bmatrix} 5 \\ 3 \\ 0 \end{bmatrix}$$

j.
$$\begin{bmatrix} 5 & 7 & 0 \\ 3 & -2 & 1 \\ -2 & 3 & -1 \end{bmatrix} \begin{bmatrix} x \\ y \\ z \end{bmatrix} = \begin{bmatrix} 19 \\ 1 \\ 12 \end{bmatrix}$$

k.
$$\begin{bmatrix} 3 & 0 & 2 & -7 \\ 0 & 1 & -2 & 0 \\ 5 & 5 & 0 & -3 \\ 0 & 0 & 10 & -3 \\ 1 & 0 & -1 & -1 \end{bmatrix} \begin{bmatrix} v \\ w \\ x \\ y \end{bmatrix} = \begin{bmatrix} 13 \\ 0 \\ -5 \\ 15 \\ 2 \end{bmatrix}$$

l.
$$\begin{bmatrix} 4 & 0 & 0 & 0 \\ 4 & 1 & 0 & 0 \\ 4 & 2 & 1 & 0 \\ 4 & 3 & 2 & 1 \end{bmatrix} \begin{bmatrix} w \\ x \\ y \\ z \end{bmatrix} = \begin{bmatrix} -1 \\ -3 \\ -6 \\ -10 \end{bmatrix}$$

pp. 587–588   13-4 EXERCISES

1. $\begin{bmatrix} -2 & -4 \\ -8 & -6 \end{bmatrix}$ **2.** $\begin{bmatrix} 15 & -25 \\ -10 & 5 \end{bmatrix}$ **3.** $\begin{bmatrix} 14 & -14 \\ -14 & 14 \end{bmatrix}$

4. $\begin{bmatrix} 12 & 12 \\ 12 & 12 \end{bmatrix}$ **5.** $\begin{bmatrix} t & 3t \\ 2t & 6t \end{bmatrix}$ **6.** $\begin{bmatrix} 3p & 3p \\ -p & -p \end{bmatrix}$

7. $\begin{bmatrix} 2 & -9 & -6 \\ 3 & -3 & -4 \\ -2 & 2 & -1 \end{bmatrix}$ **8.** $\begin{bmatrix} 1 & 2 & -5 \\ -1 & 0 & 1 \\ -2 & 3 & -1 \end{bmatrix}$

9. $[-22]$ **10.** $[-36]$ **11.** $[-36]$ **12.** $[-9]$

13. $\begin{bmatrix} 1 & 3 \\ -6 & 17 \end{bmatrix}$ **14.** $\begin{bmatrix} -8 & 8 \\ 3 & -3 \end{bmatrix}$ **15.** $\begin{bmatrix} 0 & 0 \\ 0 & 0 \end{bmatrix}$ **16.** $\begin{bmatrix} 0 & 0 \\ 0 & 0 \end{bmatrix}$

17. $[-14 \quad -11 \quad -3]$ **18.** $[25 \quad 25]$ **19.** $[-13 \quad -1 \quad -4]$

20. $\begin{bmatrix} -15 \\ 5 \end{bmatrix}$ **21.** $\begin{bmatrix} 3 & 3 \\ -1 & -1 \end{bmatrix}$ **22.** $\begin{bmatrix} -3 & 5 \\ 2 & -1 \end{bmatrix}$

23. $\begin{bmatrix} -5 & 4 & 3 \\ 5 & -9 & 4 \\ 7 & -18 & 17 \end{bmatrix}$ **24.** $\begin{bmatrix} 14 & 12 & 16 \\ -2 & -2 & -6 \\ 5 & 5 & -9 \end{bmatrix}$ **25.** $\begin{bmatrix} -7 \\ -18 \end{bmatrix}$

26. $[9 \quad -9]$ **27.** Not possible **28.** Not possible

29. $\begin{bmatrix} 3 & -2 & 4 \\ 2 & 1 & -5 \end{bmatrix} \begin{bmatrix} x \\ y \\ z \end{bmatrix} = \begin{bmatrix} 17 \\ 13 \end{bmatrix}$ **30.** $\begin{bmatrix} 3 & 2 & 5 \\ 4 & -3 & 2 \end{bmatrix} \begin{bmatrix} x \\ y \\ z \end{bmatrix} = \begin{bmatrix} 9 \\ 10 \end{bmatrix}$

31. $\begin{bmatrix} 1 & -1 & 2 & -4 \\ 2 & -1 & -1 & 1 \\ 1 & 4 & -3 & -1 \\ 3 & 5 & -7 & 2 \end{bmatrix} \begin{bmatrix} x \\ y \\ z \\ w \end{bmatrix} = \begin{bmatrix} 12 \\ 0 \\ 1 \\ 9 \end{bmatrix}$

32. $\begin{bmatrix} 2 & 4 & -5 & 12 \\ 4 & -1 & 12 & -1 \\ -1 & 4 & 0 & 2 \\ 2 & 10 & 1 & 0 \end{bmatrix} \begin{bmatrix} x \\ y \\ z \\ w \end{bmatrix} = \begin{bmatrix} 2 \\ 5 \\ 13 \\ 5 \end{bmatrix}$

33. $3A + 2B = \begin{bmatrix} 9 & 3 & 0 \\ 18 & 12 & 0 \\ 6 & 9 & 3 \end{bmatrix} + \begin{bmatrix} 4 & 2 & 0 \\ 6 & 6 & 18 \\ 12 & 8 & 12 \end{bmatrix}$

$= \begin{bmatrix} 13 & 5 & 0 \\ 24 & 18 & 18 \\ 18 & 17 & 15 \end{bmatrix}$

$B - 2A = \begin{bmatrix} 2 & 1 & 0 \\ 3 & 3 & 9 \\ 6 & 4 & 6 \end{bmatrix} - \begin{bmatrix} 6 & 2 & 0 \\ 12 & 8 & 0 \\ 4 & 6 & 2 \end{bmatrix} = \begin{bmatrix} -4 & -1 & 0 \\ -9 & -5 & 9 \\ 2 & -2 & 4 \end{bmatrix}$

34. $AI = \begin{bmatrix} 3\cdot 1 + 2\cdot 0 & 3\cdot 0 + 2\cdot 1 \\ -1\cdot 1 + 5\cdot 0 & -1\cdot 0 + 5\cdot 1 \end{bmatrix} = \begin{bmatrix} 3 + 0 & 0 + 2 \\ -1 + 0 & 0 + 5 \end{bmatrix}$

$= \begin{bmatrix} 3 & 2 \\ -1 & 5 \end{bmatrix}$

$IA = \begin{bmatrix} 1\cdot 3 + 0\cdot(-1) & 1\cdot 2 + 0\cdot 5 \\ 0\cdot 3 + 1\cdot(-1) & 0\cdot 2 + 1\cdot 5 \end{bmatrix} = \begin{bmatrix} 3 + 0 & 2 + 0 \\ 0 - 1 & 0 + 5 \end{bmatrix}$

$= \begin{bmatrix} 3 & 2 \\ -1 & 5 \end{bmatrix}$

35. Since $AI = IA = A$, I is a multiplicative identity.

36. $\begin{bmatrix} \frac{3}{72} & \frac{-12}{72} & \frac{27}{72} \\ \frac{30}{72} & \frac{-36}{72} & \frac{14}{72} \end{bmatrix} = \frac{1}{72}\begin{bmatrix} 3 & -12 & 27 \\ 30 & -36 & 14 \end{bmatrix}$

37. The product does not exist.

38. Yes, the product does exist. A 5×5 matrix multiplied by a 5×6 matrix will yield a 5×6 matrix.

39. Suppose A has m rows and n columns.
Since AB exists, B must have n rows.
Since BA exists, and A has m rows, B must have m columns.
So B must be n by m. AB is then a square $m \times m$ matrix, BA is a square $n \times n$ matrix.

40. **a.** $(A + B)(A - B) = AA - AB + BA - BB$
$= A^2 - AB + BA - B^2$
This will equal $A^2 - B^2$ only if $AB = BA$.

$AB = \begin{bmatrix} -1\cdot 1 + 0\cdot 1 & -1\cdot 1 + 0\cdot 2 \\ 2\cdot 1 + 1\cdot 0 & 2\cdot -1 + 1\cdot 2 \end{bmatrix}$

$= \begin{bmatrix} -1 + 0 & -1 + 0 \\ 2 + 0 & -2 + 2 \end{bmatrix} = \begin{bmatrix} -1 & -1 \\ 2 & 0 \end{bmatrix}$

$BA = \begin{bmatrix} 1\cdot(-1) + -1\cdot 2 & 1\cdot 0 + (-1)\cdot 1 \\ 0\cdot(-1) + 2\cdot 2 & 0\cdot 0 + 2\cdot 1 \end{bmatrix}$

$= \begin{bmatrix} -1 + -2 & 0 + -1 \\ 0 + 4 & 0 + 2 \end{bmatrix} = \begin{bmatrix} -3 & -1 \\ 4 & 2 \end{bmatrix}$

$AB \neq BA$, hence, $(A + B)(A - B) \neq A^2 - B^2$.

b. $(A + B)(A + B) = AA + AB + BA + BB$
$= A^2 + AB + BA + B^2$
This will equal $A^2 + 2AB + B^2$ only if $AB + BA = 2AB$.

$AB = \begin{bmatrix} -1 & -1 \\ 2 & 0 \end{bmatrix} \quad BA = \begin{bmatrix} -3 & -1 \\ 4 & 2 \end{bmatrix}$

$AB + BA = \begin{bmatrix} -4 & -2 \\ 6 & 2 \end{bmatrix}$

$2AB = \begin{bmatrix} -2 & -2 \\ 4 & 0 \end{bmatrix}$

So $AB + BA \neq 2AB$, hence
$(A + B)(A + B) \neq A^2 + 2AB + B^2$.

41. $A + B = \begin{bmatrix} a & c \\ b & d \end{bmatrix} + \begin{bmatrix} e & g \\ f & h \end{bmatrix} = \begin{bmatrix} a + e & c + g \\ b + f & d + h \end{bmatrix}$

$= \begin{bmatrix} e + a & g + c \\ f + b & h + d \end{bmatrix} = B + A$

42. $(A + B) + C = \begin{bmatrix} a + e & c + g \\ b + f & d + h \end{bmatrix} + \begin{bmatrix} p & r \\ q & s \end{bmatrix}$

$= \begin{bmatrix} (a + e) + p & (c + g) + r \\ (b + f) + q & (d + h) + s \end{bmatrix}$

$= \begin{bmatrix} a + (e + p) & c + (g + r) \\ b + (f + q) & d + (h + s) \end{bmatrix}$

$= \begin{bmatrix} a & c \\ b & d \end{bmatrix} + \begin{bmatrix} e + p & g + r \\ f + q & h + s \end{bmatrix}$

$= A + (B + C)$

43. $A - B = \begin{bmatrix} a & c \\ b & d \end{bmatrix} - \begin{bmatrix} e & g \\ f & h \end{bmatrix} = \begin{bmatrix} a - e & c - g \\ b - f & d - h \end{bmatrix}$

$= \begin{bmatrix} a + (-e) & c + (-g) \\ b + (-f) & d + (-h) \end{bmatrix}$

$= \begin{bmatrix} a & c \\ b & d \end{bmatrix} + \begin{bmatrix} -e & -g \\ -f & -h \end{bmatrix} = A + (-B)$

44. $(-1)A = -1\begin{bmatrix} a & c \\ b & d \end{bmatrix} = \begin{bmatrix} -a & -c \\ -b & -d \end{bmatrix} = -A$

45. $k(A + B) = k\begin{bmatrix} a + e & c + g \\ b + f & d + h \end{bmatrix} = \begin{bmatrix} k(a + e) & k(c + g) \\ k(b + f) & k(d + h) \end{bmatrix}$

$= \begin{bmatrix} ka + ke & kc + kg \\ kb + kf & kd + kh \end{bmatrix} = \begin{bmatrix} ka & kc \\ kb & kd \end{bmatrix} + \begin{bmatrix} ke & kg \\ kf & kh \end{bmatrix}$

$= k\begin{bmatrix} a & c \\ b & d \end{bmatrix} + k\begin{bmatrix} e & g \\ f & h \end{bmatrix} = kA + kB$

46. $(k + m)A = (k + m)\begin{bmatrix} a & c \\ b & d \end{bmatrix} = \begin{bmatrix} (k + m)a & (k + m)c \\ (k + m)b & (k + m)d \end{bmatrix}$

$= \begin{bmatrix} ka + ma & kc + mc \\ kb + mb & kd + md \end{bmatrix}$

$= \begin{bmatrix} ka & kc \\ kb & kd \end{bmatrix} + \begin{bmatrix} ma & mc \\ mb & md \end{bmatrix}$

$= k\begin{bmatrix} a & c \\ b & d \end{bmatrix} + m\begin{bmatrix} a & c \\ b & d \end{bmatrix} = kA + mA$

47. $(x^2 - 3y)(x^2 - 3y) = x^4 - 6x^2y + 9y^2$

48. $x^2(9y^2)\frac{1}{x^3}\left(\frac{1}{y^2}\right) = \frac{9x^2y^2}{x^3y^2} = \frac{9}{x}$

49. $\left(\frac{8m^3}{27n^6z^7}\right)^{2/3} = \sqrt[3]{\left(\frac{8m^3}{27n^6z^7}\right)^2} = \sqrt[3]{\frac{64m^6}{27\cdot 27n^{12}z^{14}}}$

$= \frac{4m^2}{9n^4z^4\sqrt[3]{z^2}} = \frac{4m^2}{9n^4z^4\sqrt[3]{z^2}}\cdot\frac{\sqrt[3]{z^4}}{\sqrt[3]{z^4}}$

$= \frac{4m^2z\sqrt[3]{z}}{9n^4z^6} = \frac{4m^2\sqrt[3]{z}}{9n^4z^5}$

50. The possible rational roots are $\pm 8, \pm 4, \pm 2, \pm 1, \pm\frac{1}{2}$.

51. By Descartes' Rule of Signs:
$P(x) = 2x^4 + 3x^3 + 6x^2 + 12x - 8$ will have 1 positive real root.
$P(-x) = 2x^4 - 3x^3 + 6x^2 - 12x - 8$, so $P(x)$ will have 3 or 1 negative real roots.

52. By synthetic division:

$\begin{array}{r|rrrrr} -2 & 2 & 3 & 6 & 12 & -8 \\ & & -4 & 2 & -16 & 8 \\ \hline & 2 & -1 & 8 & -4 & 0 \end{array}$ -2 is a root.

$\begin{array}{r|rrrr} \frac{1}{2} & 2 & -1 & 8 & -4 \\ & & 1 & 0 & 4 \\ \hline & 2 & 0 & 8 & 0 \end{array}$ $\frac{1}{2}$ is a root.

For $2x^2 + 8 = 0$, $x^2 = -4$
so $x = \pm 2i$

$P(x) = 0$ when $x = \frac{1}{2}, -2, 2i, -2i$.

53. $P(3) = 2(3)^4 + 3(3)^3 + 6(3)^2 + 12(3) - 8$
$= 2(81) + 3(27) + 6(9) + 36 - 8$
$= 162 + 81 + 54 + 36 - 8$
$= 325$
$P(-1) = 2(-1)^4 + 3(-1)^3 + 6(-1)^2 + 12(-1) - 8$
$= 2 - 3 + 6 - 12 - 8$
$= -15$
$P(0) = 2(0)^4 + 3(0)^3 + 6(0)^2 + 12(0) - 8$
$= -8$
$P\left(\frac{1}{2}\right) = 2\left(\frac{1}{2}\right)^4 + 3\left(\frac{1}{2}\right)^3 + 6\left(\frac{1}{2}\right)^2 + 12\left(\frac{1}{2}\right) - 8$
$= 2\left(\frac{1}{16}\right) + 3\left(\frac{1}{8}\right) + 6\left(\frac{1}{4}\right) + 12\left(\frac{1}{2}\right) - 8$
$= \frac{1}{8} + \frac{3}{8} + \frac{6}{4} + 6 - 8$
$= 2 + 6 - 8$
$= 0$

54. Let $w =$ the width;
$w + 12 =$ the length.
$$w(w + 12) = 325$$
$$w^2 + 12w - 325 = 0$$
$$(w + 25)(w - 13) = 0$$
$$w = -25 \quad \text{or} \quad w = 13$$
The width is 13 m and the length is $(13 + 12)$ or 25 m.

pp. 589–590   **13-5 TRY THIS**

a. $AB = \begin{bmatrix} 5 \cdot (-4) + -3 \cdot (-7) & 5 \cdot (-3) + -3 \cdot 5 \\ -7 \cdot (-4) + 4 \cdot (-7) & -7 \cdot 3 + 4 \cdot 5 \end{bmatrix}$

$= \begin{bmatrix} -20 + 21 & 15 - 15 \\ 28 - 28 & -21 + 20 \end{bmatrix}$

$= \begin{bmatrix} 1 & 0 \\ 0 & -1 \end{bmatrix}$ No, A and B are not inverses.

b. $AB = \begin{bmatrix} 3 \cdot \frac{3}{8} + 1 \cdot \left(-\frac{1}{8}\right) + 0 \cdot \left(-\frac{2}{8}\right) & 3 \cdot \frac{1}{8} + 1 \cdot \left(-\frac{3}{8}\right) + 0 \cdot \frac{2}{8} & 3 \cdot \left(-\frac{2}{8}\right) + 1 \cdot \frac{6}{8} + 0 \cdot \frac{4}{8} \\ 1 \cdot \frac{3}{8} + (-1) \cdot \left(-\frac{1}{8}\right) + 2 \cdot \left(-\frac{2}{8}\right) & 1 \cdot \frac{1}{8} + (-1) \cdot \left(-\frac{3}{8}\right) + 2 \cdot \frac{2}{8} & 1 \cdot \left(-\frac{2}{8}\right) + (-1) \cdot \frac{6}{8} + 2 \cdot \frac{4}{8} \\ 1 \cdot \frac{3}{8} + 1 \cdot \left(-\frac{1}{8}\right) + 1 \cdot \left(-\frac{2}{8}\right) & 1 \cdot \frac{1}{8} + 1 \cdot \left(-\frac{3}{8}\right) + 1 \cdot \frac{2}{8} & 1 \cdot \left(-\frac{2}{8}\right) + 1 \cdot \frac{6}{8} + 1 \cdot \frac{4}{8} \end{bmatrix}$

$= \begin{bmatrix} \frac{9}{8} - \frac{1}{8} + 0 & \frac{3}{8} - \frac{3}{8} + 0 & -\frac{6}{8} + \frac{6}{8} + 0 \\ \frac{3}{8} + \frac{1}{8} - \frac{4}{8} & \frac{1}{8} + \frac{3}{8} + \frac{4}{8} & -\frac{2}{8} - \frac{6}{8} + \frac{8}{8} \\ \frac{3}{8} - \frac{1}{8} - \frac{2}{8} & \frac{1}{8} - \frac{3}{8} + \frac{2}{8} & -\frac{2}{8} + \frac{6}{8} + \frac{4}{8} \end{bmatrix}$

$= \begin{bmatrix} 1 & 0 & 0 \\ 0 & 1 & 0 \\ 0 & 0 & 1 \end{bmatrix}$

$BA = \begin{bmatrix} \frac{3}{8} \cdot 3 + \frac{1}{8} \cdot 1 + \left(-\frac{2}{8}\right) \cdot 1 & \frac{3}{8} \cdot 1 + \frac{1}{8} \cdot (-1) + -\frac{2}{8} \cdot 1 & \frac{3}{8} \cdot 0 + \frac{1}{8} \cdot 2 + \left(-\frac{2}{8}\right) \cdot 1 \\ -\frac{1}{8} \cdot 3 + \left(-\frac{3}{8}\right) \cdot 1 + \frac{6}{8} \cdot 1 & -\frac{1}{8} \cdot 1 + \left(-\frac{3}{8}\right) \cdot (-1) + \frac{6}{8} \cdot 1 & -\frac{1}{8} \cdot 0 + \left(-\frac{3}{8}\right) \cdot 2 + \frac{6}{8} \cdot 1 \\ -\frac{2}{8} \cdot 3 + \frac{2}{8} \cdot 1 + \frac{4}{8} \cdot 1 & -\frac{2}{8} \cdot 1 + \frac{2}{8} \cdot (-1) + \frac{4}{8} \cdot 1 & -\frac{2}{8} \cdot 0 + \frac{2}{8} \cdot 2 + \frac{4}{8} \cdot 1 \end{bmatrix}$

$= \begin{bmatrix} \frac{9}{8} + \frac{1}{8} - \frac{2}{8} & \frac{3}{8} - \frac{1}{8} - \frac{2}{8} & 0 + \frac{2}{8} - \frac{2}{8} \\ -\frac{3}{8} - \frac{3}{8} + \frac{6}{8} & -\frac{1}{8} + \frac{3}{8} + \frac{6}{8} & 0 - \frac{6}{8} + \frac{6}{8} \\ -\frac{6}{8} - \frac{2}{8} + \frac{4}{8} & -\frac{2}{8} + \frac{2}{8} + \frac{4}{8} & 0 + \frac{4}{8} + \frac{4}{8} \end{bmatrix}$

$= \begin{bmatrix} 1 & 0 & 0 \\ 0 & 1 & 0 \\ 0 & 0 & 1 \end{bmatrix}$

Yes, $AB = BA = I$.

---

c. It does not exist. The determinant is 0.

d. $A^{-1} = \frac{1}{2 + 3} \begin{bmatrix} 2 & -3 \\ 1 & 1 \end{bmatrix} = \begin{bmatrix} \frac{2}{5} & -\frac{3}{5} \\ \frac{1}{5} & \frac{1}{5} \end{bmatrix}$

e. $A^{-1} = \frac{1}{15 + 15} \begin{bmatrix} 5 & -5 \\ 3 & 3 \end{bmatrix} = \begin{bmatrix} \frac{5}{30} & -\frac{5}{30} \\ \frac{3}{30} & \frac{3}{30} \end{bmatrix} = \begin{bmatrix} \frac{1}{6} & -\frac{1}{6} \\ \frac{1}{10} & \frac{1}{10} \end{bmatrix}$

pp. 591–592   **13-5 EXERCISES**

1. Yes   **2.** No   **3.** No   **4.** Yes

5. $\begin{bmatrix} -3 & 2 \\ 5 & -3 \end{bmatrix}$ **6.** $\begin{bmatrix} 2 & -5 \\ -1 & 3 \end{bmatrix}$ **7.** $\begin{bmatrix} 2 & -3 \\ -7 & 11 \end{bmatrix}$

8. $\begin{bmatrix} -3 & 5 \\ 5 & -8 \end{bmatrix}$ **9.** $\begin{bmatrix} \frac{2}{11} & \frac{3}{11} \\ -\frac{1}{11} & \frac{4}{11} \end{bmatrix}$ **10.** $\begin{bmatrix} 0 & 1 \\ -1 & 0 \end{bmatrix}$

11. Does not exist.   **12.** $\begin{bmatrix} \frac{1}{4} & 0 \\ 0 & 1 \end{bmatrix}$ **13.** Does not exist.

14. $A^{-1} = \frac{1}{\frac{1}{8} - 0} \begin{bmatrix} \frac{1}{4} & 0 \\ -1 & \frac{1}{2} \end{bmatrix} = 8 \begin{bmatrix} \frac{1}{4} & 0 \\ -1 & \frac{1}{2} \end{bmatrix} = \begin{bmatrix} 2 & 0 \\ -8 & 4 \end{bmatrix}$

15. $A^{-1} = \dfrac{1}{0.1 - 0.15}\begin{bmatrix} 0.2 & -0.1 \\ -1.5 & 0.5 \end{bmatrix} = -\dfrac{1}{0.05}\begin{bmatrix} 0.2 & -0.1 \\ -1.5 & 0.5 \end{bmatrix}$

$= -20\begin{bmatrix} 0.2 & -0.1 \\ -1.5 & 0.5 \end{bmatrix} = \begin{bmatrix} -4 & 2 \\ 30 & -10 \end{bmatrix}$

16. $A^{-1} = \dfrac{1}{xy}\begin{bmatrix} y & 0 \\ 0 & x \end{bmatrix} = \begin{bmatrix} \dfrac{1}{x} & 0 \\ 0 & \dfrac{1}{y} \end{bmatrix} \quad x, y \neq 0$

17. $A^{-1} = \dfrac{1}{-xy}\begin{bmatrix} 0 & -x \\ -y & 0 \end{bmatrix} = \begin{bmatrix} 0 & \dfrac{1}{y} \\ \dfrac{1}{x} & 0 \end{bmatrix} \quad x, y \neq 0$

18. $A^{-1} = \begin{bmatrix} \dfrac{1}{x} \end{bmatrix} \quad x \neq 0$

19. $A^{-1} = \dfrac{1}{\dfrac{5}{121} + \dfrac{6}{121}}\begin{bmatrix} \dfrac{5}{11} & \dfrac{2}{11} \\ -\dfrac{3}{11} & \dfrac{1}{11} \end{bmatrix} = 11\begin{bmatrix} \dfrac{5}{11} & \dfrac{2}{11} \\ -\dfrac{3}{11} & \dfrac{1}{11} \end{bmatrix} = \begin{bmatrix} 5 & 2 \\ -3 & 1 \end{bmatrix}$

20. Let $A = \begin{bmatrix} 0 & 0 \\ a & b \end{bmatrix}$. Then $|A| = 0$, hence, A^{-1} does not exist.

Let $A = \begin{bmatrix} 0 & a \\ 0 & b \end{bmatrix}$. Then $|A| = 0$, hence, A^{-1} does not exist.

21. Let $A = \begin{bmatrix} a & a \\ b & b \end{bmatrix}$. Then $|A| = ab - ba = 0$, hence, A^{-1} does not exist.

Let $A = \begin{bmatrix} a & b \\ a & b \end{bmatrix}$. Then $|A| = ab - ab = 0$, hence, A^{-1} does not exist.

22. Let $A = \begin{bmatrix} a & b \\ ka & kb \end{bmatrix}$. Then $|A| = akb - kab = 0$, hence, A^{-1} does not exist.

Let $A = \begin{bmatrix} a & ka \\ b & kb \end{bmatrix}$. Then $|A| = akb - bka = 0$, hence, A^{-1} does not exist.

23. $(x^2 - 9y^4)(x^2 + 9y^4) = (x + 3y^2)(x - 3y^2)(x^2 + 9y^4)$

24. $(a + 5b)(a + 5b) - c^2$
$(a + 5b)^2 - c^2$
$((a + 5b) - c)((a + 5b) + c) = (a + 5b - c)(a + 5b + c)$

25. $(2m - 3n)(3m - 2n)$

26. $((((a^{-2}b)^{-1})^4)^{-1/2})^2$

$\left(\left(\left(\left(\dfrac{b}{a^2}\right)^{-1}\right)^4\right)^{-1/2}\right)^2$

$\left(\left(\left(\dfrac{1}{\dfrac{b}{a^2}}\right)^4\right)^{-1/2}\right)^2$

$\left(\left(\left(\dfrac{a^2}{b}\right)^4\right)^{-1/2}\right)^2 = \left(\left(\dfrac{a^8}{b^4}\right)^{-1/2}\right)^2 = \left(\dfrac{1}{\sqrt{\dfrac{a^8}{b^4}}}\right)^2 = \left(\dfrac{1}{\dfrac{a^4}{b^2}}\right)^2$

$= \left(\dfrac{b^2}{a^4}\right)^2 = \dfrac{b^4}{a^8}$

27. $\sqrt[3]{27y^3z^9 \cdot 2y} = 3yz^3\sqrt[3]{2y}$

28. $\left(\dfrac{16x^4y^{-3}}{y^5z^{-4}}\right)^{3/4} = \sqrt[4]{\left(\dfrac{16x^4z^4}{y^8}\right)^3} = \sqrt[4]{\dfrac{8 \cdot 8 \cdot 8 \cdot 8x^{12}z^{12}}{y^{24}}} = \dfrac{8x^3z^3}{y^6}$

29. $\left(\dfrac{-4^{-2}m^3n^{-2}}{2^{-3}m^{-1}n^2}\right)^{-3} = \left(\dfrac{-\dfrac{1}{16}m^4}{\dfrac{1}{8}n^4}\right)^{-3} = \left(\dfrac{-m^4}{2n^4}\right)^{-3} = \left(-\dfrac{2n^4}{m^4}\right)^3$

$= \dfrac{8n^{12}}{m^{12}}$

30. $\dfrac{3r}{5r} + \dfrac{3s}{5s} - \dfrac{6rs}{10rs} = \dfrac{3}{5} + \dfrac{3}{5} - \dfrac{6}{10} = \dfrac{12}{10} - \dfrac{6}{10} = \dfrac{6}{10} = \dfrac{3}{5}$

31. A square of $P = 120$ m
$P = 4s$
$4s = 120$ m
$s = 30$ m
3 m $\times$ 30 m; 900 m^2

p. 592   **13-5 PROBLEM FOR PROGRAMMERS**

```
10   REM  Chapter 13 Problem
20   INPUT "Enter row 1 or 2 × 2 matrix ";A,B
30   INPUT "Enter row 2 of 2 × 2 matrix ";C,D
40   X = D / (A * D - B * C)
50   Y =  - B / (A * D - B * C)
60   W =  - C / (A * D - B * C)
70   Z = A / (A * D - B * C)
80   PRINT "Inverse matrix = ",X,Y
90   PRINT  TAB( 20),W,Z
100  IA = A * X + B * W
110  IB = A * Y + B * Z
120  IC = C * X + D * W
130  ID = C * Y + D * Z
140   PRINT "Verification: A*A^-1 = " ,IA,IB
150   PRINT TAB( 25),IC,ID
160   GOTO 20
```

pp. 594–596   **13-6 TRY THIS**

a. $\begin{bmatrix} 1 & 0 & 1 & | & 1 & 0 & 0 \\ 2 & 1 & 0 & | & 0 & 1 & 0 \\ 1 & -1 & 1 & | & 0 & 0 & 1 \end{bmatrix}$

$\begin{bmatrix} 1 & 0 & 1 & | & 1 & 0 & 0 \\ 0 & 1 & -2 & | & -2 & 1 & 0 \\ 0 & -1 & 0 & | & -1 & 0 & 1 \end{bmatrix} \begin{matrix} \\ -2①+② \\ -1①+③ \end{matrix}$

$\begin{bmatrix} 1 & 0 & 1 & | & 1 & 0 & 0 \\ 0 & 1 & -2 & | & -2 & 1 & 0 \\ 0 & 0 & -2 & | & -3 & 1 & 1 \end{bmatrix} \begin{matrix} \\ \\ ②+③ \end{matrix}$

$\begin{bmatrix} 2 & 0 & 0 & | & -1 & 1 & 1 \\ 0 & 1 & 0 & | & 1 & 0 & -1 \\ 0 & 0 & -2 & | & -3 & 1 & 1 \end{bmatrix} \begin{matrix} 2①+③ \\ ②-③ \\ \end{matrix}$

$\begin{bmatrix} 1 & 0 & 0 & | & -\dfrac{1}{2} & \dfrac{1}{2} & \dfrac{1}{2} \\ 0 & 1 & 0 & | & 1 & 0 & -1 \\ 0 & 0 & 1 & | & \dfrac{3}{2} & -\dfrac{1}{2} & -\dfrac{1}{2} \end{bmatrix} \begin{matrix} \dfrac{1}{2}① \\ \\ -\dfrac{1}{2}③ \end{matrix}$

$A^{-1} = \begin{bmatrix} -\dfrac{1}{2} & \dfrac{1}{2} & \dfrac{1}{2} \\ 1 & 0 & -1 \\ \dfrac{3}{2} & -\dfrac{1}{2} & -\dfrac{1}{2} \end{bmatrix}$

b. $\begin{bmatrix} 1 & 2 & 3 & | & 1 & 0 & 0 \\ 4 & 5 & 6 & | & 0 & 1 & 0 \\ 7 & 8 & 9 & | & 0 & 0 & 1 \end{bmatrix}$

$\begin{bmatrix} 1 & 2 & 3 & | & 1 & 0 & 0 \\ 0 & 3 & 6 & | & 4 & -1 & 0 \\ 0 & 6 & 12 & | & 7 & 0 & -1 \end{bmatrix} \begin{matrix} \\ 4①-② \\ 7①-③ \end{matrix}$

Row 3 is a multiple of row 2.

$\begin{bmatrix} 3 & 0 & -3 & | & -5 & 2 & 0 \\ 0 & 3 & 6 & | & 4 & -1 & 0 \\ 0 & 0 & 0 & | & 1 & -2 & 1 \end{bmatrix} \begin{matrix} \\ \\ 2②-③ \end{matrix}$

There is no way to obtain a nonzero element for a_{33}. A^{-1} does not exist.

c. $\begin{bmatrix} 4 & -2 \\ 1 & 5 \end{bmatrix}\begin{bmatrix} x \\ y \end{bmatrix} = \begin{bmatrix} -1 \\ 1 \end{bmatrix}$

$A^{-1} = \dfrac{1}{20 - (-2)}\begin{bmatrix} 5 & 2 \\ -1 & 4 \end{bmatrix} = \begin{bmatrix} \dfrac{5}{22} & \dfrac{2}{22} \\ -\dfrac{1}{22} & \dfrac{4}{22} \end{bmatrix}$

$$\begin{bmatrix} \frac{5}{22} & \frac{2}{22} \\ -\frac{1}{22} & \frac{4}{22} \end{bmatrix} \begin{bmatrix} 4 & -2 \\ 1 & 5 \end{bmatrix} \begin{bmatrix} x \\ y \end{bmatrix} = \begin{bmatrix} -1 \\ 1 \end{bmatrix} \begin{bmatrix} \frac{5}{22} & \frac{2}{22} \\ -\frac{1}{22} & \frac{4}{22} \end{bmatrix}$$

$$\begin{bmatrix} 1 & 0 \\ 0 & 1 \end{bmatrix} \begin{bmatrix} x \\ y \end{bmatrix} = \begin{bmatrix} -\frac{5}{22} + \frac{2}{22} \\ \frac{1}{22} + \frac{4}{22} \end{bmatrix}$$

$$\begin{bmatrix} x \\ y \end{bmatrix} = \begin{bmatrix} -\frac{3}{22} \\ \frac{5}{22} \end{bmatrix};$$

$$\left(-\frac{3}{22}, \frac{5}{22}\right)$$

d. $\begin{bmatrix} 1 & 3 & -4 \\ -2 & 2 & -5 \\ 0 & 1 & -6 \end{bmatrix} \begin{bmatrix} x \\ y \\ z \end{bmatrix} = \begin{bmatrix} -14 \\ 0 \\ 0 \end{bmatrix}$

$$AX = B$$

Find A^{-1}.

$$\left[\begin{array}{ccc|ccc} 1 & 3 & -4 & 1 & 0 & 0 \\ -2 & 2 & -5 & 0 & 1 & 0 \\ 0 & 1 & -6 & 0 & 0 & 1 \end{array}\right]$$

$$\left[\begin{array}{ccc|ccc} 1 & 3 & -4 & 1 & 0 & 0 \\ 0 & 8 & -13 & 2 & 1 & 0 \\ 0 & 1 & -6 & 0 & 0 & 1 \end{array}\right] \quad 2①+②$$

$$\left[\begin{array}{ccc|ccc} 8 & 0 & 7 & 2 & -3 & 0 \\ 0 & 8 & -13 & 2 & 1 & 0 \\ 0 & 0 & 35 & 2 & 1 & -8 \end{array}\right] \quad \begin{array}{l}8①-3② \\ ②-8③\end{array}$$

$$\left[\begin{array}{ccc|ccc} 40 & 0 & 0 & 8 & -16 & 8 \\ 0 & 280 & 0 & 96 & 48 & -104 \\ 0 & 0 & 35 & 2 & 1 & -8 \end{array}\right] \quad \begin{array}{l}5①-③ \\ 35②+13③\end{array}$$

$$\left[\begin{array}{ccc|ccc} 1 & 0 & 0 & \frac{1}{5} & -\frac{2}{5} & \frac{1}{5} & \frac{1}{40}① \\ 0 & 1 & 0 & \frac{12}{35} & \frac{6}{35} & \frac{13}{35} & \frac{1}{280}② \\ 0 & 0 & 1 & \frac{2}{35} & \frac{1}{35} & -\frac{8}{35} & \frac{1}{35}③ \end{array}\right]$$

$$A^{-1} = \begin{bmatrix} \frac{1}{5} & -\frac{2}{5} & \frac{1}{5} \\ \frac{12}{35} & \frac{6}{35} & \frac{13}{35} \\ \frac{2}{35} & \frac{1}{35} & -\frac{8}{35} \end{bmatrix}$$

$$x = A^{-1}B$$

$$= \begin{bmatrix} \frac{1}{5} & -\frac{2}{5} & \frac{1}{5} \\ \frac{12}{35} & \frac{6}{35} & \frac{13}{35} \\ \frac{2}{35} & \frac{1}{35} & -\frac{8}{35} \end{bmatrix} \begin{bmatrix} -14 \\ 0 \\ 0 \end{bmatrix} = \begin{bmatrix} -14\left(\frac{1}{5}\right) \\ -14\left(\frac{12}{35}\right) \\ -14\left(\frac{2}{35}\right) \end{bmatrix} = \begin{bmatrix} -\frac{14}{5} \\ -\frac{24}{5} \\ -\frac{4}{5} \end{bmatrix}$$

The solution is $\left(-\frac{14}{5}, -\frac{24}{5}, -\frac{4}{5}\right)$.

pp. 596–597   **13-6 EXERCISES**

1. $A^{-1} = \begin{bmatrix} -1 & 1 & 0 \\ -1 & 0 & 1 \\ 6 & -2 & -3 \end{bmatrix}$ **2.** $A^{-1} = \begin{bmatrix} -\frac{2}{5} & \frac{3}{5} & \frac{1}{5} \\ \frac{3}{5} & \frac{3}{5} & \frac{1}{5} \\ -\frac{2}{5} & \frac{8}{5} & \frac{1}{5} \end{bmatrix}$

3. $A^{-1} = \begin{bmatrix} -\frac{4}{3} & -\frac{5}{3} & 1 \\ -\frac{4}{3} & -\frac{8}{3} & 1 \\ \frac{1}{3} & \frac{2}{3} & 0 \end{bmatrix}$ **4.** $A^{-1} = \begin{bmatrix} \frac{3}{8} & -\frac{1}{4} & \frac{1}{8} \\ -\frac{1}{8} & \frac{3}{4} & -\frac{3}{8} \\ -\frac{1}{4} & \frac{1}{2} & \frac{1}{4} \end{bmatrix}$

5. $A^{-1} = \begin{bmatrix} -\frac{1}{2} & \frac{1}{2} & \frac{1}{2} \\ 1 & 0 & -1 \\ \frac{3}{2} & -\frac{1}{2} & -\frac{1}{2} \end{bmatrix}$

6. Does not exist
7. $(2, 2)$
8. $(4, 3)$
9. $(-2, 3)$
10. Dependent system
11. $(3, -3, -2)$
12. $(124, 14, -51)$

13. $\left[\begin{array}{ccc|ccc} x & 0 & 0 & 1 & 0 & 0 \\ 0 & y & 0 & 0 & 1 & 0 \\ 0 & 0 & z & 0 & 0 & 1 \end{array}\right] = \left[\begin{array}{ccc|ccc} 1 & 0 & 0 & \frac{1}{x} & 0 & 0 \\ 0 & 1 & 0 & 0 & \frac{1}{y} & 0 \\ 0 & 0 & 1 & 0 & 0 & \frac{1}{z} \end{array}\right]$

So, $A^{-1} = \begin{bmatrix} \frac{1}{x} & 0 & 0 \\ 0 & \frac{1}{y} & 0 \\ 0 & 0 & \frac{1}{z} \end{bmatrix}$, $x, y, z, \neq 0$

14. $\left[\begin{array}{cccc|cccc} 1 & 2 & 3 & 4 & 1 & 0 & 0 & 0 \\ 2 & 3 & 4 & 1 & 0 & 1 & 0 & 0 \\ 3 & 4 & 1 & 2 & 0 & 0 & 1 & 0 \\ 4 & 1 & 2 & 3 & 0 & 0 & 0 & 1 \end{array}\right]$

$$\left[\begin{array}{cccc|cccc} 1 & 2 & 3 & 4 & 1 & 0 & 0 & 0 \\ 0 & -1 & -2 & -7 & -2 & 1 & 0 & 0 \\ 0 & -2 & -8 & -10 & -3 & 0 & 1 & 0 \\ 0 & -7 & -10 & -13 & -4 & 0 & 0 & 1 \end{array}\right] \quad \begin{array}{l}-2①+② \\ -3①+③ \\ -4①+④\end{array}$$

$$\left[\begin{array}{cccc|cccc} 1 & 0 & -1 & -10 & -3 & 2 & 0 & 0 \\ 0 & -1 & -2 & -7 & -2 & 1 & 0 & 0 \\ 0 & 0 & -4 & 4 & 1 & -2 & 1 & 0 \\ 0 & 0 & 4 & 36 & 10 & -7 & 0 & 1 \end{array}\right] \quad \begin{array}{l}①+2② \\ \\ -2②+③ \\ -7②+④\end{array}$$

$$\left[\begin{array}{cccc|cccc} 4 & 0 & 0 & -44 & -13 & 10 & -1 & 0 \\ 0 & -2 & 0 & -18 & -5 & 4 & -1 & 0 \\ 0 & 0 & -4 & 4 & 1 & -2 & 1 & 0 \\ 0 & 0 & 0 & 40 & 11 & -9 & 1 & 1 \end{array}\right] \quad \begin{array}{l}4①-③ \\ 2②-③ \\ \\ ③+④\end{array}$$

$$\left[\begin{array}{cccc|cccc} 40 & 0 & 0 & 0 & -9 & 1 & 1 & 11 \\ 0 & -40 & 0 & 0 & -1 & -1 & -11 & 9 \\ 0 & 0 & -40 & 0 & -1 & -11 & 9 & -1 \\ 0 & 0 & 0 & 40 & 11 & -9 & 1 & 1 \end{array}\right] \quad \begin{array}{l}10①+11④ \\ 20②+9④ \\ 10③-④ \\ \end{array}$$

$$\left[\begin{array}{cccc|cccc} 1 & 0 & 0 & 0 & -\frac{9}{40} & \frac{1}{40} & \frac{1}{40} & \frac{11}{40} & \frac{1}{40}① \\ 0 & 1 & 0 & 0 & \frac{1}{40} & \frac{1}{40} & \frac{11}{40} & -\frac{9}{40} & -\frac{1}{40}② \\ 0 & 0 & 1 & 0 & \frac{1}{40} & \frac{11}{40} & -\frac{9}{40} & \frac{1}{40} & -\frac{1}{40}③ \\ 0 & 0 & 0 & 1 & \frac{11}{40} & -\frac{9}{40} & \frac{1}{40} & \frac{1}{40} & \frac{1}{40}④ \end{array}\right]$$

$$A^{-1} = \frac{1}{40}\begin{bmatrix} -9 & 1 & 1 & 11 \\ 1 & 1 & 11 & -9 \\ 1 & 11 & -9 & 1 \\ 11 & -9 & 1 & 1 \end{bmatrix}$$

Algebra and Trigonometry

15. $\begin{bmatrix} 3 & 2 \\ 7 & 5 \end{bmatrix} X = \begin{bmatrix} 3 & 2 \\ 11 & 8 \end{bmatrix}$

$AX = B$, so $X = A^{-1}B$

$A^{-1} = \dfrac{1}{15-14}\begin{bmatrix} 5 & -2 \\ -7 & 3 \end{bmatrix} = \begin{bmatrix} 5 & -2 \\ -7 & 3 \end{bmatrix}$

$X = \begin{bmatrix} 5 & -2 \\ -7 & 3 \end{bmatrix}\begin{bmatrix} 3 & 2 \\ 11 & 8 \end{bmatrix}$

$X = \begin{bmatrix} 15-22 & 10-16 \\ -21+33 & -14+24 \end{bmatrix}$

$X = \begin{bmatrix} -7 & -6 \\ 12 & 10 \end{bmatrix}$

16. Say $A = \begin{bmatrix} 1 & 2 \\ 3 & 4 \end{bmatrix}$

$\left[\begin{array}{cc|cc} 1 & 2 & 1 & 0 \\ 3 & 4 & 0 & 1 \end{array}\right]$

$\left[\begin{array}{cc|cc} 1 & 2 & 1 & 0 \\ 0 & -2 & -3 & 1 \end{array}\right]$ $-3①+②$

$\left[\begin{array}{cc|cc} 1 & 0 & -2 & 1 \\ 0 & -2 & -3 & 1 \end{array}\right]$

$\left[\begin{array}{cc|cc} 1 & 0 & -2 & 1 \\ 0 & 1 & \frac{3}{2} & -\frac{1}{2} \end{array}\right]$ $-\frac{1}{2}②$

Multiplying $\begin{bmatrix} 1 & 2 \\ 3 & 4 \end{bmatrix}\begin{bmatrix} -2 & 1 \\ \frac{3}{2} & -\frac{1}{2} \end{bmatrix} = \begin{bmatrix} 1 & 0 \\ 0 & 1 \end{bmatrix};$

The technique works.

17. By definition of the inverse of a matrix,
$A^{-1}A = I$ and $(A^{-1})(A^{-1})^{-1} = I$.
So, $A^{-1}A = A^{-1}(A^{-1})^{-1}$.
So, $A(A^{-1}A) = A[A^{-1}(A^{-1})^{-1}]$.
By the associative property of multiplication of matrices,
$(AA^{-1})A = (AA^{-1})(A^{-1})^{-1}$
$IA = I(A^{-1})^{-1}$
$A = (A^{-1})^{-1}$

18. $\left[\begin{array}{ccc|ccc} 0 & t & t & 1 & 0 & 0 \\ t & 0 & t & 0 & 1 & 0 \\ t & t & 0 & 0 & 0 & 1 \end{array}\right]$

$\left[\begin{array}{ccc|ccc} t & 0 & t & 0 & 1 & 0 \\ t & t & 0 & 0 & 0 & 1 \\ 0 & t & t & 1 & 0 & 0 \end{array}\right]$ ② Interchanging
③ rows
①

$\left[\begin{array}{ccc|ccc} t & 0 & t & 0 & 1 & 0 \\ 0 & t & -t & 0 & -1 & 1 \\ 0 & t & t & 1 & 0 & 0 \end{array}\right]$ $-①+②$

$\left[\begin{array}{ccc|ccc} t & 0 & t & 0 & 1 & 0 \\ 0 & t & -t & 0 & -1 & 1 \\ 0 & 0 & 2t & 1 & 1 & -1 \end{array}\right]$ $-②+③$

$\left[\begin{array}{ccc|ccc} 2t & 0 & 0 & -1 & 1 & 1 \\ 0 & 2t & 0 & 1 & -1 & 1 \\ 0 & 0 & 2t & 1 & 1 & -1 \end{array}\right]$ $2①-③$
$2②+③$

$\left[\begin{array}{ccc|ccc} 1 & 0 & 0 & -\frac{1}{2t} & \frac{1}{2t} & \frac{1}{2t} \\ 0 & 1 & 0 & \frac{1}{2t} & -\frac{1}{2t} & \frac{1}{2t} \\ 0 & 0 & 1 & \frac{1}{2t} & \frac{1}{2t} & -\frac{1}{2t} \end{array}\right]$ $\frac{1}{2t}①$
$\frac{1}{2t}②$
$\frac{1}{2t}③$

$A^{-1} = \begin{bmatrix} -\frac{1}{2t} & \frac{1}{2t} & \frac{1}{2t} \\ \frac{1}{2t} & -\frac{1}{2t} & \frac{1}{2t} \\ \frac{1}{2t} & \frac{1}{2t} & -\frac{1}{2t} \end{bmatrix} = \frac{1}{2t}\begin{bmatrix} -1 & 1 & 1 \\ 1 & -1 & 1 \\ 1 & 1 & -1 \end{bmatrix}$

19. $AX = B$, so $X = A^{-1}B$
First find A^{-1}
$-3\,-0\,-0\ \mid\ -9\,-9\,-0$

$\left[\begin{array}{ccc|ccc} 2 & -2 & 4 & 1 & 0 & 0 \\ -3 & 1 & -4 & 0 & 1 & 0 \\ 1 & 0 & 3 & 0 & 0 & 1 \end{array}\right]$

$\left[\begin{array}{ccc|ccc} 1 & 0 & 3 & 0 & 0 & 1 \\ -3 & 1 & -4 & 0 & 1 & 0 \\ 2 & -2 & 4 & 1 & 0 & 0 \end{array}\right]$ Interchanging
① and ③

$\left[\begin{array}{ccc|ccc} 1 & 0 & 3 & 0 & 0 & 1 \\ 0 & 1 & 5 & 0 & 1 & 3 \\ 0 & -2 & -2 & 1 & 0 & -2 \end{array}\right]$ $3①+②$
$-2①+③$

$\left[\begin{array}{ccc|ccc} 1 & 0 & 3 & 0 & 0 & 1 \\ 0 & 1 & 5 & 0 & 1 & 3 \\ 0 & 0 & 8 & 1 & 2 & 4 \end{array}\right]$ $2②+③$

$\left[\begin{array}{ccc|ccc} 8 & 0 & 0 & -3 & -6 & -4 \\ 0 & 8 & 0 & -5 & -2 & 4 \\ 0 & 0 & 8 & 1 & 2 & 4 \end{array}\right]$ $8①-3③$
$8②-5③$

$\left[\begin{array}{ccc|ccc} 1 & 0 & 0 & -\frac{3}{8} & -\frac{3}{4} & -\frac{1}{2} \\ 0 & 1 & 0 & -\frac{5}{8} & -\frac{1}{4} & \frac{1}{2} \\ 0 & 0 & 1 & \frac{1}{8} & \frac{1}{4} & \frac{1}{2} \end{array}\right]$ $\frac{1}{8}①$
$\frac{1}{8}②$
$\frac{1}{8}③$

$X = A^{-1}B$

$X = \begin{bmatrix} -\frac{3}{8} & -\frac{3}{4} & -\frac{1}{2} \\ -\frac{5}{8} & -\frac{1}{4} & \frac{1}{2} \\ \frac{1}{8} & \frac{1}{4} & \frac{1}{2} \end{bmatrix}\begin{bmatrix} 8 & 4 & 2 \\ -3 & 0 & 3 \\ 2 & -1 & -5 \end{bmatrix}$

$= \begin{bmatrix} -\frac{7}{4} & -1 & -\frac{1}{2} \\ -\frac{13}{4} & -3 & -\frac{9}{2} \\ \frac{5}{4} & 0 & -\frac{3}{2} \end{bmatrix}$

20. $\begin{array}{r} 2y + 3x = 18 \\ -9y - 3x = -39 \\ \hline -7y = -21 \\ y = 3 \end{array}$
$2(3) + 3x = 18$
$3x = 12$
$x = 4$
$(4, 3)$

21. $\begin{array}{r} 4y + 3x = 24 \\ 15y - 3x = 147 \\ \hline 19y = 171 \\ y = 9 \end{array}$
$4(9) + 3x = 24$
$3x = -12$
$x = -4$
$(-4, 9)$

22. $\dfrac{\sqrt{(u+v)(u^2 - uv + v^2)}}{\sqrt{u+v}}$

$= \sqrt{\dfrac{(u+v)(u^2 - uv + v^2)}{(u+v)}}$

$= \sqrt{u^2 - uv + v^2}$

23. $\dfrac{5}{(8-\sqrt{6})} \cdot \dfrac{(8+\sqrt{6})}{(8+\sqrt{6})} = \dfrac{40 + 5\sqrt{6}}{64 - 6} = \dfrac{40 + 5\sqrt{6}}{58}$

24. $\dfrac{3}{(4-3i)} \cdot \dfrac{(4+3i)}{(4+3i)} = \dfrac{12 + 9i}{16 - 9i^2} = \dfrac{12 + 9i}{16 + 9} = \dfrac{12 + 9i}{25}$

$= \dfrac{12}{25} + \dfrac{9}{25}i$

25. $\dfrac{\sqrt[3]{2u^4}}{\sqrt[3]{6v^4}} \cdot \dfrac{\sqrt[3]{36v^8}}{\sqrt[3]{36v^8}} = \dfrac{\sqrt[3]{72u^4v^8}}{6v^4} = \dfrac{\sqrt[3]{8u^3v^6 \cdot 9uv^2}}{6v^4}$

$= \dfrac{2uv^2\sqrt[3]{9uv^2}}{6v^4} = \dfrac{u\sqrt[3]{9uv^2}}{3v^2}$

26. $\sqrt[3]{108} - 2\sqrt{75} + \sqrt{98} = \sqrt[3]{27 \cdot 4} - 2\sqrt{25 \cdot 3} + \sqrt{49 \cdot 2}$

$= 3\sqrt[3]{4} - 10\sqrt{3} + 7\sqrt{2}$

27. $2x - 6 < 5x - 9$
$-6 < 3x - 9$
$3 < 3x$
$1 < x$

28. $-1 < x + 2 \leq 6$
$-3 < x \leq 4$

29.
Let $x + 2 =$ the 1st score,
$x =$ the 2nd score,
$(x + 2) + 6 =$ the 3rd score.
$(x + 2) + x + ((x + 2) + 6) = 244$
$3x + 10 = 244$
$3x = 234$
$x = 78$
1st score $= 80$
2nd score $= 78$
3rd score $= 86$

30. Let $P_1 = (250, 150)$ and $P_2 = (380, 202)$.

Then, $m = \dfrac{202 - 150}{380 - 250} = \dfrac{52}{130} = 0.4$

$y = 0.4x + b$
$150 = 0.4(250) + b$
$50 = b$
So, $y = 0.4x + 50$
If $x = 300$, then $y = 0.4(300) + 50$
$y = 120 + 50$
$y = 170$
The cost of renting the car is $170.

p. 599   13-7 TRY THIS

a. $[2.25 \quad 3.15]\begin{bmatrix} 400 & 250 & 600 \\ 180 & 300 & 250 \end{bmatrix}$

$= [2.25 \cdot 400 + 3.15 \cdot 180 \quad 2.25 \cdot 250$
$+ 3.15 \cdot 300 + 2.25 \cdot 600 + 3.15 \cdot 250]$
$= [1467 \quad 1507.50 \quad 2137.50]$
So, profit is
A: $1467
B: $1507.50
C: $2137.50

pp. 600–601   13-7 EXERCISES

1. A: $248.50
B: $298.75
C: $370
D: $180

2. A: $428.75
B: $818.75
C: $968.75

3. Hawks: 29 points
Eagles: 32 points
Angels: 31 points
Tornadoes: 36 points
Cyclones: 43 points
Zephyrs: 38 points
Jays: 40 points
Dynamos: 37 points

4. $\begin{bmatrix} 13 & 4 & 12 & 21 & 9 & 0 & 0 \\ 3 & 12 & 25 & 19 & 0 & 0 & 1 \\ 10 & 10 & 8 & 4 & 9 & 11 & 0 \\ 0 & 0 & 5 & 15 & 21 & 11 & 2 \\ 26 & 17 & 7 & 2 & 3 & 1 & 1 \\ 0 & 0 & 0 & 0 & 1 & 19 & 33 \\ 18 & 27 & 11 & 0 & 1 & 0 & 0 \end{bmatrix} \begin{bmatrix} 10 \\ 8 \\ 6 \\ 4 \\ 3 \\ 2 \\ 1 \end{bmatrix}$

$= \begin{bmatrix} 130 + 32 + 72 + 84 + 27 + 0 + 0 \\ 30 + 96 + 150 + 76 + 0 + 0 + 1 \\ 100 + 80 + 48 + 16 + 27 + 22 + 0 \\ 0 + 0 + 30 + 60 + 63 + 22 + 2 \\ 260 + 136 + 42 + 8 + 9 + 2 + 1 \\ 0 + 0 + 0 + 0 + 3 + 38 + 33 \\ 180 + 216 + 66 + 0 + 3 + 0 + 0 \end{bmatrix} = \begin{bmatrix} 345 \\ 353 \\ 293 \\ 177 \\ 458 \\ 74 \\ 465 \end{bmatrix}$

So the ranking is
Riverside	465
Kennedy	458
Northpoint	353
Third Avenue	345
Don Ramos	293
St. Cecilia	177
Washington	74

5. $\begin{bmatrix} 2 & 3 & 5 \\ 1 & 3 & 4 \\ 4 & 2 & 1 \end{bmatrix} \begin{bmatrix} x \\ y \\ z \end{bmatrix} = \begin{bmatrix} 82.50 \\ 69.00 \\ 48.50 \end{bmatrix}$

$A \quad\quad X \;=\; B$
$X = A^{-1}B.$ Find A^{-1}

$\begin{bmatrix} 2 & 3 & 5 & | & 1 & 0 & 0 \\ 1 & 3 & 4 & | & 0 & 1 & 0 \\ 4 & 2 & 1 & | & 0 & 0 & 1 \end{bmatrix}$

$\begin{bmatrix} 1 & 3 & 4 & | & 0 & 1 & 0 \\ 2 & 3 & 5 & | & 1 & 0 & 0 \\ 4 & 2 & 1 & | & 0 & 0 & 1 \end{bmatrix}$ Interchanging ① and ②

$\begin{bmatrix} 1 & 3 & 4 & | & 0 & 1 & 0 \\ 0 & -3 & -3 & | & 1 & -2 & 0 \\ 0 & -10 & -15 & | & 0 & -4 & 1 \end{bmatrix}$ $\begin{array}{l} -2① + ② \\ -4① + ③ \end{array}$

$\begin{bmatrix} 1 & 0 & 1 & | & 1 & -1 & 0 \\ 0 & -3 & -3 & | & 1 & -2 & 0 \\ 0 & 0 & -15 & | & -10 & 8 & 3 \end{bmatrix}$ $\begin{array}{l} ① + ③ \\ -10② + 3③ \end{array}$

$\begin{bmatrix} 15 & 0 & 0 & | & 5 & -7 & 3 \\ 0 & 15 & 0 & | & -15 & 18 & 3 \\ 0 & 0 & -15 & | & -10 & 8 & 3 \end{bmatrix}$ $\begin{array}{l} 15① + ③ \\ -5② + ③ \end{array}$

$\begin{bmatrix} 1 & 0 & 0 & | & \frac{1}{3} & -\frac{7}{15} & \frac{1}{5} \\ 0 & 1 & 0 & | & -1 & \frac{6}{5} & \frac{1}{5} \\ 0 & 0 & 1 & | & -\frac{2}{3} & \frac{8}{15} & \frac{1}{5} \end{bmatrix}$

$X = \begin{bmatrix} \frac{1}{3} & -\frac{7}{15} & \frac{1}{5} \\ -1 & \frac{6}{5} & \frac{1}{5} \\ -\frac{2}{3} & \frac{8}{15} & \frac{1}{5} \end{bmatrix} \begin{bmatrix} 82.5 \\ 69 \\ 48.5 \end{bmatrix} = \begin{bmatrix} 5 \\ 10 \\ 8.5 \end{bmatrix}$

Item 1 — $5, Item 2 — $10, Item 3 — $8.50
Item 1 — 7 purchased @ $5 = $35
Item 2 — 8 purchased @ $10 = $80
Item 3 — 10 purchased @ $8.50 = $85

6. First find A^{-1}.

$$\begin{bmatrix} 36 & 25 & 11 & | & 1 & 0 & 0 \\ 29 & 16 & 27 & | & 0 & 1 & 0 \\ 25 & 18 & 51 & | & 0 & 0 & 1 \end{bmatrix}$$

$$\begin{bmatrix} 36 & 25 & 11 & | & 1 & 0 & 0 \\ 0 & 149 & -653 & | & 29 & -36 & 0 \\ 0 & -23 & -1561 & | & 25 & 0 & -36 \end{bmatrix} \quad \begin{matrix} 29①-36② \\ 25①-36③ \end{matrix}$$

$$\begin{bmatrix} 5364 & 0 & 17{,}964 & | & -576 & 900 & 0 \\ 0 & 149 & -653 & | & 29 & -36 & 0 \\ 0 & 0 & -247{,}608 & | & 4392 & -828 & -5364 \end{bmatrix} \quad \begin{matrix} 149①-25② \\ 23②-149③ \end{matrix}$$

$$\begin{bmatrix} 149 & 0 & 499 & | & -16 & 25 & 0 \\ 0 & 149 & -653 & | & 29 & -36 & 0 \\ 0 & 0 & -247{,}608 & | & 4392 & -828 & -5364 \end{bmatrix} \quad 149/5364①$$

$$\begin{bmatrix} 36{,}893{,}592 & 0 & 0 & | & -1{,}770{,}120 & 5{,}777{,}028 & -2{,}676{,}636 \\ 0 & 36{,}893{,}592 & 0 & | & 4{,}312{,}656 & -8{,}373{,}204 & 3{,}502{,}692 \\ 0 & 0 & -247{,}608 & | & 4392 & -828 & -5364 \end{bmatrix} \quad \begin{matrix} 247{,}608①+499③ \\ 247{,}608②-653③ \end{matrix}$$

$$\begin{bmatrix} 6878 & 0 & 0 & | & -330 & 1077 & -499 \\ 0 & 6878 & 0 & | & 804 & -1561 & 653 \\ 0 & 0 & 6878 & | & -122 & 23 & 149 \end{bmatrix} \quad \begin{matrix} ①/5364 \\ ②/5364 \\ -③/36 \end{matrix}$$

$$A^{-1} = \frac{1}{6878}\begin{bmatrix} -330 & 1077 & -499 \\ 804 & -1561 & 653 \\ -122 & 23 & 149 \end{bmatrix}$$

or

$$A^{-1} = \begin{bmatrix} 0.04798 & 0.15659 & -0.07255 \\ 0.11689 & -0.22696 & 0.09494 \\ 0.01774 & 0.00334 & 0.02166 \end{bmatrix}$$

Solve for wholesale costs per item.

$$\frac{1}{6878}\begin{bmatrix} -330 & 1077 & -499 \\ 804 & -1561 & 653 \\ -122 & 23 & 149 \end{bmatrix} \times \begin{bmatrix} 140.5 \\ 157.25 \\ 299.25 \end{bmatrix}$$

$$= \frac{1}{6878}\begin{bmatrix} -46{,}365 + 169{,}358.25 - 114{,}395.75 \\ 112{,}962 - 245{,}467.25 + 149{,}700.25 \\ -17{,}141 + 3616.75 + 34{,}158.25 \end{bmatrix}$$

$$= \frac{1}{6878}\begin{bmatrix} 8597.5 \\ 17{,}195 \\ 20{,}634 \end{bmatrix}$$

$$= \begin{bmatrix} 1.25 \\ 2.5 \\ 3 \end{bmatrix}$$

So,
	Wholesale
Silky	$1.25
Face It	$2.50
Incan	$3.00

Solve for

$$\frac{1}{6878}\begin{bmatrix} -330 & 1077 & -499 \\ 804 & -1561 & 653 \\ -122 & 23 & 149 \end{bmatrix} \times \begin{bmatrix} 206.25 \\ 228.75 \\ 329.75 \end{bmatrix}$$

$$= \frac{1}{6878}\begin{bmatrix} -68{,}062.5 \\ -357.078.75 \\ 49{,}132.75 \end{bmatrix}$$

$$= \frac{1}{6878}\begin{bmatrix} 13{,}756 \\ 24{,}073 \\ 29{,}231.5 \end{bmatrix} = \begin{bmatrix} 2 \\ 3.5 \\ 4.25 \end{bmatrix}$$

So,
	Retail
Silky	$2.00
Face It	$3.50
Incan	$4.25

7.
$$\begin{bmatrix} 0 & 1 & 3 & 2 \\ 1 & 0 & 2 & 1 \\ 3 & 2 & 0 & 2 \\ 2 & 1 & 2 & 0 \end{bmatrix}\begin{bmatrix} 0 & 1 & 3 & 2 \\ 1 & 0 & 2 & 1 \\ 3 & 2 & 0 & 2 \\ 2 & 1 & 2 & 0 \end{bmatrix} = \begin{bmatrix} 14 & 8 & 6 & 7 \\ 8 & 6 & 5 & 6 \\ 6 & 5 & 17 & 8 \\ 7 & 6 & 8 & 9 \end{bmatrix}$$

The element a_{12} represents the two flight routes between Peoria and Detroit. $a_{12} = 0 \cdot 1 + 1 \cdot 0 + 3 \cdot 2 + 2 \cdot 1$

$0 \cdot 1$ indicates that there is no two-flight route with Peoria as the intermediate stop.

$1 \cdot 0$ indicates that there is no route with Detroit as the intermediate stop.

$3 \cdot 2$ indicates that there are 6 routes with St. Louis as the intermediate stop.

$2 \cdot 1$ indicates that there are 2 routes with Denver as the intermediate stop.

8. $\quad -10 \le 3x - 5 \le -1$
$\quad -10 + 5 \le -1 + 5$
$\quad -5 \le 3x \le 4$

$$-\frac{5}{3} \le x \le \frac{4}{3}$$

9. $|x| \le 5$
$\quad -5 \le x \le 5$

10. $\quad -8 > 3y - 4 > 8$
$\quad -8 + 4 > 3y > 8 + 4$
$\quad -4 > 3y > 12$

$$-\frac{4}{3} > y > 4$$

11. Let s = the last test score.
$\quad 82 + 77 + 91 + s \ge 340$
$\quad 250 + s \ge 340$
$\quad s \ge 90$

p. 603   COLLEGE ENTRANCE EXAMS

1. Since (i) if $b > 0$ but (ii) if $b < 0$.
$\qquad ab > bc \qquad\qquad ab < bc$ (D)

2. $n < m$
So $8765n < 8765m$ (A)

3. $ef < f$
$$f < \frac{f}{e} \quad (e > 1)$$
$$ef > f > \frac{f}{e} \quad \text{(A)}$$

4. Since (i) if $a - 3 > 0$,   but (ii) if $a - 3 < 0$.
$\quad (a-3)(a+6) > (a-3) \qquad (a-3)(a+6) < (a-3)$ (D)

5. Since (i) if $x + y > 0$,   but (ii) if $x + y < 0$
$\qquad w(x+y) > (x+y) \qquad w(x+y) < (x+y)$ (D)

6. $40 \times 10^{x-2} = 40 \times \dfrac{10^x}{10^2} = \dfrac{40}{10^2} \times 10^x = 0.04 \times 10^x$ (C)

7. $0.06(m + n) = 0.06m + 0.06n$ and
$0.06m + 0.07n > 0.06m + 0.06n$ (A)

8. Since (*i*) if $a > b$, then $a + 1 > b + 1$ and $\dfrac{a}{b} < \dfrac{a+1}{b+1}$.

Since (*ii*) if $a < b$, then $a + 1 < b + 1$ and $\dfrac{a}{b} > \dfrac{a+1}{b+1}$.   (D)

9. $(2a)(3b) = 6ab$ (C)

10. Since, for example,
(*i*) if $m = n$, then $m + n > m - n$, and (*ii*) if $m > n$
m, n both > 0, then $m + n < m - n$.   (D)

p. 605   PROBLEM SOLVING: APPLICATION

1. a. $\begin{bmatrix} -2 & 1 \\ \frac{3}{2} & -\frac{1}{2} \end{bmatrix} \begin{bmatrix} 40 \\ 96 \end{bmatrix} = \begin{bmatrix} -80 + 96 \\ 60 - 48 \end{bmatrix} = \begin{bmatrix} 16 \\ 12 \end{bmatrix}$

$\begin{bmatrix} -2 & 1 \\ \frac{3}{2} & -\frac{1}{2} \end{bmatrix} \begin{bmatrix} 51 \\ 103 \end{bmatrix} = \begin{bmatrix} -102 + 103 \\ 76.5 + 51.5 \end{bmatrix} = \begin{bmatrix} 1 \\ 25 \end{bmatrix}$

$\begin{bmatrix} -2 & 1 \\ \frac{3}{2} & -\frac{1}{2} \end{bmatrix} \begin{bmatrix} 4 \\ 10 \end{bmatrix} = \begin{bmatrix} -8 + 10 \\ 6 - 5 \end{bmatrix} = \begin{bmatrix} 2 \\ 1 \end{bmatrix}$

$\begin{bmatrix} -2 & 1 \\ \frac{3}{2} & -\frac{1}{2} \end{bmatrix} \begin{bmatrix} 36 \\ 84 \end{bmatrix} = \begin{bmatrix} -72 + 84 \\ 54 - 42 \end{bmatrix} = \begin{bmatrix} 12 \\ 12 \end{bmatrix}$

So, the decoded message is:
16 12 1 25 2 1 12 12
P L A Y B A L L
PLAY BALL

b. $\begin{bmatrix} -2 & 1 \\ \frac{3}{2} & -\frac{1}{2} \end{bmatrix} \begin{bmatrix} 29 \\ 77 \end{bmatrix} = \begin{bmatrix} -58 + 77 \\ 43.5 - 38.5 \end{bmatrix} = \begin{bmatrix} 19 \\ 5 \end{bmatrix}$

$\begin{bmatrix} -2 & 1 \\ \frac{3}{2} & -\frac{1}{2} \end{bmatrix} \begin{bmatrix} 22 \\ 58 \end{bmatrix} = \begin{bmatrix} -44 + 58 \\ 33 - 29 \end{bmatrix} = \begin{bmatrix} 14 \\ 4 \end{bmatrix}$

$\begin{bmatrix} -2 & 1 \\ \frac{3}{2} & -\frac{1}{2} \end{bmatrix} \begin{bmatrix} 43 \\ 99 \end{bmatrix} = \begin{bmatrix} -86 + 99 \\ 64.5 - 49.5 \end{bmatrix} = \begin{bmatrix} 13 \\ 15 \end{bmatrix}$

$\begin{bmatrix} -2 & 1 \\ \frac{3}{2} & -\frac{1}{2} \end{bmatrix} \begin{bmatrix} 24 \\ 62 \end{bmatrix} = \begin{bmatrix} -48 + 62 \\ 36 - 31 \end{bmatrix} = \begin{bmatrix} 14 \\ 5 \end{bmatrix}$

$\begin{bmatrix} -2 & 1 \\ \frac{3}{2} & -\frac{1}{2} \end{bmatrix} \begin{bmatrix} 73 \\ 171 \end{bmatrix} = \begin{bmatrix} -146 + 171 \\ 109.5 - 85.5 \end{bmatrix} = \begin{bmatrix} 25 \\ 24 \end{bmatrix}$

So, the decoded message is:
19 5 14 4 13 15 14 5 25 24
S E N D M O N E Y X
X is a dummy.
SEND MONEY

2. Answers will vary.

3. P E A C E   A S S U R E D
16 5 1 3 5   1 19 19 21 18 5 4

$\begin{bmatrix} 1 & -2 & 3 \\ -3 & 2 & 4 \\ 5 & -1 & -2 \end{bmatrix} \begin{bmatrix} 16 \\ 5 \\ 1 \end{bmatrix} = \begin{bmatrix} 16 - 10 + 3 \\ -48 + 10 + 4 \\ 80 - 5 - 2 \end{bmatrix} = \begin{bmatrix} 9 \\ -34 \\ 73 \end{bmatrix}$

$\begin{bmatrix} 1 & -2 & 3 \\ -3 & 2 & 4 \\ 5 & -1 & -2 \end{bmatrix} \begin{bmatrix} 3 \\ 5 \\ 1 \end{bmatrix} = \begin{bmatrix} 3 - 10 + 3 \\ -9 + 10 + 4 \\ 15 - 5 - 2 \end{bmatrix} = \begin{bmatrix} -4 \\ 5 \\ 8 \end{bmatrix}$

$\begin{bmatrix} 1 & -2 & 3 \\ -3 & 2 & 4 \\ 5 & -1 & -2 \end{bmatrix} \begin{bmatrix} 19 \\ 19 \\ 21 \end{bmatrix} = \begin{bmatrix} 19 - 38 + 63 \\ -57 + 38 + 84 \\ 95 - 19 - 42 \end{bmatrix} = \begin{bmatrix} 44 \\ 65 \\ 34 \end{bmatrix}$

$\begin{bmatrix} 1 & -2 & 3 \\ -3 & 2 & 4 \\ 5 & -1 & -2 \end{bmatrix} \begin{bmatrix} 18 \\ 5 \\ 4 \end{bmatrix} = \begin{bmatrix} 18 - 10 + 12 \\ -54 + 10 + 16 \\ 90 - 5 - 8 \end{bmatrix} = \begin{bmatrix} 20 \\ -28 \\ 77 \end{bmatrix}$

So, the encoded message is:
9 −34 73 −4 5 8 44 65 34 20 −28 77

4. $D = \dfrac{1}{4 \cdot 12 - (-1 \cdot 3)} \begin{bmatrix} 12 & -3 \\ 1 & 4 \end{bmatrix} = \dfrac{1}{51} \begin{bmatrix} 12 & -3 \\ 1 & 4 \end{bmatrix} = \begin{bmatrix} \frac{12}{51} & -\frac{3}{51} \\ \frac{1}{51} & \frac{4}{51} \end{bmatrix}$

$\begin{bmatrix} \frac{12}{51} & -\frac{3}{51} \\ \frac{1}{51} & \frac{4}{51} \end{bmatrix} \begin{bmatrix} 51 \\ 0 \end{bmatrix} = \begin{bmatrix} 12 \\ 1 \end{bmatrix}$

$\begin{bmatrix} \frac{12}{51} & -\frac{3}{51} \\ \frac{1}{51} & \frac{4}{51} \end{bmatrix} \begin{bmatrix} 126 \\ 147 \end{bmatrix} = \begin{bmatrix} \frac{1512 - 441}{51} \\ \frac{126 + 588}{51} \end{bmatrix} = \begin{bmatrix} \frac{1071}{51} \\ \frac{714}{51} \end{bmatrix} = \begin{bmatrix} 21 \\ 14 \end{bmatrix}$

$\begin{bmatrix} \frac{12}{51} & -\frac{3}{51} \\ \frac{1}{51} & \frac{4}{51} \end{bmatrix} \begin{bmatrix} 36 \\ 93 \end{bmatrix} = \begin{bmatrix} \frac{432 - 279}{51} \\ \frac{36 + 372}{51} \end{bmatrix} = \begin{bmatrix} \frac{153}{51} \\ \frac{408}{51} \end{bmatrix} = \begin{bmatrix} 3 \\ 8 \end{bmatrix}$

$\begin{bmatrix} \frac{12}{51} & -\frac{3}{51} \\ \frac{1}{51} & \frac{4}{51} \end{bmatrix} \begin{bmatrix} 31 \\ 56 \end{bmatrix} = \begin{bmatrix} \frac{372 - 168}{51} \\ \frac{31 + 224}{51} \end{bmatrix} = \begin{bmatrix} \frac{204}{51} \\ \frac{255}{51} \end{bmatrix} = \begin{bmatrix} 4 \\ 5 \end{bmatrix}$

$\begin{bmatrix} \frac{12}{51} & -\frac{3}{51} \\ \frac{1}{51} & \frac{4}{51} \end{bmatrix} \begin{bmatrix} 51 \\ 0 \end{bmatrix} = \begin{bmatrix} 12 \\ 1 \end{bmatrix}$

$\begin{bmatrix} \frac{12}{51} & -\frac{3}{51} \\ \frac{1}{51} & \frac{4}{51} \end{bmatrix} \begin{bmatrix} 115 \\ 35 \end{bmatrix} = \begin{bmatrix} \frac{1380 - 105}{51} \\ \frac{115 + 140}{51} \end{bmatrix} = \begin{bmatrix} \frac{1275}{51} \\ \frac{255}{51} \end{bmatrix} = \begin{bmatrix} 25 \\ 5 \end{bmatrix}$

$\begin{bmatrix} \frac{12}{51} & -\frac{3}{51} \\ \frac{1}{51} & \frac{4}{51} \end{bmatrix} \begin{bmatrix} 55 \\ 152 \end{bmatrix} = \begin{bmatrix} \frac{660 - 456}{51} \\ \frac{55 + 608}{51} \end{bmatrix} = \begin{bmatrix} \frac{204}{51} \\ \frac{663}{51} \end{bmatrix} = \begin{bmatrix} 4 \\ 13 \end{bmatrix}$

So, the decoded message is:
12 1 21 14 3 8 4 5 12 1 25 5 4 13
L A U N C H D E L A Y E D M
M is a dummy.
LAUNCH DELAYED

5. First find A^{-1}

$\begin{bmatrix} 1 & -2 & 3 & | & 1 & 0 & 0 \\ -3 & 2 & 4 & | & 0 & 1 & 0 \\ 5 & -1 & -2 & | & 0 & 0 & 1 \end{bmatrix}$

$\begin{bmatrix} 1 & -2 & 3 & | & 1 & 0 & 0 \\ 0 & -4 & 13 & | & 3 & 1 & 0 \\ 0 & 9 & -17 & | & -5 & 0 & 1 \end{bmatrix}$ 3①+② −5①+③

$\begin{bmatrix} -2 & 0 & 7 & | & 1 & 1 & 0 \\ 0 & -4 & 13 & | & 3 & 1 & 0 \\ 0 & 0 & 49 & | & 7 & 9 & 4 \end{bmatrix}$ −2①+② 9②+4③

$\begin{bmatrix} 14 & 0 & 0 & | & 0 & 2 & 4 \\ 0 & 196 & 0 & | & -56 & 68 & 52 \\ 0 & 0 & 49 & | & 7 & 9 & 4 \end{bmatrix}$ −7①+③ −49②+13③

$\begin{bmatrix} 1 & 0 & 0 & | & 0 & \frac{1}{7} & \frac{2}{7} \\ 0 & 1 & 0 & | & -\frac{2}{7} & \frac{17}{49} & \frac{13}{49} \\ 0 & 0 & 1 & | & \frac{1}{7} & \frac{9}{49} & \frac{4}{49} \end{bmatrix}$ $\frac{1}{14}$① $\frac{1}{196}$② $\frac{1}{49}$③

$$\text{So, } A^{-1} = \begin{bmatrix} 0 & \dfrac{7}{49} & \dfrac{14}{49} \\[6pt] -\dfrac{14}{49} & \dfrac{17}{49} & \dfrac{13}{49} \\[6pt] \dfrac{7}{49} & \dfrac{9}{49} & \dfrac{4}{49} \end{bmatrix}$$

DECODE MESSAGE

$$\frac{1}{49}\begin{bmatrix} 0 & 7 & 14 \\ -14 & 17 & 13 \\ 7 & 9 & 4 \end{bmatrix}\begin{bmatrix} 25 \\ 48 \\ 32 \end{bmatrix} = \begin{bmatrix} 16 \\ 18 \\ 15 \end{bmatrix}$$

$$\frac{1}{49}\begin{bmatrix} 0 & 7 & 14 \\ -14 & 17 & 13 \\ 7 & 9 & 4 \end{bmatrix}\begin{bmatrix} 8 \\ 21 \\ 0 \end{bmatrix} = \begin{bmatrix} 3 \\ 5 \\ 5 \end{bmatrix}$$

$$\frac{1}{49}\begin{bmatrix} 0 & 7 & 14 \\ -14 & 17 & 13 \\ 7 & 9 & 4 \end{bmatrix}\begin{bmatrix} 1 \\ -2 \\ 15 \end{bmatrix} = \begin{bmatrix} 4 \\ 3 \\ 1 \end{bmatrix}$$

$$\frac{1}{49}\begin{bmatrix} 0 & 7 & 14 \\ -14 & 17 & 13 \\ 7 & 9 & 4 \end{bmatrix}\begin{bmatrix} 26 \\ -20 \\ 73 \end{bmatrix} = \begin{bmatrix} 18 \\ 5 \\ 6 \end{bmatrix}$$

$$\frac{1}{49}\begin{bmatrix} 0 & 7 & 14 \\ -14 & 17 & 13 \\ 7 & 9 & 4 \end{bmatrix}\begin{bmatrix} 33 \\ 9 \\ 69 \end{bmatrix} = \begin{bmatrix} 21 \\ 12 \\ 12 \end{bmatrix}$$

$$\frac{1}{49}\begin{bmatrix} 0 & 7 & 14 \\ -14 & 17 & 13 \\ 7 & 9 & 4 \end{bmatrix}\begin{bmatrix} 57 \\ 47 \\ 64 \end{bmatrix} = \begin{bmatrix} 25 \\ 17 \\ 22 \end{bmatrix}$$

```
16  18  15   3   5   5   4
 P   R   O   C   E   E   D
```

```
3   1  18   5   6  21  12  12  25  17  22
C   A   R   E   F   U   L   L   Y   Q   V
```

Q and V are dummies. The message is
PROCEED CAREFULLY.

pp. 606–608   CHAPTER 13 SUMMARY AND REVIEW

1. 2×3 2. 3×1

3. $\begin{bmatrix} 3 & -2 & 7 \\ 5 & 3 & -1 \end{bmatrix}$ 5①$-$3② $\begin{bmatrix} 3 & -2 & 7 \\ 0 & -19 & 38 \end{bmatrix} -\dfrac{1}{19}$②

$\begin{bmatrix} 3 & -2 & 7 \\ 0 & 1 & -2 \end{bmatrix}$ 2②$+$① $\begin{bmatrix} 3 & 0 & 3 \\ 0 & 1 & -2 \end{bmatrix}$ $\begin{aligned} 3x &= 3 \\ x &= 1 \\ y &= -2 \quad (1, -2) \end{aligned}$

4. $\begin{bmatrix} 3 & -1 & 1 & 5 \\ 2 & -1 & 4 & -3 \\ 1 & 2 & -1 & 1 \end{bmatrix}$ $\begin{matrix}③\\ \\①\end{matrix}\begin{bmatrix} 1 & 2 & -1 & 1 \\ 2 & -1 & 4 & -3 \\ 3 & -1 & 1 & 5 \end{bmatrix}$

$\begin{matrix}-2①+②\\-3①+③\end{matrix}\begin{bmatrix} 1 & 2 & -1 & 1 \\ 0 & -5 & 6 & -5 \\ 0 & -7 & 4 & 2 \end{bmatrix}$

$-7②+5③\begin{bmatrix} 1 & 2 & -1 & 1 \\ 0 & -5 & 6 & -5 \\ 0 & 0 & 22 & -45 \end{bmatrix}$

$z = -\dfrac{45}{22}$ $-5y + 6\left(-\dfrac{45}{22}\right) = -5$ $x + 2y - z = 1$

$-5y - \dfrac{135}{11} = -\dfrac{55}{11}$ $x + 2\left(-\dfrac{16}{11}\right) - \dfrac{45}{22} = 1$

$-5y = \dfrac{80}{11}$ $x - \dfrac{64}{22} - \dfrac{45}{22} = \dfrac{22}{22}$

$y = -\dfrac{16}{11}$ $x = \dfrac{41}{22}$

5. $\begin{bmatrix} -2 & 0 \\ 1 & -4 \end{bmatrix}$ 6. $\begin{bmatrix} -4 & 10 \\ 7 & 0 \end{bmatrix}$

7. $3(4) - (-2)(1) = 14$ 8. $(-2)(-3) - 0 = 6$

9. $x = \dfrac{\begin{vmatrix} 9 & -5 \\ -7 & 1 \end{vmatrix}}{\begin{vmatrix} 2 & -5 \\ -3 & 1 \end{vmatrix}} = \dfrac{9 - 35}{2 - 15} = \dfrac{-26}{-13} = 2;$

$y = \dfrac{\begin{vmatrix} 2 & 9 \\ -3 & -7 \end{vmatrix}}{\begin{vmatrix} 2 & -5 \\ -3 & 1 \end{vmatrix}} = \dfrac{-14 + 27}{2 - 15} = \dfrac{13}{-13} = -1$

$(2, -1)$

10. $x = \dfrac{\begin{vmatrix} 10 & -1 \\ -4 & 5 \end{vmatrix}}{\begin{vmatrix} 4 & -1 \\ -3 & 5 \end{vmatrix}} = \dfrac{50 - 4}{20 - 3} = \dfrac{46}{17};$

$y = \dfrac{\begin{vmatrix} 4 & 10 \\ -3 & -4 \end{vmatrix}}{\begin{vmatrix} 4 & -1 \\ -3 & 5 \end{vmatrix}} = \dfrac{-16 + 30}{20 - 3} = \dfrac{14}{17}$

$\left(\dfrac{46}{17}, \dfrac{14}{17}\right)$

11. $3\begin{vmatrix} -1 & 1 \\ 1 & -1 \end{vmatrix} - 2\begin{vmatrix} 1 & 1 \\ 0 & -1 \end{vmatrix} - 3\begin{vmatrix} 1 & -1 \\ 0 & 1 \end{vmatrix}$

$= 3(0) - 2(-1) - 3(1) = 2 - 3 = -1$

12. $-2\begin{vmatrix} 0 & 0 \\ -1 & 1 \end{vmatrix} - 2\begin{vmatrix} -1 & 0 \\ 3 & 1 \end{vmatrix} - 4\begin{vmatrix} -1 & 0 \\ 3 & -1 \end{vmatrix}$

$= -2(0) - 2(-1) - 4(1) = 2 - 4 = -2$

13. $|D| = \begin{vmatrix} 3 & -2 & -1 \\ 2 & 1 & 1 \\ -1 & 3 & -2 \end{vmatrix} = -6 + 2 - 6 - (1 + 8 + 9)$

$= -10 - 18 = -28$

$|D_x| = \begin{vmatrix} -1 & -2 & -1 \\ 8 & 1 & 1 \\ 5 & 3 & -2 \end{vmatrix} = 2 - 10 - 24 - (-5 + 32 - 3)$

$= -32 - 24 = -56$

$|D_y| = \begin{vmatrix} 3 & -1 & -1 \\ 2 & 8 & 1 \\ -1 & 5 & -2 \end{vmatrix} = -48 + 1 - 10 - (8 + 4 + 15)$

$= -57 - 27 = -84$

$|D_z| = \begin{vmatrix} 3 & -2 & -1 \\ 2 & 1 & 8 \\ -1 & 3 & 5 \end{vmatrix} = 15 + 16 - 6 - (1 - 20 + 72)$

$= 25 - 53 = -28$

$x = \dfrac{-56}{-28} = 2 \qquad y = \dfrac{-84}{-28} = 3 \qquad z = \dfrac{-28}{-28} = 1$

14. $|D| = \begin{vmatrix} 2 & -2 & -1 \\ -4 & 1 & -3 \\ -2 & -3 & 1 \end{vmatrix} = 2 - 12 + 12 - (-2 + 8 + 18)$

$= 2 - 24 = -22$

$|D_x| = \begin{vmatrix} 3 & -2 & 1 \\ 1 & 1 & -3 \\ 0 & -3 & 1 \end{vmatrix} = 3 - 3 - (-2 + 27) = 0 - (25) = -25$

$|D_y| = \begin{vmatrix} 2 & 3 & 1 \\ -4 & 1 & -3 \\ -2 & 0 & 1 \end{vmatrix} = 2 + 18 - (-2 - 12)$

$= 20 - (-14) = 34$

$|D_z| = \begin{vmatrix} 2 & -2 & 3 \\ -4 & 1 & 1 \\ -2 & -3 & 0 \end{vmatrix} = 0 + 4 + 36 - (-6 - 6)$

$= 40 - (-12) = 52$

$x = \dfrac{-25}{-22} = \dfrac{25}{22} \qquad y = \dfrac{34}{-22} = -\dfrac{17}{11} \qquad z = \dfrac{52}{-22} = -\dfrac{26}{11}$

15. $-3A = \begin{bmatrix} 9 & 0 \\ -6 & 3 \end{bmatrix}$ 16. $4A = \begin{bmatrix} -12 & 0 \\ 8 & -4 \end{bmatrix}$

17. $AB = \begin{bmatrix} -3 & 0 \\ 2 & -1 \end{bmatrix}\begin{bmatrix} 2 & 1 & -1 \\ -1 & 0 & 2 \end{bmatrix} = \begin{bmatrix} -6 & -3 & 3 \\ 5 & 2 & -4 \end{bmatrix}$

18. $BC = \begin{bmatrix} 2 & 1 & -1 \\ -1 & 0 & 2 \end{bmatrix}\begin{bmatrix} -2 & 0 & 3 \\ -1 & 1 & 1 \\ 0 & 2 & 0 \end{bmatrix} = \begin{bmatrix} -5 & -1 & 7 \\ 2 & 4 & -3 \end{bmatrix}$

19. Does not exist.

20. $\begin{bmatrix} 5 & 2 & -4 \\ -3 & -4 & -2 \\ 6 & 7 & 5 \end{bmatrix}\begin{bmatrix} x \\ y \\ z \end{bmatrix} = \begin{bmatrix} 0 \\ 6 \\ 15 \end{bmatrix}$

21. $A^{-1} = \dfrac{1}{4-3}\begin{bmatrix} 2 & -3 \\ -1 & 2 \end{bmatrix} = \begin{bmatrix} 2 & -3 \\ -1 & 2 \end{bmatrix}$

22. Does not exist.

23. $\left[\begin{array}{ccc|ccc} 2 & 0 & 1 & 1 & 0 & 0 \\ 1 & -1 & 2 & 0 & 1 & 0 \\ 1 & 1 & 2 & 0 & 0 & 1 \end{array}\right]$ $\begin{array}{c} -2②+① \\ -2③+① \end{array}$

$\left[\begin{array}{ccc|ccc} 2 & 0 & 1 & 1 & 0 & 0 \\ 0 & 2 & -3 & 1 & -2 & 0 \\ 0 & -2 & -3 & 1 & 0 & -2 \end{array}\right]$ $\begin{array}{c} 1/2① \\ 1/2② \end{array}$

$\left[\begin{array}{ccc|ccc} 1 & 0 & \frac{1}{2} & \frac{1}{2} & 0 & 0 \\ 0 & 1 & -\frac{3}{2} & \frac{1}{2} & -1 & 0 \\ 0 & -2 & -3 & 1 & 0 & -2 \end{array}\right]$ $2②+③$

$\left[\begin{array}{ccc|ccc} 1 & 0 & \frac{1}{2} & \frac{1}{2} & 0 & 0 \\ 0 & 1 & -\frac{3}{2} & \frac{1}{2} & -1 & 0 \\ 0 & 0 & -6 & 2 & -2 & -2 \end{array}\right]$ $-1/6③$

$\left[\begin{array}{ccc|ccc} 1 & 0 & \frac{1}{2} & \frac{1}{2} & 0 & 0 \\ 0 & 1 & -\frac{3}{2} & \frac{1}{2} & -1 & 0 \\ 0 & 0 & 1 & -\frac{1}{3} & \frac{1}{3} & \frac{1}{3} \end{array}\right]$ $\begin{array}{c} -\frac{1}{2}③+① \\ \frac{3}{2}③+② \end{array}$

$\left[\begin{array}{ccc|ccc} 1 & 0 & 0 & \frac{2}{3} & -\frac{1}{6} & -\frac{1}{6} \\ 0 & 1 & 0 & 0 & -\frac{1}{2} & \frac{1}{2} \\ 0 & 0 & 1 & -\frac{1}{3} & \frac{1}{3} & \frac{1}{3} \end{array}\right]$

$A^{-1} = \begin{bmatrix} \frac{2}{3} & -\frac{1}{6} & -\frac{1}{6} \\ 0 & -\frac{1}{2} & \frac{1}{2} \\ -\frac{1}{3} & \frac{1}{3} & \frac{1}{3} \end{bmatrix}$

24. $\left[\begin{array}{ccc|ccc} 3 & 1 & 2 & 1 & 0 & 0 \\ 1 & 0 & 1 & 0 & 1 & 0 \\ -2 & -1 & 1 & 0 & 0 & 1 \end{array}\right]$ $\begin{array}{c} -3②+① \\ 2①+3③ \end{array}$

$\left[\begin{array}{ccc|ccc} 3 & 1 & 2 & 1 & 0 & 0 \\ 0 & 1 & -1 & 1 & -3 & 0 \\ 0 & -1 & 7 & 2 & 0 & 3 \end{array}\right]$ $\begin{array}{c} 1/3① \\ ③+② \end{array}$

$\left[\begin{array}{ccc|ccc} 1 & \frac{1}{3} & \frac{2}{3} & \frac{1}{3} & 0 & 0 \\ 0 & 1 & -1 & 1 & -3 & 0 \\ 0 & 0 & 6 & 3 & -3 & 3 \end{array}\right]$ $1/6③$

$\left[\begin{array}{ccc|ccc} 1 & \frac{1}{3} & \frac{2}{3} & \frac{1}{3} & 0 & 0 \\ 0 & 1 & -1 & 1 & -3 & 0 \\ 0 & 0 & 1 & \frac{1}{2} & -\frac{1}{2} & \frac{1}{2} \end{array}\right]$ $②+③$

$\left[\begin{array}{ccc|ccc} 1 & \frac{1}{3} & \frac{2}{3} & \frac{1}{3} & 0 & 0 \\ 0 & 1 & 0 & \frac{3}{2} & -\frac{7}{2} & \frac{1}{2} \\ 0 & 0 & 1 & \frac{1}{2} & -\frac{1}{2} & \frac{1}{2} \end{array}\right]$ $-\frac{2}{3}③+①$

$\left[\begin{array}{ccc|ccc} 1 & \frac{1}{3} & 0 & \frac{1}{6} & \frac{1}{3} & -\frac{1}{3} \\ 0 & 1 & 0 & \frac{3}{2} & -\frac{7}{2} & \frac{1}{2} \\ 0 & 0 & 1 & \frac{1}{2} & -\frac{1}{2} & \frac{1}{2} \end{array}\right]$ $-\frac{1}{3}②+①$

$\left[\begin{array}{ccc|ccc} 1 & 0 & 0 & -\frac{1}{3} & \frac{3}{2} & -\frac{1}{2} \\ 0 & 1 & 0 & \frac{3}{2} & -\frac{7}{2} & \frac{1}{2} \\ 0 & 0 & 1 & \frac{1}{2} & -\frac{1}{2} & \frac{1}{2} \end{array}\right]$

$A^{-1} = \begin{bmatrix} -\frac{1}{2} & \frac{3}{2} & -\frac{1}{2} \\ \frac{3}{2} & -\frac{7}{2} & \frac{1}{2} \\ \frac{1}{2} & -\frac{1}{2} & \frac{1}{2} \end{bmatrix}$

25. $\begin{bmatrix} 3 & -2 & 7 \\ 5 & 3 & -1 \end{bmatrix}$ $5① - 3②$ $\begin{bmatrix} 3 & -2 & 7 \\ 0 & -19 & 38 \end{bmatrix}$ $-\frac{1}{19}②$

$\begin{bmatrix} 3 & -2 & 7 \\ 0 & 1 & -2 \end{bmatrix}$
$y = -2$
$3x = 7 + 2(-2)$ $(1, -2)$
$3x = 3$
$x = 1$

26. $\begin{bmatrix} 2 & 3 & 6 \\ 1 & 2 & 2 \end{bmatrix}$ $-2②+①$ $\begin{bmatrix} 2 & 3 & 6 \\ 0 & -1 & 2 \end{bmatrix}\begin{bmatrix} 2 & 3 & 6 \\ 0 & 1 & -2 \end{bmatrix}$
$y = -2$
$2x = 6 - 3(-2)$
$2x = 12$
$x = 6$
$(6, -2)$

27.
$\begin{bmatrix} .08 & .05 & .20 \end{bmatrix}\begin{bmatrix} 40 & 30 & 20 \\ 50 & 30 & 60 \\ 40 & 40 & 60 \end{bmatrix} = \begin{bmatrix} 7.2 \\ 7 \\ 28 \end{bmatrix}$

Pens $7.20, pencils $7.00, erasers $28.00

p. 609   CHAPTER 13 TEST

1. 3×2

2. $\begin{bmatrix} 2 & -5 & 1 \\ 3 & 2 & -2 \end{bmatrix}$ $3① - 2②$ $\begin{bmatrix} 2 & -5 & 1 \\ 0 & -19 & 7 \end{bmatrix}$
$-19y = 7$

$y = -\frac{7}{19}$

$2x = 1 + 5\left(-\frac{7}{19}\right)$

$2x = -\frac{16}{19}$

$x = -\frac{8}{19}$

$\left(-\frac{8}{19}, -\frac{7}{19}\right)$

3. $\begin{bmatrix} 1 & 0 \\ 5 & -3 \\ 2 & 0 \end{bmatrix}$

4. $3 - 8 = -5$

5. $x = \dfrac{\begin{vmatrix} 3 & -2 \\ -4 & -5 \end{vmatrix}}{\begin{vmatrix} -4 & -2 \\ 3 & -5 \end{vmatrix}} = \dfrac{-15-8}{20-(-6)} = \dfrac{-23}{26}$

$y = \dfrac{\begin{vmatrix} -4 & 3 \\ 3 & -4 \end{vmatrix}}{\begin{vmatrix} -4 & -2 \\ 3 & -5 \end{vmatrix}} = \dfrac{16-9}{26} = \dfrac{7}{26}$

$\left(-\dfrac{23}{26}, \dfrac{7}{26}\right)$

6. $3\begin{vmatrix} 1 & 0 \\ -1 & -3 \end{vmatrix} + 0 + (-2)\begin{vmatrix} -2 & 1 \\ 1 & -1 \end{vmatrix}$

$= 3(-3) + (-2)(2-1) = -9 - 2 = -11$

7. $|D| = \begin{vmatrix} 2 & -3 & 1 \\ 1 & -2 & 3 \\ 3 & 1 & -1 \end{vmatrix} = 4 - 27 + 1 - (-6+3+6)$

$= -22 - 3 = -25$

$|D_x| = \begin{vmatrix} 2 & -3 & 1 \\ 0 & -2 & 3 \\ -1 & 1 & -1 \end{vmatrix} = 4 + 9 - (2+6) = 13 - 8 = 5$

$|D_y| = \begin{vmatrix} 2 & 2 & 1 \\ 1 & 0 & 3 \\ 3 & -1 & -1 \end{vmatrix} = 18 - 1 - (-2-6) = 17 - (-8) = 25$

$|D_z| = \begin{vmatrix} 2 & -3 & 2 \\ 1 & -2 & 0 \\ 3 & 1 & -1 \end{vmatrix} = 4 + 2 - (-12+3) = 6 - (-9) = 15$

$x = -\dfrac{5}{25} = -\dfrac{1}{5} \quad y = -\dfrac{25}{25} = -1 \quad z = -\dfrac{15}{25} = -\dfrac{3}{5}$

8. $-2A = \begin{bmatrix} -4 & 2 & 0 \\ 0 & -2 & 8 \end{bmatrix}$

9. $\begin{bmatrix} -3 & 2 & 0 \\ 1 & 1 & 1 \\ 0 & -1 & 0 \end{bmatrix}\begin{bmatrix} 2 & 3 & -1 \\ -1 & 0 & 1 \\ 1 & 1 & -2 \end{bmatrix} = \begin{bmatrix} -8 & -9 & 5 \\ 2 & 4 & -2 \\ 1 & 0 & -1 \end{bmatrix}$

10. $\begin{bmatrix} 2 & 3 & -1 \\ -1 & 0 & 1 \\ 1 & 1 & -2 \end{bmatrix}\begin{bmatrix} -3 & 2 & 0 \\ 1 & 1 & 1 \\ 0 & -1 & 0 \end{bmatrix} = \begin{bmatrix} -3 & 8 & 3 \\ 3 & -3 & 0 \\ -2 & 5 & 1 \end{bmatrix}$

11. $\begin{bmatrix} 2 & -1 & 3 \\ 3 & 2 & -1 \\ 1 & -3 & 4 \end{bmatrix}\begin{bmatrix} x \\ y \\ z \end{bmatrix} = \begin{bmatrix} 5 \\ 1 \\ 0 \end{bmatrix}$

12. $A^{-1} = \dfrac{1}{0+5}\begin{bmatrix} 0 & -1 \\ 5 & 3 \end{bmatrix} = \dfrac{1}{5}\begin{bmatrix} 0 & -1 \\ 5 & 3 \end{bmatrix} = \begin{bmatrix} 0 & -\dfrac{1}{5} \\ 1 & \dfrac{3}{5} \end{bmatrix}$

13. $\begin{bmatrix} 1 & 2 & 0 & | & 1 & 0 & 0 \\ 0 & -2 & 1 & | & 0 & 1 & 0 \\ -1 & 1 & -1 & | & 0 & 0 & 1 \end{bmatrix}$ $\begin{array}{l} -1/2 \,②\\ \\ ① + ③ \end{array}$

$\begin{bmatrix} 1 & 2 & 0 & | & 1 & & 0 & 0 \\ 0 & 1 & -\dfrac{1}{2} & | & 0 & -\dfrac{1}{2} & 0 \\ 0 & 3 & -1 & | & 1 & & 0 & 1 \end{bmatrix}$ $-3②+①$

$\begin{bmatrix} 1 & 2 & 0 & | & 1 & & 0 & 0 \\ 0 & 1 & -\dfrac{1}{2} & | & 0 & -\dfrac{1}{2} & 0 \\ 0 & 0 & \dfrac{1}{2} & | & 1 & & \dfrac{3}{2} & 1 \end{bmatrix}$ $\begin{array}{l} ②+③ \\ \\ 2③ \end{array}$

$\begin{bmatrix} 1 & 2 & 0 & | & 1 & 0 & 0 \\ 0 & 1 & 0 & | & 1 & 1 & 1 \\ 0 & 0 & 1 & | & 2 & 3 & 2 \end{bmatrix}$ $-2②+①$

$\begin{bmatrix} 1 & 0 & 0 & | & -1 & -2 & -2 \\ 0 & 1 & 0 & | & 1 & 1 & 1 \\ 0 & 0 & 1 & | & 2 & 3 & 2 \end{bmatrix}$ $A^{-1} = \begin{bmatrix} -1 & -2 & -2 \\ 1 & 1 & 1 \\ 2 & 3 & 2 \end{bmatrix}$

14. $[2 \quad 0 \quad 1]\begin{bmatrix} 8 & 5 & 7 & 9 & 4 \\ 8 & 8 & 6 & 5 & 6 \\ 0 & 3 & 3 & 2 & 6 \end{bmatrix} = \begin{bmatrix} 16 \\ 13 \\ 17 \\ 20 \\ 14 \end{bmatrix}$
16 pts	Fireballs
13 pts	Blue Angels
17 pts	Tigers
20 pts	Dynamites
14 pts	Rangers

CHAPTER 14

p. 610   READY FOR SEQUENCES, SERIES, AND MATHEMATICAL INDUCTION?

1. 20   **2.** 60   **3.** 15   **4.** 125   **5.** 32   **6.** $-\dfrac{1}{30}$

7. $5, 8, 11$ **8.** $2, 11, 26$ **9.** $-3, 9, -27$

10. $\dfrac{1}{2}, \dfrac{1}{4}, \dfrac{1}{8}$

pp. 613–614   14-1 TRY THIS

a. $a_1 = 2^1 - 1 = 1$
$a_2 = 2^2 - 1 = 3$
$a_3 = 2^3 - 1 = 7$
$a_{10} = 2^{10} - 1 = 1023$
$a_{15} = 2^{15} - 1 = 32{,}767$

b. $a_1 = (-1)^1(1)^2 = -1$
$a_2 = (-1)^2(2)^2 = 4$
$a_3 = (-1)^3(3)^2 = -9$
$a_{10} = (-1)^{10}(10)^2 = 100$
$a_{15} = (-1)^{15}(15)^2 = -225$

c. $a_1 = 0$ **d.** $a_1 = 4$
$a_2 = 0 + 4 = 4$ $a_2 = 4 - 2 = 2$
$a_3 = 4 + 4 = 8$ $a_3 = 2 - 2 = 0$
$a_4 = 8 + 4 = 12$ $a_4 = 0 - 2 = -2$
$a_5 = 12 + 4 = 16$ $a_5 = -2 - 2 = -4$

e. These are multiples of 2: $a_n = 2n$.

f. $a_n = (-1)^n(n)$

g. These are cubes of n:
$a_n = n^3$.

h. These are powers of 2 starting with zero:
$a_n = 2^{n-1}$.

i. $S_1 = \dfrac{1}{2}$ $= \dfrac{1}{2}$

$S_2 = \dfrac{1}{2} + \dfrac{1}{4}$ $= \dfrac{3}{4}$

$S_3 = \dfrac{1}{2} + \dfrac{1}{4} + \dfrac{1}{8}$ $= \dfrac{7}{8}$

$S_4 = \dfrac{1}{2} + \dfrac{1}{4} + \dfrac{1}{8} + \dfrac{1}{16} = \dfrac{15}{16}$

j. $\displaystyle\sum_{n=1}^{3}\left(2 + \dfrac{1}{n}\right) = 2 + \dfrac{1}{1} + 2 + \dfrac{1}{2} + 2 + \dfrac{1}{3}$

$= 7 + \dfrac{1}{2} + \dfrac{1}{3}$

$= 7\dfrac{5}{6}$

k. $\displaystyle\sum_{n=1}^{4}(5^n - 1) = 5^1 - 1 + 5^2 - 1 + 5^3 - 1 + 5^4 - 1$

$= 5 + 25 + 125 + 625 - 4$
$= 776$

l. $2 + 4 + 6 + 8 + 10 = 2(1) + 2(2) + 2(3) + 2(4) + 2(5)$

$= \displaystyle\sum_{n=1}^{5} 2n$

m. $2 - 3 + 4 - 5 + \cdots = (-1)^2(1+1) + (-1)^3(2+1) + \cdots$

$= \displaystyle\sum_{n=1}^{\infty} (-1)^{n+1}(n+1)$

pp. 615–616   14-1 EXERCISES

1. $4, 7, 10, 13; 31; 46$ **2.** $2, 5, 8, 11; 29; 44$

3. $\dfrac{1}{2}, \dfrac{2}{3}, \dfrac{3}{4}, \dfrac{4}{5}, \dfrac{10}{11}; \dfrac{15}{16}$ **4.** $2, 5, 10, 17; 101; 226$

5. $-1, 0, 3, 8; 80; 195$ **6.** $0, \dfrac{3}{5}, \dfrac{4}{5}, \dfrac{15}{17}; \dfrac{99}{101}; \dfrac{112}{113}$

7. $2, 2\dfrac{1}{2}, 3\dfrac{1}{3}, 4\dfrac{1}{4}; 10\dfrac{1}{10}; 15\dfrac{1}{15}$

8. $1, -\dfrac{1}{2}, \dfrac{1}{4}, -\dfrac{1}{8}; -\dfrac{1}{512}; \dfrac{1}{16,384}$

9. $2, 5, 17, 65, 257$ **10.** $-3, -11, -27, -59, -123$

11. $8, 6, 5, 4\dfrac{1}{2}, 4\dfrac{1}{4}$ **12.** $3, 3, 0, -3, -3$

13. $a_n = 2n - 1$ **14.** $a_n = 3^n$ **15.** $a_n = \dfrac{n + 1}{n + 2}$

16. $a_n = \sqrt{2n}$ **17.** $a_n = (3)^{n/2}$ **18.** $a_n = n(n + 1)$

19. $a_n = -3n + 2$ **20.** $a_n = n - 1$

21. $S_1 = \dfrac{1}{3}, S_2 = \dfrac{1}{2}, S_3 = \dfrac{7}{12}, S_4 = \dfrac{5}{8}$

22. $S_1 = -1, S_2 = 2, S_3 = -3, S_4 = 4$

23. $S_1 = 4, S_2 = 11, S_3 = 21, S_4 = 34$

24. $S_1 = -3, S_2 = 6, S_3 = -21, S_4 = 60$

25. $\dfrac{1}{2} + \dfrac{1}{4} + \dfrac{1}{6} + \dfrac{1}{8} + \dfrac{1}{10} = \dfrac{137}{120}$

26. $\dfrac{1}{3} + \dfrac{1}{5} + \dfrac{1}{7} + \dfrac{1}{9} + \dfrac{1}{11} + \dfrac{1}{13} = \dfrac{43,024}{45,045}$

27. $2 + 4 + 8 + 16 + 32 = 62$

28. $\sqrt{7} + \sqrt{9} + \sqrt{11} + \sqrt{13} = \sqrt{7} + 3 + \sqrt{11} + \sqrt{13}$

29. $\log 7 + \log 8 + \log 9 + \log 10$
$= \log(7 \cdot 8 \cdot 9 \cdot 10) = \log 5040$

30. $0 + \pi + 2\pi + 3\pi + 4\pi = 10\pi$

31. $\displaystyle\sum_{n=1}^{6} \dfrac{n}{n + 1}$ **32.** $\displaystyle\sum_{n=1}^{5} 3n$ **33.** $\displaystyle\sum_{n=1}^{6} (-1)^n 2^n$ **34.** $\displaystyle\sum_{n=1}^{5} \dfrac{1}{n^2}$

35. $\displaystyle\sum_{n=2}^{\infty} (-1)^n n^2$ **36.** $\displaystyle\sum_{n=3}^{\infty} (-1)^{n+1} n^2$

37. $a_1 = \dfrac{1}{2(1)} \log 1000$ $a_2 = \dfrac{1}{2(2)} \log 1000^2$

$\quad = \dfrac{1}{2} \cdot 3$ $= \dfrac{1}{4} \cdot 2 \cdot \log 1000$

$\quad = \dfrac{3}{2}$ $= \dfrac{2}{4} \cdot 3$

                             $= \dfrac{3}{2}$

$a_3 = \dfrac{1}{2(3)} \log 1000^3$ $a_4 = \dfrac{1}{2(4)} \log 1000^4$

$\quad = \dfrac{1}{6} \cdot 3 \log 1000$ $= \dfrac{1}{8} \cdot 4 \log 1000$

$\quad = \dfrac{1}{2} \cdot 3$ $= \dfrac{1}{2} \cdot 3$

$\quad = \dfrac{3}{2}$ $= \dfrac{3}{2}$

$a_5 = \dfrac{1}{2(5)} \log 1000^5$

$\quad = \dfrac{1}{10} \cdot 5 \cdot \log 1000$

$\quad = \dfrac{1}{2} \cdot 3$

$\quad = \dfrac{3}{2}$

38. $a_1 = (\sqrt{-1})^1$ $a_2 = (\sqrt{-1})^2$ $a_3 = (\sqrt{-1})^3$
$\quad = \sqrt{-1}$ $= (i)^2$ $= i^3$
$\quad = i$ $= -1$ $= -i$
$a_4 = (\sqrt{-1})^4$ $a_5 = (\sqrt{-1})^5$
$\quad = i^4$ $= i^5$
$\quad = 1$ $= i^4 \cdot i$
                      $= 1 \cdot i$
                      $= i$

39. $a_1 = \ln(1)$ $a_2 = \ln(1 \cdot 2)$ $a_3 = \ln(1 \cdot 2 \cdot 3)$
$\quad = 0$ $= \ln 2$ $= \ln(6)$
              $= 0.693$ $= 1.792$
$a_4 = \ln(1 \cdot 2 \cdot 3 \cdot 4)$ $a_4 = \ln(1 \cdot 2 \cdot 3 \cdot 4 \cdot 5)$
$\quad = \ln(24)$ $= \ln(120)$
$\quad = 3.178$ $= 4.787$

40. $S_n = \left(1 + \dfrac{1}{1}\right)^1 + \left(1 + \dfrac{1}{2}\right)^2 + \left(1 + \dfrac{1}{3}\right)^3 + \left(1 + \dfrac{1}{4}\right)^4$

$\qquad + \left(1 + \dfrac{1}{5}\right)^5 + \left(1 + \dfrac{1}{6}\right)^6$

$\quad \approx (1 + 1)^1 + (1.5)^2 + (1.\overline{3})^3 + (1.25)^4 + (1.2)^5$
$\qquad + (1.1\overline{6})^6$

$\quad \approx 2 + 2.25 + 2.3703702 + 2.4414063 + 2.48832$
$\qquad + 2.5216255$

$\quad \approx 14.071724$

41. $S_n = (\sqrt{1 + 1} - \sqrt{1}) + (\sqrt{2 + 1} - \sqrt{2})$
$\qquad + (\sqrt{3 + 1} - \sqrt{3}) + (\sqrt{4 + 1} - \sqrt{4})$
$\qquad + (\sqrt{5 + 1} - \sqrt{5}) + (\sqrt{6 + 1} - \sqrt{6})$
$\quad = \sqrt{2} - \sqrt{1} + \sqrt{3} - \sqrt{2} + \sqrt{4} - \sqrt{3} + \sqrt{5}$
$\qquad - \sqrt{4} + \sqrt{6} - \sqrt{5} + \sqrt{7} - \sqrt{6}$
$\quad = -\sqrt{1} + \sqrt{7}$
$\quad = -1 + \sqrt{7}$
$\quad \approx 1.645751$

42.   1st month = 1 pair   6th month = 8 pairs
      2nd month = 1 pair   7th month = 13 pairs
      3rd month = 2 pairs   8th month = 21 pairs
      4th month = 3 pairs   9th month = 34 pairs
      5th month = 5 pairs   10th month = 55 pairs
                          11th month = 89 pairs
                          12th month = 144 pairs
                                 233 rabbits

43. $S_1 = \dfrac{1}{2}$

$S_2 = \dfrac{1}{2} + \dfrac{1}{6} = \dfrac{2}{3}$

$S_3 = \dfrac{1}{2} + \dfrac{1}{6} + \dfrac{1}{12} = \dfrac{3}{4}$

$S_4 = \dfrac{1}{2} + \dfrac{1}{6} + \dfrac{1}{12} + \dfrac{1}{20} = \dfrac{4}{5}$

The pattern appears to be $S_n = \dfrac{n}{n + 1}$. Note that

$\dfrac{n}{n + 1} = 1 - \dfrac{1}{n + 1}$. Thus $S_n = 1 - \dfrac{1}{n + 1}$.

44. $a_n = a_{n-1} + a_{n-2}$

45.

$$\begin{bmatrix} 3 & -1 & 2 \\ -1 & 2 & 1 \\ 3 & 5 & 2 \end{bmatrix} + 3\begin{bmatrix} 4 & 5 & 6 \\ 3 & 0 & 7 \\ 2 & 9 & 8 \end{bmatrix}$$

$$= \begin{bmatrix} 3 & -1 & 2 \\ -1 & 2 & 1 \\ 3 & 5 & 2 \end{bmatrix} + \begin{bmatrix} 12 & 15 & 18 \\ 9 & 0 & 21 \\ 6 & 27 & 24 \end{bmatrix}$$

$$= \begin{bmatrix} 3 + 12 & -1 + 15 & 2 + 18 \\ -1 + 9 & 2 + 0 & 1 + 21 \\ 3 + 6 & 5 + 27 & 2 + 24 \end{bmatrix}$$

$$= \begin{bmatrix} 15 & 14 & 20 \\ 8 & 2 & 22 \\ 9 & 32 & 26 \end{bmatrix}$$

46.

$$t \begin{bmatrix} 4 & 5 & 6 \\ 3 & 0 & 7 \\ 2 & 9 & 8 \end{bmatrix} + \begin{bmatrix} 3 & -1 & 2 \\ -1 & 2 & 1 \\ 3 & 5 & 2 \end{bmatrix}$$

$$= \begin{bmatrix} 4t & 5t & 6t \\ 3t & 0t & 7t \\ 2t & 9t & 8t \end{bmatrix} + \begin{bmatrix} 3 & -1 & 2 \\ -1 & 2 & 1 \\ 3 & 5 & 2 \end{bmatrix}$$

$$= \begin{bmatrix} 4t + 3 & 5t - 1 & 6t + 2 \\ 3t - 1 & 2 & 7t + 1 \\ 2t + 3 & 9t + 5 & 8t + 2 \end{bmatrix}$$

47.

$$AC = \begin{bmatrix} 12 - 3 + 4 & 15 + 18 & 18 - 7 + 16 \\ -4 + 6 + 2 & -5 + 9 & -6 + 14 + 8 \\ 12 + 15 + 4 & 15 + 18 & 18 + 35 + 16 \end{bmatrix}$$

$$= \begin{bmatrix} 13 & 33 & 27 \\ 4 & 4 & 16 \\ 31 & 33 & 69 \end{bmatrix}$$

48.

$$AB = \begin{bmatrix} 18 - 5 + 8 \\ -6 + 10 + 4 \\ 18 + 25 + 8 \end{bmatrix} = \begin{bmatrix} 21 \\ 8 \\ 51 \end{bmatrix}$$

49. Not possible

50.

$$CB = \begin{bmatrix} 24 + 25 + 24 \\ 18 + 28 \\ 12 + 45 + 32 \end{bmatrix} = \begin{bmatrix} 73 \\ 46 \\ 89 \end{bmatrix}$$

pp. 617–621   14-2 TRY THIS

a.
$3 - 2 = 1$
$4 - 3 = 1$
$a_1 = 2, d = 1$

b.
$4 - 1 = 3$
$7 - 4 = 3$
$a_1 = 1, d = 3$

c.
$14 - 19 = -5$
$4 - 9 = -5$
$a_1 = 19, d = -5$

d.
$9\frac{1}{2} - 10 = -\frac{1}{2}$

$7\frac{1}{2} - 8 = -\frac{1}{2}$

$a_1 = 10, d = -\frac{1}{2}$

e.
$a_{13} = 2 + (13 - 1)(4)$
$= 2 + 12(4)$
$= 2 + 48$
$= 50$
$a_{13} = 50$

f.
$a_n = 2 + (n - 1)(4)$
$286 = 2 + 4n - 4$
$286 = 4n - 2$
$288 = 4n$
$72 = n$
$a_n = 286 \Rightarrow n = 72$

g.
$a_7 = a_1 + (7 - 1)d$
$79 = a_1 + 6d$ ①
$a_{13} = a_1 + (13 - 1)d$
$151 = a_1 + 12d$ ②
$79 = a_1 + 6d$
$\underline{-151 = a_1 + 12d}$
$-72 = -6d$
$12 = d$
$a_1 + 6d = 79$
$a_1 + 6 \cdot 12 = 79$
$a_1 + 72 = 79$
$a_1 = 7$
$a_1 = 7; d = 12; 7, 19, 31, 43, \cdots$

h.
$a_4 = 3 + 3 \cdot d$
$24 = 3 + 3d$
$21 = 3d$
$7 = d$
$3, \underline{10}, \underline{17}, 24$

i.
$S_{200} = \frac{200}{2}(1 + 200)$
$= 100(201)$
$= 20{,}100$
The sum is 20,100.

j.
$S_{473} = \frac{473}{2}(1 + 473)$

$= \frac{473}{2}(474)$

$= 473(237)$
$= 112{,}101$
The sum is 112,101.

k.
$S_{15} = \frac{15}{2}[2a_1 + (n - 1)d]$

$= \frac{15}{2}(2 \cdot 1 + 14 \cdot 2)$

$= \frac{15}{2}(2 + 28)$

$= \frac{15}{2}(30)$

$= 15(15)$
$= 225$
The sum is 225.

l. 5, 14, 23

$\sum_{n=1}^{10} 9n - 4$

$S_{10} = \frac{10}{2}[2 \cdot 5 + 9 \cdot 9]$

$= 5(10 + 81)$
$= 5(91)$
$= 455$
The sum is 455.

pp. 622–623   14-2 EXERCISES

1. $a_1 = 2, d = 5$ **2.** $a_1 = 1.06, d = 0.06$

3. $a_1 = 7, d = -4$ **4.** $a_1 = -9, d = 3$

5. $a_1 = \frac{3}{2}, d = \frac{3}{4}$ **6.** $a_1 = \frac{3}{5}, d = -\frac{1}{2}$ **7.** $a_{12} = 46$

8. $a_{11} = 0.57$ **9.** $a_{17} = -41$ **10.** $a_{14} = -\frac{17}{3}$

11. a_{27} **12.** a_{33} **13.** a_{102} **14.** a_{46}

15. $a_1 = 8; d = -3; 8, 5, 2, -1, \cdots$

16. $a_1 = \frac{1}{3}; d = \frac{1}{2}; \frac{1}{3}, \frac{5}{6}, \frac{4}{3}, \frac{11}{6}, \cdots$

17. $2, 7, 12, 17, 22$ **18.** $8, 11, 14, 17, 20, 23$

19. 2550   **20.** 2500   **21.** 670   **22.** -210 **23.** 432

24. -264 **25.** 855   **26.** 630

27.
$S_{30} = \frac{30}{2}(30 + 1)$

$= 15(31)$
$= 465$
465 poles

28.
$S_{31} = \frac{31}{2}(10 + a_n)$

$a_{31} = 10 + 30 \cdot 10$
$= 10 + 300$
$a_{31} = 310$

$S_{31} = \frac{31}{2}(10 + 310)$

$= \frac{31}{2}(320)$

$= 31(160)$
$= \$49.60$
Saved $49.60

29.
$S_n = \frac{n}{2}(2 \cdot 1 + (n - 1)2)$

$= \frac{n}{2}(2 + 2n - 2)$

$= \frac{n}{2}(2n)$

$= n^2$

30.
$a_1, a_1 + d, a_1 + 2d$
$a_1 + a_1 + 2d = 10$
$a_1 + d = 5$
$a_2 = a_1 + d \Rightarrow a_2 = 5$
$a_1 \cdot a_2 = 15$
$a_1 \cdot 5 = 15$
$a_1 = 3$
$3, 5, 7$

31.
$S_n = 459 = \frac{n}{2}(1 + 50)$

$918 = n(51)$
$18 = n$ terms
16 means
$a_{18} = 1 + 17d$
$50 = 1 + 17d$
$49 = 17d$

$\frac{49}{17} = d$

32.
$(4x + y) - (3x + 2y) = d$
$(4x - 3x) + (y - 2y)$
$x + (-y) = d$
$a_1 = 3x + 2y$
$d = x - y$

33.
$a_2 + d + d = 10p + q$
$4p - 3q + 2d = 10p + q$
$2d = 6p + 4q$
$d = 3p + 2q$
$a_1 = a_2 - d$
$= 4p - 3q - 3p - 2q$
$= p - 5q$
$a_1 = p - 5q; d = 3p + 2q$

34. $a_1 = \$8760$
$a_2 = \$7961.77$
$a_3 = \$7163.54$
$a_4 = \$6365.31$
$a_5 = \$5567.08$
$a_6 = \$4768.85$
$a_7 = \$3970.62$
$a_8 = \$3172.39$
$a_9 = \$2374.16$
$a_{10} = \$1575.93$

35. $S_{10} = \dfrac{10}{2}(8760 + 1575.93)$
$= 5(8760) + 5(1575.93)$
$= 43{,}800 + 7879.65$
$= 51{,}679.65$
$S_n = \$51{,}679.65$

36. Answers may vary.

Harmonic Seq: $1, \dfrac{1}{2}, \dfrac{1}{3}, \dfrac{1}{4}, \cdots$

37. a_6
$20 = 5 + 5d$
$15 = 5d$
$3 = d$
$20, 17, 14, 11, 8, 5$ arithmetic sequence

$\dfrac{1}{5}, \dfrac{1}{8}, \dfrac{1}{11}, \dfrac{1}{14}, \dfrac{1}{17}, \dfrac{1}{20}$

38. p, m, q form an arithmetic sequence, therefore, $m = p + d$ and $q = p + 2d$. The sum of a_1 and a_3 would be
$p + q = p + (p + 2d)$.

But $m = \dfrac{p + q}{2}$, so $m = \dfrac{p + d}{2} = \dfrac{p + (p + 2d)}{2}$,

$m = \dfrac{2p + 2d}{2}$ or $m = p + d$.

39. $S_n = a_1 + a_2 + a_3 + a_4 + \cdots + a_n$
$= \underbrace{a_1 + (a_1 + d) + (a_1 + 2d) + \cdots + (a_1 + (n-1)d)}_{n \text{ times}}$

$\therefore S_n = a_1 n + d + 2d + 3d + \cdots + (n-1)d$
$S_n = a_1 n + d(1 + 2 + 3 + \cdots + n - 1)$

$S_n = a_1 n + d\left(\dfrac{(n-1)(n)}{2}\right)$

$S_n = \dfrac{n}{2}(2a_1 + d(n-1))$

$S_n = \dfrac{n}{2}(a_1 + a_1 + d(n-1))$

$S_n = \dfrac{n}{2}(a_1 + a_n)$

40. $S_n = a_1 + a_2 + a_3 + \cdots + a_n$
$S_n = a_1 + (a_1 + d) + (a_1 + 2d) + \cdots + (a_1 + (n-1)d)$
$S_n = a_1 n + d(1 + 2 + 3 + \cdots + (n - 1))$

$S_n = a_1 n + d\left(\dfrac{(n-1)(n)}{2}\right)$

$S_n = \dfrac{n}{2}(2a_1 + (n-1)d)$

41. $x = x$
$y = x + d$
$z = x + 2d$
$x + y + z = x + x + d + x + 2d$
$x + y + z = (x + d) + (x + d) + (x + d)$
$x + y + z = 3y$

42. ① n is odd.

Middle term: $a_{(n+1)/2} = a_1 + d\left(\dfrac{n+1}{2} - 1\right)$

$= a_1 + d\left(\dfrac{n-1}{2}\right)$

$S = \dfrac{n}{2}(2a_1 + (n-1)d)$

$\dfrac{S}{n} = \dfrac{\dfrac{n}{2}(2a_1 + (n-1)d)}{n}$

$= \dfrac{2a_1 + (n-1)d}{2}$

$= a_1 + d\dfrac{(n-1)}{2} = a_{(n+1)/2}$

② n is even.
Two middle terms:

$a_{n/2} = a_1 + \left(\dfrac{n}{2} - 1\right)d$ and $a_{(n/2)+1} = a_1 + \left(\dfrac{n}{2} + 1 - 1\right)d$

$= a_1 + \dfrac{dn}{2}$

$a_{n/2} + a_{(n/2)+1} = \left(a_1 + \dfrac{dn}{2} - d\right) + \left(a_1 + \dfrac{dn}{2}\right)$

$= 2a_1 + dn - d$
$= 2a_1 + d(n - 1)$

$S = \dfrac{n}{2}(2a_1 + (n-1)d)$

$\dfrac{2S}{n} = \dfrac{2n}{2n}(2a_1 + (n-1)d)$

$= 2a_1 + (n-1)d = a_{n/2} + a_{(n/2)+1}$

43. $|x| \ge 5$
$x \le -5$ or $x \ge 5$

44. $|3y - 4| < 8$
$-8 < 3y - 4 < 8$
$-4 < 3y < 12$

$-\dfrac{4}{3} < y < 4$

45. $|A| = -2(3) - 5 = -11$

46. $|B| = 3(2)(2) - 3(1)(5) - (-1)(-1)(2) + (-1)(3)(1)$
$+ 2(-1)(5) - (2)(3)(2)$
$= 12 - 15 - 2 - 3 - 10 - 12 = -30$

47. $A = \begin{vmatrix} -2 & 1 \\ 5 & 3 \end{vmatrix}, |A| = -2 \cdot 3 - 5 \cdot 1 = -11$

$A^{-1} = -\dfrac{1}{11}\begin{bmatrix} 3 & -1 \\ -5 & -2 \end{bmatrix} = \begin{bmatrix} -\dfrac{3}{11} & \dfrac{1}{11} \\ \dfrac{5}{11} & \dfrac{2}{11} \end{bmatrix}$

48.
$\begin{bmatrix} 3 & -1 & 2 & | & 1 & 0 & 0 \\ -1 & 2 & 1 & | & 0 & 1 & 0 \\ 3 & 5 & 2 & | & 0 & 0 & 1 \end{bmatrix}$

$\begin{bmatrix} -1 & 2 & 1 & | & 0 & 1 & 0 \\ 3 & -1 & 2 & | & 1 & 0 & 0 \\ 3 & 5 & 2 & | & 0 & 0 & 1 \end{bmatrix}$ Interchanging ① and ②

$\begin{bmatrix} -1 & 2 & 1 & | & 0 & 1 & 0 \\ 0 & 5 & 5 & | & 1 & 3 & 0 \\ 0 & 11 & 5 & | & 0 & 3 & 1 \end{bmatrix}$ $3① + ②$ $3① + ③$

$\begin{bmatrix} -5 & 0 & -5 & | & -2 & -1 & 0 \\ 0 & 5 & 5 & | & 1 & 3 & 0 \\ 0 & 0 & 30 & | & 11 & 18 & -5 \end{bmatrix}$ $5① - 2②$ $11② - 5③$

$\begin{bmatrix} -30 & 0 & 0 & | & -1 & 12 & -5 \\ 0 & -30 & 0 & | & 5 & 0 & -5 \\ 0 & 0 & 30 & | & 11 & 18 & -5 \end{bmatrix}$ $6① + ③$ $-6② + ③$

$\begin{bmatrix} 1 & 0 & 0 & | & \dfrac{1}{30} & -\dfrac{2}{5} & \dfrac{1}{6} \\ 0 & 1 & 0 & | & -\dfrac{1}{6} & 0 & \dfrac{1}{6} \\ 0 & 0 & 1 & | & \dfrac{11}{30} & \dfrac{3}{5} & -\dfrac{1}{6} \end{bmatrix}$ $-\dfrac{1}{30}$ ① $-\dfrac{1}{30}$ ② $\dfrac{1}{30}$ ③

$B^{-1} = \begin{bmatrix} \dfrac{1}{30} & -\dfrac{2}{5} & \dfrac{1}{6} \\ -\dfrac{1}{6} & 0 & \dfrac{1}{6} \\ \dfrac{11}{30} & \dfrac{3}{5} & -\dfrac{1}{6} \end{bmatrix}$

49. $f(x) = x^3 + 8$
$f(x) - 8 = x^3$
$x = \sqrt[3]{f(x) - 8}$
$f^{-1}(x) = \sqrt[3]{x - 8}$

50. $f(x) = \sqrt[3]{x + 1}$
$x + 1 = [f(x)]^3$
$x = [f(x)]^3 - 1$
$f^{-1}(x) = x^3 - 1$

51. $f(x) = x^3$
$x = \sqrt[3]{f(x)}$
$f^{-1}(x) = \sqrt[3]{x}$

52. $f(x) = 3^x$
$\log_3 f(x) = \log_3 3^x$
$x = \log_3 f(x)$
$f^{-1}(x) = \log_3 x$

53. $f(x) = \log_3 x$
$3^{f(x)} = 3^{\log_3 x}$
$3^{f(x)} = x$
$f^{-1}(x) = 3^x$

54. $7^x = 5$
$\log_7 7^x = \log_7 5$
$x = \log_7 5$

55. $x^5 = 7$
$\log_x x^5 = \log_x 7$
$5 = \log_x 7$

56. $5^7 = x$
$\log_5 5^7 = \log_5 x$
$7 = \log_5 x$

57. $A = B + 10$
$B = C + 10$
$A + B + C = 180$
Substituting, $A = (C + 10) + 10$
$= C + 20$
$(C + 20) + (C + 10) + C = 180$
$3C + 30 = 180$
$3C = 150, \quad C = 50$
$B = 50 + 10 = 60$
$A = 60 + 10 = 70$
$m\angle A = 70°, m\angle B = 60°, m\angle C = 50°.$

pp. 624–627   14-3 TRY THIS

a. $\dfrac{25}{5} = r$ **b.** $-\dfrac{9}{3} = -3$ **c.** $-\dfrac{12}{48} = -\dfrac{1}{4}$

$r = 5$ $r = -3$ $r = -\dfrac{1}{4}$

d. $\dfrac{18}{54} = \dfrac{1}{3}$ **e.** $a_6 = 3(-5)^5$ **f.** $a_3 = a_1 r^{n-1}$

                 $= 3(-3125)$ $20 = 5(r)^2$

$r = \dfrac{1}{3}$ $a_6 = -9375$ $4 = r^2$

                                        $2 = r$

                                  mean $= 10$

g. $a_{25} = 400(1.01)^{24}$
$= 400(1.2697346)$
$= \$507.89$

h. $S_6 = \dfrac{3(1 - 5^6)}{1 - 5}$ **i.** $S_{10} = \dfrac{2\left(1 - \left(-\dfrac{1}{2}\right)^{10}\right)}{1 - \left(-\dfrac{1}{2}\right)}$

$= \dfrac{3(-15,624)}{-4}$ $= \dfrac{2\left(1 - \dfrac{1}{1024}\right)}{\dfrac{3}{2}}$

$= \dfrac{-46,872}{-4}$

$= 11,718$ $= \dfrac{4}{3}\left(\dfrac{1023}{1024}\right)$

                                  $= \dfrac{341}{256}$

j. $S_5 = \dfrac{3(1 - 3^5)}{1 - 3}$ **k.** $\dfrac{1\left(1 - \left(\dfrac{2}{3}\right)^4\right)}{1 - \dfrac{2}{3}} = \dfrac{1 - \dfrac{16}{81}}{\dfrac{1}{3}}$

$= \dfrac{3(-242)}{-2}$

$= 363$ $= \dfrac{65}{81} \cdot \dfrac{3}{1}$

                                   $= \dfrac{65}{27}$

pp. 628–629   14-3 EXERCISES

1. 2   **2.** $-\dfrac{1}{3}$ **3.** -1 **4.** 0.1   **5.** $\dfrac{1}{x}$ **6.** $\dfrac{m}{2}$

7. 243   **8.** $\dfrac{81}{64}$ **9.** 1250   **10.** 162   **11.** 3, 12, 48

12. 4, 8, 16, 32   **13.** $\dfrac{1}{4}, \dfrac{1}{8}, \dfrac{1}{16}, \dfrac{1}{32}, \dfrac{1}{64}$

14. $\dfrac{1}{9}, \dfrac{1}{3}, 1, 3, 9, 27$ **15.** $1015.79   **16.** $1489.35

---

17. 762   **18.** $10\dfrac{1}{2}$ **19.** $\dfrac{547}{18}$ **20.** $\dfrac{33,333}{5000}$ **21.** $\dfrac{1 - x^8}{1 - x}$

22. $\dfrac{1 - x^{20}}{1 - x^2}$ **23.** $\dfrac{63}{32}$ **24.** 510   **25.** 21,844   **26.** $\dfrac{121}{81}$

27. a. The 6th rebound is the 7th valve in the sequence.

$a_n = 16\left(\dfrac{1}{4}\right)^n$

$a_7 = 16\left(\dfrac{1}{4}\right)^6 = \dfrac{16}{4096} = \dfrac{1}{256}$ ft

b. $S_7 = \dfrac{16\left(1 - \left(\dfrac{1}{4}\right)^7\right)}{1 - \dfrac{1}{4}} = \dfrac{16\left(\dfrac{16,383}{16,384}\right)}{\dfrac{3}{4}}$

$= \dfrac{\dfrac{16,383}{1024}}{\dfrac{3}{4}}$

$= \dfrac{65,532}{3072}$

However, all of the distances except a_1 are doubled.

Total distance $= 16 + 2\left(\dfrac{65,532}{3072} - 16\right)$

$= 16 + 2\left(\dfrac{16,380}{3072}\right) = 26\dfrac{169}{256}$ ft

28. $a_5 = 100,000(1.1)^5$
$= 100,000(1.61051)$
$= 161,051$

29. a. $S_n = \dfrac{1000(1 - 1.08^5)}{1 - 1.08}$

$= \dfrac{1000 - 1000(1.4693281)}{-0.08}$

$= \dfrac{1000 - 1469.3281}{-0.08}$

$= \dfrac{-469.3281}{-0.08}$

$= \$5866.60$

b. $S_n = \dfrac{200 - 200(1.13)^5}{1 - 1.13}$

$= \dfrac{200 - 200(1.8424352)}{-0.13}$

$= \dfrac{200 - 368.48704}{-0.13}$

$= \dfrac{-168.48704}{-0.13}$

$= \$1296.05$

30. $\displaystyle\sum_{k=1}^{n} x^k$

$S_n = \dfrac{1 - 1(x)^n}{1 - x} = \dfrac{1 - x^n}{1 - x}$

31. a. $a_3 = 4(r)^2$ **b.** $a_3 = 2(r)^2$ **c.** $a_3 = \dfrac{i}{2}(r)^2$

$9 = 4r^2$ $6 = 2r^2$ $\dfrac{1}{3} = \dfrac{1}{2}r^2$

$\dfrac{9}{4} = r^2$ $3 = r^2$ $\dfrac{2}{3} = r^2$

$\dfrac{3}{2} = r$ $\sqrt{7} = r$ $\sqrt{\dfrac{2}{3}} = r$

                       $2\sqrt{3}$ $\dfrac{\sqrt{6}}{3} = r$

$4 \cdot \dfrac{3}{2} = 6$ $\dfrac{\sqrt{6}}{3} \cdot \dfrac{1}{2} = \dfrac{\sqrt{6}}{6}$

d. $\sqrt{5} - \sqrt{2} = (\sqrt{5} + \sqrt{2})(r)^2$

$$r = \sqrt{\frac{\sqrt{5} - \sqrt{2}}{\sqrt{5} + \sqrt{2}}}$$

$$a_2 = (\sqrt{5} + \sqrt{2})\sqrt{\frac{\sqrt{5} - \sqrt{2}}{\sqrt{5} + \sqrt{2}}}$$

$$= \sqrt{(\sqrt{5} + \sqrt{2})(\sqrt{5} - \sqrt{2})}$$

$$= \sqrt{5 - 2} = \sqrt{3}$$

32. The terms of a geometric sequence have the following form: a_1, a_1r, a_1r^2, a_1r^3, a_1r^4. The product of these terms is $a_1{}^5r^{10}$. We know $a_1r^2 = 4$. So, $a_1{}^5r^{10} = (a_1r^2)^5 = 4^5a = 1024$.

33. $1, r, r^2, \ldots$ becomes
$C, Cr, Cr^2, \ldots$

$$\frac{Cr^{n+1}}{Cr^n} = \frac{C}{C} \cdot \frac{r^{n+1}}{r^n} = 1. \ r = r$$

r is the common ratio, so the sequence is geometric.

34. $1, r, r^2, \ldots$ becomes
$1 + C, r + C, r^2 + C, \ldots$

$$\frac{C + r^{n+1}}{C + r^n} \text{ is not constant. Not geometric.}$$

35. a. $\dfrac{a_n}{a_{n-1}} = r$ so $\dfrac{a_n{}^2}{a_n{}^2 - 1} = r^2$

Hence $a_1{}^2, a_2{}^2, \ldots$ is geometric with ratio r^2.

b. $\dfrac{a_n}{a_{n-1}} = r$ so $\dfrac{a_n{}^{-3}}{a_n{}^{-3} - 1} = r^{-3}$

Thus $a_1{}^{-3}, a_2{}^{-3}, a_3{}^{-3}, \ldots$ is geometric with ratio r^{-3}.

36. $S_n = \dfrac{(0.01) - (0.01)(2)^{20}}{1 - 2}$

$$= \frac{0.01 - (0.01)}{-1}$$

$$= \frac{0.01 - 10,485.76}{-1}$$

$$= 10,485.75$$
10,485.75 in.

37. $S_n = \dfrac{1000 - 1000(1.14)^{41}}{1 - 1.14}$

$$= \frac{1000 - 215,327.21}{-0.14}$$

$$= \frac{-214,327.21}{-0.14}$$

$$= 1,530,908.6$$
Since \$1000 is not invested in the 41st year, the answer is \$1,529,908.60.

38. Let one geometric series be $a_1, a_1r, a_1r^2, \ldots, a_1r^n \ldots$, the other $a_2, a_2R, a_2R^2, \ldots, a_2R^n \ldots$. The new series is $a_1a_2, a_1a_2rR, a_1a_2r^2R^2, \ldots, a_1a_2r^nR^n \ldots$. Let $a_1a_2 = b$ and $rR = q$. The new series is $b, bq, bq^2, \ldots, bq^n \ldots$, which is a geometric series.

39. Let $y = xr$ and $z = xr^2$.

Then $\dfrac{1}{2y} - \dfrac{1}{y - x} = \dfrac{1}{2xr} - \dfrac{1}{x(r - 1)}$

$$= \frac{1 + r}{2xr(1 - r)}$$

$$\frac{1}{y - z} - \frac{1}{2y} = \frac{1}{xr - xr^2} - \frac{1}{2xr}$$

$$= \frac{1 + r}{2xr(1 - r)}$$

Since the differences are the same, the terms make up an

arithmetic sequence with $d = \dfrac{1 + r}{2xr(1 - r)}$.

40. If 0 is a term of a geometric sequence, the next term must be $r \cdot 0 = 0$, the next after that $r \cdot 0 = 0$, etc. Previous terms cannot be nonzero for the common ratio to be the same. Thus every term must be 0. But the common ratio of this sequence is

$\dfrac{0}{0}$, which is undefined, so this sequence is not geometric.

41.
$$x^2 + y^2 - 25 = 0$$
$$y^2 + 8x - 40 = 0, \text{ or } y^2 = 40 - 8x$$
$$x^2 + (40 - 8x) - 25 = 0$$
$$x^2 - 8x + 15 = 0$$
$$(x - 5)(x - 3) = 0$$

$x = 5$ or $x = 3$
$y^2 = 40 - 8(5)$ or $y^2 = 40 - 8(3)$
$y^2 = 40 - 40$ $\quad y^2 = 40 - 24$
$y^2 = 0$ $\quad\quad\quad y^2 = 16$
$y = 0$ $\quad\quad\quad y = \pm 4$
$(5, 0), (3, 4), (3, -4)$

42. $xy - 25 = 0$
$\quad y - x = 0$, or $x = y$
$x(x) - 25 = 0$
$\quad\quad x^2 = 25$
$\quad\quad x = \pm 5$
$(5, 5), (-5, -5)$

43. $A = \dfrac{1}{2}b \cdot h$

$27 = \dfrac{1}{2}(h - 3)(h)$

$54 = h^2 - 3h$
$0 = h^2 - 3h - 54$
$0 = (h - 9)(h + 6)$
$h = 9$ or $h = -6$
Height cannot be negative, so the height is 9 cm.

p. 631   **14-4 TRY THIS**

a. $r = \dfrac{16}{4} = 4, |r| > 1$; No

b. $r = \dfrac{-30}{5} = -6, |r| > 1$; No

c. $r = \dfrac{1}{3}, |r| < 1$; Yes

d. $\dfrac{3}{2}$

$a_1 = 1, r = \dfrac{1}{3}$ $S_n = \dfrac{1}{1 - \dfrac{1}{3}} = \dfrac{1}{\dfrac{2}{3}} = \dfrac{3}{2}$

e. $\dfrac{16}{5}$

$a_1 = 4, r = -\dfrac{1}{4}$ $S_n = \dfrac{4}{1 - \left(-\dfrac{1}{4}\right)} = \dfrac{4}{\dfrac{5}{4}} = 4 \cdot \dfrac{4}{5} = \dfrac{16}{5}$

pp. 632–633   **14-4 EXERCISES**

1. No   **2.** Yes   **3.** Yes   **4.** No   **5.** Yes   **6.** Yes

7. Yes   **8.** No   **9.** 8   **10.** $\dfrac{49}{4}$ **11.** 2   **12.** $\dfrac{16}{3}$

13. $\dfrac{160}{9}$ **14.** 10

15. $0.\overline{7} = 0.7 + 0.07 + \cdots$
$a_1 = 0.7, r = 0.1$

Hence $0.\overline{7} = \dfrac{0.7}{1 - 0.1} = \dfrac{0.7}{0.9} = \dfrac{7}{9}$

16. $0.\overline{3} = \dfrac{0.3}{1 - 0.1} = \dfrac{0.3}{0.9} = \dfrac{3}{9} = \dfrac{1}{3}$

17. $0.\overline{21} = 0.21 + 0.0021 + \cdots$
$a_1 = 0.21 \quad\quad r = 0.01$

$0.\overline{21} = \dfrac{0.21}{1 - 0.01} = \dfrac{0.21}{0.99} = \dfrac{21}{99} = \dfrac{7}{33}$

18. $0.\overline{63} = \dfrac{0.63}{1 - 0.01} = \dfrac{0.63}{0.99} = \dfrac{7 \cdot 9}{11 \cdot 9} = \dfrac{7}{11}$

19. $5.\overline{15} = 5.1 + 0.051 + 0.00051 + \cdots$
$a_1 = 5.1 \quad\quad r = 0.01$

$5.\overline{15} = \dfrac{5.1}{1 - 0.01} = \dfrac{5.1}{0.99} = \dfrac{510}{99} = \dfrac{170}{33}$

20. $4.\overline{125} = 4 + 0.125 + 0.000125 + \cdots$

$$0.\overline{125} = \frac{0.125}{1 - 0.001} = \frac{0.125}{0.999} = \frac{125}{999}$$

$$4.\overline{125} = \frac{4 \cdot 999 + 125}{999} = \frac{3996 + 125}{999} = \frac{4121}{999}$$

21. The ball is dropped 12 m, and each rebound is $\frac{1}{3}$ of the previous

distance. Since a rebound up is equal to the distance the ball falls to bounce again,

$$S_n = 12 + (4 + 4) + \left(\frac{4}{3} + \frac{4}{3}\right) + \left(\frac{4}{9} + \frac{4}{9}\right) + \cdots$$

$$= 12 + 8 + \frac{1}{3}(8) + \frac{1}{9}(8)$$

$$= 12 + \frac{8}{1 - \frac{1}{3}}$$

$$= 12 + \frac{8}{\frac{2}{3}}$$

$$= 12 + 12 = 24 \text{ m}$$

22. $\dfrac{2}{1 - r} = 3$ $2, \dfrac{2}{3}, \dfrac{2}{9}, \dfrac{2}{27}, \dfrac{2}{81}$

$$2 = 3 - 3r$$
$$-3r = -1$$
$$r = \frac{1}{3}$$

23. $a_1 = 16^2 = 256$. We use the Pythagorean theorem to find the value of r. The length of a side of square 2 is
$\sqrt{8^2 + 8^2} = \sqrt{128} = 2\sqrt{32} = 8\sqrt{2}$.

$$r = \frac{a_2}{a_1} = \frac{(8\sqrt{2})^2}{256}$$

$$= \frac{128}{256}$$

$$= 0.5$$

$$S = \frac{256}{1 - 0.5}$$

$$= \frac{256}{0.5}$$

$$= 512 \text{ cm}^2$$

24. $S_1 = 2$

$$S_2 = 2 + \frac{1}{2} = 2.5$$

$$S_3 = 2 + \frac{1}{2} + \frac{1}{6} = \frac{8}{3} = 2.\overline{6}$$

$$S_4 = 2.\overline{6} + \frac{1}{24} = 2.708\overline{3}$$

$$S_5 = 2.708\overline{3} + \frac{1}{120} = 2.71\overline{6}$$

$$S_6 = 2.71\overline{6} + \frac{1}{720} = 2.71805\overline{5}$$

$$S = e$$

25. $0.010101\ldots$

$$= 2^{-2} + 2^{-4} + 2^{-6} + \cdots = \frac{1}{4} + \frac{1}{16} + \frac{1}{64} + \cdots$$

$$S = \frac{\frac{1}{4}}{\left(1 - \frac{1}{4}\right)} = \frac{\frac{1}{4}}{\frac{3}{4}} = \frac{1}{3}$$

3 is 11 in binary, so $\dfrac{1}{11}$ is the answer in binary.

26. The sum of each group is greater than $\dfrac{1}{2}$. Thus, the series is

greater than $1 + \dfrac{1}{2} + \dfrac{1}{2} + \cdots$, which does not converge.

27. $\pm 80, \pm 40, \pm 20, \pm 16, \pm 10, \pm 8, \pm 5, \pm 4, \pm 2, \pm 1$

28. Positive, 1; Negative, 4 or 2 or 0

29. $P(x) = x^5 + 2x^4 - 15x^3 - 12x^2 - 76x - 80$
$P(2) = 32 + 2(16) - 15(8) - 12(4) - 76(2) - 80$
$\qquad = -336$
$P(5) = 3125 + 2(625) - 15(125) - 12(25) - 76(5) - 80$
$\qquad = 1740$
$P(0) = -80$
$P(-5) = -3125 + 2(625) - 15(-125) - 12(25) - 76(-5)$
$\qquad - 80 = 0$

30. From #27, -5 is one root
$P(x) = (x + 5)(x^4 - 3x^3 - 12x - 16)$
1 is not a root

$$\begin{array}{r|rrrr}
-1 & 1 & -3 & 0 & -12 & -16 \\
 & & -1 & 4 & -4 & 16 \\
\hline
 & 1 & -4 & 4 & -16 & 0
\end{array}$$

-1 is a root
$P(x) = (x + 5)(x + 1)(x^3 - 4x^2 + 4x - 16)$
$\qquad = (x + 5)(x + 1)(x^2(x - 4) + 4(x - 4))$
$\qquad = (x + 5)(x + 1)(x - 4)(x^2 + 4)$
The roots are $-5, -1, 4, 2i$ and $-2i$.

31. x-intercepts: $-5, -1, 4$
roots: $-5, -1, 4, 2i, -2i$

32.

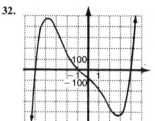

33. $1^2 - 7 = 1 - 7 = -6$
$2^2 - 7 = 4 - 7 = -3$
$3^2 - 7 = 9 - 7 = 2$
$12^2 - 7 = 144 - 7 = 137$
$-6, -3, 2, 137$

34. $10(1) + 17 = 10 + 17 = 27$
$10(2) + 17 = 20 + 17 = 37$
$10(3) + 17 = 30 + 17 = 47$
$10(12) + 17 = 120 + 17 = 137$
$27, 37, 47, 137$

p. 633   GRAPHING SEQUENCES

a.

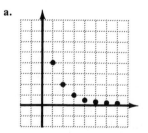

b.

c.

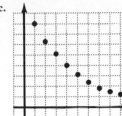

p. 633   PROBLEM FOR PROGRAMMERS

```
10   REM   Chapter 14 Problem
20   INPUT "Enter first 3 terms of geometric
     series ";A1,A2,A3
30   IF  ABS (A1 / A2 - A2 / A3) > .000001 THEN
     PRINT "Not a geometric series!": GOTO 70
40   R = A2 / A1
50   IF R >= 1 THEN PRINT "Sum is not finite!":
     GOTO 70
60   PRINT "Sum = ",A1 / (1 - R)
70   END
```

p. 635   14-5 TRY THIS

a. A. Show true for $n = 1$; $\dfrac{1(1+1)}{2} = \dfrac{1 \cdot 2}{2} = 1$

B. Assume true for $n = k$;

$$1 + 2 + 3 + 4 + \cdots + k = \frac{k(k+1)}{2}$$

Show true for $k + 1$; $1 + 2 + 3 + 4 + \cdots + k + k + 1$

$$= \frac{k(k+1)}{2} + k + 1 = \frac{k(k+1)}{2} + \frac{2(k+1)}{2}$$

$$= \frac{k(k+1) + 2(k+1)}{2} = \frac{(k+1)(k+2)}{2}$$

$$= \frac{(k+1)[(k+1)+1]}{2}$$

b. A. Show true for $n = 1$; $2^{1+1} - 1 - 2 = 4 - 1 - 2 = 1$
B. Assume true for $n = k$;
$1 + 3 + 7 + 15 + \cdots + (2^k - 1) = 2^{k+1} - k - 2$
Show true for $n = k + 1$;
$1 + 3 + 7 + 15 + \cdots + (2^k - 1) + (2^{k+1} - 1)$
$= 2^{k+1} - k - 2 + 2^{k+1} - 1$
$= 2 \cdot 2^{k+1} - k - 1 - 2$
$= 2^{(k+1)+1} - (k+1) - 2$

p. 636   14-5 EXERCISES

1. a. $\dfrac{1}{2} \cdot 1(1 + 5) = \dfrac{6}{2} = 3$

b. Assume true for $n = k$, show true for $n = k + 1$.
$3 + 4 + 5 + \cdots + (k + 2) + (k + 3)$

$$= \frac{k(k+5)}{2} + k + 3$$

$$= \frac{k(k+5) + 2(k+3)}{2} = \frac{k^2 + 7k + 6}{2} = \frac{(k+1)(k+6)}{2}$$

$$= \frac{1}{2}(k+1)[(k+1)+5]$$

2. a. $1(1 + 2) = 1 \cdot 3 = 3$
b. Assume true for $n = k$, show true for $n = k + 1$.
$3 + 5 + 7 + \cdots + (2k + 1) + (2k + 3)$
$= k(k + 2) + (2k + 3)$
$= k^2 + 4k + 3 = (k + 1)(k + 3)$
$= (k + 1)[(k + 1) + 2]$

3. a. $-\dfrac{1(1+3)}{2} = \dfrac{-4}{2} = -2$

b. Assume true for $n = k$, show true for $n = k + 1$.
$-2 - 3 - 4 - \cdots - (k + 1) - (k + 2)$

$$= \frac{-k(k+3)}{2}$$

$$-(k+2) = \frac{-k(k+3) - 2(k+2)}{2}$$

$$= \frac{-(k^2 + 5k + 4)}{2}$$

$$= \frac{-(k+1)(k+4)}{2}$$

$$= -\frac{1}{2}(k+1)[(k+1)+3]$$

4. a. $\dfrac{4}{3}(4^1 - 1) = \dfrac{4}{3}(3) = 4$

b. Assume true for $n = k$, show true for $n = k + 1$.

$$4 + 4^2 + \cdots + 4^k + 4^{k+1} = \frac{4(4^k - 1)}{3} + 4^{k+1}$$

$$= \frac{4(4^k - 1) + 3 \cdot 4^{k+1}}{3} = \frac{4}{3}(4^k - 1 + 3 \cdot 4^k)$$

$$= \frac{4}{3}[(1 + 3)4^k - 1] = \frac{4}{3}(4^{k+1} - 1)$$

5. a. $\dfrac{1(1+1)(2 \cdot 1 + 1)}{6} = 1$

b. Assume true for $n = k$, show true for $n = k + 1$.
$1^2 + 2^2 + 3^2 + \cdots + k^2 + (k + 1)^2$

$$= \frac{k(k+1)(2k+1)}{6} + (k+1)^2$$

$$= \frac{(k+1)(2k^2 + 7k + 6)}{6}$$

$$= \frac{(k+1)(k+2)(2k+3)}{6} = \frac{(k+1)(k+2)[(2(k+1)+1]}{6}$$

6. a. $\dfrac{1^2(1+1)^2}{4} = 1$

b. Assume true for $n = k$, show true for $n = k + 1$.
$1^3 + 2^3 + 3^3 + \cdots + k^3 + (k + 1)^3$

$$= \frac{k^2(k+1)^2}{4} + (k+1)^3 = \frac{k^2(k+1)^2 + (k+1)^3}{4}$$

$$= \frac{(k+1)^2[k^2 + 4(k+1)]}{4} = \frac{(k+1)^2(k^2 + 4k + 4)}{4}$$

$$= \frac{(k+1)^2(k+2)^2}{4} = \frac{(k+1)^2[(k+1)+1]^2}{4}$$

7. a. $\dfrac{1}{1+1} = \dfrac{1}{2}$

b. Assume true for $n = k$, show true for $n = k + 1$.

$$\frac{1}{1 \cdot 2} + \frac{1}{2 \cdot 3} + \cdots + \frac{1}{k(k+1)} + \frac{1}{(k+1)(k+2)}$$

$$= \frac{k}{k+1} + \frac{1}{(k+1)(k+2)} = \frac{k(k+2)}{(k+1)(k+2)}$$

$$+ \frac{1}{(k+1)(k+2)} = \frac{(k+1)^2}{(k+1)(k+2)} = \frac{(k+1)}{(k+2)}$$

$$= \frac{(k+1)}{[(k+1)+1]}$$

8. a. $\dfrac{1}{2}(3 \cdot 1 + 1) = 2$

b. Assume true for $n = k$, show true for $n = k + 1$.
$2 + 5 + 8 + \cdots + (3k - 1) + [3(k + 1) - 1]$

$$= \frac{k(3k+1)}{2} + [3(k+1) - 1] = \frac{3k^2 + 7k + 4}{2}$$

$$= \frac{(k+1)(3k+4)}{2} = \frac{1}{2}(k+1)[3(k+1)+1]$$

9. a. $\dfrac{1(9-1)}{2} = 4$

b. Assume true for $n = k$, show true for $n = k + 1$.
$$4 + 3 + 2 + \cdots + (5 - k) + [5 - (k + 1)]$$
$$= \dfrac{k(9-k)}{2} + (4 - k) = \dfrac{-k^2 + 7k + 8}{2}$$
$$= \dfrac{(k+1)(-k+8)}{2} = \dfrac{1}{2}(k+1)[9 - (k+1)]$$

10. a. $\dfrac{3\left(1 - \dfrac{1}{3}\right)}{2} = \dfrac{3\left(\dfrac{2}{3}\right)}{2} = 1$

b. Assume true for $n = k$, show true for $n = k + 1$.
$$1 + \dfrac{1}{3} + \dfrac{1}{9} + \cdots + 3^{1-k} + 3^{1-(k+1)}$$
$$= \dfrac{3}{2}\left(1 - \left(\dfrac{1}{3}\right)^k\right) + 3^{-k} = \dfrac{3\left(1 - \left(\dfrac{1}{3}\right)^k\right) + 2\left(\dfrac{1}{3}\right)^k}{2}$$
$$= \dfrac{3 - \dfrac{3}{3}\left(\dfrac{1}{3}\right)^k}{2} = \dfrac{3}{2}\left(1 - \left(\dfrac{1}{3}\right)^{k+1}\right)$$

11. a. $2 \cdot 1 + 3 = 5;\ 1(1 + 4) = 5$

b. Assume true for $n = j$, show true for $n = j + 1$.
$$\sum_{k=1}^{j} (2k + 3) + [2(j + 1) + 3] = j(j + 4) + (2j + 5)$$
$$= j^2 + 6j + 5 = (j + 1)[(j + 1) + 4]$$

12. a. $2^1 = 2;\ 2(2^1 - 1) = 2$

b. Assume true for $n = j$, show true for $n = j + 1$.
$$\sum_{k=1}^{j} 2^k + 2^{j+1} = 2(2^j - 1) + 2^{j+1} = 2^{j+1} - 2 + 2^{j+1}$$
$$= 2(2^{j+1}) - 2 = 2(2^{j+1} - 1)$$

13. We check the first domino to see if it is knocked over. If we assume all dominoes before the nth domino are knocked over, and verify the nth domino is knocked over, then we can assume all dominoes are knocked over.

14. a. $1 + \dfrac{1}{1} = 1 + 1$

b. Assume true for $n = k$, show true for $n = k + 1$.
$$\left(1 + \dfrac{1}{1}\right)\left(1 + \dfrac{1}{2}\right)\cdots\left(1 + \dfrac{1}{k}\right)\left(1 + \dfrac{1}{k+1}\right)$$
$$= (k + 1)\left(1 + \dfrac{1}{k+1}\right) = k + \dfrac{k}{k+1} + 1 + \dfrac{1}{k+1}$$
$$= \dfrac{k^2 + 3k + 2}{k+1} = \dfrac{(k+1)(k+2)}{k+1} = (k + 1) + 1$$

15. a. $1^5 = \dfrac{1^2 \cdot 2^2 \cdot 3}{12}$

b. Assume true for $n = j$, show true for $n = j + 1$.
$$\sum_{k=1}^{j} k^5 + (j + 1)^5 = \dfrac{j^2(j+1)^2(2j^2 + 2j - 1)}{12} + (j + 1)^5$$
$$= \dfrac{(j+1)^2[2j^4 + 2j^3 - j^2 + 12(j+1)^3]}{12}$$
$$= \dfrac{(j+1)^2(2j^4 + 14j^3 + 35j^2 + 36j + 12)}{12}$$
$$= \dfrac{(j+1)^2(j+2)^2(2j^2 + 6j + 3)}{12}$$
$$= \dfrac{(j+1)^2(j+2)^2(2(j+1)^2 + 2(j+1) - 1)}{12}$$

16. $\displaystyle\sum_{k=1}^{n} k^3 - \sum_{k=1}^{n} k^2 = \dfrac{n(n^2-1)(3n+2)}{12} = \dfrac{n(n-1)(n+1)(3n+2)}{12}$

a. $1 - 1 = 0$

b. Assume true for $n = j$, show true for $n = j + 1$.
$$\sum_{k=1}^{j} k^3 - \sum k^2 + (j + 1)^3 - (j + 1)^2$$

$$= \dfrac{j(j^2 - 1)(3j + 2)}{12} + (j + 1)^3 - (j + 1)^2$$

$$\sum_{k=1}^{j+1} k^3 - \sum_{k=1}^{j+1} k^2$$

$$= \dfrac{(j + 1)[j(j - 1)(3j + 2) + 12(j + 1)^2 - 12(j + 1)]}{12}$$

$$= \dfrac{(j + 1)(j)(3j^2 + 11j + 10)}{12}$$

$$= \dfrac{(j + 1)(j)(j + 2)(3j + 5)}{12}$$

$$= \dfrac{(j + 1)(j + 1 - 1)(j + 1 + 1)(3(j + 1) + 2)}{12}$$

17. $P(x) = x^5 + x^4 - 16x - 16$
$= x^4(x + 1) - 16(x + 1)$
$= (x^4 - 16)(x + 1)$
$= (x^2 + 4)(x^2 - 4)(x + 1)$
$= (x^2 + 4)(x + 2)(x - 2)(x + 1)$
For $P(x) = 0$, $x = \pm 2i, -2, 2, -1$

18.
$$
\begin{array}{r|rrrrr}
3 & 1 & 1 & 0 & 0 & -16 & -16 \\
  &   & 3 & 12 & 36 & 108 & 276 \\
\hline
  & 1 & 4 & 12 & 36 & 92 & \big|\ 260
\end{array}
$$
$P(x) = Q(x) \cdot D(x) + R(x)$
$P(x) = (x - 3)(x^4 + 4x^3 + 12x^2 + 36x + 92) + 260$

19. $d = \sqrt{[5 - (-5)]^2 + (-5 - 5)^2}$
$= \sqrt{10^2 + 10^2}$
$= \sqrt{100 + 100}$
$= \sqrt{200}$
$= 10\sqrt{2}$

20. $(\log 10, 3)$ and $(4, 7)$
$(1, 3)$ and $(4, 7)$
$d = \sqrt{(1 - 4)^2 + (3 - 7)^2}$
$= \sqrt{(-3)^2 + (-4)^2}$
$= \sqrt{9 + 16}$
$= \sqrt{25}$
$= 5$

21. $x^2 - 25 = 0$
$x^2 = 25$
$x = \pm 5$

22. $x^3 = 27$
$x = 3$

23. $x^4 - 81 = 0$
$(x^2 + 9)(x^2 - 9) = 0$
$(x^2 + 9)(x + 3)(x - 3) = 0$
$x = \pm 3i, \pm 3$

p. 638 14-6 PROBLEM SOLVING: STRATEGIES

1. Strategy: Make a table; look for a pattern; write an equation.

	Salary before cut	Salary after cut	Increase needed	Percent of increase
(a)	$10,000	$8,000	$2,000	25%
(b)	$20,000	$16,000	$4,000	25%
(c)	$30,000	$24,000	$6,000	25%
(d)	x	$0.8x$	$0.2x$	25%

(a) $2000 = r(8000)$ **(b)** $4000 = r(16,000)$
$\quad\ 25\% = r$ $\qquad\qquad 25\% = r$
(c) $6000 = r(24,000)$ **(d)** $0.2x = r(0.8x)$
$\quad\ 25\% = r$ $\qquad\qquad 25\% = r$
Percent of increase needed will be 25%.

2. Strategy: Make an organized list
Consider the situation where there are fewer treats.

6 treats	7 treats	8 treats	
222	223	224	233
	232	242	323
	322	422	332

In general:

Number of treats	Number of ways to divide them
6	1
7	$3 = 1 + 2$
8	$6 = 1 + 2 + 3$
$\vdots$	
16	$1 + 2 + 3 + \cdots + (16 \cdot 5)$
	$= \dfrac{11(12)}{2} = 66$

She could distribute them 66 ways.

3. Strategy: Simplify the equations

$$ab + ac = 44$$
$$ab + bc = 50 \longrightarrow -ab - bc = -50$$
$$\underline{ac + bc = 54 \longrightarrow \quad ac + bc = \quad 54}$$
$$ac - ab = \quad 4$$
$$ac = \quad 4 + ab$$

$$ab + (4 + ab) = 44$$
$$2ab = 40$$
$$ab = 20 \longrightarrow 20 + bc = 50$$
$$bc = 30 \longrightarrow ac + 30 = 54$$
$$ac = 24$$

$ab = 20$	$ac = 24$	$bc = 30$
$1 \cdot 20$	$1 \cdot 24$	$1 \cdot 30$
$\longrightarrow 2 \cdot 10$	$\longrightarrow 2 \cdot 12$	$2 \cdot 15$
$\longrightarrow 4 \cdot 5$	$3 \cdot 8$	$3 \cdot 10$
	$\longrightarrow 4 \cdot 6 \longleftarrow$	$5 \cdot 6 \longleftarrow$

Since 2 and 4 are the only common factors between ab and ac, a must equal 2 or 4. With these restrictions, b may equal 10 or 5 and c may equal 12 or 6. With the information given by $bc = 30$, we can rule out $b = 10$ and $c = 12$. Since $b \neq 10$, $a \neq 2$.
The values are: $a = 4$, $b = 5$, $c = 6$ or $a = -4$, $b = -5$, $c = -6$.

4. Strategy: Make an organized list

$2^3 + 12^3 = 1736$	$8^3 + 12^3 = 1843$	$5^3 + 12^3 = 1853$
$2^3 + 11^3 = 1339$	$8^3 + 11^3 = 1512$	$5^3 + 11^3 = 1456$
$2^3 + 10^3 = 1008$	$8^3 + 10^3 = 1241$	$5^3 + 10^3 = 1125$
$4^3 + 12^3 = 1792$	$1^3 + 10^3 = 1001$	$7^3 + 12^3 = 1674$
$4^3 + 11^3 = 1395$	$1^3 + 11^3 = 1332$	$7^3 + 11^3 = 1343$
$4^3 + 10^3 = 1064$	$1^3 + 12^3 = 1729$	$7^3 + 10^3 = 1072$
$6^3 + 12^3 = 1944$	$3^3 + 12^3 = 1755$	$9^3 + 10^3 = 1729$
$6^3 + 11^3 = 1547$	$3^3 + 11^3 = 1358$	
$6^3 + 10^3 = 1216$	$3^3 + 10^3 = 1027$	

The code number is 1729, which is $9^3 + 10^3$ and $1^3 + 12^3$.

5. Strategy: Write an equation
x = number of correct items
$2x$ = number of points for the corrections
$20 - x$ = number of incorrect items
$$2x - (20 - x) = 16$$
$$x - 20 + x = 16$$
$$3x = 36$$
$$x = 12$$
$$20 - x = 8$$
The person had 12 items correct on the test.

6. Strategy: Look for a pattern.
$10 = 2^1 \cdot 5^1$ and 10 has 4 factors: 1, 2, 5, 10
$12 = 2^2 \cdot 3^1$ and 12 has 6 factors: 1, 2, 3, 4, 6, 12
$20 = 2^2 \cdot 5^1$ and 20 has 6 factors: 1, 2, 4, 5, 10, 20

If you add 1 to each exponent of the factors in the prime factorization and take their product, you get the number of factors of the number.

We want to construct a prime factorization with exponents that yield 8 factors using this pattern.
$$2^7 = 128$$
$$2^3 \cdot 3 = 24$$
$$2 \cdot 3^3 = 54$$
$$3^7 = 2187$$
The smallest positive integer with 8 different positive factors is 24.

1. $0, \dfrac{1}{3}, \dfrac{2}{4}, \dfrac{3}{5}; \dfrac{9}{1}; \dfrac{14}{16}$

2. $0, 1\dfrac{1}{2}, 2\dfrac{2}{3}, 3\dfrac{3}{4}; 9\dfrac{9}{10}; 14\dfrac{14}{15}$

3. $2, -2, -\dfrac{2}{3}, -\dfrac{2}{5}, -\dfrac{2}{7}$

4. $n^2 - 1$ 5. $\dfrac{n+1}{n}$ 6. $3 + 9 + 27$ 7. $\displaystyle\sum_{n=1}^{6} 4n(-1)^{n+1}$

8. $a_1 = 3$; $d = 1\dfrac{1}{2}$,

and

$$a_{10} = 3 + 9\left(\dfrac{3}{2}\right) = 3 + \dfrac{27}{2} = 16\dfrac{1}{2}$$

9. $3 + (n - 1)\dfrac{3}{2} = 24$

$$(n - 1)\dfrac{3}{2} = 24$$
$$(n - 1) = 14$$
$$n = 15 \qquad 15^{\text{th}} \text{ term}$$

10. $7, 12, 17$ 11. $\dfrac{30}{2}(1 + 30) = 15(31) = 465$

12. $a_1 = 3 - 15 = -12$
$a_2 = 6 - 15 = -7$
$d = 3$

$$S_{20} = \dfrac{20}{2}[2(-12) + 19(3)] = 10[-24 + 57] = 10(33) = 330$$

13. $r = -2$ 14. $a_7 = 4(-2)^6 = 4(64) = 256$

15. $4(-2)^{n-1} = -512$
$(-2)^{n-1} = -128$
$n - 1 = 7$
$n = 8 \qquad 8^{\text{th}} \text{ term}$

16. $36, 18$

17. $S_6 = \dfrac{2\left(1 - \left(\dfrac{1}{2}\right)^6\right)}{1 - \dfrac{1}{2}} = \dfrac{2\left(\dfrac{63}{64}\right)}{\dfrac{1}{2}} = \dfrac{63}{16} = 3\dfrac{15}{16}$

18. $S_7 = \dfrac{-3 + 3(-3)^7}{4} = -1641$

19. $a_1 = 1$ $r = -2$ $|r| > 1$ No sum

20. $a_1 = 3.2$ $r = .5$ $|r| < 1$ Has a sum

21. $S = \dfrac{20}{1 - \dfrac{1}{2}} = \dfrac{20}{\dfrac{1}{2}} = 40$

22. $S = \dfrac{10}{1 + \dfrac{1}{5}} = \dfrac{10}{\dfrac{6}{5}} = \dfrac{50}{6} = 8\dfrac{1}{3}$

23. **a.** True for $n = 1$
    b. Assume true for $n = k$
    Show that statement is true for $n = k + 1$.
    $$1 + 4 + 7 + \cdots + (3k - 2) + [3(k + 1) - 2]$$
    $$= \dfrac{k(3k - 1)}{2} + [3(k + 1) - 2]$$
    $$= \dfrac{3k^2 - k + 6k + 2}{2}$$
    $$= \dfrac{3k^2 + 5k + 2}{2}$$
    $$= \dfrac{(k + 1)(3k + 2)}{2}$$
    $$= \dfrac{(k + 1)[3(k + 1) - 1]}{2}$$

1. $\frac{1}{3}, \frac{1}{5}, \frac{1}{7}, \frac{1}{9}; \frac{1}{21}; \frac{1}{31}$

2. $-3, \frac{3}{2}, \frac{3}{5}, \frac{3}{8}, \frac{3}{11}$

3. $a_n = \frac{(-1)^n}{n}$

4. $1 + 2 + 4 + 8 = 15$

5. $\sum_{n=1}^{7} (3n - 9)$

6. $a_1 = -4$, $d = 2\frac{1}{2}$, and $a_{20} = -4 + 19\left(\frac{5}{2}\right) = -4 + \frac{95}{2} = 43\frac{1}{2}$

7. $\quad 41 = -4 + (n - 1)\frac{5}{2}$

$\qquad 45 = (n - 1)\frac{5}{2}$

$\quad (n - 1) = 18$
$\qquad n = 19 \qquad 19^{\text{th}} \text{ term}$

8. $3\frac{1}{5}, 4\frac{2}{5}, 5\frac{3}{5}, 6\frac{4}{5}$

9. $S_{84} = \frac{84}{2}(1 + 84) = 42(85) = 3570$

10. $a_1 = 5$
$a_2 = 3$
$d = -2$

$S_{30} = \frac{30}{2}(10 + 29(-2)) = 15(10 + -58) = 15(-48) = -720$

11. $\frac{2}{3}$

12. $a_6 = 24\left(\frac{2}{3}\right)^5 = 24\left(\frac{32}{243}\right) = \frac{256}{81}$

13. $S_6 = \dfrac{24 - 24\left(\frac{2}{3}\right)^6}{1 - \frac{2}{3}} = \dfrac{24 - 24\left(\frac{64}{729}\right)}{\frac{1}{3}} = 3\left[24 - \frac{1536}{729}\right]$

$\qquad = 3\left[\frac{15,960}{729}\right] = 65\frac{55}{81}$

14. $24\left(\frac{2}{3}\right)^{n-1} = \frac{1024}{729}$

$\left(\frac{2}{3}\right)^{n-1} = \frac{1024}{17,496}$

$n - 1 = 7$
$\qquad n = 8$

15. $\frac{1}{8}, \frac{1}{4}, \frac{1}{2}, 1, 2$

16. $S_6 = \dfrac{\frac{2}{3} - \frac{2}{3}\left(\frac{1}{2}\right)^6}{\frac{1}{2}} = 2\left[\frac{2}{3} - \frac{1}{96}\right] = 2\left[\frac{63}{96}\right] = \frac{63}{48} = \frac{21}{16}$

17. $S_5 = \dfrac{-2 - (-2)\left(-\frac{1}{2}\right)^5}{\frac{3}{2}} = \left[-2 - \frac{1}{16}\right]\frac{2}{3} = \frac{2}{3}\left[-\frac{33}{16}\right] = -\frac{11}{8}$

18. $r = 2 \qquad$ No

19. $r = -\frac{1}{3} \qquad S = \dfrac{81}{1 + \frac{1}{3}} = \frac{3}{4}(81) = \frac{243}{4} = 60\frac{3}{4}$

20. a. $2 = 2(1)^2$
$\quad 2 = 2$

b. Assume true for $n = k$, show true for $n = k + 1$.
$2 + 6 + 10 + \cdots + (4k - 2) + [4(k + 1) - 2]$
$= 2k^2 + 4(k + 1) - 2$
$= 2k^2 + 4k + 2$
$= 2(k^2 + 2k + 1)$
$= 2(k + 1)^2$

CHAPTER 15

1. $\frac{1}{12}$ **2.** $\frac{1}{495}$ **3.** $\frac{11}{850}$ **4.** $9x^2 + 6x + 1$

5. $4 - 12x + 9x^2$ **6.** $x^3 - 3x^2 + 3x - 1$

7. $x^4 + 8x^3 + 24x^2 + 32x + 16$

a. $2 \cdot 4 \cdot 3 = 8 \cdot 3 = 24$ **b.** $4 \cdot 2 \cdot 8 = 8 \cdot 8 = 64$
c. $_3P_3 = 3 \cdot 2 \cdot 1 = 6$ **d.** $_5P_5 = 5 \cdot 4 \cdot 3 \cdot 2 \cdot 1 = 120$
e. $_6P_6 = 6 \cdot 5 \cdot 4 \cdot 3 \cdot 2 \cdot 1 = 720$
f. $_6P_6 = 6 \cdot 5 \cdot 4 \cdot 3 \cdot 2 \cdot 1 = 720$
g. $9! = 9 \cdot 8 \cdot 7 \cdot 6 \cdot 5 \cdot 4 \cdot 3 \cdot 2 \cdot 1 = 72 \cdot 42 \cdot 120 = 362,880$
h. $18!$ **i.** $10 \cdot 9!$ **j.** $11 \cdot 10 \cdot 9 \cdot 8!$

k. $_7P_3 = \dfrac{7!}{(7 - 3)!}$ **l.** $_{10}P_4 = \dfrac{10!}{(10 - 4)!}$

$\qquad = \dfrac{7 \cdot 6 \cdot 5 \cdot 4!}{4!}$ $\qquad = \dfrac{10 \cdot 9 \cdot 8 \cdot 7 \cdot 6!}{6!}$

$\qquad = 210$ $\qquad = 5040$

m. $_8P_2 = \dfrac{8!}{6!}$ **n.** $_{11}P_5 = \dfrac{11!}{6!}$

$\qquad = \dfrac{8 \cdot 7 \cdot 6!}{6!}$ $\qquad = \dfrac{11 \cdot 10 \cdot 9 \cdot 8 \cdot 7 \cdot 6!}{6!}$

$\qquad = 56$ $\qquad = 55,440$

o. $_{10}P_6 = \dfrac{10!}{4!}$ **p.** $_7P_7 = 7! = 5040$

$\qquad = 10 \cdot 9 \cdot 8 \cdot 7 \cdot 6 \cdot 5$ $\qquad 5040 \cdot \frac{4}{7} = 2880$
$\qquad = 151,200$

1. 24   **2.** 120   **3.** 720   **4.** 5040   **5.** 336

6. 280   **7.** 720   **8.** 120   **9.** 24   **10.** 2   **11.** 5040

12. 40,320   **13.** 720   **14.** 5040   **15.** 40,320

16. 362,880   **17.** 120   **18.** 720   **19.** 1   **20.** 1

21. $9 \cdot 8!$ **22.** $13 \cdot 12!$ **23.** $a \cdot (a - 1)!$

24. $m \cdot (m - 1)!$ **25.** $27 \cdot 26 \cdot 25 \cdot 24 \cdot 23 \cdot 22!$

26. $13 \cdot 12 \cdot 11 \cdot 10 \cdot 9 \cdot 8 \cdot 7 \cdot 6 \cdot 5!$

27. 24   **28.** 2520   **29.** 604,800   **30.** 720   **31.** 380

32. 870   **33.** 336   **34.** 840   **35.** 120; 60   **36.** 120; 720

37. $_6P_4 = 360$ **38.** $_5P_3 = 60$ **39.** 20,160   **40.** 604,800

41. $9 \cdot 9 \cdot 8 \cdot 7 \cdot 6 \cdot 5 \cdot 4 = 544,320$

42. a. $5! = 5 \cdot 4 \cdot 3 \cdot 2 \cdot 1 = 120$ **b.** $2^5 \cdot 5! = 32(120) = 3840$

43. Answers may vary.
a. 11! which equals 39,916,800
b. 69! which equals 1.7112245×10^{98}

44.
$$_nP_5 = 7 \cdot {}_nP_4$$
$$\frac{n!}{(n-5)!} = \frac{7n!}{(n-4)!}$$
$$n!(n-4)! = 7n!(n-5)!$$
$$(n-4)(n-5)! = 7(n-5)!$$
$$n-4 = 7$$
$$n = 11$$

45.
$$_nP_4 = 8 \cdot {}_{n-1}P_3$$
$$\frac{n!}{(n-4)!} = \frac{8(n-1)!}{(n-1-3)!}$$
$$n!(n-4)! = 8(n-1)!(n-4)!$$
$$n(n-1)! = 8(n-1)!$$
$$n = 8$$

46.
$$_nP_5 = 9 \cdot {}_{n-1}P_4$$
$$\frac{n!}{(n-5)!} = \frac{9(n-1)!}{(n-1-4)!}$$
$$n!(n-5)! = 9(n-1)!(n-5)!$$
$$n(n-1)! = 9(n-1)!$$
$$n = 9$$

47.
$$_nP_4 = 8 \cdot {}_nP_3$$
$$\frac{n!}{(n-4)!} = \frac{8n!}{(n-3)!}$$
$$n!(n-3)! = 8n!(n-4)!$$
$$(n-3)(n-4)! = 8(n-4)!$$
$$n-3 = 8$$
$$n = 11$$

48. When $n = 3$ we have $3! = 6 < 8 = 2^3$. For 4, we have $4! = 24 > 16 = 2^4$. From this point on, each additional factor on the left is larger than 2, while the new factors on the right are always two. Hence, the left side grows faster.

49. $2 \cdot 4 \cdot 6 \cdots \cdot (2n) = 2^n n!$
$2(1) \cdot 2(2) \cdot 2(3) \cdot 2(4) \cdots (2)(n)$
$= 2 \cdot 2 \cdot 2 \cdots 2 \cdot 1 \cdot 2 \cdot 3 \cdots n$
$= 2^n \cdot n!$
Two is taken as a factor of each term in lines 2 and 3.

50. If $n > 1$, n will always contain 2 as a factor, which will make $n!$ even.

51. If $n > 4$, $n!$ will end in zero because $n!$ will contain a 2 and a 5, which will multiply and end in zero.

52. $x^3 + 20x^2 + 133x + 294 = 0$
$294 = 2 \cdot 3 \cdot 7 \cdot 7$
Some possible roots are ± 2, ± 3, ± 6, ± 7.
Use synthetic division to test:

$$\begin{array}{r|rrrr} -6 & 1 & 20 & 133 & 294 \\ & & -6 & -84 & -294 \\ \hline & 1 & 14 & 49 & 0 \end{array}$$

$(x+6)(x^2 + 14x + 49) = 0$
$(x+6)(x+7)^2 = 0$
$x = -6$ or $x = -7$

53.
$$x^4 + 27x^2 = 324$$
$$x^4 + 27x^2 - 324 = 0$$
$$(x^2 - 9)(x^2 + 36) = 0$$
$$x^2 = 9 \quad \text{or} \quad x^2 = -36$$
$$x = \sqrt{9} \qquad\quad x = \sqrt{-36}$$
$$x = \pm 3 \qquad\quad x = \pm 6i$$

54. $30x^2 - 61x + 30 = 0$
$(6x - 5)(5x - 6) = 0$
$$x = \frac{5}{6} \quad \text{or} \quad x = \frac{6}{5}$$

55. $a_{17} = a_1 + 16(3)$
$1 = a_1 + 48$
$-47 = a_1$
$a_{50} = -47 + 49(3)$
$a_{50} = -47 + 147$
$= 100$

56.
$a_3 = a_1 + 2d \qquad a_{13} = a_1 + 12d$
$0 = a_1 + 2d \qquad 33 = a_1 + 12d$
$-a_1 = 2d$
$a = -2d \quad \rightarrow \quad 33 = -2d + 12d$
$33 = 10d$
$3.3 = d$

57. $a_{50} = a_1 + 49(3)$
$1 = a_1 + 147$
$-146 = a_1$
$a_{17} = -146 + 3(16)$
$= -146 + 48$
$= -98$

58. $a_{515} = a_1 + 514d$
$-(222 = a_1 + 514d)$
$a_{555} = a_1 + 554d$
$\underline{444 = a_1 + 554d}$
$222 = 40d$
$5.55 = d$

59. $S = \frac{33}{2}[2(0) + 32(3)] - 3$
$= \frac{33}{2}(\overset{16}{\cancel{32}}(3) - 3)$
$= 99(16) - 3$
$= 1584 - 3$
$= 1581$

60. $S = \frac{22}{2}[2(-20) + 21(2)] + 20$
$= 11[-40 + 42] + 20$
$= 22 + 20$
$= 42$

61. $S = \frac{44}{2}[2(-40) + (43)(4)] + 40 + 36 + 32$
$= 22[-80 + 172] + 108$
$= 22(92) + 108$
$= 2024 + 108$
$= 2132$

62. $\sum_{n=2}^{22} \left(\frac{1}{2}\right)^n = \frac{1}{4} + \frac{1}{8} + \cdots ; r = \frac{1}{2}$
$$S_n = \frac{\frac{1}{4}}{1 - \frac{1}{2}} = \frac{1}{4} \div \frac{1}{2} = \frac{1}{2} \quad \text{or} \quad 0.5$$

63. $\sum_{n=3}^{33} 3^n; S_n = \frac{27(1 - 3^{31})}{1 - 3} \approx 8.34 \times 10^{15}$

64. $\sum_{n=4}^{44} \left(\frac{1}{4}\right)^{n-4}; S_n = \frac{1\left(1 - \frac{1}{4^{41}}\right)}{\frac{3}{4}} \approx \frac{4}{3}$

65. $A + B + C = 86$
$A + B \qquad = 59 \rightarrow A = 59 - B$
$A + \qquad C = 58 \rightarrow A = 58 - C$
$59 - B + B + C = 86$
$59 + C = 86$
$C = 27$
$A = 58 - 27 = 31$
$31 = 59 - B \rightarrow B = 28$
$A = 31; B = 28; C = 27$

66. $(5000, 13000) (7500, 1450)$
$$\frac{1450 - 1300}{7500 - 5000} = \frac{150}{2500} = .06$$
$1300 = 5000(.06) + b$
$b = 1000$
$E = 1000 + 0.06g$
b. $E = 1000 + 0.06(8500) = \$1510$

pp. 651–653   **15-2 TRY THIS**

a. 26^5 **b. (1)** $52 \cdot 51 = 2652$ **(2)** $52^2 = 2704$

c. $P = \frac{7!}{2!3!} = \frac{7 \cdot 6 \cdot 5 \cdot 4 \cdot 3!}{2 \cdot 3!} = 7 \cdot 6 \cdot 5 \cdot 2 = 420$

d. $P = \frac{(2 + 3 + 2)!}{2!3!2!} = \frac{7 \cdot 6 \cdot 5 \cdot 4 \cdot 3!}{3! \cdot 2 \cdot 2} = 7 \cdot 6 \cdot 5 = 210$

e. $\frac{8!}{8} = \frac{8 \cdot 7 \cdot 6 \cdot 5 \cdot 4 \cdot 3 \cdot 2}{8} = 7 \cdot 6 \cdot 5 \cdot 4 \cdot 3 \cdot 2 = 5040$

1. 1296; 360   **2.** 16,807; 2520   **3.** 11,880   **4.** 6720

5. 648; 180   **6.** 9604; 1440   **7.** 648; 180   **8.** 9604; 1440

9. $80 \cdot 26 \cdot 9999 = 20{,}797{,}920$ **10.** 6   **11.** 6

12. 45,360   **13.** 34,650   **14.** 50,400   **15.** 151,200

16. 45,360   **17.** 180   **18.** 64,864,800   **19.** 1260

20. 420   **21.** 24   **22.** 120   **23.** 5040   **24.** 362,880

25. **a.** 120
    b. 625
    c. 24
    d. 6

26. $\dfrac{9!}{2!\,2!\,2!\,3!} = \dfrac{9 \cdot 8 \cdot 7 \cdot 6 \cdot 5 \cdot 4 \cdot 3!}{2 \cdot 2 \cdot 2 \cdot 3!}$
$= 9 \cdot 7 \cdot 6 \cdot 5 \cdot 4$
$= 7560$

27. $\dfrac{5!}{2!} - 4!$

(4! will start with 0)

$= \dfrac{5 \cdot 4 \cdot 3 \cdot 2}{2} - 4!$

$= 5 \cdot 4 \cdot 3 - 24 = 36$

28. $\dfrac{5!}{2!} = 60$

$60 \cdot \dfrac{2}{5} = 24$

29. Multiply the left side of the equation by $(n - r)!$
$n \cdot (n - 1) \cdots (n - r + 1) \cdot (n - r)! = n!$
Multiply the right side of the equation by $(n - r!)$

$\dfrac{n!}{(n - r)!} \cdot (n - r)! = n!$

If $ac = bc$ and $a, b, c \neq 0$ then $a = b$, so the two forms are equivalent.

30. There are $(5 - 1)! \div 2!$ or 12 permutations.

31. $(9 - 2)! = 7 \cdot 6 \cdot 5 \cdot 4 \cdot 3 \cdot 2 \cdot 1 = 5040$

32. $n - 1$ **33.** $2n - 1$ **34.** $1 \cdot 2 \cdot 3 \cdot 6! = 4320$

35. $_nP_r = \dfrac{n!}{(n - r)!}$

$= \dfrac{n(n - 1)(n - 2)(n - 3) \cdots (n - r + 1)(n - r)!}{(n - r)!}$

$= n(n - 1)(n - 2) \cdots (n - r + 1)$

36. $P(x) = x^4 + 2x^3 - 13x^2 - 14x + 24$

$$
\begin{array}{r|rrrrr}
-1 & 1 & 2 & -13 & -14 & 24 \\
   &   & -1 & -1 & 14 & 0 \\
\hline
   & 1 & 1 & -14 & 0 & \;24
\end{array}
$$ -1 is not a root of $P(x)$

$$
\begin{array}{r|rrrrr}
-2 & 1 & 2 & -13 & -14 & 24 \\
   &   & -2 & 0 & 26 & -24 \\
\hline
   & 1 & 0 & -13 & 12 & \;0
\end{array}
$$ -2 is a root of $P(x)$

$$
\begin{array}{r|rrrrr}
-3 & 1 & 2 & -13 & -14 & 24 \\
   &   & -3 & 3 & 30 & -48 \\
\hline
   & 1 & -1 & -10 & 16 & \;-24
\end{array}
$$ -3 is not a root of $P(x)$

$(x + 2)(x^3 - 13x + 12)$
$(x^2 + 1)$ is not a factor of $(x^3 - 13x + 12)$ so i is not a root of $P(x)$.

37. $P(x) = x^4 + 2x^3 - 13x^2 - 14x + 24$

$$
\begin{array}{r|rrrrr}
-1 & 1 & 2 & -13 & -14 & 24 \\
   &   & -1 & -1 & 14 & 0 \\
\hline
   & 1 & 1 & -14 & 0 & \;24
\end{array}
$$ $(x + 1)$ is not a factor of $P(x)$.

$$
\begin{array}{r|rrrrr}
-2 & 1 & 2 & -13 & -14 & 24 \\
   &   & -2 & 0 & 26 & -24 \\
\hline
   & 1 & 0 & -13 & 12 & \;0
\end{array}
$$ $(x + 2)$ is a factor of $P(x)$.

$$
\begin{array}{r|rrrrr}
-4 & 1 & 2 & -13 & -14 & 24 \\
   &   & -4 & 8 & 20 & -24 \\
\hline
   & 1 & -2 & -5 & 6 & \;0
\end{array}
$$ $(x + 4)$ is a factor of $P(x)$.

38. $P(x) = x^4 + 2x^3 - 13x^2 - 14x + 24$

$$
\begin{array}{r|rrrrr}
5 & 1 & 2 & -13 & -14 & 24 \\
  &   & 5 & 35 & 110 & 480 \\
\hline
  & 1 & 7 & 22 & 96 & \;504
\end{array}
$$ $P(5) = 504$

$$
\begin{array}{r|rrrrr}
0 & 1 & 2 & -13 & -14 & 24 \\
  &   & 0 & 0 & 0 & 0 \\
\hline
  & 1 & 2 & -13 & -14 & \;24
\end{array}
$$ $P(0) = 24$

$$
\begin{array}{r|rrrrr}
-4 & 1 & 2 & -13 & -14 & 24 \\
   &   & -4 & 8 & 20 & -24 \\
\hline
   & 1 & -2 & -5 & 6 & \;0
\end{array}
$$ $P(-4) = 0$

$$
\begin{array}{r|rrrrr}
-5 & 1 & 2 & -13 & -14 & 24 \\
   &   & -5 & 15 & -10 & 120 \\
\hline
   & 1 & -3 & 2 & -24 & \;144
\end{array}
$$ $P(-5) = 144$

39. $P(x) = x^4 + 2x^3 - 13x^2 - 14x + 24$
$= (x + 2)(x^3 - 13x + 12)$
$= (x + 2)(x + 4)(x^2 - 4x + 3)$
$= (x + 2)(x + 4)(x - 1)(x - 3)$
$x = -2, -4, 1, 3$

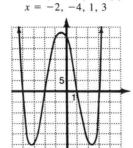

40. $S_n = \dfrac{8}{1 - \dfrac{1}{2}}$

$= \dfrac{8}{\dfrac{1}{2}}$

$= 16$

41. $S_n = \dfrac{\dfrac{1}{2}}{1 - \dfrac{1}{2}}$

$= \dfrac{1}{2} \div \dfrac{1}{2}$

$= 1$

42. 9, 27, 81
$a_5 = 3r^4$
$243 = 3r^4$
$81 = r^4$
$3 = r$

43. $x^4 = x^2 r^4$
$x^2 = r^4$
$(x^{1/2})^4 = r^4$
$x^{1/2} = r$
$x^{5/2}, x^3, x^{7/2}$

44. $2(l + w) = 56$ $l \cdot w = 192$
$l + w = 28$ $(28 - w)w = 192$
$l = 28 - w$ $28w - w^2 = 192$
$w^2 - 28w + 192 = 0$
$(w - 16)(w - 12) = 0$

16 cm, 12 cm

a. **(1)** 1   **(2)** 4   **(3)** 6   **(4)** 4   **(5)** 1

b. $\dbinom{10}{8} = \dfrac{10!}{8!\,(10 - 8)!} = \dfrac{10 \cdot 9}{2} = 45$

c. $\dbinom{10}{2} = \dfrac{10!}{2!\,(10 - 2)!} = \dfrac{10 \cdot 9}{2} = 45$

d. $\dbinom{n}{1} = \dfrac{n!}{(1 - n)!} = n$

e. $\dbinom{12}{5} = \dfrac{12!}{5!\,(12 - 5)!} = \dfrac{12 \cdot 11 \cdot 10 \cdot 9 \cdot 8}{1 \cdot 2 \cdot 3 \cdot 4 \cdot 5} = 792$

f. $\dbinom{9}{0} + \dbinom{9}{1} + \dbinom{9}{2} + \cdots + \dbinom{9}{9}$ or 512

1. 126   **2.** 91   **3.** 1225   **4.** 9880   **5.** 495

6. 2002 **7.** $\dfrac{n(n-1)(n-2)}{6}$ **8.** $\dfrac{n(n-1)}{2}$

9. 8855 **10.** 210 **11.** 72 **12.** 90

13. 28, 56 **14.** 21, 35 **15.** 1200 **16.** 112

17. $\dbinom{58}{6} \cdot \dbinom{42}{4}$ **18.** $\dbinom{63}{12} \cdot \dbinom{37}{8}$

19. $\dbinom{8}{3} = \dfrac{8 \cdot 7 \cdot 6 \cdot 5!}{3 \cdot 2 \cdot 5!} = 8 \cdot 7 = 56$

20. $\dbinom{n}{n-1} = \dfrac{n(n-1)!}{(n-1)!(1!)} = n$

21. $\dbinom{n}{n} = \dfrac{n!}{n!} = 1$

22. $\dbinom{n+1}{n} = \dfrac{(n+1)(n)!}{n!\,1!} = n+1$

23. $\dbinom{n+1}{n-1} = \dfrac{(n+1)(n)(n-1)!}{(n-1)!\,2!} = \dfrac{n(n+1)}{2}$

24. $\dbinom{n+1}{3} = 2\dbinom{n}{2}$

$\dfrac{(n+1)(n)(n-1)(n-2)!}{3!\,(n-2)!} = \dfrac{2 \cdot n(n-1)(n-2)!}{2! \cdot (n-2)!}$

$(n+1)(n)(n-1) = n(n-1) \cdot 3 \cdot 2$

$n+1 = 3 \cdot 2$

$n = 5$

25. $\dbinom{n}{n-2} = 6$

$\dfrac{n(n-1)(n-2)!}{(n-2)!\,2!} = 6$

$n(n-1) = 12$

$n^2 - n - 12 = 0$

$(n-4)(n+3) = 0$

$n = 4 \text{ or } -3 \qquad n \geq 0, \text{ so } n = 4$

26. $\dbinom{n+2}{4} = 6\dbinom{n}{2}$

$\dfrac{(n+2)(n+1)n(n-1)(n-2)!}{4 \cdot 3 \cdot 2 \cdot (n-2)!} = \dfrac{6 \cdot n(n-1)(n-2)!}{2!\,(n-2)!}$

$(n+2)(n+1)n(n-1) = 24 \cdot 3n(n-1)$

$n^2 + 3n + 2 = 72$

$n^2 + 3n - 70 = 0$

$(n+10)(n-7) = 0$

$n = -10 \text{ or } 7 \qquad n \geq 0, \text{ so } n = 7$

27. $\dbinom{n}{3} = \dbinom{n-1}{n} \cdot \dbinom{n}{1}$

$\dfrac{n(n-1)(n-2)(n-3)!}{3 \cdot 2 \cdot (n-3)!} = \dfrac{(n-1)(n-2)!}{1!\,(n-2)!} \cdot \dfrac{n(n-1)!}{(n-1)!}$

$\dfrac{n(n-1)(n-2)}{6} = n(n-1)$

$n-2 = 6$

$n = 8$

28. $\dbinom{n}{r} = \dfrac{n!}{r!\,(n-r)!} = \dfrac{n!}{(n-r)!\,r!} = \dfrac{n!}{(n-r)!\,[n-(n-r)]!} = \dbinom{n}{n-r}$

The number of combinations of a set of n objects taken r at a time is equal to the number of combinations of a set of n objects taken $n - r$ at at time.

29. Each vertex forms a line with any other vertex. Two vertices are needed for each line.

$\dbinom{n}{2} = \dfrac{n!}{2!\,(n-2)!} = \dfrac{n(n-1)}{2}$

Since the figure is an n-gon, n of these lines are sides. The number of diagonals is

$\dfrac{n(n-1)}{2} - n = \dfrac{n(n-1)}{2} - \dfrac{2n}{2} = \dfrac{n(n-3)}{2}$

30. $\dbinom{5}{2}\dbinom{3}{2}\dbinom{2}{2}\dbinom{6}{2}\dbinom{5}{2}\dbinom{8}{2}\dbinom{7}{2}\dbinom{3}{2}\dbinom{2}{2}\dbinom{4}{2}$

$= \dfrac{5! \cdot 3! \cdot 2! \cdot 6! \cdot 5! \cdot 8! \cdot 7! \cdot 3! \cdot 2! \cdot 4!}{2(3!) \cdot 2!\,1! \cdot 2!\,0! \cdot 2!\,4! \cdot 2!\,3! \cdot 2!\,6! \cdot 2!\,5! \cdot 2!\,1! \cdot 2!\,0! \cdot 2!\,2!}$

$= \dfrac{7.2815 \times 10^{18}}{1.5288 \times 10^{11}} = 4.7628 \times 10^7, \text{ or } 47,628,000 \text{ ways}$

31. $3A + B = 3\begin{bmatrix} 2 & 1 & 4 \\ 3 & 0 & 7 \\ 4 & 5 & 6 \end{bmatrix} + \begin{bmatrix} 1 & 1 & 1 \\ 1 & 2 & 2 \\ 2 & 1 & 0 \end{bmatrix}$

$= \begin{bmatrix} 6 & 3 & 12 \\ 9 & 0 & 21 \\ 12 & 15 & 18 \end{bmatrix} + \begin{bmatrix} 1 & 1 & 1 \\ 1 & 2 & 2 \\ 2 & 1 & 0 \end{bmatrix}$

$= \begin{bmatrix} 7 & 4 & 13 \\ 10 & 2 & 23 \\ 14 & 16 & 18 \end{bmatrix}$

32. $|A| = \begin{bmatrix} 2 & 1 & 4 \\ 3 & 0 & 7 \\ 4 & 5 & 6 \end{bmatrix} \rightarrow 2\begin{bmatrix} 0 & 7 \\ 5 & 6 \end{bmatrix} - \begin{bmatrix} 3 & 7 \\ 4 & 6 \end{bmatrix} + 4\begin{bmatrix} 3 & 0 \\ 4 & 5 \end{bmatrix} = 0$

33. $|B| = \begin{bmatrix} 1 & 1 & 1 \\ 1 & 2 & 2 \\ 2 & 1 & 0 \end{bmatrix} \rightarrow \begin{bmatrix} 2 & 2 \\ 1 & 0 \end{bmatrix} - \begin{bmatrix} 1 & 2 \\ 2 & 0 \end{bmatrix} + \begin{bmatrix} 1 & 2 \\ 2 & 1 \end{bmatrix} \rightarrow$

$-2 + 4 - 3 = -1$

34. $B^{-1} = \begin{bmatrix} 1 & 1 & 1 \\ 1 & 2 & 2 \\ 2 & 1 & 0 \end{bmatrix} \left| \begin{array}{ccc} 1 & 0 & 0 \\ 0 & 1 & 0 \\ 0 & 0 & 1 \end{array}\right. \rightarrow$

$\begin{bmatrix} 1 & 1 & 1 \\ 0 & -1 & -1 \\ 0 & -3 & -4 \end{bmatrix} \left| \begin{array}{ccc} 1 & 0 & 0 \\ 1 & -1 & 0 \\ 0 & -2 & 1 \end{array}\right. \rightarrow$

$\begin{bmatrix} 1 & 1 & 1 \\ 0 & -1 & -1 \\ 0 & 0 & -1 \end{bmatrix} \left| \begin{array}{ccc} 1 & 0 & 0 \\ 1 & -1 & 0 \\ -3 & 1 & 1 \end{array}\right. \rightarrow$

$\begin{bmatrix} 1 & 0 & 0 \\ 0 & -1 & -1 \\ 0 & 0 & -1 \end{bmatrix} \left| \begin{array}{ccc} 2 & -1 & 0 \\ 1 & -1 & 0 \\ -3 & 1 & 1 \end{array}\right. \rightarrow$

$\begin{bmatrix} 1 & 0 & 0 \\ 0 & 1 & 0 \\ 0 & 0 & 1 \end{bmatrix} \left| \begin{array}{ccc} 2 & -1 & 0 \\ -4 & 2 & 1 \\ 3 & -1 & -1 \end{array}\right.$

$B^{-1} = \begin{bmatrix} 2 & -1 & 0 \\ -4 & 2 & 1 \\ 3 & -1 & -1 \end{bmatrix}$

35. $BA = \begin{bmatrix} 1 & 1 & 1 \\ 1 & 2 & 2 \\ 2 & 1 & 0 \end{bmatrix}\begin{bmatrix} 2 & 1 & 4 \\ 3 & 0 & 7 \\ 4 & 5 & 6 \end{bmatrix} = \begin{bmatrix} 9 & 6 & 17 \\ 16 & 11 & 30 \\ 7 & 2 & 15 \end{bmatrix}$

36. $AB^{-1} = \begin{bmatrix} 2 & 1 & 4 \\ 3 & 0 & 7 \\ 4 & 5 & 6 \end{bmatrix}\begin{bmatrix} 2 & -1 & 0 \\ -4 & 2 & 1 \\ 3 & -1 & -1 \end{bmatrix} \rightarrow \begin{bmatrix} 12 & -4 & -3 \\ 27 & -10 & -7 \\ 6 & 0 & -1 \end{bmatrix}$

37. $f(x) = x^{2/3}$

$x = f(x)^{2/3}$

$x^3 = f(x)^2$

$x^{3/2} = f(x)$

$x^{3/2} = f^{-1}(x)$

$f^{-1}(x) = x^{3/2}, \ x \geq 0$

38. $f(x) = 3^x$

$x = 3^{f(x)}$

$x = f(x) \log 3$

$f^{-1}(x) = \log_3 x; \ x \geq 0$

39. $f(x) = 3x + \dfrac{3}{2}$

$x = 3f(x) + \dfrac{3}{2}$

$x - \dfrac{3}{2} = 3f(x)$

$\dfrac{1}{3}x - \dfrac{1}{2} = f^{-1}(x)$

40. $|5 + 12i| = \sqrt{25 + 144} = 13$

41. $|6 + 8i| = \sqrt{36 + 64} = 10$

42. $|15 - 8i| = \sqrt{225 + 64} = 17$

43. $|3x + 4| \le 10$
$-10 \le 3x + 4 \le 10$
$-14 \le 3x \le 6$
$-\dfrac{14}{3} \le x \le 2$

44. $|-8x + 9| < 1$
$-1 < -8x + 9 < 1$
$-10 < -8x < -8$
$\dfrac{10}{8} > x > 1$

$1 < x < \dfrac{5}{4}$

45. Perimeter: $2(l + w) = 44$
$l + w = 22$
$l = 22 - w$
Area: $\quad l \cdot w = 120$
$(22 - w)w = 120$
$22w - w^2 = 120$
$-w^2 + 22w - 120 = 0$
$w^2 - 22w + 120 = 0$
$(w - 12)(w - 10) = 0$
$w = 12 \quad \text{or} \quad 10$
12 m, 10 m

pp. 661–662   15-4 TRY THIS

a. $(x - 3)^8$

4th term $= \dbinom{8}{3} x^{8-3}(-3)^3$

$= \dfrac{8 \cdot 7 \cdot 6 \cdot 5!}{5! \cdot 3 \cdot 2} x^5(-3)^3$

$= 56x^5(-27)$
$= -1512x^5$

b. $(y^2 + 2)^{10}$

6th term $= \dbinom{10}{5}(y^2)^{10-5}(2)^5$

$= \dfrac{10 \cdot 9 \cdot 8 \cdot 7 \cdot 6 \cdot 5!}{5! \cdot 5 \cdot 4 \cdot 3 \cdot 2} \cdot y^{10}(32)$

$= 252y^{10}(32)$
$= 8064y^{10}$

c. $(x^2 - 1)^5 = (x^2)^5 + \dbinom{5}{1}(x^2)^4(-1)^1 + \dbinom{5}{2}(x^2)^3(-1)^2$

$+ \dbinom{5}{3}(x^2)^2(-1)^3 + \dbinom{5}{4}(x^2)^1(-1)^4 + \dbinom{5}{5}(x^2)^0(-1)^5$

$= x^{10} + 5(-1)x^8 + 10x^6(1) + 10x^4(-1)$
$+ 5x^2(1) + (-1)$
$= x^{10} - 5x^8 + 10x^6 - 10x^4 + 5x^2 - 1$

d. $\left(2x + \dfrac{1}{4}\right)^4 = (2x)^4 + \dbinom{4}{1}(2x)^3\left(\dfrac{1}{y}\right) + \dbinom{4}{2}(2x)^2\left(\dfrac{1}{y}\right)^2$

$+ \dbinom{4}{3}(2x)^1\left(\dfrac{1}{y}\right)^3 + \dbinom{4}{4}(2x)^0\left(\dfrac{1}{y}\right)^4$

$= 16x^4 + 32\dfrac{x^3}{y} + 24\dfrac{x^2}{y^2} + 8\dfrac{x}{y^3} + \dfrac{1}{y^4}$

e. 2^{50} **f.** 2^{10}

pp. 662–663   15-4 EXERCISES

1. $15a^4b^2$ **2.** $21x^2y^5$ **3.** $-745,472a^3$ **4.** $3,897,234x^2$
5. $-1,959,552u^5v^{10}$ **6.** $30x\sqrt{x}; 30x\sqrt{3}$
7. $m^5 + 5m^4n + 10m^3n^2 + 10m^2n^3 + 5mn^4 + n^5$
8. $a^4 - 4a^3b + 6a^2b^2 - 4ab^3 + b^4$
9. $x^{10} - 15x^8y + 90x^6y^2 - 270x^4y^3 + 405x^2y^4 - 243y^5$
10. $729c^6 - 1458c^5d + 1215c^4d^2 - 540c^3d^3 + 135c^2d^4 - 18cd^5 + d^6$
11. $\dbinom{n}{0} - \dbinom{n}{1} + \dbinom{n}{2} - \dbinom{n}{3} + \cdots + \dbinom{n}{n}(-1)^n$
12. $\dbinom{n}{0} + \dbinom{n}{1}3 + \dbinom{n}{2}9 + \dbinom{n}{3}27 + \cdots + \dbinom{n}{n}3^n$
13. $99 + 70\sqrt{2}$ **14.** $17 - 12\sqrt{2}$ **15.** 128 **16.** 64
17. 2^{26}, or $67,108,864$ **18.** 2^{24}, or $16,777,216$

19. $\dbinom{4}{0}(\sqrt{2})^4 + \dbinom{4}{1}(\sqrt{2})^3(-i)^1 + \dbinom{4}{2}(\sqrt{2})^2(-i)^2$

$+ \dbinom{4}{3}\sqrt{2}(-i)^3 + \dbinom{4}{4}(-i)^4$

$= 1 \cdot 2^2 + 4 \cdot 2\sqrt{2} \cdot (-i) + 6 \cdot 2 \cdot i^2 - 4\sqrt{2}(i^3) + 1(i)^4$
$= 4 - 8\sqrt{2}i + 12(-1) + 4\sqrt{2}i + i^4$
$= 4 - 8\sqrt{2}i - 12 + 4\sqrt{2}i + i$
$= -7 - 4i\sqrt{2}$

20. $\dbinom{6}{0}1 + \dbinom{6}{1}1^5i^1 + \dbinom{6}{2}1^4i^2 + \dbinom{6}{3}1^3i^3 + \dbinom{6}{4}1^2i^4$

$+ \dbinom{6}{5}1i^5 + \dbinom{6}{6}i^6$

$= 1 + 6i + 15i^2 + 20i^3 + 15i^4 + 6i^5 + i^6$
$= 1 + 6i - 15 - 20i + 15 + 6i - 1$
$= \qquad\quad - 8i$

21. $\dbinom{n}{0}a^n + \dbinom{n}{1}a^{n-1}(-b) + \dbinom{n}{2}a^{n-2}(-b)^2 + \cdots + \dbinom{n}{n}a^0(-b)^n$

$= \dbinom{n}{0}a^n - \dbinom{n}{1}a^{n-1}b + \dbinom{n}{2}a^{n-2}b^2 - \cdots + \dbinom{n}{n}(-b)^n(a - b)^n$

$= \sum_{r=0}^{n}\dbinom{n}{r}(-1)^r a^{n-r}b^r$

22. $\dfrac{(x + h)^n - x^n}{h}$

$= \dfrac{\left[\dbinom{n}{0}x^n + \dbinom{n}{1}x^{n-1}h + \cdots + \dbinom{n}{n-1}xh^{n-1} + \dbinom{n}{n}h^n\right] - x^n}{h}$

$= \dfrac{x^n + \dbinom{n}{1}x^{n-1}h + \cdots + \dbinom{n}{n-1}xh^{n-1} + \dbinom{n}{n}h^n - x^n}{h}$

$= \dbinom{n}{1}x^{n-1} + \dbinom{n}{2}x^{n-2}h + \cdots + \dbinom{n}{n-1}xh^{n-2} + \dbinom{n}{n}h^{n-1}$

$= \sum_{r=1}^{n}\dbinom{n}{r}x^{n-r}h^{r-1}$

23. The product $(x + y)(x + y)(x + y) = x^3 + x^2y + x^2y + x^2y$
$+ xy^2 + xy^2 + xy^2 + y^3$.
There are 3 ways to select 1 term of the form x^2y.

24. $\sum_{r=0}^{8}\dbinom{8}{r}x^{8-r}3^r = (x + 3)^8 = 0$

$(x + 3)^8 = 0$
$x + 3 = 0$
$x = -3$

25. $\sum_{r=0}^{4}\dbinom{4}{r}5^{4-r}x^r = (5 + x)^4 = 64$

$(5 + x)^4 = 64$
$5 + x = (8^2)^{1/4}$
$5 + x = 8^{1/2}$
$x = \pm\sqrt{8} - 5$

26. $\sum_{r=0}^{5}\dbinom{5}{r}(-1)^r x^{5-r}3^r = (x - 3)^5 = 32$

$(x - 3)^5 = 32$
$x - 3 = 3$
$x = 5$

27. $\dbinom{n}{r} = \dbinom{n-1}{r-1} + \dbinom{n-1}{r}$

$\dfrac{n!}{r!(n-r)!} = \dfrac{(n-1)!}{(r-1)!(n-1-r+1)!} + \dfrac{(n-1)!}{r!(n-1-r)!}$

$\dfrac{n!}{r!(n-r)!} = \dfrac{(n-1)!}{(r-1)!(n-r)!} + \dfrac{(n-1)!}{r!(n-r-1)!}$

$= \dfrac{(n-1)!(r) + (n-1)!(n-r)}{r!(n-r)!}$

$= \dfrac{(n-1)!(r + n - r)}{r!(n-r)!}$

$= \dfrac{(n-1)!n}{r!(n-r)!}$

$= \dfrac{n \cdot (n-1)!}{r!(n-r)!}$

$$= \frac{n!}{r!\,(n-r)!}$$

28. (A) Check for $n = 1$.

$$(a+b)^1 = \binom{1}{0}a^1 + \binom{1}{1}b^1$$

$$a + b = a + b$$

(B) Assume true for $n = k$.

$$(a+b)^k = \binom{k}{0}a^k + \binom{k}{1}a^{k-1}b$$
$$+ \cdots + \binom{k}{k-1}ab^{k-1} + \binom{k}{k}b^k$$

Show true for $n = k + 1$.

$$(a+b)^k(a+b) = \left[\binom{k}{0}a^k + \binom{k}{1}a^{k-1}b\right.$$
$$\left. + \cdots + \binom{k}{k-1}ab^{k-1} + \binom{k}{k}b^k\right](a+b)$$

$$(a+b)^{k+1} = \binom{k}{0}a^{k+1} + \binom{k}{1}a^k b$$
$$+ \cdots + \binom{k}{k-1}a^2 b^{k-1} + \binom{k}{k}ab^k$$
$$+ \binom{k}{0}a^k b + \binom{k}{1}a^{k-1}b^2$$
$$+ \cdots + \binom{k}{k-1}ab^k + \binom{k}{k}b^{k+1}$$

$$= \binom{k}{0}a^{k+1} + \left[\binom{k}{1} + \binom{k}{0}\right]a^k b$$
$$+ \cdots + \left[\binom{k}{k} + \binom{k}{k-1}\right]ab^k + \binom{k}{k}b^{k+1}$$

$$= \binom{k}{0}a^{k+1} + \binom{k+1}{1}a^k b$$
$$+ \cdots + \binom{k+1}{k}ab^k + \binom{k}{k}b^{k+1}$$

$$= \binom{k+1}{0}a^{k+1} + \binom{k+1}{1}a^k b$$
$$+ \cdots + \binom{k+1}{k}ab^k + \binom{k+1}{k+1}b^{k+1}$$

Note: $\binom{k}{0} = \binom{k+1}{0}$ and $\binom{k}{k} = \binom{k+1}{k+1}$.

Therefore, by A and B the statement

$$(a+b)^n = \binom{n}{0}a^n + \binom{n}{1}a^{n-1}b + \cdots + \binom{n}{n-1}ab^{n-1} + \binom{n}{n}b^n$$

is true for all natural numbers n.

29. $P(x) = x^4 - 8x^3 + 24x^2 - 32x + 16$
Possible roots are $\pm 1, \pm 2, \pm 4, \pm 8, \pm 16$.

30. $P(x) = 0$

2	1	−8	24	−32	16
		2	−12	24	−16
	1	−6	12	−8	0

$P(2) = 0$

No other possible rational roots work.

31. $P(x) = x^4 - 8x^3 + 24x^2 - 32x + 16$

−3	1	−8	24	−32	16
		−3	33	−171	609
	1	−11	57	−203	625

$P(-3) = 625$

−1	1	−8	24	−32	16
		−1	9	−33	65
	1	−9	33	−65	81

$P(-1) = 81$

0	1	−8	24	−32	16
		0	0	0	0
	1	−8	24	−32	16

$P(0) = 16$

2	1	−8	24	−32	16
		2	−12	24	−16
	1	−6	12	−8	0

$P(2) = 0$

30	1	−8	24	−32	16
		30	660	20,520	614,640
	1	22	684	20,488	614,656

$P(30) = 614,656$

32.

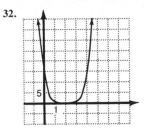

33. $\dfrac{1}{2+2i} \cdot \dfrac{2-2i}{2-2i} = \dfrac{2-2i}{4-4i^2} = \dfrac{2-2i}{4+4} = \dfrac{2(1-i)}{8}$

$$= \frac{1-i}{4} = \frac{1}{4} - \frac{1}{4}i$$

34. $\dfrac{1}{x-2i} \cdot \dfrac{x+2i}{x+2i} - \dfrac{2i}{x^2+4}$

$$= \frac{x+2i}{x^2-4i^2} - \frac{2i}{x^2+4}$$

$$= \frac{x+2i}{x^2+4} - \frac{2i}{x^2+4}$$

$$= \frac{x+2i-2i}{x^2+4}$$

$$= \frac{x}{x^2+4}$$

35. $_{10}P_{10} = 10 \cdot 9 \cdot 8 \cdot 7 \cdots 1 = 3,628,800$

36. $_{69}P_{69} = 69 \cdot 68 \cdot 67 \cdots 1 = 1.71 \times 10^{98}$

37. $x =$ part at 15%
$$x(0.15) + (12,000 - x)(0.09) \geq 1200$$
$$0.15x + 1080 - 0.09x \geq 1200$$
$$0.06x + 1080 \geq 1200$$
$$0.06x \geq 120$$
$$x \geq 2000$$

The most at 9% is $\$10,000$.

p. 663   PROBLEM FOR PROGRAMMERS

```
10   REM   Chapter 15 problem
20   INPUT "For (ax + by)^n; Enter a, b, n ";
     A,B,N
30   FOR J - 0 TO N
40   K = 1
50   IF J = 0 GOTO 120
60   FOR I = 0 TO J - 1
70   K = K * (N - I)
80   NEXT I
90   FOR I = 1 TO J
100  K = K / I
110  NEXT I
120  K = K * A ^ (N - J) * B ^ J
130  IF K = 0 GOTO 190
140  IF J < > 0 AND K > 0 THEN PRINT " + ";
150  IF J < > 0 AND K < 0 THEN PRINT " - ";
160  IF K < > 1 THEN   PRINT ABS (K);
170  IF J < > N THEN   PRINT "x";:
     IF (N - J) > 1 THEN   PRINT "^";N - J;
180  IF J < > 0 THEN   PRINT "Y";: IF J > 1 THEN
     PRINT "^";J;
190  NEXT J
200  IF N = 0 THEN PRINT 1
210  END
```

pp. 664–665   15-5 TRY THIS

a. $P(\text{prime}) = P(2, 3, 5) = \dfrac{3}{6} = \dfrac{1}{2}$

b. $P(\text{getting 3 diamonds}) = \dfrac{\dbinom{13}{3}}{\dbinom{52}{3}}$

$$= \dfrac{\dfrac{13 \cdot 12 \cdot 11 \cdot 10!}{10! \cdot 3 \cdot 2}}{\dfrac{52 \cdot 51 \cdot 50 \cdot 49!}{49! \cdot 3 \cdot 2}} = \dfrac{26 \cdot 11}{26 \cdot 17 \cdot 50} = \dfrac{11}{850}$$

c. 36 outcomes, 6 ways of getting 7

$$P(\text{total of } 7) = \dfrac{6}{36} = \dfrac{1}{6}$$

pp. 665–666   15-5 EXERCISES

1. $\dfrac{1}{4}$ **2.** $\dfrac{1}{13}$ **3.** $\dfrac{1}{13}$ **4.** $\dfrac{1}{4}$ **5.** $\dfrac{1}{2}$ **6.** $\dfrac{1}{2}$ **7.** $\dfrac{2}{13}$

8. $\dfrac{2}{13}$ **9.** $\dfrac{2}{7}$ **10.** $\dfrac{5}{7}$ **11.** 0 **12.** $\dfrac{11}{4165}$ **13.** $\dfrac{11}{4165}$

14. $\dfrac{5}{36}$ **15.** $\dfrac{1}{18}$ **16.** $\dfrac{60}{143}$ **17.** $\dfrac{28}{65}$ **18.** $\dfrac{245}{1938}$ **19.** $\dfrac{30}{323}$

20. $_{52}P_5 = \dfrac{52 \cdot 51 \cdot 50 \cdot 49 \cdot 48 \cdot 47!}{47! \cdot 5 \cdot 4 \cdot 3 \cdot 2} = 2{,}598{,}960$

21. a. $13 \cdot 48 = 624$ **b.** $\dfrac{624}{2{,}598{,}960} = \dfrac{1}{4165}$

22. For any event, the event must either occur or not occur. Thus, $P(A) + P(\text{not } A) = 1$, so $P(A) = 1 - P(\text{not } A)$.

23. a. There are 13 letters from which to choose the one which will be duplicated: $\dbinom{13}{1}$. There are 4 colors from which to choose 2 balls of the same letters: $\dbinom{4}{2}$. There are 12 remaining letters from which to choose 3 different letters for the remaining 3 balls: $\dbinom{12}{3}$. There are 4 colors from which to choose 1 ball of a given letter: $\dbinom{4}{1}$. This last step is done for 3 letters: $\dbinom{4}{1}\dbinom{4}{1}\dbinom{4}{1}$. The number of such 5-ball choices is

$\dbinom{13}{1}\dbinom{4}{2}\dbinom{12}{3}\dbinom{4}{1}\dbinom{4}{1}\dbinom{4}{1}$.

$= \dfrac{13!}{12!} \cdot \dfrac{4!}{2 \cdot 2} \cdot \dfrac{12!}{3! 9!} \cdot \dfrac{4!}{3!} \cdot \dfrac{4!}{3!} \cdot \dfrac{4!}{3!}$

$= 13 \cdot 3 \cdot 2 \cdot \left(\dfrac{12 \cdot 11 \cdot 10}{3 \cdot 2}\right) \cdot 4 \cdot 4 \cdot 4$

$= 13 \cdot 12 \cdot 11 \cdot 10 \cdot 4 \cdot 4 \cdot 4 = 1{,}098{,}240$

b. The probability of this occurring is

$\dfrac{1{,}098{,}240}{2{,}598{,}960} = 0.423$

24. a. $\dbinom{13}{2} = $ number of ways to choose 2 different letters from the 13.

$\dbinom{4}{2} = $ number of ways to choose the same specific letter twice.

$\dbinom{13}{2}\dbinom{4}{2}\dbinom{4}{2} = $ number of ways of choosing two of the same letter and two of a second letter.

$\dbinom{11}{1} = $ number of ways to choose one letter from the remaining 11.

$\dbinom{4}{1} = $ number of ways to choose the same specific letter once.

$\dbinom{11}{1}\dbinom{4}{1} = $ number of ways to choose a fifth different letter after the two pairs have been chosen.

$\dbinom{13}{2}\dbinom{4}{2}\dbinom{4}{2}\dbinom{11}{1}\dbinom{4}{1} = 123{,}552$

b. $\dfrac{123{,}552}{2{,}598{,}960} = 0.048$

25.
$4y = x^2 - 8x + 4$
$4y + 16 = x^2 - 8x + 16 + 4$
$4y + 12 = (x - 4)^2$
$4(y + 3) = (x - 4)^2$
Vertex: $(4, -3)$
Line of symmetry: $x = 4$
Focus: $(4, -2)$
Directrix: $y = -4$

26. $y^2 + 4y + 4 = 16x - 68 + 4$
$(y + 2)^2 = 16(x - 4)$
Vertex: $(4, -2)$
Line of symmetry: $y = -2$
Focus: $(8, -2)$
Directrix: $x = 0$

27. $_{15}P_5 = \dfrac{15 \cdot 14 \cdot 13 \cdot 12 \cdot 11 \cdot 10!}{10!}$
$= 360{,}360$

28. $_8P_4 = \dfrac{8 \cdot 7 \cdot 6 \cdot 5 \cdot 4!}{4!}$
$= 1680$

29. $_9P_3 = \dfrac{9 \cdot 8 \cdot 7 \cdot 6!}{6!}$
$= 504$

30. $_{22}P_2 = \dfrac{22 \cdot 21 \cdot 20!}{20!}$
$= 462$

31. $x = $ amount in A;
$5000 - x = $ amount in B
$0.1x + 0.08(5000 - x) \geq 450$
$0.1x + 400 - 0.08x \geq 450$
$400 + 0.02x \geq 450$
$0.02x \geq 50$
$x \geq \$2500$

$\$2500$

pp. 668–669   15-6 TRY THIS

a. $P(\text{even or divisor of } 10) = \dfrac{3}{6} + \dfrac{3}{6} - \dfrac{1}{6} = \dfrac{5}{6}$

b. $P(\text{ace or red card}) = \dfrac{26}{52} + \dfrac{4}{52} - \dfrac{2}{52} = \dfrac{28}{52} = \dfrac{7}{13}$

c. $P(\text{both heads}) = \dfrac{1}{2} \cdot \dfrac{1}{2} = \dfrac{1}{4}$

d. $P(D \text{ and odd}) = \left(\dfrac{1}{6}\right)\left(\dfrac{3}{6}\right) = \dfrac{1}{12}$

$P(\text{vowel and } 6) = \dfrac{2}{6} \cdot \dfrac{1}{6} = \dfrac{2}{36} = \dfrac{1}{18}$

pp. 670–671   15-6 EXERCISES

1. $\dfrac{15}{22}$ **2.** $\dfrac{17}{22}$ **3.** $\dfrac{6}{11}$ **4.** $\dfrac{5}{6}$ **5.** $\dfrac{1}{2}$ **6.** $\dfrac{5}{6}$ **7.** $\dfrac{2}{3}$

8. 1 **9.** $\dfrac{1}{2}$ **10.** Answers may vary. **11.** $\dfrac{4}{13}$ **12.** $\dfrac{11}{26}$

13. $\dfrac{9}{13}$ **14.** $\dfrac{1}{36}$ **15.** $\dfrac{1}{12}$ **16.** $\dfrac{1}{12}$ **17.** $\dfrac{1}{8}$ **18.** $\dfrac{1}{8}$

19. $\dfrac{5}{24}$ **20.** $\dfrac{1}{3}$

21. $P(\text{first marble red}) = \dfrac{3}{7}$ $P(\text{first marble green}) = \dfrac{4}{7}$

$P(\text{second marble red}) = \dfrac{3}{7} \cdot \dfrac{2}{6} + \dfrac{4}{7} \cdot \dfrac{3}{6} = \dfrac{6}{42} + \dfrac{12}{42} = \dfrac{18}{42} = \dfrac{3}{7}$

22. $P(A \cup \overline{A}) = 1$
$P(A \cap \overline{A}) = 0$

23. $P(\text{correct hats}) = \dfrac{1}{5} \cdot \dfrac{1}{4} \cdot \dfrac{1}{3} \cdot \dfrac{1}{2} \cdot \dfrac{1}{1} = \dfrac{1}{120}$

24. a. $P(\text{yellow or white}) = \dfrac{150 + 100 + 300 + 200}{1000} = \dfrac{750}{1000}$

$\qquad\qquad\qquad\qquad\qquad = 0.75$

b. $P(\text{neither blue nor red}) = \dfrac{300}{1000} = 0.30$

25. $P(\text{poodle or shaggy hair}) = \dfrac{150}{400} + \dfrac{150}{400} - \dfrac{50}{400} = \dfrac{250}{400} = \dfrac{5}{8}$

26.

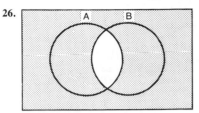

27. Let A = at least one is not a king.
$\quad\ B$ = at least one will be red.
Note: $\overline{A \cup B} = \overline{A} \cap \overline{B}$
$P(A \cup B) = 1 - P(\overline{A \cup B}) = 1 - P(\overline{A} \cap \overline{B})$
$\overline{A}$ = both are kings.
$\overline{B}$ = neither is red.
The probability of drawing a black king on the first draw is

$\dfrac{2}{52} = \dfrac{1}{26}$.

The probability of *then* drawing another black king is $\dfrac{1}{51}$.

$P(A \cap B) = \dfrac{1}{26} \cdot \dfrac{1}{51} = \dfrac{1}{1326}$

Thus $P(A \cup B) = 1 - \dfrac{1}{1326} = \dfrac{1325}{1326}$

28. $\dfrac{1}{11} \cdot \dfrac{1}{10} \cdot \dfrac{1}{9} \cdot \dfrac{2}{8} \cdot \dfrac{1}{7} \cdot \dfrac{1}{6} \cdot \dfrac{2}{5} \cdot \dfrac{1}{4} \cdot \dfrac{1}{3} \cdot \dfrac{1}{2} \cdot 1$

$= \dfrac{4}{39,916,800} = \dfrac{1}{9,979,200}$

29. $\quad A$ = draw a pair of socks in 3 draws.
$\quad P(A) = 1 - P(\overline{A})$

$P(\overline{A}) = \dfrac{6}{7} \cdot \dfrac{4}{6} = \dfrac{4}{7}$

Note:

$P(\text{sock 2 does not match sock 1}) = \dfrac{6}{7}$

$P(\text{if sock 1 and 2 are different, then sock 3 is different}) = \dfrac{4}{6}$

$P(A) = 1 - \dfrac{4}{7} = \dfrac{3}{7}$

30. Sandra has 1 chance out of 15 remaining; $\dfrac{1}{15}$

31. Focus $(-8, -2)$, vertex $(-4, -2)$
$\quad (y - k)^2 = 4p(x - h)$
$\quad\quad (h, k) = (-4, -2)$
$\quad (h + p, k) = (-8, -2) \Rightarrow p = -4$
$\quad (y + 2)^2 = 4(-4)(x + 4)$
$\quad (y + 2)^2 = -16(x + 4)$

32. Focus $(-4, -2)$, vertex $(-4, -3)$
$\quad (x - h)^2 = 4p(y - k)$
$\quad\quad (h, k) = (-4, -3)$
$\quad (h, k + p) = (-4, -2) \Rightarrow p = +1$
$\quad (x + 4)^2 = 4(1)(y + 3)$
$\quad (x + 4)^2 = 4(y + 3)$

33. Vertex $(4, -2)$, containing the point $(5, 2)$
$4p(y + 2) = (x - 4)^2 \qquad 4p(x - 4) = (y + 2)^2$
$4p(2 + 2) = (5 - 4)^2 \qquad 4p(5 - 4) = (2 + 2)^2$
$\qquad 16p = 1 \qquad \text{or} \qquad 4p = 16$

$\qquad p = \dfrac{1}{16} \qquad\qquad\qquad p = 4$

$4\left(\dfrac{1}{16}\right)(y + 2) = (x - 4)^2 \qquad 4(4)(x - 4) = (y + 2)^2$
$\qquad\qquad\qquad\qquad\qquad 16(x - 4) = (y + 2)^2$

$\dfrac{1}{4}(y + 2) = (x - 4)^2$

34. $\quad 4p(y + 3) = (x - 4)^2 \quad$ or $\quad 4p(x - 4) = (y + 3)^2$
$\quad 4p(-2 + 3) = (2 - 4)^2 \qquad\qquad 4p(2 - 4) = (-2 + 3)^2$
$\qquad\quad 4p = 4 \qquad\qquad\qquad\qquad\quad -8p = 1$
$\qquad\qquad p = 1$
$4 \cdot 1(y + 3) = (x - 4)^2 \qquad\qquad\qquad p = -\dfrac{1}{8}$
$\quad 4(y + 3) = (x - 4)^2$

$\qquad\qquad 4\left(-\dfrac{1}{8}\right)(x - 4) = (y + 3)^2$

$\qquad\qquad\qquad -\dfrac{1}{2}(x - 4) = (y + 3)^2$

35. a. $y = \dfrac{1}{2}x \qquad$ **b.** $y = 2x \qquad$ **c.** $y = \dfrac{4}{7}x$
$\qquad\qquad\qquad\qquad\qquad y = mx$
$\quad y = mx \qquad\quad -4 = m(-2) \qquad y = mx$
$\quad 3 = m(6) \qquad\quad 2 = m \qquad\qquad 4 = m \cdot 7$

$\quad \dfrac{1}{2} = m \qquad\qquad\qquad\qquad\qquad\quad \dfrac{4}{7} = m$

---

pp. 673–675 　　15-7 TRY THIS

a. Theoretical probability is $2(.75)(.25) = 0.375$.

b. Theoretical probability is $\dfrac{4!}{2!\,2!}\left(\dfrac{1}{2}\right)^4 = 0.375$.

c. Theoretical probability is 0.625.
d. Theoretical probability is 0.8.

pp. 675–676 　　15-7 EXERCISES

Answers may vary. Theoretical probabilities are given.

1. 0.64　**2.** 0.25　**3.** 0.563　**4.** 0.0625　**5.** 0.313

6. 0.156　**7.** 0.06　**8.** 0.52　**9.** 0.22　**10.** 0.92

11. 0.55　**12.** 0.03　**13.** 0.13　**14.** 0.97　**15.** 0.14

16. 0.40　**17.** 0.0746　**18.** 0.328　**19.** 0.08　**20.** 0.048

21. Answers may vary.　**22.** 2.5　**23.** 0.42

24. 0.08　**25.** 0.083

26. Each set of 10 digits includes all digits. It is unlikely that 5 sets of 10 digits would be randomly generated with no repetitions.

27. 0.34

28. If 5 keys are successfully placed, the 6th must be correct.

29. $\dfrac{(x - 3)(x + 3)}{(x + 3)(x + 3)} \div \dfrac{(x + 7)(x - 3)}{(x - 7)(x + 3)}$

$\dfrac{(x - 3)}{(x + 3)} \times \dfrac{(x - 7)(x + 3)}{(x + 7)(x - 3)} = \dfrac{x - 7}{x + 7}$

30. $a^4 = 7$　　**31.** $e^8 = u$　　**32.** $\log_{14} 196 = 2$

33. $\ln t = t + 1$

p. 677 　　BONUS TOPIC

1. 0.23　**2.** 0.74

3. $(p + (1 - p))^n = \dbinom{n}{0}p^n(1 - p)^0 + \dbinom{n}{1}p^{n-1}(1 - p)^1$

$\quad + \cdots + \dbinom{n}{n}p^0(1 - p)^n$ but $p + (1 - p) = 1$, so

$(p + (1 - p))^n = 1^n = 1$.
Thus, the sum of the terms of the binomial expansion is 1.
The probability of r successes in a sample size n, for $r = 0$ to $r = n$ is 1.

a. ≈0.29   **b.** ≈0.42   **c.** ≈0.08   **d.** ≈0.94

1. 0.64   **2.** 0.13   **3.** 0.38   **4.** 0.05   **5.** 0.52

6. 0.80   **7.** 0.47   **8.** 0.05   **9.** 0.18   **10.** 0.06

11. 0.504   **12.–16.** Answers may vary.

These programs may be used for Exercises 17–19 and 21–24.

17. $P \approx 0.4$

```
10   INPUT "TRIALS? ";T
20   FOR N = 1 TO T
30   FOR I = 1 TO 5
40   LET X =  INT (6 * RND (1))
50   IF X = 0 OR X = 1 THEN  PRINT "R ";
60   IF X = 2 OR X = 3 OR X = 4 THEN  PRINT "B";
70   IF X = 5 THEN  PRINT "Y ";:F = 1
80   NEXT I
90   IF F = 0 THEN  PRINT "SUCCESS";
100  PRINT :F = 0
110  NEXT N
```

18. $P \approx 0.33$

```
10   INPUT "TRIALS? ";T
20   FOR N = 1 TO T
30   FOR I = 1 TO 5
40   LET X =  INT (6 * RND (1))
50   IF X = 0 OR X = 1 THEN  PRINT
     "R ";:F = F + 1
60   IF X = 2 OR X = 3 OR X = 4 THEN
     PRINT "B ";
70   IF X = 5 THEN  PRINT "Y ";
80   NEXT I
90   IF F = 1 THEN  PRINT "SUCCESS";
100  PRINT :F = 0
110  NEXT N
```

19. $P \approx 0.16$

```
10   INPUT "TRIALS? ";T
20   FOR N = 1 TO T
30   FOR I = 1 TO 7
40   LET X =  INT (2 * RND (1))
50   IF X = 0 THEN  LET A$ = A$ + "W"
60   IF X = 1 THEN  LET A$ = A$ + "L"
70   NEXT I
80   PRINT A$;" ";
90   IF A$ = "LLLWWWW" OR A$ = "WWWLLLL" THEN
     PRINT "SUCCESS";
100  PRINT :A$ = ""
110  NEXT N
```

20. $P = 2(0.5)^7 \approx 0.016$

21. $P \approx 0.21$

```
5    DIM A(30)
10   INPUT "TRIALS? ";T
20   FOR N = 1 TO T
30   FOR I = 1 TO 5
40   LET X = INT (30 * RND (1)): IF A(X) = 1
     THEN 40
45   A(X) = 1
50   IF X < 10 THEN  PRINT "R";:R = R + 1
55   IF X > = 10 THEN  PRINT "B";:B = B + 1
70   NEXT I
80   IF R > B THEN  PRINT " SUCCESS";:S = S + 1
100  PRINT  :R = 0:B = 0
105  FOR J = 0 TO 29:A(J) = 0: NEXT J
110  NEXT N
120  PRINT "EXPERIMENTAL PROBABILITY ";S / T
```

22. Any number between 250 and 365; for Feb. 29, between 1000 and 1431.

```
10   INPUT "TRIALS? ";T
12   N = N + 1
```

```
13   IF N > T THEN 40
15   K = K + 1
20   LET X =  INT (365 * RND (1)): IF X = 0 THEN
     PRINT K:S = S + K:K = 0: GOTO 12
30   GOTO 15
40   PRINT "FOUND ";T;" WITH BIRTHDAY AFTER
     ASKING ";S;"PEOPLE"
50   PRINT "AVERAGE ";S / T;" PEOPLE"
```

23. $P \approx 0.33$

```
10   INPUT "TRIALS? ";T
20   FOR N = 1 TO T
30   FOR I = 1 TO 16
40   LET X =  INT (2 *  RND (1))
50   IF X = 0 THEN  PRINT "W";:LS = 0:
     WS = WS + 1: IF WS > LW THEN LW = WS
55   IF X = 1 THEN  PRINT "L";:WS = 0:
     LS = LS + 1: IF LS > LL THEN LL = LS
70   NEXT I
80   IF LW < 4 AND LL < 4 THEN  PRINT "
     SUCCESS";:S = S + 1
100  PRINT :LS = 0:WS = 0:LW = 0:LL = 0
110  NEXT N
120  PRINT "EXPERIMENTAL PROBABILITY ";S / T
```

24. $P \approx 0.57$

```
10   INPUT "TRIALS? ";T
20   FOR N = 1 TO T
30   I = I + 1
40   LET X =  INT (10 *  RND(1))
50   IF (X < = 6 AND X < = 2) OR (X < = 6 AND
     I > = 6) OR (X < = 2 AND I > 2 AND I < 6)
     THEN A$ = A$ + "W": W = W + 1: GOTO 70
55   A$ = A$ + "L":L = L + 1
70   IF W < > 4 AND L < > 4 THEN 30
80   PRINT A$;" ";
90   IF W = 4 THEN PRINT "SUCCESS";:S = S + 1
100  PRINT :A$ = "":L = 0:W = 0:I = 0
110  NEXT N
120  PRINT "EXPERIMENTAL PROBABILITY ";S / T
```

25. $\dfrac{a + 2}{a(a + 3)} \cdot \dfrac{(a - 3)(a - 2)}{(2 - a)(2 + a)} = -\dfrac{1(a - 3)}{a(a + 3)} = \dfrac{3 - a}{a(a + 3)}$

26. $\dfrac{x(x + 3)(8x - 5)}{(x + 3)(x + 4)} \cdot \dfrac{(x + 4)(x + 5)}{(x + 5)(8x - 5)} = x$ **27.** $6^{12/6} = 6^2 = 36$

1. Message   Corrected

0 0 **0** 1 1	0 0 0 1 1
1 0 **0** 1 0	1 0 0 1 0
1 1 0 0 1	1 1 **1** 0 1
0 1 1 0 0	0 1 1 0 0

2.

1 1 **0** 0 0	1 1 0 0 0
0 0 **0** 1 1	0 0 0 1 1
0 1 1 0 1	0 1 **0** 0 1
1 0 **0** 1 0	1 0 0 1 0

3.

0 0 1 0 0	0 **1** 1 0 0
1 1 0 1 1	1 1 0 1 1
1 1 0 1 1	1 1 0 1 1
0 1 1 0 0	0 1 1 0 0

4.

0 0 0 0 **0**	0 0 0 0 0
1 1 0 0 0	1 1 0 0 0
0 0 0 1 **1**	0 0 0 1 1
1 1 0 1 0	1 1 0 1 **1**

5.

1 0 0 0 1	No error
0 1 0 0 1	
1 0 1 0 0	
0 1 1 0 0	

6. $T = 1 - [(0.9)^{20} + 20(0.1)(0.9)^{19}]$
   $\approx 1 - [0.122 + 0.270]$
   $\approx 1 - 0.392$
   ≈ 0.608

7. $T = 1 - [(0.99)^{20} + 20(0.01)(0.99)^{19}]$
$\approx 1 - [0.818 + 0.165]$
$\approx 1 - 0.983$
≈ 0.017

8. $T = 1 - [(0.999)^{20} + 20(0.001)(0.999)^{19}]$
$\approx 1 - [0.98019 + 0.01962]$
$\approx 1 - 0.99981$
≈ 0.00019

9. $T = 1 - [(0.9999)^{20} + 20(0.0001)(0.9999)^{19}]$
$\approx 1 - [0.9980019 + 0.0019962]$
$\approx 1 - 0.9999981$
≈ 0.0000019

10. $T = 1 - [(0.9175)^{20} + 20(0.0825)(0.9175)^{19}]$
$\approx 1 - [0.1787 + 0.3213]$
$\approx 1 - 0.5$
≈ 0.5

11. $T = 1 - [(0.99)^{110} + 110(0.01)(0.99)^{109}]$
$\approx 1 - [0.3310 + 0.3678]$
$\approx 1 - 0.6988$
≈ 0.3012

12. $T = 1 - [(0.95)^{110} + 110(0.05)(0.95)^{109}]$
$\approx 1 - [0.0035 + 0.0205]$
$\approx 1 - 0.024$
≈ 0.976

pp. 685–686   CHAPTER 15 SUMMARY AND REVIEW

1. $3 \cdot 4 \cdot 2 = 24$ **2.** $4 \cdot 3 \cdot 2 \cdot 1 = 24$

3. $6 \cdot 5 \cdot 4 \cdot 3 \cdot 2 \cdot 1 = 720$

4. $8 \cdot 7 \cdot 6 \cdot 5 \cdot 4 \cdot 3 \cdot 2 \cdot 1 = 40{,}320$ **5.** $1! = 1$

6. $0! = 1$ **7.** $14(13!)$ **8.** $\dfrac{7!}{4!} = 5 \cdot 6 \cdot 7 = 210$

9. $\dfrac{10!}{2!} = 3 \cdot 4 \cdot 5 \cdot 6 \cdot 7 \cdot 8 \cdot 9 \cdot 10 = 1{,}814{,}400$

10. $6^4 = 1{,}296$ **11.** $\dfrac{8!}{3!\,2!} = \dfrac{4 \cdot 5 \cdot 6 \cdot 7 \cdot 8}{2} = 3360$

12. $7! = 5040$ **13.** $\binom{15}{5} = \dfrac{15!}{5!\,(10!)} = 3003$

14. $\binom{5}{2} = \dfrac{5!}{2!\,3!} = \dfrac{4 \cdot 5}{2} = 10$ **15.** $\binom{10}{7} = \dfrac{10!}{7!\,3!} = \dfrac{8 \cdot 9 \cdot 10}{6} = 120$

16. $-48{,}384x^5$

17. $32x^5 - 320x^4 + 1280x^3 - 2560x^2 + 2560x - 1024$

18. $2^8 = 256$ **19.** $P(E) = \dfrac{26 \cdot 25}{52 \cdot 51} = \dfrac{25}{102}$

20. The way to get a 5 is $(1, 4)\ (2, 3)\ (3, 2)\ (4, 1)$ or $4\left(\dfrac{1}{6}\right)^2 = \dfrac{1}{9}$.

21. $P(\text{King}) = \dfrac{4}{52} = \dfrac{1}{13}$

$P(\text{heart}) = \dfrac{13}{52} = \dfrac{1}{4}$ $\dfrac{1}{13} + \dfrac{1}{4} - \dfrac{1}{52} = \dfrac{17}{52} - \dfrac{1}{52} = \dfrac{16}{52} = \dfrac{4}{13}$

$P(\text{heart King}) = \dfrac{1}{52}$

22. $P(\text{Green}) = \dfrac{6}{10}$ **23.** 0.65

$\dfrac{6}{10} \cdot \dfrac{6}{10} = \dfrac{9}{25}$

p. 687   CHAPTER 15 TEST

1. $4 \cdot 4 \cdot 2 = 32$ **2.** $5 \cdot 4 \cdot 3 \cdot 2 \cdot 1 = 120$

3. $7! = 5040$ **4.** $0! = 1$ **5.** $11 \cdot 10!$

6. $\dfrac{9!}{5!} = 6 \cdot 7 \cdot 8 \cdot 9 = 3024$

7. $5! = 120$

8. $\dfrac{7!}{2!\,2!} = 1260$

9. $(5 - 1)! = 4! = 24$

10. $\binom{14}{9} = \dfrac{14!}{5!\,9!} = 2002$ **11.** $\binom{8}{3} = \dfrac{8!}{3!\,5!} = 56$

12. $240x^4$ **13.** $81x^4 - 216x^3 + 216x^2 - 96x + 16$

14. $2^6 = 64$ **15.** $\dfrac{13}{52} \cdot \dfrac{12}{51} \cdot \dfrac{11}{50} = \dfrac{11}{850}$

16. The ways to get seven are $(1, 6)\ (2, 5)\ (3, 4)\ (4, 3)\ (5, 2)\ (6, 1)$.

So, $6 \cdot \dfrac{1}{6} \cdot \dfrac{1}{6} = \dfrac{1}{6}$

17. $P(\text{Queen}) = \dfrac{4}{52} = \dfrac{1}{13}$

$P(\text{diamond}) = \dfrac{13}{52} = \dfrac{1}{4}$ $\dfrac{1}{13} + \dfrac{1}{4} - \dfrac{1}{52} = \dfrac{17}{52} - \dfrac{1}{52} = \dfrac{16}{52} = \dfrac{4}{13}$

$P(\text{diamond Queen}) = \dfrac{1}{52}$

18. $P(\text{Red}) = \dfrac{3}{9} = \dfrac{1}{3}$

$\dfrac{1}{3} \cdot \dfrac{1}{3} \cdot \dfrac{1}{3} = \dfrac{1}{27}$

19. 0.25 using 0 and 1

CHAPTER 16

p. 688   READY FOR STATISTICS AND DATA ANALYSIS

1. 0.9609 **2.** 0.7218

3. $6.0934 - 10$ or -3.9066

4. $5.1733 - 10$ or 4.8267

5. 0.6152 **6.** -3.2806

7. 2.4131

8. $\dfrac{1}{2} + \dfrac{2}{2} + \dfrac{3}{2} + \dfrac{4}{2} + \dfrac{5}{2} + \dfrac{6}{2} + \dfrac{7}{2} + \dfrac{8}{2} = 18$

9. $3 + 9 + 27 + 81 + 243 = 363$

10. $-\dfrac{3}{4} - \dfrac{1}{4} + \dfrac{3}{4} + \dfrac{11}{4} = \dfrac{10}{4} = 2.5$

pp. 690–692   16-1 TRY THIS

a.

Stem	Leaf
12	2, 6, 6, 1, 5, 0, 9, 7, 3, 8, 6, 5, 3
13	2, 2, 5, 7, 2, 2, 2, 1
14	3, 8, 5, 3, 8, 4, 3
15	4, 4, 3, 3
16	4, 4
17	3

b.

Stem	Leaf
1	77
2	98, 93, 89
3	89, 09, 91, 93, 12, 85, 31, 38, 54, 21
4	39, 66, 86, 38, 41
5	01
6	65, 11

c.

Interval	Frequency	Rel f
14–15	3	0.08
16–17	2	0.05
18–19	2	0.05
20–21	4	0.11
22–23	5	0.13
24–25	3	0.08
26–27	4	0.11
28–29	2	0.05
30–31	1	0.03
32–33	4	0.11
34–35	3	0.08
36–37	2	0.05
38–39	2	0.05
40–41	1	0.03

pp. 692–693   16-1 EXERCISES

1.

Stem	Leaf
0	0, 4, 3, 2, 6
1	1
2	9, 5, 2
3	5, 4
4	1, 6, 7, 6, 9, 6, 1
5	4, 9, 4
6	0

2.

Stem	Leaf
4	9, 9, 9, 6, 8
5	6, 6, 5, 8, 9, 7, 6, 5, 4, 3, 8, 6
6	3, 1, 0, 3, 0, 8, 5, 7, 3, 1, 4, 4

3.

Stem	Leaf
3	9, 8
4	5, 6, 8, 9, 0, 8, 9, 9
5	5, 6, 9, 6, 9
6	5, 7, 7, 7, 8, 9, 8, 5, 8, 9, 5, 7
7	0, 1, 0, 2, 0

4.

Stem	Leaf
12	5, 5
13	6, 6, 9, 8, 6
14	8, 7, 6, 2, 8
15	8, 2, 4, 6
16	4, 9, 4, 5, 8
17	2, 4, 9, 4, 6, 4
18	3, 9, 5, 9
19	0, 6, 2
20	6, 7
21	5, 2, 3, 5
22	4, 5
23	9, 8
24	
25	4

5.

Interval	Frequency	Rel f
801–900	1	0.025
901–1000	5	0.125
1001–1100	1	0.025
1101–1200	0	0
1201–1300	6	0.15
1301–1400	8	0.2
1401–1500	7	0.175
1501–1600	8	0.2
1601–1700	4	0.1

6.

Interval	Frequency	Rel f
24.6–25.0	2	0.07
25.1–25.5	2	0.07
25.6–26.0	7	0.25
26.1–26.5	2	0.07
26.6–27.0	5	0.18
27.1–27.5	4	0.14
27.6–28.0	4	0.14
28.1–28.5	1	0.04
28.6–29.0	1	0.04

7.

Interval	Frequency	Rel f
9.001–10.000	1	0.03
10.001–11.000	2	0.07
11.001–12.000	6	0.21
12.001–13.000	6	0.21
13.001–14.000	4	0.134
14.001–15.000	0	0
15.001–16.000	2	0.07
16.001–17.000	1	0.03
17.001–18.000	2	0.07
18.001–19.000	1	0.03
19.001–20.000	4	0.134

8.

Interval	Frequency	Rel f
61–65	2	0.05
66–70	7	0.17
71–75	5	0.12
76–80	9	0.21
81–85	1	0.02
86–90	13	0.31
91–95	0	0
96–100	4	0.1
101–105	1	0.02

9. If the diagrams were rotated 90° counterclockwise, it would approximate a bar graph.

10. A stem-and-leaf diagram can be constructed quickly but it is not as informative as a frequency distribution. A frequency distribution takes longer to construct.

11. Scan the tally column until you find the median entry. The average height of the 20 waterfalls is 1900 ft.

12. $P(\text{at least 1500 hours}) = 0.2 + 0.1 = 0.3$

13. $x^2 - 4x - y^2 - 10y = 30$
Center: $(2, -5)$
Vertices: $(-1, -5)$, $(5, -5)$
Foci: $(2 - 3\sqrt{2}, -5)$, $(2 + 3\sqrt{2}, -5)$
Asymptotes: $y + 5 = \pm(x - 2)$
$x^2 - 4x + 2^2 - (y^2 + 10y + 25) = 30 + 4 - 25$
$(x - 2)^2 - (y + 5)^2 = 9$
$$\frac{(x - 2)^2}{9} - \frac{(y + 5)^2}{9} = 1$$

14. $16y^2 + 96y - 25x^2 - 50x = 281$
Center: $(-1, -3)$
Vertices: $(-1, -8)$, $(-1, 2)$
Foci: $(-1, 3 - \sqrt{41})$, $(-1, -3 + \sqrt{41})$
Asymptotes: $y + 3 = \pm\frac{5}{4}(x + 1)$
$16(y^2 + 6y + 9) - 25(x^2 + 2x + 1) = 281 - 25 + 144$
$16(y + 3)^2 - 25(x + 1)^2 = 400$
$$\frac{(y + 3)^2}{25} - \frac{(x + 1)^2}{16} = 1$$

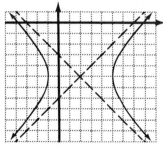

15. MULTIDIMENSIONAL

$$P = \frac{16!}{2!\,2!\,3!\,2!} = \frac{16!}{48} = 4.35891 \times 10^{11}$$

16. NANOSECOND $P = \dfrac{10!}{3!\,2!} = \dfrac{10!}{12} = 302,400$

17. TERRITORIALISM $P = \dfrac{14!}{2!\,3!\,3!} = \dfrac{14!}{72} = 1.2108 \times 10^9$

18. a. $y = \dfrac{m}{x}$ **b.** $y = \dfrac{m}{x}$ **c.** $y = \dfrac{m}{x}$

$3 = \dfrac{m}{6}$ $-4 = \dfrac{m}{-2}$ $4 = \dfrac{m}{7}$

$18 = m$ $8 = m$ $28 = m$

$y = \dfrac{18}{x}$ $y = \dfrac{8}{x}$ $y = \dfrac{28}{x}$

pp. 694–698   16-2 TRY THIS

a. $n = 37 \displaystyle\sum_{i=1}^{37} xi = 7006$ $\bar{x} = \dfrac{7006}{37} = 189.4$ pounds

b. The mode is 78.

c. $\dfrac{29 + 34}{2} = 31.5$

d.
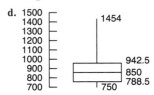

pp. 698–699   16-2 EXERCISES

1. Mean = 831, median = 794, mode = 794

2. Mean = 73.6, median = 74, mode = 74

3. Mean = 99.97, median = 98.7, mode = 98.6

4. Mean = 61.3, median = 54.9, mode = none

5. Mean = 273.6, median = 106, mode = none

6. Mean = 14.1, median = 16, mode = 20

7.

8.
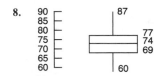

9.
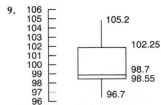

10.
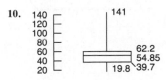

11.
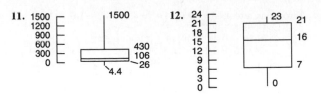

12.

13. Mean: $\displaystyle\sum_{i=1}^{21} x_i = 4519.1$ $\bar{x} = \dfrac{4519.1}{21} = 215.2$

The mean decreases from 273.6 to 215.2 light years.
median: 85
The median decreases from 106 to 85 light years.

14. Answers may vary   **15.** No

16. a. Ex: 1, 5, 6, 6   mean = 4.5   median = 5.5   mode = 6
   b. Ex: 1, 1, 7, 8, 9   mode = 1   mean = 5.2   median = 7
   c. Ex: 1, 2, 3, 9, 9   median = 3   mean = 4.8   mode = 9

17. $\displaystyle\sum_{i=1}^{18} x_i = 3656$ $\bar{x} = 203.1$

Trimming percentage $= \dfrac{4}{22} = 18.2\%$

18. Since it is the only element of this value, the mode will not be affected.

19.
$$x^2 - 2x + 4y^2 - 16y = -13$$
$$x^2 - 2x + 1 + 4(y^2 - 4y + 4) = -13 + 1 + 16$$
$$(x - 1)^2 + 4(y - 2)^2 = 4$$
$$\frac{(x-1)}{4} + \frac{(y-2)^2}{1} = 1$$

$a = 2, b = 1,$
$c = \sqrt{a^2 - b^2} = \sqrt{4 - 1}$
   $= \sqrt{3}$
Center: $(1, 2)$
Vertices: $(3, 2), (-1, 2), (1, 1), (1, 3)$
Foci: $(1 - \sqrt{3}, 2), (1 + \sqrt{3}, 2)$

20.
$$16x^2 - 64x + 25y^2 + 150y = 111$$
$$16(x^2 - 4x + 4) + 25(y^2 + 6y + 9) = 111 + 64 + 225$$
$$16(x - 2)^2 + 25(y + 3)^2 = 400$$
$$\frac{(x-2)^2}{25} + \frac{(y+3)^2}{16} = 1$$

$a = 5, b = 4$
$c = \sqrt{a^2 - b^2}$
   $= \sqrt{25 - 16} = \sqrt{9} = 3$
Center: $(2, -3)$
Vertices: $(7, -3), (-3, -3), (2, 1), (2, -7)$
Foci: $(-1, -3), (5, -3)$

21. $[x - (3 - 2i)][x - (3 + 2i)](x - \sqrt{6})(x + \sqrt{6})$
   $= (x^2 - 3x - 2ix - 3x + 2ix + 13)(x^2 - 6)$
   $= (x^2 - 6x + 13)(x^2 - 6)$
   $= x^4 - 6x^2 - 6x^3 + 36x + 13x^2 - 78$
$f(x) = x^4 - 6x^3 + 7x^2 + 36x - 78$

pp. 700–702   16-3 TRY THIS

a. The highest temperature is 13°C, the lowest temperature is 8°C, so the range is 5°C.

$$\bar{x} = \frac{\displaystyle\sum_{i=1}^{n} x_i}{n} = \frac{71}{7} \approx 10 \cdot 14 \text{ mean}$$

$|10 - 10.14| = 0.14, \ |12 - 10.14|$
       $= 1.86, \ |9 - 10.14| = 1.14$
$|8 - 10.14| = 2.14, \ |13 - 10.14| = 2.86$

$$\frac{\displaystyle\sum_{i=1}^{7} |10.14 - x_i|}{7} = \frac{9.42}{7} \approx 1.3 \text{ mean deviation}$$

b. Deviations are: 13.4, −0.6, 4.4, −8.6, 7.4, −5.6, −15.6, 0.4, 3.4, 13.4, −3.6, −8.6.

$\sigma^2 = (179.56 + 0.36 + 19.36 + 73.96 + 54.76 + 31.36$
$\quad + 243.36 + 0.16 + 11.56 + 179.56 + 12.96 + 73.96)/12$

$= \dfrac{880.92}{12} \approx 73.4$

c. $\sqrt{73.4} \approx 8.57$

pp. 702–703   16-3 EXERCISES

1. Range = 1642,
mean deviation = 537.7,
variance = 366,337.49,
standard deviation = 605.3

2. Range = 8.41,
mean deviation = 2.39,
variance = 8.27,
standard deviation = 2.88

3. Range = 5.9,
mean deviation = 1.68,
variance = 4.01,
standard deviation = 2.00

4. Range = 9.1,
mean deviation = 2.03,
variance = 6.81,
standard deviation = 2.61

5. Range = 34,
mean deviation = 9.9,
variance = 120.4,
standard deviation = 10.97

6. Range = 1.4,
mean deviation = 0.45,
variance = 0.25,
standard deviation = 0.50

7. {20, 22, 30, 36}
mean deviation: 6
standard deviation: 5.74

{20, 22, 30, 1000}
mean deviation: 22
standard deviation: 74.46

The mean deviation is affected less.

8. a. B
b. A
c. cannot be determined
d. B

9. $\sigma^2 = \dfrac{\sum\limits_{i=1}^{n} x_i^2 - \dfrac{\left(\sum\limits_{i=1}^{n} x_i\right)^2}{n}}{n}$

(1) $\sigma^2 = \dfrac{28{,}845{,}891 - \dfrac{(15{,}869)^2}{10}}{10}$

$= 366{,}337.49$

(2) $\sigma^2 = \dfrac{278.233 - \dfrac{2147.3956}{12}}{12}$

≈ 8.27

(3) $\sigma^2 = \dfrac{6425.85 - \dfrac{63{,}857.29}{10}}{10}$

≈ 4.01

(4) $\sigma^2 = \dfrac{364.91 - \dfrac{3398.89}{12}}{12}$

≈ 6.81

(5) $\sigma^2 = \dfrac{1{,}489{,}550 - \dfrac{(4564)^2}{14}}{14}$

≈ 120.4

(6) $\sigma^2 = \dfrac{735.28 - \dfrac{7327.36}{10}}{10}$

≈ 0.25

The variances are the same.

10. $S = \sqrt{\dfrac{\sum\limits_{i=1}^{n} (\overline{x} - x_i)^2}{n - 1}}$

(1) $S = \sqrt{\dfrac{\sum\limits_{i=1}^{10} (1586.9 - x_i)^2}{9}}$

$= \sqrt{\dfrac{\begin{array}{c}(7726.41 + 3191112.01 + 661131.61 \\ + 146765.61 + 586602.81 + \\ 661131.61 + 397026.01 + 194392.81 \\ + 687075.21 + 2410.81)/9\end{array}}{}}$

$= \sqrt{\dfrac{7403284.9}{9}}$

$= \sqrt{822587.21}$

≈ 906.97

(2) $S = \sqrt{\dfrac{\sum\limits_{i=1}^{12} (3.86 - x_i)^2}{11}}$

$= \sqrt{\dfrac{99.2834}{11}}$

≈ 3.00

(3) $S = \sqrt{\dfrac{\sum\limits_{i=1}^{10} (25.27 - x_i)^2}{9}}$

$= \sqrt{\dfrac{40}{9}}$

≈ 2.11

(4) $S = \sqrt{\dfrac{\sum\limits_{i=1}^{12} (4.86 - x_i)^2}{11}}$

$\approx \sqrt{\dfrac{121.69}{11}}$

≈ 3.33

(5) $S = \sqrt{\dfrac{\sum\limits_{i=1}^{14} (326 - x_i)^2}{13}}$

$= \sqrt{\dfrac{1686}{13}}$

≈ 11.39

(6) $S = \sqrt{\dfrac{\sum\limits_{i=1}^{10} (8.56 - x_i)^2}{9}}$

$= \sqrt{\dfrac{2.544}{9}}$

≈ 0.53

The new calculation is higher.

11. $m = \dfrac{2 - (-6)}{4 - (-2)}$

$m = \dfrac{8}{6} = \dfrac{4}{3}$

12. $\sqrt{(-2 - 4)^2 + (-6 - 2)^2}$
$\sqrt{(-6)^2 + (-8)^2}$
$\sqrt{36 + 64} = \sqrt{100} = 10$

13. $\left(\dfrac{-2 + 4}{2}, \dfrac{-6 + 2}{2}\right)$

$\left(\dfrac{2}{2}, -\dfrac{4}{2}\right) = (1, -2)$

p. 703   STATISTICS KEYS

$\overline{x} = 12.25$ $r_n = 8.0428540$

p. 705–707   16-4 TRY THIS

a. 16%   **b.** 84%   **c.** −1.25
d. 2.5   **e.** −0.4   **f.** 0
g. 0.9505   **h.** 0.7580   **i.** 0.0062

j. $p = 0.1056$, ≈ 11 times in 100

1. 34%   **2.** 2.5%   **3.** 81.5%   **4.** 2.50%   **5.** 95%

6. 16%   **7.** 1.7   **8.** 2   **9.** -0.75 **10.** -0.1

11. 0.0367   **12.** 0.0082   **13.** 0.0274   **14.** 0.0075

15. 0.9980   **16.** 0.6664   **17.** 0.0446   **18.** 0.7486

19. 0.2742   **20.** 0.0668   **21.** 1.32   **22.** -2.02

23. -1.25 **24.** -1.97 **25.** 0.35   **26.** 0.15

27. 0.2258   **28.** 0.0793   **29.** 0.2511   **30.** 0.3086

31. 0.9817   **32.** 0.3067   **33.** 0.0990   **34.** 0.5992

35. 0.7745   **36.** 0.6687   **37.** 0.6915   **38.** 0.1151

39. 0.0062   **40.** 0.6171

41. Yes; 4, 5, and 6 are within 1 standard deviation of the mean and account for 66% of the data. 2, 3, 4, 5, 6, 7, and 8 are within 2 standard deviations of the mean and account for 98% of the data. This is close to the normal distribution.

42. 50% of the data lie within x standard deviations of the mean, so 25% lie in each tail. Use table 7 to find the z-value that gives an area of 0.25. $z = -0.67$ gives 0.2514, $z = -0.68$ gives 0.2483. 0.25 is between these values, so $z \approx -0.675$. Half of the data lie between -0.675 and 0.675 standard deviations of the mean, so $x \approx 0.675$.

43. $P(z > 2 \text{ or } z < -2) = 0.0456$. 4.56%

44. a. 5000, 50   **b.** 0.955

45. $(x + 2y)^5 = 1(x)^5 + 5(x)^4(2y) + 10(x)^3(2y)^2 + 10(x)^2(2y)^3$
$\qquad\qquad + 5(x)(2y)^4 + (2y)^5$
$x^5 + 10x^4y + 40x^3y^2 + 80x^2y^3 + 80xy^4 + 32y^5$

46. $\left(y - \dfrac{1}{2}x\right)^4$

$= 1(y)^4 + 4(y)^3\left(-\dfrac{1}{2}x\right) + 6(y)^2\left(-\dfrac{1}{2}x\right)^2 + 4(y)\left(-\dfrac{1}{2}x\right)^3$

$\quad + \left(-\dfrac{1}{2}x\right)^4$

$= y^4 - 2y^3x + \dfrac{3}{2}y^2x^2 - \dfrac{1}{2}yx^3 + \dfrac{1}{16}x^4$

47. $(x - 1)^3 = x^3 - 3x^2 + 3x - 1$

48. $(p + q)^6$ **49.** $(x - 3)^7$

$\dbinom{6}{2}p^4q^2 \quad \dbinom{6}{6}q^6 \qquad \dbinom{7}{2}x^5(-3)^2 \qquad\qquad \dbinom{7}{6}x(-3)^6$

$\dfrac{6 \cdot 5 \cdot 4 \cdot 3 \cdot 2!}{4 \cdot 3 \cdot 2 \cdot ! \cdot 2 \cdot 1} \qquad \dfrac{7 \cdot 6 \cdot 5 \cdot 4 \cdot 3 \cdot 2!}{5! \cdot 2 \cdot 1}x^5(9) \quad \dfrac{7 \cdot 6!}{6!}x(729)$

$\text{3rd} = 15p^4q^2; \qquad 21x^5(9) \qquad\qquad 5103x$
$\text{7th} = q^6 \qquad\qquad \text{3rd} = 189x^5;$
$\qquad\qquad\qquad\qquad\quad \text{7th} = 5103x$

50. $d = mr^2$
$\quad 80 = m(60)^2 \qquad d = \dfrac{1}{45}(75)^2$
$\quad 80 = 3600m$
$\quad \dfrac{8}{360} = \dfrac{1}{45} = m \qquad = \dfrac{1}{45}(5625)$
$\quad 125m \qquad\qquad\qquad = 125$

51. $f(x) = x^4 - x^3 - 21x^2 + 9x + 108$

52. $f(x) = x^4 + 8x^3 + 24x^2 + 32x + 16$

1. a. no   **b–e.** Answers will vary.
   c. Give each person in the community a number. Use the table to select 20 numbers.

d. 1. This is not random, as not all people go to health food stores.
   2. Not random, as not all people have telephones.
   3. Not random, as this interviews people affected by the question.

e. Interview 4000 voters under age 35, 2000 voters aged 35–44, 2000 voters aged 45–54, 1500 voters aged 55–64, and 5000 voters over age 65.

1. Not a random sample because each student at the high school did not have an equal chance of participating.

2. Not a random sample because each person in the community did not have an equal chance to participate.

3. Not a random sample because each student did not have a chance to be selected.

4. Not a random sample because individuals not living in cities did not have an opportunity to participate.

5. Not a random sample because there are 99 possible selections for the first number, 100 for the second, and 101 for the third.

6. Each student could be assigned a number from 1 to 431, then 15 numbers between 1 and 431 could be selected using a random number table or random number generator.

7. The scientist could have given each mouse a number between 1 and 30, then used a random number table to select 5 numbers between 1 and 30.

8. This is only representative of people that read the advice column. It may be biased because not everyone reads the advice column.

9. This is only representative of people that walk past the county court building. This may be biased because not everyone will walk past the building.

10. This could be a representative sample if the survey only concerned owners of personal computers that participated in this network. It could be biased because individuals who spend a lot of time on their computers have a better chance of being selected.

11. This is only representative of individuals who attend wrestling meets.

12. This is only representative of individuals who are involved with cardiac problems. This survey would be biased because people that are in such close contact with cardiac problems will know more about them.

13. This is representative of people who live in densely populated areas. It would be biased because it does not include voters living in rural areas.

14. By giving each student in the school a number, then using either a random number table or a random number generator to choose 20% of the population from each grade.

15. By randomly selecting 33 people from Kent County, 134 people from New Casle County, and 33 from Sussex County.

16. By first dividing the lists of names into lists by political wards, and randomly selecting 24% of the names from the first ward, 33% from the second, 23% from the third, and 20% from the fourth.

17. Assign each of the 20,000 people a number, then use a random number generator to select 12 people.

18. The selection process was representative, random and unbiased.

19. Roosevelt won by a landslide. Poorer people could not afford the luxuries of telephones, clubs, or mail, and many were illiterate. They favored Roosevelt but were not represented in the poll.

20. $(x + 6)(x^2 - 6x + 36)$

21. $(y + 1)^3$

22. $(x + 2)(x^3 + 3x^2 + x - 9)$

23. 4 oz of Happy Trail
   8 oz of Mountain Top Trail

24. $y = 4x^2$

a. We expect 15 sixes. $\chi^2 = \frac{16}{15} + \frac{16}{75} = \frac{96}{75} = 1.28$

b. No, $\chi^2 = 11.58$, which is greater than 9.21, the table value for 3 possible outcomes at the 1% level.

c. $\chi^2 = 11.36$; it is significant at both the 5% and 1% levels. We would conclude that there is a difference between the pairs of lanes at these levels, and reject the null hypothesis.

pp. 718–720   16-6 EXERCISES

1. $\frac{2}{25} = 0.08$ **2.** $\frac{24}{25} = 0.96$

3. $\frac{9441}{80} = 118.0125$ **4.** $\frac{133585}{240} = 556.6$

5. a.

Difference	(Difference)^2	$\dfrac{\text{(Difference)}^2}{\text{Expected}}$
2	4	$\frac{1}{3}$
2	4	$\frac{1}{3}$
−4	16	$\frac{4}{3}$
−6	36	3
−3	9	$\frac{3}{4}$
9	81	$\frac{27}{4}$

$\chi^2 = 12.5$

b.

Difference	(Difference)^2	$\dfrac{\text{(Difference)}^2}{\text{Expected}}$
1	1	$\frac{1}{12}$
−1	1	$\frac{1}{12}$
2	4	$\frac{1}{3}$
4	16	$\frac{4}{3}$
−4	16	$\frac{4}{3}$
−2	4	$\frac{1}{3}$

$\chi^2 = 3.5$

7.

Difference	(Difference)^2	$\dfrac{\text{(Difference)}^2}{\text{Expected}}$
8	64	$\frac{16}{3}$
4	16	$\frac{16}{15}$
0	0	0
3	9	$\frac{3}{7}$
−4	16	$\frac{16}{21}$
−8	64	$\frac{32}{9}$
−1	1	$\frac{1}{15}$
−2	4	$\frac{1}{3}$

$\chi^2 = 11.546$

8.

Difference	(Difference)^2	$\dfrac{\text{(Difference)}^2}{\text{Expected}}$
−3	9	$\frac{9}{5}$
4	16	2
12	144	$\frac{144}{11}$
2	4	$\frac{2}{7}$
−3	9	$\frac{9}{17}$
−12	144	$\frac{36}{5}$

$\chi^2 = 24.906$

9. $\chi^2 = 31.83$; We reject the null hypothesis at the 1% level of significance.

10. $\chi^2 = 24.655$; We reject the null hypothesis.

11. No

12. Same follower expected 5 times.
±1 number expected 10 times.
Others expected 35 times.

13. Small expected values have too much effect on the value of χ^2. We can group the data so that expected values are greater than 5.

14. $\frac{27}{8}$ **15.** $\frac{9}{4}$ **16.** $\frac{3}{2}$

p. 721   PROBLEM SOLVING: APPLICATION

1. Math 2.41, Science 2.27, History 2.77, English 2.58, Social Studies 2.38, Languages 2.60, Total 2.51

2. Chi-square scores are: Math 34.4, Science 4.1, History 51.8, English 43.7, Social Studies 12.3, Languages 12.6, Total 90.3. Grades for Math, History, English, and the total are significantly different from expecteds for any level of significance. Grades for Social Studies and Languages are significant at 2.5% or more. Science grades do not differ from expected values at 10% or more.

3. No, they are not symmetric about the mean.

4. 2.35

5. You could show histograms, give median and mode grades, and break down the data further to see why the grades deviated from expected grades.

6. $r = 1.16$

pp. 722–725   CHAPTER 16 SUMMARY AND REVIEW

1.

Stem	Leaf
4	9
5	3, 0
6	7, 3, 3, 5
7	3, 7, 8, 1, 4, 6, 2, 3, 4, 7, 0, 2
8	2, 0, 1, 0, 0, 0, 3
9	2, 3, 6, 0, 1

2.

Interval	Frequency	Rel f
30–39	14	0.4375
40–49	13	0.40625
50–59	1	0.03125
60–69	3	0.09375
70–79	0	0
80–89	1	0.03125

3. Mean 935, mode 720, median 720

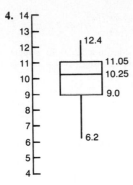

5. $27 - 14 = 13$

6. mean = 111.2, mean deviation = 13.7

7. mean 38.5, variance 195.8

8. mean 256.76, standard deviation 27.8

9. The score of 19 is one standard deviation away from the mean. The percent of students is $100 - 50 - 34 = 16\%$.

10. $\dfrac{90 - 120}{37.5} = -.8$

11. $\dfrac{50,000 - 40,000}{8,000} = 1.25 \quad p(z > 1.25) = 0.1056$

12. No, this is not random because students are not chosen independently.

13. Assign each doctor a number between 1 and 200. Then randomly select five numbers between 1 and 200.

14. Randomly choose 56 freshmen, 72 sophomores, 48 juniors, and 24 seniors.

15.

	Expected	Observed
Winner	200	223
Nonwinner	800	777

$\chi^2 = \dfrac{529}{200} + \dfrac{529}{800} = 3.3063$

16. $3.3063 < 3.84$; accept the null hypothesis

17. $\chi^2 = \dfrac{225}{70} + \dfrac{4}{70} + \dfrac{841}{70} + \dfrac{64}{70} + \dfrac{676}{70} + \dfrac{4}{70} + \dfrac{400}{70} = 31.63$; reject the null hypothesis.

p. 725   CHAPTER 16 TEST

1.

Stem	Leaf
4	0, 3, 4, 4, 7
5	1, 6, 6, 2, 3, 6
6	8, 7, 3
7	0

2.

Interval	Frequency	Rel f
39–41	1	0.07
42–44	3	0.2
45–47	1	0.07
48–50	0	0.0
51–53	3	0.2
54–56	3	0.2
57–59	0	0.0
60–62	0	0.0
63–65	1	0.07
66–68	2	0.13
69–71	1	0.07

3. Mean 54, mode 56, median 53

5. $70 - 40 = 30$

6. 7.73

7. Variance 86.27

8. Standard deviation 9.29

9. 85 is one standard deviation away. Thus, $100 - 50 - 34 = 16\%$ of the students will get A's.

10. $\dfrac{29 - 31}{1.25} = -1.6$

11. $\dfrac{38 - 40}{1.6} = -1.25 \quad p(x < -1.25) = 0.1056$

12. This is not a random sample because each person in the population (individuals that own Leopard XX cars) does not have an equal chance of being selected.

13. Assign all the athletes a number, then randomly select 25 numbers.

14. Select 54 students from Martin Luther King High, 37 from Wayne High, and 59 from Jordan High.

15.

	Expected	Observed
big prize	20	29
no prize	40	31

$\chi^2 = \dfrac{81}{20} + \dfrac{81}{40} = 6.075$

16. $6.075 > 3.84$; we reject the null hypothesis.

17. $\chi^2 = \dfrac{361}{150} + \dfrac{1225}{150} + \dfrac{484}{150} + \dfrac{1444}{150} = 23.4$

$\chi^2 > 11.3$; reject the null hypothesis.

CHAPTER 17

p. 726   READY FOR TRIGONOMETRIC FUNCTIONS?

1. 19, 9   **2.** $3t^2 - 10t - 8$ **3.** $24(a - 2b)(a + 2b)$

4. $3xy(x - 3y)(x - 2y)$ **5.** $\dfrac{a + 2}{-2}$ **6.** $\dfrac{2}{x}$

7. $\dfrac{-2c^2 + c + 7cd - d}{(2c + 1)(2c - 1)}$ **8.** $3, -4$ **9.** $\dfrac{2}{3}, -4$

10. $x = \dfrac{1 \pm i\sqrt{11}}{2}$ **11.** $x = \dfrac{-1 \pm \sqrt{5}}{2}$

12. $f(-x) = (-x)^3 - (-x) = -x^3 + x = -(x^3 - x) = -f(x)$

13. $g(-x) = 2(-x)^2 - (-x)^4 = 2x^2 - x^4 = g(x)$

pp.729–731   17-1 TRY THIS

a. $\sin \theta = \dfrac{\text{side opposite } \theta}{\text{hypotenuse}} = \dfrac{4}{5}$

$\cos \theta = \dfrac{\text{side adjacent to } \theta}{\text{hypotenuse}} = \dfrac{3}{5}$

$\tan \theta = \dfrac{\text{side opposite } \theta}{\text{side adjacent to } \theta} = \dfrac{4}{3}$

b. $\cos P = \dfrac{q}{r}$

$\cos 45 = \dfrac{12}{r}$ substituting

$\dfrac{\sqrt{2}}{2} = \dfrac{12}{r}$ using $\cos 45 = \dfrac{\sqrt{2}}{2}$

$r = 12\sqrt{2}$ ft

c. $\cot \theta = \dfrac{\text{side adjacent to } \theta}{\text{side opposite } \theta} = \dfrac{4}{3} \approx 1.33$

$\sec \theta = \dfrac{\text{hypotenuse}}{\text{side adjacent to } \theta} = \dfrac{5}{4} = 1.25$

$\csc \theta = \dfrac{\text{hypotenuse}}{\text{side opposite } \theta} = \dfrac{5}{3} \approx 1.67$

d. $\dfrac{\text{side adjacent to } \theta}{\text{hypotenuse}} = \dfrac{8}{17}$

$8^2 + b^2 = 17^2$
$b^2 = 289 - 64$
$b^2 = 225$
$b = \pm 15$

We choose the positive square root since we are finding length. We use $a = 8$, $b = 15$, and $c = 17$ to find the five other ratios in the triangle.

$\sin \theta = \dfrac{15}{17}$ $\csc \theta = \dfrac{17}{15}$

$\cos \theta = \dfrac{8}{17}$ $\sec \theta = \dfrac{17}{8}$

$\tan \theta = \dfrac{15}{8}$ $\cot \theta = \dfrac{8}{15}$

pp. 732–733   **17-1 EXERCISES**

1. $\sin \theta = \dfrac{7}{25}$, $\cos \theta = \dfrac{24}{25}$, $\tan \theta = \dfrac{7}{24}$

2. $\sin \theta = \dfrac{24}{25}$, $\cos \theta = \dfrac{7}{25}$, $\tan \theta = \dfrac{24}{7}$

3. $\sin \theta = \dfrac{8}{17}$, $\cos \theta = \dfrac{15}{17}$, $\tan \theta = \dfrac{8}{15}$

4. $\sin \theta = \dfrac{15}{17}$, $\cos \theta = \dfrac{8}{17}$, $\tan \theta = \dfrac{15}{8}$

5. $a = 3$ **6.** $b = 9\sqrt{3}$ **7.** $b = 2$ **8.** $c = 3\sqrt{2}$

9. $\cot \theta = \dfrac{27}{7} \approx 3.43$; $\sec \theta = \dfrac{25}{24} \approx 1.04$; $\csc \theta = \dfrac{25}{7} \approx 3.57$

10. $\cot \theta = \dfrac{7}{24} \approx 0.29$; $\sec \theta = \dfrac{25}{7} \approx 3.57$; $\csc \theta = \dfrac{25}{24} \approx 1.04$

11. $\cot \theta = \dfrac{15}{8} \approx 1.88$; $\sec \theta = \dfrac{17}{15} \approx 1.13$; $\csc \theta = \dfrac{17}{8} \approx 2.13$

12. $\cot \theta = \dfrac{12}{5} = 2.4$; $\sec \theta = \dfrac{13}{12} \approx 1.08$; $\csc \theta = \dfrac{13}{5} = 2.6$

13. $\sin \theta = \dfrac{\sqrt{3}}{2}$; $\cos \theta = \dfrac{1}{2}$; $\cot \theta = \dfrac{\sqrt{3}}{3}$; $\sec \theta = 2$; $\csc \theta = \dfrac{2\sqrt{3}}{3}$

14. $\sin \theta = \dfrac{\sqrt{2}}{2}$; $\tan \theta = 1$; $\cot \theta = 1$; $\sec \theta = \sqrt{2}$; $\csc \theta = \sqrt{2}$

15. $\cos \theta = \dfrac{\sqrt{3}}{2}$; $\tan \theta = \dfrac{\sqrt{3}}{3}$; $\cot \theta = \sqrt{3}$; $\sec \theta = \dfrac{2\sqrt{3}}{3}$; $\csc \theta = 2$

16. $\sin \theta = \dfrac{\sqrt{3}}{2}$; $\cos \theta = \dfrac{1}{2}$; $\tan \theta = \sqrt{3}$; $\cot \theta = \dfrac{\sqrt{3}}{3}$; $\csc \theta = \dfrac{2\sqrt{3}}{3}$

17. A 30-60-90 triangle will have, with respect to the 30° angle, sides in these ratios: opposite side 1, adjacent side $\sqrt{3}$, hypotenuse 2. If $\theta = 30°$, then

$\sin \theta = \dfrac{1}{2}$ $\cos \theta = \dfrac{\sqrt{3}}{2}$ $\tan \theta = \dfrac{1}{\sqrt{3}} = \dfrac{\sqrt{3}}{3}$

$\cot \theta = \dfrac{\sqrt{3}}{1} = \sqrt{3}$ $\sec \theta = \dfrac{2}{\sqrt{3}} = \dfrac{2\sqrt{3}}{3}$ $\csc \theta = \dfrac{2}{1} = 2$

18. A 60° angle is associated with these sides in a 30-60-90 triangle: opposite side $\sqrt{3}$, adjacent side 1, hypotenuse 2. If $\theta = 60°$, then

$\sin \theta = \dfrac{\sqrt{3}}{2}$ $\cos \theta = \dfrac{1}{2}$ $\tan \theta = \dfrac{\sqrt{3}}{1} = \sqrt{3}$

$\cot \theta = \dfrac{1}{\sqrt{3}} = \dfrac{\sqrt{3}}{3}$ $\sec \theta = \dfrac{2}{1} = 2$ $\csc \theta = \dfrac{2}{\sqrt{3}} = \dfrac{2\sqrt{3}}{3}$

19. A 45-45-90 triangle has sides in the following ratios: hypotenuse $\sqrt{2}$, legs 1. If $\theta = 45°$ then

$\sin \theta = \dfrac{1}{\sqrt{2}} = \dfrac{\sqrt{2}}{2}$ $\cos \theta = \dfrac{\sqrt{2}}{2}$ $\tan \theta = 1$

$\cot \theta = 1$ $\sec \theta = \dfrac{\sqrt{2}}{1} = \sqrt{2}$ $\csc \theta = \sqrt{2}$

20. $\dfrac{\sin \theta}{\cos \theta} = \dfrac{\text{opposite}}{\text{hypotenuse}} \div \dfrac{\text{adjacent}}{\text{hypotenuse}}$

$\phantom{\dfrac{\sin \theta}{\cos \theta}} = \dfrac{\text{opposite}}{\text{hypotenuse}} \cdot \dfrac{\text{hypotenuse}}{\text{adjacent}}$

$\phantom{\dfrac{\sin \theta}{\cos \theta}} = \dfrac{\text{opposite}}{\text{adjacent}} = \tan \theta$

21. **a.** $\cot 60° = \dfrac{b}{28}$ **b.** $\csc 60° = \dfrac{x}{28}$

$\dfrac{\sqrt{3}}{3} = \dfrac{b}{28}$ $\dfrac{2\sqrt{3}}{3} = \dfrac{x}{28}$

$b = \dfrac{28\sqrt{3}}{3}$ ft $x = \dfrac{56\sqrt{3}}{3}$ ft

22. Let H = height of tree.

$\tan 30° = \dfrac{H}{120}$

$H = 120 \tan 30° = 120\left(\dfrac{\sqrt{3}}{3}\right)$

$H = 40\sqrt{3}$ m

23. Draw the altitude, from a to the 120° angle. The two triangles formed are 30-60-90 triangles with the length of the hypotenuse = 5 and the length of the side opposite the 60° angle = $\dfrac{a}{2}$. Then

$\sin 60° = \dfrac{\left(\dfrac{a}{2}\right)}{5} = \dfrac{a}{10}$

$a = 10 \sin 60° = 10\left(\dfrac{\sqrt{3}}{2}\right)$

$a = 5\sqrt{3}$

24. $\sqrt[3]{16x^4} \cdot \sqrt[3]{256x^6 y^6} = \sqrt[3]{16^3 x^{10} y^6} = 16x^3 y^2 \sqrt[3]{x}$

25. $5\sqrt{13} - 18\sqrt[4]{7} + 8\sqrt{13} + 11\sqrt[4]{7}$
$= (5\sqrt{13} + 8\sqrt{13}) + (-18\sqrt[4]{7} + 11\sqrt[4]{7})$
$= 13\sqrt{13} - 7\sqrt[4]{7}$

26. $\dfrac{\sqrt{b}}{\sqrt{b} + \sqrt{a}}\left(\dfrac{1}{b + \sqrt{ab}}\right)^{-1} = \dfrac{\sqrt{b}}{\sqrt{b} + \sqrt{a}}(b + \sqrt{ab})$

$= \dfrac{\sqrt{b}(\sqrt{b} - \sqrt{a})}{(\sqrt{b} + \sqrt{a})(\sqrt{b} - \sqrt{a})} \cdot (b + \sqrt{ab})$

$= \dfrac{(b - \sqrt{ab})(b + \sqrt{ab})}{b - a} = \dfrac{b^2 - ab}{b - a} = \dfrac{b(b - a)}{b - a} = b$

27. $a^{2/5} b^{3/4} = a^{8/20} b^{15/20} = (a^8 b^{15})^{1/20} = \sqrt[20]{a^8 b^{15}}$

28. $b^{-3/4} c = c\left(\dfrac{1}{b}\right)^{3/4} = \sqrt[4]{\dfrac{c^4}{b^3}} = c\sqrt[4]{\dfrac{1}{b^3} \cdot \dfrac{b}{b}} = \dfrac{c}{b}\sqrt[4]{b}$

29. $(4096)^{1/3}(4096)^{1/4} = (2^{12})^{1/3} \cdot (2^{12})^{1/4} = 2^4 \cdot 2^3 = 128$

30. $\log_{10} 10^4 = 4$ **31.** $3^{\log_3 \pi} = \pi$

32. Let x = time to fill the tank.

$$\frac{x}{6} + \frac{x}{4} = 1$$
$$4x + 6x = 24$$
$$10x = 24$$
$$x = 2\frac{2}{5} \text{ hours}$$

pp. 734–739   17-2 TRY THIS

a. first quadrant   **b.** third quadrant
c. fourth quadrant   **d.** third quadrant
e. $365 - 360 = 5°$, first quadrant
f. $740 - 360 = 380$, $380 - 360 = 20°$; first quadrant

g. $\sin \theta = -\frac{1}{2}$

$\cos \theta = \frac{\sqrt{3}}{2}$

$\tan \theta = -\frac{1}{\sqrt{3}} = -\frac{\sqrt{3}}{3}$

h. For $-30°$ angle the terminal side lies in the fourth quadrant. Thus the cosine and secant values are positive; the other four function values are negative.

i. $\sin 180° = \frac{y}{r} = \frac{0}{r} = 0$ $\sin 270° = \frac{-y}{r} = \frac{-r}{r} = -1$

$\cos 180° = \frac{-x}{r} = \frac{r}{r} = -1$ $\cos 270° = \frac{x}{r} = \frac{0}{r} = 0$

$\tan 180° = \frac{y}{-x} = \frac{0}{-r} = 0$ $\tan 270° = \frac{-y}{x} = \frac{-r}{0}$ Undefined

j. $360° - 330° = 30°$
k. $180° - 150° = 30°$
l. $2370° = 6(360°) + 210°$
$210° - 180° = 30°$
The terminal side of $2370°$ angle is in the third quadrant. Thus, the tangent is positive, and the sine and cosine are negative. The reference angle is $30°$.

$\sin 2370° = -\frac{1}{2}$

$\cos 2370° = -\frac{\sqrt{3}}{2}$

$\tan 2370° = \frac{\sqrt{3}}{3}$

m. $-765° + 2(360°) = -45°$
An angle of $-765°$ has its terminal side in the fourth quadrant. Thus, the cosine is positive, and the sine and tangent are negative. The reference angle for $-45°$ is $45°$.

$\sin -765° = -\frac{\sqrt{2}}{2}$

$\cos -765° = \frac{\sqrt{2}}{2}$

$\tan -765° = -1$

n. $-2340 + 6(360) = -180$
An angle of $-2340°$ has the same terminal side as a $180°$ angle.
$\sin -2340° = 0$
$\cos -2340° = -1$
$\tan -2340° = 0$

pp. 739–740   17-2 EXERCISES

1. First   **2.** Fourth   **3.** Third   **4.** Third   **5.** First
6. Third   **7.** Second   **8.** Second   **9.** Second
10. Third   **11.** Fourth   **12.** Second

13. $\sin \theta = -\frac{3}{5}$; $\cos \theta = -\frac{4}{5}$; $\tan \theta = \frac{3}{4}$

14. $\sin \theta = \frac{5}{13}$; $\cos \theta = -\frac{12}{13}$; $\tan \theta = -\frac{5}{12}$

15. $\sin \theta = -\frac{3}{5}$; $\cos \theta = \frac{4}{5}$; $\tan \theta = -\frac{3}{4}$

16. $\sin \theta = -\frac{\sqrt{2}}{2}$; $\cos \theta = -\frac{\sqrt{2}}{2}$; $\tan \theta = 1$

17. $\sin \theta = \frac{\sqrt{3}}{2}$; $\cos \theta = \frac{-1}{2}$; $\tan \theta = -\sqrt{3}$

18. $\sin \theta = -\frac{1}{2}$; $\cos \theta = \frac{\sqrt{3}}{2}$; $\tan \theta = \frac{-\sqrt{3}}{3}$

19. All function values are positive.

20. Cosine and secant values are positive, the other four function values are negative.

21. Cosine and secant values are positive, the other four function values are negative.

22. Tangent and cotangent values are positive, the other four function values are negative.

23. All function values are positive.

24. Sine and cosecant values are positive, the other four function values are negative.

25.

θ	cot θ	sec θ	csc θ
0	undefined	1	undefined
90°	0	undefined	1
180°	undefined	−1	undefined
270°	0	undefined	−1

26. 45°   **27.** 30°   **28.** 60°   **29.** 45°   **30.** 60°   **31.** 45°
32. −1   **33.** 0   **34.** Undefined   **35.** Undefined   **36.** 1
37. Undefined   **38.** $-\frac{\sqrt{2}}{2}$ **39.** $-\frac{\sqrt{2}}{2}$ **40.** $\frac{1}{2}$ **41.** $-\frac{\sqrt{3}}{2}$
42. $\sqrt{3}$ **43.** $\frac{\sqrt{3}}{3}$ **44.** $\sqrt{2}$ **45.** $-\sqrt{2}$ **46.** 1   **47.** 1
48. $\frac{1}{2}, -\frac{\sqrt{3}}{2}, -\frac{\sqrt{3}}{3}$ **49.** $-\frac{\sqrt{3}}{2}, -\frac{1}{2}, \sqrt{3}$
50. $-\frac{\sqrt{2}}{2}, -\frac{\sqrt{2}}{2}, 1$ **51.** 0, −1, 0   **52.** 0, 1, 0

53. $\sin 30° = \frac{1}{2} = 0.5$ $\cos 30° = \frac{\sqrt{3}}{2} \approx 0.866$

$\tan 30° = \frac{1}{\sqrt{3}} \approx 0.577$ $\cot 30° = \sqrt{3} \approx 1.732$

$\csc 30° = \frac{2}{1} = 2$

$\sec 30° = \frac{2}{\sqrt{3}} \approx 1.155$

54. $\sin 60° = \frac{\sqrt{3}}{2} \approx 0.866$ $\cos 60° = \frac{1}{2} = 0.5$

$\tan 60° = \frac{\sqrt{3}}{1} \approx 1.732$ $\cot 60° = \frac{1}{\sqrt{3}} \approx 0.577$

$\sec 60° = \frac{2}{1} = 2$ $\csc 60° = \frac{2}{\sqrt{3}} \approx 1.155$

55. $\sin 120° = \frac{\sqrt{3}}{2} \approx 0.866$ $\cos 120° = -\frac{1}{2} = -0.5$

$\tan 120° = \frac{\sqrt{3}}{-1} \approx -1.732$ $\cot 120° = \frac{-1}{\sqrt{3}} \approx -0.577$

$\sec 120° = \frac{2}{-1} = -2$ $\csc 120° = \frac{2}{\sqrt{3}} \approx 1.155$

56. $\sin 225° = \frac{-1}{\sqrt{2}} \approx -0.707$ $\cos 225° = \frac{-1}{\sqrt{2}} \approx -0.707$

$\tan 225° = \frac{-1}{-1} = 1$ $\cot 225° = \frac{-1}{-1} = 1$

$\sec 225° = \frac{\sqrt{2}}{-1} \approx -1.414$ $\csc 225° = \frac{\sqrt{2}}{-1} \approx -1.414$

57. $\sin -1020° = \sin 60° = \dfrac{\sqrt{3}}{2} = 0.866;$

$\cos -1020° = \cos 60° = \dfrac{1}{2} = 0.500;$

$\tan -1020° = \tan 60° = \sqrt{3} = 1.732;$

$\cot -1020° = \cot 60° = \dfrac{\sqrt{3}}{3} = 0.577;$

$\sec -1020° = \sec 60° = 2 = 2.000;$

$\csc -1020° = \csc 60° = \dfrac{2\sqrt{3}}{3} = 1.155;$

58. $\sin 2295° = \sin 45° \approx 0.707;$
$\cos 2295° = -\cos 45° \approx -0.707$
$\tan 2295° = -\tan 45° = -1;\ \cot 2295° = -\cot 45° = -1$
$\sec 2295° = -\sec 45° \approx -1.414;$
$\csc 2295° = \csc 45° \approx 1.414$

59. $\sin \theta = -\dfrac{8}{17} \qquad \csc \theta = -\dfrac{17}{8}$

$\cos \theta = -\dfrac{15}{17} \qquad \sec \theta = -\dfrac{17}{15}$

$\tan \theta = \dfrac{-8}{-15} = \dfrac{8}{15} \qquad \cot \theta = \dfrac{-15}{-8} = \dfrac{15}{8}$

60. $\sin \theta = \dfrac{4}{7} \qquad\qquad \csc \theta = \dfrac{7}{4}$

$\cos \theta = -\dfrac{\sqrt{33}}{7} \qquad \sec \theta = -\dfrac{7}{\sqrt{33}} = -\dfrac{7\sqrt{33}}{33}$

$\tan \theta = -\dfrac{4}{\sqrt{33}} = -\dfrac{4\sqrt{33}}{33} \qquad \cot \theta = -\dfrac{\sqrt{33}}{4}$

61. $\sin \theta = -\dfrac{15}{39} = -\dfrac{5}{13} \qquad \csc \theta = -\dfrac{13}{5}$

$\cos \theta = \dfrac{36}{39} = \dfrac{12}{13} \qquad \sec \theta = \dfrac{13}{12}$

$\tan \theta = -\dfrac{15}{36} = -\dfrac{5}{12} \qquad \cot \theta = -\dfrac{12}{5}$

62. $\tan \theta = \dfrac{2}{\sqrt{5}}$. Since the terminal side is in quadrant III,

$\tan \theta = \dfrac{-2a}{-\sqrt{5}\,a}$ where a is a positive constant. The

hypotenuse is then
$$\sqrt{(-\sqrt{5}\,a)^2 + (-2a)^2} = \sqrt{5a^2 + 4a^2} = \sqrt{9a^2} = 3a$$

$\sin \theta = \dfrac{-2a}{3a} = -\dfrac{2}{3}$

$\cos \theta = \dfrac{-\sqrt{5}\,a}{3a} = -\dfrac{\sqrt{5}}{3} \qquad \cot \theta = \dfrac{-\sqrt{5}\,a}{-2a} = \dfrac{\sqrt{5}}{2}$

$\sec \theta = \dfrac{3a}{-\sqrt{5}\,a} = -\dfrac{3}{\sqrt{5}} = -\dfrac{3\sqrt{5}}{5}$

$\csc \theta = \dfrac{3a}{-2a} = -\dfrac{3}{2}$

63. The valve cap and center are on a line parallel to the ground, 26″ above the ground. After rotating 390°, or 360° + 30°, the cap is 30° above that line, forming a 30-60-90 triangle with the center and its former position. The hypotenuse is 24.5″, $\sin 30° = \dfrac{1}{2}$ so the vertical distance to the line is $\dfrac{1}{2}(24.5)$, or 12.25″. The distance to the ground is then $12.25 + 26 = 38.25″$.

64. $x^2 + (-y)^2 = 36$ **65.** $x(-y) = 25$
     $x^2 + y^2 = 36$ $-xy = 25$
   Yes   No

66. $\log_9 x = \dfrac{3}{2}$ **67.** $x^2 = \dfrac{1}{25}$

     $x = 9^{3/2}$ $x = \pm\dfrac{1}{5}$
     $x = 27$

68.
$$x^4 = 625$$
$$x^4 - 625 = 0$$
$$(x^2 - 25)(x^2 + 25) = 0$$
$$x^2 = 25 \quad\text{or}\quad x^2 = -25$$
$$x = \pm 5 \quad\text{or}\quad x = \pm 5i$$

69. $P(\text{red or king}) = P(\text{red}) + P(\text{king}) - P(\text{red and king})$
$$= \dfrac{26}{52} + \dfrac{4}{52} - \dfrac{2}{52} = \dfrac{7}{13}$$

70. $P(\text{spade or ace}) = P(\text{spade}) + P(\text{ace}) - P(\text{spade and ace})$
$$= \dfrac{13}{52} + \dfrac{4}{52} - \dfrac{1}{52} = \dfrac{4}{13}$$

71. $P(\text{club or face}) = P(\text{club}) + P(\text{face}) - P(\text{club and face})$
$$= \dfrac{13}{52} + \dfrac{12}{52} - \dfrac{3}{52} = \dfrac{11}{26}$$

72. Let x = rate in still water.
$$\dfrac{90}{r+3} = \dfrac{60}{r-3}$$
$$90r - 270 = 60r + 180$$
$$30r = 450$$
$$r = 15 \text{ mi/h}$$

pp. 741–746   **17-3 TRY THIS**

a. $225° = 225° \cdot \dfrac{\pi \text{ radians}}{180°}$

$= \dfrac{225°}{180°}\pi \text{ radians}$

$= \dfrac{5}{4}\pi \text{ radians}$

b. $300° = 300° \cdot \dfrac{\pi \text{ radians}}{180°}$

$= \dfrac{300°}{180°} \cdot \pi \text{ radians}$

$= \dfrac{5}{3}\pi \text{ radians}$

c. $-315° = -315° \cdot \dfrac{\pi}{180°}$

$= -\dfrac{315°}{180°} \cdot \pi$

$= -\dfrac{7}{4}\pi \text{ radians}$

d. $\dfrac{4\pi}{3} \text{ radians} = \dfrac{4\pi}{3} \text{ radians} \cdot \dfrac{180°}{\pi \text{ radians}}$

$= \dfrac{4\pi}{3\pi} \cdot 180°$

$= 240°$

e. $\dfrac{5\pi}{2} \text{ radians} = \dfrac{5\pi}{2} \text{ radians} \cdot \dfrac{180°}{\pi \text{ radians}}$

$= \dfrac{5\pi}{2\pi} \cdot 180°$

$= 450°$

f. $-\dfrac{4\pi}{5} \text{ radians} = -\dfrac{4\pi}{5} \text{ radians} \cdot \dfrac{180°}{\pi \text{ radians}}$

$= -\dfrac{4\pi}{5\pi} \cdot 180°$

$= -144°$

g. $s = r\theta = 10 \text{ cm} \cdot \dfrac{11\pi}{6} \approx 57.6 \text{ cm}$

h. $\theta = \dfrac{s}{r} = \dfrac{15 \text{ cm}}{2.5 \text{ cm}} = 6 \text{ radians}$

i. $\sec 60° = \csc(90° - 60°) = \csc 30° = \dfrac{1}{\sin 30°} = \dfrac{1}{\frac{1}{2}} = 2$

j. $\cot 30° = \tan(90° - 30°) = \tan 60° = \sqrt{3}$

k. $\csc 45° = \sec(90° - 45°) = \sec 45° = \dfrac{1}{\cos 45°}$

$= \dfrac{1}{\frac{\sqrt{2}}{2}} = \sqrt{2}$

l. $d = 12$ cm $\omega = \dfrac{2\pi(10)}{\sec} = \dfrac{20\pi}{\sec}$

$r = 6$ cm
$v = r\omega$

$= 6 \text{ cm} \cdot \dfrac{20\pi}{\sec}$

$\approx 6 \cdot 20(3.14)$ cm/sec
≈ 377 cm/sec

m. 3 ft/sec = 36 in./sec

$\omega = \dfrac{v}{r} = \dfrac{36 \text{ in./sec}}{10 \text{ in.}} = 3.6$ radians/sec

pp. 746–748   17-3 EXERCISES

1. $\dfrac{\pi}{6} \approx 0.52$ **2.** $\dfrac{\pi}{12} \approx 0.26$ **3.** $\dfrac{5\pi}{9} \approx 1.74$

4. $\dfrac{10\pi}{9} \approx 3.49$ **5.** $\dfrac{5\pi}{12} \approx 1.31$ **6.** $\dfrac{7\pi}{12} \approx 1.83$

7. $\dfrac{2\pi}{3} \approx 2.09$ **8.** $\dfrac{4\pi}{3} \approx 4.19$ **9.** $-\dfrac{16\pi}{9} \approx -5.58$

10. $-\dfrac{25\pi}{18} \approx -4.36$ **11.** $-\dfrac{17\pi}{36} \approx -1.48$

12. $-\dfrac{35\pi}{36} \approx -3.05$ **13.** 57.3°   **14.** 114.6°   **15.** 1440°

16. −2160°   **17.** 135°   **18.** 225°   **19.** 20.9 cm

20. 10.5 m   **21.** 5.7   **22.** 6   **23.** $\sqrt{3}$ **24.** $\dfrac{2\sqrt{3}}{3}$

25. $\dfrac{2\sqrt{3}}{3}$ **26.** 2   **27.** 1   **28.** $\sqrt{2}$ **29.** $\dfrac{\sqrt{3}}{3}$

30. 2   **31.** 0   **32.** 3150 cm/min   **33.** 54 m/min

34. 52.3 cm/sec   **35.** 41.0 cm/sec   **36.** 1047 mi/h

37. 66,626 mi/h   **38.** 68.8 radians/sec   **39.** 1429 radians/h

40. 10 mi/h   **41.** 11.4 mi/h   **42.** $\dfrac{5}{6} \cdot 2\pi = \dfrac{5\pi}{6} \approx 5.233$

43. a. $\dfrac{x}{100} = \dfrac{48}{90}$ **b.** $\dfrac{x}{100} = \dfrac{153}{90}$

$x = 53.33$ $x = 170$

c. $\dfrac{x}{100} = \dfrac{\frac{\pi}{8}}{\frac{\pi}{2}}$ **d.** $\dfrac{x}{100} = \dfrac{\frac{5\pi}{2}}{\frac{\pi}{2}}$

$x = 25$ $x = 142.86$

44. a. $\dfrac{x}{90} = \dfrac{100}{1600}$ **b.** $\dfrac{x}{90} = \dfrac{350}{1600}$

$x = 5.6°$ $x = 19.7°$

45. Circumference of the earth $= 2\pi r$
$\approx 2\pi$ (6400 km) or $\approx 2\pi$ (4000 mi)

$1° = \dfrac{1}{360}$ of the circumference

$\approx \dfrac{1}{360}(2\pi)(6400)$ or $\approx \dfrac{1}{360}(2\pi)(4000)$

≈ 111.6 km or 69.8 mi

46. $1° = 60$ nautical miles
Circumference $= 360 \cdot 60 = 21{,}600$ nautical miles

Radius $= \dfrac{c}{2\pi} = \dfrac{21{,}600}{2\pi} \approx 3439$ nautical miles

47. We know that $\sin \theta = \cos(90° - \theta)$ for $0 \le \theta \le 90°$.
Consider $90° < \theta \le 180°$. Then $\sin \theta = \sin(180° - \theta)$ and
$\cos \theta = -\cos(180° - \theta)$. Since $180° - \theta$ is an acute angle,
$\sin(180° - \theta) = \cos(90° - (180° - \theta)) = \cos(\theta - 90°)$.
Now consider $\cos(90° - \theta)$. Since θ is in the second quadrant,
$90° - \theta$ is a negative angle in the fourth quadrant. The reference
angle is thus the absolute value of the angle. Since
$90° - \theta$ is negative, $|90° - \theta| = -(90° - \theta) = \theta - 90°$.
Thus, $\cos(90° - \theta) = \cos(\theta - 90°) = \sin \theta$ for $90° < \theta \le 180°$.

Using similar arguments for the third and fourth quadrants,
you can show that $\sin \theta = \cos(90 - \theta)$ for all θ.

48. Use the diameter of the earth as arc length.
$r = 24{,}000$

$\alpha = \dfrac{8000}{24{,}000} = \dfrac{1}{30}$ radians

49. $\dfrac{7.2\pi}{180} \approx 0.1257$ radians

radius $= \dfrac{s}{\theta} \approx \dfrac{500}{0.1257} \approx 3978$

circumference $= 2\pi r \approx 2\pi(3978)$
$\approx 25{,}000$ miles

50. $(-x)^2 + y^2 = 36$ **51.** $(-x)y = 25$
$x^2 + y^2 = 36$ $-xy = 25$
Yes   No

52. $y = (-x)^4 + 3(-x)^2 - 2 = x^4 + 3x^2 - 2$; Yes

53. $f(x) = x^3$ **54.** $f(x) = 3^x$
$(f^{-1}(x))^3 = x$ $3^{f^{-1}(x)} = x$
$f^{-1}(x) = x^{1/3}$ $f^{-1}(x) = \log_3 x,\ x \ge 0$

55. $f(x) = \sqrt{x^4 - 1}$
$x = \sqrt{[f^{-1}(x)]^4 - 1}$
$x^2 + 1 = [f^{-1}(x)]^4$
$f^{-1}(x) = \sqrt[4]{x^2 + 1}$

56. $\log_7 343 = \log_7 7^3 = 3$ **57.** $7^{\log_7 e} = e$

58. $S = \dfrac{a}{1 - r}$ **59.** $S = \dfrac{1}{1 - 0.1}$ **60.** mean = 3.25,
median = 3.5,
mode = 4

$S = \dfrac{1}{1 - \left(-\frac{1}{5}\right)}$ $= \dfrac{1}{0.9}$

$S = \dfrac{5}{6}$ $= \dfrac{10}{9}$

p. 748   CALCULATOR INVESTIGATION

0.4794

pp. 750–752   17-4 TRY THIS

a. $\sin 15°20' \approx 0.2644$ **b.** $\cot 64°50' \approx 0.4699$
c.   410°20'
$\underline{-360°0'}$
50°20'
The reference angle is 50°20'.
We find $\cos 50°20' \approx 0.6383$. In quadrant four the cos is positive
so $\cos 410°20' \approx 0.6383$.
d.   260°40'
$\underline{-180°00'}$
80°40'
The reference angle is 80°40'.
We find $\sin 80°40' \approx 0.9868$. In quadrant three the sin is negative
so $\sin 260°40' \approx -0.9868$.
e. $\sec B = 1.655$ and $0 \le B \le 90°$ implies $B = 52°50'$ from Table 5.
f. $37.45° = 37° + (0.45 \times 1°)$
$= 37° + (0.45 \times 60')$
$= 37° + 27'$
$37.45° = 37°27'$

g. $43°55' = 43° + 55'$

$$= 43° + \frac{55°}{60}$$

$$\approx 43° + 0.917°$$

$43°55' \approx 43.917°$

h. The difference between sin 38°40' and sin 38°50' is 0.0023.

$0.6248 + 0.7(0.0023)$

$= 0.6248 + 0.00161$

$= 0.62641$

$\sin 38°47' \approx 0.6264$

i. The difference between cot 27°40' and cot 27°50' is 0.013.

$1.907 - 0.5(0.013) = 1.907 - 0.0065$

$= 1.9005$

$\cot 27°45' \approx 1.9005$

j. $\sin 21°20' = 0.3638$; $\sin 21°10' = 0.3611$

$0.3638 - 0.3611 = 0.0027$

$0.3624 - 0.3611 = 0.0013$

$21°10' + \frac{13}{27}(10') \approx 21°10' + 4.81' = 21°14.81'$

Thus, $\theta \approx 21°15'$

k. $\cot 31°40 = 1.621$; $\cot 31°50' = 1.611$

$1.621 - 1.611 = 0.01$

$1.614 - 1.611 = 0.003$

$31°50' - \frac{3}{10}(10)$

$31°50' - 3' = 31°47'$

$\theta \approx 31°47'$

pp. 753–754   17-4 EXERCISES

1. 0.2306   **2.** 0.6648   **3.** 0.5519   **4.** 0.3118

5. 0.5467   **6.** 1.550   **7.** 1.127   **8.** 1.063

9. −0.7969   **10.** −0.3987   **11.** 0.6383   **12.** −0.1161

13. 0.5392   **14.** −1.729   **15.** 3.689   **16.** −1.063

17. 81°10'   **18.** 3°20'   **19.** 45°50'   **20.** 64°10'

21. 13°40'   **22.** 39°50'   **23.** 46°39'   **24.** 85°12'

25. 67°3'   **26.** 38°27'   **27.** −48°57'   **28.** −94°48'

29. 412°33'   **30.** 714°6'   **31.** 45.42°   **32.** 36.28°

33. 76.88°   **34.** 12.38°   **35.** −68.78°   **36.** −113.37°

37. 225.55°   **38.** 414.12°   **39.** 0.4775   **40.** 0.5977

41. 0.5889   **42.** 0.1642   **43.** 0.4494   **44.** 0.7186

45. 39°43'   **46.** 31°8'   **47.** 45°44'   **48.** 54°45'

49. 74°53'   **50.** 20°3'   **51.** $37.71 \cdot \frac{\pi}{180} = 0.2095\pi$

52. $12.73 \cdot \frac{\pi}{180} = 0.0707222\pi$ **53.** $214.6 \cdot \frac{\pi}{180} = 1.1922222\pi$

54. $73.87 \cdot \frac{\pi}{180} = 0.4103889\pi$ **55.** $1.303 \cdot \frac{\pi}{180} = 74.694267°$

56. $2.347 \cdot \frac{180}{\pi} = 134.54140°$ **57.** $37.89 \cdot \frac{\pi}{180} = 2172.0382°$

58. $7.005 \cdot \frac{180}{\pi} = 401.56051°$ **59.** $8.206\pi \cdot \frac{180}{\pi} = 1477.08°$

60. $-14.13\pi \cdot \frac{180}{\pi} = -2543.4°$ **61.** $0.7532\pi \cdot \frac{180}{\pi} = 135.576°$

62. $-1.205\pi \cdot \frac{180}{\pi} = -216.9°$

63. $\tan 29°43' = \tan 29.72° = 0.5708$

64. $\cot 73°21' = \cot 73.35° = \tan(90 - 73.35) = 0.2991$

65. $\sin 213.56° = -0.5582$

66. $\tan -545°29' = \tan -545.48° = -0.0960$

67. $\cot -2.556° = \tan(90° - (-2.556°)) = -22.4013$

68. $\cos 4.223° = 0.9973$

69. If $\cot A = 11.546$, $\tan A = \frac{1}{11.546}$; 0.0864

70. Press INV or 2ndF key, then tan; 1.5052

71. Press INV or 2ndF key, then sin; −0.0089

72. Press INV or 2ndF key, then tan; −1.5478

73. Enter 1.706, press the $\frac{1}{x}$ key, press INV or 2ndF key and then cos key.

74. Convert to decimal degrees, press the sin key, then press the $\frac{1}{x}$ key.

75. $\sin \theta \approx \theta$ for small angles.   **76.** $\tan \theta \approx \theta$ for small angles.

77. $61°38'22'' = 61 + \frac{38}{60} + \frac{22}{3600} = 61.63944°$

78. $\log \sin 57° \approx \log 0.8387 \approx -0.7639$

$\sin \theta$ must be positive, so the domain is

$360k < \theta < 180 + 360k$, k an integer

79. $\tan 16' = \frac{x}{9.3 \cdot 10^6}$

$x = 8.65690 \times 10^5$, diameter

80. $(-x)^2 + (-y)^2 = 36$ $y^2 + x^2 = 36$

$\quad x^2 + y^2 = 36$ $x^2 + y^2 = 36$

$\quad\quad$ Yes $\quad\quad\quad$ Yes

81. $(-x)(-y) = 25$ $y \cdot x = 25$

$\quad xy = 25$ $xy = 25$

$\quad\quad$ Yes $\quad\quad$ Yes

82. $4(-x - 3)^2 + (-y - 3)^2 = 25$ $4(y - 3)^2 + (x - 3)^2 = 25$

$4(x + 3)^2 + (y + 3)^2 = 25$

$\quad\quad$ No $\quad\quad\quad\quad\quad$ No

83. $-f(x) = (-x)^3 - (-x) = -x^3 + x$ $x = (f(x))^3 - f(x)$

$f(x) = x^3 - x = -f(x)$

$\quad\quad$ Yes $\quad\quad\quad\quad\quad$ No

84. $x = \dfrac{\begin{vmatrix} 9 & 2 \\ 16 & 4 \end{vmatrix}}{\begin{vmatrix} 4 & 2 \\ 7 & 4 \end{vmatrix}} = \dfrac{9 \cdot 4 - 2 \cdot 16}{4 \cdot 4 - 2 \cdot 7} = 2$

Use substitution to find y, $\left(2, \frac{1}{2}\right)$

85. $x = \dfrac{\begin{vmatrix} 0 & 1 & 1 \\ 2 & 1 & 2 \\ -5 & 2 & 0 \end{vmatrix}\begin{matrix} 0 & 1 \\ 2 & 1 \\ -5 & 2 \end{matrix}}{\begin{vmatrix} 1 & 1 & 1 \\ 2 & 1 & 2 \\ 1 & 2 & 0 \end{vmatrix}\begin{matrix} 1 & 1 \\ 2 & 1 \\ 1 & 2 \end{matrix}}$

$= \dfrac{0 + -10 + 4 + 5 - 0 - 0}{0 + 2 + 4 - 1 - 4 - 0} = \dfrac{-1}{1} = -1$

$y = \dfrac{\begin{vmatrix} 1 & 0 & 1 \\ 2 & 2 & 2 \\ 1 & -5 & 0 \end{vmatrix}\begin{matrix} 1 & 0 \\ 2 & 2 \\ 1 & -5 \end{matrix}}{1} = -2$

Find z by substitution; $z = 3$

$(-1, -2, 3)$

86. $|5 - 2x| > 7$

$5 - 2x > 7 \quad$ or $\quad 5 - 2x < -7$

$-2x > 2 \quad$ or $\quad -2x < -12$

$x < -1 \quad$ or $\quad\quad x > 6$

87. $|3 + 7x| \geq -11$

Absolute value is always positive.

All real numbers

f. $\cos\left(\theta - \dfrac{\pi}{2}\right) \equiv \sin\theta,\ \theta = 0$

$\cos\left(0 - \dfrac{\pi}{2}\right) = \cos\left(-\dfrac{\pi}{2}\right) = 0 = \sin 0$

g. $\cot\left(\theta + \dfrac{\pi}{2}\right) \equiv \dfrac{\cos\left(\theta + \dfrac{\pi}{2}\right)}{\sin\left(\theta + \dfrac{\pi}{2}\right)}$

$\equiv \dfrac{-\sin\theta}{\cos\theta}$

$\equiv -\tan\theta$

Thus, $\cot\left(\theta + \dfrac{\pi}{2}\right) \equiv -\tan\theta$

pp. 767–768   **17-6 EXERCISES**

1. $\cos\theta \equiv \dfrac{\sin\theta}{\tan\theta}$ **2.** $\sin\theta \equiv \dfrac{\cos\theta}{\cot\theta}$

3. $\csc\theta \equiv \pm\sqrt{1 + \cot^2\theta}$ **4.** $\tan\theta \equiv \pm\sqrt{\sec^2\theta - 1}$

5. $\cot\theta \equiv \pm\sqrt{\csc^2\theta - 1}$ **6.** $\sec\theta \equiv \pm\sqrt{1 + \tan^2\theta}$

7. $\tan\theta \equiv \pm\sqrt{\dfrac{1}{\cos^2\theta} - 1}$ **8.** $\csc\theta \equiv \pm\sqrt{\dfrac{1}{1 - \cos^2\theta}}$

9. $\sin\left(\dfrac{\pi}{4} - \dfrac{\pi}{2}\right) = \sin -\dfrac{\pi}{4} = -\dfrac{\sqrt{2}}{2} = -\cos\dfrac{\pi}{4}$

10. $\cos\left(0 - \dfrac{\pi}{2}\right) = \cos -\dfrac{\pi}{2} = 0 = \sin 0$

11. $\sin\left(\dfrac{\pi}{2} - \dfrac{5\pi}{4}\right) = \sin -\dfrac{3\pi}{4} = -\dfrac{\sqrt{2}}{2} = \cos\dfrac{5\pi}{4}$

12. $\cos\left(\dfrac{\pi}{2} - \dfrac{\pi}{3}\right) = \cos\dfrac{\pi}{6} = \dfrac{\sqrt{3}}{2} = \sin\dfrac{\pi}{3}$

13. $\tan\left(\theta - \dfrac{\pi}{2}\right) = \dfrac{\sin\left(\theta - \dfrac{\pi}{2}\right)}{\cos\left(\theta - \dfrac{\pi}{2}\right)} = \dfrac{-\cos\theta}{\sin\theta} = -\cot\theta$

14. $\cot\left(\theta - \dfrac{\pi}{2}\right) = \dfrac{\cos\left(\theta - \dfrac{\pi}{2}\right)}{\sin\left(\theta - \dfrac{\pi}{2}\right)} = \dfrac{\sin\theta}{-\cos\theta} = -\tan\theta$

15. $\sec\left(\dfrac{\pi}{2} - \theta\right) = \dfrac{1}{\cos\left(\dfrac{\pi}{2} - \theta\right)} = \dfrac{1}{\sin\theta} = \csc\theta$

16. $\csc\left(\dfrac{\pi}{2} - \theta\right) = \dfrac{1}{\sin\left(\dfrac{\pi}{2} - \theta\right)} = \dfrac{1}{\cos\theta} = \sec\theta$

17. $\sin 25° = \cos 65° = 0.4226$
$\cos 25° = \sin 65° = 0.9063$
$\tan 25° = \cot 65° = 0.4663$
$\sec 25° = \csc 65° = 1.103$
$\csc 25° = \sec 65° = 2.366$
$\cot 25° = \tan 65° = 2.145$

18. $\sin 58° = \cos 32° = 0.8480$
$\cos 58° = \sin 32° = 0.5299$
$\tan 58° = \cot 32° = 1.600$
$\sec 58° = \csc 32° = 1.887$
$\csc 58° = \sec 32° = 1.179$
$\cot 58° = \tan 32° = 0.6249$

19. $\sin(\theta + \pi) = \sin\left(\theta + \dfrac{\pi}{2} + \dfrac{\pi}{2}\right) = \cos\left(\theta + \dfrac{\pi}{2}\right) = -\sin\theta$

20. $\sin(\theta - \pi) = \sin\left(\theta - \dfrac{\pi}{2} - \dfrac{\pi}{2}\right) = -\cos\left(\theta - \dfrac{\pi}{2}\right) = -\sin\theta$

21. $\cos(\pi - \theta) = \cos\left(\dfrac{\pi}{2} + \dfrac{\pi}{2} - \theta\right) = -\sin\left(\dfrac{\pi}{2} - \theta\right) = -\cos\theta$

22. $\sin(\pi - \theta) = \sin\left(\dfrac{\pi}{2} + \dfrac{\pi}{2} - \theta\right) = \cos\left(\dfrac{\pi}{2} - \theta\right) = \sin\theta$

23. $\cos(\theta + 2k\pi) = \cos\theta$ **24.** $\sin(\theta + 2k\pi) = \sin\theta$

25. $\cos(\theta - \pi) = \cos - (\pi - \theta) = \cos(\pi - \theta) = -\cos\theta$

26. $\cos(\theta + \pi) = \cos\left(\theta + \dfrac{\pi}{2} + \dfrac{\pi}{2}\right) = -\sin\left(\theta + \dfrac{\pi}{2}\right) = -\cos\theta$

27. $\sin^2\dfrac{\pi}{8} + \cos^2\dfrac{\pi}{8} = 1;\ \cos\dfrac{\pi}{8} = \sqrt{1 - (0.38268)^2} \approx 0.92388$

28. $\cos\dfrac{5\pi}{8} = \sin\left(\dfrac{\pi}{2} - \dfrac{5\pi}{8}\right) = \sin -\dfrac{\pi}{8} = -\sin\dfrac{\pi}{8} = -0.38268$

29. $\sin\dfrac{5\pi}{8} = \sin\left(\dfrac{\pi}{8} + \dfrac{\pi}{2}\right) = \cos\dfrac{\pi}{8} = 0.92388$

30. $\sin -\dfrac{3\pi}{8} = -\sin\dfrac{3\pi}{8} = -\cos\left(\dfrac{\pi}{2} - \dfrac{3\pi}{8}\right) = -\cos\dfrac{\pi}{8} = -0.92388$

31. $\cos -\dfrac{3\pi}{8} = \cos\dfrac{3\pi}{8} = \sin\left(\dfrac{\pi}{2} - \dfrac{3\pi}{8}\right) = \sin\dfrac{\pi}{8} = 0.38268$

32. $\cos -\dfrac{\pi}{8} = \cos\dfrac{\pi}{8} = 0.92388$

33. $\sin\left(\dfrac{\pi}{2} - \theta\right) \equiv \cos\theta;\ \cos\left(\dfrac{\pi}{2} - \theta\right) \equiv \sin\theta$

$\tan\left(\dfrac{\pi}{2} - \theta\right) \equiv \dfrac{\sin\left(\dfrac{\pi}{2} - \theta\right)}{\cos\left(\dfrac{\pi}{2} - \theta\right)} \equiv \dfrac{\cos\theta}{\sin\theta} \equiv \cot\theta$

$\sec\left(\dfrac{\pi}{2} - \theta\right) \equiv \dfrac{1}{\cos\left(\dfrac{\pi}{2} - \theta\right)} \equiv \dfrac{1}{\sin\theta} \equiv \csc\theta$

$\csc\left(\dfrac{\pi}{2} - \theta\right) \equiv \dfrac{1}{\sin\left(\dfrac{\pi}{2} - \theta\right)} \equiv \dfrac{1}{\cos\theta} \equiv \sec\theta$

$\cot\left(\dfrac{\pi}{2} - \theta\right) \equiv \dfrac{\cos\left(\dfrac{\pi}{2} - \theta\right)}{\sin\left(\dfrac{\pi}{2} - \theta\right)} \equiv \dfrac{\sin\theta}{\cos\theta} \equiv \tan\theta$

b. The function of an angle is equal to the cofunction of its complement.

For Exercises 34–37, answers may vary.

34. $\theta = 30°;\ \dfrac{1 - \sin 30°}{\cos 30°} = \dfrac{\cos 30°}{1 + \sin 30°};$

$\dfrac{\dfrac{1}{2}}{\dfrac{\sqrt{3}}{2}} = \dfrac{\dfrac{\sqrt{3}}{2}}{\dfrac{3}{2}}$

$\dfrac{\sqrt{3}}{3} = \dfrac{\sqrt{3}}{3}$

35. $\theta = 60°;\ \dfrac{1 - \cos 60°}{\sin 60°} = \dfrac{\sin 60°}{1 + \cos 60°}$

$\dfrac{\dfrac{1}{2}}{\dfrac{\sqrt{3}}{2}} = \dfrac{\dfrac{\sqrt{3}}{2}}{\dfrac{3}{2}}$

$\dfrac{\sqrt{3}}{3} = \dfrac{\sqrt{3}}{3}$

36. $x = \dfrac{\pi}{2};\ \csc\dfrac{\pi}{2} - \cos\dfrac{\pi}{2}\cot\dfrac{\pi}{2} = \sin\dfrac{\pi}{2}$

$1 - 0 \cdot 0 = 1$

$1 = 1$

37. $x = \dfrac{\pi}{4}$; $\sec \dfrac{\pi}{4} - \sin \dfrac{\pi}{4} \tan \dfrac{\pi}{4} = \cos \dfrac{\pi}{4}$

$$\sqrt{2} - \dfrac{\sqrt{2}}{2} \cdot 1 = \dfrac{\sqrt{2}}{2}$$

$$\dfrac{\sqrt{2}}{2} = \dfrac{\sqrt{2}}{2}$$

38. $6x^2 - 13x + 6 = (3x - 2)(2x - 3)$

39. $x^4 - 65 = (x^2 + 25)(x^2 - 25) = (x^2 + 25)(x + 5)(x - 5)$

40. $6xy^2(4x^2 - 9y^2) = 6xy^2(2x - 3y)(2x + 3y)$

41. Use Factor Theorem and synthetic division
$x^3 + 15x^2 + 74x + 120 = (x + 4)(x + 5)(x + 6)$

42.
$$\begin{array}{r} x^2 - 3x + 2 \\ x - 1 \overline{)\, x^3 - 4x^2 + 5x - 2} \\ \underline{-x^3 + \; x^2} \\ -3x^2 + 5x \\ \underline{3x^2 - 3x} \\ 2x - 2 \\ \underline{-2x + 2} \end{array}$$

43.
$$\begin{array}{r} x^3 - x^2 + x - 1 \\ 3x + 4 \overline{)\, 3x^4 + x^3 - x^2 + x - 4} \\ \underline{-3x^4 - 4x^3} \\ -3x^3 - x^2 \\ \underline{3x^3 + 4x^2} \\ 3x^2 + x \\ \underline{-3x^2 - 4x} \\ -3x - 4 \\ \underline{3x + 4} \end{array}$$

44. $\left(\dfrac{-32a^{12}b^{-3}c^7c^4}{a^2b^2c^2d^2}\right)^{3/5} = \left(\dfrac{-2^5 a^{10} c^5 d^2}{b^5}\right)^{3/5}$

$$= \dfrac{(-2)^3 a^6 c^3 d^{6/5}}{b^3} = \dfrac{-8a^6 c^3 d \sqrt[5]{d}}{b^3}$$

45. $\left(\dfrac{-125n^7 m^{-7} l^7}{343 n^3 m^2 l}\right)^{5/3} = \left(\dfrac{-5^3 n^4 l^6}{7^3 m^9}\right)^{5/3}$

$$= \dfrac{(-5)^5 n^{20/3} l^{10}}{7^5 m^{15}} = \dfrac{-3125 n^6 l^{10} \sqrt[3]{n^2}}{16807 m^{15}}$$

46. $\sqrt{\dfrac{\sqrt{2}}{2}} = \left(\dfrac{\sqrt{2}}{2}\right)^{1/2} = \left(\dfrac{2^{1/2}}{2}\right)^{1/2} = 2^{-1/4}$

$$= \sqrt[4]{\dfrac{1}{2} \cdot \dfrac{2^3}{2^3}} = \dfrac{\sqrt[4]{8}}{2}$$

47. $\sin \alpha = \dfrac{12}{13}$ $\sin \theta = \dfrac{5}{13}$ $\cot \alpha = \dfrac{5}{12}$ $\cot \theta = \dfrac{12}{5}$

$\cos \alpha = \dfrac{5}{13}$ $\cos \theta = \dfrac{12}{13}$ $\sec \alpha = \dfrac{13}{5}$ $\sec \theta = \dfrac{13}{12}$

$\tan \alpha = \dfrac{12}{5}$ $\tan \theta = \dfrac{5}{12}$ $\csc \alpha = \dfrac{13}{12}$ $\csc \theta = \dfrac{13}{5}$

48. $\cot 30° = \dfrac{\sqrt{3}}{a}$ $\cos 30° = \dfrac{\sqrt{3}}{b}$

$\sqrt{3}a = \sqrt{3}$ $\dfrac{\sqrt{3}}{2}b = \sqrt{3}$

$a = 1$ $b = 2$

49. $\tan 45° = \dfrac{\sqrt{2}}{a}$ $\sin 45° = \dfrac{\sqrt{2}}{b}$

$1a = \sqrt{2}$ $\dfrac{\sqrt{2}}{2}b = \sqrt{2}$

$a = \sqrt{2}$ $b = 2$

a.

Amplitude = 2

b.

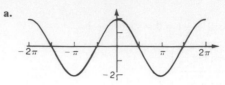

Period = π

c.

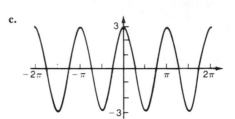

Amplitude = 3, period = π

p. 771   17-7 EXERCISES

1. $A = \dfrac{1}{2}$

2. $A = \dfrac{1}{2}$

3. $A = 3$

4. $A = 3$

5. $A = \dfrac{1}{3}$

6. $A = \dfrac{1}{3}$

7. $A = 4$

8. $A = 4$

9. $A = 2$

1, 3, 5

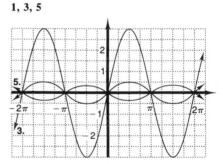

2, 4, 6.

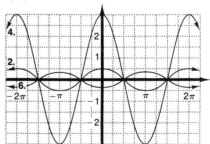

7, 8, 9.

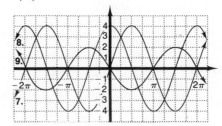

10. $\frac{2\pi}{3}$

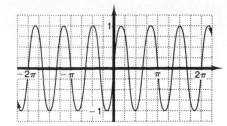

11. $\frac{2\pi}{3}$

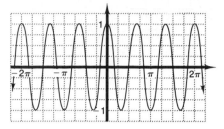

12. 4π **12, 14.**

13. 4π

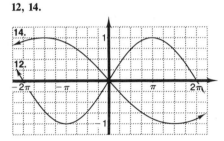

14. 6π

15. 6π

13, 15.

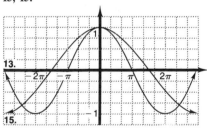

16. π **16, 17.**

17. π

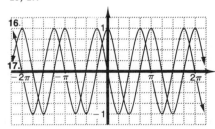

18. $\frac{2\pi}{3}$

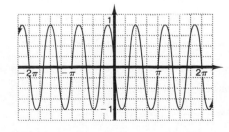

19. $A = 2$,   **19, 21.**
period $= \pi$

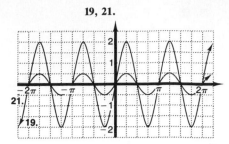

20. $A = 2$,
period $= \pi$

21. $A = \frac{1}{2}$,
period $= \pi$

22. $A = \frac{1}{2}$,   **20, 22.**
period $= \pi$

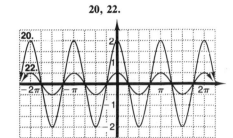

23. $A = 2$;   **23, 24.**
period $= 4\pi$

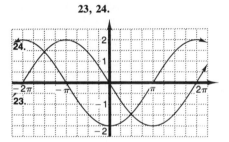

24. $A = 2$;
period $= 4\pi$

25. $A = \frac{1}{2}$;   **25, 27.**
period $= \pi$

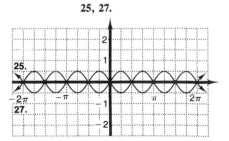

26. $A = \frac{1}{2}$;
period $= \pi$

27. $A = \frac{1}{2}$;   **26.**
period $= \pi$

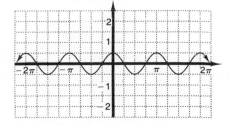

28, 29.

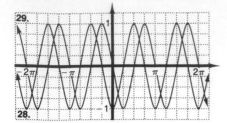

30.

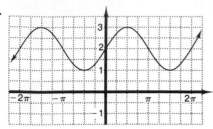

31. $y = -4 \sin \frac{1}{3}\theta$

32. $A = 2$; period $= \pi$

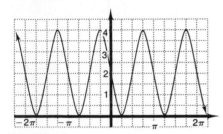

33. $A = \frac{1}{2}$; period $= 4\pi$

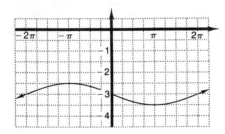

34. $P(x) = x^3 + 6x^2 + 11x + 6$; no change in sign; no positive real roots
$P(-x) = -x^3 + 6x^2 - 11x + 6$; three changes in sign; 1 or 3 negative real roots

35. $P(-1) = 0$: $x + 1$ is a factor
$P(2) = 100$: $x - 2$ is not a factor
$P(1) = 24$: $x - 1$ is not a factor

36. $P(-2) = 0$; Yes
$P(0) = 6$; No
$P(3) = 120$; No

37. $P(-5) = (-5)^3 + 6(-5)^2 + 11(-5) + 6$
$= -125 + 6(25) - 55 + 6$
$= -24$
$P(-3) = (-3)^3 + 6(-3)^2 + 11(-3) + 6$
$= -27 + 6(9) - 33 + 6$
$= 0$
$P(2) = 2^3 + 6(2)^2 + 11(2) + 6$
$= 8 + 24 + 22 + 6$
$= 60$
$P(4) = 4^3 + 6(4^2) + 11(4) + 6$
$= 64 + 96 + 44 + 6$
$= 210$

38. From #35, $(x + 1)$ is a factor.
From #36, $(x + 2)$ is a factor.
From #37, $(x + 3)$ is a factor.
$P(x) = (x + 1)(x + 2)(x + 3)$: x-intercepts are where
$P(x) = 0$: $(-1, 0), (-2, 0), (-3, 0)$

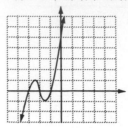

pp. 772–773   **17-8 TRY THIS**

a. $\sin x(\cot x + \csc x) = \sin x \cot x + \sin x \csc x$
$$= \sin x\left(\frac{\cos x}{\sin x}\right) + \sin x\left(\frac{1}{\sin x}\right)$$
$$= \cos x + 1$$

b. $\sin^3\theta + \sin \theta \cos^2\theta = \sin \theta(\sin^2\theta + \cos^2\theta)$
$$= \sin \theta(1)$$
$$= \sin \theta$$

c. $\dfrac{1 - \cos^2 x}{\cos\left(\dfrac{\pi}{2} - x\right)} = \dfrac{\sin^2 y}{\sin x} = \sin x$

d. $\cot^2 x + \cot x = 12$
$\cot^2 x + \cot x - 12 = 0$
$(\cot x + 4)(\cot x - 3) = 0$
$\cot x + 4 = 0$ or $\cot x - 3 = 0$
$\cot x = -4$ or $\cot x = 3$

pp. 773–774   **17-8 EXERCISES**

1. $\sin^2 x - \cos^2 x$ **2.** $\tan^2\theta - \cot^2\theta$

3. $\sin x - \sec x$ **4.** $\cos x + \csc x$

5. $\sin \theta + \cos \theta$ **6.** $\sin y - \tan y$

7. $\cot x - \tan x$ **8.** $\tan x + \cot x + 2$

9. $1 - 2 \sin y \cos y$ **10.** $1 + 2 \sin \theta \cos \theta$

11. $\sec^2\theta + 2 \tan \theta$ **12.** $\csc^2 x + 2 \cot x$

13. $\cos x(\sin x + \cos x)$ **14.** $\csc x(\sec x - \csc x)$

15. $(\sin y - \cos y)(\sin y + \cos y)$

16. $(\tan y - \cot y)(\tan y + \cot y)$ **17.** $\cos^2 x$

18. $\cot \theta + \cos \theta$ **19.** $\sin^2\theta - \cos^2\theta$

20. $-(\tan^2 x + \sec^2 x)$ **21.** $3(\cot y + 1)^2$

22. $4(\sin y + 1)^2$ **23.** $(\csc^2\theta + 5)\cot^2\theta$

24. $(\tan^2 x - 3)\sec^2 x$ **25.** $\tan x$ **26.** $\cot x$

27. $\dfrac{2}{9} \cos \theta \cot \theta$ **28.** $5 \tan x \sin x$ **29.** $\cos x - 1$

30. $\sin x + 1$ **31.** $\cos x + 1$ **32.** $\sin \theta - 1$

33. $\tan x = -7$ or $\tan x = 3$ **34.** $\sec x = 5$ or $\sec x = 2$

35. $\sin \theta = -\dfrac{1}{2}$ or $\sin \theta = \dfrac{3}{4}$ **36.** $\cos x = -\dfrac{1}{3}$

37. $\cot x = 1$ or $\cot x = -10$ **38.** $\csc \theta = 2$ or $\csc \theta = -5$

39. No solution   **40.** $\tan \theta = 3 \pm \sqrt{13}$

41. $\csc x = \dfrac{3 + \sqrt{41}}{4}$ **42.** $\sin x = -\dfrac{1}{2}$

43. $\csc \theta - \cos \theta \cot \theta \equiv \sin \theta$

$$\dfrac{1}{\sin \theta} - \cos \theta \dfrac{\cos \theta}{\sin \theta}$$

$$\dfrac{1}{\sin \theta} - \dfrac{\cos^2\theta}{\sin \theta}$$

$$\dfrac{1 - \cos^2\theta}{\sin \theta}$$

$$\dfrac{\sin^2\theta}{\sin \theta}$$

$$\sin \theta \;\Big|\; \sin \theta$$

44. $\sec \theta - \sin \theta \tan \theta \equiv \cos \theta$

$$\dfrac{1}{\cos \theta} - \sin \theta \dfrac{\sin \theta}{\cos \theta}$$

$$\dfrac{1}{\cos \theta} - \dfrac{\sin^2\theta}{\cos \theta}$$

$$\dfrac{1 - \sin^2\theta}{\cos \theta}$$

$$\dfrac{\cos^2\theta}{\cos \theta}$$

$$\cos \theta \;\Big|\; \cos \theta$$

45. $\dfrac{1 - \sin \theta}{\cos \theta} \equiv \dfrac{\cos \theta}{1 + \sin \theta}$

$$\dfrac{\cos \theta}{1 + \sin \theta} \cdot \dfrac{(1 - \sin \theta)}{(1 - \sin \theta)}$$

$$\dfrac{\cos \theta(1 - \sin \theta)}{1 - \sin^2\theta}$$

$$\dfrac{\cos \theta(1 - \sin \theta)}{\cos^2\theta}$$

$$\dfrac{1 - \sin \theta}{\cos \theta} \;\Big|\; \dfrac{1 - \sin \theta}{\cos \theta}$$

46. $\dfrac{1 - \cos \theta}{\sin \theta} \equiv \dfrac{\sin \theta}{1 + \cos \theta}$

$$\dfrac{\sin \theta}{1 + \cos \theta} \cdot \dfrac{1 - \cos \theta}{1 - \cos \theta}$$

$$\dfrac{\sin(1 - \cos \theta)}{1 - \cos^2\theta}$$

$$\dfrac{\sin(1 - \cos \theta)}{\sin^2\theta}$$

$$\dfrac{1 - \cos \theta}{\sin \theta} \;\Big|\; \dfrac{1 - \cos \theta}{\sin \theta}$$

47. No: $\sin\left(\dfrac{\pi}{2} + \dfrac{\pi}{2}\right) = \sin \pi = 0$

$\sin \dfrac{\pi}{2} + \sin \dfrac{\pi}{2} = 1 + 1 = 2$

48. $\sqrt{\sin^2 x \cos x} \, \sqrt{\cos x} = \sqrt{\sin^2 x \cos^2 x} = |\sin x \cos x|$

49. $(2 - \sqrt{\tan y})(\sqrt{\tan y} + 2) = 4 - |\tan y|$

50. $\sqrt{\dfrac{\sin x}{\cos x}} = \dfrac{\sqrt{\sin x}}{\sqrt{\cos x}} \dfrac{\sqrt{\cos x}}{\sqrt{\cos x}} = \dfrac{\sqrt{\sin x \cos x}}{\sqrt{\cos^2 x}} = \dfrac{\sqrt{\sin x \cos x}}{|\cos x|}$

51. $\sqrt{\dfrac{1 + \sin x}{1 - \sin x}} = \sqrt{\dfrac{(1 + \sin x)(1 - \sin x)}{(1 - \sin x)(1 - \sin x)}} = \dfrac{\sqrt{1 - \sin^2 x}}{|1 - \sin x|} = \dfrac{|\cos x|}{|1 - \sin x|}$

52. Use rational root theorem and synthetic substitution, possible roots: $\pm\{1, 2, 3, 4, 5, 6, 10, 20, 30, 60\}$
$P(-3) = 0;\ P(-4) = 0;\ P(-5) = 0;\ (x + 3)(x + 4)(x + 5)$

53. Use rational root theorem and synthetic substitution, possible roots: $\pm\{1, 2, 4, 8, 16\}$
$P(-2) = 0;\ (x + 2)^4$

54. $45° \cdot \dfrac{\pi}{180°} = \dfrac{\pi}{4}$ **55.** $72° \cdot \dfrac{\pi}{180°} = \dfrac{2\pi}{5}$

56. $-270° \cdot \dfrac{\pi}{180°} = -\dfrac{3\pi}{2}$ **57.** $210° \cdot \dfrac{\pi}{180°} = \dfrac{7\pi}{6}$

58. $\dfrac{2\pi}{3} \cdot \dfrac{180°}{\pi} = 120°$ **59.** $\dfrac{7\pi}{4} \cdot \dfrac{180°}{\pi} = 315°$

60. $-\dfrac{5\pi}{6} \cdot \dfrac{180°}{\pi} = -150°$ **61.** $\dfrac{\pi}{6} \cdot \dfrac{180°}{\pi} = 30°$

62.
$A = kr^2 \qquad A = \dfrac{128.6}{40.96} \cdot (9.2)^2$
$128.6 = k(6.4)^2$
$k = \dfrac{128.6}{40.96} \qquad A = 265.7 \text{ cm}^2$

pp. 776–778   CHAPTER 17 SUMMARY AND REVIEW

1.

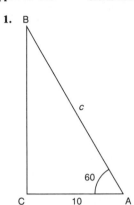

$\cos 60° = \dfrac{10}{c}$

$c = \dfrac{10}{\cos 60°} = 20$

2. $\sin \theta = \dfrac{1}{2} \qquad$ or $\quad \sin \theta = -\dfrac{1}{2}$

$\cos \theta = \dfrac{\sqrt{3}}{2} \qquad\quad \cos \theta = -\dfrac{\sqrt{3}}{2}$

$\cot \theta = \sqrt{3} \qquad\quad \cot \theta = \sqrt{3}$

$\sec \theta = \dfrac{2\sqrt{3}}{3} \qquad\quad \sec \theta = -\dfrac{2\sqrt{3}}{3}$

$\csc \theta = 2 \qquad\qquad \csc \theta = -2$

3. First **4.** Third **5.** Second **6.** Third

7. $\sin \theta = -\dfrac{4}{7}$, $\cos \theta = \dfrac{\sqrt{33}}{7}$, $\tan \theta = -\dfrac{4\sqrt{33}}{33}$,

$\cot \theta = -\dfrac{\sqrt{33}}{4}$, $\sec \theta = \dfrac{7\sqrt{33}}{33}$, $\csc \theta = -\dfrac{7}{4}$

8. 30° **9.** 30° **10.** 40° **11.** Undefined **12.** 1

13. $\dfrac{\sqrt{2}}{2}$ **14.** $45° = 45° \cdot \dfrac{\pi \text{ radians}}{180°} = \dfrac{\pi}{4}$

15. $150° = 150° \cdot \dfrac{\pi \text{ radians}}{180°} = \dfrac{5\pi}{6}$

16. $270° = 270° \cdot \dfrac{\pi \text{ radians}}{180°} = \dfrac{3\pi}{2}$

17. $-60° = -60° \cdot \dfrac{\pi \text{ radians}}{180°} = \dfrac{-\pi}{3}$ **18.** $\dfrac{7\pi}{6} \cdot \dfrac{180°}{\pi \text{ radians}} = 210°$

19. $\dfrac{-\pi}{3} \cdot \dfrac{180°}{\pi \text{ radians}} = -60°$ **20.** $4\pi \cdot \dfrac{180°}{\pi \text{ radians}} = 720°$

21. $\csc 45° \equiv \sec 45° = \dfrac{1}{\cos 45°} = \sqrt{2}$

22. $\cot 30° = \tan 60° = \sqrt{3}$ **23.** $\sin 90° = \cos 0° = 1$

24. $v = rw$
$30 = 60\ w$

$w = \dfrac{1}{2}$ radians/sec

25. 0.1449 **26.** 0.8526 **27.** 0.5147

28. 0.6730 **29.** 24°35′ **30.** 47°48′

31.

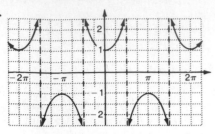

32. $\tan\dfrac{\pi}{4} = \dfrac{\sin\frac{\pi}{4}}{\cos\frac{\pi}{4}} = \dfrac{\frac{\sqrt{2}}{2}}{\frac{\sqrt{2}}{2}} = 1$

33. $\sin\left(\dfrac{\pi}{2} - \dfrac{\pi}{4}\right) = \sin\dfrac{\pi}{4} = \dfrac{\sqrt{2}}{2} = \cos\dfrac{\pi}{4}$

34. $\cot\theta = \pm\sqrt{\csc^2\theta - 1}$

35. $\csc\theta = \pm\sqrt{1 + \cot^2\theta} = \pm\sqrt{1 + \dfrac{1}{\tan^2\theta}}$

$= \pm\sqrt{1 + \dfrac{1}{\sec^2\theta - 1}}$

$= \pm\sqrt{1 + \dfrac{\cos^2\theta}{1 - \cos^2\theta}}$

$= \pm\sqrt{\dfrac{1}{1 - \cos^2\theta}}$

36. $\cot\left(\theta - \dfrac{\pi}{2}\right) = \dfrac{1}{\tan\left(\theta - \frac{\pi}{2}\right)}$

$= \dfrac{\cos\left(\theta - \frac{\pi}{2}\right)}{\sin\left(\theta - \frac{\pi}{2}\right)}$

$= \dfrac{\sin\theta}{-\cos\theta}$

$= -\tan\theta$

37. $\sin 15° = 0.2588$ **38.** $\cos 15° = 0.9659$

39. $\tan 15° = 0.2679$ **40.** $\cot 15° = 3.732$

41. $\sec 15° = 1.035$ **42.** $\csc 15° = 3.864$

43. $A = 3$

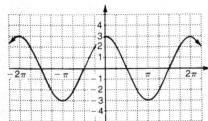

44. period = π

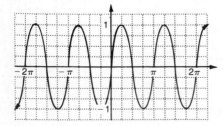

45. $\cos\theta(\tan\theta + \cot\theta) = \cos\theta\tan\theta + \cos\theta\cot\theta$

$= \sin\theta + \dfrac{\cos^2\theta}{\sin\theta}$

$= \dfrac{\sin^2\theta + \cos^2\theta}{\sin\theta}$

$= \dfrac{1}{\sin\theta}$

$= \csc\theta$

46. $3\tan^2\theta - 2\tan\theta - 2 = 0$

$\tan\theta = \dfrac{2 \pm \sqrt{4 + 24}}{6}$

$\tan\theta = \dfrac{2 \pm 2\sqrt{7}}{6}$

$\tan\theta = \dfrac{1 \pm \sqrt{7}}{3}$

p. 779   **CHAPTER 17 TEST**

1. 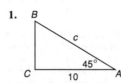 $\cos 45° = \dfrac{10}{c}$

$c = \dfrac{10}{\cos 45°}$

$c = 10\sqrt{2}$ cm

2. $\cos\theta = \dfrac{2\sqrt{5}}{5}$

$\tan\theta = \dfrac{1}{2}$

$\cot\theta = 2$

$\sec\theta = \dfrac{\sqrt{5}}{2}$

$\csc\theta = \sqrt{5}$

3. $\sin\theta = -\dfrac{8}{17}$, $\cos\theta = \dfrac{15}{17}$, $\tan\theta = -\dfrac{8}{15}$

$\cot\theta = -\dfrac{15}{8}$, $\sec\theta = \dfrac{17}{15}$, $\csc\theta = -\dfrac{17}{8}$

4. $-\dfrac{\sqrt{2}}{2}$ **5.** 0 **6.** $-225° \cdot \dfrac{\pi\text{ radians}}{180°} = \dfrac{-5\pi}{4}$

7. $\dfrac{-3\pi}{2} \cdot \dfrac{180°}{\pi\text{ radians}} = -270°$ **8.** $r = rw$
$(75)(15) = 1125$ cm/sec

9. 0.8444 **10.** 1.391 **11.** 38°45′ **12.** 53°5′

13. $\sin 36° = 0.5878$, $\cos 36° = 0.8090$,
$\tan 36° = 0.7265$, $\cot 36° = 1.376$,
$\sec 36° = 1.236$, $\csc 36° = 1.701$

14. $A = 4$

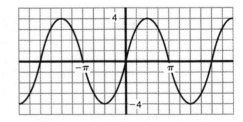

15. Period = π

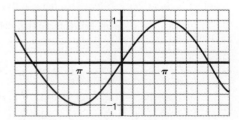

16. $\dfrac{\csc\theta\sin^2\theta + \csc\theta\cos^2\theta\tan\theta}{\sin\theta + \cos\theta} = \dfrac{\sin\theta + \cos\theta}{\sin\theta + \cos\theta} = 1$

17. $6\sec^2\theta - 5\sec\theta - 2 = 0$

$\sec\theta = \dfrac{5 \pm \sqrt{25 + 48}}{12}$

$= \dfrac{5 \pm \sqrt{73}}{12}$

$\sec\theta = \dfrac{5 + \sqrt{73}}{12}$

18. $\sec\theta = \pm\sqrt{1 + \tan^2\theta}$

$= \pm\sqrt{1 + \dfrac{\sin^2\theta}{\cos^2\theta}}$

$= \pm\sqrt{\dfrac{1}{\cos^2\theta}}$

$= \pm\sqrt{\dfrac{1}{1 - \sin^2\theta}}$

19. $\cot\left(\dfrac{\pi}{2} - \theta\right) = \dfrac{1}{\tan\left(\dfrac{\pi}{2} - \theta\right)}$

$= \dfrac{\cos\left(\dfrac{\pi}{2} - \theta\right)}{\sin\left(\dfrac{\pi}{2} - \theta\right)}$

$= \dfrac{\sin\theta}{\cos\theta}$

$= \tan\theta$

20. $2\sin^2\theta - 3\sin\theta + 1 = 0$

$(2\sin\theta - 1)(\sin\theta - 1) = 0$

$2\sin\theta - 1 = 0 \quad\text{or}\quad \sin\theta - 1 = 0$

$\sin\theta = \dfrac{1}{2} \quad\text{or}\quad \sin\theta = 1$

$\theta = 30°,\ 150°,\ 90°$

CHAPTER 18

p. 780 READY FOR TRIGONOMETRIC IDENTITIES AND EQUATIONS?

1. 81 **2.** $9|c|$ **3.** $\dfrac{\sqrt[3]{100mn^2}}{5n}$ **4.** $-\dfrac{63 + 4\sqrt{15}}{33}$

5. $\sqrt{a^2 + b^2}$ **6.** 13 **7.** $f^{-1}(x) = \dfrac{1}{3}x + \dfrac{2}{3}$

8. $f^{-1}(x) = x^2 - 4x + 1$ **9.** $\pm\sqrt{\dfrac{\sin^2\theta}{1 - \sin^2\theta}}$

10. $\pm\dfrac{\sqrt{1 - \cos^2\theta}}{\cos\theta}$ **11.** $\pm\dfrac{\sqrt{\csc^2\theta - 1}}{\csc^2\theta - 1}$ **12.** $\dfrac{1}{\cot\theta}$

13. $\pm\sqrt{\sec^2\theta - 1}$

pp. 782–786 18-1 TRY THIS

a. $\cos\left(\dfrac{\pi}{2} - \dfrac{\pi}{6}\right) = \cos\dfrac{\pi}{2}\cos\dfrac{\pi}{6} + \sin\dfrac{\pi}{2}\sin\dfrac{\pi}{6}$

$= 0\left(\dfrac{\sqrt{3}}{2}\right) + 1\left(\dfrac{1}{2}\right)$

$= 0 + \dfrac{1}{2}$

$= \dfrac{1}{2}$

b. $\cos 105° = \cos(150° - 45°)$

$= \cos 150°\cos 45° + \sin 150°\sin 45°$

$= -\cos 30°\cos 45° + \sin 30°\sin 45°$

$= -\dfrac{\sqrt{3}}{2}\cdot\dfrac{\sqrt{2}}{2} + \dfrac{1}{2}\cdot\dfrac{\sqrt{2}}{2}$

$= -\dfrac{\sqrt{6}}{4} + \dfrac{\sqrt{2}}{4}$

$= \dfrac{\sqrt{2} - \sqrt{6}}{4}$

c. $\cos 75° = \cos(30° + 45°202$

$= \cos 30°\cos 45° - \sin 30°\sin 45°$

$= \dfrac{\sqrt{3}}{2}\cdot\dfrac{\sqrt{2}}{2} - \dfrac{1}{2}\cdot\dfrac{\sqrt{2}}{2}$

$= \dfrac{\sqrt{6}}{4} - \dfrac{\sqrt{2}}{4}$

$= \dfrac{\sqrt{6} - \sqrt{2}}{4}$

d. $\sin\left(\dfrac{\pi}{4} + \dfrac{\pi}{3}\right) = \sin\dfrac{\pi}{4}\cos\dfrac{\pi}{3} + \cos\dfrac{\pi}{4}\sin\dfrac{\pi}{3}$

$= \dfrac{\sqrt{2}}{2}\cdot\dfrac{1}{2} + \dfrac{\sqrt{2}}{2}\cdot\dfrac{\sqrt{3}}{2}$

$= \dfrac{\sqrt{2}}{4} + \dfrac{\sqrt{6}}{4}$

$= \dfrac{\sqrt{2} + \sqrt{6}}{4}$

e. $\tan 105° = \tan(45° + 60°)$

$= \dfrac{\tan 45° + \tan 60°}{1 - \tan 45° + \tan 60°}$

$= \dfrac{1 + \sqrt{3}}{1 - 1(\sqrt{3})}$

$= \dfrac{1 + \sqrt{3}}{1 - \sqrt{3}}\left(\dfrac{1 + \sqrt{3}}{1 + \sqrt{3}}\right)$

$= \dfrac{4 + 2\sqrt{3}}{-2} = -2 - \sqrt{3}$

pp. 786–787 18-1 EXERCISES

1. $\cos A\cos B + \sin A\sin B$ **2.** $\cos A\cos B - \sin A\sin B$

3. $\dfrac{\sqrt{2} + \sqrt{6}}{4}$ **4.** $\dfrac{\sqrt{6} - \sqrt{2}}{4}$ **5.** $\dfrac{\sqrt{2} - \sqrt{6}}{4}$ **6.** $\dfrac{\sqrt{2} + \sqrt{6}}{4}$

7. $-\dfrac{\sqrt{3}}{2}$ **8.** $-\dfrac{\sqrt{3}}{2}$ **9.** $\dfrac{-\sqrt{2} - \sqrt{6}}{4}$ **10.** $\dfrac{-\sqrt{2} - \sqrt{6}}{4}$

11. $-\dfrac{\sqrt{2}}{2}$ **12.** $-\dfrac{\sqrt{2}}{2}$ **13.** $\sin P\cos Q + \cos P\sin Q$

14. $\sin P\cos Q - \cos P\sin Q$ **15.** $\dfrac{\tan P - \tan Q}{1 + \tan P\tan Q}$

16. $\dfrac{\tan P + \tan Q}{1 - \tan P\tan Q}$ **17.** $\dfrac{\sqrt{2} + \sqrt{6}}{4}$ **18.** $\dfrac{\sqrt{6} - \sqrt{2}}{4}$

19. $2 - \sqrt{3}$ **20.** $-2 - \sqrt{3}$ **21.** $\dfrac{\sqrt{6} - \sqrt{2}}{4}$

22. $\dfrac{\sqrt{2} + \sqrt{6}}{4}$ **23.** $2 + \sqrt{3}$ **24.** $2 - \sqrt{3}$ **25.** $\dfrac{\sqrt{6} - \sqrt{2}}{4}$

26. $\dfrac{\sqrt{6} + \sqrt{2}}{4}$ **27.** $\dfrac{\sqrt{2}}{2}$ **28.** $\dfrac{1}{2}$ **29.** $2 + \sqrt{3}$

30. $-2 - \sqrt{3}$ **31.** $2 - \sqrt{3}$ **32.** -1

33. $\sin\left(-\dfrac{5\pi}{2}\right)\cdot\sin\dfrac{\pi}{2} + \cos\dfrac{\pi}{2}\cos\left(-\dfrac{5\pi}{2}\right) = \cos\left(-\dfrac{5\pi}{2} - \dfrac{\pi}{2}\right)$

$(-1)(1) + (0)(0) = \cos\left(-\dfrac{6\pi}{2}\right)$

$= \cos(-3\pi)$

$-1 = \cos(-3\pi)$

34. $\sin\dfrac{\pi}{3}\cdot\sin\left(-\dfrac{\pi}{4}\right) + \cos\left(\dfrac{-\pi}{4}\right)\cdot\cos\dfrac{\pi}{4} = \cos\left(\dfrac{\pi}{3} - \left(-\dfrac{\pi}{4}\right)\right)$

$\dfrac{\sqrt{3}}{2}\cdot\dfrac{-\sqrt{2}}{2} + \dfrac{\sqrt{2}}{2}\cdot\dfrac{1}{2} = \cos\left(\dfrac{\pi}{3} + \dfrac{\pi}{4}\right)$

$-\dfrac{\sqrt{6}}{4} + \dfrac{\sqrt{2}}{4} = \cos\dfrac{7\pi}{12}$

$\dfrac{-\sqrt{6} + \sqrt{2}}{4} = \cos\dfrac{7\pi}{12}$

35. $\cos A \cos B + \sin A \sin B = \cos(A - B)$

36. $\cos A \cos B - \sin A \sin B = \cos(A + B)$

37. $\cos(\alpha + \beta) + \cos(\alpha - \beta) = \cos \alpha \cos \beta - \sin \alpha \sin \beta$
$\qquad\qquad\qquad\qquad\qquad + \cos \alpha \cos \beta + \sin \alpha \sin \beta$
$\qquad\qquad\qquad\qquad = \cos \alpha \cos \beta + \cos \alpha \cos \beta$
$\qquad\qquad\qquad\qquad = 2 \cos \alpha \cos \beta$

38. $\cos(\alpha + \beta) - \cos(\alpha - \beta) = \cos \alpha \cos \beta - \sin \alpha \sin \beta$
$\qquad\qquad\qquad\qquad\qquad - [\cos \alpha \cos \beta + \sin \alpha \sin \beta]$
$\qquad\qquad\qquad\qquad = \cos \alpha \cos \beta - \sin \alpha \sin \beta$
$\qquad\qquad\qquad\qquad\quad - \cos \alpha \cos \beta - \sin \alpha \sin \beta$
$\qquad\qquad\qquad\qquad = -2 \sin \alpha \sin \beta$

39. $\tan(A - B)$ **40.** $\tan(A + B)$

41. $\tan(20° + 32°) = \tan 52°$ **42.** $\tan(35° - 12°) = \tan 23°$
$\qquad\qquad\qquad\; = 1.2799$ $\qquad\qquad\qquad\qquad\qquad\; = 0.425$
$\qquad\qquad\qquad\; = 1.280$

43. $\sin(\alpha + \beta) + \sin(\alpha - \beta) = \sin \alpha \cos \beta + \cos \alpha \sin \beta$
$\qquad\qquad\qquad\qquad\qquad + \sin \alpha \cos \beta - \cos \alpha \sin \beta$
$\qquad\qquad\qquad\qquad = 2 \sin \alpha \cos \beta$

44. $\sin(\alpha + \beta) - \sin(\alpha - \beta) = \sin \alpha \cos \beta + \cos \alpha \sin \beta$
$\qquad\qquad\qquad\qquad\qquad - [\sin \alpha \cos \beta - \cos \alpha \sin \beta]$
$\qquad\qquad\qquad\qquad = \sin \alpha \cos \beta + \cos \alpha \sin \beta$
$\qquad\qquad\qquad\qquad\quad - \sin \alpha \cos \beta + \cos \alpha \sin \beta$
$\qquad\qquad\qquad\qquad = 2 \sin \beta \cos \alpha$

45. $\sin \dfrac{\pi}{3} \cdot \cos \pi + \sin \pi \cdot \cos \dfrac{\pi}{3} = \sin\left(\dfrac{\pi}{3} + \pi\right)$

$\qquad\qquad\qquad\qquad\qquad\qquad\quad = \sin \dfrac{4\pi}{3}$

$\qquad\qquad\qquad\qquad\qquad\qquad\quad = -\dfrac{\sqrt{3}}{2}$

46. $\sin \dfrac{\pi}{2} \cdot \cos \dfrac{\pi}{3} - \sin \dfrac{\pi}{3} \cdot \cos \dfrac{\pi}{2} = \sin\left(\dfrac{\pi}{2} - \dfrac{\pi}{3}\right)$

$\qquad\qquad\qquad\qquad\qquad\qquad\quad = \sin\left(\dfrac{\pi}{6}\right)$

$\qquad\qquad\qquad\qquad\qquad\qquad\quad = \dfrac{1}{2}$

47. $\cot(\alpha + \beta) = \dfrac{1}{\tan(\alpha + \beta)}$

$\qquad\qquad\quad = \dfrac{1}{\dfrac{\tan \alpha + \tan \beta}{1 - \tan \alpha \tan \beta}}$

$\qquad\qquad\quad = \dfrac{1 - \tan \alpha \tan \beta}{\tan \alpha + \tan \beta}$

$\qquad\qquad\quad = \dfrac{1 - \dfrac{1}{\cot \alpha} \cdot \dfrac{1}{\cot \beta}}{\dfrac{1}{\cot \alpha} + \dfrac{1}{\cot \beta}}$

$\qquad\qquad\quad = \dfrac{\cot \alpha \cot \beta - 1}{\cot \beta \cot \alpha} \cdot \dfrac{\cot \beta \cot \alpha}{\cot \beta + \cot \alpha}$

$\qquad\qquad\quad = \dfrac{\cot \alpha \cot \beta - 1}{\cot \beta + \cot \alpha}$

48. $\cot(\alpha - \beta) = \dfrac{1}{\tan(\alpha - \beta)}$

$\qquad\qquad\quad = \dfrac{1}{\dfrac{\tan \alpha - \tan \beta}{1 + \tan \alpha \tan \beta}}$

$\qquad\qquad\quad = \dfrac{1 + \tan \alpha \tan \beta}{\tan \alpha - \tan \beta}$

$\qquad\qquad\quad = \dfrac{1 + \dfrac{1}{\cot \alpha} \cdot \dfrac{1}{\cot \beta}}{\dfrac{1}{\cot \alpha} - \dfrac{1}{\cot \beta}}$

$\qquad\qquad\quad = \dfrac{\cot \alpha \cot \beta + 1}{\cot \alpha \cot \beta} \cdot \dfrac{\cot \alpha \cot \beta}{\cot \beta - \cot \alpha}$

$\qquad\qquad\quad = \dfrac{\cot \alpha \cot \beta + 1}{\cot \beta - \cot \alpha}$

49. $\sin\left(\dfrac{\pi}{2} - x\right) = \sin \dfrac{\pi}{2} \cos x - \cos \dfrac{\pi}{2} \sin x$

$\qquad\qquad\qquad = 1 \cdot \cos x - 0 \cdot \sin x$

$\qquad\qquad\qquad = \cos x$

50. $\sin\left(x - \dfrac{\pi}{2}\right) = \sin x \cos \dfrac{\pi}{2} - \cos x \sin \dfrac{\pi}{2}$

$\qquad\qquad\qquad = \sin x \cdot 0 - \cos x \cdot 1$

$\qquad\qquad\qquad = -\cos x$

51. $\cos\left(\dfrac{\pi}{2} - x\right) = \cos \dfrac{\pi}{2} \cos x + \sin \dfrac{\pi}{2} \sin x$

$\qquad\qquad\qquad = 0 \cdot \cos x + 1 \cdot \sin x$

$\qquad\qquad\qquad = \sin x$

52. $\cos\left(x + \dfrac{\pi}{2}\right) = \cos x \cos \dfrac{\pi}{2} - \sin x \sin \dfrac{\pi}{2}$

$\qquad\qquad\qquad = \cos x \cdot 0 - \sin x \cdot 1$

$\qquad\qquad\qquad = -\sin x$

53. $\sin 45° + \sin 30° \approx 0.7071 + 0.5 = 1.2071$
$\qquad\qquad\quad \sin 75° \approx 0.9659$

54. $\cos 45° - \cos 30° \approx 0.7071 - 0.8660 \approx -0.1589$
$\qquad\qquad\quad \cos 15° \approx 0.9659$

55. $\sin 2\theta = \sin(\theta + \theta)$
$\qquad\quad = \sin \theta \cos \theta + \cos \theta \sin \theta$
$\qquad\quad = 2 \sin \theta \cos \theta$
$\cos 2\theta = \cos(\theta + \theta)$
$\qquad\quad = \cos \theta \cos \theta - \sin \theta \sin \theta$
$\qquad\quad = \cos^2 \theta - \sin^2 \theta$
$\tan 2\theta = \tan(\theta + \theta)$

$\qquad\quad = \dfrac{\tan \theta + \tan \theta}{1 - \tan \theta \tan \theta}$

$\qquad\quad = \dfrac{2 \tan \theta}{1 - \tan^2 \theta}$

56. $\sin(\theta + \phi) = \sin \theta \cos \phi + \cos \theta \sin \phi$
$\qquad\qquad\quad \approx (0.6249)(0.1102) + (0.7807)(0.9939)$
$\qquad\qquad\quad \approx 0.0689 + 0.7759$
$\qquad\qquad\quad \approx 0.8448$

57. $\cos(\theta + \phi) = \cos \theta \cos \phi - \sin \theta \sin \phi$
$\qquad\qquad\quad \approx (0.7807)(0.1102) - (0.6249)(0.9939)$
$\qquad\qquad\quad \approx 0.0860 - 0.6211$
$\qquad\qquad\quad \approx -0.5351$

58. $\tan(\theta + \phi) = \dfrac{\sin(\theta + \phi)}{\cos(\theta + \phi)} = \dfrac{0.8448}{-0.5351} = -1.5789$

59. $\sin(\sin x + \sin y) = \sin(u + v)$
$\qquad\qquad\qquad\quad = \sin u \cos v + \cos u \sin v$
$\qquad\qquad\qquad\quad = \sin(\sin x) \cos(\sin y) + \cos(\sin x) \sin(\sin y)$

60. $\cos(\cos x + \cos y) = \cos(\cos x) \cos(\cos y)$
$\qquad\qquad\qquad\qquad\quad - \sin(\cos x) \sin(\cos y)$

61. $\sin(x + y + z) = \sin[(x + y) + z]$
$\qquad\qquad\qquad = \sin(x + y) \cos z + \cos(x + y) \sin z$
$\qquad\qquad\qquad = (\sin x \cos y + \cos x \sin y) \cos z$
$\qquad\qquad\qquad\quad + [\cos x \cos y - (\sin x \sin y)] \sin z$
$\qquad\qquad\qquad = \sin x \cos y \cos z + \cos x \sin y \cos z$
$\qquad\qquad\qquad\quad + \cos x \cos y \sin z - \sin x \sin y \sin z$

62. $\dfrac{2}{(q + 1)(q - 1)} - \dfrac{1}{q(q - 1)} = \dfrac{2q - q - 1}{q(q + 1)(q - 1)}$

$\qquad\qquad\qquad\qquad\qquad\qquad = \dfrac{q - 1}{q(q + 1)(q - 1)}$

$\qquad\qquad\qquad\qquad\qquad\qquad = \dfrac{1}{q(q + 1)}$

63. $\dfrac{1 - m}{1 - \dfrac{1}{m}} = \dfrac{1 - m}{\dfrac{m - 1}{m}}$

$$= 1 - m \cdot \left(\frac{m}{m-1}\right)$$
$$= -m$$

64. $\dfrac{\dfrac{4}{x-5} + \dfrac{2}{x+2}}{\dfrac{-3x}{(x-5)(x+2)} + \dfrac{3}{x-5}} = \dfrac{\dfrac{6x-2}{(x-5)(x+2)}}{\dfrac{6}{(x-5)(x+2)}}$

$$= \frac{2(3x-1)}{6}$$
$$= \frac{3x-1}{3}$$
$$= x - \frac{1}{3}$$

65. $\sqrt{\dfrac{2}{3}} + \sqrt{\dfrac{3}{2}} = \dfrac{\sqrt{6}}{3} + \dfrac{\sqrt{6}}{2}$
$\qquad = \dfrac{2\sqrt{6} + 3\sqrt{6}}{6}$
$\qquad = \dfrac{5\sqrt{6}}{6}$

66. $\sqrt[3]{9}\ \sqrt[6]{9} = 3^{2/3} \cdot 3^{1/3}$
$\qquad = 3^{3/3}$
$\qquad = 3$

67. 0.3488 **68.** 0.8 **69.** 0.8420 **70.** 5.9758

71. $(v^{2/5})^{5/2} = (9)^{5/2}$
$\qquad v = 9^{5/2}$
$\qquad = \sqrt[2]{9^5}$
$\qquad = 243$

72. $x^{2/3} - x^{1/3} - 12 = 0$
$\qquad (x^{1/3} - 4)(x^{1/3} + 3) = 0$
$\qquad\qquad x^{1/3} = 4 \quad \text{or} \quad x^{1/3} = -3$
$\qquad\qquad\quad x = 64 \quad \text{or} \quad x = -27$

73. $\dfrac{19.6}{4} = \dfrac{s}{225}$
$\qquad 4s = 19.6 \cdot 225$
$\qquad\ s = 1102.5$
The object falls 1102.5 meters.

pp. 788–791　　18-2 TRY THIS

a. $\sin 2\theta = 2 \sin \theta \cos \theta$
$\qquad = 2\left(\dfrac{3}{5}\right)\left(\dfrac{4}{5}\right)$
$\qquad = \dfrac{24}{25}$

b. $\sin 2\theta = 2 \sin \theta \cos \theta$
$\qquad = 2\left(-\dfrac{5}{13}\right)\left(\dfrac{12}{13}\right)$
$\qquad = -\dfrac{120}{169}$
$\cos 2\theta = \cos^2\theta - \sin^2\theta$
$\qquad = \dfrac{25}{169} - \dfrac{144}{169}$
$\qquad = -\dfrac{119}{169}$; θ is in the second quadrant.

$\tan 2\theta = \dfrac{2 \tan \theta}{1 - \tan^2\theta} = \dfrac{2\left(-\dfrac{12}{5}\right)}{1 - \left(-\dfrac{12}{5}\right)^2} = \dfrac{\dfrac{-24}{5}}{\dfrac{-119}{25}} = \dfrac{120}{119}$

c. $\cos 3\theta \equiv \cos(2\theta + \theta)$
$\qquad \equiv \cos 2\theta \cos \theta - \sin 2\theta \sin \theta$
$\qquad \equiv (\cos^2\theta - \sin^2\theta) \cos \theta - 2 \sin \theta \cos \theta \sin \theta$
$\qquad \equiv \cos^3\theta - \sin^2\theta \cos \theta - 2 \sin^2\theta \cos \theta$
$\qquad \equiv \cos^3\theta - 3 \sin^2\theta \cos \theta$
$\qquad\qquad$ OR
$\qquad \equiv (1 - 2 \sin^2\theta) \cos \theta - 2 \sin \theta \cos \theta \sin \theta$
$\qquad \equiv \cos \theta - 2 \sin^2\theta \cos \theta - 2 \sin^2\theta \cos \theta$
$\qquad \equiv \cos \theta - 4 \sin^2\theta \cos \theta$
$\qquad\qquad$ OR
$\qquad \equiv (2 \cos^2\theta - 1) \cos \theta - 2 \sin \theta \cos \theta \sin \theta$
$\qquad \equiv 2 \cos^3\theta - \cos \theta - 2 \sin^2\theta \cos \theta$

d. $\cos 15° = \cos \dfrac{30°}{2}$
$\qquad = +\sqrt{\dfrac{1 + \cos 30°}{2}}$
$\qquad = +\sqrt{\dfrac{1 + \sqrt{3}/2}{2}}$
$\qquad = \sqrt{\dfrac{2 + \sqrt{3}}{2} \cdot \dfrac{1}{2}}$
$\qquad = \dfrac{\sqrt{2 + \sqrt{3}}}{2}$

e. $\tan 45° = \tan \dfrac{90°}{2}$
$\qquad = \dfrac{\sin 90°}{1 + \cos 90°}$
$\qquad = \dfrac{1}{1 + 0}$
$\qquad = 1$

p. 792　　18-2 EXERCISES

1. $\dfrac{24}{25}, -\dfrac{7}{25}, -\dfrac{24}{7},$ II **2.** $\dfrac{120}{169}, \dfrac{119}{169}, \dfrac{120}{119},$ I

3. $\dfrac{24}{25}, \dfrac{7}{25}, \dfrac{24}{7},$ I **4.** $\dfrac{24}{25}, -\dfrac{7}{25}, -\dfrac{24}{7},$ II

5. $\dfrac{24}{25}, -\dfrac{7}{25}, -\dfrac{24}{7},$ II **6.** $\dfrac{24}{25}, \dfrac{7}{25}, \dfrac{24}{7},$ I

7. $\dfrac{\sqrt{2 + \sqrt{3}}}{2}$ **8.** $\dfrac{\sqrt{2 - \sqrt{3}}}{2}$ **9.** $2 + \sqrt{3}$

10. $\sqrt{2} + 1$ **11.** $\dfrac{\sqrt{2 + \sqrt{2}}}{2}$ **12.** $\dfrac{-\sqrt{2 - \sqrt{2}}}{2}$

13. $\dfrac{\sqrt{2 + \sqrt{2}}}{2}$ **14.** $\dfrac{\sqrt{2 - \sqrt{2}}}{2}$ **15.** $\sqrt{2} - 1$

16. $1 - 2 \sin^2 \dfrac{x}{2} = \cos 2\left(\dfrac{x}{2}\right)$
$\qquad\qquad\qquad\qquad = \cos x$

17. $2 \cos^2 \dfrac{x}{2} - 1 = \cos 2\left(\dfrac{x}{2}\right)$
$\qquad\qquad\qquad\qquad = \cos x$

18. $2 \sin \dfrac{x}{2} \cos \dfrac{x}{2} = \sin 2\left(\dfrac{x}{2}\right)$
$\qquad\qquad\qquad\qquad = \sin x$

19. $2 \sin 2x \cos 2x = \sin 2(2x)$
$\qquad\qquad\qquad\qquad = \sin 4x$

20. $\cos^2 \dfrac{x}{2} - \sin^2 \dfrac{x}{2} = \cos 2\left(\dfrac{x}{2}\right)$
$\qquad\qquad\qquad\qquad\quad = \cos x$

21. $2 \sin^2 \dfrac{x}{2} + \cos x = 2\left(\sqrt{\dfrac{1 - \cos x}{2}}\right)^2 + \cos x$
$\qquad\qquad\qquad = 2\left(\dfrac{1 - \cos x}{2}\right) + \cos x$
$\qquad\qquad\qquad = 1 - \cos x + \cos x$
$\qquad\qquad\qquad = 1$

22. $\cos^4 x - \sin^4 x = (\cos^2 x - \sin^2 x)(\cos^2 x + \sin^2 x)$
$\qquad\qquad\qquad\quad = (\cos^2 x - \sin^2 x) \cdot 1$
$\qquad\qquad\qquad\quad = \cos 2x$

23. $(\sin x + \cos x)^2 - \sin 2x = \sin^2 x + 2 \sin x \cos x$
$\qquad\qquad\qquad\qquad\qquad\qquad + \cos^2 x - 2 \sin x \cos x$
$\qquad\qquad\qquad\qquad\qquad = 1$

24. $(\sin x - \cos x)^2 + \sin 2x = \sin^2 x - 2 \sin x \cos x$
$\qquad\qquad\qquad\qquad\qquad\qquad + \cos^2 x + 2 \sin x \cos x$
$\qquad\qquad\qquad\qquad\qquad = 1$

25. $2 \sin x \cos^3 x + 2 \sin^3 x \cos x = 2 \sin x \cos x$
$\qquad\qquad\qquad\qquad\qquad\qquad (\cos^2 x + \sin^2 x)$
$\qquad\qquad\qquad\qquad\qquad = 2 \sin x \cos x \cdot 1$
$\qquad\qquad\qquad\qquad\qquad = 2 \sin x \cos x$
$\qquad\qquad\qquad\qquad\qquad = \sin 2x$

26. $2 \sin x \cos^3 x - 2 \sin^3 x \cos x = 2 \sin x \cos x$
$\qquad\qquad\qquad\qquad\qquad\qquad (\cos^2 x - \sin^2 x)$
$\qquad\qquad\qquad\qquad\qquad = \sin 2x \cdot \cos 2x$

27. $\sin 4\theta = \sin 2(2\theta)$
$\qquad\quad = 2 \sin 2\theta \cos 2\theta$
$\qquad\quad = 2 \cdot 2 \sin \theta \cos \theta(\cos^2\theta - \sin^2\theta)$
$\qquad\quad = 4 \sin \theta \cos^3\theta - 4 \sin^3\theta \cos \theta \qquad$ OR
$\qquad\quad = 2 \cdot 2 \sin \theta \cos \theta(1 - 2 \sin^2\theta)$
$\qquad\quad = 4 \sin \theta \cos \theta - 8 \sin^3\theta \cos \theta \qquad$ OR

$$= 2 \cdot 2 \sin\theta\cos\theta(2\cos^2\theta - 1)$$
$$= 8\sin\theta\cos^3\theta - 4\sin\theta\cos\theta$$

$$\cos 4\theta = \cos 2(2\theta)$$
$$= \cos^2 2\theta - \sin^2 2\theta$$
$$= (\cos^2\theta - \sin^2\theta)^2 - 4\sin^2\theta\cos^2\theta$$
$$= \cos^4\theta - 2\cos^2\theta\sin^2\theta + \sin^4\theta - 4\sin^2\theta\cos^2\theta$$
$$= \cos^4\theta + \sin^4\theta - 6\sin^2\theta\cos^2\theta$$

OR

$$= 1 - 2\sin^2 2\theta$$
$$= 1 - 2(4\sin^2\theta\cos^2\theta)$$
$$= 1 - 8\sin^2\theta\cos^2\theta$$

OR

$$= 2\cos^2 2\theta - 1$$
$$= 2(2\cos^2\theta - 1)^2 - 1$$
$$= 2(4\cos^4\theta - 4\cos^2\theta + 1) - 1$$
$$= 8\cos^4\theta - 8\cos^2\theta + 2 - 1$$
$$= 8\cos^4\theta - 8\cos^2\theta + 1$$

28. $\sin^4\theta = \sin^2\theta \cdot \sin^2\theta$

$$= \frac{\cos 2\theta - 1}{2} \cdot \frac{\cos 2\theta - 1}{2}$$

$$= \frac{\cos^2 2\theta - 2\cos 2\theta + 1}{4}$$

$$= \frac{\cos 4\theta + 1}{2 \cdot 4} - \frac{2\cos 2\theta}{4} + \frac{1}{4}$$

$$= \frac{1}{8}(\cos 4\theta + 1 + 4\cos 2\theta + 2)$$

$$= \frac{1}{8}(3 - 4\cos 2\theta + \cos 4\theta)$$

29. $\cos^4\theta = \cos^2\theta \cdot \cos^2\theta$

$$= \frac{\cos 2\theta + 1}{2} \cdot \frac{\cos 2\theta + 1}{2}$$

$$= \frac{1}{4}(\cos^2 2\theta + 2\cos 2\theta + 1)$$

$$= \frac{1}{4}\left(\frac{\cos 4\theta + 1}{2} + 2\cos 2\theta + 1\right)$$

$$= \frac{1}{8}(\cos 4\theta + 1 + 4\cos 2\theta + 2)$$

$$= \frac{1}{8}(\cos 4\theta + 4\cos 2\theta + 3)$$

30. $\tan 2\theta = \tan(\theta + \theta) = \dfrac{\tan\theta + \tan\theta}{1 - (\tan\theta)(\tan\theta)}$

$$= \frac{2\tan\theta}{1 - \tan^2\theta}$$

31.
$$f(x) = \sqrt[3]{x^2 + 1}$$
$$x = \sqrt[3]{y^2 + 1}$$
$$x^3 = y^2 + 1$$
$$x^3 - 1 = y^2$$
$$\sqrt{x^3 - 1} = y$$
$$\sqrt{x^3 - 1} = f^{-1}(x)$$

32. $f(x) = \log_4 x$
$$4^x = y$$
$$4^x = f^{-1}(x)$$

33. $f(x) = e^x$
$$y = e^x$$
$$\ln_e y = x$$
$$\ln_e x = y$$
$$\ln_e x = f^{-1}(x)$$

34.
$$f(x) = 2x - 6$$
$$y = 2x - 6$$
$$x = 2y - 6$$
$$x + 6 = 2y$$
$$\frac{1}{2}x + 3 = y$$
$$\frac{1}{2}x + 3 = f^{-1}(x)$$

35.

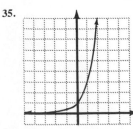

36.
$$x^2 + (x - 2)^2 = 10^2$$
$$x^2 + x^2 - 4x + 4 = 100$$
$$2x^2 - 4x - 96 = 0$$
$$x^2 - 2x - 48 = 0$$
$$(x - 8)(x + 6) = 0$$
$$x = 8 \quad \text{or} \quad x = -6$$

x cannot be negative, so the sides are 8 cm and $8 - 2$ or 6 cm.

p. 794   18-3 TRY THIS

a. $\cot^2 x - \cos^2 x \equiv \cos^2 x\,\cot^2 x$

$$\begin{array}{c|c} \dfrac{\cos^2 x}{\sin^2 x} - \cos^2 x & \cos^2 x\,\dfrac{\cos^2 x}{\sin^2 x} \\ \hline \dfrac{\cos^2 x - \cos^2 x\,\sin^2 x}{\sin^2 x} & \\ \dfrac{\cos^2 x(1 - \sin^2 x)}{\sin^2 x} & \\ \dfrac{\cos^2 x\,\cos^2 x}{\sin^2 x} & \end{array}$$

b. $\dfrac{\sin 2\theta + \sin\theta}{\cos 2\theta + \cos\theta + 1} \equiv \tan\theta$

$$\begin{array}{c|c} \dfrac{2\sin\theta\cos\theta + \sin\theta}{\cos^2\theta - \sin^2\theta + \cos\theta + 1} & \dfrac{\sin\theta}{\cos\theta} \\ \hline \dfrac{2\sin\theta\cos\theta + \sin\theta}{\cos^2\theta - \sin^2\theta + \cos\theta + \sin^2\theta + \cos^2\theta} & \\ \dfrac{2\sin\theta\cos\theta + \sin\theta}{2\cos^2\theta + \cos\theta} & \\ \dfrac{\sin\theta(2\cos\theta + 1)}{\cos\theta(2\cos\theta + 1)} & \\ \dfrac{\sin\theta}{\cos\theta} & \end{array}$$

pp. 794–795   18-3 EXERCISES

1. $\csc x - \cos x\,\cot x \equiv \sin x$

$$\begin{array}{c|c} \dfrac{1}{\sin x} - \cos x\,\dfrac{\cos x}{\sin x} & \sin x \\ \hline \dfrac{1 - \cos^2 x}{\sin x} & \\ \dfrac{\sin^2 x}{\sin x} & \\ \sin x & \end{array}$$

2. $\sec x - \sin x\,\tan x \equiv \cos x$

$$\begin{array}{c|c} \dfrac{1}{\cos x} - \sin x\,\dfrac{\sin x}{\cos x} & \cos x \\ \hline \dfrac{1 - \sin^2 x}{\cos x} & \\ \dfrac{\cos^2 x}{\cos x} & \\ \cos x & \end{array}$$

3. $\dfrac{1 + \cos\theta}{\sin\theta} + \dfrac{\sin\theta}{\cos\theta} \equiv \dfrac{\cos\theta + 1}{\sin\theta\cos\theta}$

$$\begin{array}{c|c} \dfrac{1 + \cos\theta}{\sin\theta} \cdot \dfrac{\cos\theta}{\cos\theta} + \dfrac{\sin\theta}{\cos\theta} \cdot \dfrac{\sin\theta}{\sin\theta} & \dfrac{\cos\theta + 1}{\sin\theta\cos\theta} \\ \hline \dfrac{\cos\theta + \cos^2\theta + \sin^2\theta}{\sin\theta\cos\theta} & \\ \dfrac{\cos\theta + 1}{\sin\theta\cos\theta} & \end{array}$$

4. $$\frac{1}{\sin\theta\cos\theta} - \frac{\cos\theta}{\sin\theta} \equiv \frac{\sin\theta\cos\theta}{1-\sin^2\theta}$$

$\dfrac{1}{\sin\theta\cos\theta} - \dfrac{\cos\theta}{\sin\theta}\cdot\dfrac{\cos\theta}{\cos\theta}$	$\dfrac{\sin\theta\cos\theta}{\cos^2\theta}$
$\dfrac{1-\cos^2\theta}{\sin\theta\cos\theta}$	$\dfrac{\sin\theta}{\cos\theta}$
$\dfrac{\sin^2\theta}{\sin\theta\cos\theta}$	
$\dfrac{\sin\theta}{\cos\theta}$	

5. $$\frac{1-\sin x}{\cos x} \equiv \frac{\cos x}{1+\sin x}$$

$\dfrac{1-\sin x}{\cos x}\cdot\dfrac{\cos x}{\cos x}$	$\dfrac{\cos x}{1+\sin x}\cdot\dfrac{1-\sin x}{1-\sin x}$
$\dfrac{\cos x - \sin x\cos x}{\cos^2 x}$	$\dfrac{\cos x - \cos x\sin x}{1-\sin^2 x}$
	$\dfrac{\cos x - \sin x\cos x}{\cos^2 x}$

6. $$\frac{1-\cos x}{\sin x} \equiv \frac{\sin x}{1+\cos x}$$

$\dfrac{1-\cos x}{\sin x}\cdot\dfrac{\sin x}{\sin x}$	$\dfrac{\sin x}{1+\cos x}\cdot\dfrac{1-\cos x}{1-\cos x}$
$\dfrac{\sin x - \cos x\sin x}{\sin^2 x}$	$\dfrac{\sin x - \sin x\cos x}{1-\cos^2 x}$
	$\dfrac{\sin x - \cos x\sin x}{\sin^2 x}$

7. $$\frac{1+\tan\theta}{1+\cot\theta} \equiv \frac{\sec\theta}{\csc\theta}$$

$\dfrac{1+\dfrac{\sin\theta}{\cos\theta}}{1+\dfrac{\cos\theta}{\sin\theta}}$	$\dfrac{\dfrac{1}{\cos\theta}}{\dfrac{1}{\sin\theta}}$
$\dfrac{\dfrac{\cos\theta+\sin\theta}{\cos\theta}}{\dfrac{\sin\theta+\cos\theta}{\sin\theta}}$	$\dfrac{\sin\theta}{\cos\theta}$
$\dfrac{\sin\theta}{\cos\theta}$	

8. $$\frac{\cot\theta-1}{1-\tan\theta} \equiv \frac{\csc\theta}{\sec\theta}$$

$\dfrac{\dfrac{\cos\theta}{\sin\theta}-1}{1-\dfrac{\sin\theta}{\cos\theta}}$	$\dfrac{\dfrac{1}{\sin\theta}}{\dfrac{1}{\cos\theta}}$
$\dfrac{\dfrac{\cos\theta-\sin\theta}{\sin\theta}}{\dfrac{\cos\theta-\sin\theta}{\cos\theta}}$	$\dfrac{\cos\theta}{\sin\theta}$
$\dfrac{\cos\theta}{\sin\theta}$	

9. $$\frac{\sin x+\cos x}{\sec x+\csc x} \equiv \frac{\sin x}{\sec x}$$

$\dfrac{\sin x+\cos x}{\dfrac{1}{\cos x}+\dfrac{1}{\sin x}}$	$\dfrac{\sin x}{\dfrac{1}{\cos x}}$
$\dfrac{\sin x+\cos x}{\dfrac{\sin x+\cos x}{\cos x\sin x}}$	$\cos x\sin x$
$\cos x\sin x$	

10. $$\frac{\sin x-\cos x}{\sec x-\csc x} \equiv \frac{\cos x}{\csc x}$$

$\dfrac{\sin x-\cos x}{\dfrac{1}{\cos x}-\dfrac{1}{\sin x}}$	$\dfrac{\cos x}{\dfrac{1}{\sin x}}$
$\dfrac{\sin x-\cos x}{\dfrac{\sin x-\cos x}{\cos x\sin x}}$	$\cos x\sin x$
$\cos x\sin x$	

11. $$\frac{1+\tan\theta}{1-\tan\theta}+\frac{1+\cot\theta}{1-\cot\theta} \equiv 0$$

$\dfrac{1+\dfrac{\sin\theta}{\cos\theta}}{1-\dfrac{\sin\theta}{\cos\theta}}+\dfrac{1+\dfrac{\cos\theta}{\sin\theta}}{1-\dfrac{\cos\theta}{\sin\theta}}$	0
$\dfrac{\dfrac{\cos\theta+\sin\theta}{\cos\theta}}{\dfrac{\cos\theta-\sin\theta}{\cos\theta}}+\dfrac{\dfrac{\sin\theta+\cos\theta}{\sin\theta}}{\dfrac{\sin\theta-\cos\theta}{\sin\theta}}$	
$\dfrac{\cos\theta+\sin\theta}{\cos\theta-\sin\theta}+\dfrac{\sin\theta+\cos\theta}{\sin\theta-\cos\theta}$	
$\dfrac{\cos\theta+\sin\theta}{\cos\theta-\sin\theta}-\dfrac{\cos\theta+\sin\theta}{\cos\theta-\sin\theta}$	

12. $$\frac{\cos^2\theta+\cot\theta}{\cos^2\theta-\cot\theta} \equiv \frac{\cos^2\theta\tan\theta+1}{\cos^2\theta\tan\theta-1}$$

$\dfrac{\cos^2\theta+\dfrac{\cos\theta}{\sin\theta}}{\cos^2\theta-\dfrac{\cos\theta}{\sin\theta}}$	$\dfrac{\cos^2\theta\dfrac{\sin\theta}{\cos\theta}+1}{\cos^2\theta\dfrac{\sin\theta}{\cos\theta}-1}$
$\dfrac{\dfrac{\cos^2\theta\sin\theta+\cos\theta}{\sin\theta}}{\dfrac{\cos^2\theta\sin\theta-\cos\theta}{\sin\theta}}$	$\dfrac{\cos\theta\sin\theta+1}{\cos\theta\sin\theta-1}$
$\dfrac{\cos^2\theta\sin\theta+\cos\theta}{\cos^2\theta\sin\theta-\cos\theta}$	
$\dfrac{\cos\theta(\cos\theta\sin\theta+1)}{\cos\theta(\cos\theta\sin\theta-1)}$	
$\dfrac{\cos\theta\sin\theta+1}{\cos\theta\sin\theta-1}$	

13. $$\frac{1+\cos 2\theta}{\sin 2\theta} \equiv \cot\theta$$

$\dfrac{1+2\cos^2\theta-1}{2\sin\theta\cos\theta}$	$\dfrac{\cos\theta}{\sin\theta}$
$\dfrac{\cos\theta}{\sin\theta}$	

14. $$\frac{2\tan\theta}{1+\tan^2\theta} \equiv \sin 2\theta$$

$\dfrac{2\dfrac{\sin\theta}{\cos\theta}}{1+\dfrac{\sin^2\theta}{\cos^2\theta}}$	$2\sin\theta\cos\theta$
$\dfrac{2\dfrac{\sin\theta}{\cos\theta}}{\dfrac{\cos^2\theta+\sin^2\theta}{\cos^2\theta}}$	
$2\dfrac{\sin\theta}{\cos\theta}\cdot\dfrac{\cos^2\theta}{\cos^2\theta+\sin^2\theta}$	
$2\sin\theta\cos\theta$	

15. $\sec 2\theta \equiv \dfrac{\sec^2\theta}{2 - \sec^2\theta}$

$$\begin{array}{c|c}
\dfrac{1}{\cos 2\theta} & \dfrac{\dfrac{1}{\cos^2\theta}}{2 - \dfrac{1}{\cos^2\theta}} \\[3ex]
\dfrac{1}{2\cos^2\theta - 1} & \dfrac{\dfrac{1}{\cos^2\theta}}{\dfrac{2\cos^2\theta - 1}{\cos^2\theta}} \\[4ex]
 & \dfrac{1}{2\cos^2\theta - 1}
\end{array}$$

16. $\cot 2\theta \equiv \dfrac{\cot^2\theta - 1}{2\cot\theta}$

$$\begin{array}{c|c}
\dfrac{\cos 2\theta}{\sin 2\theta} & \dfrac{\dfrac{\cos^2\theta}{\sin^2\theta} - 1}{2\dfrac{\cos\theta}{\sin\theta}} \\[4ex]
 & \dfrac{\dfrac{\cos^2\theta - \sin^2\theta}{\sin^2\theta}}{2\dfrac{\cos\theta}{\sin\theta}} \\[4ex]
 & \dfrac{\cos^2\theta - \sin^2\theta}{\sin^2\theta} \cdot \dfrac{\sin\theta}{2\cos\theta} \\[3ex]
 & \dfrac{\cos 2\theta}{\sin 2\theta}
\end{array}$$

17. $\dfrac{\sin(\alpha + \beta)}{\cos\alpha\cos\beta} \equiv \tan\alpha + \tan\beta$

$$\begin{array}{c|c}
\dfrac{\sin\alpha\cos\beta + \cos\alpha\sin\beta}{\cos\alpha\cos\beta} & \dfrac{\sin\alpha}{\cos\alpha} + \dfrac{\sin\beta}{\cos\beta} \\[3ex]
 & \dfrac{\sin\alpha\cos\beta + \cos\alpha\sin\beta}{\cos\alpha\cos\beta}
\end{array}$$

18. $\dfrac{\cos(\alpha - \beta)}{\cos\alpha\sin\beta} \equiv \tan\alpha + \cot\beta$

$$\begin{array}{c|c}
\dfrac{\cos\alpha\cos\beta + \sin\alpha\sin\beta}{\cos\alpha\sin\beta} & \dfrac{\sin\alpha}{\cos\alpha} + \dfrac{\cos\beta}{\sin\beta} \\[3ex]
\dfrac{\sin\alpha\sin\beta + \cos\alpha\cos\beta}{\cos\alpha\sin\beta} & \dfrac{\sin\alpha\sin\beta + \cos\alpha\cos\beta}{\cos\alpha\sin\beta}
\end{array}$$

19. $\dfrac{\tan\theta + \sin\theta}{2\tan\theta} \equiv \cos^2\dfrac{\theta}{2}$

$$\begin{array}{c|c}
\dfrac{\dfrac{\sin\theta}{\cos\theta} + \sin\theta}{2\dfrac{\sin\theta}{\cos\theta}} & \dfrac{1 + \cos\theta}{2} \\[4ex]
\dfrac{\dfrac{\sin\theta + \sin\theta\cos\theta}{\cos\theta}}{2\dfrac{\sin\theta}{\cos\theta}} & \\[4ex]
\dfrac{\sin\theta + \sin\theta\cos\theta}{2\sin\theta} & \\[3ex]
\dfrac{1 + \cos\theta}{2} &
\end{array}$$

20. $\dfrac{\tan\theta - \sin\theta}{2\tan\theta} \equiv \sin^2\dfrac{\theta}{2}$

$$\begin{array}{c|c}
\dfrac{\dfrac{\sin\theta}{\cos\theta} - \sin\theta}{2\dfrac{\sin\theta}{\cos\theta}} & \dfrac{1 - \cos\theta}{2} \\[4ex]
\dfrac{\dfrac{\sin\theta - \sin\theta\cos\theta}{\cos\theta}}{2\dfrac{\sin\theta}{\cos\theta}} & \\[4ex]
\dfrac{1 - \cos\theta}{2} &
\end{array}$$

21. $\cos^4 x - \sin^4 x = \cos 2x$

$$\begin{array}{c|c}
(\cos^2 x - \sin^2 x)(\cos^2 x + \sin^2 x) & \cos^2 x - \sin^2 x \\
\cos^2 x - \sin^2 x &
\end{array}$$

22. $\dfrac{\cos^4 x - \sin^4 x}{1 - \tan^4 x} = \cos^4 x$

$$\begin{array}{c|c}
\dfrac{\cos^4 x - \sin^4 x}{1 - \dfrac{\sin^4 x}{\cos^4 x}} & \cos^4 x \\[4ex]
\dfrac{\cos^4 x - \sin^4 x}{\dfrac{\cos^4 x - \sin^4 x}{\cos^4 x}} & \\[3ex]
\cos^4 x &
\end{array}$$

23. $\dfrac{\tan 3\theta - \tan\theta}{1 + \tan 3\theta \tan\theta} \equiv \dfrac{2\tan\theta}{1 - \tan\theta}$

$$\begin{array}{c|c}
\tan(3\theta - \theta) & \tan 2\theta \\
\tan 2\theta &
\end{array}$$

24. $\left(\dfrac{1 + \tan\theta}{1 - \tan\theta}\right)^2 \equiv \dfrac{1 + \sin 2\theta}{1 - \sin 2\theta}$

$$\begin{array}{c|c}
\left(\dfrac{\cos\theta + \sin\theta}{\cos\theta - \sin\theta}\right)^2 & \dfrac{1 + \sin 2\theta}{1 - \sin 2\theta} \\[3ex]
\dfrac{\sin^2\theta + 2\sin\theta\cos\theta + \cos^2\theta}{\sin^2\theta - 2\sin\theta\cos\theta + \cos^2\theta} & \\[2ex]
\dfrac{1 + \sin 2\theta}{1 - \sin 2\theta} &
\end{array}$$

25. $\sin(\alpha + \beta)\sin(\alpha - \beta) \equiv \sin^2\alpha - \sin^2\beta$

$$\begin{array}{c|c}
(\sin\alpha\cos\beta + \cos\alpha\cos\beta) & \\
\quad (\sin\alpha\cos\beta - \cos\alpha\sin\beta) & \\
\sin^2\alpha\cos^2\beta - \cos^2\alpha\sin^2\beta & \\
\sin^2\alpha(1 - \sin^2\beta) - [(1 - \sin^2\alpha)\sin^2\beta] & \\
\sin^2\alpha - \sin^2\alpha\sin^2\beta - \sin^2\beta + \sin^2\alpha\sin^2\beta & \\
\sin^2\alpha - \sin^2\beta & \sin^2\alpha - \sin^2\beta
\end{array}$$

26. $\cos(\alpha + \beta)\cos(\alpha - \beta) \equiv \cos^2\alpha - \sin^2\beta$

$$\begin{array}{c|c}
(\cos\alpha\cos\beta - \sin\alpha\sin\beta) & \\
\quad (\cos\alpha\cos\beta + \sin\alpha\sin\beta) & \\
\cos^2\alpha\cos^2\beta - \sin^2\alpha\sin^2\beta & \\
\cos^2\alpha(1 - \sin^2\beta) - [(1 - \cos^2\alpha)\sin^2\beta] & \\
\cos^2\alpha - \cos^2\alpha\sin^2\beta - \sin^2\beta + \cos^2\alpha\sin^2\beta & \\
\cos^2\alpha - \sin^2\beta & \cos^2\alpha - \sin^2\beta
\end{array}$$

27. $\cos(\alpha + \beta) + \cos(\alpha - \beta) \equiv 2\cos\alpha\cos\beta$

$$\begin{array}{c|c}
\cos\alpha\cos\beta - \sin\alpha\sin\beta + \cos\alpha\cos\beta & \\
\quad + \sin\alpha\sin\beta & \\
2\cos\alpha\cos\beta & 2\cos\alpha\cos\beta
\end{array}$$

28. $\sin(\alpha + \beta) + \sin(\alpha - \beta) \equiv 2\sin\alpha\cos\beta$

$$\begin{array}{c|c}
\sin\alpha\cos\beta + \cos\alpha\sin\beta + \sin\alpha\cos\beta & \\
\quad - \cos\alpha\sin\beta & \\
2\sin\alpha\cos\beta & 2\sin\alpha\cos\beta
\end{array}$$

29. Answers will vary.

30. $\log(\cos x - \sin x) + \log(\cos x + \sin x) \equiv \log(\cos 2x)$

$\log(\cos x - \sin x)(\cos x + \sin x)$ | $\log(\cos 2x)$
$\log(\cos^2 x - \sin^2 x)$
$\log(\cos 2x)$

31. If $I_1 = I_2$, then $\sin \theta = \dfrac{I_1 \cos \phi}{\sqrt{I_1^2 \cos^2\phi + I_1^2 \sin \phi^2}}$

$= \dfrac{I_1 \cos \phi}{\sqrt{I_1^2(\cos^2\phi + \sin^2\phi)}}$

$= \dfrac{I_1 \cos \phi}{\sqrt{I_1^2}}$

$= \cos \phi$

32. $\dfrac{1}{\omega C(\tan \theta + \tan \phi)} \equiv \dfrac{\cos \theta \cos \phi}{\omega C \sin(\theta + \phi)}$

$\dfrac{1}{\omega C\left(\dfrac{\sin \theta}{\cos \theta} + \dfrac{\sin \phi}{\cos \phi}\right)}$

$\dfrac{\cos \theta \cos \phi}{\omega C(\sin \theta \cos \phi + \sin \phi \cos \theta)}$

$\dfrac{\cos \theta \cos \phi}{\omega C \sin(\theta + \phi)}$

33. $\dfrac{E_1 + E_2}{2} = \dfrac{1}{2}\left[\sqrt{2}E_t \cos\left(\theta + \dfrac{\pi}{p}\right) + \sqrt{2}E_t \cos\left(\theta - \dfrac{\pi}{p}\right)\right]$

$= \dfrac{1}{2}\left[\sqrt{2}E_t\left[\cos \theta \cos \dfrac{\pi}{p} - \sin \theta \sin \dfrac{\pi}{p}\right.\right.$

$\left.\left. + \cos \theta \cos \dfrac{\pi}{p} + \sin \theta \sin \dfrac{\pi}{p}\right]\right]$

$= \dfrac{1}{2}\left[\sqrt{2}E_t \cdot 2 \cos \theta \cos \dfrac{\pi}{p}\right]$

$= \sqrt{2}E_t \cos \theta \cos \dfrac{\pi}{p}$

and

$\dfrac{E_1 - E_2}{2} = \dfrac{1}{2}\left[\sqrt{2}E_t \cos\left(\theta + \dfrac{\pi}{p}\right) - \sqrt{2}E_t \cos\left(\theta - \dfrac{\pi}{p}\right)\right]$

$= \dfrac{1}{2}\left[\sqrt{2}E_t\left\{\left[\cos \theta \cos \phi - \sin \theta \sin \dfrac{\pi}{p}\right]\right.\right.$

$\left.\left. - \left[\cos \theta \cos \dfrac{\pi}{p} + \sin \theta \sin \dfrac{\pi}{p}\right]\right\}\right]$

$= \dfrac{1}{2}\left[\sqrt{2}E_t \cdot -2 \sin \theta \sin \dfrac{\pi}{p}\right]$

$= -\sqrt{2}E_t \sin \theta \sin \dfrac{\pi}{p}$

34.

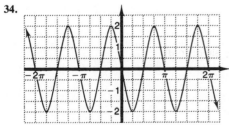

35.

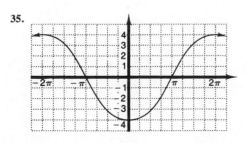

36.

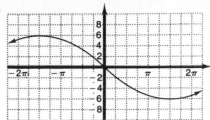

37. $8^{2/3} = x$
$\sqrt[3]{8^2} = x$
$4 = x$

38. $\sqrt{x^4} = \sqrt{1}$
$x^2 = \pm 1$
$x^2 = \pm 1$ or $x^2 = -1$
$x = \pm 1$ or $x = \pm i$

39. $(20 - x)^2 + (15 + x)^2 = 625$
$400 - 40x + x^2 + 225 + 30x + x^2 = 625$
$2x^2 - 10x = 0$
$2x(x - 5) = 0$
$x = 5$

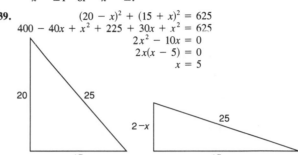

pp. 796–799   18-4 TRY THIS

a. $y = \cot^{-1} x$

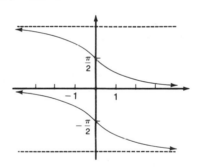

Not a function

b. $\arccos \dfrac{\sqrt{2}}{2}$

$\dfrac{\pi}{4} + 2k\pi; \dfrac{7\pi}{4} + 2k\pi$

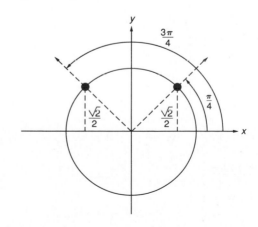

c. $\sin^{-1}\dfrac{\sqrt{3}}{2}$

$\dfrac{\pi}{3} + 2k\pi; \dfrac{2\pi}{3} + 2k\pi$

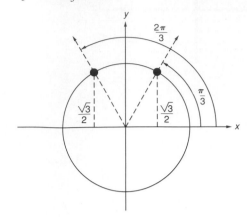

d. $\sin^{-1}0.4226$
$25° + 360°k$
$155° + 360°k$

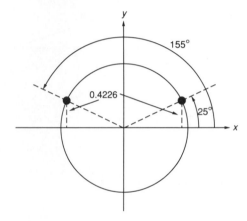

e. $\arctan -1$

$\dfrac{3\pi}{4} + k\pi$

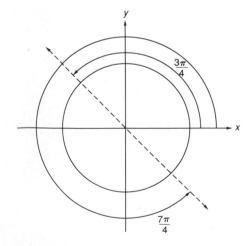

f. $\dfrac{\pi}{3}$ **g.** $\dfrac{3\pi}{4}$ **h.** $\dfrac{3\pi}{4}$ **i.** $-\dfrac{\pi}{4}$

pp. 799–800   18-4 EXERCISES

1. $\dfrac{\pi}{4} + 2k\pi, \dfrac{3\pi}{4} + 2k\pi$ **2.** $\dfrac{\pi}{3} + 2k\pi, \dfrac{2\pi}{3} + 2k\pi$

3. $\dfrac{\pi}{4} + 2k\pi, -\dfrac{\pi}{4} + 2k\pi$ **4.** $\dfrac{\pi}{6} + 2k\pi, -\dfrac{\pi}{6} + 2k\pi$

5. $\dfrac{5\pi}{4} + 2k\pi, -\dfrac{\pi}{4} + 2k\pi$ **6.** $\dfrac{4\pi}{3} + 2k\pi, -\dfrac{\pi}{3} + 2k\pi$

7. $\dfrac{3\pi}{4} + 2k\pi, \dfrac{5\pi}{4} + 2k\pi$ **8.** $\dfrac{5\pi}{6} + 2k\pi, \dfrac{7\pi}{6} + 2k\pi$

9. $\dfrac{\pi}{3} + k\pi$ **10.** $\dfrac{\pi}{6} + k\pi$ **11.** $\dfrac{\pi}{4} + k\pi$

12. $\dfrac{\pi}{6} + k\pi$ **13.** $\dfrac{5\pi}{6} + k\pi$ **14.** $\dfrac{2\pi}{3} + k\pi$

15. $\dfrac{3\pi}{4} + k\pi$ **16.** $\dfrac{5\pi}{6} + k\pi$ **17.** $0 + 2k\pi$

18. $\dfrac{\pi}{3} + 2k\pi, -\dfrac{\pi}{3} + 2k\pi$

19. $\dfrac{\pi}{2} + 2k\pi$ **20.** $\dfrac{\pi}{6} + 2k\pi, \dfrac{5\pi}{6} + 2k\pi$

21. $23° + k \cdot 360°, 157° + k \cdot 360°$

22. $74° + k \cdot 360°, 106° + k \cdot 360°$

23. $39° + k \cdot 360°, 141° + k \cdot 360°$

24. $61° + k \cdot 360°, 119° + 360 \cdot k$

25. $36°58' + k \cdot 360°, 323°02' + k \cdot 360°$

26. $22°06' + k \cdot 360°, 337°54' + k \cdot 360°$

27. $21°25' + k \cdot 360°, 338°35' + k \cdot 360°$

28. $74°8' + k \cdot 360°, 285°52' + k \cdot 360°$

29. $20°10' + k \cdot 180°$ **30.** $47°30' + k \cdot 180°$

31. $38°20' + k \cdot 180°$ **32.** $64°30' + k \cdot 180°$

33. $31° + k \cdot 360°, 329° + k \cdot 360°$

34. $46° + k \cdot 360°, 314° + k \cdot 360°$

35. $9°10' + k \cdot 360°, 170°50' + k \cdot 360°$

36. $64°10' + k \cdot 360°, 115°50' + k \cdot 360°$

37. $\dfrac{\pi}{4}$ **38.** $\dfrac{\pi}{6}$ **39.** $\dfrac{\pi}{3}$

40. $\dfrac{\pi}{4}$ **41.** $-\dfrac{\pi}{3}$ **42.** $-\dfrac{\pi}{6}$

43. $\dfrac{3\pi}{4}$ **44.** $\dfrac{5\pi}{6}$ **45.** $-\dfrac{\pi}{6}$ **46.** $-\dfrac{\pi}{3}$

47. $\dfrac{2\pi}{3}$ **48.** $\dfrac{5\pi}{6}$

49.

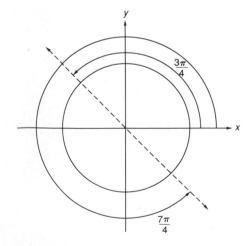

$\dfrac{3\pi}{4} + K\pi$

50.

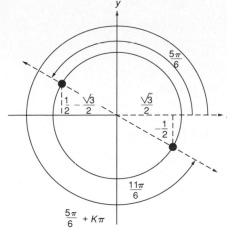

$\dfrac{5\pi}{6} + K\pi$

51.

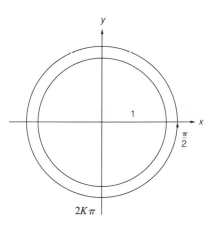

$2K\pi$

52.

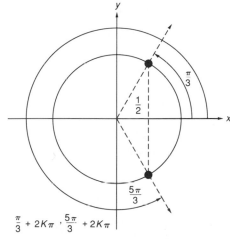

$\dfrac{\pi}{3} + 2K\pi , \dfrac{5\pi}{3} + 2K\pi$

53.

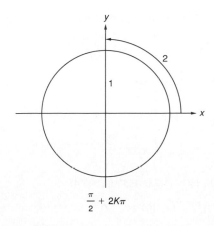

$\dfrac{\pi}{2} + 2K\pi$

54.

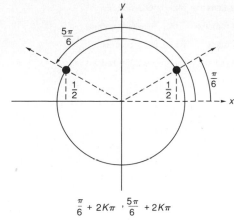

$\dfrac{\pi}{6} + 2K\pi , \dfrac{5\pi}{6} + 2K\pi$

55. Arcsin $-\dfrac{\pi}{2} \le s \le \dfrac{\pi}{2}$

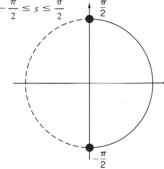

56. Arccos $0 \le s \le \pi$

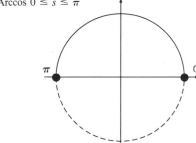

57. Arctan $-\dfrac{\pi}{2} < s < \dfrac{\pi}{2}$

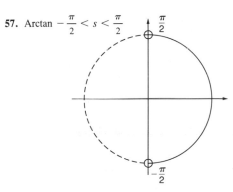

58. Arccot $0 < s < \pi$

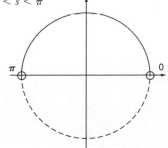

59. 0.2356 radians   **60.** 0.4683 radians

61. −0.6894 radians   **62.** −0.9600 radians

63. 2.6675 radians   **64.** 1.8675 radians

65. −0.3869 radians   **66.** −0.2356 radians

67. 2.9583 radians

68. a. $\cos^{-1}\left(\dfrac{4}{5}\right)^{4} = 66°$

   b. If $r = R$, the angle must be $0°$.

69. $\cos^{-1}(0.9010) = \dfrac{\pi}{7}$

70. $\tan^{-1}(\sqrt{3}) = -\dfrac{\pi}{3}$

71. $\tan 1.3371 = -4.2$

72. $\sin\dfrac{\pi}{3} = \dfrac{\sqrt{3}}{2}$

73.

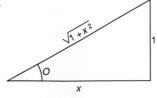

$\sin\theta = \dfrac{1}{\sqrt{1+x^2}}$

$ = \dfrac{\sqrt{1+x^2}}{1+x^2}$

74. $\sin^{-1}(-1) = -\dfrac{\pi}{2}$

75. $2500 = -12.5(100) + b$
$b = 3750$
$y = -12.5x + 3750$

76. $4^x = 10$
$x\log 4 = \log 10$
$x = \dfrac{\log 10}{\log 4}$
$ = \dfrac{1}{0.602}$
$ = 1.66$

77. $x^4 + x^3 - x - 1 = 0$
$x^3(x + 1) - (x + 1) = 0$
$(x^3 - 1)(x + 1) = 0$
$(x - 1)(x^2 + x + 1)(x + 1) = 0$
$\quad x = 1 \quad or$
$\quad x = -1 \quad or \quad x^2 + x + 1 = 0$
$\qquad x = \dfrac{-1 \pm \sqrt{1 - 4}}{2}$
$\qquad x = \dfrac{-1 \pm i\sqrt{3}}{2}$

78. $x^6 = 10$
$6\log x = \log 10$
$\log x = \dfrac{\log 10}{6}$
$\log x = 0.1667$
$\quad x = \pm1.468$

79. In one hour, they are 13 km apart. Draw a diagram.

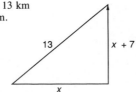

$x^2 + (x + 7)^2 = 13^2$
$2x^2 + 14x + 49 = 169$
$2x^2 + 14x - 120 = 0$
$x^2 + 7x - 60 = 0$
$(x - 5)(x + 12) = 0$
x cannot be negative
$x = 5, \; x + 7 = 12$
Phil 5 km/h, Bob 12 km/h

pp. 801–802   18-5 TRY THIS

a. $4\sin^2 x = 1$

$\sin^2 x = \dfrac{1}{4}$

$\sin x = \pm\dfrac{1}{2}$

$\sin x = \dfrac{1}{2}; \; \sin x = -\dfrac{1}{2}$

$x = \dfrac{\pi}{6} + 2k\pi \text{ or } \dfrac{5\pi}{6} + 2k\pi; \; x = \dfrac{7\pi}{6} + 2k\pi \text{ or } \dfrac{11\pi}{6} + 2k\pi$

b. $2\cos 2x = 1$

$\cos 2x = \dfrac{1}{2}$

$2x = \dfrac{\pi}{3} + 2k\pi \quad \text{or} \quad \dfrac{5\pi}{3} + 2k\pi$

$x = \dfrac{\pi}{6} + k\pi \quad \text{or} \quad \dfrac{5\pi}{6} + k\pi$

If $0 \le x \le 2\pi$

$x = \dfrac{\pi}{6}, \dfrac{5\pi}{6}, \dfrac{7\pi}{6}, \dfrac{11\pi}{6}$

c. $\qquad 8\cos^2\theta + 2\cos\theta = 1$
$\quad 8\cos^2\theta + 2\cos\theta - 1 = 0$
$(4\cos\theta - 1)(2\cos\theta + 1) = 0$
$4\cos\theta - 1 = 0 \qquad \text{or} \quad 2\cos\theta + 1 = 0$
$\qquad \cos\theta = \dfrac{1}{4} \qquad \text{or} \qquad \cos\theta = -\dfrac{1}{2}$
$\qquad \cos\theta = 0.2500 \quad \text{or} \qquad \cos\theta = -0.5000$
$\theta = 75°30' \text{ or } 284°30'; \; \theta = 120° \text{ or } 240°$

d. $\quad 2\cos^2\phi + \cos\phi = 0$
$\cos\phi(2\cos\phi + 1) = 0$
$\cos\phi = 0 \quad \text{or} \quad 2\cos\phi + 1 = 0$
$\qquad\qquad\qquad\qquad \cos\phi = -\dfrac{1}{2}$
$\phi = 90° \text{ or } 270°; \; \phi = 120° \text{ or } 240°$

pp. 802–803   18-5 EXERCISES

1. $\dfrac{4\pi}{3}, \dfrac{5\pi}{3}$ or 240°, 300°   **2.** $\dfrac{5\pi}{6}, \dfrac{11\pi}{6}$ or 150°, 330°

3. $\dfrac{\pi}{6}, \dfrac{5\pi}{6}, \dfrac{7\pi}{6}, \dfrac{11\pi}{6}$ or 30°, 150°, 210°, 330°

4. $\dfrac{\pi}{4}, \dfrac{3\pi}{4}, \dfrac{5\pi}{4}, \dfrac{7\pi}{4}$, or 45°, 135°, 225°, 315°

5. $\dfrac{\pi}{6}, \dfrac{5\pi}{6}, \dfrac{3\pi}{2}$ or 30°, 150°, 270°

6. $\dfrac{2\pi}{3}, \pi, \dfrac{4\pi}{3}$ or 120°, 180°, 240°   **7.** $0, 2\pi$ or 0°, 360°

8. $\dfrac{3\pi}{2}$ or 270°   **9.** $\dfrac{\pi}{6}, \dfrac{5\pi}{6}$ or 30°, 150°

10. $\dfrac{\pi}{6}, \dfrac{5\pi}{6}$ or 30°, 150°   **11.** 123°41′, 303°41′

12. 14°29′, 165°31′   **13.** 109°28′, 120°, 240°, 250°32′

14. $30°, 150°, 270°$ **15.** $0, \dfrac{\pi}{2}, \pi, \dfrac{3\pi}{2}, 2\pi$

16. $\dfrac{\pi}{4}, \dfrac{\pi}{2}, \dfrac{5\pi}{4}, \dfrac{3\pi}{2}$ **17.** $0, \pi, 2\pi$ **18.** $0, \dfrac{2\pi}{3}, \pi, \dfrac{4\pi}{3}, 2\pi$

19. $\dfrac{3\pi}{4}, \dfrac{7\pi}{4}$ **20.** $\dfrac{\pi}{6}, \dfrac{\pi}{3}, \dfrac{5\pi}{6}, \dfrac{5\pi}{3}$ **21.** $\dfrac{\pi}{4}, \dfrac{\pi}{2}, \dfrac{3\pi}{4}, \dfrac{5\pi}{4}, \dfrac{3\pi}{2}, \dfrac{7\pi}{4}$

22. $0, \dfrac{\pi}{4}, \dfrac{3\pi}{4}, \pi, \dfrac{5\pi}{4}, \dfrac{7\pi}{4}, 2\pi$ **23.** $0, \dfrac{\pi}{2}, \pi, \dfrac{3\pi}{2}, 2\pi$

24. $0, \dfrac{\pi}{2}, \pi, \dfrac{3\pi}{2}, 2\pi$ **25.** $0, 2\pi$ **26.** $0, \dfrac{\pi}{2}, \pi, \dfrac{3\pi}{2}, 2\pi$

27. $\dfrac{\pi}{6}, \dfrac{5\pi}{6}, \pi$ **28.** $\dfrac{2\pi}{3}, \dfrac{4\pi}{3}, \dfrac{3\pi}{2}$ **29.** $\dfrac{\pi}{6}, \dfrac{5\pi}{6}, \dfrac{7\pi}{6}, \dfrac{11\pi}{6}$

30. $\dfrac{\pi}{4}, \dfrac{3\pi}{4}, \dfrac{5\pi}{4}, \dfrac{7\pi}{4}$ **31.** $1.7682, 4.9098, 1.1071, 4.2487$

32. $\dfrac{\pi}{4}, \dfrac{5\pi}{4}, 2.0344, 5.176$

33.
$$\cot(\pi - x) + \sin\left(x - \dfrac{\pi}{2}\right) = 1$$
$$\cos \pi \cos x + \sin \pi \sin x + (-\cos x) = 1$$
$$(-1)\cos x + 0(\sin x) - \cos x = 1$$
$$-2\cos x = 1$$
$$\cos x = -\dfrac{1}{2}$$
$$\text{so, } x = \dfrac{2\pi}{3}, \dfrac{4\pi}{3}$$

34.
$$\sin(\pi - x) + \cos\left(\dfrac{\pi}{2} - x\right) = 1$$
$$\sin \pi \cos x - \cos \pi \sin x + \cos\left(-x + \dfrac{\pi}{2}\right) = 1$$
$$0(\cos x) - (-1)\sin x + \cos\left(-\left(x - \dfrac{\pi}{2}\right)\right) = 1$$
$$\sin x + \cos\left(x - \dfrac{\pi}{2}\right) = 1$$
$$\sin x + \sin x = 1$$
$$2\sin x = 1$$
$$\sin x = \dfrac{1}{2}$$
$$\text{so, } x = \dfrac{\pi}{6}, \dfrac{5\pi}{6}$$

35.
$$2\cos x + 2\sin x = \sqrt{6}$$
$$\dfrac{2}{2\sqrt{2}}\cos x + \dfrac{2}{2\sqrt{2}}\sin x = \dfrac{\sqrt{6}}{2\sqrt{2}}$$
$$\dfrac{\sqrt{2}}{2}\cos x + \dfrac{\sqrt{2}}{2}\sin x = \dfrac{\sqrt{3}}{2}$$
$$\cos \dfrac{\pi}{4}\cos x + \sin \dfrac{\pi}{4}\sin x = \dfrac{\sqrt{3}}{2}$$
$$\cos x \cos \dfrac{\pi}{4} + \sin x \sin \dfrac{\pi}{4} = \dfrac{\sqrt{3}}{2}$$
$$\cos\left(x - \dfrac{\pi}{4}\right) = \dfrac{\sqrt{3}}{2}$$
$$\text{so, } x - \dfrac{\pi}{4} = \dfrac{\pi}{6}, \dfrac{11\pi}{6}$$
$$\text{so, } x = \dfrac{\pi}{6} + \dfrac{\pi}{4}, \dfrac{11\pi}{6} + \dfrac{\pi}{4}$$
$$\text{so, } x = \dfrac{5\pi}{12}, \dfrac{25\pi}{12}$$
$$\text{so, } x = \dfrac{5\pi}{12}, \dfrac{\pi}{12}$$

36. $2\cos x + 2\sin x = \sqrt{2}$

$$\dfrac{2}{2\sqrt{2}}\cos x + \dfrac{2}{2\sqrt{2}}\sin x = \dfrac{\sqrt{2}}{2\sqrt{2}}$$
$$\dfrac{\sqrt{2}}{2}\cos x + \dfrac{\sqrt{2}}{2}\sin x = \dfrac{1}{2}$$
$$\cos \dfrac{\pi}{4}\cos x + \sin \dfrac{\pi}{4}\sin x = \dfrac{1}{2}$$
$$\cos x \cos \dfrac{\pi}{4} + \sin x \sin \dfrac{\pi}{4} = \dfrac{1}{2}$$
$$\cos\left(x - \dfrac{\pi}{4}\right) = \dfrac{1}{2}$$
$$\text{so, } x - \dfrac{\pi}{4} = \dfrac{\pi}{3}, \dfrac{5\pi}{3}$$
$$\text{so, } x = \dfrac{\pi}{3} + \dfrac{\pi}{4}, \dfrac{5\pi}{3} + \dfrac{\pi}{4}$$
$$\text{so, } x = \dfrac{7\pi}{12}, \dfrac{23\pi}{12}$$

37.
$$\sqrt{3}\cos x - \sin x = 1$$
$$\dfrac{\sqrt{3}}{2}\cos x - \dfrac{1}{2}\sin x = \dfrac{1}{2}$$
$$\cos \dfrac{\pi}{6}\cos x - \sin \dfrac{\pi}{6}\sin x = \dfrac{1}{2}$$
$$\cos\left(x + \dfrac{\pi}{6}\right) = \dfrac{1}{2}$$
$$\text{so, } x + \dfrac{\pi}{6} = \dfrac{\pi}{3}, \dfrac{5\pi}{3}$$
$$\text{so, } x = \dfrac{\pi}{3} - \dfrac{\pi}{6}, \dfrac{5\pi}{3} - \dfrac{\pi}{6}$$
$$\text{so, } x = \dfrac{\pi}{6}, \dfrac{3\pi}{2}$$

38.
$$\sqrt{2}\cos x - \sqrt{2}\sin x = 2$$
$$\dfrac{\sqrt{2}}{2}\cos x - \dfrac{\sqrt{2}}{2}\sin x = 1$$
$$\cos \dfrac{\pi}{4}\cos x - \sin \dfrac{\pi}{4}\sin x = 1$$
$$\cos\left(x + \dfrac{\pi}{4}\right) = 1$$
$$\text{so, } x + \dfrac{\pi}{4} = 0, 2\pi$$
$$\text{so, } x = 0 - \dfrac{\pi}{4}, 2\pi - \dfrac{\pi}{4}$$
$$\text{so, } x = \dfrac{7\pi}{4} \left(-\dfrac{\pi}{4} \text{ is not between 0 and } 2\pi\right)$$

39. Answers may vary

Example: $6\cos\left(x - \dfrac{\pi}{3}\right) = 1$

40. $|\sin x| = \dfrac{\sqrt{3}}{2}$

$$\sin x = \pm\dfrac{\sqrt{3}}{2}$$
$$\text{so, } x = 60°, 120°, 240°, 300°$$

41. $\cos x = \pm\dfrac{1}{2}$

$$\text{so, } x = 60°, 120°, 240°, 300°$$

42. $\sqrt{\tan x} = \sqrt[4]{3}$
$$\tan x = (\sqrt[4]{3})^2$$
$$\tan x = \sqrt{3}$$
$$\text{so, } x = 60°, 240°$$

43. $12\sin x - 7\sqrt{\sin x} + 1 = 0$
Let $\sqrt{\sin x} = t$.
So $12t^2 - 7t + 1 = 0$
$(4t - 1)(3t - 1) = 0$

So, $t = \dfrac{1}{4}, \dfrac{1}{3}$

So, $\sqrt{\sin x} = \dfrac{1}{4}, \dfrac{1}{3}$

So, $\sin x = \dfrac{1}{16}, \dfrac{1}{9}$

So, $x = 3°35', 6°23', 173°37', 176°25'$

44. $16 \cos^4 x - 16 \cos^2 x + 3 = 0$

Let $\cos^2 x = t$.

$16t^2 - 16t + 3 = 0$

$(4t - 3)(4t - 1) = 0$

So $t = \dfrac{3}{4}, \dfrac{1}{4}$

So, $\cos^2 x = \dfrac{3}{4}, \dfrac{1}{4}$

So, $\cos x = \pm\dfrac{\sqrt{3}}{2}, \pm\dfrac{1}{2}$

So, $x = 30°, 60°, 120°, 150°, 210°, 240°, 300°, 330°$.

45.
$$\text{Arccos } x = \text{Arccos } \dfrac{3}{5} - \text{Arcsin } \dfrac{4}{5}$$

$$\cos(\text{Arccos } x) = \cos\left(\text{Arccos } \dfrac{3}{5} - \text{Arcsin } \dfrac{4}{5}\right)$$

$$x = \cos\left(\text{Arccos } \dfrac{3}{5}\right)\cos\left(\text{Arcsin } \dfrac{4}{5}\right)$$
$$+ \sin\left(\text{Arccos } \dfrac{3}{5}\right) \cdot \sin\left(\text{Arcsin } \dfrac{4}{5}\right)$$

$$x = \dfrac{3}{5} \cdot \left(\dfrac{3}{5}\right) + \left(\dfrac{4}{5}\right) \cdot \dfrac{4}{5}$$

$$x = \dfrac{9}{25} + \dfrac{16}{25}$$

So $x = 1$

46. $P(x) = x^4 + x^3 + 7x^2 + 9x - 18$

```
1│ 1   1   7   9   -18
   |    1   2   9    18
   1   2   9  18 │   0

-2│ 1   2   9       18
   |   -2   0      -18
   1   0   9 │      0
```

So, $x^4 + x^3 + 7x^2 + 9 - 18 = (x - 1)(x + 2)(x^2 + 9)$.
So, the zeros are $1, -2, 3i,$ and $-3i$.
The x-intercepts are $1, -2$.

47. $P(-5) = (-5)^4 + (-5)^3 + 7(-5)^2 + 9(-5) - 18$
$= 625 - 125 + 175 - 45 - 18$
$= 612$
$P(-3) = (-3)^4 + (-3)^3 + 7(-3)^2 + 9(-3) - 18$
$= 81 - 27 + 63 - 27 - 18$
$= 72$
$P(0) = (0)^4 + (0)^3 + 7(0)^2 + 9(0) - 18$
$= -18$
$P(2) = (2)^4 + (2)^3 + 7(2)^2 + 9(2) - 18$
$= 16 + 8 + 28 + 18 - 18$
$= 52$
$P(4) = (4)^4 + (4)^3 + 7(4)^2 + 9(4) - 18$
$= 256 + 64 + 112 + 36 - 18$
$= 450$

48. From #46
$P(x) = (x^2 + 9)(x + 2)(x - 1)$

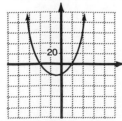

49.
$$\sqrt{x + 2} = x + 2$$
$$x + 2 = x^2 + 4x + 4$$
$$x^2 + 3x + 2 = 0$$
$$(x + 2)(x + 1) = 0$$
$$x = -2, -1$$

50.
$$z^4 + 7z^2 - 144 = 0$$
$$(z^2 + 16)(z^2 - 9) = 0$$
$$(z^2 + 16)(z + 3)(z - 3) = 0$$
$$z = \pm 4i, -3, 3$$

51. $_6P_6 = 6! = 6 \cdot 5 \cdot 4 \cdot 3 \cdot 2 \cdot 1 = 720$

52. $_{10}P_5 = \dfrac{10!}{5!} = 10 \cdot 9 \cdot 8 \cdot 7 \cdot 6 = 30,240$

53. $_9P_4 = \dfrac{9!}{5!} = 9 \cdot 8 \cdot 7 \cdot 6 = 3024$

54. $\dbinom{9}{4} = \dfrac{9!}{4!\,5!} = \dfrac{9 \cdot 8 \cdot 7 \cdot 6}{4 \cdot 3 \cdot 2 \cdot 1} = \dfrac{3024}{24} = 126$

55. $\dbinom{10}{5} = \dfrac{10!}{5!\,5!} = \dfrac{10 \cdot 9 \cdot 8 \cdot 7 \cdot 6}{5 \cdot 4 \cdot 3 \cdot 2 \cdot 1} = \dfrac{30240}{120} = 252$

pp. 804–807   **18-6 TRY THIS**

a. $\text{cosine} = \dfrac{\text{adjacent}}{\text{hypotenuse}}$ $\text{sine} = \dfrac{\text{opposite}}{\text{hypotenuse}}$

$\cos 35° = \dfrac{b}{67}$ $\sin 35° = \dfrac{a}{67}$

$b = 67 \cdot \cos 35°$ $a = 67 \cdot \sin 35°$
$b \approx 67 \cdot 0.8192$ $a \approx 67 \cdot 0.5736$
$b \approx 54.8864$ $a \approx 38.4312$
$a \approx 38.43$ and $b \approx 54.89$

b. $4^2 + 6^2 = C^2$
$16 + 36 = C^2$
$52 = C^2$
$\sqrt{52} = C$
$7.211 = C$

$\tan \angle B = \dfrac{4}{6} = \dfrac{2}{3} \approx 0.6667$

$\arctan 0.6667 \approx 33°41'$ by interpolation

$\tan \angle A = \dfrac{6}{4} = \dfrac{3}{2} = 1.5$

$\arctan 1.5 \approx 56°19'$ by interpolation

c. $\tan 32.3° = \dfrac{x}{120}$

$x = 120(\tan 32.3°)$
$\approx 120(0.632)$
≈ 75.84

d. $\sin \theta = \dfrac{6.5}{13.6} \approx 0.4779$

$\arcsin 0.4779 \approx 28°30'$

e. $\cos 5°15' = \dfrac{x}{241.3}$

$x = 241.3(\cos 5°15')$
$\approx 241.3(0.9958)$
≈ 240.3 ft

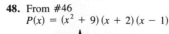

f.
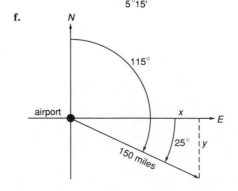

x = distance east of the airport
y = distance south of the airport
$\angle A = 115° - 90° = 25°$
$x = 150(\cos 25°) \approx 150(0.9063)$
≈ 135.6 km
$y = 150(\sin 25°) \approx 150(0.4226)$
≈ 63.4 km

pp. 807–809   18-6 EXERCISES

1. $m\angle B = 53°50'$, $b = 37.2$, $c = 46.1$

2. $m\angle B = 2°20'$, $b = 0.40$, $c = 9.74$

3. $m\angle A = 77°20'$, $a = 436.5$, $c = 447.4$

4. $m\angle A = 20°10'$, $a = 46.6$, $c = 135.3$

5. $m\angle B = 72°40'$, $a = 4.2$, $c = 14.2$

6. $m\angle B = 11°20'$, $a = 6686$, $c = 6819$

7. $m\angle A = 66°50'$, $b = 0.0148$, $c = 0.0375$

8. $m\angle B = 42°30'$, $a = 35.6$, $b = 32.6$

9. $m\angle A = 20°40'$, $b = 0.0129$, $c = 0.0138$

10. $m\angle B = 1°10'$, $a = 3949$, $b = 80.4$

11. $m\angle A = 33°30'$, $a = 0.0247$, $b = 0.0373$

12. $m\angle A = 7°40'$, $a = 0.131$, $b = 0.973$

13. $m\angle A = 33°40'$, $c = 21.6$, $m\angle B = 56°20'$

14. $m\angle A = 26°30'$, $m\angle B = 63°30'$, $c = 22.4$

15. $m\angle A = 53°10'$, $m\angle B = 36°50'$, $b = 12.0$

16. $m\angle A = 19°30'$, $m\angle B = 70°30'$, $b = 42.4$

17. $a = 3.57$, $m\angle A = 63°20'$, $m\angle B = 26°40'$

18. $a = 439$, $m\angle A = 77°10'$, $m\angle B = 12°50'$

19. 47.9 ft   20. 9.59 ft   21. 239 ft   22. 171.5 ft

23. 1°40'   24. 10°20'   25. 30°10'   26. 60°20'

27. 18,572   28. 274.4   29. 328 ft   30. 609.9 ft

31. 109 km   32. 201 km   33. 25.9 cm   34. 29.5 cm

35. 8.33 cm   36. 96.7   37. 355 ft   38. 44.9 ft

39. 7.2 km   40. 4.67 km   41. 3.45 km   42. 225 ft

43.

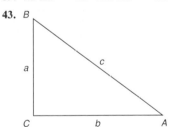

$\sin A = \dfrac{a}{c}$

Area $= \dfrac{1}{2} b \cdot a$

$= \dfrac{1}{2} b \cdot c \sin A$

44. $\tan 2(13°30') = \dfrac{2 \tan 13°30'}{1 - \tan^2(13°30')}$

$= \dfrac{2(0.2401)}{1 - (0.2401)^2} \dfrac{0.4802}{0.9424}$

$= 0.5096$

$x = 20(\tan 13°30')$ $x + y = 20 \tan 2(13°30')$
$= 20(0.2401)$ $= 20(0.5096)$
$= 4.802$ $= 10.192$
$y = 5.3895$

45. The line of sight from a height h above the earth to the horizon is tangent to the earth. The observer, horizon point, and earth's center form a right triangle. The right angle is between the radius and the line of sight. The formula is
$d = \sqrt{(r + h)^2 - r^2}$ or $\sqrt{h^2 + 2hr}$
$r \approx 3960$ miles $\approx 20{,}909{,}000$ feet.
$r + h = r + 1000 \approx 20{,}910{,}000$ feet. (This length is the hypotenuse.) The length d of the short side is
$d \approx \sqrt{(2.091 \times 10^7)^2 - (2.0909 \times 10^7)^2}$
$\approx \sqrt{4.182 \times 10^{10}} \approx 2.045 \times 10^5$ or 204,500 ft
$d \approx 38.7$ miles

46. $x^3 + 24x^2 + 191x + 504 = 0$

$\underline{-7}\ |\ 1\ +24\ +191\ \ +504$
$\ \ \ \ \ \ \ \ \ \ -7\ \ \ -119\ \ \ -504$
$\ \ \ \ \ \ 1\ \ \ 17\ \ \ \ 72\ |\ \ \ \ \ 0$ -7 is a root
$x^3 + 24x^2 + 191x + 504 = (x + 7)(x^2 + 17x + 72)$
$= (x + 7)(x + 8)(x + 9)$
$x = -7$ or $x = -8$ or $x = -9$

47. $25x^2 = -49$

$x^2 = \dfrac{-49}{25}$

$= \pm \dfrac{7}{5} i$

48. $\sqrt[3]{4y + 7} = 3$
$4y + 7 = 27$
$4y = 20$
$y = 5$

p. 754   PROBLEM FOR PROGRAMMERS

```
10   REM Chapter 17 Problem
20   ST$ = " is undefined":E$ = " = "
30   PI = 3.141592654
40   INPUT "Enter number    ";N
50   PRINT "Arcsin of ";N;: IF N > 1
     THEN PRINT ST$: GOTO 70
60   PRINT E$; ATN (N / SQR (1 - N ^ 2)) *
     180 / PI;" degrees"
70   PRINT "Arccos of ";N;: IF N > 1
     THEN PRINT ST$: GOTO 90
80   PRINT E$; ATN ( SQR (1 - N ^ 2) / N) *
     180 / PI;" degrees"
90   PRINT "Arctan of ";N;E$; ATN (N) *
     180 / PI;" degrees"
100  PRINT "Arccot of ";N;E$; ATN (1 / N) *
     180 / PI;" degrees"
110  PRINT "Arcsec of ";N;: IF N < 1
     THEN PRINT ST$: GOTO 130
120  PRINT E$; ATN (1 / (N * SQR (1 - 1 /
     N ^ 2))) * 180 / PI;" degrees"
130  PRINT "Arccsc of ";N;: IF N < 1
     THEN PRINT ST$: GOTO 150
140  PRINT E$; ATN (N * SQR (1 - (1 /
     N ^ 2))) * 180 / PI;" degrees"
150  END
```

pp. 811–814   18-7 TRY THIS

a. $m\angle B = 180° - (41° + 52°)$
$= 180° - 93°$
$= 87°$

$\dfrac{c}{\sin c} = \dfrac{a}{\sin A}$

$c = \dfrac{a \sin c}{\sin A}$

$= \dfrac{6.53(\sin 52°)}{(\sin 41°)}$

$\approx \dfrac{6.53 \times 0.7880}{0.6561}$

≈ 7.84

$$\frac{b}{\sin B} = \frac{a}{\sin A}$$

$$b = \frac{a \sin B}{\sin A}$$

$$= \frac{6.53(\sin 87°)}{\sin 41°}$$

$$\approx \frac{6.53 \times 0.9986}{0.6561}$$

$$\approx 9.94$$

b. $m\angle A = 180° - (119° + 2°)$
$\quad = 180° - 121°$
$\quad = 59°$

$$\frac{a}{\sin A} = \frac{b}{\sin B}$$

$$a = \frac{b \sin A}{\sin B}$$

$$= \frac{9 \sin 59°}{\sin 2°}$$

$$\approx \frac{9(0.8572)}{(0.0349)}$$

$$\approx 221.05$$

$$\frac{c}{\sin C} = \frac{b}{\sin B}$$

$$c = \frac{b \sin C}{\sin B}$$

$$= \frac{9 \sin 119°}{\sin 2°}$$

$$\approx \frac{9(0.8746)}{(0.0349)}$$

$$\approx 225.54$$

c. This is Case I. There are no solutions.
d. This is Case IV. We look for $m\angle B$.

$$\frac{b}{\sin B} = \frac{a}{\sin A}$$

$$\sin B = \frac{b \sin A}{a} = \frac{3 \sin 53°08'}{4}$$

$$\approx \frac{3(0.800)}{4}$$

$$\approx 0.6$$

$\sin B \approx 0.6$, thus, arcsin $0.6 \approx 36°52'$ or $143°08'$. Since $a > b$, we know there is only one solution. An angle of measure $143°08'$ cannot be an angle of this triangle since $143°08' + 53°08' > 180°$.
$m\angle C = 180° - (36°52' + 53°08')$
$\quad = 180° - 90°$
$\quad = 90°$

$$\frac{c}{\sin C} = \frac{a}{\sin A}$$

$$c = \frac{a \sin C}{\sin A} \approx \frac{4 \sin 90°}{\sin 53°08'}$$

$$c \approx \frac{4(1)}{0.8} \approx 5$$

e. This is Case III. We look for $m\angle A$.

$$\frac{a}{\sin A} = \frac{b}{\sin B}$$

$$\sin A = \frac{a \sin B}{b} = \frac{25 \sin 33°}{20} \approx \frac{25(0.5446)}{20} \approx 0.6808$$

$0 \le A \le 180$
$A \approx$ arcsin $0.6808 \approx 43°$ or $137°$.
This gives two possible solutions.
Possible solution 1:
$m\angle A \approx 43°$
$m\angle C \approx 180° - (43° + 33°)$
$\quad\quad \approx 180° - 76°$
$\quad\quad \approx 104°$

We can now find c.

$$\frac{c}{\sin C} = \frac{b}{\sin B}$$

$$c = \frac{b \sin C}{\sin B} = \frac{20 \sin 104°}{\sin 33°} \approx \frac{20(0.9703)}{0.5446} \approx 35.6$$

Possible solution 2:
$m\angle A \approx 137°$
$m\angle C \approx 180° - (137° + 33°)$
$\quad\quad \approx 180° - 170°$
$\quad\quad \approx 10°$

$$c = \frac{b \sin C}{\sin B} = \frac{20 \sin 10°}{\sin 33°} \approx \frac{20(0.1736)}{(0.5446)} \approx 6.4$$

f. This is case IV. We look for $m\angle C$.

$$\frac{c}{\sin C} = \frac{b}{\sin B}$$

$$\sin C = \frac{c \sin B}{b} = \frac{10 \sin 38°}{20} \approx \frac{10(0.6157)}{20} \approx 0.3079$$

$0° \le C \le 180°$
$m\angle C \approx$ arcsin $0.3079 \approx 18°$ or $162°$.
An angle of measure $162°$ cannot be an angle of this triangle because $162° + 38° > 180°$.
$m\angle A \approx 180° - (18° + 38°)$
$\quad\quad \approx 180° - 56°$
$\quad\quad \approx 124°$

$$\frac{a}{\sin A} = \frac{b}{\sin B}$$

$$a = \frac{b \sin A}{\sin B} \approx \frac{20 \sin 124°}{\sin 38°} \approx \frac{20(0.8290)}{(0.6157)} \approx 26.9$$

g. Area $= \dfrac{1}{2} bc \sin A$

$$= \frac{1}{2}(5)(8) \sin 25$$

$$\approx 20 \cdot 0.4226 \approx 8.452 \text{ square units}$$

pp. 815–816 18-7 EXERCISES

1. $m\angle C = 50°$, $c = 16.3$, $a = 18.4$
2. $m\angle C = 70°$, $a = 29.5$, $c = 37.3$
3. $m\angle C = 96°$, $b = 15.2$, $c = 20.3$
4. $m\angle C = 80°$, $a = 74.2$, $c = 113.7$
5. $m\angle C = 17°$, $a = 26.3$, $c = 10.5$
6. $m\angle A = 30°$, $b = 27.7$, $c = 16.0$
7. $m\angle A = 121°$, $a = 33.4$, $c = 14.0$
8. $m\angle B = 26°$, $a = 17.2$, $c = 8.9$
9. $m\angle B = 68°50'$, $a = 32.3$, $b = 32.3$
10. $m\angle A = 16°$, $a = 13.2$, $c = 34.2$
11. $m\angle A = 12°20'$, $m\angle C = 17°40'$, $c = 4.25$
12. $m\angle C = 48°40'$, $m\angle B = 101°20'$, $b = 11.8$ or $m\angle C = 131°20'$, $m\angle B = 18°40'$, $b = 3.84$
13. $m\angle A = 20°20'$, $m\angle B = 99°40'$, $b = 34.1$
14. $m\angle A = 38°40'$, $m\angle C = 96°20'$, $c = 23.9$
15. $m\angle B = 56°20'$, $m\angle C = 87°40'$, $c = 40.8$ or $m\angle B = 123°40'$, $m\angle C = 20°20'$, $c = 14.2$
16. $m\angle B = 41°10'$, $m\angle A = 95°50'$, $a = 40.8$
17. $m\angle C = 44°40'$, $m\angle B = 19°$, $b = 6.25$
18. $m\angle B = 28°30'$, $m\angle C = 103°40'$, $c = 37.1$
19. $m\angle B = 44°20'$, $m\angle A = 74°30'$, $a = 33.3$
20. $m\angle A = 41°10'$, $m\angle C = 80°10'$, $c = 37.6$
21. 30 22. 51 23. ≈ 0.0868 24. ≈ 651
25. $\approx 5.438 \text{ m}^2$ 26. $\approx 51.08 \text{ m}^2$

27. $180 - (112 + 42) = \angle B = 26°$

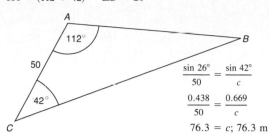

$$\frac{\sin 26°}{50} = \frac{\sin 42°}{c}$$

$$\frac{0.438}{50} = \frac{0.669}{c}$$

$$76.3 = c; \ 76.3 \text{ m}$$

28. $\angle ADC = 180 - 71 = 109°$
$\angle CAD = 180 - (109 + 37) = 34°$

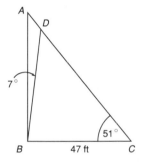

$$\frac{\sin 37°}{w} = \frac{\sin 34°}{25}$$

$$\frac{0.602}{w} = \frac{0.559}{25}$$

$$w = 26.9 \text{ ft}$$

29. $\angle CBD = 90 - 7 = 83°$
$\angle BDC = 180 - (51 + 83) = 46°$

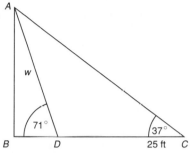

$$\frac{\sin 51°}{p} = \frac{\sin 46°}{47}$$

$$\frac{0.777}{p} = \frac{0.719}{47}$$

$$p = 50.8 \text{ ft}$$

30. $\angle BDC = 180 - 23 = 157°$
$\angle BCD = 180 - (10 + 157) = 13°$

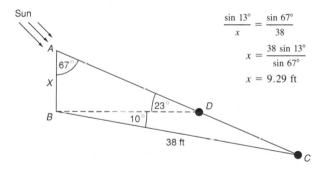

$$\frac{\sin 13°}{x} = \frac{\sin 67°}{38}$$

$$x = \frac{38 \sin 13°}{\sin 67°}$$

$$x = 9.29 \text{ ft}$$

31. $\angle CBD = 90 - 85 = 5°$
$\angle ABD = 283 - 270 - 5 = 13°$, so $\angle ABC = 13 + 5 = 18°$
$\angle BAD = 90 - 13 = 77°$

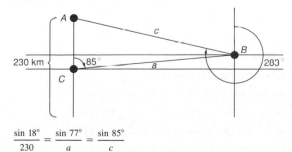

$$\frac{\sin 18°}{230} = \frac{\sin 77°}{a} = \frac{\sin 85°}{c}$$

$$\frac{0.03090}{230} \approx \frac{0.9743}{a} \neq \frac{0.9962}{c}$$

$$a \approx 724.98, \ c \approx 741.51$$
$$a + c \approx 1466.49 \text{ km}$$

32. $\angle ABC = 90° - 31°20' = 58°40'$
$\angle BAC = 90° + 10°40' = 100°40'$
$\angle C = 180° - 58°40' - 100°40' = 20°40'$

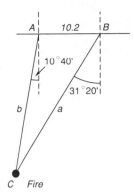

$$\frac{\sin 100°40'}{a} = \frac{\sin 20°40'}{10.2} = \frac{\sin 58°40'}{b}$$

$$\frac{0.984}{a} = \frac{0.353}{10.2} = \frac{0.854}{b}$$

$$a = 28.4 \text{ km}, \ b = 24.7 \text{ km}$$

33. $\angle ABC = 90° - 65°10' = 24°50'$

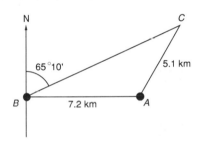

$$\frac{\sin 24°50'}{5.1} = \frac{\sin C}{7.2} = \frac{\sin A}{a}$$

$$\frac{0.420}{5.1} = \frac{\sin C}{7.2} = \frac{\sin 118°50'}{a}$$

$$\angle C = 36°22' \text{ or } 143°39'$$
$$\angle A = 118°48' \text{ or } 11°31'$$
$$a = 10.6 \text{ km or } 2.42 \text{ km}$$

34. Given: $\square ABCD$

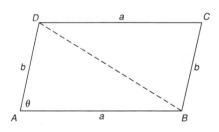

1. $\square ABCD$	Given
2. $\angle A \cong \angle C$	Opp $\angle$'s $\square$ are $\cong$
3. $\overline{AD} \cong \overline{BC}$ $\quad$ $\overline{AB} \cong \overline{DC}$	Opp sides $\square$ are $\cong$
4. Area $\triangle ABD = \frac{1}{2} ab \sin A$	Area formula
$\quad$ Area $\triangle CDB = \frac{1}{2} ab \sin C$	
$\quad$ Area $\triangle CDB = \frac{1}{2} ab \sin A$	Substitution
5. Area $\square ABCD = ab \sin A$	Addition property of equality

35. Given: quad. ABCD

Prove: Area $= \frac{1}{2}(a + b)(c + d) \sin \theta$

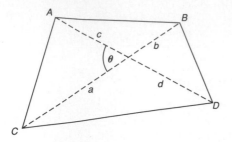

1. Figure—quad. ABCD	Given
2. Area $= \frac{1}{2} ac \sin \theta + \frac{1}{2} bd \sin \theta$	Area Formula
$+ \frac{1}{2} cb \sin(180 - \theta) + \frac{1}{2} ad \sin 180 - \theta$	
3. Area $= \frac{1}{2}(bd + ac + ad + bc)\sin \theta$	
4. Area $= \frac{1}{2}(a + b)(c + d) \sin \theta$	

36.

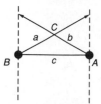

The paths of the two objects are straight and the distance between them is decreasing, so their paths cross, forming a vertical angle, $\angle C$. The straight line distance between the objects thus forms side c of a triangle with the two paths as sides a and b. $\angle A$ is then the bearing (the angle formed by sides b and c). Since the bearing is constant and $\angle C$ is constant, $\angle B$ is constant and, as the objects advance, the triangles formed are similar. By the law of sines,

$\frac{a}{\sin A} = \frac{b}{\sin B} = \frac{c}{\sin C}$. So when c decreases to 0,

$\frac{a}{\sin A} = \frac{b}{\sin B} = \frac{0}{\sin C} = 0$, a and b must be 0, thus the objects collide.

37. $(216a^{-6}b^3c^{-6}d^4)^{2/3} = 36a^{-4}b^2c^{-4}d^{8/3}$

$$= \frac{36b^2d^2\sqrt[3]{d^2}}{a^4c^4}$$

38. $(2 - i)^2(2 - i)^2$
$(4 - 4i + i^2)(4 - 4i + i^2)$
$(3 - 4i)(3 - 4i)$
$9 - 24i + 16i^2$
$-7 - 24i$

39. $\left| \frac{1}{2} - \frac{\sqrt{3}}{2}i \right| = \frac{1}{4} + \frac{3}{4} = 1$

40. $\frac{i}{(1 + i)} = \frac{i}{(1 + i)} \cdot \frac{(1 - i)}{(1 - i)}$

$= \frac{i - i^2}{1 - i^2}$

$= \frac{i + 1}{2} = \frac{1}{2} + \frac{1}{2}i$

41. $\sum_{n=-4}^{4} (4n + 6) = \frac{9}{2}(-10 + 22)$

$= \frac{9}{2}(+12)$

$= 54$

42. $\sum_{n=-3}^{3} \left(\frac{1}{2}\right)^n = 8 + 4 + 2 + 1 + \frac{1}{2} + \frac{1}{4} + \frac{1}{8} = 15.875$

43. $\sum_{n=1}^{10} (-4)^{n-1} = 1 - 4 + 16 - 64 + 256 - 1024 + 4096$

$- 16,384 + 65,536 - 262,144$
$= -209,715$

44. $S = 0.7 + 0.07 + 0.007 + \cdots = 0.777\cdots = 0.\overline{7} = \frac{7}{9}$

45. $(x + 4i)(x - 4i)(x + \sqrt{6})(x - \sqrt{6}) = f(x)$
$(x^2 + 16)(x^2 - 6) = f(x)$
$x^4 + 10x^2 - 96 = f(x)$

46.
$(x - 1)(x - 2)(x - 1 + 2i)(x - 1 - 2i) = f(x)$
$(x^2 - 3x + 2)(x^2 - x - 2ix - x + 1 + 2i + 2ix - 2i - 4i^2) = f(x)$
$(x^2 - 3x + 2)(x^2 - 2x + 5) = f(x)$
$(x^4 - 2x^3 + 5x^2 - 3x^3 + 6x^2 - 15x + 2x^2 - 4x + 10 = f(x)$
$x^4 - 5x^3 + 13x^2 - 19x + 10 = f(x)$

pp. 818–819   18-8 TRY THIS

a. Find the third side. From the law of cosines,
$a^2 = b^2 + c^2 - 2bc \cos A$
$\approx 18^2 + 28^2 - 2(18)(28) \cdot (-0.5299)$
≈ 1642
$a \approx \sqrt{1642} \approx 40.5$
Next, we use the law of sines to find a second angle.

$\frac{b}{\sin B} = \frac{a}{\sin A}$, $\sin B = \frac{b \sin A}{a} = \frac{18 \sin 122}{40.5}$

$\approx \frac{18(0.8480)}{40.5} \approx 0.3769$

$m\angle B \approx 22°10'$
$m\angle C \approx 180° - (122° + 22°10')$
$\approx 180° - (144°10')$
$\approx 35°50'$

b. $\cos B = \frac{a^2 + c^2 - b^2}{2ac} = \frac{25^2 + 20^2 - 10^2}{2(25)(20)} = 0.925$

$m\angle B \approx 22°20'$

$\cos A = \frac{b^2 + c^2 - a^2}{2bc} = \frac{10^2 + 20^2 - 25^2}{2(10)(20)} = -0.3125$

$m\angle A \approx 108°10'$
$m\angle C \approx 180° - (108°10' + 22°20')$
$\approx 180° - (130°30')$
$\approx 49°30'$

pp. 819–820   18-8 EXERCISES

1. $c = 12.0$, $m\angle A = 20°40'$, $m\angle B = 24°20'$

2. $m\angle C = 28°10'$, $a = 47.6$, $m\angle B = 35°50'$

3. $a = 14.9$, $m\angle C = 126°20'$, $m\angle B = 23°40'$

4. $c = 11.4$, $m\angle A = 22°20'$, $m\angle B = 37°40'$

5. $a = 24.8$, $m\angle C = 26°20'$, $m\angle B = 20°40'$

6. $c = 13.7$, $m\angle A = 71°30'$, $m\angle B = 48°30'$

7. $b = 74.8$, $m\angle C = 11°50'$, $m\angle A = 95°30'$

8. $a = 55.6$, $m\angle B = 30°30'$, $m\angle C = 125°$

9. $m\angle B = 46°30'$, $m\angle A = 29°$, $m\angle C = 104°30'$

10. $m\angle C = 76°10'$, $m\angle B = 61°$, $m\angle A = 42°50'$

11. $m\angle C = 86°20'$, $m\angle B = 58°50'$, $m\angle A = 34°50'$

12. $m\angle B = 52°40'$, $m\angle A = 44°$, $m\angle C = 83°20'$

13. $m\angle A = 36°10'$, $m\angle B = 43°30'$, $m\angle C = 100°20'$

14. $m\angle A = 37°20'$, $m\angle B = 37°20'$, $m\angle C = 105°20'$

15. $m\angle A = 73°40'$, $m\angle B = 51°50'$, $m\angle C = 54°30'$

16. $m\angle A = 24^\circ10'$, $m\angle B = 30^\circ40'$, $m\angle C = 125^\circ10'$

17. $m\angle A = 25^\circ40'$, $m\angle B = 126^\circ$, $m\angle C = 28^\circ20'$

18. $m\angle A = 33^\circ40'$, $m\angle B = 107^\circ$, $m\angle C = 39^\circ20'$

19.

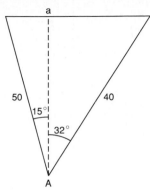

$a^2 = 50^2 + 40^2 - 2(50)(40)(0.682)2500 + 1600 - 2728$
$a^2 = 1372$
$\quad a \approx 37.04$, or ≈ 37 nautical miles

20.

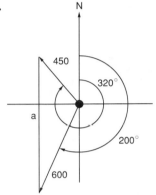

$a^2 = 450^2 + 600^2 - 2(600)(450)(\cos 120^\circ)$
$\quad = 202,500 + 360,000 - 540,000(-5)$
$\quad = 832,500$
$\quad a \approx 912.4$, or ≈ 912 km

21.

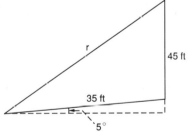

$r^2 = 35^2 + 45^\circ - 2(35 \cdot 45)\cos 95^\circ(-0.087)$
$\quad = 1225 + 2025 + 274.05$
$\quad = 3524.05$
$\quad r = 59.36$, or ≈ 59.4 ft

22.

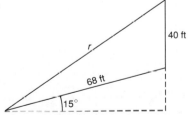

$r^2 = 40^2 + 68^2 - 2(68)(40)\cos 105^\circ$
$\quad = 1600 + 4624 + 1408.96$
$\quad = 7632.9$
$\quad r = 87.36$, or ≈ 87.4 ft

23.

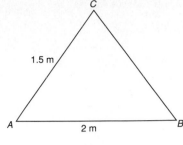

$a = 5.5 - (1.5 + 2) = 2$

$\cos A = \dfrac{1.5^2 + 2^2 - 2^2}{2(1.5)(2)}$

$\quad = \dfrac{2.25 + 4 - 4}{6}$

$\quad = 0.375$

$m\angle A = 68^\circ$; $m\angle C = 68^\circ$; $m\angle B = 44^\circ$

24.

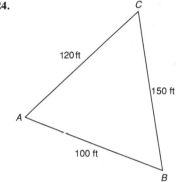

$\cos A = \dfrac{120^2 + 100^2 - 150^2}{2(120)(100)}$

$\quad = \dfrac{14,400 + 10,000 - 22,500}{24,000}$

$\quad = \dfrac{1900}{24,000} \approx 0.0792$

$\cos^{-1} 0.0792 \approx 85^\circ30'$

$\dfrac{\sin 85^\circ30'}{150} = \dfrac{\sin C}{100}$

$\quad m\angle A = 85^\circ30'$; $m\angle C = 41^\circ40'$; $m\angle B = 52^\circ50'$

25. $c^2 - 60^2 + 46^2 \quad 2(60)(46)\cos 45^\circ$
$\quad = 3600 + 2116 - 3903$
$\quad c = 42.57$, or ≈ 42.6 ft

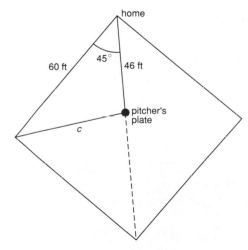

26. $c^2 = 90^2 + 60.5^2 - 2(90)(60.5)\cos 45°$
$= 8100 + 3660.25 - 7700$
$= 4060$
$c \approx 63.7$ ft

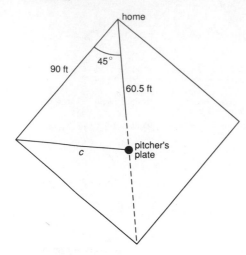

27.

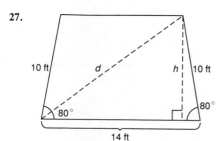

a. $d^2 = 14^2 + 10^2 - 2(14)(10)\cos 80°$
$= 14^2 + 10^2 - 2(14)(10)(0.174)$
$= 196 + 100 - 48.72$
$= 247.28$
$d = 15.725$, or ≈ 15.73 ft

b. $\dfrac{x}{\sin 41°9'} \approx \dfrac{15.7}{\sin 100°}$

$x \approx 10.49$
Area of trapezoid = Area of 2 triangles

$A = \dfrac{1}{2}(10)(14)(\sin 80°) + \dfrac{1}{2}(10)(x)(\sin 100°)$

$= 68.94 + 5(10.49)\sin 100°$
≈ 120.59 ft^2

28.

$\sin A = \dfrac{10}{75}$ 　　　　$CD \approx 105.67$

$A \approx 7.66°$ 　　　$\tan \angle CBD = \dfrac{105.67}{10}$
$\angle ABC \approx 82.34°$
$AC \approx 74.33$ 　　　　$\angle CBD = 84.59°$
　　　　　　　　　$x = 180° - 84.59° - 82.34°$
　　　　　　　　　$x \approx 13°5'$

29. $a^2 + b^2 + c^2 = 2abc\left(\dfrac{\cos A}{a} + \dfrac{\cos B}{b} + \dfrac{\cos C}{c}\right)$

30. $90° - 78° = 12°$, $90° - 72° = 18°$

$\tan 12° = \dfrac{a}{h}$; $\tan 18° = \dfrac{b}{h}$

$a = h\tan 12°$; $b = h\tan 18°$
$h\tan 12° + h\tan 18° = 5042$
$0.2126h + 0.3249h = 5042$
$0.5375h = 5042$
$h \approx 9380$ ft

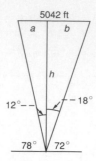

31. Area $= \dfrac{1}{2}ab\sin\theta = \dfrac{1}{2}a^2\sin\theta$, where a is the length of each congruent side and θ is the included angle. Since $\sin\theta = 1$ at $\theta = 90°$, area will be a maximum of $\dfrac{1}{2}a^2$ at $\theta = 90°$.

32. $\dfrac{\cos A}{a} + \dfrac{\cos B}{b} + \dfrac{\cos C}{c}$

$= \dfrac{bc\cos A + ac\cos B + ab\cos C}{abc}$

$= \dfrac{2(bc\cos A + ac\cos B + ab\cos C)}{2abc}$

$= \dfrac{a^2 + b^2 + c^2}{2abc}$

33. $\dfrac{1}{4}x + \dfrac{1}{6}x + \dfrac{1}{8}x = \dfrac{13}{12}$ 　　**34.** $300x + 20x - 4x = -1264$
　　　　　　　　　　　　　　　　　　　　$316x = -1264$
$6x + 4x + 3x = 26$ 　　　　　　　　　$x = -4$
$13x = 26$
$x = 2$

35. $2^{3x} = 2^6$ 　　**36.** $16^x = 1$ 　　**37.** $x^3 = 1000$
$3x = 6$ 　　　　　$x = 0$ 　　　　　$x = 10$
$x = 2$

38. $\dfrac{3x^4}{6x} - \dfrac{2x^2}{6x} + \dfrac{12x}{6x} = \dfrac{x^3}{2} - \dfrac{x}{3} + 2$

39. $1\underline{|}\quad 4\quad 0\quad -2\quad 3\quad 4$
　　　　　　　$4\quad 4\quad 2\quad 5$
　　　$\overline{\quad 4\quad 4\quad 2\quad 5\quad 1}$
$4x^3 + 4x^2 + 2x + 5$ R: 1

40.
$$x^2 - 3\overline{)x^5 + 2x^3 - x^2}$$
$\quad\quad\quad\dfrac{x^3 + 5x - 1}{}$
$\quad\quad\underline{-x^5 + 3x^3}$
$\quad\quad\quad\quad 5x^3$
$\quad\quad\quad\underline{-5x^3 \quad\quad + 15x}$
$\quad\quad\quad\quad\quad -x^2 + 15x$
$\quad\quad\quad\quad\quad\underline{-x^2 \quad\quad + 3}$
$\quad\quad\quad\quad\quad\quad\quad +15x - 3$

41. $(x^4 - 4y^2)(x^4 + 4y^2)$
$(x^2 - 2y)(x^2 + 2y)(x^4 + 4y^2)$

42. $(x^2 - 9)(x^2 - 4)$ 　　　　**43.** $2(c^2 - 14c - 15)$
$(x + 3)(x - 3)(x + 2)(x - 2)$ 　　　$2(c - 15)(c + 1)$

pp. 822–824　　18-9 TRY THIS

a. $\sqrt{2}(\cos 315° + i\sin 315°)$
$a = \sqrt{2}\cos 315° = 1$
$b = \sqrt{2}\sin 315° = -1$
Thus, $\sqrt{2}(\cos 315° + i\sin 315°) = 1 - 1(i) = 1 - i$

b. $1 - i$
$a = 1, b = -1$
$r = \sqrt{1^2 + (-1)^2} = \sqrt{2}$

$\sin\theta = -\dfrac{1}{\sqrt{2}} = -\dfrac{\sqrt{2}}{2}$ and $\cos\theta = \dfrac{1}{\sqrt{2}} = \dfrac{\sqrt{2}}{2}$

Thus, $\theta = \dfrac{7\pi}{4}$, or 315°.

$$1 - i = \sqrt{2} \text{ cis } \frac{7\pi}{4} \quad \text{or} \quad 1 - i = \sqrt{2} \text{ cis } 315°$$
$$= \sqrt{2}(\cos 315° + i \sin 315°)$$
$$= \sqrt{2}\left(\cos \frac{7\pi}{4} + i \sin \frac{7\pi}{4}\right)$$

c. $(5 \text{ cis } 25°)(4 \text{ cis } 30°) = 5 \cdot 4 \text{ cis}(25° + 30°)$
$$= 20 \text{ cis } 55°$$

d. $\dfrac{10 \text{ cis } \dfrac{\pi}{2}}{5 \text{ cis } \dfrac{\pi}{4}} = \dfrac{10}{5} \text{ cis}\left(\dfrac{\pi}{2} - \dfrac{\pi}{4}\right) = 2 \text{ cis } \dfrac{\pi}{4}$

e. $(1 - i)^{10} = (\sqrt{2} \text{ cis } 315°)^{10} = (\sqrt{2})^{10} \text{ cis } 10(315°)$
$$= 2^{10/2} \text{ cis } 3150°$$
$$= 32 \text{ cis } 270°$$

f. $(\sqrt{3} + i)^4 = (2 \text{ cis } 30°)^4 = 2^4 \text{ cis } 4(30°)$
$$= 16 \text{ cis } 120°$$

g. $(2i)^{1/2} = (2 \text{ cis } 90°)^{1/2} = 2^{1/2} \text{ cis}\left(\dfrac{90°}{2} + k \cdot \dfrac{360°}{2}\right)$,

where $k = 0, 1$.
$$= \sqrt{2} \text{ cis}(45° + 180°k),$$
where $k = 0, 1$.

Thus, the roots are $\sqrt{2} \text{ cis } 45°$ and $2 \text{ cis } 225°$, or $1 + i$ and $-1 - i$.

h. $(8i)^{1/3} = (8 \text{ cis } 90°)^{1/3} = 8^{1/3} \text{ cis}\left(\dfrac{90°}{3} + k\dfrac{360°}{3}\right)$,

where $k = 0, 1, 2$.
$$= 2 \text{ cis}(30° + 120°k),$$
where $k = 0, 1, 2$.

Thus, the roots are $2 \text{ cis } 30°$, $2 \text{ cis } 150°$, and $2 \text{ cis } 270°$, or $\sqrt{3} + i$, $-\sqrt{3} + i$, and $-2i$.

pp. 825–826   **18-9 EXERCISES**

1. $\dfrac{3\sqrt{3}}{2} + \dfrac{3i}{2}$ 2. $\dfrac{5}{2} + \dfrac{5\sqrt{3}}{2}i$ 3. $-2\sqrt{2} + 2i\sqrt{2}$

4. $-3\sqrt{3} + 3i$ 5. $-10i$ 6. $12i$ 7. $\dfrac{5\sqrt{2}}{2} - \dfrac{5\sqrt{2}}{2}i$

8. $\dfrac{5}{2} - \dfrac{5\sqrt{3}}{2}i$ 9. $2 + 2i$ 10. $-2 + 2i$ 11. $2\sqrt{3} + 2i$

12. $\dfrac{5}{2} + \dfrac{5\sqrt{3}}{2}i$ 13. $-2 - 2i$ 14. $2 - 2i$

15. $\sqrt{2} \text{ cis } \dfrac{3\pi}{4}$ or $\sqrt{2} \text{ cis } 135°$ 16. $\sqrt{2} \text{ cis } \dfrac{5\pi}{4}$ or $\sqrt{2} \text{ cis } 225°$

17. $2 \text{ cis } \dfrac{\pi}{6}$ or $2 \text{ cis } 30°$ 18. $2 \text{ cis } \dfrac{5\pi}{6}$ or $2 \text{ cis } 150°$

19. $20 \text{ cis } \dfrac{11\pi}{6}$ or $20 \text{ cis } 330°$ 20. $20 \text{ cis } \dfrac{5\pi}{6}$ or $20 \text{ cis } 150°$

21. $2 \text{ cis } \dfrac{\pi}{2}$ or $2 \text{ cis } 90°$ 22. $3 \text{ cis } \dfrac{\pi}{2}$ or $3 \text{ cis } 90°$

23. $5 \text{ cis } \pi$ or $5 \text{ cis } 180°$ 24. $10 \text{ cis } \pi$ or $10 \text{ cis } 180°$

25. $4 \text{ cis } \dfrac{3\pi}{2}$ or $4 \text{ cis } 270°$ 26. $5 \text{ cis } \dfrac{3\pi}{2}$ or $5 \text{ cis } 270°$

27. $4 \text{ cis } 0$ 28. $2\sqrt{2} \text{ cis } \dfrac{5\pi}{12}$ 29. $40 \text{ cis } 0$ 30. $2\sqrt{2} \text{ cis } \dfrac{7\pi}{12}$

31. $8 \text{ cis } \dfrac{2\pi}{3}$ 32. $12 \text{ cis } \dfrac{\pi}{3}$ 33. $\text{cis } \dfrac{\pi}{2}$ 34. $\text{cis } \dfrac{3\pi}{2}$

35. $\dfrac{\sqrt{2}}{2} \text{ cis } \dfrac{7\pi}{12}$ 36. $\dfrac{\sqrt{2}}{2} \text{ cis } \dfrac{23\pi}{12}$ 37. $2 \text{ cis } \dfrac{3\pi}{2}$ 38. $3 \text{ cis } \dfrac{11\pi}{6}$

39. $8 \text{ cis } \pi$ or $8 \text{ cis } 180°$ 40. $81 \text{ cis } 0$ or $81 \text{ cis } 0°$

41. $64 \text{ cis } \pi$ or $64 \text{ cis } 180°$ 42. $32 \text{ cis } \pi$ or $32 \text{ cis } 180°$

43. $8 \text{ cis } \dfrac{3\pi}{2}$ or $8 \text{ cis } 270°$ 44. $8 \text{ cis } \dfrac{\pi}{2}$ or $8 \text{ cis } 90°$

45. $-8 - 8i\sqrt{3}$ 46. $-8 + 8i\sqrt{3}$ 47. $-8 - 8i\sqrt{3}$

48. -64 49. i 50. -1 51. 1 52. $\dfrac{1}{2} - \dfrac{\sqrt{3}}{2}i$

53. $\sqrt{2} \text{ cis } 60°$ and $\sqrt{2} \text{ cis } 240°$ or $\sqrt{2} \text{ cis } \dfrac{\pi}{3}$ and $\sqrt{2} \text{ cis } \dfrac{4\pi}{3}$

54. $\sqrt{2} \text{ cis } 105°$ and $\sqrt{2} \text{ cis } 285°$ or $\sqrt{2} \text{ cis } \dfrac{7\pi}{12}$ and $\sqrt{2} \text{ cis } \dfrac{19\pi}{12}$

55. $\text{cis } 30°$, $\text{cis } 150°$, and $\text{cis } 270°$ or $\text{cis } \dfrac{\pi}{6}$, $\text{cis } \dfrac{5\pi}{6}$, and $\text{cis } \dfrac{3\pi}{2}$

56. $\text{cis } 90°$, $\text{cis } 210°$, and $\text{cis } 330°$ or $\text{cis } \dfrac{\pi}{2}$, $\text{cis } \dfrac{7\pi}{6}$, and $\text{cis } \dfrac{11\pi}{6}$

57. $2 \text{ cis } 0°$, $2 \text{ cis } 90°$, $2 \text{ cis } 180°$, and $2 \text{ cis } 270°$ or $2 \text{ cis } 0$, $2 \text{ cis } \dfrac{\pi}{2}$, $2 \text{ cis } \pi$, and $2 \text{ cis } \dfrac{3\pi}{2}$

58. $2 \text{ cis } 45°$, $2 \text{ cis } 135°$, $2 \text{ cis } 225°$, and $2 \text{ cis } 315°$ or $2 \text{ cis } \dfrac{\pi}{4}$, $2 \text{ cis } \dfrac{3\pi}{4}$, $2 \text{ cis } \dfrac{5\pi}{4}$, and $2 \text{ cis } \dfrac{7\pi}{4}$

59. $(1 + 0i)^3 = (1 \text{ cis } 0)^3 = 1^3 \text{ cis } 3 \cdot 0 = \text{cis } 0$
$$= \cos 0 + i \sin 0$$
$$= 1 + i(0)$$
$$= 1$$
$\left(-\dfrac{1}{2} + \dfrac{\sqrt{3}}{2}i\right)^3 = \left(1 \text{ cis } \dfrac{2\pi}{3}\right)^3 = 1^3 \text{ cis } 3\left(\dfrac{2\pi}{3}\right) = 1 \text{ cis } 2\pi$
$$= 1 \cos 2\pi + i \sin 2\pi$$
$$= 1(1 + i \cdot 0)$$
$$= 1$$
$\left(-\dfrac{1}{2} - \dfrac{\sqrt{3}}{2}i\right)^3 = \left(1 \text{ cis } \dfrac{4\pi}{3}\right)^3 = 1^3 \text{ cis } 3 \cdot \dfrac{4\pi}{3} = 1 \text{ cis } 4\pi$
$$= 1$$

60. $-1 + 0i = (1 \text{ cis } 180°)^{1/3} = 1^{1/3} \text{ cis } \dfrac{180°}{3} + 0 = 1 \text{ cis } 60°$
$$= \dfrac{1}{2} + \dfrac{\sqrt{3}}{2}i$$
$$= 1^{1/3} \text{ cis } \dfrac{180°}{3} + \dfrac{1 \cdot 360°}{3} = 1 \text{ cis } 180°$$
$$= -1 + 0i \qquad = -1$$
$$= 1^{1/3} \text{ cis } \dfrac{180°}{3} + \dfrac{2 \cdot 360°}{3} = 1 \text{ cis } 300°$$
$$= \dfrac{1}{2} - \dfrac{\sqrt{3}}{2}i$$

61. $1^{1/4} = (\text{cis } 0°)^{1/4}$
$$= \text{cis } 0°, \text{cis}\left(\dfrac{360°}{4}\right), \text{cis}\left(\dfrac{2 \cdot 360°}{4}\right), \text{cis}\left(\dfrac{3 \cdot 360°}{4}\right)$$
$$= \text{cis } 0°, \text{cis } 90°, \text{cis } 180°, \text{cis } 270°$$
$$= 1, i, -1, -i$$

62. $|z \cdot w| = |r_1 r_2 \text{ cis}(\theta_1 + \theta_2)|$
$$= |r_1 r_2 \cos(\theta_1 + \theta_2) + r_1 r_2 i \sin(\theta_1 + \theta_2)|$$
$$= \sqrt{r_1^2 r_2^2 \cos^2(\theta_1 + \theta_2) + r_1^2 r_2^2 \sin^2(\theta_1 + \theta_2)}$$
$$= \sqrt{r_1^2 r_2^2} = r_1 r_2$$
$|z| \cdot |w| = |r_1 \text{ cis } \theta_1| \cdot |r_2 \text{ cis } \theta_2|$
$$= |r_1 \cos \theta_1 + r_1 i \sin \theta_1| \cdot |r_2 \cos \theta_2 + r_2 i \sin \theta_2|$$
$$= \sqrt{r_1^2 \cos^2\theta_1 + r_1^2 \sin^2\theta_1} \cdot \sqrt{r_2^2 \cos^2\theta_2 + r_2^2 \sin^2\theta_2}$$
$$= \sqrt{r_1^2} \cdot \sqrt{r_2^2} = r_1 r_2$$

63. $\left|\dfrac{z}{w}\right| = \left|\dfrac{r_1}{r_2} \text{ cis}(\theta_1 - \theta_2)\right|$
$$= \left|\dfrac{r_1}{r_2} \cos(\theta_1 - \theta_2) + \dfrac{r_1}{r_2}i \sin(\theta_1 - \theta_2)\right|$$
$$= \sqrt{\dfrac{r_1^2}{r_2^2} \cos^2(\theta_1 - \theta_2) + \dfrac{r_1^2}{r_2^2} \sin^2(\theta_1 - \theta_2)}$$
$$= \sqrt{\dfrac{r_1^2}{r_2^2}} = \dfrac{r_1}{r_2}$$

$$\left|\frac{z}{w}\right| = \left|\frac{r_1 \operatorname{cis} \theta_1}{r_2 \operatorname{cis} \theta_2}\right| = \left|\frac{r_1 \cos \theta_1 + r_1 i \sin \theta_1}{r_2 \cos \theta_2 + r_2 i \sin \theta_2}\right|$$

$$= \frac{\sqrt{r_1^2 \cos^2 \theta_1 + r_1^2 \sin^2 \theta_1}}{\sqrt{r_2^2 \cos^2 \theta_2 + r_2^2 \sin^2 \theta_2}} = \frac{\sqrt{r_1^2}}{\sqrt{r_2^2}} = \frac{r_1}{r_2}$$

64. $(68.4321)^{1/3} = (68.4321 + 0i)^{1/3}$
$$= (68.4321 \operatorname{cis} 0°)^{1/3}$$
$$= \sqrt[3]{68.4321} \operatorname{cis} 0°, \ \sqrt[3]{68.4321} \operatorname{cis}\left(\frac{360°}{3}\right),$$
$$\sqrt[3]{68.4321} \operatorname{cis}\left(\frac{2 \cdot 360°}{3}\right)$$
$$= \sqrt[3]{68.4321}, \ \sqrt[3]{68.4321} \operatorname{cis} 120°,$$
$$\sqrt[3]{68.4321} \operatorname{cis} 240°$$

65. $(\operatorname{cis} 0°)^4$
$$= \operatorname{cis} 4 \cdot 0$$
$$= \operatorname{cis} 0$$
$$= \cos 0 + i \sin 0$$
$$= 1 + 0 = 1$$

66. $(\cos \theta + i \sin \theta)^{-1} = (1 \cdot \operatorname{cis} \theta)^{-1}$
$$= 1^{-1} \operatorname{cis}(-\theta)$$
$$= 1 \operatorname{cis}(-\theta)$$
Since $\cos \theta = \cos(-\theta)$ and $\sin \theta = -\sin(-\theta)$, we have $\operatorname{cis}(-\theta) = \cos \theta - i \sin \theta$.

67. $\begin{bmatrix} i & 0 \\ 0 & -i \end{bmatrix} = \begin{bmatrix} i & 0 \\ 0 & -i \end{bmatrix}\begin{bmatrix} i & 0 \\ 0 & -i \end{bmatrix}\begin{bmatrix} i & 0 \\ 0 & -i \end{bmatrix}$

$$= \begin{bmatrix} -1 & 0 \\ 0 & -1 \end{bmatrix}\begin{bmatrix} i & 0 \\ 0 & -i \end{bmatrix}$$

$$= \begin{bmatrix} -i & 0 \\ 0 & i \end{bmatrix}$$

68. $180°$ **69.** $720°$ **70.** $-60°$ **71.** $105°$ **72.** $\frac{11}{12}\pi$

73. $\frac{5\pi}{12}$ **74.** $\frac{\pi}{8}$ **75.** $-\frac{\pi}{2}$ **76.** $\quad x^4 - 1 = 0$
$$(x^2 - 1)(x^2 + 1) = 0$$
$$x^2 = 1 \quad \text{or} \quad x^2 = -1$$
$$x = \pm 1 \quad \text{or} \quad x = \pm i$$

77. $x^4 + x^3 - 8x^2 - 2x + 12 = 0$

$$\underline{2|} \quad 1 \quad\ 1 \quad -8 \quad -2 \quad\ 12$$
$$\qquad\qquad 2 \quad\ 6 \quad -4 \quad -12$$
$$\underline{-3|}\ 1 \quad\ 3 \quad -2 \quad -6\ |\quad 0 \qquad \text{2 is a root}$$
$$\qquad\qquad -3 \quad\ 0 \quad\ 6$$
$$\qquad 1 \quad\ 0 \quad -2 \quad\ 0 \qquad\quad \text{-3 is a root}$$
$$x^2 - 2 = 0$$
$$x^2 = 2$$
$$x = \pm\sqrt{2}$$
$$2, -3, \pm\sqrt{2}$$

78. $2x^3 - 3x^2 - 11x + 6 = 0$

$$\underline{-2|} \quad 2 \quad -3 \quad -11 \quad\ 6$$
$$\qquad\qquad\quad -4 \quad\ 14 \quad -6$$
$$\qquad\quad 2 \quad -7 \quad\ 3\ |\ 0 \qquad \text{-2 is a root}$$
$$2x^2 - 7x + 3 = 0$$
$$(2x - 1)(x - 3) = 0$$
$$x = \frac{1}{2} \quad \text{or} \quad x = 3$$
$$-2, \frac{1}{2}, 3$$

79. Radon-222 has a half-life of 3.8 days. Sample = 50 mg
$$N = N_0 e^{-kt}$$
$$25 = 50 e^{-k(3.8)}$$
$$k = 0.182$$
$$N = N_0 e^{-0.182t}$$
a. $N = 50 e^{-0.182(1)} = 41.68$ mg, or ≈ 41.7 mg
b. $N = 50 e^{-0.182(7)} = 13.98$ mg, or ≈ 13.9 mg
c. $N = 50 e^{-0.182(14)} = 3.91$ mg, or ≈ 3.9 mg

1. Since ST is tangent to the earth's surface, we know $\angle CTS$ is a right angle, thus,
$$\cos \theta = \frac{4000}{4558}$$
$$\approx 0.8776$$
Thus, $\theta \approx 0.5$ radians.

It follows that $\frac{d}{4000} \approx 0.5$ or $d \approx 2000$ miles. Hence, the maximum distance between the two tracking stations is about 4000 miles.

2. Since ST is tangent to the moon's surface, we know $\angle CTS$ is a right angle, thus,
$$\cos \theta = \frac{1080}{1150} \approx 0.9391$$
Thus, $\theta \approx 0.3507$ radians.

It follows that $\frac{d}{1080} \approx 0.3507$ or $d \approx 379$ miles. Hence, the maximum distance between the two tracking stations is about 758 miles.

3. From the example on p. 829 we see that each pair of tracking stations could be a maximum of 3006 miles apart.

Thus, $\frac{25,000}{3006} \approx 8.32$, so 9 stations are needed.

4. The tracking stations should be $\frac{25,000}{7} \approx 3571.4$ miles apart.

Thus, $d \approx \frac{3571.4}{2} \approx 1785.7$ miles.

$$\frac{d}{4000} \approx 0.4464 \text{ radians}$$
$$\cos(0.4464) \approx 0.902$$
$$\frac{4000}{0.902} \approx 4435$$

The orbit needs to be raised to at least 435 miles.

5. a. $\frac{25,000}{10} = 2500$ miles apart
$$d = 1250 \text{ miles}$$
$$\frac{d}{4000} = \frac{1250}{4000} = 0.3125 \text{ radians}$$
$$\cos(0.3125) \approx 0.9516$$
$$\frac{4000}{0.9516} \approx 4203.6$$

The lowest orbit possible is 203.6 miles.

b. $\frac{25,000}{6} \approx 4166.7$ miles apart
$$d \approx 2083.3 \text{ miles}$$
$$\frac{d}{4000} \approx \frac{2083.3}{4000} \approx 0.5208$$
$$\cos(0.5208) \approx 0.8674$$
$$\frac{4000}{0.8674} \approx 4611.5$$

The lowest orbit possible is 611.5 miles.

1. $\cos x \cos y - \sin x \sin y$

2. $\tan(45° - 30°) = \dfrac{\tan 45° - \tan 30°}{1 + \tan 45° \tan 30°}$

$$= \frac{1 - \dfrac{\sqrt{3}}{3}}{1 + \dfrac{\sqrt{3}}{3}} = \frac{3 - \sqrt{3}}{3 + \sqrt{3}} = 2 - \sqrt{3}$$

3. $\sin 75° = \sin(45° + 30°) = \sin 45° \cos 30° + \cos 45° \sin 30°$

$$= \frac{\sqrt{2}}{2} \cdot \frac{\sqrt{3}}{2} + \frac{\sqrt{2}}{2} \cdot \frac{1}{2}$$

$$= \frac{\sqrt{6}}{4} + \frac{\sqrt{2}}{4} = \frac{\sqrt{6} + \sqrt{2}}{4}$$

4. $\cos\left(\frac{\pi}{3} + \frac{\pi}{4}\right) = \cos\frac{\pi}{3}\cos\frac{\pi}{4} - \sin\frac{\pi}{3}\sin\frac{\pi}{4}$

$$= \frac{1}{2} \cdot \frac{\sqrt{2}}{2} - \frac{\sqrt{3}}{2} \cdot \frac{\sqrt{2}}{2}$$

$$= \frac{\sqrt{2}}{4} - \frac{\sqrt{6}}{4} = \frac{\sqrt{2} - \sqrt{6}}{4}$$

5. $\tan\left(\frac{\pi}{3} - \frac{\pi}{4}\right) = \dfrac{\tan\frac{\pi}{3} - \tan\frac{\pi}{4}}{1 + \tan\frac{\pi}{3}\tan\frac{\pi}{4}} = \dfrac{\sqrt{3} - 1}{1 + \sqrt{3}} \cdot \dfrac{1 - \sqrt{3}}{1 - \sqrt{3}}$

$$= \frac{2\sqrt{3} - 4}{-2} = 2 - \sqrt{3}$$

6. $\sin 2\theta = 2\sin\theta\cos\theta$

$$= 2 \cdot \frac{3}{5} \cdot \frac{4}{5}$$

$$= \frac{24}{25}$$

$\cos 2\theta = 1 - 2\sin^2\theta$

$$= 1 - 2\left(\frac{9}{25}\right) = \frac{7}{25}$$

$\tan 2\theta = \dfrac{2\tan\theta}{1 - \tan^2\theta}$

$$= \frac{2\left(\frac{3}{4}\right)}{1 - \left(\frac{9}{16}\right)} = \frac{\frac{3}{2}}{\frac{7}{16}} = \frac{24}{7} \qquad \text{Quadrant I}$$

7. $\tan\theta = \frac{4}{3}$

$\tan 2\theta = \dfrac{2\tan\theta}{1 - \tan^2\theta} = \dfrac{\frac{8}{3}}{1 - \frac{16}{9}} = \dfrac{\frac{8}{3}}{-\frac{7}{9}} = -\frac{24}{7}$

$\sin 2\theta = 2\sin\theta\cos\theta = 2\left(\frac{4}{5}\right)\left(\frac{3}{5}\right) = \frac{24}{25}$

$\cos 2\theta = 1 - 2\sin^2\theta = 1 - 2\left(\frac{16}{25}\right) = -\frac{7}{25} \qquad \text{Quadrant II}$

8. $\cos 15° = \cos\left(\frac{30}{2}\right)° = \pm\sqrt{\dfrac{1 + \cos 30°}{2}}$

$$= \pm\sqrt{\frac{2 + \sqrt{3}}{4}}$$

$$= \pm\frac{1}{2}\sqrt{2 + \sqrt{3}} \quad \text{or} \quad \frac{\sqrt{2} + \sqrt{6}}{4}$$

9. $\sin\frac{\pi}{8} = \sin\dfrac{\frac{\pi}{4}}{2} = \pm\sqrt{\dfrac{1 - \cos\frac{\pi}{4}}{2}} = \pm\sqrt{\dfrac{1 - \frac{\sqrt{2}}{2}}{2}}$

$$= \pm\frac{\sqrt{2 - \sqrt{2}}}{4}$$

10. $\tan 2\theta \equiv \dfrac{2\tan\theta}{1 - \tan^2\theta}$

$\tan(\theta + \theta)$	
$\dfrac{\tan\theta + \tan\theta}{1 - \tan\theta\tan\theta}$	
$\dfrac{2\tan\theta}{1 - \tan^2\theta}$	$\dfrac{2\tan\theta}{1 - \tan^2\theta}$

11. $\frac{\pi}{6} + 2k\pi, \frac{5\pi}{6} + 2k\pi$ **12.** $\frac{3\pi}{4} + 2k\pi, \frac{5\pi}{4} + 2k\pi$

13. $-\frac{\pi}{4}$ **14.** $\frac{\pi}{6}$

15. $\sin x(\sin x - 7) = 0$

$\sin x = 0 \quad$ or $\quad \sin x - 7 = 0$

$x = 0, \pi, 2\pi \qquad \sin x = 7$

16. $\sin 2x - \cos x = 0$

$\sin 2x = \cos x$

$2\sin x\cos x = \cos x$

$2\sin x = 1$

$\sin x = \frac{1}{2}$

$x = \frac{\pi}{6}, \frac{5\pi}{6}$

also, where $\cos x = 0$

$x = \frac{\pi}{2}, \frac{3\pi}{2}$

17. $m\angle B = 90° - 42°30' = 47°30'$

$\sin 42°30' = \dfrac{1200}{C}$

$C = 1776$

$\tan 42°30' = \dfrac{1200}{b}$

$b = 1310$

18. $(7.3)^2 + b^2 = (8.6)^2$

$b = 4.55$

$\sin A° = \dfrac{7.3}{8.6}$

$m\angle A = 58°10'$

$\sin B° = \dfrac{4.55}{8.6}$

$m\angle B = 31°50'$

19. $m\angle A = 90° - 51°10' = 38°50'$

$\cos 51°10' = \dfrac{30.5}{C}$

$C = 48.6$

$\tan 51°10' = \dfrac{b}{30.5}$

$b = 37.9$

20.

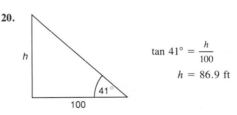

$\tan 41° = \dfrac{h}{100}$

$h = 86.9 \text{ ft}$

21.

$\cos 8°30' = \dfrac{x}{3750}$

$x = 3708.8 \text{ mi}$

22. $\dfrac{25}{\sin 80°} = \dfrac{a}{\sin 40°} \qquad a = 16.3$

$m\angle C = 180 - 40 - 80 = 60$

$\dfrac{25}{\sin 80°} = \dfrac{c}{\sin 60°} \qquad c = 22$

23. $m\angle A = 180° - 118°20' - 27°40' = 34°$

$$\frac{0.974}{\sin 118°20'} = \frac{c}{27°40'} \qquad c = 0.514$$

$$\frac{0.974}{\sin 118°20'} = \frac{a}{\sin 34°} \qquad a = 0.619$$

24. $\dfrac{5}{\sin 72°} = \dfrac{4}{\sin B°} \qquad m\angle B = 49°30'$

$m\angle C = 180° - 72° - 49°30' = 58°30'$

$$\frac{5}{\sin 72°} = \frac{c}{\sin 58°30'} \qquad c = 4.48$$

25. $b^2 = (3.7)^2 + (4.9)^2 - 2(3.7)(4.9)\cos 135°$
$\quad b = 7.96$

$$\frac{7.96}{\sin 135°} = \frac{3.7}{\sin A°} \qquad m\angle A = 19°10'$$

$$\frac{7.96}{\sin 135°} = \frac{4.9}{\sin C} \qquad m\angle C = 25°50'$$

26. $\qquad 25 = 64 + 81 - 2(72)\cos A$
$\quad 144 \cos A = 120$

$$\cos A = \frac{5}{6}$$

$\qquad m\angle A = 33.55° \approx 33°33'$

$$\frac{5}{\sin 33°33'} = \frac{8}{\sin B°} \qquad m\angle B = 62°09'$$

$\qquad m\angle C = 180 - 33°33' - 62°09' = 84°18'$

27. $a = \dfrac{1}{2}(5)(9)\sin 65°$

$\quad a = 20.4$

28. $a = 2 \cos 135°$
$\quad b = 2 \sin 135°$
$\quad -\sqrt{2} + i\sqrt{2}$

29. $a = 1, \ b = 1$
$r = \sqrt{1^2 + 1^2} = \sqrt{2}$

$$\sin \theta = \frac{1}{\sqrt{2}} \qquad \cos \theta = \frac{1}{\sqrt{2}}$$

$$\theta = \frac{\pi}{4} \quad \text{or} \quad 45°$$

$$1 + i = \sqrt{2} \operatorname{cis} \frac{\pi}{4} \quad \text{or} \quad \sqrt{2} \operatorname{cis} 45°$$

30. $2(\cos 120° + i \sin 120°)$
$\quad a = 2 \cos 120°$
$\quad b = 2 \sin 120°$
$\quad -1 + i\sqrt{3}$

31. $1 + i = \sqrt{2} \operatorname{cis} \dfrac{\pi}{4}$

$$\left(\sqrt{2} \operatorname{cis} \frac{\pi}{4}\right)^{1/3} = (\sqrt{2})^{1/3} \operatorname{cis}\left(\frac{45°}{3} + k \cdot \frac{360°}{3}\right)$$

$$= \sqrt[6]{2} \operatorname{cis}(15° + k \cdot 120°)$$

$\qquad k = 0 \qquad \sqrt[6]{2} \operatorname{cis} 15°$
$\qquad k = 1 \qquad \sqrt[6]{2} \operatorname{cis} 135°$
$\qquad k = 2 \qquad \sqrt[6]{2} \operatorname{cis} 255°$

p. 833   CHAPTER 18 TEST

1. $\sin(x - y) = \sin x \cos y - \cos x \sin y$

2. $\cos\left(\dfrac{\pi}{2} + \dfrac{\pi}{3}\right) = \cos \dfrac{\pi}{2} \cos \dfrac{\pi}{3} - \sin \dfrac{\pi}{2} \sin \dfrac{\pi}{3}$

$$= 0 - 1\left(\frac{\sqrt{3}}{2}\right)$$

$$= -\frac{\sqrt{3}}{2}$$

3. $\tan 105° = \tan(60° + 45°) = \dfrac{\tan 60° + \tan 45°}{1 - \tan 60° \tan 45°}$

$$= \frac{\sqrt{3} + 1}{1 - \sqrt{3}} \cdot \frac{1 + \sqrt{3}}{1 + \sqrt{3}}$$

$$= \frac{4 + 2\sqrt{3}}{-2} = -2 - \sqrt{3}$$

4. $\sin(45° - 30°) = \sin 45° \cos 30° - \cos 45° \sin 30°$

$$= \left(\frac{\sqrt{2}}{2}\right)\left(\frac{\sqrt{3}}{2}\right) - \left(\frac{\sqrt{2}}{2}\right)\left(\frac{1}{2}\right)$$

$$= \frac{\sqrt{6}}{4} - \frac{\sqrt{2}}{4}$$

$$= \frac{\sqrt{6} - \sqrt{2}}{4}$$

5. $\sin 2\theta = 2 \sin \theta \cos \theta$

$$= 2\left(\frac{3}{5}\right)\left(\frac{4}{5}\right)$$

$$= \frac{24}{25}$$

$\cos 2\theta = 1 - 2 \sin^2\theta$

$$= 1 - 2\left(\frac{9}{25}\right)$$

$$= \frac{7}{25} \qquad \theta \text{ in Quadrant I}$$

$$\tan 2\theta = \frac{\sin 2\theta}{\cos 2\theta} = \frac{24}{25} \div \frac{7}{25} = \frac{24}{7}$$

6. $\sin 2\theta = 2 \sin \theta \cos \theta$

$$= 2\left(\frac{3}{5}\right)\left(-\frac{4}{5}\right)$$

$$= -\frac{24}{25}$$

$\cos 2\theta = 1 - 2 \sin^2\theta$

$$= 1 - 2\left(\frac{9}{25}\right)$$

$$= \frac{7}{25}$$

$$\tan 2\theta = \frac{\sin 2\theta}{\cos 2\theta} = -\frac{24}{7} \qquad \text{Quadrant IV}$$

7. $\sin \dfrac{\pi}{12} = \sin\left(\dfrac{\frac{\pi}{6}}{2}\right)$

$$= \pm \sqrt{\frac{1 - \cos \frac{\pi}{6}}{2}}$$

$$= \pm \sqrt{\frac{2 + \sqrt{3}}{4}}$$

$$= \pm\frac{1}{2}\sqrt{2 + \sqrt{3}}; \ \frac{1}{2}\sqrt{2 + \sqrt{3}} \quad \text{checks}$$

8. $\sin\left(\dfrac{\frac{7\pi}{4}}{2}\right) = \pm \sqrt{\dfrac{1 - \cos \frac{7\pi}{4}}{2}}$

$$= \pm \sqrt{\frac{1 - \cos \frac{7\pi}{4}}{2}}$$

$$= \pm \sqrt{\frac{2 - \sqrt{2}}{4}}$$

$$= \pm\frac{\sqrt{2 - \sqrt{2}}}{2}; \ \frac{\sqrt{2 - \sqrt{2}}}{2} \quad \text{checks}$$

9. $\tan \theta = \dfrac{\sin 2\theta}{1 + \cos 2\theta}$

$\tan \theta \ \Big| \ \dfrac{2 \sin \theta \cos \theta}{1 + \cos^2\theta - \sin^2\theta}$

$\qquad \dfrac{2 \sin \theta \cos \theta}{2 \cos^2\theta}$

$\qquad \dfrac{\sin \theta}{\cos \theta}$

$\qquad \tan \theta$

256 *Algebra and Trigonometry*

10. $\dfrac{\pi}{3} + 2k\pi, \dfrac{5\pi}{3} + 2k\pi$ **11.** $\dfrac{\pi}{6}$

12. $2\cos^2 x + 3\cos x + 1 = 0$

$$\cos x = \dfrac{-3 \pm \sqrt{9-8}}{4}$$

$$= \dfrac{-3 \pm 1}{4}$$

$$\cos x = -1 \qquad x = \pi$$

$$\cos x = -\dfrac{1}{2} \qquad x = \dfrac{2\pi}{3}, \dfrac{4\pi}{3}$$

13. $1 - \sin^2 x = 1 + \sin^2 x$
$0 = 2\sin^2 x$
$0 = \sin^2 x$
$x = 0, \pi, 2\pi$

14.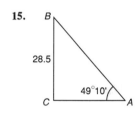

$(9.2)^2 + 6^2 = (10.1)^2$
$b = 4.16$

$\tan \angle B = \dfrac{4.16}{9.2}$

$m\angle B = 24°20'$

$\sin \angle A = \dfrac{9.2}{10.1}$

$m\angle A = 65°40'$

15.

$m\angle B = 90° - 49°10' = 40°50'$

$\sin 49°10' = \dfrac{28.5}{C}$

$C = 43.6$

$\cos 49°10' = \dfrac{b}{43.6}$

$b = 33.0$

16.

$\tan 15° = \dfrac{1454}{x}$

$x = 5426 \text{ ft}$

17. $m\angle A = 180° - 117°10' - 26°50' = 36°$

$$\dfrac{0.9763}{\sin 117°10'} = \dfrac{C}{\sin 26°50'}$$

$$C = 0.495$$

$$\dfrac{0.9763}{\sin 117°10'} = \dfrac{a}{\sin 36°}$$

$$a = 0.645$$

18. $\dfrac{9}{\sin 50°} = \dfrac{10}{\sin B°}$

$m\angle B = 58°20'$
$m\angle C = 180° - 50° - 58°20' = 71°40'$

$\dfrac{9}{\sin 50°} = \dfrac{c}{\sin 71°40'} \qquad c = 11.2$

19. $b^2 = (3.8)^2 + (4.6)^2 - 2(3.8)(4.6)\cos 132$
$b = 7.68$

$\dfrac{7.68}{\sin 132°} = \dfrac{3.8}{\sin A} \qquad m\angle A = 21°30'$

$\dfrac{7.68}{\sin 132°} = \dfrac{4.6}{\sin C} \qquad m\angle C = 26°30'$

20. $81 = 100 + 169 - 260 \cos A$
$m\angle A = 43°40'$

$\dfrac{9}{\sin 43°40'} = \dfrac{10}{\sin B} \qquad m\angle B = 50°10'$

$m\angle C = 180° - 43°40' - 50°10' = 86°10'$

21. $a = 3\cos 120°$
$b = 3\sin 120°$

$-\dfrac{3}{2} + \dfrac{3\sqrt{3}}{2}i$

22. $a = 1$
$b = -1$
$r = \sqrt{1 + (-1)^2} = \sqrt{2}$

$\cos\theta = \dfrac{1}{\sqrt{2}} \qquad \sin\theta = \dfrac{-1}{\sqrt{2}}$

$\sqrt{2} \text{ cis } \dfrac{7\pi}{4}$

23. $(2 \text{ cis } 150)^3 = 2^3 \text{ cis}(450)$
$= 8(\cos 90° + i\sin 90°)$
$= 8i$

24. $\sin x = \dfrac{1}{4}(2\sqrt{2})$

$\sin x = \dfrac{1}{2}\sqrt{2}$

$x = 45° + 360°k$
$\quad 135° + 360°k$

p. 834–837   CHAPTERS 1–18 CUMULATIVE REVIEW

1. $|-2 - 14| - |-4 - 7| - (-14) = 16 - 11 + 14 = 19$

2. $-5|4 + (-14)| - 3|-28 - 1| = -5(10) - 3(29) = -137$

3. $4x - 3[4x + 25] = 2x - 5$
$-8x - 75 = 2x - 5$
$-70 = 10x$
$-7 = x$

4. $\dfrac{2}{3}x + \dfrac{3}{4} = 2x - 22 + \dfrac{7}{4}$

$\dfrac{84}{4} = \dfrac{4}{3}x$

$\dfrac{63}{4} = x$

$15\dfrac{3}{4} = x$

5. $10 < 5a$ **6.** $5.3x < 5.3$ **7.** $-15 < 3x < 39$
$\quad 2 < a$ $\quad\quad x < 1$ $\quad -5 < x < 13$

8. $4 - y \le 10$ and $y - 4 \le 10$
$\quad -y \le 6 \qquad\qquad\quad y \le 14$
$\quad\quad y \ge -6$
$\quad -6 \le y \le 14$

9. $(20{,}000, 4380)\ (15{,}000, 3690)$

$m = \dfrac{4380 - 3690}{20{,}000 - 15{,}000} = \dfrac{690}{5000} = 0.138$

$4380 = (0.138)(20{,}000) + b$
$\quad b = 1620$
$0.138m + 1620 = c$
$0.138(1000) + 1620 = \$1758$

10. $60a - 12b = -132$
$\underline{\quad 4a + 12b = 4\quad}$
$\quad\quad 64a = -128$
$\quad\quad\quad a = -2$
$5(-2) - b = -11$
$\quad\quad -b = -1$
$\quad\quad\quad b = 1 \quad (-2, 1)$

11. $a + b - 4c = -22 \qquad a + b - 4c = -22 \qquad a = -1$
$\quad -b - c = -9 \qquad\qquad b + c = 9 \qquad\qquad b = 3$
$\quad 3b - 7c = -33 \qquad\quad -10c = -60 \qquad\quad c = 6$
$\qquad\qquad\qquad\qquad\qquad\qquad\qquad\qquad\qquad (-1, 3, 6)$

12. $-10x^4 + 8x^3 - 4x^2 - 8x + 5$

13. $4x^3y - 8xy + 5x^2y - 10y$

14. $(2x - 1)(2x - 1)(2x - 1) = (4x^2 - 4x + 1)(2x - 1)$
$\qquad\qquad\qquad\qquad\qquad\qquad = 8x^3 - 12x^2 + 6x - 1$

15. $3(4x^2 - 44xy + 121y^2) = 3(2x - 11y)(2x - 11y)$

16. $\left(\dfrac{1}{3}x^3 - 7y\right)\left(\dfrac{1}{3}x^3 + 7y\right)$

17. $2x^2(x + 3) - 8(x + 3) = (2x^2 - 8)(x + 3)$
$= 2(x + 2)(x - 2)(x + 3)$

18. $x(6 - x) = 0$
$x = 0$ or $6 - x = 0$
$6 = x$

19. $x^2 - 9x + 8 = 0$
$(x - 8)(x - 1) = 0$
$x = 8, 1$

20. $\dfrac{(x + 6)(x - 2)}{3(x - 2)(x - 2)} = \dfrac{x + 6}{3(x - 2)}$

21. $\dfrac{5a - 2}{a + 3} \cdot \dfrac{(a + 3)(a - 3)}{(5a - 2)(5a + 2)} = \dfrac{a - 3}{5a + 2}$

22. $5a - 15 = a + 2$
$4a = 17$
$a = \dfrac{17}{4}$

23. $15m + 30 - 15m = 2m(m + 2)$
$30 = 2m^2 + 4m$
$0 = 2(m^2 + 2m - 15)$
$0 = 2(m + 5)(m - 3)$
$m = -5, 3$

24. $2\sqrt[4]{2}$ **25.** $3|x|\sqrt{10x}$

26. $(2\sqrt{6})(5\sqrt{3}) = 10 \cdot 3\sqrt{2} = 30\sqrt{2}$

27. $\sqrt{(x + 3)^2} = |x + 3|$

28. $10\sqrt[3]{4} - 6\sqrt[3]{4} - 5\sqrt[3]{4} = -\sqrt[3]{4}$

29. $14 + 2\sqrt{35} - 3\sqrt{35} - 15 = -1 - \sqrt{35}$

30. $-1 + i$ **31.** $-40 - 24i - 20i + 12 = -28 - 44i$

32. $\dfrac{2 + i}{3 - 2i} \cdot \dfrac{3 + 2i}{3 + 2i} = \dfrac{6 + 3i + 4i - 2}{13} = \dfrac{4 + 7i}{13}$

33. $9x^2 = 2$
$x^2 = \dfrac{2}{9}$
$x = \pm\dfrac{\sqrt{2}}{3}$

34. $x = \dfrac{3 \pm \sqrt{9 + 36}}{2} = \dfrac{3 \pm \sqrt{45}}{2} = \dfrac{3 \pm 3\sqrt{5}}{2}$

35. $y = x^{1/3}$ $\quad 2y^2 - y - 28 = 0$
$(2y + 7)(y - 4) = 0$
$y = 4 \qquad x = 64$
$y = -\dfrac{7}{2} \qquad x = -\dfrac{343}{8}$

36. $A = kr^2$
$400 = k \cdot \left(\dfrac{100}{\pi}\right)$
$k = 4\pi$
$A = (4\pi)(4)$
$= 16\pi$

37. $4(-y)^2 = 2x - 1$
$4y^2 = 2x - 1 \qquad x\text{-axis}$

38. $5(-x)^2 - 2y^2 = 6 \qquad y\text{-axis}$
$5x^2 - 2(-y)^2 = 6 \qquad x\text{-axis}$

39. $(-y)^3 - x^3 = 7$
$-y - x^3 = -7 \qquad \text{not } x\text{-axis}$
$y^3 - (-x)^3 = -7$
$y^3 + x^3 = -7 \qquad \text{not } y\text{-axis}$

40. 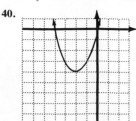 **41.**

Axis: $x = -2$;
Vertex: $(-2, -4)$;
Min.: $= -4$

Axis: $x = 1$;
Vertex: $(1, 3)$;
Max.: $= 3$

42. $\left(\dfrac{6 + 4}{2}, -\dfrac{7 + 5}{2}\right) = (5, -1)$ **43.** Center: $(-1, -3)$;
Radius: 2

44. Center: $(-1, -3)$;
Vertices: $(-1, 2), (-1, -8)$;
Foci: $(-1, -3 + \sqrt{41}), (-1, -3 - \sqrt{41})$

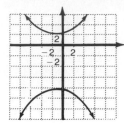

Asymptotes: $y + 3 = \dfrac{5}{4}(x + 1)$,
$y + 3 = -\dfrac{5}{4}(x + 1)$

45.

$\begin{array}{r|rrrr} 3 & 1 & 0 & 0 & -27 \\ & & 3 & 9 & 27 \\ \hline & 1 & 3 & 9 & 0 \end{array}$

$Q: x^2 + 3x + 9 \qquad R: 0$

46. $6 + 7i, \dfrac{1}{2} - \sqrt{11}$ **47.** $\dfrac{1}{2}, \dfrac{1 + \sqrt{5}}{2}, \dfrac{1 - \sqrt{5}}{2}$

48. $2y + 3x - 7 = 0$ **49.** $x = 2y^2 + 3$ **50.** $f^{-1}(x) = \dfrac{x}{2}$

51. $\log_{10} 3 = 0.4771$ **52.** $\log_3 y = x$ **53.** $\log_x z = y$

54. $3x + 5 = 2$
$3x = -3$
$x = -1$

55. $\log \dfrac{x + 9}{x} = 1$
$\dfrac{x + 9}{x} = 10$
$x + 9 = 10x$
$9 = 9x$
$1 = x$

56. $(3^2)^{y^2} \cdot 3^{5y} = 27$
$3^{(2y^2 + 5y)} = 3^3$
$2y^2 + 5y = 3$
$2y^2 + 5y - 3 = 0$
$(2y - 1)(y + 3) = 0$
$y = \dfrac{1}{2}, -3$

57. $\begin{bmatrix} -3 & 6 & 30 \\ 9 & -12 & 24 \\ 0 & 15 & -3 \end{bmatrix}$ **58.** $\begin{bmatrix} 28 & -7 \\ 58 & 15 \\ -29 & -15 \end{bmatrix}$

59. $\begin{bmatrix} -\dfrac{3}{16} & \dfrac{13}{48} & \dfrac{7}{24} \\ \dfrac{1}{64} & \dfrac{1}{192} & \dfrac{19}{96} \\ \dfrac{5}{64} & \dfrac{5}{192} & \dfrac{-1}{96} \end{bmatrix}$

60. $(-4) + 0 + 150 - [0 + (-6) + (-40)]$
$146 + 46 = 192$

61. $x = \dfrac{\begin{vmatrix} 10 & -2 \\ 20 & 1 \end{vmatrix}}{\begin{vmatrix} 7 & -2 \\ 9 & 1 \end{vmatrix}} = \dfrac{10 + 40}{7 + 18} = \dfrac{50}{25} = 2$

$y = \dfrac{\begin{vmatrix} 7 & 10 \\ 9 & 20 \end{vmatrix}}{\begin{vmatrix} 7 & -2 \\ 9 & 1 \end{vmatrix}} = \dfrac{140 - 90}{7 + 18} = \dfrac{50}{25} = 2 \qquad (2, 2)$

62. $(-1)^n(n + 1)$ **63.** $7 - 3(n - 1)$
where $n = 17$
$7 - 3(17 - 1) = -41$

64. $3^2 + 3 + 1 + \dfrac{1}{3} + \dfrac{1}{3^2} + \dfrac{1}{3^3} = 13\dfrac{13}{27}$ **65.** $\dfrac{27}{4}$

66. $\dfrac{9!}{4!} = 15{,}120$ **67.** $5 \cdot 4 \cdot 3 \cdot 2 = 120$ **68.** $\dfrac{8!}{4!\,4!} = 70$

69. $(2a + 3y)^4 = \dbinom{4}{0}(2a)^4(3y)^0 + \dbinom{4}{1}(2a)^3(3y)^1 + \dbinom{4}{2}(2a)^2(3y)^2$

$$+ \binom{4}{3}(2a)(3y)^3 + \binom{4}{4}(2a)^0(3y)^4$$
$$= 16a^4 + 96a^3y + 216a^2y^2 + 81y^4$$

70. $P(\text{black}) = \dfrac{26}{52}$ $P(\text{King}) = \dfrac{4}{52}$ $P(\text{black King}) = \dfrac{2}{52}$

$$\dfrac{26}{52} + \dfrac{4}{52} - \dfrac{2}{52} = \dfrac{28}{52} = \dfrac{7}{13}$$

71. $P(\text{even}) = \dfrac{3}{6}$ $P(\text{multiple 3}) = \dfrac{2}{6}$ $P(6) = \dfrac{1}{6}$

$$\dfrac{3}{6} + \dfrac{2}{6} - \dfrac{1}{6} = \dfrac{4}{6} = \dfrac{2}{3}$$

72.

Stem	Leaf
1	6, 7, 3
2	3, 4, 9, 8, 7, 3, 3, 9, 7, 2, 3, 2
3	1, 3, 1, 4

73. Answers may vary.

Interval	Tally	Frequency
13–15	I	1
16–18	II	2
19–21		0
22–24	IIII II	7
25–27	II	2
28–30	III	3
31–33	III	3
34–36	I	1

74. Mean: 25, mode: 23, median: 24

75.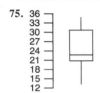

76. $34 - 13 = 21$ **77.** 4.6 **78.** 31.1 **79.** 5.6

80. IV **81.** III **82.** III **83.** II

84. Cosine and secant are positive; the other four are negative.

85. $100° \cdot \dfrac{\pi \text{ radians}}{180°} = \dfrac{5\pi}{9}$ **86.** $\dfrac{2\pi}{3} \cdot \dfrac{180°}{\pi \text{ radians}} = 120°$

87.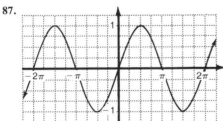

88. $\cos\left(\dfrac{\pi}{2} - \theta\right)$

$$= \cos\dfrac{\pi}{2}\cos\theta + \sin\dfrac{\pi}{2}\sin\theta$$
$$= 0 + 1\sin\theta$$
$$= \sin\theta$$

89.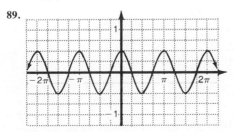

$A = \dfrac{1}{2}$

period $= \pi$

90. $\tan x \sin x(\cot y - \csc y)$
$= \sin y - \tan y$

91. $\cos(\alpha + \beta) + \cos(\alpha - \beta) = \cos\alpha\cos\beta - \sin\alpha\sin\beta$
$$+ \cos\alpha\cos\beta + \sin\alpha\sin\beta$$
$$= 2\cos\alpha\cos\beta$$

92. $\cos^2\dfrac{x}{2} - \sin^2\dfrac{x}{2}$

$$= \cos^2\dfrac{x}{2} - \left(1 - \cos^2\dfrac{x}{2}\right)$$
$$= -1 + 2\cos^2\dfrac{x}{2}$$
$$= -1 + 2\left(\dfrac{1 + \cos 2\left(\dfrac{y}{2}\right)}{2}\right)$$
$$= \cos x$$

93.
$$\dfrac{1 - \cos x}{\sin x} = \dfrac{\sin x}{1 + \cos x}$$

$\dfrac{(1 - \cos x)(1 + \cos x)}{(\sin x)(1 + \cos x)}$	$\dfrac{(\sin x)(\sin x)}{(1 + \cos x)(\sin x)}$
$\dfrac{(1 - \cos x)(1 + \cos x)}{1 - \cos^2 x}$	$\dfrac{(\sin x)(\sin x)}{\sin^2 x}$
$\dfrac{\sin^2 x}{\sin^2 x}$	$\dfrac{\sin^2 x}{\sin^2 x}$

94. $\dfrac{\pi}{6} + 2k\pi, \dfrac{5\pi}{6} + 2k\pi$

95. $(1 - \sin^2 x) - 1 = 2\sin x$
$$\sin^2 x + 2\sin x = 0$$
$$\sin x(\sin x + 2) = 0$$
$$\sin x = 0$$
$$x = 0, \pi, 2\pi$$

96. $\tan^2 x + 2\tan x - 1 = 0$
$$\tan x = \dfrac{-2 \pm \sqrt{4 + 4}}{2} = \dfrac{-2 \pm 2\sqrt{2}}{2} = -1 \pm \sqrt{2}$$
$$x = \dfrac{\pi}{8}, \dfrac{5\pi}{8}, \dfrac{9\pi}{8}, \dfrac{13\pi}{8}$$

97.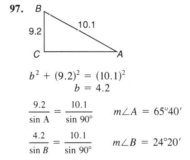

$$b^2 + (9.2)^2 = (10.1)^2$$
$$b = 4.2$$
$$\dfrac{9.2}{\sin A} = \dfrac{10.1}{\sin 90°} \qquad m\angle A = 65°40'$$
$$\dfrac{4.2}{\sin B} = \dfrac{10.1}{\sin 90°} \qquad m\angle B = 24°20'$$

98.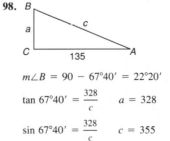

$$m\angle B = 90 - 67°40' = 22°20'$$
$$\tan 67°40' = \dfrac{328}{c} \qquad a = 328$$
$$\sin 67°40' = \dfrac{328}{c} \qquad c = 355$$

99. $\dfrac{7}{\sin 150°} = \dfrac{3}{\sin A} \qquad m\angle A = 12°20'$
$$m\angle C = 180° - 150° - 12°20' = 17°40'$$
$$\dfrac{7}{\sin 150°} = \dfrac{c}{\sin 17°90'} \qquad c = 4.25$$

100. $36 = 49 + 100 - 140\cos A \qquad m\angle A = 36°10'$
$$100 = 36 + 100 - 120\cos B \qquad m\angle B = 43°30'$$
$$m\angle C = 180° - 36°10' - 43°30' = 100°20'$$

101. $a = -\sqrt{3}$ $b = -1$
   $r = \sqrt{3+1} = 2$

   $\cos\theta = -\dfrac{\sqrt{3}}{2}$ $\sin\theta = -\dfrac{1}{2}$

   $2\,\text{cis}\left(\dfrac{7\pi}{6}\right)$

102. $a = \dfrac{1}{2}$ $b = \dfrac{\sqrt{3}}{2}$

   $r = \sqrt{\dfrac{1}{4} + \dfrac{3}{4}} = 1$

   $\cos\theta = \dfrac{1}{2}$ $\sin\theta = \dfrac{\sqrt{3}}{2}$

   $1\,\text{cis}\left(\dfrac{\pi}{3}\right)$

103. $a = 10\cos 270 = 0$
   $b = 10\sin 270 = -10$
   $0 + (-10i) = -10i$

104. $a = 4\cos 135° = 4\left(-\dfrac{\sqrt{2}}{2}\right)$

   $b = 4\sin 135° = 4\left(\dfrac{\sqrt{2}}{2}\right)$

   $-2\sqrt{2} + 2i\sqrt{2}$

COMPUTER-ASSISTED PROBLEM SOLVING

p. 839   PROBLEM 1

ANSWER TO PROBLEM

```
RUN
MAKE WINDOWS 30 INCHES BY 30 INCHES
```
A square creates a window with greatest area.

ANSWER TO EXTENSION

Replace the following lines.
```
20 FOR H = 1 TO 69
30 W = 70 - H
RUN
MAKE WINDOWS 35 INCHES BY 35 INCHES
```
The cost is $35 \cdot \$1.50 + 35 \cdot \$0.95 = \$85.75$.

pp. 839–840   PROBLEM 2

ANSWER TO PROBLEM

```
RUN
THE RADIUS SHOULD BE 1.71999999 INCHES
THE HEIGHT SHOULD BE 1.72239774 INCHES
```
For a cup with minimum surface area, the radius should be 1.72 in. and the height should be 1.72 in.

ANSWER TO EXTENSION

Replace the following line.
```
50 A = 2 * 3.14 * R * H + 1.25 * 3.14 * R ^ 2
RUN
THE RADIUS SHOULD BE 1.59999999 INCHES
THE HEIGHT SHOULD BE 1.99044589 INCHES
```
For a cup with lowest cost, the radius should be 1.6 in. and the height should be 2.0 in.

pp. 840–841   PROBLEM 3

ANSWER TO PROBLEM

```
RUN
ENTER X1,Y1,?14,20
POINT OR SLOPE? POINT
```

```
ENTER X2,Y2, ?35,-6
THE POINT SLOPE EQUATION IS
Y = -1.23809524X + 37.3333333
RUN
ENTER X1,Y1 ?-12,5
POINT OR SLOPE? SLOPE
ENTER SLOPE -2.5
THE POINT SLOPE EQUATION IS
Y = -2.5X - 25
```

ANSWER TO EXTENSION

Add the following lines.
```
107 IF F = 1 THEN STOP
108 F = 1
110 M = -1  M: PRINT
    "FOR THE LINE PERPENDICULAR TO THIS ONE":
    GOTO 55
```
For a.,
```
FOR THE LINE PERPENDICULAR TO THIS ONE
THE POINT SLOPE EQUATION IS
Y = .807692308X + 8.69230769
```
For b.,
```
FOR THE LINE PERPENDICULAR TO THIS ONE
THE POINT SLOPE EQUATION IS
Y = .4X + 9.8
```

p. 841   PROBLEM 4

ANSWER TO PROBLEM

```
RUN
1 COWS, 17 SHEEP, 82 PIGS
2 COWS, 14 SHEEP, 84 PIGS
3 COWS, 11 SHEEP, 86 PIGS
4 COWS, 8 SHEEP, 88 PIGS
5 COWS, 5 SHEEP, 90 PIGS
6 COWS, 2 SHEEP, 92 PIGS
```
There are six different combinations, all of which are solutions.

ANSWER TO EXTENSION

Replace the following lines.
```
20 FOR X = 1 TO 11
30 FOR Y = 1 TO 16
70 IF .09 * X + .06 * Y + .01 * Z = 100 THEN
   PRINT X;" PENS, ";Y;" ERASERS, ";Z;" PAPER
   CLIPS"
RUN
2 PENS, 6 ERASERS, 92 PAPER CLIPS
```
Only 1 combination satisfies the conditions of the problem.

p. 842   PROBLEM 5

ANSWER TO PROBLEM

```
RUN
INPUT THE WIDTH OF THE GUTTER 8
TURN UP 1.99999998 INCHES ON EACH SIDE
THE CROSS-SECTIONAL AREA IS 7.99999995 SQUARE
INCHES
```
Turn sides up 2.00 in.

ANSWER TO EXTENSION

Replace the following lines.
```
40 AREA = X * (WIDTH / 2 - X)
70 PRINT "THE DUCT SHOULD BE ";BESTX; " BY ";
   WIDTH / 2 - BESTX;" INCHES"
RUN
INPUT THE WIDTH OF THE AIR DUCT 15
THE DUCT SHOULD BE 3.74999994 BY 3.75000006
INCHES
THE CROSS-SECTIONAL AREA IS 14.0624999 SQUARE
INCHES
```
The dimensions are 3.75 in. by 3.75 in., a square.

ANSWER TO PROBLEM

```
RUN
HE SHOULD LAND AT A POINT 4.70000001
MILES FROM THE STORE
THE TRIP WILL TAKE 2.60000753 HOURS
```

He should land 4.7 miles from the store.
The trip will take 2.6 hours, or 2 hours
36 minutes.

ANSWER TO EXTENSION

Replace the following lines.

```
30 FOR X = .1 TO 5 STEP .1
50 W = 5 - X
60 T = R / 3 + W / 4
70 IF T < TIME THEN TIME = T:C = 5 - X
RUN
HE SHOULD LAND AT A POINT 1.60000001 MILES FROM
THE STORE
THE TRIP WILL TAKE 1.91143788 HOURS
```

He should land 1.6 miles from the store. The trip will take 1.9 hours,
or 1 hour 54 minutes.

ANSWER TO PROBLEM

```
RUN
THE SPEEDBOAT SHOULD AIM 5.1 MILES AHEAD OF THE
SHIP
```

ANSWER TO EXTENSION

Replace the following lines.

```
30 SHIPD = 12 * T
40 SPDBTD = 15 * T
50 IF SPDBTD > = SQR (9 ^ 2 + SHIPD ^ 2)
   THEN 70
RUN
THE SPEEDBOAT SHOULD AIM 13.2 MILES AHEAD OF
THE SHIP
```

ANSWER TO PROBLEM

```
RUN
INPUT THE NUMBER OF HOURS .5
472.743056 PEOPLE ON THE MAIN FLOOR AT THE END
OF .5 HOURS
57.1180556 PEOPLE IN THE LOUNGE
170.138889 PEOPLE IN THE BALCONY

RUN
INPUT THE NUMBER OF HOURS 1
411.685897 PEOPLE ON THE MAIN FLOOR AT THE END
OF 1 HOURS
88.3080754 PEOPLE IN THE LOUNGE
200.006028 PEOPLE IN THE BALCONY

RUN
INPUT THE NUMBER OF HOURS 5
400.000221 PEOPLE ON THE MAIN FLOOR AT THE END
OF 5 HOURS
99.999988 PEOPLE IN THE LOUNGE
199.999793 PEOPLE IN THE BALCONY
```

ANSWER TO EXTENSION

Replace the following line.

```
20 M = 450:L = 150:B = 100

RUN
INPUT THE NUMBER OF HOURS .5
433.420139 PEOPLE ON THE MAIN FLOOR AT THE END
OF .5 HOURS
97.4826389 PEOPLE IN THE LOUNGE
169.097222 PEOPLE IN THE BALCONY
```

```
RUN
INPUT THE NUMBER OF HOURS 1
410.858079 PEOPLE ON THE MAIN FLOOR AT THE END
OF 1 HOURS
95.8217292 PEOPLE IN THE LOUNGE
193.320192 PEOPLE IN THE BALCONY

RUN
INPUT THE NUMBER OF HOURS 5
399.999968 PEOPLE ON THE MAIN FLOOR AT THE END
OF 5 HOURS
100.000085 PEOPLE IN THE LOUNGE
199.999949 PEOPLE IN THE BALCONY
```

After 5 hours the number of people on each floor is the same as
before.

ANSWER TO PROBLEM

```
RUN
A FARE OF 115 CENTS WOULD PROVIDE THE MOST
REVENUE
```

ANSWER TO EXTENSION

Replace the following line.

```
30 DEF FN RD(F) = 30 * F
40 FOR F = 1 TO 300
RUN
A FARE OF 187 CENTS WOULD PROVIDE THE MOST
REVENUE
```

ANSWER TO PROBLEM

```
RUN
THE SHORTEST SEGMENT IS 11.1803406 UNITS IN
LENGTH
THE ENDPOINTS ARE (0, 10.001) AND
(4.99800095,0)
```

ANSWER TO EXTENSION

Replace the following lines.

```
30 FOR Y = 13.001 TO 50 STEP .1
40 X = 4 * Y / (Y - 13)
80 PRINT "THE SHORTEST LADDER IS ";MINDIST;
   " FEET"
90 PRINT "PLACE THE LADDER ";XCRDNT - 4;" FEET
   FROM THE FENCE"
RUN
THE SHORTEST LADDER IS 22.8341155 FEET
PLACE THE LADDER 8.81206563 FEET FROM THE FENCE
```

ANSWER TO PROBLEM

```
RUN
INPUT TWO X-VALUES AND THE ACCURACY -10, 10, 1
-7 IS A ROOT
-2 IS A ROOT
ONE ROOT IS APPROXIMATELY 3.5

RUN
INPUT TWO X-VALUES AND THE ACCURACY 3, 4, .1
ONE ROOT IS APPROXIMATELY 3.55

RUN
INPUT TWO X-VALUES AND THE ACCURACY 3.5,
3.6, .01
3.5 IS A ROOT
```

The roots between -10 and 10 are -7, -2, and 3.5.

ANSWER TO EXTENSION

Replace the following lines.

```
 20 DG = 4
170 DATA 1, 9.734, -17.511, -304.052, -332.563
```

Computer-Assisted Problem Solving

```
RUN
INPUT FIRST, LAST, AND ACC -10, 10, .001
ONE ROOT IS APPROXIMATELY -7.00050324
ONE ROOT IS APPROXIMATELY -6.99950323
ONE ROOT IS APPROXIMATELY -1.23350229
ONE ROOT IS APPROXIMATELY  5.50049844
```

pp. 847–848   PROBLEM 12

ANSWER TO PROBLEM

```
RUN
HE SHOULD TURN .700000003 MILES FROM
THE CORNER.
```

He should turn 0.7 miles from the corner.

ANSWER TO EXTENSION

Replace the following lines.
```
LIST
20 MNMT = 1 / 3
40 T1 = ( SQR (X ^ 2 + 4)) / 8
50 T2 = (3 - X) / 15
RUN
HE SHOULD TURN 0 MILES FROM THE CORNER.
```
He should stay on the street.

pp. 848–849   PROBLEM 13

ANSWER TO PROBLEM

```
RUN
THE ELEMENTS OF THE INVERSE MATRIX ARE
-11 -4  6
  2  0 -1
  2  1 -1
```

ANSWER TO EXTENSION

Replace the following line.
```
360 DATA 2, 1, 2, 1, 0, -2, 0, 5, -8
RUN
THE ELEMENTS OF THE INVERSE MATRIX ARE
-5    -9  1
-4    -8  1
-2.5  -5  .5
```
Using the inverse matrix, we find $x = 1.1$, $y = -3.2$, $z = 5.3$.

pp. 849–850   PROBLEM 14

ANSWER TO PROBLEM

```
RUN
INPUT THE NUMBER OF YEARS
3
IN 3 YEARS 43.362715% WILL BE WITH COLONIAL
34.35132% WILL BE WITH NATIONAL 22.285965% WILL
BE WITH WILDERNESS

RUN
INPUT THE NUMBER OF YEARS
10
IN 10 YEARS 41.769731% WILL BE WITH COLONIAL
32.7450018% WILL BE WITH NATIONAL 25.4852672%
WILL BE WITH WILDERNESS
```

ANSWER TO EXTENSION

Replace the following lines.
```
50 NC = C * .05:NN = N * .05:NW = W * .07
55 C2 = C * .08
60 C = C - NC - C2 + NN + NW
70 N = N - NN + C2
RUN
INPUT THE NUMBER OF YEARS
3
IN 3 YEARS 38.31457% WILL BE WITH COLONIAL
39.680165% WILL BE WITH NATIONAL 22.005265%
WILL BE WITH WILDERNESS
```

```
RUN
INPUT THE NUMBER OF YEARS
10
IN 10 YEARS 32.3111923% WILL BE WITH COLONIAL
44.5460319% WILL BE WITH NATIONAL 23.1427758%
WILL BE WITH WILDERNESS
```

pp. 850–851   PROBLEM 15

ANSWER TO PROBLEM

```
RUN
INPUT NUMBER OF TRIALS 1000
PROBABILITY IS 7E-03
```
Answers may vary.

ANSWER TO EXTENSION

Replace the following lines.
```
150 IF CARD$ (C1) = "KING OF HEARTS" AND RIGHT$
    (CARD$ (C2),6) <> "HEARTS" AND LEFT$
    (CARD$ (C2),4) <> "KING" THEN S = S + 1
160 IF CARD$ (C2) = "KING OF HEARTS" AND RIGHT$
    (CARD$ (C1),6) <> "HEARTS" AND LEFT$
    (CARD$ (C1),4) <> "KING" THEN S = S + 1
RUN
INPUT NUMBER OF TRIALS
1000 THE PROBABILITY IS 0.29
```
Answers may vary.

pp. 851–852   PROBLEM 16

ANSWER TO PROBLEM

```
RUN
MEAN = 16
THE SORTED MARGINS ARE:
3 4 4 5 7 9 10 10 12 16 17 17 18 19 19 21 22 25
29 32 36
MEDIAN = 17
MODE = 17
VARIANCE = 82.2727273
STANDARD DEVIATION = 9.07043148
```

ANSWER TO EXTENSION

For Super Bowl 23, suppose Seattle wins by 8 points. The following lines would need to be changed.
```
20 DIM MARGIN (23)
30 (ADD, 8 TO THE CURRENT LINE)
40 (CHANGE 22 TO 23)
50 (CHANGE 22 TO 23)
80 (CHANGE 21 TO 22)
120 (CHANGE 22 TO 23 AND 21 TO 22)
130 MEDIAN = MARGIN(12): PRINT "MEDIAN =";
    MEDIAN
140 (CHANGE 22 TO 23)
170 (CHANGE 22 TO 23)

RUN
MEAN = 15.6521739
THE SORTED MARGINS ARE:
3 4 4 5 7 8 9 10 10 12 16 17 17 17 18 19 19 21
22 25 29 32 36
MEDIAN = 17
MODE = 17
VARIANCE = 82.2173913
STANDARD DEVIATION = 9.06738063
```
Answers may vary.

pp. 852–853   PROBLEM 17

ANSWER TO PROBLEM

```
RUN
JOE SHOULD RUN AT AN ANGLE OF 33.8216561
DEGREES TO HIS STREET
```

ANSWER TO EXTENSION

Replace the following lines.

```
30 TM = (.125 + .125 * TAN (ANG)) / 24
40 TJ = (.125 / COS (ANG)) / 17

RUN
JOE SHOULD PEDAL AT AN ANGLE OF 41.8471338
DEGREES TO HIS STREET
```

pp. 853   PROBLEM 18

ANSWER TO PROBLEM

```
RUN
THEY WERE CLOSEST AFTER 2.9 HOURS THEY ARE
THEN 54.0023148 MILES APART.
```

ANSWER TO EXTENSION

Replace the following lines.

```
10 MIN = 100:TIME = 0
30 X = 86.6 - T * 17
40 Y = 50 - T * 10

RUN
THEY WERE CLOSEST AFTER 5.09999999 HOURS
THEY ARE THEN 1.00498745 MILES APART.
```